Twentieth-Century Literary Criticism

Guide to Gale Literary Criticism Series

For criticism on	Consult these Gale series
Authors now living or who died after December 31, 1959	*CONTEMPORARY LITERARY CRITICISM (CLC)*
Authors who died between 1900 and 1959	*TWENTIETH-CENTURY LITERARY CRITICISM (TCLC)*
Authors who died between 1800 and 1899	*NINETEENTH-CENTURY LITERATURE CRITICISM (NCLC)*
Authors who died between 1400 and 1799	*LITERATURE CRITICISM FROM 1400 TO 1800 (LC)* *SHAKESPEAREAN CRITICISM (SC)*
Authors who died before 1400	*CLASSICAL AND MEDIEVAL LITERATURE CRITICISM (CMLC)*
Authors of books for children and young adults	*CHILDREN'S LITERATURE REVIEW (CLR)*
Dramatists	*DRAMA CRITICISM (DC)*
Poets	*POETRY CRITICISM (PC)*
Short story writers	*SHORT STORY CRITICISM (SSC)*
Black writers of the past two hundred years	*BLACK LITERATURE CRITICISM (BLC)*
Hispanic writers of the late nineteenth and twentieth centuries	*HISPANIC LITERATURE CRITICISM (HLC)*
Native North American writers and orators of the eighteenth, nineteenth, and twentieth centuries	*NATIVE NORTH AMERICAN LITERATURE (NNAL)*
Major authors from the Renaissance to the present	*WORLD LITERATURE CRITICISM, 1500 TO THE PRESENT (WLC)*

ISSN 0276-8178

Volume 81

Twentieth-Century Literary Criticism

**Excerpts from Criticism of the
Works of Novelists, Poets, Playwrights,
Short Story Writers, and Other Creative Writers
Who Lived between 1900 and 1960,
from the First Published Critical
Appraisals to Current Evaluations**

Jennifer Baise
Editor

Thomas Ligotti
Associate Editor

GALE

DETROIT · LONDON

STAFF

Jennifer Baise, *Editor*

Thomas Ligotti, *Associate Editor*

Susan Trosky, *Permissions Manager*
Kimberly F. Smilay, *Permissions Specialist*
Sarah R. Chesney, Steve Cusack, Kelly A. Quin, *Permissions Associates*
Sandy Gore, *Permissions Assistant*

Victoria B. Cariappa, *Research Manager*
Michele P. LaMeau, Andrew Guy Malonis, Barbara McNeil, Gary J. Oudersluys, Maureen Richards, *Research Specialists*
Julia C. Daniel, Jeffrey Daniels, Tamara C. Nott, Tracie A. Richardson, Norma Sawaya,
Cheryl L. Warnock, *Research Associates*
Corrine Stocker, *Research Assistant*

Mary Beth Trimper, *Production Director*
Deborah L. Milliken, *Production Assistant*

Gary Leach, *Graphic Artist*
Randy Bassett, *Image Database Supervisor*
Robert Duncan, Michael Logusz, *Imaging Specialists*
Pamela Reed, *Imaging Coordinator*

Library of Congress Catalog Card Number 76-46132
ISBN 0-7876-2741-0
ISSN 0276-8178

Printed in the United States of America
10 9 8 7 6 5 4 3 2 1

Contents

Preface   vii

Acknowledgments   xi

Preface

Since its inception more than fifteen years ago, *Twentieth-Century Literary Criticism* has been purchased and used by nearly 10,000 school, public, and college or university libraries. *TCLC* has covered more than 500 authors, representing 58 nationalities, and over 25,000 titles. No other reference source has surveyed the critical response to twentieth-century authors and literature as thoroughly as *TCLC*. In the words of one reviewer, "there is nothing comparable available." *TCLC* "is a gold mine of information—dates, pseudonyms, biographical information, and criticism from books and periodicals—which many libraries would have difficulty assembling on their own."

Scope of the Series

TCLC is designed to serve as an introduction to authors who died between 1900 and 1960 and to the most significant interpretations of these author's works. The great poets, novelists, short story writers, playwrights, and philosophers of this period are frequently studied in high school and college literature courses. In organizing and excerpting the vast amount of critical material written on these authors, *TCLC* helps students develop valuable insight into literary history, promotes a better understanding of the texts, and sparks ideas for papers and assignments. Each entry in *TCLC* presents a comprehensive survey of an author's career or an individual work of literature and provides the user with a multiplicity of interpretations and assessments. Such variety allows students to pursue their own interests; furthermore, it fosters an awareness that literature is dynamic and responsive to many different opinions.

Every fourth volume of *TCLC* is devoted to literary topics. These topic entries widen the focus of the series from individual authors to such broader subjects as literary movements, prominent themes in twentieth-century literature, literary reaction to political and historical events, significant eras in literary history, prominent literary anniversaries, and the literatures of cultures that are often overlooked by English-speaking readers.

TCLC is designed as a companion series to Gale's *Contemporary Literary Criticism*, which reprints commentary on authors now living or who have died since 1960. Because of the different periods under consideration, there is no duplication of material between *CLC* and *TCLC*. For additional information about *CLC* and Gale's other criticism titles, users should consult the Guide to Gale Literary Criticism Series preceding the title page in this volume.

Coverage

Each volume of *TCLC* is carefully compiled to present:

- criticism of authors, or literary topics, representing a variety of genres and nationalities

- both major and lesser-known writers and literary works of the period

- 6-12 authors or 3-6 topics per volume

- individual entries that survey critical response to each author's work or each topic in literary history, including early criticism to reflect initial reactions; later criticism to represent any rise or decline in reputation; and current retrospective analyses.

Organization of This Book

An author entry consists of the following elements: author heading, biographical and critical introduction, list of principal works, excerpts of criticism (each preceded by an annotation and a bibliographic citation), and a bibliography of further reading.

- The **Author Heading** consists of the name under which the author most commonly wrote, followed by birth and death dates. If an author wrote consistently under a pseudonym, the pseudonym will be listed in the author heading and the real name given in parentheses on the first line of the biographical and critical introduction. Also located at the beginning of the introduction to the author entry are any name variations under which an author wrote, including transliterated forms for authors whose languages use nonroman alphabets.

- The **Biographical and Critical Introduction** outlines the author's life and career, as well as the critical issues surrounding his or her work. References to past volumes of *TCLC* are provided at the beginning of the introduction. Additional sources of information in other biographical and critical reference series published by Gale, including *Short Story Criticism, Children's Literature Review, Contemporary Authors, Dictionary of Literary Biography,* and *Something about the Author,* are listed in a box at the end of the entry.

- Some *TCLC* entries include **Portraits** of the author. Entries also may contain reproductions of materials pertinent to an author's career, including manuscript pages, title pages, dust jackets, letters, and drawings, as well as photographs of important people, places, and events in an author's life.

- The **List of Principal Works** is chronological by date of first book publication and identifies the genre of each work. In the case of foreign authors with both foreign-language publications and English translations, the title and date of the first English-language edition are given in brackets. Unless otherwise indicated, dramas are dated by first performance, not first publication.

- Critical excerpts are prefaced by **Annotations** providing the reader with information about both the critic and the criticism that follows. Included are the critic's reputation, individual approach to literary criticism, and particular expertise in an author's works. Also noted are the relative importance of a work of criticism, the scope of the excerpt, and the growth of critical controversy or changes in critical trends regarding an author. In some cases, these annotations cross-reference excerpts by critics who discuss each other's commentary.

- A complete **Bibliographic Citation** designed to facilitate location of the original essay or book precedes each piece of criticism.

- Criticism is arranged chronologically in each author entry to provide a perspective on changes in critical evaluation over the years. All titles of works by the author featured in the entry are printed in boldface type to enable the user to easily locate discussion of particular works. Also for purposes of easier identification, the critic's name and the publication date of the essay are given at the beginning of each piece of criticism. Unsigned criticism is preceded by the title of the journal in which it appeared. Some of the excerpts in *TCLC* also contain translated material. Unless otherwise noted, translations in brackets are by the editors; translations in parentheses or continuous with the text are by the critic. Publication information (such as footnotes or page and line references to specific editions of works) have been deleted at the editor's discretion to provide smoother reading of the text.

- An annotated list of **Further Reading** appearing at the end of each author entry suggests secondary sources on the author. In some cases it includes essays for which the editors could not obtain reprint rights.

Cumulative Indexes

- Each volume of *TCLC* contains a cumulative **Author Index** listing all authors who have appeared in Gale's Literary Criticism Series, along with cross references to such biographical series as *Contemporary Authors* and *Dictionary of Literary Biography.* For readers' convenience, a complete list of Gale titles included appears on the first page of the author index. Useful for locating authors within the various series, this index is particularly valuable for those authors who are identified by a certain period but who, because of their death dates, are placed in another, or for those authors whose careers span two periods. For example, F. Scott Fitzgerald is found in *TCLC,* yet a writer often associated with him, Ernest Hemingway, is found in *CLC.*

- Each *TCLC* volume includes a cumulative **Nationality Index** which lists all authors who have appeared in *TCLC* volumes, arranged alphabetically under their respective nationalities, as well as Topics volume entries devoted to particular national literatures.

- Each new volume in Gale's Literary Criticism Series includes a cumulative **Topic Index,** which lists all literary topics treated in *NCLC, TCLC, LC 1400-1800,* and the *CLC* yearbook.

- Each new volume of *TCLC,* with the exception of the Topics volumes, includes a **Title Index** listing the titles of all literary works discussed in the volume. In response to numerous suggestions from librarians, Gale has also produced a **Special Paperbound Edition** of the *TCLC* title index. This annual cumulation lists all titles discussed in the series since its inception and is issued with the first volume of *TCLC* published each year. Additional copies of the index are available on request. Librarians and patrons will welcome this separate index; it saves shelf space, is easy to use, and is recyclable upon receipt of the following year's cumulation. Titles discussed in the Topics volume entries are not included *TCLC* cumulative index.

Citing Twentieth-Century Literary Criticism

When writing papers, students who quote directly from any volume in Gale's literary Criticism Series may use the following general forms to footnote reprinted criticism. The first example pertains to materials drawn from periodicals, the second to material reprinted from books.

[1]William H. Slavick, "Going to School to DuBose Heyward," *The Harlem Renaissance Reexamined,* (AMS Press, 1987); excerpted and reprinted in *Twentieth-Century Literary Criticism,* Vol. 59, ed. Jennifer Gariepy (Detroit: Gale Research, 1995), pp. 94-105.

[2]George Orwell, "Reflections on Gandhi," *Partisan Review,* 6 (Winter 1949), pp. 85-92; excerpted and reprinted in *Twentieth-Century Literary Criticism,* Vol. 59, ed. Jennifer Gariepy (Detroit: Gale Research, 1995), pp. 40-3.

Suggestions Are Welcome

In response to suggestions, several features have been added to *TCLC* since the series began, including annotations to excerpted criticism, a cumulative index to authors in all Gale literary criticism series, entries devoted to criticism on a single work by a major author, more extensive illustrations, and a title index listing all literary works discussed in the series since its inception.

Readers who wish to suggest authors or topics to appear in future volumes, or who have other suggestions, are cordially invited to write the editors.

Acknowledgments

The editors wish to thank the copyright holders of the excerpted criticism included in this volume and the permissions managers of many book and magazine publishing companies for assisting us in securing reproduction rights. We are also grateful to the staffs of the Detroit Public Library, the Library of Congress, the University of Detroit Mercy Library, Wayne State University Purdy/Kresge Library Complex, and the University of Michigan Libraries for making their resources available to us. Following is a list of the copyright holders who have granted us permission to reproduce material in this volume of *TCLC*. Every effort has been made to trace copyright, but if omissions have been made, please let us know.

COPYRIGHTED EXCERPTS IN *TCLC*, VOLUME 81, WERE REPRODUCED FROM THE FOLLOWING PERIODICALS:

American History Illustrated, v. IX, December, 1974. Copyright © American History Illustrated magazine. Reproduced by permission of Cowles Enthusiast Media, Inc. (History Group), A Primedia Publication.—*Boundary 2: An International Journal of Literature and Culture*, v. 22, Fall, 1995. Copyright © 1995 by Duke University Press, Durham, NC. Reproduced by permission.—*Children's Literature Association Quarterly*, v. 8, Summer, 1983. Reproduced by permission.—*Cine-Tracts*, v. 3, Winter, 1981 for "Film Body: An Implantation of Perversions" by Linda Williams. Reproduced by permission of the author.—*Cinema Journal*, v. XVI, Fall, 1976. University of Texas Press, 1976. © 1976, Society for Cinema Studies. Reproduced by permission of the publisher.—*Commentary*, v. 76, December, 1983 for "The Greatest Living American Philosopher" by Josiah Lee Auspitz. Copyright © 1983 by the American Jewish Committee. All rights reserved. Reproduced by permission of the publisher and the author.—*Encounter*, v. 75, July-August, 1990 for "The Resurgence of Pessimistic Pragmatism: Charles Peirce's Legacy" by Lewis S. Feuer. © 1990 by the author. Reproduced by permission of the author.—*International Philosophical Quarterly*, v. XXXII, June, 1992 for "Realism and Idealism in Peirce's Cosmogony" by Douglas R. Anderson. Reproduced by permission of the publisher and the author.—*Journal of Popular Film and Television*, v. 15, Fall, 1987. Copyright © 1987 Helen Dwight Reid Educational Foundation. Reproduced with permission of the Helen Dwight Reid Educational Foundation, published by Heldref Publications, 1319 18th Street, NW, Washington, DC 20036-1802.—*Journal of the History of Philosophy*, v. XIII, October, 1975. Reproduced by permission.—*Menckeniana*, No. 118, Summer, 1991. Reproduced by permission of the Enoch Pratt Free Library.—*Monatshefte*, v. LXVII, Spring, 1975. Reproduced by permission of The University of Wisconsin Press.—*Mosaic*, v. 23, Winter, 1990. © Mosaic 1990. Acknowledgment of previous publication is herewith made.—*Partisan Review*, v. 64, Winter, 1997 for "'We Pragmatists...': Peirce and Roy in Conversation" by Susan Haack. Copyright © 1997 by Partisan Review. Reproduced by permission of the author.—*Popular Music*, v. 9, October, 1990 for "'Everybody's Lonesome for Somebody': Age, the Body, and Experience in the Music of Hank Williams" by Richard Leppert and George Lipsitz. Reproduced by permission of the Cambridge University Press and the authors.—*Prooftexts*, v. 2, September, 1982. © 1982. Reproduced by permission of The Johns Hopkins University Press.—*Revue des Langues Vivantes*, v. XXXVI, 1970, for "Clarence Darrow's Contribution to Literary Naturalism: 'An Eye for an Eye'" by R. Baird Shuman. Reproduced by permission of the author.—*South Atlantic Quarterly*, v. 84, Winter, 1985; v. 94, Winter, 1995. Copyright © 1985, 1995 by Duke University Press, Durham, NC. Both reproduced by permission.—*Studies in Short Fiction*, v. 30, Fall, 1993. Copyright ©1993 by Newberry College. Reproduced by permission.—*The American Scholar*, v. 63, Autumn, 1994. Copyright © 1994 by the United Chapters of the Phi Beta Kappa Society. Reproduced by permission of the publishers.—*The Antioch Review*, v. 13, March, 1953. Copyright © 1953 by the Antioch Review Inc. Reproduced by permission of the Editors.—*The Atlantic*, v. 206, September, 1960 for "The Peripatetic Reviewer" by Edward Weeks. Reproduced by permission of the Literary Estate of Edward Weeks.—*The Henry James Review*, v. 14, 1993. © 1993. Reproduced by permission of The Johns Hopkins University Press.—*The Journal of Religion*, v. 67, October, 1987; v. 75, April, 1995. Both reproduced by permission.—*The Kenyon Review*, v. IX, Autumn, 1947. Copyright © 1947 by Kenyon College. All rights reserved. Reproduced by permission.—*The Monist*, v. 63, July, 1980; v. 65, April, 1982; v. 75, October, 1992. Copyright © 1980, 1982, 1992 The Monist, La Salle, Illinois 62301. All reproduced by permission.—*The New York Times Book Review*, September 20, 1925; March 9, 1997. Copyright © 1925, 1997 by The New York Times Company. Both reproduced by permission.—*The Review of Metaphysics*, v. XXXIII, March, 1980; v. XLVIII, September, 1994. Copyright ©1980, 1994 by The Review of Metaphysics. Both reproduced by permission of the publisher.—*Transactions of the Charles S. Peirce Society*, v. XXVIII, Fall, 1992. Reproduced by permission.

COPYRIGHTED EXCERPTS IN *TCLC*, VOLUME 81, WERE REPRODUCED FROM THE FOLLOWING BOOKS:

Bithell, Jethro. From *Modern German Literature, 1880-1950*, Methuen & Co., Ltd., 1939. Reproduced by permission.—Brakhage, Stan. From *Film Biographies*. Turtle Island, 1977. Copyright © 1977 by Stan Brakhage and the

John Beresford

1873-1947

(Full name John Davys Beresford) English novelist and short story writer.

INTRODUCTION

An early and prolific writer in science fiction and fantasy fiction, Beresford is credited with creating the first significant fictional characterization of a superhuman mind trapped in a world of pedestrian intellect. He was particularly drawn to the world of psychic phenomena and human psychic pathology, and his writings contain thematic plots and incidents relating to altered perspectives, transcendental experiences, dreams, revelations, and fate. Scanning a continuum from intellectual realism to philosophical idealism, Beresford also used his imaginative fancy to subtly instruct his readers on his cherished beliefs and views. These included (and he could argue equally for each), several forms of religion and non-religion, mysticism, faith healing, women's rights, vegetarianism, and social pacifism.

Biographical Information

Beresford, the second son of a church minister and his wife, was born on March 7, 1873, in Castor, North-hamptonshire, England. His childhood was greatly affected when he suffered infantile paralysis which left him physically impaired, walking with difficulty for the remainder of his life. Having been advised by his father that his career options were thus limited by his disability, he passed through formal and informal education without inspiration, eventually settling for a career in architecture at his father's suggestion. However, he remained uninspired and left his London apprenticeship for a job as a bookseller. During this time, he was increasingly exposed to scientific and philosophical books which stimulated his interest in psychology and the psychic sciences. Cultivating friendships with numerous writers, actors and artists (with whom he collaborated on early works), he began writing fantasy fiction and achieved immediate fame. He eventually wrote more than sixty books, numerous short stories, and plays, most of which were respectfully received, but none achieving the critical acclaim as had attended those first literary efforts. He died in Bath, England, in 1947, at the age of seventy-three, survived by his wife and four children.

Major Works

Beresford's autobiographical trilogy, comprising *The Early History of Jacob Stahl* (about the coming of age of a young crippled boy) (1911), *A Candidate for Truth* (1912), and *The Invisible Event* (1915), established immediate literary success. But clearly, Beres-ford's *The Hampdenshire Wonder* (1911) was his most powerful and evocative novel. The story focuses on a young genius alienated by a world of non-comprehending lesser minds unable to communicate with him. This theme, of superior intellect impeded, mutated or destroyed by fundamentalist bigotry and narrow-mindedness, recurred in many of Beresford's subsequent works. Good examples of Beresford's creative best include a collection of stories, *Nineteen Impressions* (1918) and his novel *Goslings* (1913). Another collection of stories, *Signs and Wonders* (1921) searched more deeply into the world of altered minds and psychic phenomena. *God's Counterpoint* (1918) and *An Imperfect Mother* (1920) are additional examples of psychoanalytical novels. Beresford's physical disability contributed to his belief in faith-healing and metaphysics, subjects treated in *The Camberwell Miracle* (1933) and *The Case for Faith-Healing* (1934). His unfinished autobiography was never published.

Critical Reception

Following the publication of his first novels, Beresford gained the respect and attention of such literary greats as D. H. Lawrence, Virginia Woolf, and Bernard Shaw. However, he became increasingly disenchanted with the pressure to continually produce new writings for financial survival. His creativity reached a plateau, and his writings often contained redundant, didactic themes and ideas. Although his work was technically well written, most critical attention remained focused on his earliest novels, which were the more imaginative and captivating, and but for which Beresford might have slipped into literary oblivion.

PRINCIPAL WORKS

The Early History of Jacob Stahl (novel) 1911
The Hampdenshire Wonder (novel) 1911
A Candidate for Truth (novel) 1912
Goslings (novel) 1913
H.G. Wells (nonfiction) 1915
The Invisible Event (novel) 1915
God's Counterpoint (novel) 1918
Nineteen Impressions (stories) 1918
An Imperfect Mother (novel) 1920
Revolution: A Novel (novel) 1921
Signs and Wonders (stories) 1921
All or Nothing (novel) 1928
Real People (novel) 1929
The Meeting Place and Other Stories 1929
The Camberwell Miracle (novel) 1933
Peckover (novel) 1934
The Case for Faith-Healing (nonfiction) 1934
What I Believe (novel) 1938
The Idea of God (novel) 1940
What Dreams May Come (novel) 1941
A Common Enemy (novel) 1942
The Riddle of the Tower (with E. Wynne-Tyson) 1944
The Gift (with E. Wynne-Tyson) 1947

CRITICISM

The Bookman (essay date 1911)

SOURCE: A review of *Jacob Stahl*, in *The Bookman*, June, 1911, p. 144.

[*In the following review, the anonymous critic praises the "bioscopic methods" of Beresford in* Jacob Stahl, *but notes that Beresford fails to fully develop his cast of characters.*]

There is another Richmond in Mr. Arnold Bennett's field, for *Jacob Stahl* goes by rights side by side on the shelf with *The Old Wives' Tale* and *Clayhanger*. Jacob, in whose veins runs mixed blood that includes a little German and a little Jew, falls out of his perambulator in early infancy and injures his spine. He begins to walk when he is fifteen, thanks altogether to the ministrations of a delightful Aunt Hester. Too delicate a plant for the rough and tumble of school, he derives instruction of a slender and disordered character from a tutor, and is eventually articled to an architect. He is weak-willed but imaginative, and though his womenkind have spoilt him more than a little he is yet a person with ideals, in marked contradistinction to his brother. Eric, on the other hand, is vigorous alike mentally and physically, but with a knowledge that "two and two must and ever will make four, a fact for which there is no palliation and no excuse needed," but of a comprehension unable to include an emotional two or a temperamental four. Eric makes a practical success of life. Not so Jacob, or not in this volume at least, though the "Early History" of the title-page seems to promise a sequel. The anti-climax that arrests the course of his first love-story, an episode of the tale that, for all the boldness of its unconventionality, shows singular mastery and restraint in the treatment, puts a sudden end to his lackadaisical way of life in Ashby Sutton, and Jacob descends on London with the rather hazy intention of becoming a successful architect. His introduction to new aspects of "life" takes place under the tutelage of Tony Farrell, a faithfully portrayed example of a not very attractive type. Mr. Beresford, who makes his sudden and unheralded appearance on the stage of authorship with a literary equipment that is almost startling in its completeness, disposes his narrative after the bioscopic methods of Mr. Wells and the already noticed Mr. Bennett. Not yet perhaps can he boast the cultivated dexterity displayed by these authors in handling a whole group of characters, and he is less at pains to picture the influence of his protagonist on an assorted group of men and women than their collected influence on him. Thus, while Jacob as the central figure bulks ever larger, his companions dwindle, and the resultant picture, though it remains life, is still life a little distorted. Jacob has all the limelight. He plays an actor-manager's part. In only one other person does Mr. Beresford allow himself to become really deeply interested. She is called Aunt Hester.

The Bookman (essay date 1911)

SOURCE: A review of *The Hampdenshire Wonder* in *The Bookman*, September 11, 1911, pp. 263-64.

[*In the following review, the anonymous critic offers praise for Beresford's characterization in* The Hampdenshire Wonder.]

Mr. Beresford, we take it, was unknown until six months ago, when he produced *Jacob Stahl*. Now *Jacob* was an admirable example of the bioscopic method, but it never could have prepared any of us for the advent of this amazing Wonder-child. Figure to yourself a professional cricketer who bowls better than any one else in the world, and has suddenly the misfortune to lose a finger. A man of remarkable character in many ways, he concentrates his will on having a son who shall be born without habits. The idea is, you must know, that the son will learn everything that his father can teach him and will furthermore, being born without habits, find himself enabled to start where his father left off, and become an even better bowler. Ginger Stott meets the ideal mother for such a child, and Victor arrives. Here we dive into extravagance at once, but of so remarkable a character that it keeps us almost spell-bound. What follows [in *The Hampdenshire Wonder*] is philosophy, psychology, poetry, allegory, what you will. It is strangely sad, some might find parts of it even repellent. For Ginger's scheme has gone agley, and he has fathered, not the bowler that the world has waited for, but a strange creature with a huge head, the habit, its only one, of complete silence (it never cries and never answers questions), and the power of making you feel, when it looks at you, that you are utterly insignificant. To his bitterly disappointed father Victor is a "blarsted freak," and no more, but the mother (a wonderfully clever and sympathetic study) knows better. For the Wonder has been born ages before the world was ready for him or his kind. With the realms of imagination, of art, music, and poetry dead to him, he yet bears the heavy burden of all knowledge. His lonely childhood, and the effect of his extraordinary personality on the various types of humanity that figure in his little world, are sketched with amazing skill. The parson hates him, his father fears him, Challis, the dilettante squire, is interested in him in a dilettante and scholarly fashion. The village idiot, recognising that here is the only creature he has met having no spiritual kinship with the people about him, tries to make friends with the Wonder, and persecutes him with a kind of loathsome adoration. Only Victor's mother understands. It is difficult to review such a book. Who wants to be referred to the most powerful and moving of its scenes should read, first, the account of the Wonder's birth, where the half-demented father and the crotchety doctor squabble in the cottage parlour the while, upstairs, Intelligence is being born into the world. And there is the scene in the squire's library where the Wonder, having sampled learning as we understand it and known an awful disappointment, tries once, and only once, to tell the two scholars who are questioning him what he is and what is the end of all knowledge. It would, of course, be impossible to let the Wonder grow up. The uncertain manner of his death is finely suggested, and Mr. Beresford is here at his best in the tragic picture of the mother. The book ends, very fittingly, with a remarkable essay on the uses of mystery.

Ludwig Lewisohn (essay date 1920)

SOURCE: "Creation and Analysis," in *The Nation*, Vol. 111, No. 2872, 1920, pp. 74-75.

[In the following review, Lewisohn finds An Imperfect Mother *absorbing and interesting, but faults the novel's concentration on scientific information.]*

Mr. J. D. Beresford explained, in two recent articles of very high interest, the uses to which the novelist could put the discoveries of the Freudian psychology. The problem is an extraordinarily fascinating one. For whatever criticism may be made in detail, there is no doubt that Freud has discovered a very great truth which, like all great truths, is simple enough: Repressed impulses and impressions passively received do not glide through, but become, for better or worse, permanent elements in the affected soul. So soon as we know this the activities of our memory undergo a change in character. Moments that were before but faintly lit leap dazzlingly out of the dim past and help us to account for all we are and do. Now Mr. Beresford's method [in *An Imperfect Mother*] is not to attribute to his characters a self-knowledge illuminated by psycho-analysis. But he explains the life of Stephen Kirkwood through a "slight departure from the normal" which was due "to a severe nervous shock in his early childhood." So far, so good. But it seems to us that Mr. Beresford has actually made his fable richer than he claims and that the nervous shock in question is not really necessary to account for what follows. The case is common. A woman of some artistic gifts and morbidly keen sensibilities, distinctly over-sexed, has married a grubby little shop-keeping person. The two daughters resemble their father. The boy, the youngest, is fine and sensitive and has from the start, to use Freud's drastic term for a thing commonly of infinite subtlety, the Œdipus complex. But almost at the same moment of his adolescence there flashed into Stephen's soul the first perfectly pure yet indescribably tingling influence from a girl, and his mother elopes with a musician. Hence it is not in the least surprising that Margaret Weatherly's smile, her lingering, her momentary preference for him, sink permanently into his subconsciousness, that there occurs an unconscious substitution of her for his mother, which is admirably brought out by the incident of the mother's shocking laugh and the much later laughter of Margaret that recalls it, and that Stephen is lastingly and perfectly contented when he marries Margaret. And Mr. Beresford is quite right in asserting that the happiness of that marriage is not due either to Margaret's beauty or to any special sympathy or understanding that unites these two. That particular marriage simply meant to Stephen the complete abreaction of all his sex-impulses from childhood on. Hence his content. The story is woven with great delicacy and with unobtrusive skill and is remarkably interesting. Yet it is doubtful whether really great fiction would thrive on so much scientific awareness. In the richest creative efforts these things will be organic and immanent as they are in life. It is better for the critic to discover them than for the author to have put them in.

R. Brimley Johnson (essay date 1922)

SOURCE: "J. D. Beresford," in *Some Contemporary Novelists (Men)*, Leonard Parsons, 1922, pp. 97-119.

[In the following essay, Johnson presents an overview of Beresford's writing career.]

There is always an obvious danger in labels; though the temptation to grouping, since one must compare, becomes at times well-nigh irresistible. Mr W. L. George has divided modern novelists into "self-exploiters, mirror-bearers, and commentators": of whom those with most promise "stand midway between the expression of life and the expression of themselves; indeed, they try to express both, to achieve art by criticising life; they attempt to take nature into partnership."

Mr Beresford, certainly, is both a conventional novelist—in the accepted sense of the storyteller—and a modern analytic: at once reflecting and critical. He works through both mediums—self-expression and imagination or, more strictly, invention. He is, both ways, somewhat laboured, after the manner of his day, but he does not neglect either dramatic effects or firm characterisation.

Jacob Stahl, whom one assumes himself, is elaborately set out in *three* novels; and there is really no reason why he should not continue the subject indefinitely, after the manner of Miss Richardson: because "Jacob was ever at the beginning of life." He could never settle in a groove.

On the other hand, *God's Counterpoint* is a genuine creation. Philip, perhaps, is not *quite* human; but the conception has a very marked originality, is consistently maintained, and produces pure drama. It touches, moreover, upon the pre-occupation with sex in a spirit that is both independent and sincere.

In *Housemates* I fancy that we may recognise Stahl—under a new name; in circumstances which, if similar, are yet sufficiently diverse. It is not, in fact, the *same* man: but one with many of the same characteristics, offering very similar occasions for sympathy.

The Hampdenshire Wonder stands plainly apart, as mere fantasy. Here Mr Beresford plays with psychology as Wells and others have played with science: carrying invention beyond reality, whence to philosophise upon the abstract.

His later story, *The Jervaise Comedy,* is frankly a trifle: wooing the spirit of comedy to expose pride. It is a clever enough piece of work, but might have been written by many, almost at any time.

These Lynnekers is no less pure observation than *God's Counterpoint;* but less concentrated and, in one sense, more ordinary. It is based, in fact, on that time-honoured framework of opposition between the hero and his family: they are all slaves to the herd instinct, he alone taking an independent, superior line of conduct. *The House in Demetrius Road,* too, stands alone as a study in personality—ruined by drink, with the devotion accorded the "real" man.

Whatever his mood, however, Mr Beresford writes with assurance. He is not, I imagine, overweighted—like so many of our young writers—with a sense of his own responsibility towards life and art. He has no very obstinate theories upon social questions, no startling ideas about fiction. Writing to-day he can, of course, scarcely escape conscious craftsmanship, hardly avoid the discussion of marriage or sex. But he uses, and accepts, both as incidental to competent work. Being, above all things, a clever professional novelist, he has taken for atmosphere the spirit of his age, using it without pose or passion.

As already implied, Mr Beresford is, perhaps, most original in *God's Counterpoint.* This is the story of an idealist, a Galahad among the quagmires of modernity. Philip Maning has strange, strict ideas about women; which, in fact, amount to mental disease or obsession. Inheriting from a savagely Puritan father elementary conceptions of sin, he mixes the old monastic conception of the "devil in women" with fanatic worship of the Woman. To him, all questions, or aspects, of sex were "thrust into one definite category, labelled 'beastliness.' He had no other word for it, and that one very well indicates his attitude. To him these things were unclean, and even at school he had begun to practise a fastidious cleanliness in his person." Here, as indeed everywhere, he is morbidly oppressed by the sense of sin. A true Calvinist, he dreads all spontaneous emotion, which he calls a temptation of the Evil One. Unclean visions haunt his suppressed nature during the night hours, seriously disturbing his mental balance.

Only a strong character could have survived such a confusion of moral values. Luckily, Philip *is* strong; and, curiously enough, a man of imagination. In consequence, over the ordinary affairs of life he governs himself sternly, but remains attractive, and wears his unique "goodness" with charm. He is, in fact, really impressive—extorting affectionate respect; and the Holy of Holies whereinto he lifts good women shines fair and beautiful. They are, obviously, above sex.

After the preliminary home life, carefully analysed, Philip enters the world through the medium of a somewhat unusual publishing office. Robert Wing "saw literature in terms of 'what suited the public.' . . . It was his affair to provide 'pure' literature for the millions who were sick and tired of eternal immorality." His pet authors did not proclaim or denounce. Their object "might be defined as the effort to prove that to be good was not necessarily to be dull." Himself a hypocrite, and personally sensuous, Wing naturally welcomed the amazing seriousness and sincerity of Philip as a business asset of great value. He believed, with all his soul, what the other professed. And the combination—with humorous interludes—worked well for a time.

Then our hero fell in love: or perhaps one should rather say—imagined that he had found the ideal woman. Evelyn naturally disapproved of his attitude towards her from the beginning, but loved him, trusting familiarity would make him normal. However, his firm shyness and delicate idealism remained unshaken, and all advances towards real intimacy and understanding came from her. Philip dreaded, first marriage itself, and then—more fastidiously—its consummation. Even when half convinced and yielding to the genuine love between them, he felt (or at least soon came to feel) that he had lowered his own ideal and degraded her. They were driven apart.

After which came, inevitably, spiritual collapse. Meeting the ordinary female butterfly, a creature of light passions and totally unmoral, Philip indulged infidelities which would never have tempted a more normal and healthy-minded loving husband.

But "only his body was scarred." The real Philip emerges once more; still an idealist but now also a man. This time he woos his wife humbly yet passionately; and she, being a woman, understands. Because now "he can teach her to love," she trusts the future.

If morbidity here be slightly strained or exaggerated, Mr Beresford redeems the fault by a fine optimism. Philip and Evelyn challenge and conquer fate by sheer courage and strong faith. It is a triumph of character, revealing the best possible to man. For once the perversities of introspection and self-analysis do not produce tragedy, because at bottom the man has a clean heart and a brave soul.

Dickie in *These Lynnekers* begins life with somewhat the same attitude. Sex seemed vaguely "shameful" to him as a boy; and "always, the confinement of a house had had the effect of presenting love in the shape of something to be despised and desperately fought against, something secret and unclean."

But such questions did not, for him, represent life as a whole; they seldom invaded his consciousness, and then quite incidentally. His pre-occupation was, rather, "holding his own" in the practical affairs of life, against the prevailing atmosphere of a curiously ineffective family type.

All the Lynnekers had charm—and prejudices. They were born to drift—pleasantly—towards disaster. They were "the County," and for them, always, "everything went on just the same." Only Dickie, and one of his sisters, were not like that. She married "unsuitably," and drifted to Canada; he, facing the world, saved the family—crowning success by a happy marriage.

Mr Beresford contrives his plot, however familiar its framework, with considerable ingenuity. His hero is a fine, healthy-minded personality: not quite typical, but yet fairly normal. His father and mother are dramatically contrasted, yet harmonious. They and the family all possess strongly-marked individuality. The novel, in fact, is thoroughly interesting, thoroughly competent;

and every way an artistic achievement. But it does not invite detailed criticism.

Personally I am disposed to regard *The Jervaise Comedy* as a slighter effort in the same manner. We have here again a complacently "superior" family group; also disturbed by the "independence" of one member—here, a daughter, who insists on marrying the chauffeur. There is a touch of farce and melodrama in this episode, and though Melhuish, who tells the tale, claims to experience a "form of conversion" in his own love affair, no one troubles very seriously about his changed heart. This, in fact, is no more than a pleasant comedy, pleasantly planned, and well told.

It is permissible, maybe, to regard *The House in Demetrius Road* as one more study in genius and egoism. Greg, indeed, is not precisely an artist, at war with his own imagination, but he has—clearly enough—the potentialities of exceptional greatness and a commanding personality. He combines intimate charm with almost intolerable selfishness and aggressive discourtesy. He is the complete bully.

He is not, however, on ordinary occasions wholly responsible for his own words or deeds, being practically ruined by drink. A less dominating personality would have entirely collapsed before this story begins. It is concerned with the heroic attempt at cure by his secretary and his sister-in-law; two young people of spiritual enthusiasm who fall in love with each other at sight, but are prepared, in the event, for complete self-sacrifice in their devotion to a most thorny endeavour.

Mr Beresford has given us a very graphic picture of exaltation—following effort and hope, reaction—following failure and despair. The cure, in fact, is (for a time) thoroughly successful; but Greg's insane jealousy—at any division of allegiance—brings about the inevitable relapse, and the lovers are practically driven to desertion: holding that they have, after all, a right to happiness.

It would be difficult to imagine a horror revealed more dramatically; a character wasted more utterly; a sacrifice rewarded with more justice. The narrative carries conviction, and rivets our attention throughout.

We all, naturally, read Mr Beresford himself into the *Stahl* trilogy; and certain "confessions" of that hero regarding his literary career rather suggest that our novelist attaches particular importance to his essays in the "fantastic"; but I do not find *The Hampdenshire Wonder* at all convincing. Mr Beresford has been compared to "a man who has overcome a stammer," and so speaks with undue "precision and deliberateness . . . is almost too self-possessed."

In the interpretation of Victor Stott, the Wonder, the "stammer" has conquered him. That incredible infant, whose intelligence o'ertops humanity in the ratio of some millions to one, and who knows everything, condescends occasionally, indeed, to interpret life, but always, to my mind, remains halting and obscure. Mr Beresford appears to be altogether lost among the philosophies. Really, he does not know what to do with the "Wonder" he has created; and ordinary mankind is far more interesting. Victor's father and mother, in fact, are really remarkable people. The pre-natal pre-occupations which are supposed responsible for the phenomenon, are ingeniously suggested, and their attitude towards their uncanny offspring is well thought out. But Victor, being inhuman, fails to interest the plain man. As Challis, the travelled philosopher, remarked: "Take my advice, leave him alone. . . . And meanwhile leave us our childish fancies, our little imaginings, our hopes—children that we are—of these impossible mysteries beyond the hills."

I have very much the same feeling about *The Goslings:* though, obviously, the author intends here to present a philosophy of life. Having imagined that the whole of Europe (and to a lesser degree, also, America) is devastated by a terrible plague which carries off practically the whole male population, he describes for us a world of women, who are driven to nature for mere sustenance—literally earned by the sweat of their brow. They are also, inevitably, deprived of all protection or guidance from the habits and customs of civilisation, thrown back on their own initiative, and compelled to establish a new code of practical morality. Mr Beresford's sympathies are, it is clear, with those who welcome the change and have no yearnings after a return to the old order of things.

The occasion affords him an opportunity for several suggestive criticisms of convention, but as no reform of the social organism is likely to be affected by such means, I am, personally, not interested in the argument. It all seems in some way unreal, almost inhuman. It lacks even adventure.

Mr Beresford's slim volume of short stories called *Signs and Wonders* belongs to the same group, and reveals similar characteristics. The **"Night of Creation,"** however, is an effective ghost-story if somewhat overweighted with comment; and there is one suggestive and interesting, though purely conjectural, idea that recurs in all his most cryptic presentations of "other worlds," where "things happen" in the sky: "The people of that incredibly distant world, walking, as they always do, with their gaze bent upon the ground, are probably unable to see the signs and wonders that blaze across the sky. They, like ourselves, are so pre-occupied with the miserable importance of their instant lives."

This, I take it, variously expressed in Mr Beresford's different visions of the unseen, may be interpreted as a hint of purgatory. In other words, he would surmise, or suggest, that man is no more ready, after death than before, to realise the full Revelation; scarcely, in fact, more spiritual; still intent upon material trivialities. Though somewhat crudely illustrated, the theory has

this justification; that it supports our hope of a gradual, and by no means complete, change through death; a *continuous* spiritual growth towards infinity. Yet the most daring, because most definitely dramatic, of these "guesses at truth," is also—without question—the most real and convincing. **"The Miracle"** offers a fine illustration of spirituality. Eager to reach the essential spirit personality of her dying husband, "poised out of time and space, away somewhere in the void," a wife finds herself wandering among wraiths of humanity, "peering vaguely downwards with bent head and eyes," till one moves "definitely towards her, drawn by the power of her longing." By her own effort she "would compel him to come with her." And "as she came slowly out of some remote distance to a realisation of herself," the "living dead man," given up by "all the specialists," was "sitting up in his bed . . . boastful to be alive again." Love triumphant cries: "I've brought you back, and I am going to hold you here." Mr Beresford has convinced us that so it was.

There are also, in this volume, several attempts at normal character-sketching, based on effects of the war; but they are, for the most part, too vague or general for edification. Like so many of his contemporaries, Mr Beresford is really hampered by the strength of isolated emotions, lacking aim or cohesion. They do not achieve either reasonable criticism or constructive purpose.

He would have spared us the careful record of George Wallace, who wrote a book "without having put pen to paper," had he remembered Henry James and the exquisite pathos of "The Madonna of the Future."

Housemates, on the other hand, though written five years later than the second instalment of *Jacob Stahl,* reads almost like a "study" for that elongated autobiography. The hero, indeed—unlike Jacob—remains an architect: but superficially his apprenticeship is very similar, and his character develops along much the same lines. He is a hesitating, over-modest dreamer of dreams, prone to self-depreciation and self-analysis, yet conscious of power and, by fits and starts, given to startling self-assertion. He is, indeed, completed and dismissed with comparative brevity; but not, therefore, less fully realised or presented. After the usual beginning of a struggle with poverty, and a rude awakening to the complications of real life, he becomes most "unsuitably" engaged and, discovering his mistake, drifts into a boarding-house—where he meets his affinity. He is, as it were, more concentrated than Jacob. The one passion, which from the first proves itself true love, absorbs the man; takes him in hand, transfigures him.

Inwardly, *Housemates,* is pure romance, and wholly satisfying as romance. The personalities of its hero and heroine are individual and strong. But its constructive details fall far below Mr Beresford's usual standard. The minor characters are either commonplace or unreal; the incidents are dull, and Helen's grotesque attempt at supreme self-sacrifice in the cause of friendship strikes a thoroughly false note. It is sheer perverse cant.

We must, however, finally judge Mr Beresford from *The Early History of Jacob Stahl, A Candidate for Truth,* and *The Invisible Event.* The hero himself develops into a successful novelist, the reviews quoted (in *The Invisible Event*) of his first book are taken verbatim from those which actually appeared of *Jacob Stahl,* and therefore his theories of fiction must be assumed the author's. These are mainly expressed in dialogue, or argument, with one Meredith, a fairly successful novelist whom Jacob admires, but criticises.

Meredith declares that modern "realism is not art . . . the realism of Dickens and his school consists, not in reporting the slang and cant phrases of the day, but in inventing a form of speech which shall definitely represent a type to the mind of the reader . . . the artist must bring something to his work, must define something more than a mere replica of his subject. He must express an attitude—the artist crystallises all the elements of an idea into one masterpiece. Nature never does that—not even in humanity."

On the other hand, Jacob wants "data, clearly defined premises; in life I want actuality, as a stimulus for my imagination. Give me correct drawing in a picture or in a novel, and I can work inwards or outwards—whichever it is—from that. But hazy outlines don't provide me with the material I'm looking for."

Elsewhere, Stahl consenting, Meredith proclaims the realist as one who does not "concentrate on the larger emotions—quite the reverse; he finds the common feelings and happenings of everyday life more representative. You may have a big scene, but the essential thing is the accurate presentation of the commonplace."

Jacob will not admit that life should be transmuted by the author's temperament, "translating all your impressions into a sort of phantasmagoria, a sort of general effect." He prefers putting a little piece of life, as he knows it, under the microscope, and not relating it to the whole; indifferent about whether "anything can come of it." Always he seeks to be realistic without being definite . . . to work it all out with the most convincing exactitude.

What, then, does Mr Beresford make of his realism; which is, certainly, a devotion to commonplace detail, though untainted—it seems—with any marked obsession on sex?

The three novels are, undoubtedly, built upon minute observation. They record the surface of life—with immense elaboration. We meet Jacob in a perambulator, and leave him "to face new beginnings" in his forty-first year. On broad lines his was not a particularly eventful life. He fails as an architect; succeeds, once he achieves concentration, as a novelist; has one early love affair, falls under the influence of a soul-fisherman, and marries twice. There are, in reality, few changes of scene, and not a long list of dramatis personæ, but everything moves with extreme deliberation, and is most thoroughly thought out. Jacob himself has a passion for comment, is very sensitive to impressions, and all is told through his mind.

So far, indeed, Mr Beresford conforms to the "new" realism. His observation is not confined to the surface, he does analyse thought. But he retains the method of the materialist, including a vast array of *facts* experienced, things *said,* action and furniture. He works on the old principle, from the outside.

From all which emerges, however, a very vivid, lifelike, and interesting personality. One may say that, with his touch of genius, Jacob is not abnormal. His eternal self-questionings do not kill charm, or even simplicity. Though always thinking and talking about himself, seeing all life and all people as they react on himself, we love the man. Contrary to all appearance, he has moral backbone. There, indeed, lies the secret.

Mr Beresford has shown us a weak creature; almost grotesquely unpractical, offensively modest, idly irresolute, selfishly egotistical. Easily captured by two impossible women, foolishly worshipping a plaster saint, he shuffles through a vast sea of misfortune, seemingly without aim or purpose, obviously destined to final, complete failure. We grow utterly weary, indeed, of his perpetual fumbling for something he calls himself.

Only the *real* Jacob was "ever at the beginning of life"; the very end of his long story is a new beginning; "virtue lies only in the renewal of effort." Five words—"you didn't think so once"—were the "epitome of his life." The mass of mankind regarded them as a reproof, he as high praise; and that was the essential difference.

In other words, he remained always a child, ready and eager for new ideas, new experience; willing to change. There is, indeed, some appearance of finality, or perhaps one would say fulfilment, in the third novel. Speaking according to convention, real love makes a man of him. When stimulated and steadied by the understanding and sympathy of Betty Gale, something real, strong, and unselfish comes to the surface. The vision materialises. We see then that Jacob was, all the while, not only seeking an ideal, but, after his queer fashion, living up to it. After all, the real man was essentially simple-minded, singularly affectionate, fundamentally spiritual. Vigour and will, too, were hidden, not killed.

Because she, too, had innate nobility, the woman accepted, proudly and happily, the last great test. For though she had raised him to both artistic achievement and material success, sure of no more backsliding, still he was not content. He must strive always; always change, develop, wonder, and search.

For still he "lacks sight of some definite, guiding motive that shall one day, he hopes, give form and purpose to the whole." He would still describe himself, in Emerson's words, as a "candidate for truth."

It is not, I take it, Mr Beresford's ambition to offer conclusions about life. Reproduction is his ideal; and the work is masterly. It is an absolutely true picture, very much alive, sincere, thorough, and sane.

There is, however, one issue wherein his passion for exact realism seems to have led him astray; and very possibly it is just this mistaken consistency which may account for a certain heaviness of manner in parts of the story which tries our patience. I have mentioned that Jacob Stahl was slow in thought, and hesitating in action. Nearly always, moreover, he found a difficulty in expressing himself. But Mr Beresford has set himself to write *through* Jacob. Therefore he, too, is perpetually fumbling for words, offering us all the stages by which Jacob first thinks of an idea; then doubts and questions it, finally making some half-dozen attempts to tell someone else about it, or put it in a book. We have, further, re-statements (often the final expression) from friend or wife; which he accepts or rejects.

In fact, Mr Beresford has no scruple whatever against worrying out his thoughts on paper and letting us watch the process. "He can refine emotion until it becomes a fidget." Faith in the "letter" of realism injures some of his best work. Modern novelists, like the rich, talk too much.

He has returned, however, in *An Imperfect Mother* to the manner of *God's Counterpoint.* Here there is no hesitation, no worrying over the analysis of a soul. Stephen, the hero, is a clearly conceived, well-defined character, at once resolute and sympathetic, fixed yet sensitive: true to type with a most marked outline. His "imperfect" mother is no less firmly drawn. In the beginning she had been everything to him—as he remained to her: only a certain waywardness of the artistic brilliancy in the woman baffled his direct youthfulness, and at the crisis of her life misunderstanding proved him inadequate. Then while he developed with rare moral courage and brain vigour to a fine maturity, she found life—as her folly made it—strangely hollow and unsatisfying.

Only where Stephen encountered fate in the person of a half-spoilt beauty wholly adorable, his mother again played providence to her handsome son. Claiming at first his undivided devotion, she came gradually to recognise that the most loving of chains can hold no man against his will. Then the imperfect one reached heroism. Putting aside all jealousy of youth seeking after youth, taking a back seat with seeming gaiety, she made the supreme sacrifice of helping him whom her heart yearned for as hers and hers only; to the attainment of what she knew would separate them for ever. Literally she gave him away.

"In future she would be—just his mother; a useful, elderly relation who was expected to be sympathetic and kind on all occasions; no doubt he would still be polite to her."

Up to a point the boy realised her self-sacrifice; but he could never understand *why* she wanted more than he was ready to give. Her final attitude seemed to him just right. She was "going to be sensible": that was his summary of the affair.

Wherefore because he loved wisely, because his lady, for all her imperious frivolity, admired the "man," they took and held the great gift of love. Joy to youth, sorrow for age, is Mr Beresford's conclusion; and it is reached here through a fine record of average humanity. There is not even the slight strain towards the abnormal we found in *God's Counterpoint,* and yet the characters are perfectly individual, thoroughly alive, and unusually attractive.

I am disposed to think that the story pleases one so entirely, in part because it is in a sense so ordinary. There is no search after subtlety, no superfluity of wonder, no startling discoveries about man's soul. This is not, indeed, Mr Beresford himself looking out at us, giving himself away. He had to *go inside* these people: to observe them, study their personality. But on the other hand he was not misled by appearances, he "got" there. He has given us, in fact, no superficial realism; but a chapter of truth about men and women.

Revolution has an especially profound interest for the present generation. Mr Beresford has here revealed, with sincere conviction, one striking aspect of the effects that experience of the trenches may produce on a sensitive soul. Paul Leaming is, most literally, "possessed" by one idea, one spiritual endeavour, to which he is ready to sacrifice even his own honour. He will, so far as his influence may be strained to extend, prevent bloodshed, subdue the desire to kill, replace violence by brotherly love. He has seen the blood-lust, he knows how easily men slip back into the savage—once they have handled death; torn, or seen others tear, into human flesh. The vision of what may be, once evil passions prevail, haunts his imagination, day and night, as some ghastly nightmare.

Wherefore he thinks, feels, and acts—almost as Christ taught; is what Tolstoy would have us be. To afford occasion for his overmastering gospel, Mr Beresford imagines that English Labour has actually achieved—what the reactionaries are always whispering it desires and, if not crushed, will accomplish: overthrown the government, secured the army, repudiated the constitution, set up Soviets. Obviously, the "Revolution" begets violence. Paul is spurred to give expression to the faith that is in him. He does not at first, indeed, tackle the whole nation, plead with humanity at large. But in his own small village; where he can influence the Lord of the Manor, and can—in some measure—spiritualise the yokels; he instantly plans, preaches, and—for a time—evolves an almost complete, Tolstoyan community. He abolishes (in one small English parish not easily approached from the outer world) private property, distributes food through a democratically elected committee, and revives something approaching the mediaeval.

Soldiering, however, had produced different effects upon the brutal villager who leads the revolutionaries; and Paul is not quick enough to prevent him murdering the hot-headed Mr Leaming, senior, and one other obstinate farmer, whom no reasoning will convince. Only because the Idealist will neither punish nor revenge; since he is ready to let God judge even Jem Oliver; offering brotherhood over his father's corpse; the "miracle" happens.

This is a daring, very suggestive, and most truthful, imaginative feat. Paul's character is drawn with patient, unfaltering intensity. One only hopes that many who have shared his experiences may feel like him, and be able—should similar tests arrive—to prove equally heroic. This is the one lesson worth learning from Armageddon, the one faith all should proclaim with the holy passion of inspired conviction.

I am not sure, however, if Mr Beresford has not rather weakened the force of his message by other traits prominent in Paul. He is one, we read, who had been long mentally paralysed by shellshock. He has a habit of falling into a sort of trance; losing control of himself, not seeing or hearing what is happening to those around him. At such times he realises the mystic meanings of Nature, yearns towards abstract beauty, and gains spiritual confidence, hope for man, and a new faith in God. This may well be the natural soul-complement of his Tolstoyan mind, but accompanied, as we find it, by a lapse to physical inertia and mental groping, it certainly provokes the philistine comment that, after all, Paul is not quite sane: "a dear, fine fellow—but just a little— you know." All of which, to my mind, lessens the great value of what Mr Beresford, I presume, has here set out to teach.

In the closing chapters, a counter-revolution is manœuvred, and the reactionaries bring back the old order: using methods of drastic revenge, wholesale shooting, and what we have learnt to call "reprisals"—which, even among his own people, Paul could not prevent. He is roused, at last, to a sense of national responsibility; and Mr Beresford leaves him full of hope, bound for London "to form a society or something." He had not lost faith in the vision: "he must spend himself in the love of his own kind; and in doing that he must surely express his certainty that the salvation of every living being was finally assured. For was not every man and woman his spiritual equal, and was not he himself assured of some ultimate transfiguration by which he would break the bonds of a physical confinement?"

Once more, I feel, Mr Beresford suffers from not having made up his own mind. He cannot, himself, realise his hero's vision. The problem, the situation, is stated with

vigour and truth, far more so as regards its influence on varied types than I have here space to indicate. But, like all the moderns, he cannot really see his way out, he has no clear conception of a new world, not even a certain sense of its aim or direction.

Probably, **"The Convert"** (in *Signs and Wonders*) is a "study" for this prophecy; though, curiously enough, its actual plot-structure is almost identical with that of Mr Cannan's "Pugs and Peacocks." The scholar-hero of both novelists is shaken out of himself by a world-upheaval, that, destroying his "whole life's work," robs him of "every happiness and satisfaction he ever had." In both cases the brilliant "back-number" steps down boldly to face realities, "hand-in-hand with creative youth"—in the person of a charming, though downright girl-reformer.

The Prisoners of Hartling, closely recalling ***Demetrius Road,*** belongs to Mr Beresford's small group of achievements, and need not be added to his more voluminous experiments.

J. B. Priestley (essay date 1923)

SOURCE: "Fiction," in *The London Mercury*, Vol. VIII, No. 44, June, 1923, p. 208.

[*In the following review, Priestley assesses that, despite some overly conventional elements,* Love's Pilgrim *is a worthy literary effort.*]

Foster Innes is the heir to a barony; he has a club-foot, and is extremely sensitive and reserved, and very much under the influence of a somewhat selfish and worldly mother. He it is who tells the story of his pilgrimage as a lover. He meets Tertia, a cool and pretty flirt, and adores her to no purpose. Then during the War he has a brief but unsatisfactory affair with Nita, who is round-eyed and clinging and engaged to half-a-dozen subalterns at once. Then his family almost but not quite throw him into the arms of Grace, a motherly young person, who unfortunately chooses to fall in love with someone else. Finally, Innes meets the daughter of a new tenant and at last finds in her the woman he can love and who can return his love. But now there are other difficulties, for the girl's father has only just been acquitted of murdering his wife, and he is still living under a cloud. The family objects to such a match, and Innes is now prepared to relinquish his claim to the title and estate rather than lose the girl. Eventually, in a highly dramatic last few chapters, in which the girl's older sister confesses to have committed the murder herself and is promptly killed by the fall of a tree, everything comes right. Innes is happy at last; he saw "the deep, calm soul that loved me selflessly—the Claire that was faithful unto death—and beyond." I quote these phrases because they have a familiar ring; we have met them, or something very much like them, many a time; and indeed, I have outlined the story itself for much the same reason, to show with what familiar situations Mr. Beresford has chosen to deal [in *Love's Pilgrim*]. He has boldly chosen material that is almost the common stock-in-trade of the novelist, the sensitive lame hero, the rather selfish mother, the first disillusionment in love, the heroine of low degree, and all the rest of it, and has trusted his sound craftsmanship and his analytical skill to carry him through. The result is a story that is by no means one of the best things he has done but that is also by no means one of those tired productions that even our best novelists give us every other season or so. Mr. Beresford's sincerity and strong hold upon realities, which have successfully steered him past the reefs and sandbanks of his intellectual crotchets more than once, do not play him false; his actual narrative throughout is attractive and his characterisation, more lightly touched in than usual, is excellent; and if the rather melodramatic finish, the sudden confession of murder, the storm, the blasted elm, and so forth, appears somewhat out of key, too much in the nature of an experiment, at least the powerful forward sweep of the story, moving from cool analysis to drama, carries the reader along with it, and suggests that the last word on Mr. Beresford's art cannot be spoken yet for a while.

A. St. John Adcock (essay date 1923)

SOURCE: "John Davys Beresford," in *Gods of Modern Grub Street: Impressions of Contemporary Authors*, Frederick A. Stokes Company, 1923, pp. 33-39.

[*In the following essay, Adcock surveys thematic elements in Beresford's major works.*]

There seems to be something in the atmosphere of the manse and the vicarage that has a notable effect of developing in many who breathe it a capacity for writing fiction. Not a few authors have been cradled into literature by the Law, Medicine and the Army, but as a literary incubator no profession can vie with the Church. If it has produced no poet of the highest rank, it gave us Donne, Herrick, Herbert, Crashaw, Young, Crabbe, and a multitude of lesser note, and if it has yielded no greater novelists than Sterne and Kingsley, it has fostered a vast number that have, in their day, made up in popularity for what they lacked in genius.

Moreover, when the parsons themselves have proved immune to that peculiarity of the clerical environment, it has wrought magically upon their children, and an even longer list could be made, including such great names as Goldsmith, Jane Austen and the Brontes, of the sons and daughters of parsons who have done good or indifferent work as poets or as novelists.

Most of the novelists moulded by such early influences have leaned rather to ideal or to glamorously or grimly romantic than to plainly realistic interpretations of life and character, and J. D. Beresford is so seldom romantic, or idealistic, so often realistically true to secular and unregenerate aspects of human nature, that, if he did not draw his clerical characters with such evident inside knowledge, you would not suspect that in his beginnings he had been subject to the limitations and repressions that necessarily obtain in an ecclesiastical household.

He was born in Castor rectory, and his father was a minor canon and precentor of Peterborough Cathedral, and, if it pleases you, you can play with a theory that the stark realism with which he handles the facts, even the uglier facts, of modern life is either a reaction from the narrow horizon that cramped his youthful days, or that the outlook of the paternal rectory was broader than the outlook of rectories usually is.

After an education at Oundel, and at King's School, Peterborough, he was apprenticed, first to an architect in the country, then to one in London; but before long he abandoned architecture to go into an insurance office, and left that to take up a post with W. H. Smith & Son, in the Strand where he became a sort of advertising expert and was placed at the head of a bookselling department with a group of country travellers under his control.

Before he was half-way through his teens, he had been writing stories which were not published and can never now be brought against him, for he is shrewdly self-critical and all that juvenilia has been ruthlessly destroyed. He was contributing to *Punch* in 1908, and a little later had become a reviewer on the staff of that late and much lamented evening paper the *Westminster Gazette*. Among the destroyed juvenilia was more than one novel. In what leisure he could get from his advertising and reviewing, he was busy on another which was not destined to that inglorious end. For though *Jacob Stahl* was rejected by the first prominent publisher to whom it was offered, because, strangely enough, he considered it old-fashioned, it was promptly accepted by the second, and its publication in 1911 was the real beginning of Beresford's literary career. Had it been really old-fashioned, it would have delighted the orthodox reading public, which is always the majority, but its appeal was rather to the new and more advanced race of readers, and though its sales were not astonishing, its mature narrative skill and sound literary qualities were unhesitatingly recognized by the discriminating; it gave him a reputation, and has held its ground and gone on selling steadily ever since. One felt the restrained power of the book, alike in the narrative and in the intimate realization of character; its careful artistry did not bid for popularity, but it ranked its author, at once, as a novelist who was considerably more than the mere teller of a readable tale.

Jacob Stahl was the first volume in a trilogy (the other two being *A Candidate for Truth* and *The Invisible Event*)—a trilogy which unfolds a story of common life that might easily have been throbbing with sentiment and noisy with melodramatic sensation; in Mr. Beresford's reticent hands, however, it is never overcharged with either, but is touched only with the natural emotions, subdued excitements, unexaggerated poignancies of feeling that are experienced by such men and women as we know in the world as we know it.

Meredith, in *The Invisible Event,* rather grudgingly praises Jacob Stahl's first novel, *John Tristram,* as good realistic fiction of the school of Madame Bovary. "It's a recognized school," Meredith continued. "I don't quite know any one in England who's doing it, but it's recognized in France, of course. I don't quite know how to define it, but perhaps the main distinction is in the choice of the typical incidents and emotions. The realists don't concentrate on the larger emotions, you see— quite the reverse; they find the common feelings and happenings of everyday life more representative. You may have a big scene, but the essential thing is the accurate presentation of the commonplace." "Yes, I think that is pretty much what I *have* tried to do," commented Jacob. "I think that's what interests me. It's what I know of life. I've never murdered any one, for instance, or talked to a murderer, and I don't know how it feels, or what one would do in a position of that sort."

That is perhaps a pretty fair statement of Beresford's own aim as a novelist; he prefers to exercise his imagination on what he has observed of life, or on what he has personally experienced of it. And no doubt the *Jacob Stahl* trilogy draws much of its convincing air of truthfulness from the fact that it is largely autobiographical. In the first volume, the baby Jacob, owing to the carelessness of a nursemaid, meets with an accident that cripples him for the first fifteen years of his existence; and just such an accident in childhood befell Mr. Beresford himself. In due course, after toying with the thought of taking holy orders, Jacob becomes an architect's pupil. *A Candidate for Truth* shows him writing short stories the magazines will not accept, and working on a novel, but before anything can be done with this, the erratic Cecil Barker gets tired of patronizing him and, driven to earn a livelihood, he takes a situation in an advertising agency and develops into an expert at writing advertisements. Then, having revised and rewritten his novel, he is dissatisfied with it and burns it. He does not begin to conquer his irresolutions and win some confidence in himself until after his disastrous marriage and separation from his wife, when he comes under the influence of the admirable Betty Gale, who loves him and defies the conventions to help him make the best of himself. Then he gets on to the reviewing staff of a daily newspaper, and writes another novel, *John Tristram,* and after one publisher has rejected it as old-fashioned, another accepts and publishes it, and though it brings him little money or glory, it starts him on the road to success, and he makes it the first volume of a trilogy.

Where autobiography ends and fiction begins in these three stories is of no importance; what is not literally true in them is so imaginatively realized that it seems as truthful. Philip of *God's Counterpoint,* who was injured by an accident in boyhood is a pathological case; there are surrenderings to the morbid and abnormal in *Housemates,* one of the somberest of Beresford's novels, and in that searching and poignant study in degeneracy, *The House in Demetrius Road;* but if these are more powerful in theme and more brilliant in workmanship they have not the simple, everyday actuality of the trilogy; they get their effects by violence, or by the subtle analysis of bizarre, unusual or unpleasant attributes of humanity, and the strength and charm of the Stahl stories, are that, without subscribing to the conventions, they keep to the common highway on which average men and women live and move and have their being. This is the higher and more masterly achievement, as it is more difficult to paint a portrait when the sitter is a person of ordinary looks than when he has marked peculiarities of features that easily distinguish him from the general run of mankind.

Although, in his time, Mr. Beresford was an advertising expert he has never acquired the gift of self-advertisement; but he found himself and was found by critics and the public while he still counted as one of our younger novelists and had been writing for less than a decade.

He has a subdued humor that is edged with irony, and can write with a lighter touch, as he shows in *The Jervaise Comedy* and some of his short stories; and though one deprecates his excursions into eccentricities of psychology, for the bent of his genius is so evidently toward portraying what Meredith described to Stahl as the representative "feelings and happenings of everyday life," one feels that he is more handicapped by his reticences than by his daring. He is so conscious an artist that he tones down all crudities of coloring, yet the color of life is often startlingly crude. An occasional streak of melodrama, a freer play of sentiment and motion would add to the vitality of his scenes and characters and intensify their realism instead of taking anything from it; but his native reticence would seem to forbid this and he cannot let himself go. And because he cannot let himself go he has not yet gone beyond the Jacob Stahl series, which, clever and cunninger art though some of his other work may be, remains the truest and most significant thing he has done.

Frank Swinnerton (essay date 1950)

SOURCE: "The Novelists of the Next Generation," in *The Georgian Literary Scene—1910-1935: A Panorama,* Farrar, Straus and Company, 1950, pp. 228-41.

[*In the following essay, Swinnerton praises the "practised and finished craft" of Beresford's work.*]

> But today writers and painters no longer speak from Sinai-clouds. Rather, from the pavement-edge, packed closer than the vendors of penny-toys.
>
> —*Oliver Onions: Little Devil Doubt.*

I turn now to two men who belong more directly than any of the women I have named to the school which was modern in 1910. The major works of both are in the key of Wells and Bennett. *Little Devil Doubt,* by Onions, and the *Jacob Stahl* trilogy of Beresford are alike in the sense that both skim the lives of young men who, with artistic impulses, have their misadventures in business, and especially in the business of advertising. Drawing was Onions's first love; and architecture Beresford's. Both knew from experience what the insides of business offices are like. Both were rueful as to what happens in business offices; and as to what happens to young men whose ambition surpasses performance. There is in the work of both this air of ruefulness; but with Onions it has an accompaniment of joyless jocularity and with Beresford that of a melancholy smile. Onions is harsh, Beresford sad.

It is somewhat the same with the two men as with their work; for Onions has a grimness of demeanour which throws out a suggestion of force and resentment, whereas Beresford, who was early crippled as the result of an unfortunate accident, regarded the world with thoughtful sweetness but without vivacity. Both were realists, in the sense that if they contemplated any scene or circumstance they did it without sentimentality: their reactions to it, though not identical, were in accord. Having seen the world of pushing and unscrupulous men, they did not hide it from themselves by any curtain of false emotion. There it is, they said: what are you going to do about it? Neither would fake an attitude. The strength of both lay rather in associative memory than in imagination.

Onions, a Yorkshireman, was once for a period in control of an Art Department in the Amalgamated Press (publishers of many magazines and weekly periodicals founded by Alfred Harmsworth, Lord Northcliffe), and his first book was published at the beginning of the century. It was a collection of chats in the manner of *The Dolly Dialogues,* but it did not achieve the lightness of the original. He then wrote a number of short stories, many of them powerful and some of them dealing with uncanny themes, which he has collected into volume form as *Tales of a Far Riding, Widdershins,* and *Draw in Your Stool.* But until the nineteen-forties, when he had a new flowering, and achieved a new reputation, with some remarkable historical tales, his chief books were the two semi-autobiographical studies of ambitious young men, *Little Devil Doubt* and *Good Boy Seldom,* and the brief masterpiece of grimness, *In Accordance with the Evidence.* This last, which he injudiciously followed with sequels called *The Debit Account* and *The Story of Louie,* remains in its own genre unsurpassed.

It was begun as a short story; and it grew by the demands of its material to the length of a brief novel. It arose from the notion that a young student of shorthand, bent upon murdering a rival, might obtain from that rival, under pretence of speed-exercise and subsequent transcription, a confession of suicide. He would thus clear his own path, and escape detection. The ruse suc-

ceeds; the tale, being told in the first person singular, is an exercise in that harsh vigour for which Onions's character yields all the stuff. *In Accordance with the Evidence* is not a pretty book; the manner of it is even common and gritty, as such a theme demands that it should be; but it is like no other book, and it bears rereading after its dénouement has lost all surprise. It has, that is to say, a permanent quality.

The remaining realistic works of Onions lack momentum; one reads them with respect for their veracity, but one is conscious that the author is not a natural creator of illusion. He has no magic. And in the case of *Little Devil Doubt* and *Good Boy Seldom,* both of which are very sincere books based upon experience, the biographical method has a serious defect. It has always, in the work of every writer who has essayed it, had this defect. A novelist using, with however much skill and finesse, the skeleton of his own life and memory, tends to leave his central figure a colourless nonentity, a something to which experiences occur. For himself, that central figure is filled in by substantial memory—by egotism; but for the reader the central figure, a name only, represents vacuum. He has traits, but no character. He may suffer; but he is not objectively present. That is a cause of loss of interest in the progress of the book; for unless every detail has importance of its own (which it has for the writer) the book ceases to hold attention. It is the same whether the book is a narrative or an introspective study of personality; for unless the author deliberately creates for his chief actor a personality larger than life, there is nothing upon which the reader can fix his eye or his imagination. *Little Devil Doubt* and *Good Boy Seldom* are iridescent to the author, because they are charged with the colours of living memory: to the reader, who unfortunately, however eager, has no comparable self-identification, they are dead because recognition of truth is an insufficient challenge to sympathy.

This criticism, in effect, could be levelled with almost as much force at the *Jacob Stahl* trilogy of Beresford, which has the advantage, however, that Beresford does make recognizable persons of those with whom Stahl is brought into contact. Whether these are men or women, they are seen—shall we say?—with greater malice than any of Onions's characters; with clearer incisiveness. Moreover, there is an attempt to create the personality of Jacob Stahl: the other people in the tales do react to such a man, and criticize him as if he were there. We come to believe that however lacking he may be in the positives of human nature, at least he is rich in negatives. But if you take away from *The Early History of Jacob Stahl, A Candidate for Truth,* and *The Invisible Event* the plain veracity with which they tell what happened to Jacob Stahl, I wonder how much is left for the imagination to dwell upon?

As if in response to that criticism, for he gave a truthful answer to any question one put to him, Beresford only once after the publication of *The Invisible Event* returned to the personal memoir. He probably saw its weakness as clearly as anybody could do. He experimented with other technical methods, and went so far as to tell a couple of mystery stories; but while his most vigorous novel is probably *The House in Demetrius Road* (also his greatest success, ruined by the outbreak of the First World War), his most characteristic books were those in which he sought to express in the form of fiction some of the philosophical conceptions of the modern world. He was always a reader of philosophy, was always interested in current ideas. His books tended more and more to present these ideas, and his reflections upon intellectual tendencies, in the form of stories. What Rose Macaulay did with mirth and ridicule, Beresford did meditatively and with greater respect for the thoughts of others. Where Rose Macaulay dismissed what her rather old-fashioned mind did not much relish, Beresford absorbed it all without for a moment changing his expression of resigned calm. "What is happening in the world?" he asked; and by the world he meant the universal mind. And instead of answering, as Rose Macaulay might briskly do, "A lot of nonsense," he inclined his ear gravely, patiently for an answer.

He wanted to know whatever men thought. His thirst for such knowledge was unquenchable. That early book of his, *The Hampdenshire Wonder,* which some suppose to be the tale of a monster, is in reality a dream fantasy, the tale of a child who fulfilled Beresford's own ambition, to be as full of knowledge as the *Encyclopædia Britannica.* Health and temperament and circumstance were against him in the personal quest for omniscience. A delicate boyhood, with its lasting effect upon his constitution, greatly delayed his maturity. Failure in muscular energy accounted for the absence of all boisterousness from his work. Because of such delicacy, Beresford's early reading was desultory, and it was only after other ways of life had been tried that he became at last a writer and systematic reader. First he planned to be an architect; but, tiring of architecture, he wrote advertising copy. Novel-writing was, if not an after-thought, a slowly-developed aim, and it was not until he was nearly forty that he joined the ranks of those who were known in the 1910's as "the younger generation of novelists."

Even then, in 1911, when he was influenced by the vogue for which *The Way of All Flesh, Tono-Bungay,* and *Clayhanger* had been original models, he was far from being one of the joyous amateurs. On the contrary, he had less profusion than mastery. His hand was firm; he was not adventurous; it was his own story that he candidly related. And the story? The man? Not without significance are the facts that he was at one time an expert chess-player and that his chief hobby was joinery. Architecture; chess; joinery; all of them crafts of form and adjustment and rule. Beresford wrote many books; and not one of those books was casual or untidy or tumultuous. All were written with precision and scrupulousness; all are reflective and without colour. If one cannot read them with excitement, one does at least read them with respect and deep admiration of the skill, the practised and finished craft of their opening, development, and resolution.

FURTHER READING

Bibliography

Gerber, Helmut E. "J. D. Beresford: A Bibliography." In *Bulletin of Bibliography and Magazine Notes*, 21, 1956.
　　Comprehensive listing of works.

Criticism

Chevalley, Abe. "J. D. Beresford." *The Modern English Novel*, pp. 228-35. New York: Haskell, 1973.
　　Offers discussion of Beresford's techniques, themes and fictional characters.

Shanks, Edward. Review of "All or Nothing." In *The London Mercury* XVII, No. 101 (March 1928): 592-94.
　　Briefly discusses Beresford's style and strengths in writing themes which reach beyond reality.

Stableford, Brian. "J. D. Beresford." In *Supernatural Fiction Writers: Fantasy and Horror*, Vol. 1, pp. 457-61. New York: Scribners, 1985.
　　Discusses Beresford alone and in comparison with other contemporaneous writers.

The following sources published by Gale contain further coverage of Beresford's life and career: *Contemporary Authors,* Vols. 112, 155; *Dictionary of Literary Biography,* Vols. 162, 178.

David Bergelson

1884-1952

(Full name David Rafailovich Bergelson) Russian novelist, short story writer, and playwright.

INTRODUCTION

Often cited by critics as one of the foremost Yiddish authors, David Bergelson is known for his intense, brooding characters who act against a backdrop of broad social change. Early novels and short stories such as the highly acclaimed *Arum Vokzal* (1909) address the decay of Jewish institutions, symbolized by the *shtetl* or traditional village, and the birth of a new way of life in the cities of eastern Europe. These works are most noted, however, for the intensity with which the author depicts his characters, and for his moody portraits of troubled lives. After World War I, Bergelson's focus shifted from the personal to the social, and from the death of the past to the birth of the future. His work from 1926 onward reflected his increasing enthusiasm for the new Communist system in Russia; and in the view of many critics, his tendency toward propaganda blunted the impact of his later writing. Bergelson's language of choice gives his writing added significance: linguistically related to German, Yiddish was once spoken by some 11 million Jews, but by the 1990s had become all but extinct. The Holocaust dealt the language its most severe blow; ironically, much of the remaining damage was done by the Stalinist regime that Bergelson supported, which wiped out Yiddish in part through outright murder of Jews (Bergelson's own fate), and in part through forced assimilation. Bergelson has come to be considered one of the leading stylists of the language's late period, along with Sholem Aleichem, I. L. Peretz, and Mendele Mocher Sforim.

Biographical Information

Bergelson was born in the town of Okhrimovo, in the Ukraine, in 1884. The youngest child in a family of Hasidic Jews, he lost both of his parents before the age of fifteen: his father, a well-to-do merchant, died when Bergelson was nine years old, and his mother when he was fourteen. In his late teen years, he lived with older brothers in Kiev, Odessa, and Warsaw, and augmented his religious education in the Old Testament and Talmud with readings in Russian, Hebrew, and Yiddish literature. He also played the violin and around this time began to write, initially in Hebrew. Later, with the short story "Der Toyber" (The Deaf One) in 1907, which would be adapted as a successful play two decades later, he inaugurated a

career of writing in Yiddish. Unable to find a publisher for his novella *Arum Vokzal* (At the Depot), Bergelson self-published it by subsidizing the printing costs; released in Warsaw in 1909, the book gained him widespread praise from critics. The subsequent half-decade was one of the most fruitful periods of Bergelson's career, yielding a number of acclaimed works such as *Nokh Alemen* (1913; *When All Is Said and Done*); but with the coming of World War I, Bergelson fell silent for a number of years. In 1919 he published *Opgang* (Departure), and soon began to take an interest in Communism. He did not settle in Bolshevik Russia initially, but traveled widely; upon his return to his homeland in 1926, however, he fully committed himself to the Communist cause. From 1929 to 1934, he again went on a series of journeys, including a visit to the United States. The mid-1930s found the Soviet Union at the height of the Stalinist terror—and, ironically, at the height of the leader's popularity, particularly with intellectuals abroad. Bergelson threw himself with zeal into the task of building socialism, doing his part with novels, plays, and stories which advanced Soviet themes. This era also saw the publication of *Birobidzhan Dertzeilungen* (1934; *The Jewish Autonomous Region*), in which Bergelson offered a highly positive portrayal of an area to which Stalin had resettled a large number of Jews. In later years, Bergelson began to be disillusioned with the Stalinist system, and in his last significant work, the play *Prince Reuveni* (1946), he seemed to promote the idea of a Jewish homeland. In 1949, as Stalin embarked on another wave of terror—this one particularly anti-Semitic in character—the secret police arrested Bergelson. He was executed three years later in Siberia.

Major Works

The decade that followed the beginning of World War I marked a great divide in Bergelson's career. This time of transition separated a short early period, in which Bergelson wrote much of his most acclaimed work, from a much longer phase that followed his "conversion" to Communism in the mid-1920s. His later writings included several notable works, but the author's enthusiasm for the cause of socialism tended to override the serious character portrayal that had gained him notoriety with *Arum Vokzal*. That first novella set the tone for much of Bergelson's early writing: brooding and impressionistic, it offered quite a different view of *shtetl* life than the romanticized image presented by other Yiddish writers such as Sholom Asch. The depot serves as the locus of the novel's action, a place which draws to it characters such as Rubinshteyn, a failed businessman who nurtures a fantasy life as a bulwark against the frustrations of his daily existence. As its title indicates, *When All Is Said and Done* (sometimes rendered as "The End of Everything") centers around a farewell of sorts. Mirel Hurvitz, raised in the traditional fashion, finds that her upbringing offers her little help for adulthood: forced into an unhappy marriage by her father's financial problems, she faces a world bereft of solace. Bergelson carried this notion of leavetaking, of bidding farewell to the past, into a larger context with his novel *In a Fargrebter Shtot* (1913; In a Backwoods Town) and the novella *Opgang*. The former offers a negative portrayal of a small town through the medium of satire, and the latter is a dark portrait of another community haunted by suicide. The last book of Bergelson's early phase, *Opgang* was followed by several pieces of historical fiction set in the Russian Civil War (1918-20), when the Bolsheviks consolidated their control over the country. Among these books was *Midas Hadin* (1926; Measure of Justice). With *Penek* (1932), Bergelson—by then a committed Communist—presented the first in a set of coming-of-age novels known collectively by the name of the second book, *Baym Dnieper* (1936; At the Dnieper). Together they depict the growth of the boy Penek, a semiautobiographical character who rejects traditional Jewish ways to serve the cause of revolution. After Bergelson returned to Russia for the last time, he visited the Jewish Autonomous Region of Birobidzhan, and wrote a set of short stories so complimentary to the regime that the Soviets published an English translation as *The Jewish Autonomous Region*. But his *Prince Reuveni*, a drama presented more than ten years later, reflected growing antipathy toward Stalinism: ostensibly a propaganda piece urging Jews to help build socialism, it has been seen as a subversive exhortation to support the quest for a Jewish homeland—a decidedly anti-Stalinist notion. Few of Bergelson's works have been translated into English: hence Golda Werman's *The Stories of David Bergelson: Yiddish Short Fiction from Russia* (1996) offers a substantial contribution to the body of the author's work available to English-speaking readers.

PRINCIPAL WORKS

Arum Vokzal (novella) 1909
Nokh Alemen [*When All Is Said and Done*] (novel) 1913
In a Fargrebter Shtot (novel) 1913
Opgang (novella) 1919
Midas Hadin (novel) 1926
Penek (novel) 1932
Baym Dnieper (novel) 1936
Birobidzhan Dertzeilungen [*The Jewish Autonomous Region*] (short stories) 1934
Prince Reuveni (drama) 1946
The Stories of David Bergelson: Yiddish Short Fiction from Russia (short stories) 1996

CRITICISM

Soviet Literature (essay date 1947)

SOURCE: "Selections from a Jewish Classic Writer," in *Soviet Literature*, September, 1947, pp. 63-64.

[*In the following essay, published before Bergelson's arrest, a Soviet publication presents the author as a hero of socialist literature.*]

David Bergelson is a distinguished Jewish writer of the modern school whose novels rank with the classics of Jewish literature.

Bergelson's books are a product of a life's close scrutiny of complex social relations. His first short stories were published in the dark days of reaction that followed the defeat of the Russian revolution of 1905 and describe the life of the *nouveaux-riches* and their hangers-on in remote provincial towns, their cynical double dealing in human feelings and relations, stagnant traditions which corrupt the human soul. His works are permeated with bitter contempt for "petty shopkeepers", as Gorky called this group of society, and great compassion for his heroes, young people, hopelessly perishing in a contaminating and inhuman world.

In one of his best pre-revolutionary works *Mirele* (1910), the writer depicts the life and fate of Mirele, a girl from a "pauper aristocratic" family, whose youth is sold by her parents, marrying her off to the scion of a rich family in order to improve their financial status. Mirele longs for a happiness of her own, however small and pathetic, but in the long run, she surrenders to an inevitable fate, with all her desires thwarted and her hopes frustrated.

European critics draw a parallel between Bergelson's Mirele and Flaubert's Emma Bovary.

David Bergelson was born in the 90's of the last century in a provincial town of the Kiev district where he spent his boyhood and youth, and the impoverished Gurovitzes, the upstart Burnesses, Mireles, maimed by their upbringing and the truth-seeking students Libokesses, the heroes of his writings, were all familiar to him from his childhood days.

But all Bergelson's heroes, the humiliated and crippled miller (*The Deaf*), and his daughter, dishonoured by his employer's son and forced in the end to take her own life, the provincial student-democrats, the heartbroken Mirele—none of them was able to find a way out from the conditions imposed upon them by their environment.

And only after the October Revolution, as was appropriately pointed out by Isaak Dobrushin, critic and historian of Jewish literature, in his introduction to Bergelson's *Selected Works*, "did Bergelson find that his favourite heroes had at last come upon the right track, which he had so unavailingly sought for them throughout the years of his literary work."

In the obscurity of a provincial town Bergelson perceived the man of tomorrow in a toolmaker, Leiser, the son of the town doctor, who takes up arms in the struggle for his people's happiness. And in contrast Bergelson tells of a young man *(Eternal Slave)* who emigrated from tsarist Russia and returns as an "American tourist." He comes back with a bank account and with the notion that "a city without the rich is—how should one put it—like weekdays without a holiday."

But life in his native town had changed, the townsfolk were employed in honest labour and a life of social activity, and the rich, with whom he wanted to mingle, had disappeared without trace. And even the youngsters harkening to the "American wisdom" of the tourist jeered and taunted this spectre from another world.

It is only after the Revolution that Bergelson's heroes begin to comprehend social relations and deliberately bind their life with the interests of their liberated country.

Even their outward appearance has changed. His heroes now are "sturdy fellows" with "laughing eyes" like Happy Wind Velvell, foreman of a carpenter's brigade in the Soviet Autonomous Region of Birobijan, or the collective farmers, workers and builders—they are all people of labour. In yesterday's "apron-string kids," the writer discovers today a readiness for heroic deeds backed by selfless perseverence and great will power; and these newly-acquired inner qualities allow Godashvili, the Caucasian Jew of *In the Mountain Gorge,* to score a victory in unequal contest with the fascists in World War II.

The theme of the mutual friendship of the peoples is prominent in Bergelson's post-revolutionary stories.

This sentiment brings together a taciturn railwayman Makar and Meyer Shlain, an evacuée who settled down at a remote railway junction *(By the Light of the Fires).* Thanks to the thoughtful consideration of this Russian, who hides his feelings under a mask of unfriendliness— Meyer Shlain steps into a new life by the light of fires of the post-war construction works.

Bergelson's style of writing has always been distinguished by lyricism and profound and intricate psychological pattern.

Charles A. Madison (essay date 1968)

SOURCE: "Dovid Bergelson: Novelist of Psychological Refinement," in *Yiddish Literature: Its Scope and Major Writers,* Frederick Ungar Publishing Company, 1968, pp. 426-48.

[In the following excerpt, Madison presents an overview of Bergelson's life and work.]

Dovid Bergelson was born near Kiev in 1884. His father, already elderly, was a Hasid, well versed in He-

brew religious tradition, a wealthy merchant in lumber and wheat. The most prominent citizen in town, he frequently entertained neighboring businessmen and pious scholars. Dovid, a precocious child, readily absorbed the talk at his father's table as well as the personal peculiarities of the participants. At the age of four he began going to *kheder,* and for the next decade studied Hebrew books on Judaism. In 1901, with both his parents dead, he went to Kiev to live with a much older brother. By that time he was already reading Russian and Hebrew books and felt quite at home in his new and comparatively enlightened environment. He had also been practicing writing for several years and was giving much of his time to a novel in Hebrew—which was never published—undeterred by the awareness that his older brothers and sisters ridiculed his literary ambition.

After preliminary efforts at Yiddish composition, Bergelson completed **"The Deaf One"** in 1906 and *About the Depot* two years later. None of his early attempts to see his work in print were successful; editors either rejected his stories or did not even trouble to acknowledge them. When he sent a manuscript to Peretz, he received no reply. Encouraged, however, by friends who were also fledgling writers, Bergelson went to Warsaw, then a center of Yiddish publishing, and arranged for publication of *About the Depot* by assuming part of the cost. The brief narrative, issued in 1909, was generally acclaimed as a fresh and vivid portrayal of Jewish middlemen and a positive addition to the burgeoning Yiddish literature. A first review stated: "It has a mood, a feeling—and it is difficult to grasp its origin, its magic." Another critic hailed Bergelson as "an artist of both wisdom and talent, with a style of his own, with his own view of the world." All were surprised to learn that the author was in his twenties, as the story gave the impression of long familiarity with habits and attitudes of Jewish merchants and *luftmenschen* and of seasoned insight and understanding.

In this story the depot is the center of activity for neighboring businessmen, brokers, agents, porters, and hangers-on. Among them are men of shrewdness and enterprise as well as futile ne'er-do-wells, the serious and the wits, the smug rich and the anxious and ingratiating poor. For a little while after the train arrives there is a great deal of bustle and excitement; when the train leaves, life about the depot lapses into its trivial drabness. The narrative is concentrated on Rubinshteyn, an intelligent and well-educated young man who has no head for business and is frustrated at every turn. Although aware of his incompetence and his inability to stand up against shrewd and aggressive competitors, he feels impelled to make a show of business activity. In time he loses the capital with which he started. His personal life is no more satisfying. His first wife, who was beautiful and whom he loved deeply, died shortly after their marriage; his second wife is homely, sickly, and clumsy, and he soon leaves her and lives in a peasant's house near the depot. He is daily aggravated by failure and the mockery of unsympathetic observers.

Angered one day by one of these men, he slaps him, is sued, and has to spend a fortnight in prison. When released, he resumes his listless, daydreaming, hate-ridden existence.

About the Depot is an impressionistic prose narrative. It depicts Jewish life in the small town neither romantically, as did Sholom Asch, nor naturalistically in the manner of S. Weissenberg, but with a sensitivity of mood and an incisiveness of feeling. Shortly after the book's appearance Bergelson explained his method of writing in a letter to S. Niger:

> This is how I write: First is born the mood of the story together with the main character (the latter almost always not quite clearly) and so affects the soul that it becomes almost unbearable. . . . With the mood comes a strange yearning for that unique aspect of the world which brings in the protagonist and the mood. My entire aim thereafter is to express this mood together with the life and events which occur around it and (if one might say it) in it.

What he succeeded in doing was to infuse the dreariness of their environment into the characters he depicted; the atmosphere of repression, fear, and weariness prevailing in Russia during the 1900's weighted the pages of this and later stories—yet was brightened by a style of acute sensitivity and verbal scintillation.

"The Deaf One," a long short story which he later successfully dramatized under the title ***The Bread Mill,*** reveals Bergelson's strong sympathy for the poor and oppressed. A deaf mill-hand, uneducated and not very bright, is painfully sensitive of his lack of hearing. Broadboned and middle-aged, with a scarred, strained face, he is anxious to know what the other workers are saying but is ashamed to expose his deafness by asking. When spoken to, he makes believe he hears and replies noncommittally. He falls from a height when a rope breaks and is laid up. His daughter, who works as a servant in the miller's house, visits him and her hard weeping troubles him, since he knows that she has been annoyed by the miller's wanton son. Soon after she commits suicide and he is called to the scene.

> Someone pulled his sleeve and showed him the ceiling. He looks: a rope hangs there from a hook. He now understands that she had hanged herself and he wants to ask, "Why?" but doesn't ask. He takes a look at the old Jewess who stands at the head of the corpse, her face in pain, hunched, her toothless mouth open, her head thrown back with eyes closed and face awry. She wept presumably with a heart-rending voice, but he is deaf and doesn't hear. He also makes a wry face, also tries to cry, but can't.

Bereaved and distraught, unable to sleep, eager to avenge himself on the greedy miller and his worthless son, he becomes almost deranged. When he sees a cow outside his window, he assumes it to be the miller's and cuts off its tail with an axe—only to learn the next

morning that the cow belonged to a poor dairywoman. Written in the wake of the abortive revolution of 1905 and amid widespread restlessness, the story stresses the abuse and exploitation of the poor by the callous rich, but intimates that the workers are developing a spirit of rebellion—even though in the futile and stuttering manner of the deaf one.

The End of Everything (1913) was Bergelson's first major novel. It was serialized in Wilno's *Die Yiddishe Welt* (*The Jewish World*) and was highly lauded on publication. Sensitively impressionistic in treatment, acutely psychological in character analysis, almost Chekhovian in mood, the narrative stresses the disintegration of Gdaliah Hurvitz, a wealthy and learned Jew, the rise of the gross and aggressive businessmen, and the pathetic chaos of generations in transition. Most of all, however, it concentrates on the fate of the intelligent, well-educated, and handsome Mirel Hurvitz, who cannot adjust herself to a world governed by coarseness and cupidity. The only daughter of refined and respectable parents in the grip of financial decline, she suffers from frozen feelings which make her behavior pathetically foggy.

Her impulses and moods hasten her disintegration. She breaks her engagement to a youth deeply in love with her but continues to interest herself in the affairs of his family; she permits a lame student to accompany her on long walks and yet treats him shabbily; she has a high regard for her father but cannot get along with her conventional and silently accusing mother. Sometimes she wonders what makes her behave the way she does. "She smiles and is silent, as if on purpose. . . . Someone might think she has much to say and keeps quiet because she is too wise." She does not know what she wants, what is troubling her, but is keenly aware that "her life sinks in dullness."

After much hesitation she agrees to marry the son of a rich man in order to bolster her father's financial precariousness, for she cannot see him depressed by it. "His sad appearance shattered her. Always she had believed that he, her father, is strong and can do everything, in order to be proud and not let herself down. And now she saw him for the first time helpless and with the mien of a lost bankrupt." At the celebration of her betrothal, repelled by her fiancé and his half-drunk father, she leaves them and locks herself in her room. Eager to break the engagement yet unable to let her father down, she is moody and restless. "It seemed to her that she did not live like other people, that she was always alone, on the outside of life, in *tohu-vohu*, and wanders as if lost from childhood in an evanescent, confused dream, which has no beginning and no end."

Marriage does not alleviate her sadness and boredom. The prospect of the same shallow banalities day after day frightens her. Anxious for some form of release, she thinks of suicide. Rejecting her husband's advances one night, she wakes the next morning feeling "something heavy and repulsive weighting her spirit, just as if her heart were dipped in something filthy. And outside a cloudy sky showed a new dreary Sunday and spread its sole boring thought: a new week . . . a dreary week . . . an empty week."

A visit home only intensifies her depression. On her return a divorce is agreed upon and she insists on going through an abortion. Alone and miserable, she feels "as if someone stood bent over her head, choking her, reminding her: 'You have destroyed your life . . . and it is lost, forever lost.'" She goes away, and no one knows where.

Mirel Hurvitz is the first girl in Yiddish literature to behave not like a traditional Jewess but like a unique individual at once emancipated and fettered to subconscious ties of the past. Her sense of refinement and intellectual sensitivity, sharpened by generations of pious and learned ancestors, kept her from acquiescing in the coarseness and shallowness of her contemporaries. No man pleased her completely—so few matched her qualities or stirred her emotions—and her behavior toward her husband, who is good and well-intentioned, if foolish, is at once cruel and unmerited. Yet she is unquestionably a great fictional creation. Bergelson reveals the inner goodness of her being, her deep maladjustment, her futile striving to rise out of the emotional morass in which she found herself. Like her father, she has neither the will nor the strength to make amends and permits herself to drift to perdition. Her moodiness and misery are depicted with keen sympathy and psychological insight. In her failure to adjust is reflected the dispirited and doleful attitude of the Jewish youth in Russia after the failure of the 1905 revolution. Bergelson was not unaware of the novel's literary excellence: "The book is *Jewish*," he wrote to Niger. "I love it and it seems to me *to have a soul*. At the end one may become reflective, but one can also take the Book of Psalms and pray for the souls of both Gdaliah and Mirel."

In *A Coarsened City* (1914), Bergelson provides another aspect of the social satire that characterized his first decade as a writer. Heretofore he had depicted his own intimate environment; now he dealt objectively with people as he observed them with the perspicuity of the novelist. Burman, a student who did not complete his course, is appointed government rabbi in a neglected, sleepy border town. He is soon affected by the lazy and languid atmosphere. "He sat in his bachelor quarters. There everything was dirty and gray: gray the walls and the balcony, gray the pile of dusty legal tomes, which looked upon him so sadly—as if they wished to lead him in the right direction and say critically: 'Burman, you're going around idle, Burman. . . . You'll have a bad end.'"

The grandson of a man of wealth, recently deceased, comes from another town to claim his inheritance. Unlike his grandfather, he refuses to give the charity expected of him, and behaves in other ways to antagonize the people. He is refused the office of collector of the meat tax, held by his grandfather, and in the ensuing quarrel the butchers beat him up and he dies. Other aspects of the town are equally coarse and common: marriages are mercenary events; women indulge in sordid affairs; businessmen try to get the best of one another. Burman becomes resigned: "The world is mud, as I am a Jew." Even the few educated men and women lack sensitivity and refinement; the general dullness prevails. Thus the narrative becomes a stinging satire on the lack of idealism and decency in certain sections of the burgeoning bourgeoisie of prewar Russia.

World War I depressed Bergelson and inhibited his literary activity. In 1933 he recalled:

> During the war I wrote almost nothing for a variety of reasons: the war oppressed me, and it seemed as if belles lettres had become superfluous. There was also no possibility of publication, as the Czarist government had stopped all Yiddish printing. I was not even in the mood to complete the things I had already begun. This general crisis made me feel that with *Departure* I would write my last book, that I had no more to say, no more to write.

The revolution of 1917 revived his spirit and his literary activity. He became one of the founders of the Kiev League for Culture. He also participated in the editing of *The Yiddish Almanac,* in which **"The Deaf One"** appeared, and in anthologies which included the writings of both established and new authors. The civil war and the resulting pogroms caused him much grief—he lost an unpublished novel in the pogrom that occurred where he then lived. A visit to Moscow in 1920 did not quiet his perturbation and he left for Berlin a year later. There he and Nister tried to edit a periodical. At that time he arranged to contribute stories to the New York *Forverts* and the Warsaw *Folkszeitung.*

For several years he was subject to intellectual dichotomy. As an idealist and skeptic he was both repelled by the social injustices of capitalism and equivocal about the promises of Bolshevism. In 1926 he persuaded himself that the Soviet Union was the only place in which Yiddish literature could develop into full efflorescence. He left *Der Forverts* and began to write for the communist *Freiheit.* He also started to edit the short-lived pro-Russian monthly, *In Shpan (In Harness),* and urged Yiddish writers the world over to "orient themselves toward Moscow," asserting that the only hope of Jewry was "the emerging Jewish center in the Soviet Union." On a visit to Moscow he accepted co-editorship of *Emes (Truth),* declaring himself a Soviet writer and in favor of the dictatorship of the proletariat. He continued to live abroad, however, and late in 1928 came to the United States, where he remained for six months. Neither America nor Western Europe gave him the peace of mind he craved, and he came to believe that only in Russia could he function naturally as a writer—drawing on the rooted Jewish environment of his characters. With the capitalist world in a state of economic collapse and Europe in the darkening shadow of fascism, he decided in 1933 to return to his native land. In the interim he had written and published several volumes of fiction.

Departure, begun in 1913 and published in 1921, is like *The End of Everything* a work of lyrical and moody wistfulness. It, too, depicts the decline of the traditional Jewish way of life and the resulting restiveness of the younger generation. The style is again at once incisive and tentative, so that the atmosphere of doubt prevails throughout the action. Sated and dull philistines mingle with lonely and unhappy intellectuals in a world undergoing painful transition.

The story begins with Melekh's death in Rakutne, presumably by suicide. His friend Khaim Moshe comes to town to ascertain its cause. Melekh had been a revolutionary, had served two years in prison, and had come to Rakutne to open a drug store. The townspeople are naturally very inquisitive; whatever occurs to one is soon known to all. Thus when Ethel, a student, shuts herself up in her room and remains silent for two months, everyone speculates as to the cause. This curiosity is increased when it is learned that Melekh had visited her and that the next day she broke her seclusion and silence and called upon Melekh in his drug store.

There is the town's rich merchant, Ezriel Pozner:

> He had the velvety face of a respectably genteel priest and had the habit of testing the health of his lungs with a gentle cough. Once he had weak lungs—a long time ago. Now they are fully covered with yellow eggnogs and with eggs. And his face is the same—it smelled with yellow-egg cake, with butter cookies, and with sweat.

His daughter Eva is a handsome, enigmatic girl thoroughly bored: "When you add the new part to the old town there are about 9000 persons in Rakutne," she said, "yet thus far it has not produced a single interesting individual." She was also supposed to have had an affair with Melekh, and letters by her were found in his possession. Yet none in the town wish to talk about Melekh's death or about those with whom he had associated. Khaim Moshe finds few clues. The young people he meets are dissatisfied yet yearn for nothing definite; they either run away from love or find it beyond their reach. Nothing really happens throughout the narrative; Melekh's suicide is not resolved, and none of the characters emerge clearly defined. The end is inconclusive, yet with obvious intimations. As one remarks: "Everything has cloth on the outside and lining on the inside, and there is something in between," and that something is left for the reader to discern.

Storm Days (1928) is a collection of stories about the revolution and the civil war. The chaotic conditions of the period are described graphically and in detail. Soldiers abandon the front, and on their way home rob and beat up Jews to get what they want. There are no officers to discipline them, and none feels responsible; each man is for himself, and everything is haphazard and disorderly. When Petlura's hooligans arrive, they make merry by shooting up towns and raping women. Anti-Petlurists then take over, but to them Jews are bourgeois enemies to be treated accordingly.

In **"Behind the Burning Town"** an ugly young man cannot keep from lusting after a girl despite the danger from approaching anti-communists. In **"On the 101st Mile"** the presence of a Red Army youth stationed at a telephone post dominates the behavior of a group of Jews who sympathize with neither side. **"Among Emigrants"** tells of a highly disturbed youth who comes to Berlin to assassinate the leader in a pogrom and ends in suicide. **"A Strong Ending"** is a particularly well-told story about a young communist writer who, as he describes caustically the sinfulness of an attractive young neighbor, becomes so enamored of her that he gives the narrative an unexpected ending. **"Ruins"** tells how two young sons of a wealthy family impoverished by the revolution take up farming, much to their parents' dismay. These and other tales are written in a minor key, with relative objectivity and literary finesse.

Divine Justice, completed in 1925 and published five years later, has its setting in a border village during the civil war period. Although in Bolshevik control, conditions remain fluid and anti-communists as well as smugglers are actively seeking to destroy the Red Army unit. All groups are depicted through the eyes of several characters. Filipov, the Bolshevik leader, represents the rigid morality of the revolution. He suffers from festering boils and is overworked, but he persists in carrying out his assignment without flinching. He seeks to outsmart the smugglers—most of them poor Jews bribed by rich ones to do their dirty work—and to suppress the Social Revolutionaries and anti-communist bandits. Since he lacks an adequate contingent, he is accused by his associates of being too proud to ask for help—although he had already requested it and been refused. In the struggle that ensues, Filipov is killed and is avenged by the aroused workers of the vicinity.

Bergelson treats the communists sympathetically, yet realistically. All characters are delineated with intuitive understanding as human beings moved primarily by motives of idealism or survival. Their life in the thick of civil war—hectic, hard, dangerous, zigzagging—is described vividly, imaginatively, and effectively.

Two volumes of short stories followed: *Out of the World and In It* (1929) and *Air Current* (1930). Varied in content and setting as well as in point of view, the stories present a host of characters in telling situations. **"Sisters,"** for instance, is about a serious-minded girl of 28, about to take her medical examination. She misses one of her texts and finds it in possession of her much younger sister, and in it a love note arranging for a date. She scolds the adolescent for taking up with strange men and decides to meet the lover and warn him to leave her sister alone. She finds him to be a painter, an attractive fellow, and as he gets closer to her and embraces her, she begins to feel guilty toward her younger sister. In **"Enemies"** two brothers, neighbors and wealthy merchants before the revolution, had quarreled and remained enemies for 29 years. When the daughter of one of them is to be married, the father calls out to the brother next door: "Come to the wedding, come I say. . . . We quarrelled when we were still merchants. . . . Now a merchant is dirt. . . . "

Air Current contains mostly stories about the civil war and its immediate aftermath. In **"A Story about the Rich"** ten wealthy Jews are arrested by the Red Guard for not paying the assessed tax. Unwilling to part with their possessions, they face the threat of being shot. When their fellow townsmen learn of this danger they seek to save the lives of the prisoners by contributing what they have of value to make up the fines. An old sick mother of a poor worker who had been mistreated by one of the prisoners also makes her contribution and says of him: "He was of course a murderer against my Itzi. In the middle of winter he threw him out of his mill. But to be shot? . . . Here, I brought you my silver cup." Later the Jews learn that the threat to shoot was only a means of getting valuables, and the ten are released that evening—much to the chagrin of Itzi, who is now minus his one silver cup.

"Rebirth" tells of a very conscientious young doctor who had volunteered in World War I and was wounded. When the civil war started, he enlisted in the Red Army and sent his wife and child to her parents. During a pogrom his wife was refused shelter by a Polish doctor with whom the husband had been friends, and she and her child were killed. When the doctor learns of the fate of his family he cannot continue to treat the same kind of Ukrainians who had murdered his dear ones and obtains leave to go home. On the way he thinks only of shooting the Polish doctor. When he is about to carry out his act of revenge, the sight of the crawling Pole begging for mercy gives him a feeling of ugliness. "'Here,' he said and put the revolver back in his pocket. 'I give you alms—your stinking little life. . . . Not out of pity, but because I'd feel ugly to shoot you, so keep it.'" Soon after he meets the leader of the Jewish self-defense and is told that when his men used up their bullets, none would take any of them into shelter for fear of reprisal; although Red Army soldiers are no angels, he has no choice but to join the party. The doctor finds himself similarly placed and rejoins his regiment.

In **"Citizen Wolie Brenner"** old Brenner, very proud of his communist daughters, becomes angry when his former employer, who had lost status under communism, proposes a marriage between his bourgeois grandson and one of Brenner's daughters. The former employer cannot understand Brenner's indignation. "After all," he says, "you were once in my employ." "If you don't understand," the old man shouts back, "it's even worse. I am no longer your 'employee.' You don't have any employees any more. . . . And I tell you, if you still think of me as an 'employee' then, then . . . get out!"

One of the best civil war stories, **"Hershel Toker,"** concerns a young Jew caught by White Guard officers at the border. He is considered a Bolshevik spy and incarcerated in a ward filled with sufferers from spotted typhus. He is questioned repeatedly about his companion,

a girl, who had succeeded in escaping, and is not believed when he maintains that he does not know anything about her. Much to the annoyance of his interrogator he becomes infected with typhus. In his delirium he is happy with the successful escape of his companion and with reminiscence of his friends. He feels vaguely that someone is helping him but cannot tell who. When he is dying the orderly, a secret Bolshevik sympathizer, covers him with a large red flag—to the consternation of the officers.

Penek (1932), the first volume of *At the Dnieper,* is a quasi-autobiographical novel about a boy very much like himself both in character and milieu. Born into a wealthy and highly prestigious family, he is an unwanted child of elderly parents, with a considerable gap between him and the next sibling. Precocious, mischievous, sensitive, early aware of the inequalities between rich and poor and intuitively partial to the underdog, he is driven to the side of the humble by the overt hostility of his mother and the older children. Only his father, Mikhel Levin, a learned, pious, and successful merchant, treats him with kindness, but he is often away on business and has little time for the boy. The mother, a commonplace and coddled woman, had not wanted another child and feels resentment toward her youngest. As soon as he is able to walk he is left mostly to the care of the kitchen servants. Penek retaliates by being contrary and troublesome. Only seven years old, but already quite aware of the intricacies and inequalities of life, he finds the companionship he craves in the hovels of the town's poor. They appeal to him as being much more interesting than his own family. Restive, intellectually alert, he wants to see and know everything, and soon familiarizes himself with the affairs of and gossip about almost every family in town.

Unlike his mother, who becomes panicky at the least feeling of pain, his father is of a stoical nature and does not yield to minor ailments. Years before, when he needed an eye operation, he refused to take ether. "I don't need a sleeping drug. I mean—I'll think a little and won't feel the pain." Now his illness is serious and persistent, and this draws Penek closer to him. Anything out of the ordinary, like illness or death, gives the boy much to think about.

Always eager to do the poor a favor, he no sooner hears his oldest sister Sheyndel say that the floors need painting than he hurries over to the town painter, who is penniless and badly in need of work, and brings him to the house. But Sheyndel has a city painter in mind and tells the man she has nothing for him. At this point the ailing father intervenes and tells her to let the painter do the job. Stubborn, she settles by giving him only two of the lesser floors.

Mikhel Levin is portrayed sympathetically, though not without the warts of his wealth. The town's leading citizen, he is shown to be good-natured, modest, and generous. His boyhood friend Yeshiah, a poor but scholarly person, does not hesitate to contradict and criticize him, but every Thursday he is given three rubles "for the Sabbath." Once in a while, when on a trip, Levin forgets to arrange for the stipend. Yeshiah on such occasions says nothing but thinks: "Of course, forgot. . . . How else?—a rich man!" And on reflection he has the satisfaction of concluding that no matter how learned and pious a rich man may be, he remains a pig. And in fact Levin forgets his friend in his will.

The house servants are friendly to Penek, and he spends much time with them. They protect him and see that his mischief and misbehavior remain unknown to the family. Yet when the cook sees him steal food to give to a poor friend, she remarks to her assistant: "Do you see or not? . . . Now he's still all right, with a heart, since he's only ten years old. . . . But let him grow up and he'll be as wormy as the others in the house."

Penek is not long in learning the mystery of procreation and his father's part in it. "Penek felt: he suddenly lost all respect for his father. It means that his father is a common, ordinary man. . . . One would have thought that he was an angel. . . . He was annoyed with all the pious Jews who make believe they're angels." He begins to wonder who is a truthful person, and if piety is a cover for lust. He notes another aspect of adult hypocrisy when a smooth-tongued fellow begins to court the assistant cook, for it is obvious to him that the man is only after her hard-accumulated dowry. When this happens, Penek feels sad.

Penek is most at home in the slum. He loves to see people happy and tries to help them in every way he can. Not eager to study, he nevertheless goes through the routine because he knows his poor teacher depends on the tuition for his lessons. But if he neglects Hebrew lore, he makes sure to learn everything about the people of the town—about their children, their wives, their worries—all of whom he knows as he knows himself—"one could even ask him in his sleep and he will say at once how each one feels in his heart and thinks in his head."

The elder Levin is a long time dying, and the poor of the town comment: "A poor man dies quietly, but when a rich man dies the heavens split." Three doctors are called from the nearby city, but they can do nothing for him and he suffers intense pain until he dies. Meantime the ailing and crippled poor gather before the house, hoping that the doctors might help them, but Sheyndel refuses to send the doctors out to them and Penek feels that "this won't be forgiven."

At the Dnieper: Young Years (1940) continues the narrative of the Levin family, again with emphasis on Penek, but broadened to include the social and political agitation of the 1900's. The older Levin's children are coarser and less able than their father, without his piety or generosity, each one interested only in getting as much as possible out of the family inheritance. They move to Kiev, where the older sons unsuccessfully seek to pursue their business enterprise and their mother devotes herself to arranging marriages for the older children. Penek continues to be neglected and disdained, much to his indifference, as he becomes interested in the growing revolutionary movement and makes his initial attempts at authorship. He finds new friends and revives old acquaintances from his native town, especially with Manya, a girl who has attracted him from boyhood.

In this volume Bergelson writes more consciously from a communist standpoint. He is acidulous concerning the attitude of wealthy Jews toward anti-Semitism, as may be seen from his description of one of them, a rich jeweler active in civic affairs:

> He is blondish, corpulent, with the delicate, modest face of a person who is confident that he does only good. His feet are thickish, as those of a sea captain who is seldom on land; his lips are full, feminine, very naked, bright red, as if frequently kissing the good friends he has all over the world—good friends among Jews, among Christians, good friends without end and without number.

He gains friends among the important officials by gifts of costly jewelry and exploits these connections in his efforts to mitigate the agitation against Jews—to his own enhanced prestige as a man of influence and good will.

Penek enters casually but more and more fully into the activities of the revolutionists. He makes friends with poor workers in crowded tenements, learns about Lenin and the split in the Socialist party in 1903. That year the Kishinev pogrom deeply depresses him. Disgusted and distressed by this show of gentile brutality, he is forced to reflect on the history of the Jews:

> A deep shame lay on him like a heavy burden, as if upon him alone were attached all the badges of shame which he recalled in Jewish history. For over 17 centuries none can tolerate him, Penek. He is persecuted, his behavior and origin mocked at, he is ever being driven. No plague but is tried out on him, no hatred and abuse that are not used against him. "Penek" he is only to friends; in the world at large his name is "Zhid" [sheeny]. . . . Under the weight of that shame he that morning wrote: "Twenty centuries of Jewish oppression have today burdened me."

His grief makes him chagrined with the petty complacency of his family. He wonders whether it is physical or spiritual failure on his part to have reached his eighteenth year in the midst of anti-Semitism and not to have been aware of it. He decides to leave home and goes to the slum, where he sees frightened Jews beaten by drunken peasants.

Fear of a widespread pogrom becomes aggravated when the body of a little Christian girl is found under the house of a Jew. Three Jews are at once arrested, and priests begin preaching revenge. Wealthy, public-spirited Jews feel an obligation to defend the prisoners, to expose the hoax of blood accusation, but their intent and actions concern only the immediate incident and not the underlying factors bringing it about. When conditions worsen, many of them close their homes and leave for foreign parts.

Penek's first story, with its setting in slum tenements, is published and praised by a prestigious critic. Instead of elation, however, he feels as if he has suddenly lost his youthful self and experiences a sense of guilt. He takes a more active part in the work of the revolutionists and becomes antipathetic to the Jewish nationalists who place the interests of the Jews above those of the nation as a whole. Yet when he and Manya visit the home of a prominent Jew and learn of the imminence of a planned pogrom, he "suddenly felt most strongly the endless repetition of centuries and the agedness of the Jews—how many times during the centuries people in Jewish homes have sat as they were now sitting, worried and waiting for it to begin. . . . "

The next morning, when a radical demonstration was to be repressed by the police with a pogrom, a member of the Jewish self-defense hands Penek a package of guns and knives for distribution. Penek cannot help reflecting: "Bennie Gurland's quick mind can think only of Jews who suffer from pogroms. All other world events do not concern him." The thought that both Zionists and socialists seek to use him makes him feel dishonest and troubled. At a mass meeting in a synagogue he helps the revolutionists scatter propaganda leaflets and is arrested along with many others. The end of the volume indicates that Bergelson had no doubt planned to continue the narrative, but nothing further is known to have been written.

From a fictional standpoint the first volume is undoubtedly a major novel. Life in a Jewish town is depicted with exceptional vividness—mirroring the penurious and pernicious condition of the mass of the people and the slow death of the petty-bourgeois merchant class. Many of the characters are trenchantly alive, and Penek is portrayed with notable creativity and keen insight. In the second volume, which in addition to further sensitive delineation of Penek and others also dwells at length on the politics of the time as well as on the problem of anti-Semitism, Bergelson occasionally writes with the prejudice of the propagandist. The narrative as a whole, however, sparkles and soars with overriding fictional excellence. As Niger has pointed out, the propaganda passages become like driftwood on a floating expanse of intense creativity.

Bergelson returned to Russia convinced that the future of Jewish life would develop best under the benign aegis of communism. Niger describes this optimism: "The new Bergelson is new in the sense that he wants to persuade us and himself that his dissatisfaction with the world is a class feeling, that there are no ugly and fine individuals, only ugly and fine social classes; he is new in the sense that he strives to become an optimist, a believer."

Bergelson was in this euphoric state of mind when, shortly after his return, he was asked to visit Birobidjan and write about it. After observing the place and the people for two months he published *Birobidjan* (1934), a highly favorable account of how the newcomers were developing their Jewish region and becoming healthy and satisfied human beings in the process. He deals harshly with the few malingerers and skeptics, especially in the person of Yudel Lifshits, who is delineated as a destroyer rather than a builder. Of the devoted and determined pioneers, former indigent workers or *luftmenschen,* he wrote with idyllic praise: how two of them, for instance, strike out in the primeval forest to establish a place of settlement, chop down trees, build huts, dig wells, and develop homesteads. Of one he writes: "His face is lit, his gaze is lit—in Shimke's eyes candles are burning. For the first time in his life Shimke experiences the taste of good fortune, of real luck." The hardships these pioneers encounter are not minimized. Of the stinging insects that infest the forest and make life miserable he states: "They rise like clouds out of each dank place and attack—not like flies but like dogs who are curious to taste human flesh and human blood." The keynote of the narrative is stated by Mendel Saks, one of the prominent pioneers, in a speech celebrating the completion of a hamlet: "We, the hardworking poor, were never short of hard times. . . . Of those hard times we gained nothing, really nothing; now, from several hard months with the Soviet government we have a settlement in the forest . . . that's what we have!" Underneath this thin layer of sugarcoating Bergelson has written a work of creative fiction, with beautiful descriptions of pristine nature and a number of characters who are artistically realized in the course of the story.

During the ensuing 15 years Bergelson exerted himself, eagerly yet tragically, to be a loyal communist, to find acceptance and approbation in the eyes of both his fellow writers and government censors. He craved affection, and now and then demeaned himself to gain it—at great cost to his conscience and self-respect. He began to decry religion, to criticize deviation from official policy, to praise the pursuit of communism, and to chastise such "bourgeois" writers as Sholem Asch and Bialik. In the spirit of will-to-believe he spoke and wrote about himself as if his return to Russia had rejuvenated him and brought him a long-desired exaltation. To Opatoshu he wrote in 1935: "Here I feel happy and free and young and needed and appreciated, full of energy to work, happy about myself, about Markish's rise during the past two years, and about the surge of our Soviet-Yiddish literature." He became interested in getting his novels and stories published in Russian translation and began to speak of likely Jewish assimilation in the Soviet Union without the tragic overtones a Yiddish writer would normally employ. When no government honors came to him in the late 1930's, he was deeply aggravated and suspected malice and false innuendo on the part of envious writers.

The tragic destruction of Jews in the Nazi-occupied areas grieved Bergelson as much as it did all Jewish writers, but he dared not express his distress in his writing. When Germany invaded the Soviet Union and the government relaxed its censorship, he actively partook in the formation of the Jewish Anti-Fascist Committee and became one of the editors of *Einigkeit.* He wrote a play that year, *We Want to Live,* which was later performed in the United States, Argentina, Rumania, and in a Hebrew version in Tel Aviv. A number of his stories appeared in various periodicals and were collected in a book.

Prince Reuveni, a drama of the well-intentioned impostor who sought to ameliorate the lot of the Jews in the 16th century, which Bergelson completed in 1946 and which was published in New York and produced in Moscow and Warsaw, reveals his entwined Jewishness and communism. Reuveni is presented as a Bolshevik leader who seeks to save the Jews from Christian oppression not by prayer but by fighting. He cunningly acts his role as distant prince to gain his ends, and almost fools the Pope and some cardinals—only to be discovered and killed. In fighting back he discards his princely robe, dons the rags of a Jew, and calls his fellow Jews to battle. Wounded unto death, he is told that Portugal will deal fairly with his group if it will submit. "Tell the Portuguese," he replies, "'the people will die, but will not submit—that's the kind of people it is.'" And to his good friend Shabsi the clown he says: "Don't worry about me. I taught the people how to fight—that is a lot, Shabsi, a lot." So it is, and so it became in present-day Israel, but that was not the lesson of the sages or the practice of the Jews through the centuries of persecution.

For all his efforts to conform and demonstrate his loyalty to the Stalin regime, Bergelson was arrested early in 1949 and executed in August, 1952. Some years later his name was exonerated and in the next issue of the Russian *Short Literary Encyclopedia* the sketch about him reappeared with the following addendum: "He was repressed illegally. Rehabilitated after his death." Some of his work was reissued in Russian translation, and a 762-page volume of his selected writings in Yiddish was published in 1961.

Two posthumous volumes of his stories appeared abroad: *New Stories* (1949) in Buenos Aires, and *Two Worlds* (1953) in New York. Most of these stories are first-rate and treat incidents and events related to the holocaust. **"Between Mountains"** is about three German soldiers who, lost in the Caucasian mountains, come upon a young Jewish native, whose father had been tortured to death by the Nazis, and force him to direct them to the main highway. Despite their threats he keeps leading them astray and deeper into the mountains. When their food begins to run low one of the soldiers attempts to hide some of it, which leads to quarreling and results in one being killed, a second escaping, and the third, wounded, left to die by the liberated Jewish youth. Each of the four characters is vividly delineated; their thoughts and individual differences emerge in sharp and memorable outline.

In **"The Witness"** an old Jew, shabbily attired and obviously very perturbed, arrives in a town at the end of World War II to be "a witness"—he being the only survivor in his village. "The Jew's darkened face reminded one of a charred piece of wood saved from the flames of a fire. He gave one the feeling, it seems, of the smoke of charred bones. . . . He can just about walk, so weakened is everything in him that is still alive." He meets a girl who is also a lone survivor and insists on dictating his experiences to her. He speaks in Yiddish and she writes his words down in Russian. When she asks him if her translation is accurate, he replies: "You ask my opinion? What can I tell you? . . . the suffering was in Yiddish. . . . " When he tells her of a very beautiful girl whom the Nazis had made a Jewish artist paint in the nude before sending her to the gas chamber, he cannot control his tears. Asked why he wept, he explains that it is because the Nazis had burned such beauty. Later he faints out of sheer weakness and is thought dying, but he revives, realizes what has happened, and says: "How can I die? . . . I am a witness!" Here Bergelson intimates his deep Jewishness, permitted him only when writing about the Nazis. The pathos of the incident is the more poignant because it is written with the controlled delicacy of sentiment and in a prose of pure radiance.

"Chapters of a Longer Work" is set in prewar Soviet Russia. Professor Kalmans of the University of Chicago, an expert in agriculture, is visiting Russia on his sabbatical in order to see his native town again and to be of help in any way he can. At 51 he is still a bachelor, having early been disappointed in love. In Moscow he learns that Eva, the girl whom he had once loved, is now a widow and living in Birobidian. He goes there, is quite pleased with the progress being made by Jewish settlers, and gives them advice on how to plan a commune of 5000 people, to which they react skeptically. "From all this the professor realized that these people have their own plans and their own ways of life—ordinary people.' Then he meets Eva and is again thrilled at the sight of her.

> He could not now express his thoughts. No doubt they related to this: life had favored him and had brought him here to Eva. And here he sits near her and repeatedly observes her fire-red ear lobe with such a thought in his dead heart and with such pleasure—that she is in her 41st year exactly as he had known her, a nice one!

Bergelson was perhaps the most refined master of Yiddish prose. His diction was delicately polished, and both vibrant and lyrical. He described every nuance of thought and feeling with melodic exactness and suggestive overtones. There is a tantalizing tentativeness about his writing, giving his style the aura of deftness and promise: an unuttered perception seen between the lines and enjoyed as an intimacy between author and reader. He achieved this style by deep cultivation of his native gift—by remaining a prisoner at his desk. As he once said: "I rise in the morning and immediately begin to work. I sit down at my desk like a bitter pauper, but after laboring honestly until evening I rise from my written pages with a feeling of a bit of a rich man." Often, however, he tore up a day's work when he thought it did not convey what he had wished to express.

A novelist is of course judged by his ability to create living characters. In this respect Bergelson excels. Mirel and Penek are only the most successful of the numerous men and women who throb with fictional reality in the unfolding of his stories. Impressionistic, psychologically analytical, richly intuitive, he probed human motives and emotions to their inner recesses, bringing forth human beings palpitating with feeling and bursting with life. Even in his later years, when he felt impelled to demonstrate his communist orthodoxy, he seldom strayed from genuine dedication to his art. For no matter how wobbly he sometimes behaved personally—and his yearning for affection and approval occasionally made him say and do things he inwardly regretted—he was a dedicated writer once he sat down at his desk and put pen to paper.

Seth L. Wolitz (essay date 1982)

SOURCE: "Notes and Readings," in *Prooftexts,* Vol. 2, No. 3, September, 1982, pp. 313-21.

[*In the following essay, Wolitz contrasts Isaac Bashevis Singer's 1931 short story "Yordim" with Bergelson's 1919 story of the same name.*]

> I wouldn't say I feel myself a part of the Yiddish tradition. Somehow I always wanted to write in my own way, and I never felt that I was somebody's disciple . . . I would almost say that I tried to create my own tradition, if one could use such words.
>
> I. B. Singer

Isaac Bashevis Singer launched an open attack on Dovid Bergelson's last major work, ***Baym Dnieper (At the Dnieper),*** in the November 1932 issue of *Globus,* the Warsaw journal in which three months later would appear Singer's now famous *Satan in Goray.* Singer, a young ambitious author, had many bones to pick with Bergelson, the most sophisticated Yiddish writer of the day: his established fame, his admired literary style and composition, his new Marxist aesthetics, and his boring repetitiveness: "Once again the same old setting—how often repeated in his work—a stingy rich Jewish household in the Ukraine."[1] The master had become stale and worse, a hack, "in order, finally, to become a 'revolutionary' writer" (*Globus,* 56). Penek, Bergelson's child hero in ***Baym Dnieper,*** according to Singer, was unconvincing and revealed a Bergelson losing his grip on his masterful ability to draw persuasive characterizations. "Bergelson, as a consistent realist and objective painter, sought, first of all, to capture the personality of the human being" (*Globus,* 58). "His heroes [are] mature, fully ripened, not ones just beginning to grow. A child is not a personality . . ." (*Globus,* 59). Singer's criticism, with fifty years hindsight, goes straight to the

mark. Bergelson was attempting by 1932 to create art by the formulae of socialist realism—unsuccessfully—for as Singer aptly observed: "There are no faceless men in Bergelson, therefore, Bergelson has been unable to portray the masses" (*Globus,* 59). Singer could only have written such rewarding criticism of Bergelson after having closely studied his works up to ***Baym Dnieper***—and most likely in the 1929 Kletskin edition of Bergelson's collected works. No Yiddish prose writer in 1930 could have avoided Bergelson's oeuvre. Sholem Asch and Opatoshu might have enjoyed greater popularity, but for the critical world, Bergelson in the 1920s served as the yardstick of Yiddish literary accomplishment. His conscious absence from Warsaw based on personal, literary and ideological reasons did not free Tlomatske 13—the Yiddish PEN Club—from his spell. Singer had to test himself against the living Yiddish literary giant. That his critique of 1932 articulates so well Bergelson's aesthetics, its heights and limitations, at the same time that Singer was composing his first major work, the gothic novel, *Satan in Goray,* which is at the polar opposite of Bergelson's impressionist masterpiece, ***Nokh alemen (When All is Said and Done,*** 1913), suggests that Singer had tested himself against the master, had absorbed Bergelson's lessons and was now able to pursue his own resonant voice.

Where did this contest take place? And what were the initial results? It is my hypothesis that the 1931 publication of *Yordim* ("The Newly Impoverished") by Singer in the Warsaw *Literarishe bleter* was the gauntlet Singer cast down to his peers, saying, in effect, that he was a serious contender for Bergelson's laurels. By daring to use the title of one of Bergelson's finest short stories, *Yordim,* and the favorite subject matter of early Bergelson, "the same old setting . . . a stingy rich household," Singer challenged Bergelson, his peers and his own literary powers.

Bergelson had begun his short story *Yordim* in 1910 but it was not published until 1919 in Kiev. It appears today as both a preparation and a wonderful distillate of ***Nokh alemen.*** *Yordim* are those sad people who, like Mme. Ranevskaya in the *Cherry Orchard,* have become impoverished and like parvenus, in the opposite direction of course, do not adjust well or cope with their new objective reality. Bergelson made this subject his very own: Mirl Hurvits and her father Reb Gedalye are the archetypal Bergelsonian characters of this futile condition in Yiddish literature. To challenge Bergelson on his very own territory might be foolhardy but necessary for a young, ambitious and original artist. And Yiddish literature could provide its own precedent: Vaysenberg challenging Asch's *Dos shtetl* with his own *Shtetl!* The *Yordim* of Singer, his fifteenth printed story, pays its compliments to Bergelson's ***Yordim*** and goes its own way.

Both stories are hardly plotted. Rather they are built on patterning and formally presented in a triptych. Bergelson's story begins with a depiction of the impoverished family whose condition is accented by the tears of the daughters languishing without hope of marriage. The second section introduces some possible hope. The rich brother in the large city invites the younger sister, Tsivye, to his home for a month. Ostensibly he is arranging a marriage. The sister departs and returns a month later, miserable. She had danced at someone else's wedding. In section three, the pattern repeats. The brother sends a telegram inviting the family to see him at the railroad station as he travels on to Europe. Ostensibly he is bringing the bridegroom with him. The delighted family peers into the train which idles a few moments—just enough time to allow the blind father to touch his son's kidskin gloves. The family then returns empty-handed to its misery. The short story makes a perfect circle with its patterned repetition of phrasing and symbolic, precise description. Abstractly, it is a perfect rondo. Its circular lyric structure captures all of Bergelson's social and psychological perceptions depicted through an adroit shifting narrational perspective.

Singer accepts the challenge of creating a tripartite story, with the givens of the family structure and the thin plotting sequences regarding a possible marriage. Could it be accidental that both fathers are blind, that both sons are rich and live in the city and are barely considerate of the family and that the daughters are quietly longing for husbands? In Singer's story, he constructs the following argument. In part one, the Margolis family, having cancelled a seven-year engagement with the unworthy suitor of their daughter, has fallen on hard times following World War I and has moved to indigent housing in Warsaw. The son, in part two, hardly aids the family and the father must seek work until he becomes, suddenly, completely blind. The daughter, unable to adjust to the city, retreats into the house but makes the acquaintance of her neighbor, Shmontses, a poor writer with slight demonic features. Could Shmontses be her possible bridegroom? Act III begins with a *coup de théâtre*, Shmontses is getting married to an old flame. Reb Margolis, meanwhile, has retreated into his hasidic world, abandoning his sick wife and daughter. Ite, the daughter, takes to wandering the street aimlessly, and encounters her brother by chance, who chides her for being out. She returns exhausted and prepared to die. The final paragraph passes into the fantastic as dowry money, Shmontses, a curtained mirror and screaming women surround poor Ite who recedes into an erotic death. Singer has succeeded in following the external tripart form of Bergelson's story and even the thin marriage plotting sequences of absence, hope, and despair. Where Bergelson intends circular structure to reflect the static inescapable ennui of the *yordim*, who live trapped in muted, dreaded, frustration, Singer uses linear, melodramatic narrative to convey the process of collapse: becoming *yordim*. Bergelson presents a synchronic impression and expects his reader to intuit the implications through repetitive circularity as in Beckett's *Waiting for Godot*. Singer prefers the direct sequential storyline structured like a well-made play with a causal exposition, motivic development and dramatic denouement. The two authors agree in their perceptions of the

yordim; they differ sharply, however, in their compositional methods.

Both authors stress the result of economic disaster: the social, psychological, familial, personal, and general spiritual impoverishment. Both authors are teaching the reader to experience atrophy. Whereas Singer emphasizes the *process of decline* into total atrophy through the enchaining events along a linear grid, Bergelson emphasizes the simultaneity of the various modalities of atrophy. This creates in Eco's term, "over-coding" which effectuates the static stifling atmosphere for which Bergelson is so famous. Chronological time transmogrifies into psychological time. The narrative therefore is related in an unbounded subjective present tense in which past, present and future become fused. "While Tsivye gnaws away at her unfortunate life, she stops eating and drinking."[2] Singer on the other hand, keeps narration in strict historical time. His linear narrative begins in the past tense: "For weeks on end Reb Oyzer Margolis paced back and forth in front of his house, rolled cigarettes and sealed them."[3] Whereas Bergelson makes the endless present a concentrate of atrophy, Singer must fall back upon the looser *flegn* form, the repetitive past. "Before Reb Oyzer used to (*flegn*) show signs of opening his mouth, Ely used to (*flegn*) be well on the other side of the door" (698). Bergelson, therefore, seeks a static present to express implicitly the atrophied condition of the personage. Singer, less subtly, makes explicit the chronological process of atrophy.

The creation of the psychological present serves as the basis of Bergelson's narrational strategy. Repetition becomes Bergelson's major structural device to arrest the flow of time. Use of the repeated word, sentence, monologue, dialogue or event creates circularity, the inescapable present, and translates aesthetically the psychology of atrophy. The present becomes a weight pulling down the characters into quiescence. Unanswered questions are raised, sentences are cut off. Every character turns to the formulaic distress call, *Reboynesheloylem*, (169, 170, 172, 174, 178) and silence. Nothing can change: "In the following summer Tsivye will again wander about . . . and old Fuzis will then once again rest . . ." (178). The self deteriorates in the suspended present. "Tsivye, do you know what you are doing, Tsivye? Not that she's thinking about these words, she is only remembering them" (170). The use of the third person in place of the first person singular in monologues and dialogues—a unique Bergelsonian stylistic device—reveals the self alienation and atrophy.

Bergelson's narrator prefers to slip into the narrated monologue (*style indirect libre*) in order to maximize the subjective perspectives of the character upon the reader. By assimilating the competing perspectives the reader penetrates the character and comprehends directly the ennui, alienation and atrophy of the characters trapped in limited space and endless time. The stylistic collusion of reader, narrator and character goes to the heart of Bergelson's aesthetic methodology.

> A letter arrives from Shmuel, the rich son, that
> Tsivye must come . . .
>
> It's clear as day: it's about a possible marriage;
> the bridegroom isn't just anybody if he pleases
> Shmuel . . . (172).

In the quotation, the narrated monologue fuses narrator and old man Fuzis. The reader at first accepts the given facts and perspective. But later it becomes evident that all is not "clear as day"; but to the contrary, a misinterpretation has occurred. The reader has been duped by accepting the subjective perspective of Fuzis as objective. Such is an example of Bergelson's narrational manipulation of collusion.

Singer's narrator in *Yordim* maintains an omniscient and slightly ironic distance from his creations. The narrator uses the past tense as if he were presenting a case history. He pauses at the end of each narrational sequence with a piquant, characteristic phrase of direct discourse to convince the reader of the reliability of his character portrayal and thereby hopes to seduce the reader into accepting the narrator's omniscience. One declarative sentence follows the next.

> His wife, Menukhe, . . . became from day to day
> more shriveled and more jaundiced. She laid in bed
> in her curled wig . . . and did not stop taking bitter
> medicines and complained in a harsh voice and with
> thin flattened lips:—Sodom! I have always said that
> we're in the midst of Sodom. (698)

The narrator is interested only in relating, not in showing. By maintaining a detached tone and single perspective, the narrator restricts the main characters from dominating his narration. The ironic ending of Singer's story, I hope to show, will support this thesis. Singer's narrational strategies, in *Yordim* are basically unsophisticated and simplistic.

In both of these short stories, space and place function to draw the reader to the social psychological collapse of the *yordim*. The authors, however, use setting differently. Singer continuously shrinks the living space of his characters: From owning a nice house and dry goods store in the shtetl they descend to a few dirty rooms in Warsaw and finally are limited to their bed. Their physical space mimics their continuous impoverishment. The vacant dry goods store with its mice, spiders, and eerie red light in which we met Ite, the daughter, presages the Warsaw rooms and the fantastic conclusion. This *Lower Depths* setting increases with demonic presence as the atrophy grows greater. Singer, evidently, also used place for melodramatic effect. Bergelson rarely describes place and avoids place name for greater generalization. He uses space symbolically. The three rooms of the characters are all the living space they have left. The traditional function of each room has been turned against them: The salon must remain empty with its decayed fig tree, the dining room and its table is for eating one's heart out, the bedroom with its bed is not for love but for sobs, tears and death. Space is

sepulchral here and the characters are cut off from pregnant life observed through the glass window which tempts, torments and incarcerates. Even the walls are not innocent; they smell with the memory of their old wealth and distillery "in which they had once been immured" (170). Confined with no exit they are entrapped in timeless hell. The city where the rich brothers live in both stories, beckons like Moscow to the three sisters of Chekhov—and with knowledge of the city comes despair. The narrowing space reflects their atrophy. If place is imprisonment for both authors then Singer shrinks it more to capture the process of impoverishment whereas Bergelson activates confined space to gnaw at the flesh forever.

Yordim are also families collapsing into individual isolation. The sons in both stories are successful businessmen already matriculated from shtetl life. Their last pieties are the rubles sent home each month. Singer has roughened the subtext brother, Shmuel, considerably to capture the Warsaw vulgarian, Elye. Bergelson prefers irony to open moral scorn. As the train stops for a bare moment at the backwater station, the blind father who has not seen his son for twelve years can only finger his rich son's kid gloves. The patriarchs look to their sons in vain. The city sons have broken away. The inversion of wealth has diminished the male of the family. "Once, he, Kalmen Fuzis, was the bright one. Now his children take him, Kalmen, to be a fool" (171). The fullest bitterness emerges when he complains to the visiting parasite "they're worthless, his two daughters" (170).

Blindness is not only hubris, the sin of pride, but an excision from the world and family he can no longer face. Bergelson captures with exquisite humor the multiple impoverishment to the head of the family. When Kalmen asks his hanger-on about life, answers Yekusiel:

> "What's there to say? It's tough . . . to be a
> pauper."
>
> And the old man loses all at once his honor, he
> doesn't know whom Yekusiel means, himself or
> the impoverished Fuzis." (171),

Such sensibility, nuance, wit and pathos were not yet in Singer's repertoire. Reb Oyzer Margolis is too much a pearl of a man with a Jobean descent. Singer catalogues the process of his fall through his progressive blindness. Reb Oyzer appears first with golden glasses and nearsighted lenses. After moving to Warsaw as a formerly wealthy man, his eyes begin to fail. Teaching in the Talmud Torah, he has to bring the text up to his glasses. That night he goes blind. From this point on, Reb Oyzer abandons his beloved bedridden wife—a comic relief figure—and gives himself only to Hasidism. The family is abandoned. Blindness as spiritual death here is hardly subtle. (Nor the nearsightedness of cleaving to Hasidism!) Singer paces the narrative too briskly in order to focus on the process of family decline. He was trying to press a novella into a short story. Bergelson maintains an *andante* with minimum incident. At the two prospects of marriage in Bergelson's tale, the family perks up each time then falls back into silence marred by isolated sobbings.

The central victims, the real *yordim,* in this study are the daughters. They will never marry. Tsivye, Kalmen's daughter, articulates her reality and the theme of both works. "We're rotting here . . . without shrouds on. We are putrifying alive" (169). The daughters are already in their thirties. The atrophy which begins with financial reverses affects their fulfillment as women. Bergelson tortures these helpless women with false hopes. By the desperate clutching twice, once at a letter and once at a telegram out of the ordinary from the brother, Tsivye hopes against hope to escape her void. Yet nowhere in any message does her brother talk of marriage. Bergel-son's narration cleverly invites the reader to lend an ear to the subjective foolishness of blind Reb Kalmen—twice, once after each message. First: "Didn't one know earlier that he [Samuel] would seek out a bridegroom for her?" (173). And the second time: "Isn't he bringing the bridegroom with him right here into the house? He's probably not traveling alone" (175). After two defeats, Tsivye can only fall back into inescapable total atrophy. But Bergelson does not conclude his short story on Tsivye. Her victimization is the cruelist because she is fully conscious of her condition. Bergelson, we will see, has even more to say about atrophy.

Singer must have become aware that the circular structure with the letter and telegram episodes in Bergelson was a most economical means to depict the total sociopsychological reality. Bergelson's formal artistry and psychological genius for specificity in character must have appeared too formidable. To outflank Bergelson, Singer added to the victimization of Ite on the sociopsychological plane the moral erotic plane in which Ite became the plaything caught between the forces of good and evil. She is an innocent to be tested.

Once embarked on this course, Singer found his *metier.* The process of testing her permitted his demonic fantasy to break out of the realistic entrapment imposed by Bergelsonian aesthetics. Ite is a *yoyred* who has discovered the chaos of this world. She is aware that she has become in Sartrian terms *de trop.* Desperate for security in a world that has robbed her and her family, she is all alone. Marriage is the only solution and seems elusive. Elye, the brother, doesn't help but taunts. She has resisted and rejected the modern material world he represents with his cheap free-love salon parties to which he invites her. At this point a demonic figure is introduced: Shmontses, the nickname given to him by Ite. He is an unpublished author seeking to seduce her—if not the reader—through words, through his manuscripts which "smelled of disinfectant and death" (719). Language becomes the flowers of evil to test her virtue and morality. The words have erotic intent but her dreams warn her unconsciously of their latent meaning.

Her innocence or virtue ultimately shames the devilish writer to break his unresolved sexual conquest when she

repeatedly complains to him in direct discourse: "Yes, Shmontses, we are not fit for this world! From the likes of us today, they make sport" (719).

But the devil never gives up. Shmontses' sudden marriage must rob her of even friendship which he offered. He has acted cruelly like her brother and the original fiancé. She retreats to her window and desperately stares out upon the world. In Bergelson's *Yordim,* Rokhl, too, "stands with her face pressed to the window pane and stares" (170). This is clearly a parody for, as Singer wrote a year later, "This standing by the window is a Bergelson mannerism. Almost all his protagonists stand by a window" (*Globus,* 56). At last tempted by the world, her virtue still intact, Ite wanders in the streets (chaos) to watch the prestidigitators— the entertainers (displacements of Shmontses) who turn chaos to harmony—a sweet seduction. But she cannot abide life crushing in upon her.

The final paragraph of Singer's story is also his finest moment in the narration. The heroine exhausted by this floating world retreats to her bed and delusions. She is approaching stasis. Her erotic frustrations, the economic, social, familial and personal impoverishment she has borne are still held in check by her moral self-respect which can hardly resist any longer. In her fantasmagoria she demands justice from her former bridegroom as Shmontses appears in a room surrounded by covered mirrors and the presence of women wailing from a prayer book. Ite seems to resist him while apparently floating off, bed and all, in some erotic death to a better world. By positing the hasidic saw that the descent contains the rise, the author turns her into a woman of moral valor. Singer, as a traditional story teller, eschews open endings. His closure completes plot and character development.

Bergelson ends his story on a repeated dialogue between Reb Kalmen and his hanger-on. The repetition completes the formal pattern of circular structure and concludes the work in a pessimistic vision of endless atrophy—but with a wry smile.

"Once upon a time, right, Yekusiel?"

"Once, Reb Kalmen."

"And gone, Yekusiel, right? Gone with the wind."

"Day dreams, Reb Kalmen."

Bergelson's closure based on circular pattern is modernist, open-ended. The suspended narrative permits the reader to complete the obvious: so shall the characters live until death. The daring, witty and telling ending, a play-on-words, *nekhtike teg* (yesterdays)—actually the Yiddish idiom, "nothing of the kind" or "nonsense"— breaches the last stronghold of the impoverished *gvir:* his glorious past! Only atrophy ensues.

Singer would not be outshined at the coda. He, too, could spin a linguistic web and challenge Bergelson. In the last scene, a fantasmagoria, Shmontses (whose nickname means "foolish talk") appears demonically at Ite's deathbed with a ladle in his hand, "in his deadly reddish hand quivered a copper ladle" (720). In her delirium his writings have become hypostatized by the ladle. Singer plays with the Yiddish idiom, *Er makht fun a vort a kvort*—literally, "he makes a ladle from a word" or, in idiomatic English, "He can spin a yarn." Mr. "Foolish talk" is seducer/deceiver. But Singer enriches the linguistic field with a further allusion and delusion. A wailing woman intones prayers from the book, *Mayne-loshn* (720), which is Hebrew for "answer of the tongue." The title proffers Shmontses' response to Ite's earlier comment, "we are not fit for this world": He brings death. The *Mayne-loshn,* a traditional collection of prayers, is recited over the dead, particularly at the grave site. The *Mayne-loshn* is also an old slang term in Yiddish meaning "glib tongue"—or its Yiddish personification, Shmontses. Not only is the devil, Shmontses the writer, a *Mayne-loshn* for seduction, but implicated by extension, is narration, the text. If Bergelson has his play-on-words, Singer has it triplefold. The naive reader may be taken in by the melodramatic ending of Ite's gothic death, but Singer invites his knowledgeable reader to partake, as well, of the text as verbal game.

Singer insists upon the fictiveness of the work. He rejects the "consistent realist and objective painter" Bergelson and his impressionistic aesthetics. For Singer, art should not be mere mimesis. The conscious introduction of fantasy represents a break with the almost pure naturalist school of prose writers in Warsaw between the World Wars. Singer was adhering to the other tradition in Yiddish prose from Nahman of Braslav continuing through Peretz's hasidic tales to Der Nister: fantasies which are ethical parables in disguise.

The Ite-Shmontses aborted relationship may be drawn on the Tsivye-unknown *khosn* model but Singer also uses his two characters as wry allegories of good and evil. Bergelson places Tsivye and her sister as personality types trapped in social quicksand. Singer, by turning social psychological portraiture into a moral test, a teasing Gretchen-Faust replay with fantasmagoria, argues for his literary aesthetic: *invention* not *imitation.* Singer failed, therefore, to write successful parody of Bergelson's *Yordim.* He could not "spoof" characteristics of Bergel-son's theme, structure, settings, characters, situations and language and at the same time construct an original story using these givens. By introducing the *yene-velt* (otherworldly) element, and reorienting the subject matter to a moral erotic encounter, Singer established his own "characteristics." Singer, furthermore, could not make use of the varied techniques for effective mimesis under Bergelson's command if only because he wished to show Bergelson's aesthetics were limited to description whereas his own were freer and loftier. Bergelson's aesthetics based ultimately on verisimilitude, in short, were rejected. The youthful Singer, with his single, lean and linear narration, his fantasy and erotic allusions used the challenge of Bergelson's literary armature as the means to free himself of the "anxiety of influence."

Unlike the *Barber of Seville* by Paisiello being superseded by Rossini's *Barber of Seville,* Bergelson's original *Yordim* remains the masterpiece. Singer's *Yordim* is charming juvenalia. He did spin a new text out of Bergelson's model but it is formally inferior and different in resolution and tone. Singer emerges basically as a *dertseyler,* (a storyteller); Bergelson appears as a sophisticated novelist at heart. Singer learned in the contest two important facts: (1) that Bergelson's aesthetics were surely not his, and (2) that Bergelson's range of narrative techniques were beyond him.

Bergelson was a full-fledged modernist whereas Bashevis Singer was a young artist groping towards neo-conservatism. In 1931, who could have predicted Bergelson would die before a firing squad of Bolsheviks and Singer would gain a Nobel Prize?

NOTES

[1] Isaac Bashevis Singer, "On Dovid Bergelson's *Baym Dnieper*" [Yiddish], *Globus* No. 5 (Nov. 1932): 56-65. Subsequent references to this review have been incorporated into the text; translations are my own.

[2] Dovid Bergelson, *Yordim,* in *Ale verk,* II (Buenos Aires, 1961): 169. Subsequent references have been incorporated into the text; translations are my own.

[3] Isaac Bashevis Singer, *Yordim, Literarishe bleter* 8, No. 36 (4 Sept. 1931): 697; the story concludes in No. 37 (11 Sept. 1931). Subsequent references have been incorporated into the text; translations are my own.

Golda Werman (essay date 1996)

SOURCE: "Introduction," in *The Stories of David Bergelson: Yiddish Short Fiction from Russia,* Syracuse University Press, 1996, pp. xiii-xxxii.

[*In the following excerpt, Werman examines Bergelson's legacy as a Yiddish writer, and reviews a number of his short works.*]

On a mild December evening in Jerusalem in 1993, I attended a memorial meeting for the Yiddish writers and other artists who were murdered by Stalin after World War II. The event was very well attended; every seat in the library of the Russian Immigrant Society's Zionist Forum was occupied, and many people stood in the aisles and at the back of the crowded, overheated room, fanning themselves with envelopes, handkerchiefs, anything that came to hand. The Russians had not forgotten their brothers who were murdered during the dark days of Stalin's reign for the crime of keeping Yiddish culture alive.

The invited speakers sat in a semicircle at the front of the hall, facing the audience. Above them hung a portrait of Solomon Mikhoels, the famous actor and director of the Moscow State Yiddish Theater and leader of the Jewish community; he was killed in 1948 in a staged automobile accident, a favorite means of execution by the KGB. On a shelf at the far side of the reading room, a large photo of David Bergelson, the foremost modern Yiddish stylist, looked down on his Russian compatriots. He was imprisoned in 1948, under gruesome conditions, and was never heard from again. His family was not allowed to visit him or to send him letters. They were merely informed that he was shot on August 12, 1952, which was his sixty-eighth birthday. Many other Yiddish writers were executed on the same day.

Bergelson's son, Lev Bergelson, sat at the center of the semicircle. A famous chemist, he had recently immigrated to Israel from Moscow, where he was a member of the Russian Academy of Science, an almost unheard of honor for a Jew. Now he is a professor at the Hadassah Medical School in Jerusalem and at the National Institutes of Health in Bethesda, Maryland. At his left sat Natalia Mikhoels, Solomon Mikhoels's daughter; she and her sister immigrated to Israel in the seventies after years of struggle with the Soviet authorities for an exit visa. At Lev Bergelson's right was the violinist Lavia Hofstein, daughter of the renowned Yiddish poet David Hofstein, who was shot on the same fateful day as David Bergelson, and for the same crime of writing in Yiddish. His widow, Feyge, was too ill to attend the ceremony, but people remembered her fondly. In the seventies, soon after settling in Tel Aviv, she wrote a lovely Yiddish memoir about her life with the poet, their good years together and their suffering under Stalin.

Seated next to Lavia was the son of the Yiddish lyric poet Shmuel Halkin, whose poems of yearning for Zion so outraged the communist authorities that he was forced to recant publicly. This ended his career as a poet, and he switched to the safer profession of translating classical writers—Shakespeare, Gorki, and Pushkin—into Yiddish. Despite his discretion, Halkin was arrested in 1948 and sent to a remote area of Siberia where conditions were very harsh; in 1955, desperately ill and broken in spirit, he was allowed to return home for medical treatment. He died a few years later.

Two buxom, middle-aged women sat next to each other at Natalia's left: one, a former Yiddish actress, had been trained by the great Mikhoels himself; the other, a librarian, was in the process of cataloging the archives of Mikhoels's Yiddish Theater.

The program began with a girls' choir singing a medley of Yiddish songs, followed by the actress reading one of Hofstein's Yiddish poems. And that ended the sound of Yiddish for the evening—no one else uttered a Yiddish word. The master of ceremonies introduced the speakers in Russian, the speakers addressed the audience in Russian, all the announcements were in Russian, and all the questions from the audience were in Russian. Yiddish, it seems, was reserved for ceremonial rites: little girls crooning *tumba-la-laika* and aging actresses declaiming

Yiddish verse, nostalgic concessions to a remembered past. Serious discourse, however, requires a living language, and the speakers no longer thought and functioned in Yiddish—not even those who grew up in Yiddish-speaking homes, in families that were dedicated to Yiddish culture.

It is estimated that before World War II eleven million people throughout the world spoke Yiddish, and many read Yiddish literature. Publishing houses printed Yiddish books for every age and on every subject, the Yiddish theater flourished, popular Yiddish movies were produced, and Yiddish newspapers provided their readers with poetry, essays, stories, even novels in serialized form. And these were endlessly discussed—in the streets, at home, and in the coffeehouses. Today, the Yiddish language is tottering at the edge of death, despite some efforts to revive it, and the number of its speakers can be counted in the thousands rather than in millions. Poland, the former center of Yiddish culture, no longer has Jews. Russia's Yiddish was essentially wiped out by Stalin. The Jews of the West lost Yiddish somewhere on the road to their brilliant acculturation, and all that remains is nostalgia. Yiddish literature is now rarely read in the original.

David Bergelson (1884-1952) is therefore all but unknown to those who do not read Yiddish, for only a few of his writings—some short stories and a novel—have been translated into English. Yiddishists consider him the successor to the three classic modern Yiddish authors—Mendele Mocher Sforim, Sholem Aleichem, and I. L. Peretz—but, unlike them, Bergelson wrote for a cultured, highly educated audience, not for the masses.

His great predecessors had forged a literature out of their lives and dreams, when life was simpler, the lines more clearly drawn. Their world was the shtetl, and they knew it intimately; they were connected to its institutions, understood the people, recognized the enemy. By Bergelson's time the world had changed. The Revolution of 1905, which raised people's hopes for a better life, created an exodus to the industrialized cities and to America, and the shtetl inevitably declined. Of those who remained, in that heady period between the two socialist revolutions, many no longer accepted the values and traditions that had served their parents and grandparents so well. They did not want their lives anchored to the synagogue and to the study house.

Yet they had not managed to create better lives for themselves. The freedom to doubt, they soon learned, created more problems than it solved, and the newly open social structure was not so easy to penetrate. They were not yet attuned to the world of industry and competition, and the coldness and indifference of the big city frightened them. The individual who had once been part of a community, connected to its institutions and committed to its values, was now alone and experienced the angst and pain of alienation from society. Bergelson captures the dreariness of the uncommitted life and portrays characters who suffer from ennui and depression as a result of the loosening ties to the shtetl and to religion.

Bergelson's view is not narrow, however, and his focus is not solely on Jewish concerns. Although his setting is the declining shtetl, his theme is the suffering of lonely, alienated people everywhere. His characters suffer from the same malaise that afflicts the many alienated in our own inhospitable world. Bergelson is more interested in psychology than in theology. Suicide, as he describes it, is an emotional tragedy, a tragedy of the human condition, not a sin.

Bergelson is particularly impressive in his sensitive psychological probing of women, more vulnerable now in their new roles and with their increased freedom. In a style that is both lyrical and precise, using rhythmic repetitions and innovative dialogue but never an extra word or syllable, Bergelson uncovers the woman's soul and reveals her basic nature—the tenderness as well as the determination. And always there is a heavy atmosphere of gloom and oppression over her, the gloom of the dying shtetl.

He had learned much from the Russians. To depict the new world of the declining shtetl and the disaffected in that society, Bergelson had to free himself from the forms and themes of the Yiddish writers who preceded him. In the process of liberating himself from the anxiety of influence, he created a style that is unique, innovative, and original. He used the language of the old Yiddish writers, molded to suit his more worldly and contemporary concerns; and he followed the Russian writers—Tolstoy, Turgenev, Dostoyevsky, Gorki, Andreyev—in creating characters with emotional depth. From Chekhov he learned about mood and atmosphere

The style, however, is his own. Bergelson uses echoes and patterns of repetition as lyrical devices to elicit the reader's emotional response; he makes use of internal dialogue to reveal the thoughts behind the words of his heroes; and he analyzes the psychological state of his characters to a degree unprecedented in Yiddish literature. He enjoys the small moves, the details of existence, the little twists and turns that make the quotidian interesting. But he is a realist, and therefore his vision of life is essentially tragic.

His shtetl is hazy and there is the dolor of death all around, but it is a real world. His shtetl is not peopled by warm and deeply religious Jews, as in Sholem Aleichem, nor is it a society so filled with poverty and superstition that it invariably chokes its inhabitants, as in Mendele Mocher Sforim. He portrays the Yiddish-speaking intelligentsia after the failed Revolution of 1905 as frightened and confused, often aimless, talking late into the night as a substitute for action. They are no longer religious and no longer feel the pull of the shtetl community, yet they are too unsure of themselves to leave.

David Bergelson was born on August 12, 1884, in Okhrimovo, near Uman in the Ukraine. He was the youngest child in a Hasidic family. His father, a successful wood merchant, died when David was a boy of nine. His mother, a cultured woman who loved Yiddish literature, saw to it that David was tutored in secular subjects, including modern languages, while he attended the local *heder*, the traditional religious boys' school, where he studied Bible, history, and Talmud. When David was fourteen his mother died and he went to live with his older brothers in the big cities of Kiev, Odessa, and Warsaw. He read widely: Hebrew and Russian literature, world literature in translation, Yiddish literature; and, like every good Jewish-Russian lad, he played the violin.

His earliest writings were in Hebrew and Russian, but he switched to Yiddish in 1907 with his story **"The Deaf One" ("Der Toyber")**; thereafter he used Yiddish exclusively. His first novella, *At the Depot (Arum Vokzal),* written in 1908, won him immediate critical acclaim. During the next two years he wrote some of his best stories, including **"Remnants" ("Droyb")** and **"Impoverished" ("Yordim")**, both included in this volume. One of his most popular works is the children's book, *Fayvel's Tales (Fayvel's Mayses),* which adults soon adopted as their own. With the publication of his novel, *When All is Said and Done (Nokh Alemen)* in 1913, his reputation as a major Yiddish writer was firmly established; the critics declared him an outstanding talent, original, brilliant, and authentic, and predicted that his innovative style would have an important impact on modern Yiddish letters. During this period he began work on his novella *Departing (Opgang),* also included in this volume. It was not published until 1920. Many other works were published during this early, fertile period, including *Joseph Schur* (1913) and *In a Backwoods Town* (1914). In 1928 the short novel *Civil War* was printed in a collection of stories. A list of Bergelson's works that have been translated into English appears at the end of this book.

Bergelson's early works were written at a time when Yiddish literature flourished in the Soviet Union and Yiddish books sold in the hundreds of thousands. He was optimistic about the future of Yiddish letters but felt that new forms were needed. In an early article entitled **"Literature and Society,"** he declared that there was an organic tie between society and literature, the social forms being the bricks and mortar of a writer's work. The Revolution created a new society that did not fit the old forms, yet there were no new forms to replace them.

To meet the need for fresh styles, Bergelson and other Yiddish writers who were interested in experimenting with new forms founded a literary society in 1912, in Kiev, called *The League for Jewish Culture.* The group included the famous writers Der Nister, Peretz Markish, David Hofstein, and Leib Kvitko, among others. All were grounded in the Jewish sources; but they had studied Russian and European literature, too. Symbolism and Impressionism fascinated them, and they experimented with the techniques of these literary movements in an attempt to divert Yiddish literature away from the traditional forms. One of the group's major accomplishments was the publication of a two-volume miscellany called *Our Own* (Eygns), which appeared between 1918 and 1920 under Bergelson's editorship. It emphasized poetry, but other forms of literature and criticism were also represented.

Yiddish literature continued to thrive in the early years of the Bolshevik government. Between 1917 and 1921 some 850 Yiddish books were printed; many new Yiddish newspapers appeared; literary journals published Yiddish stories, poems, and criticism; and the Yiddish theater reached new heights of excellence under the direction of Solomon Mikhoels. Yiddish writers were supported financially, and there was enough flexibility to allow them to experiment with new styles.

Beginning in the 1920s, however, things began to change. Material shortages caused by the civil war made it difficult for writers to concentrate on creative work. Furthermore, Bolshevik restraints were becoming more and more intolerable as writers were forced to follow the vague dictates of socialist realism. Many Yiddish authors emigrated, among them Kadya Molodovsky, Der Nister, and Leib Kvitko. Bergelson had already left for Berlin in 1921, where he worked for the Yiddish newspaper, the *Forward,* contributing an article or a story each week. But he was restless and traveled widely, settling in Denmark for a time, and in Poland. In the United States he lectured to large audiences in New York, Baltimore, Chicago, Philadelphia, and other cities, reading from his works in progress.

He was very critical of the state of Yiddish culture in the United States. Writers for the popular Yiddish newspapers and for the stage pandered to a poor, mainly uneducated audience. Intellectuals, including the group of poets who called themselves Die Yunge (The Young Ones)—Mani Leib, Reuven Ayzland, Zishe Landau, David Ignatoff, and others—received little remuneration or recognition. They were mainly poor laborers who wrote whenever they could snatch an hour or two from their work. Bergelson identified with their poetic aims; they, too, sought to create a new and vital literature that was not based on the old, folkloristic traditions. But he found their low status and poverty intolerable. In Russia poets were respected—and subsidized.

Over the years Bergelson had become ever more convinced that communism was the only hope for mankind. In keeping with his communist sympathies, he left his job at the *Forward* in 1926 for a position with a lower salary at the communist newspaper *Freiheit,* and he published novels that supported the aims of the revolution. *Measure of Justice (Midas Hadin),* written in 1925, is about an officer in the political police; though a decent enough person in many ways, he has no pangs of conscience when he orders people shot. The killings are not the acts of an individual but part of the historical process. The revolution creates its own justice.

The first volume of *By the Dnieper,* published in 1932, when he was in Germany, has a ten-year-old hero named Penek who despises the bourgeois values of his home and prefers to associate with the servants and the people in the poorer parts of town. He has never respected his father, a Jewish scholar, and he spouts the usual formulas in praise of the communist revolution. The second volume, written after Bergelson returned to the Soviet Union, deals with Penek grown into a revolutionary.

Bergelson returned to Moscow in 1933, convinced that the new social order would encourage Yiddish writers. Indeed, he believed that there would be a great blossoming of Yiddish literature in the Soviet Union. Other equally optimistic Yiddish writers returned with him, including the poets Leib Kvitko and Peretz Markish, the novelist Moshe Kulbak, and the critic Max Erik. On the way to Moscow, Bergelson visited the autonomous Jewish area of Birobidzhan, where Yiddish was to have been the official language; he wrote *Birobidzhan Stories* after this visit.

Jewish writers did flourish in Moscow, but very briefly. Mikhoels's Yiddish Theater, which had reached the highest standards of art and had made a major contribution to Russian culture, was a great source of pride for the Jews. Yiddish writers were supported with generous royalties and given good housing. However, very quickly things changed. Moshe Litvakov, a fanatically loyal communist who was the editor-in-chief of the leading Yiddish newspaper, *Truth* (Der Emes), was arrested. Moishe Kulbak and Itze Kharik, both famous Yiddish writers, were imprisoned; Kharik was executed, and Kulbak died in a slave labor camp in 1940. Other Yiddish writers were sent to concentration camps or tortured in prison.

The atmosphere was unbearable for Yiddish writers. They were treated with the greatest suspicion; every word they wrote was censored. The strictures of socialist realism were so vague that anything Jews wrote could be considered illegitimate, depending on the mood or the prejudices of the examiner. According to the doctrine of socialist realism, art belonged to the people and had to be intelligible even to the least educated. Because the function of literature was to depict truth, and because the communist party was the source of all truth, only the writer who adhered closely to the party line was a true representative of art. No individual expression was possible in this system, nor was an opinion that differed from the party line or a view of life that might raise questions or doubts in the reader.

To further squelch Yiddish writers, a new term of opprobrium was invented: "cosmopolitanism." Because Russian culture was supposedly undermined by the Jewish content in Yiddish writings, Yiddish works were censored more and more scrupulously for Jewish content. Anything that touched on Jewish culture and the Jewish past was considered separatist and nationalistic, even including folklore or jokes. All Hebrew had to be excised from the Yiddish language, and every trace of religion, including all references to the Bible, had to be removed from Yiddish works. Such strictures not only left the language dull and colorless but also stopped up major sources of inspiration for Yiddish writers.

With these severe restrictions Bergelson could not even consider returning to his innovative experiments. If he wanted to write at all, he had to write politically correct books, not stories about his own experiences. As a result, the quality of his writing declined seriously; he could not abide by the strictures of socialist realism, vague as they were, and continue to write delicate, lyrical stories that explored the motives and responses of the individual. In the process of writing propaganda and pandering to the communist censors, his style became unrefined, even coarse.

None of the returning writers had foreseen the black future that awaited Yiddish in the Soviet Union. Stalin exterminated half a million Jews and shut down all Jewish cultural institutions, including 750 schools that taught Yiddish. It was obvious that the Yiddish language would meet the same fate as Hebrew and be annihilated root and branch.

When the Germans invaded Russia, Bergelson's dormant Jewish feelings could no longer be contained. He wrote a play, *Prince Reuveni,* in which he talks about the ancient dream of a Jewish homeland, using the Inquisition as a barely disguised metaphor for life in the Soviet Union. This was a daring move. Other Yiddish writers were similarly brought back to their Jewish roots, even including the fanatic communist Itzik Fefer and the poet Peretz Markish, who had written paeans of praise to Stalin.

The year 1948 was horrendous for Jewish artists. Isaac Babel, who wrote in Russian, was executed. Mikhoels was murdered, and his theater was closed a year later. Bergelson and other Yiddish writers were arrested, as were almost all the intellectuals who had served Stalin on the Jewish Anti-Fascist Committee. By 1952 most of the Yiddishists had been killed, and even simple Jews were so frightened that they destroyed their own Yiddish books.

. . . . .

The stories in this volume of Bergelson's writings all belong to his early period, when he believed in the integrity of the artist and expressed himself freely, unbound by socialist realism. They reveal Bergelson as a penetrating psychologist who feels the pain of his characters, victims of the human condition who are undermined by fate. His profound understanding of human nature is set off by the lyrical qualities of his prose style, exemplary for his time and still cogent and compelling today. In order to demonstrate these qualities I have chosen the stories **"Remnants"** and **"Impoverished"** and the novella *Departing.*

"Remnants" is the story of an orphaned servant, Beyla Henya, who is born to every disadvantage that a young woman in the shtetl can have. She is not only poor but also profoundly ugly, with deep pockmarks and crossed eyes. To disguise her physical deformities she covers her face with a white kerchief, and to endure the pain of her difficult existence she develops pride—and hope. In a triumph of the human spirit, she forcefully reorganizes her perceptual field and refuses to see her situation for what it is; instead, she dreams of marrying a respectable man one day. She never speaks.

In Beyla Henya, Bergelson has created the modern feminist ideal: a strong-willed, stubborn, spunky woman who knows what she wants and is not afraid to reach for it. She will not submit to her husband in a loveless marriage. She does not let the harsh circumstances of her life destroy her. And she stubbornly clings to her dream until it comes true; she finally marries a respectable man who is as silent as she is.

Bergelson's point of view is modern enough to please the most fastidious feminist critic, yet the story was written at the turn of the century and concerns the lives of simple, unsophisticated people living in a shtetl. Bergelson gives the characters a realistic, visual presence by using concise, trenchant details: Beyla Henya's rich relative wears a black worsted shawl; the husband's sister wears a peasant's kerchief; Beyla Henya and her husband eat out of the same dish; a man urinates in the street, his coat covered with the whitewash he has just brushed against. And lest the fairytale ending seem far-fetched, Bergelson emends it with an ironic twist that qualifies the happy outcome and makes the narrative wholly plausible.

"Impoverished" is a story about two unmarried sisters, Zivia and Rochl, who live with their blind father in a decaying house that smells of mold and death. The house is unstable, sinking ever deeper into the ground, a metaphor for the family's grave-like existence. Poverty has brought the sisters low—psychologically, socially, and spiritually. They are helplessly locked into their fate.

The father lies on the couch all day, bored to death, dreaming of the old days when he was rich. Rochl, the older sister, has given up on life. Zivia is depressed, but she has occasional bursts of energy when she cleans the house from top to bottom, desperately trying to fight her own death by bringing the house to life again. Shmiel, the successful brother, never visits.

And there is silence. Zivia never speaks at all during her bouts of depression; she can't even bear to be spoken to. The sisters don't have anything to say to each other because nothing ever happens to them. The old man mumbles into his beard, and when he talks too much, his daughters silence him. The wealthy brother has no interest at all in communicating with his family.

How, one might ask, can a story built on words portray silence? Eschewing the dramatist's footnote, "there was silence," Bergelson's artistry allows him to illustrate the silence in the fabric of his descriptions. The reader senses the silence, is weighed down and oppressed by it. To see and feel how Bergelson handles silence is sufficient reason to read the stories.

It is telling to compare Bergelson's use of silence in the two stories. In **"Remnants"** the silence is innocent and unaffected. The old teacher has almost forgotten how to speak since his wife died. He would like to talk to Beyla Henya after their marriage but can't because he doesn't know her name; and Beyla Henya can't overcome her shyness to speak to him. The silence between them is gentle, suggesting sympathy and even love. We sense silence here as understanding, a form of communication. When the old teacher finally breaks his silence to praise Beyla Henya's cooking, "a delicious dish, a wonderful pumpkin," she experiences the greatest happiness she has ever known. She continues to maintain her silence, however, until he dies. Then she finally gives voice to her feelings and cries out, "You liked pumpkin . . . so I made you pumpkin."

The silence in **"Impoverished"** is not the innocent silence of **"Remnants."** It is oppressive and harsh—a mark of Zivia's depression, of Shmiel's indifference, and of the sisters' cruelty to their father. The sisters speak mainly to themselves, crying out in their bitterness. "Dear God in Heaven, what does Zivia want from my life?" Rochl cries helplessly. "God in Heaven, we're rotting here before we're even in our shrouds," wails Zivia. This is not communication, nor is it intended to be. The father sighs and mumbles to himself, "Oh, dear God and Father, King of the Universe," but no one listens; he might as well be silent. Shmiel, the rich son, remains distant and silent, never so much as adding a note to the check he sends each month to his father and sisters. When his train passes through the shtetl, Shmiel has nothing to say; he merely extends his gloved hand out of the window and touches his father lightly.

In the novella ***Departing,*** we are quickly made to understand that life is suffused with pain and can have no meaning. Once we accept these givens, Bergelson asks, "Is suicide a legitimate solution to the hurt and a remedy for the vacuum?" Suicide, as a theme, had been taboo in Yiddish literature. Bergelson, the first to deal with the subject, acted on his belief that every aspect of life was proper material for an author. He fashioned a highly innovative and artistic novella, full of surprising dialogues with the dead man, along with romance and love. Bergelson understands suicide as stemming from psychological poverty and a lack of values rather than from hunger and physical pain.

Melech, a gifted and charming young man, dies suddenly, and his friend Chaim Moshe, a teacher of mathematics, comes to the shtetl to investigate the cause. During his careful and painstaking search, Chaim Moshe discovers that Melech took poison. Chaim Moshe carries on a continuous debate with himself and with the

dead Melech on the question of suicide: is it an acceptable solution to a life devoid of meaning?

The background of the novella is the dying shtetl and the dissolution of values: "Clouds chase each other across the blue sky and their shadows below play the same game in the street and in the marketplace. But in heaven everything is pure gold; below the imitation is tainted and unclean." One of the characters, Esther Fich, a student who returns reluctantly to the shtetl every summer, puts it succinctly, "Nobody ever dies here—they just fade away." The void left by the breakup of the old, established way of life, by the weakening of a religion-based life-style that gave meaning to community, is not easily filled, even by economic success. The big city, to which Chaim Moshe and his friend Melech had turned for a life of excitement and promise, failed to satisfy the young men. It is too impersonal, too empty and devoid of meaning.

Bergelson presents a wide variety of shtetl characters, among whom the women are the most memorable. One of them is Ethel Kadis, whose engagement to Melech gave her a reason to live. His death leaves her with "the look of a woman who knows deep down that life is mocking her, but . . . pretends indifference." Another is Chava Poyzner, whose solution to an empty life is to marry rich and leave the dying shtetl. The most sympathetic of the women is Channeke Loyber, who tenderly cares for her little motherless brother and whose love for Chaim Moshe ultimately saves him from suicide.

The men include Praeger, the principal of the local school, who has nothing but loathing for all the respectable people in the shtetl. Although a highly educated and successful teacher, he is spiteful and vindictive, spewing out his anger on anyone he feels is above him in status. To forget his problems he drinks, mainly with low-life characters. And there is Dr. Grabay, a former communist party orator who now stacks away his money. He has not much else to live for; his wife has left him and their little daughter for another man.

Chaim Moshe, who returns to the shtetl to find out why Melech died so suddenly, is a modern intellectual—precise, logical, and unbendingly hard on himself. In his debates with himself and with the imagined, reincarnated Melech, Chaim Moshe accuses his friend of giving in to the world. They had both agreed to live by the principle of "the silent protest." But Melech was not satisfied; he wanted happiness. His act of suicide is a betrayal, according to Chaim Moshe, who claims to have no illusions about life.

The novel begins on a cold, rainy day with Melech's funeral. Chaim Moshe discovers Melech's suicide, decries it—and, coming full circle, contemplates suicide as a solution for his own problems. But he is saved by love. The novel ends as the sun rises to the promise of a beautiful day.

Silence is again a major theme. In the city the two friends would repeat over and over again, "The silent protest, the eternal silent protest." Bergelson does not explain the meaning of the motto; instead he describes the friends as destined to walk the city like strangers, seeing and hearing everything and saying nothing. Melech has impressed everyone with his shy smile and his silence, and people loved him. They believed that his silence indicated great wisdom and knowledge. But, in fact, he fooled them all, committing suicide under their noses with small doses of poison while making them all believe that he was ill.

Not even silence can be trusted, Bergelson tells us—not in so many words, rather through the plot and the characters. And the other side of the scale is balanced with our realization that suicide, successful as a solution or not, is the ultimate silence. Man, Chaim Moshe tells us, dies alone. When his time comes, he *wants* to die alone; his funeral will be at night, and no one will come. Here is his final, silent protest.

But there is another silence, Bergelson informs us, a silence that is louder than speech, that is truer and more trustworthy. Channeke, who loves to talk, becomes increasingly silent as her love for Chaim Moshe grows. She looks into his eyes and feels that he knows everything she knows, that he has always known. And her sad blue eyes speak to Chaim Moshe's heart more than words do. At the end of the book, when Channeke comes to Chaim Moshe's room just as he is contemplating suicide, she offers him her silent love. It is perfectly understood. Chaim Moshe, the intellectual, falls silent, too, in the face of love. "Oh, Channeke" is all he says, and all that need be said.

We might ask, as Bergelson undoubtedly does, how can a novelist, a wordsmith, deal so successfully with silence. The irony is obvious and charges Bergelson's language with electric sparks. Do words have meaning? Can acting, even suicide, relieve the angst of a dying, aphonic society? Bergelson illuminates the other side of the moon in his treatment of Channecke. She is portrayed as silent and deferential, but with great native intelligence and emotional depth—she knows what she wants. Channeke understands intuitively that Chaim Moshe is contemplating suicide and acts to intercept that plan.

Bergelson's writings challenge the interpretive skills of the reader, just as his artistry plucks sympathetic chords.

. . . . .

A word about the translation. It has been said that every translation of literature produces a new literary work. The translator's attempt to uncover the writer's intended meaning forces her to engage in the tricky art of interpretation, with all its tantalizing—and egoistic—allures. And, in attempting to render some essence of the original language into the new language, the trans-

lator is again in peril. Style cannot be transferred from one language to another; at best the translator may come up with an equivalent in the new language that reproduces the sense of the original.

Bergelson depends on poetic effects to establish mood and meaning: his Yiddish syntax is complex; his language is both rich and precise; and he uses musical devices, including sound patterns and repetition. The problems of capturing the rhythms of the original language in another tongue are legion. When rendered faithfully, these constructions often grind painfully on the English reader's ear. Since my goal was to make Bergelson's work live in English as it does in Yiddish, I had to make compromises. I had to render Bergelson's flowing Yiddish into readable English and, at the same time, keep as close to the essence of Bergelson's work as I could without making the translation sound foreign.

Not the least of my problems was that Bergelson's language is a perfect match for a phenomenon not clearly represented in the experience of readers of English. These works all take place against the background of the dying shtetl, which casts a pall over everything. It is almost impossible to render Bergelson's rhythms and his haunting, elegiac descriptions into English. Yet these are precisely the stylistic devices that create the gloomy atmosphere that Bergelson aimed for, evoking empathy and enabling the reader to see and feel what Bergelson saw and felt. No translation can do justice to the moody, dark atmosphere created by Bergelson and the language he uses to further his aims; there is no strict counterpart in English to the compelling music of Bergelson's Yiddish.

Great works, however, are more easily translated than inferior works. Bergelson helped by handling the interaction of the background and the action very gently, very delicately. At the end the reader says, "That's right, that's the way it is," and puts down the book with a sigh.

Rachel Stoll (essay date 1997)

SOURCE: "The Stories of David Bergelson," in the *New York Times Book Review*, March 9, 1997, p. 19.

[*In the following essay, a review of an English translation of Bergelson's stories, Stoll treats the tales as images of a long-vanished world and culture.*]

In his brief foreword to this collection of stories, [The stories of David Bergelson: Yiddish Short Fiction From Russia] Aharon Appelfeld calls David Bergelson "the most important Yiddish writer, following the three classical authors who established modern Yiddish literature: Mendele Mocher Sforim, I. L. Peretz and Sholem Aleichem." Born in 1884 to a Hasidic family in Ukraine, Bergelson worked assiduously for the cause of Communism; nevertheless, he was arrested under Stalin and sent to a prison camp, where he died in 1952. This new volume contains two short stories and one novella from his early period when, according to the fine introduction by Golda Werman, the book's translator, Bergelson still "believed in the integrity of the artist and expressed himself freely, unbound by socialist realism." His presentation of shtetl life is similar to Aleichem's only in its genius, for Bergelson's vision is an altogether tragic one. In these pages the shtetl, which is gasping its last breath, is anything but a warm and inviting place, a colorful society in which familial love and fervent faith flow freely. Instead, its men are hunchbacked, its women pockmarked; here everyone is stifled and unfulfilled. In the novella that takes up most of the book, a young man who has left the shtetl and the religion of his youth for the freedom of a nearby city returns to "the desultory ordinariness of Rakitne" to investigate the mysterious death of a friend, a charming man who "always looked as if he wanted to say something, as if he was just about to tell the world what he knew." It turns out that the friend killed himself, an act that accorded with his phi-losophy of living in "silent protest" and a fact that the community refuses to face. "The town itself," we are told, "is old and decrepit, a dead town."

FURTHER READING

Criticism

Goldin, Judah. "The Contemporary Jew and His Judaism." In *Spiritual Problems in Contemporary Literature*, edited by Stanley Romaine Hopper, pp. 207-23. New York: Harper & Brothers, 1957.
    Examines the rejection of Judaism in favor of socialism by Jewish writers including Bergelson, whose "The Revolution and the Zussmans" Goldin compares to Jacob Glatstein's "Citizen God."

Clarence Darrow

1857-1938

(Full name Clarence Seward Darrow) American novelist, autobiographer, essayist, speech writer, and philosopher.

INTRODUCTION

Darrow is considered one of the most renowned trial lawyers and eloquent orators in American history. His legal prowess manifested itself in speeches that are considered masterpieces of emotional manipulation. Darrow argued some of the most controversial cases in U.S. history; his fame arose from his ability to influence both juries and public opinion. Darrow is also esteemed for his writings on various subjects, especially those relating to philosophy and human behavior. These written works were composed with an eye towards rhetoric and public approval. According to Darrow, human beings perform criminal acts out of an innate tendency rather than free will, and thus moral responsibility does not exist. This belief formed the basis of Darrow's personal philosophy as well as his work as a defense attorney. In addition to his nonfiction, Darrow wrote several novels that are considered fine if minor examples of literary realism.

Biographical Information

Darrow was born in the small agricultural town of Kinsman, Ohio, to parents whose strong philosophical beliefs were mirrored in Darrow's own life and work. His father, a theological seminarian who later lost his religious faith, subscribed to an intellectual skepticism and awareness of social injustice unusual for their community. The Darrows housed runaway slaves and were active in the abolition movement. While Darrow admired his father's beliefs and sense of social duty, he vowed to be more financially successful.

He attended the University of Michigan Law School but left after a year. Nonetheless, he passed the bar examination and, in 1878, began to practice law near Kinsman. In 1887, with a young family to support, Darrow moved to Chicago. There, he became general counsel to the Chicago and Northwestern Railway. Though Darrow fared well as an attorney, he left the railroad in 1895 because he found it reprehensible to represent the railroad against employees who had been hurt. While Darrow's labor career was highly successful, he found his greatest achievement in several controversial cases, most notably the Loeb and Leopold trial in 1924 and the Scopes trial in 1925. Richard Loeb and Nathan Leopold, two affluent young men, confessed to the brutal murder of a young boy. Darrow found the case intriguing because the killers had no motive save thrill-seeking. In their defense, Darrow pleaded guilty, held that

the youths were led astray by an internal force beyond their control, and asked only that their lives be spared. Because of Darrow's compelling courtroom arguments, Loeb and Leopold received life in prison rather than the death penalty. The next year, Darrow defended John Scopes, a Tennessee schoolteacher arrested for teaching evolution rather than creationism. In this case, Darrow argued that he was defending not just Scopes, but the pursuit of intellectual freedom. In so doing, he succeeded in convincing the jury that the prosecutor, the noted statesman William Jennings Bryan, was both bigoted and ignorant. In Darrow's last years, he wrote essays and spoke on a variety of subjects including agnosticism, the death penalty, and what he regarded as humanity's inherently dishonest nature. Darrow died in 1938.

Major Works

Darrow's legal career took precedence over his literary one, even when he devoted more time to writing in later life. He composed in a number of genres, including essays and novels. Throughout his works, a realistic style prevails. His first novel, *Farmington* (1904), is a fictionalized account of his rural childhood. In this book, Darrow sets forth his personal philosophy, including the need to revolt against an outdated, unsympathetic society. The story of a small town childhood, *Farmington* is nostalgic but unsentimental. In many of his writings, Darrow strove for the human touch, and novels such as *An Eye for An Eye* (1905), indicate his concern for the oppressed. Like other writers of the era, he attacks wealthy society for its collective lack of social responsibility. *Crime: Its Cause and Treatment* (1922) delineates Darrow's theory of criminal behavior. According to Darrow, crime is purely the result of environment and heredity, and should be treated as if it were a disease. Darrow's autobiography, *The Story of My Life* (1932), vividly describes his courtroom experiences. Here, Darrow contends that his belief in universal justice served as the motivating force for the often-controversial cases he accepted.

PRINCIPAL WORKS

A Persian Pearl and Other Essays (essays) 1899
Easy Lessons in Law (essays) 1902
Resist Not Evil (philosophy) 1902
Farmington (novel) 1904
An Eye for An Eye (novel) 1905
Crime: Its Cause and Treatment (nonfiction) 1922
The Prohibition Mania: A Reply to Professor Irving Fisher and Others (treatise) 1927
Infidels and Heretics: An Agnostic's Anthology (essays) 1929
The Story of My Life (autobiography) 1932

CRITICISM

New York Times Book Review (essay date 1904)

SOURCE: "The Heart of a Boy," in the *New York Times Book Review*, October 8, 1904, p. 676.

[*In the following review of* Farmington, *the anonymous critic calls the book "insidiously iconoclastic," noting Darrow's use of point of view and his stark honesty.*]

[*Farmington*] is a book insidiously iconoclastic. Under the innocent guise of telling as much of the truth about his boyhood's real feelings as he dares, Mr. Darrow sets about undermining a number of cherished notions and traditional beliefs. As Mr. Shaw says, he "spoils the attitude" of the orthodox writers about childhood, insisting (in all love and tenderness) on the tragedy of the attempt of parents to mold the life of their offspring, to instill virtue into them by precept, to make them pore over books when all the bounding life of youth calls for out-of-doors and play. In the manner of the telling, and in the spirit behind the telling, is a reminiscence of Heine in those autobiographical scraps of his, something of the same feeling of the tragedy of the joys of youth missed and gone, something of the same serio-comic attitude toward other people's meddlings. In fact, the book is very charming, and in much very true. Not a man who has been a real country boy, or who has been cheated by his elders (always with the best motives) of being all the boy he might have been—but, if he has grown up to be ripe enough, will seem to find himself again in many of Mr. Darrow's pages.

Behind the seeming simplicity and frankness of the story of how the boy really felt toward his parents, toward the other grown-ups, toward other boys, toward girls, (in the days before the glamour of romance began to distort real values,) toward his tasks, of how dimly he understood what he was taught, of how little he has remembered of all he learned, and of how much less he has ever had any use for of what he was urged to learn, some of us will see a theory of life and education with which we will not entirely agree. But there is far more truth than untruth in the picture; so much truth at times that you are a bit afraid. The book is not exactly glad reading to people who are past the turning point between youth and age, yet to these it will appeal most. By the way, the probability is that, as you set out to read, you will think for several pages that the book is silly. That's while the author is getting you into the child's point of view. Once there it is different, as what we have said above will prove. Our impression is that Mr. Darrow has shown real art in the handling of one of the most difficult forms of literature. The reader can, however, judge for himself; he ought at least to give himself the chance to judge.

It may be well to add that the book purports to be simply a collection of what John Smith, the son of a miller, (a miller who had hoped to be something else and bookish) in a small Puritan town, can remember of his boyhood impressions and the effects upon him of advice, discipline, and education of the kind universal a generation ago, and still more or less orthodox. A visit of John (now turned of forty) to his native town starts the train. The recollections are rambling and disconnected, and most evidently autobiographical.

Sara Andrew Shafer (essay date 1904)

SOURCE: "Through the Eyes of a Boy," in *The Dial*, Vol. 33, October 16, 1904, pp. 237-38.

[*In the following review, Shafer offers high praise for* Farmington.]

Since Mr. Howells's delightful idyll of boyhood, *A Boy's Town*, there has perhaps been no worthier companion volume than Mr. Darrow's *Farmington.* If one were born a boy, and has lived long enough to be able to look back and understand what it was to be young, and what his youth has meant to him ever since, he will find his real self again in these limpid pages. And if he be lucky enough to have begun life in the country, or in a village which was so small as to be almost the same thing, tucked in beside a millstream that divided two high hills, he will see with his waking eyes the places and the people that come to him in dreams,—dreams that are perhaps the best part of his life.

In Farmington there was a church, a district school, a square, a burying-ground, and a mill. In the church, long hours of torture were spent by restless urchins, who were in great awe of the minister, and were surprised when they discovered later that he was a real man like others whom they knew. In the school-house, the little ruffians made life wretched for the teacher, and had as much fun and wasted as little time over their studies as was possible for them to do. They read the highly moral tales of the old readers, they declaimed the threadbare old orations, and they governed themselves and each other according to the primal code of morals known to boys for many generations. In the village square they played the games suggested by the changing year; and along the stream, in the woods, fields, and over the hills, they had the endless varieties of fun and learned the thousand things which go to form the mind and character of country-bred children. Through the burying-ground they went only when they could prove the safety that lies in numbers, and when the sun shone on the tombstones which figured in their plan of life like sentient things. It is, however, when speaking of the village mill, which was the boy's home as well, that Mr. Darrow is at his best. He has touched the simple life that flowed through and around it with a touch so wistful and so tender that the reader can only guess if there was a smile on his lips as he wrote, or if they were pressed together to keep back the tears.

Not much character-drawing is attempted in this little book; and in this reserve Mr. Darrow shows much wisdom. People are not often clearly differentiated by the minds of children, who accept their social surroundings with as little question as they do their physical environment. A few figures stand out with boldness, however, and if they are drawn with simple lines, the lines have a vigor and directness that give them quite enough of both light and shade. The well-known ne'er-do-weel who lives in every village in every land has rarely been better drawn than in the light sketch of 'Ferman Henry,' whose counterpart may be found in 'Sam Lawson' in Mrs. Stowe's memorable 'Old Town Folks.' 'Aunt Mary' is another auld acquaintance whom one is not likely to forget,—the woman who lived in bondage to a heartless idol called Neatness, whose cult she ever preached to an unheeding generation. 'Squire Allen,' the 'great man of the village,' was so very great that it was quite inconceivable how so small a place could hold him; and the loungers and scandal-mongers of the blacksmith's and shoemaker's shops,—we have seen them all before.

The crowning glory of the book is the portrait of the boy's father,—the gentle, honest, unworldly old miller, who put aside the fervid longings of his own spirit in order that he might feed and clothe the children who thronged about his hearth; who, loving honor, loving integrity, loving justice, above all else loved learning, in the beautiful old sense of the word. One rarely hears it so used in these hurried times, and perhaps it is the mission of the little book to open the eyes of a restless later day to the old and deep well-spring of contentment that lies behind it. Here is a bit of this filial and tender portrait:

> Above the little porch that shelters the front door is my father's study window. I look in and see him sitting at his desk with his shaded lamp; before him is his everlasting book, and his pale face and long white hair bend over the infatuating pages with all the confidence and trust of a little child. For a simple child he always was, from the time when he first saw the light until his friends and comrades lowered him into the sandy loam of the old churchyard. I see him through the little panes of glass, as he bends above the book. The chapter is finished and he wakens from his reverie into the world in which he lives and works; he takes off his iron-framed spectacles, lays down his book, comes downstairs and calls me away from my companions with the old story that it is time to come into the house and get my lessons. For the hundredth time I protest that I want to play,—to finish my unending game; and again he tells me no, that John Stuart Mill began studying Greek when he was only three years old. And with heavy heart and muttered imprecations on John Stuart Mill, I am taken away from my companions and my play, and set down beside my father with my book. I can feel even now my sorrow and despair, as I leave my playmates and turn the stupid leaves. But I would give all that I possess to-day to hear my father say again, as in that far-off time, 'John Stuart Mill began studying Greek when he was only three years old.'

Farmington is not a book to be taken from the public library, or even to be borrowed from an obliging friend. It is not a book for the limited express, or the smoking-room of an inn. It is a book to own,—to read by the winter's fire, and re-read under a summer tree; a book to be kept on the shelf where the oldest favorites live. It is a book for boys, for women,—but above all, it is a book for men who have once been boys.

Arthur Evans Wood (essay date 1923)

SOURCE: A review of 'Crime: Its Cause and Treatment', in *Political Science Quarterly*, Vol. XXXVIII, No. 2, June, 1923, pp. 342-45.

[*In the following review, Wood calls* Crime: Its Cause and Treatment *a "remarkable book."*]

Mr. Darrow could probably write a book on any subject, provided that he were given a little spare time to consult what the professors call "secondary sources". As a matter of fact, on the subject of criminology he himself comes very near to being an original source of information. I mean that his experience as a lawyer in criminal trials gives him a vantage ground from which he is able to make a great number of significantly true observations regarding the penal law and its operations. He is impressed, as all students of the question must be, with the futility of the vengeful and punitive motives that too generally prevail in the treatment of offenders. The arbitrary character of penal codes; the unscientific and often corrupting aspect of court procedure; the folly of capital punishment, of "expert" testimony, of a mere increase in the number of criminal laws, and of old-fashioned notions of moral responsibility are all laid bare in choppy, sententious paragraphs such as a smart, busy lawyer of radical leanings should be expected to write in moments taken from his lunch hour or his sleep. He sees the criminal law, not as a divine revelation, but as a tradition that is badly adapted to scientific knowledge and to modern conditions. When one reflects that it took fifteen years of agitation to get the American Bar Association to appoint a committee on the revision of the criminal law, one realizes how valuable as a stalwart recruit to progressive ideas in this field is Mr. Darrow. His treatise will probably secure a wider circulation than a more scholarly one that presented similar ideas with less emotional interest. The classic work on the revision of the criminal law in accordance with modern knowledge and needs still remains to be written. Meanwhile, Mr. Darrow's book helps things along in the right direction. A few more such diatribes, and a few more surveys of actual criminal proceedings, such as we have in the Cleveland Crime Survey, may arouse even the leaders of the bar.

But the author is not content to limit his discussion to the legal aspects of the problem of crime. He plunges with a layman's confidence into a discussion of the psychology of crime. The pages are fairly littered with glands, reflexes, complexes, mechanism, and other terms familiar to us in the literature of the behaviorists. There appears to be a good deal of confusion, if not of inaccuracy, in his treatment of this sort of data. The fundamental viewpoint is sound, that crime has its genesis in both heredity and environment; but there is no careful analysis of the precise relationship between these two factors. The determinism is crude, showing no differences between human behavior problems and those of the lower animals.

Mr. Darrow's statement that "One thing only seems to be sure. Human nature does not change", ignores entirely the selective power of the environment to accentuate this or that trait in accordance with the survival needs of a particular environment or epoch. The author might better have left the doctrine of unchangeable human nature to the orthodox economists, whose dogmatism on this subject is somewhat losing its hold.

We read again, "A defective mechanism either inherited or acquired through imperfectly balanced glands will inevitably produce an imperfect mind and defective conduct. *This it is bound to do because the body is the mind"*. This passage should make the psychiatrists wish that their subject were as inaccessible to laymen as the doctors have succeeded in making the traditional medicine. Whatever be the relationship between mind and body it is certainly part of elemental psychology that they are not identical. Moreover, whether any diseased condition of mind or of body will produce defective conduct depends upon the environment. Except in extreme cases there is nothing "inevitable" about the sequence at all.

We are informed that "One's character must be fixed before birth whether Nature marks it on the head or not". In view of Cooley's more scientific statement, this doctrine belongs with other discarded theories of the "born criminal".

Finally, after being thoroughly immersed in the deterministic conception of things, we are told in an amazing chapter on "Luck and Chance" that these "are the chief of all factors that really affect man." This is so because we live in a pluralistic universe. An infinite number of "mechanisms" clash in utter chaos, but there is no Mechanism. The implications here may or may not be respectable philosophy; they certainly have no bearing upon criminological theory. The most charitable thing one can say is that the practice of law prevents a man from speculating effectively in two fields that are somewhat remote from his daily job. If chance is the all-controlling factor, why complain? Why, forsooth, write books on behalf of a greater measure of justice and rationality in our dealings with criminals? The doctrine of social control, which Mr. Darrow is disposed to treat ironically, implies that many of the fortuitous elements in human experience so far as they involve disaster, such as disease, misfortune and crime, can be largely eliminated. The author, of course, knows this; and yet he reveals a strange sense of despair that is not in accord with the constructive parts of his book. Since he has carried the discussion into the realm of ultimates one is moved to reflect that social idealism, in which the book abounds, requires some sort of confidence in the general drift of things, call it religion or what you may.

It is probably an ill-reputed "academic mind" that causes one to wish for a bit more order in the discussion. The chapter headings make good jumping-off places, but give no indication as to where one will land. The scenery is always interesting, though one imagines with difficulty just how one has arrived. But I suppose that it is not just to require armchair philosophy to be sequential.

Altogether it is a remarkable book, aglow with sympathy for those who are driven hither and yon by forces which are apparently beyond their control. The radicals will take to it, of course; but in spite of its incidental vagaries it has a grip and "punch" that will appeal to conservative groups that maintain the balance of power in social life.

T. V. Smith (essay date 1932)

SOURCE: A review of 'The Story of My Life', in *The Journal of Political Economy,* Vol. XL, No. 4, August, 1932, pp. 557-58.

[*In the following review, Smith lauds the compassion and individuality evident in Darrow's The Story of My Life.*]

It might be expected that the life of Clarence Darrow would furnish materials of professional interest to economists. He got his public start in Chicago as an adherent of Henry George, in whose *Progress and Poverty* he early felt he had found "a new social gospel that bade fair to bring about the social equality and opportunity that has always been the dream of the idealist." While still young, he became general attorney for the Chicago and Northwestern Railway Company. This position he resigned on the occasion of the American Railway Union Strike in 1894 to defend Debs, then head of the union involved. This proved the beginning of a long connection with important labor cases, including an appointment by Roosevelt on the arbitration board to settle the coal strike of 1902 and ending with—with, his friends hope, some distant future case. An intimate of Altgeld, a corporation counsel for the city of Chicago, an Illinois state legislator for one term, a participator in criminal cases involving both life and property where social issues were being redirected by the outcome, Darrow has heard for nearly half a century the creaking of the rustiest hinges of our industrial joints. But what he has learned therefrom and written in his autobiography does not fall inside the special interests of economists.

For it has been the individual's fortune that has lured him into his great cases, and it has been the dramatic episodes that have caught and held his attention even in the labor disputes. Attracted into criminal law by (the then) Judge John P. Altgeld's book, *Our Penal Code and Its Victims,* Darrow has studied the victims of capitalism as have few other men of our time, and has evolved a very simple social philosophy which, beginning with the victims, ends where, or almost where, it begins. His significance lies in the moral, rather than in the economic, field; for out of sympathy for the distressed and out of tolerance for the erring, he has erected criteria of justice which, it may be hazarded, no social order could meet with any success. Capitalism where he knows it best, in its legal provisions for justice, is so intolerable that he declares that "no man is looking for justice, and, in fact, no one knows what the word means." But socialism would be worse than capitalism, and communism worse than that, and fascism under Mussolini worst of all. Capitalism does still do theoretical homage to individuality and liberty, whereas in other social isms even the theory is set against what Mr. Darrow most cherishes. Philosophical anarchism, which he once espoused but does not recall in this book, is the only social system that could command his admiration.

Which is to say that, confronting society, Mr. Darrow is without hope for the individual. The poor have always been at a disadvantage and will always be, and there is nothing in general that can be done about it. But there remains compassion for such individual cases as come one's way, and this Mr. Darrow does not so much prescribe as merely practice. He says,

> In my rather extensive experiences I never knew any one who did not want sympathy for himself, neither do I know any justice that is not entwined with sympathy. . . . The word "justice" has become associated with fear and foreboding, and is in tune with horrifying words like "stern," "impartial," and "deserve." Real justice can be neither stern nor forbidding in its attitude, but must radiate mercy and charity, and cannot be measured alike to all.

Reacting against law as retributive and in favor of scientific treatment as remedial, Mr. Darrow buttresses his ethics of sympathy with a materialistic metaphysics and a Schopenhauerian pessimism to defend the unfortunate individual against whatever opposes him, even though it be the apparent rights and values of everybody else. And yet who knows for a fact that he is wrong in supposing that if justice is to be, it must begin other than in punishment of individuals?

A great old Stoic of the Roman sort with compassion for men, ataraxy for himself and pride in the family that begot him and in the family he begot—Clarence Darrow here towers above the details of the book, interesting and important though they are, as one of the most unique and striking of our domestic individualities.

Alan Hynd (essay date 1952)

SOURCE: "Clarence Darrow," in *Defenders of the Damned,* Thomas Yoseloff Ltd., 1952, pp. 65-122.

[*In the following essay, Hynd details Darrow's defense of "hopeless" cases.*]

The old Criminal Courts Building in Chicago was the habitat of the greatest aggregation of hard-drinking reporters, assorted malefactors, shyster lawyers, heartless prosecutors, and book-throwing judges ever assembled in one American legal arena. It is difficult, in retrospect, to point the finger at the most colorful performer in the all-star cast. Some spectators to the show would choose Hildy Johnson, the old Hearst reporter (the central character in the play *The Front Page*) who one day hid an escaped murderer in his roll-top desk in the pressroom. But when it comes to nominating the most colorful lawyer ever to gain acquittals for murderers, pickpockets, second-story specialists, dippers into the public till, madams of brothels and their horizontal merchandise, it is Clarence Seward Darrow, hands down.

Darrow was the master courtroom strategist. Although he was accused only once of jury bribing during more than half a century of trial work, he was so adept at smelling out legal loopholes, clothing guilty clients in the garments of innocence, and mesmerizing juries, that he accomplished more, with a legal framework, than mouthpieces who were out-and-out crooks. Darrow was a staunch advocate of that legal tenet that holds that a man is innocent until proved guilty. Although he often knew in his own mind that a client was dripping with guilt, he felt justified in pulling all the legal levers to gain an acquittal. It was his conviction that the law was an imperfect instrument. The forces that drove a man to murder or to theft, or a woman to shoplifting or prostitution, were, to Darrow's mind, a bewildering mixture of heredity and environment—far beyond the comprehension of the average judge or jury. Who, then, was to say that this man should go to the gallows, or that this woman should go to the workhouse?

As a boy in a small Ohio town, Clarence Darrow had seen innocent men convicted of offenses they had never committed because they did not have proper legal representation—and he had never forgotten it. As a man, he knew of cases where mitigating circumstances should have gotten killers off with prison terms or even acquittals, rather than executions, but their lawyers had not been as clever as the coldly ambitious prosecutors. And so Darrow was dedicated to the proposition that no murderer he represented would be executed. And he never swerved from his course. He went to the bar for more than one hundred murderers in his time, and not a single one of them ever hit the hemp. More than that, at least a third of them got off scot-free.

The Darrow who was so well known around the Criminal Courts Building—the scowling, shuffling, unkempt, magnetic Darrow who kept prosecutors awake nights—was exemplified in one murder case he handled—that of a Milquetoasty little man who chopped up his fat wife so that he could give his undivided attention to another woman. Here, if ever there was one, was a client whose ultimate end should be the gallows. But the little man had a well-filled sock, and Darrow, after examining its contents, decided to take the case.

So far as the evidence went, Darrow knew he didn't have a prayer. The prosecutor had the little man dead to rights. So there was no way of finding a loophole through the evidence. But there was always the jury—good men and true, perhaps, but not necessarily very bright. Darrow's only chance was somehow to put the defendant on an even, sympathetic basis with some of the jurors.

So Darrow saw to it when the jury was being picked that he got as wide a variety of men as possible—carpenters, storekeepers, old men, young men, single men, married men, fellows who liked baseball, soccer, basketball, fishing, and hunting.

The murderer had once kept a small store, he had liked to go to soccer matches, and he had liked to fish. Since

Darrow had seen to it that two of the jurors kept small stores and half of them were soccer fans and that several liked to fish, the case was all set up for Darrow before the prosecutor even started to introduce the evidence. Darrow couldn't, of course, expect an acquittal. What he was after was a disagreement. If he could get one disagreement, he could get another, and another, and the case would be kicked around until it got lost.

After the prosecution evidence was in, Darrow didn't put his client on the stand. Instead, he carefully rehearsed the little murderer to sit meekly at the defense table, a picture of docility, while he summed up. Darrow addressed his remarks to the small storekeepers, the soccer fans, and the fishermen, and to hell with the others. He pictured his little client as having acted in self-defense against an overpowering woman.

"And then he cut her up," Darrow said, "out of sheer fright. Why, gentlemen, take a look at this poor little man. Does he look to you to be the kind of a man who would have so much as an evil thought? Just look at his pinched face and undernourished little body. Why, this brute of a woman that he was forced to kill to save his own life—why, gentlemen, she wouldn't even *feed* him. I tell you, gentlemen, I am defending this little man for nothing—he has no money, but that does not matter to me in this instance—I am defending him so that he can go back to his little business and eke out enough to keep body and soul together—and perhaps go to a soccer game once in a while and maybe do a little fishing, too."

It is easy to imagine what went on in the jury room. "The little sonofabitch ought to swing," we can hear a nonsporting carpenter saying to a small storekeeper who liked to fish.

"He should like hell," we can hear the storekeeper answering. "He would never do a thing like that unless he was driven into it. Why, he likes soccer and fishing. *I* like soccer and fishing. You goin' to stand there and tell me that I could cut up *my* wife?"

So of course Darrow got his disagreement. It was the same essential story at the little cut-up's second trial—and the same disagreement. Then Darrow, following the same line, got still a third disagreement. By that time the boys in the prosecutor's office were beginning to see how somebody *could* get mad enough to commit murder. They accepted a manslaughter plea, and, if Darrow had taken the time to carry the case further, would probably have settled for a breach of the peace.

There was once quite a stink in Chicago about some dental students cheating in their examinations by somehow getting hold of the answers in advance. A detective for a go-getting prosecutor learned that the son of an examiner had gotten hold of the answers from papa's briefcase and, realizing that he had practically struck gold, had gone out and sold the answers to the boys about to take the exams.

One of the purchasers had been foolish enough to pay the examiner's son by check, so when the gumshoe from the prosecutor's office laid hands on the canceled check, the jig was up. The answer seller, indicted for his illegal hustling, yelled for Darrow, who grabbed the case because the defendant's old man could afford to pay a handsome fee to get his son off the hook.

The prosecutor put the guilty purchaser on the stand. "You admit," he said, "that you paid the defendant here the sum of money represented by this check so that he would supply you with the answers?" The witness, who looked as if he wished he had bitten his tongue off for admitting *any*thing, answered, "Yes."

While the witness was admitting this and that—all of it driving the defendant closer to a conviction—Darrow noticed that the fellow had an apparently painful right arm. And so, when it came time to cross-examine him, Darrow asked how he had hurt his arm.

"In jail," said the witness.

"In jail?" repeated Darrow. "You mean when you were taken to jail after they arrested you in this case?"

"Yes," answered the witness.

Darrow detected what he felt was an eagerness on the part of the witness to talk about what had happened to him in jail. He shot a side glance at the prosecutor and the prosecutor was looking the other way.

"Were you *beaten* in jail?" asked Darrow.

"Yes, I was," said the witness.

"Who beat you?" Somebody from the prosecutor's office had.

"Why?" asked Darrow.

"To make me confess that I paid for the examination answers."

"That," said Darrow, "will be all. *Quite* all."

Now Darrow turned to the jury. He didn't say a word. He just raised his eyebrows. That's all he had to do.

Darrow picked up his hat and coat when the jurors filed out to deliberate on their verdict. "Where are you going?" asked the defendant's father. "Aren't you going to stay to hear the verdict?"

"Why should I?" asked Darrow. "They can't do anything but bring in an acquittal." And of course he was right.

One day a woman—a widow supporting her three children—called at Darrow's office and asked if he would defend her. She had just been indicted for perjury. She

didn't have any money to spend, but that did not always matter to Darrow. He had a genuine sympathy for little people in trouble and he was almost savage in his efforts to win acquittals for first offenders—and this woman would be a first offender.

The widow had a job as secretary to an insurance adjuster—her sole means of supporting herself and her children. It seemed that the insurance adjuster had been playing ball with an arson ring and had been accused of complicity in a plot whereby the ring had collected important money on a big fire. When brought to trial for his part in the conspiracy, the adjuster's only possible out was to prove that he had been away from Chicago the day of the fire. He hadn't been, of course, so he asked his secretary—the widow who had now come to Darrow to defend her—to lie for him by saying that he had been out of Chicago on business the day of the fire and that she had accompanied him. And so she testified to the lie when the adjuster was brought to trial, believing her employer to be innocent and willing to lie to save him—and to save her job.

The woman's testimony resulted in an acquittal for the adjuster. But the prosecutor, boiling mad at the adjuster's getting off through what he suspected was perjured testimony, put a dick on the case and learned that the woman had been in Chicago the day of the fire and had, therefore, lied on the stand when her employer was tried. Thus she was indicted for perjury.

Darrow's sympathy was aroused by the woman's story. He agreed to take the case for nothing. A couple of weeks later he went to Springfield, to the office of Governor Frank Lowden, an old friend. "Frank," he said, "I need a pardon for a client of mine—a widow with three children to support. She is in trouble simply because she tried to help her employer and save her job."

Then Darrow unfolded the whole story. Governor Lowden was touched. He telephoned to the chairman of the parole board and explained the situation. "Clarence," he said when he hung up, "the chairman of the parole board wants to see you."

Now Darrow explained the whole thing—well, *practically* the whole thing—to the chairman of the parole board. The chairman listened sympathetically. "I agree with you, Mr. Darrow," he said. "No good purpose has been served by the conviction of this woman. She is an innocent victim of circumstances." The chairman was jotting notes on a pad. "Now, Mr. Darrow, just what was the date of this woman's conviction?"

"Oh," said Darrow, "she hasn't been convicted yet. Her trial doesn't come up until next week."

The chairman blinked. This was a new one on him. It is still, in fact, probably the only instance known in which a lawyer has made an application for parole before his client has even gone to trial. But Darrow was assured by the chairman that the predicament of his client would be given prompt and sympathetic consideration once she was convicted.

Darrow saw to it that the story reached the papers. Some of the jurors at the widow's trial read of Darrow's visit to the governor. Since Darrow was fighting so hard for this woman, she must be *innocent*. Anyway, what would be the use of convicting her if the pardon board was all set to throw a conviction out the official window? That, in substance, was obviously how the jury felt. They acquitted the woman on the first ballot.

Such, then, was one side of Clarence Seward Darrow—the courtroom wizard and legal magician. But behind his razzle-dazzle surface—the surface, practically, of a shyster—was a great humanitarian. Some people said he had a split personality, that he led a double life. He alone knew the truth. When he wasn't producing nightmares for prosecuting attorneys, he was grinding away at good causes—important causes, too. He was for the little man all the way, he was for religious freedom though he had no religion of his own, and he despised, with all his heart, intolerance. Some of the things he accomplished didn't hit the front pages as his murder cases did, but they were far more important, affecting the life of every man, woman, and child in the United States today.

The first case that brought Darrow to national attention had its genesis the night of December 30, 1905, when Frank Steunenberg, ex-governor of Idaho, opened the front gate of his home in Caldwell and thus pulled a wire that set off an infernal machine that killed him. Steunenberg, who had started as a printer and become a small-time newspaper publisher, had been a great champion of the workingman. He had, in fact, been elected to the governorship largely through the support of the Western Federation of Miners—a rootin', tootin' hell-raising crew.

But the cordial relationship between Steunenberg and the miners' union had deteriorated during Steunenberg's gubernatorial regime. The Federation had called a strike in the mines in the Coeur d'Alene district and the governor had declared martial law to protect the mines—a move that the Federation regarded as a breach of faith on the part of the man they had helped put in office.

Pinkerton's National Detective Agency, hired by the mine owners to find the murderer, got a free-lance killer by the name of Harry Orchard in their sights and nabbed him. He told how he had made the bomb, shadowed Steunenberg, and planted the infernal device at an hour when he knew for sure that the prospective victim would be the next person to open the gate to his home.

It was what Orchard added to the Steunenberg part of his confession that brought Darrow into the case. Orchard said that he had been hired to murder the ex-governor by two officials of the Western Federation of

Miners—Charles H. Moyer, the president, and William D. Haywood, the general secretary—and by a man named George Pettibone, an all-around champion of the workingman.

Moyer, Haywood, and Pettibone were quickly arrested and charged with the murder. The Western Federation of Miners summoned Darrow to defend the three accused men. Darrow quickly reduced the problem to its fundamentals. The state of Idaho would rely on the word of one man—Harry Orchard—to convict for murder three men who, whatever else they might have been, just weren't the murdering type.

While each side was preparing for the battle in the courtroom, Orchard was wined and dined and his biological urge catered to, all at the state's expense. The state knew how valuable he was to its case, and so did Orchard, so that everybody understood one another. Meantime, Darrow looked into Orchard's past. The man had committed more than a hundred murders for hire.

Testifying for the prosecution, Orchard was like an actor playing his first big part. He hammed it for a couple of days—dwelling on the details of his crime with the passion and gestures of a Shakespearean actor doing Hamlet's soliloquy. Darrow sat there studying the man and making notes.

When Darrow got hold of Orchard for cross-examination he tripped him up on dates, geography, and contradictions in his own testimony. Then Darrow dwelled on the fact that Orchard had committed more than a hundred murders. Everybody in the courtroom—including the jurors—was revolted. When it came time to address the jury, Darrow simply asked the good men and true if they felt like being responsible for jeopardizing the lives of three men on the testimony of the most heinous killer in criminal annals.

And then Darrow got down to real business—the business of ignoring the evidence and stabbing deep into the emotions of the twelve men who sat there listening to him. He made one of the great summations of his life that night in Idaho. The conviction of the defendants, he told the jury, would be a mortal blow to the cause of the workingman. "I speak," said Darrow, his voice taking on warmth, "for the poor, for the weak, for the weary, for that long line of men who, in darkness and despair, have borne the labors of the human race. Their eyes are upon you—upon you twelve men of Idaho—tonight." Darrow paused, lifted his head, and looked through a window of the courtroom into the blackness.

He began to speak now just loud enough for the jurors to hear him, and his voice was hoarse. "Out on our broad prairies, where men toil with their hands, out on the wide ocean where men are tossed and buffeted on the waves, through our mills and factories, and down deep under the earth, thousands of men and women and children—men who labor, men who suffer, women weary with care and toil—these men and these women and these children will kneel tonight and ask their God to guide your hearts." And now Darrow looked down from the sky and at the jurors again. He paused just long enough to search the face of each man. Then he said, "Yes, gentlemen, their eyes are upon you tonight."

Acquittal.

The general public pictured Darrow, because of his attire, as resembling a fugitive from Skid Row, a sort of grown-up ragamuffin. Actually, because of his wife—his second wife—he wore better-than-average clothes. It was what he did to his clothes during the course of a day that made him look unkempt—that and the fact that he looked upon a barber's chair with approximately the same degree of enthusiasm as a murderer looked upon the electric chair.

Darrow was never at ease if his black bow tie was correctly in place; he seldom got through a day without stuffing his coat pockets with miscellany having to do with the legal problem that was occupying him at the moment. If, in a cheap restaurant or lunchroom for a quick bite between morning and afternoon court sessions, some gravy from a hot roast-beef sandwich found its way from the plate to his vest, it stayed there.

Once Darrow was trying a case in which the opposing counsel was J. Hamilton Lewis, he of the pink whiskers, who later went to the United States Senate. Lewis was a regular fop when it came to clothes and was known as the Chesterfield of the Middle West—lavender suits, with cravats and spats to match—because he was as smooth in deportment as in dress.

During the case in which he opposed Darrow, Lewis would appear in court each morning, fresh out of a bandbox—cane, yellow gloves, and all, his pink whiskers glistening in the shafts of early sunlight. When the judge appeared, Lewis would make a production of the event. He would bow from the waist, pay his respects to His Honor, do likewise to the jury, and then favor Darrow with similar Chesterfieldian courtesy.

Darrow would look with jaundiced eye on the Lewis performances. Something had to happen. One morning Darrow, not having got home until very late the night before, arrived, spectacularly unkempt, half an hour late for the opening of court. The judge sitting impatiently on the bench, raised his eyebrows by way of inquiring for an explanation. Darrow, who usually reserved for most judges an attitude just short of open contempt, astonished everyone by making a Lewisian production of his apology to His Honor, and to the jury. Then, turning to the stiffly outraged Lewis, he outstretched his arms. "And as for *you,* sweetheart," he growled, "*kiss* me."

Darrow held a strong fascination for women as well as for men. "The damned fools," he once told a friend, "either want to press my pants or go to bed with me."

The man was right. Between marriages, he met a sob sister on a Chicago newspaper who did both.

Clarence Seward Darrow was born on April 18, 1857, in the village of Kinsman in the rolling farmlands of Ohio, the fifth of eight children. He was to say in later life that it was obvious that he personally had nothing to do with getting born and that had he known about life in advance and been given a choice in the matter he would most likely have declined the adventure.

Clarence's father, Amirus Darrow, a brilliant and scholarly man, had studied for the Methodist ministry, but had given it up for carpentry. The end of all wisdom, he had concluded, was the fear of God, and the beginning of doubt was the beginning of wisdom. Thus Clarence became an agnostic.

So far as he was ever able to recall, Clarence Darrow was fourteen when he decided to become a lawyer. The village tinsmith, who was also the village justice of the peace, lived right across the street from the Darrows. His Honor dispensed justice, if it could be called that, after he had climbed down from the roofs for the day. Clarence, sitting on his front porch of a soft summer evening, would hear the sounds of squabbles from His Honor's chambers. When, finally, he decided to investigate, he was fascinated.

More often than not, the litigants acted as their own counsel, for the legal problems for the most part consisted of such matters as who was responsible for a broken window or who, during a heated discussion, had splattered tobacco juice in the other man's face first. Once in a while, though, in a more serious fight, a genuine lawyer would come from a nearby town. The visiting mouthpiece was usually something of a dandy, occasionally even wearing striped pants, and young Darrow decided then and there that if *he* were to have anything to do with deciding the merits of the litigation he would lean *away* from the fellow in the striped pants.

Darrow observed something else at these more serious litigations before the justice of the peace. Right did not always win; justice did not always triumph. On more than one occasion, Darrow saw the litigant he thought to be in the right have the case go against him because the other litigant had imported a dressy, fast-talking, fast-thinking mouthpiece. Clarence was never to forget that.

The big time in Kinsman was Fourth of July. Clarence's father and another carpenter would construct a wooden stand in the village square and come the Fourth it would be populated by out-of-town windbags talking about patriotism. Although only a kid, Clarence could tell that the orators for the most part had about as much sincerity as an auctioneer, yet the peasants who stood in the hot sun around the stand were deeply impressed. What young Darrow observed at these patriotic celebrations helped, too, to shape his destiny. It became an article of faith with him that people were, for the most part, stupid, and would believe practically anything if it were dished up in an appetizing form—and he was to prove it in courtrooms over and over again.

Darrow's regular education ended after he had finished the equivalent of one year of high school. The panic of 1873, which struck when he was sixteen, made it imperative that he go to work. He taught rural school for three years, but, sticking to his ambition to be a lawyer, studied law books not only at night but during school hours while the class dolt was shifting from one foot to another trying to recall who it was who discovered America.

By the time he had put away enough money from his schoolteaching to go to law school, Darrow was nineteen. He was a medium-sized fellow, loose-jointed, big-boned, and quizzical of eye. His face was broad, his brow was high, and usually it was partially obscured by a shock of hair that kept coming down in front. He had spent a good deal of time in the midwestern sun during summer vacations from schoolteaching, playing baseball, his favorite daytime pastime, and his face was already deeply lined. When, on his eightieth birthday, he was interviewed by a reporter for *The New York Times* he asked the reporter, "Do I look old?" The reporter answered, "Mr. Darrow, you have *always* looked old."

The young Darrow spoke slowly with a midwestern drawl. His voice wasn't so unusual as what was behind it. It was rich with sincerity, whether he was expressing a political opinion around the village cracker barrel or, while engaged in a favorite after-dark occupation, announcing that he would put the green ball in the side pocket. He smoked cigarets and once in awhile a cigar, and he took a drink with the boys, but liquor was never to be a weakness. He had, at the age of twenty, always been so occupied with one thing or another, that he had never had time to look twice at a girl. Darrow spent two years studying law—one year at a law school in Ann Arbor, Michigan, and another year in a law office in Youngstown, Ohio. Then, at the age of twenty-one, he tacked up a shingle in a little place called Andover, only ten miles from his birthplace.

Young Darrow never got off the ground in Andover. In two years of practice there his talents were confined to legal litigations in which the dairy farmers of the community became involved. The farmers took their milk to the butter and cheese factories of the region. Somewhere between the cows and the factories, the milk acquired a high water content. Church membership by the farmer culprits had no effect whatsoever on these cases of dilution since it was so easy to pour a bucketful of water into a milk can that many otherwise upright men could not resist. Darrow usually got the milk waterers off because in those days there was no scientific way of establishing the degree of richness of the cow juice and Darrow was just the boy to make the most of that.

So, when he was twenty-three, Darrow moved to the town of Ashtabula, some twenty-five miles further on.

There he was elected city solicitor at a salary of $75 a month, with the right to take his own cases on the side. One case that he handled in Ashtabula cast shadows of coming events, revealing, as it did, Darrow's sympathy for the underdog, his disregard for money, and his tenacity of purpose.

A teen-age boy had attended a wealthy farmer during the farmer's illness and, as payment, had been given a horse harness worth $15. The farmer, upon recovering his health, decided, for some reason, he wanted the harness back. The boy refused to return it. He was brought to trial before a justice of the peace. He got Darrow to defend him, putting up Darrow's fee of $5.

The jury disagreed and the case had to be tried a second time. The boy had run out of money by now and Darrow said he would defend him for nothing. At the second trial the case was decided against the boy and the justice of the peace ordered him to return the harness to the man. "Don't do it," Darrow instructed his client. "We'll take the case to the Court of Common Pleas." There Darrow, still working for free, won the case.

Now the farmer carried the litigation to the Court of Appeals. There the verdict of the lower court was reversed and Darrow and the boy were back where they had started—all on the original $5. Much time had passed by now and Darrow had established himself in Chicago. There he carried the case to the State Supreme Court and, eight years after the Indian giver had first instituted legal action, the reversal of the Court of Appeals was reversed and the verdict in Darrow's client's favor was allowed to stand.

It was while practicing in Ashtabula that Darrow, who by this time had an eye for the girls and who had come to know his way around a hay ride, fell in love. He married a highly moral young lady named Ohl—Jessie Ohl—whose family had been friendly with his family. In a year or so they had a son, Paul—Darrow's only child.

The little family lived in a rented house and the years began to roll on. When he was about thirty, and had become the most prominent man in Ashtabula, Darrow decided to buy a house. As a result of that decision, his whole life was changed. Had it not been for this, Darrow might have lived out his days as a country lawyer, growing up with a country town, and then at the end being buried in a little hillside cemetery.

Darrow was about to close a deal for a house when the wife of the seller backed out. Darrow suddenly decided to move to Chicago. He lived there in a cheap flat on the South Side and rented desk space in a downtown firetrap.

During his first decade in Chicago, the going was tough. There were more lawyers in the town than there was business for them and Darrow accomplished nothing to raise himself above the level of ambulance chaser. He grabbed any sort of case that came along—collecting bad bills for merchants, representing little people in accident cases, and so on.

One of Darrow's first clients in the early years was a snappy trigger-brained fellow named Joe Weil, later to be known to every police department in the English-speaking world as the Yellow Kid, confidence man *de luxe*. Weil had just given somebody a fast shuffle and the mark squawked. Darrow, deceived into thinking that he might be able to steer an intelligent fellow like Weil straight for the future, went into court with the Yellow Kid and convinced the jury that his poor misguided client, brimming over with the zest of youth, had merely perpetrated a prank—a serious prank, to be sure—but just a prank none the less.

The jury acquitted Weil. "All right, Joe," said Darrow, "now your whole life lies ahead of you. Never let me see you in trouble again." In later years when Weil, now notorious for his confidence work, ran afoul of the wrong kind of mark and faced another jolt in *durance vile*, he called on Darrow to defend him. Darrow turned down the Kid. He didn't like Weil. "Anyway," Darrow later said, "you can't cure con men. It's in their blood."

Even in his earlier years Darrow seemed to have a sixth sense that defined for him in advance just how much he could get out of a jury. Often he played it all the way, for an acquittal; sometimes he knew he would be getting the best for his client if he voided the death penalty and got a prison term.

One man, freshly jailed for murder, hollered for Darrow. The man had just murdered his landlord for raising his rent—an act that aroused considerably less sympathy then than it would today. Darrow went to see the prisoner. The man's appearance was against him; he would have made a splendid exhibit many years later when Darrow, spearheading the defense in the Scopes "monkey trial," embraced the theory that man and the apes were descended from a common ancestral species. The prisoner offered Darrow a large fee—but there was a catch to it. Darrow had to get him off; cheating the gallows wouldn't be enough. Darrow said he thought the very best he could get would be a prison term. No soap. The ape man got another mouthpiece—and the gallows.

A couple of elderly peddlers, smart characters, went into the business of buying used barrels from one department of a big meat-packing plant and selling the same barrels back to another department of the same plant at more than double the price—a practice which, from the viewpoint of certain gentlemen in business with the United States government later, was years ahead of its time. The dodge was so successful that the peddlers, smelling bigger money, began to mix phantom barrels in with the real barrels. A checker for the packing company took up residence among the barrels and over a period of weeks jotted down in a large notebook columns of figures—all designed to disclose that the packing company was being swindled. So the packing company yelled for the law, the peddlers were placed on trial, and there was Darrow to defend them—knowing they were dripping with guilt but wondering how to clothe them in innocence.

The figures jotted down by the man who had resided in the barrels constituted the state's principal evidence against the culprits. The book containing the figures was offered in evidence. Darrow, examining the book, saw that the figures, though meaningful to the man who had made them, and also meaningful to the state, were just a meaningless jumble to him. He knew, though, that he dared not question the man who had put down the figures; the eavesdropper from the barrel colony would no doubt be able to make them clear to the jurors if put through a cross-examination. So Darrow allowed the book to pass into evidence without objection so that the jurors, seeing it for the first time, would be as confused by it as he was.

Right after Darrow waived objection to the book, the judge declared a noon recess. Darrow was not going to put the defendants on the stand; he couldn't afford to. So after the noon recess each side would sum up, the judge would charge the jury, and the twelve citizens would retire to deliberate on the verdict.

A friend of Darrow's happened to be in the same elevator with the jurors when they were going down for lunch. He overheard one of them asking another why Darrow hadn't objected to the introduction of the book. "Must be something fishy about that book," answered the second juror. "Maybe Darrow is going to spring a surprise when he sums up."

When his friend tipped him to the overheard conversation, Darrow knew the verdict was as good as in the bag.

"Gentlemen," he said to the jurors, "maybe you are smarter than I am and can make something out of the figures in that book. But I'll be darned if I can. All I know is that those figures can be twisted around to make a point of practically anything."

All Darrow asked was that the jurors study the figures carefully, see if they could make any sense whatsoever out of them, then search their hearts and determine whether, on the basis of the figures, they were justified in sending the two defendants—"these poor, ragged men, trying to keep body and soul together in the short time remaining to them on this troubled planet"—to prison. And of course the jurors decided to acquit the defendants—thus clearing the way for the two poor, ragged old men to devote themselves, in the short time remaining to them on this troubled planet, to better and bigger swindles.

As Darrow became more widely known, and occasionally collected a big fee for a civil action or through a criminal action in which he resorted to courtroom stratagems such as that which got the two old barrel dealers off, his home life began to come apart at the seams. His wife, Jessie, had failed to keep pace with him. They were divorced.

Darrow took up with a mistress—a physically and mentally stimulating woman with auburn hair. They played house for a while and then she began to have visions of making it legal. But she had picked the wrong man. Darrow by this time had become an apostle of free love. Marriage, he believed, was for morons.

Darrow became, in the courtrooms, an authentically unkempt figure, as would any man who slept in his clothes. "Counsel," a judge said to him one morning, "looks very tired." Said Darrow, "Your Honor would be tired, too, if he went through what I went through last night." But Darrow's unkempt appearance was at least partly window dressing. He had noticed that jurors frequently felt antagonized by a mouthpiece far above them on the sartorial level. The average juror had shiny pants that were pressed twice a year; Darrow's slovenly attire put him in the juror's class.

Darrow was trying one case where he didn't have a prayer. His client, a stockyard worker, had chopped his wife's head off. As the case wore on, Darrow could have chopped his own head off for taking it. He had made a mistake about the defendant. He had felt sorry for the man when he had asked to be defended; now he realized his client was a fiend incarnate. But there he was, stuck with it, and with a reputation to defend—a reputation that was already marking him as a lawyer who had never had a client executed. What to do?

It happened that the lawyer for the state prided himself on his attire; not only that, he positively looked down on men who were careless in dress. So that night Darrow rubbed the elbows of his jacket with sandpaper until they were threadbare and carefully scuffed up his shoes. Next morning his appearance was too much for the prosecutor. He said nothing, but the way he looked Darrow up and down was practically audible. Darrow, playing his role with Shakespearean emphasis, hung his head a little, but, sneaking an eye-corner view of the jurors, saw that they, brothers under the unkempt attire, were sorry for him. It was all over but the verdict. The jury acquitted the beheader.

By the time he was in his early forties, Darrow had arrived at the decision that picking a jury was the most important part of any case. "Get the right men in the box," he said, "and the rest is window dressing." Darrow seldom accepted a German or a Swede for a jury. A German, he held, was too bullheaded, and a Swede too stubborn. Some historians credit Darrow with originating, in a sour moment, the joke that the only thing dumber than a dumb Irishman was a smart Swede. Irishmen and Jews, when Darrow could get them, were his favorite jurors; both, he held, were highly emotional and easily moved to sympathy. The perfect jury, to his way of thinking, was one comprising six Irishmen and six Jews. "Give me that combination in the box," he once said, "and I could get Judas Iscariot off with a five-dollar fine." As a general rule, Darrow preferred older jurors to younger ones. An older man had seen more of life, he thought, than a younger one. Thus an older man would be more sympathetic with the jams other men got into and have a better understanding of the motivating forces that had culminated in the trouble.

When an important case was coming up, Darrow assigned investigators to look into the lives of prospective jurors. Sometimes this was an extensive and prolonged procedure, depending on the importance of the impending case. Thus, before he even went into the courtroom on a really big case he had what amounted to a dossier on all the veniremen—their likes and dislikes, their prejudices, their foibles, what lodges they belonged to, and so on.

But Darrow went even further than that. When questioning a prospective juror who was, because of advance information, completely acceptable to him, Darrow would ask the man questions that had no bearing whatever on his acceptable characteristics, thus throwing the prosecution off the track.

Occasionally, Darrow would handle a civil case, especially if it was against a big public-utilities company. He hated big corporations and was always willing to take a crack at them, even at his own expense, just for the hell of it.

He became nevertheless, the great apostle of compromise in big damage suits. He always looked at three sides of every litigation—the litigant's side, the defendant's side, and his own side. Intuitively he knew when compromise was the better part of valor. He saw little use in getting into a fight when staying out of it would prove more profitable. Better to get five thousand dollars by writing a few letters to the lawyers on the other side than to spend weeks preparing a case. But if the big companies insisted on going into the ring, Darrow would go in there swinging.

One time a man walked into Darrow's office and asked him to take a case against a public-utilities company. The man had been injured by falling debris. Darrow, in the offhand way be had, scribbled some notes about the case on a piece of paper and stuffed the paper in his pocket. Some weeks later the public-utilities company sent Darrow a letter saying they were willing to settle with Mr. So-and-So for such-and-such a sum.

Darrow was mystified. "What the hell's this about?" he asked his secretary. The secretary said she was sure she didn't know. Then Darrow recalled the man who had been in his office some weeks previously. "Good Christ!" he said, "I never got around to doing anything about that case. I wonder what has happened?"

What had happened was that the litigant had telephoned the public-utilities company right after seeing Darrow, informing it that Darrow was on the case. The company's lawyers, construing Darrow's silence to mean that he was up to something that would just about ruin them, had decided to get the case cleaned up as quickly as possible and had thus voluntarily offered him a settlement. Darrow took it, keeping only a small percentage of the take for himself.

There is no record of how much money Darrow averaged in a year. Unquestionably, he had a few $100,000 years in the days when a dollar wasn't a dime with the tax taken out. Yet he never had any money. In fact, he was usually in debt. He contributed large sums to various causes he was interested in and never said anything about it. He was always good for a handout to unfortunates who shuffled into his office. Sometimes in saving some cornered moron from the noose he laid out large sums of his own in investigations pertinent to the case with never a prayer for so much as a dollar for a fee. And to top it all off, Darrow was an unfortunate market speculator. He was a sucker for a fast-talking gold-brick salesman who caught him between trials. He once said that he had almost enough phony stock certificates to paper his apartment.

Darrow's offices and his places of abode were just as casual as the man was. He had one desk—a great big battered affair—that he took with him when he moved from office to office. The desk was usually piled high with papers and he could seldom find what he was looking for.

He lived in apartments most of his life. They were so sparsely furnished, and the carpeting so nearly threadbare, that one visiting New York lawyer, going into a Darrow apartment for the first time, thought for a moment that he had stumbled into the wrong place.

Darrow liked nothing better in an accident case than to cross-examine a doctor testifying for the other side—a doctor who would say that the accident victim who was suing, though confined to a wheelchair, would no doubt be up and around in good time. His favorite device in dealing with such a sawbones ran thusly:

"You came here from out of town to testify for the company, Doctor?"

"Yes, Mr. Darrow."

"And you had a nice trip?"

"Yes, Mr. Darrow."

"How much are you getting for testifying, Doctor—over and above the expenses of your trip?"

"Three hundred dollars, Mr. Darrow."

Darrow would thereupon turn to the jury, raise his eyebrows and, still looking at the jury rather than at the witness, growl, "That will be all, Doctor."

Darrow liked to joust not only with doctors for the other side but with *any* expert for the opposition. He had a strong affinity for puncturing balloons. Once he was representing a sea captain named Erickson—John Erickson—charged with criminal negligence in a maritime disaster. Erickson had been the captain of a Great Lakes steamer, the *Eastland,* which, while lying at a dock in Chicago, preparatory to embarking on a cruise with hundreds of holiday-makers, capsized with a frightful loss of life—one of the worst civilian disasters in American history. Although the ship had just been officially inspected and found seaworthy, the public hue and cry reached such a crescendo that somebody had to be made responsible. So Captain Erickson, a man with an unblemished maritime record, was nominated for occupancy of a prison cell.

The principal witness for the state was a university professor—a man hardly given to false modesty. In his cross-examination of the professor, Darrow, having boned up on ship construction, put the witness through a long series of questions having to do with the construction of a ship. The professor knew all the answers.

"What the hell are you doing, Clarence?" whispered an associate counsel. "You're building the man up."

"That's exactly what I want to do," answered Darrow, "the better to knock him down."

When the professor had been properly built up, Darrow asked him who, in his opinion, was the world's foremost authority on ship construction.

"Why," answered the professor, "*I* am."

"And who," inquired Darrow, "would you say was the *second* greatest authority on ship construction?" The professor named a naval architect in Scotland.

"And the third greatest authority?" The professor said there was no such animal; only he and the man in Scotland really knew all there was to know about ship construction.

"I see," said Darrow. "Then the defendant here—Captain Erickson—would hardly be in the same class as you and that man in Scotland when it comes to knowing all there is to know about ship construction."

"That's right, sir."

"Then Captain Erickson couldn't possibly have known enough about ship construction to have known that, in spite of officially approved examinations of the *Eastland,* it would tip over when the weight of all those poor people was concentrated on one side of it."

"That's right, sir."

"Then Captain Erickson couldn't possibly have been responsible for the *Eastland* disaster?"

"That," said the expert, before he realized what was coming out of his mouth, "is right, sir." And that, of course, acquitted Captain John Erickson of the *Eastland* disaster.

When he needed expert medical opinion for his own side, Darrow firmly believed that he could find a doctor who would testify to practically anything. That is to say, a man could be the picture of health—a condition to which ninety-nine doctors would subscribe—yet that hundredth medical practitioner would take the view that the man was on the brink of eternity.

Darrow had occasion to look around for that hundredth doctor in the case of a client who had, while in a position of public trust, freely availed himself of the contents of the public till. The man was in such fine physical and mental shape that he could have passed the stiffest of insurance examinations, but, as Darrow saw the case, the only way to save the crook from prison was to convince a jury that he was a physical and mental wreck.

So Darrow hunted around until he found a doctor who wasn't doing so well in his practice. Would the doctor like to make a nice fee for testifying to the poor condition of his client? *Would* he!

At the trial, Darrow didn't let on to the prosecution what his defense would be. In fact, he misled the prosecution into thinking that he was going to attack their evidence—black-and-white bank statements proving the defendant was a thief—by yelling objections or making furious notes when the monetary testimony went in.

Then Darrow put his doctor on the stand. "Would you say," Darrow asked the sawbones, "that the defendant here is in fairly sound physical and mental health?" The doctor looked shocked—shocked that such a thing could be so much as thought of. The defendant was far from being in sound physical and mental health. He was, in fact, a physical wreck and, mentally, a candidate for the nut house. "You mean, Doctor," asked Darrow, "that the defendant hasn't long to live?"

"Hasn't long to *live?*" repeated the witness. "Why, I wouldn't be a bit surprised if he never left this courtroom alive." Now the doctor went into the horrible details. Darrow looked at the defendant; the rascal although bubbling with health, seemed to be wracked by pain and riddled with disease. Now Darrow looked at the jury. He raised his eyebrows but he didn't speak. He didn't have to. The jurors, having heard the dire tidings, were filled with consuming sympathy for the defendant. And of course they acquitted the man.

Darrow was defending another crook one time—a cripple—and, though the fee was good, he didn't have much of a case. He didn't, in fact, have *any* case. Here again was a man about to draw a one-way ticket to the big house. But Darrow kept pondering the fact that the man was a cripple and wondering how he could put such a misfortune on a favorable basis. Finally he got an idea.

He sent an investigator to look into the backgrounds of the panel of good men and true from which the jury would be drawn. He wanted to find out who among the prospective jurors had any cripples in their families. His investigator quickly found that one juror had a crippled brother. That juror was quickly accepted by Darrow.

The state's case against the crippled defendant was one of those open-and-shut affairs. Once again Darrow had to throw the legal aspects of the problem into the discard and put it on an emotional basis. In his summation, he shaped his remarks almost entirely for the benefit of the juror who had the crippled brother. Would these good men and true find it in their hearts to send this poor, deformed man to prison—no matter what he had done? And so on and so on and so on. By the time Darrow was through, not only the juror with the crippled brother was touched, but most of the men in the box were in tears. The crippled crook was quickly acquitted.

Another time Darrow was defending a man who had skipped out on a loan shark. This one would be easy. Well he knew that most people have, at one time or another, felt the screws being put to them for nonpayment of a loan. Again he sent an investigator out to find out which members of the jury panel had been hounded by a friendly loan outfit. At least half of them had. So, when the case went to trial, the prosecution was trying a dead beat and Darrow was trying the loan shark. Darrow of course won.

As his reputation spread, Darrow, although best known for his courtroom legerdemain, engaged in greatly diversified work. Bernarr Macfadden, the great physical culturist, was constantly holding cracked-wheat derbies in which non-meat eaters, wearing only loin cloths and running shoes, periodically panted through twenty-five miles of countryside, to show the marvelous dietary benefits of cracked wheat. Occasionally, during these exhibitions, some narrow-minded rural cops would pull in a physical culturist for indecent exposure and Macfadden would yell for Darrow. Darrow would usually get the trouble settled somehow or other, using every trick short of the dodge that a naked runner, purple with cold, had not really been naked at all but had been wearing a tight-fitting blue-serge suit.

One night, while Darrow was giving a lecture in Chicago, he kept looking at a pretty red-haired girl down front. He had by now been playing the field for some time, and playing it well, all the while preaching the benefits of free love. But this night, as he looked at the red-haired girl in the audience (she seemed to be in her middle twenties, some twenty years younger than he) something happened to him. He fell in love.

The girl was sitting with friends of Darrow's—the John H. Greggs, Gregg being the originator of the Gregg system of shorthand. Darrow telescoped his speech, got down off the platform, and shoved his way through his admirers to the Greggs.

"John," he said, "give me an introduction to the young lady."

Gregg, who knew Darrow quite well, drew him to one side. "It won't do you any good, Clarence," he said. "She's engaged."

"To hell with that," said Darrow. "I'm going to marry that girl. Introduce me."

Gregg introduced Darrow to Ruby Hamerstrom—a brilliant, soundly educated and socially conscious young lady. "Let's go out somewhere," Darrow said to Miss Hamerstrom. "I've fallen in love with you."

Ruby Hamerstrom laughed. "You must be crazy, Mr. Darrow," she said.

"Maybe I am," said Darrow, "but that doesn't alter the fact that I'm in love with you. Let's go out somewhere."

Ruby Hamerstrom was part Swedish and had a mind of her own. She didn't go out with Darrow. Next day he began to phone her and send her telegrams and flowers. She fought a delaying action for weeks. One night she told her fiancé about Darrow. "Well," said the fiancé, "why don't you see him, explain once and for all that we're about to be married, and he'll stop annoying you."

That proved to be the worst advice any fiancé has ever given any fiancée. Ruby Hamerstrom saw Darrow and, overcome by the man's combination of charms, fell in love with him and married him. She remained with him to the end—the great love affair of Darrow's life.

The curtain ascended on a perilous period in the career of Clarence Darrow when, about one o'clock of a morning in the spring of 1910, somebody set off a dynamite blast in the building of the *Los Angeles Times*. In the resultant explosion and fire, twenty-one *Times* employees were killed. William J. Burns, one of the cleverest detectives this country has ever produced, was assigned to track down the killers. Darrow loved Burns as Cain loved Abel and *vice versa*. Burns got on the right trail immediately. The crime, he knew, was the result of labor strife. Various unions were trying to make Los Angeles a closed-shop city, and the *Times* was the mouthpiece of the open-shop opposition. The *Times* was published by an old fire-eater—General Harrison Gray Otis, a Civil War hero with a fierce countenance and handsome goatee—who baited the unionists. The general had small cannon mounted in strategic spots throughout the *Times* plant. "Let the bastards start something," he used to growl as he prowled the premises, "and, by God, I'll finish it!"

Burns soon smelled out the masterminds of the plot— two really bad boys named McNamara—brothers J. J. and J. B. Then he located another cog in the murder machine—a fellow named Ortie McManigal. McManigal confessed every detail of the plot, implicating the McNamara brothers and others, and the McNamaras were arrested and charged with the twenty-one deaths.

Samuel Gompers, the head of the American Federation of Labor, asked Darrow to defend the McNamaras. The fee was big and Darrow was short of money.

The first thing Darrow did was to try to establish the fiction that all the McNamara brothers had meant to do, when planting the dynamite, was to *scare* the nonunion workers in the *Times* plant. It wasn't the dynamite that caused all the havoc, but a gas explosion and fire that followed the comparatively harmless blast.

He hired architects and engineers to make a small reproduction of the *Times* building, inside and out, and proposed to go into court and prove to the jury that the dynamite itself could not possibly have caused the deaths.

But William J. Burns, playing the other side of the street, was too smart for Darrow this time. He dug up evidence showing that the dynamite that the McNamaras had ordered from a powder-manufacturing company in the San Francisco Bay area had been especially powerful at their specifications.

Darrow hired a private eye—a fellow named Bert Franklin—for the twin purposes of spying on Burns and what he was up to, and to get lines on the lives and habits of the prospective jurors who would sit in judgment on the McNamaras. Burns caught on to what Darrow was doing and put counterspies to work on Franklin. Darrow, learning of this, put counterspies on the counterspies, then Burns, ever apace, put counterspies on the counterspies who were counterspying on the original spies. It was some fun. The spying and counterspying reached such proportions that Darrow knew when Burns was in need of a laxative and Burns knew what Darrow would have for breakfast in the morning even before Darrow knew himself.

Then an odd thing happened. Nobody knows to this day how it came about. Although the prosecution had enough on the McNamara brothers to hang them and then electrocute their corpses, the prosecution decided to accept pleas of guilty from both brothers. Consequently, J. J., the elder brother, drew life, and the younger one got off with fifteen years. The country was amazed. Everybody, especially Burns, wondered how Darrow had pulled it.

Then somebody in the district attorney's office put Franklin, Darrow's head spy, in the sights. Franklin was arrested and shown some rubber hose. He said that Darrow had paid him to purchase two prospective jurors. Franklin had, in fact, paid four hundred dollars to one of them. So Darrow was indicted for conspiracy to corrupt two jurors. He would be tried twice—once for each allegedly purchased juror. This was pretty bad business. Darrow was now in the fifty-third year of his life—no longer a kid who could brush off a charge like that and live long enough for people to forget it.

Darrow, the great lawyer, now needed a lawyer to defend him. He chose the man who is remembered to this day as the most flamboyant mouthpiece in the history of American jurisprudence—Earl Rogers, a blindingly brilliant, strikingly handsome, and exceedingly corrupt attorney who was drunk half the time.

Rogers built up a pretty good case for his client Darrow. He would show that Franklin, Darrow's accuser, was a man whose word had long been regarded as worthless. The trouble was that the bottle got in the way of the defense that Rogers was constructing for Darrow. So Rogers made things brief, then turned the Darrow defense over to Darrow himself.

All during the trial, Darrow had been a beaten man. Now the old magic came back to him, and the inner fires suddenly burned white. He dramatized his whole life while the jury sat entranced. He had made many mistakes in his life, he told the jury, but crookedness had never been one of them. Was the jury, then willing to destroy him—and all the poor souls he hoped to save from injustice before he died—on the word of this scoundrel Franklin? Anyway, what good would be accomplished by sending him to prison? He was, he pointed out, already under sentence of death—even as every man who sat before him in the jury box was sentenced to death. The jurors seemed shocked. Darrow smiled sadly. Every man, he pointed out, in the words of Oliver Wendell Holmes, was sentenced to death for the crime of living.

The jury acquitted him. One down, one to go.

While Darrow was awaiting trial on the charge of conspiracy to corrupt the second juror, an old acquaintance appeared—a scowling, big-boned fellow named George Bissett. A few years before this, Bissett had been a client of Darrow's in Chicago. Darrow had gotten him off for killing a cop in a barroom pistol duel on the plea that the cop had fired first. Bissett had vowed then that he would never forget Darrow. And he hadn't. He had ridden the rods from the Midwest to do what he could for Darrow after reading how this character Franklin was saying those things about Darrow.

Darrow was touched. "What do you propose to do, George?" he asked Bissett.

"Kill the sonofabitch," said Bissett. "I brought some dynamite to blow up his house."

Darrow invoked all his eloquence to dissuade Bissett from his play. It was no dice. Bissett was a true friend. Nobody was going to get away with doing anything to the man who had got him off that murder rap.

Somebody (could it have been Darrow?) tipped the police that George Bissett should be picked up as a vagrant. And so Bissett was pinched and shipped back to the Midwest where he was murdered for playing too fast and too loose with the wrong woman. Darrow caught his breath and went on trial for the second charge. Rogers was up to his old failings again. One day he was in court, the next he wasn't. This time the jury disagreed. Then the charge against Darrow was dropped.

As the years rolled by, Clarence Seward Darrow, now the best-known lawyer in Chicago, had more cases offered to him than he could possibly handle. He moved from office to office, sometimes in partnership with others, sometimes by himself. But even when he was in partnership, a partner was usually reduced to the status of the fifth wheel on the wagon. If a case came into the office that required intensive research over dry statutes, Darrow would pass it on to a partner. But if something cropped up that had the makings of a big courtroom show, Darrow would grab it.

Once an out-of-state evangelist walked into his office and asked if Darrow would defend him on a young lady's charge that he was the father of her unborn child.

"Well, *are* you?" asked Darrow.

"I don't know," said the evangelist. "I *could* be, but I would have to be sure." Darrow asked the preacher how he was fixed for paying the expenses of an investigation into the complainant's background, in addition to the Darrow fee. Money was no object; the evangelist was loaded. Darrow got the impression that the man of God had been short-circuiting some of the collection money, but that was no skin off his teeth.

A couple of Darrow investigators learned that the young lady who had succumbed to the evangelist had been quite a girl and that any one of a dozen or more young studs in the town where she lived could very well have been responsible for her condition. What the girl really had her eye on was part of that short-circuited collection money. So Darrow sent an emissary to the girl's father, pointing out that he would be forced to subpoena several of the local boys to testify to their relations with his daughter if the girl went through with her suit. So the matter was settled out of court for a few hundred dollars.

Not long afterward, the evangelist was spreading the word of God in a Chicago suburb and Darrow, being in the vicinity, attended a service. There was his ex-client, up in the pulpit exhorting the sinners to repent, warning that Judgment Day was in the offing. Next day, Darrow made a notable remark to one of his partners about evangelists. There lies buried in the heart of every evangelist, he said, the wreck of a confidence man.

Although Darrow had never patronized brothels— "Why," he once said, "should I *pay* for it?"—he had a strong affinity for madams and their girls. "After all," he used to say, "they're serving a good purpose and giving value for value received. What's so wrong about that?" And so he was always glad to defend a madam, or a girl, or a group of girls, feeling, in that big heart of his, that they were victims of circumstances.

Once, then, he was defending a madam and half a dozen of her little doves, who had been caught in a raid by a couple of hard-hearted cops. One particular cop was to be the principal witness, so Darrow looked into him. "Don't worry," he said to a lawyer he was sharing an office with at the time, "the case is as good as won."

When the cop—a righteous-looking man with a wife and family—was through testifying to what he had come upon in the den of iniquity, Darrow went to work on him, slowly, gently, deceptively. "You have testified here that the lady who runs this establishment offered you a bribe and that you spurned it. Is that right?" It was. "Of course you wouldn't do such a thing as accept a bribe from anybody."

"No, sir, I certainly would not."

"You have, then, been offered many bribes when raiding these houses of ill fame, as you choose to call them, but you have turned down every dollar that was ever offered to you. Is that right?" It was right.

"Now," Darrow went on, "let me ask you something else. While you have raided a good many of these places, you have not always been successful in gaining entrance and thus obtaining evidence. Is that so?" That was so.

"Do you happen to have a record of the establishments where you were unsuccessful in gaining entrance—and the dates when you tried to gain entrance?" No, the officer did not have such data.

"Well," said Darrow, "I have. Maybe I can refresh your memory." Darrow, through a pipeline right in the police department, began to reel off a list of joints that had been unsuccessfully approached by the witness and the dates of the official failures. The witness clearly recalled each dud raid and the date it had been made.

Now Darrow began to question the cop about how much pay he got, how much it cost him to live, how much, if anything, he saved, and what other income he had, if any, aside from his police pay. The cop practically broke into tears as he told Darrow how difficult it was for him to make ends meet on his police pay—his only source of income.

Darrow, who had, through devious methods of his own, established a pipeline in the bank where the witness had an account, reeled off the records of the cop's deposits. The prosecutor started to scream that the cop's bank account had nothing to do with the case. Darrow maintained that it did. The judge allowed him to proceed.

What Darrow divulged, in reading the dates and deposit figures from the bank, was that the cop had made a sizable deposit after each unsuccessful raid. The inference was clear. In his summation, Darrow threw the issue at hand—the charge that the madam and the girls had been caught in carnal pursuits in violation of the law—right out the window. Before he was through, the jury thought the cop was on trial for being a crook. And out the window went the state's hope of a conviction.

A week after the trial, when the madam and the girls were back in business at the old stand, they sent Darrow a dozen American Beauty roses.

Some students of Clarence Seward Darrow are of the opinion that, all things considered, the man lived his shining hours in the summer of 1923 when, at the age of sixty-six, he appeared in the village of Dayton, the seat of Rhea County, in the Cumberland hills of Tennessee, as chief counsel for the defense in what the newspapers were to call the Monkey Trial. For it was in the Monkey Trial that Darrow, fighting against the bigoted opponents of man's right to think for himself, let go with a round-house wallop from which they have not, to this day, come up off the floor.

The state of Tennessee had passed a law which made it a crime for any schoolteacher to teach evolution, which adheres to the Darwin theory that man is allied biologically to the apes and monkeys. The proponents of the antimonkey law held that the Bible was to be taken literally: that Eve was made out of Adam's rib, that God made the world in six days, and that Jonah was swallowed by the whale. Although many religious men believed then, as they do today, that such statements in the Bible were not to be taken literally, but were only allegorical, certain brethren, called Fundamentalists, insisted that every statement in the Good Book was to be accepted as incontrovertible black-and-white fact.

So along came a young teacher in the high school of the town of Dayton, Tennessee—fellow named John T. Scopes—who believed in Darwin's theory rather than the theory of the Bible Fundamentalists. Scopes, a reddish-haired young man with the shyness, the eyeglasses, and the sober mien of the scholar, decided to put the antimonkey law to a test. He proceeded to tell his students that man was a cousin of the monkeys. And so he was arrested as a law violator and indicted.

William Jennings Bryan, the country's leading Fundamentalist and one of the most powerful and colorful figures of the era, had been the man behind passage of the antimonkey law. And so Bryan, a lawyer among his many other accomplishments, was naturally chosen to spearhead the prosecution of young Scopes. Since Bryan stood for everything that Darrow didn't stand for, Darrow did something he had never done in his life. He *asked* to get into a case. He said he would willingly go to Tennessee to defend Scopes, at his own expense, just to tangle with Bryan.

As Darrow saw the over-all picture, if Bryan wasn't defeated at the Scopes trial he would, through his nation-wide prestige, ram antimonkey laws through the legislatures of practically every state in the Union. That, as Darrow saw it, would be a mortal blow to freedom of thought.

The battle between Darrow and Bryan was to be a battle of two giants. Bryan—a big, bald-headed man with a benign countenance and golden voice—was a master spellbinder with a tremendous following. At the time of the Scopes trial, he was sixty-two, three years younger than Darrow. Starting out as a Missouri lawyer, he had embraced politics and, at the age of thirty-six, had so stirred the Democratic National Convention with his famous Cross of Gold speech that he had been nominated for the presidency. He ran on a platform of free and unlimited coinage of silver for the poor farmers and the poor workingmen and almost got into the White House. He ran again four years later, but was again defeated.

But Bryan, a tough adversary behind his benign exterior, was not through with politics—not by a country mile. At the Democratic Convention of 1912, he threw his weight behind Woodrow Wilson, and, as a result, broke a convention deadlock that got Wilson, an ex-Princeton professor and governor of New Jersey, the nomination and the presidency. Wilson appointed Bryan Secretary of State.

All the while, Bryan had been a lecturer on the Chautauqua Circuit, going out each year, grinding away at one cause or another. Always an opponent of drink, strong *or* weak, he began to stump for a prohibition law. He used to send out postal cards by the thousands, each bearing his signature, and requesting that the recipient sign his name above Bryan's. The catch was that above both signatures was a pledge that the recipient would never drink again. Darrow, getting hold of one of these postals once in awhile, would regard it sourly. "If I could only get enough of these," he once said, "I'd give them to some saloonkeeper so he could paper the toilet with them."

When, largely through Bryan's efforts, the Volstead Act was slipped into the nation's legal machinery like a Mickey in a drink, Bryan, ever the feverish guardian of his fellow man's welfare, began to cast an eye on any and all teaching that deviated from the literal truth of the Bible. He publicly offered a hundred dollars to anyone who could prove he was descended from an ape, and he embarked on a personal-appearance tour before legislatures in various parts of the country, pleading that the lawmakers pass statutes forbidding the teaching of evolution—or the Darwinian theory—in the public schools.

Bryan succeeded finally in ramming an antimonkey bill through the legislature of Tennessee. At first, nobody outside the state thought much about it. Then along came Scopes to join the issue between Bryan and Darrow.

Just as the trial of Bruno Richard Hauptmann for the murder of the Lindbergh baby turned the town of Flemington, New Jersey, into a three-ring circus, so did the monkey trial in Dayton, a decade earlier, convert that settlement into a big carnival. A couple of hundred reporters, both star and ordinary, all sorts of feature writers, and the flash-camera lads imposed a severe strain on Dayton hotel facilities and on the output of the local bootleggers.

Sidewalk preachers, most of them regional clerics but some from distant points, set up shop on the main street and shouted their exhortations from early morning until their voices gave out. At night, clusters of the faithful would go down to the river, and, out of their senses with religious fervor, jump into the waters and roll around, shouting hallelujahs.

The presiding judge at the trial—a little man named John Raulston—was a product of the Tennessee hills and a Fundamentalist all the way through. Darrow knew he wouldn't have an easy time.

The prosecution, with Bryan spearheading the attack, had pretty smooth sledding. Bryan established that Scopes had taught the theory that all life had begun in the sea and had, through the eons, assumed various forms until it emerged as man. While cross-examining Scopes, Bryan, a cagey old character, would leave the legal line to go off on a religious tangent, bringing cheers from the spectators and howls of disapproval from Darrow.

Darrow, sitting in his shirt sleeves and hitching his thumbs to a pair of bright scarlet suspenders bought especially for the trial, would, while listening to Bryan, scrutinize the courtroom spectators. One morning he riveted his gaze on a mountain boy who had such long hair that Darrow couldn't determine whether or not the lad's head came to a point on top. He nudged an associate counsel. "Take a good look at that fellow," he said. "If he's not proof that Darwin was right I hope never to leave this courtroom alive."

Darrow had lined up scientific men from all parts of the country to testify that there was scientific basis for Darwin's theory. Bryan fired his big gun when he objected to the introduction of such evidence—Darrow's most important evidence. The judge upheld the objection. Darrow blew a fuse. Then the judge blew one. Bryan looked on like a cat that had just finished a saucer of cream.

Darrow was cited for contempt. Next day, after he had cooled off, he apologized—as much, that is, as he was capable of apologizing. The judge accepted his apology and the trial resumed.

Now it was Darrow's turn to pull a fast one. He decided to execute a legal maneuver seldom seen in a courtroom. He called to the stand as a witness the chief counsel for the other side—William Jennings Bryan himself. The move made the lead headline in practically every newspaper in the land.

Darrow knew what he was doing. From the moment he had entered the Scopes case, he had assigned researchers to go into Bryan's past. Thus he knew that while Bryan was an authority on many subjects, he had only a sketchy knowledge of ancient history and science. He knew, too, that Bryan's forebears had been devout Fundamentalists and that Bryan, having been steeped in Fundamentalism since birth, had never so much as researched a single statement in the Bible.

So there was Bryan, up there on the stand, waving a palm-leaf fan to protect himself from the midsummer heat, and Darrow, in shirt sleeves and red suspenders, about to begin his attempt to take him apart.

Darrow got right down to the fundamental of Fundamentalism. He asked Bryan if he believed that Jonah had been swallowed by a whale. Bryan said he did. And did Brother Bryan believe that Joshua had made the sun stand still? Brother Bryan did.

"Do you know how long ago the Flood was—the Flood mentioned in the Bible?"

"Yes," said Bryan. "Two thousand, three hundred and forty-eight years B.C."

Bryan looked very confident. But then Darrow inquired whether Bryan knew that a number of civilizations dated back to more than 5,000 years before the birth of Christ—that the ancient civilizations of China were at least 6,000 or 7,000 years old. Bryan appeared puzzled. He had never studied up on such civilizations. Nor had he studied up on geology. Then he regained his ground and made a crack that is still good today. "I am, Mr. Darrow," he said, "more interested in the Rock of Ages than in the age of rocks."

Darrow scowled. Now he asked Bryan if he had ever made any attempt to learn how many people there had been in China 6,000 years ago. "No," came the answer. "And you, Mr. Darrow, are the first man I have ever met who has had any interest in the subject."

Darrow looked shocked. Did Bryan mean to say, he inquired, that he, Darrow, was the first man Bryan had ever met who had been interested in geology and primitive man? Bryan said he had meant to say precisely that. Darrow turned to look at the spectators. Then, turning back to Bryan, he asked, "Where, sir, have you been all your life?"

"Not," roared Bryan, "near *you*."

It went on and on, for hour after hour in the stifling heat of midsummer Tennessee. Bryan's answers were solid and surefire when they had anything to do with a state-

ment anywhere in the Bible. But when Darrow asked him to back up some of the statements in the light of modern knowledge and science, Bryan just sat there, looking, for the first time in his life, completely stumped.

As the questioning went on, Darrow played with Bryan like a cat with a mouse. Regardless of the outcome of the trial itself, Darrow knew that he had Bryan where he wanted him. Bryan was game all the way through, but, for the first time in his life, he had met more than his equal in an argument. The trouble was he just didn't know the answers to the questions Darrow asked about evolution and science. When the questioning came to an end, Darrow was daisy-fresh. Bryan was soaked with perspiration and looked like a very old man.

Darrow knew what the verdict would be before it was brought in. But he knew something else: the press had been on his side and the American public at large—excepting, of course, the Fundamentalists—had come to regard the Tennessee anti-evolution statute as something ridiculous, not to be repeated in their own communities, and had in its collective mind a picture of William Jennings Bryan as a top-drawer bigot.

And so, when the jury brought in a verdict of guilty—that Scopes had taught evolution against a state statute—Darrow was not in the least surprised. The verdict had by now become comparatively unimportant. What was important was that Darrow's handling of the case had awakened the country to an existing evil. The bigots, led by Bryan or his successor, would never now be able to make it a national crime to teach evolution in the public schools.

Scopes was fined $100 by the judge; the verdict was to be reversed by the State Supreme Court on technical grounds, and the case was never to be retried.

Bryan hung around Dayton after the trial was over. Many men who don't drink liquor become gluttons. Bryan was such a man. He drowned his sorrow over his loss of the verbal battle in food. He sat down one steaming morning to a breakfast consisting of a large stack of hot cakes drenched in syrup, half a dozen fried eggs, three thick slabs of ham, a couple of pounds of fried potatoes, seven corn muffins, and six cups of coffee with cream and sugar. Then William Jennings Bryan laid down and died.

Darrow, who had gone to the mountains for a few days before returning to Chicago, took the news of Bryan's death quite calmly.

"They say that Mr. Bryan died of a broken heart," a reporter said to Darrow, "and that you were the cause of it."

Darrow snorted. "Broken heart, hell," he said. "He died of a busted belly."

Darrow was asleep in his Chicago apartment one night in the beginning of June, 1924, when he was awakened by the arrival of four hysterical visitors—relatives of two poor little rich boys who had just confessed to one of the most heartless murders in the history of American crime. Richard (Dickie) Loeb and Nathan Leopold, Jr., sons of two of Chicago's wealthiest and most illustrious families, had, for a thrill, kidnaped and murdered a 14-year-old boy named Bobby Franks and then attempted to collect ransom on the corpse.

The city, and then the entire country, was genuinely shocked. Leopold, nineteen, tall and darkly handsome, and Loeb, small of stature and not very good-looking, came from a gold-plated environment. They drove around in foreign cars, carried hundred dollar bills in their pockets, kicked servants around, abused waiters in the tony spots, and did everything else that spoiled kids could possibly do. Surfeited with life, they had become queeries. Finally, looking for even another kind of thrill, they had cooked up a kidnaping and murder.

The leader of the visitors to Darrow's home that night was an uncle of Dickie Loeb. "Clarence," he said, "the families of the boys have authorized me to offer you one hundred thousand dollars if you can save the lives of Dickie and Nathan. That's all we ask of you—to save them from hanging. We realize that nothing more can be done." The deal was: ten thousand dollars down and the rest when the two necks were saved.

Whatever Darrow may have claimed publicly about Leopold and Loeb, he must have known, when he took the case, that they were a couple of young monsters. They had not the slightest remorse over what they had done. Worse, they seemed to be enjoying the black limelight that was beating down on them. "Bring us another kid," Leopold said to one of the jailors, "and we'll show you how we did it." Darrow was, purely and simply, out after that hundred-grand fee.

Darrow could smell danger. Thus it didn't take him very long to decide to plead the murderers guilty and avoid a jury trial. Had a jury had the slightest say in the matter, Leopold and Loeb would have swung as surely as the sun came up. They had committed not one but two offenses punishable by death—murder and kidnaping. So Darrow decided, in that instinctive way he had of measuring a situation, to put the entire responsibility for the fate on the killers on one man—the judge who would sentence them following their pleas of guilty.

A judge was, under his black robes, just as human as a juror or anyone else. Darrow knew from long experience that many a juror who had voted for a death penalty would not have done so had his decision alone decided the issue. But when there were eleven other men serving on a panel, a juror would be more likely to vote for the death penalty—especially in a case like this—because he would be only one-twelfth responsible, rather than wholly responsible, when the trap was sprung. But no judge, Darrow felt, relished the prospect of sentencing a person to death when he alone was making the decision and could just as easily sentence the defendant to life.

Now Darrow began to look around for the right kind of a judge for what he had in mind. A lawyer can't always get just the judge he wants, but sometimes he can find legitimate ways through the labyrinth of jurisprudence to get his man. So Darrow went to work behind the scenes and came up with Judge John Caverly—a brilliant and humane jurist. Now he was all set. He was ready to go into his act—an act that would culminate in a two-day speech designed to tear Judge Caverly's heart to shreds. There was just one thing to be done beforehand—make sure to keep Leopold and Loeb in line. The two killers were still smirking out loud, enjoying the whole business. "Now listen, you two," said Darrow. "Wipe those smiles off your faces when you go into that courtroom or they'll hang you, just as sure as hell."

Both sides produced alienists, as psychiatrists were called in those days—Darrow to indicate that his clients were just good boys at heart, the victims of unfortunate forces beyond their control, and the state of Illinois to point out that Leopold and Loeb were young fiends incarnate. Despite Darrow's warnings to his clients, and the tongue-lashings he gave them outside of the courtroom, Leopold and Loeb looked upon the court proceedings as a one-ring circus. They clowned and hammed through every session and the newspaper photographers caught them at it. Public opinion, strongly against the poor little rich boys at first, became stronger than ever. Courtroom spectators were revolted. Darrow was talking to himself. His clients were, in effect, insuring their own execution.

Now Darrow, his work cut out for him, began his summation. It was the same old story, new to every judge and jury who came under the Darrow spell. He began slowly, low and rich of voice, friendly of visage. He could feel the hostility in the courtroom, and in the judge. And then, somewhere along the line, that strange alchemy that happened to Clarence Darrow when the magic was upon him came to pass. Although he was sixty-seven, the years seemed to melt away. He was young and strong again and presently his words began to penetrate the hostility all around him. He was speaking not as a lawyer, trying to save the lives of two murderers, but as an apostle of goodness, pleading that the judge, in all his wisdom, temper justice with mercy. He was representing not two murderers, but two boys who had taken a human life because they were mentally and morally sick, the victims of powerful, complicated, and unseen forces that reached far back into time.

Darrow, a great believer in a certain school of thought among theatrical men that one way to achieve an effect on an audience is to exhaust it, had taken that tack now. His instincts told him, at the end of his first day of talking, that he had filled the judge with emotion. Now, as he began the second day, he decided to wring His

Honor out. He went on and on about his two unfortunate clients—victims of cosmic forces—now and then sneaking a look at them and, to himself, no doubt cursing the day they were born.

Why had Leopold and Loeb killed Bobby Franks after kidnaping him? Why, because of a perfectly ridiculous Illinois statute that he himself had fought against when it had been passed a few years before—the statute that made kidnaping an offense punishable by death. Why, these poor boys, these foolish, unfortunate boys, hadn't stopped to think, when they kidnaped Bobby Franks as a prank, that they were making themselves candidates for the noose. But then, when they realized that they had, in their childish, foolish way, committed an offense punishable by death, they had been driven by panic and thus had killed their victim so that he could not testify against them. Actually, then, Leopold and Loeb had been driven into a crime they would never have dreamed of committing by this foolish law that had made a boyish prank a capital offense.

That covered, Darrow went to work on the judge himself. The judge, he pointed out, was a fine man, a great jurist, a credit to all Chicago—remarks that could not help pleasing the listener. Surely, His Honor would not wish to cloud a distinguished career by sentencing these boys to die. "Your Honor," Darrow said, squinting at Judge Caverly, "if these two boys hang, *you* must order them to hang. It will be entirely up to *you,* Your Honor. There must be no division of responsibility here, Your Honor. The sentencing of these boys to die must be an act on *your* part and on your part alone. Such a sentencing must be your own cold, deliberate, premeditated act, without the slightest chance to shift any part of the responsibility. Your Honor alone stands between these boys and the trap door of the scaffold."

His Honor chose to duck the responsibility of sending those two poor boys to the scaffold. He gave them life imprisonment instead.

Now Darrow sat around his office waiting for the Leopold and Loeb families to kick in with the ninety thousand dollars. Nothing happened. So he sent the paymaster for the families a gentle note. No answer. Another note. Still no answer. Another note. Another dose of silence. Darrow thought of suing. Then a fiscal agent for the two families appeared in his office with the fee, but in three checks of thirty thousand dollars each. Two other lawyers had assisted Darrow in the case and were entitled to some of the money but not, as Darrow saw it, to two-thirds of it. But rather than get into a public hassle about dough he settled on the terms of the Loeb and Leopold families. Ever afterward, when some newspaper reporter would interview him and ask him to talk about his celebrated cases, Darrow would duck the Leopold-Loeb case. Somehow, when he thought of it, he felt a headache coming on.

In the year of 1925, when Clarence Darrow was in the sixty-eighth year of his life, there came to pass a happening in Detroit that altered his plans to withdraw from the turmoil of the legal arena. There appeared in Detroit a young colored physician, a Dr. Ossian Sweet, with his wife and infant son. This Sweet was quite a man, in any color. Coming up from his native Florida where the cards had been stacked against him, he had become a bellhop on the lake steamers between Detroit and Chicago. Somehow he had got together enough money to pay his tuition through the medical school of Howard University in Washington. Then he had gone to Europe to study in Vienna and later to specialize in gynecology and pediatrics at the Curie Institute in France. Coming to Detroit, he practiced in a colored district where he became so renowned in his specialties that white patients frequently crossed the color line to avail themselves of his skill.

In 1925, Dr. Sweet moved to the corner of Charlevoix and Garland Streets, then a district of foreign-born workers. White residents threatened him. He appealed to the police. The Detroit Police Department, then honeycombed with Ku Kluxers, ignored him. Sweet sent his wife and baby away and, with his two brothers, Otis, a dentist, and Henry, a medical student, and eight friends, stocked up with ammunition and stood by for a battle.

One night a mob gathered outside and stoned and set fire to the house. The doctor was seriously injured by a rock. Now his younger brother—the one he was sending through medical school—let go with his rifle. A man in the mob fell dead. The cops pinched the eleven Negroes on a murder charge.

Called to defend them, Darrow hired tipsters to infiltrate the neighborhood of the violence and find out what they could. Meantime he went into seclusion and absorbed every piece of literature he could lay hands on relating to the history of the Negro. He traced the Negro people through the corridors of time from their earliest known beginnings up through the centuries right into Detroit. He became deeply stirred by the black man's long history of unjust treatment, tragedy, and oppression.

By now the tipsters had established pipelines right into the prosecutor's office. They learned that the prosecution was going to try to show that the shooting from within Dr. Sweet's house had been utterly unprovoked, that there had not been, in fact, any mob outside of the doctor's house. The doctor, the prosecution was going to contend, lived at a busy street intersection and although it may have been slightly more crowded than usual the night of the shooting, the people who were there were bent on ordinary pursuits, certainly not assembled with malice aforethought.

Now Darrow assigned his tipsters to knocking down the prosecution's case before it was really built up. They located several motorists who said that on the night of the shooting there had been such a large crowd around the Sweet home that the cops had to reroute traffic.

Darrow made hamburgers out of the state's witnesses—a sickening parade of first-degree perjurers, some of whom pictured the corner of Charlevoix and Garland Streets that night as having been about as crowded as Death Valley. Others represented themselves as hardy souls who had been abroad in the wilderness bent on locating stray pets. Darrow lay in wait, like a tiger, for the state's witnesses to finish their stories. Then he pounced on them and clawed them to ribbons.

Now Darrow put Dr. Sweet on the stand. The physician, like Darrow, had studied the history of the Negro; he had also studied the history of mob violence in which Negroes had been victims. He told of his inward terror of a certain type of white man ever since, during his days as a medical student in Washington, he had seen a crowd of supremists roaming the streets, in the very shadow of the White House, on the prowl for a Negro who had committed a crime. All of which established the state of mind of Dr. Sweet and the ten other Negroes in the house when the mob began to stone the place.

Darrow had probed into the past of the jurors. Several of the jurors selected by the state whom he had been unable to block were Ku Kluxers. That meant the best Darrow could hope for was a disagreement. So, in his summation he addressed his remarks to two jurors who, his scouts had learned, hated Ku Kluxers. He got his disagreement.

Now the state tried young Henry Sweet—the fellow who had actually fired the shot—alone. Again Darrow found a couple of jurors who were opposed to the Kluxers. There was a third juror he couldn't quite make up his mind about. When the jury was filing out, the man looked at Darrow with a small enigmatic smile on his face. "I would give ten years of my life," Darrow whispered to an assistant, "to know how that fellow is going to vote." It was to work out that the little man with the enigmatic smile turned on the smile again when he reached the jury room with his fellow jurors. He had brought with him a box of nickel cigars.

"I'm going to smoke these," he said to the foreman. "You and the others go ahead and talk things over. I'll just be sitting in the corner there, smoking."

"But," said the foreman, "you've got to consider the evidence with us."

"I don't need to consider it," said the smiling man. "My mind's made up. When the rest of you have agreed to acquit, I'll vote your way."

The verdict was acquittal for Henry Sweet. Then the state dismissed the charges against his two brothers and the other defendants. The Sweet case became a legal and civic milestone in the Negro people's progress in the twentieth-century United States—one that is still talked about in the law schools.

Darrow hated prohibition. Once, while lecturing against it in a Chicago suburb, he spotted Al Capone in the audience. He knew what Capone had come for. Not, certainly, to hear him speak against the evils of prohibition, but to size him up as a possible mouthpiece. Darrow had heard that the T-Men—the Treasury sleuths—had come to Chicago to dig up evidence on Capone as an income-tax violator, everything else having failed to trap the Big Boy. Capone would thus be in need of top-grade legal assistance. It would be natural for the gangster, loaded as he was, to seek out the best talent to be had.

Sure enough, Darrow was visited in his office a couple of days later by a sharply dressed fellow whose eyes were a day's march from his cheekbones.

"The Boss would like to see you, Mr. Darrow," said the visitor.

Darrow, shuffling some papers, didn't look up. "You mean Capone?" he asked.

"Yeah," said the visitor.

"I'm not interested in seeing Capone," said Darrow.

"But he says you can name your own figure, Mr. Darrow—anything."

Now Darrow looked up. He said, "Capone is helping to ruin this whole country with that stuff of his that is being sold to nice decent kids. You go back and tell the sonofabitch that there ain't enough money in the world for me to have anything to do with him."

In the late Twenties, Darrow and his wife went to Europe. When they came back he decided he'd had enough of the law. He had invested his Leopold-Loeb money in the market and seemed to be pretty well fixed. He settled down to reading, writing pamphlets, and lecturing occasionally for causes he favored, and just loafing.

Then, in 1929, when Darrow was seventy-two, he was practically wiped out financially by the stock-market crash. He began to take cases again—practically any kind of case. He established connections in Washington and began to represent racketeers who had fallen afoul of the income-tax statutes. He went into court and got a few murderers off—or at least got them prison jolts instead of the noose. He was in a pretty bad way.

Darrow had reached his seventy-fifth year when, in 1932, he found himself suddenly stimulated by front-page newspaper stories coming out of Honolulu. Lieutenant Thomas H. Massie of the submarine service of the United States Navy, stationed at Pearl Harbor, and his wife, Thalia, went to a drink-and-dance affair at a night club one hot night and during the course of the evening got into one of those husband-and-wife spats usually forgotten in the morning.

Mrs. Massie, an attractive woman of twenty-three, some four years her husband's junior, decided to leave the party and walk home alone. It was around midnight. In the course of her walk, she was obliged to traverse the same route as that taken by local prostitutes catering to servicemen in the district. Mrs. Massie was halfway home when a car drew up and she was abducted by five men. She was driven to a remote spot and raped by all five. The girl's assailants she described as being a Hawaiian and four men apparently of mixed breed.

From the very beginning, this was more than just another rape case—vicious and depraved though rape is in itself. This was a *race* case. The racial problem in the islands had begun long years previously when, according to the way Darrow later put it, the white man had come to Hawaii, taught the yellow and brown men to look upward to pray, and then, when the prayer was finished and the yellow and brown men looked down again, their land had been stolen from them.

There were, in the Honolulu police department, some Orientals who didn't see much, if anything, wrong with what the five men had done to the white woman. In the twelve months prior to the attack on Thalia Massie, almost fifty native women in and near Honolulu had been raped by United States sailors, who were apparently not in a position to pay for their fun, and some of the women had been hospitalized. So the investigation into the attack on Mrs. Massie was being kicked around in the hope that it would get lost in the shuffle when the resident Navy brass and the white population demanded, and got, effective action.

The five rapists were arrested and quickly identified by Mrs. Massie. The leader of the gang was a bad egg by the name of Joe Kahahawai who was none the less a local hero because of his all-around athletic prowess; the four others were of Hawaiian, Japanese, and Chinese ancestry.

The case against the five men was tried before an all-Oriental jury. What was expected to happen happened. The jury couldn't agree on a verdict and the five blackguards were released until such time as they might be tried again.

Lieutenant Massie, a Virginian, and his mother-in-law—Mrs. Granville Fortescue, a haughty society dowager with moxie to spare—cooked up a little plot. Together with two sailors—fellows named Jones and Lord—Massie picked Kahahawai, the athlete, off a downtown street and drove him to a bungalow that had been rented by Mrs. Fortescue. There the two sailors pinioned Kahahawai against a wall while Massie, pointing a revolver at the culprit, demanded that he spill his story.

The Hawaiian spoke just four words: "Yeah, we done it." Massie fired one shot—practically involuntarily, Darrow was to claim—and killed the Hawaiian.

Massie and the two sailors wrapped up the body and dumped it in Mrs. Fortescue's car. Leaving one of the sailors behind in the bungalow to clean up the blood, the others headed for a promontory where they could throw the corpse into the sea. Meantime, however, the cops had gotten wind that Kahahawai had been kidnaped and they were on the prowl for the abductors. Thus the law overtook Mrs. Fortescue's car before its occupants had a chance to dispose of the corpse.

When Lieutenant Massie, Mrs. Fortescue, and the two sailors were charged with murder, the cleavage between the whites and those of the other races in Hawaii widened and deepened. Since there were roughly ten Orientals to every white man in Honolulu, the jury that would sit at the trial of the four defendants would be preponderantly Oriental. And since the murder victim had been an Oriental, even a moron would not be puzzled if asked to prognosticate the verdict.

Clarence Darrow got a telephone call from a representative of the Fortescue family. The caller wanted Darrow to go to Hawaii to represent the four defendants. "We will pay all your expenses, Mr. Darrow," said the caller, "and we are perfectly willing to pay you a fee of twenty-five thousand dollars in advance." Darrow took it on.

As Darrow saw the problem, even from the distance, the Massie case would stand or fall on an emotional rather than a legal level. By the time he landed in Hawaii, the four defendants had been indicted by an all-white grand jury, not for murder, but for second-degree murder. The lessened degree of the offense that had been decided upon by the white grand jurors only added fuel to the already roaring fire of resentment among the Oriental population.

Darrow got six white men on the jury. So he felt at the outset that the worst he would achieve would be an even break—a disagreement. In distilling the whole case to its fundamentals he concluded that the law was on the side of the prosecution and that life, and the human qualities that preserve it, were on his side. This was, as Darrow later put it, a conflict between the dead letter of the law and the living emotions upon which all life rests.

And so, deciding to pull out every last emotional stop, he put the defendants on the stand. There was no conflict in the evidence; nothing was to be denied. Instead, the defendants were to dwell on the emotional reasons for what they had done. The two sailors, for example, had acted out of loyalty to their superior officer. The husband had gone temporarily insane when the leader of the men who had ravaged his wife looked right at him and admitted what he had done. Mrs. Fortescue had acted out of mother love, the strongest instinct in the animal kingdom.

Mrs. Massie herself took the stand. She not only told of the attack. She told how the attackers had made her pregnant and that she had had to have an abortion performed.

When Darrow began his summation, after five weeks of the trial, he was an old and haggard man. As he moved into his task—a task that was to consume four hours—that same strange thing happened that had more than once happened before. The lines seemed to vanish from his face, and the ravages of age appeared to be lifted from his bent shoulders. His voice, cracked up to now, was somehow suddenly mended. He hitched his thumbs in his suspenders and ambled up and down in front of the jurors. He felt that the white men were with him. He concentrated his remarks on the Orientals in the box. He pleaded not only for his clients but for all humanity in the Hawaiian islands. He asked for justice among the white and the brown and the yellow men, for an end to the cancerous internal strife.

His voice was high and low, by turn harsh and mellow. He was the maestro of old, playing on the human emotions. And then, toward the end of the four hours, a curious transformation occurred. The years suddenly came back and enveloped him, lining his face, bending his back and cracking his voice. He was to say later that he suddenly realized that he was not going to get an acquittal. He saw in the faces of the Orientals on the jury the fathomless mysteries of the Orient. "I knew," he said to an associate counsel, "that I was not registering on those bastards."

The jury was out for two days. It brought in a verdict of manslaughter, with a recommendation for mercy. The judge handed each of the four defendants a ten-year jolt in prison. But Darrow had so raised a storm of public opinion, principally by putting Mrs. Massie on the stand, that the governor, not a bad judge of public opinion, commuted the ten-year sentences to one hour.

Now came an unusual development. The prosecuting authorities—the very authorities Darrow had just beaten—asked him to come over to their side and help prosecute the four living men who had assaulted Mrs. Massie. For anybody but Darrow such a request would have posed no dilemma. Here he was being given a chance to mete out justice to the men whose reprehensible actions had brought about the situation he had just defended. But Darrow didn't have to think long in order to decide about the request.

"No thanks," he said. "I've been defending people for half a century and I don't intend to start prosecuting them now."

As a matter of fact, Darrow talked the Massies into dropping their charges against the four attackers.

The Massie affair was his last big trial. Except for a few small scattered cases, his courtroom career was over.

Clarence Darrow died in March 1938, near the end of his eighty-first year. For two days and two nights people passed his bier in a Chicago funeral parlor—including ex-clients, clients, and prospective clients. Detectives kept an eye on the mourners. More than one of them was picked up. One dip, whom Darrow had once defended, was caught in the act of relieving a fat man of his wallet.

Ray Ginger (essay date 1953)

SOURCE: "Clarence Seward Darrow: 1857-1938," in *The Antioch Review,* Vol. 13, No. 1, March, 1953, pp. 52-66.

[*In the following essay, Ginger provides an overview of Darrow's life and works.*]

The career of Clarence Darrow sprawls unpredictably through eight decades of American life. He appeared as defense attorney in courtrooms from New York to Los Angeles, from Minnesota to Tennessee, and finally in Hawaii. Among his clients were labor leaders charged with conspiracy, a superintendent of schools accused of graft, professional stick-up men, a school teacher accused of violating an anti-evolution law, more than fifty persons indicted for murder in the first degree, public-utility corporations seeking privileges from the state. His living was always earned from the practice of law, but his interests ranged far wider. He lectured and debated incessantly, on topics as diverse as Prohibition and the League of Nations. Often he stepped onto the political stage, sometimes as spokesman for the disinherited, frequently as mere ward heeler.

Parallel to these changes of role ran changes of costume and mood. His attitudes ranged from brutal disdain to tender compassion. His altruism was continuously marred by a quest for luxury and influence. Despite his denunciation of "the narrow, crooked lane which men call Wall Street," he speculated in stocks and bonds with childish abandon. This chaos of contradictions is the chief problem posed by the life of Darrow. And Darrow made some astute comments on human behavior that suggest the key to a solution.

His genius for biography was a basic cause of Darrow's success as a trial lawyer. Goaded by the need to understand his client, he probed into the background of the crime, shuffled the evidence stubbornly, worried over it. His offhand and subtle technique for examining witnesses drew out the relevant facts. But his full powers appeared only in the summation to the jury, when he tried to interpret the lives of the participants. A final argument by Darrow reveals the same meticulous pondering of detail as a novel by Theodore Dreiser. Darrow, tracing the life of a defendant, shows it as a continuum in which each event has its antecedents and consequences. Nothing happens without sufficient reason; causation is always cumulative. Even Loeb and Leopold, when Darrow had finished his analysis of their careers, were no longer seen as monsters. This ability to make his clients understandable, to make the most terrifying crimes comprehensible, was Darrow's lasting gift to American social thought.

In trying to generalize about human behavior, Darrow argued that a person's life is a complicated web, which cannot be "easily explained or brought under one fixed and general rule." But a unity always permeates the diversity. "Whatever the surface indications to the superficial mind, there is or can be no real inconsistency in the complete life of any human being. . . ." Thus Darrow himself, for all his seeming contradictions, was still "that mysterious incomprehensible entity, a human life." His personality was unified by a stubborn adherence to the ways of the rural Midwest. But those individualist values were ill adapted to an industrial society. This emergent order demanded its own ideals, and Darrow would not succumb. He was too anarchistic to conform, and too quick-footed to be crushed. But he bore the scars.

Born into a society of independent men, he lived to see his country pass under the sway of vast impersonal bureaucracies. The process was brutal, and he was trapped in it. The stresses and conflicts in his society became internalized as conflicts in his character. His actions were erratic. He became a misfit as his world changed under his feet. Thus Darrow must be understood as a product of the age when industrial capitalism was born into the rural Midwest. By the scope of his interests, by his alertness to ideological and material currents, he is admirably suited to serve as index to that transformation.

Clarence Darrow was born April 18, 1857, near the tiny village of Kinsman in northeastern Ohio. His father, Amirus, was a cabinet-maker and undertaker, scratching out a scanty living for his large family. The youthful training of Amirus at a theological seminary hurt his chances, paradoxically, at Kinsman, since it had inclined him strongly toward agnosticism. Even when the penalties of ostracism were visited upon his children, Amirus would not accommodate his ways. He was a lettered, other-worldly man, who lived most fully when cloistered of an evening with his books on European philosophy. In the affairs of this earth he was barely competent. His son Clarence always manifested the same dreamy, listless indifference to business matters. Seemingly the boy acquired his bias against diligence from Amirus.

But Clarence worked slavishly to improve this bent. At school he labored over baseball rather than books. His first paid job stimulated a prompt and permanent retreat from toil. When his father suggested that he go to work, Clarence hired out on a farm. The first day he pitched hay. It was hard. The second morning he was sent out to the fields with a pan of kerosene to kill potato-bugs. The stooping hurt his back; the bugs were fat and messy. He flung the pan away and went home. He then began an earnest quest for some way to live without working. He taught school a while, went to Allegheny College for a year. But the depression of 1873 forced him to leave college and go back to Kinsman, where he persistently avoided any steady job. When the traveling court came to town and met in the tinshop, he went down to listen to the rural advocates berate each other. This occupation seemed to him much easier than killing potato-bugs. "So that day and a half of hard work," he said later, "made me a lawyer." He managed to go to law school at the University of Michigan, but he did nothing notable there, and after a year he returned to Ohio to read law by himself.

Admitted to the bar in 1878, he practiced law a while around Kinsman. But after his marriage to Jessie Ohl in 1880, he removed to the neighboring town of Andover, where his son Paul was born in 1883. Soon he moved again to the larger town of Ashtabula. Here he played poker and politics, became city solicitor, heard about Henry George from the cashier of a local bank. Motivated mainly by chance and whim, he left Ashtabula in 1887 for Chicago, where his older brother Everett was teaching school. Now in his thirtieth year, Darrow had done nothing to distinguish himself. He seemed just another young lawyer from a small town, largely self-educated, more sensitive to ideas and moods than to the main chance, having little ambition and a like degree of promise.

These early years, however, are not unimportant. He had entered a vocation that was to affect his entire life. If Darrow became a lawyer because he despised a mundane routine, the law strengthened this tendency in his character. A lawyer is typically involved in dozens or even hundreds of cases. Thus he cannot take up one task, hew to it until it is wholly finished, and then proceed in an orderly way to the next item. He has to root and grab, doing something here, a little there, all the while trying to preserve an air of mature and studious reflection. The flow of his exertions is beyond his control; the tempo of his day depends on the whim of a client, the lottery of the court docket. The overwhelming temptation is to relax and go where the wind blows. Darrow—it was typical of him—relaxed. When he was at his office in Chicago, he never knew whether he would work or not, or at what case, or in what field of the law, or for how long. And yet, since he had partners and clerks, he could leave Chicago for weeks or years, to work on a case in Idaho, write a novel in Colorado, inspect at close range the beauteous women of the Holy Land. Through the world he went, drifting. He survived by virtue of his wit, his flair for dramatics, his studied oratory, his deep perceptions about people. But few men have been less disciplined than Clarence Darrow, and a legal career let him get by that way. Although American society has been routinized, the legal profession has given ground slowly. A lawyer with Darrow's gifts could win cases, make money, and still do about what he pleased.

Because Darrow worried so hard to master the career of each client, he became further obsessed with individualism. Often he veered toward the atomistic theory of society, seeing each man in isolation, neglecting the field in which he moved. And because many of his clients, especially in later years when his work was largely in criminal law, had been dominated by circumstances, he came to deny the very possibility of rational choice. The world seemed to be under the sway of inscrutable forces, deterministic or blindly accidental.

The influence of his clients on a lawyer can hardly be overemphasized. From 1888 to 1894, Darrow represented chiefly the city of Chicago and large corporations. From the Pullman boycott to the McNamara trial in 1911, his main clients were trade union leaders. After 1912 he used his energies chiefly to defend murderers and habitual criminals. And Darrow was not the same man in these three periods. In his character there was continuity, but there was also change. His own attitudes and beliefs were colored by the clients with whom he associated. When he defended Eugene Debs and Bill Haywood and Jim McNamara, he had to reckon with men who had made deliberate judgments; but he could scarcely explain Dickie Loeb and Thalia Massie and Richard Pethick and Louise Van Keuren on that basis. And Darrow had to have a philosophy that would justify his clients; otherwise he could never have won a trial. The success of any attorney depends on his ability to build a constituency. He is always, in a sense, running for office. He must convince trade unionists that he understands their problems and motives; criminals, that he understands them too. Otherwise he gets no clients. In Darrow's case, this opportunistic motive to speak for a group of clients was reinforced by his genuine sensitivity to their hardships.

However much he might modify his philosophy, Darrow clung to certain mannerisms that were his by early habituation. He slouched and shambled and drawled. He used a loose and casual rhetoric. Avoiding all suggestion of trickery, he appeared as a frank and guileless man. Thus he cultivated his native character-type, the rural Midwesterner. It approximated an all-American personality as no possible substitute could have done. This made it possible for Darrow to argue cases in dozens of widely separated jurisdictions. His success is remarkable, since few professions are so wholly parochial as the law. It is not just a matter of knowing local law, local procedures, the peculiarities of the local judges. Darrow always retained associate counsel who had this knowledge from the community. More important is the hostility that invariably greets the appearance of a lawyer who did not grow up in the county where he practices—a Chicago attorney in a Los Angeles courtroom inevitably provoked resentment. In many cases, Darrow was an outlander facing the home talent on the prosecution side. He labored to overcome this handicap in every trial by showing the judge and jurors that he was not an alien at all, that he was one of them.

During the trial of Henry Sweet in Detroit (1926), Darrow used all his homespun devices. He needed them. He was a white lawyer, from another city, defending a Negro charged with the murder of a white man. And in this instance the murdered man had been trying to prevent a Negro family from moving into a white commu-

nity. In Detroit, where the Klan was strong, many persons regarded it as death in the line of duty. The judge was white; so were all the jurors. Darrow worked carefully to ingratiate himself with the court. Referring to a woman who had testified for the defense, he rambled off in time and space: "As I looked at her on the witness stand, . . . I could almost feel the years slipping away from me and leaving me a boy again in the simple country town where I was born; I could see my mother and her companions who swept their own houses, did their own washing and baked their own bread and made clothes for the children; they were kind, simple, human and honest." By such techniques Darrow tried to appear likeable and candid; he then argued that his client had merely done what any upstanding man would do under the circumstances. Henry Sweet was acquitted.

His roving episodic career brought Darrow into contact with hundreds of forceful men, but only John Peter Altgeld got his full devotion. While Darrow was still in Ashtabula he read Altgeld's *Our Penal Machinery and Its Victims,* which codified his aversion to the processes of American criminal law. Soon after Darrow moved to Chicago, he entered into a warm and durable friendship with Altgeld, then a county judge. Darrow proved an astute student of the ways of politics. After Altgeld helped him into a place in the city law department, he reciprocated by tireless efforts to manipulate his sponsor into the United States Senate. In 1892 he served as street-corner orator and confidential agent in Altgeld's successful race for the governorship, and he fought desperately but vainly four years later to secure Altgeld's re-election. Later Altgeld became senior partner in Darrow's prosperous law firm in Chicago. This accurately measures Darrow's reverence for Altgeld—never again did any name appear on the door of a law office above the name of Clarence S. Darrow.

In 1902 Altgeld died. Thereafter Darrow never accepted another man as leader, and few as friend. Most of his acquaintances are best described as a casual, indeed transient, audience for his anecdotes and reflections. He talked to them, but he told no secrets. Except for his son Paul and his second wife, Ruby Hamerstrom Darrow, his most stable associations were with William Carlin and William H. Holly. Carlin came to Darrow's office to read law soon after 1900, and they remained together for thirty-five years. But the difference in age and experience kept the relation from being one between peers. Holly and Darrow knew each other over four decades, but they were partners only briefly in the 1920's and intimate friends only toward the end of Darrow's life.

Others of Darrow's partnerships ended in tragedy, particularly his association with Edgar Lee Masters from 1903 to 1911. Masters was a hard-working lawyer with a fine ability for research and briefing, but he lacked the personality to attract clients or convert jurors. Moreover, his chief interest lay in literature rather than law. He entered the partnership with Darrow in hope of quick riches, so that he could retire to his writing. This hope was frustrated by Darrow's refusal to work consistently at any task, even making money. Masters opposed Darrow's decision in 1906 to abandon his Chicago practice to defend Bill Haywood in Idaho, and his resentment mounted as Darrow remained away for two years.

Masters was repeatedly nettled by the self-indulgent ways of his senior partner. Once he prepared a case which Darrow was to argue before the jury. The case was called, the jury sworn, but Darrow was inexplicably absent. Masters blundered through the oral argument and ended up with a split jury. The next morning Darrow was at the office when Masters arrived. Darrow asked about the outcome of the trial, without even a suggestion that his own absence needed any explanation. Masters admitted that he had lost four jurors. "Well," Darrow reflected, "I suppose if I had been there we would have won all of them," and he lumbered off into his own office. Days later he remarked that he had missed the trial by going to Cincinnati to give a lecture.

The climax came in 1911, when Darrow again left Chicago to defend Jim McNamara in Los Angeles. An enraged Masters left the firm. By this time he hated Darrow. Without ever mentioning Darrow's name, Masters wrote into his *Across Spoon River* a spitefully abusive picture of "my partner." Darrow never deigned to notice the attack, and his own autobiography makes no reference to Masters. Although Darrow's disdain for mankind was usually good-natured, it prompted him to keep everybody at a distance. He would never admit to concern about Masters' charges that he was immoral, crooked, a parasite on his associates, and guilty of suborning jurors in the McNamara case.

This rather contemptuous toleration of humanity Darrow bolstered with a mechanistic view of the universe. In debates on the question "Is Man a Machine?" he took the affirmative without hesitation. One could scarcely blame a machine for its mistakes, he argued, but one should not expect rational behavior. Darrow's pseudo-scientific support for this appraisal of mankind was derived from his interpretation of the researches of two biologists, Ernst Haeckel and Jacques Loeb. Haeckel contended that an essential unity exists between inorganic and organic nature, and that the evolution of species has proceeded in a mechanical, wholly predictable manner. From this philosophy and his researches in comparative zoology, he derived the recapitulation theorem. He also claimed that his two major principles—the ubiquitous law of evolution, the strict constancy of matter and force—disproved the existence of God, the soul, and free will.

Loeb was led to a mechanistic view of the lower forms of life by his experiments with tropisms. The reactions of plants and protozoa, he concluded, are rigidly physiochemical and deterministic. But, like Dreiser, Darrow carelessly overlooked Loeb's qualification. At a critical point in the evolutionary process, animals had developed the faculty of associative memory. The result-

ant ability to learn from experience reached its highest pitch (to date) in man. Thus Loeb admitted into biology the principle of levels of organization of matter. Not only is man different from inorganic machines; he is also different from monkeys.

Darrow had acquired from his father an interest in science and philosophy, and he always showed an awareness of these topics. His favorite brother-in-law, J. Howard Moore, distilled a brew of mysticism and Darwinism into books about biology. Darrow took the lead in organizing the Biology Club in Chicago, a discussion group that heard lecture-series by such eminent scientists as Anton J. Carlson, Charles Judson Herrick, Fay-Cooper Cole, and Frederick Starr. But Darrow never progressed to the point of intense and rigorous study; he was content with the dabbling of the dilettante. Eschewing Jacques Loeb's books and scholarly articles, he got his information from popularized versions in the daily newspapers. This insured that nothing would upset his own deterministic pessimism. "I may be an idiot," he told a Senate committee in 1935, "but I am not a cheerful idiot." The same note recurred in letters to his friends, like his bland comment to Fremont Older: "Of course I know . . . that one's thoughts and philosophy have nothing whatever to do with his conduct. His reactions are purely mechanistic and cannot be changed." He explained the labor boycott in similar fashion: "I boycott people because I do not like them. I know they are just as good as I am and just as bad, but they don't mix with my chemistry. There is no chemical affinity with me."

However congenial he found this view of the world, he could not hold it consistently. It was too harsh, and the contrary evidence ran strong. So he calmly supplemented it with the vitalism of Nietzche and Schopenhauer, both of whom he praised in public lectures. Sometimes he even doubted that valid knowledge of nature was possible. In his funeral oration in 1916 for J. Howard Moore, he argued: "Man does not live by truth, but by the illusions that his brain conceives." And already in 1901 he had contended: "It may be that only the ideal really is. All the facts of life are not what are, but what seems to us to be."

These two philosophies—mechanical materialism and idealism—figure in Darrow's legal arguments, but they are even more prominent in his other activities. Philosophy and religion were favored topics for his lectures and debates, and he was infatuated with the role of platform orator. When his exuberant speculation on the stock market came to disaster in 1929, he began to debate for pay, whereas previously he had done it for fun. Throughout his life he spoke publicly two or three times a week: campaign speeches, debates, lectures, impromptu talks. On the stage he gave an impression of slow-witted somnolence—huge, shambling, a lock of hair dangling across his forehead and over his eyes. But behind this façade he perfected many biting replies. Once in a debate about free will with a clergyman, his opponent closed by quoting from

Henley's "Invictus." Darrow strolled out to the front of the stage. "The minister claims to be master of his ship," he drawled sardonically. "Why, hell, he isn't even deck-hand on a raft."

This talent for repartee made Darrow a brilliant political orator. Calvin Coolidge, he commented, had achieved the impossible; he had made Warren Harding seem like a great president. But Darrow's role in politics was not limited to speeches in the spotlight; he also moved effectively in the shadows. Soon after his arrival in Chicago he was consorting with that specialist in chicanery, Hinky-Dink Kenna. He participated in Altgeld's plot to capture a seat in the Senate in 1890, and he was one of those rare reformers who knew how to work with the machine.

But for Darrow politics also involved principle. He tried valiantly in the 1890's to cement the labor-Populist alliance in Illinois. When that effort collapsed, he went back to the liberal wing of the Democratic Party. He was restless there, especially after Altgeld died, and he often bolted. He went to the state legislature as a public ownership man, almost ran for mayor as an independent. Always shuffling back and forth, in 1924, he went so far as to campaign for LaFollette in some states, for John W. Davis in others. It was Al Smith all the way in 1928; and then, reluctantly, Roosevelt. Disillusionment with the New Deal came quickly, and soon Darrow was contributing money to the Socialist Party.

He cavorted on the fringes of radicalism for forty years. In 1894 he deserted his railroad clients to serve as counsel for Eugene Debs in the cases resulting from the Pullman boycott, and thereafter his relations with Debs were always affectionate. When Debs became leader of the Socialist Party, Darrow played with the notion of following him. But he paused, uncommitted. Although he liked many socialist ideas, he thought that socialism was too simple a doctrine to cover all the complexities of the world. He called it "a dope," like morphine or religion. And temperamentally he had no liking for the majority rule of the Socialist Party; he wanted individual rule, each man to himself. The policy of accepting discipline from anybody else was outrageous. In 1913 he told an audience that "the only party I have ever found devoted to the working man is the Socialist party." But he would not join because it was "too dictatorial" and did not permit enough "personal judgment and independence." The socialists would not tolerate his aberrations, and he would not stifle them: "If I belonged to the Socialist party, I would be tried for heresy."

Darrow's fractious ways could not be molded to group effort, and he was never willing to keep his dissents to himself. He knew that organized and cooperative pressure is the effective technique in modern society, but the practical consequences of this knowledge were repugnant to him. In 1905 he resigned from the Dunne administration in Chicago because the mayor was following a course he disapproved. He threatened to withdraw from the Haywood case when an associate counsel questioned his judgment. A recalcitrant individualist, he went his own way even though it condemned him to impotence. And his way was often determined by whim. He could support a policy in the morning, oppose it in the afternoon.

These contradictory urges are nowhere more apparent than during the first World War. Darrow declared in 1914 that he would not "fix the blame as between these countries, even if I could." But the socialists were wrong in saying that capitalism caused the war. "War in itself is a natural state of man. Whether man will ever get beyond it is another question." The only hope of preventing war lay in altering man's physiochemical reactions, so the outlook was bleak indeed. But by 1917 he was convinced that the Allies were right, that Germany was a menace, and that the United States should enter the war. Darrow, because of his standing with liberals and trade unionists, was a valuable convert to the camp of preparedness. He toured the country, urging an unqualified support of the American war effort. "If President Wilson had not defied Germany he would have been a traitor," said an eloquent Darrow at Madison Square Garden, "and any man who refuses to back the President in this crisis is worse than a traitor." Furiously denying the socialist calumnies, he exploded: "Our friends the pacifists tell us that this war is the creation of Wall Street; in other words, that it is a rich man's war. How any sane man can make such a claim as this, I do not see." Thus on September 15, 1917.

Meanwhile Darrow was speculating on the stock market, using tips that he received from Samuel Insull and other associates in the patriotic committees which he had joined. He had found respectability at last. In the summer of 1918 he went to England and France on a propaganda mission, ardently describing their sacrifices in the columns of American newspapers. He also wrote from London on August 12 to his son Paul, now manager of a gas company in Colorado: "Of course I know that the Electric Co. affects you, but they will no doubt need a raise & I think you ought to have one. Things will be high for a long time after the war & we ought to be making some money if we can."

Darrow was slow to reverse his evaluation of the war, but by 1926 he suggested that perhaps the whole episode was a hoax. Even honest men can be deceived by slogans of their own making, he realized, so that they grind savagely onward to a result that was no part of their intention.

Such reflections often led to despair about the chances of shaping events, and Darrow then withdrew to write about them. His literary output was substantial: two autobiographical works, a novel, an anthology, books about Prohibition and crime, short stories, numerous reviews and essays. Although he could write brilliantly, his creations seldom seem finished. Vacation output, they bear the mark. Climaxes are burked; trivia dramatized. Focus and tempo are neglected. A superb piece of realism like **"The Breaker Boy"** is still loose in structure and stained with touches of melodrama. Darrow was no more disciplined at writing than at other tasks. But *An Eye for an Eye,* with all its rough edges, is a perceptive and truly gripping story of a murder, and few idylls of childhood are more engaging than *Farmington.* The better works range far and cut deep. In *The Story of My Life* moods shift superbly: tender tributes to Altgeld and Debs, an indignant attack on conspiracy laws, the dreamy premonitions of death at the close of the book.

This extraordinary diversity of attitudes was central to Darrow's appeal for juries—nearly everybody could find something likeable about him. His long-time acquaintance, William Allen White, called him "a cynic, a sophisticate, and a Sybarite," and the words are apt. Still, the impression created is badly askew. Darrow was as much sentimentalist as cynic, and he was given to sudden enthusiasms. Much of his sophistication eventuated in a conscious effort to seem the plain rural advocate, plucking continually at his galluses. He was never predictable, and he confronted the world by turns with tears, jests, and compassionate action. The solemnity of *An Eye for an Eye* is no more typical than the rollicking detachment of **"The Black Sheep."** His comment about Lincoln Steffens applies well to Darrow himself—his jokes always became serious, and his serious remarks turned into jokes.

Thus Darrow misled both his contemporaries and later historians about the Scopes trial at Dayton, Tennessee. Because he played the trial like a farce, it has been regarded as a farce. But Darrow did not so regard it. His own writings at the time made it clear that he was fighting a grim battle to defend science against mystical dogma. He tried to win the case by exposing the absurdities of fundamentalism as a philosophy, but fundamentalism as a reactionary force he found far from amusing. By trying the case in the headlines, Darrow crippled the campaign against the teaching of evolution. This meant more to him than any narrow legal victory, because he knew that operative rights are seldom equivalent to statutory rights.

The essence of civil liberties, to Darrow, was to preserve and extend the range of activities in which each person could follow his own preferences. Into this battle he hurled his purest efforts. He despised coercion, whether by churches, by governments, or by public opinion. When a riot against Negroes occurred at Springfield in 1908, he saw and said that the respectable white citizens had stimulated and unleashed the mob. His final argument for Henry Sweet is a forthright denunciation of white supremacy. And in 1927 he appeared before Negro audiences in Alabama to speak against lynching, thus prompting hysterical accusations that he had incited to riot. The Ku Klux Klan generously offered to "ride the agnostic out of town on a rail."

But Darrow would not give up his battle for the rights of any individual, all individuals. Any law that unnecessarily abridged these rights—and that meant most laws—was a standing provocation. A revealing anecdote tells how Darrow, while on a lecture tour during Prohibition, was interviewed in a hotel by two newspapermen. Toward the end of the session, one reporter produced a flask and suggested that they have a short drink. Darrow drank a glass of the raw whiskey. Then, coughing and red-faced, he rasped out: "Damn it, I take every chance I can to break this law, but my throat just won't stand for it. You younger men will have to carry on the fight." Not only Prohibition, but Sunday-closing laws, censorship, conspiracy laws, labor injunctions, segregation statutes, capital punishment, were all insulting and tyrannical. The right of any citizen to speak his mind without fear of reprisals, the right of others to hear free discussion, the right of wage-earners to organize, the right of Negroes to live wherever they wanted—these were absolute freedoms that admitted no qualification. Even the clear-and-present-danger test was an unjustified abridgement of these basic liberties.

Darrow showed tenacity and courage in translating these precepts into practice. He stood up for the leaders of the American Railway Union although nearly every influential voice in America was crying for their blood. When the Chicago police began an indiscriminate round-up of anarchists after McKinley's assassination, Darrow was on vacation in New Hampshire, but he wrote Jane Addams his offer of help. He was really tested after his client, Jim McNamara, pleaded guilty to the dynamiting of the Los Angeles *Times* in 1911. Twenty men had died in the explosion, and even the trade union leaders who had supported McNamara now demanded that he be punished to the full limit of the law. Darrow himself was indicted for subornation of jurors in the case. But he would not desert Jim McNamara, and when he was on trial he doggedly explained that Jim McNamara was a fine man who had not meant to kill anybody. During the World War, Darrow went to Washington to protest the denial of postal privileges to the socialist press. In 1919 he went again to the capital to petition for the freedom of Eugene Debs, serving a ten-year sentence for violation of the Espionage Act. The postwar frenzy against radicals saw Darrow defend Ben Gitlow in New York, eleven anarchists in Milwaukee, Arthur Person in Rockford, eighteen communists in Chicago. After he had retired from the practice of law, he took up the case of a youthful murderer, fought it through court after court for three years to prevent an execution, and lost everywhere he went. But he thundered and wept and begged until the governor commuted the sentence to life imprisonment. Thus did Darrow stand between the vindictiveness of America and its prospective victims. It was his greatness.

But exceptions are plentiful. How to explain, for instance, his scorn of women? He lauded without measure the views of Nietzsche and Schopenhauer on the female personality. His opposition to woman suffrage was a cause for boasting that he had resisted this brash innovation. He argued that women had "been less affected by the progress of civilization than man" and that they were "more governed by emotion than the male." He thought, in brief, that women showed to best advantage when rearing children and knitting socks.

Such deviations must be seen in terms of Darrow's total dilemma. His nostalgia is suggestive—a mood that became more frequent and embittered as the years passed. His recurrent pilgrimages to Kinsman in his old age were the physical counterpart of a craving for the past. His world had died, and he almost knew it. The world of the free market, whether in goods, ideas, or activities, had yielded to bureaucracy and manipulation. He often mentioned the difference. "The world's the same as it was fifty years ago—only the conditions of life have changed," he told a reporter in 1933. "The organizations of the capitalists make it so. They dictate the whole thing." Sensing the thrust of social change, still he denied its verdict. The foundations of individualism had splintered and fallen, but he remained committed to the pristine democracy of Kinsman. The effective subjugation of women was a part of those rural folkways. But so was the ideal of an equal chance and a fair fight. Darrow's struggle for individual freedoms was an effort to realize that ideal, to make of it a vibrant way of life. In describing the law court as an arena where gladiators fought it out, he used a significant image. Two gladiators face to face: that was his ultimate value.

His focus was always on the individual. In 1931 he wrote to Brand Whitlock that his autobiography was nearly finished. "He said a funny thing in his letter," Whitlock reported to a friend: "he said that everybody was writing his autobiography nowadays; that everybody was standing on the street corner beating a bass drum and crying: 'For God's sake, look at me for a minute!'" Darrow thought the sin of modern society was that it seldom heeded the individual. He also knew that they were neglected because the lone individual had become negligible for the major affairs of life, but the knowledge made him uncomfortable, so he denied it.

He just could not conform to the new orbits of society. Loathing discipline, he rambled through reform movements all his life, scratching at the wall of reaction and irrationality. He struck some strong blows, but his efforts seldom caused a lasting change. No single person can sustain enough pressure to move encrusted privilege and prejudice very far from the path. Never appealing beyond himself to any group or class, he had to rely on his unsupported wits and eloquence. So his energies were often dissipated in spectacular engagements which had little meaning for the long run. That was his way. But it was a losing way.

Darrow was asked, two years before he died, what advice he would give to young attorneys. "Cultivate individuality," he urged. "Let the other fellows go their way. Don't do what others do." Thus he had lived. But he doubted that others would follow his advice, and he was not sure it would matter much if they did. "Nothing's

perfect," he observed later in the same interview. "There is no such thing. But what are you going to do with the world anyway!"

Horace G. Rahskopf (essay date 1961)

SOURCE: "The Speaking of Clarence Darrow," in *American Public Address: Studies in the Honor of Albert Craig Baird,* edited by Loren Reid, University of Missouri Press, 1961, pp. 29-53.

[*In the following essay, Rahskopf discusses Darrow's speeches and public addresses.*]

Students of public address are interested in "the American gadfly," as T. V. Smith dubbed Clarence Darrow, because speech was the principal medium by which he carried on his work. Darrow was not only a successful court room pleader; he was also a brilliant conversationalist and popular lecturer and debater, with a wide following drawn by his striking non-conformist views and his forthright, yet charming and human, manner of utterance. Though he aspired to be a writer and actually produced a considerable body of essay and narrative material, his success and reputation as speaker greatly overmatched his standing as author. He loved to talk; speech was the life-blood of his intellectual and social life.

THE CAREER AND ITS SETTING

Darrow's career spanned the transition from the individualistic, agrarian, frontier America of the nineteenth century to the capitalistic, industrial, urban America of the twentieth century. The industrial revolution which shook the nation in the decades after the Civil War led to concentration of economic power and severe labor-management conflicts which continued well into the new century. Back of the economic struggles lay fundamental intellectual differences between the new and dominant philosophy of pragmatism and the older idealism, between the new materialistic science and the more traditional religious fundamentalism. Liberal religion attempted to incorporate the new scientific attitudes into Christian belief, but the masses of people, especially in the South, adhered to fundamentalism. By the time Darrow appeared on the scene the battle lines were drawn not only in economics and industry but in social and religious life as well.

In the waning years of the nineteenth century, Chicago was probably the dominant center of the rising swirl of conflict in the nation. The city was a lusty, booming, young giant which had the economic growth, racial complexity, industrial strife, political corruption, social reform, and cultural and artistic progress to make a complete cross-section of Middle America. The place "offered a study in contrasts: squalor matching splendor, municipal boodle contending with civic spirit; the very air now reeking with the foul stench of the stockyards, now fresh-blown from prairie or lake" [Arthur M.

Schlesinger, *The American as Reformer,* 1950]. A series of violent industrial disputes reached their climax in the horror of the Haymarket affair (1886).

Into this maelstrom of activity came the young man from Kinsman via Ashtabula and rented desk room in an office for the practice of law. The city ignored him, but he did two things which broke the barriers and set him on his way: he sought out judge, later governor, John P. Altgeld; and he began to make speeches. The friendship with Altgeld became strong and abiding and motivated the younger man deeply. The opportunities for speaking were numerous, and Darrow took them as they came—at study clubs, before civic organizations, and in political rallies. He joined the select Sunset Club as well as the Henry George Single Tax Club, and campaigned for the Democratic party. As a result he was invited to speak at a Democratic free trade convention in February, 1889. His address, **"The Workingmen and the Tariff,"** captivated the assembly. In that event a career was born. The newcomer was appointed to civic office and advanced rapidly. When Eugene Debs was arrested for leading his American Railway Union to strike in sympathy with employees of the Pullman Palace Car Company in 1894, Darrow felt obliged to resign his position as railroad attorney to defend the despised radical. The criminal trial was dismissed, but Debs was sentenced to prison for contempt of court. The event sealed the destiny of Clarence Darrow. He returned to private practice and found that "more and more of the distressed and harassed and pursued came fleeing to my office door."

During the years that followed the Pullman strike Darrow became known primarily as a labor attorney. By the time World War I broke out, however, labor had won substantial improvements in wages and conditions of work and the vengeful attitude of the public towards unions had declined. The war period and years immediately following, moreover, brought forward new problems to which Darrow turned his attention. Temporarily and with misgivings he abandoned his pacifism and his belief in non-resistance to support the struggle against German militarism. During this time there was a wave of "anti-red" hysteria, national prohibition was enacted, racial tensions increased, a new criminology was developed, and the nineteenth century conflict between naturalism in science and fundamentalism in religion continued. In the courtroom and on the public platform Darrow fought for civil and constitutional rights, racial tolerance, humane attitudes toward crime and criminals, and freedom of thought and education.

The total number of his public speeches is impossible to count. A contemporary estimated that he appeared in 2000 trials. The number of lectures, debates, and platform speeches must be estimated in even larger thousands. In cities where he tried cases he was usually invited to lecture on some of the literary or social topics in which he was interested. As early as 1908 he was speaking against prohibition. In 1912 he made a tour of

the Pacific Northwest. In 1928 and in 1930-1931 after returning from Europe he made extended tours under management of George G. Whitehead of the Redpath Lyceum Bureau. Many of the engagements of these tours were symposia on religion which pitted the great agnostic against representatives of Protestant, Catholic, and Jewish faiths from the local communities. Darrow once remarked that there was scarcely a city of any size in the United States in which he had not spoken at least once and in all the larger cities many times, and that "probably few men in America have ever spoken to so many people or over so long a stretch of time."

DARROW'S PHILOSOPHY—HIS MESSAGE

Contradictory though it may seem, Darrow the iconoclast and debunker was largely a product of his time. The experiences of childhood burned into his soul a sensitivity to the struggles of the common people. As he grew into manhood his mind was shaped by the philosophy of his era. He took from pragmatism something of its faith in science and in human endeavor as well as its plain down-to-earth approach to problems. He believed that the universe operated according to a rigid cause-and-effect determinism; and that man, as part of the natural order, had neither free will nor moral responsibility.

Over against this philosophy of determinism was a practical commitment to complete intellectual freedom. Clarence Darrow "determined" to hold his mind unfettered and to fight for freedom for everyone else. His realism was of the type which took a critical look at everything. Darrow once remarked to a fellow attorney, "I can say with perfect honesty that I have never knowingly catered to anyone's ideas, and I have expressed what was within me, regardless of consequences." Though he lectured on socialism and sometimes worked for the Socialist program, he never could convince himself it was consistent with individual liberty. The standard assumptions and codes of his day gained no favor in his view just because they were traditional.

The conflict between determinism and freedom was only one, although probably the most fundamental, of the paradoxes in Darrow's life. Like many another great personality, he was a bundle of inconsistencies. He regarded the human being as a machine, yet he was a deep and friendly humanitarian. He professed to despise reformers and reform organizations, yet in his own legalistic way he was a zealot for human welfare. He was a realist and pragmatist, yet idealist enough to defy the dominant wealth and power of his time in the interests of the working class. He was a Tolstoyan pacifist who did not believe in force or violence; yet he had learned that sometimes conflict was inevitable, and when it arose for a cause in which he believed, was ready to take his part. He denied the criminal's responsibility for crime, but held all other men responsible. He denied the validity of moral judgments, yet passed judgment on society. He urged justice for the criminal in spite of his conviction that the inexorable operation of heredity and environment made attainment of justice beyond the power of individual will or purpose. As his biographer has said, Clarence Darrow "was a sentimental cynic. He was a gullible skeptic. He was an organized anarchist. He was a happy pessimist. He was a modest egocentric. He was a hopeful defeatist. . . . He didn't like life; it was all a silly mess, yet he squeezed the last drop of juice out of it" [Irving Stone, *Clarence Darrow for the Defense,* 1941].

In spite of these inconsistencies there were deep and abiding elements of stability in Darrow's life and career. He was constant in his efforts for freedom of thought, personal liberty, and human welfare. His typical role was that of opposition speaker. In public debate he usually took the negative. In court he was never a prosecutor. This feature of his speaking seems to follow inevitably from both sides of the conflict between freedom and determinism. On one side the commitment to freedom of thought prevented him from attaching himself permanently to any specific cause. He was, therefore, free to move quickly from opposition to opposition. His negative role seemed to follow also from his deterministic concept of life. The forces which "determined" his "peculiar organism" had put him in the stance of defender. Many of his greatest cases were undertaken because of a compelling inner sense of obligation. He defended strikers, radicals, communists, and members of racial minorities in face of bitter social condemnation. For Darrow this was not merely the lawyer's customary professional obligation to give every man his defense before the law, but the result of passionate conviction that the social order created injustices for the poor and weak. "When the cry is loudest," he said, "the defendant needs the lawyer most." In all his speaking Darrow was dissenter, champion of the underdog, and critic of the social order.

So strong was this feeling of social protest in him that at times he skirted the borders of anarchism. He restrained no censure of laws or Constitution or anything in the established order if it seemed to him a threat to welfare of the masses of people. In his times of greatest bitterness he condemned all government as arbitrary power exercised by a dominant ruler or ruling class to keep the mass of men in subjection and exploit them. In his prime at the age of forty-six he wrote: " . . . nature, unaided by man's laws can evolve social order . . . in new countries amongst unexploited people, suggestions of order and symmetry regulated by natural instincts and common social needs are ample to show the possibility at least of order or a considerable measure of justice without penal law. It is only when the arrogance and avarice of rulers and chiefs make it necessary to exploit men that these rulers must lay down laws and regulations to control the actions of their fellows."

Back of this lay his reading of Paine, Voltaire, and Tolstoy. Back of this lay the Haymarket riots, the Pullman strike, and the defense of the Woodworkers at Oshkosh. The next year (1904) he spoke to the prisoners in the Cook County jail, telling them that "if every man and woman and child in the world had a chance to make a decent, fair, honest living, there would be no jails and no lawyers and no courts." He opposed the open shop because he considered it a means of exploiting workers. His opposition to prohibition was a dissent against legislative restriction of the liberty of the individual. His efforts to secure equal rights for racial minorities, especially the Negroes, was a challenge to hatred, prejudice, and discrimination. The era was a time of social protest. Clarence Darrow, idealist grown acrid, though not its chief promulgator, was one of its chief heralds.

At no point, however, did the social protest appear more strongly than in his views on crime. He was a passionate exponent of the new criminology that advocated reformation instead of punishment. The sources of this conviction were in part the influences of his childhood, in part the example of Altgeld, in part Darrow's own mechanistic philosophy. The criminal, he thought, was a victim of circumstance, usually inferior by heredity, deprived of normal opportunities in life, frustrated and desperate, punished hatefully by society, and therefore often hating society. Continued violation of the legal code followed inevitably. The act, the so-called crime, "had an all-sufficient cause for which the individual was in no way responsible." The definition of crime in Darrow's view, "can never mean anything except the violation of law when the violator is convicted, [and] . . . has no necessary reference to the general moral condition of man." He pleaded that society should treat the criminal with the same compassion it showed for the sick and maimed.

Opposition to capital punishment, of course, was central in the attitude toward crime. This opposition was reinforced by his abhorrence of death, his memories of the executions following the Haymarket riots, and many tense moments of waiting for verdicts in courtrooms with knowledge that the word "guilty" probably would mean death to his client. His logical reasons for opposing the death penalty were that it did nothing to remedy the causes of crime and tended to brutalize society. As a practical policy, he argued, crime "can be diminished . . . only by finding the causes and intelligently treating these causes rather than rending and destroying in anger and hate."

Through all of Darrow's philosophy ran a deep current of pessimism. A pessimist he defined as one "who looks at life as it is . . . [who] doesn't necessarily think that everything is bad, but . . . looks for the worst." He argued that civilization is a failure, that the human race is not getting anywhere, that life is not worth living. Darrow's pessimism was also founded on the conviction that man is fundamentally dishonest. Honest men "find themselves doubted, distrusted, and outcast. . . . They are obliged to conform or die." And again he wrote, "The number of homeless men and women, ruined fortunes, idle workmen . . . is evidence of the ease with which adroit men can defraud and cheat and transfer the property of the world into the hands of the few." His final and conclusive basis for pessimism, however, was the frustration of death. "All roads lead to futility and oblivion," he said. "The constant cries and pleadings of the ages have brought back no answering sound to prove that death is anything but death"; and he added, "while this makes less of man, it . . . covers his deeds with the cloak of charity which is the ultimate garment of the great Unknown."

This doubt about getting answers to life's basic questions was the key to Darrow's religious attitudes. He was considered by many to be the greatest agnostic of his day, and proudly took the designation literally—one who "doubts the verity of accepted religious creeds or faiths." He did not quite deny the reality of God. He simply found the evidence for God's existence insufficient to convince him, and claimed the right to say so while leaving others free to draw their own conclusions. He found no evidence of purpose or design in the world; and asked, "Isn't it a bit more modest and less foolish to answer, as I do, that I know nothing about it . . . ?"

On some other articles of religious faith, however, Darrow was adamant. He could not reconcile the cruelty and violence he saw everywhere in nature with the belief that a merciful and kind Supreme Being was ruler of the universe. He refused to accept the literal interpretation of the Bible as a supernatural book, because such authoritarian reverence for the Scriptures seemed to him a narrow and bigoted denial of intellectual freedom and a contradiction of the facts of science. He went to Dayton, Tennessee, not primarily to defend John Thomas Scopes, but to wage war on this denial.

Belief in immortality also seemed to him utterly impossible. He found no evidence that memory of this life persists after death, nor could he believe that mind and personality exist outside the physical body, which after death completely disintegrates and is mingled with other elements and absorbed into other life forms. This denial of spirit, he admitted, took some of the glamor and illusion from life and some of man's egotism, but added that "peace and comfort, when gained at the sacrifice of courage and integrity, are purchased at too high a price." He believed in facing life fearlessly, even though it seemed futile and meaningless.

Actually, however, Darrow was not entirely devoid of religious faith. He was, as Charles Edward Russell once remarked, too sensitive to keep out all faith. In spite of his refusal to believe in a God who permits men to suffer pain and misfortune, he was not able to follow completely his postulate of impersonal, cause-and-effect materialism. In grief at the passing of his friend he could say: "If there shall be a great, wise, humane judge, before whom the sons of men shall come, we can hope for nothing better for ourselves than to pass into that infinite presence as the comrades and friends of John Pardon Altgeld." He wrote of "infinite bubbles poured out by the great creative power." In some of his noblest

moments as speaker he proclaimed a law of love and human brotherhood. This was the religion he practiced, but he did not call it Christian. For him Christianity was still synonymous with the fundamentalist beliefs he could not accept. In their stead he lived a creed of benevolence, which he professed to derive, not from any sentiment or religious faith, but from his belief in a universe of law. "People who believe in a universe of law," he said, "never condemn or hate individuals." His humanitarian life was also derived in part from rejection of belief in immortality. "When we abandon the thought of immortality," he said, "we cast out fear and gain a certain dignity and self-respect. We regard our fellow-travelers as companions . . . traveling the same route to a common doom. No one can feel this universal relationship without being gentler, kindlier, and more humane toward all the infinite forms of beings that live with us, and must die with us." Here appears the crowning contradiction of Darrow's career: the mechanist and determinist who believed man to be utterly irresponsible, nevertheless lived a responsible life of kindness and tolerance and service to humanity.

In the words of his poetic contemporary and associate,

> This is Darrow,
> Inadequately scrawled, with his young, old heart,
> And his drawl, and his infinite paradox,
> And his sadness, and kindness,
> And his artist sense that drives him to shape his
>   life
> To something harmonious, even against the
>   schemes of God.
>
> [Edgar Lee Masters, "The Man
>   with an Old Face"]

SPEAKING METHODS

Throughout most of his life Clarence Darrow strove for a direct and thoughtful kind of discourse; and though he once remarked that oratory is a disease of youth, his career exemplified that better meaning of the word suggested in John P. Altgeld's comment that "The orator must be absolutely independent. . . . Great manhood must go with great oratory."

Because of his abhorrence of artificiality, Darrow never submitted himself, at least so far as any records show, to rigorous training in the use of voice and action. He professed to believe that when he really had something to say he could make himself understood. Here was a mechanist in philosophy declaring a think-the-thought method of training. His disgust with early school exercises in declamation blinded him to Altgeld's advice that delivery requires as much attention to voice and action as is given by a singer. Darrow's manner of speaking was indeed effective in its own peculiar way, but there is little evidence that this effectiveness came out of any deep understanding of the processes involved or was anything more than the fortunate result of years of trial and error experience on the platform.

Likewise in preparation of thought Darrow did not subject himself to intensive discipline. His was a free-wheeling and independent genius which followed its own methods. Although the speeches on favorite themes had the advantage of continued study and frequent repetition as the years passed, the popular lecturer depended primarily on his general fund of knowledge and almost never made specific and intensive preparation for any speech. In the courtroom the prolonged activity of examining witnesses and gathering evidence served in part as substitute for study and writing, and Darrow's prodigious memory enabled him to recall and use readily without written notes all the detailed facts of a case in a plea of several hours' length.

This attorney held legal technicalities in contempt and studied philosophy, psychology, biology, and history more than he studied law. He usually emphasized, therefore, those broader issues of a case which lay beyond the immediate guilt or innocence of the particular defendant. This method first appeared significantly in the defense of Eugene Debs when Darrow accused the General Managers' Association of conspiracy to use the government as a cloak to conceal its infamous treatment of labor and argued that the injunction had been used illegally by a court of equity to deny the right of trial by jury. In like manner many of Darrow's greatest cases were but "episodes in the great battle for human liberty." The crimes charged against his clients he presented as inevitable social consequences of the long struggle for justice. At Dayton, Tennessee, Darrow and his colleagues looked upon the entire proceeding as part of the battle for intellectual freedom; Scopes' guilt or innocence was all but lost sight of in the struggle over admissibility of expert testimony on the relation between evolution and Christianity. Again, the trials of Loeb and Leopold in Chicago and of the Sweets in Detroit were not simply murder cases. At Darrow's hands the former became part of the campaign against capital punishment and an extended statement of the philosophy of humanitarianism, and the latter a test of a man's right to defend his home and person.

Darrow, however, was also a master of courtroom strategy. He could doodle over cross-word puzzles at the counsel table to create an impression of casual indifference. Although noted for careless dress, he knew how to change from the shirt-sleeve and suspender aura of Dayton, Tennessee, to a correct and sophisticated appearance in metropolitan Detroit. He could bait a prosecuting attorney to distraction and confuse witnesses by repeated heckling. He knew that delay in starting a trial often gave passions time to cool, that prolonging a case gave the jury opportunity to develop a friendly feeling for the defendant, that a light touch of humor could sway a jury more than argument. On one occasion he brought a defendant's infant daughter into court. On a higher plane of strategy he met the perfect hanging case in the Loeb-Leopold trial by combining a plea of guilty with extended testimony of alienists.

Out of his experience Darrow developed definite opinions about the kind of jurors advantageous to a defense.

He preferred men (no women wanted) who were imaginative, idealistic, able to laugh and to put themselves in another man's place. Whenever possible he avoided prohibitionists and religious people because, he said, they believed in sin and punishment and might be vindictive; but if he had to accept them on a jury he much preferred Roman Catholics, with Methodists second choice. The wealthy and ultra-respectable he also avoided because they were inclined to regard themselves as guardians of the law. Germans he thought too bull-headed, Swedes too stubborn, Scotsmen too inhuman in feeling. Irishmen and Jews he found most sympathetic and susceptible to emotional appeals. He always sought to find jurors who were the same sort of men as his client or who themselves had been in trouble, and old men instead of young because the experiences of life tended to make them more charitable.

In keeping with these viewpoints Darrow's methods of persuasion and proof were based on his belief that man is not primarily rational, but imaginative and emotional. "If a jury wants to save the client," he said, "they can find a good reason why they should, and will. The problem is to bring about a situation where court and jury want a lawyer's client to win." His basic means of proof, therefore, were more largely motivational than logical.

The most frequent appeal was to the common humanity of all men. Even after the bitterness of the anthracite coal strike in Pennsylvania he could say of the operators: "If they will learn to come to us as brothers, . . . they will find that we will extend the right hand of fellowship. . . . I wish they could understand that back of the black hands of these, their servants, . . . are consciences, intellects, hearts and minds as true as in any man who ever lived." In most of his labor cases he pleaded for sympathy for "thousands of men, and of women and children . . . weary with care and toil." To a jury of white men called upon to judge the motives of Negroes defending their home he said, "Put yourselves in their place. Make yourselves colored for a little while . . . before any of you would want to be judged, you would want your juror to put himself in your place." Most of the argument in defense of Loeb and Leopold was a plea for "every other boy who in ignorance and darkness must grope his way through the mazes which only childhood knows," for "understanding, charity, kindness, and . . . for a time when hatred and cruelty will not control the hearts of men."

Closely related to this appeal for human brotherhood, in fact often mingled with it, was reference to man's love of liberty. Clarence Darrow regarded labor organizers as leaders in the struggle to free men from economic slavery. By subtle analogy Thomas I. Kidd was one with such men as Garrison, Kelley, Foster, and Pillsbury of an earlier generation who worked for freedom of slaves in the underground railroad. In his first self-defense Darrow spoke to the members of the jury as men who valued their own liberty; and he argued the case of Arthur Person as "one that reaches down to the foundation of your freedom and mine." The champion of justice defended others who, like Person, were arrested in the post-war raids against subversive organizations, not to defend their views as such, but because they had "the same right to their belief under the laws of this country as you have to yours," and because "you can only be free if I am free." He excoriated fiercely those prosecutors who had broken into houses and made arrests without warrants and urged the jury to stand for "the right of men to think; . . . to speak boldly and unafraid; . . . to be master of their souls; . . . to live free and to die free."

The great agnostic occasionally used appeals to religious sentiment. This practice raises a challenging question: What should we think of an agnostic who in impassioned defense argument referred to the "infinite God of the infinite universe," pleaded for recognition of the God in men, made extended analogy from the Sermon on the Mount, quoted Scripture to support argument, declared he did not believe in "tinkering with the work of God," and spoke of the Infinite Being who gave him light to see his duty? Were such appeals to religion merely devices of rhetoric? Possibly! Darrow must have used them with some awareness of their potential effect on audiences. In view of the man's lifelong idealism, however, any critic should hesitate to impugn his sincerity. At least one other interpretation of this religious material is possible. Darrow's agnosticism and his pessimism were intellectual convictions based on such facts of life as he could observe directly. He freely acknowledged, however, that instincts and emotions more fundamental than intellect keep man alive. Perhaps his uses of religious material came out of these deeper instincts and emotions of his life, broke through the surface crust of cynicism, and like his humanitarianism were evidences of a submerged religious belief which he scoffed at intellectually but which he could not entirely obliterate? In his moments of most impassioned pleading when issues of human welfare were at stake, these hidden springs inevitably overflowed. The religion of the heart which this man lived may well be regarded as one of the sources of his emotional power with audiences.

In fact Darrow's character and personality were generally his most powerful persuaders, and the strength of his beliefs was a major source of that power. He gave his clients a deep personal and emotional commitment. The great courtroom pleas were great primarily because motivated by depth of conviction.

The influence of a personality on audiences is difficult to assess, but we should at least notice some of the ways Darrow used to enhance his credibility with listeners. He was well aware that an attorney's every look and gesture could influence a jury; and he, therefore, made it a rule seldom to quarrel with judge or opposing lawyers or witnesses. Though he could be ruthless in challenge and intense in question, as he was in the Haywood and Scopes trials, his methods of cross-examination were typically casual and easy-going, "in the spirit of browsing along the way." Juries he complimented, de-

fied, or challenged as subject and occasion required. Frequently he expressed confidence in them. His most significant personal approach was to put responsibility directly on them:

> I will submit this case squarely to this jury to see what you are going to do in the cause of freedom of speech. . . .
>
> You can only convict yourselves in the face of the civilized world . . . ; you are trying the jury system.
>
> There is no power on earth can relieve you of your obligation. This jury alone stands between this boy and the gallows.
>
> Bill Haywood can't die unless you kill him. You must tie the rope. You twelve men of Idaho, the burden will be on you.

The most dramatic of all this attorney's personal proofs were his attacks on opponents. Although he was often blunt and forthright on the public platform, he could also be courteous and friendly. Indeed some of his strongest opponents, even on issues like prohibition and capital punishment about which he felt deeply, came to be his close friends. In court, however, he gave no quarter and asked none. His exposures of false or distorted testimony were merciless, as when he showed that George Baer had misrepresented wages paid the miners, that George Paine had lied about child labor in his mills, and that the prosecution had coached some of the seventy witnesses who testified that no mob was at Doctor Sweet's house, although all seventy admitted being there. Prosecutors he frequently branded as the tools of vested interests or of the mob, and some prosecution arguments as disgraceful even among savage tribes. Of prosecutor Gray in the bribery trial in Los Angeles, 1913, he said, "I will guarantee that Chandler has visited Gray's pen a great many times and poured many a pail of swill down his trough."

When issues were tensely drawn, Darrow's power of invective, ridicule, and sarcasm could be terrible to encounter. Who would have wanted to be Mill Owner Paine or District Attorney Quartermass, or Special Counsel Houghton on that autumn afternoon, 1898, in Oshkosh, Wisconsin, when the defender of labor stood up to speak in behalf of Thomas I. Kidd charged with conspiracy to injure the business of the Paine Lumber Company because he directed a strike of woodworkers for abolition of woman and child labor, recognition of the Union, better wages and a weekly pay day? On that day, especially, Clarence Darrow was one of God's angry men, and his anger overflowed in bitter and scathing denunciation:

> Fie on you for hypocrites and cowards, who would combine every manufacturer in the city of Oshkosh, not into a "union," but into an "association." A body of employers living from the unpaid labor of the poor is an "association." A body of their slaves is a "labor union." George M. Paine says, "I will not

meet your union; I will not meet your committee. If one of you have anything to say, come to me alone and talk." And they did go alone, and what did they get? . . .

Herman Daus went to his employer. . . . Eight or ten years' experience, and getting a dollar and a quarter a day; . . . only about a dollar a day for the number of days that a man must live, for he must live Sundays as well as other days, unless perhaps he is so religious that he can go to Brother Houghton's Sunday School and needs no food except his teachings. Seven dollars and a half a week for a man who had worked at dangerous machinery for ten years, and they had promised him a raise; and he went singly, singly the way this great corporation desired to have a man meet them; singly—the cowards. I do not know whether he carried his cap in his hand; . . . I do not know whether he said "Your lordship." . . . But he did decently ask for a raise. And what did they say? They said, "Go to hell, God damn you. . . ." These high-toned gentlemen, who come into this court of justice with kid gloves and well-brushed clothes, who can study manners at foreign courts, and send their children to foreign lands to be educated; and yet, when a poor laborer asks them for something more than seven dollars and a half a week, they tell him to go to hell. Well, he would not have far to go, Mr. Paine. . . .

And this is the man, Mr. District Attorney, for whom you prostituted the great State of Wisconsin, for whom you prostitute the office that you hold, to whom you have turned over this State to do the work of a bloodhound to track innocent men to jail.

For such a vitriolic pleader, logical reasoning served more as a framework and foundation for his proof than as a primary means of its development. The basis of his logic lay in his philosophy of life. He believed, as we have seen, that the universe operated as a rigid cause and effect determinism; his basic method of reasoning, therefore, was causal. The most pervasive of these causal arguments, both in court and on the lecture platform, was that actions of men are not the result of their own will and intention but arise from forces of heredity and environment. On this principle Loeb and Leopold were victims of their backgrounds, the McNamara brothers were but performing the inevitable consequences of generations of mistreatment of labor, the inhumanity of employers was the primary cause of all labor conflicts, and the Sweets were compelled to shoot in self-defense by fear ingrained in their race through generations of mobbing and lynching.

These broad outlines of causal reasoning were developed and amplified not only by more detailed casual inferences, but also by inductive forms of argument. Sometimes Darrow would use analogy with brilliant effect, but the more frequent form of his inductive inferences was broad generalization based on a body of detailed facts. In the courtroom Darrow's marshalling of evidence was typically exhaustive and precise. Anyone who reads the analysis of wages and conditions in the mines

before the Anthracite Coal Commission, or the extended accounts of labor history in the Haywood trial and in the self-defense pleas of 1912 and 1913, or the assembling of testimony to show the abnormal mental condition of Loeb and Leopold, must inevitably come away with renewed respect for the intellect which could marshal and reduce to order so vast an array of detail and argue issues so broadly against a backdrop of history and social conditions.

By contrast, Darrow the platform lecturer and debater was often negligent, inexact, and even flippant in his use of facts and inferences. He derided statistics, but sometimes resorted instead to unsupported assertion and sweeping generalization. Occasionally his only source was personal experience, which though wide and challenging could hardly be conclusive. For want of citations he could dispose of a point with a terse, "Every intelligent man knows," or "Is there anyone who doesn't know?" In a debate with Will Durant on the mechanistic nature of man Darrow begged the entire question by defining "mechanism" so as to include both purpose and growth, two of the main characteristics of organisms; and then used glaring examples of *non sequitur* by arguing that man is a machine because (1) the human body is imperfect and because (2) we do not know where or how the first form of life began. In some of the debates on prohibition the defender of personal liberty implied that drinking alcoholic beverages was responsible for "all the poetry and literature and practically all the works of genius that the world has produced," clinched the argument by asking what kind of a poem you would get out of a glass of ice water, and in reply to the dangers of drunken driving quipped, "Then let's get rid of automobiles." Audiences laughed with such flippancy and even applauded the statement that "in civilization men read more books and get less out of them than they do in savagery." No wonder Darrow asserted that men are not motivated primarily by reason, although in fairness we should add that he often admitted lack of knowledge and conceded points made by opponents.

In style of discourse his striking qualities were amplification and cumulation, mingled with humor, sometimes subtle and again caustic, and with frequent sprinklings of sarcasm and irony. There was a Ciceronian echo in his use of amplification. He would hold an idea up, turn it over and around by restatement, repetition, rhetorical questions, and accumulation of vivid details, until it was expanded to full-bodied significance.

During some of his earlier years Darrow affected an ornate style, which arose from his admiration for the great Robert Ingersoll. A typical example was the opening of the address at the Free Trade Convention:

When the untutored savage—nature's eldest child— first occupied the earth and freely roamed where he would, and took as he wished, his wages were the full amount that his strength and cunning enabled him to gather from the elements of nature—the earth, the sea, the air—from which all productions are originally drawn. In those primitive days, ere yet the soil had been parcelled out to individual owners, and before the accumulated earnings of by-gone days had ripened into capital, each was his own employer and his wages, fixed by nature, were the full product of his toil. . . .

By 1905, however, Darrow was setting the stylistic tone of his mature career: "As the man possessed of vital truth will not waste a moment of his precious time on vacant forms, so, too, when he tells his truth to the listening world, he will waste no time in the effort for effect." The application of this philosophy is evident in the preponderance of one-syllable words and short, simple sentences in the discourses of his middle and later years. Sometimes in the more impassioned pleas he would build a series of clauses through mounting sequence to strong climax. The choice and management of words, however, were always clear, usually plain and simple, seldom ornate. His diction at its best had the same rich and noble music that Hamlin Garland noted in *Farmington*. Most of Darrow's illustrations were from the common experiences of daily life. Such embellishment as occurred consisted primarily of references to literature. In almost all of his defense pleas he quoted poetry, and sprinkled them generously, too, with references to prose writers, philosophers, and dramatists. He carried his love of literature even into the intense struggles of the courtroom.

Let us look at Darrow, the speaker, in action. He sits slumped down on the end of his spine, sometimes preoccupied, often motionless. When the time comes to speak, he rises and ambles slowly and deliberately to the speakers' stand or close to the jury rail, his broad shoulders slightly rounded, massive head thrust forward, hair disarrayed with one unruly lock hanging down over the right side of the broad forehead, the homely, deeply-lined, Lincolnesque face stern, and the cavernous, blue-grey eyes kindly.

He begins quietly in a pleasant, drawling baritone, without fanfare. The voice is often too low to hear easily beyond the front rows, but can change from barely audible whisper to resounding power. For the most part he speaks slowly and thoughtfully with restrained modulation and conversational quality, giving the impression of utter simplicity and sincerity combined with a kind of whimsey. His greatest defense pleas, nevertheless, reveal him as a man of deep emotion, the voice often fading away at the end into silence so intense and throbbing that one can scarcely tell where the sound ceases and stillness begins.

Darrow's bodily action is a little ungainly; he may lean on the desk and at times shuffle awkwardly. Perhaps he will point a long finger to emphasize a remark, or make a sweeping backhand motion across the body with his right hand, or thrust his left hand deep in his trousers' pocket, or even hook his thumbs in the galluses and snap them. As the fires of conviction warm up, he may pound one fist in the other hand, or use some windmill gestures of the arms, or wrap them around his body and glare at the listeners. His whole frame may reverberate with the intensity of his emotion. The face is an expressive map of varied feelings. The more eloquent gestures, however, are with the shoulders. They "can express more hatred and contempt, or sympathy and understanding, or cynicism and despair in one hunch . . . than one could ever imagine possible if he did not see it." " . . . the shoulders . . . dominate the room, . . . insult the prosecutor, snub the judge, flatter the jury, comfort the defendants, joke with the newspaper men and clown for the crowd. . . ."

The whole effect was more than sincerity or directness or what teachers of speech call "audience contact." Though one man might consider Darrow's bitterness and cynicism repellent, and another call him a "gaunt, loose-skinned, fiery-eyed rebel," or describe him as "gloomy, blunt and sardonic," or refer sarcastically to his acting ability, his infinite capacity for friendship nevertheless shone through his rough exterior and broke down whatever hostility might be in the listeners. Whether reading to a few friends at his fireside, or talking to twelve men in a jury box, or lecturing in a great auditorium, he created a sense of intimacy which took the listeners into a friendly circle. There was a nameless charm about the man which enchanted the souls of listeners and carried them away captive. Therein lay the heart of Clarence Darrow's power as a speaker.

SUMMARY AND EVALUATION

What then shall we think of him? Obviously no simple answer is possible, nor even any single answer. He was many-sided and contradictory, a rebel and an eccentric, who by his speaking shattered the intellectual patterns of his time. It is difficult if not impossible to steer a middle course of judgment between, on the one hand, those caustic critics who condemned his convictions and purposes, and on the other hand, the hero-worshippers who spoke only fulsome praise.

Darrow's immediate effectiveness as a speaker was demonstrated repeatedly—in the courtroom by number of verdicts won, on the lecture platform by wide popularity and return engagements. At his great defense pleas crowds milled outside the doors, listeners often wept. At his lectures and debates large audiences listened intently and applauded, and returned to listen and applaud again.

His speaking had limitations, however. Here was a man whose neglect of disciplined study of speech method robbed him of his highest development as a speaker; whose power in logical proof was sometimes dissipated by carelessness in preparation and in use of evidence and inference; and whose greatest skills were emotional appeal and vituperation of opponents. Here, too, was a man whose idealism was weakened by pessimism and sense of futility. In its way the materialistic determinism to which he adhered was as much out of balance as was religious fundamentalism. If Bryan was a bigot, Darrow was a cynic, and there may be some question which presents the greater liabilities to society. If one violates freedom of thought, the other lacks constructive purpose.

When we have said all this, however, we have not plumbed the basic values of the Darrow career. Here was a man who by personal charm and wit could captivate an audience; who could analyze evidence with devastating effect, and reason with broad, philosophic insight; whose speech was so thoughtful, direct, and honest, and so powerful in its conviction and in blazing appeals to imagination and emotion that many who listened were moved profoundly. Here, also, was a man of ideals carried into action, a fearless man and magnificent humanitarian, who spoke out against the dominant powers of his day. He was the type of intellectual radical every country needs for its own good. He stood for fundamental rights when they were unpopular. Under his leadership education and science took the initiative against militant ignorance. As one of Darrow's younger contemporaries [Paul Y. Anderson] said in honor of his seventieth birthday:

> To a smug generation he has been a dash of vinegar. Upon an age satisfied with its superiority, he has played the hose of his skepticism. In an era when wealth and position are unduly exalted, he has made himself the champion of the outcast and disinherited of the earth. Among a people prone to swallow what is handed to them, he has exercised his corrosive common sense. In a time when liberty languishes, he carries on the good fight.

R. Baird Shuman (essay date 1970)

SOURCE: "Clarence Darrow's Contribution to Literary Naturalism: 'An Eye for an Eye,'" in *Revue des Langues Vivantes,* Vol. XXXVI, No. 4, 1970, pp. 390-400.

[*In the following essay, Shuman examines naturalistic elements in* An Eye for an Eye, *in particular as they highlight Darrow's concern for individualism and revolt.*]

The most renowned criminal lawyer in the history of American jurisprudence is undoubtedly Clarence Seward Darrow. Admitted to the Bar in 1875, when he was only eighteen years old, Darrow had established himself and gained a national reputation before the turn of the century by winning an acquittal for Eugene V. Debs in the American Railway Union strike case of 1894.

However, Darrow, who was to live until 1938, gained his most substantial reputation during the last half of his long life for his involvement in such illustrious and sensational contests as the Leopold and Loeb case (1924); the Scopes trial (1925), in which his opponent was William Jennings Bryan; and the Scottsboro case (1932), which he undertook and won in his seventy-fifth year.

For half a century, Darrow was a much-touted public speaker and debater. He was known to lecture audiences across the country and had early gained the reputation of being an intellectual spellbinder. His insights regarding the law and his criticism of the legal system aroused in those who heard him the desire for legislative change, the fruits of which many in the present generation are enjoying. Darrow was passionately concerned with individual rights, as his novel *An Eye for an Eye* clearly indicates. His compassion for the little man was unbounded, for he realized with John Donne that no man is an island; justice which is not extended to all, eventually is available to none.

I

Darrow had a strongly developed ethical sense, arrived at through years of deeply analytical social theorizing. His ethical code was an individualistic one based upon his conception of right rather than upon the legalistic codes by which his society operated. He felt that many of these codes were patently wrong, and he set about to expose the inequities which resulted from them. Darrow had a fine legal mind, but he did not have a legalistic mind. It is perhaps well that he never attended law school but instead read for the Bar, for a conventional nineteenth century legal education would probably have discouraged him from doing the sort of philosophizing about the law which accounts for his emergence as the most outstanding advocate of his age.

II

Many people who are familiar with Clarence Darrow's legal career are unaware that the famed "attorney for the damned" for some time carried on a parallel career in the field of letters. During the last decade of the nineteenth century, when he was practicing law in Chicago and was intimately involved with the labor movement of that period, Darrow seriously thought of turning from his legal practice to enter the field of letters on a more thoroughgoing basis than would be possible to one who maintained an active practice. The literature of the age, both the realism of such writers as William Dean Howells, Hamlin Garland, and Brand Whitlock, and the naturalism of such young literary iconoclasts as Harold Frederic, Stephen Crane, and, at the turn of the century, Jack London, Frank Norris, Theodore Dreiser, and Upton Sinclair, struck at the very heart of many of the problems which brought about the criminal actions with which Darrow daily contended as a lawyer. And Darrow, with his unbridled imagination and singular insight and sensitivity, often approached his law cases with the attitudes of a novelist more than with those of a lawyer. William Allen White was quite correct when he asserted in his *Autobiography* that "Darrow was off the same emotional piece of goods as Bryan . . . Darrow let off steam by romance."

Darrow was well versed in literature and was much concerned with literary realism. He wrote a number of literary essays, some of which were published by Elbert Hubbard's Roycroft Press in 1899 under the title *A*

Persian Pearl and Other Essays. Darrow was also one of the early literary defenders of the poetry of Walt Whitman and produced a thoughtful and far-sighted essay on the work of the oft-maligned poet.

William Randolph Hearst employed Clarence Darrow as counsel when the Chicago *Evening American* was to be incorporated, and Darrow immediately began to contribute essays to his employer's newspaper under the title **"Easy Lessons in Law."** Writing was a natural outlet for Darrow. He was a rapid and sure writer. Like Upton Sinclair, his social concerns took precedence over his artistic concerns; however, *An Eye for an Eye,* like *The Jungle,* is sustained at a high interest level despite some of its artistic inadequacies. The book has considerable forward thrust and great social impact. When one compares *An Eye for an Eye* to Dreiser's *An American Tragedy,* which appeared two decades later, he may well stand in awe of Darrow's primacy in dealing with some of the deterministic elements which went almost unchanged into the Dreiser novel. Of course, one can not and should not imply that Dreiser was dependent upon Darrow for these elements; many of them appear in *Sister Carrie,* which predates *An Eye for an Eye* by five years, and merely point out the fact that American writers were becoming increasingly concerned with the social problems which confronted the United States in the first decade of the twentieth century.

Before the publication of *An Eye for an Eye* in 1905, Darrow published an autobiographical work, *Farmington* (1904), which is appealingly written and which provides valuable insights into Darrow's early life as well as into the development of his set of values. Written by Darrow during a trip to Europe in 1903, *Farmington* is in the form of an autobiographical novel and essentially is concerned in theme with the revolt against the village as Oscar Cargill points out in *Intellectual America. Farmington* has never received wide acclaim and is known to few modern readers.

III

An Eye for an Eye is not wholly a naturalistic novel. The naturalist observes at first hand, records as objectively as he is able the details of his observations, and—again as objectively as he is able—presents a literary report of these observations. Few of America's literary naturalists have been able to maintain the scientific detachment, the consistent objectivity which naturalism in its purest form demands. Even Frank Norris loses his detachment in the final pages of *The Octopus,* perhaps the most artistically successful naturalistic novel in the American literary canon.

When viewed with the bulk of naturalistic novels which were produced in America around the turn of the century, *An Eye for an Eye* must be classified as being essentially naturalistic with strong romantic overtones. It is not unusual that a naturalistic novel should have such overtones; indeed, Frank Norris demonstrates con-

vincingly in "A Plea for Romantic Fiction" that naturalism is more nearly akin to the spirit of romanticism than to the spirit of realism even though it has imbibed some of the spirit of each.

Philip Rahv in "Notes on the Decline of Naturalism" writes, "I would classify as naturalistic that type of realism in which the individual is portrayed not merely as subordinate to his background but as wholly determined by it—that type of realism, in other words, in which the environment displaces its inhabitants in the role of the hero." This classification, while perhaps not a universally acceptable one, certainly would place *An Eye for an Eye* in the running with other naturalistic books of its period. It is, by Rahv's definition, the sort of naturalism which tends toward "the exposure of socio-economic conditions (muckraking)." In this respect, *An Eye for an Eye* is comparable to *The Jungle, Sister Carrie, Maggie: A Girl of the Streets, The Octopus,* and *McTeague.*

Naturalism was a literary form used by writers who were concerned with revolt. Willard Thorp has noted that in the naturalistic novel "there was unconscious revolt, . . . revolt against contrived novels of the genteel writers," as well as revolt against the socio-economic conditions which created the situations about which most naturalists wrote. Both of these forms of revolts are seen abundantly in the novel at hand.

IV

In *An Eye for an Eye,* Darrow fires a number of broadsides against the establishment. Four of these broadsides are consistently sustained and repeated throughout the novel, and they are in keeping with the social criticisms of other literary naturalists of the period.

First and most importantly, Darrow strikes hard at the working conditions which bring about the brutalization, the dehumanization of the poor. One reads today a great deal about breaking the so-called "cycle of poverty" which affects America's dwellers in ghetto areas. Sixty odd years ago, Darrow and many of his literary contemporaries were writing and lecturing about this very problem. Jim Jackson, Darrow's protagonist in *An Eye for an Eye,* is purported to be a good fellow basically. He is about to be hanged for killing his wife, but the reader is shown the obverse side of this desperate felon's personality, and he sees a concerned and loving father, a man who, though impoverished himself, has the humanity to give a half peck of potatoes to a starving woman and to take a blanket from his own bed on a cold winter's night to cover his freezing horse.

Jim has arrived on Death Row through a series of coincidences and mischances. His story, which he himself tells virtually in monologue form, is almost wholly one-sided; but, because of the use of the monologue form, the one-sidedness is quite acceptable and believable to the reader.

Jim, at the age of fourteen, began to work in the Chicago stockyards, and here began the process of his dehumanization: "I never liked that work: I used to see so much killin'. At first I felt sorry for the cattle and the hogs, and especially for the sheep and calves—they all seemed so helpless and innocent—but after I'd been there awhile, I got used to seein' their throats cut and seein' blood around everywhere . . .".

When he could abide the stockyards no longer, Jim became a switchman, work from which he was eventually driven when a friend and fellow switchman was run down and killed before his eyes. From this job, quite by happenstance, he became a potato peddler because he happened to meet Sol Goldstein, a potato peddler who was being forced by ill-health to sell out. The implication of what Darrow presents here is that Jim is trying to escape the brutalizing effects of his first two jobs. However, fate conspires against him ultimately, and purely environmental factors turn him into a murderer.

Another step in Jim's dehumanization comes when he marries a waitress with whom he is not in love—and, indeed, one may well wonder whether Jim is capable of being in love. Although he had known his future wife for some time, he had never really noticed her "until that time she got that red waist and done her hair up with them red ribbons." His marriage, like his entire life, is without zest and vitality. He realizes that divorce would be his wisest out; but divorces cost more money than the hapless Jim can lay his hands upon, so he must stay with his wife.

Circumstances are the deterministic forces which cause Jim to marry his wife and to stay married to her. It is a web of circumstances and coincidences which lead to her death at his hands. Jim, peddling his potatoes on a bitterly cold day, has had too much to drink, for petty politicians wooing constituents have been buying rounds of drinks in various saloons on Jim's route. As the day draws to an end, Jim, cold and dejected because he has sold almost none of his potatoes and because he has heard that the alderman is not planning to distribute his usual free turkeys on Thanksgiving, which is only three days off, is about to warm himself with yet another drink, when he decides instead to buy a steak and take it home for dinner. His wife cooks the steak improperly and this leads to a fight in which she goads Jim into hitting her: "Why don't you do it! Kill me! Kill me! You miserable dirty coward! Kill me!"

Quite by accident, the coal scuttle and poker are in the living room rather than in the kitchen where they are usually kept. Were the poker not within arm's reach, presumably Jim would think better of what he is doing, and the fatal blow would not be struck.

Darrow's second broadside is a generalized one against the legal system which, after the murder, began to grind resolutely against Jim. Jim's previous encounters with the legal profession had made him distrustful of it.

Once, oppressed by debts which he could not pay, Jim had sought advice from a lawyer, " . . . but he didn't tell me anything that done me any good and I had to pay him ten dollars out of my next month's wages, so that made me all the worse off." Again, when he sought a divorce, he went to a lawyer who " . . . said it would cost fifty dollars, but I hadn't any fifty dollars. So we made up our minds to try it again."

Now that Jim is in the most serious trouble of his life, his case is to be defended by an inexperienced, court-appointed attorney who, while bright and sincere, is no match for the prosecuting attorney who, like his counterpart in *An American Tragedy,* is hell bent on obtaining a conviction which will enhance his chances of being appointed to a judgeship. The reader is told early in the book "that the good lawyers charged so much that [one] couldn't have them, and the ones who came to the jail did more harm than good." And when Jim's attorney finally is appointed by the court, Jim can only say, "It didn't seem quite fair, though, that I should have a lawyer that hadn't never had a case. I didn't believe they'd take a young feller who was just out of medicine-college and set him to cut off a leg all by himself."

The judge and the jury are presented as being against Jim from the start. His conviction is assured, and although his crime was not technically first degree murder, since there was no premeditation, Jim is tried on this charge, found guilty, and sentenced to be hanged largely because an anti-crime crusade is going on in Chicago at the time of the trial. It is interesting again to note a parallel with *An American Tragedy* in which Clyde, though guilty of manslaughter, is tried and convicted on a charge of first degree murder supported on only the flimsiest of circumstantial evidence.

Of those connected with the law, only Jim's jailers and his inexperienced lawyer are presented sympathetically. The jailers, of course, are close to Jim's social class, part of the proletariat. The lawyer, at times—though not always—Darrow in thin disguise, goes so far as to ante up fifty dollars of his own money in an attempt to get a Supreme Court review of Jim's case; but the cards are stacked so completely against Jim that this effort leads to nothing except additional expense and the building up of false hopes.

The third broadside, one with strong contemporary overtones, especially in view of recent landmark decisions of the Supreme Court, has to do with the issue of trial by newspaper. The popular press had publicized the Jackson murder case so much that it was all but impossible to impanel an impartial jury—the judge as much as admitted this. Long before Jim had even been captured, the daily press, by portraying him as a monster, had in its way tried and convicted him.

Further, the courts were sensitive to popular opinion which was significantly shaped by the daily press, so Jim could not expect justice which, in this case, would have been a conviction on a charge of second degree murder. Jim's lawyer said that " . . . he'd have me plead guilty and the judge would most likely give me a life sentence, only since this crusade against crime the judges dassent do that; there was so much said about it in the newspapers, and they was all 'fraid of what the papers said."

Finally, Darrow hurled a number of broadsides against the rich, much as Sinclair did in *The Jungle.* These broadsides were rather ill-defined; however, they represented that gap in understanding which existed between those broadly classified as "the rich" and the likes of Jim whose ideals and aspirations are not dramatically different from those upon whom the gods have smiled.

An Eye for an Eye is replete with examples of this particular concern, but the examples are almost incidental. One of them occurs when Jim's friend, Hank Clery—to whom Jim's story is being told—asks about some noise outside the prison and Jim replies, "Oh, the people drivin' past in their carriages to the theatre. You know all the northside swells drive down Dearborn Avenue past the jail. I wonder if they ever think of us in here, or if they know what is going to be done tomorrow."

Of course, some of them knew because " . . . there was always some awfully nice dressed ladies settin' up there with the judge ever' day, and they had a sort of glass in their hands, and they'd hold it up in front of their eyes and look at me through the glass just like the judge looked at the paper."

Earlier in the novel, Jim also enunciates a problem which has always been prevalent in ghetto neighborhoods and which has recently been brought to public attention. In peddling his potatoes, he is forced by the wholesaler to take inferior grades, some of which have been nipped by frost, at regular prices. And he sells only to the poor because the rich " . . . won't even let you drive in their high-toned streets even after you've paid a license. If you want to sell anything, you've got to go among the poor people. Of course they can't buy very much, but then they pay more for what they get." He continues, "It's queer ain't it, the way things are fixed; them as works hardest has to pay the most for what they eat, and gets the poorest stuff at that."

Essentially, this fourth major concern points up the fact that the poor do not understand the rich even though, as Will and Ariel Durant have said in *The Lessons of History,* "By and large the poor have the same impulses as the rich, with only less opportunity or skill to implement them." As in *The Jungle,* the rich are portrayed as the ogres who thrive upon the misery of the poor. Darrow and Sinclair would have weakened their cases had they shown, for example, how the rich would very soon be poor if they did not foreclose on mortgages or take back items on which installments had not been paid as agreed. Dreiser, in a book like *Sister Carrie,* could present a more balanced picture of the rich because he

permitted Carrie to become successful. Of course, in the final pages of *Sister Carrie,* Carrie, now affluent, is rather indifferent to the sufferings of the poor; and in this indifference, she has assumed the posture of her new class—at least as this class is often presented by the naturalistic writers.

V

Darrow drew upon many generalized sources—the social conditions of his times, his professional exposure to many of these conditions, his liberal stance in general—in writing *An Eye for an Eye* during a two week period when he was vacationing in the Colorado Rockies. However, he also had in mind a number of specific sources, the most notable of these being the celebrated Chris Merry murder case.

Merry, a leader in the notorious Henry Street Gang in Chicago shortly before the turn of the century, kicked his invalid wife, Pauline, to death on November 19, 1897. He, like Jim Jackson, fled but was apprehended in Kentucky on December 19, 1897 and was brought to trial within the month. He was found guilty of first degree murder on January 21, 1898 and was sentenced to be hanged on February 18, less than three months after the murder had been committed. He received a last minute stay of execution from Governor Tanner of Illinois, but was ultimately hanged at the expiration of the stay.

Darrow was well aware of the Merry case since he lived in Chicago at the time and the newspapers gave great play to the crime and to the ensuing trial and execution. The parallels between it and the Jim Jackson case are striking, although Darrow exercises literary license freely in his redaction of the basic story. However, one may note, for example, the striking similarity between the final paragraph in the Chicago *Daily News'* report (February 17, 1898) of Merry's stay of execution and Darrow's telling about the building of the gallows in *An Eye for an Eye:*

> Work on the gallows on which Chris Merry was to perish had been begun. Jailer Whitman superintended the work and it was carried on with swiftness. That portion constructed before the news of the stay was received will not be torn down, but will be allowed to stand in anticipation of need at the expiration of the respite.

Darrow gave Jim Jackson only the hope, tenuous as it was, of a stay of execution. He apparently chose not to give Jim the stay which Chris Merry had received in part because this would have disturbed the temporal unity of the book and in part because he wished to emphasize the fact that the legal machinery to which Jim had recourse was, in essence, unavailable to him because of his poverty.

The theme of *An Eye for an Eye,* as the title clearly indicates, is vengeance. Darrow, who looked upon any purely punitive measures—and most especially capital punishment—as primitive and ineffective, is attempting to show that deterministic factors have put Jim where he is and that the only cure for the sort of crime which Jim had committed is to find a way of curing the malignancy which is eating away at society. One of Jim's speeches emphasizes this point:

> Why I was readin' about a murder and how a feller was found guilty and sentenced to be hung just before I killed her. And do you s'pose I thought anything about it? If there'd been forty scaffolds right before my eyes I'd have brought down that poker just the same.

Darrow reinforces his idea that capital punishment is not a deterrent to murder by referring to another specific source, a speech which he made in 1902 to the prisoners in the Cook County Jail, the substance of which Jim relates:

> That feller that talked to us in jail said the real reason why they hung people and locked 'em up was to get even with 'em, to make 'em suffer because they'd done somethin'. He said all the smart men who'd studied books claimed that hangin' and punishin' didn't keep other people from doin' things.

This philosophy was very much in keeping with that of Illinois' memorable reform governor, John Peter Altgeld, whom Darrow much respected, and who enunciated a point of view strikingly similar to Darrow's in both *Our Penal Code and Its Victims* (1884) and in a speech entitled "What Shall We Do with Our Criminals?" which he delivered before the Sunset Club of Chicago in 1902.

In *Crime: Its Cause and Treatment* (1922), Darrow systematically stated many of the beliefs which appeared somewhat embryonically in his address to the Cook County prisoners and three years later in *An Eye for an Eye.* The essence of what he felt, drawn from his address to the Cook County prisoners, is that

> The people here can no more help being here than the people outside can avoid being outside. I do not believe that people are in jail because they deserve to be. They are in jail simply because they cannot avoid it on account of circumstances which are entirely beyond their control and for which they are in no way responsible.

Several times within this novel, this precise view is promulgated and it is really a part of the literary naturalist's credo; determinisms outside one's control make his life what it is.

VI

If Darrow has any claim to a niche in literary history, this claim is established on the basis of his ideas rather than upon his literary virtuosity. In reviewing *An Eye for an Eye* in *Bookman.* Grace Isabel Colbron wrote:

> If to create an illusion, to attain the effect aimed at, completely and entirely, is literary art, then Mr. Darrow's work is literary art of the highest, in spite of an apparent neglect of all the canons of literary art.

This quotation from Miss Colbron's review assesses quite accurately the literary stature of the Darrow novel.

Speaking pragmatically, Darrow was a great attorney, although significant legal thinkers have found considerable fault, and quite justifiably so, with his grandstand tactics. Yet one must nod in agreement with Leroy Clark, Professor of Law at New York University, when he says, "My impression is that the most creative things in the law usually sound unacceptable and unlikely." Lawyers like Darrow have opened many new furrows in little plowed legal fields.

In *An Eye for an Eye* one finds the seeds which were to germinate into full flower in such books as *An American Tragedy* and *In Cold Blood.* Darrow, taking a Darwinian view of man, was far in advance of his time as *An Eye for an Eye,* viewed historically, clearly testifies.

Thomas M. Lessl (essay date 1988)

SOURCE: "The Scopes Trial: 'Darrow vs. Bryan' vs. 'Bryan vs. Darrow'," in *Oratorical Encounters: Selected Studies and Sources of Twentieth-Century Political Accusations and Apologies,* edited by Halford Ross Ryan, Greenwood Press, 1988, pp. 17-27.

[*In the following essay, Lessl analyzes the styles of argument used by Darrow and his opponent William Jennings Bryan in the famous Scopes trial.*]

The concept of the speech set offers the critic a systemic understanding of public discourse, an understanding that focuses the critic's attention not only upon the rhetorical texts of concern, but also upon one or more additional messages that are their progenitors. From this perspective apologies are by definition tied to some other message(s) of accusation already extant within a common persuasive field.

Reflecting on a speech set, it immediately becomes clear that accusation and apology can be thought of in two ways—as types of utterances but also as types of roles played in a rhetorical situation. As roles, these pairings are manifested at differing levels of formality. The formality of a speaking situation will determine the rigidity or flexibility of accusatory and apologetic roles. Thus, as accusatory discourse, the charges against Martin Luther set forth in Pope Leo X's bulls *Exsurge Domine* and *Decet Romanum* were highly formal and adhered closely to their purposes of calling Luther into account for his doctrines. Those who enter into a discursive exchange within the role definitions set out in a court of law must at least ostensibly play those parts that have been set out for them. But in the informal speech set, the roles of accuser and apologist are defined by situational aspects and are easily reversed.

Yet even in judicial contexts, where the roles of accuser and apologist are formally set out, one still finds certain elements that do not conform to the formally mandated roles. Thus, there was much in Martin Luther's defense at the Diet of Worms that cannot be regarded as apologetic. Because the doctrines he defended at the Diet were opposed to orthodox teaching, Luther was in effect raising accusations against the Roman church that it ultimately, though not immediately, would have to address. In the case of the Scopes trial, the judicial protocol, with its usual construction of rhetorical roles, was superseded by the immensity of the issue that was there deliberated. Indeed, if judicial procedure had been strictly followed the trial could not have lasted more than a few hours.

Clearly, it is meaningful to talk about accusation and apology as paired sets of utterances, but it is equally clear that there is more than one way in which the observer, and indeed participants, can interpret such groupings of rhetorical acts. Both sides in any sort of dispute will often simultaneously claim that they are merely defending their position, while their opponents are the ones making all the accusations. This was certainly true in the Scopes trial. The opponents in this somewhat circus-like moment in American judicial history each behaved in a manner an outsider would regard as accusatory, while simultaneously maintaining that they came to Dayton, Tennessee, on an apologetic mission—to halt some injustice being perpetrated by the other. If the critic, as an outside observer of such an exchange, regards one set of utterances as accusatory and another set as apologetic, he or she is making an important critical determination likely to influence immensely the reader's understanding of the rhetorical event. This essay will demonstrate that *kategoria* and *apologia* may designate both classes of utterances and symbolically constructed roles that, at least in certain circumstances, are subject to reversal. The role definitions one gives to a rhetorical exchange will ultimately determine whether the individual utterances are judged apologetic or accusatory.

The roles of accusation and apology are only firmly established by formality. When one disregards form, it becomes clear that these are reversible rhetorical postures. These interpretations are crucial to those involved in the exchange, for with the roles of accuser and apologist go certain relational implications that potentially contribute to or diminish the *ethos* of a speaker. For those involved, the outcome of a rhetorical interchange hinges on the ability of the combatants to define the audience's perceptions of their postures in a manner favorable to their own interests. In the Scopes affair, each side entered the case determined that its own speech should be viewed as apologetic. The rhetorical behavior displayed by each side seems to indicate the

desire of each to be perceived by the public as a victim of the other's wrongdoing. Thus, both sides wished that the observing public would define the sequence of events at Dayton so that the other would be cast as the accuser and they the apologist. Darrow and Bryan both hoped to rally political and popular sympathy around their respective causes. Neither party to this affair wished to be perceived as the aggressor. Thus, both actors in this dramatic trial attempted to help the observing public view these combative interchanges so that he would appear an innocent defender of the faith, rather than a vindictive or even malicious inquisitor.

The Scopes trial, July 10-21, 1925, came about as a consequence of the opportunism of some citizens of Dayton, Tennessee, and the desire of the American Civil Liberties Union (ACLU) to put the state's new "monkey law" to the test. John Thomas Scopes, a retiring young substitute teacher, whose education was actually in physics rather than biology, volunteered to be arrested and brought to trial for teaching evolution. Eager to draw, as one resident would proclaim, "a lot of big fellows" into Dayton for the fight, William Jennings Bryan was immediately solicited by the prosecution. With Bryan's head thus ready for the ax, Clarence Darrow, for the first time in a career in which he had never actively sought a client, found himself soliciting to work without pay as Scope's attorney. Clearly the two most familiar principals in this episode, Darrow and Bryan, came as representatives of two respectively different worlds. Bryan, through his odd blend of populism and fundamental Christianity, spoke for rural Americans as an exponent of the agrarian values, traditions, and beliefs that had long been threatened by the gradual advancement of industrialism. Darrow, a Chicagoan, lived willfully submerged in the gray urban wastelands Bryan had come to despise. He stood for modernism, not only as an ideologue, but also as one of the first prominent rhetoricians to throw off the spacious religiosity of nineteenth-century oratory in favor of a secularized speech that ran much closer to the ground.

As speech sets, the rhetorical transactions that unfolded at Dayton were addressed only intermittently to policy issues. The principals, Darrow and Bryan, were equally as concerned with defending their respective ways of life as with the immediate legality of Tennessee's anti-evolution law. Darrow had a reputation for using court cases as platforms for expressing his views on larger political and philosophical questions, endangering often by doing so the well-being of his clients. At Dayton, Darrow found an opportune moment. Here the whole nation and many outside the United States would be watching as he, with his cold sarcastic talons of rational skepticism, tore open the outward flesh of fundamentalist Christianity and exposed to the world the bigotry and ignorance he believed lay beneath. The real issues that prompted the ACLU to put up its offer to fund any test case of Tennessee's anti-evolution law were lost when it was decided that Clarence Darrow would be chief counsel for the defense. The ACLU committee that selected the defense team, which was comprised not only of Darrow, but also two very bright New York lawyers, Dudley Field Malone and Arthur Garfield Hays as well as John R. Neal, a very competent local attorney, knew that Darrow's reputation as a radical and agnostic would distract attention from the issues it wished to draw out in this trial. Darrow was chosen only at the insistence of Scopes himself, and over the protests of Felix Frankfurter, a future U.S. Supreme Court justice, who wanted a conservative attorney with more traditional religious orientations. In almost every respect, Clarence Darrow represented what anti-evolutionists claimed about the influence of Darwinism. Darrow not only was a fervent believer in Darwinism, he had also achieved notoriety by applying a social version of the same in arguing those criminal cases that had by this time made his name a household word. Darrow's was not an authentic version of social Darwinism; it was something more cautious than that, a crudely deterministic interpretation of human misconduct that ultimately removed all responsibility for criminal behavior from the individual to the environment. In Darrow's hands the trial became something different than it likely would have been in the hands of any other attorney.

William Jennings Bryan, who had not practiced law in over twenty-five years, was equally an odd choice to head the prosecution. Although it is difficult to imagine how the prosecution might have avoided its inevitable humiliation, Bryan, acting in the trial more as a figurehead of the fundamentalist movement than as an attorney, had primed himself supremely for the bitter inquisition he was to suffer at Darrow's hands. His presence at the trial was a consequence both of his fundamentalist religion and his populist political thinking. Bryan rationalized that anti-evolutionary statutes, such as Tennessee's Butler Act, were just because they were regulatory laws and symbolic decrees that voiced the authoritative directives of the popular will. Bryan had in fact made it quite well known that he was against the inclusion of penalties in any of the anti-evolution laws of concern. Bryan did not come to the trial to punish John Scopes. Like Darrow, he came to put his cause, that of religion, in the limelight, defending it against the accusations of Darrow and the whole modern world that looked on.

The Scopes trial was not a simple court case but a platform on which the foremost representatives of two prominent ideologies could fight their rhetorical battles. At this level, the accusatory and apologetic roles were not concretely set out. Consequently, as a speech set, the rhetorical events that occurred in Dayton, Tennessee, in July of 1925 can be perceived in a number of ways depending on the eyes through which one chooses to view the interactive sequence. The critic can explicate the event from the perspective of either of the participants, or from the perspective of an outsider looking in on the event. The relativity of the participants' perspectives is evidenced in the critical texts. These artifacts reveal an understanding of how the conflict was understood by those embroiled within it.

DARROW VS. BRYAN

The most obvious but also the least useful way to treat the set is as a judicial transaction. As a trial, this episode was formally cast with Clarence Darrow as the apologetic spokesman of the American Civil Liberties Union, defending John Thomas Scopes against the accusation that he had violated the state's anti-evolution act. However, in order to best understand the meaning of this trial, the critic might regard its judicial aspects as superficial. On the surface, it might seem that since Clarence Darrow came into the trial as the counsel for the accused Scopes, his would be an apologetic rhetoric. The defense team did in fact endeavor to defend Scopes, but they did so mostly by making accusations concerning the propriety of monkey laws. Darrow's defense was largely an attack against the statute, the "foolish, mischievous, and wicked act" Scopes had violated, and the climate of opinion harkening "back into the sixteenth century" that had brought it into existence. Darrow and Malone chose to say little directly in defense of Scopes, perhaps because formally he had violated the law; rather they turned against his accusers, publicly belittling the brand of fundamental Christianity, the "narrow, ignorant, bigoted shrew of religion" that William Jennings Bryan represented. But while saying much that was accusatory, Darrow and his flock claimed that theirs was an apologetic role. By declaring the statute "as brazen and as bold an attempt to destroy learning as was ever made in the Middle Ages," an indignity different only from its medieval precursors in that the state had not provided "that they shall be burned at the stake," Darrow suggested that his and his defendant's roles were analogous to those of the suffering martyr or righteous heretic before the inquisition.

The same depiction of the trial was offered by the other defense attorneys, as well as by Darrow's sarcastic friend H. L. Mencken, who covered most of the trial as a reporter. With their lacerating cynicism, Mencken's writings about the trial offered a most brutal attack against the character of the "yokels" and "yaps" who supported Bryan's prosecution. But in rendering judgment on the affair as a whole, Mencken seemed to view his friends' efforts as a defensive response to what he called an "inquisition." Similarly, Arthur Garfield Hays, one of the team of lawyers who worked on the Scopes defense, would later in his biographical account of these judicial deliberations allude to such persecutions as the burning of Giordano Bruno and Galileo's indictment before the inquisition as forerunners of the Scopes trial.

The above disclosures were all public utterances reflecting the perceived role Darrow and his assistants wished the observing public to give them. Darrow's private letters, however, reveal his real accusatory intentions. In a letter to H. L. Mencken, who missed the last day of the trial and the cross-examination of Mr. Bryan, Darrow proclaimed "I made up my mind to show the country what an ignoramus he [Bryan] was and I succeeded." Although there is ample evidence that Darrow came into the trial on the attack, he endeavored at every public juncture to make it appear that the scientific community, represented by educators such as John Scopes, was in a defensive posture, a victim of the most heinous brand of authoritarian bigotry.

BRYAN VS. DARROW

The accusatory intentions that Bryan brought with him to the Scopes trial can be seen in his perception of events on the eve of his being offered the job of chief prosecutor in the case: "We cannot afford to have a system of education that destroys the religious faith of our children. . . . There are about 5,000 scientists, and probably half of them are atheists, in the United States. Are we going to let them run our schools? We are not." Much like the arguments contemporary fundamentalists raise against secular humanists, Bryan's charge was that a minority of modernist scientists were foisting atheism upon an unwilling majority.

Although a fundamentalist in every sense, Bryan had only recently become outspoken against Darwinism. The main reason for this change in attitude seems to have been a growing conviction, resulting from his many campus speaking engagements, that Darwinism was directly tied to a loss of faith among college students. Bryan's growing convictions about the sinister influence of Darwinism were bolstered by his reading of literature proclaiming not only that Darwinism was untenable, but that it was also at the root of numerous modern plagues: it had made possible the Nietzschean rule of force that led to militant German nationalism, and it now threatened to erode the bases of American morality as well. When the Scopes case was announced, Bryan threw himself at it. He was, after all, the very personification of that brand of rural piety the people of Tennessee were trying to protect. In this regard, Bryan did not come to the trial chiefly as an accuser. Although he came to decry Darwinism, Bryan clearly regarded this activity as requisite to his defense of the faith. Bryan came to accuse evolutionary science of impiety, but only, so he thought, in order that these accusations would vindicate the Christian religion. For the constituent religious population that Bryan represented, the evolutionists were the accusers. It was they who were making a fraud out of the Christian faith. Just as much as Darrow and his colleagues, the prosecutors in this case regarded themselves as victims of a powerful accusatory tribunal.

The prosecution came to Dayton to accuse the scientific community and modernists in general of what Bryan conceived of as a great democratic impiety—that of imposing the will of a small minority upon the majority of Christians. Bryan had been attacking evolutionists in his speeches for several years. Like these speeches, most of what Bryan said during the course of the trial was, on the face of it, accusatory. At the same time, Bryan portrayed his role in the trial as apologetic. Seemingly assured of his own historic importance, Bryan proclaimed in 1923 that in his campaigns against those who teach evolution he was "trying to save the Christian Church from those who are trying to destroy her faith!" Seeming to attribute unwarranted grandeur to his role, Bryan, on the eve of the trial, cast himself as savior of the church: "The contest between evolution and Christianity is a duel to the death. If evolution wins in Dayton, Christianity goes—not suddenly, of course, but gradually—for the two cannot stand together."

Yet despite Bryan's claims that he was saving the church from the onslaughts of evolutionism, to a large degree his defenses amounted to a series of charges accusing evolutionists of all sorts of misrepresentation and impiety. Bryan's only lengthy speech of the trial began on an apologetic note by responding to the charges of bigotry and ignorance that had been previously raised by the defense. But after these issues were settled, Bryan turned against evolutionary scientists, charging that "they would undermine the faith of these little children in that God who stands back of everything and whose promise we have that we shall live with Him forever by and by. They shut God out of the world." And then in the best remembered portion of Bryan's argument, he attempted to appropriate the reasoning used by Darrow himself in his defense of Loeb and Leopold in 1924. Bryan charged that evolution was the "doctrine that gives us Nietzsche, the only great authority who tried to carry this [evolution] to its logical conclusion." In his defense of Loeb and Leopold, Darrow had claimed that the great German's influence had inspired Leopold to commit murder. Bryan extended the rudiments of this borrowed argument by charging that the introduction of evolutionary theory in American education would lead to a brand of destructive nihilism such as was inspired by Nietzsche.

It is quite clear that what to the defense was accusatory rhetoric was regarded by Bryan as defensive. Similarly, those utterances of the prosecution that Bryan took to be an accusatory affront to the Christian religion were to Darrow and his colleagues merely apologetics for evolution and freedom of education. Ultimately, at the close of the trial, Darrow would seem the accuser and Bryan the apologist. This was due in part to Darrow's frustrations with other means of making his point and to Bryan's remarkable willingness to act as Darrow's victim in cross-examination. As a whole, the Scopes trial may be fairly regarded as an ongoing transactive barrage of accusations and apologies emanating mutually from both sides. This is especially clear in a number of statements uttered by each in those climactic moments of the trial during which Darrow had Bryan on the witness stand. Here each of these rivals struggled to make himself appear the apologist:

> BRYAN: The purpose is to cast ridicule on everybody who believes in the Bible, and I am perfectly willing that the world shall know that these gentlemen have no other purpose than ridiculing every Christian who believes in the Bible.
>
> DARROW: We have the purpose of preventing

bigots and ignoramuses from controlling the education of the United States and you know it, that is all.

BRYAN: Your Honor, I think I can shorten this testimony. The only purpose Mr. Darrow has is to slur at the Bible, but I will answer his question. I will answer it all at once, and I have no objection in the world, I want the world to know that this man, who does not believe in a God, is trying to use a court in Tennessee—

DARROW: I object to that.

BRYAN: [continuing] to slur at it, and while it will require time, I am willing to take it.

DARROW: I object to your statement. I am examining you on your fool ideas that no intelligent Christian on earth believes.

Viewed as a speech set, this rhetorical head-butting that went on before Judge J. T. Raulston of the Eighteenth Judicial Criminal Court of Tennessee can be viewed as a struggle between two parties both striving to establish alternate understandings of their rhetorical roles. The defense, under Darrow's leadership, tried to depict Scopes and the scientific community he represented at the trial as victims of religious backwardness and bigotry. Similarly, although the prosecution was formally committed to strive for Scope's conviction, it tried to depict itself in the role of defender of a persecuted religious faith. The offensive portions of each side's rhetoric during the trial were devoted to bolstering a depiction of the other as aggressor and archfiend.

CONCLUSION

In considering the possible interpretations of a sequence of utterances, the critic can explicate how the participants made sense of the interchange by defining in the texts those evidences of the participants' understandings of the accusatory and apologetic roles. But because these role designations are subject to the relativity of individual perceptions, the critic must also strive to understand the rhetorical meanings of these deliberate orderings.

At Dayton, Darrow regarded himself as a liberal fighting against political aggressors he believed were using fundamentalist religion as a cover for bigotry and backwardness. In court, Darrow assuredly acted the accuser, trying at every turn to ridicule Bryan's antediluvian beliefs, but his own depictions of the ongoing dialogue showed the extent to which he wished to be regarded as apologist. Bryan similarly tried to heap scorn upon evolution as a vain hypothesis perpetrated against the faith of our fathers. At the same time, he, like Darrow, cast himself in the trial as an apologist, as a noble prophet and defender of the faith. Both sides in this controversy seemed bent not so much on winning in court, but on shaping the perceived sequencing of the speech set so that its own side would appear the victim of the other's aggression.

The critic might predict that in the midst of public controversy, the speaker who appears the apologist has a notable rhetorical advantage over the one who appears to be the accuser. Accusation will likely be perceived as an act of aggression, a willful act suggestive of maleficence. Indeed, such a predisposition is built into our judicial system where the accuser is burdened with the obligation of proof. A preference for the apologetic role is also reflected in our Judeo-Christian religions that caution their disciples to avoid accusation at all costs but encourage them always to be prepared to defend the faith. In the same sacred texts, "accuser" is one of the names for Satan. In our culture, accusation can be a dirty business. The apologist, on the other hand, might be viewed in a more favorable light. Self-defense in our culture can be a justification for homicide; it may be an act of aggression, but it is one performed reluctantly for the sake of righteousness. The apologist has the rhetorical advantage, initially at least, of being perceived as an innocent, as the passive target of the other's rage.

These cultural preferences were reflected in the Scopes trial where both sides engaged in accusation while claiming that they were apologists. Clearly, two alternate orderings of the rhetorical sequence are here at work, two ways in which the combative dialogue of this trial can be perceived. Such a view of this event reveals a secondary level, not of content, but of relational meaning that was subtly but competitively negotiated in rhetorical combat.

David B. Jezioro (essay date 1991)

SOURCE: "H. L. Mencken and Clarence Darrow: A Divine Alliance," in *Menckeniana,* No. 118, Summer, 1991, pp. 1-7.

[*In the following essay, Jezioro discusses the connection of Darrow and H. L. Mencken during the Scopes trial.*]

During the sensational 1925 Scopes "Monkey Trial," H. L. Mencken and Clarence Darrow formed an alliance—unknown to them—that may have been made in heaven. If a white-bearded-old-man God was out there directing events, then the Scopes trial surely was his handiwork. Not that God would have wanted any side to win—he's beyond simple popularity—but rather, to make a point, and to observe the spectacle cheerful in the knowledge the human race is always good for a laugh.

It is the comedy of human nature that people assume deathly serious positions on any side of a given issue, polarized—only—by the rhetoric describing it. In 1925 in Dayton, Tennessee, the issue concerned the correct view of where we came from. Genesis poetically described the origin of "Man." Darwin dryly observed the origin of the "species." As usual, metaphor gave way to precision as both languages struggled to explain the same miracle of creation. God understood this. People chose up sides.

The relevancy of Scopes' trial exists to this day. Pick a hotly contested topic. Creationist philosophy? Abortion? School prayer? Crime? The American family? They all contain connotations of God—lack of God—and even lately, how "Her" will be done. Any hint of a wrongly used semantic term can derail a presidential election, launch independent prosecutors scurrying, bankrupt congressional committees, tie up courts, and set dog upon cat. Women rush to elbow their way toward immaculate conceptions as men retreat to play survivalist games in Montana with suspiciously serious grins on their faces. In all of it there is a touch of some cosmic practical-joker flicking us into action with each bump of a simple truth.

But reality doesn't exist in cosmic form. The Scopes trial was a rousing courtroom drama that later inspired the 1955 Lawrence and Lee award winning Broadway play, and 1960 Stanley Kramer motion picture, *Inherit the Wind.* The title was drawn from the passage in Proverbs and colors the actual event in a spiritual cloud. The trial's principal characters were evocatively captured with Mencken ("Hornbeck") and Darrow ("Drummond") allied by a common cause in the trial. Vastly different in personality, they end their association in a final climactic scene with "Drummond" pitying "Hornbeck" in his self-imposed aloneness, without anybody being there "when they pull the grass up over your head." "Hornbeck," true to Mencken's style, wryly replies: "You're wrong, Henry, you'll be there . . . you're the type. Who else would defend my right to be lonely?"

Some Mencken critics would agree with this view of the "Sage," and Darrow enthusiasts would readily recognize their hero's incorruptible passion for defense. But it lies in the spirit of the stage, and the actual event, that a continuum between art and life synthesizes through cosmic strings suggesting a universal meaning to be explained.

God chose Mencken and Darrow for the Dayton job for the same reason one shouts "fire" when smelling smoke. God had enough friends to carry his messages. He needed some outside opinions to make his point. Darrow doubted God, and Mencken dismissed him outright. They rode the biblical wind into Dayton knowing enough not to fight with phantoms. They didn't come to fight God, just people's ideas of God. Alone, they weren't enough. Together, they made a formidable twosome as one, and with their particular talents for logic and the syntax of language, they could shatter the wall of complacent intellects that freely assumed a literal interpretation of Genesis—as Law! They could form a composite personality of the supreme "infidel" by buoying their separate weaknesses with their separate strengths. In Mencken and Darrow, God chose his angel perfectly. The thunder of this proto-heretic would carry on the wind through Dayton—and now the bump.

Tennessee farmer John Butler was suddenly touched by a divine civic spirit to save the children of Tennessee from the bestial teachings of Darwin. Moved so, he got himself elected to the State assembly from his district, immediately drew up a bill and placed it in the rotation, and then disappeared forever from view. God then nudged the House toward action by telling them the Senate would kill the bill—so the House passed it! He told the Senate the Governor would veto it—so the Senate ratified it! God whispered to the Governor that the People wanted it—so the Governor signed it. And that's how the great Tennessee anti-evolution law came to be. Having supplied the bump, God sat back to enjoy as the wind gathered into a squall.

In Robinson's drugstore in downtown Dayton George Rappelyea, a local mining engineer, reacted to the news of the law with: "You can't teach biology without teaching Darwin!" John T. Scopes, twenty-four-year-old substitute biology teacher, agreed: "Impossible!" And F. E. Robinson, store owner and chairman of the local school board—also in agreement—telephoned the Chattanooga *News* declaring: "We've just arrested a man for teaching evolution!" The drugstore rebels, with Scopes agreeing to be a test case, wired the American Civil Liberties Union (ACLU) requesting assistance. The ACLU, having already publicly announced their intent to fight the law, immediately replied assuring "financial aid, legal advice, and publicity."

William Jennings Bryan, former secretary of state and three-time presidential candidate, had been predicting that more states would follow Tennessee's lead. As a leading evangelist of the Christian Fundamentalists who supported the law, and affectionately and derisively known as the "Great Commoner," Bryan volunteered to prosecute the case for the State and was accepted. His presence at the trial elevated the matter into a celebrity event.

Clarence Darrow blamed Bryan for the Tennessee law, and as a relentless defender of free thought, wired Scopes' attorney offering to assist in "your defense of Professor Scopes." Darrow was once a close friend of Bryan's and even campaigned for the man, but now loathed Bryan's cartoon caricature of his former greatness in this religious crusader image. Concerned over the turn of events, Scopes, Rappelyea, and attorney John Neal travelled to New York City to meet with the executive committee of the ACLU.

According to Roger Baldwin, then ACLU director, the committee was divided on whether the defense question should be that of First Amendment rights or separation of Church and State. Further controversy surrounded the hiring of Darrow, as some saw him as too opportunistic and radical. In the end it was Scopes who decided in favor of Darrow by stating the circus had already come to Dayton with the entry of Bryan. Said Scopes, the town was filled with "screwballs, con men, and characters." "If it's going to be a gutter fight, I'd rather have a good gutter-fighter."

Darrow's gutter-fighter credentials were formidable and deceptive. He was the best known and most controversial lawyer of his day. Over six feet tall, he was a hulking figure with stooped shoulders and a craggy face topped with greying hair, that had become a virtual trademark of the man's reputation. Full of vitality and curiosity—his nature was basically hedonistic—he commanded the company of good friends and good times. He exuded freedom, ability, and compassion, but in reality could be cynical, moody, and melancholic. His was a pity for all humankind, but drew a line between sentimentality and pragmatism. He appealed to logic and reason with a talent for persuasion, and disarmed judges and juries alike with his devilishly rational defense arguments while attacking prosecutors' "thirst for blood."

It was Darrow's deepest passion to defend those whose civil rights were in peril, paradoxically preaching a gospel of Christian mercy while eschewing any religious beliefs. His religion was the sanctity of life and saw that "the earth is the home, and the only home, of man, and I am convinced that whatever he is to get out of existence he must get while he is here." Darrow's defense of Scopes, as well as his antipathy toward Bryan, elevated the trial's status one more step into the gutter fight that Scopes had envisioned.

But Darrow was bound by the constraints of the courtroom—Mencken was not. Like Darrow, Mencken held some strong opinions on religion, only his were more succinct, precise, somewhat outspoken. Said he: "Religion is fundamentally opposed to everything I hold in veneration—courage, clear thinking, honesty, fairness . . . . In brief, it is a fraud."

Mencken's greatest fame was as an essayist and social critic, and an outspoken skeptic in all matters of society and religion. His well manicured fire-plug appearance may have belied his stature as one of America's premium men of letters, but satisfied the image of his chosen profession, "journalism pure and simple—dead almost before the ink which printed it is dry."

Born in 1880, by the time he was twenty-five years of age Mencken had become managing editor of the Baltimore *Evening Sun.* In 1924 he co-founded the *American Mercury,* and had hit his stride. The 1920s saw a dawning of a new age. Changing values and a changing society saw people turning to his columns to read, to laugh, and to cuss. If Darrow were a bleeding heart, Mencken was a bull-dog snapping and chomping on the carrion of hypocrisy:

> It is still socially dangerous for an American man
> to have a reputation as virtuous. Theoretically he
> who preserves his chemical purity in the face of
> all temptations is a noble and upright fellow and
> a delight of the heavenly hierarchy; actually, he is
> laughed at by women and viewed with contempt
> by men.

Mencken loathed American democracy's solution to any problem by taking a vote on it. He viewed theology as "moonshine, wind-music, and bunk," and negated the Christian principle of Absolute Truth with "there is no truth to be discovered; there is only error to be exposed." He described the puritan Fundamentalists as "Methodists," and saw their purification of the "hapless Scopes" as part of their "haunting fear that someone, somewhere, may be happy."

For Mencken the trial in Dayton was the culmination of a war he had begun in 1917 against the backward thinking "boobs" he described in his "Sahara of the Bozart" that appeared that year in the New York *Evening Mail.* Darrow already knew the quarry in Dayton, and certainly agreed with Mencken's blunt counsel: "Nobody gives a damn about that yap schoolteacher; the thing to do is make a fool out of Bryan."

. . . . .

3000 AT APE TRIAL GET THRILL

—Louisville (KY) *Courier-Journal:*
July 21, 1925

Not since the destruction of the Jerusalem Temple had God sat agape at the antics of human frenzy. Quiet little Dayton became a combination carnival, revival-meeting, and world event. Hot dog and lemonade stands crowded with vendors, IWWs, Fundamentalists, anarchists, freethinkers, and over 100 newspaper reporters, each intent on leaving his mark on history. Banners greeted visitors with: "Read Your Bible," "Where Will You Spend Eternity," and "Your OLD Man's A Monkey." Demonstrations littered every avenue with themes on "The Resurrection," "The Damnation," and the "saving of girls in sin."

Bryan arrived several days before the trial and was feted by the Progressive Club with a dinner. Warming for battle, he weighed in against the evolutionists: "The contest between evolution and Christianity is a duel to the death . . ." Darrow's arrival two days later was similarly treated—for impartiality—but even his folksiest manner couldn't break the icy chill of suspicion and reserve. Mencken arrived by car from Chattanooga, to get a feel for the countryside, and happened upon Bryan speaking before a crowd of admirers. He introduced himself by commenting on an article he wrote for the *Nation* that upheld the constitutionality of the anti-evolution law. Bryan, his great red bald head covered by a pith-helmet, squealed joyfully to his listeners, "This Mencken is the best newspaper man in the country." Mencken, surprised at Bryan's good natured salute, returned the compliment by offering his admiration for Bryan's pongee shirt, "cut sleeveless and low at the neck."

Mencken's delight with Dayton prompted him to write his friend, Dr. Raymond Pearl: " . . . the thing is genuinely fabulous. I have stored up enough material to last me twenty years." But the arrival in town of local mountain farmers, known for their brand of swift justice, cast a pall over an already growing concern by the townfolk. On this Mencken wired Baltimore:

On the eve of the great contest Dayton is full of sickening surges. Five or six weeks ago when the infidel Scopes was first laid by the heels, there was no uncertainty in all this smiling valley . . . Here was an opportunity to get Dayton . . . on the map . . . . Today, with the worst buffooneries to come, it is obvious to even town boomers that getting on the map, like patriotism, isn't enough . . . is prayer made any more efficacious by giving a circus first? Coming to this thought, Dayton begins to sweat.

This pleased God. Mencken was warming to his divine mission—a moment in time to do God's bidding. Mencken's directness was precisely the heavenly tool necessary to complement Darrow's smooth but devilishly passionate rationale. It required Mencken's unsubtle postmark in the chronicle of time, and the moment came on the second day of the trial.

The trial opened on Friday, July 10, 1925 with a prayer. The honorable Judge John T. Raulston ("jest a reg'lar mountin'er jedge") heard some opening motions before adjourning the court for the weekend. On Monday a cool morning breeze gave way to stifling afternoon heat, leaving Darrow, Bryan, and the other attorneys in shirtsleeves. The jury had been dismissed while arguments were heard regarding the wording of the indictment. Darrow cited cases to build his argument that the State's constitution was committed to a doctrine of education—his words were sarcastic—a condition made difficult by the wording. He said that he found it hard to turn his mind back to the sixteenth-century, and entered into an emotionally building cautionary argument, "If today . . ." But he was cut short by Judge Raulston's call for adjournment. "I will not take long, Your Honor," Darrow said as he continued while Judge Raulston sat uneasy,

> I will tell you that if you can take a thing like evolution and make it a crime to teach it in the public school, tomorrow you can make it a crime to teach it in the private schools, and the next year you can make it a crime to teach it to the hustings or in the church. At the next session you may ban books and newspapers. Soon you may set Catholic against Protestant and Protestant against Protestant, and try to foist your own religion on the minds of men. If you can do one you can do the other. Ignorance and fanaticism is ever busy and needs feeding.

That evening Mencken took his turn completing the heavenly circuit, and wired the Baltimore *Evening Sun*:

> The net effect of Clarence Darrow's great speech yesterday seems to be precisely the same as if he had bawled it up a rainspout in the interior of Afghanistan . . . you have but a dim notion of it who have only read it. It was not designed for reading, but for hearing. The clangtint of it was as important as the logic. It rose like a wind and ended like a flourish of bugles. The very judge

on the bench, toward the end of it, began to look uneasy. But the morons in the audience, when it was over, simply hissed it.

The moment! The entirety of the trial's meaning neatly capsulated and frozen in time. The whole purpose presented directly and articulately by Darrow's "speech" and Mencken's crushing conclusion on it. The dangerous folly of relentless unexamined belief. Don't listen—hiss. Darrow is the bad guy—boo the bad guy. Don't hear the danger. He's one of "them;" not one of "us."

And Mencken didn't have to explain it—only describe it in its pure and simple form. The deadly enemy—us. It wasn't necessary for anyone to understand it, just so it was on the table—so to speak—the self-motivated unconscious calamity of humankind's windy old troubled house. Our pride!

The moment passed without notice. Mencken and Darrow were released from their heavenly grip to pursue the remainder of their inglorious goals. God had made his point and, as usual, left it hanging in the air to be sensed like a flower's faint aroma on a summer breeze. The ongoing miracle of Creation is not steady and progressive but accentuated by fits and spurts—like some Darwinian natural selection. A moment here—a signifying phrase there, " . . . blessed are the peacemakers!" The rest is but a swirling eddy around such moments from which mortal understanding slowly evolves. Dayton was for now the product of history to be drawn upon in enlightened hindsight.

By the sixth day of the trial the defense saw its expert witnesses—prominent scientists and biblical scholars—denied their testimony that a literal interpretation of the Bible was not sound reasoning. Frustrated by an apparent bias by the Court Darrow exploded, arguing the prosecutor's favored status and "a bare suggestion of anything that is perfectly competent on our part should be immediately overruled!" Stung by this criticism, Judge Raulston coolly replied, "I hope you do not mean to reflect upon the court?" Darrow angrily fired back, "Well, Your Honor has the right to hope!"

Court: "I have the right to do something else perhaps!"

Darrow: "All right, all right."

Surprising to everyone in the courtroom, Judge Raulston adjourned for the weekend without citing Darrow for contempt. But this was the final nail. Mencken and many of the other reporters saw the trial as being virtually over, and Mencken filed this last dispatch from Dayton before leaving forever: "All that remains of the Great State of Tennessee against the infidel Scopes is the business of bumping off the defendant." But Mencken was wrong.

On Monday a series of headlines flashed out of Dayton with lightning speed. Darrow was held in contempt and fined $5,000.00. He apologized and the court accepted it as a demonstration of Christian charity. Darrow then stunned the court by calling Bryan as a defense witness as an expert on the Bible. The courtroom exploded as Darrow's trap was set and sprung and as Bryan overruled his assistants and took the stand.

The examination of Bryan by Darrow has become one of the most unique and dramatic scenes ever enacted in a courtroom. Even God returned his gaze to Dayton to watch this one. A debate on the literal interpretation of the Bible—as a matter of law.

For over two hours Darrow and Bryan feigned and parried with the semantics and rhetoric found in Genesis. From Jonah's digestion by the "whale" to Eve's pre-natal development in Adam's rib-canal, Bryan maintained a relentless belief in the Bible's literalness. The examination was dotted by pronounced laughter from the courtroom throughout Bryan's absurd disclosures on the stand. Seeing his serious views being mocked, Bryan finally turned to the court in exasperation: "Your Honor, I think I can shorten this testimony. The only purpose Mr. Darrow has is to slur the Bible . . . I want the world to know that this man, who does not believe in God, is trying to use the court in Tennessee . . ." "I object to that," Darrow demanded! But Bryan's fervor carried him on to finish, " . . . to slur at it, and while it would require time, I am willing to take it."

"I object to your statement," Darrow said. "I am examining you on your fool ideas that no intelligent Christian on earth believes." At this Darrow and Bryan stood locked in a deadly gaze at the other as Judge Raulston adjourned the court until nine o'clock the next morning.

The next day Darrow—again—surprised the court by requesting the jury be instructed to return a verdict of guilty. Since the evidence the defense had to offer was considered inadmissible, it left no choice but to carry the matter to a higher court. The jury had been sequestered during the great Darrow and Bryan debate, and missed the public high point of the trial. Duly instructed, they found Scopes "guilty," and he was subsequently fined $100.00. For the first time in his trial Scopes spoke: "Your Honor, I feel that I have been convicted of an unjust statute. I will continue in the future, as I have in the past, to oppose this law in any way that I can . . . I think the fine is unjust."

Unjust indeed! It was a slap in the face of every pounding heart that was caught up in the hysteria. An ironic conclusion that was capped with a bellowing cosmic laugh. The final insult from on high came the following year when Scopes' conviction was overturned by the Tennessee Court of Appeals on a technicality, unrelated to the titanic issues that were confronted in Dayton—the judge had fixed the fine instead of the jury.

Four days after the trial, Bryan and his wife had dinner with the Raulstons. Following dinner Bryan retired to take a nap and never woke up. Immediate conjecture had it that Darrow's relentless courtroom examination, aggravated by the audience's laughter, had caused the old populist warrior's death. Darrow publicly declared: "I am pained to hear of the death of William Jennings Bryan . . . I differed with him on many questions, but always respected his sincerity and devotion." Privately, Darrow told friends, "Now wasn't that man a god-damned fool." Alluding to Bryan's downfall, Darrow bluntly chided: "Broken heart nothing. He died of a busted belly."

Mencken's tribute was: "Has it been marked by historians that the late William Jennings Bryan's last secular act on this earth was to catch flies . . ." A questionable eulogy, surely, but Mencken would finally conclude on the Scopes trial in 1926, in his "Prejudices: Fifth Series," where he described Bryan as: " . . . thirsting savagely for blood. All sense departed from him. He bit right and left, like a dog with rabies . . . . He came into life a hero, a Galahad, in bright and shining armor. He was passing out a poor mountebank."

Inherit the Wind portrayed Scopes as a helpless victim. In life Scopes was a perpetrator and active player in the Dayton event. Bryan's characterization was that of a pompous buffoon, doomed in his search for God, "too high up and too far away." But it was Bryan's "Brady" who first invokes the Biblical warning captured in the play's title—a cautionary for all of us who seek truth as a literal fact of life rather than as a spiritual method in the quest for human meaning. Such meaning can only be gathered in by the living of life, or, like Bryan, we shall find in our troubled houses the windy inheritance.

The wind that blew through Dayton is still blowing. Then it was Bryan and Darrow and Mencken and Scopes. Who has taken their place today? Who wants to assume their watch of lonely vigils and uncertain outcomes? Bryan was sacrificed on the altar of his own static beliefs. Scopes never taught biology again in Tennessee. Mencken and Darrow proclaimed victory and went on to greater glories.

Darrow wrote Mencken that he was sorry his comrade had missed "my examination of Bryan." "I made up my mind to show the world what an ignoramus he was and I succeeded." Mencken, too, was sorry he missed Bryan placing in the Court record the fact that "man was not a mammal."

Despite their lifelong affront to religion, and their larger-than-life stature, Mencken and Darrow remained none-the-less simple mortal men. At the age of seventy-five Darrow admitted that he was "still fighting to stay on earth." Aside from his public self, Darrow's truly personal thoughts are lost to history. One can only surmise at what it was he stared at from his Chicago Hyde Park apartment window in his waning years.

Mencken's religions opinions remained permanent to the end. But, also, what of his inner feelings? Biographer Carl Bode (*Mencken*, 1969) offers a slight insight from a Mencken friend, Marcella DuPont: " . . . he had deeply wanted to believe but had been unable to . . . once, that when he shared a room with Frank Kent, Kent had always knelt to say his prayers before going to bed. Then Mencken watched sardonically but later wished that as a child he had been taught to pray that way."

Mencken, Darrow—religious? Certainly not in the orthodox sense we think of religion. But, surely, within them breathe a divine spirit inherent in all of us. It's in Genesis! That so much energy and effort was used by them in maintaining their autonomy, alone, stands as a testimony to religion's power and reality. Their spirits were defined with mortal constructs explained with mortal words. Semantics! Their alliance in Dayton seemed touched by something more permanent than mere human intellect—almost a soulful connection.

This connection carried through their lives and swept them through the trial's maelstrom, soaring them into the popular culture of a nation—like a great and timeless wind. You can still hear their interplay on the waning breezes if you're quiet enough: "You're wrong, Henry, you'll be there . . . . You're the type. Who else would defend my right to be lonely . . ."

Exit stage right smiling—God is.

FURTHER READING

Bibliography

Hunsberger, Willard D. *Clarence Darrow: A Bibliography*. Metchuen, N.J.:   , 1981, 215 p.
   A comprehensive primary and secondary bibliography.

Criticism

Kunstler, William M. "Clarence Seward Darrow." In *The Case for Courage*, pp. 201-36. New York: William Morrow and Company, 1962.
   Proposes that Darrow's preference for controversial, potentially unpopular cases made him a hero.

McMahon, Mary Sheila. "King Tut and the Scopes Trial." In *Transforming Faith: The Sacred and Secular in Modern American History*, edited by M. L. Bradbury and James B. Gilbert, pp. 87-104. New York: Greenwood Press, 1989.
   Juxtaposes the discovery of King Tutankhamen's tomb and the Scopes trial as examples of contemporary culture in 1925.

Wolfe, Don M. "On the Ways of Man: Darrow, Steffens and Broun." In *The Image of Man in America*, pp. 264-86. Dallas: Southern Methodist University Press, 1957.
   Compares journalists Heywood Broun, Lincoln Steffens and Darrow and their differing perceptions of human nature.

The following source published by Gale contains additional coverage of Darrow's life and career: *Contemporary Authors*, Vol. 164.

Surendranath Dasgupta

1887-1952

Indian philosopher and historian.

INTRODUCTION

In such works as his five-volume *History of Indian Philosophy* (1922-55), Dasgupta attempted a comprehensive study of the philosophies and belief systems that have animated the Indian subcontinent for millennia. Though far from pedestrian in his approach, Dasgupta presented his topic in a such a manner that an educated westerner could comprehend the outlines of Hinduism, Buddhism, and their many attendant schools of thought. Long after his death, Dasgupta's influence continued in the West through his disciple Mircea Eliade (1907-1986), who in the 1960s helped to popularize his ideas within a climate of growing interest in Yoga and eastern mysticism. In addition to his work as a philosopher and historian, Dasgupta was a scholar of the ancient Sanskrit language, and his consultation of original texts—many of them thousands of years old—gave his writing particular authority.

Biographical Information

Dasgupta was born in Calcutta in 1887, at the height of British rule over India. He attended Calcutta University, and later obtained his doctorate from Cambridge University in England with a dissertation entitled *A Study of Pantanjali*, which examined the writings of a Yogic philosopher. Returning to India, he served for a decade (1911-20) as professor of Sanskrit at Chittagong College, in modern-day Bangladesh. During a two-year period as guest lecturer at Cambridge, he brought out *A History of Indian Philosophy*, Volume 1, in 1922. The next volume was published a decade later, its writing delayed by health problems which persisted for much of Dasgupta's life. By 1932, the year he published Volume 2 of the *History*, he had written two other influential works, *Yoga as Philosophy and Religion* (1924) and *Hindu Mysticism* (1927). From the early 1920s until the end of World War II, Dasgupta taught at various universities in Calcutta. His posts included a professorship in European philosophy at Indian Education Service Presidency College from 1924 to 1931, interrupted by a stint as Harris Foundation Lecturer at the University of Chicago in 1926; and a term as principal of Sanskrit College from 1933 to 1942. During this time, he published *Yoga Philosophy in Relation to Other Systems of Indian Thought* (1930), *Indian Idealism* (1933), Volume 4 of his *History*, and a number of other works. In 1945 he took a position as professor of philosophy at Benares University, where he would continue for the remaining years of his life. The last significant work of Dasgupta's career came in 1947, with the publication of *A History of Sanskrit Literature, Classical Period*, which he edited with S. K. De. At the time of his death in 1952, he was working on a fifth volume of the *History of Indian Philosophy*, which his wife, Surama, completed and edited. It was published in 1955 as *Southern Schools of Saivism*.

Major Works

Presented in four volumes during his lifetime, with a fifth completed by his wife after his death, *A History of Indian Philosophy* is the most significant and enduring of Dasgupta's works. Original both in its scope and in its use of Sanskrit texts as primary resource material, Dasgupta's *History* is a vast work befitting the gargantuan scale of its subject, not to mention the degree of unfamiliarity with which the typical western reader approaches that topic. Volume 1 inaugurates a three-volume discussion of Vedanta, a system to which Dasgupta appeared to show partiality. Developed by Sankara (A.D. 788-820), Vedanta or Advanta Vedanta is a monistic system which teaches that the apparent separation between the self and other selves, and the self and the divine, is an illusion. Dasgupta, in the views of some critics, tended to interpret unrelated belief systems—particularly Buddhism—through the prism of Vedanta. In fact the concentration of these volumes is primarily Hindu, with Buddhism, Jainism, and other religions accorded secondary significance. Hence Volume 2, in addition to its development of Vedanta principles, discusses ancient Hindu medicine and the *Bhagavad Gita*, which is perhaps the central text of the Hindu faith. In Volume 3, Dasgupta expounds on various dualistic and pluralistic (as opposed to monistic) philosophies, along with aspects of legal and ethical systems. Dasgupta was writing Volume 5 at the time of his death; hence the book, which his wife completed and published in 1955, is much shorter than the others. Subtitled *Southern Schools of Saivism*, it deals specifically with a belief system which flourished on India's Malabar Coast, and which may have been influenced by early Christianity. In a number of other works, Dasgupta dealt with specialized topics in Indian philosophy and religious belief. His *Hindu Mysticism* explores six varieties of mystical practice, including Yoga, a topic which he developed more fully in two other books. *Yoga as Philosophy and Religion* provides an introduction to that form of meditation and mysticism, which would become a familiar concept to westerners after the 1960s but which at the time of the book's publication in 1924 was still an extremely exotic idea to western readers. Dasgupta developed his topic further with *Yoga Philosophy in Relation to Other Systems of Indian Thought*, wherein he presented Yoga not merely as a method of meditation, but as an independent philosophical system. With *Indian Idealism*, he attempted to compress the wide-ranging discussions of *A History of Indian Philosophy* into a single volume less than three hundred pages long. His use of Sanskrit texts made Dasgupta's work particularly significant; and in addition to his work as a philosopher, he made a vital contribution to the history of that language by serving as co-editor of *A History of Sanskrit Literature, Classical Period.*

PRINCIPAL WORKS

A History of Indian Philosophy, 5 vols. (history and philosophy) 1922-55*
Yoga as Philosophy and Religion (philosophy) 1924
Hindu Mysticism (philosophy) 1927
Indian Idealism (philosophy) 1933
Yoga Philosophy in Relation to Other Systems of Indian Thought (philosophy) 1933
A History of Sanskrit Literature, Classical Period [editor, with S. K. De] (history) 1947

*Volume 5 was completed and edited by Surama Dasgupta.

CRITICISM

F. W. Thomas (essay date 1922)

SOURCE: A review of *A History of Indian Philosophy,* in the *Hibbert Journal,* Vol. 20, No. 80, 1922, pp. 796-99.

[*In the following essay, a review of the first volume in* A History of Indian Philosophy, *Thomas examines ways in which Dasgupta offers fresh insights on an ancient subject.*]

The outlines of the chief Indian systems have been for now about a century accessible to European readers in the essays of the great scholar Colebrooke. It may be said that even to-day it is hardly necessary to seek such outlines in any other quarter. For an acquaintance with the Indian manner of discussing philosophical questions we may refer to a delightful group of writings which are now generally neglected. These are works of Christian apologists, contending on more or less equal terms with Indian disputants. These apologists—they belonged to the middle of the nineteenth century—were men of sound philosophic culture, and those among them who were of Indian birth were in several instances thoroughly at home in their native systems and methods. Thus from such books as K. M. Banerjea's *Dialogues on the Hindu Philosophy* (1861), Ballantyne's *Christianity contrasted with Hindu Philosophy* (London, 1859),

FitzEdward Hall's *Rational Refutation of the Hindu Philosophical Systems by N. N. Sastri Gore* (1862), and the anonymous *Dialogue of the Knowledge of the Supreme Lord* (Cambridge, 1886), we obtain a clear insight into the views which their authors were combating, even if, from later advances in European thought, it may sometimes appear that they were dealing with ideas more subtle than their own.

At the present day the interest of European philosophers in Indian ideas cannot be said to be keen. The time of Schopenhauer's enthusiasm for the Upanishads is gone; and the only attempt to incorporate the Indian contribution in a general history of philosophy, that of Deussen, is felt to be infected with a slight suspicion of "Schwärmerei.' Modern philosophers are, in fact, a little impatient of Indian analogies and anticipations. The fault is not entirely on the side of the popularising theosophists, neo-Buddhists, and Vedantists, or of books eloquent in Eastern terminologies and too prone to blur the sharp outlines of European doctrines in their zeal for comparison. The feeling is deeper. Behind the philosophy of modern Europe there are the great advances of modern science, with its refined ideas, its methods of enormous power, and its immense masses of verified fact. The recent developments of mathematical logic, mathematical theories of the infinite, physical and psychological methods—the doctrines which live in this milieu are too unequally matched with systems based upon an embryonic science, an intuitive psychology, and for the most part on too intimate terms with religion. Moreover, the Indian philosophies have hitherto been known in Europe chiefly from translations of relatively easy or secondary texts, in many cases literary or religious. It is not realised that the Indian pandit is, in spite of his limitations, a logician and metaphysician in his bones, that he is fertile and dauntless in speculation, that he wields a language of unrivalled suppleness in discrimination, and has worked out a logical terminology of heroic and almost mathematical consistency.

Another awkward feature of Indian philosophies is that they generally profess to be disciplines also. Their truths are not only to be heard and understood; they are to be realised by meditation. The Vedantin holds that by means of meditation and practice he can reach successively wider intuitions, and the Yogin that by asceticism he can attain the power of seeing the atoms and so forth. This is, in fact, rather a poser for our European thinkers, who would generally admit that various passions and biases are an obstacle to the acquisition of truth, and might in some cases allow that civilisation and science are based upon renunciation in various stages, but would hardly in modern times agree that systematic spiritual discipline would much facilitate the realisation of the highest truths. They would be apprehensive of auto-suggestion; but they would hardly claim to have tried the method.

Professor Dasgupta's work [*A History of Indian Philosophy*] is the first attempt at a comprehensive exposition of the Indian philosophies generally. Max Müller's *Six Systems of Indian Philosophy* was the work of a brilliant scholar at home in Indian literature and in philosophic thinking also. But it would be idle to pretend that he was familiar with any of the more technical works, in the same way as was Colonel Jacob, whose *Handful of Popular Maxims* is a mine of information on practical points of logic and dialectics. Much work has been done of late years in connection with Buddhist logic, metaphysic, and epistemology, and we have accurate translations by Thibaut, Dr Ganganath Jha, and others of important works belonging to other systems. For Indian logic generally we have an excellent essay in German by Professor Jacobi of Bonn, a useful treatise (especially as regards the syllogism) by a Japanese scholar Sugiura (Philadelphia, 1900), and a really systematic exposition in Professor Suali's *Introduzione allo studio della Filosofia Indiana* (Paris, 1913), not to mention more recent books. But Professor Dasgupta's work is of much ampler design than any of these. He is thoroughly at home in all the important and difficult texts, and he has received a training in European philosophy. His intelligence is alert and candid, and he has the historical sense. We can sincerely commend both his method, which is that of exposition, eschewing all comparisons with European ideas, and his style, which is untrammelled, full, direct, and flowing. From this book the English reader can obtain an accurate idea of the questions which have occupied the Indian philosophers and of their manner of dealing with them. The short introductory chapter stating the present position of these studies is really admirable.

Professor Dasgupta's work is based upon primary sources, and in some large matters he develops independent views. In regard to Buddhism he points out that the doctrine of *Sunyata,* or "the void," the entire denial of any measure of substantiality, whether in the object or in the subject, was prior to Nagarjuna, who merely systematised it. The theory of *Tathata* or an absolute experience, which presents such an interesting analogy to Dr Bradley's views, really arose and fell with Asvaghosha; and the *alaya-vijñana,* or "repository cognition" of the Vijñanavadins, which among other functions serves partly the same purpose, is in some texts acknowledged to be merely a concession to the weakness of the public, which was frightened by an unmitigated sensationalism. Of that wonderfully poetic doctrine, the Sankhya, Professor Dasgupta brings to light an early form, elicited from the medical work of Charaka, and showing agreement with an outline known from the Mahabharata. He also lays stress upon a view evidenced in several passages, but surely unorthodox, according to which the three attributes of the Sankhyan primordial substance *prakriti* are substantial, so that the *prakriti* itself becomes a mere state, adjectival. The account of the Nyaya-Vaiseshika philosophy is excellent, and the view that these systems are somehow connected with the Mimamsa, so largely occupied with the principles of theological and legal exegesis, seems to contain an element of truth. For it is reasonable to hold that in India,

as in Greece, logic arose from grammatical and exegetic studies. Of course there are other elements in this philosophy, such as its categories and its atomic doctrines, for which we must find another origin. The system may claim a special interest at the present time by reason of its affinities with mediæval scholasticism and modern realisms. We cannot review Professor Dasgupta's treatment of all the systems. He gives a good outline of Jainism, with its doctrine of limited truths or aspects, the *Syadvada;* and in his account of the Vedanta, where he points out that primarily Sankara is more a theologian than a philosopher, he is original in drawing attention to the logical category of "the indeterminate," which was an important development of the later and more difficult works. This later literature will be the subject-matter of a second volume, which will include also the sectarian philosophies, Vaishnava, Saiva, etc., and which can hardly fail to be of at least equal extent.

Professor Dasgupta's work will not dispense the student who wishes to inspect the different doctrines in their precise bearings from seeking them *in situ* in their systematic expositions. The like may, of course, be said in regard to any compendium of European philosophies. The distinguishing feature here is that so large a proportion of the original texts is at present inaccessible except in Sanskrit. Professor Dasgupta admits that, and explains why, he has not given us a history strictly so called; but we get a historical perspective. If we may hope for some revision in a later edition, it is in regard to some points of scholarship. What is meant by the "touch of untouch," on p. 423, we cannot guess; nor do we follow the translation of the sentence in which it appears. "Arising after getting" (p. 93) is not a good rendering of *pratitya-samutpada* ("arising in relation to something else"). To find in the Pali *asava* any reference to "intoxicants" was possible only so long as the real etymology was unknown; and in giving "bio-motor force" as the equivalent of *prana* (p. 250), or *vayu* (p. 262), which properly denote air-currents supposed to perform physiological functions in the body, Professor Dasgupta is yielding to decidedly tendencious influences.

It has been said that what modern Europe at this date requires from ancient and oriental cultures is not their ideas (which may be supposed to have been anticipated or absorbed), but their intuitions. Even if that were true, justice demands that the ideas should be accorded their rightful historical position: and, apart from that again, it is a matter of human and also scientific interest to know what these matters were and how they arose. Europe and America supply a rather good market for the inferior products of Indian thought: why not for the best? But a mere Indianist may also perhaps venture to inquire whether in this sphere all the ideas have been absorbed. It may turn out that idealism in its Platonic or Hegelian form was never even approached in India; but most other views have been suggested, adumbrated, or worked out by Indian thinkers in their way; and at the present time, when logic and epistemology are so much in the foreground, it may be interesting to inquire what

Indian doctrines there were concerning validity and truth, how far the Indian thinkers grasped the pragmatic idea, what use they made of their *apeksha-buddhi* "awareness of relation," what Kumarila meant by his doctrine that knowledge was not directly known, but inferred from a "knownness" in the object, or how the Vedanta deals with that last inquiry addressed to any philosophy, professing to be not only beautiful, but true, namely, how far the system is consistent with the fact of its exposition or discussion.

E. J. Thomas (essay date 1924)

SOURCE: A review of *A History of Indian Philosophy,* in *International Journal of Ethics,* Vol. 34, No. 4, July, 1924, pp. 403-05.

[*In the following essay, Thomas presents* A History of Indian Philosophy *as the first book of its kind.*]

The study of the history of Indian culture in Europe has been a continuous struggle for more light. Again and again conclusions have been reached that have had to be abandoned. But Indian philosophy was fortunate in having as its first expounder H. T. Colebrooke, one of the earliest but at the same time one of the ablest of the Indianists. His work, however, was confined to the six orthodox systems, and to these only in their classical form. It is only gradually that the means have been made accessible to the West for studying the continuous history of the thought of some 3,000 years, from the Vedic culture as crystallized in the Upanishads, and developed in the orthodox and unorthodox systems derived directly from these either as true heirs or in conscious opposition.

Dr. Dasgupta's work [*A History of Indian Philosophy*] is the first comprehensive treatment of the subject as a whole. He has the advantage of being able to embrace the point of view of Western scholarship with a masterly knowledge at first hand of the Indian treatises. Thus he is not hampered by the prejudices and guesses due to a half-knowledge of the texts, but approaches his work with an insight into Hindu thought that only a Hindu can possess. The beginnings of philosophical and cosmological speculation are indeed a problem for the Hindu as well as for the Western scholar. The Upanishad thought, says Hillebrandt, is to be placed in the region of a primitive folk psychology, not at the side of Kant or Schopenhauer. This is not surprising when we reflect that it had developed its fundamental speculations before Thales had stepped out of the fossilized mythology of the sixth century. But there are no cataclysmal revolutions of thought, and we can trace from this period the lines of speculation of the various schools. The authoritative works of these schools—the Sutras—are centuries later than the Upanishads. It is here where the author has specially shown his competence as historian, as well as his philosophical acumen. There has, for example, been much dispute about the earlier forms of the Samkhya philosophy. Evidently

what is wanted here is a knowledge of all the early works that make any reference to it. We do not expect the philosopher to read works on medicine or grammatical commentaries. But this is what Dr. Dasgupta has done, and he has been the first to point out important historical evidence for several systems in the medical work known as *Caraka,* and in the great commentary of Patanjali on Panini's grammar. Besides this he has used the later philosophical works and commentaries down to modern times. This thoroughness increases our confidence in his judgment when he comes to discuss the evolution of the philosophical principles. His conclusions are based directly on the evidence and on what he knows to be historically possible. The same sobriety and respect for facts is shown in his treatment of Vedanta. In the West this system (really a group of schools) is often supposed to mean merely Sankara's treatment of it, and this treatment is even supposed to be typical of Indian philosophy as a whole. And yet the charge is made by the Hindus themselves that Sankara was a crypto-Buddhist. This charge Dr. Dasgupta shows is largely justified. The chief principle in which his teaching differs from that of other Vedantic schools was drawn from the Buddhists. Buddhist philosophy is very fully treated. Before now we have had the exposition of the later schools, which the discoverers thought represented primitive Buddhism, and then Pali Buddhism came to the front and threw the other into the shade. The author puts them into their right relations. The earlier Pali Buddhism never developed much philosophy, indeed it was not primarily a philosophy, and as the author points out, it never influenced the main course of Indian thoughts. It was the later development that came into conflict with the orthodox schools and had such an influence on Sankara. The author has wisely refrained from putting any pressure on Indian thoughts to make them appear as European, and has tried to choose words which have not been made dangerous by the acquirement of technical senses. At the same time he has added the original Sanskrit terms, so that his interpretation can be tested at every step. This invites a serious effort of thought on the part of the Western reader, but it is inevitable, if he does not wish to be put off with a hollow substitute adapted to mental indolence.

In one respect the author has modified his practice when he comes to deal with the Samkhya and Nyaya physics. Here he follows Dr. B. N. Seal's terminology. Dr. Seal has no doubt thrown much light on this subject, but we should have preferred to have the author's own method of stating the necessarily crude physics in all their crudeness. But crudeness is a relative term; the atomic theory was certainly much closer to modern science than anything in Leucippus or Aristotle. This is, however, a subsidiary matter. The fact that physics is included at all illustrates the difficulty of early philosophy in freeing itself from matters that are really beyond its province. Owing to the continuity of Indian thought we have in the present volume an account of its philosophy in its full development down to modern times. It covers in fact all that is usually thought to constitute Indian Philosophy. But there are still other important schools and movements that the author intends to treat in a second volume. One of these is particularly important as being the chief Indian exponent of a monistic system aiming to solve the problem of plurality. This is Ramanuja's Vedanta. The Samkhya was pluralistic enough. Each of its infinite number of souls is eternal, and reaches salvation by recognizing its distinctness from the ever evolving and dissolving world of matter. In its pluralism it appealed to experience, and Sankara could only explain the plurality by calling it illusion, that is, by denying it. A system that denies experience appears to be near to bankruptcy. But Ramanuja sought to satisfy the monistic impulse as well as to account for plurality. How far he was able to do this is one of the subjects that we look forward to seeing discussed in the author's second volume.

Edward J. Thomas (essay date 1925)

SOURCE: A review of *Yoga as Philosophy and Religion,* in *International Journal of Ethics,* Vol. 35, No. 3, April, 1925, p. 324.

[*In the following essay, a review of* Yoga as Philosophy and Religion, Thomas *offers a brief explanation of Yoga's place in relation to the Sankhya philosophy, and to Charles Darwin's evolutionary theory.*]

Although the philosophy expounded in this book [*Yoga As Philosophy and Religion*] is the one Indian system that has real parallels with modern scientific thought, there has never been any adequate treatment of it in English apart from the author's previous studies. Even the term Yoga is generally understood rather in its application to Vedantic pantheism. Metaphysically the Yoga and Sankhya philosophies are only two different modifications of one common system of ideas, and the work involves a discussion of both. It may at first sight seem strange that the atheistic Sankhya, and the Yoga that makes devotion to God the easiest means of salvation, could be combined. In both of them the universal cosmic matter is *prakrti* with its three constituents in equilibrium. When the equilibrium is disturbed, the evolution of the universe begins, materially as well as mentally, for "matter on the one hand, mind, the senses, and the ego on the other are regarded as nothing more than two different kinds of modifications of one primal cause, the *Prakrti.*" This would surely have pleased Herbert Spencer, but what would he have said at finding behind all this an infinity of souls (*purushas*)? These are ultimates, spiritual atoms inserted in a system of evolving and involving matter. The aim of the souls is not union with God, for there is no Brahma apart from the totality of souls, but complete dissociation from matter. The doctrines which the Yoga system added to this are not so important as may appear at first sight. The Yoga God is no First Cause or Final End, but merely one great *purusha,* who is free from matter, and who benignly aids other souls in attaining the same purpose. How far this change was due to practical religion, or

how far it was felt to be logically necessary, might be further discussed. There are several important chapters on evolution, but they have little to do with the modern theory. It is not clear why Darwin should be mentioned. Surely he never expounded any "general form of the evolutionary process," but confined himself to biology. We are told that accidental variation is a "seeming departure from the causal chain." What evolutionist would admit that? Western evolution starts from the mind and matter that we know, but Yoga never had a transmutation theory at all. It had the theory of the elaboration of an *Urstoff,* and this, whatever Spencer and Haeckel may say, does not yet constitute science for the evolutionists. The fact of a God in Yoga, who if not the ultimate reality is at least a person who can be prayed to, has opened the way to a great development of ethical theory and mystical practices. These practices can only be exercised under the training of a teacher, but the psychical states can be described, and the chapters thereon form a most illuminating account of the chief form of Indian mysticism. The whole work forms an authoritative exposition of the subject by one who is a complete master of all the original authorities.

H. L. Mencken (essay date 1927)

SOURCE: *American Mercury,* Vol. 12, No. 46, October, 1927, p. 253.

[*In the following essay, Mencken subjects* Hindu Mysticism to the *same skeptical treatment as fundamentalist Christianity—and finds both wanting.*]

Here is a little book [*Hindu Mysticism*] by the professor of philosophy at Presidency College, Calcutta, which offers salubrious reading to those persons who still labor under the delusion that the Hindus are privy to a store of wisdom hidden from Western eyes, and that their religion is, in some vague way, more refined and civilized than Christianity. Professor Dasgupta, it appears, shares that notion himself, but he is too honest a man to conceal the facts that blow it up. Those facts he arranges neatly in six chapters. They show conclusively that the theology of even the most enlightened Hindus is almost as barbaric and nonsensical as the theology of the Swedenborgians or Seventh Day Adventists. It is grounded firmly upon a bibliolatry precisely similar to the Christian bibliolatry—nay, upon one that is far worse. The Christian Fundamentalist at least tries to make himself believe that the Bible is a record of actual human experiences, and that its mandates do no violence to that wisdom which has come out of human trial and error. But the Hindu accepts the Vedas as completely transcendental—and yet completely binding. "They are not a body of facts, but a body of commands and prohibitions. . . . They do not represent commands of the inner conscience or of the spirit within us; they do not give us any food for the spirit. They represent an objective and unalterable law. . . . " In other words, they represent balderdash. Who manufactured that balderdash? The gods? Not at all. The gods seem to be bound by the Vedas quite as tightly as their worshippers. Let a devotee perform the monkeyshines ordained, and he can laugh at the gods. Those monkeyshines are "more powerful than the gods"; if they are carefully performed the magic will work, gods or no gods. And what do they consist of? Of "the utterance or chanting of the Vedic hymns with specially prescribed accents and modulations, the pouring of melted butter in the prescribed manner into the sacrificial fire, the husking of rice in a particular way, the making and exact placing of cakes." I spare you more.

Dr. Dasgupta has an interesting chapter on the practises of the Yoga sect—interesting not only because that sect attains to heights of imbecility unsurpassed even in India, but also because its blowsy nonsense has made many converts in America. They are chiefly concentrated in Los Angeles the damned, and include thousands of unhappy and half-witted women who have passed through the stages of High Church Episcopalianism, Christian Science and the New Thought. The essence of the Yoga revelation is that an adept, by the double device of thinking profoundly and breathing deeply, can throw off the trammels of the body and become a sort of gaseous angel, purged of sin and as happy as the boy who killed his father. This benign process goes on in Los Angeles in dark rooms heavy with incense, the while the police outside chase bootleggers and mop up the blood of murdered movie Lotharios. The banker's widow from the Mortgage Belt, closeted in such shades with a *yogin,* comes out flapping her wings and convinced that her rheumatism is much better. The *yogin* on his part, feeling the feathery weight of a $10 bill in his hand, returns from the empyrean to enter it upon his books. The thing threatens to spread: the *yogins,* working eastward, have already reached the western suburbs of Dallas and Kansas City. And why not? The United States is the original home of suckers. It houses more ecclesiastics than even Italy or Spain, and they are of much higher virtuosity. Once the principles of Hindu mysticism were known among us, it would flourish as the devil-chasing of Billy Sunday, or the Four-Square Gospel of Aimée Semple McPherson, D.D. All that is needed is propaganda. Unfortunately, Dr. Dasgupta's book is too intelligent. It must be translated into Brisbanese.

E. J. Thomas (essay date 1927)

SOURCE: A review of *Hindu Mysticism: Six Lectures on the Development of Indian Mysticism,* in *Mind,* Vol. XXXVI, No. 144, October, 1927, p. 520.

[*In the following essay, a review of* Hindu Mysticism, *Thomas finds in that mysticism an erotic quality usually lacking in its Christian counterpart.*]

The religions of India have suffered at the hands of Western exponents even more than its philosophies, and yet there is no doubt that a rich field awaits the psy-chologist who will put aside the prejudices both of the missionary and the atheist. No single Indian word appears to correspond to the term mysticism, but Dr. Dasgupta makes it clear [in *Hindu Mysticism: Six Lectures on the Development of Indian Mysticism*] that Indian religions have developed the same phenomenon. It is "the belief that God is realised through ecstatic communion with him". He then widens this definition by describing the goal as the realisation of ultimate truth (which need not necessarily be thought of as a God), and by making the realisation to be attainable not by reason, but by some other means of certitude, this latter point being really implicit in the idea of ecstatic communion.

The author distinguishes five main types of mysticism. These are rather historical stages of development. Some of them have a special importance for the Western investigator, for he will find here the uncurbed exercise of tendencies that were repeatedly suppressed in Christian circles. Bossuet might restrain Madam Guyon from looking upon herself as the Woman clothed with the Sun, but there was nothing to prevent the upanishadic mystic from shouting:—

> Ha-vu! ha-vu! ha-vu!
>
> I am food, I am food, I am food!
>
> . . . Before the gods, at the navel of the immortal
>
> He that gives me, even he has aided me.
>
> I am food, I eat the food-eater,
>
> I have overcome the whole world.

The Inquisition was always on the lookout to check eroticism from masquerading as the love of God, but nothing restrained Krishna-worship from symbolising this love by means of the most unbridled form of sexual union. These things show what mysticism everywhere is liable to, and Dr. Dasgupta is honest enough not to ignore them, but he has much to tell us of the nobler side both of the older theistic developments as well as of the modern religious movements and saints like Tukaram, the Maratha, and Chaitanya, his own Bengali countryman.

Not the least striking feature of his lectures is the moderation and dignity and sense of spiritual values with which he has treated the subject. It would savour of impertinence to discuss how far a Hindu has fairly expounded a fundamental expression of Hindu thought, but his words ring absolutely true, as we should expect from one who has an unrivalled knowledge of all stages of the literature and the living religions. He has further expressed himself in such a way that Western students will be able to agree upon a common basis of material and ideas for investigation, whatever final conclusions are reached. This augurs well for the more elaborate treatment that he promises.

James Bissett Pratt (essay date 1931)

SOURCE: A review of *Yoga Philosophy in Relation to Other Systems of Indian Thought,* in *Journal of Philosophy,* Vol. 28, No. 4, February 12, 1931, pp. 106-07.

[*In the following essay, Pratt gives* Yoga Philosophy *a generally favorable review, but faults Dasgupta for an occasional tendency to blur distinctions between eastern and western systems of thought.*]

Dr. Dasgupta, Professor of Philosophy in Presidency College, Calcutta, and at one time Lecturer in the University of Cambridge, is known in this country partly through his visit and his lectures here in 1926, partly from his books, particularly his semi-popular *Hindu Mysticism* and his learned *History of Indian Philosophy.* The volume under review [*Yoga Philosophy in Relation to Other Systems of Indian Thought*], though published in 1930, was the first of Professor Dasgupta's books to be written, having been prepared eleven years ago as his doctor's thesis for the University of Calcutta. Chapter VII of his *History of Indian Philosophy* is in part based upon this book, hence the general thesis which his new book supports was announced by him in 1922. This thesis in itself is not very striking, and will not arouse much opposition among Sanskrit scholars; yet it is well worth stating. It is, namely, the rejection of a fairly common notion that Yoga is in itself only a form of psychical discipline and a belief in a personal god tacked on to the preëxisting Sankhya philosophy. Dasgupta's view is that Yoga is properly called a philosophy, and that the truly philosophical teachings embodied in it are not simply borrowed, but were an intrinsic part of Yoga development. "My supposition is," he writes, "that we have lost the original Sankhya texts, whereas the systems that pass now by the name of Sankhya and Yoga represent two schools of philosophy which evolved through the modifications of the original Sankhya School." Thus it would be better not to speak of Sankhya and Yoga, but of the Kapila Sankhya and the Patanjali or Yoga Sankhya. "Yoga did not borrow its materials from Kapila Sankhya, but being itself a modification from the original stock, has as much right to pass by the name of Sankhya as the Kapila Sankhya."

This problem of the relation of the Yoga to the Sankhya will perhaps be of interest only to technical students. To the reader whose interest is chiefly philosophical the value of Dasgupta's book will be its clear and sympathetic exposition of the Yoga-Sankhya philosophy: its first beginnings in the Upanishads, its development in the centuries just before and just after the Christian era, its treatment of physical nature and its interpretation of the various sensa as physical rather than psychical, its doctrine of the self, the Sankhya atheism and Yoga theism. Yoga psychology, ethics, and methods of concentration. The deep Sanskrit scholarship and the wide reading in Western philosophy with which Professor Dasgupta is equipped is a constant source of astonishment to the reader, and the author's ability to translate Eastern thoughts into Western terms makes this book one of great helpfulness to the Western philosopher. Only occasionally has Professor Dasgupta gone perhaps a bit too far in his attempt to assimilate Indian ideas to European categories. Though it is not true that "never the twain shall meet," it still is a fact that "East is East, and West is West," and not a few popularizers of Eastern thought slur over very fundamental contrasts in point of view, method of thought, and fundamental concepts. Dasgupta's *History of Indian Philosophy* was peculiarly free from this natural but misleading tendency. Not quite so much can be said for the book now under review. Yet slips of this kind are rare, and the book may be commended both for its sound scholarship and clear exposition and for its real philosophical insight.

Edward L. Schaub (essay date 1931)

SOURCE: A review of *Yoga Philosophy,* in *International Journal of Ethics,* Vol. XLI, No. 3, April, 1931, pp. 402-04.

[*In the following essay, a review of* Yoga Philosophy, *Schaub outlines a definition of that philosophy by contrasting it with other modes of thought.*]

Though Yoga represents one of the most striking, if not most characteristic, expressions of the Hindu spirit, the Western world has had less opportunity to acquire reliable knowledge concerning it than it has, for example, concerning the Vedanta and the Sankhya systems. The present volume, therefore, is directed to the meeting of a real need. It will be welcomed with peculiar eagerness because of the high reputation which its author has already gained through his scholarly volume entitled *A History of Indian Philosophy* and his illuminating work on *Hindu Mysticism.*

Yoga Philosophy, though only recently off the press, was written prior to the works that established Professor Dasgupta's reputation in his chosen field. The treatise was prepared some ten years ago as a Doctor's dissertation. The author now brings it out with an expression of regret that other duties, along with ill health, have made impossible such modifications as would have added to its exhaustiveness and clarified its historical perspectives. Should a revised edition of the book ever be undertaken there is a further consideration which, to the present reviewer, seems even more urgent. From first to last the pages as they now stand are replete with Sanskrit terms which, in the absence of a glossary, will inevitably remain obscure, if not entirely meaningless, to the vast majority of readers. True, the English equivalents of these terms are often inserted in the text, but such is not invariably the case, and in other instances the equivalents are given only upon the first appearance of the terms, a practice which at best puts an impossible strain upon the memories of readers and overlooks the fact that many might wish to turn to later chapters without reading the earlier.

There is little excuse for the prevalent view that Yoga is but a set of practices for the attainment, through concentration, of parapsychic powers or of ecstasy. Yoga is a comprehensive system of thought, as well as of practice, belonging, indeed, among the six orthodox philosophical systems of India. It is as such that the present volume presents it: its origins (which, in common with those of the closely related Kapila Sankhya, Professor Dasgupta believes to lie in Sankhya texts now lost); its relations to other systems (for to "understand the full significance and value of the doctrines of any Indian system of thought, it is necessary that these should be taken in connection with the corresponding doctrines of other Indian systems" [p. 4]); its ontology, cosmology, theology, physics, psychology, ethics, and finally its practice. This last-mentioned subject may not be omitted for the reason that the Yoga, "unlike other systems, does not base its claims merely on the consistency of its speculative reasonings but also on a system of practices by which the speculative results at which it arrived can be verified. In fact the history of Yoga philosophy shows that the speculative part of the theory was probably supplemented latterly because it supplied a rational groundwork and basis to the body of Yoga practices" (p. 7).

In respect to the ethics of Yoga there is a close similarity with Buddhism, whether regard is had to the sources of the ethical task or to its goal and the appropriate methods for the attainment thereof. Self-conscious life is thought to spell frustration and misery. Even when pleasure is won this is seen to be but veiled pain once the cost of winning it is considered, and the suffering which ensues from its loss. To acquire a true knowledge of self is not merely a metaphysical task but likewise an ethical obligation. Such knowledge leads to a realization that *avidya,* ignorance or untruth, is the root of all evil. The ideal to which *advidya* leads is that of hedonism. This springs from an egoism, whether this be one of a narrow sort or one in which others are identified by the self with itself; in either case the guiding principles of action are desire for pleasure or life and antipathy to pain. Salvation comes through knowledge of the identity of the self with the ultimate cosmic principle. Prerequisite thereto, however, is a definite system of renunciation and self-culture, conformable to the code, on the one hand, of "the ordinary civic duties, such as truthfulness, right conduct, righteousness, obedience to parents and teachers, making gifts, etc.," and, on the other, to the "much more advanced code, namely, that of controlling the senses and of keeping the mind in a state of steady meditation" (p. 293).

According to Yoga, *prakrti,* the source of the material and content aspect of conscious life, involves not merely inclinations to pursue pleasure but likewise "a tendency to turn away from pleasure and seek to discover our own true nature" (p. 298). With this tendency man may identify himself and, by the selection of appropriate associations and teaching, and through habitual attachment to the good, he may augment its potency and insure its triumph. If allured by the opposite tendency, he will be greatly aided by meditation upon its evil effects. "All men therefore have with them the power of being good and of attaining salvation, and though the fear of being immoral may forever be removed in the case of an emancipated person, the hope of redemption is never lost to man however degraded his present condition may be" (p. 301).

The ultimate goal of man, in the teaching of Yoga, may be reached only through the destruction of *prakrti,* which is the matrix of all feelings, and through the emancipation of the soul from all bondage to matter. The self then acquires its transcendent being, which is characterized by absolute homogeneity, by a freedom of the spirit which is absolute and therefore devoid of action and its consequences, as well as of conscious processes or states.

George W. Briggs (essay date 1932)

SOURCE: A review of *A History of Indian Philosophy,* in *Journal of Philosophy,* Vol. 29, No. 21, October 13, 1932, pp. 575-81.

[*In the following essay, written after the publication of volume two of* A History of Indian Philosophy, *Briggs provides an overview of both the first and the second volumes.*]

With the publication of volume two of this important ***History of Indian Philosophy,*** the second impression of the first appears. It is now ten years since Dr. Surendranath Dasgupta, Principal of the Sanskrit College in Calcutta, issued the first volume of this work. At once it took its place in the front rank of treatises on the history of Indian philosophy, a position which it still holds.

Volume One covers a good deal of the ground usually brought into view in an account of Indian philosophy, including, as it does, expositions of the philosophical ideas of the *Vedas,* the *Brahmanas,* and the early *Upanisads;* the philosophies of the Buddhists and Jains; the Samkhya and the "Patanjali Samkhya"; the Nyaya, the Vaisesika, and the Mimamsa; and, in part, the Vedanta. The author inserts, just before taking up the history of the development of philosophical thought in Buddhism, an interesting and illuminating chapter entitled "General Observations on the Systems of Indian Philosophy." Each chapter exhibits clearly the growth of Indian thought.

The special points of view in volume one are already familiar to students of Indian philosophy. The *Upanisads* present, not a system, but a collection of the speculations of numerous thinkers scattered over several centuries. The creative period in Indian philosophy lies behind the Christian Era (B.C. 700-200), with the early *Upanisads* in the first two centuries of that age. To the second century B.C. belong the *Vaisesika-* and the *Yoga-sutras.* The *Brahmasutras* and the *Purva Mimamsa* were written about 200

B.C. The Buddhist and the Jain systems arose in the fifth century B.C. Each of the systems had a long history, centuries of speculation, debate, and exposition, before it was formulated. A statement from the former review of the first volume, in this *Journal,* Vol. XXI (1924), pp. 77-80, will suffice to call attention to other features of the work. "Among points of special interest in this volume, the reviewer may observe that Dasgupta seems rather cool toward the view that Buddhism was largely indebted to the Samkhya; the discussion, for the first time, of the Samkhya system of Caraka; the position that Kapila's Samkhya was theistic; the theory that the Vaisesika represents an old Mimamsa school; the relation of the Purva Mimamsa to Nyaya-Vaisesika and Samkhya-Yoga; the contrast between Buddhism and *Upanisads,* between Brahmanism, Buddhism, and Jainism, between Nyaya-Vaisesika and Samkhya-Yoga."

The treatment of the Vedanta, as set forth in the first volume, is incomplete, being limited to a partial survey of the history of the Sankara school, with the use of the method of Padmapada as interpreted by Prakasatman. In the second volume of his **History,** the author devotes a further chapter (of 227 pages) to writers belonging to the school of Sankara. The chapter contains many valuable illustrations of the speculation and didactic employed by these men, written with balance and with much breadth of knowledge. All the great names, and some obscure ones, belonging to the school, are introduced. These include Mandana, Suresvara, Padmapada, and Vacaspati Misra, belonging to the age of Sankara, followed by Sarvajñatma Muni, Anandabodha Yati, Sríharsa, and Citsukha, notable names in the succeeding centuries. Eight pages are given to "The Dialectic of Nagarjuna and the Vedanta Dialectic," and eighteen to "Dialectical Criticisms of Santaraksita and Kamalasila as Forerunners of Vedanta Dialectic." This is followed by eleven pages on the "Dialectic of Sankara and Anandajñana." The remainder of the chapter is taken up with expositions of points of view of Vimuktatman, Ramadvaya, Vidyaranya Nrsimhasrama Muni, Apaya Diksita, Prakasananda, and Madhusudana Sarasvati. In the early pages of the chapter is found an illuminating discussion of "Thought and its Object in Buddhism and in Vedanta."

While the philosophical elements in the various Puranas are to be reviewed in a later volume of his **History,** still, the author devotes the second chapter of his second volume to the *Yoga-vasistha-Ramayana.* For this he gives the following reasons: "The philosophical view with which it is concerned, and which it is never tired of reiterating, is so much like the view of Sankara and of Vijñanavada Buddhism, that its claim to treatment immediately after Sankara seems to me to be particularly strong. Moreover, the various interpretations of the *Vedanta-sutra* which will follow are so much opposed to Sankara's view as to make it hard to find a suitable place for a treatment like that of the *Yoga-vasistha* unless it is taken up immediately after the chapter dealing with Sankara." The poem, consisting of 23,734

verses, belongs to the seventh or eighth century (A. D.). Dr. Dasgupta's is the first adequate exposition in English of this important work. Some of its positions are set forth in the following quotations and notes:

"There is in reality no perceiver, perceived, or perceptions, no vacuity (*sunya*), no matter, no spirit or consciousness, but pure cessation or pure negation, and this is what we mean by Brahman." "The world as such never existed in the past, nor exists now, nor will exist hereafter; so it has no production or destruction in any real sense. But yet there is the appearance, and its genesis has somehow to be accounted for. The ultimate entity is . . . of the nature of pure cessation." The order of evolution of appearance is due to pure accident. And the creations are all ideal and as such have no reality apart from their being as mere appearance. "All that appears as existent does so only as a result of the conceptual activity of thought."

As for the doctrine of emancipation, "To a person who has a perfect realization of the nature of the world-appearance, as being mere conceptual creation from the Brahman and having no existence at all, there is no sorrow in this world-appearance nor any such quality which is different from Brahman." Emancipation can be attained in the life of a person or after his death. In the former case "he is absolutely unattached to anything, but is not cut off from society and can seemingly take part in everything without losing his mental balance in any way."

"One of the special features of the *Yoga-vasistha* is the special emphasis that it lays upon free-will and its immense possibilities, and its power of overruling the limitations and bondage of past *karmas.*" "The *Yoga-vasistha* not only holds that *paurusa* (mental and physical exertions made in properly advised ways) can conquer and annul *daiva,* but it even goes to the extreme of denying *daiva* and calling it a mere fiction, that, properly speaking, does not exist at all." "*Prana* (the movement of the intellect as *ahamkara*) is essentially of the nature of vibration (*spanda*), and mind is but a form of *prana* energy, and so by the control of the mind the five *vayus* are controlled." "The unreal and illusory manifestations of the reality, are produced by the operation of this inner activity of the characterless spirit, which is in itself nothing but subject-objectless pure consciousness. But this inner and immanent movement does not seem to have any dialectic of its own, and no definite formula of the method of its operation for its productions can be given; the imaginary shapes of ideas and objects, which have nothing but a mere perceptual existence, are not due to a definite order, but to accident or change (*kakataliya*). Such a conception is indeed very barren, and it is here that the system of the *Yoga-vasistha* is particularly defective. Another important defect of the system is that it does not either criticize knowledge or admit its validity, and the characterless entity which forms its absolute is never revealed in experience."

The subject, "Speculations of the Medical Schools," which forms the third chapter of volume two, is included in the *History* for the following reasons: "In ancient India, Biology had not grown into a separate science; whatever biological ideas were current in India were mixed up with medical, osteological and physiological speculations, the only branches of study in ancient India which may be regarded as constituting an experimental science."

So far as texts are concerned, "We thus find that Ayurveda was regarded by some as a Veda superior to the other Vedas and represented by their followers as a fifth Veda, as an *upa-veda* of the *Atharva-veda,* as an independent *upa-veda,* as an *upanga* of the *Athara-veda* and lastly as a *vedanga.*" Of the Ayar-veda we now possess the treatises of Caraka and Susruta.

Aside from the discussions on physiological topics, including sections on "The Foetus and the Subtle body," and "Foetal Development," the chapter is interesting as showing how use is made of logical definition and method for diagnosis and to determine the nature of disease and of its cure.

"The ideal of the good life in Caraka is not the same as that of the different systems of philosophy which are technically called the Science of Liberation (*moksa-sastra*). The fundamental idea of a good life is that a life should be so regulated that the body and mind may be free from diseases, that it should not run into unnecessary risks of danger through carelessness, that it should be virtuous, pure and moral; that it should be a prudent and wise life which abides by the laws of polite society and of good and loyal citizens, manifesting keen alertness in thought and execution and tending constantly to its own good—good for all interests of life, body, mind and spirit."

"Medicines may, however, in the case of those who are not cursed by the commission of sins of great enormity, prolong the normal length of life. It is here that Caraka and his followers differ from all other theories of *karma* that flourished on the soil of India."

In the fourth and last chapter of volume two, Dr. Dasgupta discusses the philosophy of the *Bhagavad Gita.* His exposition is based upon the contention that the *Gita* has a system all its own, not one growing out of an attempt to synthesize Samkhya and Vedanta philosophies. This is because the *Gita* is a book of high antiquity, antedating Buddhism. "The *Gita* may have been a work of the Bhagavata school, written long before the composition of the *Maha-bharata,* and may have been written on the basis of the Bharata legend, on which the *Maha-bharata* was based. It is not improbable that the *Gita,* which summarized the teaching of the Bhagavata School, was incorporated into the *Maha-bharata* during one of its revisions, by reason of the sacredness that it had attained at that time."

Some of the author's expositions are of special interest. The philosophy of the *Gita* "is diametrically opposite to that of Sankara." "The *yoga* of the *Gita* is quite different from the *yoga* of Patañjali, and it does not seem at all probable that the *Gita* was aware of Patañjali's *yoga* or the technical terms used by him." The word *samkhya* is used in the *Gita* "in the sense of path of knowledge or of philosophical wisdom."

One or two sentences may be quoted from the author's excellent exposition of *dharma.* "The word *dharma* in the *Gita* does not mean what Jaimini understood by the term, viz., a desirable end or good enjoined by the sacrifices. . . . The word seems to be used in the *Gita* primarily in the sense of an unalterable customary order of class-duties or caste-duties and the general approved course of conduct for the people, and also in the sense of prescribed schemes of conduct. The meaning of *dharma* as "old customary order" is probably the oldest meaning of the word. . . . The central meaning of the word *dharma* in the *Gita* is therefore the oldest Vedie meaning of the word, which is a much earlier meaning than the latter day technical meaning of the word as found in the Mimamsa. *Dharma* does not in the *Gita* mean sacrifices (*yajña*) or external advantages, as it does in the Mimamsa, but the order of conventional practices involving specific caste-divisions and caste-duties."

There are also in this chapter carefully developed studies of such terms as *prakrti, purusa, avyakta,* and *karma.*

The section entitled "The Ethics of the Gita and the Buddhist Ethics" is full of interest. "The *Gita* bases its ethics mainly on the necessity of getting rid of attachment and desires from which proceeds greed and frustration of which produces anger." "A man should always follow his own caste-duties, which are his own proper duties, or *sva-dharma.*" The reply to the charge that war implies injury to living beings is "that the proper way of performing actions is to dissociate one's mind from attachment." "To give up work can be significant only if it means the giving up of all desires for the fruits of such actions." "The *samadhi* of the *Gita* is not a mere concentration of the mind on some object, but communion with God, and the wisdom, or *prajña,* of the *Gita* is no realization of any philosophic truth, but a fixed and unperturbed state of mind, where the will and intellect remain unshaken in one's course of duty, clear of all consequences and free from all attachments, and in a state of equanimity which cannot be shaken or disturbed by pleasures or sorrows." "Morality from this point of view (of the unattached mind) becomes wholly subjective, and the special feature of the *Gita* is that it tends to make all actions non-moral by cutting away the bonds that connect an action with its performer."

"The *Gita* is probably the earliest document where a definite statement is made regarding the imperishable nature of existent things and the impossibility of that which is non-existent coming into being. . . . " "The main purpose of the *Gita* is not to find out how one can tear asunder the bonds of *karma* and stop rebirth, but to prescribe a true rule of the performance of one's duties."

Three passages under the heading "God and Man" must suffice to complete this rapid survey of the chapter. "The earliest and most recondite treatment regarding the nature and existence of God and His relation to man is found in the *Gita*." "This doctrine of the incarnation of God, though not dealt with in any of the purely speculative systems, yet forms the corner-stone of most systems of religious philosophy and religion, and the *Gita* is probably the earliest work available to us in which this doctrine is found. The effect of its introduction and of the dialogue form of the *Gita,* in which the man-god Krsna instructs Arjuna in the philosophy of life and conduct, is that the instruction regarding the personality of God becomes concrete and living." "For the God of the *Gita* is not a God of abstract philosophy or theology, but a God who could be a man and be capable of all personal relations."

These volumes impress the reader with their solidity and scope. The work is thoroughgoing, clearly set forth, revealing the erudite and mature scholar. The notes, mostly in Sanskrit, constitute a mass of documentation, showing that the chief sources for the preparation of such a *History* as this have been fully surveyed. While the author is conversant with the history of Western philosophy, still, he does not attempt to explain Indian and Western systems in terms of each other. All the while he is bent on writing a thorough and impartial history of *Indian* philosophy. The whole weight of his learning and labor is imposed upon the Indian point of view. In this respect his *History* stands practically alone, and it is for this reason that it is of such great importance.

Thirty-four pages of volume one and eighty-six pages of volume two are occupied with an exhaustive index of both Sanskrit and English references. The book-work is excellent and both volumes are remarkably free from errors.

The author announces that volume three, which is well along towards completion, will contain a fairly elaborate account of the principal dualistic and pluralistic Indian systems, "such as the philosophy of the Pañca-ratra, Bhaskara, Yamuna, Ramanuja and his followers, Madhava and his followers, the *Bhagavata-purana* and the Gaudiya school of Vaisnavism." Volumes four and five will deal "with the philosophy of Vallabha and some other lesser known schools of Vaisnavism, the philosophy of the Puranas, Tantras, the different schools of Saivas, Saktas, Indian Ascetics, the philosophy of right and law and the religious systems that have found their expression in some of the leading vernaculars of India."

This great work is planned on very broad and inclusive lines and bids fair to become the authoritative work in English on the history of Indian philosophy. Volumes one and two speak in the highest terms for the promise of those which are to follow.

F. Otto Schrader (essay date 1934)

SOURCE: A review of *Indian Idealism,* in *Philosophy: Journal of the British Columbia Institute of Philosophy,* Vol. 9, No. 36, October, 1934, pp. 493-94.

[*In the following essay, Schrader compares and contrasts that volume with* A History of Indian Philosophy.]

The author of this work [*Indian Idealism*], Principal of the Sanskrit College, Calcutta, will be remembered from our detailed review, in Vol. VIII of **Philosophy,** of the second and latest volume of his monumental **History of Indian Philosophy.** The work before us contains with but few alterations the lectures delivered by him years ago as the Readership Lectures of the Patna University and is published as a "first attempt to put together some of the most important strands of Indian idealistic thought within a small compass."

The six chapters (conveniently divided into numbered sections) deal respectively with (I) Beginnings of Indian Philosophy, (II-III) Upanishadic Idealism, (IV-V) Buddhist Idealism, and (VI) The Vedanta and Kindred Forms of Idealism.

It goes without saying that for the most part the contents of the work read like an abstract from the author's **History,** yet the treatment of the subject-matter as well as the latter itself are not quite the same. We have here a more decided attempt at presenting the history of Indian philosophy as a connected whole, and side-looks to Western thinkers, purposely avoided in the **History,** are not wanting (Bradley, the English Nagarjuna!). The principal Upanishads are individually described, not synthetically as in the **History.** This latter work being still in progress, a few systems not found in its published volumes had to be taken into account. Of these the ancient Vaisnavite philosophy called Pañcaratra, as represented by the Ahirbudhnya-Samhita, has thus for the first time found a place in a history of philosophy. Special importance has been rightly attached to it, because it is the systematic elaboration of the philosophy of the Bhagavadgita. Being "quite uninfluenced by the later philosophical speculations," this "best reconciliation of the apparently irreconcilable strands of Upanishadic thought" is dealt with, after the Gita as the first attempt of that kind, in the second chapter on Upanishadic idealism, and is tentatively called the *idealism of dynamic pantheism,* a somewhat queer label, indeed, which, however, well indicates the two tendencies synthesized in this system.

That Buddhist idealism has been given considerably more room than the one allotted to the idealistic systems of the Brahmins will surprise no one who knows the great indebtedness of the latter to the former. The Buddhists are the founders of scientific philosophy in India. The philosophy of the Buddha himself is described by our author according to the scholastic view (Theravada), *i.e.* as *pluralist phenomenalism,* at the end of the second chapter on Upanishadic idealism, which is indeed its proper place. But just for the latter reason a few hints would have been desirable as to those uneffaced vestiges in the Buddhist scripture which show the Buddha in much closer contact with Upanishadic idealism than the scholiasts, and to which long ago the writer of these lines and in recent years Mrs. Rhys Davids have called attention.

The last chapter has become too short. Tantrik idealism, *e.g.,* has been dealt with in a rather too sketchy way, as also the Kashmirian Trika philosophy with its superb literature cannot be sufficiently explained on two pages only; and the little section (29) of less than one page on the Ekajiva-vada is not proportional to the interest that attaches to the only systematic attempt at *solipsism* made in India.

It is a pity that the friends of the author mentioned in the Preface who have seen the work through the press are all of them Indians. An Englishman could have helped to improve the language and would have pointed out not a few passages and terms (such as *viksepa-sakti,* p. 193) which are not likely to be understood by the general Western reader. We have also found some misprints and inconsistencies which must disappear in a future edition. But this is not meant as a discouragement. Every reader, we feel sure, will draw profit from this highly interesting work, the use of which is facilitated by an excellent summary covering seventeen pages.

S. Bhattacharya (essay date 1949)

SOURCE: "On Indian Philosophy," in *Eastern World,* Vol. 111, No. 9, September, 1949, pp. 25-26.

[*In the following essay, a review of the fourth volume in the* History of Indian Philosophy *series, Bhattacharya examines that work with reference to a number of Sanskrit terms and Hindu ideas.*]

The present volume [*A History of Indian Philosophy,* Volume IV] incorporates "Indian Pluralism" and, as the author says in the preface, "it deals with the philosophy of the Bhagavata-purana, the philosophy of Madhva and his followers, the philosophy of Vallabha and the philosophy of the Gaudiya school of Vaisnavism." The Bhagavata and Ramanuja are the modern protagonists of pre-Sankara theistic streams known as the Bhagavata and the Pancaratra schools respectively. Thoughts of Madhva, Vallabha and Caitanya are largely inspired by the Bhagavata. Yet conditioned monism (*visistadvaita*) of Ramanuja, pure monism (*suddhadvaita*) of Vallabha and unthinkable duality-nonduality (*acintya-bhedavheda*) of Caitanya indicate the momentum of that great thinker Sankara on the post-Sankara world even outside his own fold. Sankara benefited them all also indirectly, by striking at the root of Buddhistic agnosticism. The only system which could save itself from Sankara's sweeping influence was that of Madhva. Ramanuja and Nimbarka, another sect based on the Bhagavata, being treated in

previous volumes, Madhva, Vallabha and Caitanya are considered in the present work.

It is a pity that Professor Dasgupta did not devote "much space to the philosophy of the Bhagavata-purana." The reason adduced at the preface that "much of its philosophical views has already been anticipated" in his previous volumes is not very convincing. The Bhagavata with an individuality of its own deserved full consideration specially in view of its dominating influence upon almost all devotional sects that came under its purview. Even the scrappy treatment is mostly a special pleading in the light of Jivagosvamin, one of the exponents of Gaudiya school.

Professor Dasgupta displays remarkable scholarship in the treatment of Madhva and his followers. Madhva flourished when Sankara and his illustrious exponents like Vacaspati, Prakasatman, Suresvara and others had already written their works. The creative stage of Sankara's philosophy developed analytical solidarity in a "long series of attacks and counter-attacks between the members of two important schools of thought" (p. 94). Madhva was an uncompromising pluralist. In Madhva, and later in his followers, the qualities of a theologian were combined with the intolerance of an unsparing disputant. And he was gifted with a rare prolificacy to put his qualities into practice. He commented on the Rg. Veda and most of the Upanisads and also gave an allegorical interpretation of the Mahabharata. In his Karma-nirmaya he held out the final import of the Brahmanas to consist in Visnu and wrote a number of ritualistic manuals for the benefit of his followers. As a Vaisnava he pinned his faith to the Samkhya doctrine of creation, with its corollaries, the theory of transformation (*parinama-vada*) and the theory of existence of the effect prior to the operation of conditions (*sat-karya-vada*). As a dialectician he chose to side with the Vaisesikas from whom he has taken categories (with amendments), invariable concomitance (*vyapti*), ratiocination (*tarka*) and epistemological process of inference, to name only a few. He has also drawn upon Mimamsa in his delineation of the source of valid knowledge (*pramana*) and also in connection with verbal testimony (*sabda*).

Professor Dasgupta has admirably handled these topics and the value of his treatment has been considerably enhanced by the comparative method which he has brought to bear upon the subject. On the one hand he draws the borderline between Sankara and Madhva, between Ramanuja and Madhva on the other. In dealing with the source of valid knowledge (*pramana*) he has placed at our disposal the views of the Buddhists and the Jains. He has traced with singular acuteness how the subjective view of Prabhakara and the Jainas has coalesced with the objective view of Nyaya in Vyasatirtha's exposition of the source of valid knowledge. He has focussed the views of Mimamsakas and the logicians to the question of self-validity of knowledge (*svatah-pramanya*). It is also interesting to notice how Vyasatirtha contributed to the view of Udayana on ratiocination (*tarka*) in preference to the views of other logicians.

Professor Dasgupta is at his best in the treatment of Madhva dialectics which he rightly holds as "almost unrivalled in the whole field of Indian thought." Vyasa tirtha wrote *Nyayamrta* which was refuted by Madhusudana in his *Advaita-siddhi*. Ramacarya in his *Nyayamrtatarangini* supported Vyasatirtha against Madhusudana. Then came Gauda-brahmananda and he unsparingly criticised Ramacarya in his *Gaudabrahmanandi,* a commentary on *Advaita-siddhi* by Madhusudana. Professor Dasgupta has summed up the views of respective parties without, however, mentioning *Gaudabrahmananda,* and he is inclined to give the finishing touch with the view of Madhusudana. The whole discussion has many-sided interest. The subject-matter represents the first formidable challenge to the views of Sankara, on behalf of a stubborn pluralist. Further, thanks to the meticulous care of Professor Dasgupta, the whole matter has been comprehensively presented, for the first time, I believe, to the English reading public.

Dr. Ganganatha Jha had attempted to break through the almost invulnerable structure of dialectical language which "New Logic" has brought to its train, under the auspices of Gangesa Upadhaya, by translating *Khandana-khanda-khadya* of Sri-harsa into English. Professor Dasgupta has improved upon that though he could not altogether avoid being cryptic. On the whole he has been able to present the subject with an appreciable amount of clarity and has put up the viewpoint of Madhva against the central doctrines of Sankara, including the doctrine of superimposition (*adhyasa*), the doctrine of inscrutability (*aniryacaniya*), the absolute monism, the doctrine of nescence (*avidya*) and its definitions and evidences.

As regards Vallabha he has indicated the "important contributions of the members of his school." He has clearly brought out Vallabha's doctrine of independence (*syabhaya*) of the absolute, by virtue of which Vallabha wanted to explain away the inconsistency between his theological dualism and metaphysical monism. The Vallabha school has accentuated the emotional aspect of devotion, and considering irresistibility as a characteristic of emotion, it has subdivided devotion into *maryada* and *pusti,* the former requiring spiritual discipline and the latter being spontaneous. Further, this school has recognised devotion, for the first time, as a sentiment (*rasa*) in the sense the poeticians have used the term. Professor Dasgupta has fairly brought these aspects out. But unfortunately he neglected the philosophy of Visnusvamin though we appreciate the difficulties he would have had to encounter in doing justice to him, for he has left no extant book expounding his views.

The treatment of Professor Dasgupta is more analytic than synthetic, though in the present volume his analytical calibre has matched at times his comparative approach. Sometimes he has not furnished us with relevant

references and he seems to have followed his own isolated course of treatment though books covering the same field have appeared before his publication. There are a few instances which bear testimony to his tendency of over-simplification. He interprets *jnatata* as a mental state of cognition (p. 169) whereas it is an entity extraneous to knowledge and is supposed to inhere in an object of cognition and generated by the cognition of that particular object (vide *Bhakta-cintamani,* p. 13, Chow. Sans. Series, Benares, 1934). Similarly *phala-vyapyatva* is pervasion (i.e., revelation) by consciousness, which is occasioned by the identification of the two types of consciousness, viz., consciousness conditioned by the mental mode and consciousness conditioned by the external object, the identification being based upon the concurrence of the mental mode and the external object, during the epistemological process of cognition; and not simply "the product of the activity of a mental state" (p. 310). Nor has "God—three powers Brahman, Paramatman and Bhagavan" (421), but they are three representations of God. He has conformed to his familiar method of presentation, which is substantially oriental. His exposition is selective, based as it is on some specific books in respective subjects. He interprets the Bhagavata in the light of *Sat-Sandarbha of Jiva,* bases the doctrines of Madhva on *Madhva-Bhasya* and *Nyayamrta,* expounds Vallabha according to *Tattvadipa* and *Bhakti-martanda,* assesses Jiva by his *Sat-Sandarbha* and, finally sizes up Baladeva by his *Govinda-Bhasya* and *Siddhanta-ratna,* yet on the whole he has shown the scholarly way for posterity to work upon these subjects and has thus done pioneering work of sustaining interest. We hope to see his fifth volume published during his lifetime.

A. C. Bouquet (essay date 1958)

SOURCE: A review of *A History of Indian Philosophy,* in *Philosophical Quarterly,* Vol. 8, No. 30, January, 1958, pp. 79-80.

[*In the following essay, a review of the fifth and final volume of* A History of Indian Philosophy, *Bouquet pays tribute to Dasgupta's wife, Surama, and makes a few points regarding the south Indian philosophy of Saivism.*]

This, the final volume in Dr. Dasgupta's *magnum opus,* [*A **History of Indian Philosophy,** Volume 5: The Southern Schools of Saivism*] has been edited and issued, after his death, by his wife, Surama Dasgupta. It is, of course, shorter than the others, and it is possible that the author, if he had lived on, might have expanded it further. As it stands, it owes much to the reverent and devoted labours of one who was the constant and loving companion and disciple of the great scholar, and who has regarded it as a great task and a sacred obligation to bring his labours to their due termination.

The philosophical theology of Saivism in Southern India has not perhaps received as much attention from students as that of the northern schools, but it deserves consideration, partly because it is the intellectual side of *bhakti* (emotional devotion), partly because of the question it inevitably arouses in our minds, as to the interrelation between it and the ancient Christian communities of the Malabar coast. Granted that it remains essentially Hindu, it is impossible to read our author's exposition of such a system as that of Srikantha (8th century A.D.) and his commentator, Appaya Diksita (A.D. 1550) without asking one's self: "Is this philosophical theism, with its doctrine of *annugraha* or grace, a wholly independent production, or is it the consequence of a religious thought-wave which swept eastward and westward, and which finds expression along Christian lines in the Mediterranean world, but along Hindu lines in the southern wedge of the Indian sub-continent? Or did the Saivite theologians, whether consciously or unconsciously, borrow something from their Christian neighbours?"

One notes that Dr. Dasgupta does not think that evidence confirms that the oldest form of Saivism is to be found in the prehistoric religion of South India. This has sometimes been urged, but it seems to me far more likely that early Saivism belongs to the proto-Dravidian invaders of India, and not to the pre-Dravidian aboriginals (whether australoid or negrito), who preceded them as the inhabitants of the South. Indeed, I think that on page 155, when the author wrote "pre-Aryan, Dravidian", he meant to write "pre-Aryan, pre-Dravidian".

FURTHER READING

Biography

Dasgupta, Surama. *An Ever-Expanding Quest of Life and Knowledge.* New Delhi: Orient Longman, 1971, 290 p.
 A personal and professional biography of Dasgupta by his wife, herself a writer and editor.

Criticism

Brett, G. S. "Book Reviews." *International Journal of Ethics* XLV, No. 1 (October 1934): 102-07.
 A comparative review of Dasgupta's *History* (Volume 1) and *Indian Idealism*, along with works by two other Indian writers—including another history of Indian philosophy.

Carr, H. Wilden. Review of *A History of Indian Philosophy*, Volume 1. *Mind* XXXII, No. 125 (January 1923): 93-100.
 A detailed review of Dasgupta's *History* which outlines distinctions and similarities between western and Indian thought.

Review of *Indian Idealism*. *Journal of Philosophy* XXXI, No. 3 (1 February 1934): 79.
 A short and highly favorable review of "an exceptionally useful volume for western students."

Review of *Hindu Mysticism*. *Monist* XXXVIII, No. 1 (January 1928): 160.
 A short review praising Dasgupta's "brief, though doubtless authoritative, description of the various forms of Indian mysticism."

Review of *Yoga Philosophy in Relation to Other Systems of Thought*. *Monist* XLI, No. 2 (April 1931): 315.
 A generally favorable review which nonetheless faults Dasgupta for his "very free use of Sanskrit philosophical terms instead of their English equivalents."

Smith, C. Ryder. "From My New Shelf." *London Quarterly* (July 1955): 236-37.
 A short review of Dasgupta's *Religion and the Rational Outlook* alongside books on Christianity.

Widgery, Alban G. Review of *Yoga Philosophy*. *Philosophical Review* 41, No. 3 (January 1932): 325.
 A short review which treats *Yoga Philosophy* as an amplification of themes first presented in *A History of Indian Philosophy*.

The following source published by Gale contains additional coverage of Dasgupta's life and career: *Contemporary Authors,* Vol. 157.

Bruno Frank

1887-1945

German novelist, dramatist, and poet.

INTRODUCTION

Frank was an eclectic writer whose forte was the historical novel. A respected lyric poet before World War I, he achieved success as a novelist, short story writer, and playwright, both in Germany and abroad. Writing in the liberal humanist tradition, his penchant for drawing model characters, whose sufferings, sorrows, and conflicts are viewed as singular and outstanding, hearkened back to the work of such nineteenth-century novelists as Leo Tolstoy, Ivan Turgenev, Gustave Flaubert, and Friedrich Hölderlin.

Biographical Information

Frank was born into a well-to-do family of German-Jewish bankers in Stuttgart. He was awarded a doctoral degree in language and literature at the University of Tübingen in 1912, traveled extensively in France and southern Europe, and served on both the Western and Eastern fronts during World War I until illness forced his release from the service. He subsequently spent several years as a free-lance writer in Bavaria. In 1924, he settled in Munich and married Elisabeth Pallenberg-Massary, the daughter of the actress Fritzi Massary and stepdaughter of the comedian Max Pallenberg. He lived the life of a successful writer in Munich until 1933, when he left Germany on the day following the burning of the Reichstag. After residing in exile in Austria, England, France, and Switzerland, he immigrated to the United States in 1937. He settled in Hollywood and died of a heart attack at his home in Beverly Hills one month after the collapse of the Third Reich, at the age of fifty-eight.

Major Works

Frank's literary career can be divided into roughly three periods, demarcated by his youth, his move to Munich in 1924, his exile abroad in 1933, and his death in 1945. His poetry career was concentrated in his early years, and his best dramatic work was produced in his middle period. Among his most successful plays were *Zwölftausend* (1927; *Twelve Thousand*, 1928), and the comedy *Sturm im Wasserglas* (1930; *Storm in a Teacup*, 1936). After 1929, he viewed his participation in drama as a potential for commercial, rather than artistic success, and his dramatic production virtually ceased after his exile in 1933. His novel *Tage des Königs* (1924; *The Days of the King*, 1927), about Frederick the Great, is considered a masterpiece in the historical-novel genre. In exile he continued to write novels, as well as criticism and screenplays. The most significant work to emerge from Frank's years in exile was the biographical novel *Cervantes* (1934; *A Man Called Cervantes*, 1934).

Critical Reception

Despite his Jewish background, Frank possessed a profound sense of German-ness reflective of his nineteenth-century orientation. Bavaria was his adopted region, and his special love was the Prussian hero, whose image he affirmed again and again in his work. Critics saw his predilection for psychological analysis and for evoking atmosphere and mood as suited more to the narrative and lyrical genres, rather than drama. The Schopenhauer concept of sympathy forms the basis for his subtle character studies, and he is at his best when treating the fates of historical characters, particularly pre-eminent personalities who, by their greatness and distinction, represent a source of consolation to a suffering world. Frank's later works can be classed with those of such exiled liberal authors as Lion Feuchtwanger, Klaus Mann, and Hans Habe. His artistic design was, through recourse to the European cultural past, to superimpose an atmosphere of order and harmony upon the political and social disruption of the time.

PRINCIPAL WORKS

Tage des Königs [*The Days of the King*] (novel) 1924
Zwölftausend: Schauspiel in drei Akten [*Twelve Thousand: A Play in Three Acts*] (drama) 1927
Politische Novelle [*The Persians Are Coming*] (novel) 1928
Sturm im Wasserglas [*Storm in a Teacup*] (drama) 1930
Cervantes: Ein Roman [*A Man Called Cervantes*] (novel) 1934
Der Reisepass: Ein Roman [*Closed Frontiers: A Study of Modern Europe*] (novel) 1937
The Magician, and Other Stories (novella and short stories) 1946

CRITICISM

Jethro Bithell (essay date 1939)

SOURCE: "The Historical Novel," in *Modern German Literature, 1880-1950*, Methuen & Co., Ltd., 1939, pp. 381-87.

[*In the following essay, Bithell identifies elements of classical Liberalism in Frank's historical novels.*]

Bruno Frank has expressionistic humanity and a fine Jewish culture, but in style and outlook he is a solid, sensible Liberal, almost old-fashioned (by comparison) in his directness of expression. His historical novel *Die Tage des Königs* (1924) is a scholarly well-documented study of Frederick the Great, who also dominates the scene in *Trenck, Roman eines Günstlings* (1926), a lively picture of Prussian rococo. Bruno Frank's enlightened Liberalism shines out from *Politische Novelle* (1928), a discussion rather than a story, which rejects the plea that antagonism between France and Germany is a necessary evil and in its vivid pen-pictures of Briand (as Dorval) and of Stresemann (as Carmer) shows how elementary the idea of permanent peace really is. His *vie romancée* of *Cervantes* (1935) is a thorough de-bunking; there is topical interest in the satirical account of the decrees for the prevention of blood-pollution at a time when there was not a grandee's family in Spain but Jewish blood flowed in his veins. *Don Quixote* is shown to be the product of utter disillusionment, not so much of sex (though Dulcinea is depicted as a literal portrait of the country girl Cervantes marries) as of the hopeless misgovernment of Spain. *Chamfort erzalht seinen Tod* (1937) is the *vie romancée* of this French aphorist. *Der Reisepass* (1937) is yet another denunciation of the Nazi régime by an emigré (to the United States). Several of Bruno Frank's dramas were successful on the English stage; of these *Zwölftausend* (1927) throws a lurid light on the sale by a German princeling of 12,000 of his subjects to England as cannon fodder. *Sturm im Wasserglas* (1930)—James Bridie's *Storm in a Teacup* (1937)—is uproarious in its picture of a platitudinous dictator engrossed in self and dead to human pity. *Nina* (1931) is a study of a guttersnipe transformed to a film-star; for love of her husband she sacrifices her glamorous career, which is taken over by a double. *Die Tochter* (1943) is based on the life of the mother of the author's wife, a cabaret artiste who is half Jew and half Pole, and of her father, an Austrian officer; the ground theme is anti-Semitism. Bruno Frank is most effective where his allusions are transparent—e.g. the theatre director in his Novelle *Der Magier* (1929) resembles Max Reinhardt; where he handles merely pathological problems he has no incisiveness—e.g. in his drama *Die Schwestern und der Fremde* (1918), in which a physically cold intellectual humanitarian satisfies the desires of a girl doomed by consumption, but, when she dies, tells her robust sister, who wishes to fill the gap, that he is an icy monster.

Wentzle Ruml III (essay date 1947)

SOURCE: A review of *The Magician*, in the *Kenyon Review*, Vol. IX, No. 4, Autumn, 1947, pp. 616-21.

[*In the following review, Ruml considers Frank's examination in* The Magician *of the place of fate in human life, finding Frank's handling of his topic to amount to an insubstantial "gimmick."*]

Bruno Frank is most concerned with irony and fate, not simple elements as people commonly think of them but rather multiplied, twisted and reversed. His characters might be anyone; you can call them universal or not people at all. Relationships between people are not important; relationships might as well not exist. People are important only in one relationship, and that is the relationship with fate, usually told by Frank in terms of an object which turns out to be a symbol of fate.

When a woman's suitcase is accidentally substituted for his own, a business man is first mentally seduced by his image of the owner, then realises that his feeling only expresses his desire for adventure, rebellion against the middle-class, middle-aged life he leads; finally, when the man's wife arrives and finds the contents of the suitcase, Frank twists fate by having her believe the business man, miraculously, in his simple statement that no woman has been there. Similarly, when a German law student, in the army, steals sixteen thousand francs from a French corpse on the battlefield, the theft determines the course of his life: it pays for his education; its guilt drives him into criminal law, makes him a renowned reviser of the field; his preoccupation with his work makes his wife leave him; and, when the Nazis drive him from Germany and he goes to France to return the sixteen thousand francs to heirs, he finds only that the French corpse was what used to be called a scoundrel and that the sole surviving heir is a French proto-Nazi.

It is easy enough to say that no story would begin without chance, but in these stories fate provides not only the beginning but almost every development. Characters, ideas, theories are not important; fate controls everything about all mankind.

Within limits, this singleness of concern is quite reasonable. But there is a difficulty, illustrated in these two stories and in the others of *The Magician.* The trouble lies in the fact that Frank does not have much to say about fate. One story might as well be any other. With Pritchett and DeJong there was a sense of variation and real development on a solid base; with Frank there is only minor verbal variation and a great sense of sameness. For Frank, having not much to say, must rely upon what is called the "gimmick," the conscious device on which a piece of work turns, the element of novelty which is expected to make a piece different from, and more interesting than, others of similar kind. The suitcase and the stolen money are obviously gimmicks; others, in other stories, include a beetle, a watch that shows the phases of the moon, and so on.

If you have been sufficiently impressed by the gimmick approach in radio programs, motion pictures, and many books, you may find Frank repugnant. In this case, I should like to suggest that we are living in a gimmick culture, in which most of us survive by turning our attention to form rather than to substance, to brilliance of technique rather than to what is being said and the suitability of the technique to it. These notions are not especially attractive to me, either, but the fact remains that Frank's gimmick sense is a more prevalent symptom of our society than the more desirable sensibilities of either Pritchett or DeJong.

Thomas A. Kamla (essay date 1975)

SOURCE: "Bruno Frank's 'Der Reisepass': The Exile as an Aristocrat of Humanity," in *Monatshefte*, Vol. LXVII, No. 1, Spring, 1975, pp. 37-47.

[*In the following essay, Kamla analyzes Frank's protagonist Ludwig in* Der Reisepass *as the embodiment of liberal humanist values and the implications of his princely status as an exemplary liberal.*]

The tradition of liberal humanism, to which the bourgeois writer was heir, underwent a re-evaluation in some cases after 1933. In their journalistic contributions and artistic works the liberal authors in exile addressed themselves to issues involving social forces and ideologies that would lend realistic substance to a literary heritage that had fostered individual freedom of expression. Lion Feuchtwanger, Klaus Mann, and Hans Habe saw, if only for reasons of expediency, in the collective struggle of Communism the one viable ideological force that could pose an effective threat to militant imperialism. Habe and Feuchtwanger include in their exile novels (*Drei über die Grenze* and *Exil*) separate historical sections showing their discontent with the political apathy of an emigration that had continued to persist in its old ways, unable to suppress private differences and join together in opposition to a common enemy. In his first exile novel (*Flucht in den Norden*), Klaus Mann is equally critical of certain reactionary tendencies displayed by various social elements in the countries of asylum. All three writers attempt to counteract the problem of individualism and non-committed humanism by introducing antipodal figures as bearers of a progressive, collective ideology.

In *Der Reisepass*, Bruno Frank describes a rather unique exponent of the Hitler opposition. His narrative, centering on the actions of Prince Ludwig of Camburg-Saxony,[1] a descendant of a deposed ruling hierarchy, sheds unusual light on the way an exiled liberal writer might confront the politically inept tradition that facilitated Hitler's rise to power. The episodes characterizing various functionaries of the Weimar government as republicans in form, but as monarchists in principle, reveal an acute perception of the situation as it existed in the 1920's. In the person of Steiger, Ludwig's private

tutor and dedicated servant throughout the Republic and in exile, we see exemplified that unpolitical, regressive state of mind typifying a large segment of the officialdom at that time.

By way of opposition to this condition, Frank creates Ludwig, an enlightened prince who rejects the former privileges of rank and nobility to which some government officials and intellectuals still aspire. In this character the author erects a model of moral decency. Ludwig is the dethroned aristocrat who possesses noble, humane sensibilities, a *princely* figure in whom *bourgeois* democratic values of equality and liberty are fostered. Whereas other writers in exile sought to reconcile the concept of humanity to existing reality, Frank goes to the other extreme, embodying this idea in a single figure standing apart from the rest of society. Ludwig becomes Frank's representative of liberal humanism. The "real" spokesmen of the bourgeois class, on the other hand, are portrayed as disillusioned monarchists or fatalistic, resigned exiles.

Klaus Mann and Ludwig Marcuse both intimated a certain dismay over their colleague's selection of a prince as protagonist in their reviews of the novel following its appearance in 1937. Since their intention is to bestow more praise than criticism, however, they pay mere lip service to what really constitutes the central issue of the work. Marcuse describes *Der Reisepass* as "einen etwas problematischen Roman," "ein tolles Wagnis," and considers "manche Partie des Frankschen Experiments" to be "recht fragwürdig."[2] Klaus Mann dispenses momentarily with the usual benevolent tone pervading his reviews when he in turn states: "Es muss Franks Absicht gewesen sein,—und wir möchten sie fast als eine dichterische Laune bezeichnen,—uns als antifaschistischen Kämpfer diesen Prinzen-Jüngling vorzuführen: diesen Ausnahmefall, dieses nicht-typische Exemplar."[3]

Needless to say, Frank's creation of a *verbürgerlichter Prinz* in the novel is more than simple "Laune." His concern for the defense of human values was just as strongly felt as that of his literary peers. But the author goes about this task in a most perplexing way. *Der Reisepass* follows Frank's earlier novel in exile *Cervantes* (1934). In the persons of Ludwig and Steiger, he constructs a relationship that is just the reversal of the lord-servant model in the Spanish writer's famous work. The ideas embodied in the Don Quixote-Sancho Pansa dualism do a complete about-face in *Der Reisepass.* Here it is the servant, Steiger, who entertains illusions of grandeur about a ruling aristocracy, and it is the nobleman who holds such fantasies to be obsolete. Appearance and reality, idealism and practicality, have reversed hands in a contemporary reworking of a historical model.

One is prompted to inquire into the rationale for such a portrayal of contemporary society. We noted that Frank creates an aristocrat as a model of humanity. Ludwig's exceptional qualities are hardly representative of the members of his dethroned class. His father, Duke Phillip, had occupied himself solely with a collection of rare coins following his deposition; the brother, Prince August, had aligned himself with the Nazi Party; the European nobility attending the mother's funeral in the early 1920's did so for reasons of ceremony, not out of empathy; Ludwig's fellow conspirators in the planned coup d'état, all of whom were deposed nobles and bourgeois sympathizers of the monarchy, were eventually released from prison through personal connections with the upper ranks of the Nazi Regime. Only Steiger, the most zealous spokesman for the coup, which was to have been spearheaded by Ludwig (the "Volksfürst aus altem Blut"[4]), remains imprisoned to be freed by the prince himself.

The rationale underlying the reversal of the Don Quixote-Sancho Pansa *Weltanschauung* ties in with Frank's criticism of Germany's political complacency in the years leading up to the maelstrom of 1933. The satirical emphasis in Cervantes' work rests with unmasking the fruitlessness of an aristocrat's desire to uphold an ideal of chivalry that had since faded into oblivion. His servant, however, is a figure out of the sixteenth century who has surpassed the age of compliant bondage. In **Der Reisepass,** Frank does not resort to satire as an artistic device for exposing the incongruities of his period. Rather he allows the anachronism of a bourgeoisie espousing an attitude of servility to speak for itself. Observed in a broader historical perspective, this anachronism had its inception with the establishment of the Weimar Republic in which the Wilhelminian monarchy was overthrown in form but not in spirit.

In the figure of Ludwig, Frank symbolizes a person whose actions are predicated on the principle of democracy and justice. Ludwig, however, is not a typical member of the bourgeoisie, but a nobleman reduced to these ranks. Frank refrains from drawing his main character from established middle class ranks, for it was they who had in part enabled Hitler to rise to power in the first place. He therefore creates in Ludwig an ideal of the bourgeois class as it *should* be in contrast to Steiger, who represents this class as it is. In showing this servant figure as a venerator of rank and authority, powerless to stand on his own feet, seeking security in the comforting arms of a benevolent protector, Frank exposes a social frame of mind extending beyond Steiger and having its roots in a class that had failed to put into practice the democratic principles upon which the Republic was founded.

The three delegates of the Republic, who shamefully present Ludwig's father with his deposition papers in 1918, are a case in point:

> Nach kaum zehn Minuten war der Staatsakt vorbei. Die drei Herren wandelten genierten Schrittes über den menschenleeren Schlossplatz. Dann blieben sie stehen. Der in der Mitte tastete in seiner Mappe umher, als fürchte er etwas verloren zu

haben, nahm dann ein Papier hervor, entfaltete es, und alle drei steckten die Köpfe zusammen und blickten hinein. Es war dem zehnjährigen Prinzen auf seinem Balkon klar, dass dies der unterzeichnete Thronverzicht war (19-20).

Here Frank is not unmasking the delusions of an outmoded aristocracy, but those of a democracy which falters in its self-assurance. With the Republic's downfall in 1933, Frank apparently could salvage little that was honorable from the bourgeoisie itself. The Republic had failed to thwart Hitler's climb to power, and it is its representative members that he intends to expose. In drawing on an outsider so to speak, a prince who willingly strips himself of title and rank, who commits himself to the principle of justice and humanity at personal risk, who makes countless sacrifices to help others, Frank sets up an image of a democratic people as he conceives it ought to be.

This characterization becomes problematic when Ludwig and Steiger are joined together in exile. Even as a youth in Germany, Ludwig had made it clear to his tutor that privileges of rank no longer played a role in his life. In exile he looks upon Steiger as simply a friend and companion whose daring escape from a concentration camp he had planned out of humane motives when he stole back to Germany from Prague under an assumed name. But Steiger fails to get the picture. Experiences in a concentration camp and then in exile in no way induce a changed outlook. He continues to regard his rescuer as the great protector, the concerned noble who never abandons his subjects. Ludwig recognizes the absurdity of such behavior, but lacks an understanding of the serious political consequences that could result from this benign attitude. Unable to enlighten his old teacher, he simply humors him. The conflicting outlooks contained in the lord-servant dualism never really interact. Lacking the critical consciousness of the *born* democratic humanist, Ludwig cannot rationalize his principle of humanity.

Consequently, Steiger demonstrates no awareness of the reality of his changed existence. Expatriation, lack of passport, material hardship—these circumstances have no effect on him as long as his prince is at his side. While Ludwig provides for the daily necessities by engaging his services as a language instructor, Steiger remains the dutiful servant who takes it for granted that his needs will be met by his lord. He still addresses Ludwig in the third person; he is ashamed of dining with his prince at the same table; and he becomes jealous when Ludwig spends an undue amount of time with Ruth, because he fears in this union a severance of the close relationship between lord and servant. Steiger's home becomes a dream world in which he envisions his prince as the infallible overseer:

> Eine kindliche Dienstbereitschaft war in seinem Wesen, zugleich etwas Zeremonielles. Und Ludwig fühlte, dass er ihn da nicht beirren dürfe. Steiger setzte sich sogar widerstrebend an den

Tisch, den er gedeckt hatte. Er wäre lieber hinter Ludwigs Stuhl stehen geblieben, als herzoglicher Obermundschenk und Truchsess. Es war eine letzte Zuflucht für seine Träume. Wie er einst den Umgang mit dem jungen Prinzchen nie hatte zur Selbstverständlichkeit werden lassen, so brachte er es jetzt fertig, im Zusammenleben auf ein paar Quadratfuss Raum die Distanz zu wahren. In seinem mitgenommenen Geist hatte sich ein Programm und eine Legende gebildet: die Legende vom vertriebenen Fürsten, dem nur ein einziger treuer Diener noch folgt, um ihm Ehren und Hof zu ersetzen (288).

Frank gives as a possible reason for Steiger's retreat from reality the horrors of the concentration camp and the misery of exile itself. At the British Ministry of Interior, where Ludwig intercedes on his friend's behalf, the impression is conveyed that Steiger's sense of servitude might illustrate a psychological condition stemming from his traumatic experiences: "Steiger sass daneben, mit jenem Ausdruck ergebener Gläubigkeit, der Ludwig teils rührte teils mit einer unbestimmten Reue erfüllte. Ihm war klar geworden, dass der Freund unter den Schlägen seiner Erlebnisse Schaden genommen hatte" (277). Further on, reference is made to "die Vereinfachung bis zum Kindlichen, die unterm Druck der Erlebnisse mit ihm vorgegangen war" (297).

Admittedly, such harrowing experiences could have produced these regressive symptoms. The state of dejection, for example, to which Rotteck, Ludwig's former university professor, has resigned himself in Prague does intimate a psychological reaction to an abrupt change of existence. Viewing Steiger's situation on a broader scale, however, one spanning the political and social turmoil of the Weimar Republic, we find that he had repeatedly sought solace in the old system when present conditions became too uncomfortable. An authority on the genealogy of the Saxon Dynasty, he had always entertained notions about the Camburg House one day achieving a place in history equal to that of the Habsburgs and Hohenzollerns. In his opinion, the establishment of the Republic merely presented an undesirable obstacle to a form of rule which he thought to be inevitable. To the young prince he exclaims: "Meinen Sie, diese deutsche Republik werde ewig stehen—eine Republik, die selber nicht wagt, sich bei Namen zu nennen, eine Republik ohne Mut, ohne Glanz, ohne wirklichen Drang zur Gerechtigkeit. Die Leute pfeifen ja in den Versammlungen, wenn man ihre Staatsform erwähnt" (28). Steiger's reverence for the old order reaches its climax in a conspiracy entered into with other loyal monarchists to overthrow Hitler's regime. More out of sympathy for the desire of the conspirators to rid Germany of the present threat than for the monarchy they wished to see reinstated afterwards, Ludwig agrees to act as a symbolic inspiration to those who would bring about the coup d'état. On this and other occasions throughout the novel he asserts his aristocratic rank for reasons of expediency only. He does not adhere in principle to the reestablishment of a political structure which he knows to be passé.

The question to be raised is: What kind of future does Frank perceive in this manner of portrayal? At the end of the novel we are left with an unresolved antithesis between two varying mentalities—a democratic and a monarchistic one. Does the future lie with the Ludwigs or the Steigers? Obviously Frank places his faith in the former. This bourgeois prince represents for him the democratic ideals of a people, a nation that has rid itself of stagnant philistinism, of smug conventionality and political lassitude. Yet, where Frank is adept at pointing out the socio-political fallacies of his society, he fails to confront this picture with a realistic counterproposal. Ludwig remains the extreme individualist throughout the work. Despite his self-sacrifice and acts of humanity, he stands out as a figure who, representing neither the aristocracy nor the bourgeoisie, admits of no social classification. By depicting him as an exemplary figure in way of criticism against the reaction of certain members of the intelligentsia, Frank in effect creates his own escape mechanism and accordingly betrays an attitude which in itself stands apart from reality. His sympathies very likely do not lie with the dispirited Rotteck, whom he casts as a contrast figure to Ludwig. In spite of the prince's concern for the injustice suffered by others, Frank still places him on a pedestal, showing him as a paragon of virtue who appears self-secure in the knowledge of his own humanity.

Indeed, the abstract cliché—"preservation of German spirit and culture"—that is frequently heard in conjunction with literature in exile seems most appropriate in Frank's case. For it takes on such humanistic connotations in *Der Reisepass* that one is inclined to view the author's hero in the framework of Germany's idealistic heritage. Ludwig's initial entrance into exile amounts to nothing but an incredible contrivance on Frank's part to involve his hero in a classical conflict between necessity and freedom, duty and inclination. Ludwig is escorted by the Gestapo to the Czech border, where he is set free with the understanding that his return will mean execution for his fellow conspirators. The following state of exile in Prague thus becomes an individual moral issue. A conflict develops in Ludwig whereby he must choose between action and passivity. Frank does not perceive Ludwig's exile as a political arena from which he could use the freedom allotted him in purposeful anti-Nazi activity. This is clearly evidenced by his unwillingness to align himself with the emigrant newspaper, *Das freie Wort*. He approaches Breisach, the editor, not to provide him with needed information about the truth of Fascist brutality, but to enlist his aid in securing a falsified passport for his return to Germany. The freedom Ludwig senses in exile, tantamount to non-activity, conflicts with his sense of betrayal of those who still remain imprisoned:

> Andere hatten für ihn geplant und gehandelt. Andere waren für ihn ereilt worden. Ihm schnürten Fesseln die Hände zusammen. Aber er würde diese Fesseln zerreissen. Er hatte denen, die für ihn litten, Hilfe zu bringen oder für sie unterzugehen.

. . . Jetzt war er zu nichts Anderem mehr auf der Welt. Wohin er um sich blickte, er ersah für sich keine mögliche Existenzform. Aber am unmöglichsten erschien dies: irgendwo unterzukommen und im Warmen zu vegetieren, während jene Männer Qualen ausstanden und vielleicht starben (183).

To intensify the antagonism between freedom and necessity, Frank introduces the element of guilt incurred by Ludwig through his passionate relationship with Rotteck's wife, Susanna. Now he has no other alternative but to return to Germany in order to atone for his weakness, his flaw: "Er konnte mit einer Tat bezahlen. Eine Tat wurde von ihm gefordert, Einsatz seines Lebens zum klaren, fest umrissenen Zweck" (203). By arranging for Steiger's escape (the other conspirators had already been released through the intervention of "private" contacts in the Regime), Ludwig executes his obligation to humanity, a daring act requiring personal courage and self-sacrifice, but completely removed from the political scene. Ludwig's return to Germany is not undertaken as an anti-Fascist venture. No ideological significance is attached to it. Frank's reason for devising this plan arises in the final analysis from a desire to heighten the image of his hero as a humanitarian, one who, needless to say, is wanting in the social conscience required to concretize this abstraction.

We gain a deeper understanding into Frank's penchant for drawing model characters when we consider his view of history, as reflected through Ludwig's research on the life and work of the Spanish painter, Goya. Nothing against the portrayal of great historical personalities. But when their sufferings, sorrows, and conflicts are viewed as singular and outstanding, as something to be appreciated and relived, then it becomes apparent how rooted Frank is in the historicity of the nineteenth century. Ludwig's art history professor, Johannes Rotteck, an expert on portraiture, stands in decided contrast to Steiger, the idealistic historian on dynastic genealogy, by virtue of his solely empirical approach to his subject matter. Ludwig's admiration for Rotteck's monumental "Geschichte des Portraits in Europa" sets the positivistic tone he will initially employ in his study of Goya:

Ein ungeheures Tatsachenwissen war hier mit römischer Klarheit geordnet. Die Meister lebten, und die sie dargestellt hatten, lebten auch. Ein leerer Name stand nirgends. Nirgens war deklamiert, nirgends fand sich ein bequemer Gemeinplatz, nirgends wurde, nach der Art so vieler neudeutscher Gelehrten, feierlich die Wolke umarmt. Alles war Substanz, Wirklichkeit, Fleisch und Leben. Ein illusionsloser Menschenbetrachter redete hier. Ihm war Kunst nicht eine losgelöste, zu Häupten schwebende Erscheinung, zu der man emporgedrehten Auges aufschaut, sie war Daseinsextrakt, Aufschrei, Trost und Nahrung. Jedes seiner Kapitel malte solid eine neue Phase der europäischen Gesellschaft. Man wusste, wie in jedem Jahrhundert in Paris, Siena oder Ulm die Menschen sich fortgebracht, wie sie geliebt, wie sie einander geehrt oder verfolgt hatten. Alles

erschien so simpel, so selbstverständlich, man glaubte, schloss man das Buch, es nacherzählen zu können (47-48).

The drawback to Rotteck's seemingly sound scrutiny of historical events and personages does not become evident until he reaches exile. Here the problems implicit in a view of history that is inclined to cyclical analysis come to light. The positivist, who rejects speculative, abstract suppositions, perceives history in terms of linear development as opposed to dynamic process. In Rotteck's case, this non-idealistic, factual outlook has blinded him towards the existence of change arising from conflicting forces in history. Because he envisions the reigning barbarism in Germany as a modern rendition of the fall of Rome, a new Dark Ages will perforce emerge, echoing in a period of renewed primitivism:

Werden sie kommen, die anderen Zeiten? Nicht für uns, Ludwig. Machen wir uns doch nichts vor. Dieser Einbruch der Werwölfe und Stinktiere ist keine Episode. Ganz so wie wir haben Andere gesessen, als Rom sank, vor einem Jahrtausend und einem halben. In ihren schönen Säulenhöfen haben sie gesessen . . . und haben darauf gewartet, dass die Herren Germanen kämen und ihre Bibliotheken und Bäder zerschlügen. Und sie wussten, . . . dass nun die Finsternis kam, dunkle Jahrhunderte, dass noch die Kindeskinder ihrer Kindeskinder das Licht nicht mehr sehen würden (143-44).

Rotteck's resigned outlook no doubt can be attributed in part to the uprootedness of exile, but more importantly it is symptomatic of a static assessment of man, which sees historical epochs in recurring terms of light and darkness, humanity and barbarism.

The author's solution to the problem of Rotteck is to take the quixotic approach to history, as is shown through the exemplary figure of Ludwig. This young art historian, whose empirical method of research is modelled after that of his mentor, takes a similar view to history as his starting point. He draws a parallel between the gruesome images of war in Goya's "Desastres de la Guerra" and the present terror in Germany. The unrelenting cyclical nature of history is uttered time and again in such expressions as: "Ist dies Napoleons Zeit, Spanien, das Gemäuer vor dem schwarzen Himmel Madrid? Nichts braucht man zu wissen. Denn es ist ewig das Selbe" (305); "Vor Verwüstung und schnöder Untat, die der Bestialismus wallte und organisierte und anpries—damals und heute und immer" (306); "Es war eine ewige Gegenwart" (307); "Geschichte wiederholt sich nicht so genau. Wohl aber wiederholt sich Tyrannei und ihr Schicksal" (308); "Ewig zahlt das Volk. Ewig baumeln Verstümmelte an den Bäumen, ewig schwingt ein rasender Bauer das Beil, ewig ziehen am Strick die zum Tod Bestimmten über die Heide" (308). Ludwig's manner of viewing Goya provides us with a clue into Frank's own quixotic tendency in his general portrayal of the exile. It was stated earlier that the author does not share the pessimism and fatalism of the historian, Rotteck, who is inclined to interpret the Fascist reign of terror as just another inevitable unleashing of man's bestial instincts. Just as Ludwig enhances the image of Goya as a justification for transcending the turmoil of the period, so does Frank transcend a direct confrontation with the political realities of exile by creating *his* model hero.

Unlike his teacher, Ludwig overcomes the ugly reality of the moment by mythicizing the object of his study. He does not grow despondent over Goya's morbid depiction of historical events, as is the case with Rotteck upon describing the current reign of barbarism as being typical of a perpetual recurrence of the past. Rather he finds consolation in heightening the image of the man himself, in elevating Goya above the cruelties and horrors he saw about him and reproduced on canvas. Frank compensates for the present barbarization of the individual by constructing in Ludwig a supraindividual, who in turn exalts the exemplary personage in his study of Goya. As a consequence, we see the Spanish painter described as a "Weltherr" and "Jahrtausendgehirn" (308), a "Riesenfigur" (309), who acts as both tragic bearer and vanquisher of the misery of his age: "Da stand der Mann . . . an der Scheidung zweier Zeitalter, doppelgesichtig. Ein Gesicht nach der alten, heiteren Welt zugekehrt, sie schwelgerisch auskostend, in Bildern von klarem Glanz ihr zärtlichster Sohn. Das andere einer neuen Zeit zugewendet, der der Massen, Maschinen, keuchenden Kämpfe. Ganz für sich stand er da, inmitten einer Generation, die in seiner Kunst nur das Flache und Schwache hervorbrachte. Er spannte seine Arme aus über zwei Jahrhunderte Malerei" (309).

The image of the pre-eminent personality who, by his greatness and distinction, symbolizes a source of consolation to a suffering world is also evoked in the immediate setting of the novel. Ludwig's admiration for the unique historical person reverts back to his own situation in exile, where he seeks out actual individuals who reflect the detached nobility of an impeccable humanity. Frank's avoidance of a representative portrayal of exile, which, if undertaken realistically, could only deal with the individual as a product of an impersonal group experience, becomes clear when we observe that his ideal of humanity is magnified almost ad infinitum. The author is so intent on non-commitment to any kind of political opposition in exile, whether it be programmatic or liberal, that he overlooks greatly divergent ideologies for the sake of a common abstract principle of humanity. That Masaryk was a Social Democrat and George V a monarch seems to be of little significance to the author. It is their irreproachable humanity that counts, not the political structure they represent. Frank's historicity takes on such ahistorical connotations that these two exemplary figureheads appear in the guise of timeless overlords, whom history always manages to produce during periods of strife and turmoil.

Frank's artistic design in exile is to superimpose upon the political and social disruption of the time an atmosphere of order and harmony, to preserve those ideals of humanity and decency that are yet unspoiled by the prevailing wave of injustice. He is not content with asserting his unpolitical position in the ideal figure of his hero alone. He even transcends this ideal, picturing in the two detached statesmen model individuals to whom even the idealized Ludwig aspires.

The prince's reverence for Masaryk reflects the same tendency to escapism as was noted in his description of Goya earlier: "Ein alter Professor und Philosoph, klar, wahrhaftig und weise, aller Phrase und Pose mit Heiterkeit fern, Gründer, Schutzpatron, beinahe Gott dieses Staats, zu höchster Geltung aufgestiegen ohne die Menschlichkeit je zu verletzen, ein Blickpunkt und Trost für alle, die in einer Epoche der maulvollen Roheit und des Völkerbetrugs vor Ekel verzweifelten" (148). The consoling figure of the recently deceased George V is treated in no less reverent terms: "Ein Pfeiler, an dem sich der grobe Eigennutz bricht. . . . Ein Richtpunkt. Ein Blickpunkt. Einfach ein Mensch, auf den man Vertrauen setzt. . . . Ein vornehmer Herr, der sich genau an der Stelle hält, wo die Geschichte ihn haben will. . . . Ein britischer Edelmann. Was eigentlich konnte er einer Epoche bedeuten, die in Wehen und Krankheiten kreiste und zuckte!" (273-74) Ludwig sums up his laudation by acclaiming both as a "Sinnbild der Menschenwürde" (275).

In the last analysis, the contradistinctive relationship that Frank purports to show in Ludwig and Steiger is really not so contrastive after all. Frank does succeed in presenting a cogent picture of the "Hoheitsmentalität" of the bourgeois officialdom during the 1920's and in exile. Yet, in trying to offset this submissive mentality by one that demonstrates the true values of humanity, he creates in effect a hero who is just as divorced from reality as his servant-tutor. Frank takes such an extremely individualistic position in the novel that he loses sight of the basic social functionality of the individual. The very fact that he chooses an aristocrat as his model of humanity—however *verbürgerlicht* he may appear—intimates a tendency to picture the exceptional, the extraordinary, the "noble" in man. In actuality, the criticism that Frank levels against the regressive attitudes of the Steigers falls back upon himself when he elevates his model figure above the political-social turmoil of the period. One could even go so far as to say that Frank, however unintentionally, entertains a certain admiration for the noblesse oblige, that very frame of mind criticized in Steiger. Throughout the novel Ludwig carries the smaragd that his mother had given him as a child. This precious stone, engraved with the coat of arms of Ludwig's dynastic heritage, is a symbol of a noble blood line which serves to enhance the image Frank creates in his hero. That Ludwig sells the stone at the end to obtain money for his beloved's operation does not signify a renunciation of his cherished memories. It is an act of sheer necessity and points once again to the heightened image of the exemplary humanitarian.

The one episode illustrating most vividly Frank's desire to create a world of peace and harmony takes place in the reading room of the British Museum, where Ludwig is diligently pursuing his studies. Both Klaus Mann[5] and Ludwig Marcuse[6] have acknowledged the significance of this scene, although their sympathetic appraisal of its idyllic Biedermeier setting is wanting somewhat in objectivity. In this "totenstille Halle" (302) Frank has established a place of refuge for the many emigrants who find in the written word a source of solace and inner strength, a haven that shelters them from the discomforting realities outside: "Dreihundert Leser mochten anwesend sein, einer nahe dem andern an den langen Tischen, aber durch Mauern des Schweigens voneinander abgeschieden, jeder in seiner gesonderten Welt" (302). This picture of philological tranquility, where no sound is heard "vom rasselnden Atem der Millionen draussen" (300), where Ludwig immerses himself "in den hundertsprachigen Schächten des Geistes" (301), reveals an artistic stance that treats the emigrant scene as a sanctuary in which the cultural treasures of the past and individual humanity can be nurtured unhampered by the current perverters of this tradition.

NOTES

[1] Mrs. Liesl Frank-Lustig believes this character might have been modelled after the Prince of Hesse, who had studied art history in Munich (personal letter dated October 19, 1972). As we shall see, Frank's penchant for drawing portraiture has a direct bearing on the idealized characterization of the hero.

[2] "Fünf Blicke auf Deutschland," *Das Wort,* 7 (1937), 84-85.

[3] "Der Reisepass," *Das Neue Tagebuch,* 23 (1937), 547.

[4] Bruno Frank, *Der Reisepass* (Amsterdam, 1937), p. 107. Subsequent references to the novel appear parenthetically in the text by page number.

[5] "Der Reisepass," 547.

[6] "Fünf Blicke auf Deutschland," 85.

Erich A. Frey (essay date 1982)

SOURCE: "Thomas Mann and His Friends before the Tolan Committee (1942)," in *Exile: The Writer's Experience,* edited by John M. Spalek and Robert F. Bell, The University of North Carolina Press, 1982, pp. 203-17.

[*In the following essay, Frey discusses Frank's and Thomas Mann's testimony before the Tolan Committee in 1942, when the United States government established "military areas" to intern "suspicious persons," usually of foreign descent. A transcript of the testimony is included.*]

Thomas Mann's plea before the "Select Committee Investigating National Defense Migration, U.S. House of Representatives" stands out as a significant example of his readiness to be a spokesman and advocate for all anti-Nazi refugees in the United States during World War II. We are referring here to Mann's testimony during a hearing of that committee (known as the "Tolan Committee" after its chairman, Representative John H. Tolan), which met in the State Building in Los Angeles on 6 and 7 March 1942.[1]

The Tolan Committee hearings, which took place in Los Angeles and other cities along the West Coast,[2] were a direct result of Executive Order No. 9066, signed by President Roosevelt on 19 February 1942, authorizing the Secretary of War or his military designate to establish "military areas" and to exclude or intern any suspicious persons, that is, "enemy aliens."[3] This order, which the president (who usually favored the émigrés) had issued under pressure from the military, some California members of Congress, and the California press, caused great unrest among the German refugees. It brought about all the more uneasiness because it involved stricter registration, evening curfews, and the threat of evacuation from the West Coast. Last but not least, the order recalled feelings of insecurity and harassment in the minds of many weary refugees who had escaped from Nazi persecution a short time before.

In a telegram to Roosevelt dated several days before the president's order, Thomas Mann had already initiated his plea for the pro-American émigrés from Germany and Italy.[4] Mann happened to be exempt from the effects of this order by virtue of his status as a Czechoslovakian citizen, but the "public handling" ("öffentliche Handhabung") of the security measures did not please him one bit. In fact, he wrote to his friend Agnes Meyer, the influential publisher of the *Washington Post:* "[This handling] causes me real concern on America's account. The California press is agitating in an atrocious manner, and there are restaurants around here that are beginning to display signs saying 'enemy aliens keep out'—which is alarmingly reminiscent of 'non-Aryans keep out.'"[5] The subsequently published directives of the overzealous military commander on the West Coast, General J. L. DeWill, bear out the fact that Mann's concern was indeed justified. Before the hearings of the Tolan Committee took place, DeWitt had made preparations to evacuate all German, Italian, and Japanese "enemy aliens," although the German and Italian aliens ranked as classes three and four (behind Japanese and Americans of Japanese descent).[6] It also seems significant that the general's chief of civilian staff and coordinator concerned with the evacuation problems, Mr. Tom Clark of San Francisco, was invited to appear as a witness in Los Angeles on the very same day that the spokesmen for the German, Italian, and Japanese "enemy aliens" were making their pleas before the same committee.[7]

The invitation extended to Thomas Mann and his friend Bruno Frank was undoubtedly connected with the preceding telegram to Roosevelt, which had been drafted by Thomas Mann and cosigned by Bruno Frank, Bruno Walter, Einstein, Borgese, Sforza, and Toscanini. The Tolan Committee, incidentally, was independent of the military and was charged by Congress with probing the effect of the evacuation order on refugees from the Axis countries, based upon the evidence of the depositions made during its hearings. Because the committee was empowered to forward the proposals resulting from the hearings directly to the Executive in Washington, it may be concluded that the pleas of Thomas Mann and his associates contributed substantially to preventing the evacuation of the Germans living in California.

The chief argument of Mann's deposition, which was delivered in English during the committee's morning session on 7 March 1942, lay in the assertion that the categorical and arbitrary evacuation of all German exiles, even if it should later be revoked, was not only unjust and demoralizing for those concerned, but also that America's own moral fiber would necessarily suffer thereby.

Because the original wording of Thomas Mann's testimony has remained practically unknown and is still unlisted in previous Thomas Mann bibliographies, the full text of his and Frank's testimony is made available [later in] this article. The committee record shows clearly that the long middle part of Mann's deposition was previously prepared and that Mann read his remarks from a manuscript. The German draft of that middle part, like so many German drafts of his English letters, seems to have been lost, although one paragraph of the original draft is preserved in Thomas Mann's letter of 27 March 1942 to Ludwig Marcuse.[8] It is in this middle part that Mann informs the committee members about the telegram that he and his prominent fellow émigrés had sent to President Roosevelt in February.

Thomas Mann seems to have been quite pleased by his appearance before the Tolan Committee. He wrote to Marcuse two weeks later: "I would like to believe that the bark will prove to be worse than the bite. We have warned most strongly against sweeping measures at the outset, pointing out that they can do a great deal of irreparable harm."[9] He was particularly impressed with the receptiveness of the committee members, as can be seen from the enthusiastic remarks to his confidante Agnes Meyer: "The hearings yesterday in Los Angeles before the Washington Committee were extremely interesting. They represented a regular public court session and one of the most heartwarming American experiences since I came here."[10]

An interesting sidelight is his evaluation of Frank's testimony. Mann writes of it to Mrs. Meyer with characteristic irony: "Frank was unfortunately too emphatic and *larmoyant*, but the congressmen nevertheless seemed to enjoy the hors d'oeuvre very much."[11]

Besides Mann and Frank, two other German-born witnesses pleaded the cause of their fellow refugees before the Tolan Committee during the Los Angeles hearings on 7 March 1942. One of them was Felix Guggenheim, representing the Jewish Club of 1933, Inc., Los Angeles. He explained to the committee the British treatment of "enemy aliens," which he considered exemplary, and also submitted a prepared statement on behalf of the German-born "anti-Nazi refugees" (*Hearings,* pp. 11733-737). The other witness was Hans F. Schwarzer, who characterized himself as "a simple example of a simple citizen" and described his personal fate as a refugee from Hitlerism, who was now trying "in every way to get Americanized" (*Hearings,* pp. 11806-807).

A third émigré writer, Lion Feuchtwanger, although he did not give evidence in person, submitted a written statement to the Tolan Committee while it was holding its hearings in Los Angeles. Feuchtwanger's statement, dated 5 March 1942, was accepted for the record as "Exhibit 22." Having been classified as an enemy alien upon his arrival in the United States, he now felt that he was "menaced [sic] to be removed from [his] home in West Los Angeles" (*Hearings,* p. 11879). His plea strikes a primarily personal tone, recounting his early fight against Nazism, his close connections with government leaders of England, France, and the Soviet Union, and the unfair treatment accorded him by the Vichy regime in France. However, he ended his appeal for special consideration by pleading for "almost all of those Germans who have immigrated into the United States since 1933 and were not yet able to acquire their American citizenship," and by suggesting three major exemption categories that included virtually all of the above-mentioned German immigrants (*Hearings,* p. 11880). (See below, pp. 215-17.)

With so many representative spokesmen and prominent personalities having such political weight as Thomas Mann and his friends, the American government and the public in general took an increasingly sympathetic position toward German aliens during the weeks following the Los Angeles hearings. Several scholars who have reexamined the entire "War Relocation" program of those years repeatedly stress the effectiveness of the "politically important leaders of German and Italian descent" who "pleaded for the aliens of their nationality," and they cite this as one of the main reasons why these two ethnic groups were spared from evacuation.[12]

Aside from the racial discrimination against Asians, which undoubtedly also played a role, a research report mentions the following point in conclusion: "The Japanese aliens [in contrast to the German and the Italian aliens] had no mature leaders of their ancestry in high political, social, and financial circles applying pressure."[13]

In the end, Japanese nationals and United States citizens of Japanese ancestry were the only population groups that found no positive responses from the Tolan Committee and other United States authorities and who were evacuated from the West Coast in 1942 under extremely discriminatory circumstances.

TESTIMONY OF DR. THOMAS MANN,
1550 SAN REMO DRIVE, PACIFIC PALISADES, CALIF.,
AND DR. BRUNO FRANK,
513 NORTH CAMDEN DRIVE, BEVERLY HILLS, CALIF.

MR. ARNOLD. Dr. Mann, you and Dr. Frank need, of course, no introduction, but for the record the committee would like to have you give your name, address, and occupation so that the record might be complete.

DR. MANN. My name is Thomas Mann. I am living now in Pacific Palisades, No. 1550 San Remo Drive.

MR. ARNOLD. Doctor, will you give us for the record your occupation and a little background?

DR. MANN. I am a writer, sir; author, novelist, essayist, and lecturer.

MR. ARNOLD. Are you a native American?

DR. MANN. No, sir. I was born in Germany. I lived a long time in Munich where I studied and married. I left Germany in the year 1933 just before Hitler came to power. Then I lived 5 years in Switzerland before I came over to America.

I came over to America first in the year 1934 for a short visit and I visited America each year after that. I came over to settle definitely in this country in the year 1938.

I followed my vocation of lecturing at the University of Princeton. I did that for two winters. It was only for 1 year first, but it was prolonged for the second year.

Then I made the acquaintanceship of California and came out here to settle. We have our home in Pacific Palisades.

MR. BENDER. Dr. Mann, I would like to ask you about the Munich conference, but I won't.

One of the questions which has come to our attention during our hearings in San Francisco, Portland, and Seattle, has been the effect of the evacuation order on refugees from Axis countries. We are interested in hearing from yourself and Dr. Frank your views and observations.

The committee would like to have you proceed in your own way, Dr. Mann, and then we will hear from Dr. Frank. We understand that you happen to be a Czech.

DR. MANN. Yes.

MR. BENDER. And are not yourself affected by the recent alien-control regulation.

DR. MANN. Correct.

MR. BENDER. Would you proceed in your own way.

DR. MANN. Thank you very much.

I really feel highly honored to have the opportunity to take part in this meeting, the subject of which has been close to my heart since the problem arose. It is close to my heart not only because it is of so vital, moral, and material importance for the people it concerns, but also because only a fair solution would be worthy of this great Nation which is fighting for freedom and human dignity.

I would like to add that, certainly, the behavior of a war-waging nation against her emigrees has something to do with the good fighting spirit of that nation. It is the frightening example of France I had in mind. A nation which seeks and enjoys victory over the most intimate and most natural enemies does not seem to be in the happiest psychological condition to meet these enemies.

I realize, of course, that in times of crisis no natural inclination to generosity and kindness can be allowed to imperil the safety of the country, and certainly it is not easy to find a general solution which does justice to both sides, the refugees and the interests of the country at war. As a matter of fact, we have to face an absolutely paradoxical situation, such as perhaps never existed before. We have to deal with people who by their birth and descent, if their case is treated mechanically, fall under the category of "enemy aliens," but who are in fact the most passionate adversaries of the European governments this country is at war with, and who left their native lands in protest against the political systems ruling there, or were forced to leave it. Most of them lost the citizenship of their original countries, and even formally cannot be regarded as nationals of a country with which they do not have the slightest connection. So in this war, the idea and characteristic of "enemy alien" has lost its logical justification in the case of the German and Italian emigrees.

Perhaps it is not superfluous to add that I, personally, am not affected for the reason that when I was deprived of my German citizenship, President Benes of Czechoslovakia was generous enough to make me a Czech citizen; so I am a friendly alien, even technically, but only by chance. And I have imagination enough to understand the feelings of these victims of national socialism and fascism who were seeking refuge and freedom to breathe in this great democracy, and would be only too happy to do their share in the work of defense, but now find themselves under suspicion and subjected to special regulations which, for many of them, would mean a deadly catastrophe, the collapse of their newly and painfully rebuilt existence. For that reason, just some weeks ago I decided to join a few prominent emigrants from Italy and Germany in sending a telegram to the President of the United States, in which we expressed the same feelings and ideas I am trying to develop today. I give you the names of the signers of this telegram; they were the Italians, Arturo Toscanini, Count Carlo Sforza, and Professor Borgese, and the Germans, Bruno Walter, Albert Einstein, my friend Dr. Frank, and myself. With the exception of Toscanini, all these men are either already American citizens or friendly aliens, but all of them felt obligated to act for their countrymen, and to ask the President to bring about, in some way, a clear and practical distinction between potential fifth columnists and people who are the victims and proven opponents of the powers with which America is at war today.

I really do not feel that the difficulties for establishing such a distinction are insurmountable. Other groups of aliens like the Austrians, Czechs, and so on, have already been excepted. It is certainly not my intention to say anything against the loyalty of these groups, but so much may be said that in no other group so many reasons speak for a passionate desire for Hitler's defeat, as in the case of German and Italian refugees. So I think that where it can be incontestably proven that a person is a refugee, a victim of Nazi oppression, an exception should be made, and the questionnaire of the registration form has already given, by its point 15, the authorities the necessary material for clarification. Moreover, there can be no doubt that the Federal Bureau of Investigation has carefully observed all aliens for quite some time, and has proven to be very well informed about their behavior and intentions. Whoever is individually suspicious will doubtless be taken care of, and it should not be difficult to find out all cases needing clarification. In my opinion it would be worth while to investigate a number of cases, which certainly would not be very considerable, instead of taking radical measures against the entirety of the refugees. All of us know that the burning problem on the west coast is the question of the Japanese. It would be a great misfortune if the regulations, perhaps necessary in their case—it is not my business to talk about the Japanese problem—would be applied to the German and Italian refugees, even with the intention of revising single cases later. For, as I have already mentioned, in many cases irreparable harm would be done to perfectly harmless and loyal persons. I think this should and could be avoided, and I am certain that other members of this meeting will make more concrete and practical propositions. In speaking for the refugees it is not only their interests I am visualizing. Every day it becomes more urgent that all available forces be put into the service of the country, and there are certainly many of the refugees who instead of becoming a burden to themselves and the country could be of valuable help in the struggle until victory.

MR. BENDER. Doctor, I am appreciating that your position is rather delicate by virtue of your Czech citizenship. I would like to ask you a number of questions and if you desire to answer all right, and if not it will be perfectly all right.

Are you acquainted personally with a Dr. Fritz Baum?

DR. MANN. No; I don't know him.

MR. BENDER. Who is the husband of the daughter of Albert J. Berridge?

DR. MANN. Sorry; I don't know.

MR. BENDER. Are you acquainted personally at all with Dr. Frank Zigmund, who is a scientist and inventor? He is a Czech citizen.

DR. MANN. It seems to me that I remember the name but surely I never met him.

MR. BENDER. Do you know the Czech language, Doctor?

DR. MANN. No; I don't.

MR. BENDER. In regard to this question of alien enemies, your impression is that everybody who is labeled that way is not necessarily an enemy?

DR. MANN. No; surely not.

MR. BENDER. And you believe, from your observation, that possibly we might have additional facilities for handling that problem?

DR. MANN. I think so.

MR. BENDER. In expediting the just treatment of these cases?

DR. MANN. Yes; I think so. I am sure that some way will be found.

MR. BENDER. You believe that there are many alleged enemy aliens incarcerated in detention places that might be of service in this war effort in the event that this could be expedited?

DR. MANN. That is very probable; yes.

MR. BENDER. What percentage of the Jewish refugees are classified as enemy aliens? For example, from Germany, Czechoslovakia, Rumania, and other places.

DR. MANN. What percentage?

MR. BENDER. What percentage of them?

DR. MANN. Of Jewish descent?

MR. BENDER. Yes; that are now being held by the United States Government who might be extremely useful in this war effort in the event of such expediting?

Dr. Frank, would you care to answer that question?

DR. FRANK. Well, perhaps I can.

MR. BENDER. Doctor, before you speak, I wish you would identify yourself. It is the committee's understanding that you are an officer of a refugee organization and are deeply concerned with alien-control rulings and that you have given the problem some thought.

DR. FRANK. Yes, I have.

MR. BENDER. First, for the record, will you identify yourself?

DR. FRANK. My name is Bruno Frank. I am by profession a writer. I live at 513 North Camden Drive in Beverly Hills.

MR. BENDER. Under what circumstances did you come to this country?

DR. FRANK. I left Germany in February 1933 the very first day after the legal government was overthrown, because very probably I wouldn't have survived the second day.

MR. BENDER. We would like to have you discuss the problem that we are particularly interested in at the moment, as it affects anti-Axis refugees who happen to be citizens of enemy countries.

DR. FRANK. Yes.

MR. BENDER. Will you proceed in your own way?

DR. FRANK. I am appearing before your committee, most thankful for the honor bestowed upon me, and let me add this at once, with a deep feeling of confidence:

Ever since the question of the evacuation of enemy aliens arose, there has been much consternation and fear among the German and Italian refugees out here. Many of them remember how, in a moment of frantic confusion, the Government of France treated the exiles, and they are afraid the same things might happen again. They already see their last and only hope gone.

May I frankly say that I personally could never share these dreads for a single moment. No, the victims of that hateful oppression won't be confounded with the oppressors. The bitterest and most consistent foes of nazi-ism and fascism won't be treated the same way as Nazis and Fascists themselves. Not in this country. Not under the great President of this Republic; not under its Congress, which is the strongest remaining fortress of constitutional freedom in the world; not under its Department of Justice, whose humane and enlightened utterances we have heard; and not, certainly not, under its military men. For these are not Prussian generals shaped after the pattern of some unspeakable "Fuehrer." They are American citizens proudly wearing their uniforms in defense of the same liberties, the loss of which has driven the refugees out of their homeland.

Thus my confidence was greatly strengthened when I saw the registration questionnaire, which so clearly indicated the intentions of the American Government. For here the fullest opportunity was offered to each German or Italian refugee for stating whether he left his country because of racial, religious, or political persecution and for naming such trustworthy persons who could vouch for his loyalty. This, I feel sure, was not done without good reason and purpose.

And there is still stronger evidence. Before the war, about a year and a half ago, a number of refugees, then trapped in defeated France, were saved by a magnanimous action of your Government. Among them were eminent statesmen, scientists, artists, writers. Under the auspices of the Presidential Advisory Committee, emergency visas were granted to them, and so they were, in the nick of time, snatched from immediate peril. How then could anyone imagine that these same people, who by the American Government were recognized as stanch democratic fighters against the Nazis, should now be branded as enemy aliens by the same Government?

But, sir, I am not so much concerned about those outstanding men, when, for instance, I read that Arturo Toscanini, before going from New York to Philadelphia in order to conduct a concert for the War Relief Fund or the Red Cross, has to ask for a permit because he is technically an enemy alien—then I think this an odd story. But I am not afraid for Signor Toscanini. Not much will happen to him. A great name, or even a well-known name, shields a man from hardship.

I am concerned about the so-called average man or woman, the little fellow who, after long and terrible sufferings, having lost situation, property, and, more often than not, those dearest to him, has finally found here a haven of rest and ultimate hope.

As it is always more instructive to give a concrete and living example than to speak in generalities, let me present to you, sir, an average case among many, nothing particularly striking, but typical for those refugees who now live in deadly fear to be branded as enemies.

In a family I happen to know they have a housemaid, a Jewish girl, kind, honest, hardworking. She alone of her kin has escaped from Germany, and it is her only longing to save and to bring to these shores her old parents she was forced to leave behind.

She comes from a small town in northern Germany, where 80 Jewish families have been living for more than 600 years. It was one of the oldest communities. Now the Nazis have uprooted these people, they have burnt their synagogue to the ground, trampled underfoot and swinishly soiled their sacred books, and desecrated their graveyard. Of the 80 families 3 are left. The rest have been exterminated, dispersed, or have been "removed to Poland." What this expression means, sir, you most certainly know. It was perfectly illustrated by those horrid pictures in last week's Life magazine, showing heaps of naked, emaciated corpses, piled upon one another like so much rubbish, ready to be flung into the common pit.

The two old people over there live under the constant threat of being carried away to that hell. Get the money for leaving the country—or else—they are told. Their daughter saves every penny she makes for their passage and for the bribes—for every single one of those Nazi gangs has to be bribed separately. But each time she offers her savings, she is told it is not enough. Transportation costs have gone up, and so have the bribes.

The girl knows what a life her parents have over there. They live in one windowless room. They are not allowed to go out in the daytime. They are not allowed to burn light at night. They are not allowed to use a phone or a radio, or to ride on the train, or to sit on a bench in the park.

Don't lose patience, writes the girl (or, rather, she wrote, because now of course she cannot write any more). Don't despair. One day my money will be enough. Then you will come here. This is heaven. One lives among friends here. I shall work for you, and you will live peaceful years.

Well, sir, what should she write now, if write she could? I am no longer among friends? I am branded as an enemy now, just as the beasts who are torturing you. Forget all about it. It was but a dream. Go to Poland, and die.

No, sir, she won't have to write thus. Not here.

Your Government, sir, is acutely aware of the gulf that separates the victims from the oppressors. They have already exempted different groups from being classified as enemy aliens, for instance, the Czechs and the Austrians. Nothing could be more justified, more appropriate. And though, when exempting these groups, the Attorney General most certainly realized that among the holders of Czech passports are those so-called Sudetens, who plotted with the Nazi aggressors; and that among the holders of Austrian passports are those Austrian Nazis who opened the gates of Vienna to Hitler. These facts, most fairly, were not considered a reason for impairing the rights of the enormous majority of loyal Austrians and Czechs. If any of the suspect elements were to be found in this country, the F.B.I., I am sure, would make short shrift of them.

But, sir, the only group where even such loathsome exceptions are most unlikely to be found, are the refugees from Germany, the very victims and proven opponents of Hitler.

Nearly all of them have been deprived of their nationality, either by individual decree or by groups. This means they have been outlawed and officially robbed of all they possessed. All of them, or next to all, have, under their oath, declared that they will sever allegiance to the debased land of their origin as soon as the American law will allow them to do so. There is absolutely no relationship left between them and the Nazis, none but bitter, implacable hatred.

Never, as far as my knowledge goes, has there been one single case of a refugee conspiring with or working for the enemy. In France there have been at least 20 times more refugees than in the United States. Not a single case has occurred. And the same goes for England.

In England, as I take it from the excellent information furnished by our expert in this matter, Dr. Felix Guggenheim, examination boards were set up, which exempted all genuine refugees from restrictions. However, when the Nazis came within 20 miles of England's shores, restrictions were suddenly tightened. But, under the very bombs of the aggressors, public opinion and the House of Commons protested violently and they did not give way until the position of the refugees had been restored. Today all these exiled scientists, physicians, workers, and industrialists enthusiastically contribute to the British war effort against the common foe. And in their registration certificates, in order to identify them as allies, these words are stamped, "Victim of Nazi oppression."

Now, as I pointed out, the number of refugees in this country is very much smaller. In the Los Angeles area, for instance, where accumulation is relatively dense, there are about 4,000—that is one-fifth of 1 percent of the population. The number of 4,000 individuals is equivalent to 1,000 or 1,200 family units. The task of investigating this number, and so to avoid the tragic consequences of wrong classification, would not be a heavy one.

For, since the registration, which in my opinion came as a godsend, the exact data about any single one of these cases are in the hands of the F.B.I. The vast majority of them will be clarified at once. There might be a few border cases, especially among gentile refugees who left Nazi Germany out of sheer horror and disgust, and who, being gentiles, were not honored by the Hitler regime with expatriation.

An examination board, sir, should be set up at once. I cannot presume to suggest how such a board should be composed. The only thing I feel allowed to propose is that, in an advisory capacity, one or several aliens with a sound knowledge of the matter, and enjoying the confidence of both the authorities and their fellow refugees, should be associated to it.

Pending final regulation, a licensing system could be established in the military zone No. 1, not in any contradiction but in fullest accordance with General DeWitt's proclamation. The spot zones, naturally, designated as such, would be excluded.

But now, sir, here comes my plea, and most ardent it is. Please don't delay. Take the anguish off the minds of those harassed people as soon as ever possible.

The idea has been proffered, I am told, that at first the refugees should be evacuated as enemy aliens, and that later on, by and by, individual readmission might be granted. Sir, that would never do. Such a procedure would spell disaster. Once removed, these people would be lost. The frail roots they have taken in this soil would be cut off. They would lose their jobs, their small businesses, and, most important of all, the friendly contact they have established with their American neighbors. Should they ever come back, perhaps after many months, they would be unwelcome strangers again, looked at with suspicion as people who once have been stigmatized and taken away as potential enemies.

Not all of them, sir, would have the strength for starting afresh, not many of them. They have been through too much. I don't want to dramatize, but I know that, if such steps were taken, there would be suicides before long.

May I add one final word, sir? I could imagine some people saying: All this may be true, but this is a world war. Our country faces the gravest crisis in her history. We are sending our husbands and sons to distant shores to fight and, maybe, to die. Why should we care for a handful of foreigners?

I don't know whether anybody in this country speaks like that. I'd rather think not. But, if so, this would be the answer:

These foreigners have fought against the same hideous foe as your boys. They still bear the scars on their bodies and souls. There is hardly anyone among them who has not lost relatives and friends by the same brutish hands. No group, by its hatred of evil and its love of freedom, could be closer united in spirit to the American soldier than these very people.

MR. BENDER. Doctor, is the United States Government making sufficient use of your services, and Dr. Mann, of yours, and your associates who were in similar positions or are in similar positions to yours? Is there anything that you could assist with further that we might suggest to the United States Government that they might call on you for additional services other than those which you have already been called upon to render?

DR. MANN. Well, I am only awaiting a call from the Government. I would be absolutely at the service of the government. At present my defense work is more or less personal because I am going over the country and lecturing in many cities about the problems of the war and of the coming peace. That is my moderate contribution to the public service.

MR. ARNOLD. Dr. Mann, I might say that in my district in Illinois, about one-third of my constituents are of German descent, mostly American citizens, but several of whom, prior to Pearl Harbor, were sympathetic, apparently, with Mr. Hitler. I might utilize your services this fall in the campaign.

MR. BENDER. Recognizing the condition that you speak of, Dr. Frank and Dr. Mann, do you not think that for one of these alleged enemy aliens or any of that group to be incarcerated in these immigration detention centers, or in any other place, even in their plight, is like Heaven, compared to the alleged freedom of their existence over in Europe under Axis domination?

DR. FRANK. Yes; I certainly would prefer the life in an American prison to free life in Germany or even in France today. This, I admit. But I don't wish it for them. They wouldn't survive.

MR. ARNOLD. Thank you very much, gentlemen. We appreciate having you come here before the committee. We will take a 2-minute recess. (*Hearings,* pp. 11725-732)

EXHIBIT 22. STATEMENT BY LION FEUCHTWANGER, 1744 MANDEVILLE CANYON, WEST LOS ANGELES, CALIFORNIA

March 5, 1942

According to the regulations I had to register as enemy alien, and now, being considered an enemy alien, I see myself menaced to be removed from my home in West Los Angeles. Therefore I beg to apply to the Honorable Chairman John H. Tolan and his congressional committee by making the following statement:

Since the year 1922 I have been fighting against the spread of naziism. I have written a number of novels dealing with the rise of the Nazis and the threat to civilization by naziism. I have published articles against the Nazis in the leading reviews, magazines, and newspapers all over the world. I broadcasted against the Nazis in the capitals of the world. My anti-Nazi books have been translated into many languages, their circulation amounts to millions of copies. My material is copiously used by the underground movement against fascism in Germany, in Italy, and even in Japan. Leading papers in this country, of England, of the Soviet Union, and even of China have repeatedly declared my literary activity an efficient weapon in the struggle against the Nazis. My plays and my pictures against the Nazis have been shown to millions of people. British pilots over Germany dropped leaflets quoting from my books. The Soviet Government spread my books and my films in order to spur the fighting spirit against Nazi Germany. The President of the French Republic before the collapse, English Cabinet Ministers, the Soviet Prime Minister, and members of the Government of this country asked to meet me and to hear my opinions on the struggle against naziism.

The Nazis themselves consider me as a very dangerous enemy, according to the public speeches of the German Minister of Propaganda. Hitler himself, many other Nazi leaders and Nazi papers attacked me. I was abused in numerous Nazi broadcasts. Thus, by the threat of the Nazis, I was forced to leave Germany in November 1932 already. My Berlin home was looted as one of the first in February 1933, my library was destroyed, my books were burnt, my fortune was confiscated. Albert Einstein and I were the first to be warned by the German Government that we would lose our German citizenship. In fact, on August 23, 1933, the German Government announced officially that I, together with twenty-odd others, had lost my German citizenship.

At the outbreak of this war I lived in France and was interned on account of general measures.

This fact aroused astonishment everywhere, especially in the United States, and many newspapers elaborated their reports on my internment with ironical comments on the French authorities. And the Nazis gloated over it in their newspapers and in their broadcasts. I just published a book on my experiences in France and how I was involved in French red tape. This book, *The Devil in France,* met with much interest in this country.

Should I definitely be classified as an enemy alien and removed from my home in West Los Angeles, the consequences would be rather critical for my future work. For months, I would have to interrupt my present work on an anti-Nazi novel, and my planned activities for anti-Nazi pictures would be frustrated. There is no question that the Nazis would be pleased if they heard about such measures against me.

Many others, probably almost all of those Germans who have immigrated into the United States since 1933 and were not yet able to acquire their American citizenship, are in a similar situation. Most of these people, however, have not only nothing in common with the political structure of today's Germany, but they are the natural enemies of the present German Government. Among three groups at least of these immigrants (since 1933) the percentage of potential Nazi sympathizers is by no means higher than among the average inhabitants of this country. Those groups of the so-called German enemy aliens could be classified rather easily:

(1) All those who lost their German citizenship by edict of the German Ministry of the Interior before September 3, 1939. These people are listed by name on lists published by the German Reichsanzeiger. Only such people are named in these lists who, according to the opinion of the present German Government, have impaired the interests of the German Reich. In every single case it could easily be demonstrated how far these people proved to be Nazi enemies.

(2) All those people who could not obtain a German passport so that they were forced to travel on other identification papers.

(3) All those who can produce actual evidence of their activities against the Nazis before America's entrance into the war.

Outstanding immigrants of German descent would gladly be willing to assist the American authorities in the possible inquiry of anti-Nazi activities.

It seems obvious that the reclassification of the so-called German enemy aliens according to such or similar principles would be fair and useful. (*Hearings,* pp. 11879-880)

NOTES

[1] Mann was accompanied by his friend Bruno Frank, who testified after Mann. The next witness was Felix Guggenheim. See *Hearings before the Select Committee Investigating National Defense Migration,* House of Representatives, 77th Cong., 2nd sess. Part 31, Los Angeles and San Francisco Hearings, 6, 7, and 12 March 1942: Problems of Evacuation of Enemy Aliens and Others from Prohibited Military Zones (Washington, D.C.: U.S. Government Printing Office, 1942), pp. 11725-732. Cited hereafter as *Hearings.*

[2] The Portland and Seattle hearings took place on 26-28 Feb. and 2 March 1942, respectively. Cf. *Hearings,* Parts 30-31.

[3] *WRA: A Story of Human Conservation,* by the U.S. Department of the Interior (Washington, D.C.: U.S. Government Printing Office, 1946), p. viii.

[4] Thomas Mann, *Briefe 1937-1947,* ed. Erika Mann (Frankfurt/M: S. Fischer, 1963), pp. 236-37. Cited as *Briefe.*

[5] Unpublished letter of Mann to Agnes Meyer, 16 Feb. 1942, Beinecke Library, Yale University. Permission to quote is kindly acknowledged. Mrs. Meyer and her husband, Mr. Eugene Meyer, were Mann's closest American friends, and they helped him establish many valuable contacts with high government officials in Washington. (English translations mine.)

[6] Edward H. Spicer et al., *Impounded People* (Tucson: University of Arizona Press, 1969), p. 37.

[7] *Hearings,* p. 11773.

[8] Mann to Marcuse: "Before the Tolan Committee I said: 'I am by no means thinking only of the emigrants; I am also thinking of the fighting spirit of this country. I have the terrible example of France in mind. A nation that takes pleasure in victories over its most intimate enemies does not seem in the best psychological condition to defeat those enemies!'" See *Briefe,* p. 251, and *Hearings,* p. 11726.

[9] *Briefe,* p. 252.

[10] *Briefe,* p. 247.

[11] *Briefe,* p. 247.

[12] Spicer, p. 38.

[13] Spicer, p. 38.

FURTHER READING

Criticism

"Fiction," *London Mercury* (January 1935): 301.
    Includes a brief review of *A Man Called Cervantes.*

Shanks, Edward. "Fiction," *London Mercury* 17, No. 102 (April 1928): 708.
    Includes a brief review of *The Days of the King.*

Sloan, Vandervoort. "*Twelve Thousand,* by Bruno Frank," *Drama Magazine* 18, No. 8 (May 1928): 249.
    A brief review of the New York production of the play.

The following source published by Gale contains additional coverage of Frank's life and career: *Dictionary of Literary Biography,* Vol. 118.

George Méliès

1861-1938

French film director, producer, scenarist, art director, and actor.

INTRODUCTION

Méliès is recognized as a progenitor of the cinematic arts. During a filmmaking career that lasted less than twenty years, Méliès directed and produced more than five hundred films   most of them less than ten-minutes in duration   of which less than two hundred still exist. Several of these films, including perhaps his best-known film *La voyage dans la lune* (1902; *A Trip to the Moon*), earned him an international reputation as a creator of imaginative films that increased film audiences's desire for cinematic storytelling rather than documentary features. Méliès is credited with pioneering film-editing and lighting techniques, special effects, and narrative story-telling, as well as building the first studio designed specifically for filmmaking. His films range from science fiction and fantasy entertainments to commercials and re-enacted newsreels. Méliès was awarded the Legion d'Honneur in 1931 for his contributions to film.

Biographical Information

Méliès was the third and youngest child of a highly successful Parisian shoe manufacturer. Méliès received a classical education at the Lycee Michelet, and fulfilled three-years's of military service and a year of business and English-language study in London. While in London, Méliès frequently attended magic shows at the Egyptian Hall, where he saw many of that era's most gifted illusionists. Upon his return to Paris, Méliès's father denied his request to study painting at l'Ecole des Beaux-Arts, and Méliès began work at his father's factory.

Méliès continued interest in theater and magic, however, resulted in his presence at the 1895 Lumiere Cinematographe moving picture presentation by the Lumiere brothers at the Grand Cafe. Méliès tried to purchase the film equipment from Antoine Lumiere for 10,000 francs, but the subsequent rejection of Méliès's bid   Lumiere claimed there was no financial future in moving pictures   motivated Méliès to travel to England, where he purchased a competing system and several films in 1896. That year, Méliès began making his first films, which he screened at the Theatre Robert-Houdin, a venue that featured magic performances. In 1986, Méliès also formed the Star Film Company and began construction of the world's first film studio at Montreuil, largely to counteract the negative effects of filming in natural light. In 1988, Méliès sold his share

of the family business to his older brothers in order to pursue full-time his careers as a filmmaker and magician, and to purchase and operate the Theatre Robert-Houdin.

From 1900 to 1912, Méliès was elected president of the International Convention of Cinematograph Editors, and in 1904 he began a forty-year term as president of the Chambre Syndicale de la Prestidigitation. Méliès's brother and film producer, Gaston, opened North American distribution and production facilities for the Star Film Company in 1903. Méliès's prodigious cinematic output and increasing audience appetites for fictional adventures on film ensured him success throughout the first decade of the 1900s. By 1913, however, Méliès abandoned filmmaking due to financial ruin caused by poor business decisions by the principals of Star Film Company and competition from other film studios. During World War I, the military melted many of Méliès's films for their silver content, and Méliès's burned many more when he lost Montreuil due to financial reasons. Following the war, Méliès also lost the Theatre Robert-Houdin, and he operated a candy and toy concession at the Montparnasse train station. The Mutuelle du Cinema paid for Méliès's tenure at the retirement home where he lived his remaining days.

Major Works

Méliès developed lighting, editing, and camera techniques that enabled him to realize the needs of his films. Such cinematic devices as stop-action, parallel action, cutaway shots and cross-cutting were readily copied by many other directors of the time. His earliest film to survive, *Une Nuit terrible* (1896; *A Terrible Night*), includes cardboard bedbugs that attack the film's sleep-deprived protagonist. The stop-action effect that is often attributed to Méliès is evident in *Escamotage d'une dame chez Robert-Houdin* (1896; *The Vanishing Lady*). In stop-action, the camera is stopped and a crucial subject is substituted with another subject. Other films by Méliès include reenactments of contemporary and historical events, including *Visite sous marine du Maine* (1898; *Divers at Work on the Wreck of the Maine*), *Le Sacré d'Edouard VII* (1902; *The Coronation of Edward VII*), and *Eruption volcanique à la Martinique* (1902; *The Eruption of Mount Pelee*). Méliès also directed advertisements for such products as mustard and baby cereal. It is for his fantasies, however, that Méliès remains celebrated. Besides *La voyage dans la lune*, these films include *L'Homme à la tête de caoutchouc* (1902; *The Man with the Rubber Head*), *Le Royaume des Fées* (1903; *The Kingdom of the Fairies*), and *A la conquête du Pôle* (1912; *The Conquest of the Pole*).

PRINCIPAL WORKS

Escamotage d'une dame chez Robert-Houdin [*The Vanishing Lady*] (film) 1896
Une Nuit terrible [*A Terrible Night*] (film) 1896
Entre Calais et Douvres [*Between Calais and Dover*] (film) 1897
L'Auberge ensorcelée [*The Bewitched Inn*] (film) 1897
Aprés le bal [*After the Ball*] (film) 1897
Danse au sérail [*Dancing in a Harem*] (film) 1897
Un Homme de tête [*The Four Troublesome Heads*] (film) 1898
La lune à un mètre [*The Astronomer's Dream*] (film) 1898
Le Magicien: Illusions fantasmagorique [*The Famous Box Trick*] (film) 1898
Panorama pris d'un train en marche [*Panorama from Top of a Moving Train*] (film) 1898
La Tentation de Sainte-Antoine [*The Temptation of St. Anthony*] (film) 1898
Visite sous-marine du Maine [*Divers at Work on the Wreck of the Maine*] (film) 1898
L'Affaire Dreyfus [*The Dreyfus Affair*] (film) 1899
Cléopâtre [*Robbing Cleopatra's Tomb*] (film) 1899
L'Impressioniste fin de siecle [*An Up-to-Date Conjurer*] (film) 1899

Le Portrait mystérieux [*A Mysterious Portrait*] (film) 1899
L'Exposition de 1900 [*Paris Exposition, 1900*] (film) 1900
L'Homme orchestre [*The One-Man Band*] (film) 1900
La Malade hydrophobe [*The Man with Wheels in His Head*] (film) 1900
Les Miracle de Brahmane [*The Miracles of Brahmin*] (film) 1900
Barbe-Bleue [*Blue Beard*] (film) 1901
Le Brahaman et le papillon [*The Brahmin and the Butterfly*] (film) 1901
Le Charlatan [*Painless Dentistry*] (film) 1901
Dislocations mystérieuses [*Extraordinary Illusions*] (film) 1901
Eruption volcanique à la Martinque [*The Eruption of Mount Pelée*] (film) 1902
L'Homme à la tête de caoutchouc [*The Man with the Rubber Head*] (film) 1902
Le Sacre d'Edouard VII [*The Coronation of Edward VII*] (film) 1902
Les Trésors de Satan [*The Treasures of Satan*] (film) 1902
Le Voyage dans la lune [*A Trip to the Moon*] (film) 1902
La Bôite à malice [*The Mysterious Box*] (film) 1903
Le Chaudron infernal [*The Infernal Cauldron*] (film) 1903
L'Enchanteur Alcofrisbas [*Alcofrisbas, the Master Magician*] (film) 1903
Faust aux enfers [*The Damnation of Faust*] (film) 1903
Les Filles du Diable [*Beelzebub's Daughters*] (film) 1903
Illusions funambulesques [*Extraordinary Illusions*] (film) 1903
La Lanterne magique [*The Magic Lantern*] (film) 1903
Le Mélomane [*The Melomaniac*] (film) 1903
Le Monstre [*The Monster*] (film) 1903
L'Oracle de Delphes [*The Oracle of Delphi*] (film) 1903
La Parapluie fantastique [*Ten Ladies in One Umbrella*] (film) 1903
Le Revenant [*The Apparition*] (film) 1903
Le Royaume des Fées [*The Kingdom of the Fairies*] (film) 1903
Le Sorcier [*The Witch's Revenge*] (film) 1903
Le Tonnerre de Jupiter [*Jupiter's Thunderbolts*] (film) 1903
Le Borreau turc [*The Terrible Turkish Executioner*] (film) 1904
La Damnation du Docteur Faust [*Faust and Marguerite*] (film) 1904
La Sirène [*The Mermaid*] (film) 1904
Le Voyage à travers l'impossible [*The Impossible Voyage*] (film) 1904
Les Cartes vivants [*The Living Playing Cards*] (film) 1905
Le Diable noir [*The Black Imp*] (film) 1905
La Légende de Rip van Winkle [*Rip's Dream*] (film) 1905
Le Menuet lilliputien [*The Lilliputian Minuet*] (film) 1905

Le Palais des mille et une nuits [*The Palace of the Arabian Nights*] (film) 1905

La Fée caraboose ou le Poignard fatal [*The Witch*] (film) 1906

Les 400 Farces du Diable [*The Merry Frolics of Satan*] (film) 1906

L'Eclipse du soleil en pleine lune [*The Eclipse, or the Courtship of the Sun and the Moon*] (film) 1907

Pauvre John ou Les Aventures d'un buveur de whiskey [*Sight-Seeing through a Bottle of Whiskey*] (film) 1907

Le Tunnel sous la manche ou Le Cauchemar franco-anglais [*Tunnelling the English Channel*] (film) 1907

La Bonne Bergère et la méchante princesse [*The Good Shepherdess and the Evil Princess*] (film) 1908

Hallucinations pharmaceutiques [*Pharmaceutical Hallucinations*] (film) 1908

Le Rêve d'un fumeur d'opium [*The Dream of an Opium Fiend*] (film) 1908

La Photographie electrique à distance [*Long-Distance Wireless Photography*] (film) 1908

Hydrothérapie fantastique [*The Doctor's Secret*] (film) 1910

La Locataire diabolique [*The Diabolic Tenant*] (film) 1910

Les Hallucinations du Baron Münchausen [*Baron Münchausen's Dream*] (film) 1911

A la conquête du Pôle [*The Conquest of the Pole*] (film) 1912

Cendrillon ou la pantoufle mystérieuse [*Cinderella or the Glass Slipper*] (film) 1912

CRITICISM

Katherine Singer Kovács (essay date 1976)

SOURCE: "Georges Méliès and the 'Féerie'," in *Cinema Journal*, Vol. XVI, No. 1, Fall, 1976, pp. 1-13.

[*In the following excerpt, Kovacs examines the influence of theater in the films of Méliès.*]

Soon after the motion picture was invented, two opposing tendencies became apparent. While the Lumière brothers used the camera to record events and incidents from everyday life, Georges Méliès eschewed the realism of street scenes in favor of artificially arranged tableaux. Méliès prided himself on the fact that his scenes were invented and that he used theatrical forms and techniques.[1] For his films he borrowed from spectacle shows such as operas, melodramas, historical mimodramas, and especially *féeries*. That Georges Méliès looked to the *féerie* should not surprise us. Although it has vanished into almost complete oblivion, during its heyday in the nineteenth century, the *féerie* attracted the attention of such men as Théophile Gautier, Charles Baudelaire, and Gustave Flaubert.[2] As

the following description will reveal, this genre was the single most important theatrical influence in the development of Méliès's film style.

The *féerie* was born shortly after the French Revolution, when a new theater-going public composed primarily of uneducated spectators began to attend spectacle shows. This new public which sought thrills, excitement, and surprises in the theater enjoyed melodramas as much as *féeries*. In fact, in its earliest form the *féerie* was a type of melodrama in which acrobatics, music, and mime were the main elements.[3] Like melodramas, the plots of most *féeries* pivoted upon a struggle between forces of good and evil. But while these forces remained invisible in melodramas, in *féeries* they were incarnated onstage by gnomes and witches. The plots of *féeries* were usually adapted from fairy tales in which supernatural creatures intervened in the lives of men. These creatures used magical talismans to effectuate the sudden metamorphosis of persons or things and the rapid replacement of one decor by another before the spectator's eyes ("les changements à vue").[4]

The appearances, disappearances, and transformations which were standard fairy play practices delighted and surprised audiences who were unfamiliar with the battery of theatrical machines facilitating these changes. To them the actions which they witnessed were a sort of magic. Gautier compared them to dreams.[5]

In addition to the supernatural creatures, the same four human beings reappear in all *féeries:* the ingenue, the handsome young man whom she loves, his valet (a lazy fellow who loves to eat), and a rival (who is usually grotesque and comic). With the support or hindrance of extraterrestrial forces, these characters pursue one another through different fabulous lands which are presented in a series of independent tableaux. At the end, the hero and heroine are reunited in a grand finale called the apotheosis scene. As the music swells, beautiful girls in diaphanous costumes either descend onstage from the "heavens" or hang in the air on invisible wires.[6]

Such finales had been the obligatory ending of all *féeries* since the beginning of the century when *Le Pied de Mouton*, the first modern *féerie*, was presented.[7] The plot of this work also became the prototype for subsequent *féeries*. As the curtain rises, the young protagonist, Gusman, is wandering through a thick forest with a cavern in the back (the conventional melodramatic setting). Because the woman he loves is betrothed to another man, Gusman has come to the woods to commit suicide. But when he brings the pistols up to his temple, they fly out of his hands and explode in the air. It is Gusman's guardian angel who intervenes at this propitious moment. With a crackle of thunder a rock opens, flames shoot out, and the genie appears, accompanied by devils and serpents (act 1, scene 2). Like other characters in early melodramas and *féeries*, Gusman's angel pronounces maxims on love, virtue, duty, etc. He reminds the young man that human life is precious and insists that he has no right to contemplate suicide. Heartened by the genie's words and by his gift of a magical mutton foot, Gusman embarks upon an energetic campaign to rescue his beloved Leonora. In subsequent tableaux her chaperones change into guitarists; a cart becomes a cage;[8] portraits yawn and move; his rival is carried aloft in the air; and food is whisked from tables. At the end love triumphs and Gusman and Leonora are married.

The power of love was often the moral of these early plays. It appears in one of Guilbert de Pixérecourt's most famous *féeries, Ondine* or *La Nymphe des Eaux* (1830). This work began a vogue of plays about supernatural creatures who fall in love with mortals. Ondine is the daughter of an underwater prince. When she falls in love with a mortal being, she acquires the most precious of all gifts: a soul. As befits a play about a water sprite, *Ondine* contains many aquatic scenes.[9] The cabin where she resides at the beginning of the play changes into a rich underwater palace illuminated by brilliant lights. The finale takes place in a crystal grotto, where all of the great rivers of Europe perform a graceful ballet to celebrate the marriage of Ondine and her prince. In such scenes not only machines but also music and dance contributed to create tableaux of charm and beauty.

Mime and dance were key elements in all *féeries*. In fact, over the years *opéra-féeries* and *pantomime-féeries* eventually replaced *mélodrame-féeries* in popularity.[10] The main attraction of these works came from their ballets and the interludes of music and mime interspersed with the action.[11] Plays of this kind remained popular until around the middle of the century when vaudeville intervened and modified the form of the *féerie*.

After around 1840 *pantomime-féeries* and *opéra-féeries* were hardly ever presented. *Vaudeville-féeries* came to dominate the theatrical scene to the extent that by the late 1840s distinctions no longer were made between *vaudeville-féeries* and *féeries:* all *féeries* would henceforth be vaudeville shows.[12] The vaudeville writers who turned to *féeries* altered their tone by introducing more songs, jokes, and puns than ever before. They relied less upon ballet and song and more upon elaborate decors and startling scene changes to hold the interest of the audience.

Technical innovations made during those years considerably facilitated their task. By the late 1830s gas had been installed in most of the important Parisian theaters. Gas was one of the first powerful sources of light for the stage. It enabled scenic artists to present more realistic as well as more fantastic scenes. With the installation of gas in many theaters, set designers could exploit not only its strength and brilliance but also its potential for creating special atmospheric effects. The development of limelight further aided in the creation of special effects by enabling set designers to cross the rays of different lamps and to create a radiant yet mellow light which perfectly imitated the beams of the sun or moon. Once stage lighting could be modified and controlled, it became an important aspect of stage production, and lighting instructions were written directly into the script as an integral element of the story.

Another important advance in theatrical techniques resulted from Louis Daguerre's invention of the diorama. In 1823 it was first exhibited in a specially constructed circular room in which the audience was transported on a platform past a series of tableaux hung from the ceiling. As the spectators moved past, the illumination of each tableau was imperceptibly modified, thereby creating certain magical effects. Later Daguerre perfected double dioramas, the effect of which also depended upon lighting. On each side of a translucent canvas a different scene was painted. When light was shone on one side of the canvas, the scene on that side emerged. When light was shone from behind, the one on the back appeared.[13] In this way, one scene would melt into another. In later *féeries,* the double diorama was utilized not only to effectuate instantaneous scene changes but also to achieve special effects such as fires or sunsets. It was yet another tool enabling playwrights to dazzle and surprise the spectators.

All of these technical advances contributed to the development of the *féerie*, which attained its greatest popularity during the 1850s.[14] Although stage effects were more spectacular during this decade, *féerie* plots did not substantially change. That is to say, new techniques enhanced timeworn *féerie* tricks. We find an example of this new-old style in a work written for the Cirque-Olympique by the well-known vaudeville writer Anicet Bourgeois and two circus writers, Laurent and Laloue. Revived and imitated innumerable times, *Les Pilules du Diable* demonstrates the way in which *féerie* writers combined sophisticated stage machinery with acrobatic and dancing skills inherited from the circus.

The plot of ***Les Pilules du Diable*** is a fairly conventional one in which an impoverished artist named Albert wishes to marry Isabelle. His principal rival is a wealthy hidalgo named Sottinez, who pursues the lovers relentlessly. In one famous scene a locomotive in which Sottinez was chasing Isabelle and Albert explodes. Pieces of Sottinez's body fall strewn upon the stage. These precious remains are gathered in a basket. After some searching, the characters locate the hidalgo's head. Before the audience's eyes, they begin to piece him together. When they have finished, Sottinez renews his furious pursuit as if nothing had happened.

This scene is achieved in a simple and ingenious manner. At the moment when the locomotive explodes, the actor playing the part of Sottinez hides behind it, while different parts of a mannequin drop from the flies above the stage. They then begin to reassemble him in front of part of the set which is cut out in the shape of a man. All of the parts of the cut-out correspond exactly to the parts of the mannequin's body. When they adjust his leg, for example, they fit it into that part of the set. Meanwhile the real actor who is located behind the set surreptitiously places both the false limb and the appropriate part of the set in the wings, substituting his own real leg and then all of the other parts of his body. Since this reconstruction obliged the actor to assume awkward positions in which he could not always maintain his balance, two stagehands held him until he had passed his head through the final cut-out in the set.[15]

Although severed heads and bodies hacked to pieces were frequent sights in *féeries,* these scenes are never alarming. In all *féeries* the victims of violent action are immune to serious disability. Characters in fairy plays resemble dream figures. As they pursue never-ending endeavors, they change clothes, transform or fall down and break, only to be put back together again in the next scene. Like puppets or machines, they are comic in the Bergsonian sense.[16] Even the devil, a frequent participant in *féeries,* performs evil acts with cheerful good humor.

As the century progressed and vaudeville writers fixed the form and the conventions of the *féerie,* comedy became more important than poetry, and tableaux were more burlesque than beautiful. Authors began to devise more outlandish and elaborate settings for the *féerie.*[17] The number of tableaux increased. By the end of the Second Empire in 1870, *féeries* contained as many as 20 different sets. In addition to the palaces, huts, underground caves and moving forests which the *féerie* inherited from melodrama, it acquired some new locales such as the sun, the moon, India, China, and Turkey.

One of the theater directors most responsible for this trend was Marc Fournier, who ran the Porte Saint-Martin theater during most of the Second Empire. It was the extravagant stage sets which made his theater thrive. For each production he assembled the most elaborate decors, scenes, and tricks ever imagined. Every few weeks he changed the settings of three or four tableaux. Although eventually he went bankrupt, his grandiose shows enthralled all of Paris for many years. Partly as a result of Fournier's example, a veritable frenzy for spectacle shows gripped Parisian theaters. As other directors followed his lead, the scenes in *féeries* became more extravagant, and the number of tableaux increased. *Rothomago,* a work first presented in 1862, boasted 25 different decors. The Goncourt brothers, who attended the opening night performance, described the *féerie* in deprecating terms, considering it to be a plebeian form of entertainment.[18] Nevertheless, the people they saw in the audience that evening were among the most fashionable in Parisian society. For, to a remarkable extent, the pomp and splendor of *féeries* coincided with the tastes of the Second Empire. This was an extravagant epoch, when the emperor and empress gave lavish dances and masked balls, when ceremonies and parades were very much in style.

2

Georges Méliès was born in 1863. Even into adulthood the glitter of the Second Empire shaped his tastes. He marveled at the spectacular effects achieved in *féeries* and sought to recreate them in his magic shows at the Robert-Houdin theater. When he began to make motion pictures, it was only natural for him to use the *féerie* as a source of techniques, plots, and themes. It was also an important force in shaping Méliès's film aesthetic. For even when he substituted photographic illusions for the flaps, traps, scrims, and mirrors of the stage, Méliès's point of view remained essentially theatrical.

That Méliès's frame of reference was the stage can be seen in the sets which he designed for his films. In all of them the camera occupies the position of a spectator in the orchestra of a theater.[19] It remains in a stationary position, at a constant distance from the actors who are always shown full-length; there is no such thing as a close-up. The actors enter and exit either from the side wings or through vampire traps in the floor of the stage.[20] All of their movements are executed on one plane along the center of the stage, behind an invisible line of demarcation (corresponding to the stage apron) at a considerable distance from the flats at the back of the stage. The latter consists of backdrops painted exclusively in shades of gray.[21] To give an illusion of depth to this two-dimensional playing area, set pieces were placed in a series of grooves between the apron and the backdrop.

In one of the his most elaborate filmed *féeries,* **Le Palais des 1001 Nuits** (1905), one scene is set in a thick forest where trees fill the entire stage. When the protagonist appears, the successive rows of foliage part to reveal a crystal grotto painted on the backdrop. After the protagonist passes through, the trees slide back to their original position along grooves in the floor. As Méliès noted in his catalogue: "This decoration, which was made only after considerable labor, is a veritable marvel of achievement. It possesses a great artistic beauty."[22]

Other decors found in this film include the exotic settings of palaces, caves, temples, and throne rooms which Marc Fournier and other stage directors had popularized. The plot is also a familiar one: a poor but noble young man arrives at the rajah's court to ask for the hand of his daughter. The rajah refuses, preferring to see her marry a rich usurer named Holdfast. The desperate prince arouses the sympathy of the fairy of gold who leads him to a fabulous treasure. The prince must prove himself worthy of the fortune by fighting the skeletons, toads, and dragon who guard the vault.

The trials which the protagonist must undergo occasion such tricks as the disappearance of objects and people as well as their instantaneous transformation. Méliès employs certain *féerie* effects which had been popular since the Italian Renaissance; statues become animated;[23] strange monsters built of wood and papier mâché dance and cavort onstage;[24] gnomes and witches of frightening aspect weave wicked schemes;[25] and men play the roles of animals.[26] Special effects such as fires, snowfalls, volcanic eruptions, and explosions are accomplished by the time-tested methods of the theater. *Le Palais des 1001 Nuits* is theatrical in inspiration as well as in execution: its changes depend upon costume and stage machinery rather than upon innovative photographic techniques. And yet the film seems richer than descriptions of contemporary theater *féeries*. Perhaps this is because the camera allowed Méliès to link single illusions together in rapid succession. At the end of the film, when the prince defeats the monsters and a series of stage transformations culminate in an endless cortege of women bearing gold and silver, the number of scene changes and the rapidity with which they are executed intensify the magical experience.

Méliès did not restrict his use of *féerie* techniques to those films which were meant to be *féeries*. They recur in nearly all of his works. For example, even in some of his comic films such as *The Terrible Turkish Executioner* (1904), *Delirium in a Studio* (1907), and *The Doctor's Secret* (1910) we find the decapitation scenes which were favored by nineteenth-century *féerie* playwrights. In *The Doctor's Secret* (also known as *Hydrothérapie Fantastique*), a corpulent man who visits a doctor in order to reduce shares the fate of Sottinez in *Les Pilules du Diable*. When he is placed inside a steam cabinet which explodes, parts of his body (or rather parts of a mannequin) drop from the flies and land in different locations around the stage. The head of the real actor appears in a clock painted on the backdrop of the stage. One of the doctor's assistants removes the head from the clock while a second one carries a high-backed chair to the center of the stage. They then reassemble the patient by placing the torso, arms, legs, and head against the chair. This prop serves the same function as did the backdrop in *Les Pilules du Diable* it gives the actor a place to hide while he substitutes the appropriate parts of his body through cutouts in the chair.[27]

The traps, flaps, and dummies employed in *The Doctor's Secret* are used with equal effectiveness in a number of Méliès's films. The plot of one of his most elaborate *féeries*, *The Merry Frolics of Satan* (1906), pivots almost entirely upon these devices. In this work a young engineer named Crackford unwittingly signs a pact with Satan in return for some magic pills.[28] For the remainder of the film he is pursued by Satan who delights in playing tricks upon him: a train in which he travels falls through a bridge; the meal he sits down to eat and the table upon which it is placed disappear;[29] the inn where he hopes to find repose is invaded by apes and demons who pursue him, traversing walls, buffets, staircases, mantlepieces, etc. In this scene the stage set is a veritable web of traps, flaps, and peepholes, through which the devils "tumble over every obstacle in their way while performing astonishing acrobatic feats. All these imps finally disappear beneath the floor. . . ."[30]

When the engineer attempts to flee, his carriage is transformed into a ghostly vehicle driven by a skeleton-horse which takes him on a vertiginous ride through space. His escape attempt fails. Satan eventually whisks him away to hell where he is burned at the stake.[31]

The most spectacular scene in the film is that of the engineer's aerial voyage in the carriage. Flights through the air or the simple suspension of objects such as spaceships (*A Trip to the Moon*), balloons and helicopters (*A La Conquête du Pôle*), and chariots (*The Kingdom of the Fairies, Jupiter's Thunderbolts*) were frequent effects in Méliès's films. To show vehicles in the air, he often relied upon conventional stage techniques in which life-sized vehicles bearing the actors aloft were suspended from invisible wires hung from the flies. As they rose in the air, they disappeared out of the camera's range.

But in some of these "flights" Méliès went further than stage set designers and substituted photographic processes for the conventional wires and panoramas of *féeries*. In certain scenes, shots of the standard-size object taking off were juxtaposed with views of miniature models whirling through the heavens.[32] These models, which were superimposed upon views of the stars and the sky, rendered flights through the air with greater realism than was possible on the stage.[33]

As these examples suggest, it was quite common for Méliès to join the conventional techniques of the stage to methods of still photography. The motion picture camera, by its very nature, rendered certain stage effects and practices superfluous. Often the camera could effectuate a trick more easily and less expensively. This was certainly so in the case of instantaneous scene changes. The movable stages, elevators, and falling flaps which had evolved over the years to effectuate the rapid change of scene from one decor to the next were replaced by camera dissolves, fade-outs, and fade-ins. The simple process of opening and closing the iris of the camera also outmoded the stage practice of using layers of gauze and of dimming the lights before a scene change and of bringing them up afterwards.[34]

The way in which Méliès showed vision scenes also changed from theatrical practice. Instead of presenting spectres behind gauze at the rear of the stage or throwing them above the actors with magic lanterns, Méliès would film the apparition before or after shooting the scene on a white background, stop the camera, wind the film back, and reshoot in order to obtain superimposition. Sometimes he would place a piece of muslin gauze over the lens to give a hazy, indistinct appearance to the image.[35] Thus in *L'Enchanteur Alcofrisbas* (1903) we see ghostly creatures shrouded in sheets dance in the air; in *Le Chaudron Infernal* (1903) the barely visible forms go up in flames.

The camera also eliminated the need for trick costumes, falling flaps, dioramas, and doubles, because it was possible to stop filming at any point and to "arrange" a scene. Méliès fully exploited the possibilities inherent in the stop-action technique. This was the single most important cinematic element in his films.[36] It enabled him to effectuate instantaneous transformations by photographing an object, substituting another one in exactly the same position, and resuming the action. When the film was run, it was as if the first object instantly transformed into the second.

Méliès used stop-actions in his films not only to transform men into women and paintings into people, but also to make characters appear and disappear. The technique replaced the leap through flaps which stage actors would make for sudden appearances. It also facilitated more rapid changes of clothing than were possible with the old theatrical methods.[37] In *Knight of Black Art* (1908), the magician throws four gowns at his assistants who are immediately seen to be wearing them; in *The Mermaid* (1904), the well-dressed magician is transmogrified into an old and seedy beggar.

The stop-action technique enabled Méliès to employ other methods of trick photography in his films. In addition to using fast motion, slow motion, and reverse action photography, Méliès achieved startling effects with composite pictures.[38] These were made by covering parts of the lens, so that one or several areas of the frame would not be exposed, and photographing a scene with a black background. Méliès would then also place a blackened piece of cardboard next to the camera aperture. This cardboard was in a shape corresponding to the black backdrop where the second part of the scene would be photographed after the film had been rewound. In one tableau of *The Kingdom of Fairies* (1903) Méliès made dramatic use of this process of duplex photography by dividing the screen into two distinct pictures. A group of people stand on the balcony of a palace watching as demons carry a princess away in the air. The flight of the creatures is really a separate scene which has been superimposed upon the sky.

With the same methods Méliès achieved other new tricks,[39] including interesting variations on scenes with severed heads. In *Le Mélomane* (1903), the conductor seems to reproduce his own head six times because Méliès photographed the same head in six different positions in the same frame. In *L'Homme à la Tête de Caoutchouc* (1902), the protagonist expands the size of his own head until it explodes.[40]

It is interesting to note that in spite of the new techniques Méliès employed in his films, he did not alter the conventions of the *féerie* but remained within the genre's traditional thematic and structural limits. In all of his films stock characters such as the scientist and the devil reappear, as do familiar scenes such as dream sequences and voyages. Méliès was not interested in revitalizing the *féerie*. His use of stop-actions, superimpositions, and illusionary photography merely offered new ways of effectuating old familiar tricks. Depending upon the illusion which he wished to create, Méliès alternated between filmic and theatrical means. Each film therefore contains a mixture of scenic and photographic devices.[41]

We see the extent to which Méliès mixed traditional techniques of the *féerie* with those of the film in one of his last elaborate works, *A La Conquête du Pôle* (1912). Although this is not a *féerie* in the conventional sense, by the time the motion picture was invented playwrights were using science-fiction stories rather than fairy tales as a source for *féeries*.[42] Such machines as the car, the helicopter, and the submarine, and such locales as the moon and the North Pole had been presented on stage years before Méliès's *Conquête du Pôle*. At the beginning of the film the titles explain that Dr. Maboul has just invented an "aerobus" which will reach the North Pole. After seeing a miniature model of the vehicle (which will be used in flight later on in the picture) and the "laboratory" where it is being constructed, we witness its take-off, effectuated by means of wires hanging from the flies.

As the aerobus travels through the air, women playing the role of constellations salute it in passage in a scene created by superimpositions. When the explorers arrive at the North Pole they land in a traditional two-dimensional decor which contains cardboard icicles and painted icebergs. As they investigate the terrain they encounter the "Géant des neiges," a giant monster made of papier mâché who smokes a pipe, rolls his eyes, and swallows one of the scientists. When the others attack him, the monster spits his victim out (the latter jumps through the flap in the monster's mouth and lands onstage). The "rescue" of Maboul's party is achieved by another vehicle which first appears in miniature against the backdrop. A set piece corresponding to the central portion of the vehicle replaces the model and descends by means of wires to where the men are located. As the scientists disappear in the air, penguins and seals appear by means of the stop-action technique. This is one of the few effects achieved by photographic means in the film. Most of the others are ones which could have been realized on the stage. Thus, even among his last films, on the eve of World War I, Méliès's point of reference remained the world of the nineteenth-century spectacle show.

In the same spirit with which his nineteenth-century predecessors had adapted scientific advances such as gaslight, limelight, and dioramas for use in the theater, Méliès turned to the film; it was but another technique in the service of his first love magic. By means of film, Méliès sought to render men's dreams and imaginings with greater reality. Ultimately, when one speaks of his films the question should not be whether they are filmic or theatrical. Above all they are magical. They were designed to appeal to that same public of the poor and the uneducated who initially had flocked to the *féeries*, to the masses who were liberated by the French Revolution. This group, which first saw its dreams incarnated onstage in *féeries*, found its full form of expression in the twentieth century with film.

NOTES

[1] As Méliès wrote in an advertisement, "these fantastic and artistic films reproduce stage scenes and create a new genre entirely different from the ordinary cinematographic views of real people and real streets." See Georges Sadoul, *Georges Méliès* (Paris, 1970), p. 14.

[2] As a theater reviewer Gautier often wrote about *féeries* (see n. 5). Baudelaire's poem "L'Irréparable" was inspired by a *féerie* called *La Belle aux Cheveux d'Or.* Its heroine was played by Marie Daubrun, a woman Baudelaire loved. See "L'Irréparable," *Les Fleurs du Mal,* ed. Crépet et Blin (Paris, 1942), p. 60. Flaubert actually completed one *féerie* entitled *Le Château des Coeurs* in 1863. It was never performed on stage.

[3] Many early *féeries* were actually called *mélodrame-féeries.* Between 1800 and 1820, when approximately 60 *féeries* were presented, nearly 20 of them were described in this way. (These figures are based on entries in Charles Beaumont Wicks's four-volume bibliography of the theater entitled *The Parisian Stage,* Alabama, 1950-1964.)

[4] The most widely used method for effectuating an instantaneous scene change from one scene to another was by means of falling flaps. The scenery flat was divided into a certain number of rectangles which moved on hinges like folding doors. On one side of the rectangles set designers painted one scene, and on the other they painted a second. They then attached ropes or strings to each flap along the length of the flat and joined the strings together. At the appropriate moment the stagehands pulled the strings and made all of the flaps pivot to the reverse side, thereby changing the scene.

[5] Théophile Gautier, *Histoire de l'Art dramatique en France depuis 25 ans* (Paris, 1858-1859), III (October, 1844), pp. 281-282.

[6] These wires were painted black so as to be invisible. They ran up to pulleys attached to a carriage and through the carriage to points on the grill. The carriage rested either on a taut rope or on a special railway which could move from side to side above the stage. To begin the "flight," one of the stagehands would draw the carriage across the stage. The pulleys in the carriage would press against the wheels, thus forcing them sideways. In this way it was possible to raise an object. A movement in the opposite direction would effectuate a descent. See A. de Vaulabelle and Charles Hemardinquer, *La Science au Théâtre* (Paris, 1908), pp. 243-244.

[7] *Le Pied de Mouton* was written by a famous pamphleteer named Martainville and presented for the first time on December 6, 1806.

[8] To effectuate changes of objects such as chairs and carts, rather than entire sets, painted set pieces with hinged flaps usually were employed. By means of a simple trick line a flap could be swung over part of the set piece like the leaf of a page. The object could thereby be increased or diminished in size. It was also in this manner that small props would be made to disappear. (See J. Moyney, *L'Envers du Théâtre,* Paris, 1875, p. 89). In a number of films Méliès used set pieces with hinged flaps.

[9] Scenes with water and with ships sailing on the high seas were common in *féeries.* The sea was depicted by means of a carpet that was moved by hoops. Stagehands placed under the carpet would alternately raise and lower the hoops. At different points on the stage they also placed jointed girders cut in the form of crests which increased the illusion of moving waves. Other trusses placed further back in a stationary position simulated the high seas. When it was necessary to present boats, they were usually set on rollers along two curved wooden "railways" (called "les chemins de mer"). The curves along the path of the railway created the illusion of a boat listing. (See Vaulabelle and Hemardinquer, *La Science au Théâtre,* p. 212.)

[10] Between 1800 and 1810, 14 *mélodrame-féeries* were presented in Paris-half of the total number of *féeries.* In the next decade the number of *mélodrame-féeries* fell to four. Between 1821 and 1830 only two were presented in Paris, even though the total number of *féeries* almost doubled. (These figures are based on Wicks's entries in *The Parisian Stage.*) During the same period, and especially between 1818 and 1825, there was a dramatic increase in the number of *opéra-féerie* plays. At the Paris Opera alone, eight such works were presented. After 1830, when romantic ballet reached its apogee, the interest in *opéra-féeries* declined, and only two of these plays appeared. At the same time Deburau, the renowned mime at the Funambules theater, began to present *pantomime-féeries* which enthralled all of Paris. Under his auspices this form became extremely popular and replaced both *mélodrame-féeries* and *opéra-féeries* in importance. In fact, in the decade 1841 to 1850 the number of *pantomime-féeries* performed in Paris equalled the entire production over the preceding 40 years. Upon Deburau's death in 1848 interest in *pantomime-féeries* waned.

[11] All *féeries* had songs. Usually new words were devised for familiar tunes.

[12] Again I am basing this conclusion upon entries in *The Parisian Stage.* Before 1840 all *féeries* contained some descriptive term along with the title. One finds *folie-féeries, comédie-féeries,* or *vaudeville-féeries.* During the decade 1821 to 1830 more than one-fourth were designated as *vaudeville-féeries.* Between 1841 and 1850, out of a total of 64 plays, only six were identified as *vaudeville-féeries.* This does not suggest that the latter was becoming less popular; on the contrary, it was such a common form that it was a redundancy to use the word *vaudeville* in the title.

[13] See Louis Daguerre, "Mémoire de l'Academie des Beaux Arts," cited by Germain Bapst in his *Essai sur l'Histoire des panoramas et des dioramas* (Paris, 1891), pp. 20-21.

[14] Sadoul mentions a somewhat later period. According to him the genre peaked between 1860 and 1880 (*Georges Méliès,* p. 33).

[15] Vaulabelle and Hemardinquer, *La Science au Théâtre,* pp. 216-217.

[16] Bergson's definition of comic was "le mécanique plaqué sur le vivant." He thought that all comic situations (ranging from slapstick scenes to word plays) originated when human beings acted like machines. That is to say, when an individual was unable to adjust his responses to changes in his environment, when his movements and actions did not conform to reality, that person would seem comic. One of the examples which he used was that of a man who does not see a step and who continues to walk until he falls on his face. He seems funny because at the moment of his fall he has lost his humanity and become like a machine or a puppet.

[17] An extremely successful *féerie* called *La Biche au Bois* contributed to this trend. In this work by the Cogniard brothers grotesque and comic forms were introduced on a large scale. Prior to this time (1845) characters in *féeries* had confined their travels to allegorical or mythological lands, in the heavens or beneath the seas. This all changed with *La Biche.* In addition to investigating these conventional locales, characters in *La Biche au Bois* explore new domains, such as the kingdom of bells, the kingdom of fish, and the kingdom of vegetables where they talk with fruits and vegetables of colossal dimensions. Each of these tableaux contains a grotesque ballet in which men dress as animals and the intention is comic. It is interesting to note that the subtitle of this work, *Le Royaume des Fées,* is the same as the title of one of Méliès's filmed *féeries,* but there is no similarity in terms of the plot.

[18] Edmond and Jules de Goncourt, *Journal littéraire* (le 1er mars, 1862), p. 1026: "The spectacle shows of the Boulevard [du Crime] are a modern paradise for the people. They have the same importance in the dreams of today's masses as did Gothic cathedrals in man's imagination during the Middle Ages."

[19] Sadoul, *op. cit.,* pp. 36-38.

[20] A vampire trap is a two-leaved trap with springs constructed either on the stage floor or in the flats. It permitted a supernatural creature to disappear more rapidly than was possible with older traps without springs.

[21] As Méliès noted, the shades of gray ran the gamut from almost white to almost black. The painting was much neater than for plays. (See Sadoul, *op. cit.,* p. 100.)

[22] Méliès, *Complete Catalogue of "Star" Films* (New York, 1905), p. 76. For distribution of his films in the U.S., Méliès opened an office in New York which was run by his brother Gaston. This *Catalogue* contains detailed descriptions of all of Méliès's films, their prices, lengths, etc.

[23] Statues also become animated in other Méliès's films such as *La Statue Animée, L'Enchanteur Alcofrisbas,* and *Sightseeing through Whiskey.*

[24] Monsters appear in *A Trip to the Moon* (the Selenites), *Sightseeing through Whiskey, A La Conquête du Pôle, The Merry Frolics of Satan,* and *The Magic Lantern,* to name only a few. These creatures are all created by theatrical means (costumes, makeup, etc.).

[25] Of all of Méliès's evildoers, the devil was his favorite. Méliès himself usually played this part.

[26] Men dress as lions and tigers in *Le Palais des 1001 Nuits.* In *The Enchanted Well* a human horse walks across the stage, and giant frogs assail the protagonist.

[27] The doctor places all of the parts of the body against the chair nearly simultaneously. Then Méliès stopped the camera so that the real actor could take the place of the mannequin. Thus the performer never had to place different parts of his own body through the flaps, as his stage counterpart was obliged to do.

[28] The idea of magic pills was a common one in *féeries.* It was first used onstage in *Les Pilules du Diable.*

[29] Disappearing food was the most common trick in all *féeries.*

[30] *Complete Catalogue of "Star" Films,* p. 110.

[31] Here Méliès used the stop-action technique to substitute a dummy for the actor.

[32] Méliès used models in *A La Conquête du Pôle, A Trip to the Moon, The Astronomer's Dream,* and *The Merry Frolics of Satan.*

[33] Méliès also used superimpositions to film scenes beneath the seas.

[34] The most effective use of fade-outs, fade-ins, and dissolves is found in Méliès's *The Kingdom of the Fairies.*

[35] Albert A. Hopkins, ed., *Magic, Stage Illusions and Scientific Diversions Including Trick Photography* (New York, 1901), p. 434.

[36] In *Georges Méliès,* Sadoul includes Méliès's own description of how he accidentally discovered that the stop-action technique could be used for transformations: "One day early in my career as I was casually photographing the Place de l'Opéra, my camera jammed . . .

with unexpected results. It took me a minute to release the film and to start cranking the camera again. During that minute, the passersby, the buses, and the cars had of course moved. Later when I projected the filmstrip . . . I saw a 'Madeleine-Bastille' bus suddenly change into a hearse and some men become women. In this way the substitution trick, the so-called 'stop-action technique' was discovered, and two days later I filmed the first metamorphoses of men into women and the first instantaneous disappearances. . . . " (*Georges Méliès*, pp. 106-107).

[37] On the stage changes of clothing were executed in the following manner: When the artist came onstage he was already dressed in the costume which he would change into before the spectators. Over it went another one ("le costume à boyau") in which he would make his entrance. All the parts of this costume were sewn together: there were no seams; it was all one piece. The costume was cut from top to bottom and on each side so that it then consisted of two pieces held together by a cord. The cord was passed through rings. At the moment of transformation, the actor placed himself above a trap in the stage. A stagehand reached up and pulled on the ends of the cord so that the costume was no longer around the actor, but resting on him. At the next signal, the stagehand pulled the costume into the trap. (See Paul Ginisty, *La Féerie*, Paris, 1910, p. 228, n. 1.)

[38] Méliès used fast motion in an ingenious way in *The Astronomer's Dream*.

[39] He often juxtaposed different, sometimes incongruous objects and scenes, achieving such effects as that of a woman emerging from a hoop (*Knight of Black Art*), a figure appearing inside an enormous box (*The Mysterious Box*), and two ballerinas dancing upon the curtains of a bed (*The Ballet Master's Dream*).

[40] To make the head expand in size the actor's body was shrouded in black and he was seated upon a chair which was attached to a "railway," by means of which he could be moved closer or further away from the camera, thereby enlarging or shrinking the size of his head.

[41] Certain general trends can nevertheless be perceived. To a certain extent, the tricks which Méliès chose to present depended upon the genre in which he worked. Méliès's films ranged from simple magic shows, to burlesque scenes, to historical reenactments, to science-fiction stories, to *féeries*. When he was devising films such as *féeries* which had a narrative structure, he was inclined to adapt more conventional techniques as well as themes and subjects. When, on the other hand, he presented simple magic shows in one tableau, his tendency was to rely exclusively upon such photographic tricks as superimpositions and stop-actions. That is to say, Méliès's *féeries* contain more theatrical techniques than do his magic shows. In the latter category would be included the following films: *Knight of Black Art, Mysterious Box, Bewitched Trunk, L'Enchanteur Alcofrisbas, The Infernal Cauldron, The Mermaid, The Magic Lantern, The Magician, The Enchanted Basket.*

[42] Paul Ginisty considers 1875 to be the year when the evolution of the *féerie* towards science-fiction began. It was in that year that *Le Voyage à la Lune*, the first adaptation of Jules Verne, was presented. (Offenbach wrote the music for this work.) See Ginisty, *op. cit.*, p. 214. Between 1875 and the end of the century, when the *féerie* became virtually moribund, a number of other science-fiction *féeries* appeared, including another adaptation of Jules Verne's stories entitled *Le Voyage à travers l'Impossible*. Written by an old *féerie* playwright, Adolphe D'Ennery, this work was first presented at the Porte Saint-Martin, in November of 1885.

Stan Brakhage (essay date 1977)

SOURCE: "George Méliès," in *Film Biographies, Turtle Island,* No. 1977, pp. 15-34.

[*In the following excerpt, Brakhage explores possible biographical sources of inspiration for Méliès work.*]

Now let me say it to you simply as I can: the search for an art . . . either in the making or the appreciation . . . is the most terrifying adventure imaginable: it is a search *always* into unexplored regions; and it threats the *soul* with terrible death at every turn; and it exhausts the mind utterly; and it leaves the body moving, moving endlessly through increasingly unfamiliar terrain: there is NO hope of return from the territory discovered by this adventuring; and there is NO hope of rescue from the impasse where such a search may leave one stranded.

It is not without cause that parents shudder when a child of theirs expresses the wish to become an Artist: they will, of course, do everything in their power to protect the child from such a fate!: they will even send him to institutes which will create phony arts and phony art appreciation to distract him . . . just as they will send the young explorer to the safe jungles of Disneyland or those of the TV movie, etc. to undermine any real adventuring: the society will, in fact, distort the whole meaning of the word "appreciation" . . . confusing it with "voyeurism" . . . to tame the energies of any active involvement: for real aesthetic appreciation runs exactly the same hazards as art-creation leads as surely to what society calls "madness" as any creative making: (you may find this hard to believe, but only because we have less example of real attendance to art in our culture than of creativity . . . thus an even phonier idea of "audience" than of "artist" . . . an ideology of many millions who imagine they appreciate who are as silly in such imagination as would be a drunken group of mountain climbers scaling the papier-maché rock sets on the back-lot of a Hollywood studio.)

If you accept the full adventure of this course, you will surely lose your mortal soul!: you will be tortured by demons (physically pained by them, tickled to death by them, mentally-anguished to the point of suicidal thought): you will be stretched to the orders of angels more terrible than demonic force, set tasks by them beyond all comprehension or imaginable accomplishment: you will be changed so that your mother will never recognize you, so that your father will disown you, your friends betray you, your loved-one live in terror of you . . . :

. . . but then all these things will happen anyway so what have you to lose? . . .

You have nothing to gain either: for this, like all real adventures, is purposeless i.e.: . . . its impulse is beyond any purposeful definition its achievements are cosmic . . . comic, if you like that term better . . . but anyway, of no *reason*able order: (it is fashionable for art adventurers these days to say they are after knowledge or fun or escape even: but these terms are sheerly as symbolic a claim as the term 'gold' was for centuries of explorers): . . ."for the hell of it" will do as explanation as well as any other: for 'hell' comes first, just as in Dante's adventure: and most do, alas, get stuck there beyond rescue : hell comes first in all sequence . . . (imagine Dante entering first what he called heaven . . . : would it not, in that order, have been hellish?): and most have always got stuck early in whatever endeavor or non-endeavor: be advised then, that if you fall behind, no one will wait for you; but no one will wait for you if you move ahead either, nor where-nor-howsomever you wander: any true sense of company will occur as rarely as Maxwell's Demon: the demons of art will make you *know* this, your desperate loneliness they will make you know this and all truth by telling you lies: . . . ("He who seeks the truth must, as far as possible, doubt everything," as Descartes put it): you will wander in hallways of real objects looking as if they were mirrored.

If this all sounds like 19th century rhetoric be advised that it IS of the orders of 19th century rhetoric . . . : I am introducing George Méliès, and thus the 19th century beginning of motion picture art.

Let me then present a fictional biography of Méliès an historical novel so to speak whereat I, as demonstrator, lie to you . . . tell a tale, as it's called . . . in order to get at the truth. My story of course is based on facts: however a fact about unexplored territory cannot be anything but misleading. I present, therefore, a fiction that is IN fact: if you follow, we begin advent adventuring . . . touring the interior of a den of light, a cave of white darkness, shadow splotched with the dappled movements of illuminating black, a four-squared corridor widening from its entrance into this room the gate of that projector to an 'impossible' chamber (of the imagination) . . . the flat 'cube' of the screen . . . and branching out to become that complex of tunnels best referred to as The Labyrinth, each terminus of which, in the spirals of the spin-of-light behind every pair of eyes every single eye-gate in this room, in the gray hills and

valleys of each brain present, holds a (thus) many-headed host of terrible monsters . . . The Hydra, considered as a singularity which we all (therefore) somehow share amidst a tangle of dangerous angel hair that electrical thought-glass which cuts instinctual nerve to pieces ("doth make cowards of us all" inheriting Hamlet's problem) in this the most forbidding, and utterly foreign, land shape of all.

Young George then already defeated by some-such creatures as we can begin to imagine on the barren planet of his foetal mind . . . completely overwhelmed, torn to pieces before what-we-would-call his 'birth' begins as a child to invent a spirit-of-himself which will revenge him . . . a hero who will FREE the wickedly enchanted or otherwise destroyed pieces of his actual being, cause the monsters to dis-gorge the parts of his actuality; and young George, perhaps later then, begins to imagine a heroine who will restore him, a woman who will sew together or otherwise re-member his actual being: but he cannot quite imagine the woman as loving him, once remembered, rather than the hero of his invention cannot imagine her as anything other than heroine (to go with the hero) and/or Mother of him-George . . . cannot visualize her as other than spirit-force (unless she be Mother-again wherein he be dismembered as once before). George finds his first hopeful solution to this dilemma at a magic show whereat impossible things happen and all contradictions therefore resolve in the hands of the able magician.

George himself decides to become just such a magician; but first he must make the hero of his invention a magician. As he is *imagining* the woman (rather than inventing her) she will always be victim of this magic subject to the transformations of it: thus young George hopes to have power over her equal to her necessary ability to re-member and, as Mother then, to restore him. He must also manage some ultimate magic for his actual being which can defeat the magic he gives the hero-of-his-invention; and he begins, therefore, to create a demon-self (of himself-imagined-restored) who can tear his hero to pieces as he foetally once was; and he must of course in all this desperate plotting manage to conceal all knowledge of the demonic invention from the heroic invention until the proper time (when he is all-of-a-piece) to spring his monster-self from ambush upon his hero. He must, additionally, conceal his 'darkside' as it's called from imaginings of the heroine, because it is necessary she love the hero up-to-a-point . . . (i.e.: until she has fulfilled her remembrance of actual him a very tricky matter because demonic-George must end up as part-and-parcel with foetal-George re-membered: otherwise George will simply have invented another monster to turn on him once his rescuing hero has been defeated: and the woman in his imaginings *must* thus be very stupid and therefore easily tricked in the midst of her greatest magic or else . . . as George thinks better . . . she must be too purely good, too utterly filled with 'sweetness and light' to even recognize the bitter black monstrousness of the darkside of her own sewing;

and, even later then at hero's death she must be too naive to recognize the evil parcel as being of the parts of actual George-restored.)

Hyenas laugh rather than growl humans, too . . . : and George soon discovers humor (that term almost synonymous, sound-wise, with human . . . and meaning, in exact English sound-synonym, to trick madness i.e.: "to humour him") . . . humor as powerful magic of duplicity . . . humor, that traditional field of endeavor whereby one elicits bared teeth in the form of a smile which appears opposite of that vicious threat it thus conceals reveals deadly fangs even, the broader it spreads to say, say, 'friend' . . . breaks into the "foe's" bark of "friendly" laughter as it reaches the height of duplicity: and young George decides to master this powerful magic to most perfectly conceal his dreadful intentions, so that he can perform all his other tricks in the contradictory milieu of elicited snarls, growls, barks, and general roaring laughter of his utterly 'fooled' audience.

There is an historical reason George must master the trick of humor before all other magics: he was born in France, amid 19th-century scepticism: audiences were no longer incredulous about magic: the day of the serious
shaman was long past (for that present at least): and even the progressive magic of Science (i.e., that craftsmanship of technical witchery . . . mechanical alchemy . . . which awed a previous generation) was becoming suspect as a closed, and completely explicable, system: the late 19th century magician either laughed with the audience, conditioning thus its laughter, or was laughed off the stage: audiences were no longer subject to the traditional 'enchantment' . . . were no longer seriously 'charmed.'

George discovered that essential madness of the 19th century that needed to be "humoured" when he was in his 'teens at a time when his own incredulity was breaking under the weight of accumulated knowledge: and, by this time, he was managing to conceal his heroic and demonic inventions from any knowledge his parts had of each other, and to exclude both from any imaginings of woman; and it was, too, at this 'teen-time' he began surely studying that master stage magician of all time: the great Robert-Houdin (*not* to be confused with his American imitator half-a-century later) Houdin, the man who embodied the fullest traditional development of this centuries-old, specifically European, form of shamanism-as-entertainment . . . the man who does now represent the culmination of that form of magic whose name is synonymous with it.

George began to study this tradition because he felt the need to *prove* the magic he'd endowed his hero with in public and ultimately to stage the triumph of his hero over primal monsters before an audience . . . thus to exteriorize the battle which his foetal-self had lost on interior grounds. What he did not at first realize was that only monsters of his own making would ever appear

under his staged direction: like the shaman with his "rain dance," George hoped his mock battles would precipitate the "real" one, and that it would follow the orders of his repeated invention that his mechanical manipulations, his tricks, would transform into the orders of phenomenal magic when the actual combat began . . . and all in the secure surrounds of attendant company/audience.

All the stories of his childhood, all myths, and most so-called "fantasy" books since, had informed him that he was not alone in having the dreadful experience of foetal dismemberment: these tales constituted a history of the various partial successess and the ultimate failure so far in human confrontation, with the seemingly endless host of monsters on that alien plain (as it was usually pictured in paintings) with that distant mountain range, marking horizon, wherefrom three shadows moving toward him had presaged the primal destructive assault . . . and that craggy valley (a specialty of Medieval 'oils') where his captive being was tortured . . . and that cave where he was torn to pieces : all these images he shared, in their various forms, with many other men who had created heroes to return there for their deliverance . . . or had made maps, like vast battle plans, of the foreign territory portraits like "wanted" posters of the demons to be slain "rain dances" of language and oil paint in terrified sympathetic magic hopefully predicting the success of the hero.

And George, raised in the Christian tradition, could not help but also think that if *once* one man's hero could take upon himself these demons of 'The World,' that then they would cease to exist in their various but clearly-related forms for all men could not help but think of each member of the audience as also a symbol of the disembodied fragments of this horrible drama, which could it ever be made to surface would be recognized by each, each lending his hero to the necessary battle.

George did not consciously think all this out as he began his career as a stage magician because his further aim (of attaining some whole being again) necessitated the concealment of one part of his invented nature from another.

Because both inventions had to be concealed from the woman of his imaginings, sex was *only* conceivable to him (as most young men of his time) as an absolute private act, clouded in the utmost secrecy, fortified from any interference with his plans by every means of possession possible . . . simplified by money ('buyable,' in other words), guarded by jealousies of romantic love (most effective when engendered in the woman) and finally insured (as it *were*) by the absolute sanctification of marriage.

But these protective measures of sexual approach operative in the society around him, and the vulgar humor so desperately clouding all public reference to the private act, failed to give George any sense of integral security. His early relationships with actual girls naturally shattered his imaginings: the societal blows dealt to his complex image of woman destroyed most of his careful make-up of her, leaving only a series of bell-shaped curves reverberating in a blur of echoing multiplicity many women of doll-like features and proportions all looking and moving alike . . . the chorus line. This Bell Woman, as we'll call her, could be publicly sexual because she was only a series of residual ghosts of some destroyed original; and as such she seemed a perfect partner for the dismembered man. Her enticing movements were safely synchronized to patterns of well-known music, all individuation limited to the bell dance, and the whole reverberation of her enmeshed in the trappings of the stage. Attention to her could contract mid-dance to focus thrillingly upon the centered image of the lead dancer, or star, because this individuation was only a pale reminder of any integral original and was always backed by the chorus-line scheduled, in the dance, to shatter into echoes of her. Often the right and left of this line of blurs divided into antithetical movements, just as a bell's visual vibrations might vary to either side of some struck center: legs could kick in clear approximate of sex dance on the stage because there was no cut to fuck in all this ghostly mass: the imagined necessary power of the Bell Woman was 'number' rather than any frighteningly indivisible magic; her make-up had to be doll-like a *reductio ad absurdum* of individual feature ; and her milieu was, natch, gaity . . . a humoresque to mask the horror of this recreation or re-enactment of the destruction of woman.

But George, a very precise man, wasn't satisfied with this blur of a woman: he cross-bred her show-biz dress with the costume of a ballerina opting for some reminder, in this complex, of Tchaikovskian tragedy . . . the sad swan woman, mystery-woman, tragic heroine albeit alive and kicking. Finally, he singled her out (usually in ballet tights and that blur of hips such fluff of swan's dress engenders) for a most particular transformation of his own devising: he imagined her multiplicity in the sense that she could be turned into anything as a variety of being rather than a number of images of being . . . a transformation in quality rather than quantity himself, The Magician, controlling the various charms of this *femme fatale*. He limited her in his imagination to the tradition of stage magic: she was always thus, the "helper" of The Magician: and otherwise, he drew upon the whole mythic history of woman, from oracle of Delphi to mermaid, from goddess to witch. In her divine aspects he had the courage to give her power over men to loose demons against them . . . to turn men into beasts, etc.: but she was always putty in the hands of The Magician or almost always and could be made to jump through hoops like circus dogs, vanish in a puff of smoke at The Magician's slightest annoyance: she could be made-up out of anything . . . a dress-maker's dummy . . . the hoop she'd jump through . . . thin air itself. But whatever George's control over her, she was a magnificent imagining greater than if she

were just George's creation inasmuch as she had a divine aspect which George adored and was certainly, in all her aspects, essentially "an original:" and, as such, we will call her "George's Love."

The 19th century magic showman had to be a mechanical genius, and George Méliès was no exception to this rule: the hero of his invention that spirit-of-him created to wreak vengeance upon the demons who had destroyed his actual self before birth that hero then, came to take on aspects of The Golem . . . a kind of stone impassivity and a manner of implacable servitude the aloof presence and politesse of the stage magician, moving with rhythmic grace and machine precision through his acts and bowing to the audience he has just amazed . . . the audience he leads into the maze of awesome improbability or taking upon himself the laughter of that audience he has just amused . . . the audience whose madness he had 'humoured' by making his hero-self appear as buffoon before them. George struggled many years preparing for the dreadful eventuality of his revenge and possible salvation: and all this time the hero took the gadgets and machines of magician's trade as extensions and, finally, appendages of self . . . as knights must once have taken their swords, lances, horses. George built his own sets, gaining maximum control of the synthetic *mise en scène* which would one day (through sympathetic magic) precipitate the land shapes of original terror (the plain, the valley, the cave); and he designed all costume to wrap each moving creature in recognizable form (the oldest shamanism in the book); and he choreographed all movements to make (for the "rain dance") a puppet-master's perfect manipulability of the entire stage . . .

And he failed . . .

He achieved a wordly fame which was of no use to his desperate purpose, and wealth which couldn't bribe demons, and he won The Bell Woman in her endlessly repeating variations of being (no vibration of which offered the least hope of heroine splendor or resolution for his dismembered self).

He failed as miserably as ever a man could . . . inasmuch as he had never even approached the 'darkling plain' of his dismemberment again had made a charade instead to stand for it a distraction repeated nightly with mocking success before an endlessly howling and applauding audience of horrible heads and hands floating in a black pit beyond the illuminated space of his actual shame.

Were it not for the machine, George would probably have played-out this hopeless game for the rest of his life: but the signs of the times were kind to George and directed him beyond his own advertence, led him (in midst of his inner despair) down the most natural path of his daily existence to the door-way of friendship with a man (symbolically?) named Pathé. It would have been difficult for George (as famous 19th century Parisian magician) *NOT* to have known the French inventor Pathé: and (as we know now how difficult it would have been for George to be *anything but* a 19th century magician) we can begin to say he had a *destiny* . . . that these two men were destined to meet . . . that the signs of the times The Fates perhaps advertised them to each other in such a milieu of practicality as to insure their friendship: (how happily extricable are these Fates once one understands the simple daily warps and woofs of all their weaving). Anyway, George was one day invited to the home of his friend Pathé to view a new invention.

The inventor dimmed all light and then cast a single beam of illumination across the room to etch the black and white image of a beach and ocean against the wall. George was not surprised; he had seen 'transparencies' before. Such 'shadow images' were, in fact, centuries old: and photographs had been available since George's birth. But then, suddenly, the waves of the ocean began to move in toward the beach to splash upon them . . . a brilliant rash of white light along a line of gray texture: had Venus herself emerged from this sea, been born in that room then, George couldn't have been more excited than he was by this moving picture; for he must have immediately known this machine as a means for the Venus-birth of his own being, known it as a means of infinite transformation, known it as his Love.

His first move, in keeping with his character, was to attempt to buy it: but Pathé would have none of that said this invention was for scientific research . . . not, no! not ever to be used for entertainment. George's next action, in keep with his whole story of indomitable will, was to go home and invent it himself. Mercurially (after god of both thieves and artists) he both stole and created the Venus machine: like Prometheus he brought this god-force to 'the people' its firing light (on-off illumination of individual still images in sequences giving the illusion of movement) lit up his magician's stage and dazzled his audiences.

But George, who knew these images were *not* moving pictures knew them as 'stills' he'd photographed in a sequence of move-mirages was no more dazed by this machine's performance than by any of the other tricks of his creation . . . and thus he, alone of all those in attendance, first sensed something very strange occurring at each projecting something no one else in the entire world was to recognize consciously for twenty-some years: an eerie feeling . . . a rising of hair on the back of his neck . . . an indefinable fright to his whole nervous system though not anything he could put his mechanic's finger upon nothing logically explicable caused him increasing apprehension each time the flickering beam of light cut across his workshop room or flared over the sea of hands and faces in the darkened auditorium: it was as if some being he *hadn't* photographed was attempting to "steal the show," to usurp the screen and "upstage" all the pictured theatricality of his devising . . . by some ephemeral yet "real" act unchoreographed or simply by the power of "presence" (that in-

definable quality some actors have which makes it impossible to cast them as anything but "star.")

George often faced the projector from his position on the stage, saw the beam of widening illumination as a hallway he might almost climb, diminishing in size until he'd perhaps vanished into the tunnel of the lens: he knew from experience that any step into the light would tear his shadow off his back and hurl it against screen behind; and so at first he avoided bodily intruding upon the apparitions of this machine. But his thoughts entered the flickering corridor and dissolved in hypnotized 'light-mares' as they encountered some alien quality moving there, creeping steadily down the temporal ladders of off-on illumining, gathering fearfully in the dark pockets of all pictured forms. It began to seem to him as if some forbidden veil were being ripped open in each shift of light . . . slowly, steadily, rent by black's every insistence. The screen behind him smoked and darkened in formal patches as if the focused ray were turning it to carbon; and yet the screen seemed to repair itself continually, for these carboniferous patches shifted feverishly across the flat surface: were they smoke-hold of some hellfire, then, that burns eternally without ever consuming? No!, rather George sensed this fire of motion pictures erupts out of Time's dimension . . . and burns through an infinite number of screens, or veils films, then beyong human comprehension.

Thus George became the first man to recognize motion pictures as medium of both super-nature and underworld and instrument for unveiling the natural through reflection . . . and also the gateway for an alien world underneath the surface of our natural visual ability an underworld that erupts into "ours" through every machine which makes visible to us what we cannot naturally sense. The so-called supernatural IS as any magician knows innately tangible to the naked eye . . . its recognition-as-nature requiring only a shift of thought a sleight of hand: but the underworld HAD to be invented, as it were . . . i.e.: its very real existence had to be passed-thru invention for "us" to begin to be both aware *of* it and prey *to* its consummation.

In these recognitions George inherited the full destiny he'd been born-to before his physical birth. The instant he found his medium . . . a medium that could summon-up the unborn . . . the only medium which can exteriorize moving imagination in that instant George's life was all *before* him: he became the artist he had always been the first such in modern history to turn 'a medium' into 'an art:' he had his demons lured from under and trapped into a realm of super sense: all the monster creatures which the mechanical thought of his unborn self had loosed upon him were loosed again through the terrible machine of motion pictures: and the long awaited battle could begin.

Knowing the black areas of the ignited screen to be the most actually haunted, George created many of his ghostly photo-apparitions in white overexposing the image even, and blurring his spectral forms by shaking the camera . . . creating a counter-balancing demonology an army of super-impositions upon all shadow. Black costume demons of his design tended, in his photo-play, to be easily defeated . . . exploded, usually, in a puff of brilliant white smoke.

The hero of these movie dramas was usually himself-as-photographed, garbed in enough black the tux of the showman to permit his photo-form to move magically through the darkling planes of any composition . . . carrying, as if it were a standard, his recognizable features for a head as hero's helmet and yet sometimes disguised by the beard of an old man's role he'd created for his hero self and almost always in that aged form disguised as a 'fool,' 'buffoon,' or one utterly prey to, at least, costume-demons in a play of foolishness . . . as if George were offering devils or baiting *The* Devil with his elder self (some trap, perhaps, borrowed from Goethe's *Faust* with its humanly happy ending.) Certainly George borrowed the trappings of all western man's converse with demons in a fight of fire with fire white fire with black fire.

But because any actual monstrousness seemed to George to inhabit every area of graphic form every shade of line that made image recognizable his war spread naturally against every being and object photographed . . . the only safety of his hero-self being his ability to transform one thing into another especially into some mass of white . . . the only heroic weapon, then, the magic wand: and George's ultimate means of helping his heroic self was his ability to transform the whole structure of the battlefield at any instant the 'going' got too rough. It was this later necessity which led him to make the first splice in motion picture history the attaching of one piece of celluloid sequence of "stills" to another.

The very nature of the war, however, began to change in the middle of George's career as film-maker. If every graphic of recognizable form was 'haven' for demons, then photo-still objects became enemy's fort. Every unmoving *thing* was, after all, a deteriorating thing. And if it had lines and shading upon it (nestling dark forces), it quickly became haunted: even the image of the sun main source of light required only the lines of a 'face' upon it to make it at enmity with anything more purely white. The moon, almost synonym for movie screen, haunted George particularly because its representation demanded a 'face' . . . thus led George to some cosmic suspicion of every light in the sky: were not all stars as the first astro-watchers had seen them simply highlights vaguely indicating the shapes of enormous black creatures? Because George felt all photo-still objects as demon fortresses, he was moved as film-maker to keep everything as animated as possible (like a man stuffing old houses with as much life as he could to edge out ghosts) certainly to keep all people-shapes in continual movement in opposition to any 'set' of their surroundings . . ."on his side," so to speak. He was also determined to give inanimate objects their 'faces' . . . like

warning signs of what they harbored . . . and then often to animate those faces. He was inspired like the Greeks before him to "fill in" the spaces between stars with as much white as possible.

All Renaissance shading, giving the illusion of depth, also provided 'cover' for his enemies: thus George was obsessed to attack the whole of western painterly trappings Renaissance perspective itself: he therefore began to conceive his movie scenes as a series of movable 'flats,' offering a minimal 'vanishing point' and maximal relationship to the screen against which they would be projected. This desperate measure, against the grain of western visual development, gave George a new battle-ground (the likes of which had not been seen since the aesthetics of Florence had won over those of Siena). The nature of the battle became *anamorphic* (rather than *mythic*): the moving against the immovable: the quick against the dead. Just as he *knew* the moon must have a face (more dreadful to imagine in "the dark of the moon" than when clearly etched on white) so, too, he knew all white must have its black lines of form (though *not* necessarily spacial shadings . . . which he minimized by front lighting); and thereby he created his costume-demons as double-agents . . . spies on his side . . . demonstrating, so to speak, the defeat of all such monstrousness. George finally came to play The Devil himself again and again: and his witches came to take the very revenge that he himself desired. With masterful complexity George proceeded to play-out the war with spies and counter-spies of triumphant vision. His films became anagrams of incredible duplicity as he abrogated more and more powers of transformation to himself and his self's hero magician . . . or witch . . . or demon . . . or devil, even.

But George could not honestly bring any aspect of his dismembered being to identify with either inanimate object or depth-of-space. The 'sets' were always 'given over' to the demons . . . his only control of them being the warning sign of their visage thus visibility and "change of scene." Inevitably, therefore, George came up against cosmic disaster . . . his defeat by material itself and the space of its residence demon strata!

George, at the time of life a man just begins to feel himself as 'ageing,' would have surrendered were it not for the emergence of a new hero-image in his dreams the only hero who might possibly pass through the veils of materiality and traverse all cosmological stuffing . . . the last (for George) heroic trick in the bag: The Machine: yes! . . . the hero-as-machine old Golem again young Venus maybe too, who'd once before given him a new lease on struggle: The Machine-as-photographed . . . The Machine-as-pictured through the means of machinery something like a 'hall of mirrors' reflecting mirrors, *ad infinitum,* to confound all material sense and punch a hole in the whole of universal space.

Was it not the perfect servant or "helper" of The Magician? Was it not that absolute contradiction to confound demonology? inasmuch as The Machine *was* material, yet animate beyond any human capability . . . was there any limit to the space a machine might traverse? the master of it, himself, utterly inside its armor. Was it not a thing made up of many inanimate parts which were put together and came to 'life' then as they were fueled to intereact perfectly with each other in a miraculous entirety of moving being? The Machine was yes! kin-creator to George his bloodless (therefore humanly invulnerable) brother . . . and woman, too (for be it automobile or boat or aeroplane or rocket, even, some 'unwritten law' had always made it be lovingly called a "her"): she, any machine, was yes! the triumph of all his imagining and actual invention . . . the wildest Galatea of all Pygmalion time "let 'er rip" through Time itself, if possible, and all black space, shaking shadows off herself in each shift of gear, turn of wheel, whirl of The Magician's motivation as she/he tore through the film's cast fast as frames could touch her/his movement across the screen.

The Machine of his dreams became star of his dramas, defying all actor-scoffers knocking 'em down when they got in the way . . . knocking down walls, houses, and all such blocks or blockheads of material . . . putting out the eye of the moon . . . jostling stars, even and all the while protecting The Magician (and his friends), carrying him as gently as a baby in a cradle . . . as a baby in the womb . . . as man entombed . . .

Yes alas The Machine failed George too, finally . . . it was for all its animation a recognizable shape; and as such it fell into every trap of illumination fell, as a train, once, into the sun's mouth . . . damned those within it to the same set-to of all inanimate scenery. As a recognizable object The Machine could never be more than subject matter: thus George's photoplays still whirled shamanistically their dance flashing blacks and whites against impenetrable screen.

George desperately tried color toward the last dyeing the celluloid having images of objects (often The Machine) tinted tones that might vibrate them into another dimension of thought . . . brushed-in hues over the black and white shape on every single frame to shift the dark/light trap of photo-genesis. But he only managed to paint himself into a beautiful corner: (color is a quality of light a qualification then . . . a diminishment as surely as shadow).

The battle was over without there having actually been a fight and George was left with reels of projectionable maps of a campaign only imagined . . . a record of sympathetic magic that had failed the maker's inner tension had failed to alter for him what had already been. He had directed and acted a series of pretensions; and he had been (as all artists before him) simply used by forces beyond his imagined "2nd coming" his 'coming again' his comprehension.

No artist has ever been permitted to comprehend the work he creates: only those who do creatively attend it are permitted to second-guess its actual being . . . make game of it . . . hunt down the beasts of it in lairs of their own angelic orders. Only those who exert as much creative energy apprehending the work of art as it took to make it, can break the traps of form that whirl an almost impenetrable cocoon of habit-sense around revelation. But the audiences of George's day were having NONE of *THAT* you may be sure . . . certainly NOT any Gordion knots to be unraveled on their 'evening's out' no!, not ever . . . never, then, any reminder, please, of what each man, woman, and child had forfeited prebirth . . . not, for god's sake, any labyrinthining amidst our pleasure : let us, rather, be spirit *only,* escaping in a gas of distractive words, music and images meaning no thing whatsoever: let the gods and demons *have* of us what they will, what they have *had,* so long as our play is surely fun and free and we reasonably assured of soul's immortality.

An industry of imitators began making films like George's, but films which carried no weight of obsession, no haunt, no art. These 'escape movies' freed audiences from the strange discomforts and the apprehensions which George's elicited in even the most dense sensibility. George could not compete with his imitators and thus lost all commercial stance for his cosmic act.

Toward the last he tried to make a "come-back," as it's called, and he made a series of movie dramas which premised his primal scene of dismemberment *as if* it had been at the hands of audience on the darkling plain of the auditorium . . . as if the hands and heads of the clapping and laughing wealthy members of society black with evening dress had torn him/George to pieces . . . as indeed they had. His commercial failure at their hands had taught George lessons more immediate to his daily living than those he had learned in the womb. But these social dramas of the last years of his creating posed no war as had the fantasies of all previous making . . . George was by then too defeated in all his being to manage even imaginary battle. He used the motion picture machine finally, almost as if to write a letter to 'the worldly' pleading the cause of 'the poor' . . . asking shelter and food, *at least* for the abandoned baby or starving child he now felt himself to be. Sometimes he asked in these literaries his films had become to be invited again to the bacchanal the birthday party of all beast scene . . . the celebration of demon's day amidst the rich (those who epitomized, for George, the humans that lived most successfully with dismemberment). In other films he sometimes fancied powers of goodness that would take pity upon his orphaned self and all such outcasts of a Victorian society obviously given-over to an evil that existed on, now, moral grounds rather than fields of cosmic disorder. He envisioned all church, for instance, as just another theatre where audience gathered to escape . . . rather than attend the messages of angels. He had no hero anymore, nor invention either. All that was left to his imagination was that old 'mothering' heroine: Christian Charity. His every plot now was dedicated to arousing this spirit-of-pity in each spectator or at least to haunt every eye with this goodly ghost. His scenes now were only supports of an aesthetic propaganda for yes, these plays, though Charity advertisements, were still sufficiently "*of* an art" to establish a realm of consideration beyond George's wishes . . . were more than the moral pleadings he imagined them to be: they did, as a matter of incredible fact, anticipate the aesthetic milieu of the next great film artist, D. W. Griffith, and prophetically announce the subject which would most interfere with the light of this new art for the next twenty-five years. D. W. Griffith was to go to war in this matter and marshal pictured "fact" as his army against social indifference: but George Méliès was reduced to begging *for* sympathy . . . rather than *in* sympathetic magic . . . and had only sentiment on his side.

George's visual pleas went altogether over the heads of his audience, raining tears down out of their eyes instead of diamonds for either him or 'the poor:' he therefore failed himself once again . . . failed (as all artists do) to achieve anything reasonable to himself for the muse-force in a man only uses "reason" . . . feeds on it from inside out, destroying it while assuming its logical shape . . . feeds on the maker, turning him inside out destroys every idea he has of himself, finally even of himself-as-artist. George was luckier than many (having that 'luck' of the very hard-worker): he exhausted most of his aesthetic possibilities in his late middle age.

Magician that he was, he managed to vanish from popular sight, effected completely his disappearance from 'The World' as it's called, and attained, at least, a private life. All his failures in the realm of heroics proved useful at last in that kingdom-of-acceptance any 'daily living' is: George had identified sufficiently with every imaginable creature and condition of circumstance to manage a livelier/happier personal existence than most men even day-dream. Certainly no nightmares could ever take him by terrible surprise again. He continued to see the shifting faces in the fire's dark of his hearth and all those leering from his living-room walls, floors, furnishings the visages of all wood-work . . . the shapes in the irregularities of plaster, *etcetera:* but these had become 'familiars,' so to speak, and must often have seemed even friendly charged as they were with the nostalgia of acknowledged enmity grown old . . . : certainly they were no longer terrifying to him as they were when he was a child.

He married the proprietress of a candy store and became, thus, shopkeeper at center of children's world. He had children of his own; and he certainly did everything he could to protect them and all his candy customers too, from any fate at all like his: but still he couldn't entirely resist playing The Magician at times for them performing small parlor tricks for their amazement . . . tiny transformations reduced to the stage of his aged hands, alive with loving movement in a flutter of tricks a 'now-you-see-it/now-you-don't' amusement before the admiring eyes of a child: and he would then, more often than not, show how it was done . . . so that there should

be no sensibility trap left in the wake of his game with them.

When he was a very old man and his children fully grown and, happily, none of them artists . . . or even magicians . . . he was re-discovered, recognized, in his candy shop by a government official. His films, having a life of their own quite separate from his, had become established film classics in the meantime. Something in each of these films drew people to look at them again and again: after all the laughs had spent their force, and the films had entertained to their fullest extent, there still remained an attraction to them beyond popularity some felt-quality of power unleashed in each . . . as if they were *as in fact they are* one of the greatest untapped natural resources in the world . . . if only one could penetrate their surface and release the real energy of them. George, of course, had no such notion of them: they had failed him much as children will fail a father had failed to even make him a living, let alone to restore him to some whole being . . . ; and he was more-than-a-little surprised at the attention they belatedly brought him like some old soldier decorated twenty/thirty years after his defeat on the field of battle.

George was awarded for *god* knows what reason, the French Legion of Honor medallion . . .

. . . He died a very short time after.

Linda Williams (essay date 1981)

SOURCE: "Film Body: An Implantation of Perversions," in *Cine-Tracts*, Vol. 3, No. 4, Winter, 1981, pp. 19-35.

[*In the following excerpt, Williams asserts that Méliès's treatment of the human physical form in his films is an attempt to grant it magical and mysterious qualities—in contrast to Eadweard Muybridge who depicted the human form as sculpture.*]

In the first volume of *The History of Sexuality*, Michel Foucault writes that ever since the seventeenth century there has been in the West an increasing intensification of the body both as object of knowledge and element in the relations of power.[1] This intensification has emerged in a proliferation of discourses of sexuality which have produced a whole range of sexual behavior now categorized as perverse. For Foucault this "implantation of perversions" is the result of the encroachment of power on bodies and their pleasures.

> The implantation of perversions is an instrument-effect: it is through the isolation, intensification, and consolidation of peripheral sexualities that the relations of power to sex and pleasure branched out and multiplied, measured the body, and penetrated modes of conduct. And accompanying this encroachment of powers, scattered sexualities rigidified, became stuck to an age, a place, a type

of practice. A proliferation of sexualities through the extension of power; an optimization of the power to which each of these local sexualities gave a surface of intervention: this concatenation, particularly since the nineteenth century, has been ensured and relayed by the countless economic interests which, with the help of medicine, psychiatry, prostitution, and pornography, have tapped into both this analytical multiplication of pleasure and this optimization of the power that controls it. Pleasure and power do not cancel or turn back against one another; they seek out, overlap, and reinforce one another. They are linked together by complex mechanisms and devices of excitation and incitement.[2]

Foucault's argument offers a significant challenge to the commonly held notion that sex exists autonomously in nature, independent of any discourse on it and as a natural challenge to a power which either pretends it does not exist or prohibits it. He argues instead that sex is a fictitious causal principle that allows us to evade the true relation of power to sexuality. Thus we do not escape social determination when we have recourse to the supposedly natural pleasures of the body since the particular forms these pleasures take are themselves produced by the needs of power.

Psychoanalysis has been a major force in the deployment of a sexuality that has intensified the body as a site of knowledge and power, making this body the major arena for the discovery of the non-existent "truth" of sex. But nowhere has the deployment of sexuality, and its attendant implantation of perversions, been more evident than in the visible intensification of the body that came about with the invention of cinema. This invention itself grew out of a scientific discourse on the body in the work of Muybridge and Marey whose "chronophotography" attempted to document the previously unobserved facts of its movements. And yet, this very machinery of observation and measurement turns out to be, even at this early stage, less an impartial instrument than a crucial mechanism in the power established over that body, constituting it as an object or subject of desire, offering up an image of the body as mechanism that is in many ways a reflection of the mechanical nature of the medium itself.

THE FILM BODY AND THE BODY OF THE SPECTATOR

In his essay on "Tha Apparatus" Jean Louis Baudry argues that the cinematic apparatus considered not just as the film itself but the technical specificity of the entire cinematic process and its ideological effects brings about a state of regression and narcissism in the spectator. Baudry suggests that his regression imitates an original condition of unity with the body of the mother. In this original state of plenitude, before the separation of the subject's body from everything else in the world, the images produced by dreams and hallucinations are taken as real perceptions. Baudry suggests that the cinematic apparatus imitates aspects of this

original condition of unity by placing the film spectator before "representations experienced as perceptions" similar to those of dreams and hallucinations. Thus the cinema re-creates a form of lost satisfaction from a time when desire could be immediately satisfied through the transfer of the memory of a perception to the form of hallucination.[3]

In other words, according to Baudry, the very formation of the cinematic apparatus responds to a desire to figure a unity and coherence in the spectator that has long since been lost in the spectator-subject's entrance into the symbolic of difference. But if the "invention" of the cinema corresponds to a desire to figure a lost unity in the body of the spectator-subject, what is the effect of this invention on the primary object of this spectator-subject's vision: the human body figured in the film?

To a certain extent we know what the status of this body becomes as a relay to the body of the spectator within the already formulated institution of classical narrative films and their system of "suture."[4] To a certain extent also we already know how these films constitute the male body within the film as surrogate for the look of the male spectator and the female body as site of the spectacle.[5] But we know much less about the position of these male and female bodies in the "pre-historic" and "primitive" stages of the evolution of the cinema, before codes of narrative, editing and mise-en scene were fully established. I hope to show that this "film body," like the apparatus itself, operates to restore a lost unity in the spectator-subject, but that this unity is a more specific and perverse response to the threat of disunity posed by the visible "presence" of the body on the screen that in fact, there exists, at the very moment of the emergence of a "simulation machine"[6] capable of figuring the human body in a dream-like "representation mistaken for a perception," a dramatic re-staging within this representation of the male child's traumatic discovery of, and subsequent mastery over, sexual difference.

Both Eadweard Muybridge and Georges Méliès, two child-men whose work, in different ways and at different times, was formative of the institution and apparatus of cinema, privilege the body as pure object of truth in their work. For Muybridge this truth is scientific a matter of isolating the essential. He strips the body of clothes to better reveal its musculature and movement. He isolates it against a bare background or grid to measure it, and he tailors his frame to accommodate the body's full extension in size. For Méliès, on the other hand, the truth of the body is both magical and mysterious. He complicates and clutters his bodies with a vast array of costumes, mechanized scenery and gadgets of all sorts, and he situates all of this within a rudimentary diegesis. But for both men the naked body of the woman, whether boldly and repeatedly figured by Muybridge as in the plate from *The Human Figure in Motion*[7], or briefly and coyly glimpsed as ... [a]still from one of Méliès' rare "stag" films entitled *After the Ball*[8], poses a problem of sexual difference which it then becomes the work of the incipient forms of narrative and mise-en-scene to overcome.

EADWEARD MUYBRIDGE

As early as 1880 Muybridge had illustrated his lectures on animal locomotion with the aid of his own "zoopraxiscope" a circular glass plate that could mount up to 200 transparencies which, when revolved, could project a short sequence of movement. These projections of movement sequences, like the printed plates of *Animal Locomotion* his vast study of both human and animal movement published in 1887 repeated very short portions of motions from side, front and rear points of view. Both the published photo-sequences and the projected movements of these sequences mounted in the "zoopraxiscope" portray an image of the body as a repeatable mechanism. This body mechanism is controlled in the published work by a whole battery of machines (Muybridge employed 48 cameras in a normal set up) capable of arresting movement for further scrutiny; and it is controlled in the zoopraxiscope by a mechanism capable of reconstructing this movement as illusion. Thus with Muybridge we encounter the very moment at which the representation of the discontinuous fragments of the still photograph begins to be reconstituted as a perception (Baudry's "representation mistaken for a perception") of continuous motion.

What is striking, however, is that with this mastery of the illusion of motion, with this near restoration of the whole body in its full perceptual force, come, in Muybridge's studies of the human body, gratuitous fantasization and iconization of the bodies of women that have no parallel in the representation of the male. And this is so in spite of the enormously simplified decor and relative absence of clothing of all his subjects.

In *The Human Figure in Motion Muybridge* divides his subjects into three categories: men, women and children. In each category, sequences of movements are arranged to reveal a progression from simple to more complex motions. The male figures progress, for example, through various forms of walking, running and jumping to more complex tasks such as throwing and catching, kicking, boxing and wrestling, and finally to the performance of "Various Trades" such as carpentry and hod carrying.

Women's bodies are put through a similar progression of activities designed to reveal movement in more typically "feminine" contexts. For example, we see many sequences of women walking but only one that shows a woman running. In place of the "Throwing and Catching" activities for men, we have women more sedately "Picking Up and Putting Down" to which a very brief section on throwing has been added. On the other hand, there are many variations on the comparatively passive postures of standing, sitting and kneeling.

Some of the movements and gestures in the women's section walking, running, jumping parallel those of the men. Yet even here there is a tendency to add a superfluous detail to the women's movements details which tend to mark her as more embedded within a socially prescribed system of objects and gestures than her male counterparts. For example, the sequence of a women walking adds the inexplicable, and rather coy, detail of having her walk with her hand to her mouth, thus lending an air of mystery, an extra mark of difference which far exceeds the obvious anatomical difference between the male and female. Or, in the single instance in which a woman runs, her run is again differentiated from the male's by the gesture of grasping her left breast with her right hand. Although one could presume that this is to keep her breast from bouncing, the narcissism of the gesture is unmistakable, especially since it has no parallel among the similarly bouncing male genitals.

A frequent feature of the various male activities is some kind of simple prop that is either carried or manipulated to facilitate different muscular and kinetic activities: dumbbells, boulders, baseballs; the equipment of various combat sports such as swords for fencing; and the tools of the "Various Trades" such as spades, saws and hammers. (Many male activities show men lifting, throwing, balancing and carrying a simple round boulder which functions in a variety of situations to demonstrate the movements which manipulate it.) But when the women's gestures include props, these props are always very specific objects, never a simple weight that can be reused in many different situations. Lifting or carrying activities for women never use an abstract, non-specific object but instead, two types of baskets for her head, a jug of water, a bucket of water and a basin of water all of which engage her in specific activities of washing, watering or giving to drink.

Although these props serve the ostensible purpose of eliciting certain kinds of motor activities, and although we do encounter some equally specific props for men as well, the props associated with women's bodies are never just devices to elicit movement; they are always something more, investing her body with an iconographic or even diegetic surplus of meaning. For example, when a women lies down on a blanket placed on the ground in an activity that is identical to the series entitled "Man Lying Down", she does not only lie down. She is provided with a narrative reason for lying down and the extra prop that goes with it: she lies down in order to read a newspaper. In other variations of lying down that have no male equivalent, the woman lies down in a hammock and, finally, in a bed complete with sheets and pillows. The latter offers the bizarre sight of covering up the woman's nudity. It is complemented, in the final plate of the women's section, by the reverse spectacle of uncovering her nudity as the woman gets out of this same bed.

It does not seem entirely accidental that Muybridge chooses to conclude his section on women with this particular prop which in addition to its obvious sexual use, entirely covers and then uncovers the very body which the motion study seeks to reveal.[9] A similar game of peek-a-boo is played with a variety of materials or garments which partially cover and in that covering seem to reveal all the more the woman's body. We see this in the sequence entitled "Woman Walking Downstairs Throwing Scarf over Shoulders,", which covers only to uncover again. Thus the women are consistently provided with an extra prop which overdetermines their difference from the male. This overdetermination of difference also extends to such propless activities as walking and running or, strikingly, in a sequence in which the gratuitous gesture of difference, blowing a kiss, entirely defines her as a flirtatious object of desire.

An even greater surplus of erotic meaning runs through the group of photos which show two women in the same frame. These sequences are paralleled in the male section by such two-persons activities as boxing, fencing and wrestling which show the men performing a limited repertoire of combat sports. It would be absurd to expect women of the period to engage in similar sports. But it is interesting that even though Muybridge makes no attempt to imitate with women the motor activities of these male combat sports, he nevertheless does attempt to create activities that women can perform together. Since he must literally invent these activities, it is not surprising that we find in them extreme instances of what can already be termed a cinematic mise-en-scène.

In one almost comically incongruous "scene", an ambulant naked woman serves a cup of coffee to another seated woman who drinks it and hands it back. In another, a woman stands on a chair and pours a bucket of water over another woman seated in a large basin. This second woman reacts, as if surprised by the coldness of the water, by jumping out of the basin and running away. In both examples Muybridge has directed his female figures in what are very nearly dramatic scenes of domestic interaction taking place in a minimally defined dining room and bathroom. These scenes have a much greater degree of diegetic illusion than the less spatially situated, more purely motor activities of the men.

But even the more erotically charged are the scenes in which two women perform an atypical series of movements, as when two women dance together, or the sequence entitled "Women Turning and Holding Water Jug for Kneeling Companion". This sequence depicts the unlikely situation of a woman pouring water into the mouth of another from a large and unwieldy jug, with the added detail that she appears to spill a little water. Here, the unconventionality of the activity invests the scene with an enigmatic eroticism: why are these women playing with this large jug (no less!), and what is the nature of their relationship? The two women are defined as "companions;" none of the two-person male activities offers a similar description of the nature of the relationship between them. Another enigmatic scene, entitled "Women Sitting Down in Chair Held by Companion, Smoking Cigarette" the very length of these titles indicates their increased narrativity shows a stand-

ing woman leaning against the back of the chair of her "seated companion" gazing down on her almost longingly.

The cigarette in this last sequence offers a powerful connotation of both loose morals and, for the period, masculinity, both of which lend lesbian overtones to the scene which are completely unequaled in the comparable male activities of boxing or wrestling. For even though these male activities involve body contact, their purposeful and conventional nature does not allow the same erotic investment. The cigarette is yet another of the many gratuitous details which perversely fetishize the woman's body. But it does so with some insistence, as in an equally unmotivated, extravagantly lascivious "pose" of a single woman, or in a twosome in which both women smoke while walking arm in arm.

Of course, one could try to explain all these props and poses by the fact that most of the women Muybridge used for his photos were professional artist's models, while the male "performers" were everyday people whose movements were linked to their activities in real life, e.g., the University of Pennsylvania's "professor of physical culture," two "instructors at the Fencing and Sparing Club," etcetera. But all this really explains is the significant fact that even in the prehistory of cinema, at a time when the cinema was much more a document of reality than a narrative art, women were already fictionalized, already playing assumed roles, already not there as themselves.[11]

Robert Taft, who wrote the introduction to the current edition of *The Human Figure in Motion,* tries to explain the need for professional female models by the fact that many of the women were required to appear nude.[12] But even allowing for the fact that it was more risqué for a Victorian woman to pose nude than for a Victorian male and thus the need for professional models, we cannot use this same reasoning to account for the fact that the women are both categorically and numerically more nude than the men. Of the fourteen classes of human and animal subjects photographed by Muybridge during his stay at the University of Pennsylvania, the first three are of men in three stages of undress listed as 1) "draped," 2) "pelvis cloth" a kind of jock strap, and 3) "nude." Thus the women's intermediate level of undress, transparent drapery and semi-nude, does not perform the same function of covering the genitals as the male "pelvis cloth." In fact, it does quite the reverse, draping the female body with a transparent veil (fig. 20) or partial garment which, like the bedcovers, scarf or dress, only call attention to her nudity all the more. These transparent and partial clothes offer a variation on what Roland Barthes has described as the erotic function of all revealing clothes: the "staging of an appearance-as disappearance."[13]

The contradictory nature of the gesture which discloses the "truth" of the woman's body at the same time that it attempts to hide it is common to almost all the surplus props and gestures throughout these photo-sequences, revealing the unmistakable structure of the fetish. In its classic Freudian definition, the fetish is any object which acts as a substitute for the penis, allowing the male to continue to believe in the myth of the female phallus so as not to have to confront the threat of castration which underlies the fact of sexual difference.[14] These erotically charged substitutes often cover or connect with the part of the female body thought to have undergone castration to preserve the illusion the perverse male fantasy of a female phallus. Freud calls these substitutes a "disavowal" but he also notes that it is in the very nature of this disavowal[15] to perpetuate belief that have been abandoned, thus paradoxically reasserting the very same fears it is intended to allay.

If Muybridge's photos of naked women insist on their nakedness at the same time that they also attempt to disavow it, if, in a sense, he always gives us more to see more of her body, more of her gestures and more objects which decorate or situate her in a prototypical narrative this could be because of the male fear that this "more" is really less, that women pose the terrifying threat of "lack." The obsessive gaze at the naked female body attempts to re-assure itself in the very sight (and site) of this "lack" by the fetish-substitutes which endow her with a surplus of male-generated erotic meaning. By denying the woman any existence apart from the marks of difference, Muybridge exerts a form of mastery over that difference. But the very nature of the fetish disavowal also assures that the woman is defined entirely in terms that will perpetuate the nagging fear of the lack she represents. Her body can never by anything more than the two poles of this contradiction.

In this Freudian reading, the woman's body is reduced to the pure expression of desires produced in the male unconscious. But as Foucault notes, since it is law that constructs both desire and the lack upon which it is based, "where there is desire, the power relation is already present."[16] In other words, we find in the work of Muybridge, long before the evolution of the cores of either the primitive or the classical illusionist cinemas, at the very inception of the basic apparatus itself, a patriarchal power which places the woman's body within a perversely fetishized structure. The cinematic apparatus thus becomes, even at this early stage, an instrument in the "implantation of perversion" whose first effect is to deny the very existence of women.

We have seen that the "presence" of the woman's body on the screen generates a fetish response on the part of the male image-producer to restore the unity which this body appears to lack. This fetishization operates on the level of the cinematic signified. But as Christian Metz has shown, another form of fetishization exists on the level of the cinematic signifier. This, too, is structured upon a similar process of disavowal. However, this disavowal is of the illusory nature of the signifier itself. In other words, part of our pleasure in cinema derives from the contradiction between our belief in the perceptual

truth of the image and our simultaneous knowledge that it is only imaginary the discrepancy between the perceived illusion of presence created by the image and the actual absence of the object replaced by the image. As Metz writes:

> The cinema fetishist is the person who is enchanted by what the machine is capable of, at the theatre of shadows as such. For the establishment of his full potency for cinematic enjoyment (jouissance) he must think at every moment (and above all simultaneously) of the force of presence the film has and of the absence on which this force is constructed . . . his pleasure lodges in the gap between the two.[17]

The fetishist's pleasure in the holding of two contradictory beliefs is doubly inscribed in the early invention of the cinematic apparatus: 1) on the level of its signified when it first comes to represent women's bodies, forever arresting the look at this body with a look at the fetish which disavows the very perception of which the machine is capable, and 2) on the level of the signifier. Here it is significant that the fetish pleasure is strongest at the moment the "theatre of shadows" first emerges, when audiences like the audiences who first viewed the projection of moving bodies by Muybridge's "zoopraxiscope" are still capable of amazement at the magical abilities of the machine itself. Muybridge's apparatus, present and visible in the space of projection, hand operated by its own inventor, thus revealed more acutely than the later invention of the projector the magical power to create an illusion of motion from a succession of stills. Even though this illusion would be perfected in Lumière and Edison's later invention of celluloid film and the resulting ability to film and project much longer sequences of motion, at no time would the fetish pleasure of the signifier alone be so pronounced, until, that is, Georges Méliès that other original fetishist of the early cinema found new ways to amaze his audiences at the capabilities of the machine.

GEORGES MÉLIÈS

For Muybridge the pleasure in the cinematic signifier lodged in the ability of the projection machine to produce an illusion of movement. He himself stood outside this machine as its operator. Méliès, however, redoubles and refines this pleasure in the cinematic signifier by placing his body within the machine, casting himself in the role of the magician-scientist-jester-Mephisto who manipulates its magic. Thus he makes a spectacle of his own perverse pleasure in the tricks of which his personal "theatre of shadows" is capable. In film after film Méliès obsessively repeats the same game, playing, like the fetishist, upon the contradictory knowledge of presence and absence, making the game of presence and absence the very source of his own and the spectator's pleasure, while privileging his pleasure over that of the spectator insofar as he alone, as filmmaker behind the scene and as magician on the scene, penetrates more deeply the contradictory nature of presence and absence.

As typified by a frame from the 1902 film, *The Devil and the Statue,* his mugging delight in the game of illusion is clearly visible in each role he assumes.

But if Méliès refines and increases the fetishistic pleasure in the cinematic signifier, he also refines and increases a similar pleasure in the primary cinematic signified of the human body. As with Muybridge, the primary impetus behind Méliès' manipulation of the body is, once again, the need to master the threat of difference posed by the naked female form. And if for Muybridge this fetishization of the women's body begins to produce a level of diegetic illusion and mise-en-scene that far exceeds the levels called for in his motion studies, then a similar fetishization, running rampant in Méliès, produces even more elaborate forms of diegesis and mise-en-scene.

Long before Méliès had discovered the illusory powers of cinema, he was already engaged in an obsessive pursuit of mastery over the human body. From 1885 to 1888, before purchasing the theatre of the magician Robert-Houdin, Méliès constructed a number of robots in imitation of Robert-Houdin's own work.[18] These mechanical simulations of the human body allowed their inventor-operator complete control over their appearance and movements.

(There is a fascinating similarity here, not only between the mechanical simulation of the human body constructed in the robot and the later simulation of that body afforded by the cinema, but also between the manner of Méliès' mastery of both. According to Méliès' own account, he had seen robots on the stage of the Robert-Houdin theater and had proceeded to imitate them without any prior understanding of their mechanism.[19] Thus he re-invented an invention whose trick was the simulation of the human body. This simulation of a simulation was then repeated ten years later in 1895 when, after failing to purchase the new invention of the cinématographe from Auguste Lumière after an evening showing at the Grand Café, Méliès proceeded to re-invent it as well. Thus Méliès seems to have been fated to repeat the invention-construction of machines capable of ever more perfect and life-like simulations of the human body, and to repeat this construction through a process that was itself a simulation of an already existing mechanism.)

From the first trick of assembling a simulation of the whole body out of mechanical parts to the further trick of making the imaginary bodies projected on a screen appear and disappear, Méliès perfects his mastery over the threatening presence of the actual body, investing his pleasure in an infinitely repeatable trucage. This trucage offers two related forms of mastery over the threat of castration posed by the illusory presence of the woman's body made possible by the cinema: on the one hand, the drama of dismemberment[20] and re-integration performed on all bodies, and on the other hand the celebration of the fetish function of the apparatus itself,

particularly in its ability to reproduce an image of the woman's body.

A 1903 film entitled *Extraordinary Illusions (Illusions funambulesques)*[21] is a typical example of mastery over dismemberment and of particular interest because it combines cinematic trucage with Méliès' original obsession with the mechanized limbs of a robot. The film shows Méliès as conjurer removing from a shallow box, obviously incapable of holding what emerges from it, a pair of legs, dummy's torso and finally a head. He assembles these pieces into the body of a mechanical woman who becomes animated enough to turn her head to give the conjurer a kiss. He then tosses this mannequin into the air. Upon landing on the other side of the screen, she is transformed into a flesh-and-blood woman. The rest of the film shows the conjurer trying with some difficulty to maintain this apparition the woman has a disturbing tendency to change into a chef with a saucepan but not without a further variation on the theme of dismemberment and re-integration in which the woman is tied up in a large cloth which explodes into fragments of paper whose pieces again reform the woman. Finally, when the woman turns into a chef once again, the conjurer rips the chef to pieces and gradually vanishes himself.

Many of Méliès' early films (1898-1903) have similar rudimentary narratives based on variations of this drama of the dismemberment and re-integration of both male and female bodies. As early as 1898 *The Famous Box Trick (Illusions fantasmagorique)* shows Méliès, again as conjurer, making another magic box appear from which emerges a little boy. The body of the boy is first conjured up, cut in two by the magician's wand, then restored to its original wholeness by the creation of two boys who begin to fight among themselves. Only after the drama of morcellation and restoration does final transformation causing the boys to vanish, bring an end to the conflict.

Frequently this drama of morcellation takes place on the body of the magician-conjurer himself. In *The Melomaniac (Le Mélomane, 1903)* Méliès plays a magical music teacher who gives a music lesson using a string of five telegraph wires as his staff. To obtain notes he tears off his own head and throws it up on the staff. Since his head always grows back he is able to musically notate a performance of "God Save the King" sung by the infinitely replenishable supply of heads.

The Melomaniac is in many ways a refinement of the earlier *The Four Troublesome Heads (L'homme de têtes, 1898)* in which the magician alternately removes and regrows his own head until the group of removed heads begin to annoy him with their singing. He then makes two of them disappear and tosses the third into the air to land on top of and merge with his current head. In both these films the magician stages the morcellation of his own body with the aid of a cinematic trick; he then restores his unity with another trick to become a kind of virtuoso performer of the drama of dismemberment and integration.[22]

In those films in which morcellation of the body is not followed by re-integration, we often find that the body undergoing morcellation can be regarded as a threat to another character who functions as a more sympathetic prototype of a hero. In these films two male protagonists engage in a crude oedipal drama ending in the dismemberment of one of them and the triumph of the other. Occasionally a woman figures as prize or cause of the conflict. In *The Man with the Rubber Head* (*L'homme à la tête de caoutchouc,* 1902) a conflict between a chemist and his assistant ends when the assistant inflates the head of the chemist to the point of explosion. In true oedipal fashion it is frequently the younger of the two men who succeeds in dismembering the older one, as also in *The Cook's Revenge* (*La Vengence du gâte-sauce,* 1900). In this film a kitchen boy steals a kiss from a chamber-maid, is caught by his boss, but then decapitates this boss in the ensuing chase. The film ends with the kitchen boy using the headless body of the boss as a broom to continue his work.

In all the above films we encounter a specific use of cinematic magic first to assert then to disavow an original "lack." Even when women's bodies do not appear at all (as in *The Four Troublesome Heads* and *The Famous Box Trick*), the threat of castration posed by their bodies seems to underlie the pattern of each scenario.

In a recent *Film Quarterly* article entitled "The Lady Vanishes: Women, Magic and the Movies," Lucy Fischer argues that the primary function of women's bodies in Méliès' films and in many other "trick" films of the period is to disappear.[23] Fischer takes Méliès' 1906 film, *The Vanishing Lady,* as a paradigm for the magical treatment of women throughout the period. In this first use of a cinematic "substitution trick," a magician, played as always by Méliès, covers the body of a seated woman with a piece of cloth. When he removes the cloth not only has the lady disappeared but in her place is a skeleton.

Fisher is quite right to stress the significance of a magic which exerts power over women's bodies, decorporealizing it and reducing it to the status of a decorative object. But it is simply not accurate to privilege the disappearance of women in Méliès' films, any more than it would be accurate to privilege her magical appearance. In fact, there are probably an equal number of magical appearances and disappearances of men in these films, or of any object for that matter, since the staging of appearance and disappearance is the primary way Méliès exercises the illusory power of his simulation machine.

Fischer's ultimate point is not only that Méliès' magic makes women disappear, but that often in the process this magic acts out a drama of male envy of the female procreative power, "giving birth" to all manner of animals and objects. This latter idea is tempting in its opposition to the patriarchal notion of a female "lack,"[24] and the somewhat shaky Freudian construct of "penis envy" which sometimes accompanies it. Fischer actually reverses the process to suggest that a kind of "womb envy" is at work. But again I fear that there is not enough evidence from the films. More important than the vanishing act, more important than the imitation of procreative powers, is the construction of a scenario which gives the magician-filmmaker power over all the bodies in his domain, allowing him not simply to conjure away the woman but symbolically to re-enact, and thus master through obsessive repetition, the problem of difference, the threat of disunity and dismemberment posed by the woman's body. Like the child's symbolic re-staging of the problem of his mother's absence in the game of fort!/da!, making her disappear so that she may again, this time as a result of his own manipulation, reappear,[25] Méliès' scenarios of fetishistic disavowsal announce his own role as magician-author-metteur-en-scene with a great flourish.

Significantly, these flourishes radically exclude his own body from the voyeuristic regime that Méliès, more than any other early master of film, inaugurates. In all the early films over which Méliès presides as magician (or as some thinly disguised variant thereof), the magician usually enters the scene, bows directly to the audience, begins an act containing many hand flourishes which call attention to the magic performed, and finally bows again before exiting. No one else in the film is allowed this knowledge of the existence of the film audience. Although it is possible to attribute these flourishes to the conventions of stage magic reigning at the time, it seems significant that even after the magician disappears from his films, Méliès retains characters, like Mephistopheles in *The Damnation of Faust* or the witch in *The Kingdom of the Fairies,* who carry on the function of the magician. If Méliès persists in this acknowledgement of the distance separating audience and scene, even going against all the emerging codes of cinematic illusion to do so, and if, at the same time he animates this scene with a multitude of characters who do not seem to be aware that they are on a scene, he does so in order to share with the audience his perverse pleasure in a visible *mise-en-scène.* Like the proverbial dirty-old-man who delights in showing his obscene pictures to others, part of his pleasure is in watching us watch. But for Méliès this pleasure is further enhanced by the inclusion in his own pictures of the fetish-machine that tames the threat of the female body.

It is striking, for example, just how many of Méliès' films, especially his later ones, revolve around the functioning of an elaborate machine operated and manufactured by the fictional surrogate of the original magician. These machines, whether the clocks of the 1889 *Cinderella* or the rocket ship of *A Trip to the Moon* (1902) are often associated with or adorned by the multiplying bodies of beautiful women in scant attire. The proliferation of the machines themselves the many fantastic vehicles, futuristic laboratories, even the mechanized monsters such as the giant in *The Conquest of the Pole* (1912) are obvious ways in which Méliès celebrates and makes visible, the primary invisible machinery of the cinema itself. A great many of the machines featured in these films are, in fact, optical devices: telescopes in *A Trip to the Moon* and *The Merry Frolics of Satan* (1906), a fantastic camera in *Long Distance Wireless Photography* (1908), a magic lantern that turns out to be a motion picture projector in *The Magic Lantern* (1903). These devices allow their operator and the film spectator a privileged view of women's bodies, variously producing, reproducing, or voyeuristically spying upon them.

In *Long Distance Wireless Photography* Méliès plays the Marconi-like inventor of a magical camera capable of projecting life-size moving images of whatever is placed before it. This fantasy on the potential of the recently invented telegraph is an uncanny anticipation of the not yet invented marvel of television. Méliès the inventor-operator shows off the capabilities of his machine to an elderly couple in his laboratory. He first reproduces a life-size image of three identically-dressed women taken from a small photograph, then "televises" the movements of a live model.

In both cases Méliès celebrates the power of the apparatus to frame, tame and reduce the flesh and blood woman to the status of a two-dimensional image. In the first case it may even be significant that the live model is dispensed with entirely as Méliès creates a life size enlargement of what is already only a two-dimentional image of women's bodies. In the second case, a live model is present but a comic discrepancy between the seductive movements of the "televised" image and the less seductive behavior of the original model suggests a preference for the image over the less obliging reality of the original model.

Thus Méliès celebrates within the primary image machine of his own cinema a secondary image machine that is capable, like the first, of reproducing an image of women's bodies to the voyeuristic measure of male desire. The apparatus which makes possible "long distance wireless photography" packages the real-life bodies of women into safely preferred cheese-cake tableaux. Individual female bodies become the simple stereotypes of female-ness which uniformly differs from the male.[26] Méliès' own pleasure is that of the purveyor of images who delights in watching others watch. The "Others" who watch in this case are the elderly couple, the in-the-laboratory audience of the film's scientific demonstration. Like the doubling of the cinematic apparatus itself, this within-the-film audience duplicates the voyeuristic structure of the relationship of primary audience to filmed image.

In *A Spiritualistic Photographer* (1903), Méliès reverses the above process to bring the two dimensional photograph of a woman back to life. He performs a similar trick with the figure of the Queen on a life-size playing card in the 1905 film *The Living Playing Cards.* In all these films the device of the frame within the frame alerts us to the fact that everything we see, particularly the body of the woman, has been animated and produced by a voyeuristic, optical machine which safely situates the female object of desire both at a distance from and on a different plane from the male voyeur. Thus the image machine itself, through contiguous association with the woman's body and through its ability to reproduce that body as an image which disavows its inherent threat of lack, becomes the fetish-object par excellence of all Méliès films.

Perhaps the most complex illustration of the inscription of women's bodies within the voyeuristic and fetishistic regime of cinema occurs in Méliès' 1903 film *The Magic Lantern.* In a children's play room two clowns, a Pulcinella and a Pierrot, build a giant magic lantern to which they attach a lens. When they place a light (burning torch) in it, it projects a series of circularly framed moving images upon the wall of the playroom. The progression of these images is significant: a static landscape is followed by close-ups of a man and a woman in eighteenth century wigs flirting with one another against the background of the same landscape, finally we see the clowns themselves projected in close-up upon the wall. With this progression Méliès demonstrates the power of his toy which, like the machine in *Long Distance Wireless Photography,* is once again a metaphor for the cinematic apparatus. Thus we discover the ability of this apparatus to 1) document external reality (the landscape), 2) represent a fictional world (the characters in 18th century desss), and 3) confuse the categories of real and imaginary in a gesture of reflexivity (the projection of the clowns from the "real" world into the fictional space on the wall).

After this brief anticipation of the entire history of film art, the two clowns become curious about the internal workings of the machine producing this magic (or perhaps they are like the naive spectator who suspects that the machine itself houses the people and objects it produces). They dismantle the box to discover that it contains a whole bevy of beauties attired in long dresses and hats who do a little dance in front of the dismantled machine. This process of dismantling is repeated several times to yield a pair of women in clown suits who do another dance, exit, and then perform two more choruses of dances, this time dressed in scanty tutus.

The two clowns interrupt the dancers to battle with one another center stage. Soldiers with drawn sabres arrive to restore order. They march around the two clowns and force them to climb into the magic lantern. When the soldiers re-open the box, the clowns have been transformed into a single giant jack-in-the-box Pulcinella capable of extending itself to a height twice that of a normal human. As this jack-in-the-box moves up and down, the soldiers continue to brandish their sabres in a circle around it. Finally, the soldiers exit and all the women dancers do a circular dance around the alternating elongations and retractions of the jack-in-the-box.

Once again Méliès plays with the contrast between a two-dimensional, framed image and three-dimensional reality. And once again this contrast suggests a metaphor for the machine's ability to produce women's bodies. But while Lucy Fischer emphasizes the envious male's appropriation of female procreative powers in the construction of this machine that gives "birth" to women, I would stress instead that this spewing forth of identical female bodies only calls attention even more to the status of these bodies as totally mastered, infinitely re-producible images whose potential threat of castration has been disavowed by the fetish object of the machine with which they are associated. In other words, not only can this image machine be construed as a metaphor for the womb, but also and more powerfully, it can be construed as a metaphor for the penis in particular since, as we have seen, the fetish object is always a stand-in for the fantasy of the maternal penis.[27] In the *Magic Lantern* this fantasy penis emerges first in the proliferating bodies of the women produced by the machine and second in the phallic protrusion of the jack-in-the-box. In fact, the shift from soldiers brandishing their sabres at this jack-in-the-box to the final dance of the women around it would seem to offer yet another variation of the drama of threatened dismemberment and integration. There is probably no greater illustration of the centrality of this fetish object in all of Méliès work than this dance of worship around the undulating phallus at the center of this giant magic lantern.

CONCLUSION: THE PERVERSE IMPLANTATION

In the pre-historic cinema of Muybridge and in the primitive cinema of Méliès, the unprecedented illusion of presence of the film body acutely posed the problem of sexual difference to the male image maker. Of course painting and photography had long since set precedents for the eroticization and objectification of women's bodies.[28] In many ways Muybridge simply follows these precedents. What is particularly striking in Muybridge, however, is the extent to which a supposedly scientific study of the human body elicits the surplus aesthetic qualities of incipient diegesis and mise-en-scene in the treatment of his women subjects alone. It is as if the unprecedented perceptual reality of the female body made possible by the emerging cinematic apparatus necessitated a counterbalancing fictionalization even more powerful than what could already be found in the arts of painting and still photography.

Thus what began as a scientific impulse to measure and record the "truth" of the human body, quickly became a powerful fantasization of the body of the woman aimed at mastering the threat posed by her body. This surplus of male generated erotic meaning denies the woman any meaning apart from her marks of difference from the male. As we have seen, Méliès complicates and refines this mastery over the threat of castration through the

drama of dismemberment and re-integration performed on all bodies and through the celebration of the fetish function of the cinematic apparatus.

So if, as Baudry suggests, the cinematic apparatus in general affords the simulation of a lost unity with the body of the mother, then we find that some of the earliest representations of the female body within this apparatus aim at a more specific restoration of unity in the fetishistic disavowal of castration. But if the woman's body generates a surplus aestheticism designed to disavow difference, this surplus also severely limits the meaning of this body to the two contradictory poles of the assertion and denial of sexual difference. Like the fetish which it in some ways becomes, the woman's body arrests the male's gaze just short of the site of difference. Caught between these two poles of the fetish structure of disavowal, the woman's body is perversely trapped within the contradictory assertion and denial of the fear of castration. Thus the cinema became, even before its full "invention," one more discourse of sexuality, one more form of the "implantation of perversions" extending power over the body.

NOTES

[1] Michel Foucault, *The History of Sexuality,* translated by Robert Hurley, (New York: Pantheon Books, 1978) p. 107. Original French title: *La Volonté de savoir* (Paris: Gallimard, 1976).

[2] Foucault, p. 48

[3] *Camera Obscura,* 1 (Fall 1976) pp. 97-126. Translated into English by Jean Andrews and Bertrand August.

[4] As applied to film the term suture implies the process by which the spectator as subject fills in the discontinuities and absences of a cinematic discourse which proceeds by cuts, framings and the fundamental absence of the signifier itself. The term derives from Jacques Alain Miller's discussion of Lacan's "logic of the signifier." In Miller's extention of Lacanian theory, suture describes the way the "I" created by language is both a division and a joining. Divisions of the "I" are overcome by the imaginary projections of a unitary ego to produce the fiction of the subject. In a similar way, the spectator-subject of the cinema overcomes the disunity of the cinematic discourse. See Miller, "Suture (elements of the logic of the signifier)," and Jean-Pierre Oudart, "Cinema and Suture," both in Screen 18 (Winter/Spring 1977-78), pp. 24-47.

[5] See Laura Mulvey, "Visual Pleasure and the Narrative Cinema." Screen 16 (Autumn 1975), pp. 6-18.

[6] See Baudry, p. 122.

[7] (New York: Dover, 1955) This is the latter of the two abridgements Muybridge made of his vast and very expensive original 1887 work, *Animal Locomotion. Ani-*

mal Locomotion is an eleven folio volume of some 20,000 photos of animals and humans in movement. Muybridge later abridged this work into two smaller volumes: *Animals in Motion,* published in 1899 and *The Human Figure in Motion,* published in 1901. All the photosequences reproduced here are from this latter work.

[8] *After the Ball* (1897) stars Méliès' mistress and future wife, Jehanne d'Alcy. The still from this film is taken from a reproduction in Paul Hammond's *Marvelous Méliès* (New York: St. Martins Press, 1975) p. 113. A more recent and thorough study of Méliès is John Frazer's *Artificially Arranged Scenes* (Boston: G.K. Hall, 1974). Frazer's book contains excellent synopses of all Méliès' extant films. Other studies include: Georges Sadoul, *Georges Méliès* (Pairs: Seghers, 1961) and Maurice Bessy and Lo Duca, *Georges Méliès Mage* (Paris: Pauvert, 1961).

[9] Nor does it seem entirely accidental that Muybridge concludes the male section with what could be taken as a complimentary metaphor of male ejaculation: a man with rifle falling prone on the ground and firing. The point, however, is that while the activity with the rifle reveals the male body in movement, the activity with the bed both conceals and reveals the female body in an erotically charged state of relative stasis.

[10] See Lucy Fischer's analysis of a similarly masculine use of a cigarette in the Edison 1905 short *A Pipe Dream.* This film shows a woman who smokes playing with a miniature man in her hand. "The Lady Vanishes: Women, Magic and the Movies," *Film Quarterly* (Fall, 1979), pp. 32-33.

[11] Claire Johnston, writing with reference to an earlier article by Laura Mulvey has proclaimed the basic feminist criticism of the representation of women in film: "woman as woman" is never present. She simply comes to represent the male phallus. "Women's Cinema as Counter Cinema." *Notes on Women's Cinema,* edited by Claire Johnston. *Screen* Pamphlet 2 (London: SEFT).

[12] Robert Taft, "An Introduction: Eadweard Muybridge and His Work," in *The Human Figure in Motion,* p. x.

[13] *The Pleasure of the Text,* translated by Richard Miller (New York: Hill and Wang, 1975), p. 10.

[14] "Fetishism," *Standard Edition of the Complete Psychological Works,* Vol. 21 (London: Hogarth Press, 1968).

[15] Octave Manoni, in his book, *Clefs pour l'imaginaire ou l'autre scène* (Paris: Seuil, 1969) pp. 9-34, has emphasized the contradictory nature of this form of belief that knows itself to be false, calling it the process of "je sais bien, mais quand même . . ." (I know very well, but all the same . . .).

[16] Foucault, p. 81.

[17] Metz, "The Imaginary Signifier." Translated by Ben Brewster; *Screen* 16 (Summer 1975), p. 72.

[18] According to a letter from Méliès published in Georges Sadoul's *Georges Méliès,* p. 127.

[19] Sadoul p. 127.

[20] In his *Film Biographies,* (Berkeley: Turtle Island, 1977), Stan Brankhage has much to say about Méliès' trauma of dismemberment: "Young George . . . completely overwhelmed, torn to pieces before what-we-would-call his 'birth' begins as a child to invent a spirit-of-himself which will revenge him . . . a hero who will FREE the wickedly enchanted or otherwise destroyed pieces of his actual being, cause the monsters to dis-gorge the parts of his actuality; and young George, perhaps later then, begins to imagine a heroine who will restore him, a woman who will sew together or otherwise re-member his actual being." p. 17. Although I cannot agree with this attribution of dismemberment to "young George's" fetus, or to the supposition that a woman would "re-member" his being quite the reverse seems to be the case in both instances Brakhage does correctly identify the primary concerns of much of Méliès' cinema.

[21] Frazer lists this as the correct title of the film, p. 127. There are, however, some super 8 prints bearing the title *The Magic Box.*

[22] An even more threatening version of this same drama occurs in the 1902 film, *Up-to-Date Surgery,* in which a Doctor diagnoses indigestion in a patient, performs an operation that cuts the patient up into many pieces, reassembles these pieces in the wrong order, then finally in the right order.

[23] Fischer, p. 30.

[24] This apprehension of a female "lack" does not mean that such a lack really exists. It is a male fantasy which has been instrumental in the implantation of perversion within the cinema.

[25] Sigmond Freud, *Beyond the Pleasure Principle* (New York: Bantam, 1959) pp. 32-35.

[26] It is interesting to compare, in this connection, the enormous differentiation in the costumes of the male characters in all Méliès' films to the near uniformity of dress among the females: e.g., the scant sailor suits of the women who help the scientists board the rocket ship in *A Trip to the Moon,* or the similar uniforms of the women in *The Kingdom of the Fairies.*

[27] "Fetishism," *Standard Edition of the Complete Psychological Works,* p. 153.

[28] See John Berger, *Ways of Seeing* (New York: Penguin Books and the British Broadcasting Corporation, 1973).

[29] I would like to thank Patricia Mellencamp and Stephen Heath for suggesting the "Film Body" portion of this title and the general topic of the presence of the human figure in film.

André Gaudreault (essay date 1987)

SOURCE: "Theatricality, Narrativity, and Trickality: Reevaluating the Cinemà of Georges Méliès," in *Journal of Popular Film and Television*, Vol. 15, No. 3, Fall, 1987, pp. 111-19.

[*In the following excerpt, Gaudreault describes the narrative qualities in the service of films that do not adhere to traditional storytelling in Méliès's films.*]

> I can assert that the scenario so executed was of no importance whatsoever. . . .
>
> Georges Méliès

> So much for the scenario which, as I have already said, is the main element, the starting point of the negative. . . .
>
> Charles Pathé

The recent reevaluation of early cinema (typified by such writers as Noël Burch and the historians who contributed to the 1978 FIAF Brighton Project) bases itself on an opposition to a previous teleological concept of film history. The first generation of film historians (such as Lewis Jacobs in the United States and Georges Sadoul in France) saw early filmmakers as marking stages in the development of the later classical narrative style of filmmaking. This view led to an evolutionary and progressive model of film history that would move (for example) from Georges Méliès to Edwin Porter to D. W. Griffith, with each seen as demonstrating a further mastery of cinematic technology and form. However, this progressive model has blinded us to the unique characteristics of the work of each of these filmmakers (and others) whose aesthetic projects often differed from one to the next. Indeed, the central error of those who simply see the early cinema as the primitive precursor of the post-Griffith cinema lies in the fact that they deny this period its own specificity. This error has led to the fact that the filmmakers of this early cinema have been insufficiently studied, and distinctions among them have been too readily ignored.

This teleological view of film history has particularly distorted our understanding of the cinema of Georges Méliès. The goal of my undertaking here is to resituate Méliès' films in their historical context by exploring their most unique characteristics. Such an exploration will allow us to discover in his work certain peculiarities and aspects rarely suspected by those who hold to the traditional teleological view of film history. Thus, the work of *all* the early filmmakers from Porter to Williamson and from Zecca to Hepworth could be sub-jected to a similar analysis. It is, however, the work of Méliès, the "purest" of the early filmmakers, that provides the best exemplar simply because Méliès almost always refused every "concession": from Grivola's money to filming in natural setting.[1] This independence of which he was always so proud (and which led to his ruin), as well as his taste for artificial settings, helped lend his work its singular character.

Jean Mitry notes in his *Histoire du Cinéma:*

> Most filmmakers, hypnotised by the obvious analogy between filmic spectacle and theatrical representation, preferred to follow Méliès' formula and the path opened up by the *Film d'Art:* a succession of discontinuous "tableaux," then a succession of scenes wherein every passage from one space or one time to another was specified by an intertitle.[2]

Thus Mitry identifies Méliès' aesthetic with the Film d'Art on the basis of their mutual correspondence to theatrical representation. This identification may appear legitimate insofar as much of their production is concerned notably their use of artificial sets. However, too closely identifying Méliès and the craftsmen of the Film d'Art is dangerous, for it too easily associates Méliès' films with one of the main tendencies that supposedly characterizes early cinema: theatricality. Mitry defines the latter as follows:

> . . . theatricality, that is to say dramatic construction imitated from the theatre and produced according to a staging which is *applied* to the conditions of cinema, a concept which finds its first full achievement in the *Assassination of the Duc de Guise.*[3]

Many historians identify Méliès' style with what Mitry terms "theatricality." And although appearances may be on their side (the filmmaker's use of distanced long shots, theatrical sets, entrances and exits on "stage" right and "stage" left, etc.), this generalization often prevents them from also appreciating the *cinematic* originality of Méliès' films.

Mitry also notes another approach to filmmaking developing in this early period that he opposes to "theatricality" and terms "narrativity." He defines narrativity as "a continuity describing an action freed from the confines of theater entirely dependent on the dynamic possibilities of editing."[4] Yet, if we understand narrativity as the spatial and temporal articulations made possible through such uniquely cinematic processes as editing, I feel that it is as important an aspect of Méliès' films as of other films of the time.

We are, however, dealing with a form of narrativity quite different from that developed by Griffith and other filmmakers in the second decade of the twentieth century. Méliès demonstrates an alternative attitude toward story-telling, one less focused on the story *qua* story. He neglects those narratological aspects that mark the early films of Griffith, such as the development of psychological characters, the creation of suspense, and the illusion of realism.

It must be clearly understood that the post-1915 cinema the narrative representational cinema is the product of a concept of cinematic narrative that did not exist at the turn of the century. Not that the early filmmakers did not tell stories. Rather, they told stories using a different, more flexible form of narrative. Furthermore, it must be noted that the desire to tell stories was not the only preoccupation of the early filmmakers. They were, in fact, simultaneously pulled in different directions by a number of interests. They wanted to show objects and people in motion (the time was not far past when you could get people to pay money to see on a screen what they could have seen in real life for free). They wanted to astound and fill people with wonder at the new form of magic made possible by the motion picture camera (many films, obviously including some of Méliès', existed for that primary purpose). They wanted to show objects and lands that were beyond reach (there were numerous travelogues: "the world at your finger-tips").[5] And they also wanted to tell stories. However, there was still quite some time before the desire to tell stories first and foremost came to dominate the world of film and before one form of narrative would be preferred to all others.

If we return to Méliès, it becomes obvious that his main objective was not to create films that told stories. Quite often, as we shall see, the narrative aspect of his films remained totally secondary. As just about everyone agrees, he was bent on creating cinematic spectacle bringing to the nascent medium elaborate studio sets, make-up, costumes, trick effects, etc. But cinematic spectacle is not synonymous with "theatricality." Account must be taken of the distance that separates the world articulated by Méliès' films from both the theatrical world of the Film d'Art and the diegetically sealed world of the narrative film to come.

Consider, for example, the specific spectator/screen relationships that Méliès constructs. These are not the same as those operative in either theatrical or classically narrative cinematic texts. Here, Ingmar Bergman is helpful in reminding us there are several ways we can conceive of "illusionism" in relation to an audience:

> When I make a film I am . . . perpetrating a trick. I use a machine built around a human physical imperfection, a machine which allows me to move my audience . . . from a given feeling to its extreme opposite. . . . I am therefore either a trickster or *if the audience realizes the trick being played* an illusionist. I mystify and I have at my disposal the most precious and the most amazing of magical machines which has ever in the history of the world fallen into the hands of a mountebank. Therein lies, or ought to lie, for all those who make or sell films, the source of an irresolvable moral conflict.[6]

At the dawn of cinema, Méliès surely did not suffer Bergman's moral conflict, but his films by their very construction always already point to their illusionary and "screen" existence. Méliès' filmic system (shared by many others of the era) almost always establishes a relationship between spectators and the screen based on the *recognition* of the cinematic illusion. Spectators are never really fooled (nor meant to be) especially since many of the filmic elements in this system exist precisely in order to remind viewers that they are watching a film.

For example, in his conjuring films (which may or may not contain the beginnings of a story), Méliès maintains the scenic conventions needed for the smooth unfolding of the magic act: He enters the field of view, directly greets the spectatorial public, points out the best effects, etc. In short, he interpellates both the camera and the spectator into the text as he acknowledges their existence through direct address. In his narrative films as well, Méliès or his actors will often address the camera and, thereby, the spectator demonstrating no particular allegiance to the maintenance of diegetic illusionism, but rather to the *appreciation of illusion* itself. Similarly, Méliès' elaborate sets are so stylized that there could be no doubt as to their patent artificiality. And, finally, the universe that Méliès presents is so utterly "incredible" that there can be no mistaking its obviously constructed and "marvelous" nature. John Frazer has understood this aspect of Méliès well:

> When the actors in *A Trip to the Moon* bow and recognize the audience, it is not, as has often been suggested, merely a naive misunderstanding of the distincting between stage and screen. It is an explicit recognition and respect for the audience accustomed to the conventions of the popular stage.[7]

These asides to the audience, however, should not be seen simply as the transfer of a stage practice to the cinema in which it has no place, for many theatrical plays establish a relationship with its audience that attempts to deny the audience's real presence. Conversely, there is no reason why filmmakers should not act as if the audience were present during the filming, knowing full well they will be present during the showing.

This recognition of the audience's belated (and the camera's immediate) presence presupposes an audience/screen relationship quite different from the one that would come to dominate the Griffith and post-Griffith cinema. In fact, Griffith will turn precisely to the rules of construction of a closed and autonomous universe whose primary condition of existence is the implicit negation of the audience's presence. And in his footsteps, a long line of filmmakers for whom it is of the utmost importance that the spectator be swept away to a diegetically sealed and more or less believable universe will do the same. Noël Burch calls this system of representation based on the constitution of a closed and autonomous universe the "Institutional Mode of Representation."[8] Its characteristic work involves attempts to erase all traces of the process of enunciation that produced the text, in this way inscribing, as Alain Bergala puts it, "a narrative into a chain of images and [producing] the illusion that these images are narrating themselves."[9] This is cinematic illusionism of quite a different kind than that practiced by Méliès.

We need now consider the specific nature of Méliès' construction of narrative, the neglected question of his "narrative style." Reading the various commentaries on his work, one gets the impression not only that he was primarily concerned with cinematic spectacle, but also that this spectacle was narratively conceived; Méliès is often called the "father" of the fiction or narrative film. And yet, Méliès' movement toward narrative was initiated through and developed within the "spectacular" context of his magic act. Beginning with a singular representation of that act in *The Vanishing Lady* (1896), he rapidly moved toward filming acts with an increasing diversity of narrative elements. *Ten Ladies in One Umbrella* (1903) or *The Terrible Turkish Executioner* (1904), for example, are both magical "screen acts" embellished with an elementary narrative development. Moving from *Ten Ladies in One Umbrella* to *The Terrible Turkish Executioner,* however, Méliès introduced a more developed story in terms of action (although not necessarily more elaborate in terms of the cinematic expression of narrativity). *Ten Ladies in One Umbrella* is narratively simple in its fairground framing:

> An illusionist standing in front of a fairground stall is playing around at making his hat turn into a balloon. He then turns himself into an Ancient Greek and, with the help of his umbrella, makes ten young maidens appear all dressed in various garb. After they leave, he resumes his normal appearance and changes the balloon which had remained in a corner into a top hat.[10]

In comparison, *The Terrible Turkish Executioner* is more complex:

> In Constantinople, an executioner is ordered to behead four prisoners. The heads of the condemned men, however, rejoin their bodies and they come back to life. The prisoners take revenge by cutting the executioner in half. He manages to rejoin his two halves and chases after them.[11]

The person of the magician who justifies, supports, and explains the appearances, disappearances, and other physical impossibilities is always present on the stage in *The Vanishing Lady* and also on the stage (which is quickly transformed into a Greek backdrop) in *Ten Ladies in One Umbrella*. In *The Terrible Turkish Executioner,* however, the magician is replaced by an executioner in a public square. Moreover, *The Terrible Turkish Executioner* does not show a *magic act* involving successive appearances and disappearances, but a *fantastic action* during which impossible events occur all by themselves without the presence of some mediating *deus ex machina* that would have caused or "justified" them.

It is important, however, to point out that in this movement toward narrative, Méliès was merely repeating what he had already done on stage and what was becoming increasingly common in the theatrical magic acts of the time: the integration of a series of tricks within a fictional story rather than their discontinuous presentation with a pause between each (for applause) as many magicians and illusionists continue to do even today. According to Paul Hammond, this innovative introduction of narrative is attributable to Maskelyne in the 1880s:

> The generation separating the French and English showman had seen Maskelyne develop the use of dramatic narratives to connect and enhance the tricks performed piecemeal by Robert-Houdin.[12]

This narrative element, however, was seen as entirely secondary to the magical effects; thus, Méliès did not consider himself a story-teller. Indeed, here are his own words on the matter (written in 1932):

> In this type of film (fantasy films, flights of imagination, artistic, diabolical, fantastical or magical films), the most important thing lies in the ingeniousness and unexpectedness of the tricks, in the picturesque nature of the décors, in the artistic lay out of the characters and also in the main "hook" and the grand finale. Contrary to what is usually done, my procedure for constructing this sort of film consisted in coming up with the details before the whole; the whole being nothing other than the "scenario."[13]

He could hardly state his position more clearly. The scenario, the story line, are merely a means to an end. This view of the function of narrative is exactly the opposite of the narrative system that would become dominant. Méliès usually only tells a story in order to embellish or to tie together the presentation of his latest effects. All his films are "trick-motivated." He tells us:

> It could be said that in this case the scenario is merely the thread used to hold together "effects" which haven't much in common anyway just as the master of ceremonies in a stage review exists merely to tie together scenes with no obvious connection between them.[14]

It needs emphasizing that Méliès holds this view of narrative as functional but secondary not only in those films showing an illusionist doing tricks (*The Vanishing Lady* or *Ten Ladies in One Umbrella*) or in his short one-shot fiction films (*The Terrible Turkish Executioner*), but also in his longer fiction films. Once again Méliès has left us invaluable testimony:

> For twenty years I made fantastical films of all types and my main preoccupation was always to find for each film a new trick, a big main effect and a final apotheosis. Afterwards, I would try to select the best period for costumes in which to dress my characters . . . and once all that had been settled, I would then draw the backgrounds

for the action according to the era and the costumes that I had chosen. As for the scenario, the "fable," the "story," I only worried about it at the very end. I can assert that the scenario so executed was of *no importance whatsoever* because my sole aim was to use it as a "pretext" for the "staging," for the "tricks," or for picturesque tableaux.[15]

So much for his general approach to narrative. Méliès, however, also gave us accounts of this de-emphasis on narrative and privileging of "tricks" and "picturesque tableaux" in specific films. Thus he said of *Jeanne D'Arc* (1900):

> As a lover of the fantastic, I was especially compelled to make this film because of its trick effects, notably the apparitions to Jeanne of the Archangel Gabriel, of the Saints, and of the flight of her soul to heaven during the stake-burning scene.[16]

And of *A Trip to the Moon* (1902):

> So I thought . . . of reaching the moon in such a way as to be able to stage a number of original and amusing fairytale images both on and inside the moon all the while adding one or two artistic effects (maidens standing in for stars, comets, etc., snow effects, the bottom of the sea, etc.).[17]

Méliès' use of narrative, then, is totally accessory and the stylistic key to his films is to be found elsewhere. He sees narrativity as pretext rather than text, and it is not determinant in his cinematic imagination and production. No more so than the theatricality that is equally secondary in his work. Indeed, if I may be permitted a neologism, I would like to introduce the notion of "trickality" a concept that seems to me to best "sum up" his work.

This emphasis on "trickality," however, does not mean that Méliès' films are exempt from any number of characteristics specific to the systems of cinematic articulation that emphasize theatricality or narrativity. Indeed, film historians have generally underestimated Méliès' unique contribution to the development of narrativity and the processes of editing upon which it is founded. There are two reasons for this underestimation. The first is that, blinded by the analogy between Méliès' films and stage acts, historians have often failed to notice certain particularly developed forms of editing in his films. The second is that, blinded by their teleological understanding of film history, many historians have not seen certain editing operations that are absolutely essential to Méliès' style, but that do *not* resemble the narrative editing that would come to dominate later cinema.

One need only read Georges Sadoul, for example, to realize just how far this blindness can go. Claiming that as a general rule Méliès almost never showed the same object from two different points of view (by cutting-in, for example), Sadoul concludes that Méliès' camera never gave a mobile viewpoint on action through changes in the camera's position.

> *"The unity of point of view"* presupposes that the director has set his camera up as the eye of the spectator seated in the middle of a row of theater seats: the "man in the front row" . . . Méliès never imagined that he could leave his seat in the middle of the show to get a better look at the leading lady's smile or to follow her into the dining room when she left the living room.[18]

This characterization of Méliès' work willfully ignores dozens, hundreds, even thousands of meters of his films. In *A Trip to the Moon,* for example, Méliès systematically shifts his point of view and follows his characters as they move from the "Astronomers' Club" to the factory, then to the roof from which the "scientists" can see the foundry. What is more, in *Fairyland or the Kingdom of the Fairies* (1903), one very short shot shows us the witch drowning after the previous shot in which Prince Bel Azor has thrown her off a cliff. Indeed, all of Méliès' "feature" films contain similar examples of shifts in point of view, in no way justifying Sadoul's claim that: "The passage from one scene to another is not *editing* but a trick, a substitute for quick set changes."[19]

Given this sort of limited description, some of the most important aspects of Méliès' editorial technique have been passed over in silence. It is, in fact, particularly odd that historians have never mentioned an example of rapid editing, quite unusual for the period, which can be found in his famous *A Trip to the Moon.* The film contains a succession of four shots in less than twenty seconds! (I have had the opportunity to view over 1,500 films from the period 1895-1907 and, as far as I can recall, no other film I've viewed contains an example of such rapid editing.) The episode in question deals with the return of the rocket and is constructed in the following narrative sequence of shots:

> 1. On the moon. The rocket is near an overhang and the astronomers, pursued by the Selenites, rush toward it. Professor Barbenfouillis grabs hold of the rope and makes the rocket tip over into space. (7 seconds)
>
> 2. In space. The rocket is in free fall. (2 seconds)
>
> 3. Above the ocean. The rocket plunges into the water. (2.5 seconds)
>
> 4. At the bottom of the sea. The rocket hits bottom and rises slowly to the surface. (8 seconds)

Obviously, such rapid editing is not an everyday occurrence in Méliès' films. Nonetheless, all of his "feature-length" fiction films demonstrate a certain editorial flexibility and counter the prevailing opinion according to which Méliès "is quite content, as regards his 'feature' films, to glue end to end his twenty metre negatives as the camera cranks them out."[20]

Filmic expression has at its disposal many types of cuts (cut-ins, cuts on action, eye-line cuts, cuts in relation to the 30-degree rule, etc.) that help determine various significant visual relations between and among shots (scale, disposition of filmed subjects, angles of vision, etc.). Certain conventional rules have been formulated and come to stand as Burch's earlier cited "Institutional Mode of Representation," a mode that has emphasized the practice of matching cuts so as to make them as "invisible" as possible. This editorial rule (and others) began to appear and become institutionalized during the second decade of the twentieth century. Previously, filmmakers had relied on their intuition or had proceeded haphazardly. However, it is primarily through systematic cutting that filmmakers are able to make their stories progress. This need to move the story ahead is most acutely present in Griffith and the filmmakers who came after him. Earlier filmmakers, however, sometimes caused their stories to "stutter" through their editorial practice. Indeed, it sometimes happened that from one shot to the next the action would be repeated: There would be a temporal overlap.

Like other early filmmakers, Méliès also used such temporal overlap. Historians frequently mention *A Trip to the Moon* in which the rocket is seen to touch down "twice" on the moon's surface. *An Impossible Voyage* (1904) is also often cited: The vehicle bursts through the wall of the inn "twice." As might be expected within the context of an evolutionary and teleological view of film history, this "lack" of temporal continuity in the early ("primitive") cinema is often condemned: "Three or four snips of the scissors would have been enough to re-establish the *proper* chronology."[21] But Sadoul once again forgets that the system of early cinema did not "require" the chronological continuity that would later dominate film practice. For Méliès and the other filmmakers of his era, it was more important *to show everything* (the reaction of the people outside the inn before and during the accident of *An Impossible Voyage,* and the activity of the people seated around the table of the inn as well as their reactions to the accident) than to sweep the audience along the continuous path of the uncontrollable vehicle.

Previous historians have noted these types of examples only to point to them as "primitive." Thus, they often conclude that editing was not a crucial part of Méliès' production process or cinematic style. From reading their works, it is rather difficult to imagine Méliès in a half-darkened room examining his strips of film, carefully finding the exact spot that will have to be cut, taking his scissors, cutting the film and gluing the two ends together, checking the result, and then starting over again if necessary. And yet, that is exactly what Méliès did for almost all of his films. This is confirmed by Jacques Malthête who undertook the enormous task of reconstructing a large part of the films held by the association Les Amis de Georges Méliès. Here is what he says:

Indeed, if one were to examine carefully . . . a trick film, one would soon realise that we have

for some time been living with false notions and that film historians have missed some important facts. . . . This effect [stop motion] is always associated with a splice. . . . I know of no exception to this rule. Every appearance, disappearance or substitution was of course done in the camera but was always re-cut in the laboratory on the negative, and for a very simple reason: this trick effect . . . will not work if the rhythm is broken. But the inertia of the camera was such that it was impossible to stop on the last frame of the "shot" before the "trick," change the background or the characters, and start up again on the first frame of the "shot" after the "trick" without having a noticeable variation in speed.[22]

Fundamentally, Méliès' films are *montage films* except that and the exception is essential many of his cuts juxtapose two "shots" with the *same* framing: Before and after a stop-motion substitution, the framing remains the same. Certainly this editorial technique is quite different from the descriptive or narrative editing of later cinema that primarily relies on the *difference* of framing between cuts. But it remains editing nonetheless, especially when one considers that this type of operation led Méliès to consider and solve the basic problems of match cutting: cutting on movement, matching the positions of filmed subjects, etc. In fact, Méliès was one of the first to think of the cinema in terms of cuts! The point here is not to turn Méliès into the father of montage, the precursor of Griffith or Eisenstein. Rather, the point is to recognize that in his work and in many of the other films of the era there exists a type of editing that is all too often occulted by the privileged status that film historians regularly grant to the later form of narrative editing.

We are thus led to believe that the question of matching images must have been a major preoccupation for Méliès as well as for the other filmmakers of his time making "trick" films. One only need see a film such as *The Human Fly* (1902) to realize that this was the case. Méliès shows a Russian dancer dancing across walls as though it were the most natural thing in the world. First, we see a man walking across the floor in front of a backdrop. He is about to step onto the wall and at that very instant there occurs a cut that, it must be said, is practically invisible. The filming has been stopped, the backdrop has been laid flat across the studio floor, and the camera has been hoisted up so as to shoot the scene from a 90-degree angle directly above. Care has been taken to reframe the backdrop exactly as it had been in the previous shot/scene, and to maintain the same distance between the camera and the subject. The dancer (played by Méliès) has repositioned himself at the same spot in the scene that is now shot horizontally. The illusion is perfect and is the result of a perfect match cut. Indeed, all stop-action substitutions require this kind of meticulousness and presuppose an equally precise continuity of action. However, these cuts are used for *magical ends* rather than for the dramatic purposes found later in Griffith's editing. Nonetheless, the fact remains that these match cuts are indeed cuts resulting from a practice of editing that sometimes far outstrips what is normally thought of as editing practice of the time. *The Black Imp* (1905), for example, contains about one hundred cuts (stop-action or substitutions) within three and one-half minutes!

Méliès' use of the camera also seems ill-served by traditional historiographic thought about his work. It is often said that the viewpoint of Méliès' camera on the action is stationary. I have already discussed this matter briefly in relation to his shifting perspective in sequences of *A Trip to the Moon* and *Fairyland or the Kingdom of the Fairies.* However, allow me here to further elaborate a fairly remarkable example of Méliès' creation of the illusion of camera movement between shots within a single space that had it been shot outdoors by Porter, Zecca, or a member of the "Brighton School" would certainly have received delirious praise and have caused all teleological historians to speak of yet another cinematic "first." In *Fairyland or the Kingdom of the Fairies,* the rescue of Princess Azurine is told through a series of shots during which the camera, its position changed for each shot, literally circles the dramatic space. Here is a breakdown of the rescue (also see diagram):

1. Prince Bel Azor and his companions reach dry land and move into a natural tunnel.

2. The characters emerge at the other end of the tunnel in front of the island where Princess Azurine is held captive. The prince dives into the water. (From shot 1 to shot 2 there is a kind of cut-in.)

3. The prince reaches the island, forces open the castle door, and enters. (The camera has moved in and about 45-degrees right.)

4. Inside the castle, the prince saves the princess. (It is impossible to locate the exact position of the camera here.)

5. The prince and princess reach dry land and join up again with the prince's companions. The prince throws the witch off the top of the cliff. (The camera now stands opposite its position in shot 3.)

6. The witch drowns. (The camera is now at the bottom of the cliff although it is impossible to situate the exact shot angle.)[23]

These various examples of Méliès' editing and his illusion of a shifting point of view on the action demonstrate clearly that we need to reexamine the work of this pioneer filmmaker who pushed the logic of his system of "trickality" right up to the very end of his life for he took leave of his public under the cover of a *temporal overlap!* His last public appearance took place on 16 December 1929 at Pleyel Hall in Paris. This was the "Méliès Gala" that honored him by showing some of his recently recovered films. At the end of the screening, the audience rose to acclaim Méliès who was nowhere to

be found. The lights went down again and another film was projected on the screen. Let us leave the last description of the event to Madeleine Malthête-Méliès:

> Calling upon the method perfected by Méliès twenty-four years earlier . . . which allowed action to move from the screen to the stage . . . the Gala organisers asked him to shoot a very short film; we see him suddenly appear on the screen. . . . Lost in the streets of Paris, he is looking everywhere for Pleyel Hall . . . on the wall he sees an enormous Gala poster bearing his picture. . . . He dives head first into the poster. Suddenly, the lights go on in the hall. The screen rises and uncovers, in the middle of the stage, a frame to which is nailed the poster we have just seen. Suddenly the paper rips apart and Méliès appears in the flesh. . . . [24]

"Suddenly the paper rips apart . . . ," but still a few moments *after* the beginning of the same action had been seen on the screen. An end worthy of one of the most extraordinary of cinematic pioneers using a process that perhaps no one had yet called a mismatch.

ACKNOWLEDGMENTS

This article is an abridged and revised English version of a paper orginally given at Cerisy-la-Salle, France, in August 1981, at the symposium *Méliès et la naissance du spectacle cinématographique.* (Earlier and quite different versions have been published in French by Klincksieck in 1984 and in English by McGill University, Montréal, Working Paper Series Graduate Communication Program, in 1982). The author would like to thank both the Canada Council and the Social Sciences and Humanities Research Council of Canada for grants that enabled this research as well as attendance at the Cerisy conference.

This paper was translated from the French by Paul Attallah. This version was adapted and revised by Tom Gunning and Vivian Sobchack.

NOTES

[1] Méliès considered filming in a natural setting a concession to facility. The use of artificial and composed backgrounds was a way for him to distinguish himself from those who, having opted for facility as far as he was concerned, chose to film in natural settings. On this matter, see his 1907 article, "Les vues cinématographiques," reprinted in Georges Sadoul's *Georges Méliès* (Paris: Seghers, 1961), pp. 87-112. For the point raised here, see specifically p. 91.

[2] Jean Mitry, *Histoire du cinéma,* Vol. I (Paris: Editions Universitaires, 1967), p. 400.

[3] Mitry, p. 370.

[4] Mitry, p. 370.

[5] This is the motto of Star Films that was also used on the company's letterhead.

[6] Ingmar Bergman, quoted without any source in the 1980 program of "Cinématographe," the film club of the Collège de Ste-Foy in Québec City. (Emphasis mine.)

[7] John Frazer, *Artificially Arranged Scenes: The Films of Georges Méliès* (Boston: G. K. Hall, 1979), p. 99.

[8] Noël Burch, "Porter or Ambivalence," *Screen,* 19, No. 4 (Winter 1978-79), p. 98.

[9] Alain Bergala, *Initiation à la sémiologie du récit en images* (Paris: Ligue française de l'enseignement et de l'éducation permanente, 1977), p. 38.

[10] *Essai de reconstitution du catalogue de la Star Film,* followed by *Analyse catalographique des films de Georges Méliès recensés en France* (Bois d'Arcy: Centre National de la Cinématographie, 1981), p. 152.

[11] *Ibid.,* p 171.

[12] Paul Hammond, *Marvelous Méliès* (London: Gordon Fraser Gallery, 1974), p. 19.

[13] Quoted by Georges Sadoul in *Georges Méliès,* p. 115.

[14] Sadoul, p 115.

[15] Sadoul, pp. 115-116. (Emphasis mine.)

[16] *Catalogue de l'Exposition commémorative due centenaire de Georges Méliès* (Paris: La Cinémathéque Française, 1961), p. 28. This is a written statement that dates approximately from 1937.

[17] Quoted by Madeleine Malthête-Méliès in *Méliès l'enchanteur* (Paris: Hachette, 1973), p. 267. This is a written statement that dates from 1933.

[18] Georges Sadoul, *Histoire générale du cinéma,* Vol. 11 (Paris: Denoel, 1948), p. 141. (Emphasis mine.)

[19] Sadoul, *Histoire généerale du cinéma,* p. 142. (Emphasis mine.)

[20] Sadoul, *Georges Méliès,* p. 38.

[21] Sadoul, *Georges Méliès,* p. 56. (Emphasis mine.)

[22] Letter of 1 May 1981 to the author.

[23] I have described the succession of shots as though, across all the shots, we have been dealing with one and the same background set through which the camera had travelled while changing angles between shots. In fact, Méliès' camera remained in the same place at the back of the studio, and different drawings of the same set were laid out in front of the camera thereby producing the *illusion* of camera movement between shots. It is nonetheless surprising that Méliès should have gone to all the trouble of making five or six different backdrops for a scene whose relative unity of space might have allowed him to avoid this découpage. No other filmmaker of the period made such a meticulous découpage, not even in a *natural* setting. Thus, despite the actual fixed position of Méliès' camera, we need to reconceptualize the way we think about his work and to realize that he was deeply concerned with constituting the illusion of camera movement and a variety of ideal viewpoints.

[24] Madeleine Malthête-Méliès, *Méliès,* pp. 398-399.

Tom Gunning (essay date 1990)

SOURCE: "'Primitive' Cinema: A 'Frame-up'? or 'The Trick's on Us'," in *Early Cinema: Space, Frame, Narration,* edited by Thomas Elsaesser with Adam Barker, The British Film Institute, 1990, pp. 95-103.

[*In the following excerpt, Gunning attempts to dissassociate Méliès from the theatrical tradition, with which he often is linked, and pronounces him a pioneer in film-editing techniques.*]

> 'People will come back to that, you get sick of everything except sleeping and daydreaming. **The Trip to the Moon** will be back again . . .' (Louis-Ferdinand Céline, *Death on the Instalment Plan*).

Frank Norris' 1899 novel *McTeague: A Story of San Francisco,* contains a sequence absent from the novel's definitive film version, Erich von Stroheim's *Greed* (1925). Stroheim updated *McTeague* to the contemporary 1920s and therefore omitted Norris' topical reference to 'the crowning scientific achievement of the nineteenth century, the kinetoscope'.[1] The kinetoscope occupies the next to last place on the bill of the vaudeville programme which Mac and Trina (along with Trina's mother, Mrs Sieppe, and her brother, little Owgooste) attend to celebrate their engagement. Norris describes the effect of this featured attraction:

> The kinetoscope fairly took their breaths away. 'What will they do next?' observed Trina in amazement. 'Ain't that wonderful, Mac?' McTeague was awestruck.
>
> 'Look at that horse move his head,' he cried excitedly, quite carried away. 'Look at the cable car coming and the man going across the street. See here comes a truck. Well, I never in all my life. What would Marcus say to this?'
>
> 'It's all a drick' exclaimed Mrs Sieppe with sudden conviction. 'I ain't no fool; dot's nothun but a drick.'
>
> 'Well, of course Mamma,' exclaimed Trina; 'it's—'

But Mrs Sieppe put her head in the air. 'I'm too old to be fooled,' she persisted. 'It's a drick.' Nothing more could be got out of her than this.[2]

Although a piece of fiction, this nearly contemporaneous account of the reception of the cinematic image contains rich material for understanding the horizon of expectations in which films originally appeared. Mrs Sieppe's reaction is presented as the pig-headed response of a recent, barely assimilated immigrant (the act on this vaudeville bill that she responds to most favourably is a group of yodellers: 'Joost like der old country'[3]), which exasperates her more informed, modern and American daughter. But what Norris presents as a naive response to the projected moving image directly opposes our now dominant conception of the naive viewings of the first movies. According to current myths of early projections, the first audiences for Lumière's *Arrivée d'un train* rushed from the auditorium for fear of being demolished by the oncoming engine. Far from confusing the film image with reality, Mrs Sieppe dismisses it as mere trickery.

The conflict in Norris' clash in cultural and generational responses does not lie in whether the kinetoscope is a trick: Trina takes this as a matter of course. Trina and Mac accept the trick as a scientific wonder ('Wasn't wasn't that magic lantern wonderful, where the figures moved? Wonderful ah wonderful' McTeague intones after the show[4]). Both the suspicious and the enthralled viewers immediately place the phenomenon within the context of visual illusions, the transforming tricks and magic lanterns which vaudeville at the turn of the century exhibited with increasing frequency.[5]

That even pure actuality footage such as Norris describes could summon up such associations calls into question another myth of early film history: the Manichaean division between the films of Lumière (documentary realism) and the films of Méliès (fiction, fantasy, stylization). Clearly the fascination and even the realism of early films related more strongly to the traditions of magic theatre (with its presentation of popular science as spectacle) than to later conceptions of documentary realism. Méliès himself recognized this at his first viewing of Lumière films, proclaiming the projection, 'an extraordinary trick' ('un truc extraordinaire').[6]

Placing the first projections of moving film images within the context of the tradition of visual illusions allows us to overcome the distorting view of the reception of early actuality films as simply achievements in cinematic realism. Likewise, a close examination of the genre of film-making which explicitly continued the tradition of visual illusions, the 'trick film', allows us to call into question the very terms of our discussion of this early period, particularly the rubric 'primitive' cinema and its connotations.

The notion of the first decade of film history as a 'primitive' period has been hard to shake. Recent scholars have expressed reservations about the term and emphasized that they employ it in a non-pejorative sense.[7] The term 'primitive' persists, I believe, partly out of inertia, but also because it cradles a number of connotations which stand in need of further examination and critique. The most regrettable connotations are those of an elementary or even childish mastery of form in contrast to a later complexity (and need we add that this viewpoint often shelters its apparent reversal in the image of a cinema of a lost purity and innocence?). But the limitations of this view seem fairly obvious and I believe it is disappearing.

However, a less pejorative variation of these connotations still persists, if only from a lack of an alternate way to view this early period of development. These connotations see the earliest period of cinema as a period of lack in relation to later evolution. This lack has most often been specified as a relative absence of editing, a nearly monolithic concept of the shot unsubordinated to any editing schema. Even those who maintain the uniqueness and value of early film within a non-linear view of film history have a hard time avoiding a description of early cinema as a sort of degree zero in the evolution of montage.

It is not my purpose to deny the subordinate role of editing in early film. In fact it is precisely the role played by the single viewpoint embodied in the monolithic shot that I wish to define with more precision. There is no doubt that one of the defining aspects of early cinema (and an element of what has been called the 'non-continuous style of early film'[8]) is the relative autonomy of the single shot. However, the meaning of this phenomenon is deceptively simple, and only apparently elementary. As I shall show, this regime of the single uninterrupted shot, independent and unsubordinated to the demands of montage, is often an appearance rather than a reality, a mask for a complex but easily ignored labour, a distraction from the traces of a historically neglected practice. Or, as Mrs Sieppe would put it, a trick. In fact, we could say that the single monolithic shot functions as a trick which film audiences and historians have not seen through for decades.

The understanding of editing in early film as primitive intertwines with the myth of early film as a simple reproduction of the pre-existing art of theatre (minus the voice). According to this view, the single shot functions as a reproduction of the theatrical proscenium (the long-shot framing) and the theatrical scene (the lengthy uninterrupted shot). This understanding oversimplifies the traditions from which early cinema derives. As a variety of researchers have recently shown, early film drew on traditions as various as the forms of popular entertainments appearing at the turn of the century, and not at all restricted to the legitimate theatre. The initial reception of film projections as one in a series of visual illusions alerts us to the particular importance of what Charles Musser has called the 'tradition of screen entertainments' (the magic lantern and related projected illusions), and the magical (rather than the dramatic) theatre to a new understanding of early film.

Anyone who has seen more than a handful of early films recognizes the many violations of the stage tableau and proscenium arch framing that are found in films before 1907. The 'facial expression' genre in which characters mug at the camera in close-up or medium shot forms one dramatic example. But my point goes beyond simply establishing the varied sorts of framing found in early film. I assert that early film's tendency to rely upon the space within the frame rather than the possibilities of juxtaposition between shots involves a particular attitude towards the filmic illusion and one which is far from a Bazinian aesthetic of non-manipulation. In fact the single shot contained (seemingly) by a single framing was manufactured by certain early film-makers precisely as an illusion. And the maintenance of a single point of view relates more to a particular mode of audience address than to a passive or primitive approach to film-making.

The most commonly recognized technique of early trick films, what is frequently referred to as 'stop motion substitution', provides a proving ground. This trick lies behind the magical transformations which find their *locus classicus* in the films of Georges Méliès, but which exist, of course, in trick films of all nations and producers, and which frequently can be found in non-trick films as well. Based partly on Méliès' oversimplified and (intentionally, I believe) misleading description of his technique, this process has been explained as a stopping of the camera at a predetermined point, a profilmic rearrangement of actors or props, and then a resumption of the turning of the camera. This was certainly part of the process.

However, as John Frazer has pointed out,[9] and as Jacques Malthête has systematically demonstrated, the trick only began here.[10] Examination of the actual prints of Méliès films reveal that in every case, this stop motion technique was in fact revised through splicing. Variation in hand-cranked camera speed when stopping and starting, as well as refinements possible only at this stage, called for the actual cutting of the film at the beginning and ending of the interrupted action and the subsequent splicing of it together. Examination of positive prints of Méliès films led Jacques Malthête to declare that in Méliès there is never any trick of substitution which does not make use of splicing. For Malthête, Méliès is not simply a master of 'trucage' but also an unacknowledged master of 'collage',[11] the altering of filmic reality through the act of cutting and splicing which we normally associate with the act of editing. This for a film-maker so often criticized for under-utilizing the possibilities of editing because of his attachment to the theatrical practice.[12]

This discovery of a previously unperceived process of film cutting raises enormous problems of definitions for the film historian. Does a film like *The Terrible Turk-*

ish Executioner, which previously seemed to contain only a single shot with numerous substitution tricks due to stop motion, now demand description as a film made up of multiple shots? Is Méliès not only a master of collage, but in fact the father of montage? Although this could be subject to debate, I believe it would be equally distorting to see Méliès' trick splice as the equivalent of cuts which perform basic spatial and temporal articulations. As André Gaudreault has said in an essay which revises our view of Méliès:

> The point is not to turn Méliès into the predecessor of Griffith or Eisenstein or to turn him into the father of montage. Rather the point is to recognise that in his work and in many of the other films of the era there exists a type of editing which is all too often occulted by the privileged status that film historians regularly grant to the later form of narrative editing.[13]

What should astonish film historians here is the process of production, the painstaking technical labour this 'splice of substitution' involves, one which includes careful attention to the minutiae of 'matching' continuity and creates a particular mode of address to the spectator.

Such care taken with the problems of creating a seamless illusion of transformation should finally dispel any conception of early film-makers as primitive in relation to their technology (if anyone who has read Méliès' even incomplete description of the technical concerns surrounding the production of trick films is not already convinced).[14] But, further, it shows early film-makers were concerned with issues that traditionally they are thought to have ignored, those of precise continuity of action over a splice. The splices in Méliès' films are managed in order to maintain the flow and rhythm of acting which a mere stopping of the camera could not provide. While later classical editing can be referred to as 'invisible editing' only metaphorically, such 'substitution splices' are nearly literally invisible, having passed for the last eight decades for the most part without notice.

Does this mean that the concept of early film editing as 'non-continuous' needs to be abandoned? Although I feel the term still indicates something of the early film's alterity from later practice, it does need modification. Even if this early form of continuity editing (or splicing) does show a striking prefiguration of later ideals of matching action, it none the less serves a very different purpose and the alterity of early cinema remains evident within it. As is often the case, the insights of Noël Burch provide importance guidance. Burch refers to the lack of editing in early film in terms of 'the *autarky* and *unicity* of each frame'.[15] The clarification here is the use of the term *frame* rather than shot. Burch does not refer, of course, to the frame as a unit of celluloid, but to the framing of the shot. A consideration of Méliès' use of the 'substitution splice' shows that what is maintained is both a continuity of action *and* (in contrast to later continuity editing) a continuity of framing. It is the absolute duplication of framing over the splice which, along with the continuity of action, allows the interruption to be all but imperceptible to the viewer.

Burch has not elaborated his understanding of the unicity of the frame in exactly this way. However, his discussion of the 1902 Pathé trick film *The Ingenious Soubrette* clearly regards the continuity of framing as more important than the singleness of a shot in early cinema. This film consists of three shots which seem to frame identically the same set of a bourgeois parlour in which a maid hangs paintings on the wall. However, the second shot, which appears to reproduce faithfully the framing of the first, is in fact an overhead view of a set constructed so that the maid (ingeniously, indeed) seems simply to slide up the wall as she hangs the pictures. The film's third and final shot returns to the initial camera placement. The apparently identical framing of all three shots masks the switches in camera placement, so the film appears to be one continuous uninterrupted shot, and thus creates the illusion of the maid's seeming conquest of the laws of gravity. Burch observes that 'the overwhelming dominance of frontality and unicity of viewpoint in the Primitive Era must have made such tricks totally effective illusions. . . . '[16]

The continuity that is preserved and fostered in early cinema, then, is one of viewpoint, of framing, to make explicit a point Burch leaves implicit. This concern for a unified viewpoint of the action (an act of enframing which does not vary even as the action within it is synthetically constructed by a series of concealed splices) differs sharply from the classical continuity system based on dramatic and psychological analysis and fragmentation. In the classical system a variety of viewing angles and distances are related to a larger spatial whole and these relations are regulated by the rules of continuity editing. While the continuity system maintains a consistent spatial orientation for the viewer, the variations between shots allow a dramatic and spatial articulation of the action. In contrast, the approach of early film privileges the single viewpoint and its posture of displaying something to the audience. The substitution splice is based on maintaining the apparent continuity of this single viewpoint, rather than a dramatic articulation of a story through varied shots.

In contrast to this dramatic analysis, early film's unity of framing and viewpoint defines the primary act of film-making as one of display, of showing, of showmanship. To borrow a term from André Gaudreault's narratological treatment of cinema (and to revise its meaning a bit),[17] the film-maker of early cinema appears as a *monstrator,* one who shows, a showman. But this act of showmanship within a unity of framing differs considerably from the theatricality with which it has been identified, first by Georges Sadoul, subsequently by Jean Mitry,[18] and even by Burch. Pierre Jenn in his recent work on Méliès has launched a particularly strong attack against this conception of Méliès' 'theatricality', developing points first raised by André Gaudreault. Jenn

points out that rather than passive theatricality, this unity of viewpoint plays an essential role in concealing the process of the trick. Unity of point of view gives the illusion of a theatrical unity of time, when, in fact, the substitution splice creates a specifically cinematic synthesis of time. The framing of Méliès' composition, taken by historians as a sign of his 'primitive' theatricality, reveals itself as consciously constructed illusion designed to distract attention from the actual cinematic process at work.[19] And, at least for some film historians, it has succeeded.

The importance of framing and unity of viewpoint in early cinema need not be identified with the proscenium arch. Although the frontality of the theatrical tableau may have presented one model of framing for early film-makers, there were several other sources from which they drew both inspiration and subject matter. The screen itself as the unchanging site of projected images in the magic lantern tradition is an important one, as David Francis among others has pointed out.[20] The variety of processes used in trick slides and dissolving views, in which one element of a slide might change while the setting remained the same, offers a clear parallel to the effect of the substitution splice. Similarly the role of the frame in stereoscope cards, comic strips and postcards may have exerted as much influence as the proscenium arch on early film-makers. Further, although certainly the staging and framing in a Méliès film often (although not always, as Jenn points out[21]) recall theatrical practice, a similar concern for unity of viewpoint can be found in patently non-theatrical films as well, from the 'facial expression' films to the radically non-theatrical framings of the English Brighton School film-makers.

One of the most astounding of these early British films, *How It Feels to Be Run Over* (Cecil Hepworth, 1900), shows the essential role a single viewpoint played in the structure of certain early British films, through humorously invoking the direct address it offers the spectator. This single-shot film shows a buggy passing the camera, followed by an automobile. The auto's driver seems suddenly blinded by the buggy's dust and veers directly at the camera threatening a collision with this fixed viewpoint of camera/spectator. This collision apparently occurs, as the front of the car engulfs the field of vision and the film cuts to a section of black leader to represent this total disaster. Words then appear scratched on the leader, reading: 'Oh Dear Mother Will Be Pleased'.

Such framing and motion contrast sharply with the frontality and distance that typify the theatrical tableau. However, in spite of its non-theatrical movement, the film employs a fixed framing for its trick effect, a viewpoint that is maintained until it is literally untenable, pushing the unity of point of view in early film to a *reductio ad absurdum* which bares the device. Many other films of early cinema (e.g. Williamson's *The Big Swallow* or the many railway films of the 'phantom rides' or Hale's Tours sort) play in similar ways with unity of point of view within a non-theatrical framing. It is the framing itself, its marking of the act of display, that remains primary. The spectator is directly addressed, even confronted, by these plays with framing. In the same way the trick film maintains its unchanging frame in order to display its magical transformations directly to the audience.

We are dealing, then, with an approach to cinema which stresses film's ability to present a view, a tendency André Gaudreault and I have referred to as the 'cinema of attractions'.[22] This cinema differs from later narrative cinema through its fascination in the thrill of display rather than the construction of a story. Burch, I believe, obscures the evolution of film style when he defines the 'linchpin' of the later institutional mode of representation (his term which basically corresponds to what I have been calling the classical system of continuity) as 'spectatorial identification with a ubiquitous camera'.[23] Spectatorial identification with the viewpoint of the camera is a linchpin of early cinema as well, as *How It Feels* dramatically demonstrates. For Burch this film and others like it 'act out' the process of centring a spectator within a diegesis through camera identification, thereby establishing the central strategies of the institutional mode of representation, strategies that Burch finds more central than the development of narrative.[24]

But without an understanding of the way the classical mode of film-making subordinates cinematic techniques to the task of narration, we lose our grasp on the fundamentally integrating role the narrative plays. Coherence of story and storytelling allows the classical mode to fashion a unity from a proliferation of viewpoints and shots, through identification of the camera with an act of narration. The classical film can absorb sudden ubiquitous switches in viewpoint into an act of storytelling, creating a cinema whose role is less display than articulating a story. The continuity of classical cinema is based on the coherence of story, and the spectator's identification with the camera is mediated through her engagement with the unfolding of the story.[25]

In early film spectator relations are direct and relatively unmediated by concern with the story. As Jean Mitry has said, speaking of Méliès, 'it is not the spectator who was introduced into the space of the film, but rather the space which comes forward to present itself to him within a uniformity of theatrical framing.'[26] However, as we have seen, this unity of framing should not be identified with theatricality. Rather a more primal fascination with the act of display grounds the theatrical tableau, the medium shot of such facial expression films as Edison's *May Irwin Kiss,* the mobile vantage-point of the 'phantom railway rides', and the magical transformations contained within a single framing but created by substitution splices.

If the enunciator of early film is less a narrator than a monstrator, we must recognize the monstrator's mark in the act of framing. The frame presents the action displayed to the spectator. It is the unity of this framed viewpoint which addresses her specifically and directly, and this is the continuity the film-makers wished to preserve. However, such framing is a far from passive act, and not all due to either a primitive lack of expertise or a purist's desire to avoid manipulation. Early films are enframed rather than emplotted, and what is contained by their framing is often a result of a complex and detailed labour, one which, in the tradition of nineteenth-century illusionism, labours to efface its traces just as surely as did the later classical style.

Here again we encounter the strange intertwining of the traditions of realistic illusionism and the magic theatre. In maintaining a single point of view through his concealed substitution splices, Méliès (and other early film-makers) were drawing undoubtedly on the tradition and methods of behind-the-scenes manipulation found in the late nineteenth-century magic theatre. The detailed description that Méliès produced of the mechanisms and methods for producing visual illusions at his Théâtre Robert-Houdin (which have recently been reprinted in both the Malthête-Méliès anthology and Jenn's book) show how much these stage illusions were based on controlling the audience's view of the action either through lighting or mechanical devices. The magic theatre of the turn of the century was a technically sophisticated laboratory for the production of visual effects using recent technology to control spectators' perceptions.[27] It is this aspect of Méliès' theatrical inheritance that demands more attention from film historians, rather than a simple reference to the primitive use of proscenium framing.

For Méliès, this theatre was a theatre of illusions rather than a theatre of illusionism. But in the evolution of late nineteenth-century theatre there is a subterranean connection between these two apparently different approaches. David Belasco, for instance, could begin his career as a master of the Pepper's Ghost Illusion, yet reach his height of fame as the man who managed the perfect recreation of Child's Restaurant on stage, complete with the smell of real pancakes cooking on the griddle.[28] We might wonder with Mrs Sieppe whether managing the illusion of reality does not fundamentally correspond with the trick that produces an apparently supernatural event.

We confront here the essential paradox of the history of early film and to which Burch consistently calls our attention. It is simultaneously different from later practices an alternate cinema and yet profoundly related to the cinema that followed it. This relation must be approached avoiding the biological or progress-laden metaphors which a term like 'primitive' supplies. The substitution splice reveals a film-making praxis which is strongly concerned with continuity, but conceives of this continuity in a radically different manner from the cinema which follows. Such a move from a cinema of attractions to one of storytelling involves a change in basic spectator address which must be recognized if the logic of film history is to be traced in all its complexity.

NOTES

[1] Frank Norris, *McTeague: A Story of San Francisco* (New York: Signet, 1964), p. 79. The kinetoscope, of course, was the original name for Edison's peep-show device. However, since Norris' reference is to projected images, he is undoubtedly referring to Edison's Projecting Kinetoscope which was placed on the market in February 1897 (see Charles Musser, *Thomas Edison Papers: A Guide to Motion Picture Catalogues by American Producers and Distributors 1894-1908* (Fred-erick, Maryland: University Publications of America, 1985), p. 8.

[2] Norris, *McTeague,* pp. 85-6.

[3] Ibid., p. 85.

[4] Ibid., p. 87.

[5] See Robert C. Allen, *Vaudeville and Film 1895-1915: A Study in Media Interaction* (New York: Arno Press, 1980), pp. 57-64, 311.

[6] Anne-Marie Quévrain and Marie-George Charconnet-Méliès, 'Méliès et Freud: un avenir pour les marchands d'illusions?', in Madeleine Malthête-Méliès (ed.), *Méliès et la naissance du spectacle cinématographique* (Paris: Klincksieck, 1984), p. 235.

[7] See Kristin Thompson, in David Bordwell, Janet Staiger and Kristin Thompson, *The Classical Hollywood Cinema: Film Style and Mode of Production to 1960* (New York: Columbia University Press, 1985), p. 158.

[8] Tom Gunning, 'The noncontinuous style of early film', in Roger Holman (ed.), *Cinema 1900/1906: An Analytical Study* (Brussels: FIAF, 1982).

[9] See John Frazer, *Artificially Arranged Scenes: The Films of George Méliès* (Boston: G. K. Hall & Co., 1979), pp. 74-5.

[10] Jacques Malthête, 'Méliès, technicien du collage', in Malthête-Méliès, *Méliès.*

[11] Ibid., p. 171.

[12] See, for instance, Georges Sadoul, *Histoire générale du cinéma, Vol. II: Les pionniers du cinéma* (Paris: Denoël, 1948), p. 270.

[13] André Gaudreault, 'Theatricality, narrativity and "trickality": reevaluating the cinema of Georges Méliès', *Journal of Popular Film and Television,* vol. 15 no. 3, Fall 1987, p. 118. (This is an abridged and revised translation by Paul Attalah, Vivian Sobchak and Tom Gunning of Gaudreault's ' "Théâtralité" et "narrativité" dans l'oeuvre de George Méliès', in Malthête-Méliès, *Méliès.*)

[14] See 'Les vues cinématographiques' in Georges Sadoul (ed.), *Georges Méliès* (Paris: Seghers, 1961).

[15] Noël Burch, 'Primitivism and the avant-gardes: a dialectical approach', in Phil Rosen (ed.), *Narrative—Apparatus—Ideology* (New York: Columbia University Press, 1986), p. 486.

[16] Ibid., p. 500.

[17] André Gaudreault, 'Récit scriptural, récit théâtral, récit filmique: prolégomènes à une théorie narratologique du cinéma' (unpublished doctoral thesis, Université de Paris III, 1983).

[18] See, for instance, Jean Mitry, 'Le montage dans les films de Méliès, in Malthête-Méliès, *Méliès.*

[19] Pierre Jenn, *Georges Méliès cinéaste* (Paris: Albatros, 1984), pp. 26-9.

[20] David Francis, 'Films à trucs (1896-1901)', in Pierre Guibbert (ed.), *Les Premiers Ans du cinéma français* (Perpignan: Institut Jean Vigo, 1985), p. 144.

[21] Jenn, *Méliès,* passim. However, the strong influence of theatrical technique on Méliès should not be entirely discounted, as Jacques Malthête reminds us in 'Organisation de l'éspace scénique méliésien', in Guibbert, *Les Premiers Ans.*

[22] In 'The Cinema of Attractions: Early Film, Its Spectator and the Avant-Garde', pp. 56-62, of this volume. Also Gunning and Gaudreault, 'Early film as a challenge to film history', paper delivered at Conference in Cerisy on Film History, 1985.

[23] Burch, 'Primitivism', p. 491.

[24] See Noël Burch, 'How we got into pictures: notes accompanying *Correction Please',* *Afterimage,* 8/9, Spring 1981; and 'Narrative diegesis—thresholds, limits', *Screen,* vol. 23 no. 2, July-August 1982.

[25] I therefore state my agreement with Ben Brewster's article 'A Scene at the "Movies"', pp. 318-25 of this volume, which Burch's article in the same issue argues with. Brewster asserts the importance of narrative point of view over simple camera identification in forming the classical style.

[26] Jean Mitry, 'Le montage', p. 151 (my translation).

[27] See particularly Georges Méliès, 'Un grand succès du Théâtre Robert-Houdin', in Jenn, *Georges Méliès,* pp. 161-8.

[28] See Lise-Lotte Marker, *David Belasco: Naturalism in the American Theater* (Princeton: Princeton University Press, 1975), pp. 24-5, 61-2.

FURTHER READING

Biography

Barnouw, Erik. "The Magician and the Movies." *American Film* 111, No. 6 (April 1978): 8-13.
　　Examines the influence of French magicians on the development of French cinema.

McInroy, Patrick. "The American Méliès." *Sight and Sound* 48, No. 4 (Autumn 1979): 250-54.
　　McInroy surveys the film production work of Méliès's brother Gaston in the United States.

Stephenson, Ralph. "A Film a Day." *Films and Filming* 8, No. 3 (December 1961): 19, 40.
　　Written while Méliès's films were the subject of a Louvre Museum exhibition, the article details Méliès's life, and positions him as a major artist of the twentieth century.

Criticism

Frazer, John. *Artificially Arranged Scenes: The Films of George Méliès.* Boston: G.K. Hall & Company, 1979, 269 p.
　　Presents analysis of and illustrations from each surviving film of Méliès.

Hammond, Paul. *Marvellous Méliès.* London: Gordon Fraser Ltd., 1974, 159 p.
　　Surveys Méliès's life and work, and includes filmographies of both Méliès brothers.

William Mitchell

1879-1936

(Full name William Lendrum Mitchell) American military officer and aviator; nonfiction writer and memoirist.

INTRODUCTION

William "Billy" Mitchell helped to establish the United States Air Force, though he did not serve in that branch, and was in fact court-martialed as an Army officer in 1925. Outspoken in his advocacy of the air services as an independent part of the military, Mitchell was in the eyes of his detractors an insubordinate troublemaker—and, from the perspective of his supporters, a prophet and a visionary. Certainly the bombing of the U.S. Naval base at Pearl Harbor in 1941, five years after his death, confirmed Mitchell's warnings of American vulnerability to a Japanese air strike; and the subsequent conduct of the air war over Germany was in line with his formula for victory through strategic bombing. As a writer he was far from a brilliant stylist, but he stuck to a single point, which he presented effectively in a handful of books and some one hundred magazine articles.

Biographical Information

Mitchell was born in Nice, France, in 1879, the son of John Lendrum Mitchell, a future U.S. Senator from Wisconsin. Among his childhood friends was Douglas MacArthur, whose father had served in the Civil War alongside Mitchell's. Mitchell's early life had many of the trappings that came with an aristocratic upbringing: an education at the Racine College prep school, and a love of polo and other outdoor sports gained from time spent on a large family estate. At just fifteen years old, Mitchell entered Columbian (later renamed George Washington) University but left school in 1898 to enlist with the 1st Wisconsin Infantry. Eager to take part in the Spanish-American War, he arrived in Cuba after the hostilities had died down; soon afterward, however, he gained an assignment to the Philippines, another territory acquired by the United States from its war with Spain. While in the Far East Mitchell, who had served to that point as a private, received a commission as a lieutenant. By 1903 he was a captain in the signal corps serving in Alaska, and in 1906 he went to San Francisco to assist in the recovery of communications after the famous earthquake there. For almost three years, from 1907 to 1909, he attended the School of the Line and the Staff College at Fort Leavenworth, Kansas; and in 1912, during the U.S. conflict with Pancho Villa, served on the Mexican border. On an assignment as the youngest member of the General Staff, Mitchell analyzed the Balkan Wars of 1912 and 1913, which had helped bring on World War I. In 1915, Mitchell was

assigned to the signal corps's aviation section and learned to fly the following year, beginning an involvement with the airplane that would last the remainder of his life. Soon after America entered the war in April 1917, Mitchell—hastily promoted to the rank of lieutenant colonel—became air officer of the American Expeditionary Forces (AEF). A year later, he had become a colonel and had been put in the position of air officer of I Corps. In this capacity he became the first American aviator to fly behind enemy lines, and in September 1918 led a group of 1,500 French and American planes in what was then the largest bombing raid in history. By October he had become a brevet, or temporary, brigadier general, and he had plans for a large-scale bombing of Germany, but the war ended in November. Returning to the United States, he became assistant chief of the Air Service under General Charles T. Menoher, who was not himself a pilot. At that point, Mitchell began to undertake a campaign of writing and speaking in support of his convictions regarding the importance of air power. These ideas were revolutionary enough in the eyes of the early 1920s military leadership, but Mitchell's abrasive style helped to further alienate a number of Navy admirals who took offense to his claim that battleships were useless against air power. To prove his point, in July 1921 Mitchell arranged to have a group of flyers sink an obsolete German battleship, the *Ostfriesland*, captured in the war. They repeated the feat with the *U.S.S. Alabama,* another discontinued warship, later in the year; and again in 1923 with two other craft. These demonstrations did little to win friends for Mitchell among the Navy or Army brass, or among political leaders in Washington, and Mitchell continued his war of words in several books and dozens of magazine articles. In April 1925, he was returned to the rank of colonel and sent to a post in Texas, far from the center of power in Washington. It was a clear signal to Mitchell, but a few months later, he sent an equally clear signal of his own. After the Naval airship *Shenandoah* went down in a storm in September, killing twenty-eight men, he told the media that such incidents were "the direct result of incompetency, criminal negligence, and almost treasonable administration of the national defense by the War and Navy Departments." These remarks led to a court-martial, and Mitchell used his trial as a further platform for the presentation of his ideas. At its conclusion, he was found guilty and suspended for five years, but instead he resigned in February 1926. From the time of his resignation, Mitchell lived almost exactly a decade longer, and he spent that time campaigning for his principles, in part through a series of magazine articles. In 1946, ten years after his death, Congress awarded Mitchell a special posthumous medal in recognition of his "outstanding pioneer service and foresight in the field of military aviation"; and the next year it authorized the creation of a Defense Department, as Mitchell had envisioned, with subordinate Army, Navy, and Air Force branches.

Major Works

Mitchell's written works include *Our Air Force* (1921), *Winged Defense* (1925), and *Memoirs of World War I* (1960), as well as the biography *General Greely* (1936), the unpublished *Skyways* (1930), and some one hundred magazine articles. With the exception of the Greely biography, these works—even the wartime *Memoirs*, published long after Mitchell's death—simply serve to further reinforce the basic ideas which the author spent the last two decades of his life advancing. Among these were the convictions that America needed to build up its air power; that wars could be won or lost in the air; that airborne operations and strategic bombardment would decide the conflicts of the future; and that to meet this challenge, the United States needed to form a new Air Force Department on an equal footing with the Navy and Army, and place these three under a unified Defense Department, which would take the place of the existing War Department. His books were also notable for their publication dates, which greatly enhanced their success with the public: *Our Air Force* coincided with the *Ostfriesland* demonstration, and *Winged Defense* with the court-martial.

PRINCIPAL WORKS

Our Air Force: The Keystone to National Defense (nonfiction) 1921

Winged Defense: The Developments and Possibilities of Modern Air Power, Economic and Military (nonfiction) 1925

Memoirs of World War I: From Start to Finish of Our Greatest War (memoirs) 1960

CRITICISM

New York Times Book Review (essay date 1921)

SOURCE: "Value of the Airship in Modern Warfare," in the *New York Times Book Review,* July 3, 1921, pp. 16, 27.

[*In the following essay, a review of* Our Air Force, *the critic makes several references to Mitchell's famous tests of air power over battleships—at that time still a few days in the future.*]

The author of **"Our Air Force,"** the most distinguished aviation officer in the United States Army, knows his subject both as a specialist and as a pilot. After the battle of St. Mihiel General Pershing wrote the following appreciation of his services: "The organization and control of the tremendous concentration of air forces, including American, French, British and Italian units, which has enabled the Air Service of the First Army to carry out so successfully its dangerous and important mission, is as fine a tribute to you personally as is the courage and nerve shown by your officers a signal proof of the high morale which permeates the service under your command." The Distinguished Service Cross was conferred upon Colonel William Mitchell for "repeated acts of extraordinary heroism in action." He also received the Distinguished Service Medal. The French and British decorated him. As he was the one American flying officer who "handled large forces of aviation" against the enemy, his deserts could be recognized only by appointing him Assistant Chief of the Air Service, with the rank of Brigadier General, after the war.

William Mitchell entered the army as a volunteer in the first days of the conflict with Spain, and in less than three weeks became a Lieutenant at the age of 18. A youngster of intelligence and unusual physical activity, he always sought promotion. To qualify himself he went through the Army School of the Line and the Army Staff College, graduating with distinction from both. Aviation attracted him. He studied it intensively, and early learned to fly, becoming a skillful pilot. In his forty-first year he is still flying, asking no odds of younger men, to whom he is an example and an inspiration. In a single-seater he recently, by good judgment of atmospheric conditions, avoided the storm in which several army aviators met their deaths near Morgantown, Md. These details of General Mitchell's career are essential to an understanding of his qualifications to discuss aviation and to propose a policy for the country, especially as he takes advanced ground and asserts that the air force is "the keystone of national defense." The book is dedicated to the memory of a brother, John Lendrum Mitchell, a pilot in the United States Air Service who was killed in France.

General William Mitchell has the courage of his convictions. He has been so outspoken about the future of military aviation, both on sea and land, that his boldness has given offense in some quarters. However, he is not a prophet without honor. He realizes that "in the development of aeronautics one has to be careful that the imagination does not run into unpractical channels when a question so unlimited as aviation is considered." He adds: "Each thing in the development of aviation should be proved to a sufficient extent to warrant the entrance of the Government into it before it is attempted." General Mitchell is either in advance of his time or he misconceives and exaggerates the scope and value of aviation in modern warfare. If he seems extravagant in the following conclusion it must be remembered that there are European experts who share his belief:

> No navy will be able to exist against air attacks unless it obtains an absolute decision beforehand; and, as an air service will eventually be able to sink any warship, there will be no use in main-taining these expensive instruments for national defense.

It is not popular in the sea and land services to attack accomplished facts as unwise and deplorable, but the author does. He declares that it was a great mistake to send back to civil life 15,000 flying officers who were trained during the World War, "without any serious attempt to organize them and perpetuate their knowledge of aeronautics as a national asset, or to organize them as a reserve force to be used in any emergency that may come in the future." Nor is it the better part of valor to say that "neither the army nor the navy, nor both combined, can be expected to develop, organize and perfect a flying corps and its employment to the greatest possible limit of which that weapon is capable," when both the War and Navy Departments are set upon a policy of maintaining separate aviation corps. As the author says, aviation in this country is now split up between several Government agencies—the army, the navy, the Post Office, the Coast Guard, the Marine Corps and the Department of Agriculture. He recommends in vigorous fashion, without caring whose toes he treads upon, a unified air service to supply all these Government agencies and promote commercial aviation. But General Mitchell has plenty of support for this view. Representative Kahn of California has introduced a bill for a unified air service. The army and navy chiefs are

cold to it. President Harding has been quoted as opposed, but recently it was said that he had an open mind. At any rate, there will be an uphill fight, and a long one, before unity is attained.

It would be superfluous to reproduce the author's startling estimate of the damage that could be wrought from the air on cities as well as fleets by bombing airplanes, superfluous because tests at sea, urged by him before a Congressional committee, are now proceeding. As to the havoc upon land which he pictures, all the world knows that the truth about the raids by German aviators upon cities in Great Britain during the war was concealed as necessary to the keeping up of the morale of her people. Since those days and nights of horror there has been a wonderful advance in aviation and explosives of a power then unknown are now available for "modern warfare," not to speak of the gas deviltries of the laboratory.

General Mitchell does not write in technical terms. "He who runs may read" his exposition of the development of aeronautics since the war and understand his plan of organizing the air service. The illustrations are apt. Thus he shows an enlisted man standing between 500 and 1,000 pound airplane bombs, the larger rising above his head. One cannot help thinking what would happen at the corner of Wall and Broad Streets if such a monster were dropped by a passing plane. The loss of life and the destruction are not to be conceived; and, as the author tells us, a fleet approaching the coast with fast airplane carriers could dispatch a hundred flying machines loaded with bombs to devastate New York. The only sure, or partial, protection would be a superior defending fleet.

"Future control of the seas depends on the control of the air," says the author. This is a truism, but there are naval officers still reluctant to admit it and others who actually deny it. Theoretically, at least, General Mitchell is right when he says:

> A nation unequipped to concentrate her whole air force over the water, if the decision lies there, can just as well leave her navies tied up to the wharves, instead of sending them out to certain destruction against a hostile country equipped for this purpose.

This is not put with precision. What the author wants his readers to understand is that, however strong a nation may be in capital ships, as, for instance, the United States is, it will invite defeat if it goes to war with a nation perhaps not so formidable on the sea but stronger by a wide margin in the air. It is imperative for the United States to strengthen its naval aviation branch, even if it becomes necessary to suspend dreadnought construction for the time being. In pointing this out General Mitchell renders a great service, army man as he is. His critics in the navy may not like what they call his presumption in giving the sea service advice, but they cannot answer him except by contending that battleships would be able to take care of themselves in combat with bombing airplanes. By the time this review is published General Mitchell's theory will probably have had a certain test in sea manoeuvres proposed by himself, but in the nature of the conditions of attack it will not be accepted as conclusive. Only warfare would furnish a positive demonstration. However, it will be astonishing if the effect of dropping high explosives upon or in the vicinity of the obsolete warships selected as targets does not convince Congress that more attention must be given to the development of naval aviation.

The author sees no future for commercial aviation, which is essential to the full attainment of military aviation, until "a system of airdromes is established through the country and proper rules have been prescribed by law and are well administered, which will guarantee to the public safe transit through the air." The principle is fundamental that "commercial power in the air" insures a nation against unpreparedness for war. The most valuable chapter in the book is that entitled "What the United States should do now to establish its aeronautical position." It is urged to establish a Department of Aeronautics, and memoranda for drafting a bill are offered. Efficiency is promised and a great saving in expenditures. General Mitchell's treatment of his subject is by no means exhaustive. There are loose ends. The style might be better. But it is an honest book and planned in a spirit of patriotic service. He is a pioneer who blazes the way as a practical aviator as well as a thinker.

Henry E. Armstrong (essay date 1925)

SOURCE: "Like Armored Knights, Airmen will Monopolize War," in the *New York Times Book Review,* September 20, 1925, p. 3.

[*In the following essay, Armstrong takes issue with a number of points raised by Mitchell in* Winged Defense.]

"**Winged Defense**" is a brief for a more important place in the military establishment for aircraft than champions of the battleship in the navy and of the infantry in the army are willing to allow it. The argument is free from the spectacular, although not always free from exaggeration. There are no fulminations against the "old comptibles," that is to say, the moss-backs, who refuse to be convinced that surface ships are obsolete or who believe that the man on the ground will continue to win battles; there are no contumelious outbursts against superiors. Court-martial evidence is absent from "**Winged Defense**"—a title by the way, that may be catchy but blinks the offensive, in which the airplane is most puissant. It was reported that the Inspector General had scanned the book to detect wantonness in the former Assistant Chief of the Army Air Force. It was a waste of time.

Air power seems to have almost no limitations in the view of Colonel Mitchell. That is just where Admirals and Generals, just as sincere, differ with him. It is their contention that air power without fleets and armies cannot finish a campaign, conquer the enemy and hold territory. It may be supposed that he does not really think that air power is the beginning and the end of war. As a propagandist he may, however, justify his tactics for instance such a conception as this:

> It is probable that future wars again will be conducted by a special class, the air force, as it was by the armored knights in the Middle Ages, Again, the whole population will not have to be called out in the event of a national emergency, but only enough of it to man the machines that are the most potent in national defense.

This is a view that would make the nation with the longest purse impregnable and invincible. The author says that "this little book has been thrown together hastily." The material was Congressional hearings, articles in the public journals and personal experiences. There are traces of haste here and there, undigested ideas, snapshot conclusions. "Neither armies nor navies can exist," says Colonel Mitchell, "unless the air is controlled over them"—which is more of an admission that both can function than was to be expected of him, but in the next paragraph he declares:

> The missions of armies and navies are very greatly changed from what they were. No longer will the tedious and expensive processes of wearing down the enemy's land forces by continuous attacks be resorted to. The air forces will strike immediately at the enemy's manufacturing and food centres, railways, bridges, canals and harbors. The saving of lives, man power and expenditures will be tremendous to the winning side. The losing side will have to accept without question the dominating conditions of its adversary, as he will stop entirely the manufacture of aircraft by the vanquished.

The author says a very sober thing when he exclaims:

> What is necessary in this country is that the people find out the exact conditions concerning air power and the exact truth about what it can accomplish in time of peace as well as in time of war.

He has both feet on the ground. But he insists that "the views of the air must be heard in the national councils on an equal basis with those of the army and navy." There need be no caviling about that. He will have many supporters of his contention that there should be a single Department of National Defense and under it a Department of Aeronautics, a Department of the Army and a Department of the Navy. "The air-going people," says Colonel Mitchell, "have a spirit, language and customs of their own. They're just as different from those on the ground as those of seamen are from those of land men." It is plain that he puts the "air-going people" first as warriors, and that he thinks they should be deferred to. One may suppose he believes that the commander of all the forces in a war should have his headquarters in the air. The following prediction will arouse the General Board of the Navy:

> The surface ship, as a means of making war, will gradually disappear, to be replaced by submarines that will act as transports for air forces and destroyers of commerce.

Colonel Mitchell takes the case of Mesopotamia, or Iraq, as confirming his judgment that air forces can control territory. It is true, as he says, that the aviators "fly over the country at will, are able to put down uprisings quickly," but there is very little opposition to the mandate and certainly none in a military way to the air corps. Moreover, troops are available for punitive measures if needed. If a Turkish army were to invade Iraq in force, it would have to be expelled by infantry. "Fortunately, Congress," says the author, "has been pretty good to aviation." It is an admission to stick a pin into. The conditions of which Colonel Mitchell complains are, then, not the fault of our legislators but of the wicked old conservatives in the War and Navy Departments and in the sea and land services, who have their own axes to grind and no aeronautical "vision." The hearts of the aviators are sound, and they are keen for progress. It will rather surprise the British and French, who plumed themselves upon their achievements in the air at the front, to learn from the author that the American aviators, who used so many machines of our Allies, "knew every kink of the fighting game" and "knew they could defeat in single or combined combat any aviators of the world." Yet how often we should have had no air reconnaissance and no protection for our troops in action but for the intervention of French and British squadrons. The scores of some of their aces left no doubt of their great skill and valor. Such excesses of vainglory on Colonel Mitchell's part make one doubt whether he is always a stickler for exact statement. In another place he says that if the war had continued into 1919 the command of all air forces of the Allies would probably have been given to the Americans. One wonders why.

Colonel Mitchell tells again the fascinating story of the sinking of the surrendered German battleship Ostfriesland and other vessels by the army bombers off the Virginia Capes in 1921. It was a signal triumph for him, or rather for the Army Air Service, whatever the naval men may say about the non-war conditions under which the targets were sent to the bottom. Perhaps his account of how it was done is a little partial and somewhat boastful, but is he not speaking the stark truth when he says that "all the airplanes we had except the Martin bombers were obsolete war machines entirely unsuited for the work?" Colonel Mitchell may be pardoned his hilarity when he tells this story:

> After looking over the effect of all the different weapons used against the Alabama, one of the officers facetiously remarked that the future individual equipment of a sailor on a battleship would have to consist of a parachute to come down in when blown up into the air by our bombs and a life preserver to float on the water when he came down. He would have to wear asbestos-soled shoes, as the decks would all be hot; a gas mask to protect him from the noxious gases, and a pocket flash-lamp to find his way around the deck and interior of the ship when the electric lights went out.

This is diverting, but the issue of whether the airplane makes the capital ship obsolete is no laughing matter. Upon the right solution of the problem depends victory in the next war in which the United States is involved. No seventh son of a seventh son can tell us the day of the conflict, whether remote or near at hand. In March Rear Admiral Albert Gleaves began a talk to the Norfolk-Portsmouth Chamber of Commerce by saying that "we should have just as many airplanes as Congress will possibly provide. The battleships and other such vessels as can carry them should be equipped with them." But he added:

> Until the airplane has passed through the experimental stage in which it now is and accomplishes infinitely more than it has done up to date it cannot be said with accuracy that the battleship is either obsolete or obsolescent.

Concerning the sinking of the Ostfriesland Admiral Gleaves said that she was "anchored, undefended, abandoned. There was no counterattack. The planes flew low down from three to six thousand feet, and dropped their bombs undisturbed." He pointed out that in the case of the Iowa steaming only six and a half knots "but two hits were made out of eighty shots," and that "in the English experiments 114 bombs were dropped over the Agamemnon without making a hit." And, of course, the bombarding planes did not have to contend with an enemy in the air nor even with anti-aircraft guns, which of late have been wonderfully improved as to range and rapidity of firing. Weather conditions, the Admiral declared, would have made it impracticable for airplanes to operate in the battle of Heligoland Bight, which was fought in a fog, and they would have been greatly handicapped in the sea fight of Coronel, where the sea was very rough, rain fell and the light was bad. "What," asked Admiral Gleaves, "could airplanes have accomplished in any of the great sea battles (of the World War), which were fought at speeds of from twenty-four to twenty-eight knots, notably in the Falkland Islands fight?" He concluded: "If we, or any other nation, rely solely upon aviation for protection, it will be a fatal handicap from the beginning of the war." As a weapon the bombing plane may be terrible, but without fleets and armies its use and effectiveness are at present limited. This extract from Admiral Sir Reginald Bacon's book on the Dover Patrol should be illuminating, even to the aviation enthusiasts.

> Heavy gales and great quantities of rain were experienced during fourteen of the thirty-one days in December, 1915, and no flying was possible, while on others the conditions were such that while, protective patrols were carried out over the warships of La Panne, it was not considered feasible to undertake offensive work.

In his chapter "How Should We Organize?" Colonel Mitchell contends for a separate air department, such as England has. It

> handles all aviation matters, the central air force, the aviation assigned to the army and navy, civil aviation and commercial aviation. It maintains its airways, weather services, radio control stations, and subsidizes its passenger and cargo planes.

Colonel Mitchell has no means of knowing that "it is probable that both the army and navy will be under the air commander's orders for the defense of the islands." Such an opinion only reflects the partisan. The author would have the United States consolidate its aeronautical activities in the same way. Opposition has come from both the army and navy whenever the proposal has been made. Naval officers maintain that a sea air service independent of the department and the fleet commander would not be effective or dependable. The seaplane pilot must be first of all a sailor, trained as such and ready to take responsibility in emergencies. To be most useful he must be attached to the fleet or to a shore station, always a part of the service. He must be steeped in naval traditions. Disassociation from ships, officers and men, in fact, any isolation from them, would be embarrassing to commanders of fleets and squadrons who had battle plans to work out, and were answerable for their success to the country. Such is the naval view. The army's case is not as impressive, but any General in the field, regarding aviators as scouts as well as combatants, would find his initiative sometimes halted and his movements cramped by having to defer to an air force that took instructions only from a separate bureau or department. But there is a great deal to be said for an organization that would prevent duplication in purchases and distribution of material and generally in the supply of the sea, land and other Government services. Into details Colonel Mitchell does not go sufficiently, but haste he might plead in preparing his book to arouse his countrymen to the need of a sound and progressive air policy. He is certainly entitled to respectful attention when he says that "as a result of many years of service and an intimate knowledge of the aeronautical organization of each of the great powers" he is justified in proposing: a department of aeronautics coequal with the army and navy, a definite aeronautical policy; an organization to fit the aeronautical policy, which should include commercial aviation; a method to supply suitable personnel for all air undertakings, a single system of procurement and supply, and inspection of all air elements. **"Winged Defense"** is a thoughtful and impressive book by an officer, who, as Mr. G. P. Putnam says in "A Word About William Mitchell," "has always been a pioneer, and in aeronautics a good deal of a prophet."

Mark S. Watson (essay date 1960)

SOURCE: "Maverick Rides the Airways," in *Saturday Review,* Vol. XLIII, No. 29, July 16, 1960, pp. 21-22.

[*In the following essay, a review of* Memoirs of World War I, *Watson finds in that record of Mitchell's earlier career evidence of the defiant spirit that would later play a part in deciding the author's future.*]

General "Billy" Mitchell, a generation after his court-martial and fourteen years after his death in retirement, remains an idol of the Air Force quite as much by reason of his bold defiance of Army and Navy (it was the intemperance of his statements that brought disciplinary action) as by his pioneering in air tactics and air thinking. He was snorting defiance as early as 1917 and, costly as it proved to his career, he never stopped.

That spirit of rebellion against an establishment unready to change its ways breathes from chapter after chapter of Mitchell's memoirs of World War I *Memoirs of World War I: From Start to Finish of Our Greatest War,* published only in part in the Twenties, and now for the first time presented much as the impulsive and cocksure Mitchell had originally reconstructed them from his wartime diary. Limited to a chronicling of 1917-19, they stop short of the period when Mitchell was conducting his war on the U. S. Navy with a determination as marked as that with which he opposed the Kaiser and, naturally, this time with a far tighter tenure of the center of the stage. Even so, over and around the actual World War I events that he chronicled, Mitchell laid a gloss of judgments related to those events and, in effect, set the stage for the postwar expressions of opinion which fixed the pitch for Air Force thinking down to this day.

The British Air Marshal Trenchard's firmly expressed theories of that day (equally distasteful to his own War Office) clearly influenced the eager young American. Hit the enemy's resources hard, Trenchard urged, and waste little effort on air defense, since the airplane is not an effective defense against the airplane, anyway (for all the brilliant aerial dueling of that day) and "the sky is too large to defend." Granted that an enemy raid will have a bad moral effect on the homeland, do not be overwhelmed by that worry: rather, exploit the principle fully by first using our own air power deep in the enemy's homeland! This gospel impressed Mitchell and still inspires our Strategic Air Command.

Observations which Mitchell himself made in Britain—of Britain's ground-based airplanes unable to operate beyond the shore line, and sea-based airplanes forbidden to come within the shore line, with resultant happiness for the enemy led him to a conviction that all of a nation's air power should be under one command; likewise that all its military power, land, sea, and air alike, should be united, and united to a far tighter degree than exists even now in the Department of Defense. His enthusiasm for air power led him to extreme views about the limitations of the other armed services; thus, "an army's value lies only in holding the ground; it cannot conquer it" and "a navy's value lies only in undersea operations." Well, other prophets of the past—and the present—have been overenthusiastic.

Here, in any case, is a presentation of very advanced thinking on aviation of that day. It runs through a text that narrates with enthusiasm, rather than literary art, the World War I events which came to Mitchell's wide-roving attention. He had gone to Europe as a military observer in March, 1917, and thus was on the spot when America entered the war—"before Pershing in Europe," as he captions his opening chapter. He raced along the Western front and to England; he participated in some lively infantry and artillery actions; he studied aviation activities from factory and training school to combat, and from observation balloon to fighter-plane; he marveled at French skill with camouflage (shell-holes were simulated to deceive the German artillery-spotters, and a dead horse's carcass in no-man's-land was at length replaced by an imitation carcass of identical shape and color—actually a less odorous hiding place for a French observer).

So passionate a zealot as Mitchell could not hide either his admiration or his rages. Years after the war he continued to denounce violently many aspects of the American airplane program of 1917-18 ("a foolish and disastrous move," "scheming politicians," etc.); our training program ("under non-flying officers who knew nothing of aviation"); our first new wave of aviation officers ("almost none of whom had ever seen an airplane; a more incompetent lot of air warriors had never arrived . . . these carpetbaggers"), and their leader, General Ben Foulois, who, for all Mitchell's dislike, the present publisher remarks tartly, had been the Army's most active flyer long before Mitchell ever thought of becoming a pilot. But there are pleasant pictures of General Pershing and of numerous other wartime heroes.

There is a proud report of the first action by an American air unit, and later of the air element's mounting operations until Mitchell himself briefly commanded the largest array of American and Allied air units ever assembled up to that time. And there is a proud summary of American pioneering air accomplishments, for which no one had a larger responsibility than Mitchell.

Edward Weeks (essay date 1960)

SOURCE: "The Peripatetic Reviewer," in *The Atlantic*, Vol. 206, No. 3, September, 1960, pp. 110, 112.

[*In the following essay, a review of* Memoirs of World War I, *Weeks briefly examines Mitchell's career up to the time of the war, as well as the problematic situation of the Allied air effort which inspired his later crusade.*]

Like Admiral William S. Sims in the Navy, Brigadier General William Mitchell was an outspoken firebrand and a constant source of irritation to the old guard in the Army Signal Corps. Billy Mitchell at the age of eighteen enlisted as a private and served throughout the Spanish-American War. In 1901, now a first lieutenant in the Signal Corps, he was sent to Alaska, where he set up a primitive telegraph system. In 1909, while on leave, he made an extensive tour of the Far East, and on his return at the age of thirty-two he was appointed to the General Staff. As a General Staff officer he submitted a report in 1914 that if the Allies were allowed to float loans in this country, it would assuredly involve us in the war. He had known the Wright brothers, and in 1916 he learned to fly at his own expense; six months later he was ordered to France as a military observer for aviation, and so became the first American officer to serve with the Allies under German fire.

It was Billy Mitchell's wish to be commander of the Air Services in the newly formed A.E.F., and for a time he held this command. His plans and his predictions for the squadrons then forming at home were right-minded and prophetic. He urged that we assist the production of French planes instead of wasting time trying to devise our own American models; he made note of the fighting tactics of the French pursuit pilots, whom he greatly admired; he realized how much the French pilots were dependent upon their devoted, well-trained mechanics; he saw how the Germans scored with their weight of numbers; and, finally, he recommended that all Allied aviation should be placed under a single command instead of being trammeled by conflicting instructions from the ground forces. These ideas are some of the spear points in his posthumous volume, *Memoirs of World War I.*

It is grim to have to add that, in almost every instance, General Mitchell's recommendations were blocked by the high brass in France and in Washington. Instead of speeding up the production of Spads in the French factories, it was decided, thanks to British propaganda, that we should use the De Havilland airplane with the as yet undeveloped Liberty engine being substituted for their Rolls-Royce. The result of this blunder was that no plane of American origin ever fought in combat, and our pilots were, many of them, compelled to take to the air in French retreads, planes which in anything but an emergency would have been condemned as unfit.

General Mitchell himself was at the front constantly throughout 1917. He saw the disastrous bogging down of General Nivelle's offensive (300,000 casualties in three weeks); he participated in the strafing of German balloons; he saw aerial combats at close range and was one of the first to inspect the great Zeppelins which were brought down intact after the ill-fated raid over Britain. He spoke French and had established a confidential relationship with the commanding officers of the French Aviation when he learned to his chagrin that he was being relieved by Brigadier General Foulois, who had just arrived in France "with a shipload of aviation officers, almost none of whom had ever seen an airplane." He himself was to be given command of the air force of the 1st Army Corps, as soon as that unit could be formed. Meantime, he was to assist in teaching "the staff officers what the Air Service was all about and how it could be used," and if he sometimes seemed brusque and tactless, one can hardly wonder.

Mitchell was too good a fighter to sulk, and his re-sourcefulness as a leader was called on more and more as the American forces were built up for their vital campaigns in the summer and autumn of 1918. He never lost his capacity to look ahead or his infuriating habit of making suggestions upsetting to the old guard. "If we had been called on to fight alone," he writes, "I doubt if we could have put up as much resistance with our regular army, steeped as it was in the conservatism of peace-time methods, as with the New York City police force." "There must have been a lot of inside work somewhere by the English manufacturers to put this thing over on the Americans," he wrote when he heard that the Liberty-De Havilland deal had finally been accepted.

On his days off he went to shoot the wild boar in the forests of the Marne, and on his days on he watched Frank Luke, the Arizona cowboy, shoot down the German *saucisses* with flaming bullets and helped to build up the *esprit* and the training of his favorite bombardment squadrons—the 94th was one of them—against that great moment on the morning of September 12, 1918, when he directed the British, French, Italian, and American pilots in their victory at Saint-Mihiel.

American Heritage (essay date 1962)

SOURCE: "Billy Mitchell's Prophecy," in *American Heritage,* Vol. XIII, No. 2, February, 1962, pp. 74-75.

[*In the following essay, a writer for* American Heritage *records a series of exceedingly prescient observations made by Mitchell during a tour of Hawaii in 1923—eighteen years before the attack on Pearl Harbor.*]

In the fall of 1923, Brigadier General William "Billy" Mitchell, then Assistant Chief of the young Army Air Service, was sent on an inspection tour of the Pacific. Upon his return, Mitchell publicly voiced opinions about the inadequacies of our Pacific defenses and the very real threat of Japanese aggression that caused a furor in the War Department.

Among other things Mitchell warned that the Hawaiian Islands—and, in particular, the great naval base at Pearl Harbor—were open to a Japanese surprise air attack. He then proceeded to outline how such an attack could be made successfully. Because Mitchell failed to reckon on the development of the aircraft carrier, many details of his plan now seem unnecessarily elaborate, if not fantastic; but in the light of what happened on December 7, 1941, his total concept proved alarmingly accurate.

The prophetic words which appear below are published for the first time. They are taken from the original report that Mitchell wrote in 1924—a 525-page manuscript recently brought to light after years of obscurity in the classified files of the War Department and the National Archives.—Ed.

I. The Military Importance of the Island of Oahu

1. Assuming a state of war to be impending and with the mission of the Hawaiian Department to be the holding of the Island of Oahu for four months before the arrival of supporting troops, let us estimate what the action of Japan will be. . . . She knows full well that the United States will probably enter the next war with the methods and weapons of the former war, and will, therefore, offer the enticing morsel which all nations that have followed this system have done before. Japan also knows full well that the defense of the Hawaiian Group is based on the defense of the Island of Oahu and not on the defense of the whole group.

2. The Island of Oahu, with its military depots, both naval and land, its airdromes, water supplies, the city of Honolulu with its wharves and supply points, forms an easy, compact and convenient object for air attack. . . .

II. Possible Plan of Attack of the Hawaiian Islands and Results Thereof.

1. There is no adequate defense against air attack except an air force. This can be supplemented by auxiliaries on the ground, such as cannon, machine guns, and balloon barrages, but without air power these arrangements act only to give a false sense of security, such as the ostrich must feel when he hides his head in the sand. . . .

2. I believe, therefore, that should Japan decide upon the reduction and seizure of the Hawaiian Islands, the following procedure would be adopted. Ten submarines would be loaded with six pursuit airplanes and spares each, the airplane crates being made in two segments so that each one could be used as a barge when emptied of its cargo. These crates would be carried as deck loads, the boats would dive only for concealment. Two airplane transports would be provided, each loaded with fifty bombardment planes. These ships could be equipped with a flying-off deck laid down in sections while the transports were in use. These seacraft would be started so as to arrive at the islands of Niihau [the smallest and westernmost of the Hawaiian Islands, it is now privately owned and operated as a sheep ranch—Ed.] and Midway respectively on "D" day.

3. The submarines with the pursuit equipment aboard would land at Niihau on the evening of "D" day and, as there are only 140 people on the island, no radio station or other means of communication, except by water, probably the first information of this force, received at Honolulu, would be the appearance of the hostile aircraft. . . .

4. The pursuit ships could be set up and made ready for service during the night and be ready for duty the next morning. (Twenty submarines could carry twice as many pursuit ships as the ten mentioned above.) The force destined for Midway Island could debark its bombardment equipment from the transports, prepare the airdrome in the sand with landing mats and the necessary

auxiliaries to the aircraft. All the islands between Midway and Niihau would be occupied with observation posts and radio sets.

5. The flying time between Midway to Niihau is eleven hours. By equipping the bombers with auxiliary gas tanks in their bomb compartments a cruising ability of about sixteen hours can easily be given them. As soon as set up and tested, those ships would fly to Niihau and be ready to attack Oahu immediately afterwards. While these operations are taking place the Island of Guam would be seized. (Under these conditions the Philippines would fall of their own weight within a year or two.)

6. The distance from Niihau to Honolulu is about 150 miles, or an hour and a half flight, or a total of three hours there and back; allowing forty minutes for an attack and an additional twenty minutes for eventualities would require a maximum of four hours for one attack mission. (The present United States pursuit airplane with auxiliary gas tank has four and a half hours' fuel; the bomber, about six.)

7. The first attack would be arranged as follows: Japanese pursuit, sixty ships, organized into one group of three squadrons of twenty ships each; two squadrons to participate in combined attack with bombardment and one squadron to remain in reserve on the alert. . . . The objectives for attack are: (1) Ford Island airdrome hangars, storehouses, and ammunition dumps (2) Navy fuel oil tanks (3) Water supply of Honolulu (4) Water supply of Schofield (5) Schofield Barracks airdrome and troop establishments (6) Naval submarine station (7) City and wharves of Honolulu.

8. Attack will be launched as follows:

Bombardment

Attack to be made on Ford's Island at 7:30 A.M. . . . .

Anthony Sommer (essay date 1974)

SOURCE: "Billy Mitchell: Aviation's Prophet," in *American History Illustrated*, Vol. IX, No. 8, December, 1974, pp. 32-43.

[*In the following essay, Sommer provides an overview of Mitchell's life and legacy.*]

There was no military escort at the funeral of General William Mitchell in February of 1936. An American Legion post fired the last salute while its bugler sounded taps in the chill winter air at a small cemetery near Milwaukee, the home he had left in 1898 to begin his remarkable career as soldier and seer.

Mitchell died without seeing his dreams and predictions—and his warnings—come to pass. Within a decade, he would be vindicated.

The commander of the largest force of military aircraft ever assembled up to that time, Mitchell came away from World War I with the conviction that the "War To End All Wars" had solved little. It had, he believed, failed to establish democracy as the dominant political force in Europe. And in Germany particularly, where the seeds of the Weimar Republic were planted in barren soil, he knew the forces of militarism were still alive. He believed that unless America maintained her military aviation capability on a par with other major world powers she would be drawn unprepared into another world conflict with enemies who had learned better the lessons of the Great War.

His outspoken efforts to convince the government and the military hierarchy cost him his career but also thrust him into the national limelight where his views were eagerly accepted for publication on the value of his name alone.

In taking his case before the American public he realized he faced an audience disillusioned with the results achieved by military might, a people who had shrunk back into a dream of isolation already shattered. During the frivolities of the Twenties and the hardships of the Thirties, his writings had a pronounced effect on those initiated few involved in aviation. His views were read avidly by military aviation leaders in Europe and Japan. But in his own country, his works were ignored by the reigning conservative clique in the military and read by the general public only because Billy Mitchell was a colorful figure on the American scene.

Mitchell said as much in his **"Last Message,"** published in *Liberty* magazine in April 1936, two months after his death:

> Americans have not yet had things brought home to them as the Europeans have. Their cities have not been bombed. If we organize properly we might be able to prevent such an eventuality. To let our national defense organization fall down and become weak in policy and methods is to extend an invitation to a well-armed adversary to come and fall upon us.

William Lendrum Mitchell was born in Nice, France, December 29, 1879, the son of John Lendrum Mitchell and grandson of Milwaukee financier Alexander Mitchell. Soon after Billy's birth, John Mitchell moved his family back to Wisconsin, and by the time Billy entered the military was a United States senator.

Billy Mitchell grew up on Meadowmere, a large farm estate where he learned to hunt, fish, swim, and trap. Known for his equestrian skill in his early military career and a horse fancier all his life, he first played polo at the age of 13.

A brilliant student, Billy was graduated from Racine College, a preparatory school, and at the age of 15 became the youngest freshman at George Washington

University. He left the University in 1898 to fight against Spain with the Wisconsin Volunteers and was commissioned a second lieutenant in the Signal Corps. Mitchell expected to be sent to Cuba but he languished in Florida during the hostilities, arriving in Havana only in time to witness the formal surrender ceremonies.

Still longing for action, he requested duty in the Philippines and was ordered there in 1899 to become chief signal officer to General Arthur MacArthur, long-time family friend and father of Mitchell's closest companion, Douglas MacArthur. During the Philippine Insurrection, one of the cruelest and most savagely contested military actions in America's history, Mitchell distinguished himself with numerous examples of leadership and personal courage.

By 1901, when he received his commission in the Regular Army, Mitchell had toured China, Japan, the Middle East, and Europe. He put in for duty in Alaska where the Signal Corps was stretching a telegraph line across 2,200 miles of wilderness. During this tour Mitchell survived several near-fatal mishaps and once drove a dog sled a record 150 miles in twenty-four hours. In the same year, at the age of 23, Mitchell became the youngest captain in the United States Army.

Three years later he was sent to San Francisco to restore communications after the great earthquake and fire. In 1909 he returned to the Philippines and from there went on another tour of the Far East before being posted to Latin America.

In 1912 Mitchell, then 32, became the youngest member of the General Staff, where he spent three years analyzing the Balkan Wars. He also completed his first serious study of military aviation and concluded that to establish a separate air service would violate the principle of unity of command. He would soon reverse his thinking.

Mitchell's first exposure to aviation had come several years earlier as an observer at the 1908 Army trials at Fort Myer, Virginia. Although he witnessed the crash of a frail biplane which fatally injured Lieutenant Thomas Selfridge and seriously injured the pilot, Orville Wright, Mitchell was impressed even then with the potential of the airplane.

It was not until 1916, however, that Mitchell learned to fly—at his own expense—from a civilian instructor who taught him on weekends. A major then, he was one of the highest ranking flying officers and a natural choice for making an inspection of military aircraft in use by the French and British pilots over the Western Front. He toured Allied airfields and saw service in the trenches with French infantry locked in bloody stalemate along a front stretching for hundreds of miles.

In his report on both communications and aviation in Europe, Mitchell advocated for the first time a separate air force because of the strategic importance he saw in flying machines ranging far behind enemy lines. Although his proposal was turned down, Mitchell was still in Europe when America entered the war, and he was put in command of all United States air forces arriving at the front.

Initially there were, in fact, no American air forces. American pilots, flying French and British machines, were used as replacements in the squadrons of the Allies, and American ground forces were integrated into the lines with existing Allied infantry units.

After a bitter dispute the American commander, General John Pershing, won out and was given a separate sector of the front as his area of operations. Promoted to brigadier general, Mitchell was then able to reassemble his pilots into a single American air service. They continued to fly French and British aircraft because, despite promises to darken the skies of Europe with American aircraft, U.S. airplane manufacturers were unable to design a single aircraft of the quality then fighting over the Western Front.

Mitchell became a legend among Allied pilots, flying missions with American airmen deep behind enemy lines. He constantly visited his airfields, either flying his own plane or, when the weather was too poor, driving a purchased Mercedes racer, the fastest in France. Later the French Government presented him with a Renault racer to avoid the embarrassment of having a German car carrying an American commander behind their lines.

The end of the war cancelled Mitchell's most farsighted plan. He had assembled a fleet of Handley-Page bombers and had begun training an entire infantry division for a parachute attack behind enemy lines.

Returning to the United States, Mitchell was named assistant director of the air service on March 1, 1919 under a non-flyer, General Charles T. Menoher, who allowed Mitchell wide latitude in developing his own plans. But the General Staff had other ideas and even as Mitchell fought to improve the air service, its numbers were cut back and development of new aircraft came to a virtual standstill. American pilots continued to fly machines which had been obsolete when the United States entered the war. A sense of frustration enveloped Mitchell, but his arguments remained within aviation and military circles.

Assistant Secretary of War Benedict Crowell was one of the few high government officials who saw potential in aviation. At Mitchell's urging he headed a special mission to Europe in 1919 and its seven members called for an effort to move America from the weakest major power in aviation to the forefront. Secretary of War Newton D. Baker, however, read the report with great dismay and buried it deep in his files, where it remained suppressed until Mitchell made it public in 1925.

It became clear to Mitchell that his polite efforts were not swaying aviation's critics and the air service continued to deteriorate. In a single year, from mid-summer 1920 to mid-summer 1921, the Army Air Service lost 330 planes and 69 pilots in crashes resulting from defective aircraft.

In September 1920 Mitchell began a more emphatic program, carrying his message to a broader public but purposely choosing a rather select-readership journal, *The Review of Reviews.* He had broken out into open debate and the three pieces written for *Review of Reviews* issued a clear challenge to the military establishment and to the Navy in particular to fully test the potency of the airplane as a major weapon. Airplanes, he wrote, could sink the largest battleships.

The Navy could not ignore the dare. Tests were scheduled for June and July 1921. The air service first dispatched a submarine, a destroyer, and a light cruiser, all obsolete, to the bottom of Chesapeake Bay. For the main event, one of the most heavily armored ships in the world, the captured German battleship *Ostfriesland,* was chosen.

With Mitchell leading them, a flight of Martin MB-2 bombers swept over the bay dropping their 2,000-pound bombs in the water around the battleship. Its hull split by the concussion of the underwater blasts, the *Ostfriesland* went down in twenty-five minutes. Senior American naval observers wept at the sight.

Later that same year Mitchell's pilots similarly sank the battleship *USS Alabama.* In 1923 further tests were ordered and two other obsolete battleships, the *Virginia* and the *New Jersey,* also were sunk. Although no drastic changes in the air service came about, Mitchell was confident he had won support through public pressure to stage the tests. He had the attention of the policy-makers and, having discovered a new weapon in the art of mass persuasion, he just as quickly abandoned it, feeling there was no further need to go directly to the public.

Instead Mitchell used his Army pilots to demonstrate the capability of aviation. In May 1923 Lieutenants John A. MacReady and Oakley G. Kelly made the first non-stop transcontinental flight in twenty-seven hours. A year later Lieutenant Russell A. Maughan flew from Long Island to San Francisco in eighteen hours. On April 4, 1924 four Army planes set out to circle the globe. Two of them completed the flight September 28.

But at about the same time, in 1923, Mitchell took an extended leave to study aviation in Europe and the Far East. He came back even more convinced that America was falling too far behind. The danger of war with Japan, second only to England in aviation progress, was becoming obvious to Mitchell. Unable to convince his superiors of the mounting threat, he again presented his case before the American people.

What had been a mere flirtation with the press now turned to an earnest endeavor. After first receiving permission from President Calvin Coolidge, Mitchell offered his writings to the general circulation magazines providing him with the greatest number of readers. On December 20, 1924 *The Saturday Evening Post* ran the first of a series of articles by Mitchell openly challenging the strategy of the General Staff who believed the United States could be protected by a battleship-oriented Navy.

He expanded his readership to the Hearst newspapers where he wrote: "Every other nation is developing aviation. We are slipping backward." He told readers of *U.S. Air Service Magazine,* "Neither Armies nor Navies can exist unless the air is controlled over them."

In *Liberty* magazine Mitchell wrote:

> This will mean that you, Navy, must put on your diving suit and get out into the water, away from our shores and on the high seas. Your role of defense, close in shore, is a thing of the past. We can handle that now with our aircraft.
>
> Air power says to the Army: You must provide for holding secure all land areas. You must take off your spurs and get in a motor car. You must provide yourself with the latest weapons—cannon, mortars, machine guns, and chemicals. We will keep the enemy out of the air above you.

Predictably, reaction in the War and Navy Departments was not favorable. Mitchell's term as assistant air chief was due to expire in early 1925, and those who opposed him saw the opportunity to get Mitchell out of the inner circle of policy-makers. But the problem was complex-Mitchell was a brevet general officer. A popular war hero, he was embarrassing the military establishment while at the same time increasing his stature with the public, who gave him such titles as "Stormy Petrel" and "The Hard-Riding Cavalryman of the Skies." In his six years in office Mitchell had flown more than 200,000 miles, personally testing all new Army aircraft, barnstorming at county fairs, blazing new air routes across the country, courting the wealthy and influential at horse shows, appearing before congressional committees, and making news wherever he went.

It was finally decided to reduce Mitchell to his permanent rank of colonel and banish him to command the training school at Randolph Field, Texas. Mitchell protested to the President but Coolidge now backed his senior military officers.

At Randolph Mitchell continued writing, averaging an article a month. He had been making slow gains through his supporters in Congress, and finally a bill calling for a separate air force was passed, only to be vetoed by Coolidge.

On September 1, 1925, less than three months after Mitchell had been assigned to Randolph, a naval aircraft bound for Hawaii on a publicity flight went down at sea. The crew was rescued several days later but in the meantime the giant dirigible *Shenandoah* with a crew of forty-two was torn apart in a storm over the Ohio River Valley. Its commander, Zachary Lansdowne, one of the twenty-eight killed, had protested the flight because of bad weather and structural faults in the airship. But the *Shenandoah* was on a tight schedule of public relations appearances and senior Navy officials ordered the mission to be flown.

For a day and a night Mitchell, troubled by critics of aviation who were trying to exploit the two disasters, worked on a 6,000-word statement which his legal aide warned him would only result in retaliation by the War Department. He released it at a press conference.

"These accidents," he summed up, "are the direct result of incompetency, criminal negligence and almost treasonable administration of the national defense by the War and Navy Departments."

The reaction was almost immediate. Mitchell was to be court-martialed under Article of War 96 for "conduct of a nature to bring discredit upon the military service."

"Officers are tried under it for kicking a horse," Mitchell told a reporter. But what emerged was a series of events that were to climax Mitchell's military career and place him even more firmly in the public eye.

Whether he calculated in advance that this would happen is questionable. Once committed, however, Mitchell grabbed the opportunity of the rapidly unfolding drama to strike repeated blows for his cause. If he was to lose his military career, he would gamble it away for very high stakes.

Before Mitchell's trial there were two highly-publicized investigations and in both Mitchell was a key witness. First was the inquest into the loss of the *Shenandoah*. So many questions were raised in the press that Coolidge was forced to form a commission to look into the many charges made by Mitchell.

The hearings before the Morrow Board were heavily influenced by the administration and the War and Navy Departments. But the board was obliged to allow Mitchell to give as much testimony as he wished. Mitchell's views and those of his supporters who were paraded to the witness stand and the release of the long-concealed Crowell Report dominated both the hearings and the headlines.

There were few who doubted Mitchell would be found guilty at his court-martial, but that did little to alter the high drama of the trial set in a converted warehouse. Mitchell, attempting to focus the validity of his incriminating statement as a defense, was allowed to bring forward many airmen and air power advocates who had previously been shackled by their superiors. The trial,

which began October 28 and lasted six weeks, provided the first honest look at the state of the nation's defenses. The list of air service officers testifying for Mitchell reads like a roster of the senior air corps officers of World War II. The appearance on the stand of Zachary Lansdowne's widow and Mitchell's own moving testimony climaxed the long, detailed, and emotional appeal of aviation's supporters.

Their actions closely monitored by the national press, the court, which included Mitchell's boyhood friend Douglas MacArthur, was forced to appear impartial. Their decision, however, already had been written. Mitchell was found guilty and suspended for five years. On February 1, 1926, after twenty-eight years in the service, he resigned from the Army. His new status as a controversial figure—a martyr, in fact, to his supporters—provided him now with the freedom to pursue his crusade without restraint.

In his writings he spoke of aircraft and aerial weapons then only just being conceived, and he wrote of war in the sky on a massive scale. Mitchell predicted events which must have appeared as science fiction in an era when military pilots still flew in open cockpit biplanes with skins of stretched fabric over wood airframes held taut by stressed wire.

He told *Liberty* magazine readers in 1926 of air battles above 35,000 feet with superchargers delivering compressed air to airplane engines. Every one hundred bombers would be accompanied by two hundred pursuit planes. Airfields, he said, must be equipped to service hundreds of planes at the same time.

The United States, he wrote the same year in *Collier's,* would in the future be vulnerable to air attack unless an adequate number of pursuit aircraft defended her cities. An enemy gaining airfields in Alaska or Greenland could easily reach targets in the United States and future aircraft would be able to launch attacks on America from Europe. In the early twenties Mitchell and his pilots had flown mock bombing raids against major American cities; he concluded that crowded urban areas such as New York would suffer terrible casualties in a real attack.

While still the assistant air chief, Mitchell had claimed that antiaircraft guns were useless and provided more of a danger (from falling fragments) to people on the ground then they did to attacking airplanes. The War Department challenged Mitchell and in a test with towed targets, gunners were unable to puncture a single sleeve. Mitchell now told his readers this, adding that future aircraft may utilize "aerial torpedos" launched from bombers at great distances from their targets. He said, too, that several European nations were developing pilotless aircraft controlled by radio.

Billy Mitchell made his final trip to Europe in the fall of 1927 to attend an American Legion convention in

Paris and act as a roving correspondent for the Hearst newspapers on a tour which explored aeronautical progress in all the former combatant countries in the Great War. The titles of the articles written for the *New York American* are indicative of the dangers he saw in America's failure to keep up with Europe in aviation progress: **"Germany's Air Traffic Leads the World," "How Russia Seeks to Dominate The Air." "How Italy Is Mobilizing A Sky Army," "How Britain Is Striding Forward in the Air," "France Aims to Lead the World in the Air."**

Mitchell returned from Europe with no illusions of a lasting peace on the troubled continent. "The same influences which brought about the former conflict are at work," he wrote for Hearst readers early in 1928. "Germany, even with her wings clipped, has practically recovered her former position after 10 years of strenuous effort. She holds the central position on the stage of European politics."

Although he reported Germany was disarmed, Mitchell observed she was developing the most advanced civil airline and passenger and merchant marine in Europe. He predicted that the air and sea crews being trained could form the nucleus of an air force and navy.

He found very much alive the old German ambition to form in central Europe "one great German confederacy or empire, with a domain stretching from the North Sea and the Baltic, through to the Black Sea and the Aegean and across Asia Minor to the Persian Gulf." Conflict, he wrote in a 1928 *Collier's* article seemed inevitable. "Today Europe is armed to the teeth. There are probably more soldiers there than ever before."

On his return to America he hit hard on the central theme throughout his crusade:

> No other civilized country in the world today allows its army and navy to have control of its air power.
>
> What we need is an organization specifically charged with the defense of the land, one specifically charged with the defense of the water, and one specifically charged with the defense of the air; all of these to work under a common master, a single Department of National Defense which embraces them all.

His remarks about the Navy drew particular wrath from Rear Admiral William A. Moffett, the first chief of the Navy Bureau of Aviation and father of the aircraft carrier. Mitchell—incorrectly, as it turned out—believed aircraft carriers as vulnerable to air attack as battleships and labeled them "largely a delusion and a snare." Moffett characterized Mitchell as "unsound of mind."

But Mitchell was far from being totally wrong about the direction he believed the Navy should move. Submarines, he wrote readers of *The Saturday Evening Post,* "will be the future means of operating on the sea. In the

future, surface navies cannot be the arbiters of the communications over the ocean." If Mitchell and Moffett agreed on one area it was in a concept which never bore fruit: Both were strong advocates of the use of dirigibles. Moffett was killed in the crash of one in 1933.

Impressed by the aviation progress he had witnessed in Europe, Mitchell set out to educate his readers on the dawning potential of the airplane. An innovator himself, Mitchell had experimented with pressurized flying suits for high altitudes and to counter the effects of tight turns. In 1921 he had planned experiments with pressurized cockpits but could not find the funds. Neither concept was perfected for many years. Flying higher, faster, and farther was only a matter of advancing technology, said Mitchell in **"What About Future Flying?"** in the June 8, 1929 *Liberty* magazine:

> I do not think there is any limit to speed in the air except the point of fusion; for example, the burning of a meteorite when it hits the earth's atmosphere. I believe the pilot will be able to withstand velocities up to 1,000 miles an hour.

The earth inductor compass, gyroscopic instruments, radio direction finders, great circle courses, all were being developed in Europe, he wrote. Work was still needed on a de-icing method for wings and propellers, perhaps using the heat of the engine. Another need was a method of air-to-air refueling and the development of crash-proof gasoline tanks which could be jettisoned to prevent fires in the event of a crash.

As early as 1926 Mitchell had warned readers of the Hearst newspapers that Japan held ambitions in the Pacific. When Japan invaded Manchuria in 1932, Japanese pilots were bombing targets 1,200 miles from their air bases. In a series of *Liberty* magazine articles in 1932 Mitchell outlined with remarkable clarity the strategy of a war still a decade away. He saw a war in the Pacific dominated by aircraft and submarines, and island invasions with the sole aim of gaining land air bases from which to launch long-range bombing missions.

Isolationists branded him a jingo but Mitchell continued. In the June 25, 1932 edition of *Liberty* he asked, "Will Japan try to conquer the U.S.?" and concluded that as the only other major power on the Pacific, the United States was logically Japan's ultimate adversary. "The Japanese are working almost with desperation to make themselves the strongest military power in the world," he warned.

Mitchell predicted there would be three targets the Japanese would seek simultaneously. Hawaii and Alaska would be the major prizes. And the Philippines, the only major islands threatening the Southeast Asia coast on which Japan depended for many natural resources, would be the third. These three objectives "will undoubtedly be pounced upon at the first favorable opportunity," he wrote in mid-1932, pointing out that historically Japan never declared war before attacking. "In case of trouble, Japan will have the jump on us and could pull off the greatest surprise in military history."

A decade before Pearl Harbor, in magazines that entered a substantial portion of American households, Mitchell described the strategy for winning a war against Japan. The Japanese, he noted, were wholly dependent on raw materials from outside sources in Korea and Southeast Asia. Her link to them was the sea lanes which she controlled but which could effectively be cut by American submarines.

"Japan is in no way afraid of our naval power," Mitchell claimed. The Japanese, he wrote, controlled a vast network of island bases reaching to within 600 miles of Hawaii. From these bases long-range aircraft could attack any approaching fleet. In order to gain superiority, American forces would have to seize these islands. Once American bombers gained these island bases, Japan, with its towns built of wood and hemmed in by mountains, would provide "the greatest aerial targets the world has ever seen. Incendiary projectiles would burn their cities to the ground in short order."

Mitchell continued his pronouncements against Japan in a lengthy 1933 series in the Hearst newspapers, in many magazines, and even in *Popular Mechanics* where in 1935 he wrote, "History and destiny unmistakably point to the next contest being for the Pacific."

An early supporter of the Roosevelt Administration, Mitchell appeared for a time the choice to head a separate air force under a proposed unified department of defense. But the New Deal passed both Mitchell and air power by. Building a large submarine fleet in the Pacific and developing new airfields in Hawaii, the Philippines, and Alaska were seen as too expensive in the depths of the Depression and too militaristic in an administration committed to neutrality.

Mitchell carried on his campaign from his retreat at Boxwood, Virginia, and remained a popular speaker. His subordinates from his service years, slowly climbing to the top ranks of a peacetime air service, remained faithful. Supporters in Congress continued to plead his case but their numbers did not grow.

His health began to fail in 1935 and doctors warned him against further speaking engagements. But so long as he could hold an audience, Mitchell felt an obligation to speak his views. He died of a heart attack on February 19, 1936 in New York City at 56.

The course of World War II vindicated much of what Mitchell had argued, and during the war Congress restored his rank of brigadier general, later adding two more stars posthumously to make him a lieutenant general.

In 1947 a unified Department of Defense was created with three co-equal branches: Army, Navy, and Air Force, each "specifically charged with" defense of land, sea, and air.

Mitchell's critics, including some who shared his philosophy, contended that the bitterness he aroused may well have slowed the move toward his objectives. His tactics were direct and blunt. His writings were painfully repetitious, hammering on familiar themes, always with either direct or implied accusation of wrongdoing by those in control of the military.

Billy Mitchell is certainly best remembered for the spectacular bombing tests which made admirals weep and for gambling his career for his beliefs in his emotion-packed court-martial. But it was the 100 or more magazine articles he wrote in his last ten years following his resignation from the service which secured his place in history; in retrospect, even his most ardent critics could not deny their prophetic truth.

One of the frankest appraisals of Billy Mitchell was written by Washington journalist Clinton Gilbert, who came to know Mitchell well while covering his trial:

> What is in him is innate love of speed, of excitement, a capacity to throw himself utterly into whatever he does, reckless physical daring, self confidence, a politician's love of applause, delight in his fellow man, aristocratic contempt for dull, commonplace and ponderous caution. What isn't in him is poise, balance, sober regard for consequences, capacity to wait upon time's slow justification.
>
> He has always been cheating time. He is on more intimate terms with the future than any wise man, especially an army bureaucrat has a right to be.

FURTHER READING

Biography

Burlingame, Roger. *General Billy Mitchell: Champion of Air Defense.* New York: McGraw-Hill, 1952, 212 p.
A biography of Mitchell aided by interviews with General Carl Spaatz and others who knew him.

Davis, Burke. *The Billy Mitchell Affair.* New York: Random House, 1967, 373 p.
A detailed and thoroughly researched account of events in Mitchell's life from the end of World War I to the aftermath of his court-martial.

Gauvreau, Emile, and Lester Cohen. *Billy Mitchell: Founder of Our Air Force and Prophet without Honor.* New York: Dutton, 1942, 318 p.
An admiring wartime biography dedicated to "The Boys of the American Air Force with whom Billy Mitchell is flying in spirit in the Air War he predicted."

Hurley, Alfred H. *Billy Mitchell: Crusader for Air Power.* Bloomington: Indiana University Press, 1975, 190 p.

A revised version of a 1964 biography by Hurley, an Air Force officer, who in his introduction states that he set out to write his book as an answer to much of the "sensationalism" surrounding Mitchell.

MacArthur, Douglas. "The Country's Safety Was at Stake and I Said So." *Life* 57, No. 1 (3 July 1964): 55-56, 61-62, 64, 66, 68.

Recalls his experiences during the interwar period, including his role in Mitchell's court-martial.

Mitchell, Ruth. *My Brother Bill: The Life of General "Billy" Mitchell.* New York: Harcourt, Brace, 1953, 344 p.

Personal recollections of Mitchell by his sister.

"A Matter of Conscience." *Newsweek* 49 (27 May 1957): 37-38.

A report on attempts by the Air Force Association, a private group, to have Mitchell's court-martial declared null and void.

Criticism

Hayward, Walter. "General Greely of Arctic Fame." *New York Times Book Review* (12 April 1936): 13.

A favorable review of *General Greely: The Story of a Great American*, published shortly after Mitchell's death.

Huie, William Bradford. "Prophet and Pioneer." *Saturday Review of Literature* XXVI, No. 10 (6 March 1943): 10.

A review of *Mitchell: Pioneer of Air Power* by Isaac Don Levine which comments favorably on several aspects of the book, including its treatment of Mitchell's early career and of MacArthur's role in the court-martial.

Sandburg, Carl. "Past and Present Odd Numbers." In *Home Front Memo*, pp. 266-68. New York: Harcourt, Brace, 1942.

An approving wartime commentary on Mitchell.

Charles (Sanders) Peirce

1839-1914

American philosoper.

INTRODUCTION

Peirce founded pragmatism, a branch of philosophy that also included as its major proponents William James and John Dewey. Pragmatism—originally termed "pragmaticism" by Peirce—concerns the practical consequences of ideas, upon which Peirce elaborated: "In order to ascertain the meaning of an intellectual conception one should consider what practical consequences might conceivably result by necessity from the truth of that conception; and the sum of these consequences will constitute the entire meaning of the conception."

Biographical Information

Peirce was born to a wealthy and distinguished New England family. His father was Benjamin Peirce, a respected mathematician and member of the Harvard faculty. His mother, Sarah Hunt Mills, was the daughter of a United States senator. Peirce's older brother, James Mills, also became a member of the Harvard mathematics faculty. Peirce's parents raised their children in an unconventional fashion, imposing few if any limits on their progeny's behavior. The Peirce household was a satellite in the intellectual and cultural milieu of Cambridge, and the family entertained such nineteenth-century writers and thinkers as Ralph Waldo Emerson, Henry Wadsworth Longfellow, and Oliver Wendell Holmes. When he was twelve-years-old, Peirce read his brother's copy of Whatley's Elements of Logic, which began his lifelong fascination with logic and semiotics. He received an advanced degree in chemistry from Harvard, abandoned his family's Unitarian affiliation to join the Episcopalian Church, and married his first wife, Harriet Melusian Fay. He also initiated a lifelong dependency on such painkillers as alcohol, cocaine, morphine, and opium, which some biographers conjecture he used to offset the physical suffering of facial neuralgia (trigeminal neuralgia), a condition he shared with his father. For the next thirty years, Peirce was employed with the U.S. Coast and Geodetic Survey, a government-funded program that enabled him to travel extensively conducting solar eclipse and gravitational research. His salary, however, did not match his lifestyle, and Peirce lived the remainder of his life deeply in debt. His physically and verbally abusive behavior, public intoxication and infidelities, and eventual divorce disenchanted Peirce with Harvard faculty, and he was forever denied a teaching post there. However,

in 1872, he founded the Metaphysical Club, which included William James, Chauncy Wright, John Fiske, and Oliver Wendell Holmes, Jr. A teaching position at Johns Hopkins in 1879—where he met his student John Dewey—ended in one of a series of nervous breakdowns, and Peirce forever was unable to secure another faculty position. A U.S. Congressional investigation into misuse of funds allocated to the Coast and Geodetic Survey further besmirched his name, and Peirce lived the remainder of his life impoverished in Milford, Pennsylvania, writing philosophy, publishing book reviews, and taking care of his second wife, Juliette. He died of cancer in 1914.

Major Works

Peirce began publishing a series of articles under the topic of "Illustrations of the Logic of Science" in 1877. The second lecture in the series, "How To Make Our Ideas Clear," which is the first important work in American pragmatism. Peirce's belief that human behavior is predicated upon thought has antecedants in

Immanual Kant's *Critique of Pure Reason*, a work that he studied extensively as a young man, and attempts to reconcile the gulf between rational, scientific empiricism and Rene Descartes's dictum that human thought exists independent from outside stimuli. Peirce adopted the word 'pragmaticism" from the Greek word pragma, which means act or deed, to display that the true meanings of words derive from a general public's reasonable anticipation of its kinetic potential. Commonly understood tactile words such as "hard," for example, rely on some sort of action to convey their true meaning; hard, in this case, being something that is difficult to scratch by other substances. If an idea cannot be tested against its effects or public consequences, Peirce argued, it is rendered meaningless. Despite this, Peirce considered the communicative signs employed by humans as only an approximation of the truth that they try to convey, which he termed fallibilism. Peirce based his doctrine on fallibilism on his belief that, "there are three things which we can never hope to attain, namely, absolute certainty, absolute exactitude, absolute universality." Peirce's background in mathematics and chemistry helped him adapt pragmatism to metaphysical questions in the essay "A Neglected Argument for the Reality of God." Declaring that belief in a supreme being had heretofore relied on three systems of belief—tenacity, an irrational refusal to entertain opposing views; authority, which legislated belief upon threat of punishment or death; and reason, which Peirce felt inherently unable to explain faith because of its isolation from facts—he offered a fourth, science. Because science recognizes the existence of observable phenomena that exist regardless of human opinion, the public nature of belief systems scientifically validates the basis for religion; and because science continually adapts to new evidence, religious belief also should be open to new data; and, furthermore, public cooperation within and without the scientific community precludes any one individual corrupting religion to their own ends. Therefore, belief is predicated on thought, and action is predicated upon belief. Peirce published no major works in his lifetime and was prevented from disseminating his ideas in academic circles because of his personal behavior. He was, however, a highly influential and original philosophical thinker. His *Collected Papers of Charles Sanders Peirce* was compiled and published as eight volumes between 1931 and 1958.

PRINCIPAL WORKS

The Collected Papers of Charles Sanders Peirce (1931-58)
The Writings of Charles S. Peirce: A Chronological Edition (1982)

CRITICISM

Vincent G. Potter, S. J. (essay date 1973)

SOURCE: "'Vaguely Like a Man': The Theism of Charles S. Peirce," in *God Knowable and Unknowable*, edited by Robert J. Roth, S. J., Fordham University Press, 1973, pp. 241-54.

[*In the following essay, Potter presents a Jesuit's interpretation of Peirce's "Neglected Argument for the Reality of God."*]

Peirce's theism is not calculated to please many philosophers—at least not at first sight. His theism, he says, is "sound pragmatism," and this is not likely to attract positivists who have adopted its maxim as an expression of their own views concerning verification. His theism, he says, is a consequence of anthropomorphism—a claim not likely to delight either traditional theists or hardheaded scientists. Finally, his theism is intrinsically infected with vagueness, a disease which surely will be diagnosed as fatal by many analysts and logicians. We have failed to remark perhaps the most disturbing claim of all: Peirce's theism is supported by a form of the ontological argument! This will perhaps please no one at all.

Yet there it is in all its outrageous boldness: a theism supported by an "exact logician" trained in natural science; a theism which is the consequence of pragmatism; a theism vague and anthropomorphic, and *therefore* indubitable in the strictest sense. These are hard words and who among philosophers will hear them? The point of this paper is to help the philosopher, if he is still willing to read on, to understand the precise import of these shocking claims and perhaps suggest at least that they are not so shocking—perhaps too that in the end they are not so bad even if unusual and/or distasteful.

In a letter to William James (July 23, 1905), Peirce remarked that his own belief in theism was "good sound solid strong pragmatism" (8.262).[1] Three years later he published his well-known **"Neglected Argument for the Reality of God"** in the *Hibbert Journal* (6.452-493) where he gave a "poor sketch" of that argument and a mere "table of contents" of what would be required to show its validity. This poor sketch is in reality a rapid and terse outline of that philosophical view called "pragmaticism" which he had elaborated over the preceding half-century. The "table of contents" is nothing but a marshaling of the conclusions he had reached concerning the nature of reasoning worked out with so much labor over that same period.

In a short article, we cannot hope to do justice to Peirce's thought on this matter. We shall simply try here to expound some of his reflections which may serve as a propaedeutic to his well-known article in the hope that it will aid the reader first to understand the unusual kind of argument it is, and second to help focus properly critical evaluation. We shall not attempt an analysis of the argument itself; that alone would require an article or two. We restrict ourselves, then, to preliminaries: what Peirce had to say about God-talk in general and why in general he held what he did. Although this paper does not seek critical evaluation *in recto*, it does so *in obliquo* since it pretends not only to expound but also to explain and interpret. That explanation and interpretation intend to be a presentation of the truth of the matter as this writer sees it, while at the same time remaining faithful to Peirce. The presentation will consist of three parts: 1) traditional theism, 2) anthropomorphic theism, 3) vagueness.

1. TRADITIONAL THEISM

In a letter to William James (June 12, 1902), Peirce says that he has been reading Royce's *The World and the Individual* and finds it not in very good taste "to stuff it so full of the name of God" (8.277). The reason is that "the Absolute is strictly speaking only God, in a Pickwickian sense, that is, in a sense that has no effect" (8.277). The point of this remark seems to be that, although it may be true that God is absolute, such a characterization is altogether too abstract and formal to make of God an object of belief. An object of belief in the strict sense according to Peirce must be such that it is capable of influencing human conduct. Peirce seems to think that Royce's absolute if not allowed other attributes would be precisely incapable of such influence because it would be too abstract and empty. It is God in a Pickwickian sense, in a sense which has no effect, and so, literally, is incapable of belief. The reality (or unreality) of God as merely "the Absolute" would make no difference to human conduct. Whatever attributes over and above "absoluteness" we decide "God" must have, they must be such as to show God to be intimately related to and "concerned with" what men do. To be an object of belief the reality of God must make a difference to human conduct. The meaning of "God," then, must be rooted in human experience and at the same time must indicate in some way that that reality is not confined to space and time. Let us consider how Peirce describes the absolute reality called "God."

In the opening lines of his article on the neglected argument Peirce defines the term "God" as *the* definable proper name signifying *ens necessarium* (6.452). This reality is not only necessary but also one, personal, not immanent in creation but creating the universe (5.496; 6.505-506), omniscient (6.508), omnipotent (6.509), infallible (6.510), not subject to time (4.67), and not finite (8.262). These attributes are recognizable as the traditional ones of theistic natural theology. What is different, however, in Peirce's description is that he will not allow that God exists, in the strict sense of that term, but rather that He is real (cf. 8.262). The reason is that existence strictly belongs to the category of secondness, of brute force or interaction. Whatever belongs to secondness must be capable of action and reaction and must therefore be spatio-temporal. Conse-

quently, such a reality would be limited and finite. But this will not do for God, since He is the Creator of the three universes of which the actual—the realm of existents—is but one. God, then, must be said to be real (as opposed to unreal, fictitious, non-being) but not to exist.

The term of Peirce's argument, therefore, is a non-finite, necessary reality which can best be described in traditional theistic terms because such a description makes of that reality more than an abstract and empty Absolute. It makes of that reality something which would make a difference to human conduct if it were acknowledged as real. It is a conception which would arise from meditation upon human experience and which in turn would affect that experience insofar as it is subject to self-control. It was such considerations as these which led Peirce to try to write down a description of his argument:

> If God Really be, and be benign, then, in view of the generally conceded truth that religion, were it but proved, would be a good outweighing all others, we should naturally expect that there would be some Argument for His Reality that should be obvious to all minds, high and low alike, that should earnestly strive to find the truth of the matter; and that this Argument should present its conclusion, not as a proposition of metaphysical theology, but in a form directly applicable to the conduct of life, and full of nutrition for men's highest growth [6.457].

In a word, Peirce believes that there is no more adequate way for us to conceive of the adequate cause of the universe than as vaguely like a man (5.536). The theistic notion of God, then, is both anthropomorphic and vague. According to Peirce, it is precisely because that notion is anthropomorphic that it is believable and because it is vague that it is a notion of God.

2. ANTHROPOMORPHIC THEISM

Peirce's claim that theism must be anthropomorphic to be believable is, to say the least, unusual. One might have expected that a theist would try to avoid the charge of anthropomorphism as an objection to any theory of God. The medieval theologians were at pains to avoid precisely this sort of objection by developing at length a negative theology and a doctrine of analogous predication. Whether these attempts by some of the leading proponents of theism were successful or not is not the point here; what is important is the lengths to which defenders of theism have gone in order to avoid this sort of criticism. And yet Peirce not only does not reject the allegation, he seems to revel in it.

What, then, does he understand by anthropomorphism? Peirce contrasts his use of this term with Schiller's "humanism." Though humanism is allied with anthropomorphism and is in perfect harmony with pragmatism, it does not deal precisely with the same question since Schiller, in Peirce's view, identifies it with the "old humanism" which was not so much a scientific opinion as an aim. Pragmatism as a scientific opinion is best expressed by the term "anthropomorphism." The scientific opinion to which Peirce refers is of course the correct analysis of scientific method at which all his logical researches were directed. It is this analysis which implies theism.

> . . . if by metaphysics we mean the broadest positive truths of the psycho-physical universe . . . then the very fact that these problems can be solved by a logical maxim is proof enough that they do not belong to metaphysics but to "epistemology," an atrocious translation of *Erkenntnislehre* [5.496].

Among other things, *Erkenntnislehre* shows that man has powerful and accurate instincts besides reasoning. In fact, reasoning is nothing but a development of instinct and so is continuous with it. Instinct is more basic than reasoning, and no adequate account of reasoning and scientific research can be given without recognizing its role. This, of course, is not to say that reasoning is identical with instinct. It is not. But, according to Peirce, a correct analysis of scientific reasoning will show its roots in human instinct. Thus he can say:

> For those metaphysical questions which have such interest [human interest], the question of a future life and especially that of One Incomprehensible but Personal God, not immanent in but creating the universe, I, for one, heartily admit that a Humanism, *that does not pretend to be a science but only an instinct,* like a bird's power of flight, but purified by meditation, *is the most precious contribution that has been made to philosophy for ages* [5.496; italics mine].

Peirce argues that almost all human conceptions are at bottom anthropomorphic. This is true even of scientific hypotheses, and to say that an hypothesis is unscientific simply because it is anthropomorphic is an objection "of a very shallow kind, that arises from prejudices based upon much too narrow considerations" (5.47). According to Peirce, this is the objection of the nominalist. In opposition to these "much too narrow considerations," Peirce maintains that all man's knowledge, including all scientific and philosophical theories and hypotheses which can have any meaning, is based upon experience.

> I hold . . . that man is so completely hemmed in by the bounds of his possible practical experience, his mind is so restricted to being the instrument of his needs, that he cannot, in the least, *mean* anything which transcends those limits [5.536].

All man's conceptions, then, are anthropomorphic in the sense that they depend upon the limits of his possible experience. But to say this is like passing a law forbidding man to jump over the moon; such a law would not prevent him from jumping as high as he could. Man will continue to try to conceive of a supreme and indeed transcendent cause or agency of the entire universe, but there will be no more adequate way of

conceiving it than "as vaguely like a man." Furthermore, Peirce repeatedly recalls that the only satisfactory explanation of man's ability to form any hypothesis applicable to the universe is his affinity to the universe.

> And in regard to any preference for one kind of theory over another, it is well to remember that every single truth of science is due to the affinity of the human soul to the soul of the universe, imperfect as that affinity no doubt is. To say, therefore, that a conception is one natural to man, which comes just about to the same thing as to say that it is anthropomorphic, is as high a recommendation as one could give to it in the eyes of an Exact Logician [5.47].

Peirce's anthropomorphism, therefore, is nothing other than his metaphysical realism.

> They [the great realists] showed that the general is not capable of full actualization in the world of action and reaction but is of the nature of what is thought, but that our thinking only apprehends and does not create thought, and that that thought may and does as much govern outward things as it does our thinking [1.27].

The basic mistake of nominalism is that it violates the fundamental rule of exact logic—do not block the road to inquiry. By denying that anything is real except the actual, it at once renders all knowledge of the world inexplicable and posits an unknowable "thing-in-itself." It renders knowledge of the world inexplicable because all knowledge of the world involves generals. If generals are not real but only figments of the mind, then knowledge is not of the world. Rather it posits a mere "out-there-here-and-now" about which nothing can be said, conceived, or judged. It would be positing the utterly unintelligible and inexplicable as the ultimate explanation, thus cutting off all further questions and inquiry. For Peirce such a position turns out to be in the strictest sense meaningless in virtue of the pragmatic maxim.

> The elements of every concept enter into logical thought at the gate of perception and make their exit at the gate of purposive action and whatever cannot show its passports at both of those gates is to be arrested as unauthorized by reason [5.212].

Peirce's "anthropomorphism," it must be concluded, is but another name for his realistic pragmatism (pragmaticism).

3. VAGUENESS

Theism, it has been remarked, is only implied by anthropomorphism. The middle term, as it were, for this inference is to be found in Peirce's critical commonsensism, itself a consequence of pragmaticism (5.439). It is so, in our view, because it takes seriously the role of "instinctive mind" by which man has an affinity to nature (5.47) and to God (8.262; see 6.516).

> Our logically controlled thoughts compose a small

part of the mind, the mere blossom of a vast complexus, which we may call instinctive mind, in which this man will not say he has *faith*, because that implies the conceivability of distrust, but upon which he builds as the very fact to which it is the whole business of his logic to be true [5.212].

This "instinctive mind" through which every concept enters into logical thought Peirce elsewhere calls "Insight . . . into Thirdnesses, the general elements, of Nature." Again he refers to it as a "faculty" which man must have because otherwise there would be no accounting for his undeniable ability to guess right among the millions of possible hypotheses often enough to allow him to make genuine discoveries (5.171ff.). This is man's *il lume naturale,* the natural disposition with which man comes into the world (see 1.80, 2.750, 5.47, 5.603-604, 6.10, 5.504). Ultimately, then, instinctive mind must consist of "*in posse* innate cognitive habits, which is all that anybody but John Locke ever meant by innate ideas" (5.504).

Instinctive mind, then, is "pre-scientific"; it is the ground of reasoning both as an activity and as a developed habit; it is the affinity of the mind to reality which makes any scientific inquiry possible. Insofar as science strives for greater and greater precision in its terms and concepts, instinctive mind will escape scientific analysis. It will always remain vague and indeterminate because it is the innate source and origin of reasoning itself whose function to a large extent is to analyze and make precise what it apprehends. No attempt to inquire scientifically into instinctive mind (no matter how useful and informative such investigation may prove to be) can be adequate to the reality so investigated. Something which is vague and indeterminate will always be "left over." Not only is this true of instinctive mind but of any reality investigated by science. The real is continuous and therefore intrinsically affected by vagueness and generality, both forms of indeterminateness; this is why the real is intelligible; why it must be said to be "mind-like"; and why, finally, there is any affinity between human minds and the universe.

The point we are trying to make is that for Peirce it is a serious mistake not to take vagueness seriously. It would be even a greater mistake to think that whatever remains vague after investigation can be disregarded as unreal. And perhaps the greatest mistake of all would be to think that in principle all vagueness can be eliminated even from science in the strictest sense. These errors in understanding human knowing are found in varying forms and degrees in the several nominalistic interpretations of inquiry. Peirce's pragmaticism was meant to avoid them. Critical common-sensism and "scholastic" realism, both consequences of pragmaticism, argue for vagueness and generality as essential ontological as well as logical categories.

In an attempt to show that there is nothing contradictory in holding a common-sensism which is at the same time

critical, Peirce lists six characteristics which distinguish his position from the Scotch school. The fourth and most important of these he states as follows:

> By all odds, the most distinctive character of the Critical-Common-sensist, in contrast to the old Scotch philosopher [Reid], lies in his insistence that the acritically indubitable is invariably vague.

> Logicians have been at fault in giving Vagueness the go-by, so far as even to analyze it [5.446; see 5.505].

The recognition of vagueness as an important logical category is essential to Peirce's discussion of theism. Our ideas of the infinite are extremely vague, he writes to James, and become contradictory the moment we attempt to make them precise (8.262). It is true to say of God that He is omniscient and omnipotent if we leave these concepts vague (6.508-509). And yet these predicates "are not utterly unmeaning" for, as a matter of fact, they can be interpreted "in our religious adoration and the consequent effects upon conduct" (8.262). The vagueness of our notions of God, therefore, ought not for that reason to rule them out from rational belief. Indeed this vagueness acts as a corrective to anthropomorphism by negating the limitations of human experience and classification in the infinite reality. In a word, it is vagueness which allows our notions to be about God.

Vagueness is a form of indeterminateness. Generality is another. A subject is said to be determinate with respect to a character when that character is predicated of it universally and affirmatively. Such a subject of course would also be determinate with respect to the negative of such a character. In all other respects the subject is *indeterminate.* A sign is objectively *general* if it leaves it to the *interpreter* to supply further determinations. Thus, in the sentence "Man is mortal" the term "man" is objectively general because the answer to the question "Which man?" is "Any one you choose." A sign is objectively *vague* if it reserves *for some other possible sign* (and not for the interpreter) the function of completing the determination. Thus, in the sentence "This month a great event will happen," the term "great event" is objectively vague because the answer to the question "Which event?" is not "Any one you like" but rather "Let us wait and see" (5.447; 5.505). Now, every utterance leaves the right of further exposition to the utterer, and so every utterance is to that extent vague. Its vagueness is removed to the extent that the signs it uses are rendered general. According to Peirce it is usually the case that an affirmative predication covers generally every essential character of the predicate, while a negative predication vaguely denies some essential character (5.447). It turns out, therefore, that in every communication situation *absolute* determinateness and precision are not and cannot be attained.

> . . . honest people, when not joking, intend to make the meaning of their words determinate, so that there shall be no latitude of interpretation at

all. That is to say, the character of their meaning consists in the implications and the non-implications of their words; and they intend to fix what is implied and what is not implied. They believe that they succeed in doing so, and if their chat is about the theory of numbers, perhaps they may. But the further their topics are from such precise, or "abstract," subjects, the less possibility is there of such precision of speech [5.447; see also 2.357].

Another way of distinguishing vagueness and generality as two forms of indeterminateness is as follows: "anything is *general* in so far as the principle of excluded middle does not apply to it and is *vague* in so far as the principle of contradiction does not apply to it" (5.448; cf. 5.505). Thus, Peirce observes, a triangle in general is not isosceles, equilateral, or scalene. It is false neither that an animal (in a vague sense) is male, nor that an animal is female (5.505). Though no sign can be both vague and general in the same respect, still every sign is to some extent indeterminate and to that degree is both vague and general. The only way in which it could escape being either vague or general would be for it to be completely and absolutely determinate. According to Peirce this is simply not possible. Although every proposition actually asserted must refer to some non-general subject, still no communication between persons can be entirely non-vague. The reason for this, without going into detail, is that there is no such thing as a logical atom in the strict sense, that is, a term incapable of logical division (see 3.93). It follows, then, that none of our conceptions, even the most intellectual and scientific, is absolutely precise, that is, without some vagueness.

Peirce holds that our acritically indubitable beliefs are invariably vague. To submit such beliefs to criticism involves an attempt to render them more precise. To the extent that they are rendered more precise, Peirce admits that they are open to doubt. His point, however, is this: "Yet there are beliefs of which such a critical sifting invariably leaves a certain vague residue unaffected" (5.507). The question, then, is simply whether that vague residue itself would disappear under persevering attempts at precision.

> But the answer . . . is that it is not because insufficient pains have been taken to precise the residuum, that it is vague: it is that it is vague intrinsically [5.508].

The example of such an indubitable belief offered by Peirce is that of order in nature. A host of critics have submitted to criticism every precise statement of that order which has been proposed. Each of these precise statements is open to doubt. "As precisely defined it can hardly be said to be absolutely indubitable considering how many thinkers there are who do not believe it" (5.508). All this shows, however, is that any precise statement of nature's order is open to doubt. In fact, it is the very precision which allows room for doubt and therefore for criticism. And yet for all that "who can think that there is *no* order in nature?" (5.508). For

Peirce such a claim is literally unthinkable. Pure chaos cannot be thought; the notion of chaos itself is parasitical upon the notion of order; it is *relative* disorder, that is, relative to an order we expected to find or hoped to find. Any number of doubts can be cast upon this or that or the other characterization of nature's order, but there always remains a vague residue of that original belief which cannot be eliminated. This residue is indubitable and indeed acritical, but it is not indubitable precisely because it is acritical in the sense of simply not having been criticized. Rather it remains indubitable because it cannot be criticized since it remains essentially vague.

Peirce is convinced that there is a relatively fixed list of such original beliefs which is the same for all men. He tells us that he was not always so convinced but that experience and reflection have led him to this view. He admits to having always been strongly attracted by a form of common-sensism which holds that there is "no definite and fixed collection of opinions that are indubitable, but that criticism gradually pushed back each individual's indubitables, modifying the list, yet still leaving him beliefs indubitable at the time being" (5.509). A better understanding of vagueness, however, changed his mind. From very early on (at least from the paper **"Some Consequences of Four Incapacities"** in 1868), Peirce held that there is no first, indubitable proposition which occupies a privileged epistemic position. This basic criticism of what he took to be the "spirit of Cartesianism" is compatible with the position outlined in the preceding paragraph. Every proposition is indeed open to criticism, revision, and doubt to the extent that it is precise, i.e., non-vague. On the other hand, every proposition remains to some extent and in some respect vague. Otherwise it simply would not function as a symbol (see 2.357). Every proposition, therefore, is to be interpreted in terms of another proposition and thus *ad infinitum*.

To the extent that the vagueness of a proposition is intrinsic to it, that proposition retains an element of the indubitable. Hence every proposition is open to revision both in the sense that it can always give way to a more adequate expression and in the sense that an erroneous proposition (i.e., a false proposition) can give way to a true one. Indubitables in the sense of primitive, original beliefs are indubitable because they remain intrinsically vague not only with respect to the individual logical subjects to which they refer but also with respect to the character or characters predicated of them. No amount of analysis will render those predicates absolutely precise and determinate since they will always carry the rider "vaguely like." This rider, of course, warns the hearer or reader that some unspecified character of that predicate does not apply to the subject, and so that the subject is also vaguely *unlike* the character applied to it. Some predicates, e.g., infinite, omnipotent, etc., carry this warning in themselves since they contain in their own comprehension the negation of some general predicate (non-vague in that respect).

Perhaps all of this is not well put, and an example might be worth a thousand vague and general explanations. Let us consider Peirce's own example: there is order in nature. The logical subject of this indubitable is a non-vague, non-general reality vaguely and generally characterized in the first place by the predicate "nature" and further specified by the vague and general predicate "order." What is intended in this proposition is not at all indefinite, and consequently the subject term partakes of the nature of an index in that it functions so as to force attention on its object. Still the logical subject of a symbol is not strictly an index because it indicates its object only as a result of being intended to do so (a true index is a sign independently of anyone's intending it to be). Since only a true index can be absolutely determinate and since the subject of a proposition is only *like* an index, the logical subject of our proposition is not absolutely non-vague. This sort of vagueness attaches to the logical subject of any proposition whatsoever.

This is what Peirce means by saying that there is no logical atom. Both predicates in our example are also vague and intrinsically so. "Nature" is vague because it is understood to be the denial of "artifact" and a collective term for all such non-artifacts. More precision can be accomplished only by indicating further what "nature" is not or by pointing to objects which comprise "nature" without being nature—natural objects. The positive content of that term remains imprecise although not empty on that account. "Order" is vague because it is a relational term and can be made precise only with respect to some standard of comparison antecedently specified. What this comes to is that this or that particular order might be non-vaguely indicated but not order as such. Similarly non-order is a relative term. It indicates the absence of some anticipated kind of order. But absolute non-order is literally unthinkable and cannot be even vaguely indicated. Since non-order is not real in any absolute sense at all, it has no positive content at all. It is pure negativity—the limit notion of "no thought at all." The proposition under consideration, then, is at least doubly vague, with respect to its subject and with respect to its predicates.[2] Its predicates are vague not because of any lack of diligence on the part of analysts but of their very nature (sic!). Order is unity amid multiplicity—one and many—and of course this is *the* paradox!

Belief in the God of theism is for Peirce an original belief. It is one of the indubitables in that relatively fixed list which is the same for all men. Doubts about God's reality or about the attributes which most aptly describe Him arise from attempts at precision. Every formula about God which claims to be non-vague is to that extent open to real doubt. The ultimate ground for such doubt is the fact that insofar as such formulae succeed in being precise they are false. An infinite being is not the sort of thing which can be precisely classified. If it were, then it would fall under a genus and so would entail the possibility of many Gods (8.262). Doubts about God's reality, therefore, are in fact doubts about

various formulae meant to express that reality in relatively non-vague terms. Such doubts, however, are not about God's *reality;* indeed for Peirce such a doubt is impossible because belief in it is instinctive; it is an acritical indubitable in the sense already discussed. Doubt about it, according to Peirce, vanishes once it is recognized that all appropriate formulations of that reality are intrinsically vague. Thus Peirce claims that any argument for God's reality is really a form of the ontological argument.

NOTES

[1] References to Peirce's works are taken from *Collected Papers of Charles Sanders Peirce,* vols. I-VI, edd. Charles Hartshorne and Paul Weiss (Cambridge: The Belknap Press of Harvard University Press, 1931-1935); vols. VII-VIII, ed. Arthur Burks (Cambridge: The Belknap Press of Harvard University Press, 1958). References are by volume and paragraph.

[2] Peirce remarks that "indefiniteness and generality might primarily affect either the logical breadth or the logical depth of the sign to which it belongs" (5.448n). In the case of a proposition, logical breadth is the subject denoted and logical depth is the predicate asserted (5.471; see 2.394ff.).

Paula Rothenberg Struhl (essay date 1975)

SOURCE: "Peirce's Defence of the Scientific Method," in *Journal of the History of Philosophy,* Vol. XIII, No. 4, October, 1975, pp. 481-90.

[In the following essay, Struhl examines Peirce's "The Fixation of Belief" as a pragmatic approach to discussing religious faith.]

Peirce's classic essay **"The Fixation of Belief"** has received considerable critical attention. In spite of the numerous discussions of this essay, scholars continue to fall prey to certain unfortunate and important misinterpretations of Peirce's position here. A proper understanding of the argument contained in this essay concerning the adoption of the scientific method is extremely important for all further Peirce scholarship, and the errors made in interpreting Peirce's argument are indicative of the kinds of misinterpretations that are offered of his later work in Pragmaticism. These misinterpretations often have their roots in the failure to understand Peirce's rejection of Descartes' epistemology in general and of his methodological doubt in particular. Most recently, A. J. Ayer in his book *The Origins of Pragmatism*[1] has offered us such a misinterpretation. We would do well then, to consider once again the nature of the argument that Peirce offers in support of the Scientific Method as the *only* acceptable method for fixing belief. Where helpful we shall make reference to other thinkers in order to elucidate Peirce's position and to demonstrate the problems in Ayer's critique.

The opening lines of Peirce's essay immediately bring to mind the opening of Descartes' *Discourse on Method*. The lines in question are reproduced below so that the reader may remark on their similarity for himself.

> Good sense is mankind's most equitably divided endowment, for everyone thinks that he is so abundantly provided with it that even those with the most insatiable appetite and most difficult to please in other ways, do not usually want more than they have of this. (*Discourse*)

> Few persons care to study logic, because everybody conceives himself to be proficient enough in the art of reasoning already. But I observe that this satisfaction is limited to one's own ratiocination and does not extend to that of the other man. (**"Fixation"**)

That Peirce was deliberately patterning the very beginning of his essay after Descartes' famous lines is not difficult to hypothesize since Peirce was avowedly concerned with remedying the deficiencies of the Cartesian System. Where Descartes was concerned with providing a "Discourse on the Method of Rightly Conducting the Reasoning and Seeking Truth in the Sciences," Peirce set himself a similar task. He proposed to undertake that task under the general heading "Search for a Method," the title of one of his projected works, and under the specific title **"Fixation of Belief."** Like Descartes, Peirce recognizes the need for a method of arriving at beliefs and like Descartes he saw doubt as the crucial starting place for that method. His conception of the nature of that doubt differs strikingly however, and is responsible for the particular nature of the method Peirce proposes.

Peirce begins his essay on the fixation of belief with an attack on Descartes' method.[2] While recognizing the importance of doubt as the initiating factor in inquiry, it is Peirce's contention that the doubt proposed by Descartes is not and cannot be genuine. It is, according to Peirce, a psychological impossibility. The wholesale doubt, in so far as it cannot actually be accomplished, is particularly dangerous because it permits us to think that we have wiped the slate clean and are beginning our inquiry free of prejudice. The possibility of such a beginning is precisely what Peirce wishes to deny.

> Some philosophers have imagined that to start an inquiry it was only necessary to utter a question, whether orally or by setting it down on paper, and have even recommended to begin our studies with questioning everything! But the mere putting of a proposition into the interrogative form does not stimulate the mind to any struggle to attain belief. (5.376)

Inquiry, or the struggle after belief, *does* arise from doubt when that doubt is genuine and specific.[3] We inquire because the beliefs we have been acting upon prove unsatisfactory. As a result of beliefs we hold, we have certain expectations about our experience. When those expectations are not fulfilled we find ourselves in a state of surprise, hesitancy, confusion and discomfort. This state Peirce calls a state of doubt. Insofar as doubt is uncomfortable and unpleasant, we strive after a new belief. This striving is called "inquiry" and it has as its object, not arriving at "The Truth," but arriving at a new belief, one which will not lead to further doubt. This then, was Descartes' mistake. He failed to recognize that the end of inquiry is always simply the resolution of doubt, i.e., the attainment of belief, and not necessarily the attainment of "truth." Insofar as Peirce rejects the Cartesian conception of doubt he is free to recognize that "the settlement of opinion is the sole end of inquiry" (5.377). That this must be the case becomes clear from an analysis of the differences between the state of doubt and belief. The two conditions, Peirce assures us, are sufficiently different from each other to avoid the possibility of confusion.

> 1. The sensation of doubting is unlike the sensation of believing.

> 2. Beliefs shape our actions while doubt does not. That is, doubt does not indicate to us that some habit has been established which will guide our actions, while belief does.

> 3. Doubt is an unpleasant state from which we attempt to remove ourselves, while belief is a calm and satisfactory state which we are reluctant to leave.

It might at first appear as though almost any method for arriving at belief will do. For once we acknowledge that a belief that we can hold rather than truth is the end of inquiry, we seem not to need any special method for arriving at the belief. Peirce himself raises this very question. Given his analysis of inquiry, why, asks Peirce, "should we not attain the desired end by taking as an answer to a question any we may fancy and repeating it to ourselves until we have learnt it by heart?" His answer to this question takes us through a thorough consideration of various methods for fixing belief, namely the methods of tenacity, authority, and taste, and leads us ultimately to consideration of the Scientific Method. For Peirce's contention is that there is one method and only one method for arriving at belief that will prove satisfactory in the long run. This claim grows out of his theory of inquiry which inspite of its seeming compatibility with innumerable methods for fixing belief ultimately requires that the scientific method must be adopted. Let us turn our attention now to a discussion of the adequacies and inadequacies of the various methods of fixing belief which are open to us.

The method of taking any answer to a question that we fancy and then repeating it until we have learnt it by heart is entitled by Peirce "the Method of Tenacity." It is perhaps the most primitive means of fixing belief open to human beings and consists in fastening on a belief arbitrarily and then clinging to that belief tenaciously. It is, as Peirce notes, simple and direct and is used by a good many men affording them a "great peace of mind."

Since the attainment of such a calm and peaceful state was the goal of inquiry it would seem that this method should be a perfectly acceptable way of fixing belief. And in fact, Peirce seems to accept this conclusion at first. He tells us apropos of its practitioner that it would be "an egotistical impertinence to object that his procedure is irrational, for that only amounts to saying that his method of settling belief is not ours." Peirce follows up this observation with the injunction that we must "let him think as he pleases." However, only a sentence later we are warned that "the method of tenacity will be unable to hold its ground in practice." By this Peirce means that *in the long run* it will not effectively eliminate doubt and insure belief. While postponing a detailed examination of the failure of the method of tenacity until after we have surveyed the alternative methods for arriving at belief, we should take note now of Peirce's initial explanation of its failure. The method of tenacity, as well as several of its successors, is doomed we are told because "the social impulse is against it."

Human beings live out their lives surrounded by other men and women and at some time it will occur to each individual that the opinions held by others are perhaps equally as good of his own. This social impulse, this recognition of the existence of a community and the desire to arrive at some consistency within the community, impels him to find some method for fixing belief that will succeed for the community as opposed to the individual. "Unless we make ourselves hermits, we shall necessarily influence each other's opinions; so that the problem becomes how to fix belief, not in the individual merely, but in the community" (5.378).

Historically, the most comprehensive method for arriving at belief is what Peirce calls "the Method of Authority." Here the will of the state has supplanted the will of the individual as the legislator of "truth." The state decrees the proper opinions on all matters and takes steps to insulate the community in such a way as to remove all potential causes of doubt. In this way the individual's belief is rendered consistent with the beliefs of all other individuals in the domain of the authority. Nonetheless, and in spite of its high degree of effectiveness during various periods, this method too is doomed to failure in the long run. The method of authority will fail simply because no state will ever be capable of living up to the enormity of the task that the method of authority sets for itself. It will be impossible to insulate the community entirely and permanently against the causes of doubt. There will always be some people who are able to place their own nation's truths within the context of a broader perspective. Such people, like the individual who clings to his personal choice of beliefs arbitrarily, will at some time come to suppose that other people's opinions are equally as good as their own. It will then be necessary to find an alternative method for fixing beliefs.

This alternative method presents itself in the form of the a priori method or method of taste. Its appeal is far more extensive than that of the method of authority for it appeals to people, not as subjects of a particular authority, but as rational beings. According to this method, belief is arrived at via an exchange of views among people in such a way as to lead to the emergence of those beliefs which appeal to the natural preference of all men. The resulting beliefs will be those which are "agreeable to reason." Unfortunately in practice this method leads, not to consistency of belief throughout the community, but to a great diversity of belief and corresponding confusion.

The a priori method, then, will be rejected ultimately because it fails to perform the function expected of it. According to Peirce, "we examined into this a priori method as something which promised to deliver our opinions from their accidental and capricious element," but while the method succeeds in eliminating certain elements of caprice, it only serves to magnify others. And so this method too must be rejected and a new method sought after: "To satisfy our doubts, therefore, it is necessary that a method should be found by which our beliefs may be determined by nothing human, but by some external permanency—by something upon which our thinking has no effect" (5.384). It is the scientific method that satisfies our needs in this respect and with its emergence our search for a method comes to an end. However, before going on to elaborate the nature of the scientific method let us pause long enough to examine critically Peirce's rejection of the first three methods.

Peirce presents the various methods of fixing belief almost as though he were giving an historical account of the necessary evolution of human beings' reasoning abilities. He treats each method as a significant advance over its predecessor so that the progression is from more to less primitive methods. Each method however, is rejected for the same sort of reason; in fact, while seeming to differ markedly, each of the first three methods are remarkably similar. All three share the characteristic of offering conclusions or solutions which would never be urged or justified in terms of their relation to the problem under consideration. That is, challenges to any beliefs or conclusions arrived at via tenacity, authority or the a priori method would be met with the answers, (1) because, (2) because the authority says so, (3) because I feel it is true, respectively. The same answer would be given in defense or explanation of any belief arrived at according to each of the methods. It is this shared characteristic that tempts us to deal with all three methods as variations of the same theme. Indeed, it is in part this shared characteristic that causes Peirce to dismiss all three. Their major defect is that they fail to provide "any distinction of a right and a wrong way" (5.385). That is, in each case there are no conditions under which one could *meaningfully* claim that an individual is using the method incorrectly. The problem then becomes that several people, all using the same method (any one of the preceding three will do) can arrive at totally opposed beliefs without having any shared criterion according to which they can decide who was and who was not applying the method correctly. It is at this point that the social impulse plays a crucial role.

Peirce tells us in this essay and elsewhere[4] that "the only cause of our planting ourselves on reason is that other methods of escaping doubt fail on account of the social impulse." It is the social impulse that accounts for the seemingly inevitable ascendancy of the scientific method.

Precisely what Peirce understood by the phrase "social impulse" is open to interpretation. The expression makes its first appearance in **"Fixation of Belief"** in the following context:

> But this method of fixing belief, which may be called the method of tenacity, will be unable to hold its ground in practice. The social impulse is against it. The man who adopts it will find that other men think differently from him, and it will be apt to occur to him, in some saner moment, that their opinions are quite as good as his own, and this will shake his confidence in his belief. This conception, that another man's thought or sentiment may be equivalent to one's own, is a distinctly new step, and a highly important one. It arises from an impulse too strong in man to be suppressed, without danger of destroying the human species. (5.378)

Let us begin by noticing that Peirce wants to suggest at least two things by the phrase "the social impulse": first, that man is a social animal and tends to seek out the society of other men; second, that men recognize other men as in some sense being of equal value, which is to say that I recognize your words and your beliefs as having an equal claim to veracity as my own. Further, the meaning we attribute to this notion of "social impulse" must, it seems to me, be pursued within the context of Kant's treatment of humanity as an end in itself. From each man valuing his own life we generalize to every man valuing all life. It is appropriate to quote several line's from Kant's *Foundations of the Metaphysics of Morals* and not at all implausible, granted Peirce's profound study of Kant, to suggest that this sort of reasoning may well lie behind Peirce's conception of "the social impulse." In the course of elaborating on the categorical imperative, Kant argues that "rational nature exists as an end in itself. Man necessarily thinks of his own existence in this way; thus far it is a subjective principle of human actions. Also every other rational being thinks of his existence by means of the same rational ground which also holds for myself; thus it is at the same time an objective principle from which, as a supreme practical ground, it must be possible to derive all laws of the will."[5]

This kind of reasoning turns up again in the course of John Stuart Mill's argument for Utilitarianism as concerning itself not with the individual's happiness alone but with the greatest good for the greatest number. Mill argues, in the style of Kant, that each man thinks his own happiness and pleasure is good and thus is able to generalize and think that the happiness and pleasure of all men is worth striving for. Both of these arguments may well have contributed to the development of Peirce's conception of "the social impulse." Insofar as Peirce finds it inevitable that men will come to recognize each other, and correspondingly each other's beliefs, as having equal claim to consideration, they will, he suggests, find in the conflicting beliefs of their neighbors a basis for doubting their own beliefs. It is this tendency, man's need to seek out the society of other men rather than insulating himself from it, and his awareness that other men are of equal value, that Peirce baptizes "the social impulse."

It follows from this, that when we ask "What is the best method for fixing belief?" we are raising the question for the community and not for the individual. As we have seen, it is their failure to arbitrate for the community of mankind that causes Peirce to reject the first three methods for fixing belief. All three of the so-called methods fail to provide a criterion for correct and incorrect application of the method.

The reasoning behind Peirce's rejection of the methods is very much like the line of thought pursued by Wittgenstein in the course of his demonstration of the impossibility of a private language. Such a "language" we are told, could not possess any rules governing the application of words because there would be no conditions under which it could be maintained that the user of such a language was making a mistake. It is this very kind of element that Peirce focuses on in his critique of the first three methods for fixing belief. None of them permit us any idea of what it would mean to make a mistake with respect to the application of the method. That is, a method, like a language, must have rules that can be correctly or incorrectly applied. This carries with it the notion of public verifiability. This is why Peirce can describe the tenacious individual at such length in such glowing terms as one who has gained "great peace of mind"—which it must be remembered is the *only* goal of inquiry according to Peirce's account—without in the course of such praise committing himself to the method. This is why he can intimate that if a man sticks his head in the sand like an ostrich and refuses to see anything that might threaten his beliefs that individual can maintain his beliefs tenaciously. Such a case would not provide a counter-example to Peirce's claim that only the scientific method is actually capable of fixing belief. The method of tenacity is not a method at all, nor in fact are the methods of authority and taste actual methods in the full sense of the word. We can no more speak of a method for fixing belief used and understood by only one person than we can speak of a language used and understood by only one person. A method for fixing belief must be capable of fixing belief for the community. In order to qualify as a method it must include the possibility of making a mistake in its application. But this all three methods fail to do.[6]

The method that must be used to appease our doubt, we are to learn, must not merely permit us to arbitrate our differences, "the method must be such that the ultimate conclusions of every man shall be the same." Such, we are told, is the method of science. The primary characteristic of the method of science is that it permits a distinction between truth and falsity. Such a distinction is made possible because of what Peirce refers to as "the fundamental hypothesis" of the method of science, namely:

> There are Real things whose characters are entirely independent of our opinions about them; those Reals affect our sense according to regular laws, and though our sensations are as different as are our relations to the objects, yet, by taking advantage of the laws of perception . . . any man, if he have sufficient experience and he reason enough about it, will be led to the one True conclusion. (5.384)

Here then, we have a further reason for the rejection of the other methods of fixing belief. Not merely the social impulse, but also the existence of Reals is responsible for our pursuit of a method which permits us to reach agreement. Clearly we shall be forced to reach the scientific method insofar as its fundamental hypothesis is correct. If there are in fact "Reals," we shall be in a state of doubt and dissatisfaction from which we shall be unable permanently to remove ourselves via any method other than one which attempts to remove doubt not by suppression but by alleviation. Were this not the case, then the advantages Peirce attributes to the other three methods would make any one or all of them superior to the scientific method. Peirce assures us that the a priori method is "distinguished for its comfortable conclusions," the method of authority provides the path to peace, and the method of tenacity is distinguished by its "strength, simplicity and directness." Any one of them might be successful if all that was necessary was the suppression of doubt, but Peirce is committed to arguing that no attempt at suppressing doubt can be effective for a very long period because of the social impulse. The existence of Reals provides an explanation for the persistent operation of the social impulse in such a way as to require the scientific method.

The scientific method is strikingly different because it introduces the idea of Reality. In fact, as we have seen, the idea of Reality plays a pivotal role in Scientific Method, and this leads us to raise certain questions. "It may be asked," Peirce notes, "how I know that there are any Reals. If this hypothesis is the sole support of my method of inquiry, my method of inquiry must not be used to support my hypothesis" (5.384). He then proceeds to offer four points in support of the fundamental hypothesis of the method of science. They are somewhat repetitive but bear consideration nonetheless because of their importance.

1. Though investigation does not prove that there are Reals, it does not lead to the contrary conclusion.

2. The social impulse does not cause men to doubt the hypothesis.

3. Everybody uses the scientific method about a great many things and only ceases to use it when he does not know how to apply it.

4. Using the method has not brought people to doubt it. On the contrary, the method itself has been quite successful in settling opinion. (5.384)

These four observations constitute Peirce's defense of the hypothesis that there are Reals. In one form or another they amount to the claim that the use of the method does not call its own validity into question. One cannot experience genuine doubt with respect to the hypothesis that there are Reals.

The third point that Peirce makes in its support is somewhat perplexing, for the appeal to anything like a head count on the matter of what is true or correct is decidedly out of line with Peirce's whole approach. A. J. Ayer has called this point "triffling" and raises two points against it. (1) People are kept from using the method by factors other than ignorance as to its application. These factors include conservatism, timidity and prejudice. (2) And even were it the case that people always use the scientific method to the best of their ability, this has not always been the case and it may not be the case in the future.[7]

Since Peirce himself is so committed to the view that the truth cannot be defined in terms of the beliefs and practices of any finite group, it is incumbent upon us to find some interpretation of his point here which will be more in line with his overall approach and which will manage to avoid the kind of criticism that Ayer levels against him. The seeds for such an interpretation lie in the similarity that we can point to between the way in which Peirce argues for the hypothesis that there are Reals (especially arguments 1 and 3 taken in conjunction) and the way in which Jeremy Bentham argues in support of the Principle of Utility. And indeed, the Principle of Utility and the fundamental hypothesis of science seem to have comparable status as first principles. The reader will recall that both Bentham and Mill tell us that the Principle of Utility is not susceptible of any direct proof. This is also true of the hypothesis of the scientific method. The kind of evidence relevant to the support of both principles is the kind of evidence which demonstrates the impossibility of raising significant questions about the merits of the principles. This consists in showing that significant questions do not arise, for the most part, with respect to the actual operation of the principle. That some people never use the method is not of concern to us. But what would concern us very much is finding that people who did use it gave up using it for reasons directly traceable to the method itself. That this does not occur provides additional support for the claim that there are Reals.

The fourth point brought forward by Peirce is again similar to the others. In favor of the hypothesis that there are Reals is the point that by acting on this hypothesis we have managed to settle opinion.

Peirce concludes his support of the method and the hypothesis by maintaining that neither he nor anyone else can have a living doubt with respect to either. That is, the method does what a method is expected to do. It helps arrive at belief. The hypothesis does what an hypothesis is supposed to do, it provides a coherent account of our experience.

Ayer suggests that one is left with the impression that "Peirce is being slightly disingenuous and that in the end he comes out into the open."[8] According to Ayer, Peirce shows his hand at last when he follows a summary of the advantages that the first three methods have over the method of science with the additional observation that "after all, he wishes his opinions to coincide with the fact, and that there is no reason why the results of the first three methods do so. To bring about this effect is the prerogative of the method of science" (5.387). Using these lines as his "clue," Ayer goes on to argue that Peirce's justification of the scientific method is circular, that "what it comes to, in short, is that the method of science is victor in its own cause."[9] The argument that Ayer attributes to Peirce is that "we should investigate in order to discover what the world is like."[10] This argument, as understood by Ayer, begs the question.

Peirce of course, would give a very different answer to the questions "Why investigate? Why Experiment?" from the answer that Ayer attributes to him. Why indeed? We investigate and experiment to resolve doubt. We engage in investigation because we find ourselves in a state of irritation and frustration from which we wish to extricate ourselves. We use a method of settling belief insofar as it is successful in resolving our doubt. Peirce's claim, for the reasons already outlined in this discussion, is that only the scientific method provides for the resolution of the doubt. Clearly a good portion of doubt arises because we find ourselves and our peers holding different beliefs on the same matter. The social impulse impels us to inquire. One method and only one method will resolve doubt in such cases because only one method provides for a distinction between that which is real and that which is unreal, between that which is true and that which is false. Only one method performs the function required of a method, namely, that it arbitrate between conflicting views. This is why Peirce urges the scientific method upon us as the most effective method for fixing beliefs.

But, protests Ayer, the claim that an opinion does or does not "coincide with the facts" is only intelligible within the context of the pursuit of the scientific method. And other methods "result in beliefs which coincide with what they would lead us to accept as facts." In making this claim Ayer recognizes, and announces apparently with little hesitation, that if we use one of these alternate methods for fixing beliefs it may be necessary for us to shut out certain of our sense-experiences. In fact, he goes on to add that "it is true also that if we adhere to one of the other methods we shall find ourselves believing many things which, if we were to investigate them, we should discover to be false. But again, why should we investigate?"[11]

Peirce's response to this challenge would be that we can no more explain why we should investigate than we justify doubting, when put forward as a wholesale inquiry into our beliefs. In fact, Peirce would not answer the question "Why investigate?" by telling us that this is the best way to find out what the world is like. The question when asked apart from the specific and particular irritation of doubt has no real answer. This is precisely Peirce's point against Descartes' doubt. In any given case we investigate because of the dissatisfaction that arises from the frustration of the expectations that the belief we held lead to. "Logic depends on a mere struggle to escape doubt, which as it terminates in action must begin in emotion" (2.655). And here we have Peirce sounding very much like David Hume. It is passion and not reason that impels us to undertake inquiry. We investigate or experiment in any given case, not to find out the nature of the world (to think so was Descartes' error) but to dispel the sensation of doubt.

Ayer is quite right in observing that in order to operate with one of the other methods we would have to shut out certain of our sense-experience. Where he goes astray is in not recognizing this as something which, in the long run, will make it impossible for those other methods to be used. Surely we are all familiar with people who manage to deny what is, metaphorically, right in front of their nose. In fact recent experiments in psychology disclose that people's perception of what is literally in front of their nose can be significantly modified by the beliefs they hold. We need not deny either of these assertions for they do not significantly challenge Peirce's claim. The thesis we are considering says that, regardless of the kinds of willful or unwillful self-deception we engage in, in the long run the social impulse, that is, the pressure of interaction with other people, will be such that doubt will arise with respect to our perceptions. At the same time, the existence of Reals serves as a check on those who display what the poet Keats has titled "negative capacity," namely, "when a man is capable of being in uncertainties, mysteries, doubts, without any irritable reaching after fact and reason."[12] For the existence of Reals, of things which have a character apart from the nature we bestow upon them, makes it inevitable, in the long run, that doubt will arise with respect to "unrealistic" beliefs. We find, then, that the social impulse on the one hand and the existence of Reals on the other, operate as checks and balances on the human being as he lives out his life. They force him, in the long run, to bring his own beliefs in line with the nature of the world. Either the human race uses the scientific method or, after a period of years, it goes out of existence. These seem to be the only alternatives. Peirce wins by default. For if the existence of Reals and the social impulse in their combined operation do not force men to the scientific method and they persist in adopting the kind of approach that Ayer holds out—that of blocking out sense data and so forth in order to preserve their own beliefs—then it will be just a matter of time before the human race propels itself out of existence. The alternative then, posed by Ayer, and open to those who embrace one of the other methods, is not very viable. I may believe in invisible deities that protect my health and well-being in lieu of any and all medicine and skilled medical attention, and I may block out all evidence (friends' warnings, the worsening of symptoms of my illness)—all this is quite possible—but the end result will be not the defeat of the scientific method, but rather one less practitioner of the method of tenacity.

One element remains to be accounted for in Peirce's account of the seemingly inevitable evolution of the scientific method. Both the operation of what Peirce calls the social impulse and the existence of Reals as affecting our thoughts and acts regardless of what we may choose to think about them, require one further element if they are to function in the way that Peirce explains. What is needed is an account of the human being as a creature who desires beyond virtually everything else to render his behavior consistent. The notion of consistency and the idea that men do need to bring their beliefs in line with those of other men is of course contained in some form in this concept of social impulse. However, Peirce's theory of inquiry requires a full blown account of the role of consistency as a value in human life. It is incumbent upon him to demonstrate both that men wish to make their beliefs consistent with those of their fellow men, and that men wish to render their own set of beliefs consistent with each other. The notion of social impulse is employed to provide for the first operation and Peirce devotes much of his essays **"The Doctrine of Chances"** (which follows **"Fixation of Belief"**) and **"How to Make Our Ideas Clear"** (in the 1878 *Popular Science Monthly* series) to exploring the claim that "logic is rooted in the social principle" (2.654). The second aspect of consistency, the role of self-consistency, was not explored or developed by Peirce until 1903 when he began to devote himself to a detailed consideration of the Normative Sciences. That account, as Manley Thompson and others have rightly pointed out, provides a crucial portion of the foundation for his theory of inquiry. The theory of inquiry remains essentially incomplete until Peirce's writings on the Normative Sciences where he explores the relation between logic, ethics and esthetics. But the kernel of the position that will emerge full blown from his later writing is already present in the final paragraphs of **"Fixation of Belief"**:

> But, above all, let it be considered that what is more wholesome than any particular belief is integrity of belief, and that to avoid looking into the support of any belief from a fear that it may turn out rotten is quite as immoral as it is disadvantageous. (5.387)

NOTES

[1] San Francisco: Freeman, Cooper, 1968.

[2] The attack presented here is similar to the one offered at the beginning of "Some Consequences of Four Incapacities."

[3] Later Peirce expands his account of doubt to allow for "feigned hesitancy" and hypothesized doubts which prepare use in advance for decisions we may some day have to make.

[4] "The Doctrine of Chances," (2.655).

[5] Immanuel Kant, *Foundations of the Metaphysics of Morals* (New York: The Library of Liberal Arts Press, 1949), p. 53.

[6] It might be argued that the method of authority permits a distinction between right and wrong ways to fix belief. Peirce rejects this suggestion explicitly with what seems to me a correct observation, namely, "But the only test on that method is what the state thinks; so that it cannot pursue the method wrongly" (5.385).

[7] Ayer, *Origins,* p. 23.

[8] Ibid.

[9] Ibid., p. 24.

[10] Ibid.

[11] Ibid.

[12] John Keats in a letter to his brothers George and Thomas, dated December 21, 1817. I am indebted to William Earle for pointing out this passage to me.

J. Jay Zeman (essay date 1977)

SOURCE: "Peirce's Theory of Signs," in *A Perfusion of Signs,* edited by Thomas A. Sebeok, Indiana University Press, 1977, pp. 22-37.

[*In the following excerpt, Zeman discusses Peirce's semiotic approach to logic and science.*]

The lifetime of Charles Sanders Peirce spanned a period of tremendous change and development in human knowledge, in the sciences in general. He was a young man of twenty in the year that *Origin of Species* was published; he approached the end of his life just before Albert Einstein presented us with General Relativity. His lifetime saw the emergence of psychology as a discipline separate from philosophy, a birth attended by philosopher-psychologists such as his good friend William James. The work of Peirce, like that of the other American Pragmatists, reflects the ferment of the times.

His thought bears the imprint of science, not the science of that Nineteenth Century which, as Loren Eiseley has remarked, "regarded the 'laws' of nature as imbued with a kind of structural finality, an integral determinism, which it was the scientists' duty to describe,"[1] but rather, of science as open, as intrinsically revisable, as radically empirical. Working from the model of science in this latter sense, Peirce held that philosophy, and indeed logic itself, must ultimately return to experience for validation (2.227).[2]

As a man of science in the open sense and as a logician, Peirce concentrated heavily on what science had to teach philosophy; he emphasized the intellectual aspect of human experience; he examined habit and law; he devoted much energy to the study of logic itself, logic in the narrower sense of deductive symbolic logic as well as in the broader sense of the general theory of signs, or semiotic.

Peirce's semiotic is not a detached, independent element of his philosophy, but interpenetrates and is interpenetrated by his thought as a whole. Peirce held that all thought—indeed, I would say, all experience—is by signs; his theory of signs is, then, a theory of experience, a theory of consciousness. The examination of so central an aspect of Peirce's thought requires a preliminary view of the structure of that thought. Peirce held that logic—along with ethics and esthetics—is a normative science (5.36), and

> before we can attack any normative science, any science which proposes to separate the sheep from the goats, it is plain that there must be a preliminary inquiry which shall justify the attempt to establish such dualism (5.37).

What he proposes is a

> science of phenomenology [which] must be taken as the basis upon which normative science is to be erected and [which] accordingly must claim our first attention (5.39).

The heart of the Peircean phenomenology is Peirce's system of categories; the categories are basic to the understanding not only of Peirce's concept of normative science, but of his theory of signs and indeed of his thought as a whole.

> The *list of categories* . . . is a table of conceptions drawn from the logical analysis of thought and regarded as applicable to being. This description applies not merely to the list published by me . . . but also to the categories of Aristotle and to those of Kant (1.300).

Aristotle listed ten categories and Kant twelve; Peirce employs three. Their names are, simply enough, *first, second,* and *third,* or *firstness, secondness,* and *thirdness.*

By far the most difficult of the categories to discuss is firstness. Firstness is, among other things, the category of *feeling,* by which Peirce means

an instance of that kind of consciousness which involves no analysis, comparison or any process whatsoever, nor consists in whole or in part of any act by which one stretch of consciousness is distinguished from another, which has its own positive quality which consists in nothing else, and which is of itself all that it is, however it may have been brought about; so that if this feeling is present during a lapse of time, it is wholly and equally present at every moment of that time. . . . A feeling, then, is not an event, a happening, a coming to pass, . . . a feeling is a *state,* which is in its entirety in every moment of time as long as it endures (1.306).

Firstness, the category of feeling in this sense, is preeminently the category of the *prereflexive.* The difficult thing about talking about firsts is that when we recognize that something is grasped as a first, its firstness as firstness effectively evanesces. I cannot give you a first, I can merely point to where you might find one and subsequently recognize that you *had* found it. Significantly, the places where firsts may most easily be located and recognized have strong esthetic connections. Sitting back and enjoying a piece of music (without reflecting on the enjoyment) is close to experiencing a first.

Firstness is immediacy, firstness is the prereflexive. When reflection does occur, however, we enter the realm of secondness. Secondness is the category of the *actual existent,* and as such is the easiest of the Peircean categories to discuss. It is the category of the other recognized as other; it is the knock on the door which interrupts the musical reverie; it is the unexpected rear-end collision; it is the sudden confrontation with a person you'd rather not confront. Something is a second insofar as it is, and in particular, insofar as it is an object to a subject. Seconds are unique existences, unique in space and time. For example, specific observations as recorded in a laboratory, whether physics or psychology, are seconds. While firstness is essentially atemporal, secondness provides the discrete, distinguishable points which we order by the time sequence.

The brute thereness, the unquestionable existence of seconds might lead us to think of secondness as the category of the "really real." Peirce would consider this to be an inadequate analysis. Reality, he held, is more than a matter of discrete events occurring at given points in space-time. Reality is also a matter of the *relations between* events, and here is where his category of thirdness enters. Thirdness is the category of law, of habit, of continuity, of relatedness. Tycho Brahe's recorded observations of the positions of the planet Mars at given times are seconds. Kepler's laws, worked out to unify that body of data, are thirds. If we look back to that musical performance we earlier gave as a place to hunt for firsts, we may comment that the performance in its unreflected immediacy is firstness; in the actual space-time thereness of its individual notes it is secondness; and in the identifiable structurings relating its notes, rhythms, harmonies, it is thirdness. We shall now move away from remarks specifically about Peirce's categories; we shall see many examples of their application in what follows, which has to do with Peirce's theory of signs.

"A sign," Peirce tells us,

> . . . is something which stands to somebody for something in some respect or capacity. It addresses somebody, that is, creates in the mind of that person an equivalent sign, or perhaps a more developed sign. That sign which it creates I call the *interpretant* of the first sign. The sign stands for something, its *object* (2.228).

Peirce here is discussing the sign as it participates in semiosis, the sign relation. There are a number of ways of subdividing the matter of Peirce's semiotic; one of them is based on the fact that we may identify three *relata* in the semiosical relation as understood by Peirce: these are the sign itself, and the above-mentioned object and interpretant. The interpretant itself is a sign (2.228) which Peirce calls the "proper significate effect" of the original sign (5.475). As Charles Morris has pointed out, "Semiotic . . . is not concerned with the study of a particular kind of object, but with ordinary objects in so far (and only in so far) as they participate in semiosis."[3] I would suggest that the participation of an object in semiosis as a sign implies a dual nature for that object. On the one hand, the sign—and this includes interpretants—is an object "in the world"; it is empirically describable in terms of its effects in a variety of ways as is any object in the world—it exists, so to speak, in a "public forum." Insofar as it is in this forum, it is accessible to you in the same way that it is accessible to me. But as a sign, it also stands in a "private forum." It is accessible to me in a way which by its very nature is cut off from you—it is an "element of my consciousness" (of course, I infer that it is accessible to you too in this unique way—unique in this case to *you*). The interpretant as a sign shares this dual nature. It is an event in my body in principle observable by a variety of means, means that vary from the poker player's experienced eye to such devices as the polygraph and electroence-phalograph. But in the private forum, it *is* my consciousness. Morris speaks of the *interpreter* as a fourth component of semiosis,[4] and Peirce speaks of the interpretant as being produced "in a mind." I would like to suggest that the interpretant is not "in" a mind or an interpreter the way that peanut butter is in a jar, but rather that interpretants, or proper significate effects of signs, *constitute* the interpreter or mind; the interpreter, then, is a historically existing continuum of interpretants, and the interpretant, correlatively, is a cross section or snapshot of the interpreter—the cross section may, but need not be, at an instant of time. Incidentally, this view of the interpreter as a continuum of interpretants (which are signs) throws some light, I think, on Peirce's at first curious-appearing view that *man is a sign* (5.310ff.). There is an interesting connection here from a perhaps unexpected direction. The concept of the interpreter as historical continuum of interpretants is

closely akin to the concept of ego developed by Sartre in *The Transcendence of the Ego.*[5] The Sartrean ego emerges in the process of reflection on consciousness. In such reflection present consciousness becomes consciousness of (previous) consciousness, which (previous) consciousness is then *reflected* consciousness; the ego emerges as an object which is the unity of "consciousnesses of . . ." the multitude of "things"—material and abstract—states, qualities, and activities of which we can be conscious. The "consciousness of . . ." which can be reflected upon I see as a Sartrean analog of the interpretant; the ego which emerges in the process of reflection would then be the interpreter.

At this point we may note something of a difficulty in Peirce's discussion of the sign. 2.228, quoted above, continues:

> [A sign] stands for [its] object, not in all respects, but in reference to a sort of idea, which I have sometimes called the *ground* of the [sign].

The "sometimes" in this assertion would seem to have reference chiefly to Peirce's **"On a New List of Categories"** (1.551). Unfortunately, the **"New List"** was published in 1867, some thirty years before the passage in 2.228 was written. One suspects that we may be seeing here what Murray Murphey calls "a typically Peircean procedure: having set forth a doctrine with appropriate terminology, Peirce revises and refines the content of the doctrine while retaining the form and terminology unchanged. Thus, extensive revisions of position pass unnoticed under a shell of changeless terminology, to the utter confusion of the reader."[6] Peirce's thought underwent considerable development in those thirty years, and there is a legitimate question as to whether the 'ground' of 1897 is the same as that of 1867. A fair assumption is that Peirce himself saw a continuity between the two, because of his using the same term and his explicit reference to earlier uses of it.

Although Peirce devotes a fair amount of attention to the ground in the **"New List,"** he discusses it hardly at all in his later years, although he uses it in the perplexing fashion of 2.228; it is perhaps best to seek understanding of his later use of 'ground' by examining its employment in this passage. First of all, we note that ground, when added to object and interpretant, makes a triad; this is typically Peircean, and involves a classification by his categories, with ground, object, and interpretant as first, second, and third respectively. Peirce states:

> In consequence of every [sign] being thus connected with three things, the ground, the object, and the interpretant, the science of semiotic has three branches. The first is called by Duns Scotus *grammatica speculativa.* We may term it *pure grammar.* It has for its task to ascertain what must be true of the [signs] used by every scientific intelligence in order that they may embody any *meaning* (2.229).

So the ground of a sign is intimately associated with pure grammar, which is the study of interrelationships between signs themselves; it would appear that the ground of the sign, then, has a close connection with the sign itself. And we note that elsewhere (and elsewhen—1885) Peirce asserts that "a sign is in a conjoint relation to the thing denoted and to the mind" (3.360). In this passage Peirce explicitly makes the sign the first *relatum* in semiosis. In the analysis of Morris, the *relata* in the semiosical relation are "sign vehicle," *"denotatum,"* and "interpretant." On the basis of this analysis of semiosis, Morris distinguishes respectively three "dimensions" of semiotic—the syntactic, the semantic, and the pragmatic—the syntactic dimension corresponds to Peirce's *pure grammar.*

It is worthwhile taking a look at Peirce's assertion that pure grammar "has for its task to ascertain what must be true of the [signs] used by every scientific intelligence in order that they may embody *any meaning*" (2.229). It may seem peculiar for Peirce to speak of meaning in this context, since Peircean "meaning" has at its very center the concept of *possible effect*—the meaning of something in a definite sense is, for Peirce, its possible effects; note Peirce's "pragmatic maxim":

> Consider what effects that might conceivably have practical bearing we conceive the object of our conception to have. Then our conception of these effects is the whole of our conception of the object (5.402).

Indeed, we find Murray Murphey discussing a passage very similar to 2.229, but from the much earlier New List:

> Peirce describes speculative grammar as treating "of the formal conditions of symbols having meaning, that is of the reference of symbols in general to their grounds or imputed characters . . ." (1.559), thereby indicating how far he was from the idea of pragmatism in 1867 [which is the theory of meaning summarized in the "pragmatic maxim" (5.402) quoted above].[7]

The Peirce of the New List, of 1867, may have been far from the idea of pragmatism, but in 2.229, written about 1897 when he was well into pragmatism, he speaks of speculative (pure) grammar and meaning in almost the same terms as thirty years previously. How does the asserted relationship between pure grammar and meaning mesh with the pragmatic concept of meaning as possible effects? About 1903, Peirce answers this:

> A word has meaning for us in so far as we are able to make use of it in communicating our knowledge to others and in getting at the knowledge that others seek to communicate to us. That is the lowest grade of meaning (8.176).

A sign does not communicate *in vacuo,* but in a context, in relationship to other signs; a paradigm of such relationship is the grammatical structure of language. That there be such a grammatical structure is a necessary condition for the signs of language to be able to communicate, and so, by the above passage, to have meaning (in the sense of the lowest grade of meaning). It would be in this sense of meaning that pure grammar "has as its task to ascertain what must be true of . . . [signs] . . . in order that they may embody meaning" (2.229). The passage from 8.176 goes on to indicate that there is more to meaning than this "lowest grade":

> The meaning of a word is more fully the sum total of all the conditional predictions which the person who uses it *intends* to make himself responsible for or intends to deny.

The full meaning of meaning does indeed involve possible consequences. But insofar as relatedness to other signs is a necessary condition of a sign's communicating, speculative (or pure) grammar is the study of what must be true of signs "in order that they may embody any *meaning*" (2.229).

Speculative, or pure, grammar (of which we shall see more anon) is the first branch of Peirce's semiotic, corresponding to the "ground" of the sign—or to what Morris called the "sign vehicle."

> The second [branch] is logic proper. It is the science of what is necessarily true of the [signs] of any scientific intelligence in order that they hold of any *object,* that is, may be true. Or say, logic proper is the formal science of the truth of representations (2.229).

Peirce clearly sees logic proper here from the semantic point of view; note that Morris's "dimension of semiotic" corresponding to the *denotatum* or object of the sign is the semantic dimension.

Considerable study has been devoted to what Peirce calls "logic proper," which is a subject, or group of subjects, warranting special attention in itself. Much of the material in this area is involved and specialized, and so we shall not discuss this topic in technical detail in this paper; however, a few general remarks about his accomplishments here are in order, since he clearly considered "logic proper" to be an integral part of his theory of signs.

For Peirce, logic proper is "the formal science of the truth of representations." Another way to characterize it would be to follow Dewey, and call logic in this sense "The Theory of Inquiry." Peirce divides logic from this point of view into deductive, inductive, and abductive, or retroductive logic (hypothesis formation). The division is by the Peircean categories (though it is not completely, in this case, clear how the division works). Peirce tells us that

> Retroduction and Induction face opposite ways. . . .
> The order of the march of suggestion in retroduction is from experience to hypothesis. A great many

people who may be admirably trained in divinity, or in the humanities, or in law and equity, but who are certainly not well trained in scientific reasoning, imagine that Induction should follow the same course. . . . On the contrary, the only sound procedure for induction, whose business consists in testing a hypothesis already recommended by the retroductive procedure, is to take up the predictions of experience which it conditionally makes, and then try the experiment and see whether it turns out as it was virtually predicted in the hypothesis that it would (2.755).

Note that the concept of induction to which Peirce objects here is the same as that embodied in that essentially worthless distinction between inductive and deductive logic that continues to be perpetrated upon countless undergraduates in introductory logic, speech, and writing courses: "Inductive logic argues from particulars to generals, while deductive logic argues from generals to particulars."

An extended discussion of "logic proper," including inductive and abductive logic, would necessarily take us far afield from what is generally considered semiotic. We note that Peirce's best-known philosophical writings, the essays on the **"Fixation of Belief"** (5.358ff.) and **"How to Make Our Ideas Clear"** (5.388ff.) are studies of logic as the general theory of inquiry. This fact is illustrative of the central position of semiotic in Peirce's thought. As we have remarked, Peirce's semiotic is not an isolated, separate part of that thought, but is integral to his philosophy as a whole. In preparing a paper of so limited a scope as the present one must be, however, we must choose carefully the paths to be followed in detail. We shall not pursue inductive and abductive logic further, then, and shall take a brief look at Peirce's deductive logic, which he set out in great detail and with great skill.

First of all, Peirce saw formal deductive logic as an analytic tool; the purpose of a system of symbolic logic is "simply and solely the investigation of the theory of logic, and not at all the construction of a calculus to aid the drawing of inferences" (4.373). A calculus for Peirce is a computing aid of some kind, designed to shorten, say, the drawing of inferences; a logic, on the other hand, is supposed to break inferences down into their most basic steps and so to exhibit the deductive process involved. In a number of places, Peirce gives us what may be considered postulate sets for symbolic logic; examples are the "icons of the algebra of logic" of his 1885 **"Contribution to the philosophy of notation"** (3.359ff.), and the **"Rules of illative transformation"** of his **"Existential graphs"** (4.372-584). The 1885 "icons" include a complete axiomatization of the classical propositional calculus[8] as well as a considerable chunk of material on quantification and the logic of relatives. The later (1897 and after) transformation rules for Peirce's existential graphs are postulates for a successful and ingenious logic in a non-standard notation. The rules of transformation for the graphs include a

complete formulation not only of the classical propositional calculus, but of the full quantification theory with identity[9] as well. In addition, this later work of Peirce is loaded with suggestions that Peirce himself was unable to exploit fully, but which anticipated by decades contemporary developments in symbolic logic; notable here is a beginning development of what is effectively a "possible worlds" semantics for modal logic (4.512ff.).[10]

Although Peirce presents sets of axioms (the 1885 "icons") or rules of inference for his logics, a little examination shows that his basic orientation toward deductive logic is a *semantical* one, as we might be led to expect from his association of "logic proper" with the *object* of a sign. The icons of the algebra of logic are justified by him on what we recognize as truth-functional, and so semantic, grounds (see 3.384, for example) and the most basic sign of the systems of existential graphs, the "sheet of assertion" on which logical transformations are carried out, is "considered as representing the universe of discourse" (4.396); such representation is a semantical matter. But contemporary logic makes a distinction that Peirce did not make. It is necessary to study logic not only from a radically semantical point of view, in which propositions are thought of as being true or false, but also from a *syntactic* or *proof-theoretical* point of view, in which the deducibility of propositions from each other is studied without reference to interpretations in universes of any sort, and so without reference to truth and falsity.

Peirce failed to distinguish between logic as proof-theoretical and logic as semantical, but he can hardly be faulted for that; Gottlob Frege, who with Peirce must be considered a co-founder of contemporary logic, also failed to make the distinction[11] and even Whitehead and Russell are fuzzy about it. Indeed, a clear recognition of the necessity for distinguishing between logical syntax and semantics does not arise until later, with the developments in logic and the foundations of math which culminated in Gödel's celebrated completeness and incompleteness results of 1930 and 1931 respectively.

We have mentioned Peirce's first and second branches of semiotic. The first, pure grammar, is associated with the "ground" of the sign, or with the sign itself. The second, "logic proper," is associated with the object of the sign, for Peirce. The third branch arises because of the role of the interpretant in semiosis, and is called by Peirce

> *pure rhetoric.* Its task is to ascertain the laws by which in every scientific intelligence one sign gives birth to another, and especially one thought brings forth another (2.229).

Peirce also calls this branch of semiotic "speculative rhetoric" and sometimes "methodeutic"; this science

> would treat of the formal condition of the force of symbols, or their power of appealing to a mind, that is, of their reference in general to interpretants (8.342).

Peirce calls speculative rhetoric "the highest and most living branch of logic" (2.332). (Note that here he is using the word "logic" to refer to semiotic as a whole, rather than to deductive logic; this is a usage explicitly adopted by him in 2.227.) From Peirce's remarks on speculative rhetoric, it is clear that he considered it an important science; it also seems clear that he devoted considerable thought to it. Unfortunately, he presents no systematic study of it. About 1902, he remarks that "The practical want of a good treatment of this subject is acute" (2.105). And further,

> although the number of works upon Methodeutic since Bacon's *Novum Organum* has been large, none has been greatly illuminative. . . . THE book on the subject remains to be written, and what I am chiefly concerned to do is to make the writing of it more possible. I do not claim that the part of the present volume [never completed] which deals with Speculative Rhetoric will approach that ideal (2.109-10).

Speculative rhetoric was to be, for Peirce, "a method for discovering methods" (2.108) in human inquiry in general (2.110); the longing for such a science is deeply rooted in Peirce, and goes back to his earlier days—see, for example, 3.364, which is from the "Philosophy of notation" paper of 1885. The project, however, remains uncompleted. This "highest and most living branch of logic" is a matter of scattered treatments and vague content in Peirce's writing. It does, however, occupy a key place in the architectonic of Peirce's philosophy. An interesting, if somewhat difficult, task would be to reconstruct, based on the structure of Peirce's philosophy, what a Peircean speculative rhetoric might look like.

Of the three branches of Peirce's semiotic, then, the third, speculative rhetoric, is radically incomplete, and the second, "logic proper," when studied in detail, carries us into areas of Peirce's philosophy and symbolic logic not commonly thought of as belonging to the theory of signs. Much, perhaps most, of the material we commonly associate with Peirce's semiotic falls under the first branch of the theory of signs, speculative grammar. I now propose to discuss some of the major topics treated by Peirce under this heading.

A major thrust of Peirce's speculative grammar is a detailed and complex classification of signs. In a definite sense, even the most basic part of speculative grammar, the description of the semiosical relation itself, is a classification of signs. The interpretant is a sign (2.228), and the object is, at least often, a sign. So the description of semiosis gives us a triple viewpoint from which to observe signs in action: signs functioning as signs properly so called, signs as objects of semiosis, and signs as effects of semiosis (interpretants). Peirce elaborates the theory of sign, object, and interpretant in a variety of ways. In his "Survey of pragmaticism," written about 1906, he discussed different kinds of interpretant; the classification is again by the categories. His opening remark here, by the way, illustrates the

epistemological importance that he attached to this kind of classification:

> Now the problem of what the "meaning" of an intellectual concept is can only be solved by the study of the interpretants, or proper significate effects, of signs. These we find to be of three general classes with some important subdivisions. The first proper significate effect of a sign is a feeling produced by it. There is almost always a feeling which we come to interpret as evidence that we comprehend the proper effect of the sign, although the foundation of truth in this is frequently very slight. This "emotional interpretant," as I call it, may amount to much more than that feeling of recognition; and in some cases, it is the only proper significate effect that the sign produces. Thus, the performance of a piece of concerted music is a sign. It conveys, and is intended to convey, the composer's musical ideas; but these usually consist merely in a series of feelings (5.475).

The emotional interpretant is a very good example of a first. It is experience "at its most immediate." As such it is unreflected upon, and is *recognized* only in a "later moment." John Dewey gives, in a discussion of immediate experience, an excellent description of the kind of thing involved in the emotional interpretant:

> Immediacy of existence is ineffable. But there is nothing mystical about such ineffability; it expresses the fact that of direct existence it is futile to say anything to one's self and impossible to say anything to another. Discourse can but intimate conditions which if followed out may lead one to *have* an existence. Things in their immediacy are unknown and unknowable, not because they are remote or behind some impenetrable wall of sensation of ideas, but because knowledge has no concern with them. For knowledge is a memorandum of conditions of their appearance, concerned, that is, with sequences, coexistences, relations. Immediate things may be *pointed to* by words, but not described or defined.[12]

Note that Peirce draws his example of an emotional interpretant from esthetic experience, where we are very likely to be in significant immediate contact with the objects involved. An anecdote told of Schubert (whether apocryphal or not) illustrates the key role of the immediate, and so of the emotional interpretant, in esthetic experience. The composer had played one of his pieces on the piano, and afterwards was asked by a lady who had been listening, "Oh, Maestro, what does it *mean?*" Whereupon he sat back down at the pianoforte and played the composition again. Any answer to her question other than the providing of the immediate experience of the music would have missed the point, for the point was found precisely in the ineffable immediacy of the experience—in the Peircean emotional interpretant which was its effect.

Esthetic experience may be the *locus* where the emotional interpretant is most easily recognized, but this interpretant is by no means restricted to experience in the arts. Rather, it is an element of experience in general; in fact, "If a sign produces any further proper significate effect [beyond the emotional interpretant], it will do so through the mediation of the emotional interpretant" (5.475).

When a sign produces an effect beyond (and with the mediation of) the emotional interpretant, Peirce tells us,

> such further effect will always involve an effort. I call it [the effect, the effort] the energetic interpretant. The effort may be a muscular one, as it is in the case of the command to ground arms; but it is much more usually an exertion upon the Inner World, a mental effort (5.475).

Where the emotional interpretant is clearly a first, the energetic interpretant is a second. A key here is the word "effort." Secondness is the category of the other, of "struggle," of effort—the *action* of an effort implies the *reaction* of an other. In classroom work on this subject, I will commonly interrupt the lecture at this point with an injunction to one of the note-taking students to "Look here!" or some such. The student invariably does, often with some surprise. I point out that the overt action, the effort, involved in looking here is itself an interpretant, the energetic interpretant connected with the sign "Look here!" Peirce points out that the energetic interpretant need not be as over as that; a mere shifting of attention, for example, would count as an energetic interpretant (I would suggest, however, that any energetic interpretant is in principle observable, although instrumentation [EEG, etc.] may be required to observe it).

The energetic interpretant, however, "never can be the meaning of an intellectual concept, since it is a single act, [while] such a concept is of a general nature" (5.475). When we speak of interpretants in terms of *meanings* we enter the realm of what Peirce called the "logical interpretant." A quick characterization of the logical interpretant would be to say it is a "general concept." Peirce speaks of "first logical interpretants" (5.480) of the phenomena that suggest them as being the initial conjectures arising in problematic situations. He sees a second stage in the logical interpretant as arising when

> these first logical interpretants stimulate us to various voluntary performances in the inner world. We imagine ourselves in various situations and animated by various motives; and we proceed to trace out the alternative lines of conduct which the conjectures would leave upon to us. We are, moreover, led by the same inward activity, to remark different ways in which our conjectures could be slightly modified. The logical interpretant must, therefore, be in a relatively future tense (5.481).

We see the logical interpretant itself being classified by the categories, as having a first, a second, and—we

might expect—a third stage. Indeed, after the activity referred to in this last passage has so taken

> the form of experimentation in the inner world . . . the interpreter will have formed the habit of acting in a given way whenever he may desire a given kind of result. The real and living logical conclusion *is* that habit; the verbal formulation merely expresses it. . . . The deliberately formed, self-analyzing habit—self-analyzing because formed by the aid of analysis of the exercises that nourished it—is the living definition, the veritable and final logical interpretant (5.491).

In speaking of "logic proper," the second branch of Peirce's semiotic, we saw that an excursion of any depth into the topic would involve us in an intimate way with Peirce's philosophy; the same would doubtless be true of speculative rhetoric (that "highest and most living branch of logic"), had Peirce developed it in any detail. In our examination of the theory of the logical interpretant, we see that the same is true of speculative grammar. "The deliberately formed, self-analyzing habit . . . is . . . the veritable and final logical interpretant"; in such ways does Peirce tie this branch of semiotic in with the center of his philosophy. The concept of habit for Peirce may fairly be identified with thirdness; note that for Peirce "habit" is not restricted to our ordinary use of the word. The habits by which I deal with my environment are just one species of what Peirce calls generically "habit." Any regularity, any disposition—including, for example, the laws of physics—counts as habit, as *thirdness* for Peirce. And thirdness, habit, is preeminently the category of reality (cf. 5.93ff.). So once again do we see Peirce's semiotic as integral to his thought as a whole.

As we move into the further study of Peirce's speculative grammar, we are struck by the great wealth of material available; indeed, some wags might suggest that we would be better off a little poorer. About 1903, he tells us that

> signs are divisible by three trichotomies; first, according as the sign in itself is a mere quality, is an actual existent, or is a general law; secondly, according as the relation of the sign to its object consists in the sign's having some character in itself, or in some existential relation to that object, or in its relation to an interpretant; thirdly, according as its Interpretant represents it as a sign of possibility or as a sign of fact or as a sign of reason (2.243).

So at this point, Peirce sees the *relata* in the semiosical relation—sign, object, and interpretant—as defining three trichotomic divisions of signs; the first he calls the division into *Qualisigns, Sinsigns,* and *Legisigns* (2.244); the second, into *Icons, Indexes,* and *Symbols* (2.247); and the third into *Rhemes, Dicisigns,* and *Arguments* (2.250). These three trichotomies he sees as giving rise to ten classes of signs (2.254ff.). Several years later, in his correspondence with Lady Welby, he expands the list of *trichotomies* to ten (8.344 ff.), which gives rise, it would seem, to no fewer than *sixty-six classes* of signs.[13]

I do not propose to enter here into a discussion of this later classification of signs. Peirce himself did not complete work on the classification, and a fair amount of what he does say is conjecture. Speculative work in this area may be found in the papers of Weiss and Burks and of Sanders referred to in note 13. To give a taste of Peirce's classification of signs appropriate to the present paper, it seems sufficient to examine briefly the earlier classification of signs by the three trichotomies of 2.243ff. We shall, in this discussion, leave to the last the trichotomy which Peirce says is the one he most frequently uses (8.368), that of Icon, Index, and Symbol.

The first of the trichotomies is based on the sign "as it is in itself," and from this point of view,

> a sign is either of the nature of an appearance, when I call it a *qualisign* or secondly, it is an individual object or event, when I call it a *sinsign* (the syllable *sin* being the first syllable of *semel, simul, sin*gular, etc.); or thirdly, it is of the nature of a general type, when I call it a *legisign*. As we use the term 'word' in most cases, saying that 'the' is one 'word' and 'an' is a second 'word', a 'word' is a legisign. But when we say of a page in a book that it has 250 'words' upon it, of which twenty are 'the's', the 'word' is a sinsign. A sinsign so embodying a legisign, I term a 'replica' of the legisign. The difference between a legisign and a qualisign, neither of which is an individual thing, is that a legisign has a definite identity, though usually admitting a great variety of appearances. Thus, &, *and,* and the sound [of the printed 'and'] are all one word. The qualisign, on the other hand, has no identity. It is the mere quality of an appearance and is not exactly the same throughout a second. Instead of identity, it has *great similarity,* and cannot differ much without being called another qualisign (8.334).

As we might expect, the branch of this trichotomy most difficult to understand is that associated with firstness, the qualisign. Peirce offers some help elsewhere with the kind of thing he here calls qualisigns, indicating that they are

> objects which are signs so far as they are merely possible, but felt to be positively possible; as, for example, the seventh ray that passes through the three intersections of opposite sides of Pascal's hexagram (8.348).

As we indicated, we shall turn now to what Peirce has to say about the third trichotomy of signs, which is "In regard to its relation to a signified interpretant"; here,

> a sign is either a Rheme, a Dicent, or an Argument. This corresponds to the old division, Term, Proposition, and Argument, modified so as to be applicable to signs generally. A *Term* is

simply a class-name or proper-name. . . . A Rheme is any sign that is not true nor false . . . (8.337).

We note that in what is probably Peirce's most extended discussion of rhemes, in his work on the existential graphs (see 4.438ff.), he uses 'rheme' virtually synonymously with the way contemporary logicians use the term 'predicate.' The predicate 'x is red', for example, is a sign which cannot be spoken of as being true or false (until a quantifier or other such index is added to tell which or how many x's we are talking about). Peirce goes on about propositions:

> A *proposition* as I use that term, is a dicent symbol. A dicent is not an assertion, but is a sign capable of being asserted. But an assertion is a dicent. According to my present view . . . the act of assertion is not a pure act of signification. It is an exhibition of the fact that one subjects oneself to the penalties visited on a liar if the proposition asserted is not true. An act of judgment is the self-recognition of a belief; and a belief consists in the deliberate acceptance of a proposition as a basis for conduct (8.337).

Peirce goes on to comment that he thinks "this position is open to doubt." Perhaps, but the tentative assertion of it shows again how closely connected to his philosophy as a whole his semiotic is. The conjectures about propositions, judgment, belief, and conduct in this passage are very much those of Peirce the pragmatic philosopher. He goes on about the *argument:*

> Holding, then, that a Dicent does not assert, I naturally hold that an Argument need not actually be submitted or urged. I therefore define an argument as a sign which is represented in its signified interpretant not as a Sign of that interpretant (the conclusion) [for that would be to urge or submit it][14] but *as if* it were a Sign of the Interpretant. . . . I define a dicent as a sign represented in its signified interpretant *as if it were* in a Real Relation to its Object. (Or as being so, if it is asserted.) A rheme is defined as a sign which is represented in its signified interpretant as *if it were* a character or mark (or as being so) (8.337).

He goes on to expand on this by holding that a sign may "appeal to its interpretant" in one of three ways, depending on whether it is rheme, dicent, or argument:

> 1st, an argument only may be *submitted* to its interpretant, as something the reasonableness of which will be acknowledged.

> 2nd, an argument or dicent may be *urged* upon the interpretant by an act of insistence.

> 3rd, an argument or dicent may be, and a rheme can only be, presented to the interpretant for contemplation (8.338).

In connection with Peirce's talking about signs "being presented to the interpretant," note that this is virtually the same as being presented to the *interpreter* in a given "moment" of consciousness.

We now turn to that trichotomy of signs which Peirce felt he used most often, which indeed he saw as the most fundamental division of signs (2.275), and which is probably the best known to students of the theory of signs; this is the division of signs into *icons, indexes,* and *symbols.* Peirce tells us that

> an analysis of the essence of a sign . . . leads to a proof that every sign is determined by its object, either first, by partaking in the characters of the object, when I call the sign an *Icon;* secondly, by being really and in its individual existence connected with the individual object, when I call the sign an *Index;* thirdly, by more or less approximate certainty that it will be interpreted as denoting the object, in consequence of a habit (which term I use as including a natural disposition), when I call the sign a *Symbol* (4.531).

So this division of signs comes about because signs have objects, and is based on the way that the sign represents its object.

The key feature of an icon is that it bears a resemblance of some sort to its object, "whether any such Object actually exists or not" (2.247). The resemblance may be the extreme likeness of a photograph (2.281), or it may be more subtle; under any circumstances, "Each Icon partakes of some more or less overt character of its Object" (4.531). This partaking can be of a complex sort:

> Particularly deserving of notice are icons in which the likeness is aided by conventional rules. Thus, an algebraic formula is an icon, rendered such by the rules of commutation, association, and distribution of the symbols. It may seem at first glance that it is an arbitrary classification to call an algebraic expression an icon; that it might as well, or better, be regarded as a compound conventional sign. But it is not so. For a great distinguishing property of the icon is that by the direct observation of it other truths concerning its object can be discovered than those which suffice to determine its construction (2.279).

The icon in a very definite sense partakes of the life of its object. Once it is set down, inferences about it become inferences about the object, insofar as it is iconic. A mathematical figure of speech would be to say that the icon is a *mapping* of its object, or a morphism of it. The mapping function may be very like an identity function, as is the case with photographs viewed as icons; on the other hand, it may be complex and conventional. We have employed a mathematical analogy in speaking of icons; the reverse of this coin is that icons are of key importance in mathematics:

> The reasoning of mathematicians will be found to turn chiefly upon the use of likenesses, which are the very hinges of the gates of their science. The utility of likenesses to mathematicians consists in

their suggesting in a very precise way, new aspects of supposed states of things (2.281).

An icon represents by resembling. An index, on the other hand, need bear no resemblance to its object. The key thing about an index is that it has a direct existential connection with its object. The uses of ordinary English are reliable in our discourse about indexes; the index finger is used to point to something, for example. The pointing-to is a direct existential connection with the pointed-to, and so is an index in the Peircean sense. When *tumor, dolor, rubor* and *calor* are present, inflammation is *indicated* to the physician; swelling, pain, redness and heat are indexes of inflammation. You will find the party tomorrow night by looking for the house with the white picket fence—that fence, by its connection to the house, is an index of the house and so of the party. "Indices . . . furnish positive assurance of the reality and the nearness of their objects. But with the assurance there goes no insight into the nature of those Objects" (4.531). The fence tells you where the party is, but it does not tell you whether the party will be dull, wild, etc.

It is important, by the way, to note that signs by no means need be purely icons or indexes (or symbols, either). The sign in front of a shop is indexical by its connection with the shop. But it also may be iconic, by, say, bearing a picture of a book to indicate that the shop is a bookstore.

We have looked at icons and indexes; now,

> A Symbol is a [sign] whose Representative character consists precisely in its being a rule that will determine its Interpretant. All words, sentences, books, and other conventional signs are Symbols (2.292).

The employment of icons and indexes is a necessary condition of communication but the conceptualization that is so essential a part of human interaction with the environment rests directly on symbols:

> Symbols grow. They come into being by development out of other signs, particularly from icons, or from mixed signs partaking of the nature of icons and symbols. We think only in signs. These mental signs are of mixed nature; the symbol-parts of them are called concepts (2.300).

We have attempted in this paper to give a taste of Peirce's theory of signs. Obviously, as the taste is not the complete meal, so short a paper as this must omit much of the detail of so large a topic as Peirce's semiotic. Actually, this paper may be looked upon, in its incompleteness, as a kind of iconic representation of the semiotic of Peirce. For, as is the case with much of Peirce's later work, his classification of signs and the semiotic as a whole is by no means complete; it is as if the later Peirce had an overabundance of potentially fruitful insights, which would require another lifetime to exploit fully. However, it was Peirce who remarked that the opinion which is fated to be ultimately agreed to by all who investigate is the truth, and the object represented by this opinion is the real (5.407).

The full exploitation of what any one man begins is, for Peirce, a matter for the community of investigators to complete, and that completion may be indefinitely far away (5.408). Given Peirce's view of scientific inquiry as a community effort, with the community extended in time as well as in space, it would be unreasonable to expect him to come to closure in all that he began. Certainly his semiotic is a phase of his work which he did not complete. But he began it, and pointed out a variety of possible paths to follow, paths promising both to the Peirce scholar and to the semiotician with only a passing interest in Peirce. It is to be hoped that we will ably make use of the guideposts he left us.

NOTES

[1] Loren Eiseley, "The Intellectual Antecedents of the *Descent of Man*," in *Sexual Selection and the Descent of Man,* ed. Bernard Campbell, Chicago: Aldine, 1972.

[2] *The Collected Papers of C. S. Peirce,* vols. 1-6, ed. Charles Hartshorne and Paul Weiss. 1931-5; vols. 7-8, ed. A. W. Burks, 1958, Cambridge: Harvard. Quotations from the *Collected Papers* are referenced in the standard manner of Peirce scholarship, parenthesized within the text. The first numeral in the reference is the volume number, and the number to the right of the point is the paragraph. Thus 2.227 refers to paragraph 227 of volume 2.

[3] Charles Morris, *Foundations of the Theory of Signs,* IEUS, vol. 1, no. 2, Chicago: University of Chicago Press, 1938, p. 4.

[4] Ibid., p. 3.

[5] Jean Paul Sartre, *The Transcendence of the Ego,* tr. by Forrest Williams and Robert Kirkpatrick, New York: Noonday, 1957.

[6] Murray Murphey, *The Development of Peirce's Philosophy,* Cambridge: Harvard, 1961, pp. 88-9.

[7] Ibid., pp. 91-2.

[8] Arthur Prior, "Peirce's Axioms for the Propositional Calculus," *Journal of Symbolic Logic* 23 (1958), 135-6.

[9] Jay Zeman, "The Graphical Logic of C. S. Peirce," Doctoral Dissertation, University of Chicago, 1964.

[10] For possible world semantics, see, for example, J. Jay Zeman, *Modal Logic,* Oxford, 1973; on Peirce in this connection, see Zeman, "Peirce's Logical Graphs," *Semiotica* 12 (1974), 239-56.

[11] Gottlob Frege, "Begriffschift," *From Frege to Gödel,* ed. Jean van Heijenoort, Harvard, 1967, p. 13.

[12] John Dewey, *Experience and Nature,* Dover 1958 (originally 1925), pp. 85-6.

[13] For detailed discussions of these divisions, see Gary Sanders, "Peirce's sixty-six signs?" *Transactions of the C. S. Peirce Society* 6 (1970), pp. 3-16, and Paul Weiss and A. W. Burks, "Peirce's sixty-six signs," *The Journal of Philosophy* 42 (1945), pp. 383-8.

[14] The brackets are Peirce's.

Max H. Fisch (essay date 1978)

SOURCE: "Peirce's General Theory of Signs," in *Sight, Sound, and Sense,* edited by Thomas H. Sebeok, Indiana University Press, 1978, pp. 31-70.

[*In the following excerpt, Fisch presents a chronological ordering of Peirce's writings on symbolic logic.*]

Both the general theory of signs and certain specialized branches of it, such as symptomatology and grammar, may be traced back to the ancient Greeks. But when today's semioticians speak of the founders of their science, they seldom mention anyone earlier than Charles Sanders Peirce (1839-1914), and they mention him oftener than any later founder.

If Peirce was one of the founders, perhaps even the founder, of modern semiotic, when and how did the founding take place? What are his relevant published writings? What did he take the business of the science to be? What importance did he attach to it? How did he conceive its relations to other sciences? To logic, say; or psychology, or linguistics? And by what steps did he come to be recognized as such a founder? Has all his relevant published work been either assimilated or superseded, or are there things still to be learned from it? Is any important part of his relevant work still unpublished? In what follows I suggest approaches toward answering such questions as these.

1. A PRELIMINARY NOTE ON SPELLING AND PRONUNCIATION

Most of the vocabulary of Peirce's doctrine of signs—for examples, *representation, sign, object,* and *interpretant*—is derived from Latin, and poses no difficulty of spelling or pronunciation. But for the science itself and for what it studies, he uses English forms of two Greek terms that are more troublesome in both these respects. Now Peirce was, among other things, linguist, philologist, lexicographer, and exponent of the ethics of terminology. So if we count him a founder of our science, we shall wish to know what these terms were, and how he spelled and pronounced their English forms.

For σημείωσις—sign-action, the operation or functioning of a sign, sign-interpretation, or the act of inferring from signs—he uses two English forms, *semiosis* and *semeiosy*. The former he tells us to pronounce with the *e* and the first *i* long and with the accent on the *o* (5.484°).[1] He does not tell us where to place the accent in semeiosy (5.473), but I think he put it on the second syllable, pronouncing it "my."[2] For the plural of semiosis, he uses semioses (5.489).[3]

For σημειωτική—the art or science or doctrine or general theory of semioses—he uses *semeiotic;* much less often, *semeiotics* or *semiotic;* very rarely, *semeotic;* never *semiotics*. To tell us how to pronounce his preferred form, he marks it sēmeio'tic (Ms 318 p.15).[4]

His rationale for that spelling and pronunciation was probably twofold. (1) There is no more reason for *semeiotics* or *semiotics* than for *logics* or *rhetorics*. (2) Both the spelling and the pronunciation should (in this case, at least) be signs of etymology; that is, should make it evident that the derivation is from Greek σημεῖον, sign, not from Latin *semi-* ("half-"). There is nothing halfway about semeiotic; it is all about signs, and it is about all signs. And the *o* in semeiotic should be long because it has behind it a Greek omega, not an omicron.

In the remainder of this paper, I shall use in quotations whatever spellings Peirce there uses, but outside of quotations I shall use only semeiosis and semeiotic, and I invite the reader to pronounce them with me "See my o, sis" and "See my o tick." I cannot believe that Peirce ever pronounced the latter "semmy-AHT-ick."

2. THE FIRST FOUNDING (1865-1869)

Peirce's training was in chemistry. His career was in the service of the United States Coast Survey, 1859-1860, 1861-1891. His work for the Survey was primarily astronomical and geodetic, but it involved metrology, spectroscopy, optics, color theory, map projections, the four-color problem, and the history of astronomy and of science in general. His contributions to the annual reports of the Survey included one on the theory of errors of observations in the *Report* for 1873 and one on the economy of research in that for 1876. He deliberately diversified his researches beyond the requirements of his work for the Survey, not from ambition to contribute to as many sciences as possible, but with a view to advancing the logic of science; that is, of hypothesis and induction. His first professional publication was on the chemical theory of interpenetration; his second on the pronunciation of Shakespearian English. He was a mathematician also, but with a view to advancing the logic of mathematics, that is, of deduction.

In the spring of 1877, when he was being considered for election to the National Academy of Sciences, he submitted a list of four of his published papers in logic and asked that his eligibility be judged by these rather than by his contributions to the special sciences.[5] He was elected, and in his letter of acceptance he expressed his "gratification at the recognition by the Academy of Logic as entitled to a place among the real sciences."[6]

Many of the papers he later presented to the Academy were in logic, and at least one in semeiotic.

For five years, 1879-1884, he was part-time Lecturer in Logic at the Johns Hopkins University, while continuing his work for the Coast Survey.[7]

From time to time he gave single courses of lectures at Harvard University, at the Lowell Institute in Boston, and elsewhere. These were usually in logic, in the history of logic, or in the history of science considered from the viewpoint of the logic of science.

His first such course was given at Harvard University in the spring of 1865, under the title **"The Logic of Science."** In the first half of the first lecture he reviewed various definitions and conceptions of logic, psychological and nonpsychological. In the second half he approached his own nonpsychological definition by way of Locke's identification of logic with semeiotic, "the doctrine of signs," in the last chapter of his *Essay Concerning Human Understanding* (1690). The resulting definition of logic, Peirce said, would serve as a first approximation; but it was too broad, since, of the three kinds of representations, logic treats only of symbols. (Locke had used "representation" as a synonym of "sign," and Peirce at this time was using "representations" as his technical term for signs in general.[8])

> A second approximation to a definition of it then will be, the science of symbols in general and as such. But this definition is still too broad; this might, indeed, form the definition of a certain science, which would be a branch of Semiotic or the general science of representations, which might be called Symbolistic, and of this logic would be a species. But logic only considers symbols from a particular point of view. . . .
>
> A symbol in general and as such has three relations. . . . I define logic therefore as the science of the conditions which enable symbols in general to refer to objects.
>
> At the same time symbolistic in general gives a trivium consisting of Universal Grammar, Logic, and Universal Rhetoric, using this last term to signify the science of the formal conditions of intelligibility of symbols. [Ms 340]

On May 14, 1865, Peirce began a book called *Teleological Logic* with a chapter of definitions, in which, like Locke, he makes semeiotic one of the three most general kinds of science. With no further help from Locke, he then makes symbolistic one of the three divisions of semeiotic, as he had done in his lecture; and he makes General Grammar, General Rhetoric, and General Logic the three divisions of Symbolistic (Ms 802).

In Boston in the fall of 1866 he gave a course of twelve Lowell Lectures on "The Logic of Science; or, Induction and Hypothesis," in which the doctrine of signs was carried into somewhat greater detail (Mss 351-59, esp. 357, 359).

The first published sketch of his semeiotic was in a paper **"On a New List of Categories,"** which he presented to the American Academy of Arts and Sciences on May 14, 1867. Forty years later he described this paper as the outcome of "the hardest two years' mental work that I have ever done in my life" (1.561). He first establishes, in place of Aristotle's ten categories and Kant's twelve, a new list of three: Quality, Relation, Representation. He then uses these categories to distinguish: (1) three kinds of representations—likenesses (which he will later call icons), indices, and symbols; (2) a trivium of conceivable sciences—formal grammar, logic, and formal rhetoric; (3) a general division of symbols, common to all three of these sciences—terms, propositions, and arguments; and (4) three kinds of argument, distinguished by their three relations between premisses and conclusion—deduction (symbol), hypothesis (likeness), induction (index) (1.545-59).[9]

It is evident that Peirce is still using *representation* in the general sense in which he will later use *sign*. In effect, therefore, he is making of *sign* an ultimate and irreducible category. It would seem to follow, though he does not press the point, that we need an autonomous science or doctrine of signs. Other sciences—perhaps *any* other science—may supply indispensable data, but no synthesis of these will suffice to constitute the science.

Nevertheless, it might plausibly be objected, Peirce is a logician, and he concerns himself with semeiotic only so far as is necessary to place logic within the larger framework of that one of the three most general kinds of science that Locke, following the ancient Greeks, had distinguished. To that objection, however, it may fairly be replied that at no time of his life did Peirce set any limit to the intensity of cultivation of the larger field of semeiotic that would be advantageous for purposes of logic, even if the cultivating had to be done by logicians themselves because, for the time being, they were the only semeioticians.

In any case, it was not enough in Peirce's eyes for semeiotic to provide a pigeonhole for logic in the classification of the sciences. This became fully apparent in 1868-69 in a series of three articles in the *Journal of Speculative Philosophy:* **"Questions Concerning Certain Faculties Claimed for Man," "Some Consequences of Four Incapacities,"** and **"Grounds of Validity of the Laws of Logic: Further Consequences of Four Incapacities"** (5.213-357).

The first two papers are there for the sake of the third. The upshot of the series is a theory of the validity of the laws of logic, including those of the logic of science (that is, of hypothesis and induction) as well as those of the logic of mathematics (that is, of deduction). Yet the first paper is in the form of a medieval *quaestio*, a dis-

puted question, and the second begins with a four-point statement of "the spirit of Cartesianism," followed by an opposed four-point statement of the spirit of the scholasticism that it displaced. In respect of these four antitheses, "modern science and modern logic" are closer to the spirit of scholasticism. The first paper was "written in this spirit of opposition to Cartesianism." It was meant to illustrate as well as to commend the "multiform argumentation of the Middle Ages." It resulted in four denials.

> 1. We have no power of Introspection, but all knowledge of the internal world is derived by hypothetical reasoning from our knowledge of external facts.
>
> 2. We have no power of Intuition, but every cognition is determined logically by previous cognitions.
>
> 3. We have no power of thinking without signs.
>
> 4. We have no conception of the absolutely incognizable. [5.265]

These propositions cannot be regarded as certain, Peirce says; and the second paper puts them to the further test of tracing out some of their consequences. The third paper then constructs a theory of the validity of the laws of logic in the form of "further consequences" of these "four incapacities."

The central positive doctrine of the whole series is that "all thought is in signs" (5.253). Every thought continues another and is continued by still another. There are no uninferred premisses and no inference-terminating conclusions. Inferring is the sole act of cognitive mind. No cognition is adequately or accurately described as a two-term or dyadic relation between a knowing mind and an object known, whether that be an intuited first principle or a sense-datum, a "first impression of sense" (5.291). Cognition is a minimally three-termed or triadic relation (5.283). The sign-theory of cognition thus entails rejection not only of Cartesian rationalism but also of British empiricism.

The sign-theory of cognition leads into a semeiotic theory of the human self, "the man-sign" (5.313), and thence into a social theory of logic. "When we think, then, we ourselves, as we are at that moment, appear as a sign" (5.383); "the word or sign which man uses *is* the man himself" (5.314). "Finally, no present actual thought (which is a mere feeling) has any meaning, any intellectual value; for this lies not in what is actually thought, but in what this thought may be connected with in representation by subsequent thoughts; so that the meaning of a thought is altogether something virtual" (5.289). "Accordingly, just as we say that a body is in motion, and not that motion is in a body, we ought to say that we are in thought and not that thoughts are in us" (5.289n1). "The real, then, is that which, sooner or later, information and reasoning would finally result in, and which is therefore independent of the vagaries of me and you. Thus, the very origin of the conception of reality shows that this conception essentially involves the notion of a COMMUNITY, without definite limits, and capable of an indefinite increase of knowledge" (5.311).[10] "So the social principle is rooted intrinsically in logic" (5.354).

Along the way, with the help of his three categories, Peirce's doctrine of signs is worked out in greater detail in these three papers, and especially in the second of them.

As a first approximation, then, we may say that, if Peirce was a founder—perhaps *the* founder—of modern semeiotic, the first founding took place in the years 1865-1869. The most relevant publications were **"On a New List of Categories"** (1867) and the three papers developing the sign-theory of cognition (1868-1869). The chief occasions for the founding were that Peirce was invited to give lecture courses in "the logic of science" at Harvard in 1865 and at the Lowell Institute in 1866; that he presented five papers on logic to the American Academy of Arts and Sciences in 1867; and that the editor of the *Journal of Speculative Philosophy* challenged him in 1868 to show how, on his principles, the validity of the laws of logic could be "other than inexplicable" (5.318).

The semeiotic thus founded was semeiotic as viewed from the standpoint of logic and studied for the purposes of logic, and more particularly for those of the logic of science rather than for those of the logic of mathematics. But it was a semeiotic that *included* logic.

3. THE FIRST NON-PEIRCEAN ERECTION ON THIS FIRST FOUNDATION (1913)

So far as I am aware, nobody but Peirce himself deliberately built on this first foundation until forty-five years later. Then, in 1913, Josiah Royce, though acquainted with much of Peirce's later work, discovered in the doctrine of signs contained in these four early published papers just the foundation he needed for solving "the problem of Christianity." In a two-volume work under that title he moves toward the solution in the following four chapters:

XI Perception, Conception, and Interpretation
XII The Will to Interpret
XIII The World of Interpretation
XIV The Doctrine of Signs

The very first step toward the solution was to abandon the dyadic models of perception and conception and to adopt in their stead Peirce's triadic semeiotic model of interpretation.[11]

4. PRAGMATISM A SECOND FOUNDING? (1877-1879)

As we shall see, when modern semeioticians began in the 1920s and 1930s to recognize Peirce as a founder of their science, the Peirce they had in mind was the founder of pragmatism. Pragmatism was, at least in the

first place, a theory of meaning, and therefore a contribution to the doctrine of signs. Peirce's first published exposition of pragmatism was in a series of six **"Illustrations of the Logic of Science"** in the *Popular Science Monthly* in 1877-78.[12] A book under the same title was announced as in preparation for the International Scientific Series but never appeared. The **"Illustrations"** bore the following titles:

ILLUSTRATIONS OF THE LOGIC OF SCIENCE

First Paper.—The Fixation of Belief.
Second Paper.—How to Make Our Ideas Clear.
Third Paper.—The Doctrine of Chances.
Fourth Paper.—The Probability of Induction.
Fifth Paper.—The Order of Nature.
Sixth Paper.—Deduction, Induction, and Hypothesis.[13]

A reader coming to these papers directly from that **"On a New List of Categories"** and those on the sign-theory of cognition and the validity of the laws of logic would soon make the following observations. (a) Peirce is having another go at the validity of the laws of logic, and more particularly those of the logic of science; that is, of hypothesis and induction. (b) The upshot is not radically different; we reach the social theory of logic at the same stage (2.654); but the pragmatism that is only implicit in the earlier papers, if present there at all, is now unfolded as the lesson in logic taught by Darwin's *Origin of Species* (5.364).[14] (c) Though there is no mention of the categories or of the doctrine of signs, they are omnipresent, and the **"Illustrations"** become fully intelligible only in the light of the four papers of a decade earlier. (d) The categories are the key to the analysis of belief, doubt, and inquiry in the first paper, and to the distinction of the three grades of clarity in the second paper. (e) The sign-object-interpretant triad is the key to the maxim for attaining the third grade of clarity: "Consider what effects, which might conceivably have practical bearings, we conceive the object of our conception to have. Then, our conception of these effects is the whole of our conception of the object." (f) The whole series is thought out within the framework of the doctrine of signs. (g) Peirce has presumably suppressed the terminology and the technicalities of semeiotic so as not to put too great a strain on the readers of the *Popular Science Monthly*. (h) Perhaps the book never appeared because he decided that this suppression had been a mistake, but he did not find time for the rewriting that would have been needed to save the book from the same mistake. (i) Even so, the **"Illustrations,"** just as they appeared in the *Monthly*, constitute an anti-Cartesian *Discourse on the Method of Rightly Conducting the Reason and Searching for the Truth in the Sciences.*

Take observation (e). In the second paper Peirce applies the maxim to the scientific conceptions of hardness, weight, and force, and to the logical and metaphysical conceptions of truth and reality; and in the third and following papers he applies it to the most difficult conception of the logic of science, that of probability. Take hardness, for example. The object is the physical property designated by the sign *hard* as used both by laymen and by mineralogists. The three grades of clarity are exemplified by three kinds of interpretants of this sign. The second presupposes the first, and the third presupposes the first and the second. The first is that of familiar feel, ready use, and easy recognition; the second is that of abstract genus-and-differentia or synonym-and-antonym definition. At the very least, what is hard is not soft, and what is harder than *x* is less soft than *x*. Suppose that the second kind of interpretant, and thereby the second grade of clarity, that of distinctness, is already attained; then the rule for reaching the third involves two further steps. In the first further step we specify, in this case, the sensible effects of one thing's being harder than another; say, of a diamond's being harder than glass. Sensible effects are not effects upon our senses, but perceivable public effects. For example, diamond will scratch glass but glass will not scratch diamond. In the second further step we specify practical bearings of these effects. Practical bearings are bearings on practice or conduct; that is, on habits of action. A sensible effect has a practical bearing if it is such that to conceive ourselves as being in a certain situation and having a certain desire is to be ready to act in a certain way if such a situation should ever arise. For example, we can conceive ourselves as desiring to divide a sheet of glass, and as having no regular glass-cutting tool available, but only a diamond ring. So to conceive is already to have formed the habit of using the diamond to cut the glass in such situations. On the other hand, we can conceive ourselves as having a sheet of glass we do not want scratched; say, a mirror. The habit of action determined by the belief that diamond is harder than glass will in that case be the habit of keeping the diamond ring away from the mirror. In each of these cases, the third and final interpretant, which marks the third level of clarity, consists of conceived sensible effect, conceived desire, and habit of action *together*. At that level of clarity, interpretants such as these constitute the whole of our conception of the object represented by the sign *hard*. The mineralogists' scale of hardness is arrived at by interpreting *hard* in this way, and the scale itself is so interpreted.

Much of this, however, would have escaped a reader unacquainted with Peirce's earlier papers. If the pragmatism of 1877-79 was indeed a second founding of semeiotic, this would have been evident at the time only to a reader who had the first founding very much in mind. In both foundings, the semeiotic is one that includes logic and that serves logic.

5. PHILODEMUS AND SEMEIOSIS (1879-1883)

In 1865, the first year of the first founding, Theodor Gomperz published an edition of the Herculaneum papyrus remains of a Greek treatise on inductive logic by the Epicurean philosopher Philodemus. The papyrus lacked the title, but the one most often given it is the Latin *De signis* ("On Signs").

Peirce seems not to have made the acquaintance of this work immediately, but at the Johns Hopkins University he had a student named Allan Marquand, with whom he made an intensive study of it in 1879-80. To meet the thesis requirement for his Ph.D. degree, Marquand translated the treatise under the title "On Inductive Signs and Inferences" and wrote an introduction to it. The introduction, or an abridgment of it, was published under the title "The Logic of the Epicureans" as the first essay in a volume of *Studies in Logic* edited by Peirce in 1883.[15]

One of the most striking features of the treatise is the frequency of the term *semeiosis*. The Greek suffix *-sis* means the act, action, activity, or process of. Peirce was prepared to understand semeiosis in either of two ways: (1) from the side of the sign, as sign-action, the functioning of a sign, or (2) from the side of the interpretant, as sign-interpreting or inferring from signs. Philodemus used it primarily in the latter sense, and even more narrowly as drawing inductive inferences from inductive signs. But for Peirce sign-action and sign-interpretation were not two different kinds of semeiosis but one and the same semeiosis considered from two points of view. To act as a sign is to determine an interpretant.

Furthermore, a sign is not a kind of thing. The world does not consist of two mutually exclusive kinds of things, signs and non-signs, each with its subdivisions, yet with no subdivision of the one overlapping any subdivision of the other. There is nothing that may not be a sign; perhaps, in a sufficiently generalized sense, everything *is* a sign: "all this universe is perfused with signs, if it is not composed exclusively of signs" (5.448n1). The fundamental distinction is not between things that are signs and things that are not, but between triadic or sign-*action* and dyadic or dynamical *action* (5.473). So the fundamental conception of semeiotic is not that of sign but that of semeiosis; and semeiotic should be defined in terms of semeiosis rather than of sign, unless sign has antecedently been defined in terms of semeiosis. A quarter of a century later, in 1907, Peirce could still describe himself as "a pioneer, or rather a backwoodsman, in the work of clearing and opening up what I call semeiotic, that is, the doctrine of the essential nature and fundamental varieties of possible semiosis" (5.488).

6. SEMEIOTIC AND THE LOGIC OF MATHEMATICS (1866-1911)

Peirce wrote in 1903: "It has taken two generations to work out the explanation of mathematical reasoning" (NE 3:1119; cf. 1:256). What were the essential steps that he himself took or observed others taking? A list of some of them follows.

But first a prefatory note. It all started in 1854 with *The Laws of Thought* by George Boole, the Copernicus of modern logic (Ms 475 p.6).[16] After an introductory chapter on the nature and design of the work, Boole began the work itself with a chapter entitled "Of Signs in General, and of the Signs Appropriate to the Science of Logic in Particular; also of the Laws to which that Class of Signs are Subject." Of Peirce's five papers on logic in 1867, the first was "On an Improvement in Boole's Calculus of Logic," the fourth took off from Boole, and Peirce later showed how study of Boole led him to the "natural classification of arguments" in the second (Ms 475 pp.2-28). Now for the steps:

(1) In a privately printed paper of 1866 (at 2.801-804) and in his second and third papers of 1867 (at 2.470, 474 and 1.559) Peirce showed, as he later put it, that "all logical thought" is "an operation upon symbols consisting in substitution" but did *not* claim or assume that such substitution is "an indecomposable operation."[17]

(2) In 1870 Peirce published his **"Description of a Notation for the Logic of Relatives"** (3.45-149), with sections on the various signs (for examples, of inclusion, equality, addition, multiplication, involution). The logic of relatives became the key to the inexhaustible richness of mathematical reasoning, its ability to draw indefinitely numerous necessary conclusions from a single hypothesis, a single premiss or conjunction of premisses (NE 4:58-59).

(3) In the same year his father, Benjamin Peirce, began his *Linear Associative Algebra* with the sentence: "Mathematics is the science which draws necessary conclusions." He went on to discuss "the language of algebra"—its letters and signs and rules of composition. The first principle he states is that of "the substitution of letters," which "is radically important, and is a leading element of originality in the present investigation."

(4) During the period in which son and father were working on (2) and (3), they had frequent conversations. The son later remembered two things: (a) The father at one point seemed inclined toward the view, later embraced by Dedekind, that mathematics is a branch of logic; but the son "argued strenuously against it," and thus the father "came to take the middle ground of his definition" (NE 3:526). (b) The father as mathematician and the son as logician were both struck by the contrary nature of their interests in the same propositions and in the systems of notation in which they were represented. Take the algebra of logic for example.

> The mathematician asks what value this algebra has as a calculus. . . . The logician . . . demands that the algebra shall analyze a reasoning into its last elementary steps. Thus, that which is a merit in a logical algebra for one of these students is a demerit in the eyes of the other. The one studies the science of drawing conclusions, the other the science which draws necessary conclusions. [4.239]

(5) In the 1870s, the British mathematicians Cayley, Sylvester, and Clifford made two-way connections between mathematics and chemistry. Cayley applied his mathematical theory of "trees" to a problem in chemis-try. Sylvester and Clifford shortened to *graph* the "graphic formula" of the chemists, and, starting with the theory of invariants, they began adapting such graphs to mathematical uses.

(6) Sylvester became professor of mathematics at the Johns Hopkins University in 1876, founded the *American Journal of Mathematics* there in 1878, introduced the new term *graph* in the first issue, and said that Clifford had found "the universal pass key to the quantification of graphs."[18]

(7) Peirce joined the Hopkins faculty in 1879. As chemist, mathematician, friend of Clifford (who had died in the spring), and now younger colleague of Sylvester, he welcomed the adapting of chemical graphs to mathematical uses. To the *Journal's* first seven volumes (1878-1885) he contributed a review and four articles, as well as a new edition of his father's *Linear Associative Algebra,* with many notes and two addenda by himself.[19]

(8) Cayley was visiting lecturer at Hopkins from January to June 1882. Peirce, as usual, was attending meetings of the Mathematical Society, presenting papers to it, and taking part in discussions of papers presented by others. At its January meeting, for example, papers were presented by Cayley, Sylvester, and Peirce.[20] In the spring Peirce gave a short course of three lectures on the logic of relatives for students of mathematics.

(9) In 1883 George Chrystal gave an account of mathematics in the ninth edition of the *Encyclopaedia Britannica,* which Peirce took to be defining it as the science of making pure hypotheses, though Chrystal used the term *conception* rather than *hypothesis* (3.558). Chrystal, he said, "puts emphasis upon the definiteness of mathematical hypotheses. . . . I incline to suspect that Prof. Chrystal has confounded *definiteness* with *iconicity,* or the capability of being represented in a diagram" (NE 2:595).

(10) In 1885 Peirce published the second of his two papers **"On the Algebra of Logic,"** with the subtitle "A Contribution to the Philosophy of Notation" (3.359-403). It begins with a section on "Three Kinds of Signs"—icons, indices, and tokens—whose thesis is that "in a perfect system of logical notation signs of these several kinds must all be employed." He gives his student O. H. Mitchell credit for introducing indices, and thereby quantification, into the algebra of logic. He goes on to say that by means of tokens and indices alone "any proposition can be expressed; but it cannot be reasoned upon, for reasoning consists in the observation that where certain relations subsist certain others are found, and it accordingly requires the exhibition of the relations reasoned with in an icon." The theory of signs and the logic of relatives thus lead to the further conclusion that all deductive reasoning, including that of mathematics, involves experiment and observation (3.363). In the main body of the paper, Peirce presents in the form of twelve "icons" the algebraic foundations of a

system of material implication, including truth-table analysis and quantification. One of these "icons," the fifth (3.384), has come to be called Peirce's Law.

Every one of the icons consists of symbols (here called tokens) and *is* a symbol. Some of the elementary symbols are indices. But what Peirce wants to emphasize is the iconicity of each formula as a whole. The logic of relatives has opened the way for him to extend the notion of iconicity from quasi-geometrical graphs, whose iconicity was already obvious, to algebraic formulations of the laws of logic, whose iconicity is rendered obvious by the logic of relatives.

It follows that, just as the world does not consist of two mutually exclusive kinds of things, signs and non-signs, so there are not three mutually exclusive kinds of signs: icons, indices, and symbols. These are rather elements or aspects of semeioses that vary greatly in relative prominence or importance from semeiosis to semeiosis. We may therefore call a sign, for short, by the name of that element or aspect which is most prominent in it, or to which we wish to direct attention, without thereby implying that it has no element or aspect of the other two kinds.

(11) In 1886 A. B. Kempe published in the *Philosophical Transactions.* "A Memoir on the Theory of Mathematical Form" and sent an inscribed copy to Peirce, who annotated and indexed it. Kempe made an extensive use of graphs, and it was in part by critical study of this memoir that Peirce later arrived at his own two systems of graphs. As late as 1905, he called Kempe's "great memoir" "the most solid piece of work upon any branch of the stecheology of relations that has ever been done" (5.505).

(12) In 1889 Peirce contributed to *The Century Dictionary* the first dictionary definition of the new term *graph:*

> A diagrammatic representation of a system of connections by means of a number of spots, which may be all distinguished from one another, some pairs of these spots being connected by lines all of which are of one kind. In this way any system of relationship may be represented. Graphs are commonly used in chemistry, and have been applied in algebra and in logic.

(13) In 1894-95 Peirce drafted two textbooks: ***Elements of Mathematics*** (NE 2:1-232) and ***New Elements of Geometry Based on Benjamin Peirce's Work & Teachings*** (NE 2:233-473). In the former he describes mathematics as "the exact study of ideal states of things" and says his father's definition "comes to much the same thing" (NE 2:10). "Two kinds of icons are chiefly used by mathematicians, namely, first, geometrical *figures,* drawn with lines, and, second, *arrays* of points or letters. . . . upon which experiments and observations can be made" (NE 2:24; cf. 2:12).

(14) In 1896, in a paper **"On Quantity,** with special reference to Collectional and Mathematical Infinity,"

Peirce finally concedes that his father's definition of mathematics is defective in that it omits the framing by the mathematician of the hypotheses from which he proceeds to draw necessary conclusions (NE 4:271); and he offers a definition of his own that makes good that defect (NE 3:40-41).

> Mathematics may be defined as the study of the substance of exact hypotheses. It comprehends 1ST, the framing of hypotheses, and 2ND, the deduction of their consequences. . . . [T]he definition I here propose differs from that of my father only in making mathematics to comprehend the framing of the hypotheses as well as the deduction from them. [Ms 16 p.1; Ms 18 p.3; cf. NE 2:595][21]

(15) In *The Monist* for January 1897, with references to Clifford and Kempe by name (3.468, 479nl) and to Sylvester by implication (3.470°), Peirce presented the system of what he later called *entitative graphs.* While reading the proofs, he conceived another system, which he called *existential graphs.* Partial expositions of this second and more iconic system reached print in 1903 (4.394-417) and 1906 (4.530-72).[22]

(16) In the *Educational Review* for 1898 Peirce published **"The Logic of Mathematics in Relation to Education"** (3.553-62).

> Thus, the mathematician does two very different things: namely, he first frames a pure hypothesis stripped of all features which do not concern the drawing of consequences from it, and this he does without inquiring or caring whether it agrees with the actual facts or not; and, secondly, he proceeds to draw necessary consequences from that hypothesis. [3.559]

Peirce describes the "stripping" as "skeletonization or diagrammatization"; that is, iconization.

(17) In 1901, in a draft of **"On the Logic of Drawing History from Ancient Documents, especially from Testimonies,"** Peirce divided deductions into two kinds, corollarial and theorematic, and gave a detailed example of each, both drawn from the doctrine of multitude (NE 4:1-12). He took this to be the most important division of deductions, and his own most important discovery in the logic of mathematics (NE 4:38, 56). He had already "opened up the subject of abstraction" (NE 4:1), distinguished its two kinds, prescission and subjectification, and called the latter "the very nerve of mathematical thinking" (2.428). He now proceeded to divide theorematic reasoning into abstractional and non-abstractional (NE 4:49). Here again the theory of signs came into play. "Every subject partakes of the nature of an index. . . . The expressed subject of an ordinary proposition approaches most nearly to the nature of an index when it is a proper name. . . . Among, or along with, proper names we may put abstractions. . . ." (2.357). But this is matter for a separate long article or short book.

(18) In 1902, in the chapter of his **Minute Logic** on "The Simplest Mathematics," Peirce briefly restates the distinction between corollarial and theorematic deduction; speaks of the latter as "mathematical reasoning proper"; describes it as "reasoning with specially constructed schemata"; and says it "invariably depends upon experimentation with individual schemata," that is, with icons, whereas corollarial reasoning is largely "reasoning with words," that is, with symbols (4.233). In the same chapter, in an eleven-page passage omitted by the editors of the **Collected Papers** (at 4.261), he introduces two notations for the sixteen binary connectives of the two-valued propositional calculus. One of these may be called his box-X, the other his cursive notation. He says it was his Hopkins student Christine Ladd-Franklin "who first proposed to put the same character into four positions in order to represent the relationship between logical copulas, and . . . it was a part of her proposal that when the relation signified was symmetrical, the sign should have a right and left symmetry." Peirce's own notations simply carry out that proposal in a particular way (NE 3:272-75n at 272).[23]

(19) In his article on Symbolic Logic in Baldwin's *Dictionary of Philosophy and Psychology* in 1902, Peirce said the symbols should include graphical as well as algebraic ones, and that a system of symbols devised for the investigation of logic, as opposed to one intended as a calculus, "should be as analytical as possible, breaking up inferences into the greatest possible number of steps, and exhibiting them under the most general categories possible." "There must be operations of transformation. . . . In order that these operations should be as analytically represented as possible, each elementary operation should be either an insertion or an omission" (4.372-74).[24]

(20) In 1903, in his **Syllabus of Certain Topics of Logic,** there appeared the first published account of Peirce's existential graphs (4.394-417), including rules of transformation and code of permissions, from which it appears that in this system each elementary operation is an insertion or an omission. This is preceded by a section called **"The Ethics of Terminology"**—an ethics that applies to notations and other symbols as well as terms (2.219-26). And that is preceded by **"An Outline Classification of the Sciences"** (1.180-202). Logic is now a normative science, depending on ethics, as that does on esthetics. Above the normative sciences are mathematics and phenomenology.

> All thought being performed by means of signs, logic may be regarded as the science of the general laws of signs. It has three branches: 1, *Speculative Grammar,* or the general theory of the nature and meanings of signs, whether they be icons, indices, or symbols; 2, *Critic* . . . ; 3, *Methodeutic.* . . . Each division depends on that which precedes it. [1.191]

(21) About 1904, in his καινὰ στοιχεῖα (**"New Elements"**), Peirce presents the best restatement so far of his general theory of signs (NE 4:238-63). Symbols are now genuine signs; indices are signs degenerate in the first degree; icons are signs degenerate in the second degree. A symbol sufficiently complete always involves an index; an index sufficiently complete always involves an icon (NE 4:256). But "the icon is very perfect in respect to signification, bringing its interpreter face to face with the very character signified. For this reason, it is the mathematical sign *par excellence*" (NE 4:242).

(22) About 1905 Peirce begins **"The Rules of Existential Graphs"** (Ms 1589) with a preface and an introductory section on "The Nomenclature," in which he confesses a violation of the ethics of terminology in his previous expositions. The preface reads:

> The system of existential graphs is intended to afford a method for the analysis of all necessary reasonings into their ultimate elements. No transformations are permitted except *insertions* and *omissions,* and the formal signs are the fewest with which it is possible to represent all the operations of necessary reasonings.

(23) In 1906, in his **"Prolegomena to an Apology for Pragmaticism,"** Peirce presents the fullest and most mature accounts both of his semeiotic (4.530-51) and of his existential graphs (4.552-72) that he succeeded in publishing. A sample sentence:

> Now since a diagram, though it will ordinarily have Symbolide Features, as well as features approaching the nature of Indices, is nevertheless in the main an Icon of the forms of relations in the constitution of its Object, the appropriateness of it for the representation of necessary inference is easily seen. [4.531]

(24) Up to this point, Peirce has concerned himself primarily with the classification of arguments. From the beginning he recognizes three kinds, which he calls at first *deduction, induction,* and *hypothesis.* The last he later calls *abduction,* and finally *retroduction.* He has set the logic of mathematics (that is, of analytic, deductive, or necessary arguments) over against the logic of science (that is, of ampliative or probable arguments, either retroductive or inductive). In 1908, however, in **"A Neglected Argument for the Reality of God,"** he presents retroduction, deduction, and induction as successive stages of inquiry (8.468-73). To that extent, he absorbs the logic of mathematics into that of science. Deduction, he says, has two parts.

> For its first step must be by logical analysis to Explicate the hypothesis, i.e. to render it as perfectly distinct as possible. . . . Explication is followed by Demonstration. . . . It invariably requires something of the nature of a diagram; that is, an "Icon," or Sign that represents its Object in resembling it. It usually, too, needs "Indices," or Signs that represent their Objects by being actually connected with them. But it is mainly composed of "Symbols," or Signs that represent their Objects essentially because they will be so interpreted. Demonstration should be *Corollarial*

when it can. . . . *Theorematic* Demonstration resorts to a more complicated process of thought.

(25) The nearest thing to a retrospective summing up is in a long letter to J. H. Kehler in 1911 (NE 3:159-210), from which I quote two short passages.

> I invented several different systems of signs to deal with relations. One of them is called the general algebra of relations, and another the algebra of dyadic relations. *I was finally led to prefer what I call a diagrammatic syntax.* [162]

He gives an exposition of the syntax of his existential graphs, in the course of which he remarks that

> this syntax is truly *diagrammatic,* that is to say that its parts are really related to one another in forms of relation analogous to those of the assertions they represent, and that consequently in studying this syntax we may be assured that we are studying the real relations of the parts of the assertions and reasonings; which is by no means the case with the syntax of speech. [164f.]

In concluding this section, I trust that its twenty-five selected steps in the working out of the explanation of mathematical reasoning have made it sufficiently evident that Peirce's lifelong study of the logic of mathematics was conducted throughout within the framework of the general theory of signs.

7. THE REBIRTH OF PRAGMATISM (1898-1911)
     —A THIRD FOUNDING?

In the United States, at least, it was in 1898 that the word *pragmatism* was first used in a public address and then in print as the name of a philosophic doctrine and method. The speaker was William James, addressing the Philosophical Union at the University of California at Berkeley on "Philosophical Conceptions and Practical Results." His address appeared as the leading article in the *University Chronicle* for September. It was widely circulated, and pragmatism soon became a movement, the liveliest so far in American philosophy.[25]

Though James gave him full credit, Peirce soon felt the need of restating his own pragmatism, both to distinguish it from James's and Schiller's and to correct certain errors and omissions in his original statement of 1877-78; above all to make fully explicit the semeiotic framework within which it had been worked out. Peirce held that his own strictly limited form of pragmatism was provable, and it was only within the semeiotic framework that the proof could be made evident.[26] With this in view, he gave two series of lectures in 1903, one at Harvard University in the spring, the other at the Lowell Institute in the fall.

In 1905 he began a series of articles on pragmatism in *The Monist.* In the first, **"What Pragmatism Is,"** his own form of it was renamed *pragmaticism* (5.411-37 at 414). In the second, **"Issues of Pragmaticism,"** two

doctrines that he had defended before he first formulated his pragmatism back in the 1870s—namely, critical common-sensism and scholastic realism—were now treated as consequences of it. The chief novelty in this article is the semeiotic of vagueness, one of the characters of critical common-sensism (5.438-63 at 446-50).

These two articles were meant only to prepare the way for the proof of pragmaticism in a third article. But after the second had appeared, Peirce decided that the best way to present the proof was by means of his existential graphs. So he devoted the third article to further **"Prolegomena"** to the proof. These, as we saw in step (23) of section 6, were a restatement of his general theory of signs—the last he succeeded in getting into print—and a much fuller exposition of his system of existential graphs.

But, alas! Though there are drafts of a fourth article and promises of a fifth and sixth, the third was the last to reach print. One of the unfinished tasks of Peirce scholarship is to construct the proof, largely from manuscripts not yet published, and to show how the graphs would have functioned in the exposition of it.

In sheer volume, his writings on the theory of signs in the nine years from 1903 through 1911—many of them still unpublished—exceed those of the preceding forty years. The most striking features of these later writings are the high frequency of focus on pragmaticism and the development of a semeiotic realism out of the type-token distinction.

In any case, the semeioticians who were soon to begin thinking of Peirce as founder of modern semeiotic had in mind chiefly his published writings of this last period, rather than those of what I have called the first and second foundings.

Meanwhile a relevant change had taken place in Peirce's view of the relation between logic and semeiotic. I report that change in the following section.

8. BACK TO LOCKE: FROM LOGIC-WITHIN-SEMEIOTIC TO
     LOGIC-AS-SEMEIOTIC (1865-1911)

We have seen in section 2 that Peirce at first refused to follow Locke in identifying logic with semeiotic, and defined it rather as one of the three parts of a symbolistic which in turn was one of the three parts of semeiotic. By the mid-1880s, however, as we saw in step (10) of section 6, he had come to realize that logic requires indices and icons; that it cannot do business with symbols that are neither indexical nor iconic. About 1894, in the chapter on signs in his only finished treatise on logic (the so-called Grand Logic), he argued that in all reasoning we must use a "mixture" of icons, indices, and symbols. "We cannot dispense with any of them" (Ms 404 p.46). So the symbolistic trivium became the semeiotic trivium, with logic as its mid-science, and Peirce was halfway back to Locke.

But we have also seen in step (20) of section 6 that by 1903 he had gone the rest of the way. Logic was now semeiotic, as Locke held, and what Peirce had previously called *logic* he now called *Critic*. When and how did his conversion come about?

It was a gradual transition rather than a conversion. Even on the second half of the way back there was an intermediate stage, beginning about 1896, in which Peirce was saying such things as: "The term 'logic' is unscientifically by me employed in two different senses" (1.444). "The word logic is ambiguous. It is at once the name of a more general science and a specific branch of that science" (Ms 751 p.1). During this two-sense transitional stage, logic in its narrow sense was the mid-science of the semeiotic trivium; in its broad sense it was general semeiotic, embracing all three sub-sciences. But even the narrow sense was by no means as narrow as that which Peirce had given to logic in what I have called the first founding.

The journey back to Locke was completed when in 1902 he gave up the narrow sense altogether, identified logic unreservedly with semeiotic, and adopted Locke's term *Critic* for what he had most recently been calling "logic in the narrow sense" (NE 4.20f.). Since Critic in this sense is the critic of arguments (4.9), and since this may need to be distinguished from the critic of morals or of works of art or of craftsmanship, Peirce sometimes calls it *Critical Logic* (2.93); more often, *Logical Critic* (6.475). To one occurrence of the latter phrase, however, he adds "or let us say 'critic' simply, as long as we have to do with no other than the logical kind" (Ms 852 p.2).

It is important to note, however, that though logic is now wholly semeiotic, it is still not the whole of semeiotic. It is semeiotic variously qualified as cenoscopic[27] (Ms 499 p.[15]), formal (NE 4:20f.), general (1.444), normative (2.111), speculative (Ms 693 p.188). It is "General Semeiotic, the *a priori* theory of signs" (Ms 634 p.14); "the quasi-necessary, or formal doctrine of signs" (2.227); "the pure theory of signs, in general" (Ms L 107 p.24). In addition to cenoscopic semeiotic, there are, or may be, idioscopic studies of signs as various as the idioscopic sciences themselves—physical, chemical, biological, geological, anthropological, psychological, medical, musical, economic, political, and so on. None of these is any part of logic, though the reasonings they employ may be made matter for logical study. Take psychology for example.

> Of course, psychologists ought to make, as in point of fact they are making, their own invaluable studies of the sign-making and sign-using functions,—invaluable, I call them, in spite of the fact that they cannot possibly come to their final conclusions, until other more elementary studies have come to their first harvest. [Ms 675 pp.20f.]

Those, namely, of cenoscopic semeiotic.

The explanation Peirce most often gives of his move from logic-within-semeiotic to logic-as-semeiotic is in terms of the classification of the sciences.[28] This was always a concern with him, but increasingly so after 1890, from dissatisfaction both with the definitions of science and with the classification of the sciences that he had contributed to the *Century Dictionary*. He came to think of science no longer as knowledge already possessed or acquired and systematized, but as ongoing investigation, as what research scientists do; and therefore to identify a given science not with a particular body of knowledge but with a social group, a subcommunity of the larger community of investigators. As he wrote Lady Welby in 1908, "the only natural lines of demarcation between nearly related sciences are the divisions between the social groups of devotees of those sciences" (8.342). But of course, in attempting to place a given science, the classifier would consider not only what the subcommunities are severally doing at present, but what changes are in progress, and how far they are likely to go in the near future.

"A great desideratum," he wrote in 1909, "is a general theory of all possible kinds of signs, their modes of signification, of denotation, and of information; and their whole behaviour and properties, so far as these are not accidental" (Ms 634 p.14). The task of supplying this need must be undertaken by *some* group of investigators. Nearly all that had hitherto been accomplished in that direction had been the work of logicians. No other group was so well prepared to take on the task, or could do so with less diversion from its previous concerns.

For examples, though "a piece of concerted music is a sign, and so is a word or signal of command," and "logic has no positive concern with either of these kinds of signs," it must nevertheless "concern itself with them negatively in defining the kind of signs it does deal with; and it is not likely that in our time there will be anybody to study the general physiology of the non-logical signs except the logician," who is in any case "obliged to do so, in some measure" (Ms 499 p.[15]).

So it came about that the last of Peirce's major unfinished works, which he hoped would in the twentieth century have some measure of the success that Mill's *System of Logic* had had in the nineteenth, was *A System of Logic, considered as Semeiotic* (Ms 640 p.10; NE 3:875); considered, that is, not as the whole of semeiotic, but as the whole of cenoscopic semeiotic.

9. THE LOGIC OF MATHEMATICS AGAIN (1903)

At this point we return briefly to section 6, step (14). How could Peirce defend his father's definition so long and then so abruptly change it? Because of the change in his conception of science that we have just been tracing. As he put it in 1903,

> if we conceive a science, not as a body of
> ascertained truth, but, as the living business which
> a group of investigators are engaged upon, which
> I think is the only sense which gives a natural

classification of sciences, then we must include under mathematics everything that is an indispensable part of the mathematician's business; and therefore we must include the *formulation* of his hypotheses as well as the tracing out of their consequences. [NE 3:343]

10. VICTORIA LADY WELBY AND SIGNIFICS (1903-1911)

In May 1903 Victoria Lady Welby published *What is Meaning?,* had a copy sent to Peirce, and wrote him asking for criticism. He replied, and he reviewed the book in *The Nation* along with Russell's *Principles of Mathematics.* The correspondence thus begun lasted eight years, until her final illness.[29]

Along with the rebirth of pragmatism, his having at last a responsive correspondent was almost certainly a factor in Peirce's concentration on semeiotic in the last decade of his life, from his Harvard and Lowell lectures of 1903 onward. It may also have been a factor in the directions this concentration took, and in its characteristic emphases. Some of his best expositions are in letters to Lady Welby, and among his last creative efforts were drafts of a paper for a *Festschrift* in her honor.

After first trying *sensifics,* Lady Welby had adopted *significs* as the name for the field to which she was devoting the latter part of her life. She had contributed a brief article under that title to Baldwin's *Dictionary* in 1902. She later contributed a much longer one to the *Britannica,* in which she distinguished "three main levels or classes" of "expression-value"—"those of Sense, Meaning, and Significance." Peirce wrote her that these nearly coincided with his own division of interpretants (W111). And in a letter to James about the same time, he referred to her distinction in an illuminating passage on the sign-object and sign-interpretant relations, and on the relations between the two relations (NE 3:844).

Lady Welby wrote on December 4, 1908: "You have always been kindly interested in the work to which my life is devoted" (W65). Peirce replied on the 23rd:

But I smiled at your speaking of my having been "*kindly* interested" in your work, as if it were a divergence—I should say a *deviation,* from my ordinary line of attention. Know that from the day when at the age of 12 or 13 I took up, in my elder brother's room a copy of Whately's "*Logic,*" and asked him what Logic was, and getting some simple answer, flung myself on the floor and buried myself in it, it has never been in my power to study anything,—mathematics, ethics, metaphysics, gravitation, thermodynamics, optics, chemistry, comparative anatomy, astronomy, psychology, phonetics, economic, the history of science, whist, men and women, wine, metrology, except as a study of semeiotic. . . . [W85-86]

Or, as he put it in a postscript not mailed, "when I have myself been entirely absorbed in the very same subject since 1863, without meeting, before I made your ac-

quaintance, a single mind to whom it did not seem very like bosh" (8.376).

11. THE SOP TO CERBERUS (1908)

Responding to questions about his work in logic, Peirce wrote to Philip E. B. Jourdain on December 5, 1908:

My idea of a sign has been so generalized that I have at length despaired of making anybody comprehend it, so that for the sake of being understood, I now limit it, so as to define a sign as anything which is on the one hand so determined (or specialized) by an object and on the other hand so determines the mind of an interpreter of it that the latter is thereby determined mediately, or indirectly, by that real object that determines the sign. Even this may well be thought an excessively generalized definition. The determination of the Interpreter's mind I term the Interpretant of the sign (NE 3:886).

Less than three weeks later, in his letter of December 23 to Lady Welby, Peirce wrote:

I define a Sign as anything which is so determined by something else, called its Object, and so determines an effect upon a person, which effect I call its Interpretant, that the latter is thereby mediately determined by the former. My insertion of "upon a person" is a sop to Cerberus, because I despair of making my own broader conception understood. [W80-81]

What was that broader, that more generalized, conception? Negatively, it is apparent that it did not involve "the mind of an interpreter" or "an effect upon a person." Did it also not involve an utterer, a sign-giver? In the last account of his theory of signs which Peirce had published, as a framework within which to introduce his existential graphs, the place of the sign-utterer or sign-giver had been taken by the Graphist.

Morever, signs require at least two *Quasi-minds;* a *Quasi-utterer* and a *Quasi-interpreter;* and although these two are at one (*i.e. are* one mind) in the sign itself, they must nevertheless be distinct. In the Sign they are, so to say, *welded.* Accordingly, it is not merely a fact of human Psychology, but a necessity of Logic, that every logical evolution of thought should be dialogic (4.551).

What, then, was the sop to Cerberus? If we recall that the original motive of subsuming logic under semeiotic in 1865 was to avoid basing it on psychology, we can give a tentative and at least partial answer. The sop to Cerberus was lapsing from sign-talk into psych-talk—from semeiotic into psychology. Since Peirce was himself an experimental psychologist, perhaps the first on the American continent, and once thought of giving up logic for psychology,[30] no disparagement of psychology is implied. Certainly it was no disparagement of psychology to place it lower than semeiotic in the classification of the sciences, just as it was no disparagement of semeiotic to place that below mathematics.

If we were attempting to give a more positive and complete answer, we might well begin with Peirce's 1902 application to the Carnegie Institution for a grant to enable him to write a series of thirty-six memoirs on logic; and more particularly with his brief descriptions of Memoirs No. 11, **"On the Logical Conception of Mind,"** and No. 12, **"On the Definition of Logic."**

> If the logician is to talk of the operations of the mind at all . . . he must mean by "mind" something quite different from the object of study of the psychologist. . . . Logic will here be defined as *formal semiotic.* A definition of a sign will be given which no more refers to human thought than does the definition of a line as the place which a particle occupies, part by part, during a lapse of time (NE 4:20).

A few sentences from one of the drafts of the application offer further hints.

> We must begin by getting diagrammatic notions of signs from which we strip away, at first, all reference to the mind; and after we have made those ideas just as distinct as our notion of a prime number or of an oval line, we may then consider, if need be, what are the peculiar characteristics of a mental sign, and in fact may give a mathematical definition of a mind, in the same sense in which we can give a mathematical definition of a straight line. . . . But there is nothing to compel the object of such a formal definition to have the peculiar feeling of consciousness. That peculiar feeling has nothing to do with the logicality of reasoning, however; and it is far better to leave it out of account (NE 4:54).

If that does not answer our question, it sets us off on the right track. But we return from it to pursue the question how Peirce came to be recognized as a founder of semeiotic.

12. OGDEN AND RICHARDS: THE MEANING OF MEANING (1923)

Almost from the beginning of their correspondence in 1903, Lady Welby gave her visitors accounts of Peirce's letters, and frequently enclosed copies of extensive extracts from them in her letters to other correspondents. On May 2, 1911, she wrote Peirce that she thought she had found a disciple for him in C. K. Ogden, then still a student at Cambridge University (W138-39).

In Peirce's letters to Lady Welby, one of the most striking passages is that concerning his early reading of Whately's *Elements of Logic.* Ogden was so impressed by it that in *The Meaning of Meaning* in 1923 he and Richards made Whately and Peirce the culminating figures in the movement "Towards a Science of Symbolism"—the nominalistic movement from Ockham through Hobbes, Locke, Leibniz, Berkeley, Condillac, Horne Tooke, and Taine. (In order to pass directly from Whately to Peirce, they depart from chronology by taking up Taine before Whately.) They quote a passage

from Whately's introduction in which he professes to know nothing of any universals but signs. Signs, he says, are the instrument of thought, not merely the vehicle of expression and communication. In any case, the only logic he understands "is entirely conversant about language" and other signs. It knows nothing of "abstract ideas" or of non-semeiotic mental processes. Ogden and Richards then say:

> It was doubtless this insistence on Signs, in which few subsequent logicians have followed him, that appealed to C. S. Peirce, the most notable of all the thinkers who have approached the question of Symbolism from the logical side.

After misquoting the Whately passage from Peirce's letter to Lady Welby, they continue:

> There cannot be thought without signs, he insists; and when William James drew attention to the work of Taine as the first writer to emphasize the importance of symbol-substitution in 'thought,' the objection was put forward that already in 1867 Peirce had treated "all logical thought as an operation upon symbols consisting in substitution."[31]

They do not call Peirce a nominalist, but they suggest that his "scholastic realism" and his exclusion of psychological considerations may account for a lack of clarity at certain points in a semeiotic that was otherwise the final upshot of the nominalistic tradition they have been sketching. In an appendix they offer a thirteen-page digest of his theory of signs in the form of extracts from his published papers (chiefly from the **"Prolegomena"** of 1906) and from three of his longer letters to Lady Welby, one of which contains the Whately and the "sop to Cerberus" passages.

The Meaning of Meaning was the first book in any language from which it was possible to get a grasp of Peirce's semeiotic at first hand, in his own terms. F. P. Ramsey, reviewing the book in *Mind,* rightly said that its "excellent appendix on C. S. Peirce deserves especial mention."[32] (Ludwig Wittgenstein may have known something of Peirce through Ramsey.)

The authors misquote three passages from Royce's *The World and the Individual.* Had they also looked into *The Problem of Christianity,* its chapters on interpretation would surely have led them to Peirce's cognition series of 1868-69, in which the doctrine that all thought is in signs was most fully argued and developed.[33] This is much more fundamental than anything they do quote. Had they known of it, they would surely have asked themselves where Peirce got that doctrine, and would have given what is almost certainly the right answer: He got it from Whately at the age of twelve. But at least they were on the right track in approaching Peirce from Whately and from Whately's nominalistic predecessors. It is unfortunate that no other writer on Peirce's theory of signs has taken the same approach.

13. CHARLES MORRIS: FOUNDATIONS OF THE THEORY OF SIGNS (1938)

The movement variously called logical positivism, logical empiricism, scientific empiricism, and the unity of science movement, began in German-speaking middle Europe in the 1920s, started a westward migration in the 1930s, and for a time found its main resting place, at least in English-speaking countries, at Chicago. Its chief single monument is the *International Encyclopedia of Unified Science,* edited by Otto Neurath, Rudolf Carnap, and Charles Morris, and published by the University of Chicago Press. After an introductory monograph called "Encyclopedia and Unified Science" (by six authors—Neurath, Bohr, Dewey, Russell, Carnap, and Morris), its first systematic monograph was *Foundations of the Theory of Signs* by Morris in 1938.[34]

The position of Morris's monograph in the *Encyclopedia* was no accident. It was the outstanding feature of the very design of the *Encyclopedia.* The foundations of the theory of signs were the foundations for the unification of the sciences.

Morris had studied under George Herbert Mead and had written his dissertation on *Symbolism and Reality* in 1925. He had been "helped to identify the contours of a general theory of signs by *The Meaning of Meaning.*"[35]

The first six volumes of Peirce's **Collected Papers,** edited by Charles Hartshorne and Paul Weiss, had come out in the earlier 1930s; the first in 1931, the sixth in 1935. (Hartshorne was a colleague of Morris's at Chicago.) Morris acquired each of the six volumes as it appeared, and annotated it extensively.[36] There were semeiotic materials in all six volumes, but especially in the second and fifth. By the time Morris wrote the *Foundations,* therefore, he had examined a much more nearly adequate body of evidence for Peirce's theory of signs than had been accessible to Ogden and Richards. But the same evidence was now in the hands of many other students, and interpretations or criticisms of Peirce no longer passed unchallenged.

Morris had a student named Estelle Allen De Lacy, who wrote her dissertation in 1935 on *Meaning and Methodology in Hellenistic Philosophy,* giving prominence to Philodemus. She assisted Morris for several years in collecting materials for a history of semeiotic. This was never written, but she and her husband, Phillip De Lacy, edited and translated Philodemus's *De signis.*[37]

Morris's later work, *Signs, Language and Behavior* (1946), has an appendix with a section on Peirce, which begins: "Peirce was the heir of the whole historical analysis of signs and has himself had a major influence upon contemporary discussion." In this book, as in the *Foundations,* Morris rightly took off from semeiosis, but about the same time Dewey challenged his earlier account of "the pragmatic dimension" of semeiosis as "the relation of signs to interpreters." Morris replied to Dewey and other critics in 1948 in "Signs About Signs About Signs," which brought Peirce to the center of semeiotic controversy,[38] as Morris's two books had brought Peirce to the center of fresh construction.

Another student of Morris's, Thomas A. Sebeok, has become the most productive and influential semeiotician of the present day. A special field of his, which he will forgive me for spelling *zoösemeiotic,* is one that farmer Peirce entered now and then with his horses and dogs, but found no time to cultivate systematically.

14. THE GESTATION PERIOD (1851-1865)

Whately's *Elements of Logic* was studied in the spring semester of the junior year in Harvard College. In September 1851, when about to enter upon his junior year, Peirce's older brother Jem (James Mills Peirce) bought his textbooks for the year, including Whately. Charles, who was turning twelve that month, came into Jem's room, glanced at the new textbooks, and asked what logic was. Jem's answer led Charles to stretch himself upon the carpet there in Jem's room, with Whately open before him. As Charles wrote F. A. Woods in 1913, in a few days he got all the good he could out of it, "so that 6 years later when I was, with the rest of my class, required to answer at recitations on the book, I needed no more than a slight rereading of the lessons" (Ms L 477).

There was no other episode of his boyhood that Peirce so often recounted. In other accounts he speaks of himself as having "in a few days mastered that illuminating work" (Ms 905, canceled p.5), as having been "intent" upon reading it "on several days" (Ms 842[s]), as having "buried" himself in it (W85), as having been "delighted" with it (Ms 1606 p.11), as "poring over" it (NE 4:vi); and in at least four other accounts as "devouring" it.[39]

The logicians of Peirce's youth, however critical they were of particular points in Whately, ascribed to him the revival of logic at Oxford and elsewhere after a century or more of stagnation. As early as 1833, Sir William Hamilton wrote that by the publication of Whately's *Elements* in 1826 "a new life was suddenly communicated to the expiring study," and that the decade in which it appeared had "done more in Oxford for the cause of this science than the whole hundred and thirty years preceding."[40] In 1854 George Boole, in the preface to his *Laws of Thought,* said that for "a knowledge of the most important terms of the science, as usually treated, and of its general object . . . there is no better guide than Archbishop Whately's *Elements of Logic,*" to which "the present revival of attention to this class of studies seems in a great measure due." Augustus De Morgan in his article on logic in the *English Cyclopaedia* in 1860 wrote that Whately possessed "the talent of rendering a dry subject attractive in a sound form by style, illustration, and clearness combined. And to him is due the title of the restorer of logical study in England." Peirce's Harvard teacher, Francis Bowen, had written in the *North American Review* for October 1856:

The revival was not confined to England, but extended to the colleges in this country. The study of Whately's *Elements* here almost immediately superseded that of Hedge's *Logic,* a little compend which did not profess to give more than a few definitions of the most frequently recurring technicalities of the science.[41]

Besides the passages in his introduction from which Ogden and Richards quoted, Whately had a chapter criticizing realism, and treating conceptualism as a variant of it.[42] He made the same distinction between fact and arrangement[43] to which Peirce appealed in two of the most nominalistic passages of his *Popular Science Monthly* series: the application of the pragmatic maxim to the conception "hard" and the comment on Gray's "Elegy" (5.403 and 409 at end; cf. 7.340). In later stages of his long progress from nominalism into realism, Peirce corrected or rejected these (5.453, 457, 545; 1.27nl, 615; 8.216).

To keep from sliding into realism unawares, Whately prescribed the prophylactic measure of using "description" when tempted to say "kind" or "nature."[44] Peirce never quite lost the habit so formed, in spite of having gradually become more and more of a realist (1.27n, 204, 549n; 5.127, 483, 486; 8.251).

When Peirce recited on Whately's *Logic* in the spring of 1858, it had been the Harvard logic text, and nominalism had been "the Cambridge Metaphysics,"[45] for a quarter of a century. But the *Logic* was not the only book of Whately's on which Peirce had to recite. In the first term of his freshman year, he recited twice a week on Whately's *Lessons on Morals and Christian Evidences.* In both terms of his junior year and perhaps also in his senior year he recited on Whately's *Elements of Rhetoric,* which had a passage advocating nominalism more vigorously even than the one that Ogden and Richards quoted from the *Logic.* Here is the latter half of it:

> The full importance, consequently, of Language, and of precise technical Language,—of having accurate and well-defined "names for one's tools,"—can never be duly appreciated by those who still cling to the theory of "Ideas"; those imaginary objects of thought in the mind, of which "Common-terms" are merely the names, and by means of which we are supposed to be able to do what I am convinced is impossible; to carry on a train of Reasoning without the use of Language, or of any General-Signs whatever.

> But each, in proportion as he the more fully embraces the doctrine of *Nominalism,* and consequently understands the real character of Language, will become the better qualified to estimate the importance of an accurate system of nomenclature.[46]

The rhetoric text in Peirce's sophomore year, George Campbell's *Philosophy of Rhetoric,* inculcated similar views.

While still in college, Peirce had in his private library at least two other books of Whately's. One was *A Selection of English Synonyms,* by Whately's daughter Elizabeth Jane Whately, revised throughout by Whately himself, who said in his preface that it was "very much the best" work that had appeared on the subject, but that

> the importance of that subject itself . . . and of all that relates to language, will be much less highly estimated by those who have adopted the metaphysical theory of *ideas,* and who consider the use of language to be merely the *conveying* our meaning to *others,* than by those who adhere to the opposite—the *nominalist*—view . . . and who accordingly regard words—or some kind of *signs* equivalent to words—as an indispensable instrument of thought, in all cases, where a process of *reasoning* takes place.[47]

It was doubtless this book that prompted Peirce in October 1857, early in his junior year, to begin writing **"A Scientific Book of Synonyms in the English Language"** (Mss 1140-42).

Also in Peirce's private library was Whately's *Historic Doubts Relative to Napoleon Buonaparte,* a parody of Hume's scepticism concerning miracles. This was almost certainly the germ from which Peirce's theory of historical method developed (2.625, 634, 642, 714; 5.589; 8.194f., 380, 382; Mss 1319-20).

Peirce also read the nominalists that Ogden and Richards later reviewed on their way to Whately and Peirce. Take Horne Tooke, for example. On January 1, 1861, Peirce's "Aunt Lizzie" (Charlotte Elizabeth Peirce) gave him a copy of the 1860 edition of *The Diversions of Purley.*[48] Though Horne Tooke was a follower of Locke, his thesis was that everything Locke had said in terms of ideas should rather have been said in terms of words. Though Peirce did not jettison the language of ideas, even in the article in which his pragmatism was first put forward—**"How To Make Our Ideas Clear"** (1878)—he could write as late as 1896: "What do we mean by an idea being clear? It is not needful to inquire first what an idea is. We can dispense with the word idea, and can ask what we mean by attaching a clear signification to a word" (Ms 953 p.8).

Peirce frequently said in later years that it was the extreme nominalists such as Ockham, Hobbes, Leibniz, and Berkeley who had especially urged the doctrine that "every thought is a sign" (5.470), that "thoughts *are* signs" (4.582), that "Any concept is a sign" (8.332), but that there is nothing inherently or peculiarly nominalistic about the doctrine, and that "the realists are, for the most part, content to let the proposition stand unchallenged, even when they have not decidedly affirmed its truth" (4.582).

Of Peirce himself it may be concluded that he committed himself in youth to a theory of cognition which he knew to be *prima facie* nominalistic, and that he at first conceived himself to be a nominalist in so doing; but that, step by step over a period of forty years or more, beginning in 1868, he transformed that nominalistic doctrine into a more and more realistic one.

In any case, he remained a nominalist throughout what I have called the gestation period of his semeiotic.[49]

15. A FOURTH FOUNDING? (1976-)

Peirce's *Letters to Lady Welby* came out in 1953. Volumes 7-8 were added to the *Collected Papers* in 1958, both containing further materials on the general theory of signs, including a long draft of a letter not sent to Lady Welby and therefore not included in the 1953 edition (8.342-79). A microfilm edition of the Peirce manuscripts at Harvard University became available in 1964, and a *Catalogue* of them came out in 1967. The first of four volumes of his *Nation* reviews appeared in December 1975. Carolyn Eisele's *The New Elements of Mathematics by Charles S. Peirce* (1976) consists almost entirely of papers not previously published, and much more of this new material is relevant to semeiotic than would be guessed from the title, from the indexes, or from a casual glance through the four-volumes-in-five. A microfiche edition of the papers Peirce himself published appeared in 1977. An edition of the Peirce/Welby correspondence by Charles S. Hardwick, containing Lady Welby's letters to Peirce as well as his to her, appeared later in 1977. Several anthologies of Peirce's writings on semeiotic, both in English and in translation, are being prepared.

It remains the case, however, that Peirce's still unpublished writings on the theory of signs exceed in quantity those that have so far been published. A new and more comprehensive edition of his writings is now in preparation, to be arranged chronologically in fifteen or more volumes to appear over a period of ten or more years, plus a two-volume biography and a volume of bibliographies and indexes. The semeiotic materials appearing for the first time in this new edition will exceed in quantity those which first appeared in the eight volumes of *Collected Papers.*

There is already an extensive body of secondary literature, some of it purely expository, some of it critical; some of it continuing where Peirce left off; some of it inspired in part by Peirce but making no attempt to distinguish Peircean from non-Peircean elements in the new constructions in progress.

The continuing confusion of tongues in the semeiotic tower of Babel is such that, for some time to come, it will be worthwhile for semeioticians and Peirce scholars to study the new materials as they become available, and to attempt some of the unfinished tasks of Peircean semeiotic scholarship. Eight of these occur to me as worth mentioning here.

(1) Most needed, and perhaps even a prerequisite to the rest, is an annotated bibliography of Peirce's own rel-

evant writings, published and unpublished, followed by a bibliography of the secondary literature and by a lexicon that quotes Peirce's best definitions or explanations of the terms he uses and that gives references to other relevant passages in his writings and in the secondary literature.

(2) The present paper has briefly shown how Peirce's lifelong study of the logic of mathematics was conducted throughout within the framework of semeiotic. This is worth showing in greater detail. But Peirce's work in the logic of mathematics was for the sake of his more extensive work in the logic of the positive sciences, and it remains to be shown how that also was conducted throughout within the same framework.

(3) Peirce said that the proof of pragmaticism on which he embarked in his *Monist* series of 1905 was "the one contribution of value" that he had still to make to philosophy, "For it would essentially involve the establishment of the truth of synechism" (5.415). What, in full, was the unfinished proof? How did the theory of signs and the system of existential graphs function in it? And how would it establish the truth of synechism?[50]

(4) What, more exactly, was the "sop to Cerberus"? And what, more exactly, was that broader, that more generalized conception of sign that Peirce despaired of making understandable and understood?

(5) Suppose that Peirce had succeeded in writing *A System of Logic, considered as Semeiotic,* or rather suppose that he were writing it today, in full knowledge of developments in logic and in semeiotic since his time. What would be its distinguishing features? Imagine the *System* already published, and a competent critic writing a careful review article on it. How would the article go?

(6) As an approach to (5), consider that nearly everything that has so far been written about Peirce's general theory of signs belongs to the first of the three parts of the semeiotic trivium, leaving the second and third empty. But Peirce said his hardest and best work had been done on the third (NE 3:207).[51] Interpreters and critics of his pragmatism and of his theory of the economy of research, for examples, have either detached them from semeiotic altogether or have failed to assign them properly, as he did, to its third part, Methodeutic, as presupposing the second, Critic. To what extent has our understanding of them been thereby vitiated? What were his other contributions to Methodeutic? And how about Critic?

(7) What were the steps by which Peirce passed from a nominalistic to a more and more realistic general theory of signs? "Everybody ought to be a nominalist at first, and to continue in that opinion until he is driven out of it by the *force majeure* of irreconcilable facts" (4.1). What was the *force majeure* at each step of the way?[52]

(8) Among the recurring topics in Peirce's writings, early and late, are "first impressions of sense" and

"immediate perception." It is perhaps obvious enough that the sign theory of cognition entails rejection of the former. It is less obvious that it entails acceptance of the latter. But as late as 1905 Peirce not only claimed to have adhered from the beginning to the doctrine of immediate perception, as held by Aristotle, by Reid and Hamilton, and by Kant in his refutation of Berkeley (8.261), but said that in his own case it was viewing logic as semeiotic that led "at once" to this doctrine.[53] These matters are worth arguing out in detail, and our understanding of Peirce will remain imperfect until that has been done.

If the new materials becoming available are as illuminating as the old, and if oncoming semeioticians and Peirce scholars carry out such tasks as these, and others not less fundamental, may we not look for a fourth founding before the end of the century?

It is my belief that such a fourth founding has already begun.

NOTES

References in the form 5.484 are to the *Collected Papers of Charles Sanders Peirce* by volume and paragraph number. (Cambridge: Harvard University Press, vols. 1-6 edited by Hartshorne and Weiss, 1931-1935; vols. 7-8 edited by Burks, 1958.) References in the form "Ms 318 p.15" are to the Charles S. Peirce Papers in the Houghton Library at Harvard University, quoted by permission of the Department of Philosophy. References in the form NE 3:886 are to *The New Elements of Mathematics by Charles S. Peirce,* edited by Carolyn Eisele (4 vols. in 5, The Hague: Mouton; Atlantic Highlands, N. J.: Humanities Press, 1976), by volume and page. References in the form W75 are to the pages of *Semiotic and Significs: The Correspondence between Charles S. Peirce and Victoria Lady Welby,* edited by Charles S. Hardwick (Bloomington: Indiana University Press, 1977). Christian J. W. Kloesel has helped me by calling my attention to manuscript passages I might otherwise have missed, by criticizing drafts of this essay, and in numerous other ways.

[1] Imagine a small boy for whom shaping his letters is still fun. One day he draws a big *O* that pleases him, and he proudly calls to his older sister, "See my *O*, sis!"

[2] "See *my* O, see!"

[3] The boy puts a pair of eyes in his big *O* and says, "See, my *O* sees!"

[4] The boy draws another big *O* with a quivering or zig-zag line and says, "See my *O* tick! Hear the clock tick, but see my *O* tick!" See further Thomas A. Sebeok, "'Semiotics' and Its Congeners," in his *Contributions to the Doctrine of Signs* (Bloomington: Indiana University and Lisse: Peter de Ridder Press, 1976), pp. 47-58; and Luigi Romeo, "The Derivation of 'Semiotics' through the History of the Discipline," *Semiosis* 6:37-50 (1977).

[5] Peirce in a letter to his father without date but about April 15, 1877, in Ms L 333.

[6] Letter to J. E. Hilgard, Secretary of the Academy, August 6, 1877, in the C. S. S. Peirce folder in the Archives of the National Academy of Sciences.

[7] Max H. Fisch and Jackson I. Cope, "Peirce at The Johns Hopkins University," in *Studies in the Philosophy of Charles Sanders Peirce,* edited by Philip P. Wiener and Frederic H. Young (Cambridge: Harvard University Press, 1952), pp.277-311.

[8] He uses the singular *representamen* once, in 1.557 (1867). The plurals *representamina* and *representamens* do not yet occur. He uses both later. By 1904 he has dropped this term, but he picks it up again at least once, in 1911 (Ms 675). He continues to use *represent* and *representation,* but seldom technically.

[9] In 1.555 Peirce places these three categories between Being and Substance, making five in all; but he makes no *use* of the first and fifth *as categories.* By the time he wrote his 1870 paper on the logic of relatives, it was evident to him that, in any sense in which the central three are categories, the first and fifth are not; and they never reappear as such after 1867. They are hardly ever even mentioned in connection with the categories. In at least one account, however, Peirce explicitly says that "Being and Substance are of a different nature" (Ms L 75, Carnegie Application, "Statement," p.4 of longer draft with that heading). The best account of this matter is still that by Manley Thompson in *The Pragmatic Philosophy of C. S. Peirce* (Chicago: University of Chicago Press, 1953), pp.29-36. (Other questions concerning Peirce's theory of categories are dealt with in my essay "Hegel and Peirce," in *Hegel and the History of Philosophy,* edited by Joseph J. O'Malley, Keith W. Algozin, and Frederick G. Weiss [The Hague: Martinus Nijhoff, 1974], pp.171-93, at 173-78.)

[10] The last clause is here corrected from an errata list not found by the editors of the *Collected Papers.*

[11] Josiah Royce, *The Problem of Christianity* (New York: The Macmillan Co., 1913), vol. 2, pp.107-325. See especially vol. 1, p.xi, and vol. 2, p.114. See also the last paragraph of section 12 below.

[12] *Popular Science Monthly* 12:1-15 (November 1877), 286-302 (January 1878), 604-15 (March 1878), 705-18 (April 1878); 13:203-17 (June 1878), 470-82 (August 1878). *Collected Papers* (with later revisions and notes) 5.358-87, 388-410; 2.645-60, 669-93; 6.395-427; 2.619-44.

[13] The first two papers appeared also in French in the *Revue philosophique* 6:553-69 (December 1878), 7:39-57 (January 1879), under the titles: *La Logique de la Science, Première partie: Comment se fixe la croyance; Deuxième partie: Comment rendre nos idées claires.*

[14] To be sure, there *are* differences, but they might not strike a reader unacquainted with Bain's theory of belief. See Max H. Fisch, "Alexander Bain and the Genealogy of Pragmatism," *Journal of the History of Ideas* 15:413-44 (1954), at 438-40.

[15] See Max H. Fisch, "Peirce's Arisbe: The Greek Influence in his Later Philosophy," *Transactions of the Charles S. Peirce Society* 7:187-210 (1971), at 190-91, 203.

[16] Next in importance was Augustus De Morgan's fourth memoir on the syllogism, in 1860, which opened up the logic of relations (NE 4:125) and elaborated the syllogism of transposed quantity (4.103). A distant third was Sir William Hamilton's quantification of the predicate (1.29) and the controversy to which it gave rise (2.532-35).

[17] "Substitution in Logic," *The Monist* 15:294-95 (1905), signed by Francis C. Russell but written by Peirce. See further steps (3), (19), (20), and (22) below. See also note 31 below.

[18] *American Journal of Mathematics* 1:126n (1878).

[19] Ibid., 4:97-229 (1881); for errata see p.iv.

[20] *Johns Hopkins University Circulars* 1:178-80.

[21] For an explanation of this step, see section 9 below.

[22] See Don D. Roberts, *The Existential Graphs of Charles S. Peirce* (The Hague: Mouton, 1973).

[23] Cf. Ms 530, "A Proposed Logical Notation." (An American psychologist and logician, Shea Zellweger, is about to publish a new notation for the same connectives, which he calls "the logic alphabet." He accepts four of Peirce's criteria for a good notation, and follows Peirce in calling two of them *iconicity* and *cursiveness*. The other two, in substance contained in Peirce's box-X, he calls *frame consistency* and *eusymmetry*. Although his logic alphabet differs from Peirce's notations, he conceives his own notation as directly continuing Peirce's work.)

[24] See step (1) above and steps (20) and (22) below. Peirce submitted a long article on "Mathematical Logic" for the same *Dictionary*, but Baldwin printed only the first five words of it and the appended bibliographical note. The article included a five-step analysis of the mathematician's procedure. The account of the peculiarities of mathematical reasoning ended: "Of still greater importance is the practice of making operations and relations of all kinds objects to be operated upon" (NE 3:742-50 at 749f.).

[25] Max H. Fisch, "American Pragmatism Before and After 1898," in *American Philosophy from Edwards to Quine*, edited by Robert W. Shahan and Kenneth R. Merrill (Norman: University of Oklahoma Press, 1977), pp. 77-110.

[26] Max H. Fisch, "The 'Proof' of Pragmatism," in *Pragmatism and Purpose: Essays Presented to Thomas A. Goudge*, edited by John G. Slater, Fred Wilson, and L. W. Summer (Toronto: University of Toronto Press, forthcoming).

[27] For Peirce's use of Bentham's cenoscopic-idioscopic distinction, see 1.241f., 8.199.

[28] For Peirce's classification of the sciences as of 1902-1903, see 1.180-283. This is presented in tabular form between pages 48 and 49 of Thomas A. Goudge, *The Thought of C. S. Peirce* (Toronto: University of Toronto Press, 1950). See also the illuminating Ph.D. dissertation by Beverley E. Kent, *Logic in the Context of Peirce's Classification of the Sciences* (University of Waterloo, 1975); *Dissertation Abstracts* 36:2899-A, November 1975).

[29] Charles S. Hardwick, ed., *Semiotic and Significs: The Correspondence between Charles S. Peirce and Victoria Lady Welby* (Bloomington: Indiana University Press, 1977).

[30] Fisch and Cope (note 7 above), p.292.

[31] C. K. Ogden and I. A. Richards, *The Meaning of Meaning* (London: Kegan Paul, Trench, Trubner & Co.; New York: Harcourt, Brace & Co., 1923), p.125, referring to the article cited in note 17 above.

[32] *Mind* 33:109 (1924).

[33] See sections 2 and 3 above.

[34] Two hundred and sixty monographs were contemplated, to be collected in twenty-six volumes, but World War II and Neurath's death intervened. The ten monographs of Volume I were collected in 1955. When nine of the ten for Volume II were ready in 1969, it appeared along with a reprint of Volume I under the title *Foundations of the Unity of Science: Toward an International Encyclopedia of Unified Science*. The remainder of the project was indefinitely postponed. Meanwhile the monographs of both volumes had been appearing singly, as they became ready, beginning in 1938. Morris's monograph appeared in that year as Volume I, Number 2.

[35] Charles Morris, *Writings on the General Theory of Signs* (The Hague: Mouton, 1971), p.7. (*The Foundations* and other writings mentioned below are reprinted in this volume.)

[36] Morris has recently given a collection of his correspondence and other papers and a part of his library, including these volumes, to Indiana University-Purdue University at Indianapolis.

[37] *Philodemus: On Methods of Inference; A Study in Ancient Empiricism* (Philological Monographs published by the American Philological Association, Number X, 1941). Estelle Allen De Lacy, "Meaning and Methodology in Hellenistic Philosophy," *Philosophical Review* 47:390-409, 1938.

[38] *Philosophy and Phenomenological Research* 9:115-33 (1948). On the controversy between Morris and Dewey about Peirce see Max H. Fisch, "Dewey's Critical and Historical Studies," in *Guide to the Works of John Dewey,* edited by Jo Ann Boydston (Carbondale: Southern Illinois University Press, 1970), pp. 306-33 at 330-32.

[39] Mss 842 p.7, 848 p.9; W77; letter to Samuel Barnett, December 20, 1909, in Emory University Library.

[40] Sir William Hamilton, *Discussions on Philosophy and Literature* (New York: Harper & Brothers, 1860), p.126.

[41] In 1864 Bowen began the preface to his own *Treatise on Logic* (Boston: John Allyn): "The revival of the study of Logic, at least in England and America, as an important element of a University education, dates only from the publication of Dr. Whately's treatise on the subject, little over thirty years ago."

[42] *Elements of Logic* (New York: Harper & Brothers, 1856), Book IV, ch. V, pp.294-303, at p.299°.

[43] Ibid., pp. 296f.

[44] Ibid., pp. 294°, 298, 302, 347.

[45] Amos Bronson Alcott, writing to William Torrey Harris on April 2, 1868, and commenting on "Nominalism *versus* Realism" (*Journal of Speculative Philosophy* 2:57-61, 1868 [6.619-24]), says: "I take the author . . . to be the son of the Cambridge Mathematical Professor, and speaking the best he has for the Cambridge Metaphysics. . . ." (quoted from a typewritten transcript sent to me by Harris's daughter, Edith Davidson Harris, in 1949. She gave her Alcott-Harris collection to the Concord Free Public Library in 1952, but the entire collection, including this letter, has been missing since 1960.) In a draft of this letter among the Alcott Papers in the Houghton Library of Harvard University, Alcott puts it as follows: "I take Peirce to be the son of the Cambridge mathematics Professor, and perhaps defending as he best can the Professor's metaphysics, if not of the College." So Benjamin Peirce, too, was understood to be a nominalist.

[46] *Elements of Rhetoric* (London: John W. Parker, 1846), pp.20f.

[47] Editor's preface to Elizabeth Jane Whately, *A Selection of English Synonyms,* 4th ed., rev. (London: John W. Parker and Son, 1858). Peirce's own copies of four of the five Whately books are listed in Ms 1555. All are of editions published in Cambridge, or Boston and Cambridge; the *Napoleon* in 1832, the *Logic, Rhetoric,* and *Synonyms* in the 1850s.

[48] The call number of this copy in the Harvard University Library is 9265.11.

[49] Max H. Fisch, "Peirce's Progress from Nominalism toward Realism," *The Monist* 51:159-78 (1967), shows that he was espousing nominalism under that name in 1867, well into the period of what I have called the first founding. (Among the defects of this article are that it pays too little attention to the theory of signs, fails to mention Whately and Harvard nominalism, and ignores the gestation period altogether. Moreover, its title was misleading. It was short for "Peirce's progress toward that degree—or that extremity—of realism which he eventually reached." But it was also meant to leave room for a subsequent paper, not yet written, on "Peirce's Lifelong Nominalism.")

[50] See section 7 above and note 25.

[51] Lines 9-11 of p.207 should read: "The third branch of logic is *Methodeutic* which shows how to conduct an inquiry. This is what the greater part of my life has been devoted to, though I base it upon Critic." The preceding sentence was left unfinished. From another draft of the same letter (Ms 231): "In my own feeling, whatever I did in any other science than logic was only an exercize in methodeutic and as soon as I had the *method* of investigation thoroughly shown, my interest dropped off." From an earlier draft letter to William James (NE 3:874): "I have done a lot of work in Methodeutic that is valuable and very little of it is printed. This will be the most widely useful part of my Big Book."

[52] See section 14 above and note 49.

[53] Draft letters to James, July 22 and 26, 1905, in Ms L 224.

Peter Skagestad (essay date 1980)

SOURCE: "Pragmatic Realism: The Peircean Argument Reexamined," in *The Review of Metaphysics,* Vol. XXXIII, No. 131, March, 1980, pp. 527-40.

[*In the following excerpt, Skagestad summarizes Peirce's pragmatic approach to realism.*]

During the past decade or so, philosophers of science have increasingly recognized that the rationality and progressiveness of science cannot be fully exhibited in syntactic or semantic terms, i.e., by considering science merely as a system of symbols. The idea is rapidly gaining ground that science is fundamentally a way of dealing with the world around us and that the rationality of scientific method essentially depends on the role which it plays within our total conduct.

Two things are not implied by this pragmatic erspective (as I shall call it). It is not implied that science has to be regarded as a purely utilitarian enterprise, any more than any other aspect of human conduct has to be so regarded. Nor is it implied that, because scientific statements and inferences are means to some further end, they cannot therefore be evaluated or criticized without reference to that end. Some go so far as to assert the contrary: It is because science must be regarded from the perspective of its role within our *total* conduct, that a utilitarian perspective is insufficient.[1] Moreover, scientific statements can serve as means to their intended end only if they stand in a certain relation to the world in which we live and act. Put more specifically, these statements are attempted descriptions of an external reality, and the contribution which they make to the success of our total conduct is partially explained by the degree to which they approach the truth about this reality. In this respect, the pragmatic perspective now emerging departs from the mainstream of classical, nineteenth-century pragmatism. In the writings of James, Mach, Pearson, and others, the pragmatic perspective on science was thought to entail an instrumentalist interpretation of scientific theories. In such an interpretation, the notions of "truth" and "reality" were eliminated as superfluous metaphysical verbiage. Today, on the contrary, we see these notions rehabilitated as explanatory concepts, explaining how our manipulation of linguistic signs helps us cope successfully with the nonlinguistic world around us.

A lucid recent statement of this pragmatic realism is found in Hilary Putnam's *Meaning and the Moral Sciences*. Putnam's account of realism depends on a distinction between the use-meaning which is sufficient to understand scientific statements and the referential meaning which is required to explain how the making of scientific statements can make the contribution which it does make to the success of our total activity. Having initially sketched a slightly revised version of Wittgenstein's account of meaning as use, Putnam makes his point as follows:

> Nothing in this account of "use" says *anything* about a correspondence between words and things, or sentences and states of affairs. But it doesn't follow that such a correspondence doesn't exist. A number of tools have this feature: that the instructions for the use of the tool do not mention something that *explains* the successful use of the tool. For example, the instructions for turning an electric light on and off—"just flip the switch"— do not mention *electricity*. But the explanation of the success of switch-flipping as a method of getting lights to go on and off certainly does mention electricity. It is in this sense that reference and truth have less to do with understanding language than philosophers have tended to assume, in my opinion.[2]

From the perspective of this distinction, Putnam argues that both Wittgenstein's use-theory and his earlier picture-theory of language are correct if they are each seen as only part of a total theory.

Science is par excellence a linguistic activity which makes a notable contribution to the success of our nonlinguistic behavior. The uses to which scientists put language, and in terms of which they understand language, may well be adequately accounted for by a verificationist semantics. But this admission does not exclude realism; it may, on the contrary, be supplemented by a realist explanation of how the scientists' use of language comes to affect the results of our total activity the way it does. Realism, so understood, is an empirical hypothesis explaining the success and progress of science:

> That science succeeds in making many true predictions, devising better ways of controlling nature, etc., is an undoubted empirical fact. If realism is an *explanation* of this fact, realism must itself be an over-arching scientific *hypothesis*. And realists have often embraced this idea, and proclaimed that realism *is* an empirical hypothesis.[3]

The empirical purport of the realist hypothesis is this: by explaining past scientific progress, the hypothesis predicts future progress. Should scientific progress come to a halt, this hypothesis would be empirically refuted. What the realist hypothesis states, according to Putnam, is that science converges towards truth, in the sense of correspondence with facts. This hypothesis entails that the principle of charity is applicable to the history of science, i.e., that, even though our descriptions of the world are incommensurable in meaning with past descriptions, still those past descriptions can be understood as having the same reference as ours, so that our descriptions can be meaningfully described as *better* descriptions of the same reality. If this condition were to fail, if the principle of charity were found to be inapplicable to the history of science, then we should be compelled to accept the "meta-induction" that, just as no scientific term used in the past is now thought to refer, so no term used now will in the future be found to refer.[4] Any evidence for this meta-induction will count as evidence against realism, which thus turns out to be indeed an empirical hypothesis, belonging to the pragmatics of the language of science.

Putnam's views, if the above is a fair paraphrase of them, represent what I believe to be the most sophisticated present-day understanding of the relationship between pragmatism and realism. My argument in this paper will be that essentially the same understanding, though it was rare in the age of classical pragmatism, is to be found in the works of Charles S. Peirce. This conclusion will put contemporary philosophical discussion in an interesting historical perspective. Furthermore, it will help solve some thorny problems of Peirce-scholarship.

Peirce was an ardent defender of the hardheaded experimentalism which was fashionable among the scientists of his age. He was himself a distinguished experimenter, and his best known contribution to philosophy is the experimentalist theory of meaning summarized in his pragmatic maxim (***Collected Papers,*** 5.402). At the same time, he was a scientific and scholastic realist of a somewhat extreme kind. I have argued elsewhere that the pragmatic maxim, in at least some of its formulations, is a radically verificationist criterion of meaning, which Peirce set forth for the avowed purpose of eliminating empty metaphysical verbiage.[5] In this version, Peirce's pragmatism appears to make nonsense of abstract entities, thus conflicting with his realism. Peirce's attempt, in 1905, to derive realism from pragmaticism (as he then called it) by a kind of semantic entailment has the appearance of validity only because his premises are inconsistent, thus licensing any inference whatever. From this state one might easily conclude, as Murray G. Murphey strongly insinuates, that Peirce was a sort of sheep in wolf's clothing. According to Murphey, Peirce was "a romantic idealist of a very extreme sort," his world view was "theological and metaphysical in the extreme," and his "apparent empiricism" was "a mask."[6]

There is probably some justice to Murphey's charges. Many of Peirce's formulations, especially in the 1870s, seem to be propagandistic in intent. Likewise, his numerous paraphrases of Herschel's consensus theory of truth give a misleadingly naturalist appearance to what is essentially an absolutist conception of truth.[7] On the other hand, Peirce was never a sycophantic flatterer of the self-image of contemporary science. Confident in his own standing as a scientist and in his own right to speak on behalf of science, he did not hesitate to take on the most influential philosophical spokesmen of science in his time; thus, time and again we find him arrogantly attacking the empiricist methodologies of Kirchhoff, Bernard, and Pearson. To sort out this apparent conflict of attitudes, I wish to suggest (pace Murphey) that Peirce's empiricism was no *mere* mask, but an essential aspect of his realist metaphysics. To be precise, *some* sort of empiricism was required by Peirce's version of realism. Peirce may have mistaken his exact requirements by formulating the pragmatic maxim, at times, as a *criterion* of meaning. At other times, however, he clearly proposes pragmaticism as an empirical hypothesis of semantics, in a manner fully compatible with a realist account of the pragmatics of language (e.g., *CP,* 5.6). To put it more strongly, Peirce's pragmaticist—i.e., verificationist—semantics is essentially required for the defense of his particular brand of realism. Before turning to that doctrine, we must take a brief look at the elements of Peirce's semiotic.

Peirce devoted a great deal of his life to the development of a general theory of signs, which he called by the now standard name "semiotic." A fundamental presupposition of such a theory is our ability to distinguish the theory itself from its subject-matter. That is, we must be able to distinguish the level at which language functions—what Peirce called "sign-action" or "semiosis"—from the level at which we study the functioning of language—the level of semiotic. Science is, *inter alia,* a particular use of language; and so we may distinguish between the manner in which it presents itself to its

user—its "interpreter"—in the process of semiosis, and the manner in which that process presents itself to the student of semiotic. Moreover, within semiotic theory itself, the process of semiosis is analyzed along a trivision of dimensions, which includes within it the use-reference distinction. Peirce propounded this trivision at least as early as in his anti-Cartesian articles from 1868 (*CP,* 5.283); its clearest statement, however, is found in his manuscript "Division of Signs" from 1897:

> A sign or *representamen,* is something which stands to somebody for something in some respect or capacity. It addresses somebody, that is, creates in the mind of that person an equivalent sign, or perhaps a more developed sign. That sign which it creates I call the *interpretant* of the first sign. The sign stands for something, its *object.* It stands for that object, not in all respects, but in reference to a sort of idea, which I have sometimes called the *ground* of the representamen. . . . In consequence of every representamen being thus connected with three things, the ground, the object, and the interpretant, the science of semiotic has three branches (*CP,* 2.228-229).

Peirce then goes on to enumerate the three branches: pure grammar, logic proper, and pure rhetoric, corresponding to what we call today, respectively, syntactics, semantics, and pragmatics.[8] Of the third branch, pure rhetoric or pragmatics, Peirce says that "its task is to ascertain the laws by which in every scientific intelligence one sign gives birth to another" (*CP,* 2.229), having shortly before defined "scientific intelligence" as "an intelligence capable of learning by experience" (*CP,* 2.227). Pragmatics, we may say, is the study of how thoughts are modified by the language-user's interaction with experience. This study must take into account both what a sign refers to and how it is understood by its user. In addition, however, it examines how the user's understanding of the sign affects the realization of his aims and purposes, and how that experience in its turn modifies his understanding of the sign. The pragmatic maxim tells us only how the sign is understood by its user, what is its "ultimate logical interpretant" (*CP,* 5.477); this is a part of the story of how that understanding is modified by experience, but it is not the whole story. Moreover, it is itself an *empirical* hypothesis about meaning; not a definition or a stipulation. It is thus itself modifiable by experience and hence cannot in any meaningful sense constitute a "criterion" of meaning.

As has been convincingly argued by Bruce Altshuler, the pragmatic maxim was from the start intended to form a part of Peirce's theory of signs.[9] However, when the maxim originally appeared in print, in "How To Make Our Ideas Clear" in 1878, Peirce largely disregarded his own theory of signs and formulated the maxim as a verifiability criterion of meaning. Only in 1902, rethinking the pragmatic maxim, did Peirce explicitly assign it a role within his semiotic and suggest the beginnings of a pragmatic argument for realism:

> The doctrine appears to assume that the end of

man is action—a stoical axiom which, to the present writer at the age of sixty, does not recommend itself so forcibly as it did at thirty. If it be admitted, on the contrary, that action wants an end, and that that end must be something of a general description, then the spirit of the maxim itself, which is that we must look to the upshot of our concepts in order rightly to comprehend them, would direct us towards something different from practical facts, namely, to general ideas, as the true interpreters of our thought (*CP*, 5.3).

Here, I believe for the first time, Peirce recommends applying the pragmatic maxim to the maxim itself. The result of this, he strongly suggests, will be to show that the use-meaning explicated by the pragmatic maxim is only one gambit in a larger game. The very use of concepts defined in verifiable terms has a point only if the general concepts so defined are really instantiated, i.e., if there really are universals.

So far, to be sure, this line of argument is barely hinted at. It was to be further elaborated three years later, in the series of papers which Peirce published in the *Monist* in 1905, and in which he renamed his doctrine "pragmaticism" so as to set it apart from the instrumentalist doctrines defended by James, Dewey, Schiller, *et al.*, under the label "pragmatism." Pragmaticism, Peirce now says, makes meaning consist in conceived experimental phenomena. But this is to say that words are meaningfully employed only on the condition that experiments can actually be carried out. This, in turn, implies both an actually existing world, in which the experimenter acts and is acted upon, and something of a general description, namely the experimenter's plan and purpose, without which his actions would not constitute an experiment. Describing the various phases of an experiment, Peirce concludes:

> While the two chief parts of the event itself are the action and the reaction, yet the unity of essence of the experiment lies in its purpose and plan, the ingredients passed over in enumeration (*CP*, 5.424).

Putting this quote side by side with the one on the last page, we arrive at the following line of reasoning. An experimental scientist understands scientific statements fully in terms of their experimental consequences, in terms of action and reaction. But he is able to do this only on the condition that someone is able to formulate a general plan, within which a particular experiment will serve a purpose. And experiments have a point or purpose only to the extent that there are some general lessons to be drawn from particular experiments. That is, it is precisely because scientific statements are fully understandable in purely experimental terms that the reality of (some) universals is a precondition for the scientific use of language to have a point and purpose.

It should now be clear in what way Peirce's pragmaticism, when understood within the framework of his semiotic, not only is compatible with a realist ontology,

but positively requires to be supplemented by such an ontology. Let us see, next, precisely how Peirce's argument for realism is developed.

The most explicit brief statement of Peirce's pragmatic argument for realism is to be found in his Harvard lectures from 1903. The argument is set forth in the course of a presentation of Peirce's three categories: First, Second, and Third. First is the category of quality, feeling, immediacy, action—in short, of subjectivity. Second is the category of brute fact, perception, reaction—in short, of objectivity. Third is the category of relation, law, generality—in short of mediation between First and Second. Peirce thought of these three categories as objective and universal, i.e., as the aspects under which all experience necessarily presents itself.

In his Harvard lectures Peirce claimed that "thirdness"—i.e., lawlikeness or generality—is really found in nature, and not merely imposed on nature by the scientific investigator. To support this claim he proposed to "approach the question experimentally," by means of an experiment which he was sure his audience would regard as "a very silly experiment" (*CP*, 5.93). He then held up a stone before the audience and posed the question: How do I know that the stone will drop when I let go of it? *That* the stone will drop is not in question; the question is how I can *know* this before it actually happens. Peirce's answer is the obvious one, that he knows this by prediction from the general law that heavy objects always drop when unsupported (*CP*, 5.95). But this law may be construed in two different ways, nominalistically or realistically. In the first case, the law is just a shorthand summary of a sequence of particular events which have been observed to occur with a given regularity in the past; in the second case, the law asserts that the observed past regularity is just a particular manifestation of a universal regularity to be found in nature; that is, it asserts the reality of a universal. The point of Peirce's "silly" experiment is to decide between these two options.

Now on the first hypothesis, Peirce claims, since there is nothing more asserted by the law than the actual occurrence of certain conjunctions of events in the past, the law tells us absolutely nothing about the future. On this hypothesis, therefore, it is purely a matter of chance whether the past conjunctions of events will repeat themselves in the future; and thus it should be an even bet whether the stone will drop on this novel occasion which, on the nominalist view, does not fall within the scope of the regularity asserted by the law. But no one in his right mind would accept an even bet; both Peirce and his audience know that the stone will drop. Peirce's argument is that they can know this only on the assumption that the chance hypothesis is false, and that the opposite, realist hypothesis is true. Knowing something about the future by inference from our knowledge of past events is possible only if those past events count as evidence of a real regularity which, by virtue of being universal, applies also to the future:

The fact that I *know* that this stone will fall to the floor when I let it go, as you all must confess, if you are not blinded by theory, that I do know—and you none of you care to take up my bet, I notice—is the proof that the formula, or uniformity, as furnishing a safe basis for prediction, is, or if you like it better, *corresponds to,* a reality (*CP,* 5.96).

After dramatically dropping the stone with a triumphant "I told you so!" Peirce proceeds to draw the expected conclusion, namely:

A thousand other such inductive predictions are getting verified every day, and one would have to suppose every one of them to be merely fortuitous in order reasonably to escape the conclusion that *general principles are really operative in nature.* This is the doctrine of scholastic realism (*CP,* 5.96).

There are certain ambiguities in Peirce's formulation of this "experimental proof of realism," as it has come to be called. As has been ably pointed out by Manley Thompson, Peirce wants to do more than rhetorically illustrate a self-evident common sense belief; he is not simply anticipating G. E. Moore's proof of the existence of the external world. What he wants to do is give some sort of experimental evidence for a belief which is not self-evident, a belief which we are able to doubt, which many people do doubt, and which we may therefore seek evidence for or against. At the same time, the physical event which concludes his experiment—the fall of the stone—does not count as experimental evidence, since it is assumed at the outset as known, and assumed to be compatible with both the rival hypotheses. The nominalist hypothesis does not exclude the fall of the stone; only, it fails to predict it. So does the realist hypothesis. The fall of the stone is predicted by the law of gravity, but realism does not assert that this law is true. The realist hypothesis is only that *there are* real laws of nature; it does not say which of the presumed laws are real. So the fall of the stone proves nothing either way.

Once this is granted, Thompson is not necessarily justified in concluding that Peirce "was badly confused about the question he proposed to attack," let alone that this confusion "is fundamental to his thinking, early and late, on the issue of scholastic realism."[10] Thompson criticizes Peirce by posing the dichotomy: rhetorical illustration of common sense belief vs. experimental testing of a dubitable hypothesis. He then argues, in effect, that Peirce wants to do more than the former and does not succeed in doing the latter since all the evidence cuts both ways. Nor, he holds, can Peirce's experiment count as a thought-experiment, since there is no conceivable experimental evidence which could decide the issue.

I want to propose that there is a sense in which Peirce does offer experimental evidence for realism. What Peirce does is perform a genuine thought-experiment on a phony physical experiment, and the very phoniness of the physical experiment is part of the experimental out-

come of the thought-experiment. The fall of the stone is assumed at the outset, so the physical experiment on the stone is phony. But the fact that the fall of the stone is assumed, is not in itself assumed; the joint fact that this assumption is both made and subsequently verified constitutes the outcome of the thought-experiment. The experimental evidence for realism is the fact that everybody predicts that the stone will fall, and that it actually does fall. In this experiment, the fall of the stone is not superfluous. Its fall is compatible with nominalism, just as its failure to fall would have been compatible with realism. Still, if it had failed to fall, this would have counted as *evidence* against realism, only not as *decisive* evidence. The nonfulfillment of an inductive prediction does not overthrow realism, but the nonfulfillment of *all* inductive predictions would overthrow it; hence, *each* nonfulfillment of an inductive prediction counts as evidence against it—and each fulfillment of an inductive prediction counts as evidence in its favor.

This is not to say that there is no confusion in Peirce's formulation of the argument, only that the confusion is not so profound as to vitiate the argument in its entirety. As I have interpreted the argument, it does not *prove* the truth of realism, nor does it refute nominalism. The realist hypothesis—"there are real laws of nature"—is only superficially a singular existential statement; we cannot experimentally produce an instance of a law of nature, thereby proving that they exist. Nor is the hypothesis strictly speaking a universal statement, which can be refuted by individual counterexamples; individual events may refute this or that law of nature, but no individual event can refute the assertion that there are laws of nature. Properly analyzed, then, this is a statement embodying mixed quantifiers and, I believe, quantification over either statements or properties. It can be inductively *corroborated* through the inductive corroboration of any law of nature, and it can be inductively *disconfirmed* through the inductive refutation of *any* law of nature. Realism cannot be experimentally refuted, as can a putative law of nature; but it can be inductively overthrown through the refutation of *all* laws of nature.

In the latter case, of course, we should no longer have any empirical science, so realism cannot be scientifically refuted, and hence it is not a hypothesis *within* science. It is still an empirical hypothesis, namely, a hypothesis *about* science. What is empirical evidence *for* science does not exhaust all the empirical evidence there is. There is also empirical evidence *of* science; we know empirically that there is such a thing as science, and the scientific activity itself furnishes us with experience which we may theorize over. If, in the future course of science, all laws were to be empirically refuted, and all predictive reliability were to be lost, we should no longer have science, but we should have *empirical* evidence of the falsity of realism.

As Peirce himself puts the argument, then, it is confused, and it can be saved only by a somewhat free rendering. Peirce did not, to be sure, think that one single event proved realism; he cited as the relevant evidence the fact that a thousand inductive predictions get verified every day (*CP*, 5.96). He did, however, claim to prove the truth of realism; elsewhere, he makes claims which would render realism immune to disconfirming evidence. For instance, in a manuscript from 1909, he purports to prove that the notion of a purely chance world is self-contradictory (*CP*, 6.398-404). But if so, of course, realism becomes a necessary and a priori truth; there would then be no evidence for or against it, and any attempt at testing it experimentally would be nonsensical. This kind of apriorism, I might add, comes into irresoluble conflict with Peirce's often expressed fallibilism. In a case like this, where there appear to be inconsistencies in the texts, the principle of charity tells us to locate the unavoidable inconsistencies as close as possible to the periphery of Peirce's thought, rather than placing them right at the heart of his doctrine. Peirce's realism and anti-apriorism are both persistent and central strands in his thought, and it is desirable that any interpretation should preserve both these strands, if at all possible. In this case, it means taking the word "proof" in the sense of "inductive corroboration."

We have looked at one of the clearest and briefest statements of Peirce's pragmatic argument for realism. Let me briefly recapitulate the interpretation I have given of Peirce's line of argument. The up-shot of the pragmatic maxim is that scientists understand scientific terms only operationally, in terms of possible experiments and expected experimental outcomes. To the onlooker, studying the pragmatics of the language of science, it is evident that scientific terms can be used and understood only to the extent that certain experiments can be carried out. One condition for the execution of an experiment is the plan or purpose in the mind of the experimenter; he can, of course, manipulate lab equipment with no purpose whatever in mind, but such random manipulation does not constitute an experiment. For the experimenter to attach a purpose to his experiment, he must have reason to believe that experimental results are reproducible, i.e., that inductive predictions will tend, on the whole and for the most part, to be verified. A belief in predictive reliability is therefore a pragmatic condition for attaching an intelligible meaning to scientific terms; and this belief, in its turn, involves a belief in universal regularities, manifesting themselves in reproducible experimental phenomena. These phenomena are not in themselves sufficient evidence of such regularities; nominalism can always account for all the phenomena observed to date. But there is no point in performing experiments unless we believe that their results are indefinitely reproducible in the future. This belief, too, is logically compatible with nominalism; but realism explains why experimental results tend to be reproducible and thereby predicts that they will go on being reproducible in a higher than random proportion of cases; nominalism does not. Hence, unless the realist hypothesis were true, science would be an idle game

with no point or purpose to it. Finally, to the extent that we have empirical evidence that science is not an idle game, that it does in fact contribute to the success of our total conduct, we have *eo ipso* empirical evidence in favor of realism.

Enough has been said to show that pragmaticism, at least in its semiotic interpretation, is not an alien body in Peirce's defense of realism, but on the contrary an essential link in that defense. That defense, as we have seen, moves on the level of the pragmatics of scientific language, and within this defense pragmaticism serves the function of exhibiting the semantics of that language. Now Peirce's argument for realism is, of course, itself a process of semiosis, or sign-action; if we are to understand it in the spirit in which it is intended, we must move up to a higher level of semiotic and apply the pragmatic maxim to the level of philosophical argument, not that of scientific discourse. That is, a philosophical understanding of Peirce's realism consists in understanding it in terms of the kind of thought-experiments which philosophers may perform on the scientific activity as their subject-matter. The experimental outcomes of such experimentation will be made up of case histories from the history of science. To understand the statement that universal regularities are really to be found in nature is to understand what difference belief or nonbelief in this statement will make to the success or failure of scientists in their activity.

If one accepts this perspective, then the further debate over the truth or falsity of realism will have to be carried out in terms of the philosophical analysis of carefully collected case studies, with a view to ascertaining what effect, if any, belief in realism or nominalism, respectively, has had in advancing or retarding the progress of science. Taking his own realism in a pragmatic spirit, Peirce himself has led the way in this line of argumentation. It was his conviction that the natural science of his day was riddled with a nominalist metaphysics, which could only serve to retard scientific progress, to "block the way of inquiry" (*CP*, 1.135), as Peirce habitually put it. Among the targets of his criticism were, as I have mentioned before, some of the most prestigious and influential methodologists of science of his day, including Claude Bernard, Ernst Mach, and Karl Pearson. Bernard's nominalism, according to Peirce, was one of the gravest obstacles which Pasteur had to confront when he advanced his germ-theory (*CP*, 1.109). According to that nominalism, as it is presented in a somewhat oversimplified manner by Peirce, only symptoms mattered for medical science because only symptoms could be dealt with in actual practice, while all talk of underlying entities, such as germs, was dismissed as metaphysical obscurantism. When Peirce wrote this (ca. 1896), Bernard was long dead, Pasteur's theory had won the day, and Peirce's judgement was strictly retrospective. In the cases of Mach and Pearson, on the other hand, Peirce was able to predict that their instrumentalist views would have a retrograde effect (*CP*, 5.601; 8.135). Both predictions were shortly to be verified, when Mach denied the existence of atoms, and Pearson the existence of genes, both on purely a priori and metaphysical grounds.[11]

As I hope to have made clear, realism can be tested only through the cumulative effect of inductive confirmation or disconfirmation; there can be no question of proving it by quoting two or three instances from the history of science. Nevertheless, each such instance is relevant to the testing. Once we construe realism as a hypothesis which seeks to explain why the scientific manipulation of language affects our interaction with the world in the way it does affect it, realism becomes susceptible to discussion and criticism in the light of empirical evidence. In this way, Peirce's pragmatic realism offers us a way of avoiding the dogmatism of aprioristic metaphysics without succumbing to the dogmatism of aprioristic empiricism.

NOTES

[1] This point is persuasively made by Larry Laudan in *Progress and Its Problems* (London: Routledge & Kegan Paul, 1977), esp. pp. 224-25.

[2] Hilary Putnam, *Meaning and the Moral Sciences* (London: Routledge & Kegan Paul, 1978), p. 99.

[3] Ibid., p. 19.

[4] Ibid., p. 25.

[5] "Pragmaticism and Counterfactuals," unpublished MS.

[6] Murray G. Murphey, "Kant's Children: The Cambridge Pragmatists," *Transactions of the Charles S. Peirce Society* 4 (1968): 11, 13.

[7] E.g., in *CP*, 8.12. For Herschel's formulation, cf. John Herschel, *Preliminary Discourse on the Study of Natural Philosophy,* 2d ed. (London: Longman, Brown, Green, and Longmans, 1851), p. 10.

[8] For an elementary introduction to semiotic, including a clear statement of the three dimensions of semiosis, cf. Charles W. Morris, *Foundations of the Theory of Signs,* International Encyclopedia of Unified Science, vol. 1, no. 2 (Chicago: University of Chicago Press, 1938).

[9] Bruce Altshuler, "The Nature of Peirce's Pragmatism," *Transactions of the Charles S. Peirce Society* 14 (1978): 147-75.

[10] Manley Thompson, "Peirce's Experimental Proof of Scholastic Realism," Moore and Robin, eds., *Studies in the Philosophy of C.S. Peirce* (Second series) (Amherst: University of Massachusetts Press, 1964), p. 414.

[11] In *CP*, 1.109, Peirce ascribes to Bernard the dictum "a disease is not an entity but merely a sum of symptoms." In the reference given, Bernard puts the matter in a somewhat less simplistic manner; cf. Claude Bernard, *Leçons de pathologie expérimentale* (Paris: J.B. Baillière et Fils, 1872), pp. 17, 21. For a more nuanced but fundamentally similar view of Bernard, cf. Nils Roll-Hansen, "Critical Teleology: Immanuel Kant and Claude Bernard on the Limitations of Experimental Biology," *Journal of the History of Biology* (Spring 1976), esp. pp. 80-89.

On Mach's opposition to atomic theory, cf. Ernst Mach, *Die Leitgedanken meiner naturwissenschaftlichen Erkenntnislehre und ihre Aufnahme durch die Zeitgenossen* (Leipzig: Verlag von Johann Ambrosius Barth, 1919), pp. 10-11. English translation in S. Toulmin, ed., *Physical Reality* (New York: Harper Torchbooks, 1970), pp. 36-37. On Pearson's opposition to genetics, cf. B. Norton, "Metaphysics and Population Genetics: Karl Pearson and the Background to Fisher's Multi-factorial Theory of Inheritance," *Annals of Science* 32 (1975), esp. pp. 544-49.

William J. Gavin (essay date 1980)

SOURCE: "Peirce and the 'Will to Believe'," in *The Monist,* Vol. 63, No. 3, July, 1980, pp. 342-50.

[*In the following excerpt, Gavin examines common conclusions drawn by Peirce and William James on the nature of religious faith.*]

The multi-dimensionality of the term 'pragmatism' is by now a well-known phenomenon. Much has been made of the Peircean pragmatic theory of meaning vis-à-vis the Jamesian pragmatic theory of truth. Sometimes the contrast is made too quickly. This results in the undervaluing of important similarities between the two thinkers.

It is often said that the Jamesian position appealed to the affective dimension in life, in the sense of our having the "right to believe" in a hypothesis when the situation is unsolvable, yet forced, living, and momentous. Going further, James's metaphysics of "pure experience" involves more than just theoretical knowledge. He held the position that the human being is capable of experiencing dimensions of reality not completely reducible to the knowable, in the strong sense of that term. "Pure experience" is not an objective ground which can be demonstrated with certainty. In this sense, Jamesian metaphysics demands an element of "commitment."

In this paper, I want to suggest that these same elements, the affective and/or the will to believe play an important role in Peirce's position. More specifically, as Peirce begins to refine his pragmatic method, he reacts against two things: nominalism and personalism. Both of these have one thing in common: they emphasize the "foreground" of experience. Peirce reacts by emphasizing the "background" of experience. Science is the study of the "useless"; pragmatism defines meaning in terms of conceivable effects "in the long run." The *ongoing* scientific community becomes the basic unit of reference, etc. However, the two elements of nominalism and personalism are not collapsible. In reacting to these two different degrees of individualism, Peirce sets the stage for the question: "What is the relationship between realism and meaning?" Differently put, Peirce moved from a narrow to a broad definition of pragmatism. So much is well known. But Peirce's broader definition, which is *not* metaphysically neutral, contains an element of conviction or commitment. The relationship between meaning and realism is actually that of the relationship between epistemology and metaphysics. How does this relation function for Peirce? In my opinion, the possibilities are two: if one tries to justify Peirce's metaphysics via his pragmatic epistemology, the latter must be widened *still further,* to *include* an affective dimension or preference. If one tries to justify Peirce's epistemology via his metaphysics, here, too, an element of commitment is involved, in so far as Peirce's entire cosmological outlook is not capable of verification. Let us see how this comes about.

Peirce's pragmatism is developed within the doubt-inquiry-belief-action matrix made famous in the article **"How to Make Our Ideas Clear."** The Cartesian approach is rejected as insufficient. So is any claim to direct, intuitive knowledge. For Peirce, if two beliefs alleviate the same doubt content by producing the same habit of action, then they are identical; here is pragmatism being born. ". . . what a thing means is simply the habits it involves."[1] However, in the well-known example of the meaning of calling something "hard," Peirce initially gives a very positivistic description of the situation. "There is absolutely no difference between a hard thing and a soft thing as long as they are not brought to the test." This stance, if consistently maintained, would commit Peirce to strict operational definitions and, furthermore, to nominalism. "Generals" would be viewed as abstractions; disposition terms could not be properly defined. Ultimately, laws in science would be seen as mere duplications of physical phenomena. As such they would be expendable on *pragmatic* grounds as superfluous.[2] The scope of the difficulty becomes more obvious when one applies the pragmatic method to a term like "reality" and asks "What does it mean to say that 'x' is real?" Peirce defined real things in terms of their effect, which was to cause belief.[3] But he wanted to hold the position that ultimately some shared opinion would come about. Such a position is best stated in terms of the contrary-to-fact conditional, as indeed are the laws of science in general. Peirce, of course, realized all this and later on indicated that pragmatism was *not* to be taken in a neutral positivistic sense:

> . . . the question is, not what *did* happen, but whether it would have been well to engage in any line of conduct whose successful issue depended upon whether that diamond *would* resist an attempt to scratch it, or whether all other logical means of determining how it ought to be classed *would* lead to the conclusion which, to quote the very words of the article, would be "the belief which alone

could be the result of the investigation carried *sufficiently far*."[4]

The above text is important because it clearly indicates Peirce's emphasis upon the subjunctive; pragmatism is not neutral; it is to be associated with a metaphysical stance of scholastic realism, which advocates the reality of generals; ". . . possibility is sometimes of a real kind."[5] This broader view of pragmatism avoids the problems of operational definitions,[6] but his new non-neutral metaphysical position raises the question of whether or not it can be justified by his epistemology.[7]

It is clear that Peirce did not want to merely conflate truth and reality, as in some form of idealism. But it is also clear that he rejected the position wherein "the really real" is completely independent of all thought, forever and ever. For Peirce, such a view would "block the way of inquiry."[8] Rather does Peirce define reality as independent of what you or I or any finite group of people might think about it, but not as necessarily independent of thought in general.[9] Going further, Peirce asserts that the opinion ultimately fated to be agreed upon by the community of scientific investigators is what is meant by truth, and "the object represented in this opinion is the real."[10] From this perspective then, individual beliefs are clearly "constrained"; also present or future opinions held in a communal fashion are subject to constraint—at this very moment. Only in the ultimate case limit where a completely shared opinion is arrived at do we have co-extension of knowledge and reality. Such a position raises the question: "how do we get from here to there?" Peirce's reply is normative: we ought to get from here to there by employing the pragmatic method.[11]

But which version? Clearly the broader of the two definitions is needed. Only by employing a version of the method which allows for the reality of generals can Peirce say that, even now we are subject to constraint by a reality which exhibits independence in some sense. But can one employ the pragmatic method itself to establish that there is some conceivable difference between nominalism and realism? Can the epistemology be used to justify the metaphysical stance? Arthur Burks, in an insightful introduction to Peirce's thought, argues that it cannot.

> The sole difference between the nominalist's and the realist's conception of law has to do with potentialities; and there can be a genuine dispute between the two only if propositions involving potentialities alone have practical consequences. But clearly they do not. It can make no practical difference to say of a diamond that has not been and never will be tested whether it would or would not have been scratched if it had been tested. So long as we agree to the law "All diamonds are hard" and its practical consequence that "If this diamond *is* tested it will not be scratched," then it can make no practical difference what we hold of a diamond that is *never* tested. An untested diamond is beyond practical interest. Another way of putting the matter is to say that action is based

on actualities, not on potentialities, and that potentialities cannot affect conduct.[12]

In a footnote, Burks goes on to say that we do act on potentialities in the sense that "feelings of regret" are possible. For example, one might regret having made a particular speech, because had I not, I would have won the election. He (Burks) asserts, however, that such feelings of regret are not part of the conceivable effects of a belief. Such effects are "not consequences of the belief itself . . . but rather are consequences of holding the belief,"[13] i.e., they are emotional associations of the belief. Now it is undoubtedly true that Peirce often argued in this fashion, viz., against the sentient, the private, the merely satisfying, etc., particularly when he was reacting to James's position, which he considered too individualistic and conduct-orientated. But there also seems to be at least one instance where Peirce cannot make this distinction clearly, namely, the belief by the members of a scientific community that they are slowly and correctly arriving at a shared belief. Peirce held that the members of a (the) scientific community were driven by a "cheerful hope"[14] that their investigations would ultimately terminate in truth, if only they utilized the correct method, namely pragmatism. "We all hope that the different scientific inquiries in which we are severally engaged are going ultimately to lead to some definitely established conclusion we endeavor to anticipate in some measure."[15] Pragmatism was seen as the required method—not because it was self-justifying in an apodictic sense, but because it was self-criticizing. The "proof" of the method itself involves an application of the method. And Peirce appealed to the "facticity" of the history of scientific achievement as inductive proof that the method worked. Furthermore, if pragmatism did not actually prove a realism once and for all, it was at least compatible with the thesis that "There are real things existing independently of us." The method of pragmatism, taken in the broader sense of implying the reality of generals, was supposed to avoid the possibility of a group of scientific investigations "fixing by convention" what the truth would be, because the method forced the individuals to be constrained by experience, by independent reals. But the argument ultimately rests upon the cheerful hope that scientists will act in the manner described and prescribed by Peirce. There is nothing in the argument which would logically prohibit investigators deciding to hold some belief as paradigmatic in a Kuhnian sense. Indeed, it is at this level that Peirce's "Popperian" philosophy of science comes to the fore. Peirce believed that the "best hypothesis, in the sense of the one most recommending itself to the inquirer, is the one which can be the most readily refuted if it is false."[16] Whereas confirmation makes a hypothesis more likely, which is to say more in alignment with our preconceptions, Peirce did believe that hypotheses could be falsified. Peirce has an implicit faith in scientific method as honest, a faith capable of inductive justification, but a faith, nevertheless. Karl Popper argues in the same fashion, admitting that at any given moment "we are prisoners caught in the framework of our theo-

ries; our expectations; our past experiences; our language. But we are prisoners in a Pickwickean sense: if we try we can break out of our framework at any time. Admittedly, we shall find ourselves again in a framework, but it will be a better and roomier one, and we can at any moment break out of it again."[17] But as Kuhn has shown so well, if that were so, "there ought to be no very special difficulties about stepping into someone else's framework in order to evaluate it."[18] Kuhn's conclusion is that Popper "has characterized the entire scientific enterprise in terms that apply only to its occasional revolutionary parts",[19] and, further, that when a transfer *does* take place between paradigms, it is a "conversion experience that cannot be forced".[20] We need not take a position here on the Kuhn-Popper debate. The point is rather that Peirce himself made an act of faith in scientific method. While he believed that "the perversity of thought of whole generations may cause the postponement of the ultimate fixation"[21] of belief, ultimately, he would not accept a Kuhnian analysis. On this he was adamant. Also, the issue here cannot be dealt with merely by pointing to the history of science. It is precisely what that history is that is at issue.

We might sum the discussion up in a negative fashion by saying that Peirce's distinction between the four methods—tenacity, authority, a priori, and scientific[22]—is overdrawn. Peirce, himself, is *tenacious* in advocating the scientific method of pragmatism over all others, and he becomes more tenacious as James develops his own position. This does *not* mean that Peirce could not give good reasons for his position. His reasons were numerous, brilliant, and well-articulated. However, positively summarized, in the last analysis, Peirce's "cheerful hope" involves a Jamesian "will to believe" in a *situation* that is forced, living, and momentous.

What is the situation? Ultimately, it concerns "the really real," the known and the knowable. Peirce was willing to admit that the really real is not coextensive with the known, but *not* that "the really real" was not knowable. To take such a stance would be, in his opinion, to "block the road to inquiry." James might respond that *only* such a stance (really real—greater than knowable) keeps our theoretical concepts honest. In a vague, unfinished universe, one can avoid self-deception only if one admits the essential tentativeness of all hypotheses. This, on a meta-theoretical level, is a strategem, an attitude taken on James' part toward "the really real."

Peirce assumes the opposite strategem, or attitude, though "pragmatically" they may come to the same thing.[23] For him, it is "better" to assume the stance or hope that "the really real" is knowable—at least that this is possible. But this stance is a Peircean "will to believe." Furthermore, part of the meaning of adopting it *is* the consequences of holding it, on the part of the members of the scientific community. The "cheerful hope" cannot be expressed solely in terms of conceivable effects which would occur. Part of the "meaning" of the cheerful hope is its function as a catalyst. Otherwise an infinite regress is the result.

What then has this to do with the possibility of justifying Peirce's metaphysics in terms of his epistemology? Simply this: if one tries to make the distinction between nominalism and realism simply in terms of conceivable effects, i.e., *meaning,* such a distinction can be made if pragmatism is broadened still further, if the affective dimension is included, or better if, at least in some instances, the "consequences of belief" vs. "consequences of holding that belief" dichotomy is rejected. To do so flies in the teeth of Peirce's admitted emphasis upon the conceptual vis-a-vis the affective. But I am suggesting that at a meta-theoretical level, Peirce has no other choice. He chooses a different "belief" than James, but his choice is made ultimately in the same way. In short, Peirce's pragmatic epistemology can make room for or justify his metaphysical realism only if it is admitted that an extra-logical dimension is involved.

But this is only half the question. If Peirce's epistemology cannot justify his metaphysics without a "belief factor" can his metaphysics justify his epistemology? Here the issue is more obvious, and we can be briefer. However, the outcome is the same: an extra-logical dimension is involved.

Metaphysically, Peirce developed an objective idealism, to account for his "realist" approach to laws in science. Mind is viewed as basic and as capable of associating, of taking on habits. ". . . ideas tend to spread continuously and to affect certain others which stand to them in a peculiar relation of affectability."[24] The habits are the laws of nature. Matter from this perspective is viewed as frozen mind, as hidebound. Peirce viewed the universe as containing both a tychistic dimension and an anancastic aspect. But neither was a sufficient explanation of how things evolve. Peirce's evolutionary cosmology is "agapastic." The universe is moving from chance toward order, though at any given moment one can find aspects of both. Habits tend to spread and connect with others, in accordance with Peirce's principle of "synechism." Finally, the universe is viewed by Peirce as ". . . a vast representamen, a great symbol of God's purpose, working out its conclusions in living realities."[25] Such an outlook is remarkable for its richness and detail; yet it clearly involves an extra-logical dimension. Peirce himself viewed metaphysical outlooks as "guesses" based on current scientific facts. But his own exposition is clearly anthropomorphic. While Peirce, indeed, would have been the first to admit this,[26] it does raise questions about the self-sufficiency of a metaphysical position. But there is a bigger problem: Peirce asserted that his evolutionary outlook "constitutes a hypothesis capable of being tested by experiment."[27] Yet it is highly questionable whether the thesis that we are moving from firstness through thirdness toward secondness in accordance with the principle of cosmic love constitutes a verifiable, or better, falsifiable proposition—or ever could do so. Peirce espoused a belief in God and advocated reverie as a "base" (i.e., the humble argument) which might be partially justified by the more logical neglected argument. But as he himself held, the base is "abductive," and there is no complete logic of abduction. Finally, Peirce's agapastic evolutionary position is vehemently opposed to the "gospel of greed" and is, in his words, his "own passionate predilection. . . . Yet the strong feeling is in itself, I think, an argument of some weight in favor of the agapastic theory of evolution,—so far as it may be presumed to bespeak the normal judgment of the Sensible Heart."[28] Such references to feeling and the sensible heart seem clearly to indicate that aspects at least of Peirce's metaphysical cosmology are value-laden. To be sure, Peirce's contribution here is not a small one. But on this level also, an element of "conviction" or "commitment" is involved.

CONCLUSION

The predominant approach to Peirce is to divorce his epistemology and his metaphysics, or at least his cosmology. The latter is "generally regarded by contemporary philosophers as the black sheep or white element of his philosophical progeny."[29] By way of contrast, in his recent book *Purpose and Thought: The Meaning of Pragmatism,* John Smith has argued against any such dichotomy: " . . . The theory of science and of truth cannot, in Peirce's view, be elaborated without reference to a larger context embracing the nature of the real and its relation to the inquirer who seeks to grasp it in the form of truth."[30] In this sense, for Smith, the very success of science must be viewed in a larger context, one of ontological dimensions. The achievements of "scientific inquiry are not left in their immediacy at the level of brute fact but must be understood as manifestations of patterns of development underlying the evolution of the entire universe."[31] The purpose of this paper was to indicate, in one way, why Smith's "wholistic" approach is more adequate.[32] Specifically, the distinction between Peirce's epistemology and his metaphysics is often made in terms of the logical vs. the psychological, the objective vs. the subjective. I have tried to show that it is a mistake to employ this distinction, because on *both* the level of epistemology and that of metaphysical cosmology a so-called "psychological" element, a belief factor, is involved. In reacting to nominalism and personalism—both foreground experiences—Peirce under-estimated important differences between the two. In arguing against nominalism and for realism, Peirce espouses a position wherein *actual* possibility exists. But in reacting against the personal, the affective Peirce argues for the meaningful, and ultimately advocates a position wherein possibility can exist only as logical possibility—as *possible* possibility. This ultimately sets up the question of the relation of Peirce's theory of meaning to his theory of reality. In a sense, Peirce's theory of meaning evolves into a theory of truth, since it points toward a reality which is *not* completely "meaningful." In sum, whether one grounds Peirce's metaphysics in his epistemology or his epistemology in his metaphysics, a version of James's "will to believe" seems to be a *necessary* ingredient.

NOTES

[1] *Collected Papers of Charles Sanders Peirce,* vols. 1-6, edited by Charles Hartshorne and Paul Weiss; vols. 7-8 edited by Arthur Burks (Cambridge: Harvard University Press, 1931-57). Vol. 5, paragraph 5.400. All paragraph references are to this edition.

[2] See Carl Hempel, "The Theoretician's Dilemma," *Minnesota Studies in the Philosophy of Science: Vol. II: Concepts, Theories, and the Mind-Body Problem,* ed. H. Feigl, M. Scriven, and G. Maxwell (Minneapolis: University of Minnesota Press, 1958), pp. 37-98.

[3] 5.406

[4] 5.453

[5] Ibid., *loc. cit.*

[6] For an analysis of the problems here, see Rudolph Carnap, "Testability and Meaning," *Philosophy of Science,* III (1936) pp. 420-68 and IV (1937) pp. 1-40.

[7] This same issue arises in other areas in Peirce's writings; e.g., in "critical common sense inquiry" vis-à-vis "scientific inquiry"; and in "existential doubt" vis-à-vis "hypothetical doubt." See 1.75-76; 5.394.

[8] 1.135ff.

[9] See 5.408

[10] 5.407

[11] For an excellent analysis of this issue in Peirce, see John Smith, "Charles S. Peirce: Community and Reality," in *Themes in American Philosophy* (New York: Harper Torchbooks, 1976), pp. 80-108.

[12] Arthur Burks, "Charles Sanders Peirce: Introduction," in *Classic American Philosophers,* ed. Max Fisch (New York: Appleton-Century-Crofts, Inc., 1951), p. 51.

[13] Ibid., *loc. cit.,* footnote

[14] 5.407

[15] 7.187

[16] 1.120

[17] Karl Popper, "Normal Science and Its Dangers," in *Criticism and the Growth of Knowledge,* ed. I. Lakatos and A. Musgrave (Cambridge: Cambridge University Press, 1970), p. 56.

[18] Thomas Kuhn, "Reflections on My Critics," in *Criticism and the Growth of Knowledge,* p. 232.

[19] Kuhn, "Logic of Discovery or Psychology of Research," in *Criticism and the Growth of Knowledge,* p. 6.

[20] Thomas Kuhn, *The Structure of Scientific Revolutions,* (Chicago: Phoenix Books, University of Chicago Press, 1962), p. 150.

[21] 5.430

[22] See 5.358-87.

[23] See 5.466

[24] 6.104

[25] 5.119

[26] See, for example, 5.212; 5.536.

[27] 6.101

[28] 6.295

[29] W. B. Gallie, *Peirce and Pragmatism* (New York: Dover Publications, Inc. 1966), p. 216.

[30] John E. Smith, *Purpose and Thought: The Meaning of Pragmatism* (New Haven: Yale University Press, 1978), pp. 54-55.

[31] Ibid., p. 55.

[32] This does not necessarily mean that Smith would accept the position advocated here.

E. F. Kaelin (essay date 1982)

SOURCE: "Reflections on Peirce's Aesthetics," in *The Monist,* Vol. 65, No. 2, April, 1982, pp. 143-55.

[*In the following excerpt, Kaelin defends Peirce's aesthetics as an uncredited source of modern critical theory.*]

I

The first thing to note about Peirce's semiotic aesthetics is that Peirce himself had very little to say about it. Two articles published in the *Journal of Asthetics and Art Criticism* are concerned with determining Peirce's views on aesthetic theory. The first was by Max Oliver Hocutt, in 1962, called "The Logical Foundations of Peirce's Aesthetics."[1] This article has something less than an auspicious start, however, since its first sentence reads, "There is a sense in which it might be said that Charles Peirce had no aesthetics."[2] And since that sentence is followed in the next paragraph with one of the flattest—or, if you prefer, deadest of metaphors, to wit:

> Probably the best single explanation of this fact is that Peirce was wedded to logic and knew her to be a satisfying spouse. A contented husband is, like any other husband, frequently distracted by

charming young things—but usually only for fleeting moments. Peirce was no exception.[3]

It is nothing less than a miracle that anyone interested in aesthetics would continue reading the article. If one's interest in Peirce is stronger than one's expectation of a graceful style, however, continued reading of the argument will discover the author's opinion that Peirce's few aesthetic fragments may be said to contain three suggestions for an aesthetic theory: first, that the art object is an icon; second, that the aesthetic value of an art icon is the harmony of its intrinsic qualities; and third, that the interpretant by which a viewer responds to the art icon is a feeling or emotion. Peirce's realism is also operative in showing the relationship between these three propositions. The iconicity of the art object establishes only its sign-character; the clue to reading this sign-character is as always in the interpretant, here a feeling (the subjective correlate of "objective" properties and qualities of the work of art); and when these phenomenally objective properties are verified by a continual replication of the emotional interpretant, the object is correctly called "beautiful."

The surprise of this account of Peirce's aesthetic theory is that it recognizes that iconicity does not imply mimesis: i.e., that it does not follow from an artwork's iconic sign-quality that it must represent an object of nature. That, as will be pointed out later, has been the bane of the second generation Peirceans. Since the object referred to by the icon need not exist, a work of art may be an icon without being a realistic rendition of a portion of the natural scene:

> There is nothing in Peirce's view of art to suggest that "realism" is the only legitimate or proper art technique. Since there need be no existential counterpart for the aesthetic icon, invidious comparisons of works of art with actual things are irrelevant. The work of art must be appreciated for the qualities it possesses itself.[4]

At this juncture in the argument, Hocutt finds not *one,* but *two* "objects" that might serve as designata for the iconic art sign: first, the particular set and arrangement of the qualities *intended by the artist;* and second, the essence of beauty, defined in a straightforward Platonic sense and interpreted below as kalos or harmony. If, however, there were only the first object, no viewer other than the painter could ever judge of the artwork's inconicity; and since the second serves as check on the arbitrary subjectivity of the artistic intention, there is hardly any need to refer to the first. Hence Peirce's aesthetic theory comes down to this:

> The aesthetically valuable object is a sign which "means" what it does in virtue of possessing the characteristics of its object. It is, in short, an icon. What the aesthetic icon represents is, speaking generally, an instance of *kalos,* that is, a certain complex of qualities which appears as a simple quality because of the internal relatedness of the members of the complex. The effect on an inter-

preter of an aesthetic sign is a feeling, or rather, a complex feeling having correspondence to the complex quality which is the object of the aesthetically valuable sign.[5]

As for the supposed relationship between "logic" and aesthetics, in one sense of the term, the narrower, in which "logic" means critical logic, that science depends upon aesthetics as a first to its third (as qualities are primary to facts and laws), while in the most general sense, logic as semiotic, aesthetic theory clearly depends upon it. Or in Peirce's own words, "obsistent logic" depends upon aesthetics, but aesthetics itself depends upon "originalian logic."

Ten years later C. M. Smith in an article entitled "The Aesthetics of C. S. Peirce,"[6] points out that the Peircean aesthetic is not limited to the application of sign-theory as a specialized version of originalian logic, but is rather referred to by Peirce as "an exact science," a "normative science," "a science of ideals of what is objectively admirable," etc. Given its Platonism, however, Peirce's normative science of aesthetics is neither new nor particularly enlightening. And although in his development of the theory of signs Peirce made a number of suggestions relative to aesthetics, that theory contains few explicit references to what a complete aesthetic theory would be like. We read, for example, that an aesthetics would have as its central feature an explicit concentration on the firstness of experience, and that art has a capacity for arresting or fixing qualities and feelings, as it exhibits them for contemplation. The theory of signs merely gives a way of interpreting the sign functions of works of art.

Smith is careful to spell out the relationship of Peirce's categories of experience (firstness, secondness, and thirdness) with respect to the three elements within a sign-function: sign, object, and interpretant. According to the first trichotomous division, a sign is, for the interpretant, either a qualisign, a sinsign, or a legisign, depending upon whether it is a quality, an actual existent, or a law. According to the second trichotomy, the ground of the relation determines signs to be icons (by virtue of a similarity), indices (by virtue of an existential connection), or symbols (as determined by the habit of association, and hence as exhibiting regularity and law). Finally, in the third trichotomy, the object of the sign is, for the interpretant, presented as a rheme (qualitative possibility), a dicisign (a sign of actual existence), or an argument (a sign of law, i.e., understood "to represent its Object in its character of sign"). If aesthetics is bound, as Peirce maintained, to the immediacy of firstness, it might be said that the aesthetic sign is a rhematic iconic qualisign, i.e., a quality, or a work of art under the aspect of its qualitative wholeness, serving as a sign of a distinct qualitative possibility by virtue of a similarity between the two. Such indeed is a simple icon.

But an icon denotes its object, whether that object is known to exist or not: "The mind noting the iconic nature of a sign is stirred to sensations analogous to those that would be the effect of the possible object, but it can become aware of this analogy only through the mediation of another sign, the interpretant or 'significate effect' of a sign."[7] Thus, Hocutt's warning against interpreting the iconicity of artworks as representational of actually existent objects is reinforced by this reading of Peirce's theory. Since, moreover, the significate effects of simple icons are the only vehicles of direct communication through signs [2:279], this claim often made for artworks seems founded in semiotic theory. And, on the other hand, although works of art usually make no truth claims, a close examination of their structures may lead the viewer of art to otherwise ordinarily hidden truths concerning their objects. This is the aspect of the sign-situation that led Suzanne K. Langer to develop her theory of the art object as "a symbol" of a pattern of sentience, a form of insight into man's capacity to feel.[8]

But besides the simple icon, there are other icons, of the second and third categories: iconic sinsigns, or diagrams, having a structural similarity with their objects, e.g., the schematic of an electrical circuit as a diagram of the actual circuit; and iconic legisigns, which function as general laws or types for innumerable tokens, each of which is a sinsign of a particular kind, as, for example, the "model" of a year's production is reproduced in each automobile of a given series. Within aesthetics, the design model of a multiple-original medium like graphic printmaking may also serve as an example here.

According to still another division of icons, Peirce refers to a different triad: hypoicons, i.e., "any material image, such as a painting . . . in itself, without legend or label . . . ," [2:276] diagrams, and metaphors. If the hypoicon is the firstness of a first (a simple qualitative similarity), it may be called an image; but those which represent the relations, mainly dyadic, of the parts of a thing by virtue of similar relations in its own structure are *diagrams,* while icons illustrating the thirdness of a first, i.e., those which "represent the representative character of a representamen by representing a parallelism in something else" [2.277] are *metaphors.* Smith points out how a "tension" as the funded quality of two component qualities (let us say, the "pull" felt to exist between adjacent planes of complementary colors) may be considered an example of "the first degree of genuine thirdness" in that one quality mediates between two others. A metaphor may indeed be interpreted as representing this representative character of the tense triad of quality being taken as equivalent to a similar tension observed in another medium; perhaps even, says Smith, in the human psyche.[9]

Can this somewhat dense typological schema be applied to other "aesthetic" phenomena? Surely, claims Smith, it might serve as a guide to understanding the various interpretations given to works of art. For example, if a portrait has a name or a legend attached to it, it is an indexical rather than an iconic sign because it would stand for its object through the nameplate. Without the legend, however, the portrait would serve as an iconic sinsign, referring to the person represented in the portrait by virtue of similar physiognomic characteristics. Unfortunately for both a coherent aesthetic theory and for the aesthetic interpretation of Peirce's semiotic, the iconicity of the work of art was mostly interpreted to be of this variety. But as Hocutt had already noticed, the object of an icon need not exist, and some "portraits" may be of fictional characters, such as Paul Bunyan or Mary Poppins, whose physical characteristics are known through descriptions in other media. Such icons would still be iconic sinsigns. Next, if the painting is to be reproduced by lithographic or any other means it would then become an iconic legisign, determining what properties the "copies" of the original must possess in order to be replicas of the original.

But that is not all. Everything depends upon how the painting is attended to. If one views the total effect of the component qualities as itself a single quality, and that quality is perceived as, say, "strength," then the emotional interpretant of the image would be the same or similar to the significate effect of any other object exhibiting the same kind of strength. Lastly, if the lines and brush strokes of a given sensuous surface are perceived as "crude," stark, or powerful, they may themselves be taken as metaphors of the crudity, starkness or power of the subject they represent; and if they are, as in the case of Picasso's *Guernica* analyzed below, they are taken as a metaphor.[10] Thus, in Smith's account, there are as many interpretants as there are ways to view the phenomenal structures of a painting, and one would be misadvised to look for a single interpretant which would define necessary and sufficient properties of "works of art."

Between Hocutt, writing in 1962, and Smith, in 1972, for the same journal, the one finding the sketch of an aesthetic theory and the other, only a system for classifying the various ways works of visual art may be interpreted as signs, what is there to be chosen? Perhaps an answer may be found for this question if we consider the aesthetic writings of Peirce's followers and their critics—a task projected for the next section of this article.

II

The first of the second generation Peircean accounts of aesthetic experiences was given by Charles Morris, working, in 1939, within the tradition of the "unified science" movement.[11] The advantage of his application of the Peircean account, he thought, was the possibility of unifying science through the general theory of signs. As phenomena of firstness, and of the immediate communication of feelings, art works would best be interpreted as icons, much as has been explained for Hocutt's and Smith's account of Peirce's own theory. Morris was aware, however, that an icon may have an object that does not necessarily exist, and hence distinguished between the "denotata" and "designata" of the iconic sign;

both these terms were applied to the object referred to by the sign. What Morris added to the Peircean account was the notion of a sign-vehicle, to replace Peirce's notion of a representamen. This substitution allowed for the interpretation of a sign or, as Morris said, of sign-situations in terms of a sign-vehicle, that object which served as sign, its designata, and the interpretant.

Since works of art were, for the most part, composite signs made up of other signs, there were three dimensions of sign analysis pertinent to works of art: the relation within the sign vehicle of component signs to each other (syntactics); that between the sign-vehicle and its designatum (semantics); and that between the sign-vehicle and its interpretant (pragmatics). Although these designations are themselves only rough metaphors for various ways of reading the aesthetic sign's significance, they do correspond to three conventional interpretations of an artwork's functioning in human experience; or, if you prefer, to three different putative definitions of the working of a work of art. Formalistic aestheticians emphasize the "syntactical dimension" of an aesthetic sign's constitution; and mimetic aesthetic theorists have always emphasized the "semantic dimensions," while expressionists have found the "pragmatic dimension" the most illuminating of an artwork's characteristics for developing an aesthetic theory.

The difficulty in these analyses was to find a counter or candidate for the "semantic dimension" in obviously nonrepresentational works. This, I take it, was the crux of the debate; and it rests upon a serious mistake. For instead of assuming that nonrepresentational works constitute the limiting or boundary concept of the ideal of mimesis, the debate should have centered around the propriety of considering the iconicity of apparently pictorial art as the end or value of that form of expression. There shall be more about where the debate should have been centered later. It suffices for the moment to consider the way in which nonrepresentational works were interpreted as the limiting cases of an artwork's "iconicity."

The only modification necessary to understand Morris's use of Peircean semiotics is that "sign" has been replaced by "sign-vehicle" and that the object of a sign-vehicle may be either a designatum or a denotatum, the latter being a designatum that actually exists. A realistic scene or portrait would then have both a designatum and denotatum, whereas a scene or portrait of a purely imaginary entity or person would have only a designatum. Whichever, the (artwork) sign would have a "semantic dimension." Other works of art would seem, on the surface of the matter, to lack this dimension entirely, leaving the expressiveness of the work to be determined solely by its "syntactic dimension"; but Morris always refused to make this step with the formalistic aestheticians. His assumption is as follows: "every iconic sign has its own sign-vehicle among its denotata," and "there is sometimes no denotatum other than the aesthetic sign vehicle itself.[12] When this occurs the artwork as sign vehicle may be described as the funded quality of component qualities, and its denotatum would be the "value" of this quality as a possibility (i.e., its rheme is a possible value), actually known by the significate effect in the interpretant. In this way, even so-called nonobjective works of art may fulfill the threefold conditions for being a sign.

Although Morris's account of the semiotics of artworks influenced generations of students at the University of Chicago, it came under the stringent criticism of Richard Rudner (1951) and Charles L. Stevenson (1958).

Rudner's account is the easiest to dispense with.[13] He claimed that any theory of aesthetic value which maintained that it was both immediately experienced and at the same time mediated by a sign was manifestly inconsistent. The argument was general, aimed at Suzanne K. Langer's theory of art symbolism, as well as Morris's and all others that interpreted an artwork to be a sign.

The source of Rudner's confusion was his interpretation of immediacy as the experience of "any object valued in and for itself," which I can only take to mean "valued for its intrinsic properties." The confusion is so simple any reader of Hegel would have caught it straightaway. Immediacy is a predicate applying in the first instance to consciousness intending an object, not to the object or its values. It is only on reflection that consciousness discovers its mediated components, an ego and its objects. If Rudner had attended to the growing development of the Hegelian phenomenology, it would have been no mystery how the object of an immediately-felt consciousness "dirempts" into its two component parts, and then returns to itself in a new state of conscious immediacy following the diremption. Farfetched? Not at all. If one were to look for an historical precedent to Peirce's theory of "transuasion," no clearer model than the Hegelian movement from simple consciousness to consciousness mediated by its object and the return to a more complicated form of immediacy could be found. Indeed any object considered in itself fulfills the role of the sign-vehicle; in relationship to our consciousness of it, it exists for us, as an object of our intending (of a significant function); and the two stages are mediated by our future awareness of them as being a new object for consciousness, now in- and for-itself. When this future awareness has been fulfilled, we will have achieved a new status of immediacy, and the dialectic may continue.

C. M. Smith registers basically the same complaint against Rudner, pointing out that surely Peirce did maintain that artworks were icons, therefore signs and the objects of a mediated experience. What Rudner forgot is that an icon is a degenerate sign; that its meaning is confined to category the first. Such a sign (or an object so interpreted) states no facts, indicates no laws. And since it does not involve any thinking in the ordinary sense of this term, it may be said to have the immediate impact it does.[14] The secret is in the interpretation of the interpretant; and if we refuse Morris's own idiosyncratic interpretation of the iconic sign's denotatum, we should still be able to feel the tension between our perception of the artwork's sensuous surface and the conception of any mimetic elements found in its "depth" when the work is conventionally representational, or to feel the tensions of the component qualities of that surface if it contains no depth. All feelings are immediately felt, and some of them are interpretants.

Smith puts this last point in a slightly different way. He claims that there is only one interpretant for the entire significant relation, whether the sign itself be a quality, an existent entity, or a general law, and whether the object of that sign is a rheme, a dicisign, or argument; and that interpretant is the object of an immediate awareness once the relationship has been established between the sign and its object. Rudner, in a word, was guilty of trying to deduce possible aesthetic responses—or to eliminate impossible ones on the basis of a deduction, instead of reporting on his actual responses one by one, as they occurred.

Charles Stevenson's argument takes Morris to task for a number of reasons, most of which will likewise be found to be irrelevant.[15] Like Rudner, Stevenson throws in Langer's theory as another "symbolic theory" incapable of fulfilling the conditions of symbolism in the nonrepresentational arts. Once again we are faced immediately with the assumption that the iconicity of a representational work is paradigmatic, while nonrepresentational works are the theoretical "hard cases" straining the general theory's credibility. I have already indicated that this assumption is wrongheaded, and shall try to explain myself more fully in the last section of this article.

Stevenson does have the good sense to direct his arguments against the specific theories of Morris and Langer, rather than attempting to refute all aesthetic theories of the semiotic type; and I am still interested in Morris only, as the first and most influential Peircean. Morris, it is alleged by Stevenson, uses the term "sign-situation" so broadly that nothing of which we can become aware can fail to define a sign-situation. This would have come as a surprise to both Morris and Peirce, not because what is alleged is false, but because that is what both of them had precisely maintained. Nothing is brought to awareness without the mediacy of some sign. Why is this stated as a criticism of Peirce's and Morris's aesthetic theories, if indeed it is a fact of consciousness? If we attend to the three specific corollaries of this general remark perhaps we shall be led to understand.

First, Morris had noted that certain parts of largely complex signs set up expectations for a kind of fulfillment in other parts of the same complex sign. Why, asks Stevenson, should the initial perception be said to be a sign of eventual fulfillment? Answer: the phenomenon in question takes place at the level of the "syntactic dimension" of the signifying icon. The allegation is not made that any leading motif must resemble its anticipated resolution, but only that both in their relationship constitute a sign-vehicle whose designatum is a possible feeling (a rheme), and that the connection between this sign-vehicle and this rheme is established by the significate effect of their relationship: it is felt, in the interpretant, as a feeling. Stevenson's remark, that noting the relationship between leading motif and anticipated resolution is so "elementary" that calling it "symbolic" adds nothing to its significance,[16] must be suspect since he does not deny such relationships exist, and whether they may be truly symbolic is precisely the point mooted in his article. This latter point, then, may not be so summarily disregarded without begging the question.

His second specific quarrel is with the possibility of a sign-vehicle's having its own properties as one of its denotata. Morris introduced his notion, we remember, in order to show how a work of nonobjective art may be said to denote its own values, since values (by Morris as well as by Peirce) were thought to be properties of objects. What sticks in Stevenson's craw here is the "oddity" of the claim that something may represent itself. Don't all things resemble themselves? Why are all things then not works of art? The question is ignorant, since it abstracts from the felt qualities of the interpretant, and from the limiting firstness of aesthetic signs. All things that may be contemplated may have their aesthetic qualities, to be sure; but if they do, and there is no element of representation either of an existent thing or of a general law, then the object of that sign-relation will be a rhematic possibility. And there is no absurdity involved in stating that a complex iconic sign denotes the possibility of a subjectively-felt value precisely because the interpretant registers the feeling of that value.

Stevenson's third objection may be answered in the same way. He claims that the Peircean semiotic aesthetic (as worked out by Morris) suffers from a certain lack of specificity in the definition of the "aesthetic" interpretant, since aesthetic signs are all considered icons yet may be considered under specific circumstances as having other signific functions, say as an index or a symbol. It is of course, true that artworks may be both indices and symbols in the Peircean sense (I shall treat of that later), but if it is agreed that aesthetic value is a matter of firstness, and in its paradigmatic form of the firstness of a first, then we need not speak to the question of "the" aesthetic interpretant; any interpretant would be aesthetic which had the requisite sign-status. Certainly there is no implication that all aesthetic signs have the same interpretant; that would be absurd. Interpretants merely follow the properties of the sign. The question, posed by Stevenson, concerning the relation between the icon and its denotatum must be answered by our experiencing some kind of interpretant. The sign-vehicle possesses qualities external to the interpreting mind; its denotatum, as a mere possibility, is likewise external to any particular mind; the interpretant which notes the iconic relation between the two is an internal structure of the mind intending the sign for its values.

From my own reading of all three—Morris, Rudner, and Stevenson—I can only marvel at the effect of the latter two's criticisms. From 1951 (Rudner) and 1958 (Stevenson) to 1962 (Hocutt) and still later to 1972 (Smith), the Peircean semiotic aesthetic was thought to be dead for lack of support. True, there were in the interim few proponents of the theory, but philosophers had by then gotten out of the habit of reading Peirce's seminal work on the subject. In what follows I shall attempt to relate what I have learnt about aesthetics from reading Peirce's semiotics. If Rudner and Stevenson may be fairly said to have forgotten the interpretants of particular works of art, rereading Peirce may help us rediscover them.

III

I have in the foregoing sections of this article been concentrating on the Peircean semiotic theory as itself constituting a phenomenon of recent aesthetics. That it should have been relatively unknown even after the first publication of the **Collected Papers** comes as no surprise: Peirce's early reputation had been made as a scientist, philosopher of science, and logician, and the prejudice had it that such people are not supposed to be interested in aesthetics. Moreover, Peirce's writings contained only the barest suggestions for an aesthetic theory. It was Charles Morris's interest in the unity of science movement that led to the full scale development of a "Peircean" aesthetic, and after its formulation in 1937-38 it enjoyed a considerable vogue before becoming the object of criticism by analytical philosophers.

In the meantime, however, Suzanne K. Langer had developed her special theory of musical expressiveness (1942)[17] and the general theory of aesthetic expressiveness (1953)[18] based upon her interpretation of an artwork's "symbolic" functioning. Although there was a difference in Morris's and Langer's theory of symbolism (in Morris, the sign-vehicle was the physical artifact itself; in Langer's the phenomenal or "virtual" object served as a symbol of human feeling), the ground for the sign (or symbol) relation in both was similarity of structure in the sign and its object.

The widespread popularity of Langer's account led to the conception of "semiotic" theories of aesthetics as those which impute the sign-function to works of art. Rudner's criticism and, seven years later, those of Stevenson succeeded in bringing about the demise of interest in semiotic theory until 1962, when Hocutt in particular pointed out the logical foundations of Peirce's aesthetics. Ten years later C. M. Smith laid the groundwork for evaluating the degree to which Charles Morris had assimilated and that to which he had modified Peirce's original suggestions. In the foregoing I have treated this historical phenomenon as a series of modu-

lations upon the theme of human consciousness intending what Peirce called "the interpretant."

Most recently J. Jay Zeman (1977) took up the theme of the aesthetic sign in Peirce's semiotic,[19] but was inclined to fill in the "missing elements" of the Peircean aesthetics by appealing to analogous structures in the aesthetic theory of John Dewey.

What have I learnt from personally observing this phenomenon? First of all, that semiotic may be used as a tool for interpreting responses to works of art, and that the iconicity of a painting is not the only ground for the relationship of significance between the painting and its denotatum or designatum. Philosophers of art have most often focused on that property of paintings, but not always with an eminent degree of success. Art historians are often prone to accept the artifact as an index, i.e., an existent thing referring to the artist or to the physical process by which the artist made the artifact. The critical term "action painting," introduced into recent art history by Harold Rosenberg, illustrates an indexical reading of painting as a true symbol, as a sign of a general style, of the functioning of socio-economic or political conditions, or the national character of its maker, etc. Indeed, the very same painting may be interpreted in any of these ways.

Picasso's *Guernica,* for example, may be considered aesthetically as an icon, not of the real scene of destruction that took place during that day of the Spanish Civil War (26 April 1937), but the author's vivid imagination of that scene, rendered in stark and forceful clash of broken lines and forms, all enhanced by the extreme contrast of color limited to a single dimension, its value. As such, the painting may be experienced as the rhematic iconic qualisign it is: the object of the sign (its denotatum, per Morris) is a determinate possibility, this feeling of horror and outrage; the sign-vehicle, this organization of visual counters; the interpretant, our feeling the horror. And as Morris had correctly pointed out, there is no oddity in supposing the "same" thing to be a sign of itself in an important way, as long as one distinguishes between the features of the thing qua signifying and those of the thing qua signified.

Aestheticians get themselves in trouble only when a second degree of iconicity is discerned within the same painting, as when they point out that an imagined scene of an actual war is depicted within *Guernica.* There is nothing either wrong or wrongheaded about the same sign's possessing two denotata, even when the ground of the sign-relation is iconicity. Nothing necessitates that the structure of an icon correspond in a one-to-one relationship with the structure of its object. One subset of its properties may be analogous to one kind of object, while another subset may be analogous to still another at the same time. This is what happens in our phenomenal attention to paintings like *Guernica,* containing both "surface" and "depth" elements. The painting may depict a real event, but that event must be reduced to its visual and affective aspects to become a part of a visual work of art. The surface properties govern surface expressiveness; the depth properties (reduced to visual characteristics) govern a similar depth expressiveness. In our experience of such paintings, therefore, one set of expressive qualities reinforces the other: the work is still a rhematic iconic qualisign, for the harmonious strata of surface and depth expressiveness is itself felt as a quality, the interpretant mediating the painting perceived as a stratified quality and the determinate possibility of this same quality as a constituent feature of a possible world. Plato, of course, would have called this feature an "eidos," and contemporary phenomenologists, a "purely intentional object," but to speak in this way is to open an ontological question too long to be answered here. It is better perhaps to follow the lead of the painter, and to respond to his painting as an "arrangement in grey and black," rather than as a portrait of his mother. He, of course, had a mother; but no one except perhaps Whistler himself and his mother should care how she looked while sitting in her rocking chair.

When it was said in the earlier sections of this article that the question of a painting's representationality or nonrepresentationality has been a red herring in recent aesthetic debate, the reason was this: the problematic case of iconicity is not a nonrepresentational painting (as Stevenson tried to show), but the representational, since the temptation is to interpret such paintings as dicisigns, i.e., as making a statement about an existent object in our actual world. Cultural historians do this all the time, but then no one has ever accused a cultural historian of being an aesthetician; nor an aesthetician of being a cultural historian, although this latter possibility has brighter prospects than the former. And the reason for this is that each treats the same aesthetic objects from the point of view of different interpretants. Let it just be restated that in one of the senses of the terms involved aesthetics is, for Peirce, a necessary condition for a complete logic. Therefore, for a cultural historian to give a complete picture of this or any other epoch, he must refer ultimately to the distinctive qualities of human experience that serve as firsts to the seconds of his observations; and what is true of the objects of his signs is true of the sign-vehicles themselves.

Professor C. M. Smith has already pointed out how the same "sign" could be interpreted as a sinsign of a legisign; and if we relax the criterion of firstness for the designata of aesthetic signs, it is likewise clear that their "object" may be dicisigns or arguments. Literary works, of course, are constructed in part with dicisigns and contain many arguments; but on this matter it is most probably safer to agree with Ingarden that the statements of a literary work comport only "pseudo-judgments" and that any argument composed of pseudo-judgments can only have a pseudo-conclusion: i.e., there is no way to judge of the purported truth of a conclusion if that truth depends upon statements which are themselves not discernably true. It is for this reason that it is logically odd to claim that works of art may bear a truth value or that they demonstrate either probably or conclusively that anything whatever is true in our actually existent world. Nothing will prevent the attempt to treat works of art as a statement or an argument, but it seems apparent that all such attempts in making abstraction of the firstness of experience likewise make abstraction of anything's aesthetic qualities. That in the end is why cultural historians make poor aestheticians.

In summary, although Peirce's semiotic gives a ready system for classifying art objects, it does not give us a single clue as to how an aesthetic sign (either as a quality or an existent object—a qualisign or a sinsign) is to be described in concrete fact. That still depends upon our experience of such signs, our reflections upon them, and our ability to describe the objects of our reflection: in a word, upon a successful application of the phenomenological epoché, wherein the firstness of a first is most clearly apparent to us. Or, as Peirce would put it, we shall have to learn or relearn how to pay closer attention to the *phanerons* of our minds in order reflectively to interpret the interpretants of our aesthetic signs. This latter activity, of course, is the business of aesthetic theory; but the theory of the interpretant had become all but extinct only because aestheticians had in the first instance lost the technique of scanning their phanerons. A thorough dosage of phenomenology may help us to regain this technique. A course in phaneroscopy, anyone?

NOTES

* Read before the Edgar Henderson Memorial Symposium on The Philosophy of Charles S. Peirce, 17 May, 1980.

N.B.: All references to Peirce's *Collected Papers* are given in the conventional manner, by volume and paragraph, within the text itself.

¹ *Journal of Aesthetics and Art Criticism,* 21 (Winter, 1962): 157-66.

² Ibid., p. 157.

³ Ibid.

⁴ Ibid., p. 159.

⁵ Ibid., p. 165.

⁶ *Journal of Aesthetics and Art Criticism,* 31 (Fall 1972): 21-29.

⁷ Ibid., p. 25.

⁸ Cf. her *Philosophy in a New Key* (New York: Penguin Books, 1948), original, 1942; and *Feeling and Form* (New York: Scribner's Sons, 1953).

⁹ Smith, "The Aesthetics of C. S. Peirce," p. 26.

[10] Ibid.

[11] See his "Aesthetics and the Theory of Signs," *The Journal of Unified Science,* 8 (June, 1939): 131-50.

[12] Ibid., pp. 136, 131.

[13] "On Semiotic Aesthetics," reprinted from the *JAAC* in *Aesthetic Inquiry,* ed. Monroe Beardsley and Herbert Schueller (Belmont, CA: Dickenson Publishing Co., 1967), 93-102.

[14] Smith, "The Aesthetics of C. S. Peirce," p. 28.

[15] "Symbolism in the Nonrepresentational Arts," in *Introductory Readings in Aesthetics,* ed. John Hospers (New York: The Free Press, 1969), 185-210.

[16] Ibid., p. 188.

[17] See her *Philosophy in a New Key.*

[18] See her *Feeling and Form.*

[19] J. Jay Zeman, "The Esthetic Sign in Peirce's Semiotic," *Semiotica,* 19 (1977): 241-58.

Sandra B. Rosenthal (essay date 1982)

SOURCE: "Meaning as Habit: Some Systematic Implications of Peirce's Pragmatism," in *The Monist,* Vol. 65, No. 2, April, 1982, pp. 230-45.

[*In the following excerpt, Rosenthal concludes that Peirce's pragmatism is founded on sound ontological and epistemological thinking.*]

Peirce's pragmatic stress on meaning in terms of habits of response is, of course, well known.[1] However, the language in which it is usually expressed tends too often to conflate its epistemic and ontological dimensions,[2] thereby hiding from view its full systematic significance. The following discussion will focus on the emergence of such meanings as epistemic relational structures which embody the characteristics of the dynamics of organism-environment interaction in their very internal structure and which lead outward toward the universe, providing an experienced content which is at once epistemic and ontological.

For Peirce, meanings are to be understood as logical structures,[3] not as psychological or biological facts. Peirce does not want to give meaning an existence independent of purpose, yet he does not want to reduce meaning to the categories of psychology or biology.[4] Meanings are to be understood, for Peirce, as relational structures emerging from behavioral patterns, as emerging from the lived through response of the human organism to that universe with which it is in interaction. Or, in other terms, human behavior is meaningful be-

havior, and it is in behavior that the relational patterns which constitute conceptual meaning are rooted. What, however, is meaning as a relational pattern? A purely relational pattern devoid of sensuous criteria of recognition would be a pattern of relationships relating nothing that had reference to the world, while a pure datum, devoid of the relational pattern, could not be an object of thought. Indeed, for Peirce, sensuous recognition and conceptual interpretation represent two ends of a continuum rather than an absolute difference in kind. His view that sensuous recognition involves interpretive aspects, in some yet to be determined sense, is fairly clear cut and can be found in his view that there are no first impressions of sense.[5] However, Peirce's view that conceptualization requires imagery is open to some confusion. He states that "I will go so far as to say that we have no images even in actual perception." Yet, he objects to Kant, not because Kant requires a schema for the application of a concept to experience, but because he separates the schema from the concept, failing to recognize that a schema for the application of a concept to the data of experience is as general as the concept.[6] And, if the schema is to allow for the application of a concept to sense experience, then imagery, in some sense at least, would seem to be required.

The resolution of this difficulty lies in the definition of image which Peirce so emphatically rejects in the former statement, that is, the definition of image as an absolutely singular representation, a representation absolutely determinate in all respects.[7] Thus, Peirce accepts imagery as part of conceptual meaning, but refuses to equate such imagery with determinate, singular, representation. In the schematic aspects of conceptual meaning, then, there would seem to be found the inseparable mingling of the sensuous and the relational as the vehicle by which we think about and recognize objects in the world. It is to the relation between habit and schematic structure that the ensuing discussion will turn.

Such a relation emerges only in unifying Peirce's unsystematic analyses found scattered throughout his writings, for Peirce did not explicitly recognize until late in his career that in addition to his carefully worked out logical analysis of the sign process, or relation between representamen, interpretant, and object, his philosophy required a similarly worked out logical analysis of the internal structure of the concept or logical interpretant.[8] Peirce thus came to recognize that conceptual meaning must include within itself the emotional, energetic and logical interpretants. Or, in other terms, it must include the elements of Firstness, Secondness, and Thirdness found, in some form, in all analyses, in this case: Firstness as feeling core or sensuous content; Secondness as response or set of acts; and Thirdness as structure or resultant image.[9] Imagery, then, as part of the internal structure of meaning, is inseparably connected with sense content as Firstness and pattern of reaction as Secondness. As Peirce observes, "To predicate a concept of a real or imaginary object is equivalent to declaring that a certain operation, corresponding to the concept, if performed upon that object would . . . be followed by a result of a definite general description."[10] Or, in other terms, "How otherwise can a habit be described than by a description of the kind of action to which it gives rise, with the specification of the conditions and the motive?"[11]

Here it should be noted that it is habit which gives rise to certain kinds of action in the presence of certain kinds of conditions to yield certain kinds of results. And, if the act is dependent upon the condition or sensory content, then different sensory cues will give rise to different acts. Thus, there is not one act but an indefinite number of acts corresponding to an indefinite number of possible sensory conditions. For example, varying perspectives yield varying appearances and hence varying resulting acts. Indeed, even if one considers only one essential property, so that the application of a physical object meaning is determined solely by the presence of one property, there is the possibility of an unlimited number of possible conditions and resultant acts. Yet, this indefinite number radiates from one intended objectivity. Precisely what it means to apprehend an object or objective structure rather than an appearance only is to have "filled in" the result of a particular act with the results of other possible acts given other possible cues. Thus, in a sense there are an indefinite number of cues, acts, and resulting appearances. Yet, in another sense, though there are an indefinite number of possibilities they are all "part of" the one result, an objectivity having certain characteristics. The difference between an apprehended appearance and an apprehended object for Peirce is precisely this difference in levels of meaning organization.[12]

Thus, if we are to meaningfully assert the existence of physical objects, or in other terms, to perceive a world of objectivities, then there must be, in addition to sensory cue, act, and further sensory appearance, that which binds into a system the set of possibilities which as a system give rise to the resultant objective structure. Here it is necessary to distinguish between the logical interpretant or resultant structure, and the ultimate logical interpretant as the living habit which binds together into a systematic unity the various possibilities, thus making the logical interpretant possible. It is habit which binds into a system the set of possible conditions and possible acts which as a system gives rise to the objective structure. As Peirce states, "to say that mental phenomena are governed by law" means that "there is a living idea" which pervades mental phenomena.[13] Further, habit does more than unify three pre-existent elements. Only as habit performs its function of unifying sensory conditions and reactions does structure emerge at all. As Peirce notes, "the general idea is the *mark* of the habit."[14] And, perhaps even more significant, it is habit which determines reaction, and it is reaction which partially determines the nature of the sensory cue. Thus, it is habit, ultimately, which partially determines the nature of the sensory cue. As Peirce stresses, "Feeling which has not yet emerged into immediate con-

sciousness is already affectible and already affected. In fact, this is habit . . ."[15] Or, in other terms, "Thus, the sensation, so far as it represents something, is determined, according to logical law, by previous cognitions; that is to say, these cognitions determine that there shall be a sensation."[16]

Peirce's position can perhaps best be clarified by taking the term 'image' as 'aspect'. For example, one may say, quite correctly, that an ocean presents a turbulent image or aspect. And, while the specific empirical content of experience is best understood as one particular among many, the image of the schema for the application of a living habit to experience is best understood as the one which determines the many. Indeed, the importance of the content of the image of the schema lies in the way in which it comes into being. Such an image represents an aspect of the dispositional structural order by which it is regulated, whether the resultant image is taken at the level of appearance or of objectivity. Such an image as representing an aspect of an ordering cannot be reduced to the content of any experience, whether imagined or actual. Rather, it represents principles or possibilities in terms of which sensory content can emerge within experience.

An examination of the internal dynamics of the meanings by which objects come to conscious awareness indicates that habits are partially constitutive of immediate perceptual experience. Pure "feeling core" or pure Firstness or pure "sense content" is "there" in experience as the logically or epistemically final basis and ultimate referent for all cognitive activity. In this sense it is epistemically primitive. Further, such a "feeling core" held apart from particular experiences must be "there" as part of the image if concepts are to be applicable to experience. But, such a core is precisely the sensuous core of the schematic image, and as such partakes of the generality of the image. Neither the image nor its sensuous core can be apprehended independently of the structural orderings of habit, for their character is partially determined by the generative functioning of habit. Habit is thus the living meaning which generates acts of response in relation to criteria for grasping the situations in terms of which such activity is appropriate. And, since these meanings are constitutive of perceptual experience, both the world of perceptual objectivities and the supposed "immediate" grasp of "pure" appearance is shot through with the structural orderings of habitual modes of response. In brief, all perceptual experience is shot through with the relationship between human action and apprehended content, for such felt dispositions and tendencies to act enter into the very tone and structure of any experienced content. Thus, meanings emerge from organism-environment interaction as precise relational structures unified by habit as a rule of generation and organization, and they contain activity and temporal reference in the very heart of their logical structure. Such meanings are not reducible to the biological only, for what habit binds together into a unity is a triadic relation of factors emerging from organism-environment interaction, a triadic sign relation through which a perceptual world gives itself to conscious awareness.

Because of the epistemic dimensions of habit, then, the grasp of experienced "immediacies" cannot be divorced from the structures of objectivity, for the character of the immediacies is generated by the dispositional structural orderings which yield objectivities. "We are, of course directly aware of positive sense qualities in the percept (although in the percept they are in no wise separate from the whole object)."[17] And, just as it can be said that habit yields qualities as appearances of objectivities, "So when feeling emerges into immediate consciousness, it always appears as a modification of a more or less general object already in the mind."[18] Because of the function of habit, appearances emerge for conscious awareness only within a world of appearing objects. They are not the historic originals for the construction of objects.

The apprehension of appearance, obtained by reflective abstraction from the world of perceptual objects, is important within Peirce's pragmatic understanding of verification, for verification is not just a temporal linear affair but rather includes logical or epistemic levels. Grasp of appearance is the most fundamental level for verification in experience in the sense that it is that level most devoid of interpretive elements and, as indicating the way a thing appears as opposed to the way a thing is, is itself devoid of future reference. Indeed, this level is most devoid of interpretive elements precisely in the sense that reference to future experience contained in assertions of objectivity is withheld. In a certain sense, however, interpretation is very much in evidence, since the appearance obtained by a change of focus or abstractive attention reflects, in the very structure of its appearance, that context of objectivity which one is attempting to withhold. In this way, the appearances of the intended object serve as the verification of what is meant. Thus, while the ontological dimensions of habit lead to the expression of the validity or appropriateness of meanings in terms of the ongoing conduct of the biological organism emersed in a natural world, the epistemic dimensions of habit lead to their expression in terms of the phenomenological description of the appearance of what is meant.

It is the epistemic dimension of meaning in terms of habit which provides, further, the source of a sense of the concrete unity of objectivity as more than a collection of appearances. Just as a continuum may generate an unlimited number of cuts within itself, so a disposition as a rule of organization and generation contains within itself an unlimited number of possibilities of specific acts to be generated. As Peirce states, "a true continuum is something whose possibilities of determination no multitude of individuals can exhaust," while a habit or general idea is a living feeling, infinitesimal in duration and immediately present, but still embracing innumerable parts.[19] That such an objective concreteness

which transcends any indefinite number of appearances is built into our very sense of objectivity is evinced in Peirce's description of habit as the "living continuum" indicated above. In such an "absence of boundedness a vague possibility of more than is present is directly felt."[20] Or, as he emphasizes, a pragmatist must subscribe to the doctrine of real possibility because nothing other than this can be so much as meant by saying that an object possesses a character.[21] Habit, then, is the source of our sense of a reality of physical objectivities whose possibilities of being experienced transcend, in their very nature, the experiences in which they appear.

Thus, the conceiving mind cannot, by the very nature of meaning, be tied down to a consciousness which apprehends actualities only, for the implicit content of our concepts includes meaningful assertions about potentialities which reach out beyond that which will ever be actualized. Embodied in the actuality of our conceptual structures as dispositional, then, is a sense of a reality which transcends actual occasions of experience.

Such an understanding of meaning leads directly to process, for if one tries to reduce the process of lived time to a series of knife-edged moments, one has taken away the basis for the primitive epistemological "feel" of continuity. And, in doing this, one has ruled out of court the very possibility of the functioning of meaning as dispositional, and hence has ruled out of court the basis for a primitive epistemological "feel" of real potentialities. "There is no span of present time so short as not to contain . . . something for the confirmation of which we are waiting."[22] But this "peculiar element of the present, that it confronts us with ideas which it forces upon us . . . is something which accumulates in wholes of time and dissipates the more minutely the course of time is scrutinized."[23] Thus, such a structure of meaning grounds in lived experience a primordial grasp of time as process. What occurs within the present awareness is not the apprehension of a discrete datum in a moment of time, but rather the time-extended experiential "feel" within the passing present of a readiness to respond to more than can ever be specified. This "feel" provides the experiential basis for the meaningfulness of a process metaphysics.

Further, the dispositional theory of meaning leads to a metaphysics of realism as opposed to a nominalism, a realism not of eternal essences but a "process realism" in which there are real modes of behavior which govern what occurs. Laws cannot be understood as some shorthand for what occurs. Laws, which outrun any number of actualities are, as modes of behavior, the source of the structures emerging in what occurs. Man's habits of response are precisely lawful modes of behavior structuring emerging activities. Here, in Peirce's pragmatic understanding of meaning in terms of habit, the answer to the problem of the meaningfulness of his realism is to be found, for a disposition or habit as a rule of generation is something whose possibilities of determination no multitude of actually generated instances can exhaust. It is the awareness of habit as a disposition or readiness to respond to more than can be specified which gives a concrete meaning to the concept of a "process realism," of a real lawfulness which governs unactualized possibilities. Thus, the meaning of the potentialities or dynamic tendencies which are held to characterize the real is to be found in the awareness of the actuality of habit as that which can never be exhausted by any number of exemplifications.

Finally, the sense of unactualized possibilities embedded in meaning as dispositional brings a sense of real alternatives—they could do otherwise—into the very heart of perceptual awareness, providing an experientially meaningful basis for the rejection of deterministic hypotheses, and a directly felt sense of the spontaneous, of the pure possibilities of a nondeterministic universe. Thus, the pervasive features of the epistemic dimension of meaning as habit lead to a sense of the pervasive textures of the independently real. As Peirce observes:

> Suffice it to say once more that pragmatism is, in itself, no doctrine of metaphysics, no attempt to determine any truth of things. It is merely a method of ascertaining the meanings of hard words and of abstract concepts. All pragmatists of whatever stripe will cordially assent to that statement. *As to the ulterior and indirect effects of practising the pragmatistic method, that is quite another affair* . . . [24]

Such effects are well evidenced in Peirce's claim that:

> There are certain questions commonly reckoned as metaphysical, and which certainly are so, if by metaphysics we mean ontology, which as soon as pragmatism is once sincerely accepted, cannot logically resist settlement. These are for example, What is reality? Are necessity and contingency real modes of being? Are the laws of nature real? Can they be assumed to be immutable or are they presumably results of evolution? Is there any real chance or departure from real law?[25]

Pragmatism, then, is far more than a tool for clarifying the meanings of terms. Rather, the very tool leads to a particular ontological content. Indeed, such a content belongs not only to ontology, but also "to 'epistemology,' an atrocious translation of *Erkenntnislehre*."[26]

At this point it may be objected that though these subtle tones of experiencing within the internal structure of meaning provide a phenomenological sense of an antideterministic yet lawfully processive universe, there is no basis for the claim that they in fact are features of the metaphysically or ontologically real.[27] It is to this issue that the remaining discussion will turn.

For Peirce, as for all the pragmatists, man is a natural organism in interaction with a natural environment. One of the most distinctive and most crucial aspects of pragmatism is its concept of experience as having the character of an interaction or transaction between man and his environment. Experience is that rich ongoing transactional unity between man and his environment, and only within the context of meanings which reflect such an interactional unity does what is given emerge for conscious awareness. Indeed, such a transactional unity itself has epistemic or phenomenological dimensions, for that which intrudes itself inexplicably into experience is not bare datum, but rather evidences itself as the over-againstness of a thick world "there" for my activity. "Deceive yourself as you may, you have a direct experience of something reacting against you."[28] And, if experience is an interactional unity of man's responses to the ontologically real, then the nature of experience reflects both the responses man brings and the pervasive textures of that independent reality or surrounding natural environment.[29] There is thus, for the pragmatist in general, and for Peirce in particular, a "two directional openness" within experience. What appears opens in one direction toward the structures of the independently real or the surrounding natural environment and in the other direction toward the structures of man's modes of grasping that independently real, for what is experienced is in fact a unity formed by each in interaction with the other. The pervasive textures of experience, which are exemplified in every experience and embedded within the meanings by which we respond to the world, are at the same time indications of the pervasive textures of the independent universe which, in every experience, gives itself for our responses and which provides the touchstone for the workability of our meanings. The basic textures of experience thus lead to the outlines of the categories of metaphysics.[30] As Peirce so well states this transition from the pervasive features of meaning and experience to the pervasive features of the independently real, "that time and space are innate ideas, so far from proving that they have merely a mental existence, as Kant thought, ought to be regarded as evidence of their reality. For the constitution of the mind is the result of evolution under the influence of experience."[31] And, time as process brings with it a processive content, for "Time with its continuity logically involves some other kind of continuity than its own. Time, as the universal form of change cannot exist unless there is something to undergo change and to undergo a change continuous in time there must be a continuity of changeable qualities."[32] That such qualities cannot be taken as subjective is evidenced through the bringing together of two claims by Peirce. "Not only is consciousness continuous in a subjective sense . . . its object is ipso facto continuous. In fact, this infinitesimally spread out consciousness is a direct feeling of its contents as spread out."[33] Further, though "Everything which is present to us is a phenomenal manifestation of ourselves," this "does *not* prevent its being a phenomenon of something without us, just as a rainbow is at once a manifestation both of the sun and of the rain."[34]

Such phenomenal manifestations cannot be understood in terms of a dichotomy between appearance and reality, for Peirce stresses that his philosophy "will not admit a sharp sundering of phenomena and substrates. That which underlies a phenomenon and determines it thereby is, itself, in a measure, a phenomenon."[35] What appears within experience, then, is also the appearance of the independently real; there is no ontological gap between appearance and reality. Further, it is at the same time "to me" to whom it appears and reflects my intentional link with the externally real. Thus, Peirce can say that "Perhaps it may reconcile the psychologist to the admission of perceptual judgments involving generality to be told that they are perceptual judgments concerning our own purposes."[36] Yet, "since no cognition of ours is absolutely determinate, generals must have a real existence."[37] What appears, then, opens in one direction toward the structures of the independently real and in the other direction toward the structures of our mode of grasping the independently real. Or, in other terms, what appears within experience is a function of both in interaction and thus "mirrors" neither exactly, though it reflects characteristics of each. Man's link with his world includes, for Peirce, a vital intentionality at the level of sensibility. The externally real from a certain particular place does not, at any level of awareness, cause a reaction as does a stimulus. Rather, it has a significance, and is a being which is acted upon even as it acts upon us. The structures which come to awareness in experience are an interactional unity of such activities.

Precisely because all contents of awareness are an intentional unity of meaning and being, of knower and known, the continuity of changeable qualities which reflects both the immediacy of conscious experience and the character of the independently real is a limiting concept within experience, for "the development of mind has practically extinguished all feeling."[38] Indeed, as indicated above, though meaning contains a core of felt content, such a core is not experienceable apart from the dispositionally generated structures which present the possibilities in terms of which the sensory may appear. Thus, the grasp of experience as containing repeatable, recognizable qualities "which have been seen before and may be seen again" is a product of the vital intentionality of meaning as habit. Pure Firstness, on the other hand "is predominant, not necessarily on account of the abstractness of that idea, but on account of its self-containedness. It is not in being separated from qualities that Firstness is most predominant, but in being something peculiar and idiosyncratic."[39] Such a characterization leads Peirce to speak of Firstness in terms of qualities of feeling,[40] for what are the characteristics of feeling according to Peirce? "There is no resemblance at all in feeling, since feeling is whatever it is, positively and regardless of anything else, while the resemblance of anything lies in the comparison of that thing with something else."[41]

Pure feeling, then, as a limiting concept within experience, would seem to indicate the boundary of consciousness, the idealized moment of organism-environment interaction, and the pure concrete having, within such a moment, of the indefinitely rich universe within or upon which meaning as habit operates to create a world of perceived objects. The brute meaningless feel of qualitative immediacy is a philosophic abstraction or limiting concept analogous to that of a moment within process or a point on a line. Brute having or brute qualitative feel, devoid of the meanings implicit in dispositional modes of response, would be brute interaction at an instant. But, the concept of interaction at an instant is an abstraction from the reality of process, and brute activity is an abstraction from the continuity of a dispositional mode of response. Such pure feeling is a philosophic idealization, but not an unreal one. The felt concreteness of the continuum of changeable qualities is "there"; it is that which we always experience, but which we always experience through the web of meanings our habits have woven into it. This level of unique qualitative immediacies is important in understanding the ontological categories as they emerge from Peirce's pragmatic understanding of meaning as habit, for it indicates that Firstness in its metaphysical aspect does not indicate any sort of determinate repeatables. To allow the repeatability of appearing qualities to lead to a metaphysics which gives an independent ontological status in any sense to qualities as determinate repeatables is completely to ignore this most basic mode of Firstness,[42] and to lose a crucial key to understanding his metaphysics.

That Firstness is the most elusive and ignored of Peirce's categories has been repeatedly noted.[43] As one commentator has summarized the problem of Firstness, both "abstract qualities" and "chance variations" belong to the category of Firstness, and they seem to have in common only the fact that they are neither Seconds nor Thirds and therefore are relegated to the category of Firsts.[44] As he continues, it may well be asked why chance variations should not be assigned to some new fourth category.[45] On this view, Firstness seems to have become the systematic dump-heap for that which will not fit into the categories of Secondness and Thirdness. Yet, if Firstness is indeed first, one would expect it to provide the significant starting point for the metaphysical functions assigned to the other categories. If, as indicated by approaching Firstness through Peirce's pragmatic theory of meaning, qualitative immediacy and chance variation are intimately related, then the need for some "new fourth category" dissolves and Firstness does indeed become the significant starting point of Peirce's metaphysics, for it indicates the infinitely varied, concrete qualitative richness of a universe in process, the substratum of pure chance diversity within which random activities occur and begin to take on habits. It is this interrelationship which will be explored in the ensuing discussion.

Peirce observes that "Generality is either of that negative sort which belongs to the merely potential, as such, and this is peculiar to the category of Firstness, or it is of the positive kind which belongs to conditional necessity, and this is peculiar to the category of law."[46] Further, "The general is seen to be precisely the continuous."[47] Generality, then, must involve continuity; hence the generality of Firstness can only be fully understood when this category is viewed from the aspect of the continuity which pervades it. Here it may be objected that continuity belongs to the category of Thirdness. However, if the general is the continuous, then the negative generality of Firstness must imply a negative continuity which belongs to the category of Firstness rather than Thirdness. This negative continuity or negative generality of Firstness indicates a negative possibility or mere "may-be" which contains no positive possibility or "would-be" and which thus provides no positive range for further determinations. As Peirce states the position, "Firstness is essentially indifferent to continuity."[48] Indeed, just as feeling was seen above to refer to that qualitative element which in its purity can be related to nothing beyond itself, so the negative generality and continuity of Firstness, which forms the cosmological basis for our experience of Firstness, can be related neither to what has been nor to what will be; it has no relatedness; it contains no "would-be"; in short, it is a qualitative continuum of negative possibilities, a "substratum" of pure chance.[49]

How, then, does this view of Firstness relate to the other categories? The intimate interrelation of Secondness and Thirdness for Peirce is indicated to some extent in his statement that

> The court cannot be imagined without a sheriff. Final causality cannot be imagined without efficient causality, but no whit the less on that account are their modes of action polar contraries. The sheriff would still have his fist, even if there were no court; but an efficient cause, detached from a final cause in the form of a law would not even possess efficiency; it might exert itself, and something might follow post hoc, but not propter hoc; for propter implies potential regularity. Now without law there is no regularity; and without the influence of ideas there is no potentiality.[50]

Again, Peirce writes that the court, or the category of Thirdness, "can have no concrete being without action, as a separate object on which to work its government."[51] Thus, it can be seen that efficient causation, in the sense of actualization of a possibility, requires the rational or "ideal causality"[52] of Thirdness to provide the positive potentialities, while Thirdness, apart from its relation to Secondness is not real. Because Peirce's category of Firstness is considered confused, or, at best, elusive, the interrelation of Secondness and Thirdness is usually discussed in isolation from Firstness. This fact, combined with Peirce's emphasis on his Scholastic Realism, leads too often to an understanding of the interrelation of Secondness and Thirdness in terms of relationships appropriate to a static, substantive universe. However, when Firstness is integrated with Secondness and Thirdness from the backdrop of Peirce's pragmatic focus on habit, a different type of relationship comes to light. Such an integration can best be approached by way of Peirce's cosmology, for his cosmological account, in which the random actions and reactions of the substra-

tum of pure chance gradually tend to take on habits which in turn limit future interactions, will lead to an interrelation of the categories in terms of processive emergence.

It may be held that to view the ontological problem of the relationship of the categories in terms of the cosmological problem of the origin of the categories is to commit a sort of genetic fallacy at the metaphysical level. However, only if the emergence of Thirdness from Secondness and Firstness is recognized can the status of Thirdness be adequately understood. Furthermore, as has been so aptly noted, the sequence to be traced is not, in the initial stages, a temporal one at all. It is an objective logical sequence.[53]

At first sight there seems to be an ambivalence in Peirce's cosmological categorization of the primordial state. On the one hand, he seems to establish a type of situation which represents Firstness alone. On the other hand, he attempts to show that such a primordial state contains the germ of a generalizing tendency. The ensuing discussion will attempt to indicate the manner in which the primordial state does suggest a representation of the First category alone, yet nonetheless contains the germ of a generalizing tendency. This generalizing tendency lies in Peirce's First Category in the form of a qualitative continuum. It has been seen that Firstness is a negative generality or negative continuity in that it does not limit the future as does law. Further, Firstness is also a pure possibility in relation to Secondness, for its being as possibility is not dependent upon its actualization.[54] From the indeterminate qualitative continuum which is logically prior to both Secondness and Thirdness, anything can occur in that any two parts can interact. These random reactions occur from the brute blind force of Secondness or efficient causation acting on the substratum of pure spontaneity. And, though Firstness is essentially indifferent to its continuity, when interaction of two parts of the continuum occurs, that which interacts is continuous and provides a positive possibility of future interactions by excluding certain possibilities in its very occurrence. As Peirce illustrates:

> Let the clean blackboard be a sort of diagram of the original vague potentiality . . . I draw a chalk line on the board. This discontinuity is one of these brute acts by which alone the original vagueness could have made a step toward definiteness. There is a certain element of continuity in this line. Where did this continuity come from? It is nothing but the original continuity of the black-board which makes everything upon it continuous.[55]

Again, as Peirce notes, the discontinuity can be produced upon that blackboard only by the reaction between two continuous surfaces into which it is separated. Thus, what is a singularity or discreteness in the containing continuum is itself a positive generality in relation to the discrete cuts potentially "in" it. In brief, Secondness, or bare brute action and reaction, is a distinct analytic element within the ongoing process or evolving qualitative continuum. However, there is no such thing as disembodied interaction, and actuality as it contextually occurs in the passing present is characterized by the brute hereness and nowness of the shock of interaction or efficient causation "acting upon" the substratum of pure chance or "negative continuity" in accordance with the limitations placed upon it by the positive possibilities of Thirdness.

Here we see the manner in which acts or Secondness can be characterized both as privative, brute, blind or unintelligible, and as that which gives reality to laws and general types. Secondness, as distinct from Firstness or Thirdness, is a brute action and reaction. In this sense it is the acting compulsion of efficient causation. Secondness is a mode of behavior of the concrete qualitative continuum—the mode of behavior which is characterized by efficient causation. It is the bruteness of interaction of two parts of a qualitative process. Thus, existence is a mode of behavior of the general; it is the mode of behavior characterized by interaction. And, it is the interaction, not that which interacts, which is individual, brute, and blind. But, this brute, blind interaction of the general qualitative continuum is precisely what turns negative possibility into positive possibility, mere "may-be" into "would-be." Thus, Secondness is that which makes possible the very reality of Thirdness.

We can see now why Peirce insists that Thirdness does not contract into Secondness—Thirdness is not the kind of 'thing' that can be in Secondness. Indeed, if one insists on using spatial language, it is more accurate to say that Secondness is in Thirdness than that Thirdness is in Secondness, for a continuum may be said to contain its cuts, potential or actual, but the cuts do not contain the continuum.[56] Thus, Peirce can say that Secondness does not contain any Thirdness at all, for an "*existing* thing is simply a blind reacting thing" though "existing *things* do not need reasons; they are reasons."[57] Here, then, can be found the significance of Peirce's view that synechism and realism are intimately linked.[58] Their linkage is to be found in Peirce's process realism as it develops from his pragmatic understanding of meaning as habit.

Peirce's pragmatism thus leads to the metaphysical vision of an infinitely rich evolving universe in process, a universe which has emergence and novelty built into the very core of its being, and through any and every cross-section of which run two modes of behavior. Such a process does not contain the hard discrete exactitudes of repeatable qualities or universal classes, for such a reality is a continuum which "swims in indeterminacy."[59] For this reason, the principle of continuity, which pervades the independently real, is "fallibilism objectified."[60] Indeed, in such a processive universe, "Truly natural classes may, and undoubtedly often do, merge into one another inextricably,"[61] and thus boundary lines must be imposed, although the classes are natural.[62]

Thus, our lived perceptual experience is an intentional unity of knower and known which emerges through our

modes of grasping the independently real continuum of qualitative events which "swims" in indeterminacy. The internal structure of meaning as habit both provides the tool for "cutting the edges" of such a processive continuum and allows for a primordial experiential grasp of its continuities, real relations and real potentialities; for a sense of an anti-deterministic world in which one grasps real alternative possibilities; for the "feel" of the surd, brute, otherness of the environment to which one must successfully respond. Peirce's pragmatic understanding of meaning as habit, then, incorporates the textures of the ontologically real within the very heart of the structure of meaningful experience, bringing to a unity the knowing by man of the world and the being of man in the world.

NOTES

[1] See, for example, Charles Sanders Peirce, *Collected Papers,* vol. 1-4, ed. Hartshorne and Weiss (Cambridge, MA: The Belknap Press of Harvard University, 1931-1935); vol. 7, 8 ed. Burks (Cambridge, MA: Harvard University Press, 1958), 5.491 and 5.486. (Hereafter cited using only conventional two-part number).

[2] This distinction refers to the epistemic and ontological dimensions of *meaning* in terms of habit. There is intended at this point no reference to "habit-takings" of the universe.

[3] 4.9

[4] 8.326; 8.332. It must be emphasized that purposive biological activity, as the foundation of meaning, cannot be understood in terms of scientific contents. Rather, it is the "lived through" biological activity of the human organism and, as such, is capable of phenomenological description.

[5] 5.416, 5.213; 7.465.

[6] 5.531 (See also 7.407 for a discussion of Kant's schema in relation to Peirce's position.)

[7] 5.298-99.

[8] 8.305.

[9] Peirce refers to such an analysis both as logical and as "phaneroscopic."

[10] 6.132.

[11] 5.491. (The use of 'motive' here seems analogous to 'anticipated result'.)

[12] These two levels correspond respectively to the content of the perceptual judgment in its narrow and wide senses. These two senses of the perceptual judgment are developed by me in some detail in "Peirce's Theory of the Perceptual Judgment: An Ambiguity," *Journal of the History of Philosophy,* 7 (1969).

[13] 6.152.

[14] 7.498.

[15] 6.141.

[16] 5.291.

[17] 7.624.

[18] 6.142.

[19] 6.170, 6.138.

[20] 6.138.

[21] 5.457.

[22] 7.675.

[23] Ibid.

[24] 5.464. (Italics not in text.)

[25] 5.496.

[26] Ibid.

[27] The terms 'ontological' and 'metaphysical' are used interchangeably in this essay, although Peirce at times makes a distinction, seeming to label as 'metaphysical' issues which are pragmatically "meaningless gibberish" or at best unsolvable.

[28] 2.139.

[29] More precisely stated, the surrounding natural environment *is* the independently real as it enters into the field of interest of an active organism.

[30] Thus, Peirce's phenomenology, in providing categories as "classifications of all that is in any way present to mind in experience" provides as well the epistemic categories for analyzing the structures of meaning and the metaphysical or ontological categories for delineating "modes of being."

[31] Section 14, Article 23, p. 33 of *The Microfilm Edition of the Peirce Papers.*

[32] 6.132.

[33] 6.111.

[34] 5.283.

[35] 7.629.

[36] 5.166. Peirce's use of the term 'judgment' is of course not intended to indicate a highly intellectualized process but to emphasize that perception is not the "passive receiving" of a spectator theory of knowledge.

[37] 5.312.

[38] 6.132.

[39] 1.302.

[40] 5.444.

[41] 1.310. To think of feeling as used by Peirce in terms of psychology is to be misled by a word, for as Peirce himself emphatically states, "If by psychology we mean the positive observation science of the mind or consciousness . . . psychology can teach us nothing of the nature of feeling, nor can we gain knowledge of any feeling by introspection, for the very reason that it is our immediate consciousness." 1.308.

[42] See, for example, John Boler, *Charles Peirce and Scholastic Realism* (Seattle: University of Washington Press, 1963). Although recognizing the significance of Peirce's switch from substance to process in most areas, Boler finds that at one point at least there is for Peirce "real commonness," or repetition of form in some sense (p. 158); Boler's argument seems to hinge on the unstated assumption that Peirce's ontological category of Firstness implies repeatable, fully structured qualities.

[43] See, for example, Isabel Stearns, "Firstness, Secondness, and Thirdness," *Studies in the Philosophy of Charles Sanders Peirce,* ed. Weiner and Young (Cambridge, MA: Harvard University Press, 1952), pp. 196-97; John Boler, *Charles Peirce and Scholastic Realism,* pp. 122-23.

[44] Douglass Greenlee, "Peirce's Hypostatic and Factorial Categories," *Transactions of the Charles S. Peirce Society: A Quarterly Journal in American Philosophy,* 4 (1968): 55, 58.

[45] Ibid., p. 58.

[46] 1.427.

[47] 8, p. 279.

[48] 6.205.

[49] Perhaps this clarifies the meaning of Peirce's statement, usually interpreted as indicating an idealistic metaphysics, that "wherever chance spontaneity is found, there in the same proportion feeling exists. In fact, chance is but the outward aspect of that which within itself is feeling." 6.265.

[50] 1.213.

[51] 5.436.

[52] 1.212.

[53] Thomas Goudge, *The Thought of C. S. Peirce* (Toronto: University of Toronto Press, 1950), p. 144.

[54] 1.531.

[55] 6.203.

[56] 1.478, 5.107 (continuity); 8.208 (contraction)For Peirce, "A true continuum is something whose possibilities of determination no multitude of individuals can exhaust" (6.170). (It may be objected that there is a sense in which the cuts do contain the continuum, since the possibilities inherent in the continuum cut are partially dependent upon the possibilities inherent in the continuum from which it is cut. However, this objection depends upon viewing the cut not in its aspect of discreteness or Secondness, but in its aspect of continuity or Thirdness.)

[57] 4.36; 5.107. (Italics added.)

[58] 6.169 ff.

[59] 1.171-1.172.

[60] 1.171.

[61] 1.209.

[62] Section 427, pp. 40-41 of *The Microfilm Edition of the Peirce Papers.*

Josiah Lee Auspitz (essay date 1983)

SOURCE: "The Greatest Living American Philosopher," in *Commentary,* Vol. 76, No. 6, December, 1983, pp. 51-64.

[*In the following excerpt, Auspitz asserts that Peirce was the United States' only contribution to great philosophy, and isolates his later writing as his most profound.*]

Charles Sanders Peirce, the only American one can confidently place among the world's great philosophers, had a view of logic as a form of heroism. As he saw, it, logical thinking is virtually useless in life, where the most important matters must be settled by faith and instinct. Logicality is heroic precisely because it is unarrested by practical interests, unhindered by the everyday need to leap to judgment. It is reasoning as if for eternity and for humanity as a whole. It is not dispassionate, since a commitment to the life of the mind is itself a sublime passion, but rather disinterested and selfless. It is, in his view, founded upon an altruistic principle.

When Peirce expounded this idea in a series of articles on the philosophy of science for *Popular Science Monthly* in 1877-78 he could not know that he was fated not merely to praise the heroism of intellect but to become corban to it. He was in those days as comfortably positioned and highly regarded as a forty-year-old logi-

cian could hope to be in 19th-century America. He was widely recognized as brilliant, and more importantly, appreciated in a select international scientific circle for his accomplishments in geodesy, astronomy, mathematics, symbolic logic, and philosophy. He had the patronage of the most influential men of science of the older generation and the enthusiastic support of the leading editors of both the very learned and the semi-popular journals. He was able to write on the most esoteric subjects but also to make non-didactic philosophy interesting to the readers of the *Nation, Popular Science Monthly,* and the *North American Review.* Besides, he had a remunerative post at the Coast and Geodetic Survey, the major government employer of research scientists. To this he was about to add a lectureship at the newly founded Johns Hopkins University, where he had every prospect of training a generation of graduate students to carry on his devotion to pure inquiry.

Even on the basis of what he had written before his fortieth year, one might have said that there had not been since Pascal a writer so thoroughly grounded in science and mathematics who worked to retrieve rather than to overturn the scholastic heritage of the Middle Ages. And how much bolder an enterprise from a child of Unitarian Harvard.

No one could have then imagined that Peirce would die a shivering pauper, sustained on alms raised for him by William James, that at his death in 1914 his major works would lie uncollected and unpublished, his contact with students nil, his final and most brilliant contributions buried in letters and notebooks that would begin to receive due notice only two generations after his death. No one could have predicted that even dutiful works of scholarship devoted to him would have the effect of delaying a general appreciation of his merit.

I

But we run ahead of the story. One result of the fate that befell Charles Sanders Peirce is that we cannot assume that the educated English-speaking reader even recognizes his name. Among specialists, of course, his reputation grows—I count seven issues of major international journals devoted to Peirce in the past few years, covering such topics as semiotics, pragmatism, linguistics, philosophy of science, metaphysics, and history of mathematics. One of these, the April 1982 issue of *The Monist,* contains a bibliography listing more than 600 entries during the previous five years. And the attention Peirce receives is not merely archival. As one philosophy professor wrote recently: "I look on him not as a thinker of bygone days, but as a colleague and a coworker on issues of abiding interest."

If a philosopher can be considered among the living so long as his ideas continue to spark interest and controversy at the frontiers of inquiry, there is little doubt that Peirce will remain for some time the greatest living American philosopher. There is afoot a kind of back-door Peirceanism in which his positions are rediscovered, often without attribution, or worse still, are alleged to have been superseded in the work of critics (in different generations, Arthur O. Lovejoy, Willard Van O. Quine, and Jürgen Habermas come to mind) who fall well short of comprehending their full range.

In disparate specialties, academic fashions have moved closer to aspects of Peirce's work that previously seemed outlandish: his diagrammatic habits of thought, his use of the continuum of infinitesimals, his post-Darwinian concept of evolution, his view of science as relying on a community of inquirers, his stress on the imaginative element in scientific discovery, his penchant for combinatorial analysis, his sophisticated use of the concept of modality, his insistence on a "logic of vagueness," his admiration for Hegel and Duns Scotus, his critiques of what are now called positivism, empiricism, skepticism, and intuitionism, his meticulous lexicographic work in philosophical terminology, and, above all, his founding of the now ubiquitous discipline of semiotics. At the same time, among those who admire philosophy for its own sake, a patient scholarship has begun not only to trace the development and antecedents of the many topics he addresses but to see a common core of animating ideas that gives Peirce's work its unusual power, self-sufficiency, and coherence.

But none of this ferment has yet reached a cultivated American public. Even among professors of philosophy Peirce has been neglected both by the scientifically inclined, who have looked to Britain and Vienna for philosophical direction, and by the historically, morally, and portentously minded, who have shopped German, French, and Eastern. For example, at Peirce's alma mater, Harvard, his name has appeared in the catalogue of philosophy courses only once in the past five years, during which period no fewer than two course listings a year have advertised close readings of Wittgenstein.

At last, however, both the professoriat and a broader public will have a chance to know Charles Peirce as only a few devoted scholars have known him. Indiana University Press has now issued the first two of a projected twenty-volume collection of Peirce's writings, chronologically arranged. Though the edition bears the authoritative stamp of the Center for Scholarly Editions of the Modern Language Association, it is something more significant than the final embalming fluid for a classic author. Just as the 19th-century editions by Erdmann and Gerhardt established Leibniz as a writer who still exercises influence, so Peirce, it seems safe to say, will emerge from this collection as an active participant in current philosophical debates.

About half of the projected Indiana material has never been in print before. Peirce's known corpus would fill more than a hundred 500-page volumes, of which about one-fourth were published during his lifetime, and no book of his collected papers appeared until after his death. The Indiana volumes are thus more than the el-

egant reprinting of previously available work. They draw upon decades of scholarship in assembling, deciphering, and dating Peirce's manuscripts.

Moreover, by placing Peirce's work in chronological rather than topical order—as was the scheme followed by the Harvard University Press edition of the 1930's—the new edition will enable a wide readership to follow his philosophical progress on a variety of interconnected problems. This is as Peirce himself would have wished. He saw philosophy not as issuing in systems or settled doctrines but as the working out of a logical point of view.

The chronological selection also focuses attention on piquant historical and biographical issues. Peirce's life was closely bound up with the founding of the modern American research university, and with the beginnings of federal and foundation patronage for scientific inquiry. Yet after his dismissal in 1884 from Johns Hopkins, some dark scandal was rumored to justify his ostracism from academic life, and the very purity of his devotion to logic was repeatedly used to deny him institutional funds as an independent scholar. He had to fall back on odd jobs, support from friends, and the patronage of a few New England families still prominent in higher learning. Does his exclusion tell us anything about institutional as opposed to individual support for philosophy in the land of pragmatism?

II

We meet "Charley" Peirce in Volume I as the ultimate Harvard brat. He came from one of those Yankee families which, whatever their professed church—and the Peirce-Nichols family's drift from Calvinism to Unitarianism to Episcopalianism is typical—have made of Harvard their cathedral.

Charles Sanders Peirce was the grandson of the librarian of Harvard College and the son of America's preeminent professor of mathematics. At his father's hands, he received a "laboratory" education that, from a scientific point of view, made John Stuart Mill's seem like a genteel kindergarten. He was drilled in mathematical games and careful observation of the unreliability of his own senses. At eleven he wrote his own **"History of Chemistry"** after reading a translation by his father's sister and brother of the first German chemistry text to be used in American colleges. At fourteen he fell in love with *Whateley's Elements of Logic.* At fifteen he inherited his uncle's library of medical and chemical books. At sixteen his father supervised him in what were to be three years of regular readings in German of Kant's *Critique of Pure Reason,* so that he committed whole chunks of it to memory.

Charley entered Harvard at sixteen. He did not do well in the areas central to computing class rank—compulsory chapel, good behavior, regular recitations, and compositions on set topics (e.g., "What is your favorite virtue?"). His performance declined as he grew older and more disposed to libertine bouts in Boston. His senior year he ranked seventy-ninth in a class of ninety-one. He did, however, spend some time with his Aunt Lizzie, the German translator, on an original rendering of the Transcendental Deduction of the Categories from Kant's *Critique,* took loving notes on his father's lectures in advanced mathematics and physics, and plunged himself into Schiller's *Aesthetic Letters.*

He was graduated without honors in the class of 1859, and then spent several months on field trips in Maine and Louisiana with Alexander Dallas Bache, an old family friend who was superintendent of the United States Coast Survey. Then it was on to tutelage under another family friend, Louis Agassiz, for six months of private instruction in biological classification. He entered Harvard's Lawrence Scientific School in 1861 for formal training in chemistry and in 1863 received a B. S. degree in chemistry *summa cum laude.* In 1861, as the Civil War began, Bache appointed him to a (draft-exempt) post in the Coast Survey, as an aide to his father, who held the rank of assistant, directly below superintendent.

During the 1860's Charley remained at Harvard as a proctor, tutor, instructor, lecturer, and staff member of the Harvard Observatory. Like all other Harvard students in those days, he studied mathematics exclusively from texts written by his father, with the exception of an analytic geometry section by James Mills Peirce, his older brother.

His marriage, too, was an intramural affair. His wife, Melusina ("Zina") Fay, was the daughter of his father's Harvard classmate, an Episcopalian clergyman. Charley had to leave Unitarianism for the union, but his philosophical work had already progressed to a fascination with triadic categories that reconciled the unitarian-trinitarian dispute on a metaphysical level. Though an enthusiastic convert in his first years, he thereafter described himself as a Christian by sentiment rather than creed.

Zina, in any case, was not conventionally pious. Her real religion was separate-but-equal feminism, and her theological interests extended mainly to the person of the Holy Ghost, which she saw as the feminine aspect of the Trinity. She wrote a series of lead articles for the *Atlantic* advocating cooperative housekeeping to free women for careers, and a female parliament in which women would have their own political voice without having to compete with men. In Cambridge, she organized a school (which only her nephews attended), a Cooperative Housekeeping Society (with her father-in-law chairing its meetings), and a Committee on the Intellectual Education of Women, "by which girls might go through a course of study in some degree equivalent to that of Harvard College." In politics she advocated a form of proportional representation devised by her husband. She thus helped lay the ground for the founding of Radcliffe College and for the complex system of proportional voting which the city of Cambridge has retained to this day. Zina left Charley in Paris in 1875,

and they were legally divorced in 1883. But during their Harvard period they seemed the quintessentially busy and productive Cambridge couple.

We should pause here to note that the three great scientific teachers of Peirce's youth—his father Benjamin Peirce, Jr., Alexander Dallas Bache, and Louis Agassiz—were more than fast friends. They were the core of the "Lazzaroni," or beggars for science, lobbyists who used every opportunity to build a national scientific research establishment. They formed a socially prominent yet uncompromisingly meritocratic cabal who sought to remove any obstacles that might deter humble, talented boys from a university career. The up-and-coming American astronomer, Simon Newcomb, an immigrant from Canada, exemplified their ideal. We shall encounter him later.

The Lazzaroni openly despised "practical" studies and "leveling" trends in education, yet were expert at dealing with crass legislatures and private donors in the cause of pure research. Many of their institutions survive to this day. In 1848 they founded the American Academy for the Advancement of Science; in 1863, channeling war fever into funding for science, they helped to write the bill which chartered the National Academy of Science. Their stamping ground was the U.S. Coast Survey, later renamed the Coast and Geodetic Survey. Benjamin Peirce succeeded Bache as its superintendent and inherited from him the dutiful Julius Erasmus Hilgard, an immigrant from Germany, to run the Washington office. Hilgard, too, figures in Charley's future.

None of the Lazzaroni was a more tireless promoter of science than Benjamin Peirce. He developed elaborate plans for the Lazzaroni dream of "a truly national university," which he tried at various times to sell to the federal government, the State of New York, and the City of New York. He and Agassiz worked more successfully at moving Harvard in that direction. The two of them were able to influence the choice of two successive Lazzaroni as presidents of Harvard in the 1860's. And to this day the governing structure of Harvard University, with its various boards and visiting committees loosely coordinated by an overarching board of overseers, owes much to Benjamin Peirce's *Working Plan for the Foundation of a University* circulated in 1856.

The first Lazzaroni president of Harvard, a classicist, died after two years, the second resigned unexpectedly after six. While Peirce and Agassiz were preoccupied with blocking an older Unitarian clergyman, they got (as they wished) a scientist and a layman but (as they did not) a young chemist whose elevation to a tenured chair they had previously blocked on the novel grounds that his social connections and administrative gifts were no substitute for scientific ability. This was Charles William Eliot, thirty-five, a professor of chemistry at the newly founded Massachusetts Institute of Technology, and the son of a former mayor of Boston and treasurer of the Harvard Corporation.

Since Eliot had proctored the Harvard class of 1859 and had taught chemistry at the Lawrence Scientific School until 1863, he had ample opportunity to form what was to remain an unshakably low opinion of the character of Charley Peirce. But he also appreciated the need to placate the Peirce-Agassiz faction. Within weeks of Eliot's appointment, he topped an offer that had been made to Peirce's elder son James from the University of California. He followed with a plum for Charley, who was invited to give eleven university-wide lectures on British logicians in Eliot's first year as president and a further series his second. The year was then 1871, Charles Peirce was thirty-two, nine years married, and we are at the end of the period in which he wrote the papers collected in Volumes I and II.

Though he had been to the wilds with Alexander Bache, and made a Coast Survey trip to Europe with his brother and father to observe a solar eclipse in Sicily in 1870, he had never had to venture outside the ambit of his father's influence in Cambridge, Massachusetts. A vignette by Aunt Lizzie in family correspondence of 1867 describes a lively and lovable Charley "seated in his comfortable and handsome study" in front of the new glass-fronted bookcases of which he was inordinately proud (and which already contained a collection in medieval logic more than double that of the Harvard library). He seemed then as bright-eyed as a squirrel. He would, his aunt thought, never grow old.

III

In his own family correspondence of 1909 Peirce wrote that he did not "gain control" of his philosophical direction until 1867, when he was twenty-eight. The Indiana volumes appear to be edited with this in mind. Volume I takes an immature Charley to 1866, while Volume II covers the momentous years 1867-71, during which the young Peirce, in effect, pioneered a distinctively American and yet post-Enlightenment approach to philosophy. He announced his intention to do so obliquely but unmistakably in the seventh of a series of evening lectures on **"The Logic of Science"** at the Lowell Institute in Boston in 1866.

At that time, as indeed now, the purveying of philosophy in America was like the dry-goods business in an underdeveloped country, in which trading houses of various European nations supply the more refined native needs. The main imported brands in mid-19th-century America were German transcendental philosophy, Scottish common-sense philosophy, English association philosophy, and French positive philosophy. There was, in addition, a native so-called philosophy, which had not, however, crossed the crucial threshold between moralizing and theorizing. Peirce, therefore, while paying courteous notice to the homespun names of Edwards, Channing, Parker, and Emerson, among others, did not consider their work to be philosophy in the classical sense.

Yet New England, he thought, had three prerequisites for great philosophy: "the love of research and espe-cially of history," "the capacity for being elevated by an idea," and, above all, the proverbial Yankee ingenuity rooted in "the same mixture of enthusiasm and patience which are required to originate a philosophic theory." "But though the Yankee is thus fitted to do so much good service in philosophy, let us by no means forget that he has not done it hitherto."

Hitherto. Between 1867 and 1871 Charles Sanders Peirce would publish ten papers, on a range of seemingly disparate topics—five papers on logic and mathematics for the American Academy of Arts and Sciences, three metaphysical essays for the *Journal of Speculative Philosophy,* a further essay in symbolic notation applying the algebra of Boole to an entirely new field, and a long semipopular review of a new edition of the works of Bishop Berkeley. These pieces, all reprinted in Volume II, do not comprise a system so much as a related set of beginnings. They lay down the main lines of inquiry to which Peirce would devote his life. But more than this: the best of them, taken together, constitute at once the declaration of independence of American philosophy and the movement of that philosophy into a central position in the mainstream of Western thought.

By the end of Volume II, indeed, it is clear that Peirce has launched a philosophical enterprise remarkable in three enduring respects. First, he shifts the ground of Western philosophy to a concern with the medium about which philosophy is itself a message—language, or more generally, signs. Second, he refounds modern science in terms seen as continuous with the logic of Aristotle and the Middle Ages rather than as based on a sharp break with them. Third, he prepares the way for mapping in formal terms territories of thought that still elude textbook logic.

These undertakings are all closely related. Philosophically, the first and third of them remain the most radical and fruitful in new lines of inquiry. But it is the second—the logical reconceptualization of modern science—that provides the most accessible approach to Peirce's work during this period. Unlike the purer logical undertakings—and pure logicality, the reader will recall, is heroically incomprehensible to those of us preoccupied with daily chores—it is susceptible of historical and polemical presentation. Peirce himself delivered semi-popular polemics on the failings of the fathers of modern science from which one can, with a few philosophical short cuts and a few forward glances, extract an underlying argument.

As I have suggested, Peirce's sensibilities about science recall Pascal's, but in a very different idiom. Pascal, living through the instauration of modern science, had an acute sense of the insufficiency of scientific categories in moral conduct: he had described in belles lettres the differences between the rigorous demonstrations of "the geometrical spirit" and the refined discriminations of everyday life. Yet as a result of his religious conversion, he asserted an ultimate unity of reason and faith.

On these same questions Peirce took a more austerely logical tack. What Pascal had experienced as a personal religious crisis, Peirce was already well advanced in treating as a problem for the method and logic of science. What he sought was a unified theoretical criterion adequate to science and moral practice alike. If certain logical categories were incompatible with moral conduct, they must also be incompatible with the activity of being a scientist. Scientific inquiry, after all, was itself a form of conduct, a practice with its own shared standards and mores. Like medieval religion it rested on real, catholic assent. The difference lay in the manner of fixing belief: the medieval church invoked canonical authority, buttressed from time to time by the bonfire and rack, while science relied more on reasoned agreement. The task for Peirce, then, was not to vindicate revealed religion, but rather to make explicit the postulates of scientific inquiry, and with them to reform the philosophical habits of the scientific community.

These philosophical habits had, as Peirce saw it, been perverse from the start. For historically contingent reasons the scientific movement had adopted a jerry-built metaphysics incompatible with science itself. The so-called "new philosophy" of science had been founded on an unexamined rejection of positions associated with religious orthodoxy. Because the Church revered Aristotle, science became anti-Aristotelian; because the Church glorified faith, science embraced systematic doubt; because orthodox scholastics accepted the reality of universals, the "new philosophers" followed the unorthodox Ockham in attending to empirically verifiable particulars; because the Roman priesthood invoked the world to come, science stressed utility in the here and now.

In adopting what were, in effect, forensic positions, modern science had gotten off on the wrong philosophical foot. It was therefore stuck with logical dogmas that would ultimately block the road to inquiry. The remedy was to find for it a true logic not vitiated by what Peirce would later call "a barbaric reaction against the Middle Ages." This logic was implicit in the actual practice of science—in, as Peirce would later argue, Galileo's stress on the "natural light" of reason or Kepler's continuing struggle to readapt his initial cosmology to new empirical evidence. But the logic-in-use, the *logica utens* of modern science, had never been explicated and systematically pursued as a textbook logic, a *logica docens*.

What was then taught as the so-called philosophy of science was a bifurcated method thought to consist of induction and deduction. Each strand could be traced to one of the "church fathers" of modern science. The deductive strand was personified in Descartes, the inductive one in Bacon. The inadequacies of the one were thought to be complemented and corrected by the other. And each had associated with it a metaphysic that provided a line of philosophical retreat for the other. Deduction drew upon the supposed priority of intuition and the ultimate validity of introspective knowledge. Induction drew upon empiricism, the doctrine of the primacy of external fact. Together they gave science the semblance of a working metaphysic. How did we know which experimental facts were significant? By intuition. How did we establish that our intuitions were valid? By experiment.

For Peirce, by contrast, neither deduction nor induction nor some mysterious oscillation between them could account for the methods of science. For the two left out the crucial, creative element in scientific inquiry—successful hypothesis. In the vulgar mythology of science the bifurcated method gave rise to a misleading folklore of experimental observation. There was, for example, the tale about Galileo coming to his laws of motion by observing a lamp swinging in the cathedral of Pisa. This sort of legend lent support to the views of John Stuart Mill, who had lately proclaimed that even the axioms of geometry were founded in induction.

Now Galileo's most important experiments, as Peirce (correctly) understood them, were "thought experiments" only. They were not founded either in induction or in deduction but in the crucial *tertium quid* of scientific method: hypothesis. Peirce presented successful hypothesis as a method in its own right, and he would extend his view of it beyond science and see it as an instance of what, for the sake of parallelism with induction and deduction, he would call "abduction" or sometimes "retroduction." The term retroduction suggests a method of reasoning backward from presumptions to supporting evidence. It aims at demystifying the "intuitive leaps" that scientists rely upon.

Peirce's view of its centrality to science was not a point about method alone. It was a rejection of a deeper error that both Descartes and Bacon shared: a failure to deal with the artificiality and fallibility of the scientific construction of reality. Philosophically, the lurching from intuitionism to empiricism did not correct the metaphysical errors of the "new philosophy" but compounded them. For the two were simply two versions of the same underlying error—the attempt to establish some fixed point, unmediated by language, as an ultimate and certain foundation for knowledge. As Peirce saw it, any such certainty was meretricious.

Contra the Cartesians, he argued that there was no truth that could be established intuitively because there was no such thing as purely introspective knowledge. Even the apparently introspective methods of the mathematician were nothing of the sort. The seeming certainty of mathematics derived not from introspection or intuitive access to the absolute but from (as he would later put it) the simple fact that mathematicians reason about ideal constructs—diagrams, really—wholly within their control.

But this did not mean that the brute facts are the final authority. For Peirce also argued, against the dogmatically skeptical empiricists, that facts can have no logical priority to concepts. Every fact of which we are able to form a proposition at once involves us in a world of conceptions from which there is no exit and no extra-conceptual authority. However loudly we may assert that an extra-conceptual world patterns our thinking, our very assertion is intelligible only within a world of ideas.

In short, science is not exempted from the human predicament of abstraction. For abstraction, to put it simply, is the price of attending to one aspect of reality to the neglect of another. Since one cannot attend to everything at once, there is no escape from it. One does not get beyond abstraction by ignoring it but by having an articulated grasp of its power and limitations. For science this required, Peirce saw, a new metaphysic; for logic, a rededication to it as "the science of the conditions which enable symbols in general to refer to objects." And both the metaphysical and logical projects required a new view of the old medieval debate on the degree of reality to be accorded to universal conceptions.

IV

One of the anti-scholastic prejudices that modern science had embraced was a deep skepticism toward universals, toward general ideas. Science had adopted what was commonly called Ockham's razor (which Peirce traced to Ockham's nominalist contemporary Durand de St. Pourçain): that entities should not be multiplied unnecessarily. The class of entities that the late medieval nominalists had wished to cut out were universals. They denied that universal terms could have any reality apart from the individual things to which they referred. Universals were mere names—whence the label "nominalism." And since this view, though piously and cautiously expressed, contained suggestions subversive to a universal and catholic order, it naturally had great appeal when that order was breaking up into individual, quasi-national units. Moreover, its cash value for science was to argue for economy, for the elimination of what Hobbes called the "insignificant speech" and "empty words" of the learned doctors.

In England, especially, nominalism reigned supreme, often without any awareness of its late-scholastic origins. There it seemed, simply, part of the national character. As Peirce observed in his 1871 essay on Berkeley:

> From very early times, it has been the chief intellectual characteristic of the English to wish to effect everything by the plainest and directest means, without unnecessary contrivance. . . . In philosophy this national tendency appears as a strong preference for the simplest theories, and a resistance to any complication of the theory as long as there is the least possibility that the facts can be explained in a simpler way. And accordingly, British philosophers have always shown strong nominalistic tendencies since the time of Edward I, or even earlier.

Since Britain had, on Peirce's view, been the exclusive or shared home of every major scientific advance of the previous three centuries, its national habits of thought had penetrated the common sense of science. Men of science took for granted the nominalist doctrine that every general idea was a generalization from particulars or "cases," and could have no meaning beyond the individual things it covered. Reality was a preexisting standard that science uncovered by small incremental inductions. Such advances as hypothesis could yield were intuitive leaps beyond the existing (inductive) evidence that were later vindicated by it.

But Peirce, trained to his fingertips as a "man of science" (Whewell's neologism "scientist" was one of the few he detested), found this notion backward-looking and restrictive. Hypothesis to him was a leap not beyond reality but into it. If one wished to use a mysterious word like intuition, it had to be understood as the completion of ideas already achieved and presupposed in scientific inquiry. It depended on an element that was conceptual yet not introspective, real yet never wholly verifiable as present fact.

The hallmark of nominalism was a backward-looking view of reality. It accepted as fact only that whose existence was established. Hypothesis, by contrast, meant pursuing as real that which would be agreed upon as real by some future community of inquirers. It presupposed what Peirce would later call the doctrine of the "unsettled universal." That is, it granted a degree of reality to general ideas whose limits remained to be determined.

Hypothesis, in sum, posited a reality that would be accepted by the scientific community after inquiry had run its full course. Every (hypothetical) concept was to be judged not merely as a recapitulation of previous instances but as a forward-looking anticipation of its working-out. Its meaning consisted in all the imaginable uses to which it might be put. It stressed not what was but what would be. In so doing, hypothetical reasoning had a power well beyond random guessing. One could not account for its success without conceding some degree of reality to forward-looking general ideas. As Peirce would later put it, "no agglomeration of actual happenings can ever fill up the meaning of a 'would be.'"

But ever since Hume's critique of causation, the philosophical presumption was against a "would be" as wishful thinking. So the question still remained: could any supposedly universal conceptions, whether one took them forward or backward, be more than collections of particular aspects of individual things? Could one speak seriously of real universals? Even if one granted some basis in reality to the scientist's need for hypothesis, how far could this be extended into one's view of experience as a whole?

In addressing such questions—and we can, of course, only provide signposts toward them here—Peirce had two advantages over later logicians. Though many of them have, like him, been trained in classics, science, and mathematics, Peirce added to this a grounding in both German metaphysics and scholastic logic. Following the Germans, he put the problem of universals in terms of "the categories," those elementary conceptions that since Aristotle were held to underlie all discourse. Following the scholastics, he also cast the problem as one of "speculative grammar" (to use the title of a 13th-century treatise), an inquiry into the degree of reality to be accorded the formalities of discourse. Combining these two approaches with a scientific sensibility yielded powerful results, so powerful, in fact, that we shall have to become a bit more familiar with them to understand the logical categories reinforced both by the *logica utens* of modern science and by the American experience.

v

I have suggested that Peirce's writings during the period 1867-71 mark a coming of age not only for him but for American philosophy. I have even said that they amount to "the declaration of independence of American philosophy," words that may seem hyperbolic and loose. As it happens, I mean them quite literally.

Much as the colonies broke with their mother country by proclaiming certain English liberties to be founded in universally "self-evident truths," so Peirce broke with English nominalism over the status of universals themselves. These two declarations of independence share more than a family resemblance. They are both premised on a post-nominalist view of public discourse, in which universals are taken as living realities. In practical American politics this view reaches its apotheosis in Lincoln. Ultimately, it is at odds with the deeper logical categories of John Locke, who is both overplayed as the progenitor of all that is American and underrated for his coherence as a philosopher.

I say ultimately, because one can read Locke's political treatises very far without noticing the implacable and shrewdly couched hostility of his logical writings to anything that smacks of universalism. His nominalism coupled with his horror of "enthusiasm" repels the universalistic strain in the American regime. Scholars who have noticed this have accordingly looked elsewhere for literary influences: to Montesquieu and other writers of the French Enlightenment, to the Scottish commonsense philosophers, to Cicero, to Aquinas, to Shakespeare, Calvin, Aristotle, the Bible. As a historical matter, these are interesting leads to explore.

But if what is sought is an articulated and enduring philosophical basis for American universalism, it comes in the difficult, apolitical, post-Civil War work of Charles Peirce. And if the best American statecraft has tamed an almost Gallic universalism with a very British sense of particular and contingent practices and interests, Peirce has given us a comparable achievement in logic: a presumption in favor of universals checked and balanced with devices for making them corrigible and concrete.

Peirce's first lasting contribution to the literature of universals was a deceptively modest paper entitled **"On a New List of Categories"** presented to the American Academy of Arts and Sciences in 1867. It is cast as a technical improvement upon Kant's transcendental deduction. Kant, in revising Aristotle's list of the categories, had limited himself to those for which he could find an a-priori, transcendental basis. His revised tables reaffirmed logical categories that were by then traditional—quantity, quality, modality, and relation. Later German writers who tried to supersede him (Hegel, Fichte, Schiller) invoked some mode of experience (history, morals, art) that went beyond mere textbook logic.

One move remained inadequately explored: an approach to the categories through the notion of representation itself. It could be called, following Locke, a semiotic approach (from the Greek *sema,* a sign, as in semaphore). It had been broached by Kant in the footnote that concludes his summary of the three critiques, and more explicitly by the early Kantian Karl Leonhard Reinhold, with whose work Peirce was acquainted.

The semiotic approach (or "semeiotic," as Peirce punctiliously spelled it) preserved the approaches of the German idealists while remaining neutral among them. Since all ideas, even those declared to be a-priori, absolute, or "things-in-themselves," could be seen as signs, it was fair to ask: what categories were postulated in semiosis, the activity of signification? In casting the question in this way, Peirce reoriented philosophy from a concern with the theory of knowledge (sometimes called "epistemology," another word he disliked) to the conditions of representation.

This reorientation had the ironic advantage of using Ockham's razor to cut down the Ockhamists themselves. The nominalist presumption against general ideas was, as Peirce saw it, a mystical doctrine masquerading as a skeptical one. For if ideas in general are not the criterion by which we judge other ideas, then we must posit some incognizable reality as that criterion. But a reality beyond cognition is a metaphysical, not to say mystical, superfluity. If one values parsimony, there is, as Peirce put it in 1868, no need to posit "a reality more recondite than that represented in a true representation."

Of course, a true representation is not a simple thing. And Peirce's subtle paper of 1867 sets forth the category of representation as presupposing other categories which are, however, accessible to us only through representation itself. To put it another way, each sign is abstracted from a welter of qualities and relations which are themselves accessible to us only as signs. As a bare simplification one can speak of two orders of such ulterior relations—that between the sign and its object, and that between the sign and some interpreting mind. Absent signs, there is no relation between one mind and another or between mind and the world of external objects. All experience, in short, is mediated, and mediated experience is the sole basis of our knowledge.

Yet our mediations—which Peirce calls signs and representations—carry with them evidence of their own fallibility. Whence the central predicament of all discursive theorizing: the theorist is always trying to capture in representations a precise account of experience which from the very nature of representation he knows will remain beyond his grasp. His predicament is not different in kind from that of the artist or businessman or politician, who deal with their own worlds of representation. But since his world requires that everything be articulated, he, unlike them, must have a reasoned account of the signs he uses and the inferences he makes with them and from them. For Peirce this led, as his insights invariably did, to a three-pronged project in the study of signs ("semiotic"): first, to a ramified typology of signs and their elemental constituents ("stecheotic"); second, to an investigation of the methods by which signs earn the patent of truth among the scientific community ("methodeutic"); third, to a view of philosophy as an inquiry into the "postulates" of logical experience ("critic").

What still distinguishes Peirce's contributions in these fields is his awareness of their medieval roots. And the second distinctive component of his discussion of universals is that he sees it as a continuation of the scholastic debate between the followers of Duns Scotus and those of William of Ockham—a debate between the "realists" and the "nominalists."

His views on this debate were presented most forcefully in the 1871 review of the works of Bishop Berkeley, often considered an "idealist" voice at odds with the dominant, "empirical" spirit of British philosophy. Peirce, by contrast, saw Berkeley as a link between Hobbes and Locke, on the one hand, and Hume, on the other. And he saw all of them as playing out the nominalist themes introduced by William of Ockham. He thus used the Berkeley review to expose the dogmatic nominalism of modern English philosophy and to declare his independence from it.

Over the course of his life Peirce would systematically replace the keystones of nominalist logic with an alternative set of leading principles. Instead of the nominalist habit of assuming ideas to be discrete and to be related by the principle of association, he would employ the principle of continuity, which assumed fuzzy boundaries. Instead of taking doubt as the norm of inquiry, he would stress belief: "To make believe that one does not believe anything is an idle and self-deceptive pretense." In place of a merely parsimonious prejudice against multiplying concepts, he would propound a *general* rule for simplifying all relations of more than three terms into triadic form.

He would even provide an alternative to the algebraic notation which Boole and he had pioneered as the basis of symbolic logic. Algebraic form, after all, subtly encourages the old nominalist prejudice that logical thought, like mathematical calculation, consists in the concatenation of precisely defined elements. Toward the end of his life Peirce would devise two systems of logical graphs to give diagrammatic form to his own sense that the most powerful thinking begins with indeterminacy and moves from the vague to the precise. Within precise algebraic notation, meanwhile, he would replace the central technical device of nominalism (Ockham's "syncategorematic") with the "quantifier," a term he coined to describe the device that encourages individuation while building in a bias against isolated individuals.

On the fruitfully vague level of metaphysics, he would readapt his own notion of the "unsettled universal," which looked to the future for vindication, to cover also the ground of Hegel's "concrete universal," which was better attuned to the past. And he would rework the central concepts of Plato's *Timaeus* and Aristotle's *Metaphysics* so that they applied not to the nature of the universe directly but only mediately through the human interpretation of signs.

The result is a body of work that does not fall neatly on one or the other side of what are often portrayed as irrevocable watersheds of modern philosophy—realism versus idealism, empiricism versus transcendental speculation, mathematical precision versus anti-formalist vagueness, an epistemological versus a metaphysical approach to first philosophy. It marks Peirce as the most scientific of the German idealists, the most profound of the Scottish common-sense school, the most powerful of the neoscholastics, the most far-ranging of the modern realists, the first American.

VI

The unfolding of this astonishing development is a story for the years beyond 1867-71, and thus falls outside the volumes considered here. Still, "by their fruits shall ye know them." The best-known fruit of Peirce's youthful anti-nominalism is "pragmatism," another term he is credited with introducing. The idea is already evident in Volume II. It will make its full appearance in Volume III, as a maxim for clear thinking. Here is the way Peirce presented it in **"How to Make Our Ideas Clear,"** the second of his *Popular Science Monthly* articles of 1877-78:

> Consider what effects, which might conceivably have practical bearings, we conceive the object of our conception to have. Then, our conception of these effects is the whole of our conception of the object.

Read in its chronological place, the pragmatic maxim is, I think, indisputably not a theory of truth but of meaning, not a fancy word for anti-intellectualism but an attempt to extend our intellectual purview. It is one of a wide array of devices by which Peirce developed his post-nominalist logic of science.

Specifically, the pragmatic maxim is Peirce's counter and corollary to Ockham's (that is, Durand's) razor. For if we accept that "entities are not to be multiplied unnecessarily," the question remains: how do we know what constitutes an unnecessary entity?

The nominalist answer, as we have seen, is to rule out universals, to admit only the (universal?) principle of resemblance and association among particular cases. The pragmatic maxim, by contrast, provides a more open-minded reading of the razor. It proposes that we weed out unnecessary ideas by a principle of clarity. Presented with any idea, the pragmatic maxim leads us to ask: what practical difference could it conceivably make? If there is no conceivable difference, the idea is superfluous.

Peirce's pragmatic maxim does not build in a dogmatic presumption in favor of universals; it merely permits them to earn their own way. On pragmatic grounds, then, how do universals earn their way? What practical difference does it make whether we view universals as real possibilities or as mere associations of particulars? What difference whether we proceed with realistic or nominalistic presumptions?

For science, as we have seen, the difference is to be found in whether hypothesis is treated as a mystical exercise of "intuition" or as a method in its own right, to be studied and improved. Outside science, the practical consequences of the debate on universals are no less far-reaching. Here is the description of them with which Peirce concludes the Berkeley review:

> . . . though the question of realism and nominalism has its roots in the technicalities of logic, its branches reach about our life. The question whether the *genus homo* has any existence except as individuals is the question whether there is anything of any more dignity, worth, and importance than individual happiness, individual aspirations, and individual life. Whether men really have anything in common, so that the *community* is to be considered as an end in itself, and if so, what the relative value of the two factors is, is the most fundamental practical question in regard to every public institution the constitution of which we have it in our power to influence.

Q.E.D. Peirce's philosophical declaration of independence from nominalism provides a belated logical ground for the Declaration of Independence of the United States of America. For if, as the nominalists have it, reality only inheres in discrete individuals, it cannot be "self-evident" that, in Jefferson's words, "all men are created equal and endowed by their Creator with certain unalienable rights." Such self-evidence presupposes the reality of universals or the reality of human community, or both. The American Declaration of Independence, then, insofar as it is more than a merely opportunistic assertion of power, requires a non-nominalist logical ground. It asserts that the legitimate authority of government rests upon universal truths, accessible to common reason.

Writing after that assertion had been put to its bloodiest test in a great civil war, Peirce provided a moderate

basis for it—one that permits but does not require or encourage any further commitment to innate ideas, natural law, general will, collective conscience, or revealed religion. Unlike Locke, Peirce was not a man of politics, and it would be wrong to read him as consciously justifying an abolitionism, Civil War, or Reconstruction for which, among his close circle, only his wife Zina had any enthusiasm. But he was certainly aware that the way in which the particular, the individual, and the universal are related in logic is totemic of the relation between the individual and the community. The generalizing power of science encourages one to grant a degree of reality to universals; the American regime has required it as an article of faith. Peirce's "unsettled universal" reconciles these demands.

It is thus not surprising that Peirce's forward-looking view of the reality of universals was taken up in cruder form by other Americans. It is, for example, the central idea behind Josiah Royce's notion of progressive revelation in religion, in which the truth of Christianity is made manifest in a Community of Interpretation. It is equally pronounced in John Dewey's Great Community, in which science and democracy are seen as twin progressive forces uncovering universal principles by self-correcting procedures of public discourse.

There is about it, too, more than a faint echo of theological doctrine. A real universal is what is predestined to be accepted as such, in the way, for example, that in rabbinic tradition the whole development of the Oral Law is held to have been revealed along with the Written Law at Sinai, or in the way that in the Gospel According to St. John a preexistent Christ is held to have been present with God in the form of the Word, or (to get closer to home) in the way in which among Peirce's Puritan forebears the elect were held predestined to work themselves into that condition. And in the popular religion of Peirce's day, the notion of a universal truth both objectively real and continuously unfolding was embodied in the refrain of the "Battle Hymn of the Republic": "His truth goes marching on."

VII

None of which, to be sure, constitutes a philosophical case. Quite to the contrary: merely to suggest a theological analogue, a cultural resonance, or an institutional need for a philosophical argument is often taken, *prima facie,* as proof against it. To play fair, we should not judge a philosophical position by its agreement with some extraneous interest but, at the first threshold, by its integrity on its own terms. For Peirce the relevant terms always refer to the future.

As we have seen, around 1867 the young Peirce began to view reality as a "would-be"—as what would be agreed upon if all the evidence were known and all the possible viewpoints on it critically evaluated. For him what is called "truth" consists not in any settled doctrine but in the fated forward movement of inquiry itself. That usually irrelevant question—what is the relevance of this philosophy for us?—thus seems in Peirce's case reasonable and apt. To what extent has the progress of the past century vindicated him?

Within academic philosophy, Peirce's youthful anti-nominalism takes on, if anything, a sharper edge today. It reads as an attack on unnamed eminences—Wittgenstein and Strawson on one side of the Atlantic, Willard Quine and Nelson Goodman, the polestars of Harvard's postwar preeminence, on the other—writers who have helped to make orthodox that peculiar vacillation between worlds of fact and intuition that Peirce calls nominalism.

Right after World War II, which many thought to have been fought in part over universal ideals, Professors Quine and Goodman declared universals unreal. They were perhaps reacting against C. I. Lewis, an admirer of Peirce who had been America's reigning logician in the interwar period. They issued (in the *Journal of Symbolic Logic*) a manifesto entitled "Steps Toward a Constructive Nominalism," which reads like a parodist's version of the attitudes Peirce criticized. The authors declaim against "abstract objects" in terms that reintroduce the confusion between the "abstract" and the "general" that Peirce had taken some pains to dispel in 1867. And they candidly confess the grounds of their skepticism: "Fundamentally our refusal [to accept 'abstract objects' even in mathematics] . . . is based on a philosophical intuition that cannot be justified by appeal to anything more ultimate." The extremism of this statement necessitated many adjustments over the years, often with ideas that show a greater continuity with C. I. Lewis and thence with Peirce than the initial break would lead one to suppose. Here, then, the reader of Peirce has a head start in understanding the backing and filling of postwar academic philosophy.

Peirce's thought *circa* 1871 also puts in some perspective the work of Saul A. Kripke, often described as the leading younger logician of the analytic school. His most recent book, *Wittgenstein on Rules and Private Language* (Harvard, 1982), would appear at first glance a careful and respectful reinterpretation of Wittgenstein's later philosophy, which abandons an extreme for a more supple nominalism. In point of fact, it sets up the terms for a radical break with Wittgenstein on issues adumbrated in Peirce's Berkeley review. Walking unawares along Peirce's path, Kripke finds a common structure in the central arguments of Wittgenstein, Berkeley, and Hume. He describes this as due to "skepticism" rather than "nominalism," and he notices points of comparison with Quine, Goodman, and other latter-day nominalists ("skeptics"). He takes care to note that his interpretation of Wittgenstein came to him in the early 1960's, so that, if he does in fact make the open, Peircean break—if he sees "community" not as an independent concept but as a derivative one entailed in the character of signs themselves—it will seem roughly fair to say that in the century following the original publica-

tion of the materials in Volume II, American philosophy of logic has moved from the early Peirce to the early Peirce.

As latter-day nominalism runs its course, the caveat conveyed in Peirce's work on medieval texts is especially pertinent: crudely put, don't throw out the baby with the bathwater. Just as the achievements of scholastic logic were ignored in the first three centuries of the scientific movement, so there are now portents of a compensatory barbarism. Increasingly, academic philosophers are expected to earn their keep by pronouncing on morally meaningful topics. This has led in some quarters to a nostalgia for pre-scientific times and to a general berating of "modernity," by which is sometimes meant something much broader than the *via moderna* of the early Ockhamists: an attack also upon the humane skepticism and cultivated individuality often associated with the nominalist school. Peirce, in his willingness to entertain universals and in his insistence on methods for making them open-ended, workable, and precise, suggests a more civilized and arduous procedure for those wishing to do philosophy on nonscientific topics: instead of rejecting out of hand the entire body of modern philosophy, to understand its limitations on its own terms. Indeed, Max H. Fisch, the dean of Peirce scholarship, has suggested that Peirce's greatest future influence may lie in his bearing upon the "philosophy of institutions" other than those of modern science.

Outside the departments of philosophy there are also fruits to be plucked from the young Peirce. He puts forth a model for disciplined thought still in advance of the prevailing canons. Instead of beginning with what is precise and verifiable, one begins with what is ill-defined. Inquiry then appears not like a mosaic in which one works with tesserae already cut to size, but like the molding of an unshapen piece of clay. The discipline consists not in avoiding what is vague or grandiose but in the self-control to entertain indeterminate ideas until one can give them precise definition. Since definition itself results from a back-and-forth procedure of testing, relation, and negation, it is this procedure, not the canonical forms called induction and deduction, that is at the heart of creative work.

But unlike clay modeling, Peirce's method of thought does not stop with a settled form. Its concepts never rest in equilibrium. They are never baked into a hardened mold. Peirce's early thought lays the ground not only for an alternative to nominalism as a school of thought but to the noun as a crutch for thought. As his later correspondence has it, Peirce sought a "mode of thinking that never results in a concept that is equivalent to a noun substantive." He elsewhere notes that Gaelic lacks a subject noun, that Egyptian hieroglyphs are subversive of the Indo-European subject-predicate form, and that in biblical Hebrew and other Semitic languages nouns have obvious verbal roots and force.

In effect, Peirce is advocating a suspension of the Law of the Excluded Middle, which stipulates that anything must be either A or not A. He is proposing also a doctrine of the "continuous predicate," in which no logical relation is static. I, for one, doubt whether the equilibrium theories of modern economists, or the notion of discrete stages, periods, and social classes that are so convenient in the writing of history are compatible with thinking in Peirce's terms.

There is, finally, a way in which the young Peirce speaks to what is often called common sense—that sphere in which outworn philosophies supply counters for everyday thought. Current political discourse, for example, is structured around quasi-philosophical antinomies—"idealism" versus "realism," a "pragmatic" versus an "ideological" approach—that cannot survive a reading of Volume II. To distinguish the real from the fictitious or the external from the internal is tenable enough. But as the young Peirce shows, to distinguish the real from the ideal is a very different matter. The real, as he sees it *circa* 1871, is an idea that would be agreed upon independently of what you or I now happen to believe. In this sense the real has an inescapable ideal character, and it is a profoundly corrupting discourse that sets "realism" and "idealism" at antipodes, as if philistinism were the ultimate realism.

An ideal or conceptual basis is also at the heart of what can properly be called pragmatism. Whether used as a term of praise or derision, "pragmatism" now connotes a hearty anti-intellectualism, a robust willingness to be buffeted by the winds of fortune, to accommodate, to compromise, to succeed under the pressures of the moment. In this vulgar pragmatism, whatever succeeds is true, and if it ceases to succeed, something else must be true, until such time as it, too, can be associated with some documentable debacle, such as a lowering by two percentage points of the gross national product.

It seems almost a fresh revelation to be reminded that pragmatism, as originally set forth, is a maxim for appraising concepts rather than an excuse for playing fast and loose with them. Insofar as it bears on politics, pragmatism consists simply in understanding the meaning of a doctrine in terms of its practical effects. Thus if, for instance, a given view of the state carries with it the need for wholesale liquidation of populations, suppression of freedoms, and regimentation of everyday life, these are not, pragmatically considered, "means" to an "end"; rather, they are the "meaning" of the doctrine itself.

VIII

In Part, Peirce's precocity on a wide range of issues is a tribute to the philosophers he worked hardest to understand—the "nominalists" Kant and Ockham, the "realist" Duns Scotus. But the ranging relevance of his early thought also has an institutional cause. Boston in those days aspired to be an American Athens. Peirce had to go no farther than his father's house to meet the country's leading poets, jurists, scientists, preachers, and statesmen. And as we have already seen, his father,

aunt, uncles, and other teachers were at the very center of the Lazzaroni clique. They were all imbued with an ideal of a scientific research university fed by elite secondary schools. They sought a combination of intellectual rigor and democratic recruitment that would improve upon rather than ape the available European models. Peirce wrote for that kind of a research establishment, but without the compromises by which the contemporary version of it has been achieved. If his work, even when wrong, enters easily into the conversations of contemporary specialists, it is because he had them specifically in mind. If it goes beyond them, it is because he was not limited by their institutional blinders.

When Peirce wrote the materials in Volume II there was no such thing as a graduate department of philosophy in America. The system of our own day, in which a philosopher is employed as a scholar in some subfield of a balkanized faculty, has advantages that Peirce, with his faith in the cultivation of the specialized sciences, appreciated. In philosophy, however, the departmental system has also resulted in the sundering of elements that he united in his person. Few American philosophy departments, let alone individuals, combine his historical sense of philosophy with a dedication to precise, mathematical notation with broad speculative and scientific abilities. As a result, readings of Peirce by scholars in this or that philosophical subdivision have often missed a larger sense of what he is doing.

He was, after all, consciously recasting the logical basis of modern science, consciously developing the first systematic American philosophy, consciously justifying the vision of an ideal university as a community of ongoing inquiry, and doing so in a way that both ratified and moderated the religiously grounded universality that had triumphed in the American Civil War. All this gives his theoretical work a breadth and depth not equaled by any other American philosopher. He emerges as a post-Enlightenment writer untinged by romanticism, aestheticism, or nostalgia. Independently of the techniques pioneered, arguments made, and doctrines expounded—and the ritual admission that one "cannot do justice to them here" is especially appropriate for a writer as meticulous and difficult as Peirce—the truly exciting thing about the two volumes at hand is that they document the founding of American philosophy. They exhibit the maturation and then the first bold strokes of an epochal mind.

IX

They also set the stage for a tragedy. The bright-eyed young scholar of 1867 will become, in his own words of 1898, "an old hermit, white and wild," and in the words of William James five years later, "a seedy, almost sordid old man." His collection of medieval texts will have long since been sold to the Johns Hopkins library to raise money. He will have become involved in the 1890's in frenetic, failed, Gilded Age moneymaking schemes to float new inventions, build great canals, sell oil paintings, write bestselling texts. In the end he will be reduced to offering himself to declaim the part of King Lear before a hall in Boston for $200. His old friend William James will rescue him first by laundering private funds through the Harvard Corporation to provide him a dignified forum for a lecture series in 1903, then by direct charity.

The whole spectacle will point comfortable lessons for his tenured contemporaries: genius without character is vain; brilliance cannot be sustained without colleagues; the most important book is a balanced checkbook; slow and steady wins the race.

And not for his contemporaries alone. There is an undercurrent in much writing on Peirce that suggests he got what he deserved, that it was his own flaws that brought him down. Overprotected by his father, he was too self-centered to get on with others, too erratic to work in harness, too lacking in self-control to manage his finances. His star rose only while his father lived. After that his academic career collapsed and his work became hopelessly eccentric. His separation from university life has seemed to point a special moral about the impossibility of a life of the mind outside academe, and to this day in the institutions that blackballed him there arise exculpatory rumors of other sins made darker by being unnamed.

This account, at least insofar as it concerns his intellectual output, seems to have been rejected by the Indiana editors: of their twenty volumes, sixteen will be devoted to Peirce's post-academic period. But I also think the "tragic-flaw" account faulty in giving insufficient credit to the indifference and malevolence of others. And since this academic year marks the centenary of Peirce's firing from Johns Hopkins, in a prejudicial way that ended his university career, it is perhaps fitting to conclude by pursuing to 1884 our brief chronicle of Peirce's relation to academic life.

Documents which have not yet received public notice suggest that, whatever his personal weaknesses, Peirce was the victim at Johns Hopkins of a star-chamber proceeding set in motion by a scientific rival, Simon Newcomb, and abetted by a bureaucratic one, Julius Hilgard.

The prime mover of the piece was Simon Newcomb, described by Peirce in later years as America's leading man of science of the 19th century. Newcomb had been a protégé of Benjamin Peirce and his brother-in-law Charles Henry Davis. He had made his early career entirely within the Lazzaroni circle. Like Peirce's father, he led a publicly irreproachable life and had an institutional influence equal to his scientific achievement. He and Charles Peirce were among the extraordinary group of younger scholars and scientists assembled by Daniel Coit Gilman, the founding president of Johns Hopkins.

Hopkins in those days was the university of Lazzaroni dreams. Gilman announced that the $4-million Hopkins bequest would be devoted to pure graduate research. This bold stroke spurred other college presidents, notably Eliot at Harvard, to invest in advanced research. Peirce was hired by Gilman in 1879 as a part-time lecturer in logic, with the remainder of his time devoted to work at the Coast and Geodetic Survey. The quality and general tenor of his graduate teaching may be surmised from what was to have been the first of a series edited by him of collected papers of his students, *Studies in Logic by Members of the Johns Hopkins University* (1883). Though he was, as a personal matter, what would now be called highly neurotic, his main personal disability was a great resource to a research university. He was cursed with a systematic mind chained to an impulsive nature. Unable to find a form for all his ideas, he was forever generating insights that were immensely stimulating to others. He was for five years hired on a year's renewable contract. At the beginning of his fifth year, in September 1883, he was encouraged by Gilman to take a two-year lease on a house in Baltimore.

Before coming to Hopkins, Peirce had alerted Gilman to possible embarrassment resulting from his permanent separation from his wife. Peirce's formal divorce went through in 1883 and was followed with an immediate marriage to a French widow, who claimed to be of a partly noble background. Juliette, the new Mrs. Peirce, made a favorable initial impression on Mrs. Gilman. There was nothing in the remarriage that changed Peirce's status at Hopkins, until Newcomb took it upon himself to bring certain rumors about Peirce to the attention of a straitlaced member of the board of trustees.

The source of the rumors was Julius Erasmus Hilgard, whom we have encountered as assistant under Bache and Benjamin Peirce. Twice blocked by the elder Peirce for promotion to superintendent of the Coast and Geodetic Survey, Hilgard finally succeeded to the job, but as a bitter, broken, and sick man. He was morally outraged at young Peirce's remarriage: he knew Charley and Juliette to have been in flagrant consort prior to the divorce. Newcomb retailed this and perhaps other rumors to the Baltimore burgher in a railroad-car conversation. The trustee, horrified, reported the rumors as fact to Gilman. Newcomb then followed with a written note to Gilman confirming that the source of the rumors felt it a moral duty to supply whatever further testimony was needed.

Though there is no record of any further inquiry having been made, Peirce soon found himself severed from Hopkins without any idea of the cause. The university simply declared itself to be discontinuing instruction in logic and terminated all three faculty in the subject. It then hired two of them back under other rubrics. Unaware of Newcomb's role and never informed of the charges against him, Peirce accused Gilman of "treachery." Juliette made a special appeal in a stormy private meeting that made matters worse. Neither Gilman nor the trustees ever gave any statement of cause for their action, though they did, in the end, make restitution for the second year of rental on Peirce's house. A reputation for moral turpitude followed the Peirces during their subsequent thirty years of quiet rural life, and there are written records to attest that a bad moral character was used to deny Peirce consideration for further university posts.

Newcomb's role can be substantiated mainly from his gossip-laden correspondence with his wife, who spent 1883-85 in Europe supervising the Swiss education of the three Newcomb daughters. Those letters also reveal that Mary Hassler Newcomb, a granddaughter of the founding superintendent of the Survey, did some Peirce research of her own. She reported to her husband allegations of financial improprieties in Peirce's commissioning of the European manufacture of pendulums for the Survey. Newcomb passed these reports on to Hilgard, who tried to use them to compel Peirce's resignation. But the European source of the allegations could not (to Newcomb's annoyance) be induced to commit them to writing, and Peirce was able to demonstrate an out-of-pocket payment that Mrs. Newcomb's informant had neglected. Hilgard and Newcomb thus did not find sufficient grounds to complete the destruction of Peirce's livelihood. As a public agency, the Survey could not chop Peirce quite so neatly as Johns Hopkins, and he was still drawing his assistant's salary when Hilgard's alcoholism forced his own premature retirement. Newcomb, foreseeing Hilgard's demise, corresponded with his wife about giving up his tenured chair at Hopkins to become Hilgard's successor. But he did not need the superintendency to confirm his victory in the one-sided war for the Lazzaroni succession.

Peirce and Juliette had some inherited income, which along with his Survey job gave them a very comfortable $10,000 a year with which to retire to a newly bought house in Milford, Pennsylvania. It was his hope to live as a country gentleman/philosopher. As long as his money lasted, his wife was continually making additions to the chateau. In the early 1890's, however, Peirce lost everything in a stock-market crash, was terminated for neglecting his duties at the Survey, went through a sheriff's seizure of his house, and had to support himself by writing reviews for the *Nation* and definitions for the *Century Dictionary and Cyclopedia*. Newcomb, when the first edition of the dictionary appeared, published a needlessly captious letter criticizing some of Peirce's definitions.

By the turn of the century, when Peirce was nearly destitute, his friends encouraged him to apply to the newly formed Carnegie Institution, set up to support outstanding intellectual work in "every department of study." His application may well be the most impressive foundation-grant proposal ever submitted, both in intellectual scope and in the accompanying testimonies of support. Some two dozen letters of recommendation were filed from the leading philosophers and statesmen of the day. The president of that newly founded institution, however, was Daniel Coit Gilman, who had the secretary of the executive committee solicit an independent professional opinion from Simon Newcomb. Peirce's application was refused, on the old Johns Hopkins grounds that work in logic fell outside the defined sphere of the Carnegie Institution, which would limit itself to work in the special sciences. Under this rubric, Newcomb himself received a grant at a later date, as did one of his close associates.

X

Peirce was without rancor. He remained unflagging in his high estimation of Newcomb's contribution to science and of Gilman's institution-building role. Their failure to support him does not erase these achievements. But I am not the first to see it as raising serious questions about institutional support of what is called genius. For it is in the nature of ground-breaking work that few can identify it. Of these, fewer still command the resources to support it. And in highly theoretical fields the very activity of inquiry often carries with it incapacities in practical affairs that limit effective control to still fewer hands. If those hands are unsteadied by some extraneous passion, even a brilliant light may be extinguished. In Peirce's day, the modest resources he required were concentrated in two places—Harvard and Johns Hopkins—and both failed him.

As a result, his later life was subjected to torments beyond those already built into his work. Any critical examination of the deepest logical categories risks severing the bonds that unite the philosopher with his fellow men. Any attempt to develop an alternative to orthodox habits of thought requires a dedication and regularity that put severe strains on any but the most phlegmatic temperament. For the prickly and emotional Peirce, there was enough agony simply in pursuing his aim in life. To this were added financial uncertainty, social ostracism, and poignant contradictions: Peirce, the philosopher *par excellence* of the communal basis of inquiry, forced to work in utter isolation; the warrior against the noun substantive having to make his livelihood writing dictionary definitions; the pampered child of the Lazzaroni exiled from the university of their dreams to a cruel world of piecework and business ventures; the believer in heroic dedication to an indefinite future begging for tomorrow's bread. That he managed nevertheless to complete a body of work which, for all its many imperfections and unfulfilled projects, will provide, as it is issued over the coming years, more to raise the general standard of theoretical study than that of any living American philosopher, is one of the more inspiring stories to have taken place on this continent.

It would be comforting to think that in our own day a vast, bureaucratized, and pluralistic research establishment and the system of "peer review" prevent a repetition of Peirce's tribulations. But there are never peers to review unique work, and the very bureaucratization of intellectual labor entrenches the conventional. Moreover, the mere maintenance of overhead costs seems to require making and therefore enforcing a case for inquiry in terms of some irrelevant utility, as in books by university presidents with such titles as *Beyond the Ivory Tower* (Harvard) or *The University and the Public Interest* (Yale) or *The Uses of the University* (California). There is, however, no utilitarian formula for the propagation of genius, or even of simple intelligence, no institutional procedure more efficacious than the exercise of spacious judgment, and no rule more reliable than this: to pursue our intimations of what is important for its own sake, and when we find it in others, to support it as best we are able.

It will perhaps be clear why among friends of learning these Peirce volumes will be welcomed as more than a publishing event. They provide an occasion to retrieve a sense of clarity about fundamental concerns. Attractively produced, impeccably introduced and annotated, they pay tribute to a remarkable mind. In so doing they advance by a giant step the life of the mind to which Charles Sanders Peirce was heroically devoted:

> Sometimes we can personally attain to heroism. The soldier who runs to scale a wall knows that he will probably be shot, but that is not all he cares for. He also knows that if all the regiment, with whom in feeling he identifies himself, rush forward at once, the fort will be taken. In other cases we can only imitate the virtue.

Michael L. Raposa (essay date 1987)

SOURCE: "Peirce's Theological Semiotic," in *The Journal of Religion,* Vol. 67, No. 4, October, 1987, pp. 493-509.

[In the following excerpt, Raposa explores Peirce's religious nature as a backdrop for the entirety of his writings.]

Charles Peirce described his essay, **"A Neglected Argument for The Reality of God,"** as the "poor sketch" of an argument; he intended that it should function as a "table of contents" on the basis of which others might be able to "guess" what he had to say. I propose to fill in some of the details of that sketch, to suggest the sort of text that Peirce might have written, given the table of contents that he provided. Such a project requires a certain amount of "guesswork," but those guesses are both educated ones and fewer in number than one might expect. This is the case because Peirce's reflections on religious topics are continuous with, even integral to, his work in semiotic, metaphysics, and the normative sciences; consequently, he himself supplied, in other writings, much of the "text" for the Neglected Argument.[1]

Written and published in 1908, only six years before his death, Peirce's essay represents both the maturest form of his thought and one of the very few extended treatments of a religious topic that he produced during a lifetime of philosophizing. The small number and fragmentary nature of his religious writings, however, are by no means indices of their significance. Moreover, Peirce's philosophy as a whole seems to have been shaped and informed by certain religious beliefs and ideas; his thought will be vulnerable to misinterpretation, then, until these ideas have been rendered explicit, their function and importance ascertained. Such considerations underscore the potential hermeneutical value of Peirce's Neglected Argument.

That article actually embodies a "nest" of three arguments, only the first of which concludes that God is real. I proceed with an analysis of "Musement," the central concept in this initial, "Humble Argument." Peirce's own attempts to explicate and contextualize that notion constitute the second and third phases of his discussion. I trace the line of reasoning that he pursues in all three "arguments" before turning, in the final section of my paper, to the task of characterizing Peirce's "theological semiotic," a label that I attach to his distinctive theological method and theory of religious knowledge.

I

What does it mean to affirm that God is real? Peirce begins his inquiry by analyzing the key terms in such a claim. "God," he explains, "is the definable proper name, signifying *Ens necessarium;* in my belief Really creator of all three Universes of Experience" (6.452).[2] Here Peirce invokes his doctrine of categories; the three "universes," exhaustive of reality and comprising the objects of all possible experience, consist in, first, the realm of ideal qualities or pure possibility, second, brute actuality or existence, and third, real generality or law (see 6.455). God is their creator, but it is inappropriate to conclude, as a consequence, that God "exists." To do so would be to reduce the Deity to the category of "secondness," for Peirce, the realm of brute reaction events, devoid of generality, and, thus, of intelligibility. (From his point of view, it is inadequate to say, even about a physical object enduring in time, simply that it "exists"; since it endures, it is a "continuity of reactions," and its nature must be lawlike.) Rather, God is "real," invoking here what Peirce perceives to be Duns Scotus's notion of a *reality* as that which is what it is independently of what any mind or finite collection of minds might conceive it to be (6.453, 496).[3]

Peirce does not, in this context, say anything more precise about the divine nature and attributes. Indeed, he suggests elsewhere that the great utility of the word "God" in religious discourse derives from its *vagueness* (6.494); more readily definable metaphysical terms are to be eschewed for reasons that will become somewhat clearer as Peirce's argument unfolds. In this regard, it is important to note that his argument for the reality of God is exactly that, the description of an "argument" rather than the development of an "argumentation."

> An "Argument" is any process of thought reasonably tending to produce a definite belief. An

"Argumentation" is an Argument proceeding upon definitely formulated premises. [6.456]

Just as the concept of God is invariably vague, the argument for the reality of such a being resists precise formulation. The philosophical commentary on this "process of thought" ought to be distinguished, as supplementary argumentation, from the natural and informal line of reasoning that actually produces belief in God. Now there are a number of factors that motivate Peirce to draw this distinction, not the least of which is his concern that the rational belief in God be recognized as universally accessible. For

> If God Really be, and be benign, then, in view of the generally conceded truth that religion, were it but proved, would be a good outweighing all others, we should naturally expect that there would be some Argument for His Reality that should be obvious to all minds, high and low alike, that should earnestly strive to find the truth of the matter; and further, that this Argument should present its conclusion, not as a proposition of metaphysical theology, but in a form directly applicable to the conduct of life, and full of nutrition for man's highest growth. [6.457]

This natural expectation is fulfilled by the "Humble Argument." "Its persuasiveness is no less than extraordinary; while it is not unknown to anybody" (6.457). Nonetheless, Peirce contends, it has been strangely "neglected" by theologians, who in their attempts to supply rational support for the belief in God, have ignored the very process of reasoning that typically generates such a belief. It is this process or form of reasoning that Peirce labels "Musement" and describes as "Pure Play"; "it involves no purpose save that of casting aside all serious purpose" (6.458). Governed by no rules other than the "law of liberty," the Muser proceeds, not with the goal of "becoming convinced of the truth of religion," but simply to contemplate "some wonder in one of the Universes, or some connection between two of the three." This is essential from Peirce's point of view, that "religious meditation be allowed to grow up spontaneously out of Pure Play without any breach of continuity." For it is in the Pure Play of Musement, he explains, that "the idea of God's Reality will be sure sooner or later to be found an attractive fancy, which the Muser will develop in various ways. The more he ponders it, the more it will find repose in every part of his mind, for its beauty, for its supplying an ideal of life, and for its thoroughly satisfying explanation of his whole threefold environment" (6.456).

The Muser will recognize, on carefully considering the idea of God, that it represents the summum bonum, the threefold aesthetic, ethical, and logical ideal that, for Peirce, constitutes the ultimate object of inquiry in the normative sciences.[4] It is this ideal quality that will recommend the idea, as a highly plausible *hypothesis*, for subsequent investigation. But Peirce makes it clear that the actual belief in God will not, in most cases, be contingent on the outcome of such an investigation. The idea of God will suggest itself as being so attractive and so plausible that the Muser "will come to be stirred to the depths of his nature by the beauty of the idea and by its august practicality, even to the point of earnestly loving and adoring his strictly hypothetical God, and to that of desiring above all things to shape the whole conduct of life and all the springs of action into conformity with that hypothesis" (6.467).

To shape the "whole conduct" of one's life in conformity with a proposition, Peirce argues, is precisely to *believe* that proposition since, on his account, all beliefs are nothing other than *habits* of inference and of action. If it seems odd for Peirce to speak, in this context, about "loving" and "adoring" a "hypothetical God," it should be noted that he regarded all perceptual judgments as being hypothetical inferences; that is, to perceive anything at all involves, however unconscious, automatic, or indubitable it may be, the formation of a hypothesis. Labeling the God who is revealed in the process of Musement as "strictly hypothetical" need not conflict, then, with those claims made about the power of the experience of such a reality. The hypothetical status of an idea reflects the "stage of inquiry" at which it is being considered and does not necessarily tell one anything about its power or plausibility at that stage. But these comments anticipate Peirce's own subsequent analysis of the Humble Argument. Before turning to that analysis, some "models" for the concept of Musement ought to be considered.

Throughout most of his philosophical career, Peirce was an objective idealist; he defended the notion that all of reality is of the nature of living mind. Against the background of such a notion, he attempted to develop a cosmology that would account for both the variety of phenomena in the universe and the growth of ideas as objective "habits" or laws of nature. He speculated that the origin of both elements, variety and growth, is to be located in a primordial state of pure "firstness," of spontaneous feeling "sporting here and there in pure arbitrariness" (6.33). Regarded objectively, such feelings constitute ideal qualities, possibilities, some of which are actualized, react with one another, and, eventually, form continua of qualities. These continua are the manifestations of a generalizing tendency, of objective habits that gradually strengthen themselves (6.196 ff.). But the element of chance or spontaneity remains, breaking up old habits, serving as a catalyst and a stimulant for the development of new laws of behavior. And so, while such laws "grow" out of the chance "sporting" of qualities, their reign is never absolute, nor is the variety of phenomena in the cosmos brought, under the influence of law, to a state of perfect regularity and order.

This is, of course, a rather crude sketch of Peirce's own crude and highly speculative cosmology. Its purpose is to illustrate the fact that Peirce really did conceive of the universe as an Absolute Mind.[5] Insofar as it is a mind characterized by spontaneous feeling, it is a "sporting" consciousness, indeed, a mind at play. Peirce's thinking here is informed by the Darwinian principle of fortuitous variation; he was impressed by the manner in which Darwin had been able to show, in the biological realm, that chance could beget order, facilitate growth. But Peirce generalized that principle and gave it a much wider application. With bold and broad strokes he painted the sort of cosmic picture that has been briefly described here: the Absolute Mind "muses," forms hypotheses, performs inductions, and so "thinks" the laws of nature.

In certain respects, then, the Muser in Peirce's Humble Argument actually "imitates" a cosmological phenomenon. Furthermore, Peirce prescribes as the ideal subject matter for meditation the very phenomenon that is being imitated; it is in pondering the variety and growth in the three universes that questions about their relationship and origin will be raised. And it is within this context that the idea of God will inevitably suggest itself. Indeed, the Muser will be in direct communion with the Absolute Mind since Peirce insisted that all of reality is continuous; in fact, communication can only occur as the result of the continuous connection between ideas (6.158-63).

While Peirce's metaphysics and cosmology shed some light on the concept of Musement, he himself reported that it was a notion borrowed from Friedrich Schiller's aesthetics and that it was intended to convey nothing other than what the latter designated as *Spieltrieb*.[6] A detailed comparison of Peirce and Schiller on this issue is not possible here, but four brief observations suggest that such a comparison might be highly instructive, while underscoring the features of Schiller's work that were most likely to have attracted Peirce.

1) In the first place, the concept of a "play impulse" is formulated by Schiller within the context of a discussion of aesthetics and of the nature of the beautiful. For Peirce, aesthetics grounds ethics and logic as the most fundamental of the normative sciences; its object is to describe the *summum bonum*, that which is admirable in itself. Now it is clear that the *summum bonum* has religious connotations for Peirce and, at several points in the Neglected Argument, he stresses the fact that the idea of God is distinguished by its great beauty (6.465, 467, 487). Moreover, the beauty of the idea is a quality that both inspires the immediate belief and love of the Muser and recommends it as a hypothesis for scientific consideration.

2) Schiller contends that the contemplation of the beautiful is morally edifying "since it is only out of the aesthetic . . . state that the moral can develop."[7] Peirce, too, locates the final upshot of Musement in the realm of the ethical. The most visible and significant effects of the God hypothesis derive from its "influence over the whole conduct of life" (6.490). No belief is genuine unless it constitutes a real habit of action, and the end result of Musement has already been described as a state of belief.

3) The purposelessness and disinterestedness that characterize Schiller's *Spieltrieb* render it analogous to the ideal "scientific" attitude. Only the Muser, who has cast aside all specific interests and purposes, can be said to be "inquiring in scientific singleness of heart" (6.458). Peirce's commentary on the Humble Argument will make it clear that that process of reasoning need not, but certainly can be, identified as a legitimate stage in a scientific inquiry.

4) As such, it is the "abductive" phase of inquiry, that is to say, the process of hypothesis formation and selection. It is most interesting to speculate, in this regard, how Schiller's analysis of the play impulse might have shaped Peirce's own development of the logic of abduction. Even Schiller's language resonates with Peirce's usage. Of the two conflicting impulses that are harmonized in play, one furnishes "cases" (*Falle*), the other gives "laws" (*Gesetze*).[8] Similarly, abduction, for Peirce, is a mode of inference whereby particular instances, or "cases," are recognized as being governed by a specific law, or "rule."[9] Inquiry originates in a form of cognitive play, a "playing with" the observed facts, with various "rearrangements" of them, and with the candidate hypotheses that might render them intelligible (see 6.488). This is the plot of the next chapter in Peirce's story.

II

The meditation on the idea of God constitutes a "reasonable argument" because it produces a "truly Religious belief" in God's "Reality" and "nearness" (6.486). Why, then, does Peirce choose to supplement it with additional argumentation? Clearly, he regards this sort of commentary as being, in a sense, superfluous, lacking the "religious vitality" of the Humble Argument and serving only as an "apology," a "vindicatory description" of it (6.487). Nonetheless, for the individual who has never "seriously" engaged in Musement, these comments function as an invitation, a recommendation for that particular exercise. Furthermore, having been committed for most of his life to the scientific method as the only *ultimately valid* procedure for "fixing belief," Peirce must have been predisposed to illustrate some relation between the Humble Argument and systematic scientific inquiry.

Now Peirce is not rigorously consistent in specifying what he intends to include under the rubric of the "Neglected Argument." He sometimes indicates that this label should be applied to the Humble Argument proper (6.483-84); elsewhere, he explains that he uses the designation loosely for all three in his "nest" of arguments but that, more precisely, it refers to the second in this nest (6.487). This last account seems most accurate since Peirce does contend that it is specifically the theologians who have been guilty of "neglect," and what they have repeatedly neglected to do is carefully *describe* the Humble Argument and *defend* its reasonableness and force (6.484, 487). This would involve showing that the argument, "if sufficiently developed, will convince any normal man" precisely because "a latent tendency toward belief in God is a fundamental ingredient of the soul" and "the natural precipitate of meditation upon the origin of the Three Universes." Such is the burden of the theological argumentation that focuses the second phase of Peirce's discussion.

It is a significant burden, and Peirce's claim is quite remarkable, especially in light of his own admission that "there is very little established fact" that can be enlisted in support of it. But note immediately that it is *not* a claim about the reality of God. Rather, it is a contention about the *naturalness*, the *instinctiveness*, of the hypothesis concerning God's reality. That Peirce should choose to explicate the Humble Argument in exactly this way is a fact of some importance; for example, it suggests that any interpretation of his essay that represents it as embodying a version of the "argument from design" is a misconstrual.[10] Peirce never affirms that the order, purpose, and design manifest in the universe supply an adequate evidential basis for the logical inference (inductive or analogical) that God exists. Instead, such realities serve to focus the contemplative activity of Musement. Peirce's emphasis is on the inevitability with which the God hypothesis will tend to arise in the midst of such activity, on the special type of human "instinctiveness" that displays itself in this process. Indeed, there is good reason to suspect that the Humble Argument is Peirce's own highly idiosyncratic version of the *ontological* proof. In addition to his revealing definition of God as *Ens necessarium*, Peirce actually admitted to defending that proof in a certain form. He explains in a 1905 letter to William James that "the esthetic ideal, that which we *all* love and adore, the altogether admirable, has, *as ideal*, necessarily a mode of being to be called living. . . . Now the Ideal is not a finite existent. Moreover, the human mind and the human heart have a filiation to God" (8.262). And, in another draft of the same correspondence, "It is impossible to think that the ideal of our hearts is merely existent or limited another way, and it is impossible for a person who puts metaphysical definitions aside to think that the object of one's love is not living. The idea is a vague one, but it is only the more irresistible for that."[11]

Despite the enormous differences between Peirce and Saint Anselm of Canterbury, they both agree that careful meditation on the idea of God will lead inevitably to the conclusion that such a being must be real ("living"). But for Peirce this process of reasoning resists translation into clearly defined metaphysical terms. The God whose being is affirmed is understood only vaguely; moreover, this vagueness is mitigated at the great expense of the indubitability of the hypothesis (see 6.499). To render any vague proposition more precise is to problematize it, to specify the prediction that can be derived from it, thus making it vulnerable to falsification. This sort of precision, of course, is a legitimate goal of rational inquiry, and it surely ought to be pursued. To falsify a specific formulation of some general hypothesis, however, is not to reject the hypothesis itself but only that

precise explication of it; the vague, instinctive hypothesis is, as such, indubitable. Furthermore, one ought not to seek greater precision in one's discourse than a given subject matter allows. It would be possible to speak with perfect precision only about a reality that was completely determinate in every respect; since, for Peirce, the Absolute Mind is a continuum of the highest level of generality, it is unreasonable to expect that the vagueness of religious utterances can be drastically reduced.[12]

Now it seems to be the case that these remarks about vagueness relieve Peirce's argument of some of its burden. It is, after all, not a specific, clearly articulated idea of God that he claims will inevitably suggest itself in the process of Musement; rather, it is a vague hypothesis about a necessary being who is both the creator of the universes and the ideal that ought to govern all human thought and action. The "playful" reasoning about such a being is continuous with the love and adoration that it inspires. For Peirce, in fact, "emotion *is* vague, incomprehensible thought." "That," he explains, "is why the highest truths can only be felt."[13] And that is why the feeling responses to the idea of God are integral to Musement and not merely its side effect.

It should also be noted that Peirce is not guilty here of some form of special pleading for his religious claims. The argumentation about the instinctiveness of the God hypothesis is consistent with Peirce's contentions regarding the instinctive, commonsense beliefs that ground all scientific inquiry. Such inquiry is the rendering precise of these vague notions, but the notions themselves are generated "abductively" as hypotheses: "not only is our knowledge not exclusively derived from experience, but every item of science came originally from conjecture, which has only been pruned down by experience."[14]

Consequently, Peirce's Neglected Argument needs to be read against the background supplied by his own numerous remarks about a human "guessing instinct," a capacity that he explains as the product of evolution and natural selection.[15] It is an extremely fallible instinct, far more often wrong than right but right just frequently enough to account for the remarkable success with which scientists, in such a short period of time, have proceeded to unlock the secrets of nature. Other species clearly demonstrate instinctive capacities; on what grounds should humanity be excepted from the general rules?

> Animals of all races rise far above the general level of their intelligence in those performances that are their proper function, such as flying and nest-building for ordinary birds; and what is man's proper function if it be not to embody general ideas in art-creations, in utilities, and above all in theoretical cognition? To give the lie to his own consciousness of divining the reasons of phenomena would be as silly in a man as it would be in a fledgling bird to refuse to trust its wings and leave the nest. . . . *If we knew* that the impulse to prefer one hypothesis to another really were analogous to the instincts of birds and wasps,

it would be foolish not to give it play, within the bounds of reason; especially since we must entertain some hypothesis, or else forego all further knowledge than that which we have already gained by that very means. [6.476]

Galileo's reflections on *il lume naturale* are cited by Peirce as being compatible with and supportive of his own point of view on this issue. He confesses to having long misconstrued the former's defense of the criterion of simplicity in hypothesis selection as an appeal to *logical* simplicity; rather, Peirce now recognizes that the simpler hypothesis is the one that is "the more facile and natural, the one that instinct suggests" (6.477). Having evolved under the influence of nature, it is reasonable to assume that human beings would have become adapted to the task of understanding their environment. Translated into the terms of Peirce's objective idealism, this becomes an argument about the continuous connection between ideas, about Mind shaping minds.

The strength of Peirce's claims about Musement seems to be contingent, then, on (1) the level of vagueness that he intends to ascribe to the idea of God that arises in this process and (2) the general coherence and plausibility of his philosophy of science, especially his perspective on the instinctual basis of scientific knowledge. Unfortunately, the "sketch" that Peirce supplies here embodies no clear answer to the question about point 1. And the careful and thorough assessment of Peirce's views about science is a huge task that lies beyond the scope of this paper. Nevertheless, this second argument in his "nest" does flow directly and comfortably into the third. There, at least, a few additional remarks about the general nature of scientific inquiry will lend some clarity to Peirce's overall exposition.

The preceding analysis has already anticipated Peirce's final series of moves. The Humble Argument concluded that God is real. The "neglected" defense of that argument was fashioned around the claim that this conclusion is instinctive, the "natural precipitate" of Musement. Now Peirce makes explicit that which had already emerged as obvious. Musement is a form of abductive reasoning, the appropriate initial stage of any scientific inquiry. Abduction always involves observation, the imaginative manipulation of observed facts, and the formulation of explanatory hypotheses (6.488). Such hypotheses, subsequently, can be explicated deductively, and their validity must be tested inductively, but all inquiry receives its creative impetus from these preliminary abductive inferences. New or inventive ideas are already embodied in the hypothesis; deduction and induction merely serve to clarify and to confirm (or disconfirm) abductive insights.

If the second phase of Peirce's discussion involves the attempt to strengthen the conclusion about God's reality by underscoring its "naturalness," this third phase is designed to link the argument for that conclusion with a general logic of inquiry (see 6.491). Religious knowing will be like scientific knowing, and it will have a comparable validity, if both are the end results of the same rational process. In the case under scrutiny, however, that process seems to be short-circuited. In the first place, "so hard is it to doubt God's reality, when the Idea has sprung from Musements, that there is great danger that the investigation will stop at this first stage, owing to the indifference of the Muser to any further proof of it" (6.488).

This in itself is no indictment of the hypothesis but, rather, a very strong claim about its plausibility. More troublesome is a second observation that, owing to its obscurity or vagueness, it is virtually impossible to deduce the testable implications of the hypothesis (6.489). How could the behavior of such a divine being be predicted with enough specificity to enable one to subject the claim about its reality to experiment, to checking procedures? Peirce suggests that this "peculiarity" of the God hypothesis is counteracted by another, "which consists in its commanding influence over the whole conduct of life of its believers" (6.490). Here he is invoking the basic principle of his pragmaticism; the meaning of a conception will consist in the set of habits that it engenders, in the manner in which it determines human cognition and behavior. But it is still unclear, even assuming that the hypothesis somehow can be explicated, how the inductive phase of inquiry is to be initiated, how evidence is to be gathered for the claim about God.

Peirce might have responded to this sort of challenge, had he filled in the details of his sketch, in a number of ways. First, despite the enormous conceptual and practical difficulties, as well as the crudeness of our present state of knowledge, it is the ongoing task of philosophy to attempt to explicate the God hypothesis, and it is the goal of a truly scientific cosmology to gather evidence that can be brought to bear on that notion. Surely there are analogous examples in science of theories that, given our actual skills and expertise, cannot be immediately subjected to decisive verification or falsification.[16] Second, since the meaning of the idea of God is revealed in human conduct, a test of the reality of that being might consist in a long-range assessment of the fruitfulness, the success of behavior that conforms to this hypothesis as an ideal. If God is real, then behaving as if God were real ought to be efficacious. But this is an obscure enough proposal, and, ultimately, the "test" that Peirce would be proposing here would involve the gathering of data ranging over the entire scope of human history (see, e.g., 6.287-317).

A more practical possibility might suggest itself were one to shift one's gaze to the heart of Peirce's discussion, to the innermost "core" of his nest of arguments. That is to say, Musement itself constitutes a kind of "experiment"; Peirce carefully prescribes the ideal set of conditions under which such an experiment should be conducted and then invites the reader to test the normality of his (Peirce's) thinking and perceptions. Some evidence that this is very much what Peirce had in mind appears in an unpublished version of the Neglected

Argument, where he suggests that among the most powerful and visible effects of the God hypothesis are those wrought upon the Muser in the very process of meditation.[17] This "experiment" bears positive results if the Muser is brought to feel and to "see" that which Peirce claims can and should be felt and seen under these circumstances. In fact, the very skills that one needs to discern the "reality" and "nearness" of God are acquired in or at least sharpened by Musement.

Such an interpretation invokes a semiotic context for the Humble Argument; it is with a brief discussion of that context that this paper concludes.

III

Abduction is, on Peirce's account, the primary logic of sign interpretation. To interpret the meaning of x is to supply an explanation of x, to form a certain kind of hypothesis about it. Given the enormous amount of time and energy that he expended in the process of attempting both to formulate a general semiotic and to explicate the logic of abduction, one might suspect that the depth and significance of his contribution in these areas has yet to be fully assessed. What insights might such an assessment yield for understanding Peirce's religious thought? One way to begin to answer this question is by taking a closer look at the role that beliefs play, on Peirce's account, in hypothetical inferences.

Generally speaking, beliefs about the typical features of a certain kind of thing or phenomenon will function as habits, predisposing an individual who observes this configuration of features to infer hypothetically that the observed x is of that kind. Beliefs, both singly and in combination, serve in this fashion as the guilding "rules" of abductive reasoning. They are "models" or "laws" that are utilized, consciously or unconsciously, in the classification or explanation of specific "cases." Consider Peirce's characterization of this habit function. "Habit is that specialization of the law of mind whereby a general idea gains the power of exciting reactions. But in order that the general idea should attain all its functionality, it is necessary, also, that it should become suggestible by sensations. That is accomplished by a psychical process having the form of a hypothetic inference" (6.145). How, more precisely, does such a general idea become "suggestible by sensations?" "The mode of suggestion by which, in abduction, the facts suggest the hypothesis is by *resemblance*—the resemblance of the facts to the consequences of the hypothesis" (7.218). "Hypothesis substitutes, for a complicated tangle of predicates attached to one subject, a single conception" (2.643).

It is this resemblance between the observed configuration of facts and the pattern of expectations generated by a given belief or system of beliefs that is the source of abductive insight. When, in some instances, this resemblance is not readily apparent, it becomes necessary to "playfully" manipulate or rearrange the observed data

and to continuously suppress and highlight the various implications of hypotheses in order to test their explanatory power. Musement greatly accentuates this playful aspect of abduction; indeed, it is playful enough to allow a "latent" belief habit to exert its creative influence. However, hypothetical inferences can be immediate and unconscious, as well as indubitable. This is the case when something is simply perceived to be this or that sort of thing. It has already been noted that perceptual judgments are, for Peirce, instances of abduction (see 5.181 ff.); that is, all experience is interpreted experience. Whether it is simply a matter of "seeing" x as y or of concluding after a careful and deliberate process of reasoning that x is of the y sort, the mode of inference is essentially the same.[18]

At least two important features of Peirce's account need to be underscored at this point. In the first place, abduction is not always simply a matter of classification, whereby observed phenomena are "explained" by being located in a familiar, well-defined category. Frequently, *new* categories and classifications will have to be created in the process of reasoning itself, ideas connected, disconnected, and rearranged in very much the same way that the data must be continuously "played with" and reorganized. If successful, a strong hypothesis will emerge out of this process. That hypothesis may function to identify some x, but not in the sense that x is now recognized as a y, y being the kind of thing that one was already quite familiar with. One's idea of that *kind* of thing is itself generated in the course of abduction, as an explanatory "rule" of thought.

Since Peirce regarded feelings as being vague thoughts, they might very well be perceived as partially constituting a vague hypothesis. For example, the love of God, as a "habit of feeling" that arises in response to the reality encountered, might form part of the "explanation" of that reality. That is to say, this love could function to organize, to unify, to "explain" a "complicated tangle" of feelings. And this love, like the vague ideas that form the God hypothesis, could enable the Muser to see the three universes in a new way, as it is often the case that a phenomenon can only be clearly perceived "in the light of the hypothesis" (6.469). This is the second important feature of Peirce's account: just as he intends to connect the Humble Argument with a general logic of inquiry, the latter itself is directly linked to the logic of perception. To interpret the meaning of a sign can involve either a very extended process of reasoning or a simple matter of recognition, of "seeing" it; both are instances of abduction. Now Peirce seems to be suggesting that, as the effects of Musement accumulate, the "nearness" and "beauty" of the divine reality become more readily perceptible; in this case, meditative thinking facilitates or clarifies perception.

> Just as a long acquaintance with a man of great character may deeply influence one's whole manner of conduct, so that a glance at his portrait may make a difference, just as almost living with

Dr. Johnson enabled poor Boswell to write an immortal book and a really sublime book, just as long study of the works of Aristotle may make him an acquaintance, so if contemplation and study of the physicopsychical universe can imbue a man with principles of conduct analogous to the influence of a great man's works or conversation, then that analogue of a mind is . . . God. [6.502]

Where would such an idea, say as that of God, come from, if not from direct experience? . . . Open your eyes—and your heart, which is also a perceptive organ—and you see him. [6.493]

This is Peirce's formula, the encounter or acquaintance with a mind through the mediation of its ideas, its works, its "signs." If the world is God's "argument," God's "great poem" (5.119), then this formula becomes the basic principle of a theological semiotic; although "we cannot think any thought of God's, we can catch a fragment of His thought as it were" (6.502).

What is peculiar about such a possibility? For Peirce, all perception is sign interpretation, a matter of "reading" the phenomena encountered in any given situation as embodying a certain kind of information, of construing them as the signifiers of a certain kind of reality. The case of religious perception and of the knowledge that it yields does not differ in principle from instances of "ordinary" perception. It is peculiar only in the sense that the knowledge acquired is extremely vague and its power over the "whole conduct of life" quite extraordinary. But it is not the case, for Peirce, that religious knowledge is the result of idiosyncratic inferential processes that, because they are "unscientific," generate problematic conclusions. If religious knowledge is problematic, it must be in a way that all human knowledge is problematic and fallible,[19] and the Muser will be as unlikely to doubt what she "knows" as the ordinary perceiver will the existence of his neighbor or friend. This may seem, of course, like a preposterous claim. Peirce argues that its seeming so, however, is a consequence of the fact that those perceptual skills ("beliefs," "habits" of perception) that are adapted for the purpose of recognizing ordinary persons or objects are well developed, while for most individuals the skills required for religious "seeing" have atrophied. "Seldom do we pass a single hour of our waking lives away from the companionship of men (including books); and even the thoughts of that solitary hour are filled with ideas that have grown in society. Prayer, on the other hand, occupies but little of our time. . . . Consequently, religious ideas never come to form the warp and woof of our mental constitution, as do social ideas. They are easily doubted, and are open to various reasons for doubt, which reasons may all be comprehended as one, namely, that the religious phenomenon is sporadic, not incessant" (6.437).

Musement liberates a "latent tendency" to believe in God, to perceive God as real, a natural skill that has become dull from lack of use. What role of theological

significance, then, can the subsequent stages of inquiry play in a process that, at its earliest phase, already results in a religiously satisfying belief? Perhaps, by analogy, it is the same sort of role that literary criticism plays vis-à-vis the immediate encounter with the artwork. This second-order critical reflection and explication, this "argumentation," generally lacks the spontaneous power of the reading experience itself. It can facilitate a better understanding of the dynamics of such reading, however, perhaps motivating the critic to pursue and to cultivate that kind of experience. Moreover, careful, rigorous "study" can serve to reinforce or strengthen those perceptions that also result from a more "playful" reading (6.502).[20] So the theological clarification and defense of the God hypothesis do have a certain religious value, so long as it is continuous with and does not supplant living religious experience.[21] (Of course, Peirce insists that from a purely scientific perspective all commonsense hypotheses, no matter how indubitable, *must* be submitted to critical examination.)

If Peirce's theological semiotic is grounded in experience—indeed, rooted in prayerful communion with God—its final upshot must be located in the realm of praxis, in belief habits that shape human conduct as well as perceptions. Peirce regarded the development and strengthening of habits as a matter of induction, in this case, a matter of consistency and reasonableness in behavior, of the *practice* of virtue, of conduct repeatedly shaped and conformed to an ideal. Even as they inform human behavior, that behavior itself represents the further explication of such ideals, as well as the experimental testing of their validity. So Peirce's theory of inquiry supplies the rubrics for a complex theological method. Such a method commences with an act of interpretation—a "reading" of the signs that are presented in human experience—proceeds with the exploration and clarification of that interpretation and then with its utilization as a rule for living, a habit of action. Nor should this be regarded, exclusively, as the model for a purely "natural" theology. The pattern of abduction-deduction-induction is paradigmatic for all of human inquiry. And all sorts of beliefs, acquired as well as "natural" or instinctive, can function as habits of thought and feeling, habits of interpretation, ultimately, as habits of conduct.

Praxis should not be conceived so narrowly here, however, as to exclude the activity, the "practice" of Musement itself. How else, for example, is the "habit of love" to be nourished and deepened, if not as the result of a continuous or "incessant" acquaintance with the beloved? The birth of love itself, the first glimpse of it, the "falling in love," as it were, may constitute an "abductive" insight, the sudden recognition in a configuration of perceptions of that which is precious and lovable, like the sudden aesthetic delight in that which is perceived to be beautiful. But this experience can recur even when the habit of love is firmly entrenched, like falling in love again with a person already well loved, or having an insight that one has had before, a "sharpening" of one's vision,[22] so that Musement itself is not an activity designed simply for the religious "notice" but for the constant renewal of religious feelings and perceptions.

NOTES

[1] In a work in progress on Peirce's philosophy of religion, I am exploring Peirce's religious thought systematically, linking it to the relevant features of his "scholastic" realism, his objective idealism, and his evolutionary cosmology, as well as to insights gleaned from his work in the normative sciences and in semiotic.

[2] References to Charles Peirce's *Collected Papers,* vols. 1-6, ed. Charles Hartshorne and Paul Weiss; vols. 7-8, ed. Arthur Burks (Cambridge, Mass.: Harvard University Press, 1931-58), here follow the convention among Peirce scholars: read 6.452 as vol. 6, par. 452. Parenthetical citations in text refer to the *Collected Papers.*

[3] In "Habits and Essences," I explore Peirce's relationship to Scotus, in particular, its relevance for understanding Peirce's concept of "real generality"; see *Transactions of the Charles S. Peirce Society* 20 (Spring 1984): 147-67.

[4] Vincent Potter has supplied the most insightful and extended treatment of Peirce's work in the normative sciences in his *Charles S. Peirce on Norms and Ideals* (Amherst: University of Massachusetts Press, 1967).

[5] See Peirce, 6.199. Peirce's "synechism," his objective idealism, really does supply the necessary background against which his Neglected Argument becomes intelligible. It is not possible to examine Peirce's metaphysics thoroughly here, and it must be simply assumed, for the purposes of this discussion, that Peirce's comments about the Absolute Mind can be properly construed as "God talk." That assumption is somewhat problematic since Peirce was skeptical about the adequacy of metaphysical and cosmological notions for the task of explicating religious terms (see Peirce, 5.47, n. 1).

[6] See Charles Peirce's *Letters of Lady Welby,* ed. I. Lieb (New Haven, Conn.: Whitlock's, Inc., 1953), p. 27.

[7] Friedrich Schiller, *On the Aesthetic Education of Man,* ed. Elizabeth Wilkinson and L. A. Willoughby (Oxford: Oxford University Press, 1967), p. 165.

[8] Schiller, p. 81.

[9] See, e.g., Peirce, 2.146, 2.708 ff., 2.776, 6.145, and 8.218 ff.

[10] Donna Orange makes this mistake in her analysis of *Peirce's Conception of God* (Lubbock: Texas Tech University Press, 1984), p. 91; see Peirce's rejection of the argument from design, 6.419 ff.

[11] See Peirce's MS no. 1,224 for the variant draft of this letter. (Identification of manuscripts of Peirce's papers

from *The Charles S. Peirce Papers,* microfilm edition [Harvard University Library Photographic Service, 1966], utilizes the system established by Richard Robin in his *Annotated Catalogue of the Papers of Charles S. Peirce* (Amherst: University of Massachusetts Press, 1967).

[12] See Peirce (n. 2 above), 6.190-99; Peirce does speculate about whether God determines himself, makes himself more "precise" *in time* (6.466).

[13] Peirce, MS no. 891.

[14] Charles Peirce, *Selected Writings,* ed. P. Wiener (New York: Dover Publishers, 1958), p. 320.

[15] Compare W. Quine's hypothesis about an instinctive "spacing" capacity, also, for him, the product of evolution (Quine, "Natural Kinds," in his *Ontological Relativity & Other Essays* [New York: Columbia University Press, 1969]). Note that, for Peirce, explaining the instinct in terms of evolution does not constitute a denial of its religious origin. As his father, Benjamin Peirce, put it, evolution is the "manifestation" of God's "paternity" (see B. Peirce's *Ideality in the Physical Sciences* [Boston: Little, Brown & Co., 1881], pp. 56-57).

[16] Peirce himself was never what one would regard as a "strong verificationist." He only demanded that a hypothesis have some discernible implications, that it be testable at least in principle, and he resisted conceiving of such implications in the narrowest of empirical terms. He was also an optimist about the future of science, convinced that "God's wisdom and mercy," as revealed in nature, now "poetically divined shall be scientifically known" (see his *Selected Writings,* p. 13).

[17] See Peirce, MS no. 843, p. 70.

[18] Musement appears to illustrate something of this continuity: it begins as playful deliberation and terminates in the *perception* of God's reality (see the discussion below).

[19] And Peirce means, quite literally, that *all* human knowledge is fallible, including mathematical knowledge, which he argues is the result of "experimentation" with iconic signs, imaginary diagrams.

[20] I have, in fact, used the concept of Musement to illuminate the sort of cognitive play that constitutes our typical response to verbal artworks; see my "Art, Religion and Musement," *Journal of Aesthetics and Art Criticism* 42 (Summer 1984): 427-37.

[21] John E. Smith has insightfully explored the relation between experience and reflection in Peirce's essay; see his "The Tension between Direct Experience and Argument in Religion," *Religious Studies* 17 (1983): 487-97.

[22] In another essay, I have tried to analyze, using Peircean apparatus, the manner in which belief habits

can facilitate new insight into a phenomenon at a "deeper" level of information; see my "Boredom and the Religious Imagination," *Journal of the American Academy of Religion* 53 (March 1985): esp. 82 ff.

Lewis S. Feuer (essay date 1990)

SOURCE: "The Resurgence of Pessimistic Pragmatism: Charles Peirce's Legacy," in *Encounter*, Vol. 75, July-August, 1990, pp. 38-45.

[In the following excerpt, Feuer advances his notion that Peirce was the first philosopher to be considered a "pragmatic pessimist."]

According to John Dewey, the pragmatic philosophy arising in America as the expression of its open frontier and its business civilisation offered, to many men an open universe with indeterminate futures. "It is beyond doubt", he wrote, "that the progressive and unstable character of American life and civilisation has facilitated the birth of a philosophy which regards the world as being in continuous formation, where there is still place for indeterminism, for the new and for a real future."

To both William James and John Dewey, the existence of never-ending open possibilities of novel events, experiences, and social structures was the philosophical basis for belief in human progress. When the constraining hand of determinism was removed, and the tenet of open choices among novel routes affirmed, then American optimism rested on a cosmic ground at least as firm as that of Germanic pessimism. Pragmatism has thus been regarded as the philosophical counterpart of the optimistic, expanding, democratic, American civilisation.

As the young William James put it eloquently in 1875, ". . . the existence of a Walt Whitman confounds Schopenhauer as the existence of a Leopardi refutes Dr Pangloss". James obviously had not read Walt Whitman's descriptions of how Confederate and Union soldiers massacred each other: "Multiply the above by scores, aye hundreds—and verify it in all the forms . . . —light it with every lurid passion . . . and you have an inkling of this war."[1]

The linkage between the pragmatic principle and the notion of an expanding, advancing civilisation—whether that of an industrial or a frontier society—is, however, scarcely a logical or necessary one. (Indeed, the frontier experience was frequently less one of open alternatives than that of a harsh, cruel setting, as Josiah Royce, Bret Harte, and Mark Twain recorded.[2]) The two ideas are, in the language of Arthur O. Lovejoy, the analytic historian of ideas, separate and independent unit-ideas. If the social universe were one of diminishing resources, declining possibilities, vanishing of novel forms, and retrogression to less complex institutions as well as a more backward technology, the validity of the pragmatic philosophy would not be lessened. An asso-

ciation of the pragmatic philosophy with a pessimistic outlook toward the human prospect could be as valid for the 21st century as that with optimism was for William James at the onset of the 20th century, as he watched the San Francisco earthquake.

Moreover, the pragmatic movement was probably less the product of an open-frontier universe than an articulation of what Alexis de Tocqueville called "the philosophical method of the American":

> "I think in no country in the civilised world is less attention paid to philosophy than in the United States. The Americans have no philosophical school of their own, and they care but little for all the schools into which Europe is divided, the very names of which are scarcely known to them."

Yet curiously, added Tocqueville, almost all the Americans "use their minds in the same manner", and "have a philosophical method common to the whole people". All tried to:

> ". . . evade the bondage of system and habit, of family maxims, class opinions, and . . . national prejudice; to accept tradition only as a means of information . . . ; to seek the reason of things for oneself, and in oneself alone; to tend to results. . . ."[3]

This anti-philosophical philosophy of the Americans coincided in large part with the pragmatic principle as Charles Peirce first defined it.

Peirce—born 150 years ago, in September 1839—was the pioneer in associating pragmatism with pessimism, in formulating what we might call "a pragmatic pessimism". In the first place, he did not regard truth-discovery as necessarily or generally contributing to the *advancement* of the human race's chances for survival. To be sure, John Dewey, in his first formulation of his experimental logic, regarded the experimental method as having originated and been continued because of its contribution to the successful struggle of human organisms with their environment. At the outset, however, Peirce conceded that the discovery of truths might also tend to *diminish* the human species' chances of survival. Truths concerning themselves and their universe might conceivably impel people to destroy themselves, yet the scientist's devotion to their discovery would still hold him compulsively:

> "But let the consequences of such a belief [having a possible atheistical issue] be as dire as they may, one thing is certain: that the state of facts, whatever it may be, will surely get found out, and no human prudence can long arrest the triumphal car of truth—no, not if the discovery were such as to drive every individual of our race to suicide!"[4]

In other words, from Peirce's standpoint, the mutations toward scientific reasoning that arose in the course of man's biological evolution, contributing toward his more successful nutrition and reproduction, might also eventuate in the discovery of such truths concerning himself, his fellows, and his universe that a will to collective self-destruction might prevail.

It is curious that such thoughts of a self-destructive outcome as the collective consequence of man's advancement in science and technology affected the leaders of British empiricist thought in the 19th century. John Stuart Mill at the end of 1854, watching Italian peasants dying of hunger, wondered if "there was a conspiracy among the powers of nature to thwart human industry" and finally starve the human race. He wondered what would happen if the corn crop were blighted: "I think", he wrote, "that should be a signal for the universal and simultaneous suicide of the human race. . . . In the meantime", he added in a provisional optimism to his wife, "let us make what we can of what human life we have got. . . ."[5]

Meanwhile, the workings of sociological law, according to Mill, tended toward the dominance of mediocrity and bureaucracy; the revolutionary socialism toward which he inclined when young seemed to him finally to be impelled by a cruel hatred of individual liberty.

Herbert Spencer, the philosopher of evolution, had as early as his thirties reached the conclusion that life was not worth living, though his friends George Henry Lewes and George Eliot were shocked when he told them so. He never changed his mind on this point, and toward the end of his life told his friend and quondam literary executor Beatrice Webb, the foremost Fabian socialist woman: "If pessimism means that you would rather not have lived, then I am a pessimist."[6] By that time, however, Spencer had arrived at a sociological pessimism: that is, one grounded in sociological law rather than on his personal exhaustion with, or repugnance toward, human beings.

Spencer believed that a rhythmic movement toward social retrogression was manifesting itself in the wave of "re-barbarisation" that was under way. Brutality was spreading throughout society, he concluded, as he recorded his observations:

> ". . . the literature of the periodicals reeks with violence . . . men overpowered . . . , daggers raised, pistols levelled—these, in all varieties of combination, have appealed to our latent savagery."

The socialistic administrations helped to power by the Fabian intellectuals would, according to Spencer, inaugurate a new despotism; the worst traits of human nature—love of power, selfishness, injustice, untruthfulness—that were partially restrained by the institutions of private society, would become "irresistible" in a socialist system; a "disciplined army of civil officials" would engender with successive generations "evils far greater and less remediable".[7]

Now, by and large, Charles Peirce shared the sociological pessimism of Spencer and Mill. Though he acknowl-

edged an emotional sympathy with the French Revolutionary "sentimentalists", he expected that the social revolution in the 20th century would far exceed the cruelties attained by the French Reign of Terror:

> "The twentieth century, in its latter half, shall surely see the deluge-tempest burst upon the social order—to clear upon a world as deep in ruin as that greed—philosophy has long plunged it into guilt. No post-thermidorian highjinks then!"

In June 1894, the following year, many Americans indeed thought social revolution loomed when President Grover Cleveland called out the Federal troops to quell the strikers of the American Railway Union, led by Eugene V. Debs, against all the railroad companies operating through Chicago; trains stood immobilised, locomotives were derailed, tracks were torn up, as violent battles raged in the railroad yards.

To Lady Victoria Welby, in 1908, Peirce elaborated on the character of the retrogressive era, "going back relatively to the Dark Ages", that he believed was in the offing for American and English civilisation. ". . . we [Americans]", wrote Peirce:

> "have constantly experienced, and felt but too keenly, the ruinous effects of universal suffrage and weakly exercised government. Here are the labor-organisations, into whose hands we are delivering the government, clamoring today for the 'right' to persecute and kill people as they please. We are making them a ruling class; and England is going to do the same thing. It will be a healthful revolution; for when the lowest class insists on enslaving the upper class, as they are insisting, and that is just what their intention is, and the upper class is so devoid of manhood as to permit it, clearly that will be a revolution by the grace of God; and I only hope that when they get the power they won't be so weak as to let it slip from their hands. Of course it will mean going back relatively to the Dark Ages."

This time, Peirce hoped, "the governing class" would use common sense to maintain their rule, and not be enthralled, as the 18th-century revolutionary rationalists were, by "the hedonist delusion". For, according to Peirce, those captivated by such 18th-century notions as, presumably, the purported inalienable right to the pursuit of happiness, "will find they spell revolution of the most degrading kind".

Indeed, Peirce had become disenchanted with the egalitarian-minded liberals:

> "[Nothing] can appear to me sillier than rationalism; and folly in politics cannot go further than English liberalism. The people ought to be enslaved; only the slaveholders ought to practice the virtues that alone can maintain their rule. England will discover too late that it has sapped the foundations of culture."[8]

In short, Peirce saw none of the relationships between pragmatism and democracy that John Dewey tried to elaborate. His pessimistic outlook was that of someone who felt himself living in a closing, contracting society, with diminishing resources and declining opportunities. His socio-political pessimism was based in part on his belief that under a proletarian democracy a tyranny would prevail against scientists and intellectuals, marking a return, relatively, to the Dark Ages.

He interpreted his pessimism as a theorem derivable from the theory of probabilities. Every society must finally break down—not because of the sociological laws peculiar to that society, but because, since every society is an organised conglomeration of physical entities, the physical shufflings that are its history must in the long run involve the decay, downfall, or disintegration of that improbable organisation into more probable, mixed-up, aggregates.

In the long run—according to the theory of probabilities as Peirce conceives it—since the direction of social historic change must be from the improbable to the probable, it follows an evolution from the organised society to the more disorganised:

> "All human affairs rest upon probabilities. If man were immortal, he could be perfectly sure of seeing the day when everything in which he had trusted should betray his trust, and, in short, of coming eventually to hopeless misery. He would break down, at last, as every good fortune, as every dynasty, as every civilisation does. In place of this we have death."[9]

It is doubtful whether any social scientist would now regard Peirce's probabilistic basis for pessimism as convincing. For Peirce, in effect, assumes that human societies are analogous to conglomerations of molecules randomly bumping and colliding with each other, and that their histories are therefore derivable from statistical laws in a way similar to Rudolf Clausius's derivation of the second law of thermodynamics. But in social history we are dealing with men who act in accordance with laws of motivation, conflict, and cooperation, with drives of sexuality, power-seeking, and economic gain operating beside the emergent varieties of conduct, from the pursuit of scientific research to that of ascetic withdrawal.

If God were a shuffler of persons, like a gambler shuffling his deck of cards, Peirce's probabilistic argument for pessimism might have some ground, though he suppresses the equiprobable alternative that every logically possible Utopia would be realised; certainly Utopias should have an equiprobable status with Dystopias. And indeed, if Peirce's later metaphysics has any genuine validity, the progressive emergence of a Utopian order is the likeliest direction of human events. For, according to Peirce, the ultimate law of existence is that an energising reasonableness of law tends to spread itself throughout all entities, replacing the primordial chaos with the rule of law. This he regarded as the ultimate law of laws.[10]

At times, too, Peirce seems to suggest—as John Dewey did more emphatically in his later writings at Chicago—that the *pragmatic* logic is a kind of corollary of Darwin's theory of natural selection. That the two are in fact independent unit-ideas is clear, however, from a simple consideration. The *experimental* logic would still remain valid even if its use had resulted in the contravening of Darwin's theory. Thus, if Charles Darwin had discovered during his voyage on the *Beagle* that species had evolved very definitely in different directions even on islands where there was no tendency to overpopulation, with its consequent struggle for existence, that finding would in no way have affected the validity of scientific verification or falsification.

Curiously, Peirce never seems to have confronted the underlying threat to scientific, industrial civilisation that his fellow logician, William Stanley Jevons, had posed for Britain in 1865. In that year, Jevons—the founder of British mathematical economics—published a book called *The Coal Question*, which dared, in the midst of the Victorian expansion, to raise the question as to whether Britain might soon see its coal reserves dwindle, and its industrial civilisation decline. Within 100 years, Jevons argued from his extrapolations, Britain's rate of consumption would have seriously depleted its coal reserves. Jevons feared for the future of his country, though he hesitated "at asserting things so little accordant", as he said, "with the unbounded confidence of the present day." But this, he added, was a question of "almost religious importance".[11]

John Stuart Mill grasped at once the tremendous seriousness of Jevons's analysis. Mill, with his constitutional pessimism, could not subscribe to the technological optimism of Sir William Robert Grove, President in 1866 of the British Association for the Advancement of Science. Drawing comfort from the law of conservation of energy, Grove asserted cheerfully that new reservoirs of heat and force that were technologically practicable would be discovered, "before the coal-fields are exhausted . . . we may with confidence rely on invention being in this case, as in others, born of necessity, when the necessity arises".

It is true that William James later made it central to his pragmatic optimism to affirm that rewards, whether to the lover or the retail storekeeper, are given to him who has emotional confidence in the outcome. Mill, however (he was then serving his one term as an elected Member of Parliament), rose in the House of Commons to tell them of Jevons's book. He had read, he told the House, "the various attempts to answer Mr Jevons", but, at most, they succeeded only in adding "a few years longer" to the probable economic lifetime of the coal mines, and he pleaded for a sense of responsibility to posterity in terms so selfless that they seemed to transcend his utilitarian ethics.

When Jevons—who disagreed with many of Mill's views on logic—heard of Mill's speech, he was deeply affected: "What is this poor mind of mine with all its wavering hopes and fears, that its thoughts should be quoted and approved by a great philosopher in the parliament of so great a nation?"

Now Jevons, like Peirce, was slowly grasping at a general theme: that industrial and scientific advance, at certain stages in human evolution, was potentially self-destructive for the human race. The postulate that from Francis Bacon to Benjamin Franklin and later John Dewey had affirmed the uniform convergence between science-seeking and welfare-advancement was being shaken as replaceable by a scientific pessimism.

In the cases of both Jevons and Peirce, personal circumstances and character traits probably contributed much to the pessimistic cast or pessimistic sensitivity of their philosophies. According to John Maynard Keynes, Jevons's conclusions concerning the depletion of the British coal reserves arose in large part from "a psychological trait, unusually strong in him, which many other people share, a certain hoarding instinct, a readiness to be alarmed and excited by the idea of the exhaustion of resources".[12] Keynes, however, with his Cambridge Apostolic morality, was perhaps too easily contemptuous of the reasoning of such chapel-type personalities as W. S. Jevons and Woodrow Wilson. Moreover, both the latter had had direct experiences of poverty and men's misery that were alien to the background of the Cambridge Apostles' Circle.[13]

Jevons was indeed haunted by fear—of a pending scarcity of paper. He therefore stockpiled such a huge reserve of writing and packing paper that more than a half-century after his death his children were still using its stores. And his nature was certainly pervaded by gloom; having grown up virtually without friends or acquaintances, mostly isolated by his own choice, he was so shy that in later years he still trembled before his lecture-classes. Like Thomas Hardy's Jude Fawley, he felt that his family was "under certain curses"; he was so self-deprecatory that he averred he "should feel utterly wretched if I knew another to think me better than I was". He felt he was seeing mankind at its dominant lowest when he witnessed the Australian gold rush of 1859, with the camps to which some 30,000 diggers had been drawn within a month like iron filings to a magnet, among them "swarms of Chinese . . . ugly little Mongolians. . . ." Happily he found a job at the Melbourne Observatory helping to chart the Southern stars.[14]

More tragically, his fellow logician Charles Peirce, in his own self-torment, told President Daniel C. Gilman at the Johns Hopkins University that his physician feared "that the state of my brain was alarming" and that he might become "something like" insane. The nature of Peirce's neurosis might be partially suggested by the unusual fact that Peirce attached to his name an additional one—"Santiago"—evidently re-christening himself in gratitude to William James. What James thought of this act of psychological identification is not

thus far recorded, though he probably would have been seriously troubled by a Freudian diagnosis.

Peirce's father, Benjamin, moreover, evinced a strange cruelty toward his son. "I was forced to think hard and continuously", recalled Charles Peirce: "My father would sometimes make me sit up all night playing double dummy till sunrise without relaxing my attention." Though a transcendentalist, Benjamin Peirce had been "vehemently opposed to the abolitionists", and was not displeased when his student, Thomas Wentworth Higginson, was sent to jail.[15] Charles Peirce never served in the Union Army, nor does he seem to have mentioned Lincoln or the Civil War or the slavery issue in all his writings.

A Schopenhauerian component entered Peirce's thinking as his pessimism developed. He veered toward Schopenhauer's view of a dominant Unconscious Will, and speculated that "God probably has no consciousness". When he was much younger, his pessimism had expressed itself in a certain allegiance to the ontological atheism of Etienne Vacherot, the positivist historian of the Alexandrian School: ". . . it does seem to me", Peirce wrote, "that the spirit of science is hostile to any religion except such one as that of M. Vacherot." As an ontological atheist, Vacherot argued that a Perfect Being was necessarily non-existent; but the idea of God, added Peirce, could still fill one with adoration, even though he realised that the adored one was absent from the universe. Later, when he regarded God as probably existent, though unconscious, the whole "problem of evil" became for Peirce an unfathomable mystery, a "blasphemous" search "to define the purposes of the Most High. . . ."

Meanwhile the social future of mankind continued to fill Peirce with a pessimistic apprehension. When he listed the leading ideas of the 19th century (29 of them), although scientific ones were the majority, "Labor Unions" and "Socialism" and "Sewing Machine" were also included. As he wrote to Lady Welby in 1908, labour unions, reaching for an arbitrary power for persecuting and punishing people, were in his view the precursors of the new Dark Ages. Despite his own cosmology of an energising reasonableness spreading its laws or habits throughout the universe, Peirce acknowledged that ". . . even if there be a general march of events and ideas, the pessimists have heaped up solid arguments going to show that march ultimately brings up the nothingness from which it set out".[16]

Peirce, however, continued to seek inspiration from the history of science and its benefactions for humanity, for withstanding the scientific pessimists. He regarded the simultaneous discovery of the anaesthetic use of ether by "three different New England physicians" as the effect of a growing philanthropic spirit. Agapic influences, the ripening of sensitivity, or sentimentalism, the philanthropic spirit, were among Peirce's energising reasonable ideas; that, he argued, was why ether, hitherto used for Punchinello entertainment, had been recruited for the diminishing of human physical pain.

This was a beautiful application of his metaphysics to the history of science, but it was probably a mis-perception of the historical facts. The principal discoverer of the anaesthetic properties of ether, William Thomas Green Morton, was a small-town dentist much interested in making money, and "very much a man of this go-ahead age". He became so tried and tired in law suits and controversies over priority in discovery that he tried to kill himself in 1868, and did die a few hours later. A rival claimant, Horace Wells, had committed suicide twenty years earlier. Morton's teacher, Dr Charles T. Jackson—brother-in-law to Ralph Waldo Emerson—during many years pressed his own claim, evidently unfounded, for a part in the discovery of ether's humane properties; when his quest for fame proved fruitless, he declined into alcoholism and dishonesty, and finally became insane as he stood by Morton's grave.

The entertaining properties of ether, as Peirce observed, had indeed long been known to circus and travelling showmen who promoted "ether frolics" in Puritan America. At staid gatherings and supervised parties at which liquor was forbidden, ether could be used to achieve a brief metaquotidian voyage. A Southern claimant, Dr Crawford Long, was encouraged to his experiments in 1841 because he had seen how the use of ether at parties helped enhance the opportunities to enjoy the kisses of Southern belles. Ambition, renown, wealth, and pleasure held causal roles in the historic-scientific drama that perhaps outweighed Peirce's agapic, philanthropic spirit.[17]

The upshot of Peirce's pessimistic sociological perspectives should have been to separate him more sharply from William James's version of pragmatism. Actually Peirce's final formulation approximated to that of James, except that it was broad enough to accommodate retrenching the terms of human existence to an historical situation of diminishing possibilities; Peirce's pragmatism allows more for a closing universe.

Peirce's first formulation in 1878 had used such ambiguous terms as "effects" and "practical bearings", of which James had availed himself:

> ". . . consider what effects, which might conceivably have practical bearings, we conceive the object of our conception to have. Then, our conception of these effects is the whole of our conception of the object."

James was quite entitled to regard the psychological "effects" of a given idea on the thinker's life as part of its "practical bearings." Peirce was perturbed by the "will to believe" that emerged, and he redrew the pragmatic principle in 1905, saying:

> ". . . if one can define accurately all the conceivable experimental phenomena which the

affirmation or denial of a concept could imply, one will have therein a complete definition of the concept."

None the less, Peirce still argued that all experimental phenomena might bear on "the conduct of life". His new "pragmaticism" still retained, therefore, the terms of a moralist: ". . . pragmaticism consists in holding that the purport of any concept is its conceived bearing upon our conduct". All that was absent was James's passionate insistence on the extent to which faith can create its own verification.

Peirce had too deeply experienced personal defeat to endorse an optimistic metaphysics. His social arguments pointed toward an adaptation of pragmatism to a philosophy of wisdom in a universe that confirmed pessimist projections. However, he felt himself impelled to attack pessimists generally with *ad hominem* arguments far cruder than any which William James used. "I do not admit that pessimists are . . . thoroughly sane", he wrote. "Though the great majority of mankind are naturally optimistic", there still were, in Peirce's view, three types of pessimists. One type was made up of those who, like Leopardi, had endured some dreadful malady. A second—the misanthropes like Schopenhauer—were simply "diseased minds", while the last was mainly composed of *littérateurs,* people with lively philanthropic sympathies, "easily excited to anger at what they consider the stupid injustices of life". ". . . no individual remotely approaching the calibre of a Leibniz", added Peirce, "is to be found among them."

Those whom Peirce called *"littérateurs"* would today be called "intellectuals". Earlier he had called them "dilettanti", and, curiously, he disliked them for the same reasons Lenin had. They engaged, said Peirce, in a "very debauchery of thought"; they never wanted to settle any question, but simply to keep up an endless "literary debate" without the consummation of action which is the "only possible motive" for thinking.[18] Lenin too had excoriated the "intellectuals", who rarely wanted to make the leap from talk in discussion circles to that of revolutionary action in order to change reality.

Pessimism was for both Peirce and Lenin the philosophy of those in whom the arc from thought to act, from reflection to deed, that aimed to eliminate the problem-generating irritant, was severed or atrophied. Oddly, the world's leading intellectuals have included men of the calibre of Leibniz, and they have tried in the measure of their powers to act to influence the course of events; of such, for instance, were Einstein and Russell, and in Peirce's own time, such men as Karl Pearson and Henri Poincaré.

Rather hard put to it to dissociate pragmatism from a linkage to pessimism, Peirce towards the end of his life fell back upon what he called a **"Neglected Argument for the Existence of God"**. That resolved itself into the assertion that in our free "musements" (or free reflections and associations), we find that the wonderful varieties, simplicities, and evolving growths in natural phenomena suggest to every "normal man" the hypothesis of God's Reality; and that the criterion of simplicity that we instinctively use is evidence in us of a "divinatory power".

On the other hand, Peirce simultaneously held to a theory closer to Darwin and Freud: that "all science is nothing but an outgrowth from these two instincts", namely, hunger and sexual desire, or—in his language—"the feeding impulsion" and "the satisfaction of the reproductive impulse". And there is indeed much evidence to suggest that the criterion of verification arises primarily from the patterns imposed by the hunger drive, while preferences in the formation of hypotheses, the aesthetic elements in scientific thinking, originate more intimately from variations in sexual development.

Belief in God, Peirce then adds, "overmasters every agnostic scientist" because it is backed by "the power of the passion of love", by "one's own instinct". We avoid pessimism, and confront the miseries of existence—even at times with superhuman courage, as priests among lepers—because, according to Peirce, we recognise that the heart is an organ of knowledge: ". . . your heart . . . is also a perceptive organ—and you see him [God]." That is why, in Peirce's view, pragmatism was "going to be the dominant philosophical opinion of the twentieth century. . . ." He called "the Unknowable . . . a nominalistic heresy".[19]

Peirce's argument, however, seems one of desperation, of a determination to make a stand against the overwhelming forces of Evil and Hatred which he felt were operating in the guise of the social movements of our time. He never took seriously John Dewey's attempt to conjoin pragmatism with the democratic, political spirit, and his chief memory of Dewey was that of a moralistic graduate student who had quickly dropped out of Peirce's course in scientific logic at the Johns Hopkins University. However, because Peirce talked frequently of his philosophy as having been the outcome of his experiences as a man of the laboratory, not of the theological seminary, and because he wrote of the claims of truth as expressing the resolution of the unlimited community of scientific inquirers, he bequeathed a pragmatism that was more adapted to a political world of contracting possibilities, and an economic world of diminishing resources—a pragmatism more compatible with a long-term realistic pessimism.

Of all the varieties of pragmatism, the one explicated by Charles Peirce corresponds most to that which has had a tremendous resurgence in the last twenty years. That resurgence has been perhaps the most unusual socio-intellectual phenomenon in recent history.

For the generation after World War II, pragmatism was generally regarded as a philosophy of the past. Existentialism was much in vogue; metaphysical treatises of German Nazi and French pro-Stalinist anti-Americans were being studied; and student revolutionaries from Berlin to Berkeley to Tokyo described themselves as "existentialist Marxists". During the last fifteen years that phenomenon has been reversed, and almost every day *The New York Times* has an article reporting some statesman in Africa, Asia, Western Europe, the Soviet Union, Eastern Europe, or Latin America as describing himself or being described approvingly as a pragmatist.

For a while, I catalogued these usages—until the expanding universe of clippings threatened the geometry of my small study. In the summer of 1984, for instance, the new socialist government in France was described (20 July) as "pragmatic". Iranian moderates were characterised (23 August) as wishing to behave "more pragmatically", while spokesmen for Japan's school system (12 August) asserted that "most Japanese consider themselves pragmatists [and], pragmatically speaking, [had] produced the educated, well-disciplined work force" that helped make possible "the country's economic surge". At that summer's Republican Convention, Vice-President George Bush was reported (22 August) as "re-emphasising his pragmatic conservatism . . .", while on the preceding day a letter on the pregnancies of teen-age mothers as their chosen route toward economic independence was entitled "The Pragmatism in Becoming an Unwed Mother".

In that year, too, the nomination by the Democratic Party of Geraldine Ferraro for Vice-President of the United States was adjudged "pragmatic" in a popular Canadian newspaper (*Toronto Sun,* 20 July 1984) on the ground that she would "add 15 or 19 points" to the presidential candidate's standing. At this juncture the correspondent observed that "this year's 'in' word on the political circuit [was] 'pragmatic'."

Four years later, on 24 April 1988, *The New York Times* averred in two headlines: "PRAGMATISTS LEAD IN BUSH ECONOMICS" and "BUSH TURNS TO PRAGMATISTS FOR ECONOMIC POLICIES". More exotic, however, were the reports from China (*The New York Times,* 26 March 1988) that moderation, the re-emergence of private property, and "pragmatism" were part of the new orthodoxy that the opposition denounced as "bourgeois liberalisation": "A SENSE OF PRAGMATISM PREVAILS" said the headline. Even the official Chinese News Agency was quoted (13 April 1988) as describing the new group of state councils as "a group of technocrats, who are younger in age, pragmatic, and enthusiastic in the reform". That same day, however, the plight of homosexuals, in their constricted political choices, was sympathetically expressed: "Do you 'hold your nose and vote for Dukakis because you're a pragmatist'? I know a lot of people who will do that, but God knows not comfortably."

Meanwhile, reports had been arriving from Ho Chi Minh City in Viet Nam which were meant to conciliate Americans; the new leader of the Communist Party, Nguyen Van Linh, although 72 years old, was described

(4 February 1988) as a follower of "pragmatism" who was succeeding in removing the indurated party apparatus. In America, at that time, political analysts were worried by the rise of "the religious right"; one of them queried (1 March 1988) whether the Rev. Pat Robertson, a presidential aspirant, could "use his influence carefully, moderately and pragmatically". Two weeks earlier an article entitled "Europe Talks: Pragmatism and Fury" had described (16 February 1988) how François Chirac had had to apologise to the British Prime Minister, Margaret Thatcher, for using a coarse expletive.

Reports from the Soviet Union have, of course, for some years been describing Mikhail Gorbachov as a pragmatist; they began when Armand Hammer, who has known nearly every Soviet ruler since Lenin (and entertained John Dewey several times in Moscow during Dewey's brief visit to Russia), announced (18 June 1985) that: "I am very much impressed by [Gorbachov] as a leader— very forthright, very intelligent with a good sense of humour, very pragmatic."

It is Peirce's scientific-moral pragmatism that especially answers to the mood and needs of our newly-evolving political era. This reborn pragmatism alone has the sobriety of judgment that a time of diminishing social possibilities requires.

A recent summary article in *The New Scientist* tried to take comfort from the notion that the Greenhouse Effect would at any rate be "a more desirable state of the world, from the human point of view, than the onset of a new Ice Age might be".[20] And *The New York Times*'s editorial page (9 October 1988) pondered sombrely what the consequences would be if crop ranges shifted toward the equator and the West Antarctic ice cap melted— raising the sea and finally "forcing the evacuation of New Orleans, New York, London, and Beijing". The world would then be threatened by outbreaks of social calamities worse perhaps than those that Peirce in his most pessimistic mood ever envisaged. The most sanguinary wars among peoples struggling for land and survival might ensue; the world's civilisation would be imperilled. An anti-science movement might arise that would, like Christian anti-scientists during the latter Roman Empire, try to extirpate the scientific universities as they once did the School and Library at Alexandria.

Peirce's pragmatism, unlike William James's, recognised the pessimistic truth that faith is probably more often contravened than confirmed by its consequences; that self-fulfilling prophecies have been statistically infrequent; and that a continuous effort is required to maintain a democratic loyalty to science. Whatever the crises of the 21st century may prove to be, their consequences will be least unfavourable for mankind if they are met with a scientific pragmatic spirit.

The new scientific pragmatism will have no inner, prior commitment to any political-economic system, and its own test will be more fully experimental. Thus young

Soviet thinkers today weigh the postulates of their social system against its experimental consequences. During the 1920s and early 1930s, several remarkable essays were published by such economists as Ludwig von Mises and Friedrich von Hayek which showed on theoretical grounds that a socialist planned economy, lacking as it would a competitive market, would be unable to allocate rationally the diverse producers' and consumers' "goods"; for, in a competitive market, demand and supply tend to determine in a rational manner those quantities manufactured, and priced, and bought. They thereby predicted and explained the chronic shortages, inefficiencies, long waiting-lines, shoddy workmanship, and surly social relations that came to characterise the Soviet economy.

The rejoinder of Marxist economists and social scientists was that every social system has its own corresponding sociological laws, and that the Socialist economy would evolve its own specific method for rational allocation of productive resources. Only an experimental determination could resolve such faith in a "dialectical evolution", and it is the failure of the Soviet system to solve its problem of rational allocation after more than 70 years of effort, exhortation, and education, that has led it to begin the shelving of its ideology.

Perhaps that is why young Soviet philosophers tend to turn to Charles Peirce's works for inspiration. Twenty-five years ago I spent a fortnight or so at Tbilisi in Soviet Georgia, as a guest of the Institute of Philosophy. I found a group of young philosophers studying photographic copies of the pages of Peirce's **Collected Papers**—they could not procure American currency with which to import the books. They handled these photographed pages almost as if they were sacred scrolls.

For them, Peirce's pragmatism was not just an American mode of thought, or one born of optimism, or a by-product of Darwin's theory of natural selection; it expressed the scientific temper of mind which arises among those who, in whatever society they chance to find themselves, aspire to rationality.

NOTES

[1] John Dewey, "The Development of American Pragmatism", in *Studies in the History of Ideas*" edited by the Department of Philosophy of Columbia University (New York, 1925), vol. II, p. 374. William James, "German Pessimism", in *Collected Essays and Reviews,* New York, 1920, p. 17. Walt Whitman, "A Glimpse of War's Hell-Scenes", from *Specimen Days,* in Maxwell Geismar (eds.), *The Whitman Reader* (New York, 1955), pp. 306-309.

[2] The cowboy, celebrated in later folklore and films, was a pathetically underpaid proletarian who in his solitariness under the skies was apt to become eccentric or insane. See David Lavender, *One Man's West* (New York, 1943); Edward and Eleanor Marx Aveling, *The*

Working-Class Movement in America (2nd ed., London, 1891; reprinted New York, 1969), pp. 154-165; Philip Ashton Rollins, *The Cowboy: An Unconventional History of Civilisation on the Old-Time Cattle Range* (New York, 1936), pp. 65-67; Ramon F. Adams, ed., *The Best of the American Cowboy* (Norman, Oklahoma, 1957), p. 6.

[3] Alexis de Tocqueville, *Democracy in America* (1835, 1840), tr. Henry Reeve, rev. Francis Bowen, ed. Phillips Bradley (New York, 1945), vol. II, pp. 3-4.

[4] C. S. Peirce, "Illustrations of the Logic of Science: Fifth Paper—The Order of Nature", *The Popular Science Monthly,* vol. 13 (June 1878), p. 216. Reprinted in Charles S. Peirce, *Chance, Love, and Logic: Philosophical Essays,* ed. Morris R. Cohen (New York, 1923), pp. 129-30.

[5] F. A. Hayek, *John Stuart Mill and Harriet Taylor: Their Correspondence and Subsequent Marriage* (Chicago, 1951), p. 214.

[6] Hugh Elliot, *Herbert Spencer* (New York, 1917), pp. 46-47. Herbert Spencer had appointed Beatrice Potter as his literary executor, but then sorrowfully rescinded that decision after she married the Fabian Socialist Sidney Webb. Beatrice Webb, *My Apprenticeship* (1926, Penguin, 1938), vol. I, p. 53.

[7] Herbert Spencer, *Facts and Comments* (New York, 1902), pp. 172-73, 185-87; also David Duncan, *Life and Letters of Herbert Spencer* (1908), vol. II, pp. 137. Herbert Spencer, "The Coming Slavery" (1884), reprinted in Herbert Spencer, *The Man versus the State,* ed. Donald G. MacRae (Penguin, 1969), pp. 108-109.

[8] Charles S. Peirce, "Evolutionary Love", *The Monist,* vol. III (January 1893), p. 181; *Chance, Love and Logic,* p. 274. Irwin C. Lieb, *Charles S. Peirce's Letters to Lady Welby* (New Haven, 1953), p. 28, reprinted in Charles S. Peirce, *Selected Writings: Values in a Universe of Chance,* ed., Philip Paul Wiener (New York, 1958, reprinted 1966), p. 402.

[9] Cited in Charles S. Peirce, *Chance, Love and Logic,* p. 72. C. S. Peirce, "Illustrations of the Logic of Science: Third Paper, the Doctrine of Chances", *The Popular Science Monthly,* vol. 12 (March 1878), p. 610. Peirce at this time was already recognised by such a mathematician as William Kingdon Clifford as "the greatest living logician". See John Fiske, *Edward Livingston Youmans: Interpreter of Science for the People* (New York, 1894), p. 340.

[10] "Every evolutionism must in its evolution eventually restore that rejected idea of law as a reasonableness energising in the world (no matter through what mechanism of natural selection or otherwise). . . ." C. S. Peirce, "The Laws of Nature and Hume's Argument against Miracles", *Selected Writings,* p. 300.

[11] Jevons showed with his statistical evidence that ". . . if our consumption of coal continues to multiply for one hundred and ten years, at the same rate as hitherto, the total amount of coal consumed in the interval will be one hundred thousand millions of tons". Estimating the available coal in Britain at only 83 thousands of millions of tons within a depth of 4,000 feet, Jevons was led to conclude: ". . . we cannot long maintain our present increase of consumption . . . the check to our progress must become perceptible considerably, within a century from the present time." W. Stanley Jevons, *The Coal Question: An Inquiry Concerning the Progress of the Nation, and the Probable Exhaustion of our Coal-Mines* (2nd, revised, ed., London, 1866), pp. 241-42, 12, 13.

[12] See George Basalla, William Coleman, and Robert H. Kargon (eds), *Victorian Science* (New York), pp. 95-96. *Hansard's Parliamentary Debates,* Third Series, vol. CLXXXII (London, 1866), 12 March 1866-26 April 1866, pp. 1,524-28. W. Stanley Jevons, *Pure Logic and Other Minor Works,* ed. Robert A. Adamson and Harriet A. Jevons, (London, 1890), p. 202. John Maynard Keynes, *Essays in Biography* (New York, 1933), p. 266.

[13] See Paul Levy, *Moore: G. E. Moore and the Cambridge Apostles* (London, 1979).

[14] Harriet Ann Jevons, ed., *Letters and Journal of W. Stanley Jevons* (London, 1880), p. 60. R. D. Collison Black and Rosamond Könekamp, *Papers and Correspondence of William Stanley Jevons* (London, 1972), vol. I, pp. 38, 101, 123, 127, 129.

[15] Hugh Hawkins, *Pioneer: A History of the Johns Hopkins University, 1874-1889* (Ithaca, 1960), p. 195. Ralph Barton Perry, *The Thought and Character of William James* (Boston, 1935), vol. II, p. 436. Charles S. Peirce, *Selected Writings,* p. 417. Thomas Wentworth Higginson, *Cheerful Yesterdays* (Boston, 1898; reprinted New York, 1968), p. 51.

[16] Charles Sanders Peirce, *Collected Papers,* vol. VI, p. 334. C. S. Peirce, "Illustrations of the Logic of Science, Fifth Paper: The Order of Nature", *The Popular Science Monthly,* vol. 13 (June 1878), p. 216. Charles S. Peirce, *Chance, Love and Logic,* p. 129. Charles Sanders Peirce, *Collected Papers,* vol. VI, pp. 300, 283-84. D. Parodi, "La Philosophie de Vacherot", *Revue de Métaphysique et de Morale* (1899), Tome 7, pp. 468, 492-94. Charles S. Peirce, *Selected Writings,* pp. 262, 402. Ralph Barton Perry, *The Thought and Character of William James,* vol. II, p. 434.

[17] Betty Macquitty, *The Battle for Oblivion: The Discovery of Anaesthesia* (London, 1969), pp. 184, 144, 78, 55, 63, 39, 47, 185. George Edmund Gifford, Jr., "Charles Thomas Jackson", *Dictionary of Scientific Biography* (New York, 1973), vol. VII, pp. 44-46.

[18] Charles S. Peirce, *Selected Writings,* pp. 124, 183, 221, 377-78, 120-21.

[19] Charles Sanders Peirce, *Collected Papers,* vol. VI, pp. 319, 326, 344-47.

[20] John Gribbin, "The Greenhouse Effect", Inside Science, Number 13, *The New Scientist* (22 October 1988), vol. 120, p. 4.

Dana J. Ringuette (essay date 1990)

SOURCE: "The Self-Forming Subject: Henry James' Pragmatistic Revision," in *Mosaic*, Vol. 23, No. 1, Winter, 1990, pp. 115-30.

[In the following excerpt, Ringuette examines the influence of Peirce's brand of pragmatism on the novels of his friend, Henry James.]

In the final Preface for the New York edition of his novels and tales, Henry James took up in earnest the question of revision. Finding that he has undercut the term's "grand air," James tells of his discovery that "to revise is to see, or to look over, again," and that revising has nothing in common with a notion of *rewriting,* an act "so difficult, and even so absurd, as to be impossible." Re-writing, James confesses, remains a mystery for him, but revising and rereading are two efforts that "proved to be but one" (338-39).[1] Although this act of revision, of seeing it again, had virtually been a central preoccupation throughout the earlier Prefaces, in writing this final Preface James felt an urgency to address explicitly the question of its importance and rewards: "The interest of the question is attaching, as I say, because really half the artist's life seems involved in it—or doubtless, to speak more justly, the whole of his life intellectual" (339).

Given the critical debate over James's revisions, carried on for most of this century, it is clear that the "interest of the question" is "attaching" not only for the artist, and in the Prefaces James himself anticipates this critical dimension by repeatedly adopting the stance of the reader, as well as author, of the works. In doing so, James advances a view of fictional form as inexorably bound to the "re-vision" that proceeds from the changing, contingent influences of author and reader and work. A central concern of my essay is to examine the concept of revision in this light: to re-see its place in the theoretical paradigm of literary authority and in the critical register of commentary on and by James, and to re-see it within the context of its philosophical counterpart—specifically the "pragmaticism" of Charles Sanders Peirce.

My purpose, therefore, is not to discuss revision in terms of variant editions, emendations and particular textual changes and histories. Instead, my concern is to investigate what sense of artistic agency or authority—what sense of artistic "self"—is yielded by James's notion of "re-seeing," and to suggest what ramifications such agency would have for readers (including editors) of his works, as well as for his protagonists. Hershel Parker has advanced a forceful argument for an intensive "textual-aesthetic approach to literary study" which brings biographical, textual and esthetic evidence to bear upon editorial and interpretive issues concerning the literary work and which questions the critical assumption of "relying on the text as a constructed given" (213, 234; see also Mailloux 93-125). The biographical and textual issues involved in "revised" (that is, rewritten) texts are compelling, and the working out of these issues is important; I wish to maintain, however, that before one can know how to regard particular textual variants, a notion of artistic agency is desirable and necessary. Parker, too, seems aware of this necessity, returning throughout his study to what he calls the "creative process" of the writer (3). James's "creative process," I believe, reveals itself in his concept of revision; and, as I hope to show, the creative process, for James, simply is revision.

Revision, for James, "means in the case of a written thing neither more nor less than to re-read it" (338-39). His formulation of revision allows the works—those included in the New York edition and their "'revised' element"—an influence, as it were, quite apart from an "intention" on his part. Repeatedly within the Prefaces he acknowledges "original" intentions when composing, but consistently he backs away from articulating them. Concerning *The Awkward Age,* for example, James begins: "I recall with perfect ease the idea in which [the novel] had its origin, but re-perusal gives me pause in respect to naming it." A moment later, he says that the book "was to belong, in the event, to a group of productions, here re-introduced, which have in common, to their author's eyes, the endearing sign that they asserted in each case an unforeseen principle of growth" (98).

The phrase "unforeseen principle of growth" is one frequently cited by critics of James, often in connection with concepts of romanticism and organicism, whereby it is seen to suggest his affinities with "the tradition of Coleridge" (Hocks 13). As a "Coleridgean metaphor," the phrase is taken to connote James's perception of "the development of a work of art," a development ultimately disclosing a "dialectic of spiral return" (Fogel 15, 6). Charles Feidelson, concentrating on James's "Romantic life of imaginative consciousness," observes the "ever incomplete" nature of James's dialectic and the "ever renewed" possibilities of the "dynamic of his circular logic" (339-40). Drawing upon previous studies and finding James "a bedfellow of Coleridge," William Goetz traces a romantic "hegemony of the imagination," subsequently addressing the Prefaces and the question of "the organic connection between James's past and present selves" (61, 76, 90-91). Viewed in terms of literary authority and agency, however, the "unforeseen principle of growth" also has a decidedly pragmatistic aspect.

For an artist who for all his creative life placed such acute emphasis on the powers of observation, and who continues to do so in the Prefaces, the admission of any part of the creative process as being *unforeseen* is striking. Being "unforeseen," unexpected, this "principle of growth" cannot possibly be an assertion of the artist—it is not to be found simply in artistic volition. Conversely, neither can it be located in the agency of any of the individual works alone, because James's reference is not to works which assert, but to "productions." This usage implies that more is involved in this principle than any one single point from which agency emanates.

Moreover, this "unforeseen principle of growth" leads James toward further unexpected discoveries. James speaks of "fallibilities" and "false measurements" as he reviews his work, and he further finds "little ideas," "developed situations," long and short stories, "modest beginnings," "misplaced middles" and "the triumph of intentions," all of which seem to exert influence beyond what the artist wills into them (100). The artist, James says, must be able to bring out the "promise" of a situation, "*any* situation, that appeals," but must also recognize the situation's "reserves," that which he cannot predict or entirely determine (101). The "whole 'job'" becomes, as he says, "wonderfully amusing" (109), but what produces the "whole 'job'" is more than simply an artist imposing form upon a formless mass, more than merely the inscribing of a drama dictated by the manners and morals of one's environment.

Difficult as James finds these fallibilities and false measurements, he nonetheless welcomes the "lesson" they offer (100). James, in re-reading, finds that the works do not display the "trick of looking dead, if not buried," and "he almost throbs with ecstasy when, on an anxious review, the flush of life reappears." "Life" is discovered in the process of reading. Furthermore, re-reading reveals, as he notes, "the *quantity* of finish it [the work] stows away" (99). The "production," isolated neither in the work's "assertion" nor in the will of the artist, can be found only in the relation between work and reader, that is, in re-reading, in revision; and what it "produces" for James is a revised sense of self, not merely of the self who pens the work but also of the one who reads it. The "unforeseen principle of growth" is manifested in the act of revision.

Revision of this kind requires an understanding which extends far beyond the persistent concern about textual "revision*s*," that is, those critical readings comparing passages from the earlier works to the respective "changes" James made to those works for inclusion in the New York edition. In fact, it is the strategy of "comparison" which so cleanly, and therefore completely, misses the mark when it comes to accounting for James's sense of revision. Comparison, in this context, presupposes a static sense of similarity and difference which either unites or disunites early and late editions.

Hershel Parker has drawn attention to the fundamentally Platonic assumptions of an ideal text and "original" intentions which characterize such readings of James's revision (85-114). In the view of such critics, James in his later years was able to "fulfil his original intentions in a superior way" (96); and in a variant form of this insistence upon an "original," James is seen as having worked a "transformation" (99), a process interpreted either as James better refining *original* ideas, characters, dialogue, and so on; or as James creating another work entirely. Further, the critical insistence upon archetypes, upon "original" texts (or copy texts) from which all further ideas emanate, and upon a hard core of intention which dictates all subsequent ideas, owes something, as Parker points out, to this Platonic preconception of an ideal text and author.

In his discussion of *The Portrait of a Lady*—in the Norton Critical Edition of this novel—Anthony Mazella provides a perhaps paradigmatic example of this critical approach. Reading James's revisions as "different," "separate" and "disunited" from the earlier versions, yet nonetheless "transformed," Mazella concludes that "there are two *Portraits*, not one, and that each is a different literary experience. The Isabel Archer who faces her destiny is not the same girl in both versions, nor is the quality of her destiny the same" (619, 597). What such a reading ignores, unfortunately, is precisely the *quality* of Isabel's experience. The focus centers instead on textual differences, and the assumption is that because words change, texts become "disunited." Revision is seen to result in two different texts, two separate Isabels, because what is precluded is the "unforeseen principle of growth" that to James is the mark of "revision." One particular passage from *The Portrait* that Mazella uses to support his contention is actually instructive for suggesting the consistency that underlies James's alterations—not consistency in the sense that no changes have been made, of course, but a consistency in the effect the two versions produce.[2] Toward the end of the novel, a weary Isabel, returning to Gardencourt, contemplates the duplicitous Madame Merle. The passage in the 1881 text reads:

> The only thing to regret was that Madame Merle had been so—so strange. Just here Isabel's imagination paused, from literal inability to say what it was Madame Merle had been.

The passage from the New York edition reads:

> The only thing to regret was that Madame Merle had been so—well, so unimaginable. Just here her intelligence dropped, from literal inability to say what it was that Madame Merle had been.

In Mazella's reading, the "revision" here displays a "shift from creative contemplation (imagination) to pure mind (intelligence)" (614). While one might ignore, for the moment, the unexplained notion of "pure mind," and the possibility that imagination and intelligence for James may be related, the dichotomy discovered here is rather forced, based as it is primarily upon a violated sense of superficial consistency. The insistence upon two Isabels becomes suggestive, however, if the focus is on her experience rather than on static comparisons of texts.

We must remember the context of this passage: Isabel, returning to a dying Ralph Touchett, now seeing Osmond for the selfish brute he is, continues to see herself anew in the midst of such a relation. Her musings on Madame Merle are bound up within this seeing anew. In the 1881 passage Madame Merle had been "strange," which becomes "unimaginable" in the later edition. This is consistent with James's focus upon Isabel and her developing consciousness throughout the novel. "Strange" is ambiguous, perhaps, but what is strange for Isabel *is* unimaginable precisely because she has never before confronted a situation in which a supposed friend so flagrantly betrays another. Having no experience to draw from, Isabel's "intelligence," her knowledge "drops"; involved is a combined imaginative and literal inability to characterize what happened to her in relation to Madame Merle.

In both passages, Isabel is quite simply left dumbfounded. What is emphasized in the second passage is something the first already suggests: Isabel is as nonplussed by her inability to characterize her own perceptions (she had always prided herself on her ability in this respect) as she is by Madame Merle's deceptions (which she now realizes she could not possibly have controlled). In Isabel's developing consciousness, then, James focuses on an "unforeseen principle of growth," that is, a revision of self, which she experiences. Revision, in this sense, is as evident in the first text as it is in the second. James's textual changes serve to emphasize the revision of self which Isabel is undergoing, by showing that imagination, intelligence, and the ability to articulate experience are interrelated.

Revision for character and author and reader is a developmental principle revealing an expanding consciousness, constantly realizing growing relations. James did not tinker with characters; he simply but profoundly realized that revision is bringing out the "cross-relations," the "finish" which is present in the work—early, middle, and late (Prefaces 114, 99). Revision is for James, as Theodora Bosanquet noted, "neither substitution nor rearrangement. It [is] the demonstration of values implicit in his early work, the retrieval of countless lost opportunities for adequately 'rendering'" (58). James's effort, however, clarifies that the opportunities are never truly "lost."

Returning, then, to James's discussion of this "unforeseen principle of growth" and the revised sense of self this principle initiates, we see James reproducing a drama of sorts between himself as artist and as reader, a drama which is replayed in different forms throughout the whole of the Prefaces. And what this drama plays out is the continual subversion of a primary, intuitive, internal self in favor of an external, inferred, "produced" self. John Carlos Rowe has observed that, for James, self "comes to know itself only through the relations of its experience," making self an "incomplete circle" and a "fluid expression" (37, 34, 35). If the Jamesian self, however, arises not internally—from volition—but externally—from the confrontation of consciousness and one's environment—then self is as complete as it need be; indeed it is as complete, at any given

moment, as it can be. It is a self which is neither simply determined nor simply determining. As James illustrates with his own example, self cannot but constantly revise and "re-see" self.

Because James is concerned with an individual's relation to his or her world (in this case, his own relation to his work), that produced self, as continually forming and reforming itself, is the subject of attention. As we have just seen in James's "drama," self is the subject of revision. As we have also seen, that subject is not limited only to the self but encompasses the relation among an individual's consciousness, his/her environment (literary, in this case), and the sense of self yielded by that ongoing relationship. In this sense, then, revision denotes the "self (-)forming subject" in the two senses implied by this phrase. First, revision marks the experience of a subject (that is, subject as subject matter) forming itself: the self-forming subject. Second, self (the present nexus of developing relations) becomes subject for further revision: self forming subject. Revision produces self, at the same time that self makes possible further revision.

Self as a nexus of developing relations does away with the traditional notion of self as the static, primary core of being and cognition which alone determines significance. Self is not set in opposition to what stands outside of it because self is itself external and can be known only by its relation to other things, people and ideas.

As many commentators have observed, notably Richard A. Hocks and John Carlos Rowe, this relational quality of self intersects here with William James's understanding of consciousness as "a kind of external relation," a "function" (*Writings* 178, 170). With consciousness no longer an "aboriginal stuff or quality of being," William asserts a "radically empirical," "individualized self," which he sees as "part of the content of the world experienced." Yet, whereas this "individualized self" is an "emphasized position" or "prerogative emphasis" (284n)—suggesting the resilient dichotomy of subject and object with which William struggled—Henry's concept of revision involves a broader notion of self, mainly because self, for Henry, is an even more thoroughgoing, if more fine-drawn, relation.

Self is never an *a priori* entity whose primary function is to constitute—or even to be, as William observes, "the storm centre, the origin of co-ordinates" (284n). Rather, to Henry self is always *a posteriori* and constituted, and this because: "We are shut up wholly to cross-relations, relations all within the action itself; no part of which is related to anything but some other part—save of course by the relation of the total to life" (114).

Yet the ramifications of this configuration of self and revision extend further. In the discovery of his own "fallibilities," James does not set up an ontological hierarchy which cites author as prime mover or sole creator; nor are the works seen as unchanging "originals," as if they existed as the prime or ideal form from which revision departs. With this in mind, a reader is making a fundamental error in assuming that there is an "original" text determined univocally by authorial intention, for there is nothing univocal about any subject for James. Not only is there no "copy text" in this understanding of revision, but there is no real warrant for assuming that James, as intending author, could have produced such a definitive object if he wanted to. The subject, whether author, reader, or work, is dispersed within the same matrix of relations in which, for instance, we find characters; all are without the comforting backdrop of a conventional, autonomous, Cartesian "self."

For these reasons, re-writing—which James all but rejects—would invite extraordinary pressure by drawing all attention to the writer alone. Re-writing invokes the traditional sense of a self driven by volition, basically existing unrelated. For James, however, revision necessarily includes the language of the work itself as well as the "terms, perceptional and expressional," yielded by the act of re-seeing. James's practice shows that revision is a necessary element of reading the work and of composing it. With this abiding principle of revision, James underscores and distinguishes the interpenetrating influences of an individual's experiences, the environment within which one moves or is moved and the language, "artistic" and "intellectual," that encompasses both.

The very nature of James's realizations of revision as he presents them is revealing. That they should be "awkward," that they are sometimes unexpected, should reassure those of us who have struggled with "his" Maisie, Kate Croy and Merton Densher, Isabel Archer, Lambert Strether, Fleda Vetch, and "his" Ververs and Amerigo. James indicates explicitly in the Prefaces (not to mention his notebooks and his letters) that he too struggled and continued to struggle for greater understanding of his art and his work. Like James, we must not discount the "fallibilities," the surprises, because they are often indicative of new awareness; they become the latest manifestation of this "principle of growth" which is revision; they become "intenser lights of experience" (339).

This experience of an intenser light can be both exhilarating and unsettling, especially in the challenge revision makes to fundamental assumptions concerning the nature of self and assumptions about the agency of author, reader and work. Nonetheless, even which James's work provides a locus for understanding revision, it is precisely because revision is often unexpected and even "awkward"—is strewn with "fallibilities" and "false measurements"—that one can sympathize with James when he confesses: "When I think indeed of those of my many false measurements that have resulted, after much anguish, in decent symmetries, I find the whole case, I profess, a theme for a philosopher" (100). And indeed it is.

. . . . .

James's principle of revision finds a compelling parallel in the work of Charles Sanders Peirce, specifically in two major areas of his thought and writing: his analytic categories, and his understanding of Doubt and the struggle of inquiry toward Belief. James's predilection for consciousness allies him more closely with Peirce's "pragmaticism" (Peirce came to prefer this term) than with the "pragmatism" of William James. Peirce's abiding interest was in dispelling what was seen by him as the pervasive legacy of metaphysical assumptions, whereas William became progressively less concerned with such speculative issues and more drawn to the consequences of a "radical empiricism" for a psychology of self. That in a 1907 letter to his brother, Henry admitted that he had lately realized he had "unconsciously pragmatised" all along (cited in Matthiessen 343), does not by any means conclusively or exclusively align him with his brother's pragmatism. Indeed, William all but says this himself in his letters of the same time to Henry (338-43).

This, of course, does not preclude the possibilities of intersections of thought. Richard Hocks, in his extensive study, discerns an "interpenetrating" relationship of William's pragmatic thought and Henry's literary artistry (12; see also Rowe 34-39). Yet the insistence within William's work on a stable, "individualized self" and on the importance of freedom of the will is ultimately too limiting for the constantly revising self found in Henry. As Ross Posnock has persuasively argued, in down playing or excluding the possibilities of an "intersubjective" self or even a "social model of identity" as that proposed by George Herbert Mead, William "does not seem to consider either the possibility that his basic premise of monadic subjectivity may be too simple and constricted a model or that the self is a social construct dependent on and conditioned by others" (12). William's is fundamentally too individualized a conception of self for what we find developed in Henry (see Colapietro 62-63, 78-79). If Henry is a pragmatist, then he is one at variance with William's model; he is, to employ Peirce's refinement, a pragmaticist. The importance of Peirce's conclusions for an understanding of Henry James, then, lies precisely in the clarification they offer to the notion of revision present in James's fiction and criticism.

Peirce's earliest writings (which, interestingly enough, he later revised) focus upon his critique of the Cartesian principles of an intuitive, neutral ego and the centrality of this ego to all further speculation and knowledge. For Peirce, philosophy labored under metaphysical "make-believes," largely through the dependence upon a logic of identity. His pragmaticism refuted the premises which bolstered such a logic (5: 416).[3]

Peirce holds that identity is only one aspect within a triadic relationship which includes feeling, the qualitative relation (Firstness); and thought, the symbolic relation (Thirdness); along with identity, the quantitative relation (Secondness). Within his theory of signs, no sign to our understanding is without elements of all three relations. Whether we necessarily understand or recognize the presence of all three is dependent upon the representative function of "Thirdness," the symbolic function; but even so, for Peirce, reflection shows that the actual coming-about of this recognition, of course, requires the presence of all three categories of consciousness.

Peirce maintained that "there is but one state of mind in which you actually find yourself at the time you do 'set out'—a state in which you are laden with an immense mass of cognition already formed, of which you cannot divest yourself if you would" (5: 416). This mass of cognition from which the individual began Peirce brought together under the rubric of a *guiding principle* of inference" or as he was to call it later, the "leading principle." This "formula," "whether constitutional or acquired," made up a "habit of mind" or "habit," which "determines us, from given premises, to draw one inference rather than another" (5: 367). These "guiding principles" (like James's "unforeseen principle of growth") are what we cannot possibly be without; otherwise a question about some idea or thing could not have possibly arisen. There may be facts which are taken for granted when taking into consideration a logical question, but Peirce asserts that "though they are difficult to exhibit at the outset . . . conceptions which are really products of logical reflection, without being readily seen to be so, mingle with our ordinary thoughts, and are frequently the causes of great confusion." They are leading principles, products of inference, but are so taken for granted that we have lost sight of their semiotic beginnings. And by confusion Peirce means "that bad logical quality to which the epithet *metaphysical* is commonly applied" (5: 369). These guiding principles, moreover, are drawn from the state of belief which is a "rule for action." In other words, Peirce is simply rejecting the Cartesian notion of an intuitional, neutral self which, in order to attain an unprejudiced state, initiates all action by doubting.

Action does not begin with neutral, unprejudiced doubt; rather "settlement of opinion" which "is the sole object of inquiry" can proceed only from the "settled opinions" with which one began (5: 375; see also 5: 371). Belief, the point from which we invariably start, is "a cerebral habit of the highest kind, which will determine what we do in fancy as well as what we do in action":

> A belief-habit in its development begins by being vague, special, and meagre; it becomes more precise, general, and full, without limit. The process of this development, so far as it takes place in the imagination, is called *thought*. A judgment is formed; and under the influence of a belief-habit this gives rise to a new judgment, indicating an addition to belief. Such a process is called an *inference;* the antecedent judgment is called the *premiss* [sic]; the consequent judgment, the *conclusion;* the habit of thought, which determined the passage from the one to the other (when formulated as a proposition), the *leading principle.*
>
> (3: 160)

One's sense of subject is inferred—it is knowledge gained and made part of one's beliefs. Corresponding to James's "principle of growth," Peirce's "leading principle" is a nexus of relations which yields a subject.

Moreover, like James with his "false measurements," Peirce had his experiential illustration of this process of inference in the element of Doubt. Broadly speaking, doubt is an external element of surprise, of chance, of interruption, wherein general experience cannot account for a particular experience (see 5: 372-73). Doubt, for Peirce, arises because we cannot at any one point in time know everything. We are always involved in a process of greater, evolving knowledge. Otherwise, we would exist within a state of perfect, revealed knowledge—a state which again admits the existence of a transcendental, intuitive subject—and we would not be able to account adequately for the phenomena of ignorance and error.

Because "all positive reasoning is of the nature of judging the proportion of something in a whole collection by the proportion found in a sample," Peirce maintains that "there are three things to which we can never hope to attain by reasoning, namely, absolute certainty, absolute exactitude, absolute universality" (1: 141). The "scientific method," as Peirce labeled his enterprise, "can only rest on experience; and experience can never result in absolute certainty, exactitude, necessity, or universality." Thus, doubt denotes that "scientific spirit" which "requires a man to be at all times ready to dump his whole cartload of beliefs, the moment experience is against them" (1: 55). Hence it is that within consciousness Peirce allows that an "interruption," a "saltus" or "hesitancy," arises which begins cognition. The outgrowth of this "moment of time" is that "attention"—consciousness of "two sides of an instant"—has been focused all within a process, ultimately, that marks a "sense of learning, of acquiring, of mental growth" (1: 381).

In other words, the three elements of consciousness are brought to bear upon this new "experience," not only the subsequent, time-bound synthesis of Thirdness. That experience of hesitancy, moreover, cannot be a moment of "Belief," in the strict sense required by Peirce, because the ignorance or error it suggests is something not contained within the existent logic that makes up one's beliefs. Here, however, it is important to remember that Doubt cannot have meaning outside of the semiotic system—we could have no sense or idea of it if it were—although the object of doubt can exist as something *incredible,* that is, something not yet part of our belief, our logic. We do not doubt what we cannot but believe, says Peirce, and at the same time, we cannot attain infallibility at any time. These are simply varied ways of saying that we experience ignorance and error, that existing knowledge cannot account for everything, that there is bad logic as well as good, and that an extension of knowledge is possible (in fact, for Peirce, an ethical and moral imperative) within the system of signs.

Within concepts of First and Second, Peirce has a way of accounting for the experience of doubt as pragmatistically "subjective," yet externally derived. Although doubt might be commonly viewed as a "negative" term (so too, at first, can James's "fallibilities"), it is for Peirce more accurately speaking a contingent (but important) interruption, a hesitancy in the ongoing extension of knowledge and thus a potential and positive addition to the semiotic system (5: 373).

The pragmatistic subject present in thought is a positive effect and not a moment of absence or nothingness, precisely because it is defined in experiential terms; it arises from experience and is defined and modified through experience. What remains finally compelling about such a construal of "subjectivity" is that it can be expressed or articulated only within a sign system that is communally-based and has a history. That is, it turns the subject, commonly understood as intuitional and internal, on its head and ultimately makes it understandable only in external terms. It follows then that doubt has its origin not internally but externally, despite whatever might be felt by the person (5: 443).

In Peirce's phenomenology, the subject—and here I will begin to call it *self* as I wish to employ the term—thus takes the form of a continual reforming. While commentators have often noted that Peirce is less than explicit in his own explanation of "self," Walter Benn Michaels observes that "it is in the process of elaborating this argument [against Cartesian intuition and for inference] that Peirce is most explicit about the self" (193). Self is inferred, derived and always being interpreted by subsequent thought in the "flow of time." Self in this sense takes on less an absolute position and more a transitory, functional existence.

Self *is* a sign, not in itself, but in relation to thought; and it is "first and foremost a sign in the process of development" (Colapietro 66). That is, no self can be thought to exist *in itself,* unchanging, because on the one hand, the self which was, is being interpreted by subsequent thought—hence another self comes into life; and, on the other hand, the interpreted or evolving self can never be what it was, just as "when once past, we can never bring back the quality of feeling as it was *in and for itself.*" Self, for Peirce, like belief, is "altogether something virtual," an effect which is undergoing continual change and reformation (5: 289). Self, then, articulates belief at certain points, and in this way it stands within its own triadic relation as the third term that expresses meaning within a semiotic system which must include consciousness and community as the other two terms.

A person, for Peirce, is never a static individual, but an evolving compendium of thoughts, of signs—a sign—that "is just coming into life in the flow of time." An individual is a kind of compact community, testing and retesting, being tested and retested (5: 421).

Consciousness, then, is no longer simply conflated with self, but both become two of the triad of terms that determine meaning and significance not only in the world but in the literary text as well (which, by extension of Peirce's third category, might be considered very much the same thing). Yet such a conception of self does not lessen the impact, or take away the significance in its own right, of the object of doubt by assuming that all meaning lies only within the interpreter. As we have seen, potential cognition is just as important as that which is contingently finalized as cognition.

A Peircean analysis of self thus calls into question many of the assumptions of Jamesian critics. Such an analysis marks a shift away from self seen simply as the often paralyzed organ of desire caught up within a recalcitrant, brutally effective world of force. The question of self is not a question of being tossed about within a deterministic environment, or one of being simply the intuitive, "creative" force constantly frustrated by the political, social, economic "realities" of the world and of society. Self is never caught in the lurch, nor merely one pole of opposition, because self never exists, never functions, indeed never is knowable, outside of a triadic relation with community and consciousness. In Jamesian terms, self is indeed less a matter of being *centered,* and more a matter of being *central*—in the sense of necessary—to the whole discussion of knowledge, significance and meaning within the community and for the individual. The "center of consciousness" is not an intuitional self; rather the "center of interest" is consciousness and its relation to the community and the formation—revision—of self.

. . . . .

Although James repeatedly attests to a fundamental focus on consciousness in his fiction, it is vital to notice that this focus asserts more, indeed something other, than simply an understanding of consciousness based on the principle of identity. In his Preface to *The Princess Casamassima,* James admits: "I confess I never see the *leading* interest of any human hazard but in a consciousness (on the part of the moved and moving creature) subject to fine intensification and wide enlargement" (67). The "*leading* interest" is consciousness, but consciousness subject to "fine intensification and wide enlargement." Consciousness becomes a focus within a context of attaching concerns. The "human hazard" suggests the larger environment in which that consciousness dwells and functions.

By way of illustration, *The Portrait of a Lady* will provide an even more explicit discussion of a central consciousness. On the one hand, we have Isabel Archer, concerning whom James, in the Preface, recalls saying to himself: "Place the centre of the subject in the young woman's consciousness . . . and you get as interesting and as beautiful a difficulty as you could wish" (51). On the other hand, there are the "super-added" elements, "the things that are not herself," as James puts it, the setting in which she moves (42, 51). This still, however, does not account for the "subject" of which Isabel and her consciousness are the center and to which these elements are related. James's syntax is crucial here: the "centre of the subject" is "in the young woman's consciousness." The subject, I believe, is the intervening ground between the heroine's consciousness and community; the subject is the formation—that is, revision—of self.

James places so much emphasis on consciousness because what he wants to investigate (and indeed what he is reading and revising within the context of preparing the New York edition) is the growth of self yielded by the individual's relationship to her world. James, with Isabel as his dramatic focus, recounts a formative process of consciousness and community, and the action or drama revolves around her acquiring a cognition of self and of the function of that self-realization in further cognition. Adopting Peirce's formulation, the situation is one wherein "[her] thoughts are what [she] is 'saying to [her]self,' that is, is saying to that other self that is just coming into life in the flow of time" (5: 421). That she experiences pain along the way suggests the "interesting and beautiful difficulty" which James notes as underpinning the subject. In other words, in a setting of consciousness and cosmopolitan community, the "stuff of drama or, even more delightful word still, of 'story'" is the formation and cognition, *re*formation and *re*cognition, of self (56).

Numerous scenes might be cited here to illustrate this progressive formation of self, such as Isabel's well-known conversation with Madame Merle concerning "one's 'self'" (3: 287-88), Ralph Touchett's observation of and astonishment at Isabel's "function" (4: 143-44) and especially Isabel's late night, "meditative vigil" (4: 189-205).[4] As James observes in the Preface, it is the "remembered vision" concluding this intensely dramatic "vigil of searching criticism" (57), and the later resolution this vision presages, which indicates concisely the movement toward a recognition of self awareness. As Isabel finally gets up to go to bed at last, "she stopped again in the middle of the room and stood there gazing at a remembered vision—that of her husband and Madame Merle unconsciously and familiarly associated" (4: 205).

This reflection on an earlier, unforeseen, chance discovery of an intimacy between Madame Merle and Osmond constitutes an essential addition to the elements of belief and convention that have been at work in her preceding, excruciating contemplations. Up to and even including the reflections of this moment, community has been largely restraint, constraint, limitation: negation. Thus far, to Isabel self has been simply a radically subjective power with which one hopes to impress oneself on others and one's environment, a manifestation which Rowe calls a "fiction" and a "vulnerable romanticism" (33). Further, at the time of the discovery of intimacy, Isabel had attached no real import to the scene of Osmond sitting in the presence of a standing Madame Merle: "The impression had, in strictness, nothing unprecedented; but she felt it as something new, and the soundlessness of her step gave her time to take in the scene before she interrupted it. . . . Their relative positions, their absorbed mutual gaze, struck her as something detected. But it was all over by the time she had fairly seen it" (4: 164-65).

Now, however, this hesitation becomes, as Isabel finds later, the abiding and lasting impression that stays on beyond her musings in her midnight vigil. The impression, a stumbling upon something not yet known, signals the beginnings of a jolt to her beliefs and of the subsequent inquiry that attempts to alleviate the irritation that she feels. Thus this present arrest of attention and the painful inquiry which Isabel undergoes in her vigil promise an addition to the self—to those beliefs—which is in crisis. Isabel is quite aware that her marriage to Osmond has deteriorated, but all the same, concerning herself and her actions subsequent, no hard conclusions are drawn—only potential resolutions are indicated.

The dramatic promise of this reflection is fulfilled, however, as Isabel struggles further toward the decision that she will return to Osmond. She has moved toward a more pragmatic resolution, and in doing so has moved away from accepting only her own perception of the situation—she also finally accepts the deceit and deception of her environment as a contributing part; that is, she understands Osmond for what he is. She has attained an addition to her beliefs, and in this sense has reformed her self. Moreover, she has shown that one is in the continual reformation of self:

> Deep in her soul—deeper than any appetite for renunciation—was the sense that life would be her business for a long time to come. And at moments there was something inspiring, almost enlivening, in the conviction. It was proof of strength—it was proof she should some day be happy again. It couldn't be she was to live only to suffer; she was still young, after all, and a great many things might happen to her yet. To live only to suffer—only to feel the injury of life repeated and enlarged—it seemed to her she was too valuable, too capable, for that. Then she wondered if it were vain and stupid to think so well of herself. When had it even been a guarantee to be valuable? Wasn't all history full of the destruction of precious things? Wasn't it much more probable that if one were fine one would suffer? It involved then perhaps an admission that one had a certain grossness; but Isabel recognized, as it passed before her eyes, the quick vague shadow of a long future. She should never escape; she would last to the end.
>
> (4: 392-93)

Compressed in this passage are the progressive elements in awareness—each distinct and necessary—which she has been undergoing and experiencing throughout the novel. Each interrogates and augments the others so that they exist uncompromised, all leading toward an addition to belief, a revision of self: 1) Isabel exhibits briefly her, by now, characteristic belief in personal volition, a belief that suggests an exclusively inner identity that is "too valuable, too capable" to live in suffering; 2) this belief is offset, countered, by a recognition of the external, of the world, as a force to be reckoned with; value and preciousness fluctuate within history and in a community; 3) in turn, despite the recognition of the force and destructiveness of the world, she projects that she will have a long life—this admits a "certain grossness" and a new awareness of self, an addition to her beliefs. This admission of a "certain grossness" is certainly something that Isabel would not previously have done, even if she had earlier deferred to Osmond's "charm"; and the admission underscores the struggle of inquiry to attain belief.

Her acceptance of some kind of life with Osmond signals the re-discovery, as it were, of self and self-awareness—a hard earned, learned ability. Isabel's future does not promise a great deal, but she may produce changes effectively. She will at least surely *not* allow herself to be unwittingly "ground in the very mill of the conventional" again (4: 415). Individuality is not sacrificed, as she had feared earlier, because she now has a much better awareness of what is at stake in her relationships with others, specifically Osmond; nor is external pressure to be feared. Individuality, volition, choice, doubt, desire are not compromised by community, convention, environment, society, nor vice versa. Consciousness and community gain validity through constant interaction that underscores the self and can be cognized only by that self. In this sense, self is indeed a *realization* of the workings of consciousness and community. Self cannot be renounced; it cannot be turned away from, any more than Isabel can turn away from or discount the force of convention on her life. One might confuse the issue of self and pretend it is something other than what it is, as Isabel certainly attempts to do throughout most of the novel; but this is not renunciation: this is simply another self yielded. That James brings Isabel from a state of individualistic interiority to an individualism of interconnectedness suggests his inclination toward a self that accepts and invites continual reformation, a self that can never be "responsible *enough*," as James puts it in his final Preface (328).

The great emphasis that James places upon a process of self, community and consciousness in his characters, leads one in turn to query the role of narrative agency in this process. And, true to James's concerns, the narrator participates within this revision, finding his own sense of agency processive rather than stable. The narrator is not simply "historian," as he so stolidly in the beginning places himself, but his role changes as Isabel's realization of self comes about (cf. 3: 67-68, 69, 271, 413; 4: 21-22, 145). In addition, because both narrator and heroine are involved in this process of reforming, the reader's awareness and self-consciousness must undergo a similar process. As Nicola Bradbury observes: "the perceptions of the protagonist come to meet those of the narrator and reader" (10). James's method suggests that all are involved in the acquisition of self-awareness, and in this involvement the focus on consciousness enlarges to include all three.

The narrator is a method by which James invites the reader to witness and question a mind at work (Isabel's)—and a mind at work upon Isabel's; but this reader must also be at work upon that narrator. In this way, James forces the reader to become self-consciously aware of how one becomes aware. Such awareness signals not only that narrator and reader go through the same process as Isabel, but that no participant in the novel can effectually avoid it. Isabel Archer acts and influences action; narrator relates action, but also becomes part of it; the reader does not simply absorb, but also must take a part in creating meaning. The event, as James has said, is not plot, but neither is it character, narrator, heroine or reader alone. The event of the novel involves all at once. In this event, emphasis falls on how self moves and is moved, how it fashions and is fashioned by reality: not in the sense that it creates or attempts to create (to use Richard Poirier's title phrase) "a world elsewhere"—as Isabel might be seen attempting early on—but in the sense of a dynamic progression of consciousness and community in which self can be known only by its connections with society and yet, just as important, can add to that society through the contingent interrogations of one's world.

. . . . .

To return then, for a moment, to James's concern with "these intenser lights of experience": it follows that as author, James too must take part in this triadic course of self-awareness which also incorporates heroine, narrator and reader. Such revision encompasses "these intenser lights." As life itself is the business of continual renewal, reperusal and revision, for James it can logically only follow that the re-presentation of this business within a novel must also follow this process, and involve author and reader. That James should at different times within the Prefaces see himself as author, character and reader should be no surprise: all three necessarily pertain to a work of revision. That James should revise his works should also be no surprise—nothing could be more natural (even necessary) to an author who placed great and distinct emphasis on the consciousness of the "responsible" author. That revision is a "*living* affair" should signal that "renewals of vision" are a way of art and life, that one's language, like one's experience, is not etched once and for all in stone once it is uttered or published (341-42). There is continuity in life and art, but it is a continuity of contingency and change. For one who feels so strongly "these intenser lights of experience," to present in his work anything less than this continuity of revision would be to forsake one's "active sense of life."

NOTES

[1] All references to James's Prefaces will be to *The Art of the Novel,* Blackmur's readily available edition.

[2] For the sake of convenience, in this instance my citations from both the 1881 and New York editions of *The Portrait* will be from Mazella's article. Mazzella (614-15) quotes from page 492 of the 1881 edition and 4: 392 of the New York edition.

[3] In citing Peirce's writings, I will follow the conventional practice of providing volume and paragraph: 5:416, for example, refers to Volume 5, paragraph 416.

[4] All references to *The Portrait* will be to the New York edition (Vols. 3 and 4); citations will note volume then page number(s).

WORKS CITED

Bosanquet, Theodora. "The Revised Version." *The Little Review* 5 (1918): 56-62.

Bradbury, Nicola. *Henry James: The Later Novels.* Oxford: Oxford UP, 1979.

Colapietro, Vincent M. *Peirce's Approach to the Self: A Semiotic Perspective on Human Subjectivity.* Albany: State U of New York P, 1989.

Feidelson, Charles. "James and the 'Man of Imagination.'" *Literary Theory and Structure: Essays in Honor of William K. Wimsatt.* Ed. Frank Brady, John Palmer, and Martin Price. New Haven: Yale UP, 1973. 331-52.

Fogel, Daniel Mark. *Henry James and the Structure of the Romantic Imagination.* Baton Rouge: Louisiana State UP, 1981.

Goetz, William R. *Henry James and the Darkest Abyss of Romance.* Baton Rouge: Louisiana State UP, 1986.

Hocks, Richard A. *Henry James and Pragmatistic Thought: A Study in the Relationship Between the Philosophy of William James and the Literary Art of Henry James.* Chapel Hill: U of North Carolina P, 1974.

James, Henry. *The Art of the Novel: Critical Prefaces.* Ed. Richard P. Blackmur. 1934. New York: Scribner's, 1962.

———. *The Novels and Tales of Henry James.* 26 vols. New York: Scribner's, 1907-17.

James, William. *The Writings of William James: A Comprehensive Edition.* Ed. John J. McDermott. 1967. Chicago: U of Chicago P, 1977.

Mailloux, Steven. *Interpretive Conventions: The Reader in the Study of American Fiction.* Ithaca: Cornell UP, 1982.

Matthiessen, F. O. *The James Family.* New York: Knopf, 1947.

Mazella, Anthony J. "The New Isabel." Textual Appendix. *The Portrait of a Lady.* By Henry James. New York: Norton, 1975. 597-619.

Michaels, Walter Benn. "The Interpreter's Self: Peirce on the Cartesian 'Subject.'" *Reader-Response Criticism: From Formalism to Post-Structuralism.* Ed. Jane P. Tompkins. Baltimore: Johns Hopkins UP, 1980. 185-200.

Parker, Hershel. *Flawed Texts and Verbal Icons: Literary Authority in American Fiction.* Evanston: Northwestern UP, 1984.

Peirce, Charles Sanders. *Collected Papers of Charles Sanders Peirce.* Ed. Charles Hartshorne, Paul Weiss, and Arthur W. Burks. 8 vols. Cambridge: Harvard UP, 1931-35, 1958.

Poirier, Richard. *A World Elsewhere: The Place of Style in American Literature.* New York: Oxford UP, 1966.

Posnock, Ross. "William and Henry James." *Raritan* 8 (1989): 1-26.

Rowe, John Carlos. *Henry Adams and Henry James: The Emergence of a Modern Consciousness.* Ithaca: Cornell UP, 1976.

Douglas R. Anderson (essay date 1992)

SOURCE: "Realism and Idealism in Peirce's Cosmogony," in *International Philosophical Quarterly,* Vol. XXXII, No. 126, June, 1992, pp. 185-92.

[*In the following excerpt, Anderson explores the potential contradictions in Peirce's religious faith and his pragmatic convictions.*]

That Charles Peirce was a realist in several ways is hardly disputable; the body of work that discusses Peirce's realisms is already large and is growing steadily.[1] We know, for example, that Peirce embraced an epistemological realism displaying contempt for concern for that which is "absolutely incognizable" (CP 5.312).[2] At the same time, and perhaps more significantly, he defended a Scotistic realism that asserted the reality of generals, that is, of ideas. On the other hand, we also know that Peirce often described his metaphysics as, in part, "objective idealism" (CP 6.24, 6.163)[3]; he believed matter to be "a specialization of mind" (CP 6.268). Peirce's testimony is borne out by a number of similarities his writings share with the work of Hegel and Josiah Royce.

On the face of it, the combination of realism (as opposed to nominalism) and idealism (as opposed to materialism) seems unproblematic. Peirce's realism asserts the reality of general ideas (continua of feeling, see CP 6.151), and these ideas play a central role in the growth of reasonableness that marks his objective idealism. But if we look closely at Peirce's cosmogony and cosmology with which these ideas are associated, another kind of realism and another kind of idealism emerge as potentially in conflict.

This potential problem arises, on the one hand, from the fact that Peirce's realism demands the independence of real ideas from any particular mind: realities are precisely those things "which have an existence independent of your mind or mine or that of any number of persons" (CP 8.12, see also 5.311). On the other hand, Peirce's objective idealism is tied directly to his theism—his belief in a God that is creator of all.[4] Peirce freely acknowledged that he conceived God to be mind in a vague sense, or at least an "analogue of mind" (6.502). These two points raise the question, then, whether the real ideas that are found at the origin of the universe—and out of which the universe evolves—are independent of God such that God is a mere "friend of the forms," or whether God is in full control of the ideas such that, as Donna Orange suggests, they are "God's ideas."[5] In short, is Peirce an extreme Platonic realist or is he a neo-scholastic idealist?[6]

I. SOME DIFFICULTIES

Before establishing any kind of answer to the question I have posed, I need to present a variety of difficulties facing the inquirer. Most important, to the specific question at hand—whether Peirce is a cosmogonical realist or idealist—Peirce's writings are to some degree indifferent. That is, Peirce never raised the question precisely as I have raised it, and therefore of course never answered it in direct fashion. This indifference resulted from Peirce's belief that the notions of ultimate origin and God were inherently vague and therefore could not be adequately articulated from any finite perspective. Thus, for example, he maintained that cosmology was "decidedly a difficult subject on which to break ground for oneself" (MS 948, p. 1). Moreover, the inherent vagueness of the notions opens discussion of them to the possibility of confusion since, for Peirce, "Every concept that is vague is liable to be self-contradictory in those respects in which it is vague" (CP 6.496). This meant that Peirce had little fear of contradicting himself in his discussions of God and creation. Any exegesis of texts whose author is not concerned about self-contradiction is quite clearly potentially problematic.

Such difficulties, however, once acknowledged, need not preclude inquiry. Vagueness is a warning for caution; it is not a dead end for inquiry. Peirce himself, admitting the difficulties he faced, did not refrain from speculating at length concerning both God and the creative origin of the universe. And it is from these speculations, as well as from other central features of Peirce's philosophy, that I hope to draw some preliminary conclusions concerning the question I have posed. My hope, as the title

might suggest, is to show that Peirce sketched an account of God and of aboriginal ideas that makes him both a realist and an idealist—that he sought to mediate the dichotomy I present.

II. THE QUESTION OF TEMPORALITY

In asking whether Peirce is an idealist or a realist in his cosmogony, it is tempting to frame the question in temporal terms. Which came first, God or ideas? The question put thus becomes an unanswerable question of historical fact. But if anything is clear in Peirce's cosmological writings, it is that he recognized the inadequacy, and indeed the impossibility, of using only a temporal framework. The problem is the timing of time. While Peirce tentatively asserted that time was prior to existence (MS 944), he was set in his belief that it followed from both God and the Firsts that were the aboriginal ideas[7]: "In short, if we are going to regard the universe as a result of evolution at all, we must think that not merely the existing universe, that locus in the cosmos to which our reactions are limited, but the whole Platonic world, which in itself is equally real, is evolutionary in its origin, too. And among the things so resulting are time and logic." (CP 6.200) Thus, for Peirce, time was a creation, and a creation of the "latter" stages of creative act.

To get a sense of time's place, let me try to outline some of the features of Peirce's conception of creation. First, he seemed to argue that creation involved at least three stages.[8] The first stage of creation Peirce variously described as "the bare Nothing of Possibility" (MS 942, p. 1), "the utter vagueness of completely undetermined and dimensionless potentiality" (CP 6.193), and "the general vague nothing-in-particular-ness" (CP 6.200). This was perhaps a world of Platonic worlds, a continuum of pure and undifferentiated Firsts. As Peirce put it in a description of hyperbolic cosmology (c. 1905): "Feeling, then is assumed as the starting point; but feeling uncoordinated, having its manifoldness implicit" (MS 878, p. 12). Out of this real possibility or potentiality developed a particular chaos or world of Firsts: the Platonic world that lies behind our own specific universe (CP 6.200 and 6.208). As we proceed, we must keep in mind that Peirce held both of these initial worlds to be "conscious" in some form, because they were constituted by Firsts. For, "whatever is First is ipso facto sentient," and feeling is a vague form of consciousness (CP 6.201, see also 6.221).[9] The spontaneous relationships, what Peirce thought of as developing habits, of these Firsts, or ideas, then yielded the third stage of creation—the evolution of our real and existent universe in which time comes into play. Thus, for Peirce, "we must suppose that the existing universe, with all its arbitrary secondness, is an offshoot from, or an arbitrary determination of, a world of ideas, a Platonic world . . ." (CP 6.192). It is here of course that the importance of Secondness and habit become apparent. Insofar as time appears here in the third stage, Peirce believed that to try to use time to understand orders of relation between God and aboriginal ideas was fundamentally impossible.

A consequent problem, however, was that in discussing the issue of creation Peirce saw no alternative to using temporal terms in a nontemporal fashion:

> We have therefore to suppose a state of things before time was organized. Accordingly, when we speak of the universe as arising we do not mean that literally. We mean to speak of some kind of sequence, say an objective logical sequence; but we do not mean in speaking of the first stages of creation before time was organized, to use "before," "after," "rising," and such words in the temporal sense. But for the sake of the commodity of speech we may avail ourselves of these words. (CP 6.214)

Peirce was aware of the confusion this could lead to—especially among those who were not used to thinking mathematically—and occasionally apologized for his usage (MS 944). This constitutes, then, another result of the vagueness of the conceptions of God and origin that we must keep in mind as we proceed.

III. ANSWERS IN THE COSMOLOGY OF THE 1890's

Peirce's 1891-92 *Monist* essays may seem an odd place to look for his mature view concerning the nature of creation. On numerous occasions in his later writings, however, he referred the reader back to these essays and indicated that his understanding of the evolution of the cosmos had not changed in any significant fashion. Moreover, the many later writings that focus on God's role in creation seem to be in large part quite consistent with the earlier cosmology. These considerations, together with the fact that Peirce's most extensive cosmological writings are to be found in these *Monist* essays and in several essays from the late 1890s, suggest that it is reasonable to begin here in looking for an answer to my question. In particular, then, I will build my case around the essay **"Evolutionary Love,"** though I will pay close attention to its companion pieces and the later essays mentioned above.

In **"Evolutionary Love"** Peirce addressed what he believed to be the three possible theories to account for the evolution of the universe: tychasticism, anancasticism, and agapasticism. Peirce's explicit identification of himself as an agapasticist provides an inroad into assessing his view of the aboriginal relation of God and ideas. Moreover, his corollary rejection of the other two possibilities gives us a fairly clear sense of how he might mediate the conflict of cosmogonical realism and idealism as I have presented it.

Agapasticism is the view that agapasm or a love-driven evolution is effective in the universe—that the development of the universe was governed by agape or cherishing love: "In genuine agapasm . . . advance takes place by virtue of a positive sympathy among the created springing from continuity of mind" (CP 6.304). Moreover, Peirce freely associated this agapasm with theism. Borrowing from the gospel of John, he proceeded on the assumption that "God is love" (CP 6.287ff). But, if God is love, and if, as we saw earlier, God is mind in some sense, and the evolution of the world proceeds by love's efficacy, it seems reasonable to conclude that Peirce must come down on the side of idealism. God is that which determines ideas; or conversely, the ideas are God's ideas. Indeed, what we see here is that agapasticism involves some elements of anancasticism, the claim that necessity determines the evolution of the cosmos. Insofar as the ideas are under the sway of God's mind their development is ordered by God's reason; this is why Peirce often described evolution as the growth of reasonableness.[10] But while it may be true that Peirce was an idealist, it is not true in an unqualified way. We must examine agapasm more closely.

While Peirce willingly rejected tychasticism (the claim that chance governed evolution), he never rejected—and in fact he went to great lengths to make it clear that he did not reject—the more modest assertion of tychism. Tychism is the claim that some element of chance is operative in the universe. Thus, while agapasticism adopted an element of anancasticism, it also maintained a weak tie with tychasticism. This is of particular importance for the question at hand, for Peirce argued that it was chance alone that could account for the initial development of ideas in the cosmos. "The very first and most fundamental element that we have to assume," he maintained, "is a Freedom or Chance, or Spontaneity, by virtue of which the general vague nothing-in-particular-ness that preceded the chaos took a thousand definite qualities" (CP 6.200). Chance, however, was not to be considered some external power; rather, it reflected the autonomy of the original ideas inasmuch as they were feelings and Firsts. As Peirce put it: "Thus, when I speak of chance, I only employ a mathematical term to express with accuracy the characteristics of freedom and spontaneity" (CP 6.201). Or again, with respect to the efficacy of evolution, he argued that we can think of "the ideas as springing into a preliminary stage of being by their own inherent firstness" (CP 6.199).

This assertion of the autonomy of the initial Firsts, however vaguely conceived, precludes agapasticism from falling into necessitarianism. That is, Peirce used tychism effectively to block God's full control of the development of ideas, and consequently of the universe. Therefore, while God in some way is the source of these initial ideas, they, by virtue of chance, maintain an element of independence from God. Such independence suggests not cosmological idealism—at least not in the strict sense—but a realism of ideas. Such a realism qualifies the idealism inherent in agapasticism.

As Peirce developed **"Evolutionary Love,"** he was well aware of the tension between idealism and realism that he was creating. He took it to be a virtue, not a weakness, of his position. This is nowhere better illustrated than in his claim that anancasm and tychasm represented degenerate versions of agapasm (CP 6.303). Tychasm lacked any element of order, and anancasm, any element of chance. To make the point affirmatively, Peirce still viewed creation as an act—an act in some sense of God's will.[11] It was not an act of dominance, however, but rather one of empowerment. Insofar as God is love, for Peirce, God's creativity involved, as I have argued elsewhere, allowing "attractive ideas (qualities) to begin to develop themselves."[12] Agapasm thus asserts both God's priority and the ideas' autonomy; as Peirce put it, "The movement of love is circular, at one and the same impulse projecting creations into independency and drawing them into harmony" (CP 6.288).[13] This dual Peircean answer to the question with which I began can be seen from another angle if we turn to Peirce's later description of God as *Ens necessarium.*

IV. THE NECESSITY OF GOD'S BEING

In perhaps his best known writing on religion, **"A Neglected Argument for the Reality of God"** (1910), Peirce identified God in scholastic fashion: "The word 'God,' so 'capitalized' (as we Americans say), is the definable proper name, signifying *Ens necessarium;* in my belief Really creator of all three Universes of Experience" (CP 6.452). Once again, in view of Peirce's attribution of mind-likeness to God, we are led immediately to suppose a kind of strict idealist interpretation in which God is in complete command of ideas or aboriginal Firsts. This is especially so if we are led to consider not only the argument from contingency, but all five of Aquinas's arguments taken together. But if we follow Peirce through the **"Neglected Argument"** and examine his other later descriptions of God, we see that such an interpretation is too strong.

Once again, it is tychism that plays the central role in checking the completeness of God's control of ideas, and thus of evolution in general: "It is not that such phenomena [growth and relations in nature] might not be capable of being accounted for, in one sense, by the action of chance with the smallest conceivable dose of a higher element; for if by god be meant the *Ens necessarium,* that very hypothesis requires that such should be the case" (CP 6.465). In this way, God, *Ens necessarium,* as Peirce saw it, creates in the presence of chance. This is consistent with his earlier (1891) argument that the world proceeded by a developmental teleology. Such a teleology requires a certain intentional or self-imposed ignorance on the part of the "mind" whose telos is effective in the world. In other words, the initial autonomy of ideas—their spontaneity—loosens God's control of his own account of the outcome in the infinite future. Peirce put the point succinctly in his response to the question of God's omniscience: "I do not see why we may not assume that He refrains from knowing much. For this thought is creative." (CP 6.508)

Again, the ideas retain some element of independence of God and this independence constitutes a partial realism. This limiting of idealism is a direct denial that God—and consequently the universe—is "pure act" in the traditional sense. Peirce had encountered this issue with both Hegel and Royce, and in a 1902 review of Royce's work wrote the following: "This makes an apparent difficulty for idealism. For if all reality is of the nature of an actual idea, there seems to be no room for possibility or any lower mode than actuality, among the categories of being." (CP 8.126) The question here, then, as with the earlier cosmological writings, is what is the role of God? If God is *Ens necessarium,* in what sense is his being necessary?

The most obvious possibility, if God is not the complete determinant of all, is that His being is a necessary condition of the initial ideas. This parallels in part what was meant in the scholastic tradition. And if we remember that the dependence we are discussing is not temporal, and therefore not causal, such an interpretation makes good sense. Creation, as we saw in **"Evolutionary Love,"** is not so much a "molding" as it is an "enabling" or "empowering." God does not so much "make" the ideas as he "allows" them or, as Carl Hausman has suggested, "permits" them.[14] Nevertheless, if we consider the earlier cosmology of **"Evolutionary Love"** and **"The Logic of the Universe,"** we can make some sense of this more limited understanding of God's necessity.

In **"The Logic of the Universe"** Peirce emphasized his notion that cosmology is equivalent to "mathematical metaphysics" (CP 6.213 and MS 948). Whatever else was behind this description, it was surely in part a corollary to Peirce's belief in the inherent vagueness of creation as well as its implicit atemporality, for mathematical reasoning is precisely that kind of reasoning that allows us to think beyond the limits of both time and an existent universe. Pursuing this understanding of cosmology, Peirce was led to offer a kind of mathematical "clue" to guide us through the maze of "the beginnings of creation" (CP 6.203-204). The essence of his clue was that the originary potentiality was "general" and therefore inherently continuous (CP 6.204).

The initial vague potentiality—the residence of the ideas—is thus a continuum out of which all else develops. When Peirce asserted that "all the evolution we know of proceeds from the vague to the definite," he took this to entail "that as a rule the continuum [in this case, our synechistic universe] has been derived from a more general continuum, a continuum of higher generality" (CP 6.191). This led directly to his well known analogy of a chalk line on a blackboard. The chalk line constitutes a spontaneous development, but itself displays "a certain element of continuity" (CP 6.203). But the line's continuity, Peirce argued, "is nothing but the original continuity of the blackboard which makes everything upon it continuous" (CP 6.203). The upshot is that the initial vague potentiality, as a continuum, with its spontaneity, is that which enables all evolution and growth. But the analogy is suggestive of a further step.

Insofar as God is *Ens necessarium,* really creator of all, his being must in some analogical sense constitute the continuum of all continua; God, vaguely understood, is that which permits evolution to occur (CP 6.185). While I would not want to insist on the appropriateness of the claim, this does provide us with an interesting way of understanding God as agape. Insofar as God creates agapastically by drawing creatures into harmony and setting them into independency, we might construe agape as one way of naming the continuum that God is. It is the continuity—or generality—of love that constitutes Peirce's melding of idealism and realism. The continuum of agape grounds all other continua, but it does not specify them.

Let me try to draw these thoughts together by way of Peirce's 1898 attempt to distinguish his idealism from that of Hegel:

> Now the question arises, what necessarily resulted from that state [the initial potentiality] of things? But the only sane answer is that where freedom was boundless nothing in particular necessarily resulted.

> In this proposition lies the prime difference between my objective logic and that of Hegel. He says, if there is any sense in philosophy at all, the whole universe and every feature of it, however minute, is rational, and was constrained to be as it is by the logic of events, so that there is no principle of action in the universe but reason. But I reply, this line of thought, though it begins rightly, is not exact. A logical slip is committed; and the conclusion reached is manifestly at variance with observation. It is true that the whole universe and every feature of it must be regarded as rational, that is as brought about by the logic of events. But it does not follow that it is constrained to be as it is by the logic of events; for the logic of evolution and of life need not be supposed to be of that wooden kind that absolutely constrains a given conclusion. (CP 6.218)

If the development of the universe is not "constrained to be as it is by the logic of events," then a fortiori it is not so constrained by God. The initial Platonic realm or realm of realms, and consequently all that derives from it, remains in some part free in its spontaneity. Therefore, whereas Hegel—at least as Peirce read him—was a thoroughgoing idealist in having absolute spirit constrain all that is, Peirce tempered his idealism by yielding to the Firsts their firstness, thus making them real in precisely that degree to which they are unconstrained. At the same time, Peirce's realism in this respect is intended not so much as a limitation on God's will, but, given the world in which we find ourselves, as its only possible natural expression.

NOTES

[1] The following examples only begin to show what is available. Robert F. Almeder, *The Philosophy of Charles Peirce: A Critical Introduction* (Totowa, NJ: Rowman and Littlefield, 1980); J. F. Boler, *Charles Peirce and Scholastic Realism* (Seattle: Univ. of Washington Press, 1963);

Peter Skagestad, *The Road of Inquiry: Charles Peirce's Pragmatic Realism* (New York: Columbia Univ. Press, 1981); Robert G. Meyers, "Peirce's Doubts about Idealism," *Transactions of the Charles S. Peirce Society* 21 (Spring 1985); Sandra Rosenthal, "Temporality, Perceptual Experience, and Peirce's 'Proofs' of Realism," *Transactions of the Charles S. Peirce Society* 20 (Fall 1984).

[2] References to Peirce's work are as follows: CP=*Collected Papers of Charles Sanders Peirce*, eds. C. Hartshorne and P. Weiss (vol. I-VI) and A. Burks (vol. VII-VIII) (Cambridge: Harvard Univ. Press, 1931-58). Cited by volume and paragraph number. All manuscript (MS) numbers are according to the Robin listing: *Annotated Catalogue of the Papers of Charles S. Peirce* (Amherst: Univ. of Massachusetts Press, 1967).

[3] In a forthcoming essay, Carl Hausman highlights the "partialness" of Peirce's "objective idealism." Hausman, "Peirce's Evolutionary Realism."

[4] Among Peirce scholars there is a division concerning the seriousness with which one should take Peirce's writings on God and religion. I find myself in the camp that takes them seriously, because I can find no good reason to suggest that Peirce intended that anyone should do otherwise. For further exploration of this issue, see Thomas A. Goudge, *The Thought of C. S. Peirce* (Toronto: Univ. of Toronto Press, 1950); Michael Raposa, *Peirce's Philosophy of Religion* (Bloomington: Indiana Univ. Press, 1989); Donna Orange, *Peirce's Conception of God: A Developmental Study* (Lubbock, TX: Institute for Studies in Pragmaticism, 1984). For an assessment of Peirce's "vague" notion of God with which I shall be working, see Vincent G. Potter, "Vaguely Like a Man: The Theism of C. S. Peirce" in *God Knowable and Unknowable*, ed. R. J. Roth (New York: Fordham Univ. Press, 1973).

[5] Orange, p. 67.

[6] Clearly it is an historical fact that many, if not most, idealists take themselves in some sense to be realists. That is, ideas are not held to be unreal because they are God's. On the contrary, idealism is often viewed as a way to account for the reality of ideas. Two points, however, are in order here. First, Peirce defined the real as that which is as it is irrespective of what anyone thinks. Now, Peirce did not say whether God's mind is included among these "thinkers," but it remains a possibility that in certain respects it is. Second, while idealists say that ideas are real as God's ideas, they often make the ideas so completely dependent on God (e.g., Spinoza) that it is really God's reality, not that of the ideas, that is at stake. Such a pantheism of ideas was unacceptable to Peirce insofar as it makes God's love a self-love (see "Evolutionary Love"). It is for these reasons that I want to set out by taking the relation of cosmogonical realism and idealism in its most dichotomous form; the opposition allows us to see why Peirce wanted to maintain both in certain respects.

[7] Throughout the paper I shall refer to Peirce's three categories: Firstness, Secondness, and Thirdness. It is not possible here to provide a full account of the categories, though it may be helpful to readers not familiar with Peirce's work to know that he roughly equated them with quality, fact, and law.

[8] There is a question here whether or not Peirce identified God with the first stage of creation—I have not assumed this identification, though I take it to be a possibility. I leave the question open for now. But I have examined the argument I will present from both perspectives and have found that, while some changes result, the general point—Peirce's realism/idealism—seems to be unaffected.

[9] For a full treatment of Peirce's notion of the self, see Vincent M. Colapietro, *Peirce's Approach to the Self* (Albany: SUNY Press, 1989).

[10] See Orange, pp. 66ff.

[11] I am indebted here to an unpublished paper by Joseph McGinn. McGinn, "Creativity and Intelligibility in Peircean Cosmology."

[12] Douglas R. Anderson, *Creativity and the Philosophy of C. S. Peirce* (The Hague: Martinus Nijhoff, 1987), p. 111.

[13] See Raposa, p. 77.

[14] Carl Hausman, "Eros and Agape in Creative Evolution: A Peircean Insight," *Process Studies* 4 (1974).

Edward S. Perry, Jr. (essay date 1992)

SOURCE: "The Origin and Development of Peirce's Concept of Self-Control," in *Transactions of the Charles S. Peirce Society,* Vol. XXVIII, No. 4, Fall, 1992, pp. 667-90.

[*In the following excerpt, Perry examines the concept of self-control in Peirce's philosophy, finding it derives from Peirce's reading of Friedrich Schiller, Henry James, and Emmanuel Swedenborg.*]

The phenomenon of self-control, as described by Peirce, is "common to all grown men and women" (5.442). Its role in Peirce's philosophy, however, is anything but common. After the turn of the century it became a remarkably complex and central theme in his writings. Peirce based his theory of pragmaticism on a study of the phenomenon of self-control (5.442), it became a defining characteristic of his Logic and Ethics (1.191) and it is the modus operandi for evolution, at least "in its higher stages" (5.433). Perhaps because of its importance, Peirce called for "a review of the process of self-control in its entirety" (5.440). Unfortunately, he never conducted this review, at least not in a systematic way. There have been several important articles and books

that refer to the subject,[1] but thus far the review still remains incomplete.

One way of beginning an analysis of the complexities of Peirce's concept of self-control is to uncover the origins of the concept and trace its development in Peirce's writings. Its origins are found in his earliest writings and the concept developed in four stages.

The origins of the concept are located in Peirce's earliest, moralistic writings on character development,[2] his analysis of Friedrich Schiller's *Letters on the Aesthetic Education of Man,* and his study of the theology of Emmanuel Swedenborg and Henry James' exposition of Swedenborg's theology in *Substance and Shadow* (5.402, n.3). These early writings comprise the first stage in the development of Peirce's concept of self-control. As far as I know, Peirce did not use the term "self-control" in his philosophical writings, until 1868 (5.339n.). Still, as we shall see, the complex role that self-control plays in Peirce's mature philosophy is anticipated, to a surprising degree, in writings from as early as 1855.

It was not until the 1880s that Peirce began to regularly use the term "self-control," but at that time he associated self-control with "moral absolutisms" and "conservatism" that block the path of inquiry (e.g., 1.43-61, 1.330, 1.666, 2.198). Self-control, he concluded, is one element of "sham reasoning" (1.56-7). This marks a second stage in the development of his concept of self-control. In terms of his categories, Peirce's final understanding of self-control encompassed all three categories. Self-control involves the Firstness of freedom and self-determination, the Secondness of struggle and resistance to change and the Thirdness of habit. During this second stage, however, emphasis was placed almost entirely on the Secondness of self-control.

In the 1870s Peirce developed his future-oriented, fallibilistic, developmental theory of inquiry. In the 1880s he distinguished between, on the one hand, uncontrolled operations of the mind, which include elements of perception and instincts and, on the other hand, deliberate, purposive reasoning. These two related developments mark the beginning of the third stage. Chronologically it overlaps stage two but it is significantly different in that it provides the impetus for the fourth and final stage.

Self-control is implicit in Peirce's theory of inquiry and his uncontrolled/controlled distinction, but until he overcame his early moralistic interpretation of Ethics and his related overemphasis on the Secondness of self-control, he was unable to see how Ethics and self-control could be compatible with inquiry. It wasn't until after his turn of the century reevaluation of Ethics that self-control surfaced as a major theme in his philosophy.

Beginning in 1902, Peirce reached back to his earlier writings, including some of his first efforts, and he began to make explicit use of the concept that had always been an implicit part of his philosophy. The fourth stage consists in the integration of the concept of self-control with the rest of his philosophy. There is not a single aspect of Peirce's philosophy that is not related to his doctrine of self-control. For that reason, this paper will only concentrate on stages one through three.

STAGE ONE
Early Influences
Schiller's Aesthetic *Letters*
and Swedenborg' Cycle of Redemption

Friedrich Schiller's *Letters on the Aesthetic Education of Man* was the first philosophical work studied by Peirce (MSS 310, 619, 630, 683, 1634). It is easy to dismiss the influence of Schiller's *Letters* on Peirce's mature philosophy for if we leave aside the autobiographical references, in which Peirce only mentions the text, we find only one manuscript in which Peirce explicitly discusses Schiller's ideas, and it is a brief college theme, a response to Ruskin's contention that "The Sense of Beauty never furthered the Performance of a single Act of Duty" (W1:10-12). The theme was written in or before 1857.[3] It would be a mistake, however, to underestimate the influence of Schiller's *Letters*. According to Peirce, "it produced so powerful an impression" that it continued to have an impact on his thinking throughout his life (MS 1606, also 2.197). In 1906 he cited it as one of several sources which had an impact on his concept of self-control (5.402 n.3.) Of all the sources cited it is chronologically the first.

For Schiller, in order to unify our physical, logical and moral powers and thereby unify our nature (Schiller, 97 and W1:10-11) we must have the ability to conceive of subjective continuity and persistence through temporal alterations (Schiller, 73-75). Neither the "sensuous" nor the "formal impulse" can accomplish this. On the one hand, it cannot be accomplished "as long as sense perception governs" (Schiller, 65), for when the "sensuous impulse" dominates, we lose ourselves in the manifold of sensations, "personality is extinguished" and the individual "is not" (*ibid.*). On the other hand, according to Schiller, the result is no better when "the formal impulse holds sway." The "formal impulse" "annuls time and change; it wishes the actual to be necessary and eternal, and the external and necessary to be actual" (Schiller, 66). When the "formal impulse" dominates, we appear to be "no more in time" and "we are no longer individuals, but species" (*ibid.*).

In Peirce's early writings on temptation and character development we see ideas that are quite similar to Schiller's critique of the "sensuous impulse" (MS 891, XXXIII, XXXIX, XL, L). As a young man he must have been struck by Schiller's account, for it probably seemed like a description of his own private struggles "to acquire a sovereignty" over himself (MS 619).

The "sensuous impulse" relates to our temporality but not to continuity and persistence, the "formal impulse" gives us continuity and persistence but at the expense of temporality. If "the unity of human nature" is to be accounted for, a "third impulse" must be created (Schiller, 67-72 and W1:11). This impulse must combine the temporality and sensuality of the "sensuous impulse," with the continuity and persistence of the "formal impulse" (Schiller, 67-74). This synthesis is possible because, while the two fundamental impulses are "self-contradictory," their tendencies do not contradict one another in the same object (Schiller, 67-72 and W1:11). Therefore, in Peirce's words, "they can easily coexist, and in perfect harmony" (W1:11).

For Schiller, this synthesis results in the "play impulse." It is the result of a balancing of our "sensuous" and "formal impulses" (Schiller, 74). Here we find one of the sources of Peirce's nascent idea of self-control. According to Schiller, in order for us to harmonize the "sensuous" and "formal impulses," aspects of each must be controlled and moderated (Schiller, 72). The "play impulse" is the result of our efforts to control our tendency to lose ourselves in the contingency of the "sensual impulse," together with our efforts to control our tendency toward atemporality which is associated with the "formal impulse." Instead of losing ourselves in either the contingency of sensations (Schiller, 65-66) or the sterility of atemporal formality, we use what Peirce would later describe as self-control (cf., 8.320). That is, we use foresight and become actively involved in the creation of the form that our-future experiences would take, provided we continue to exercise control. Sculpting from a block of marble is both an example and a metaphor of this activity (Schiller, 76).

It is important to note that we must not only control the "sensuous impulse," but the "formal impulse" too. The "formal impulse" demands an annulment of time and change (Schiller, 66), but when we are guided by the "play impulse" we temper this demand and limit ourselves to the order and stability that can be found within temporal, sensuous experience (Schiller, 73-75). This is consistent with and may have been an early inspiration for Peirce's "Private Thought" of 1866: "What is not a question of a possible experience is not a question of fact" (W1-9).

What is missing in Peirce's "Private Thought" however, is the dynamic tension that we find in Schiller. For Schiller, and though absent in this "Private Thought," I think it was accepted by Peirce as well, we have an impulse or tendency toward atemporality. That is, we have a tendency toward that which is "not a question of possible experience." This tendency must be controlled just as much as our tendency toward sensuous immediacy. All too often, we think of self-control solely in terms of controlling the "sensuous impulse." But, if we trace Peirce's idea of self-control back to its roots in Schiller, we are reminded that self-control is also the means by which we temper our "formal impulse."

At this point in his exposition of Schiller's *Letters*, Peirce asks "what are [the] results with respect to morality?" (W1:11). Schiller described the state created by the "play impulse" as a state of "the utmost self-dependence and freedom" (Schiller, 69). In Peirce's words, "play" is "neither internally nor externally constrained" (W1:11). "Play" is therefore a type of freedom because the individual no longer abandons the self to be determined by the world nor is the world abandoned for an atemporal order, instead the world is drawn inside (Schiller, 69) and is ordered by our purposive thoughts and conduct.

Peirce concludes that Ruskin may have been correct if he meant that the "aesthetic state" "does not further the performance" of any single duty, but it does enable us to "do our duty" in a general way. The thrust of Schiller's *Letters* is that the "play impulse," places us in an "aesthetic state," which enables us to perceive and create Beauty in our experience (W1:11-12). Since Beauty is our ultimate telos (W1:11-12), "play" put us "in a state to do our duty." It "places the mind in a state of 'infinite determinableness' so that it can turn in any direction and is in perfect freedom" (W1:11-12).

In sum, there are two concepts which Peirce derived from Schiller that went on to play a direct role in the development of his idea of self-control: his understanding of the importance of the normative sciences, and his concept of "perfect freedom." First, and most generally, Schiller's thesis that the unity of human nature depends on the normative role of Beauty, contributed to Peirce's understanding of the foundational importance of Aesthetics (Barnouw, 607 ff.,). It is likely that this is what Peirce had in mind when he emphasized the lasting influence of Schiller on the general development of his philosophy (MSS 683 and 1606). Second, in what may be his first, explicit use of the term "self-control," Peirce related it to "perfect freedom." We therefore have a direct link from Peirce's analysis of Schiller to his use of the term "self-control." In 1868, Peirce argued that Hobbes' position that "a man always acts from a reflection upon what will please him most" is "a crude opinion" (5.339 n.). According to Peirce "Men are not always thinking of themselves" (5.339 n.). He identified the capacity to think about more than one's self and about more than one's own immediate concerns with self-control and he calls this capacity a type of freedom:

> Self-control seems to be the capacity for rising to an extended view of a practical subject instead of seeing only temporary urgency. This is the only freedom of which man has any reason to be proud; and it is because love of what is good for all on the whole, which is the widest possible consideration, is the essence of Christianity, that it is said that the service of Christ is perfect freedom. (5.339 n.)

In his analysis of Schiller, Peirce accepted Schiller's view that Beauty is our telos. In this passage he argues that "love of what is good for all on the whole" is our telos. This anticipates his later emphasis on *agape* and community. This important difference notwithstanding, the 1868 passage and the 1857 analysis of Schiller are

strikingly similar. In both, Peirce emphasizes the role that self-control plays as a necessary condition for recognizing an ideal and then thinking and acting in conformity with it.

Swedenborg

Peirce was familiar with Emmanuel Swedenborg's theology primarily through Henry James, the elder (5.402 n.3, 6.287, 6.507 and 8.263). In 1870, Peirce published a review of James' *The Secret of Swedenborg* (W2: 433-438). In 1905, he cited James the elder, his *Substance and Shadow,* and Swedenborg as being early influences that contributed to the development of his idea of self-control, particularly with respect to its relationship to Aesthetics (5.402 n.3). In addition, Peirce incorporated some of Swedenborg's terminology, for example the notion of the "vir" (see W2: 438 and 5.402 n.3), into his theory of the normative sciences (Krolikowski, 1964).

Peirce's early writings emphasized a struggle between a future-oriented, idealizing self and a self that is tempted (e.g., MSS. 891, 1629, and 1633, 1638). I believe this opposition, and the ensuing attempts to acquire "sovereignty," should be interpreted in terms of Swedenborg's cosmology which describes a cycle of alienation through incarnation followed by creative redemption. It seems likely that Peirce interpreted it in this way, at least in part. Swedenborg's theology and its influence on the development of Peirce's idea of self-control may be summarized as follows.

In his review of James' *The Secret of Swedenborg,* Peirce is very critical of James' lack of argumentation (W2: 435-436) and his confusing use of terminology (W2: 437-438). However, Peirce writes that "though deficient in argumentation, the book contains some interesting philosophical doctrines. The most prominent of these is a theory of the relation of matter to form" (W2: 436). What interests Peirce is James' account of Swedenborg's principle of individuation and its role in creation. In *Substance and Shadow,* James explains the doctrine:

> The sole possible basis of identity for the creature, the only conceivable ground for attributing distinctive character or selfhood to him, lies in his being in himself a direct contrast to the creator: empty where He is full, impotent where he is omnipotent, ignorant where He is omniscient, evil where he is good. (James, 1863, 442)

Creation for James and Swedenborg is a matter of individuation. As creatures we are independent of the Creator. Peirce stresses this independence and in a passage that anticipates his later "theory" of the self he emphasizes that:

> This distinction is no mere logical convenience or necessity, but it is a real partition, for it lies in the very *esse* of a thing . . . the creature, because he does not contain within his own self the essence

of his being, is, in himself, a mere phantom and no reality. (W2: 433)

Why must there be radical independence and differentiation between the Creator and creatures? The answer to this for Swedenborg, James and Peirce lies in the nature of the Creator. The Creator is perfect love and He is "utterly void of self-love" (James, 1863, 442). Therefore, He can only be what He is if there is something wholly other than Himself:

> It is no doubt very tolerable finite or creaturely love to love ones' own in another, to love another for his conformity to oneself: but nothing can be in more flagrant contrast with the creative Love, all whose tenderness *ex vi termini* must be reserved only for what intrinsically is most bitterly hostile and negative to itself. (James, 1863, 442)

Peirce was especially interested in this doctrine as it pertains to Man. But Peirce emphasized that Man is not entirely distinct from the Creator. Man's material, individual existence differentiates him, but Man is also spiritual and this is the source of his hope for redemption. Peirce summarizes, and apparently approves of James' view:

> In the case of man, the matter is what sets him off from God and gives him being in himself and consciousness, while the form is the Divine element in him, whereby he is brought back into harmony with his Creator; that is, it is his conscience of good and evil. The form is the element of love in man, the matter the element of self. (W2: 436)

In sum, we must control that which sets us apart and we must follow the dictates of conscience. For Swedenborg and James our material existence is what sets us apart. This is similar to the themes Peirce studied in Schiller. Schiller argued that we must control our "sensuous impulse." Here our "sensuous impulse" is associated with "the element of self" that "sets [Man] off from God."

The Swedenborgian influence is still evident when, years later, Peirce argued that self-controlled purposive thought and conduct has a significance far beyond the creation of personal habits. Using the Swedenborgian notion of the *vir,* he wrote that self-control is the means by which we participate in the on-going process of creation and the growth of concrete reasonableness:

> . . . it is by the indefinite replication of self-control upon self-control that the *vir* is begotten, and by action, through thought, he grows an esthetic ideal, not for the behoof of his own poor noodle merely, but as the share which God permits him to have in the work of creation.

> This ideal, by modifying the rules of self-control modifies action, and so experience too—both the man's own and that of others. . . . (5.402 n.3 see also 1.575, 1.588 and 1.615 from 1903 and 8.138 n.4 from 1905)

In 1859, while in the midst of struggles to control what others described as his "independent and violent," "thorny and spinous" character (Perry, 1935, I, 211 and 363), Peirce wrote the following. It says much about his own personal struggles. It also anticipates his 1868 association of self-control and Christian ethics and, most surprisingly, it anticipates the cosmological significance he would much later attribute to self-control. In addition it poetically expresses the essence of what would become his developmental teleology. In short, it reveals the extent to which later theories—which he would associate with self-control—are present in his earliest writings:

> The happiness of the Christian, what does that consist in, but in the consciousness that he is giving his infinitesimal aid to God,—is doing his mite in the work of the universe? He follows perfection, as the ocean the moon; he gets no nearer, but though he is dashed against the eternal rocks of circumstance, and, superficially, is monstrous and violent, by turns, in his eternal depths there is a tranquility which conception cannot grasp. (MS 1633, see also MS 891 from 1858)

STAGE TWO
Self-control and "sham reasoning"

In his earliest moralistic writings and until the 1890s, Peirce described Ethics as a dualistic matter concerned with what is eternally right and eternally wrong (2.198 and 1.43-1.61). As late as 1902 Peirce explained how Ethics, understood in this way, interferes with the progress of inquiry:

> It may very easily happen that the over-development of a man's moral conception should interfere with his progress in philosophy. The protoplasm of philosophy has to be in a liquid state in order that the operations of metabolism may go on. Now morality is a hardening agent. It is astonishing how many abominable scoundrels there are among sincerely moral people. The difficulty is that morality chokes its own stream . . . morality, doctrinaire conservatist that it is, destroys its own vitality by resisting change, and positively insisting, This is eternally right: That is eternally wrong. The tendency of philosophers has always been to make their assertions too absolute. Nothing stands more in the way of a comprehension of the universe and of the mind. But in morals this tendency acquires triple strength. (2.198)

For these reasons, in 1898 he wrote that Ethics is "as useless a science as can be conceived" (1.667 and see 2.198). The only praise he could muster for "ethical writers" was that "they are commonly free from the nauseating custom of boasting of the utility of their science" (1.667).

Later in 1902, he amended this view, though the seeds for this reevaluation of ethics were sown years earlier. Until this revision, however, self-control, for Peirce, was primarily a matter of Secondness, a struggle involving resistance, dualisms and a polarized consciousness.

Peirce later acknowledged that, for a while, he overemphasized his category of Secondness (8.254-6). Why Peirce emphasized Secondness during this period is a question to which we may never have an answer. Peirce's study of some of the works of Josiah Royce and F. C. S. Schiller (5.402 n.3 and 8.41) had an effect on the development of his idea of self-control during this period but I see no reason to believe that this would have led to an overemphasis on Secondness. Peirce's psychological experiments between 1882 and 1884 with Joseph Jastrow (7.21-7.35 and 7.63 ff.) indicate that he was interested in the actual, psycho-physical machinery—primarily the Secondness—which is involved in our becoming self-controlled. This could be part of the explanation. Whatever the reasons, his idea of self-control during this period may be summed up as follows.

In an 1885 review of Royce's *The Religious Aspect of Philosophy*, "self-control" was used as a technical term by Peirce; it was described as a type of volition, an internal struggle and an internal, inhibitory resistance (8.41 and also, 1.383 and 1.386). In these passages, it is clear that Peirce conceived of the phenomenon of self-control primarily in terms of his category of Secondness. In fact, Peirce explicitly distinguished self-control from continuity (8.41), which he had already recognized as the hallmark of Thirdness (1.337). Peirce writes:

> What I call volition is the consciousness of the discharge of nerve-cells . . . it does not involve the sense of time (i.e. not of a continuum) but it does involve the sense of action and reaction . . . it has an outward and an inward variety, corresponding to Kant's outer and inner sense, to will and self-control, to nerve-action and inhibition. . . . (8.41)

There are indications that, beginning in the 1880s, Peirce was already going beyond this limited view of self-control. For example, in 1883 Peirce writes:

> There is, therefore, some general rule according to which [one belief] . . . succeeds the other. But further, the reasoner is conscious of there being such a rule, for otherwise he would not know he was reasoning, and could exercise no attention or control; and to such an involuntary operation the name "reasoning" is very properly not applied. (2.696)

This passage points to changes that were taking place in his theory of cognition. In particular, it points to his distinction between uncontrolled operations of the mind and controlled reasoning. This was a critical insight, which I will return to in the concluding section. For the most part, however, his narrow and dyadic view of self-control continued into the 1890s. Peirce indirectly associated self-control with "the voice of conscience" and with compulsions from within that are of the form of "degenerate seconds" (1.365). Until 1896 and possibly as late as 1898 (1.618), Peirce identified self-control

with the inner struggles of "morality" (1.43-1.61). "Morality," which he took to be wholly anti-synechistic (1.49-1.51), "supposes self-control" (1.57).

As a result of this association, Peirce identified self-control with the absolutist side of Ethics (2.198), with the "dual distinctions" of "good and bad" (1.61) and "right and wrong" (1.330) and with "conservatism" that blocks the path of inquiry (1.50, 1.57, 1.666 and 8.158). Most revealingly—for it is in sharp contrast with his later views—during this second stage Peirce wrote that self-control is an element of "sham reasoning" (1.57).

I believe that this is an important phase in the overall development of Peirce's idea of self-control, for it highlights its Secondness. Though Peirce later put less emphasis on the Secondness of self-control he never abandoned the idea that self-control is in part a struggle involving resistance, dualisms and a polarized consciousness.

Self-control always involves a degree of Secondness and this is so in at least three ways. First, Peirce, demonstrating the influence of Swedenborg, often remarked on the continuing presence of evil in the world (e.g., 6.479-6.480). Peirce broadly defined evil as "what it is man's duty to fight" (6.479). This includes alienation, selfish tenacity, ignorance and error. Peirce went on to say that self-control is the means at our disposal for waging the fight against evil (6.480). Therefore, the Secondness of self-control will always be present as we continue to struggle to avoid self-centeredness, ignorance and error. Secondly, as Peirce explained in his doctrine of Critical Common-sensism (e.g., 5.446), there is always an element of "vagueness" in our inquiries. Secondness is present as we struggle with the inadequacies and surprises that are inevitable in a fallibilist inquiry. Thirdly, the polar consciousness which Peirce associated with the Secondness of self-control is polar in a temporal way: "the polar sense is the sense of the difference between what was before and what is after a dividing instant . . ." (1.386). Therefore, the Secondness of self-control will always be present, for we are temporal. Further, our temporality is emphasized by Peirce's pragmaticism which looks to the future to clarify the meaning of concepts. As long as we are faced with the task of breaking with a past, shaping a future, and looking to the future to determine the meaning of concepts, self-control will involve Secondness.

STAGE THREE
Peirce's Reevaluation of Ethics and Self-control

After 1902, Peirce rejected his dualistic interpretation of Ethics. Consequently he rejected the related view that self-control is the internal struggle over moral dualisms and as such, blocks the path of inquiry (2.198).

Peirce continued to believe that moral dualisms must be part of Ethics (e.g., MS 1334), but during 1902 he interpreted Ethics as being more than "doctrinaire conservatism":

We are too apt to define ethics to ourselves as the science of right and wrong. That cannot be correct . . . The fundamental problem of ethics is not, therefore, what is right, but, What am I prepared deliberately to accept as the statement of what I want to do, what am I to aim at, what am I after? To what is the force of my will to be directed? (2.198)

Peirce also reversed his position on the importance of Ethics. He no longer considered it to be "useless" (1.667) but instead he wrote that it was foundational and essential for Logic (1.191). What led to this change in his views?

There are very few clues in Peirce's writings to help us answer this question. He does tell us that:

> . . . beginning in 1883, I came to read the works of the great moralists, whose great fertility of thought I found in wonderful contrast to the sterility of the logicians—I was forced to recognize the dependence of Logic upon Ethics. (5.111)

Elsewhere he writes that "only since 1883" did he number Ethics among his "special studies" (5.129); that early in the 1880s he "began to be impressed with the importance of the theory [of Ethics]" and that beginning in 1896 or 1897 "all the intimacy" of the relation of Ethics to Logic was "revealed" (2.198). I believe this was primarily the result of internal developments in his theories including his theories of inquiry and Critical Common-sensism. To a lesser degree, he may have been influenced by others, perhaps the "great moralists." This issue is important since Peirce's reevaluation of Ethics was the proximate cause of the surfacing of the concept of self-control in his writings. Before we turn to a consideration of Peirce's theories of inquiry and his Critical Common-sensism we must first examine the possible influence of others at this juncture.

Max Fisch has shown that Peirce's study of Greek philosophy was very influential during the 1890s (Fisch, 1971). In an unpublished manuscript from that period Peirce discusses the Greek conception of the relationship of Ethics, Esthetics and Logic (Ms 434). There is superficial evidence that suggests that Peirce's explicit references to self-control were in part the result of his study of Greek philosophy. In the history of philosophy, self-control has rarely been discussed in any depth. Until Peirce's writings, the exceptions to this were Plato, Aristotle, Neoplatonic theologians who wrote about the Greek virtue of *sophrosyne* and Calvinist theologians who saw self-control as a sign of grace and a means to redemption. Although Peirce may have been indirectly influenced by the Calvinists, perhaps through his early education, I know of no explicit mention of any direct link. In fact it is much more likely that Peirce would dismiss such a source as being wholly inconsistent with his early Unitarianism and his later Tychism. On the other hand, chronologically his study of the Greeks immediately precedes the period in which self-

control became an explicit and important theme in his writings. This superficial evidence notwithstanding, it is doubtful that Peirce's study of the Greeks led to his emphasis on self-control. Peirce was always careful when introducing terms. If his idea of self-control was similar to either Aristotelian or Platonic *sophrosyne*, Peirce would have used the Greek term, as he did so many others; or, in keeping with his "ethics of terminology" (2.219 ff.,) he would have explained its derivation. Finally, I have found no evidence in Peirce's writings to indicate that he recognized or was at all interested in the philosophical complexities of *sophrosyne*. Few of his many references to Aristotle mention the *Nichomachean Ethics* in which *sophrosyne* is discussed and none of them refer to Aristotle's ideas about *sophrosyne*. Nor do any of his references to Plato, including the lengthy MS 434, discuss *sophrosyne* except in passing. While it is possible that Peirce's study of the Greeks contributed to his reevaluation of the normative sciences, there is no positive evidence to support this claim. Nor is there any evidence that Peirce based his idea of self-control on the Greek virtue of *sophrosyne*.

Another possible source of Peirce's reevaluation of Ethics and the normative sciences is his study of the writings of Johann Friedrich Herbart. Peirce had studied Herbart by 1866 (MS 357) and he refers to him in a manuscript that was probably written in the early or mid 1890s (MS 400), just before his reevaluation of Ethics. While it is difficult to know what impact Peirce's study of Herbart may have had, we do know that in 1905 Peirce gave serious consideration to Herbart's division of the normative sciences and his inclusion of Esthetics as a "branch of Ethics":

> The normative sciences are usually said to be esthetics, ethics, and logic; but Herbart and others put esthetics and ethics together, perhaps rightly . . . I do not see how there can be any rational approval or disapproval of a mere idea in itself and therefore I think there can be no esthetics until something is to be *done* with the idea. Esthetics, therefore, can be nothing but a branch of ethics. (MS 1334 but cf., 1.575)

A third possibility is suggested by Murray Murphey. He writes that Peirce's reevaluation of Ethics was a consequence of his study of William James' pragmatism:

> . . . I suspect it was James' doctrine that the truth is a species of the good which suggested to Peirce the idea of the dependence of logic on ethics. Certainly, the priority here belongs to James. . . . (Murphey, 361)

This may be true, but I know of no evidence in any of their surviving correspondences or in Peirce's manuscripts to support the claim. If Peirce was influenced by James in this matter, he did not acknowledge it, and that would be very unlike him.

I do, however, agree with another suggestion by Murphey: Peirce's reevaluation of Ethics was the result of internal pressures directing the growth of his philosophy (Murphey, 361). We will now examine this possibility in more detail.

Pragmaticism and Critical Common-sensism

Peirce developed his pragmaticism during the 1870s. Pragmaticism delivers a series of conditional propositions. On the antecedent side there are rules for behavior including rules pertaining to our thoughts and conduct in relation to an object. On the consequent side there are hypotheses about the laws governing the behavior of objects under the conditions resulting from our behaviour (Murphey, Chapter VII).

This method suggests that reasoning is subject to self-control. It only makes sense to propose conditional propositions if it is in our power to either make changes or to hold to a course of thought and action which will bear fruit in the future (see 1.598, 5.130 and 5.182). Some habit of personal development and continuity is necessary if future thoughts and conduct are to be either similar to those of the present or, more importantly for Peirce, the product of a deliberate, conscious and teleological growth. In either case, only if we are self-controlled can we predict that there will be a continuum of thought and conduct. Furthermore, only by assuming self-control can we be confident that there will be continuity between our thoughts and our conduct. That is, only if we are in control of both can we anticipate that our conduct will be deliberate and an expression of our thoughts. This continuity of thinking and conduct enables the self-controlled individual to trace into the future the purport of his or her present thoughts and conduct. This is important, for in Peirce's words ". . . it is to conceptions of deliberate conduct that Pragmaticism would trace the intellectual purport of symbols; and deliberate conduct is self-controlled conduct" (5.442).

If one is self-controlled, there is continuity between the present and the future and consequently, one need not await the future in order to have a reasonable conception of it. This was the basis upon which Peirce differentiated his pragmaticism from the pragmatisms of others (5.414-5.427, 5.453 and 5.461). The pragmatisms of James, Papini and F. C. S. Schiller for example, seem to make truth dependent on action (e.g., 8.254-256). But if one is self-controlled one can anticipate the thoughts and conduct that will follow from present thoughts. For this reason self-control places the individual in a position to consider and anticipate what conceivable practical effects would follow. This is more or less the maxim of Peirce's pragmaticism, which was first expressed by Peirce as follows:

> Consider what effects, that might conceivably have practical bearings, we conceive the object of our conception to have. Then, our conception of these effects is the whole of our conception of the object. (5.402)

Without self-control this would be impossible. And so, we can now understand why Peirce argued that his "theory of Pragmaticism" was originally based "upon a study of that experience of the phenomena of self-control which is common to all grown men and women; and it seems evident that to some extent, at least, it must always be so based" (5.442, see also Potter, 1967, 61).

What finally led Peirce to clarify his position and explicitly state the importance of self-control? One possibility is a series of experiments he conducted in the early 1880s. In 1884 Peirce and Joseph Jastrow published a paper titled "On Small Differences of Sensations" (7.21-35 and see also 7.36-48 and 7.63 ff.). The paper summarized the findings of experiments which showed that sensory stimuli too slight for us to be conscious of nevertheless influence our judgments. We draw inferences that are based in part on "sensations so faint that we are not fairly aware of having them" (7.35). Peirce believed that this might be the explanation for "the insight of females as well as certain 'telepathic' phenomena" (7.35).

The Peirce/Jastrow theory should be considered alongside Peirce's theory of perception, in particular the role played by the percept. The "blow" of the percept begins a cognitive process (7.643). The process culminates in hypotheses which are deliberately formed and are under our control (5.115 and 5.180). But the percept—functioning as a percept—is not, strictly speaking, part of the controlled, cognitive process (7.643). The percept is part of an uncontrolled "mental operation" but Peirce contrasts this with the level of cognition at which we exercise control and deliberately draw inferences (7.439-50). Once we respond to the "blow" of the percept and "fix our minds upon it and think the least thing about the percept" the percept then functions as a "percipuum" (7.643). We are conscious of the "percipuum" and it is then part of a "perceptual judgment" (7.643). Even at this point the process is not under our control (5.115). Control begins when hypotheses are formed out of "perceptual judgments" (5.180). The percept is similar to the sensory stimuli described in the Jastrow/Peirce experiment. We are conscious of neither, but they nevertheless have an effect on our deliberate judgments. They steer our judgments in one way or another and they limit the inferences that we are likely to draw.

By 1893 these findings along with Peirce's theory of instincts were included in his doctrine of Critical Common-sensism. Instincts contribute to inferences as do percepts and faint unnoticed sensory stimuli. The mental operations that are generated in these ways are identical to each other in so far as they are:

> beyond the jurisdiction of criticism. It is the part of psychology to explain their processes as it can; but, as long as they are out of the focal plane of consciousness, they are out of our control, and to call them good or bad is idle . . . Quite otherwise is it with the actions that carry out our grander

purposes. Here all must be voluntary, thoroughly conscious, based on critical reflection. Logic is wanted here, to pull inferences to pieces, to show whether they be sound or not, to advise how they may be strengthened, to consider by what methods they ought to proceed. (7.448-449)

The key distinction Peirce is making is between mental operations that are "uncontrolled" and inferences that "come under self-criticism and self-control. The latter . . . may be pronounced *good or bad;* the former could not be otherwise than they were" (7.444). Uncontrolled mental operations are not subject to criticism. Peirce describes them as "operations of thought" and "a kind of thinking" but he contrasts them with controlled inferences. As early as 1883 he had reserved the term "reasoning" for the latter (2.696 and later 1.606, 2.182, 5.108 and 5.130). Prior to these experiments Peirce had not clearly considered the importance of mental operations that could not be controlled nor critiqued. Once he did, he seems to have recognized that the hallmark of arguments and all conscious, deliberate inferences, is that they *can* be controlled and critiqued. The control and critique of reasoning then became a paramount consideration for Peirce. It is at this point that a reevaluation of Ethics became necessary.

In 1893 he argues that Logic is the means by which we critique reasoning (2.532 and 7.448-449). Since reasoning is defined as controlled thought (2.696), it follows that Logic is, at least in part, the critique of controlled thought. This is precisely how Peirce defined Logic nine years later in 1902 when he included it as one of the normative sciences (1.191). In 1893, however, he still thought of Ethics as "doctrinaire conservatism" and he associated self-control with "sham reasoning." Because of this he was apparently unable to explicitly draw the conclusions that Logic must be a normative science and that it must appeal to Ethics for its principles. The impetus for his reevaluation of Ethics was, however, in place. It was only a matter of time before he would reconsider Ethics and reevaluate his understanding of the normative sciences. Then the way was open for the surfacing of self-control in his writings and the fourth stage in its development: its integration with the whole of his philosophy.

NOTES

[1] Examples include: Anderson, 1987. Bernstein, 1964, pp. 165-189 and 1965, pp. 66-91. Colapietro, 1988. Goudge, 1969. Holmes, 1966. Murphey, 1961. Potter, 1967 and Smith, 1978.

[2] See, for example, W1:1-9, W1:101-114 and MSS 619, 891, 1629, 1633, and 1638; also Howe, 1937, pp. 94-6, also Perry, I, 1935, pp. 211, 363, 367, and Perry, II, 1935, pp. 117, 416-7, 423, 425, 436-7.

[3] There is some question about the date that this manuscript was written. The editors of the *Writings of Charles S. Peirce; A Chronological Edition,* assume the

date of composition is March 26, 1857 (W1:10 and 533). It is possible, however, that Peirce actually wrote this interpretation of Schiller in 1855 and the manuscript that was submitted by Peirce as a college theme on March 26, 1857 is a copy of an earlier manuscript that is now lost. We know that Peirce studied Schiller in 1855 and one other theme submitted in 1857 titled "What Is Your Favorite Virtue?" is a verbatim copy of a composition written by Peirce in 1854 or 1855 while he was attending the Dixwell School (MS 1629).

REFERENCES

Works by Peirce

Peirce, Charles Sanders.
1931-1935 *Collected Papers of Charles Sanders Peirce.* Volumes 1-6. Cambridge, Massachusetts: The Belknap Press of Harvard University Press. Edited by Charles Hartshorne and Paul Weiss.

1958 *Collected Papers of Charles Sanders Peirce.* Volumes 7 and 8. Cambridge, Massachusetts: The Belknap Press of Harvard University Press. Edited by Arthur W. Burks.

1975 *Charles Sanders Peirce: Contributions to the Nation, Part One: 1869-1893.* Lubbock: Texas Tech Press. Edited by Kenneth Laine Ketner and James Edward Cook.

1977 *Semiotics and Significs.* Bloomington: Indiana University Press.

1982-1986 *Writings of Charles S. Peirce: A Chronological Edition.* Volumes 1-3. Bloomington: Indiana University Press.

Works by Others

Anderson, Douglas R.
1987 *Creativity and the Philosophy of C.S. Peirce,* Dordrecht: Martinus Nijhoff.

Barnouw, Jeffrey.
1988 "'Aesthetic' for Schiller and Peirce: A Neglected Origin of Pragmatism," *Journal of the History of Ideas,* XLIX, 4, pp. 607-632.

Bernstein, Richard J.
1964 "Peirce's Theory of Perception" in *Studies in the Philosophy of Charles Sanders Peirce,* Second Series, edited by Edward C. Moore and Richard S. Robin, Amherst: The University of Massachusetts Press, pp. 165-189.

1965 "Action, Conduct, and Self-Control," in *Perspectives on Peirce,* edited by Richard J. Bernstein, New Haven: Yale University Press, pp. 66-91.

Colapietro, Vincent M.
1989 *Peirce's Approach to the Self,* Albany: State University of New York Press.

Fisch, Max H.
1971 "Peirce's Arisbe: The Greek Influence in His Later Philosophy," *Transactions of the Charles S. Peirce Society,* 7, pp. 187-210.

Gallie, W.B.
1952 "Peirce's Pragmaticism," in *Studies in the Philosophy of Charles Sanders Peirce,* edited by Philip P. Wiener and Frederic H. Young, Cambridge: Harvard University Press, pp. 61-74.

Goudge, Thomas A.
1969 *The Thought of C.S. Peirce.* New York: Dover Publications.

Hausman, Carl R.
1974 "Eros and Agape in Creative Evolution: A Peircean Insight," *Process Studies,* 4, pp. 11-25.

Holmes, Larry
1966 "Peirce on Self-Control," *Transactions of the Charles S. Peirce Society,* 2, pp. 113-130.

Howe, M.A. DeWolfe
1937 *John Jay Chapman and His Letters,* edited by M.A. DeWolfe Howe, Boston.

James, Henry, Sr.
1863 *Substance and Shadow,* Boston.

Krolikowski, Walter P.
1964 "The Peircean Vir" in *Studies in the Philosophy of Charles Sanders Peirce,* Second Series. Edited by Edward C. Moore and Richard S. Robin, pp. 257-270.

Murphey, Murray.
1961 *The Development of Peirce's Philosophy.* Cambridge: Harvard University Press.

Perry, Ralph Barton.
1935 *The Thought and Character of William James,* two volumes. Boston: Little, Brown and Company.

Potter, Vincent.
1967 *Charles S. Peirce on Norms and Ideals.* Worcester: The Heffernan Press.

Schiller, Friedrich
1794 *Briefe uber die asthetische Eizichung des Menshen.* All references are to the English translation edited by Reginald Snell, New Haven: Yale University Press, 1954.

Smith, John E.
1978 *Purpose and Thought: The Meaning of Pragmatism.* New Haven: Yale University Press.

Vincent G. Potter, S. J. (essay date 1992)

SOURCE: "Peirce on 'Substance' and 'Foundation'," in *The Monist,* Vol. 75, No. 4, October, 1992, pp. 492-503.

[*In the following excerpt, Potter presents an overview of Peirce's categories and discusses Peirce's views on substantiality and empiricism.*]

Charles S. Peirce has a great deal to contribute both to understanding and to solving many of the philosophical problems which puzzle contemporary thinkers. In fact it is probably true that in some ways philosophers of our time are in a better position to understand Peirce's thought than those of his own day. In this paper I would like to consider two puzzling notions: 1) the substantiality of things (including the "self"), and 2) the foundations of human knowledge.

1. SUBSTANCE

The substantiality of things has been challenged at least since the time of the Enlightenment. The question is whether an existing thing (like the self) is, and can be known to be, something which lasts over time and keeps its identity through change. Both the British Empiricists and the Continental Rationalists undermined the very notion of substance. The Rationalists, following Descartes' characterization of substance as a reality which is not only capable of existing in itself (*in se*) but also of existing completely independently of anything else (*a se*), so divinized the notion of substance that Spinoza's monism and Leibniz's monadism were the results. Even some Rationalists found these a strain on credulity.[1]

Hume all but eliminated the notion of substance by taking seriously Locke's characterization of it as an inert, unknowable substratum for sense qualities. Berkeley had already drawn the conclusion that material substance was self-contradictory precisely because it is inert. Nothing completely inert can either be or be a cause. He admitted, however, spiritual substance since it actively perceived ideas. Hume made short work of Berkeley's spiritual substance (the self) by showing that it cannot be known since we have no impression of it, whether an impression of sensation or of reflection. But an idea having no corresponding impression is simply without any assignable meaning. For Hume, the notion of self as substance can at best be traced to a series of impressions of reflection and so really refers to a set of perceptions. Hence the notion of self as unifying substratum of impressions is the product of either memory or imagination.[2] Hume might further have argued that whatever is completely inert is completely unknowable, since there would be no interaction whatever between the knower and what is to be known. Such an entity would be completely unintelligible and so unreal.

Peirce's account of substance attempts to do justice to the Empiricists' criticism of our knowledge of it and to the Rationalists' requirement of a principle of unity and continuity. Peirce's position on substance is connected with his discussion of the self and that position he frequently states in negative terms. Peirce, I would contend, does have the elements of a positive position on both self and substance which, even if never put together in a systematic way, is worth a second look since it suggests a notion of substance different from that criticized by the Enlightenment and one which is perhaps much sounder.[3] I suggest that we undertake a search for Peirce's view of substance by looking at his views about the self, since it is perhaps the most important example of substance.

As Vincent Colapietro has pointed out in his recent book, many passages from Peirce give the impression that his views about the self were purely negative. For example, in the 1868 essays written for the *Journal of Speculative Philosophy*, Peirce is emphasizing against the Cartesians that we have no intuition of the self or of anything else for that matter. Hence he talks about our becoming aware of the self through our ignorance and proneness to error. Again, in the 1890's Peirce, emphasizing his synechism, denies in various ways that thoughts are confined to our own individual minds. In fact, our personal minds are not "individual" at all if by that is meant isolated from other minds.[4]

The point of Peirce's negative presentation was to counter the assumption that the self in its existence is separated and isolated from all others. This is precisely Locke's assumption about substance—that it is an isolated, inert, unchanging, absolute substratum for sensible qualities. In effect, such a substance would be a logical atom.[5] Peirce holds that there can be no logical atoms. Hence the notion of self as individual, if this is understood to mean without relation to or connection with anything else, is just an illusion. Peirce's positive understanding of the self emphasizes its connectedness with other selves and with the environment. The self is real insofar as it is in continuity with everything else and yet at the same time retains its identity as this self and not that. This required Peirce to rethink both the notion of "individual" and the notion of "substance" to overcome the misconceptions of the Enlightenment.

As one might expect, the key to Peirce's ability to rethink these notions successfully is his theory of categories. It would take us too far afield to review his entire theory but it is probably enough simply to remind the reader that for Peirce, while the categories (Firstness [mere possibility], Secondness [brute fact], Thirdness [law-likeness]) are real (not merely logical) and really distinct (one is not the other), they are *not* separable in the real order. We can distinguish them but we cannot find them in reality nor experience them in isolation from one another.[6]

> These universal categories [according to Peirce] are three in number, no more and no less, absolutely irreducible to one another yet interdependent, and

directly observable in elements of whatever is at any time before the mind in any way. Firstness, Secondness, and Thirdness roughly correspond to the modes of being: possibility, actuality, and law (1.23).[7]

Consider, first, Peirce's rethinking of individuality. He distinguishes individuality in a strict sense and in a wider sense. He characterizes strict individuality as reaction and of course reaction is in the category of Secondness. On this account, strictly speaking the individual is such only at the moment of an actual reaction. But for Peirce such an actual reaction can neither exist nor be understood in isolation from everything else (otherwise Secondness would be separable from the other categories). Furthermore such an account of the individual does not square very well with our experience of physical objects and of other people as individuals lasting as individual over time. Peirce's category of Thirdness comes to the rescue, since, as the category of continuity, it allows him to characterize individuality in a wider sense as a "continuity of reactions" which constitutes a single logical subject:

> an individual is something which reacts. That is to say, it does react against some things, and is of such a nature that it might react, or have reacted, against my will. . . . It may be objected that it [the definition of individual in the strict sense] is unintelligible; but in the sense in which it is true, it is a merit, since an individual is unintelligible in that sense . . . that is to say, a reaction may be experienced, but it cannot be conceived in its character of a reaction; for that element evaporates from every general idea. According to this definition, that which alone immediately presents itself as an individual is a reaction against my will. But everything whose identity consists in a continuity of reactions will be a single logical individual. (3.613)

The notion of the self as an individual in the sense of a continuity of reactions brings us to the notion of substance since, as Colapietro points out, Peirce's substance is one and the same as continuity of reactions.[8]

By insisting upon continuity, regularity of behavior, the law-likeness of reality, Peirce in effect retains a notion of substance but one very much different from Locke's. In his well-known piece, **"A Guess at the Riddle"** (c. 1890), Peirce, speculating about the origin of things, writes:

> Pairs of states will also begin to take habits, and thus each state having different habits with reference to the different other states will give rise to bundles of habits, which will be substances. Some of these states will chance to take habits of persistency. . . . Thus, substances will get to be permanent.[9] (1.414)

The permanence of reactions is substance. Hence the notion of substance is relational. It means regularity of behavior, continuity. This is a very different notion from the Lockean hidden substratum, absolute and inert.

Peirce is right in suggesting that his use of the term is in an "old sense" (1.414 n.). After all, in the past, when various schemes of act and potency were common philosophical categories, at least some thinkers understood substance to be a co-principle of being inseparably related to accident, its corresponding co-principle. On such an account, then, substance is relational; in fact it *is* a relation. The real, existing thing (Aristotle's "first substance") is a *composite* of substance and accident related in such a way that they are distinguishable but not separable.[10] Some called this kind of relation (between co-principles of being rather than between beings) a transcendental relation (to distinguish it from the more familiar predicamental relation). This older view would maintain that substance is known in and through its accidents (i.e., its sensible manifestations and regular behavior). It would maintain that only some such scheme renders a changing thing intelligible. Finally, it would maintain that nothing unintelligible (even though perhaps as yet not understood by us here and now) is, or can be, real. These views I take to be Peirce's too.

Let me conclude my remarks on Peirce's general conception of substance by pointing out, in Colapietro's words, Peirce's distinction between existence and persistence:

[For Peirce] existence is the mode of being of an individual substance considered as a continuity of *reactions;* insofar as it is *actually* reacting against other things, it exists. Persistence is the mode of being of such a substance seen as a *continuity* of reactions; insofar as it endures throughout a series of reactions, it persists. In other words, existence . . . designates the aspect of secondness exhibited by any individual substance, while persistence . . . designates one of the ways in which it manifests thirdness (1.487). Both of these aspects of substance are relevant to the cognitive enterprise of human agents. Substances are both designatable and knowable. They are designatable by virtue of their brutally oppositional presence, whereas they are knowable by virtue of their inexhaustibly intelligible character.[11]

2. FOUNDATIONS

Peirce steadfastly maintained that human knowledge is discursive, not intuitive. This also meant that there is no immediate knowledge of anything. Hence, for Peirce, if *all* human knowledge is discursive and mediated, both the question of "first principles" and of the "foundations" of human knowledge need to be rethought in a radical way.[12]

In 1868 Peirce (just turning thirty years of age) published a series of three articles in the *Journal of Speculative Philosophy.* The views there set out remained central to his thought throughout his long career. In those articles he made a sustained attack on what he took to be the spirit of Cartesianism which, according to him, consisted in a preoccupation with removing skeptical doubt by establishing human knowledge as imme-

diate, intuitive and certain. Peirce attributed this penchant to the empiricists as well, although what they claimed to intuit were sensible rather than "clear and distinct" ideas. In place of this Cartesianism Peirce strove to put a theory according to which human knowledge is thoroughly mediated and discursive. In a preliminary draft Peirce makes the point that *what* we think is to be understood only in terms of the proper method for ascertaining *how* we think.[13] He begins, therefore, with an account of cognition, then of truth and reality, and finally of the grounding of inference.[14]

The first paper, **"Questions Concerning Certain Faculties Claimed for Man,"** centers on the issue whether we have any immediate or intuitive knowledge of ourselves, of our mental states, or of the external world. By intuition Peirce means cognition not determined by previous cognition. In the case of judgment this would be a proposition which can be a premise but is not itself a conclusion—a first principle in the traditional sense. His conclusion on this point is negative. All knowledge is inferential and mediated through signs. By introspection Peirce understands internal cognition of our internal states not determined by external cognition. He concludes that we have no such power. All knowledge of our mental states is by inference from overt behavior and not by an inward-looking.

The second paper, **"Some Consequences of Four Incapacities,"** focuses upon a theory of cognition in terms of inference and sign-mediation. The argument proceeds on the assumption that language as the external manifestation of mental activity is to be taken as a model of that activity's structure. Language is a system of signs. Peirce works out an analysis of signs and how they function. Mental activity then is viewed as "inner speech." What is more the thought-process manifested in language is inferential. Inferences are expressed in (and so can be analyzed into) a series of propositions (asserted in judgments). Judgments in turn are expressed through (and so can be analyzed into) concepts. But the thought-process which is expressed in propositions and general terms and is analyzed into judgments and concepts is continuous and inferential. It is not the case that judgments are constructed out of concepts and inferences out of judgments. So to think would be to make a mistake comparable to thinking that because a line segment can be analyzed into points it can also be constructed out of points. The linguistic representation of inference (say, in the syllogism) is static and discrete. The process itself is dynamic and continuous. Such representation is no doubt useful but it is inadequate. It would be an error to attribute to the process what is an attribute of its representation. It is this error that generates Zeno's paradoxes. Later in his career Peirce made this point very clear when he distinguished between an argument and an argumentation.[15] The former is the living inferential process; the latter is its representation in premises and conclusion.

If the human thought process is inferential, still that process is differentiated. Just as the color spectrum is continuous but differentiated, so too the inferential process is continuous but differentiated. It can be analyzed into three sorts of inference: abduction, deduction, and induction. Abduction forms hypotheses (perceptual judgment is a limiting case), deduction draws their implications, and induction tests their truth. This process is continuous and hence there is no first premise which is not itself a conclusion. What then according to Peirce grounds this inferential process?

At the close of the second article Peirce introduces three notions necessary to handle this foundational question: the notion of truth, the notion of reality, the notion of community. From one point of view truth is what is the case independently of what anyone happens to think. From another point of view truth is what is *destined* in the long run to be agreed upon by investigators. It is not the agreement which constitutes the truth but it is the truth which brings about in the long run the agreement. To put it another way, it is the *opinion* of the community which converges; that opinion is *about* reality. Reality, however, is neither an opinion nor constituted by an opinion. The persevering application of the inferential thought-process will correct error and bring about a convergence on the truth. Reality is that which is represented in the long-run agreement. Here and now it is the knowable. In the limit case of the long run it is what will be known. Here and now reality is what is intended in knowing. In the limit case it is knowledge of everything about everything. For Peirce there is no reality which is absolutely incognizable. Such a supposition is self-defeating. Truth and Reality, then, are convertible terms. These notions as merely intended by human cognition at any given time suppose the notion of a community without definite limits and capable of an indefinite increase in knowledge. To cite the last two paragraphs of this article, Peirce says:

> Finally, as what anything really is, is what it may finally come to be known to be in the ideal state of complete information, so that reality depends on the ultimate decision of the community; so thought is what it is, only by virtue of addressing a future thought which is in its value as thought identical with it, though more developed. In this way, the existence of thought now, depends on what is to be hereafter; so that it has only a potential existence, dependent on the future thought of the community. The individual man, since his separate existence is manifested only by ignorance and error, so far as he is anything apart from his fellows, and from what he and they are to be, is only a negation.
> This man,
> proud man,
> Most ignorant of what he's most assured,
> His glassy essence.[16]

The third article, **"Grounds of Validity of the Laws of Logic,"** sets out to justify inference in all its forms. Peirce begins with a consideration of deductive or necessary inference. He shows that each type of categorical syllogism is governed by the *dictum de omni* and refutes

various classical objections to syllogistic reasoning. With respect to abductive and inductive (probable) inferences Peirce disposes of any attempt to justify them by turning them into a form of deduction or by appealing to the uniformity of nature. Since both abduction and induction are inferences from part to whole, they are essentially forms of statistical inference the validity of which depends upon the fact that in the long run any item selected is as likely as any other to be included in the sample.[17] Peirce maintains that this in turn follows from the very notion of reality which he previously developed. Suppose that men could not learn from induction. The reason would be that as a general rule when they had made an induction the order of things would change. But then the real would depend on how much men should know of it. But this general rule could be discovered by induction and so it must be a law of a universe such that when the rule was discovered it would cease to operate. But this rule too could be discovered by induction, and so there would be nothing in such a universe which could not be known by a sufficiently long process of inference. But this contradicts the hypothesis that men cannot learn from induction. Finally Peirce stresses

> that logic rigidly requires, before all else, that no determinate fact, nothing which can happen to a man's self, should be of more consequence to him than everything else. He who would not sacrifice his own soul to save the whole world, is illogical in all his inferences, collectively. So the social principle is rooted intrinsically in logic.[18]

To illustrate how a continuous process can begin in time and yet have no "first" member of the series, Peirce asks his readers to suppose an inverted triangle gradually dipped into water (5.263). Clearly there is a beginning in time of its being submerged, but there is no assignable first place on the triangle where it first contacts the water. Once the triangle is immersed, the surface of the water traces a line on it at some distance, say length *a*, from the apex. Such a line can be marked wherever one pleases and there will still be an infinite number of other places between it and the apex where it could be marked: at $1/2a$ or at $1/4a$ or at $1/8a$. . . . *Because* the series is continuous, there is no "first place" which must enter the water first. The apex itself is not that "first place" since it is the triangle's boundary and marks where the triangle is not yet in the water.

Peirce suggests that we think of the triangle as representing cognition and of the water as representing what is distinct from cognition. Thus when the apex itself is at the water's surface, there is as yet no cognition. Now let each line traced by the water on the immersed triangle represent a cognition and let those lines nearer the apex represent cognitions which determine cognitions represented by lines further up the triangle. It is then clear that while every cognition is determined by a one prior to it, there is no first cognition, that is, one which is not itself so determined.

Peirce contends, therefore, that one can conceive, without contradiction, of *every* cognition being determined by another, while the whole process had a beginning in time. The term 'first cognition' or 'first principle' cannot mean "a cognition not determined by another" or "a premise which is not itself a conclusion." Whatever is to ground, or be the foundation of, cognition must be other than the "first principles" as abstractly conceived by at least some of the tradition.

It is here, I think, that the late Canadian philosopher, Bernard Lonergan, has something to offer Peirce. Lonergan holds substantially the same position as Peirce with regard to the inferential and mediated character of all human knowing.[19] His helpful proposal is that what grounds the process of cognition (continuous as it is) is intelligence *in act*. The "foundation" of knowing is not itself an *abstract* knowing, but rather a concrete seizing of intelligence in action by the intelligent knowing agent. "First principles" (Identity, Contradiction, etc.) as abstract formulae are mere tautologies which, for all we know, have no truth value for anything outside the world of lexigraphical meaning. They are what Lonergan calls "analytic propositions." They are *principles* only insofar as they are grasped as existentially instantiated and this is possible only in the concrete act of knowing. It is in the concrete act of knowing that their evidence is grasped as sufficient; that is, they are recognized as operating here and now because, whatever be the conditions of their operation, they are fulfilled here and now. If the evidence is challenged, the response is to point out a *performatory* (not merely a logical) contradiction if such evidence is rejected. To challenge and reject the first principles as existentially instantiated in any concrete act of knowing, itself requires a concrete act of knowing which instantiates the principles. For if the challenge were truly telling, it would bring intelligent acts to a stop and reduce everyone to silence. To put it another way, the very act of challenging the evidence produces the same evidence again. Notice that this response itself is an inference and is determined by another act of cognition. These concrete principles grasped in the act of knowing are the conditions of possibility of the act, not abstractly and tautologically enumerated, but grasped as fulfilled in the act of knowing itself. Hence they are *a priori* but not outside the conscious appropriation of the act of knowing. They are *transcendental,* not in the Kantian sense of an object ever beyond the knowing experience, but in the sense of the immanent structure of every act of knowing.

I would like to close my remarks by returning to the three ideas central to Peirce's theory of knowing as continuous inference. The three central ideas are: the notion of truth, the notion of reality, and the notion of community.

Peirce adds to the traditional notion of truth (what is the case independently of what any finite knower may think) an heuristic notion of truth as that upon which the community of inquirers will agree in the long run. This emphasizes the search for truth rather than its possession (although it does not deny the latter). It introduces an historical and existential dimension which

characterizes what actually goes on within the scientific community. Lonergan recognizes this implicitly when he points out that the canons of scientific method leave open the question of further relevant issues and thus make scientific inquiry a fallible and so indefinite quest.

Peirce's account of reality explicitly endorses the Scholastic insight into truth and reality as coextensive. There is nothing which cannot be known, for if there were, it would be inexplicable and so would block the road to inquiry. This is operative in Lonergan's notion of metaphysics as heuristic and of being as whatever is or can be known.[20] This insight is at the heart of both Lonergan's and Peirce's argument for God.

Finally, Peirce's account of truth and of reality requires the explicit recognition of the role of the community. This refers not just to any group of people but to the community of inquirers. Nor is this community merely a *de facto* requirement for arriving at the truth about reality. It is a necessary condition for the enterprise even to begin. This need for a community of inquirers, by the way, does not mean that there must be actually an endless community of researchers. All that is required is that the possibility of an endless community of researchers be real. As long as the possibility is real the condition is fulfilled even if as a matter of fact the community destroys itself or is destroyed.

Here I would suggest that the essential role of the community in Peirce's understanding of human inquiry rejoins Lonergan's insistence on the need for a series of personal conversions in order that there be any members of such a community dedicated to searching for the truth.[21] This includes what for Lonergan is the final and perhaps most important conversion, "falling in love." Peirce indeed could have written the following:

> When he pronounces a project worthwhile, a man moves beyond consideration of all merely personal satisfactions and interests, tastes and preferences. He is acknowledging objective values and taking the first step towards authentic human existence.[22]

Much of what Peirce proposed may be of real help in overcoming the seeming bankruptcy of contemporary thought by shifting it away from the paralyzing self-doubt of skepticism. I would like this essay to be a small contribution to that project.

NOTES

[1] Descartes, *The Principles of Philosophy,* Sec. LI in Haldane and Ross, *Philosophical Works of Descartes,* vol. I (New York: Dover, 1955).

[2] Locke, *An Essay Concerning Human Understanding,* (Fraser Edition) Bdk. II, Ch. XXIII, 2; Berkeley, *Principles of Human Knowledge,* (New York; Bobbs-Merrill, 1970), pp. 85-96 (critique of material substance); pp. 135-42 (notion of spirit); Hume, *A Treatise of Human*

Nature, (New York: Doubleday, Dolphin Books, 1961), Part IV, Sec. V & VI.

3 Several commentators have criticized Peirce for having no adequate account of the self. Among them are: Manley Thompson, *The Pragmatic Philosophy of C. S. Peirce,* (Chicago: University of Chicago Press, 1953); Richard Bernstein, *Praxis and Action,* (Philadelphia: University of Pennsylvania Press, 1971). Among those who have defended Peirce's account of the self are: Gresham Riley, *The Self, Self-Knowledge, and Pragmaticism,* Ph.D. dissertation, Yale University, 1965; "Peirce's Theory of Individual," *Transactions of the Charles S. Peirce Society,* 10 (1974), 135-63; Stanley Harrison, *Man's Glassy Essence: An Attempt to Construct a Theory of Person Based on the Writings of Charles Sanders Peirce,* Ph.D. dissertation, Fordham University, 1971; "Charles S. Peirce: Reflections on Being a Man-Sign," *Proceedings of the American Catholic Philosophical Association,* 53 (1979), 98-106; "Peirce on Persons," *Proceedings of the C. S. Peirce Bicentennial International Congress,* 1981, 217-21; Vincent M. Colapietro, *Peirce's Approach to the Self: A Semiotic Perspective on Human Subjectivity,* (Albany, NY: State University of New York Press, 1989), pp. 61-65.

4 Colapietro, *op. cit.,* pp. 61-65. References to Peirce are from *The Collected Papers of Charles Sanders Peirce,* vols. I-IV, eds. Charles Hartshorne and Paul Weiss (Cambridge, MA: The Belknap Press of Harvard University Press, 1960); Vols. VII-VIII, ed. Arthur Burks (Cambridge, MA: Harvard University Press, 1958). These will be cited by volume and paragraph number: e.g., 5.310. See the following: "Some Consequences of Four Incapacities," 1868, 5.264-314; Responses to James, c. 1891, 8.81-82; Ms. from c. 1892, 7.565 ff.; "Detached Ideas on Topics of Vital Importance," 1898, 1.616-76.

5 See, 3.611-13; 3.516.

6 I have treated Peirce's categories at some length elsewhere; see, Vincent G. Potter, S.J., *Charles S. Peirce: On Norms and Ideals* (Amherst, MA: University of Massachusetts Press, 1967), pp. 8-24.

7 *Ibid.,* p. 11.

8 Colapietro, p. 81.

9 In 1.409-16 Peirce sums up his "guess at the riddle" and shows that his system of categories is the key to his answer.

10 One such act/potency scheme looks like this:

	ACT (Pr. of perfection)	POTENCY (Pr. of Limitation)
ORDER OF EXISTENCE	esse	essence
ORDER OF ESSENCE	substantial form	prime matter
ORDER OF ACTIVITY	accident	substance

11 Colapietro, *op. cit.,* p. 83.

12 See e.g., Peirce's articles of 1868 published in the *Journal of Speculative Philosophy* (1.213-1.357).

13 See, C. F. Delaney, "The Journal of Speculative Philosophy Papers" in the new edition, *Writings of Charles S. Peirce: A Chronological Edition,* vol. 2 (Bloomington, IN: Indiana University Press, 1984), pp. xxxvi-xlii.

14 *Ibid.*

15 Pierce, "A Neglected Argument for the Reality of God," 6.456 ff.

16 5.316-17.

17 See, e.g., 2.619-44; 3.516.

18 5.354.

19 See, "Insight Revisited," *A Second Collection: Papers by Bernard J. F. Lonergan, S.J.,* eds. W. Ryan, S.J. and B. Tyrell, S.J. (Philadelphia: Westminster Press, 1974), 265-69. He remarks that rather early in his career he came to think of human knowledge "as not intuitive, but discursive with the decisive component in judgment." For Lonergan's account of judgment see *Insight: A Study of Human Understanding* (New York: Philosophical Library, 1958) *passim,* especially chs. IX and X.

20 See *Insight,* chs. XII and XIX.

21 See, e.g., Lonergan, "Theology in Its New Context," *A Second Collection,* 65-67. To show that Peirce in effect requires the same sort of thing of his searchers after truth would require a study of Peirce's understanding of the Normative Sciences and of how they are interdependent and hierarchically ordered.

22 "The Future of Christianity," *A Second Collection,* 152. Compare Peirce 6.441: "Now what is this way of life? Again I appeal to the universal Christian conscience to testify that it is simply love. As far as it is contracted to a rule of ethics it is: Love God, and love your neighbor; 'on these two commandments hang all the law and the prophets.' It may be regarded in a higher point of view with St. John as the universal evolutionary formula. But in whatever light it be regarded or in whatever direction developed, the belief in the law is the Christian faith." See also Peirce's "Evolutionary Love" (6.287-317).

Patricia A. Turrisi (essay date 1992)

SOURCE: "The Purpose of the Proof of Pragmatism in Peirce's 1930 Lectures on Pragmatism" in *The Monist,* Vol. 75, No. 4, October, 1992, pp. 521-37.

[*In the following excerpt, Turrisi concerns herself with Peirce's pragmatism and his application of pragmatism in his discussions on logic.*]

A proof of pragmatism is proposed in Peirce's 1903 lecture series on *Pragmatism as a Principle and Method of Right Thinking.* It is necessary first to define what pragmatism is, a task for which a practitioner of the pragmatic maxim would be fitted, but which, however, must be highly problematic to a potential practitioner who does not yet know its full meaning. In order to clarify its meaning, Peirce uses a method he recommends for such conundrums in his 1891 article, **"The Architecture of Theories,"** that is, "to make a systematic study of the conceptions out of which a philosophical theory may be built, in order to ascertain what place each conception may fitly occupy in such a theory and to what uses it is adapted" (CP 6.9). Peirce's systematic study of the basis of logic and pragmatism in relation to it begins to appear around 1898 and peaks in 1903 when pragmatism's definition and role within the sciences is established in these lectures.

I

The first lecture of Peirce's 1903 series on *Pragmatism as a Principle and Method of Right Thinking* introduced his audience to a variety of issues, many of which would have been familiar to a student of Peirce at the time. The significance of pragmatism in Peirce's systematic philosophy of science is one important exception. Published sources alone have not so far enabled scholars to remark adequately on the scientific nature of his pragmatism but lecture notes and correspondence furnish us with an account of his motivation for embarking on a revision of pragmatism in this regard in the latter stage of his career. By 1903, Peirce had long had regrets about the directions his pragmatic doctrine had taken due to what he sensed to be the incompleteness of its original articulation. That year, an opportunity to speak to William James's students, "well primed in pragmatism," was used to address these deficiencies in his presentation.[1] A re-definition of pragmatism in its scientific role would have to begin with a criticism of the effects conceived as a result of the "pragmatic maxim," put forth in 1878, "Consider what effects that might conceivably have practical bearings we conceive the object of our conception to have: then, our conception of those effects is the whole of our conception of the object." The "object" of his inquiry in these lectures was the very concept of pragmatism itself.

While, in Peirce's opinion, other "pragmatists" were not overly concerned about the definition of pragmatism,[2] Peirce believed the definition of any term to be a serious matter with normative value. In his **"Ethics of Terminology,"** written shortly after the Lectures on Pragmatism, he defends the notion that it becomes the duty of science to accept and preserve the name given to a conception by its inventor, stating that,

> . . . every symbol is a living thing, in a very strict sense that is no mere figment of speech. The body of the symbol changes slowly, but its meaning inevitably grows, incorporates new elements and

throws off old ones. But the effort of all should be to keep the *essence* of every scientific term unchanged and exact; although absolute exactitude is not so much as conceivable.[3]

Peirce claimed inventorship of "pragmatism" and was acknowledged as such by others as well. Users of the term "pragmatism" seemed to Peirce to have honored the term without honoring the conception

In an effort to preserve the "essence" of pragmatism, the 1903 Lectures contain an argument for Peirce's own definition, and consequently, for whatever conceivable effects are implied by it. Indeed, as a precursor for the general set of the 1903 lectures, in the 1901 *Baldwin Dictionary of Philosophy and Psychology,* Peirce's entry on pragmatism (written c. 1899) follows James's. In it, he argues against the Jamesian assumption in *Will to Believe* and *Philosophical Conceptions and Practical Results* that the end of man is action: "If it be admitted, on the contrary, that action wants an end, and that that end must be something of a general description, then *the spirit of the maxim itself,* which is that we must look to the upshot of our concepts in order rightly to apprehend them, would direct us towards something different from practical facts, namely, to general ideas, as the true interpreters of our thought." And, he argues for, what I shall demonstrate is a view consistent with his re-evaluation of pragmatism as it emerges in these lectures, a purpose for pragmatism which is scientific in nature: "[I] would venture to suggest that [the pragmatic maxim] should always be put into practice with conscientious thoroughness, but that, when that has been done, and not before, a still higher grade of clearness of thought can be attained by remembering that the only ultimate good which the practical facts to which it directs attention can subserve is to further the development of concrete reasonableness; so that the meaning of the concept does not lie in any individual reactions at all, but in the manner in which those reactions contribute to that development."[4] This statement is written specifically with James in mind, but also for such pragmatists as Schiller, whom Peirce claimed had "missed the point" and that in order to think *any* thought, one must proceed pragmatistically.[5]

Thereby, Peirce proposes an inquiry into the question, "Is pragmatism true?" Peirce wished the appeal of pragmatism to lie not only in its psychological efficacy in easing doubt, but in its logical efficacy in promoting greater scientific knowledge of reality, that is, a concrete reasonableness. The fact that he makes this inquiry at all is highly significant insofar as it is not duplicated by any other "pragmatist." Demonstration of the *truth* of pragmatism is required by Peirce because he considers it to be a *scientific maxim* and not a speculative doctrine. I will further examine the problem of what it is he considers himself to be proving about pragmatism in the second part of this paper.

However, the question of what *constitutes* a proof *per se,* in Peirce's view, is also problematic. What can "truth" mean here? What kind of proof is required to demonstrate its truth? While Fisch[6] and McCarthy,[7] each note a proof as such, an account of this proof's specific dependence on an explanation of the role of pragmatism among the sciences has never been explored.

McCarthy accounts for this dependence somewhat, but his reiteration of the "proof" primarily focuses upon the dependence of logic on ethics and esthetics and away from the systematic classification of sciences given by Peirce as a locus for the proof in Lectures I-IV. He states,

> The first lecture sets out the problem, shows that it is a problem—i.e., that there is a real question about the truth of pragmatism—and gives a plan for the subsequent inquiry. The next three lectures are taken up by the first part of the plan, the exposition of the categories—phenomenological in the second and third as well as metaphysical in the fourth. . . . *This confirms what one suspected already, viz., that the second, third and fourth lectures were intended more to familiarize the audience with Peirce's modes of thought than to contribute anything directly to the proof.* [my emphasis] In any case that is my opinion and I will have little more to say about them.[8]

But Peirce's published writings, letters and unpublished manuscripts clearly indicate that he found the "ladder of the sciences" necessary for grounding logic as a science and thereby pragmatism as a scientific maxim.

Under the inspiration of Kant, Peirce sought to build logical thought architectonically upon the whole range of the sciences. It seems unlikely that his notion of "proof" would be unaffected by his notion of the place of logic among the sciences. He wrote in 1898,

> Logic requires that the more abstract sciences should be developed earlier than the more concrete ones. For the more concrete sciences require as fundamental principles the results of the more abstract sciences, while the latter only make use of the results of the former as data; and if one fact is wanting, some other will generally serve to support the same generalization. (CP 6.1)

And:

> That systems ought to be constructed architectonically has been preached since Kant, but I do not think the full import of the maxim has by any means been apprehended. What I would recommend is that every person who wishes to form an opinion concerning fundamental problems should first of all make a complete survey of human knowledge, should take note of all the valuable ideas in each branch of science, should observe in just what respect each has been successful and where it has failed, in order that, in the light of the thorough acquaintance so attained of the available materials for a philosophical theory and of the nature and strength of each, he may proceed to the study of what the problem of philosophy consists in, and of the proper way of solv-

ing it. I must not be understood as endeavoring to state fully all that these preparatory studies should embrace; on the contrary, *I purposely slur over many points, in order to give emphasis to one special recommendation, namely, to make a systematic study of the conceptions out of which a philosophical theory may be built, in order to ascertain what place each conception may fitly occupy in such a theory, and to what uses it is adapted.* [my emphasis] (CP 6.9)

In support of this view, he gave at least three other accounts of the architectonic of scientific theories in the years 1902-1904 which agree with the account given in Lecture I of the 1903 Pragmatism series.[9] By 1902, he was ready to give a full account of his theory of reasoning. His application for a Carnegie Institution grant in 1902, **"Methods of Science,"** proposed three dozen "memoirs" which would "persuade of the scientific nature of logic" (L75). He states in Memoir No. 9 **"On the Bearing of Esthetics and Ethics Upon Logic,"**

> I show that Ethics depends essentially upon Esthetics and Logic upon Ethics. The latter dependence I had shown less fully in 1869 (*Journal of Speculative Philosophy,* vol. II, pp. 207 et seq.) But the methods of reasoning by which the truths of logic are established must be mathematical, such reasoning alone being evident independently of any logical doctrine.

and proposes to expand on mathematical methods of discovering and establishing the truths of logic in Memoir No. 14. *A Prospectus on Reasoning,* c. 1904 (MS 693a) reflects a similar orientation, but adds, as in the 1903 lectures, that the normative sciences themselves depend upon phenomenology, which is dependent upon mathematics. On November 25, 1902, subsequent to his Carnegie proposal and just prior to giving the 1903 lectures, Peirce writes to James, "I think I could satisfy you that your view of pragmatism requires some modification, that it is the logical basis and proof of it (and it can receive no sound support from psychology) and its relation to the categories that have first to be made clear before it can be accurately applied except in very simple ways."[10] And the 1903 lectures give us his most complete account of the hierarchy of the sciences in which logic falls.

In the third part of this paper, I will show the importance of the architectonic place of pragmatism to its proof and argue that the first five lectures in *Pragmatism as a Principle and Method of Right Reasoning* provide intrinsic elements of the proof, contrary to McCarthy's claim that the proof begins late in Lecture V. If the recollection of pragmatism's conceivable effects is, as Peirce suggests, an integral part of this proof, it is indeed necessary to locate it correctly in logic in *its* place among the other sciences.

II

It was clear to Peirce as well as to an array of "pragmatists" what pragmatism could do in the way of guiding practical action, if applied correctly. In the first lecture on Pragmatism, Peirce concurs with his earliest formulation of pragmatism by illustrating its efficacy in solving a paradox in a problem concerning probability. In the area of thought experiments and, indeed, in the application of these to practical conduct, pragmatism works. Peirce adds that "pragmatism is generally practised by successful men" and efficient men are distinguished from inefficient men through the practical advantage of being able to think pragmatically.

Pragmatism's *usefulness* on the level of directing its practitioners to specific conclusions is eminently demonstrable, but as he pointed out in his *Dictionary of Philosophy and Psychology* article, its general meaning is a different matter. While here Peirce regards the practical skill of using pragmatic technique as valuable but not in any great need of elucidation, by contrast, readers of William James's works prior to 1903 are treated almost exclusively to descriptions of pragmatic skills and techniques implying its value for practical action. Justifications of pragmatism even later in James's works, for example in the 1907 Lowell Lectures on Pragmatism, as was the case with those to whom James claimed to owe his theory's origin in his dedication[11] and Preface,[12] are made in terms of usefulness, under the presumption that practical utility is its own best defense.

The direction of pragmatic studies typified by James, not grounded on any greater justification than efficacy, convinced Peirce that pragmatism had gone too far without its necessary *logical* justification. And a vindication of its role as a maxim of logic would serve the end of the "spirit of pragmatism," in promoting concrete reasonableness as a general concern.

Peirce distinguishes use from justification in a criticism of his own early account:

> There is no doubt, then that pragmatism opens a very easy road to the solution of an immense variety of questions. But it does not follow from that that it is true. (CP 5.26)

In fact, the ease with which such a method "so resolves the most difficult of problems" is deceptive. In the history of science, immensely simple hypotheses which originally promised to explain much have had to be greatly modified to accommodate further reflection in order that science make progress. If pragmatism is as good as even the most successful hypotheses, it is either not as simple a hypothesis as it seems, or it is, more likely, in need of modification or at least greater justification as it stands.

Peirce vies for an examination of the status of pragmatism through its justification. He argues,

> Which is the *proof* that the possible practical consequences of a concept constitute the sum total of the concept? The [Peirce deletes the word "proof" here] argument upon which I rested the

maxim in my original paper was that *belief* consists *mainly* [my emphasis] in being deliberately prepared to adopt the formula believed in as the guide to action.

> If this be in truth the nature of belief, then undoubtedly the proposition believed in can itself be nothing but a maxim of conduct. That I believe is quite evident.

> But how do we know that belief is nothing but the deliberate preparedness to act according to the formula believed?

> My original article carried this back to a psychological principle. The conception of truth according to me was developed out of an original impulse to act consistently, to have a definite intention. . . . (301:19-21; CP 5.27-28)

But in the first lecture, Peirce admits he did address the issue of the justification of pragmatism in the 1877-1878 papers (**"The Fixation of Belief"** and **"How to Make Our Ideas Clear"**), albeit on *psychological* grounds, which he now recognizes as inadequate in terms of a *logical* proof. Specifically, the "psychological principle" that stood behind the notion that "belief is nothing but the deliberate preparedness to act" was the principle that when the irritation of doubt is sufficient, a person rendered in two by undecidedness of opinion will seek to overcome doubt. The impulse to overcome doubt, Peirce claims in 1878, is "the motive for thinking" (CP 5.397), referring to his initial analysis in 1877, that "doubt is an uneasy and dissatisfied state from which we struggle to free ourselves and pass into the state of belief, while the latter is a calm and satisfactory state which we do not wish to avoid, or to change to a belief in anything else" (CP 5.372).

Interpretations of the meaning of the pragmatic maxim arising from Peirce's arguments for it in 1878 base themselves upon his apparent identification of the definition of an apprehension with a definition of a belief, i.e., that belief is "nothing but the deliberate preparedness to act according to the formula believed." The specific difference between the accounts of 1878 and 1903 rests upon the question of whether belief, the "proof" or "argument" upon which the pragmatic maxim rests, is *"mainly"* a deliberate preparedness to act or is, in fact, *"nothing but"* a "preparedness to act."

If Peirce had held that the definition of belief carried no other possible meanings than the one above, his original definition of belief, and thereby, of the basis of the truth of the pragmatic maxim, would not have been logically defensible, even if psychologically defensible. Fortunately, the pragmatic maxim describes the *apprehension* of the meaning of a concept, and Peirce now questions whether (1) apprehension is identical to belief as he has defined belief, and (2) that belief should be defined as *merely* a propensity to act in accordance with a proposition. Peirce most definitely seems to be attempting to make a very important distinction between a concept to which one is willing to assent and a concept which one may understand, without necessarily assenting to it, i.e., a definition of concept which emphasizes its psychological acceptibility and a definition of concept which emphasizes its logical acceptability. While it may appear obvious that one needs to apprehend a concept in order to assent to it, it is by no means established that one need assent to a concept in order to apprehend it or even that apprehension of a concept need lead to a "preparedness to act." If the meaning of the apprehension of a concept is considered independently of "belief" so expressed as a propensity to act, as Peirce's plan shows it must be, it becomes possible for the first time, to evaluate pragmatism as a logical doctrine. The "proof" of pragmatism is a proof of whether, as a scientific doctrine, it belongs to a science more fundamental than psychology, to logic, or to the less fundamental, special science of psychology.

Peirce and his readers from 1878 on were persuaded of the definition of belief by the psychological principle so justifying it in 1878, that the propensity to act is preferred over the lack of such propensity and the discomfort it brings. But the question remained in 1903 how to explain why, in the first place, human beings are constituted so as to embody this particular psychological principle. The psychological condition noted itself stands in need of a justification. That is, one needs to know further how human beings come to share a tendency to want and be able to gain deliberate preparations for actions in the form of beliefs. Perhaps an explanation could be made from an evolutionary perspective, but then the question of the proof *per se* would still be whether pragmatism could be provided with any sound *logical* basis.

The reason for Peirce's hesitation in supplying an evolutionary account of the psychological "motive for thinking" that lies behind pragmatism is complex. The dependence of psychological principles upon logical ones in his architectonic classification of the sciences is itself grounded upon the notion that general psychological propensities among humans have evolved in response to logical necessities. In other words, insofar as true beliefs have been formed, they have promoted human existence in a proportion greater than beliefs that are false and so have been retained by "natural selection." In a very general manner, psychological tendencies reflect a kind of recognition of logical truths, the investigation of the conditions for the possibility of which cannot be conducted exclusively by reference to history or evolution.

III

The purpose of a proof of pragmatism is to account for the possibility that a well-known psychological condition, i.e., doubt as the motivator for thought, receives its impetus from a set of *logical* conditions and is not somehow independent or prior to the logical conditions affecting a thinker. These logical conditions are what concerns Peirce throughout the 1903 lectures and almost exclusively in the first five lectures.

It ought to be reiterated that the purpose of logic is conceived by Peirce not as a formulaic rendering of conclusions from premises, but as a means of elucidating the basic elements of reasoning.[13] Pragmatism is claimed to supply a tool by which to accomplish this purpose. But the reckoning of the elements of reasoning themselves does not proceed directly *from* logic. Rather, they are observed and recorded by logical means. In saying that "logic requires that the more abstract sciences should be developed earlier than the concrete ones" (CP 6.1), he does not mean that an abstract science *creates* a concrete one, but that the subject matter of concrete sciences only becomes a subject matter in the hand of abstract science, "for the more concrete sciences require as fundamental principles the results of the more abstract sciences" (CP 6.1). Furthermore, abstract sciences make use of the results of concrete sciences "as data" (CP 6.1).

Peirce delineates the relationship of logic to other sciences in terms of abstractness and concreteness in order to show where the data it produces is used as well as to show from whence it receives its data. The very nature of the data received and produced by logic is that which the pragmatic maxim aids in interpreting. And so it is essential to a "proof" of pragmatism, that is, a proof of its truth as a maxim of logical conduct, to identify exactly with what logical conduct is concerned.

Then and only then is it possible to "prove" whether pragmatism is or is not a facilitator of logic, or of something else or of nothing at all. Thereby, Peirce follows his own recommendation "to make a systematic study of the conceptions out of which a philosophical theory may be built in order to ascertain what place each conception may fitly occupy in such a theory, and to what uses it is adapted," in this case, the conceptions of logic as per his theory that it is the science of a species of conduct, reasoning.

To that specific end, Peirce places his proof within an architectonic of scientific knowledge. Contrary to Jeremiah McCarthy's opinion that "the second, third and fourth lectures were intended more to familiarize the audience with Peirce's modes of thought than to contribute anything directly to the proof," these lectures demonstrate the "place each conception may fitly occupy" in reference to the pragmatic maxim.[14] At any rate, the specific relatedness of Peirce's "modes of thought" to one another would have been unfamiliar to any audience since Peirce admits he has only just understood it correctly himself. Peirce is not merely reiterating his "modes of thought," but is presenting what is for him, a *new* doctrine of pragmatism's exact occupation within logic and for other "pragmatists," a renewed doctrine of the status of pragmatism within philosophy.

In contrast to "pragmatists" whose doctrines no longer bear a strong resemblance to the pragmatism developed around 1872 or so in the "Metaphysical Club,"[15] Peirce denies that pragmatism is a "sublime principle of speculative philosophy" (CP 5.18). In a deleted passage from his first lecture, he states,

> The direst fault I find with all the people who pose as pragmatists is that they all write philosophy in more or less lively styles and are sometimes even entertaining. It is plain that to be deep one must be dull. I do not know what fault these writers find with me because they never mention me; but I suspect that if they did they would find me flippant for making pragmatism to be a mere maxim of logic instead of being what they all hold it to be, a sublime principle of theoretical philosophy (301:6)

A maxim of logic would have to aid in the aim of logic. Its effects would have to serve logical ends. But the truth about the role of logic within the sciences, that is, the demarcation and foundation of logical ends, Peirce discloses, had not occurred to him at the time he originated his pragmatic doctrine.[16]

The novel idea Peirce develops and defends in these first four lectures as well as in the rest is the place of logic within the normative sciences, and theirs in reference to the science of phenomenology. In order to prove the truth of pragmatism, a maxim of a fairly abstract science, data from more concrete sciences are useful as per the general structure of architectonic set out in 1891. Thus, not only will the placement of logic within the sciences serve to elucidate the place pragmatism occupies in logic, but will outline the sources for data by which to support the generalizations of pragmatism. Peirce writes to James in November 1902, shortly before being invited to lecture on pragmatism,

> My own view in 1877 was crude. Even when I gave my Cambridge lectures [1898], I had not really got to the bottom of it or seen the unity of the whole thing. It was not until after that that I obtained the proof that logic must be founded on ethics, of which it is a higher development. Even then, I was for some time so stupid as not to see that ethics rests in the same manner on a foundation of esthetics.[17]

Lecture I restates and justifies this position and Lectures II through VI amplify it.

Continuing in this letter, Peirce summarizes the relation of the normative sciences to the universal categories.

> These three normative sciences correspond to my three categories, which in their psychological aspect, appear as Feeling, Reaction, Thought. . . . The true nature of pragmatism cannot be understood without them.

The foundation of the normative sciences is further defined and justified in his first lecture:

> But before we can attack any normative science,

any science which proposes to separate the sheep from the goats [as each of the normative sciences do in matters of thought, conduct, and admirability], it is plain that there must be a preliminary inquiry which shall justify the attempt to establish such dualism. This must be a science that does *not* draw any distinction of good and bad in any sense whatever, but just contemplates phenomena as they are, simply opens its eyes and describes what it sees. Not what it sees in the real as distinguished from figment,—not regarding any such dichotomy but simply describing the object as a phenomenon, and stating what it finds in all phenomena alike. (301:33)

This science, is of course, the science of the categories, of phenomenology, which Peirce discusses in the second, third and fourth lectures.

The architectonic is not complete, however, without resting phenomenology upon *its* ground. Phenomenology, "the most primal of all the positive sciences" rests on no other "positive science," but does depend on a "Conditional or Hypothetical Science of Pure Mathematics." A "positive science," though an "inquiry which seeks for positive knowledge, that is for knowledge as may conveniently be expressed in a *categorical proposition*" would seem to exclude normative sciences insofar as they ask "not what *is* but what *ought to be*." However, these, says Peirce, "nevertheless are positive sciences since it is by asserting positive, categorical truth that they are able to show that what they call good really is so; and the right reason, right effort, and right being of which they treat derive that character from positive categorical fact." Contrasted with positive science, the aim of Pure Mathematics is "to discover not how things actually are, but how they might be supposed to be, if not in our universe, then in some other." Peirce adds that "A Phenomenology which does not reckon with pure mathematics, a science hardly come to years of discretion when Hegel wrote, will be the same pitiful clubfooted affair that Hegel produced." This comment explains a great deal about the inclusion in the second lecture of an account of one-value, Dichotomic, Trichotomic mathematics and other kinds of Pure Mathematics in their relation to Eulerian diagrams, or existential graphs, for the logic of relations. James's view that its "lack of nonmathematical examples" was a deficiency of the lectures expressed in a letter discouraging Peirce from publishing the lectures, results from a misunderstanding of the role of "mathematical examples" in the proof.[18] Insofar as the establishment of pragmatism's dependence on the "science of hypotheses," i.e., mathematics, goes, Peirce's use of "mathematical examples" is a *proficiency* of the lectures.

Overall, the purpose for a discussion of mathematics in these lectures is to demonstrate the basis of logic in a science "independent" of logic. In Lecture II, Peirce states that the Boolean algebra of logic which, "if developed by means of arrays of letters with conventional signs to signify relations in between them" may "equally be developed by means of diagrams—composed of lines and dots, and this in various ways of which the *Eulerian diagrams* form one example while my *Existential Graphs* and *Entitative Graphs* are others" (302:5) He mentions that "no masterly presentation has ever been given" of this mathematics, but that he has attempted it several times himself (302.6-9). Ultimately, what fragments of the system Peirce has chosen to reveal in these lectures are not intended to be a re-hash of his "modes of thought," but rather an upending of conventional ideas concerning logic. He claims, "this exact logic of relatives . . . simply dynamites all our traditional notions of logic and with them Kant's Critic of the Pure Reason which was founded upon them." (302:11). This claim deserves further exploration and not as a mere tidbit about Peircean notions of logic but as a key to the architectonically arranged sciences which depend on logic and ultimately upon mathematics for their principles.

And so, the "apparently aimless beating about the bush" of which Peirce speaks in CP 5.130 at the beginning of what Jeremiah McCarthy takes to be Peirce's proof of pragmatism is actually not aimless at all, but an integral part of an inquiry into the truth of pragmatism. A look at its foundation in logic, and in turn the Normative Sciences, Phenomenology and Pure Mathematics is a look at the construction of a systematic array of sciences in which pragmatism serves as a precipitator and clarifier of the data and principles of science.

It is appropriate to include Peirce's remarks to James here in defense of purporting this "background" to be *part* of a pragmatic proof for pragmatism. He writes on November 25, 1902, comparing himself with other pragmatists: "I seem to myself to be the sole depository at present of the completely developed system which all hangs together and cannot receive any proper presentation in fragments."[19] A week later, in discussing the publication of his logic and pragmatism's dependence upon it, he states,

> Were all the parts of my system separately published, the mathematician would approve of the mathematical part, the physicist of the physical part, the ethicist would admit the ethical part to be a contribution of some weight, and so on, but the principal thing would remain unpublished; for this depends upon the way the parts are fitted together, which is not the most obvious thing, and would then wholly escape notice.[20]

These statements are not at all surprising coming from a proponent of a logic of relations whose explicit task is to discover and exhibit "the way the parts are fitted together." Peirce essentially follows through in the 1903 lectures on his promising Introduction, giving not only the "proof" summarized from Lecture V on, but a wider proof which makes intelligible the architectonically defined parameters of logic and thereby pragmatism. It is not the intention of this essay to justify every claim made by Peirce about his system. Rather, I have suggested by way of constructing the outline of the system wherein

the hypothesis of the pragmatic maxim falls, that the elaboration of its foundation constitutes a stage of its proof, that of defining its purpose and function, the clear apprehension of the "data" and principles of logic.

NOTES

[1] As 1902 waned without any positive word on Peirce's Carnegie Institution proposal for a grant to write his definitive work on logic, Peirce began to offer suggestions to James as to how he could both supplement his income and complete the logic. In March, 1903, James wrote that the Corporation of Harvard University had "voted to authorize six University lectures" by Peirce on any subject he liked. Seven lectures took place in Sever Hall and it is safe to assume that students from James's Phil. 3 course on "The Philosophy of Nature" were invited. Items 688-698 and 3394-3396 in *The Correspondence of the James Library,* 1959, in Harvard's Houghton Library contain the correspondence relating to these lectures.

[2] See MS 301, Lecture I of Peirce's 1903 Harvard Lectures on "Pragmatism as a Principle and Method of Right Thinking," *The Charles S. Peirce Manuscripts,* The Houghton Library of Harvard University.

[3] "Ethics of Terminology," *Syllabus of Certain Topics of Logic* (Boston, MA: Mudge, 1903); in P1035 of the microfiche edition published by Bowling Green: Philosophy Documentation Center, as catalogued in *A Comprehensive Bibliography of the Published Works of Charles Sanders Peirce,* 2nd rev. ed., K. L. Ketner.

[4] James Mark Baldwin, ed., *Dictionary of Philosophy and Psychology* (Gloucester, MA: P. Smith), 1960, pp. 321-22.

[5] *The Correspondence of the James Library,* The Houghton Library of Harvard University, Item 689.

[6] Max H. Fisch, "The 'Proof' of Pragmatism," *Pragmatism and Purpose: Essays Presented to Thomas A. Goudge,* ed. L. W. Sumner, John G. Slater, and Fred Wilson (Toronto: University of Toronto Press, 1981), pp. 28-40. Fisch notes (p. 40) that "the best accounts of the 'proof' so far published are those by Manley Thompson [in 1953, *The Pragmatic Philosophy of C. S. Peirce,* University of Chicago Press] and John J. Fitzgerald" [in 1966, *Peirce's Theory of Signs as Foundation for Pragmatism,* The Hague]. He observes that neither made use of unpublished manuscripts which would have led them to assign pragmatism "neither to speculative grammar nor to critic, but to methodeutic."

[7] Jeremiah McCarthy, "Peirce's Proof of Pragmatism," *Transactions of the Charles S. Peirce Society* 26 (1990): 63-113.

[8] *Ibid.,* p. 67.

[9] See "Memoir No. 1 *On the Classification of the Theoretic Sciences of Research*" in L75 (1902) in which

Peirce outlines a "catalogue of the sciences as to exhibit the most important of the relations of logical dependence among them" in order to "give, from a general survey of science, an idea of the place of logic among the sciences"; also "Syllabus of Certain Topics" in CP1.180-202 (1903), originally published by Alfred Mudge & Son, Boston, as an accompaniment to *Lectures on Logic* delivered at the Lowell Institute; and "Reason's Conscience: A Practical Treatise on the Theory of Discovery; Wherein Logic is Conceived as Semeiotic," MS 693a (c. 1904). Peirce seems to have been concerned with the relation of the sciences to one another in general as early as 1891 in "The Architecture of Theories," CP6.7-34. (See Appendix following References.)

[10] *The Correspondence of the James Library,* The Houghton Library of Harvard University, 1959, Item 690.

[11] James dedicated the published edition of *Pragmatism, A New Name for Some Old Ways of Thinking* "to the memory of John Stuart Mill, from whom I first learned the pragmatic openness of mind and whom my fancy likes to picture as our leader were he alive to-day" in *Pragmatism,* edited by Bruce Kuklick (Indianapolis, IN: Hackett Publishing Company, 1981), p. 2.

[12] The Preface to James's *Pragmatism* gives references to works by John Dewey, F. C. S. Schiller, J. Milhaud, Le Roy, Blondel, De Sailly, and a "book on Pragmatism, in the French language, to be published very soon" by Papini (in Kuklick, p. 3). Peirce is not mentioned by name, but James claims that "the founder of pragmatism himself recently gave a course of lectures at the Lowell Institute with that very word in its title—flashes of brilliant light relieved against Cimmerian darkness. None of us, I fancy, understood *all* that he said—yet here I stand, making a very similar venture." (in Kuklick, pp. 7-8).

[13] See Robert W. Burch, *A Peircean Reduction Thesis* (Lubbock, TX: Texas Tech University Press, 1991). Burch gives an account of Peirce's algebraic logic which supports the thesis that logic's purpose is to analyze and display logical relations rather than calculate arguments.

[14] McCarthy, p. 67 and Note 19, p. 111. Peirce's first four lectures reflect a complete lack of confidence in the Harvard student's grounding in logic or science, both requirements for the proof's effectiveness. See Item 698 of *The Correspondence of the James Library* in which Peirce states, in reference to the difficulties of teaching "pure theory," "I don't think even my Harvard audience was quite fit for that. What they need is logical training,—lessons, not lectures." For a discussion of lessons in logic, see Lecture II, MS 302:2. Thirty-six out of one hundred lessons in a liberal education would "suffice really to teach the leading principles of logic, and logic, the ability to think well, constitute about three-eighths of a truly liberal education. . . . A liberal education ought to be a living organism and logic may truly be said to be the heart of it. But I do not say that six lectures on a fragment of logic will have the same pro- portionate value. It will be like cutting out five-sixths of a man's heart and leaving him with the remainder. Or rather it would be that if lectures were lessons which they certainly are far from being."

[15] Edward C. Moore et al., eds., *Writings of Charles S. Peirce: A Chronological Edition,* vol. 2, (Bloomington, IN: Indiana University Press, 1984), p. xxxvi. The editors date the founding of the Metaphysical Club at Cambridge, "in which pragmatism was born" at 1872. Indeed, in a 1909 treatise on "Meaning" (MS 619) which recounts his philosophical development, Peirce attributes the origin of the doctrine of pragmatism to a club consisting of "some dozen philosophical friends" which formed "a year or two" after a spate of nine of his papers on logic were published in the years 1867-9. David Gruender's demonstration, in "Pragmatism, Science, and Metaphysics," (in *The Relevance of Charles Peirce,* The Monist Library of Philosophy, Hegeler Institute, La Salle, IL, 1983, pp. 275-76) that the earliest passage in which "something like the pragmatic principle occurs" is in Peirce's 1868 article, "Some Consequences of Four Incapacities," supports this chronology. Peirce's paper was one of four published that year by *The Journal of Speculative Philosophy* in the series, "Search for a Method."

[16] *The Correspondence of the James Library,* The Houghton Library of Harvard University, 1959, Item 689.

[17] *Ibid.*

[18] *Ibid.,* Item 3396.

[19] *Ibid.,* Item 689.

[20] *Ibid.,* Item 690.

Peter Ochs (essay date 1993)

SOURCE: "Charles Sanders Peirce," in *Founders of Constructive Postmodern Philosophy,* edited by David Ray Griffin, John B. Cobb, Jr., Marcus P. Ford, Pete A. Y. Gunter, Peter Ochs, State University of New York Press, 1993, pp. 166-78.

[*In the following excerpt, Ochs asserts that Peirce is the first postmodernist philosopher.*]

By definition, a "logic of postmodernism" would appear to be a contradiction in terms: philosophic post-modernism emerged as a critique of attempts to found philosophy on some principle of reasoning and to found reasoning on some formal guidelines for how we ought to think. Nonetheless, there are two reasons why Charles Sanders Peirce (1839-1914) ought to be labelled the logician of post-modernism—the philosopher who, more than any other, etched out the normative guidelines for postmodern thinking. The first reason is that Peirce attempted to accomplish the impossible, or at least the contradictory. He launched his philosophic career with a logical critique of "Cartesianism"—his label for the modernist attempt to found philosophy on some formal principles of reasoning. He then attempted to replace the principles of Cartesian reasoning with a set of antimodernist principles that proved themselves to be as modernist as their contraries. The second reason for giving Peirce this label is that his failures to accomplish the impossible engendered in him something he was unable to achieve wilfully: a habit of self-critical yet self-affirming thinking that was neither modernist nor antimodernist but, rather, a disciplined variety of postmodern thinking. In his later years, Peirce began to sketch out the principles of philosophic postmodernism by describing features of his own emergent habit of thinking. The sketching comes close enough to what I would label a logic of postmodernism—where the method of logic is as postmodern as the thinking it describes.

As you may have surmised already, I do not believe Peirce's postmodernism is something one can study straight-on. His postmodernism was not a position or a place, but a process, of which his modernist struggles were an essential part. We must hence begin our study with Peirce's early modernism and then move forward, to see how his mature thought emerged as a way of completing and correcting his modernist project. After offering a few comments on Peirce's comparably complex life, I begin by reviewing Peirce's early critique of philosophic modernism. His own modernism is displayed in this technical critique—which means, I am afraid, that you will be confronted immediately with some rhetorical irony as well as with a strong dose of logical and epistemological argumentation. Relief will come slowly, as I then examine selected features of the habit of thinking that emerged from the contradictory tendencies in Peirce's early work. Making a postmodern move in my own method of analysis, I adopt Peirce's habit of thinking as a prototype for post-modern philosophy—suggesting that the norms of postmodern thinking must be embedded in the intellectual drama of certain ways of living. In conclusion, I reinterpret the claims of Peirce's mature philosophy as descriptions of selected features of his postmodern thinking. Among the topics considered are Peirce's claims about the self-correcting character of pragmatic reasoning; about the reality of chance, brute force and love as principles of cosmic evolution; and about the communal context of philosophic inquiry.

A few prefatory words, then, about some of the complexities of Peirce's life. First, the theological complexities. The dominant influence in Peirce's early life was his father, the eminent Harvard mathematician Benjamin Peirce. Benjamin was a devout Unitarian who, in the words of Peirce biographer Joseph Brent, "taught mathematics as a kind of religious worship."[1] Charles retained from his father's teaching a profound conviction that we live in God's creation and that, through this creation, we have immediate contact with God, or, as

Peirce phrased it at age 24 to a philosophical audience, with reality itself:

> When the conclusion of our age comes, and skepticism and materialism have done their perfect work, we shall have a far greater faith than ever before. For then man will see God's wisdom and mercy not only in every event of his own life, but in that of the gorilla, the lion, the fish, the polyp, the tree, the crystal, the grain of dust, the atom.[2]

On the other hand, Benjamin did not engender in Charles the need to participate, in a disciplined fashion, in any particular hermeneutical or ecclesiastical system. Thus Charles wrote, near the end of his life:

> I abominate the unitarians myself, because all through my boyhood I heard in our unitarian family nothing but angry squabbles between Calvinists and Unitarians, and though the latter were less absurd than the former, I thought their church was based on mere denial and when I grew up I joined the Episcopal church, without believing anything but the general essence and spirit of it. *That* I did and do profoundly believe.[3]

Peirce's love of irony and his tendency simultaneously to affirm and to deny, or at least to criticize, are displayed as well in these excerpts from his entry into the Harvard Class-Book of 1860:

> 1839 September 10. Tuesday. Born. . . .
>
> 1844 Fell Violently in love with Miss W. and commenced my education. . . .
>
> 1847 Began to be most seriously and hopelessly in love. Sought to drown my care by taking up the subject of Chemistry—an antidote which long experience enables me to recommend as sovereign. . . .
>
> 1850 Wrote a "History of Chemistry". . . .
>
> 1853 Set up for a fast man and became a bad schoolboy. . . .
>
> 1856 SOPHOMORE. Gave up the idea of being a fast man and undertook the pursuit of pleasure.
>
> 1857 JUNIOR. Gave up the pursuit of pleasure and undertook to enjoy life.
>
> 1858 SENIOR. Gave up enjoying life and exclaimed "Vanity of vanities! All is vanity!"
>
> 1859 Wondered what I would do in life.
>
> Appointed Aid on the Coast Survey. Went to Maine and then to Louisiana.[4]

Peirce did not have the reputation of being disciplined in his personal life. In his wife's words, "All his life from boyhood it seems as though everything had conspired to spoil him with indulgence."[4a] One of the results was an uneven employment record.

Peirce's first expertise was in chemistry. In 1863 he graduated from the Lawrence Scientific School with a B. S. *summa cum laude* in Chemistry, and he continued throughout his life to call himself a chemist. Until the 1890s, however, his gainful employment was with the Coast and Geodetic Survey, for whom he served as administrator and conducted gravimetric and other basic research. At the same time, through all these years, Peirce's central intellectual foci were logic and philosophy, and his first interest was to teach these fields in the university. Peirce made major contributions to numerous subfields in the logic and philosophy of science, formal and mathematical logic, topology, semiotics, linguistics and epistemology; he was most widely recognized as the founder of pragmatism. Nevertheless, contentious and undisciplined as he was, he was unable to procure a permanent teaching position.[5]

Even William James, perhaps Peirce's truest friend and admirer, was unable to convince Harvard administrators that Peirce, one of the greatest American philosophers, merited a place on their faculty. James did succeed, however, in securing Peirce's scholarly reputation as the founder of pragmatism. In an 1898 address to the Philosophical Union at the University of California, James said,

> I will seek to define with you merely what seems to be the most likely direction in which to start upon the trail of truth. Years ago this direction was given to me by an American philosopher whose home is in the East, and whose published words, few as they are and scattered in periodicals, are not fit expression of his powers. I refer to Mr. Charles S. Peirce, with whose very existence as a philosopher I dare say many of you are unacquainted. He is one of the most original of contemporary thinkers; and the principle of practicalism—or pragmatism, as he called it, when I first heard him enunciate it at Cambridge in the early '70s—is the clue or compass by following which I find myself more and more confirmed in believing we may keep our feet upon the proper trail.[6]

In the early 1870s, Peirce and James discussed pragmatism in a Metaphysical Club that met in Cambridge, Massachusetts, for about a decade.[7] Peirce laid the foundations for his pragmatism several years earlier with his first published critique of modernism.

I. THE CRITIQUE OF MODERNISM: PEIRCE'S ANTI-CARTESIANISM

In a series of papers published in the *Journal of Speculative Philosophy* in 1867-68,[8] Peirce sought to uncover the fundamental error that misled modern philosophers since Descartes into fearing they had to discover the foundation of all reasoning and then into believing they had found it. Peirce believed that this search for foundations reasserted platonic idealism in a new, subjective key, leading the philosophers of modernity into a war with the everyday. He believed that, from Descartes on, they rightfully objected to the ecclesiastic elitism of their scholastic progenitors, but then wrongfully re-

placed it with an elitism of their own—preferring genius over hoary learning, mathematical imagination over saintliness, the systematizing capacities of a few individual reasoners over the organic life of a community of inquirers. Peirce did not object to the need to refashion ecclesial authority, nor to the benefits of genius, imagination, and system. But he argued that these are gifts to be offered in the service of everyday life and everyday community, rather than as alternatives. Without idealizing the everyday and without calling for any atavistic returns to "a time when," he was a critic of the modern intellectual rather than of ordinary life. He called for the most sophisticated development of intellectual life, but in the service of a master who valued such a life only for its contributions to our worldly existence, or at least for its potential contributions to how we will ultimately exist in this world. Later, we may name this master "God," but not in a way that is overly influenced by classical-modern spiritualism or spirit-body dualism. For now, it is best to keep this master unnamed and to take note only of the effect of Peirce's references to it. This effect is to correct what Peirce considered the hubris of modern conceptions of the self.

According to Peirce, modern philosophy tended to encourage the egoism he saw manifested in the idolatries of his age: individualism (displayed, for example, in his scholarly peers' vainglorious defense of unverified and even untestable pet theories), economic materialism (the adoration of Mammon), social Darwinism (the anti-gospel of a societal survival of the fittest), and—his most general term of opprobrium—"nominalism." In fact, he took nominalism to underlie all the other negative tendencies of modernism.

In the great medieval controversies, the realists (such as Duns Scotus) believed that our ideas of universals correspond to something real, while the nominalists (such as William of Ockham) did not, claiming, instead, that only individual entities are real and that universals are merely names (*nomen*) we use to talk about collections of individuals. For many modern philosophers, this controversy seemed an empty and interminable dispute. According to Peirce, however, modernists belittled the dispute only because they had long since opted for the nominalist position, which they treated as if it were self-evident. In other words, he treated the medieval debate as if it were still raging, albeit in different terms, and as if "nominalism" referred to the epistemological doctrine that underlay all the other tendencies of modernism ("the nominalistic *Weltanschauung* has become incorporated into what I will venture to call the very flesh and blood of the average modern mind"[9]). Labeling himself a "scholastic realist," Peirce then set out to resuscitate Scotus' doctrine as his weapon against modernism. Playing the game of philosophic debate, he confronted modern philosophy in its own terms, offering logical, epistemological and empirical arguments against the claims of modern nominalism. Peirce's most convincing arguments were pragmatic ones, however. Undercutting the terms of philosophic debate, these did not neatly fit into the theater of scholastic disputation, and Peirce did not offer them explicitly for another ten years.

In his 1867-68 papers, Peirce offered what I call his nonpragmatic argumentation. His argument was based on the premise that nominalists question the reality of universals because, assuming that we acquire our universal beliefs on the authority of parents, teachers, ecclesial leaders and so on, they question the validity of such authority. Rather than trust such authorities, nominalists rely on immediate human judgments—perceptions, sensations, intuitions—which, they believe, offer us knowledge of individual entities, but not of any universals. Trusting immediate over learned knowledge, nominalists therefore tend to favor individuality over sociality, insight and genius over wisdom, and autonomy over relationship. Peirce concluded that nominalist systems stand or fall on the strength of their explanations of how, in fact, we have immediate knowledge of the real world. He offered his nonpragmatic argumentation as a critique of such explanations.

According to Peirce, Descartes' intuitionism provided the prototype for modernist attempts to account for our capacity to know the world immediately. It was what Descartes considered the Archimedean point upon which to ground the modern project of philosophy.[10] Peirce defined intuitionism as the claim that we have cognitions of objects outside of consciousness and uninfluenced by previous cognitions, and that we know, intuitively, that we have such knowledge independently of the influence of any previous knowledge. Peirce argued that "there is no evidence that we have this faculty [of knowing that we have intuitions uninfluenced by previous cognitions], except that we seem to *feel* that we have it."[11] Were this feeling to serve as our Archimedean point, then it would itself have to deliver information about its authority as well as about whatever it is about. The very simplicity of feeling, however, precludes its fulfilling such a dual function. For Peirce, the claim *that* a feeling or an intuition is authoritative must therefore belong to subsequent interpretation, and not to the feeling or intuition itself.

Peirce argued that a more reasonable interpretation of the empirical evidence is that whatever *appears* to us to be an immediate intuition is itself the product of previous cognitions. He suggested we consider, for example,

the perception of two dimensions of space. This appears to be an immediate intuition. But if we were to *see* immediately an extended surface, our retinas must be spread out in an extended surface. Instead of that, the retina consists of innumerable needles pointing toward the light, and whose distances from one another are decidedly greater than the *minimum visible.* Suppose each of those nerve-points conveys the sensation of a little colored surface. Still, what we immediately see must even then be, not a continuous surface, but a collection of spots. Who could discover this by mere intuition? But all the analogies of the nervous system are against the supposition that the excitation of a single nerve cell can produce an idea as complicated as that of space, however small. If the excitation of no one of these nerve points can immediately convey the impression of space, the excitation of all cannot do so. . . . [H]ence, the sum of these impressions is a necessary condition of any perception produced by the excitation of all.[12]

As additional examples, he suggested that we consider the way our visual field is uninterrupted by the blind spot that appears in the middle of the retina; the way we hear pitch independently of the aural impressions that contribute to it; or the way we perceive the duration of time: "That the course of time should be immediately felt is obviously impossible. For, in that case, there must be an element of this feeling at each instant. But in an instant there is no duration and hence no immediate feeling of duration."[13] (Peirce's later arguments were consistent with the claims of Bergson, James, Husserl, Whitehead, and Heidegger that the feeling of duration is itself a duration. At this point, however, Peirce's accomplishment was merely critical. Having displayed the inadequacies of intuitionism, he tended to replace it with a conversely dogmatic logicism: the claim that, if we are to have any certainty, then the way we interpret cognitions must be guided by indubitable modes of reasoning, rather than by infallible modes of intuition.) Peirce adduced comparable evidences against the various corollaries of intuitionism, such as the claims that we have intuitive self-consciousness (even Kant knew that children lacked this)[14] and a power of introspection (we lack an intuitive faculty of identifying elements of consciousness as "inner" or "outer") and, finally, a power to think without signs. Peirce concluded that "every thought is a sign," and, because signs are general, that "generals must therefore have a real existence."[15] At this stage in his thinking, in other words, Peirce linked his critique of intuitionism with a reassertion of realism. He believed that, if there are no primary intuitions, then there must, at least, be primary modes of interpreting intuitions—what he would later call indubitable habits of belief, whose generality he would later identify with the generality of real signs or symbols.[16]

In sum, Peirce believed he had offered a critique of, and an alternative to, the nominalist foundation of modern philosophy. Having argued that intuitionism is ungrounded, he believed he had both removed the intellectual supports of modern individualism and offered good reasons in support of its contrary: a kind of socialism and, underlying it, a kind of cognitivism. This latter is the claim that, if our knowledge is not about objects outside of consciousness, then it must be about previous knowledge.

In offering his cognitivist conclusions, however, Peirce reasserted a fundamental element of the nominalist argumentation he had sought to refute. In appearance, Peirce's cognitivism offered an alternative to the nominalists' subjectivism or self-reference. Having shown that intuitions are merely private, he concluded that non-private knowledge must be non-intuitional. Having defined intuitions as cognitions that refer directly to objects outside of consciousness, he concluded that non-intuitions are cognitions that refer only to other cognitions. But how, then, do cognitions refer to objects? Did Peirce not replace intuitionism with a vicious conceptualism[17]—a system of cognitions that refers only to itself the way each intuition refers only to itself? In the next stage of his work, Peirce introduced a mode of inquiry in terms of which he could identify the logical assumptions he had shared, in 1867, with the nominalists. While they offered contrary arguments, both the nominalists and he made use of the same method of argumentation, and the fallacy of modernist thinking lay in this *method,* not merely in the claims to which the method was applied. As we will see, Peirce called this the *a priori* method of thinking. For now, we may note that one of its leading principles is the law of excluded middle ("a" or "not a"). Both Peirce and the nominalists argued as if epistemological inquiry could be divided between mutually exclusive alternatives, in this case between the logical contraries "intuitionism" or "non-intuitionism." Following this method of reasoning, if intuitionism is false then its contrary must be true; in Peirce's argument, if intuitionism is false, then cognitivism is true, defined as non-intuitionism. Such a contrary represents a mere logical possibility, however, established on merely *a priori* grounds. We would have reason to expect that cognitivism, so defined, has as little to do with actual experience as intuitionism, so defined. Peirce's task, in the next stage of his work, was to search for an epistemological option that was neither intuitionist nor non-intuitionist, but rather some third something: intuitionism's logical contradictory, rather than its contrary.

II. THE CRITIQUE OF MODERNISM: PEIRCE'S EARLY PRAGMATISM

In what would become his most famous series of papers, the **"Illustrations of the Logic of Science"** of 1877-78,[18] Peirce developed a methodological critique of modernism. While Peirce's first arguments against intuitionism were epistemological and empirical, he now offered a critique of Descartes' method of argument itself: if Descartes' claim was not based on the facts of reason and experience, then it must have been based on something else. Rather than responding to nominalistic claims on their own terms, Peirce reduced them to their governing methods, or "guiding principles," and then evaluated them within a new taxonomy of what he called the "methods of fixing belief."[19] Laying the groundwork for his emergent pragmatism, he said: before worrying out the details of nominalistic claims, let us not suppose that every claim we hear is meaningful within the terms we bring to it or even within the terms it purports to bring to us. Let us first ask: out of what environment of inquiry does it come to us?

Peirce nurtured this question through several years of spirited discussions at the Cambridge Metaphysical Club in which James first heard his ideas about pragmatism. In the Club, an informal group of lawyers (Nicholas St. John Green and at times Oliver Wendell Holmes and Joseph Warner), scientists (Chauncy Wright, Peirce himself), psychologists (James) and philosophers of religion and science (Francis Abbot and John Fiske) debated questions of morality, science, and religion after Darwin. Green introduced Peirce to the theories of Alexander Bain, the English psychologist, in particular the theory that "belief is 'that upon which a . . . [person] is prepared to act.'"[20] Peirce was struck by this notion and expanded it into the theory of doubt and belief on which he based his taxonomy of methods of fixing belief:

> Our beliefs guide our desires and shape our actions. . . . The feeling of believing is a more or less sure indication of there being established in our nature some habit which will determine our actions. . . . Doubt is an uneasy and dissatisfied state from which we struggle to free ourselves and pass into a state of belief, while the latter is a calm and satisfactory state which we do not wish to avoid, or to change to a belief in anything else. . . .
>
> The irritation of doubt causes a struggle to attain a state of belief. I shall term this struggle *Inquiry,* though it must be admitted that this is sometimes not a very apt designation. . . .
>
> The irritation of doubt is the only immediate motive for the struggle to attain belief. . . . With the doubt . . . the struggle begins, and with the cessation of doubt it ends. Hence the sole object of inquiry is the settlement of opinion.[21]

On the basis of this theory, Peirce identified four prototypical methods of fixing belief in response to doubt, of which the third one underlies Cartesian intuitionism. The first is the method of tenacity, which is simply "taking as an answer to a question any we may fancy, and constantly reiterating it to ourselves, dwelling on all which may conduce to that belief, and learning to turn with contempt and hatred from anything that might disturb it."[22] Of course, this approach cannot hold its ground for very long in social practice.

A primary method for fixing belief in the community is, instead, that of authority: to "let an institution be created which shall have for its object to keep correct doctrines before the attention of the people, to reiterate them perpetually, and to teach them to the young; having at the same time power to prevent contrary doctrines from being taught, advocated or expressed." Peirce explained that, while this method has underwritten the development of strong, "priest-ridden states," it fails wherever citizens "possess a wider sort of social feeling." Observing the relativity of their inherited doctrines among the community of nations, these citizens suffer doubts about what they have learned on the basis of authority alone. They "further perceive that such doubts as these must exist in their minds with reference to every belief which seems to be determined by the caprice either of themselves or of those who originated the popular opinions." To settle these doubts, they appeal to a method of authoritative tenacity that Peirce dubbed the "*a priori* method."

According to Peirce, this third method for fixing belief, the *a priori* method, has until now been the darling of modern western philosophic tradition: it was anticipated by Plato and favored by Ockham, Descartes, Leibniz, even Kant and Hegel.[23] Proponents of this method say: "let the action of natural preferences be unimpeded . . . and, under their influence let men, conversing together and regarding matters in different lights, gradually develop beliefs in harmony with natural causes." Let them, in other words, believe what appears to be consistent with what *they* take to be their natural dispositions. According to Peirce, Descartes' approach boils down to this method alone. Having, like the enlightened citizens, lost faith in the mere authority of scholastic tradition, Descartes turned, instead, to the authority of his own deepest inclinations, which seemed to lead him, irresistibly, to the beliefs (1) that he did not doubt that he doubted, (2) that he had an idea of a perfect Being who is perfect necessarily, and (3) that that Being could not be a deceiver. In other words, if Descartes maintained his intuitionism independently of the empirical evidence, it is because he replaced scholastic authority with a new form of dogmatism. As restated in Susan Haack's very helpful formulation, Peirce believed that Descartes quieted his overgeneralized doubts (his "unwarranted skepticism") with an overstated certainty (an "unwarranted dogmatism").[24] Peirce argued that this method fails the way the method of authority failed: those who do not happen to share a given dogma will discover that dogmas, in general, may be relative to particular dispositions. Relativism does not, however, quiet our doubts.

This brings us to the turning point in Peirce's early pragmatism. By identifying the fallacy of modernism with *a priorism* in general rather than only with the intuitionist variety of *a priorism,* Peirce opened himself to his own criticism. He could now disclaim the cognitivism of his 1867-68 papers as another variety of *a priorism,* and he could replace it with something else. But with what? I do not believe that, deep down, he was yet certain, because *a priorism* remained as close to his heart as it was to Descartes', and, however much he saw its errors, he did not yet see very clearly how to avoid them. Thus, as I will explain in a moment, he argued strongly on behalf of science, defined in a new way, as the fourth method of fixing belief. But his arguments for this new science tended to reinforce the dogmatic habits of modernism as much as they introduced postmodern paradigms. His pragmatism seemed to offer a method for undoing dogmatic habits, but, not yet fully realizing its force, he tended to promote pragmatism as if it were another, better way of completing the modernist quest for *a priori* certainty. What else could he do? I believe the solution lay in his looking more carefully within, to discern precisely which of his tendencies encouraged his *a priorism* and which of them encouraged his pragmatism. If the solution did indeed lay within, then it took

Peirce some thirty years to develop the epistemological tools he needed to get to know himself. For it was not until 1905 that Peirce made a clear break with his philosophic modernism.

Rather than lead you through all the ins and outs of Peirce's years of precise and yet equivocal argumentation, allow me to substitute a tally sheet of where, in his early pragmatism, his thinking led back to elements of modernism and where it pointed forward. The distinction between the backward and forward elements of Peirce's thinking will introduce a distinction to be made later between his modernism and postmodernism.

(1) On the subject of science as a better method of fixing belief:

Peirce's thinking led *forward* toward the view that, within its historical context, modernism is a sign of the failures of scholastic science and of the need for a new paradigm for conducting empirical inquiry. This means that modernists doubted the capacity of the Aristotelean-Church system to account for new discoveries in the natural world. To overcome the *a priorism* that they have asserted in place of scholastic authority, these modernists need, instead, to locate a method "by which our beliefs may be determined by nothing human, but by some external permanency—by something upon which our thinking has no effect." They were searching, in other words, for a new paradigm of science, based on the realist hypothesis that "there are Real things, whose characters are entirely independent of our opinions about them; . . . [which] Reals affect our senses according to regular, [knowable] laws," the investigation of which would lead anyone with sufficient experience and reason to true conclusions. This science would not proceed from induction to theory building (the intuitionist model), nor from theory to inferences deduced from it (the authoritarian model), but from hypothesis-making to the inductions through which they would be tested. Induction would be a way of calculating the probability that inquirers would experience the world in ways their hypotheses would lead them to expect. Hypothesis-making would be a way of generating expectations about portions of experience that remain as yet incompletely considered in the traditions of science inherited by modernity. These expectations would remain, at the same time, consistent with those presuppositions of scientific tradition that remain unquestioned. The clearest prototype for this way of conducting science is to be found in the emergent practice of laboratory experimentalism. We have yet to identify the analogues of laboratory experimentalism within the verities of empirical inquiry.

Peirce's thinking led *backward* toward the dogmatic view that this theory of science does not merely correct modernism within the scholastic context of its complaints, but offers, rather, the best possible model of how to conduct the enterprise of knowing. In this view, experimentalism is the answer to a series of foundational questions, among them, "If we offer hypotheses to extend knowledge beyond its present limits, on what are our hypotheses fundamentally grounded? How do we delimit the range of possibilities we might imagine?" Among the foundational answers Peirce offered is this one: "we have the good fortune of guessing correctly more often than chance would allow, because the human mind 'is strongly adapted to the comprehension of the world.'" (Peirce's foundational question is based on the modernist's assumption that, whenever we doubt or extend ourselves beyond the limits of traditional knowledge, we find ourselves stripped of normal, linguistic resources and left to confront nature itself, in the raw. We must then identify our ultimate source of knowledge: either a plenum of pure possibility or else our own instincts and sensations in their prelinguistic purity. In his answer—in this case, that our minds are adapted to the world—Peirce transformed an intriguing theory of evolutionary adaptation into the unnecessarily foundational claim that, when all else fails, our own instincts will display to us the fundamental laws of nature.[25] From the perspective of Peirce's postmodernism, however, the question need not arise in the first place, since our doubts leave intact a host of epistemic supports for inquiry, whose ultimate sources we cannot clearly identify.)

(2) On the subject of how modernists should transform their dogmatisms into patterns of inquiry that may settle their doubts:

Peirce introduced his pragmatism, formally, as a maxim about how we can make our ideas clear: "Consider what effects, that might conceivably have practical bearings, we conceive the object of our conception to have. Then, our conception of these effects is the whole of our conception of the object."[26] This pragmatic maxim meant different things, however, in Peirce's forward and backward thinking.

Peirce's thinking led *forward* to the view that the pragmatic maxim was directed specifically to modernists, offering them advice we might paraphrase this way: "You present as dogmas certain clear and distinct ideas about the world. Instead, you ought to ask yourselves either of two questions, both of which will give you the same answer. Ask from what practice of inquiry you have abstracted the ideas through which you present your dogmas. Or ask from what complex of observable behaviors you have abstracted your description of the objects signified by your dogmas. You will find that the practice of inquiry and the complex of observable behaviors are inseparable one from the other and that your dogmas are merely shorthand ways of drawing our attention to both of these. To overcome your dogmatism, go out now and tell us how the dogmas relate back to the practices and the complexes, what you specifically want to tell us about them, and what we have left to learn." Consider, for example, the nominalist dogma that we know only particulars. Applying the pragmatic maxim, nominalists might say that, in response to doubts about their inherited traditions of knowledge, they identified "universals" with the unreliable claims

of their forebears and "particulars" with whatever judgments of experience they could make themselves, without relying on such claims. In other words, offering the dogma was a way of expressing their disappointment with both their forebears' claims and their forebears' insistence that these claims be accepted on authority. We might imagine that, if pressed, erstwhile nominalists might agree to abandon their own universal claim about particulars, in exchange for a policy of testing and, if necessary, revising those traditional claims that they had specific reasons to doubt.

Peirce's thinking led *backwards* to the view that pragmatism provided an epistemological alternative to Cartesian intuitionism. In this view, modernist dogmatisms arose out of the errant assumption that knowing a thing clearly is simply a matter of getting our ideas about it in order, as if there corresponded to everything in the world some single set of ideas that represented truly what it really is. The way to correct this assumption is to replace it with the pragmatic assumption that knowing a thing means being able to anticipate how it would act or appear in given circumstances. When we claim to know something, we mean knowing in this second sense. The pragmatic maxim thus tells us what we do when we claim to know something. (The problem with this version of pragmatism is that it adopts what it calls the modernist assumption of knowledge in the very process of attempting to refute it. This version places pragmatic and modernist claims side by side, as if they were two competing views of the way humans actually know things, one view being true and the other false. This is, however, to adopt the modernist assumption that knowing something—in this case, human knowledge—clearly is to represent it as it really is. A corollary problem with this version of pragmatism is that it offers modernism a rebuttal rather than a remedy: rather than offer modernists a way of discovering the truths within or behind their claims, it suggests that they abandon these claims in favor of some others.)

(3) Finally, then, to return to the subject of Peirce's critique of modernist conceptions of the self:[27]

Peirce's pragmatism generated the metaphysical claim that the "soul" of anything, human or extrahuman, is its tendency to act in certain ways in certain circumstances. Peirce put this claim to the service of his different ways of thinking.

His thinking led *backwards* to the view that the modernist conception of the self was simply erroneous, built on a failed logic and an empty metaphysics and contributing to unethical conduct. This erroneous conception was that the human self is an incorporeal substance, ultimately unknowable, self-contained and ultimately self-referring; that it is the subject of all perceptions and cogitations; that it asserts itself, over against the material substance to which it is attached, over against the world, and over against other selves. According to this view of Peirce's, such a conception is false because it is incompatible with a pragmatic conception of the human soul. As a complex of tendencies to act, the soul must be corporeal (as well as incorporeal), knowable, relational, and other-referring; it must mediate between subjects and objects of knowing, among other selves and the world. The modernist self appears only as the negation of the actual life of such a soul. "The individual man, since his separate existence is manifested only by ignorance and error, so far as he is anything apart from his fellows, and from what he and they are to be, is only a negation."[28]

Peirce's thinking led *forward* to the view that the modernist conception of the self was an assertion of loneliness and distress, of complaint and the need for truth and love, of the plenitude of possibility as well as the fearsomeness of infinity. In this view of Peirce's, the modernist self is, indeed, an abstraction and thus an incomplete sign. But it is the sort of sign that calls for a redeeming love: the compassionate interpretation that would relink the sign to the community of interpretation in which it displayed its full meaning. Unlike Job's sorry comforters, the compassionate interpreter would not suppose that the process of relinking was an obvious affair. To relink the sign to its context of meaning would be to reintroduce the self to its community of practice, in which it would find its particular history and a more open future. Because, however, the self is a sign of inadequacies in that very community, such a reintroduction would come only through great effort, involving the reformation of community as well as the transformation of self. In the process, the community would itself appear as a self, or as an individuated part of a wider society, and its wider society would appear this way, as well. The emergent, postmodern understanding of the modern self would relink conceptions of self to conceptions of the human soul as a center of ways of acting. This relinking would not be merely a conceptual affair, but a matter of real work.

III. FROM MODERN PRAGMATISM TO POSTMODERN PRAGMATICISM

In the 1877-78 **"Illustrations of the Logic of Science,"** Peirce first offered his pragmatism to the world. In a series of articles published in *The Monist* in 1905, he threatened to take his pragmatism back. He claimed that, in the intervening years, the scholarly world had misrepresented what pragmatism really means, forcing him, at this time, to re-explain and, in fact, rename it. Speaking of himself, he wrote

> His word "pragmatism" has gained general recognition in a generalized sense that seems to argue power of growth and vitality. The famed psychologist, James, first took it up, seeing that his "radical empiricism" substantially answered to the writer's definition of pragmatism, albeit with a certain difference in the point of view. Next, the admirably clear and brilliant thinker, Mr. Ferdinand C. S. Schiller, casting about for a more attractive name for the "anthropomorphism" of his *Riddle of the Sphinx*, lit . . . upon the same

designation "pragmatism." . . . So far all went happily. But at present, the word begins to be met with occasionally in the literary journals, where it gets abused in the merciless way that words have to expect when they fall into literary clutches. Sometimes the manners of the British have effloresced in scolding at the word as ill-chosen—ill-chosen, that is, to express some meaning that it was rather designed to exclude. So then, the writer, finding his bantling "pragmatism" so promoted, feels that it is time to kiss his child good-by and relinquish it to its higher destiny; while to serve the precise purpose of expressing the original definition, he begs to announce the birth of the word *"pragmaticism,"* which is ugly enough to be safe from kidnappers.[29]

We might take Peirce's protestations with a grain of salt. As Peirce averred in a footnote, he had never previously made popular use of the term "pragmatism" in writing. In his 1907 lecture "What Pragmatism Means," James recalled that Peirce's principle of pragmatism

> lay entirely unnoticed by any one for twenty years, until I, in an address before Professor Howison's Philosophical Union at the University of California,[30] brought it forward again and made a special application of it to religion.[31] By that date the times seemed ripe for its reception. The word "pragmatism" spread, and at present it fairly spots the pages of the philosophic journals.[32]

While grateful for the publicity, and generally pleased by James' work, Peirce found James' pragmatism itself too "nominalistic" for his purposes. As John E. Smith writes, "James, with his incipient nominalism, was always hesitant about allowing concepts to have any other than a representational meaning or a surrogate function."[33] Peirce's pragmaticism was thus a response to James as well as to the "literary circles." But on what was this response based? Peirce claimed that he was returning to his "original definition." However, as I have suggested earlier, Peirce spent many years taking up his original definition in a modernist, as well as a postmodernist, way. Peirce's misinterpreters were led by the modernist (or "backward") tendency in Peirce's own writings. This all means that pragmaticism was Peirce's way of kissing good-by to the child of his own modernism, of which the nominalisms of his interpreters were mere reflections.

I belabor these autobiographical points not as a matter of mere scholarly erudition, but, rather, to suggest that the principles of Peirce's postmodernism are principles of critical self-reflection, of which Peirce's own self-corrections are prototypical. We will take "pragmaticism" to be a general label for the way Peirce sought to recover what, in our terms, was postmodern in his earlier studies of pragmatism and to elide what was not. Returning to the distinctions I made between what was *forward*-and what was *backward*-looking in Peirce's pragmatism, we may then relabel pragmaticism a restatement of the principles displayed in his forward-looking thinking. I mentioned three areas of forward thinking on Peirce's part. These areas may be viewed as various expressions of a single tendency of thinking, of which we may discern the following aspects, or sub-tendencies. (The order of presentation here is arbitrary. On this occasion, I am portraying postmodern thinking as a reflection on the way modernist thinking responds to problems in premodern "practice," which means premodern patterns of thinking-and-acting. Each of the aspects I describe represents what I am picturing to be stages or moments in this process of reflection. I am obviously asking for a little trust at this point, because I have not yet displayed the criteria I used to distinguish forward from backward, or postmodern from modern, tendencies. I am trying to display the criteria in use, before labelling them abstractly. Once you get through this, you will see what I was doing and will then have the freedom to evaluate it.)

The first aspect is the *negative or critical character* of Peirce's forward thinking, which began with the discovery of a problem in modernist thinking. Peirce's postmodern thinking began as a way of responding to problems, rather than as a way of generating ideas for their own sake. Its occasion was not wonder or curiosity or assertion, but rather the intrusion of something insistent and unpleasant: a kind of suffering. It was therefore an activity whose subject matter lay behind it, as the still unknown source of the discomforts that moved it forward.

A second aspect is the *reflexive character* of Peirce's forward thinking, which was a way of recollecting the source of discomfort out of which it arose. The negativity of Peirce's postmodernism was thus merely a reflection of the negativity of modernity. Modernist thinking *expresses* this negativity, while postmodernist thinking identifies it *as* negative: identifying the discomforts of modernity as symptoms of disruptions in modernity's antecedent traditions of practice. From this perspective, postmodernist thinking is modernist thinking reflecting on itself, its origins and its future. Peirce's later writings on *self-control* and on *semiotics* displayed his attentiveness to the phenomenon of reflexivity.[34] Reflection is an activity of *self-control,* and *semiotics* displays its logic: interpreting negative thinking as the *sign* of some antecedent problem—as *object*—and of some consequent response—as what Peirce called the *interpretant* of a sign. (On self-control, Peirce wrote that "the term 'reasoning' ought to be confined to such fixation of one belief by another as is reasonable, deliberate, self-controlled";[35] and, "the pragmaticist does not make the *summum bonum* to consist in action, but makes it to consist in that process of evolution whereby the existent comes more and more to embody [real generals, which are general conditional propositions as to the future] . . . , which is what we strive to express in calling them *reasonable.* In its higher stages, evolution takes place more and more largely through self-control. . . ."[36])

A third aspect is the contribution Peirce's forward thinking made to *solving whatever problem* stimulated it. Peirce's postmodernist thinking was a *performative activity,* which embodied its purposes in the way it actually responded to the discomforts of modernity. Its reflexivity was thus not an end in itself, but a moment in an extended process of referring the complaints of modernity back to the antecedent practices to which they refer and then forward to the reformation of practice to which it contributes. While prompted by suffering, Peirce's postmodernism was thus animated by hope.

A fourth aspect is the *reaffirmation* implicit in Peirce's forward thinking. If his postmodernism reflected the negativity of modernity, it also exhibited the relationship of modernity to its antecedent practices, which Peirce identified with the practices of scholastic philosophy and science. Peirce considered these practices to be the sources of both the problems of modernity *and* the capacity of modernity to solve those problems. He said the best way to understand this duality is to conceive of there being two levels of regularity within the practices. On one level, the practices apply to context-specific ways of acting and are thus highly informative, but subject more readily to change, since they must be responsive to the variable character of their contexts. All practices of which we are conscious belong to this first level. The second level is inhabited by all those practices of which we are not ordinarily conscious: what he would later call the original, commonsense beliefs that we share with members of our species, or perhaps with culture-specific subgroups of the species. These practices are indubitable for all practical purposes and therefore appear to be neither context-specific nor informative. Nevertheless, we must conceive of these practices as providing the rules that inform our reflections on the first-level practices.

Note that Peirce conceived of these levels of practice in a relational way: the second level was indubitably only relative to our experiences of the world. He meant that, if modernists have doubts about antecedent practices, then these are, by definition, doubts about first-level practices,[37] offered with respect to the rules of judgment and doubt provided by second-level practices.[38] He believed that his pragmatism belonged to and exhibited the rules of modernity's second-level practices: for that reason, in fact, both he and James considered pragmatism "a new name for an old way of thinking." Applying to scholastic thinking the same reflexivity he applied to modernist thinking, Peirce was prepared to identify this old way of thinking with the deeper level of the scholastics' own inherited practices. The ground of Peirce's hope lay therefore in his reaffirming the ancient or, ultimately, primeval roots of modern practices, as exhibited in chronologically successive contexts of critical thinking.[39]

A fifth aspect is the *fallibilistic character* of Peirce's forward thinking. Invoking the terminology of the Scotch commonsense realists,[40] Peirce called his reaffirmation of our indubitable beliefs his "commonsensism." He added, however, that the commonsense realists erred in imaging that the second-level practices were indubitable in any and all circumstances: "one thing the Scotch failed to recognize is that the original beliefs only remain indubitable in their application to affairs that resemble those of a primitive mode of life."[41] For example, he wrote that while we act on the belief that there are only three dimensions, "it is . . . quite open to reasonable doubt whether the motions of electrons are confined to three dimensions, although it is good methodeutic to presume that they are until some evidence to the contrary is forthcoming."[42] Peirce named his position *critical* commonsensism. All practices are potentially corrigible. "Not only is our knowledge thus limited in scope, but it is even more important that we should thoroughly realize that the very best of what we, humanly speaking, know [we know] only in an uncertain and inexact way."[43] The negativity of modernity was a sign of this uncertainty and, thus, of postmodernity's need to reform a first level of practices, as guided by a second level of practices. Peirce recognized that the second level was potentially corrigible. ("'Indubitability,' for Peirce, did not mean 'absolute certainty.' Rather, it meant 'freedom from genuine doubt.'"[44]) He also recognized that this potentiality did not preclude its functioning, now, as the condition of our knowing the real. As we will discuss later, he believed that the fallibility of human knowledge is, rather, a sign of the indefinite character of the real itself.

A sixth aspect is the role of *creativity and imagination* in Peirce's forward thinking. Peirce sought to reform first-level practices by reaffirming the reformatory guidance offered by second-level practices. To doubt the authority of one practice—for example, obedience to the church, or to the Aristotelean syllogistic—we rely on the authority of more fundamental standards of behavior or of reasoning. Peirce argued, however, that these deeper practices are not informative in themselves. They reveal themselves only *in actu* and, that means, only relative to the tasks we ask them to perform. On one level, this means that we would, following Kant, attempt to discover the fundamental practices by asking what all our other practices must presuppose. This also means, however, that our presuppositions would only be as revealing as our practices; our inquiry would be limited by the kinds of practice we know how to practice. We might expect the pragmatist to answer, "But the limit of knowledge is simply that: the limit of action!" Without officially departing from the disciplines of his pragmatism, Peirce stretched this answer to its limits by adding words that I will paraphrase, less formally, in this way: "Then again, the limit of action is the limit of *conceivable* action. In this sense, we know how to practice whatever we can conceive of practicing, and we discover more about our presuppositions the more we expand our capacities to conceive of what we *might* do on this earth, even if what we might do remains a way of reforming what we already do."

Peirce invented the term *abductive reasoning* to refer to the inquiry we undertake to generate hypotheses about how we might reform what we already do. He believed this mode of reasoning was a power as well as a skill that could be improved by practice and by discipline. And he believed that, by improving our capacity to imagine new possibilities, we deepened our capacity to display our fundamental beliefs. Of course, abductive reasoning generates mere hypotheses. Peirce argued that, to separate the fundamental from the fanciful, we had to test our hypotheses' usefulness in actually reforming our practices and, thus, resolving the real doubts and problems that stimulated our inquiry in the first place. To test them, he suggested we employ what he called the methods of deductive reasoning (to indicate precisely how, if successful, the hypotheses *would* contribute to the reform of antecedent practices) and inductive reasoning (to evaluate their success in actual practice).[45]

We have, then, a collection of six aspects of Peirce's actual practice of forward thinking, which was negative, reflexive, devoted to problem-solving, affirming of original beliefs, fallibilistic, and creative. What does this tell us? If we were modernists, we might ask, "What does philosophy have to learn from descriptions of a particular person's style of thinking? If this person were creator of our world, we might take these to be descriptions of our god's essential attributes and see in these attributes the limits toward which the activities of this world might tend. But Peirce is no god, and the most we can see in these descriptions are the attributes of his own creative activity, his own world. We learn very little about *our* various worlds, or about any world we might share." If we were the relativistic sort of postmodernists, we might admire the beauty, power, or curiosity of this person's style of thinking, all the while treating with some condescension his apparent belief that his critique of modernity told us something positive about a world we share. We would see in his style of thinking only a style of thinking, acceptable and even attractive as long as it abandoned its claim to be any more than that. In the context of this book, however, we bring to the study of Peirce's thinking the perspective of a nonrelativistic postmodernism. This means we are predisposed to accept his claim that, after the critique of modernist intuitionism and substantialism, philosophy may still have something to say about the world we share or, to reinvoke scholastic terminology, something to say about "the real." This critique means, however, that we do not expect philosophy to talk about the real the same way it did previously. In this essay, we consider the claim that Peirce displayed a new way of talking about the real. But, up to this point, all we have before us are descriptions of his postmodern manner of thinking. What do these descriptions tell us about the real?

I hesitate to trot out the "principles of Peirce's postmodernism" as an answer to this question, because I do not want to give the impression that these principles were the kinds of propositions dogmatic metaphysicians offered before Kant and, then again, among the romantic responses to Kant. Peirce's critique of Cartesianism meant that he could no longer portray himself as having arrived at certain propositions whose subjects designated reality and whose predicates designated reality's essential characters. He rejected the notion that we know reality by arriving at propositions that mirror it. His postmodern thinking implied, instead, that we know reality by imitating it in our own activity: the way a theologian would say we know God by imitating God, or the way Jesus said "Follow me and leave self behind." That is, "leave behind the *ego cogito,* whose abstractions do not imitate God or God's creation, and follow me, instead, with your *whole* being." Our descriptions of Peirce's forward thinking are not adequate representations of his whole being, but, within the limits of a philosophic study like this, they are meant at least to symbolize it. In Whitehead's terms, they represent *prehensions* of reality within the context of Peirce's work. In what we are about to learn are Peirce's terms, they represent the *interpretants* of reality within Peirce's work. This means that they belong "merely" to Peirce's life, but also that Peirce's life, like any life displayed in its wholeness, really tells us about the reality it interprets. Like all lives displayed in their wholeness, Peirce's life was more than Peirce's. If we take it up into our lives, in their wholeness, then it implicates our lives as well.

It takes an indefinitely long time to display the wholeness of a life, and, in philosophic conversation, we ask to get to the bottom of a life in a very short time. Even in its postmodern form, philosophic conversation is therefore somewhat abusive. Nevertheless, we know that, on pages like these, we are simply trying to offer brief glimpses of processes that continue to run deeply even as we describe them. We know that these glimpses do not display the realities of which they are glimpses until we have fleshed them out within our own lives. We know, then, that there is no single, privileged way in which they display their realities. Yet we also trust that, in bringing these glimpses into our various lives, as we do, we also share in some activity that is one despite the irreducible multiplicity of its appearances. The glimpses we presume to offer are offered, therefore, merely as attempts to share with one another our firm sense and our fallible understanding of the oneness that binds us together: the oneness of a process that is symbolized for us in the ways we find to identify what we share with another human life.

In the following section, I attempt to identify what we might share with Peirce's life by posing certain questions of his life that may be of interest to us in the context of this volume. Of course, Peirce is not here to answer, but our interest need not, at any rate, be merely in what Peirce would literally have said. What he literally wrote were answers to questions posed by his contemporaries, and these are not necessarily questions we are asking now. We may, instead, take the risk of imagining Peirce's responding to questions he may not have asked in the way we are asking them. We would thereby elicit answers that belong, at once, to our lives (for we posed the questions), to the life about which we are

asking (displayed through Peirce's writing), and to the specific context we are considering. For the present discussion, I will define these triply limited and triply relational answers as *the principles of a life.* This will be my way of introducing *principles* into our discussion without fearing that I have led you to associate these principles with dogmatic propositions. I will, then, present the principles of Peirce's postmodernism *as the answers I imagine the forward-thinking Peirce would have offered to a series of questions of interest to us as nonrelativistic postmodernists.*

IV. THE PRINCIPLES OF PEIRCE'S POSTMODERNISM

We begin with three preliminary questions, the answers to which constitute a first principle of postmodernism, or a principle about principles. The first question is: if, in its wholeness, any human life tells us about the reality it interprets, why would we want to learn about other lives? The answer is that every life tells us about the real, but in a finite way, which means that learning about other lives is a way to expand the limits of our own finitude and learn about reality more fully. The second question is: why would we learn more from Peirce's life than from another life? The answer is that a reflective life is one that asks questions about itself and, therefore, generates answers. Living his life in a particularly reflective way, Peirce generated a particularly informative array of answers. These answers may function as *principles of life* for those who may ask similar questions. The third question is: why would these function as principles of postmodern living in particular? According to the perspective I have adopted in this essay, the answer is that the questions Peirce asked of himself were principally questions about the burdens of his own modernist thinking. The greatest of these burdens was the gulf he sensed between his modernist thinking and the needs of everyday life, including *his* everyday life. The principles of postmodern living are ways of living in response to, hopefully as a remedy to, one's own modernism.

The primary questions we will ask the postmodern Peirce to answer are: what kind of activity is your postmodernist thinking? what does it tell us about? and, to whom does it tell this? His imagined answers will represent the principles of Peirce's postmodernism.

A. *What Kind of Activity is Peirce's Postmodern Thinking?*

Principle A1: It is a semiotic activity. I have structured this essay so far according to the most powerful principle I see embedded in Peirce's work: that postmodern thinking is a way of interpreting the meaning of modernist thinking. Peirce's most powerful instrument for articulating the process of interpretation was *semiotics,* or the science of signs he later came to identify with logic. He called the process of sign interpretation *semiosis,*[46] meaning "an action, or influence, which is, or involves, a cooperation of *three* subjects, such as a sign, its object and its interpretant, this tri-relative influence not being in any way resolvable into actions between pairs."[47] He would say that, in the process of interpretation, we interpret some entity as a *sign* that refers to its *object,* or meaning, with respect to some *interpretant,* or mode of interpretation for which the sign displays that meaning. Semiosis is thus always a relational activity involving three entities. Before considering how Peirce's postmodern thinking may appear as a process of sign interpretation, allow me to explain somewhat more technically how Peirce identified the three elements of semiosis in general.

Peirce said that his semiotics presupposed two formal sciences. The first was *mathematics,* by which he meant not merely various theories of quantity, but also what others may call formal logic: "the study of what is true of hypothetical states of things."[48] We might call this the disciplined study of creative imagination: a process of diagramming, or drawing pictures of, the elemental rules the imagination suggests to itself when left fully to its own devices. For example, a thinker may take a blank page, then draw a dot on it, then a line and a dot, then a line connecting two dots, and so on. What unseen rule guides the thinker's drawing? Peirce discovered that, giving his imagination a free voice, he was not satisfied to draw any single diagram, but was moved to construct another diagram and another: "Beginning with suitable examples and thence proceeding to others, one finds that the diagram itself, in its individuality, is not what the reasoning is concerned with. . . . In passing [rather] from one diagram to the other, the [reasoner] . . . will be supposed to *see* something, which will present this little difficulty for the theory of vision, that it is of a *general nature.*"[49] This *seeing* is a way of conceiving the rule whose urgings led the reasoner to draw the individual diagrams. Of course, the seeing is itself a kind of diagramming, which means the process can continue on and on. Peirce found that the minimal elements of any such diagramming are three: the initial act of drawing something, the repetition or iteration of the act, and the activity of linking the repetitions together.[50] The simplest way to diagram the act of diagramming would, then, be to distinguish between what Peirce called the *monadic* character of a simple act, the *dyadic* character of a repetition (one act plus one act) and the *triadic* character of the act of linkage (one plus one plus the linkage or relation).

The second science presupposed by semiotics was *phenomenology,*[51] which "treats of the universal Qualities of Phenomena,"[52] or of "the collective total of all that is in any way or in any sense present to the mind."[53] Put crudely, the phenomenologists' job is to see how much sense they can make of our experiences by supposing that the elemental characters of mathematical reasoning, or of imagination, will appear again as the most general qualities of all phenomena. Peirce thus identified the three categories of experience as Firstness, Secondness, and Thirdness. He labelled "Firsts" all phenomena that display merely monadic or simple qualities, such as simple states of consciousness, like the feeling of red-

ness. He labelled "Seconds" all phenomena that display dyadic qualities, such as divided states of consciousness, in which something inner is opposed to something outer. An example of the latter is the shock of surprise, which signals the interruption of one state by something other. He labelled "Thirds" all phenomena that display triadic qualities: these are all phenomena of mediation, relationality, or representation. Signs are paradigmatic Thirds.

Within his phenomenology, Peirce defined a sign as something that stands *for* something (its object) *to* the idea that it produces or modifies (its *interpretant*).[54] Once again, the key to Peirce's semiotic is his conception of the tri-relationality of the sign. A sign is obviously not a sign just by itself, but it is also not a sign if considered merely in relation to its object: as if a sign (*signe* for de Saussure) had a meaning (*signifié*) in general—some privileged partner out there in the universe to which it was connected independently of some third something, some mediator. For Peirce such a two-part relation would be an instance of mere Secondness, such as the rude shock of an unexpected encounter—a real event, but one as yet without any meaning. In fact, we may consider the reduction of signification to dyadic relations an emblem of modernist nominalism: an emblem of the belief that our concepts are records of merely chance or brute encounters. This belief implies that we can make whatever use we wish of such records, but that we cannot expect them to guide us. A genuine sign is, instead, a sign that has its meaning *with respect to* its interpretant. This means that meaning is not simply projected out into empty space, but is offered to some being for some reason. Meaning is an aspect of relationship. A sign relates beings together.

Technically speaking, Peirce classified phenomenology as the first sub-science of philosophy. He said the business of philosophy "is to find out all that can be found out from those universal experiences which confront every [person] in every waking hour."[55] As pragmaticist, he added that we seek to find these things out in order to solve the problems that arise in everyday experience. Within this inquiry, phenomenology sketches out the elemental qualities of everyday experience. What he called the "normative sciences"—aesthetics, ethics and logic—identify the rules of reasoning and practice we adopt in making assertions about everyday experience and, thus, in solving the problems that confront us. Metaphysics, finally, articulates a vision of the entire universe of mind and matter that we would inhabit if those rules of reasoning and practice were rules of being itself. Within this scheme, Peirce came to employ semiotics as his language of logic.[56] It is a particularly integrative language, which enables us both to perceive the elements of experience that delimit the activity of reasoning and to imagine the rules of being that issue from it.

For the semiotician, reasoning is itself a process of semiosis, the elements of which are all the possible kinds of relationship that can connect sign to sign, sign

to object, sign to interpretant, object to interpretant, sign to object to interpretant, and so on. For example, Peirce said a sign can refer to its object in any of three ways. An *icon* is a sign that refers to its object "by virtue of characters of its own, and which it possesses . . . whether any such object actually exists or not." An example is a painting, which depicts its object only by virtue of the oil, brush, canvas and imagination of the painter. An *index* is a sign that refers to its object "by virtue of really being affected by that object," as well as by sharing some quality in common with the object. An example is a weather vane, which is actually moved by the wind whose directionality it both shares and depicts. A *symbol* is a sign that refers to its object "by virtue of a law . . . which operates to cause the symbol to be interpreted as referring to that object. . . ." Not only is the symbol itself "a general type, or law . . . but the object to which it refers is [also] of a general nature."[57] Examples of symbols are linguistic terms or predicates, propositions and arguments, all of which are partial embodiments of genuine or
triadic processes of semiosis.[58]

Terms, such as "scholastic thinking," or predicates, such as "_____is an index of problems in scholastic thinking," symbolize the iconic or monadic character of a process of semiosis. Propositions, such as "Modernist thinking is an index of problems in scholastic thinking," symbolize the indexical or dyadic character of a process of semiosis. Such arguments as the following one symbolize the symbolic or triadic character of a process of semiosis:

> Modernist thinking is a way of criticizing the inadequacies of traditions of practice in general.
>
> Problems in scholastic thinking may give rise to criticisms of the inadequacies of traditions of practice in general.
>
> Modernist thinking may be an index of problems in scholastic thinking.

Such arguments, finally, presuppose the formal and material *leading principles* that enable us to reason from their premises to their conclusions. In this case, among the formal principles is the rule of abduction or hypothesis-making, which enables us to say "If A is B, and C can be signified by B, then maybe A is a sign of C." Among the material principles are theories of postmodern thinking—Peirce's theory, for example, which was a tendency of thinking that provided a context of interpretation, or interpretant, with respect to which modernist thinking appeared as a *sign* whose *meaning* was that something is wrong with the practices out of which modernist thinking emerged. Peirce diagrammed this tendency in the process of reflecting on his own modernist thinking. His pragmaticism emerged when he said, in effect, "Aha! My own merely critical thinking was an indexical *sign* that displays its *meaning* when I locate the *interpretant* that allows me to reform my precritical practices in ways hinted at in that sign.

My postmodern thinking is this interpretant." The first element of Peirce's postmodern thinking that we have considered is his semiotics, in terms of which he abstracted the elemental or formal elements of his discovery, as if to say: "As a modernist, I understood my claims as signs that referred to their objects generally, apart from any particular context of meaning. Now I understand these claims as signs that deliver their meanings *to* the particular process of interpretation I am now articulating."

Principle A2: Peirce's postmodern thinking is a method of habit-change. Using the language of Peirce's semiotics, we can identify the formal properties of his postmodern thinking, viewed as an interpretive process and as part of the interpretive processes that link together his modernist criticism and his precritical practices. However, the formality of semiotics might tempt us to overlook the bodily dimension of thinking. And studying the coherence of an interpretive process might tempt us to overlook the transformational character of postmodern thinking. The bodily dimension and transformational character of Peirce's postmodernism are displayed more fully in terms of his *theory of habit-change.*

In their Metaphysical Club sessions of the 1870s, Peirce and James paid a great deal of attention to Alexander Bain's psychological studies of human habits of reasoning. In his *Principles of Psychology,* James wrote that "when we look at living creatures from an outward point of view, one of the first things that strike us is that they are bundles of habits. . . . The habits to which there is an innate tendency are called instincts; some of those due to education would by most persons be called acts of reason."[59] He added that

> the moment one tries to define what habit is, one is led to the fundamental properties of matter. The laws of Nature are nothing but the immutable habits which the different elemental sorts of matter follow in their actions and reactions upon each other. In the organic world, however, the habits are more variable than this. . . . Organic matter, especially nervous tissue, seems endowed with a very extraordinary degree of plasticity [meaning, "the possession of a structure weak enough to yield to an influence, but strong enough not to yield all at once"]. . . . We may without hesitation lay down as our first proposition the following, that *the phenomena of habit in living beings are due to the plasticity of the organic materials of which their bodies are composed.*[60]

In the same year that James published his *Psychology,* Peirce located the riddle of existence in this plasticity. He called it the capacity of protoplasm to feel (and thus "to take on ideas"), to respond to stimuli (and thus "to react" or be moved), to allow feelings to spread (and thus "to generalize" or "to grow"), *to form habits* (and thus to acquire rules of behavior) and to forget or lose excitability (and thus to "to select" certain rules of behavior and let others go).[61] In these writings, Peirce devoted most of his attention to the phenomenon of habit-taking, or of acquiring the capacity to act in a certain way under certain circumstances.[62] We learn about the world, he said, not simply by forming ideas in response to stimuli, but by forming habits of responding to the world. This means, he concluded, that the Cartesian and Platonic picture-theory of knowledge is inadequate: the world is not something we can depict in the way we organize our ideas, but only something whose processual character we can embody, and in that sense imitate, in the ways we act.[63] In these terms, a way of thinking is a habit of thinking. If the world is viewed as a great sign, then a habit of thinking is what Peirce called the logical, or ultimate, *interpretant* of that sign. This means that we display the *meaning* of the world in the capacities we acquire to act in response to the world.

But what if our habits of thinking prove faulty? In his writings on pragmaticism, Peirce directed his attention to the phenomenon of *habit-change,* or the modification of a person's tendencies toward action. Among the sources of habit-change, he listed "experiences forced upon" the mind; acts of will or "muscular effort"; and "efforts of the imagination," which are ways of imagining how we might act in the future.[64] Peirce was most interested in the latter: those "experimentations in the inner world" that enable us to test out our habits of action without muscular effort, to examine and criticize the likely results of our efforts and, then, to recommend to ourselves alternative ways of acting. He claimed that, by repeating such recommendations to ourselves, we may be able to alter our habits of action as well as we could through physical exercise.[65]

Peirce made these claims at the same time that he was framing his pragmaticism: as if he had abstracted his theory of habit-change from his own activity of changing his merely modernist habits of thinking into postmodern ones. We might then redescribe Peirce's postmodern thinking as a method of habit-change—in particular, as a way of transforming his modernist habit of criticism into a habit of reforming precritical habits of action in response to modernist criticism. In this redescription, we would not characterize postmodern thinking as a mere habit, but, rather, as an activity of *habit-change.* Like modernist thinking, it is a critical activity; unlike it, it is a critique of mere criticism, and, thus, a reaffirmation—a *reforming* reaffirmation. From the attention Peirce paid to the various sources of habit-change, we may infer, furthermore, that Peirce understood his postmodern turn to be the result of his thought experiments more than of some transforming encounter or of some spontaneous act of will. This would mean that Peirce's postmodernism was, in sum, a reforming reaffirmation of his precritical habits of action, stimulated by his imaginative reflections on how his modernist criticisms actually influenced the ways he might act in the world.

Principle A3: Peirce's postmodern thinking is an activity of pragmatic inquiry. If we were to review the principles we have considered so far in terms of Peirce's

phenomenology, we might say that principle A1 displays the Firstness of Peirce's postmodern thinking, its formal coherence, while principle A2 displays its Secondness, its capacity to transform actual behavior. We might then look for principle A3 to display the Thirdness of Peirce's postmodernism, or the actual and coherent process of inquiry according to which Peirce sought to transform precritical practices into reformed or postcritical practices. This is the process of pragmatic inquiry *per se.*

As Peirce argued in 1878 and continued to argue in his mature work, pragmatic inquiry begins with real doubt: in John Dewey's helpful terms, it emerges out of a "problematic situation."[66] Peirce emphasized the *reality* of this doubt to distinguish his critical commonsensism from Descartes' attempt to launch inquiry out of the academic exercise of feigning doubts. "Do you call it *doubting*," he asked, "to write down on a piece of paper that you doubt? If so, doubt has nothing to do with any serious business."[67] Peirce explained that the danger of adopting what he dubbed "paper doubts" was that, in pretending to doubt what we trust (the philosophic modernist's way of "crying wolf!"), we fall into the habit of mistrusting the very principles of reasoning we need to resolve the problems that actually confront us. On the basis of his theories of signs and of habits, he argued that *real* doubt, on the other hand, is the most reliable index of our immediate contact with reality. We may summarize his argument as follows.

If our habits of thought-and-practice are ultimate interpretants of the world as a vast symbol, then we know the world intimately only through these habits. Unlike the "sense impressions" described by the nominalistic empiricists, however, these habits are not simply forced upon us through our encounters with the world. The world is, indeed, what we actually encounter through the senses, but Peirce's critique of nominalism means that we do not *know* what we encounter simply by sensing it. Our "knowledge" of the world is the way we have learned to act successfully in it, where "success" is judged by the degree to which our interactions with the world display the effects we expect them to display. But when and how do we evaluate this success? Every time I look at a tree, do I ask myself, "Is that the way I expected it would look?" First of all, "seeing" is not the right metaphor to invoke here, because the knowledge we are discussing concerns our encountering the *realities* of things and not merely their appearances. Peirce argued early on in his work that we have acquired our conception of "reality" from scholastic usage, where *realitas* referred to the *forcible* character of the world: its insistence on being something whether I like it or not or, in Peirce's pragmatic terminology, the *difference* it makes for the way I live in the world. When I look at a tree, I do not usually ask myself what difference the tree makes in how I live; this means I am not usually interested in knowing about the tree's reality. But what if a tree falls on my house? or what if I need its lumber to warm my house and cook my food? or what if we discover that the life-sustaining character of our atmosphere depends on the tree's health? or what, finally, if I discover that the kind of creature I happen to be is one that lives well only in the company of trees? In all these cases, the tree makes a great difference in how I live. And in all these cases, I say I know the tree when my interactions with it do not surprise me. When they do surprise me, I say I want to inquire further, to find out what's there. According to Peirce, my surprise is a sign that the ways I have learned to interact with the tree are inadequate: for example, that cutting down every tree for fuel is not what I wanted to do, or that assuming that this specimen belongs to the genus *Acer* was not what I wanted to assume. According to Peirce, finally, my lack of surprise is a sign that, at this moment, the tree and I share a settled relationship. A settled relationship is one I am not concerned to examine further, which suggests that, for me, my lack of surprise would not be a sign at all, because it would be something about which I would not find myself thinking.

Pragmatists have a tendency to argue that "if belief ain't broke, don't fix it"—in other words, that we must assume our beliefs are true if we have no reason to doubt them. If we follow this maxim, however, how can we distinguish between true beliefs and potentially false yet untested ones, or between knowing truly and knowing nothing? Peirce's response was embedded in his philosophic practice but not clearly explicated. It was that the only way to know whether or not our habits correspond to the world is to *act* on them and, then, to feel reassured that the habits that work as we expect them to are *reliable* sources of knowledge and to *know* that the habits that fail to work as expected are unreliable and must be reformed. Peirce would then affirm Socrates' maxim, but in this modified way: the un*lived* and thus unexamined life is not worth living. For we cannot examine habits we have not enacted, and it is up to the world and not ourselves to declare that our habits need re-examination. The first Peircean maxim is, therefore, "Engage the world actively and without prejudgment!" The second maxim is, "Examine thoroughly whatever you have reason to doubt!" The third is, "Find within the habits you have no reason to doubt the principles that will guide you in reforming those you must doubt!" Trusting these deeper habits is what Peirce called *commonsensism*. Trusting that experience might one day call even these habits into question is what Peirce called *fallibilism*. Fallibilism is not skepticism as much as it is modesty: trusting that, as powerful as is our capacity to know the world, our capacity to grow and learn more is even greater.

For the postmodernist, modernist thinking is an index of real doubt, even if it is misinterpreted by those who display it. Misinterpreting it, modernists cannot get on with the work of the second stage of pragmatic inquiry, which is to identify and examine in detail the habits of action whose inadequacies gave rise to this doubt in the first place. This is empirical inquiry, understood pragmatically. The pragmatic inquirer is, first, a historian, who examines the biographical-social-cultural contexts of modernist doubts in order to offer reasonable hypotheses about the sorts of habits that may have informed modernists' lives. The inquirer is, secondly, a transcendental critic of a Kantian sort, who asks what a modernist must have presupposed about the world in order to have offered such and such a claim and such and such a criticism. This search for presuppositions was Peirce's critical commonsensism: manifested here as an activity of recovering the foundations of belief that underlie and are often covered over by modernist criticisms and, thus, of distinguishing just what needs to be criticized from what needs to be reaffirmed in order to respond constructively to this criticism. Linking together historical and critical research, the inquirer offers reasonable hypotheses about how the modernist's claims indicate precisely what was wrong with which inherited habits of action.

The third stage of pragmatic inquiry is to recommend ways of reforming those inherited habits of action, to respond to modernist concerns without abandoning the precritical habits out of which they emerge. The work of this stage is constructive and realistic imagination. It is to imagine new ways of acting, within the contexts of inherited beliefs and habits and as constrained by the demands of problem solving. Peirce believed the constructive imagination was guided by a logic of discovery he termed *abduction*. He said the ultimate norms guiding our discoveries may be revealed through a process of "musement," or the free play of imagination as it contemplates the orders of existence.[68] This is, in fact, the same sort of play informing the mathematical imagination that, Peirce said, underlay his phenomenology.[69] Given free play, the imagination gives uninhibited expression to the fundamental categories of our existence—Firstness, Secondness, and Thirdness—in the contemplation of which inquirers may construct norms for reforming our habits of action. The product of abduction is of practical import, because it offers possibilities that might really be enacted within our contexts of action: possibilities of real habit-change, enabling us to comprehend the world as it now displays itself. For Peirce, philosophy itself is the prototypical activity of constructively re-imagining the fundamental norms of action.

I move now from the question of what Peirce's postmodern thinking is to the question of what it tells us.

B. What Does Peirce's Postmodern Thinking Tell Us About?

Principle B1: Postmodern thinking tells us about the real. This principle brings us the reward for all our preparatory work: Peirce's claim that, *without* abandoning our modern habits of criticism and our fallibilism (and therefore reverting to *pre*modernism), we may have direct knowledge of reality. Call it a postmodern *permission*. We no longer *must* maintain what Richard Bernstein has labelled "the Cartesian anxiety." We have, indeed, discovered that our inherited traditions of belief and practice are fallible, but this discovery is not grounds for abandoning all those traditions, nor for feeling guilty whenever we suspect that, beneath all our critical training, we still have faith and trust in our capacities to know more than we admit we know. For Peirce, this suspicion—which he called our "cheerful hope"—is no merely subjective feeling, but an irrepressible index of our actual relationship to the real. Faith in this sense is no infantile wish for security, but the primary manifestation of our being in relationship to something other than ourselves and greater than ourselves, and that relationship *is* knowledge. Peirce did not read Hebrew, but the ancient Israelite term for "knowledge"—*yidiah*—may convey Peirce's claim better than any of the terms he used. For the Biblical authors, "to know" is "to have intercourse with"—with the world, with one's spouse, with God. That is, it is to enter into intimate relationship with these others, retaining one's own identity while recognizing that, in one's own being, one is not alone, but with others. To have this faith-knowledge means to recognize that, as in an argument with a lover, our errors, doubts and struggles for understanding are all aspects of our relationship to a reality that remains with us even in our moments of uncertainty.

Modern philosophers make much of the distinction between epistemology and ontology. For the postmodern Peirce, these modes of inquiry are distinguishable but not clearly distinct. Seen as a semiotic activity, the process of human knowing is not self-contained but intimately related to the processes that it interprets and the processes that interpret it. To refer to "being" is to refer to the generalizable characters of all processes with which human knowledge is potentially in relationship. To refer to "reality" is, following Peirce's adaptation of scholastic usage, to refer to that which lies outside of the knower but remains in relationship with him or her—in Peirce's terms, that "which has such and such characters, whether anybody thinks it to have those characters or not"[70] *and* that which *makes a difference* in how we think, which means in how we will act.

Contrary to what he claimed, Peirce's realism is not exactly a "scholastic realism."[71] It is, rather, what we might call a pragmatic, critical, or postmodern realism—that which remains of scholastic realism once it is made to answer the criticisms of it that are implicit in modernist thinking. For example, the postmodern realist will claim, against modern nominalists, that we can encounter and accurately describe real generality in the world—that our generalizations about the world are not merely expressive of our own desires and interests. However, this is not the generality of abstract possibility we customarily attribute to Platonic forms or essences. It is, instead, the generality of reasonable predictions, which is vague in its definition and probabilistic in its reference.[72] In Peirce's words, the purposes to which semiotic thinking refers are predictions about what *would* happen if certain conditions of experience were met. Peirce's strongest response to modern nominalism is that, as a sign of what is wrong with aspects of scholastic thinking, modernist thinking itself displays the

generality of a reasonable prediction: if we were to emend scholastic thinking in such and such a way, then it would not warrant such and such a modernist objection.

The ontological implication of Peirce's postmodern thinking is, then, that human knowledge is the symbolic mode of intercourse between the processes that, from our perspective, we say take place "out there" and the processes that we say take place "in here"—the processes of human activity in the world. From the perspective of "in here," it is helpful to refer to this intercourse as a semiotic activity: viewing our thoughts as symbols of reality and viewing our efforts to connect thoughts to actions as ways of correcting and perfecting the clarity of these symbols. From the perspective of "out there," it is helpful to refer to this intercourse as a relationship among three kind of habits: "things" as habits of worldly action, our "practices" as habits of action in the world, and "thinking" as an activity of habit-change, through which the two forms of habit adjust their relations, one to the other. From these perspectives, pragmatic inquiry represents a worldly activity as much as it does a human one. As an expression of modernist practices of critical thinking, it displays to us the merely human contexts of our knowledge of reality: we do not know reality independently of the ways in which we practice our knowledge. As an expression of the postmodernist re-evaluation of modernist thinking, it reminds us that we have no reason to assume that reality could be known in any other way than this: that reality is that which, while calling attention to itself forcibly, is known fallibilistically, contextually, and relationally. As knowers, we are, in other words, part of the reality we know. In the words of the theologian Abraham Heschel, as knowers, each of us discovers that "I am that which is not mine."[73]

Principle B2: Postmodern thinking displays the realities of chance, force, and love as principles of evolution. Pragmatic realism is, thus, the principle that the elemental or indubitable characters of our own habits of thinking are also characters of the reality with which we are in relationship. The principle reflects an evolutionary conception of the adaptation of mind and world; "It seems incontestable . . . that the mind of man is strongly adapted to the comprehension of the world."[74] It is ultimately "evolution" that "made man's mind to be so constructed"[75] (although Peirce wavered on the question of whether or not natural selection was a sufficient explanation of the remarkable accuracy of our insights into Nature[76]). The upshot is that the elemental characters of our thinking are trustworthy interpretants of the reality of this world, or that, until we are shown otherwise, we expect to interact successfully with the world when our habits of action display these characters. As we have seen, Peirce discovered that he could reduce the characters of his postmodern habit of thinking to three elemental categories, which he labelled Firstness, Secondness, and Thirdness. He then found he had no reason not to assume that these categories correspond to the three elemental properties of the reality with which he was in relationship.[77]

In a series of *Monist* articles in 1892-93, Peirce claimed that the cosmos evolves in three ways: according to fortuitous variation (*tychastic* evolution), according to mechanical necessity (*anancastic* evolution), and according to creative love (*agapastic* evolution). He said "the mere propositions that absolute chance, mechanical necessity and the law of love are severally operative in the cosmos may receive the names of *tychism, anancism,* and *agapism*."[78] I find it convenient to use these three terms to refer to the three principles according to which Peirce attributed Firstness, Secondness, and Thirdness to the experiential universe.

According to Peirce's principle of *tychism,* Firstness is a sign of the objective reality of *chance,* or spontaneity, in the experiential universe:

> By thus admitting pure spontaneity or life as a character of the universe, acting always and everywhere though restrained within narrow bounds by law, producing infinitestimal departures from law continually, and great ones with infinite infrequency, I account for all the variety and diversity of the universe, in the only sense in which the really *sui generis* and new can be said to be accounted for.[79]

This *tychistic* principle is based on the point, made earlier, that the laws of nature are really habits: "the so-called immutable laws of nature . . . are not ultimate, but are the expression and indeed the outcome of tendencies, associations and habits which spread and grow."[80]

According to Peirce's principle of *anancism,* Secondness is a sign of the objective reality of brute force in the world—the direct impress of reality. Secondness displays the dyadic dimension of reality—of action/reaction, inner/outer, will and resistance—which serves as the primary index of actual existence, as opposed to essence, or merely possible being.

According to Peirce's principle of *agapism,* Thirdness is a sign of the objective reality of love in the universe: the power of ideas to attract and draw together otherwise independent or opposing actions, giving rise to communities of being whose emergence represents the end of evolutionary growth. As articulated within the vocabulary of semiotics, the attractive power of ideas is the power of symbols to elicit meaning with respect to their interpretants. In these terms, the cosmic power of love is displayed in the reality of semiosis, understood now as a cosmic process whose end is the generation of communities of interpretation. These are communities of being, with respect to which the universe is what Peirce called "a vast representamen, a great symbol of God's purpose, working out its conclusions in living realities."[81]

Peirce's metaphysics was unabashedly anthropomorphic: "I hold . . . that [humanity] is so completely hemmed in by the bounds of [its] possible practical experience, [its] mind so restricted to being the instrument of [its] needs, that [it] cannot, in the least, *mean*

anything that transcends those limits."[82] "'Anthropomorphic' is what pretty much all conceptions are at bottom. . . . It is well to remember that every single truth of science is due to the affinity of the human soul to the soul of the universe, imperfect as that affinity no doubt is."[83] Consequently, Peirce's conceiving the universe as a vast symbol meant that, observing how humans create and interpret symbols, he also conceived of this symbol as the creation of a cosmic symbol-maker—God. God is therefore known to us as the author of that process of semiosis of which any understanding we have of the universe is a symbol, and of which the multifarious processes of reality are interpretants. God as creator is therefore God as symbolizer, and we do not say "God has created the world," but "God is now creating it."[84] God is here and here and here, as source of this vast symbol whose meanings we discover anew now and now and now.

As Michael Raposa has shown in *Peirce's Philosophy of Religion,* Peirce's metaphysics is thus a metaphysical theology. Because the rules of reasoning on which it is based are semiotic rather than propositional or logocentric rules, Raposa reterms it a "theosemiotics."[85] Theosemiotics is the way we conceive of God's symbol-creating activity by analogy with humanity's symbol-creating activity, which Peirce called abductive reasoning. Within Peirce's pragmatic theory of inquiry, abduction is a way of generating hypotheses about how to reform inherited habits of action. Reasoning anthropomorphically, we may then consider God's creativity to be reformatory: the creation of new ways of being out of old ways, rather than out of "nothing." If so, the symbols God creates would be symbols of new worlds, rather than icons of old ones. These symbols would have meaning for us in the way they direct us to reinterpret our worlds of experience, rather than in the way they imitate an antecedent reality.[86] The ultimate interpretants of God's symbol-making would therefore be forms of habit-change, rather than mere forms (*eide*) or the pictures we may have of God and of God's creation.

We see, therefore, the theosemiotic significance of Peirce's postmodern thinking. As a form of habit-change, this thinking qualifies as a potential interpretant of God's symbol-making activity. To imitate God is not to make claims about what the world is, but to change one's actions in a way that represents the way God changes this world. Postmodern thinking is modern thinking that has reclaimed its transformational power by reclaiming its theological, or theosemiotic, ground.

C. To Whom was Peirce's Postmodern Thinking Addressed?

Principle C1: It was addressed to the suffering self. At the outset of this essay, we noted that Peirce first offered his pragmatism as a critique of modernist conceptions of selfhood. Still working from within modernist habits of thinking, Peirce criticized as simply false the modernist conception of the self as an incorporeal substance, ultimately unknowable, self-contained, and ultimately self-referring. As stated earlier, he argued that the self, considered as a separate existence, "is only a negation."[87] As a postmodernist, however, Peirce came close to acknowledging that, behind his earlier protestations, lay a persistently modernist conception of his own selfhood. Veiling his own loneliness and distress, his complaint and his need for truth and love, he had sought to secure for himself an existence separate from the modernist selfhood he criticized. As postmodernist, Peirce no longer required this separateness. He could confess his own modernity without despairing of it, because he had acquired the resources to redeem that modernity rather than abandon it. The early twentieth-century Jewish philosopher Franz Rosenzweig clarified this confessional dimension of postmodernism in his major work, *The Star of Redemption.*[88] As interpreted by Robert Gibbs, Rosenzweig understood the Biblical injunction "You shall love the Lord your God . . ." as a prototype of the imperative that makes human relationship possible: "love me!" "Only this command is the speech of love. Why? Because the speech of the lover must itself love."[89] In speaking the words "love me," the lover calls for a response from the beloved, calling the beloved out of his or her separateness. To respond to the call to love is, however, first to acknowledge that one was indeed separate: in need of love, but not yet called to acknowledge the need. This acknowledgment is confession:

> For Rosenzweig this confession is itself the process of atonement *[Versöhnung]*, which the soul undertakes in the presence of the lover's love. I can only come to terms with my own false self-reliance, my own illusion of completeness without love, in the presence of my lover's demand to love. And as I speak my way through this process of accepting my past as mine, as myself, even including the self that has heard the command to love, I recognize the past is not being held against me.[90]

As postmodernist, Peirce could love himself and thus recognize that his past, as modernist, was not being held against him. This is to confess the inadequacy of his self's separateness, while acknowledging, with compassion, the suffering signified by that separateness.

Interpreted this way, Peirce's postmodern thinking was addressed to the suffering self of his modernity. It was addressed to it the way a symbol is addressed to its interpretant, which means both that Peirce's thinking had *meaning with respect to* this suffering self *and* that his thinking *performed something with respect to it.* In Rosenzweig's terms, the performance was to offer it the command of love and, thus, to bring it to confess its separateness and to accept responsibility for responding to the other with whom it is in relationship. In Peirce's terms,

> The Christian religion, if it has anything distinctive . . . is distinguished from other religions by its precept about the Way of Life. . . . Now what is this way of life? Again I appeal to the universal Christian conscience to testify that it is

simply love. As far as it is contracted to a rule of ethics, it is: Love God, and love your neighbor. . . . The belief in the law of love is the Christian faith.[91]

Principle C2: Peirce's postmodern thinking is addressed to an antecedent and to a prospective community of inquirers. As a redeeming word, Peirce's postmodern thinking offered the modernist self permission to acknowledge its relatedness to others. In Peirce's words, "The Gospel of Christ says that progress comes from every individual merging his individuality in sympathy with his neighbors."[92] As a directive for undertaking corrective, pragmatic inquiry, Peirce's thinking offered the modernist self a procedure for reclaiming its relatedness and thus joining with its neighbor. The first step of this procedure is for the self to relate the narrative history of its suffering: that it belonged to an antecedent community of practitioners, that it grew dissatisfied with this community, that its dissatisfaction bred its self-isolation, and that its practices of dogmatic inquiry have veiled its history and thus reinforced its self-isolation. The self must confess its identity: "I am a modernist." The second step is for the self, now embodied as a modernist, to acknowledge her identity as a past member of that antecedent community. The modernist must declare this complex identity: "I have entered modernity as a scholastic, or a Catholic, or a Jew, or whatever I was when I left the community in anger." The third step is for this "modernist who once was . . ." to recognize that, while that community belongs only to the past, other communities may emerge from it, reformed through the kind of criticism she would offer. Rather than fear community, she may reclaim her criticism as part of the process of communal life and growth. The fourth step is for this "modernist who will belong again . . ." to locate those who would listen to her criticisms and join with her in the process of communal reformation. These may also be former members of her antecedent community: members now of what would become reformed scholastic, or reformed Catholic, or reformed Jewish, communities.

Peirce's postmodern thinking appears to be addressed, in particular, to a modernist in this fourth stage of corrective inquiry. I imagine that, not yet re-integrated into the reforming community for which she is searching, this modernist would first try to identify the attributes this community *would* have if she were to find it. Peirce's pragmaticist inquiry may then be reinterpreted as an abductive inquiry, whose purpose was to generate reasonable hypotheses about what these attributes would be.[93] Grounded in his mathematics of triadic relations,[94] Peirce's phenomenology suggested that such a community would be characterized by its Thirdness, or its mediational capacity. Peirce's discovery that symbols are paradigmatic Thirds suggests that the paradigmatic activity of a community may be interpretation. The community would offer its individual members interpretants (contexts of interpretation, for example, values, beliefs, narratives) with respect to which the world, as a vast symbol, has meaning. Individual members of the community would then be interrelated by way of these interpretants; the members would find their commonality in the common meanings these interpretants assigned to the world. Strictly within the terms of Peirce's semiotics, however, the community might appear to be *too* coherent a phenomenon, perhaps impervious to reform. Peirce's theory of habit-change suggested that the interpretation of symbols is a transformational, rather than a merely constitutive, activity—that is, that it establishes meaning by transforming prior meanings rather than by generating meaning *ex nihilo*. According to this theory, the concept of community displays different modalities, and we should be wary of reducing the concept to any one modality.

From the perspective of semiotics as a phenomenological and classificatory science, community appears in its Firstness as an interwoven collection of interpretants and, thus, of possible meanings. From the perspective of Peirce's theory of habit-change as a form of normative science, members of a community emerge as individuals when they suffer—that is, when their experiences of failed expectation breed doubts about communally secured meanings. From this perspective, community first appears in its Secondness, as an arena of oppositions between a disintegrated collection of dissatisfied individuals and what appears to them to be a mechanically or artificially collected block of outmoded signs. According to the pragmaticist, modernists tend to view community, exclusively, in either its Firstness or Secondness: describing community, in the former case, as an unachievably ideal state of epistemological and social integration; or, in the latter case, as the all-too-real source of the author-itarianism that restricts the free expression of the human spirit. Peirce's theory of habit-change, however, provides a perspective from which to view community in its Thirdness as well. This is to view community as the process through which individuals, stimulated by their doubts, undertake the cooperative, pragmatic inquiry through which imperfect communities of the past are transformed into the more perfect communities of the future. From this perspective, community is what Peirce called a community of inquiry, the reformed and reforming community of scientists. According to Peirce's pragmatic theory of inquiry, these scientists draw their principles of inquiry from out of the heritage of the communities they serve as both reformers and critics. To uncover these principles they must, ultimately, imitate the process of divine creativity itself. Otherwise put, pragmatic inquiry was, for Peirce, the ultimate interpretant of God's creative activity, and the community of pragmatic scientists constituted the reformed church.

Principle C3: Peirce's postmodern thinking is addressed to the universal church of pragmatic scientists. Peirce never tested his elaborate hypothesis about what the attributes of a reformed community *might be,* because he never located the reformed community to which he, in particular, belonged. For my own way of thinking, this means that, while he jumped ahead to a fifth step of pragmatic inquiry, Peirce failed to complete the fourth step. Others may argue that Peirce did complete the fourth step, because his own reformed community was either the community of pragmatic philosophers or, more broadly considered, the community of pragmatically minded scientists. I hesitate to accept this argument, because it is not apparent to me that any identifiable community of scientists or philosophers inherits the mantle of what Peirce took to be the Christian Church. I remain undecided on the question, however, and will, in closing, respect Peirce's own explicit claim. This claim may belong to a fifth step in pragmatic inquiry,[95] in which, already located in her reformed community, the modernist *cum* postmodernist interprets the principles of community to be principles that integrate individual communities as well as individual persons. She seeks to find her place in a universal church, conceived as a community of communities.[96] In Raposa's words, "It is the scientific community, after all, its members devoted to the discovery of 'God's truth,' that Peirce selected as the model for the Christian Church."[97] In Peirce's words:

> Man's highest developments are social; and religion, though it begins in a seminal individual inspiration, only comes to full flower in a great church coextensive with a civilization. This is true of every religion, but supereminently so of the religion of love. Its ideal is that the whole world shall be united in the bond of a common love of God accomplished by each man's loving his neighbor. Without a church, the religion of love can have but a rudimentary existence; and a narrow, little exclusive church is almost worse than none. A great catholic church is wanted.

> The invisible church does now embrace all Christendom. Every man who has been brought up in the bosom of Christian civilization does really believe in some form of the principle of love, whether he is aware of doing so, or not.

> . . . Let us endeavor, then, with all our might to draw together the whole body of believers in the law of love into sympathetic unity of consciousness. . . .

> To those who for the present are excluded from the churches, and who, in the passionate intensity of their religious desire, are talking of setting up a church for the scientifically educated, a man of my stripe must say, Wait if you can; it will be but a few years longer; but if you cannot wait, why then Godspeed! Only do not, in your turn, go and draw lines so as to exclude such as believe a little less—or, still worse, to exclude such as believe a little more—than yourselves. . . .

> A religious civilization is a somewhat idle affair unless it be sworn in as a regiment of that great army that takes life in hand, with all its delights, in grimmest fight to put down the principle of self-seeking, and to make the principle of love triumphant. It has something more serious to think about than the phraseology of the articles of war. Fall into the ranks then; follow your colonel. Keep

your one purpose steadily and alone in view, and you may promise yourself the attainment of your sole desire, which is to hasten the chariot wheels of redeeming love![98]

NOTES

[1] Joseph Brent, "A Study of the Life of Charles Sanders Peirce," Ph.D. dissertation, UCLA (May 1960), 31. This is the best source of biographical information on Peirce. I have also drawn on Max Fisch, "Introduction," *Writings of Charles S. Peirce: A Chronological Edition, 1, 1857-1866,* ed. Max Fisch et al. (Bloomington: Indiana University Press, 1982), xv-xxxv; and Murray Murphey, *The Development of Peirce's Philosophy* (Cambridge: Harvard University Press, 1961).

[2] "The Place of Our Age in the History of Civilization" (1863), cited in *Charles S. Peirce: Selected Writings (Values in a Universe of Change),* ed. Philip P. Wiener (New York: Dover Publications, 1958), 13-14

[3] C. S. Peirce to Smith, July 25, 1908, Scientific Correspondence. Cited in Murray Murphey, *The Development of Peirce's Philosophy,* 15.

[4] Charles Peirce, "My Life written for the Class-Book," in *Writings of Charles S. Peirce: A Chronological Edition, I, 1857-1866,* 1-3.

[4a] Brent, "A Study of the Life of Charles Sanders Peirce," 71.

[5] He was invited to give several lecture series at Harvard: the prestigious Lowell Lectures in 1866, when he was only twenty-five; a series of lectures on logic in 1869-70; a series on pragmatism in 1903; and another Lowell series in 1903. He held one significant position, Lecturer in Logic at the Johns Hopkins University, between 1879 and 1884.

[6] "Philosophical Conceptions and Practical Results," *University of California Chronicle* (September 1898), repr. in William James, *The Writings of William James,* ed. John J. McDermott (Chicago and London: University of Chicago Press, 1977), 347-48.

[7] See Max Fisch's account, "Was There a Metaphysical Club in Cambridge?", *Studies in the Philosophy of Charles Sanders Peirce, Second Series,* ed. Edward Moore and Richard Robin (Amherst: University of Massachusetts Press, 1964), 3-32.

[8] "Questions Concerning Certain Faculties Claimed for Man," *Journal of Speculative Philosophy* (hereafter *JSP*) 2 (1868), 103-14, reprinted in *Collected Papers of Charles Sanders Peirce,* ed. Charles Hartshorne and Paul Weiss (Cambridge: Harvard University Press, 1931-58), vol. 5, paras. 213-63 (future references to this collection will be to *CP* followed by volume and paragraph number[s], e.g., *CP* 5.213-63); "Some Conse-

quences of Four Incapacities," *JSP* 2 (1868), 140-57, repr. *CP* 5.264-317; and "Grounds of Validity of the Laws of Logic," *JSP* 2 (1868), 193-208, repr. *CP* 5.318-57.

[9] "The Universal Categories" (1903), *CP* 5.41-65, at 61.

[10] "Archimedes sought only a firm and immovable point in order to move the entire earth from one place to another. Surely great things are to be hoped for if I am lucky enough to find at least one thing that is certain and indubitable" (René Descartes, "Second Meditation," in *Discourse on Method and Meditations on First Philosophy,* trans. Donald Cress (Indianapolis: Hackett, 1980), 61.

[11] *CP* 5.214 ("Questions" [1868]).

[12] *CP* 5.223 ("Questions").

[13] Ibid.

[14] *CP* 5.227, citing Kant's *Werke,* vii (2), 11.

[15] *CP* 5.312 ("Some Consequences" [1868]).

[16] Peirce overcame his earlier dogmatic logicism by arguing for a "critical" commonsensism: the doctrine that our reasoning is guided by habits of belief that are functionally indubitable but that remain subject to future criticism.

[17] As argued by David Savan in "On the Origins of Peirce's Phenomenology," *Studies in the Philosophy of Charles Sanders Peirce, First Series,* ed. Philip P. Wiener and Frederic H. Young (Cambridge: Harvard University Press, 1952), 185-94. For a similar view, see Murphey, *The Development of Peirce's Philosophy.*

[18] "Illustrations of the Logic of Science," *Popular Science Monthly* 12-13 (1877-78), repr. *CP* 5.358-410, 6.395-427, 2.619-93.

[19] "The Fixation of Belief" (1877), *CP* 5.358-87.

[20] *CP* 5.12 (1905). See Bain's *The Emotions and the Will* (New York: Longman's Green, 1875), ch. 11.

[21] *CP* 5.371, 374, 375 ("Fixation" [1877]).

[22] *CP* 5.377 ("Fixation"). The citations to follow are from paragraphs 378-85.

[23] As Peirce adds in an 1893 note to this article; see *CP* 5.382n.1.

[24] Susan Haack, "Descartes, Peirce and the Cognitive Community," in *The Relevance of Charles Peirce,* ed. Eugene Freeman (La Salle, Ill.: The Hegeler Institute for The Monist Library of Philosophy, 1983), 238-63, at 254.

[25] I take this principle to be implicit in Peirce's 1878 answer to his own question of how induction works; or,

more precisely, how we come to offer reasonable hypotheses about what we experience. He wrote: "It seems incontestable . . . that the mind of man is strongly adapted to the comprehension of the world; at least, so far as this goes, that certain conceptions, highly important for such a comprehension, naturally arise in his mind. . . . How are we to explain this adaptation? The great utility and indispensableness of the conceptions of time, space, and force, even to the lowest intelligence, are such as to suggest that they are the results of natural selection" ("Order of Nature," *Popular Science Monthly* 13 [1878], repr. *CP* 6.395-427, at 417-18).

26 "How To Make Our Ideas Clear," *Popular Science Monthly* 12 (1878), 286-302, repr. *CP* 5.388-410, at 402.

27 See above, in the introductory paragraphs.

28 *CP* 5.317 ("Some Consequences" [1868]).

29 "What Pragmatism Is," *Monist* 15 (1905), 161-81, repr. *CP* 5.411-37, at 414 (emphasis added).

30 "Philosophical Conceptions and Practical Results" (see note 6, above).

31 In John McDermott's words, "this marked the beginning of the pragmatic movement" (from a note in his annotated bibliography of James' writings, appended to *The Writings of William James: A Comprehensive Edition,* ed. McDermott [Chicago: The University of Chicago Press, 1977], 837).

32 William James, *Pragmatism: A New Name for Some Old Ways of Thinking,* ed. Bruce Kuklick (Indianapolis: Hackett Publishing Co., 1981), 26.

33 John E. Smith, *Purpose and Thought: The Meaning of Pragmatism* (New Haven: Yale University Press, 1978), 41. Smith refers the reader to James' account of concepts in William James, *Some Problems of Philosophy* (New York and London: Longman's, Green & Co., 1911), ch. 4-6.

34 Peirce's preferred spelling for "semiotics" was *semeiotic,* but for this non-technical essay I prefer to use a spelling more readers will recognize. Peirce's triadic semiotic is to be distinguished from that dyadic semiotic originated by Ferdinand de Saussure and now influencing much semiotic work on the Continent.

35 "Issues of Pragmatism" (1905), *CP* 5.438-63, at 440.

36 "What Pragmatism Is" (1905), *CP* 5.411-37, at 432. On semiotics, see the discussion below in section IV.

37 On one occasion, he labelled these first-level practices "B-reasonings" ("Why Study Logic?" [1902], *CP* 2.119-218, at 189).

38 He labelled these "A-reasonings" (ibid.).

39 As we will discuss later, one of the central principles of Peirce's pragmaticism was that the sign of the deeper or second-level practices is their indubitability. Peirce claimed that what we *mean* by "knowing reality" is equivalent to what we know of the world when our reasoning is guided by indubitable practices of reasoning, or what he also called indubitable beliefs. Peirce therefore believed that, by reaffirming our capacity to identify fundamental practices, he was reaffirming our capacity to encounter reality directly.

40 The school of Thomas Reid (d. 1796), whose response to Hume's skepticism took what would become the non-Kantian route of affirming our "original beliefs." See Thomas Reid, *Works,* 2 vols., ed. Sir William Hamilton (Edinburgh: 1846-1863).

41 *CP* 5.445 ("Issues of Pragmaticism" [1905]).

42 Ibid.

43 "Methods for Attaining Truth" (1898), *CP* 5.574-604, at 587.

44 Richard Robin, "Peirce's Doctrine of the Normative Sciences," in *Studies in the Philosophy of Charles Sanders Peirce, Second Series,* ed. Moore and Robin, 271-88, at 272.

45 See Peirce's logic of inquiry in "A Neglected Argument for the Reality of God," *Hibbert Journal* 7 (1908), 90-112, repr. *CP* 6.467-73.

46 Peirce's preferred spelling was *semeiosis.* See note 34.

47 "A Survey of Pragmaticism" (1906), *CP,* 5.464-96, at 484. For the most recent argument in support of Peirce's claims for the irreducibility of triadic relations to dyadic or monadic relations, see Robert Burch, *A Peircean Reduction Thesis* (Lubbock: Texas Tech University Press, 1991).

48 "The Simplest Mathematics" (1902), *CP* 2.227-323, at 233.

49 "Three Kinds of Goodness" (1903), *CP* 5.120-50, at 148. In correspondence, Kenneth Ketner has pointed out that there were other kinds of diagrams in Peirce's system besides visual ones—"he admitted audio diagrams and tactile diagrams as well." See also Ketner, "Peirce's 'Most Lucid and Interesting Paper': An Introduction to Cenopythagoreanism," *International Philosophical Quarterly* 26 (1986): 375-92.

50 He called these the activities of *colligation, iteration,* and *erasure* (referring to the activity of *seeing* the general rule by attending to the general features of the repetitions and ignoring or erasing the other, nongeneral features). See *CP* 5.579 (1898), where Peirce notes that there are modes of deduction in which not all three of the elements are present: for example "in ordinary syl-

logism the iteration may be said to be absent. And that is the reason that ordinary syllogism can be worked by a machine." Ordinary syllogism, that is, lacks the creativity otherwise present in mathematical reasoning. See Kenneth Ketner, "Peirce and Turing: Comparisons and Conjectures," *Semiotica* 68/1-2 (1988), 33-61.

[51] Peirce classified phenomenology (which he came to call "phaneroscopy") as the first subscience of *philosophy*. He said that philosophy "limits itself to so much of truth as can be inferred from common experience" ("An Outline Classification of the Sciences," *CP* 1.180-202, at 184). Its second subscience was "normative science," comprised of *aesthetics, ethics,* and *logic.* Its third subscience was metaphysics.

[52] *CP* 5.122 ("Three Kinds of Goodness" [1903]).

[53] "Phenomenology: Introduction" (1905), *CP* 1.284-94, at 284.

[54] See, e.g., *CP* 1.339 (*c.* 1895).

[55] "A Detailed Classification of the Sciences" (1902), *CP* 1.203-83, at 246.

[56] *CP* 2.227 (*c.* 1897).

[57] All three references are from *CP* 2.247-49 (1903).

[58] Peirce's semiotics is, of course, a vast enterprise to which the reader is here merely introduced. See Peirce's *Semiotic and Significs: The Correspondence between Charles S. Peirce and Victoria Lady Welby,* ed. C. Hardwick (Bloomington: Indiana University Press, 1977). For some recent introductory essays, see John Dely, *Introducing Semiotic* (Bloomington: Indiana University Press, 1982), and Max Fisch, *Peirce, Semiotic, and Pragmatism* (Bloomington: Indiana University Press, 1986).

[59] William James, *The Principles of Psychology* (1890; New York: Dover, 1950), vol. 1, 104.

[60] Ibid., 104-05.

[61] See "A Guess at the Riddle" (1890), *CP* 1.354-416, esp. 385-94. Peirce claimed that these capacities can be reduced to three, corresponding to the three categories of his phenomenology: the capacity to feel spontaneously (Firstness), the capacity to react to determining stimuli (Secondness), and the capacity to form habits (Thirdness). He viewed habit-formation as the physiological manifestation of the sign-taking capacity: habits are the ultimate interpretants of the world's signs.

[62] Cf. *CP* 5.480 ("A Survey of Pragmaticism" [1905]).

[63] I believe it would be more precise to say that the world is something with whose existence we can converse, *and* whose creation we can imitate, in the ways we act.

[64] *CP* 5.478-81 ("A Survey").

[65] By way of illustration, Peirce wrote: "I well remember when I was a boy, and my brother Herbert, now our minister at Christiania, was scarce more than a child, one day, as the whole family were at table, some spirit from a 'blazer,' or 'chafing dish,' dropped on the muslin dress of one of the ladies and was kindled; and how instantaneously he jumped up, and did the right thing, and how skillfully each motion was adapted to the purpose. I asked him afterward about it; and he told me that since Mrs. Longfellow's death, it was that he had often run over in imagination all the details of what ought to be done in such an emergency. It was a striking example of a real habit produced by exercises in the imagination." (*CP* 5.487n.1 [ibid.])

[66] Peirce tended to use the terms "doubt" or "surprise," rather than the objective correlate of doubt, which, after John Dewey, I am labelling a "problem." In his 1878 papers, Peirce referred to the "doubt" that stimulates inquiry.

[67] *CP* 5.416 ("What Pragmatism Is" [1905]). Peirce continued, "But do not make believe [earlier in the paragraph, he wrote 'Dismiss make-believes']; if pedantry has not eaten all the reality out of you, recognize, as you must, that there is much that you do not doubt in the least."

[68] See p. 61, above.

[69] See the discussions of mathematics, above, in "Principle A1" (semiotics).

[70] See *CP* 5.430 ("What Pragmatism Is" [1905]), where Peirce cites Prantl, *Geschichte der Logik,* III, 91, Anm. 362.

[71] In *Peirce's Philosophy of Religion* (Bloomington and Indianapolis: Indiana University Press, 1989), 16, Michael Raposa writes that "while labelling himself as both a Scotist and a scholastic realist, . . . Peirce clearly found the medieval systems to be in need of serious repair." See also Raposa, "Habits and Essences," *Transactions of the Charles S. Peirce Society* XXV/3 (1989), 251-91; and John Boler, *Charles S. Peirce and Scholastic Realism* (Seattle: University of Washington Press, 1963).

[72] Peirce wrote that a *general* sign "turns over to the interpreter the right to complete [its] determination as he pleases" (*CP* 5.448 n. 1, "Issues of Pragmaticism" [1905]). The general indicates the character of a merely possible individual, representing the synthesis of a multitude of subjects. On the other hand, a *vague* sign "reserves for some other possible sign or experience the function of completing the determination" ("Consequences of Critical Common-Sensism" [*c.* 1905], *CP* 5.502-37, at 505). The vague denotes some of the characters of an *existent* individual, representing the synthesis of a multitude of predicates. To say that real gener-

ality is probabilistic in its reference means that the general signs that really refer to the world do not refer to discrete collections of objects, but to the probability that a certain collection would display certain characteristics. To say that real generality is vague in its definition means that general signs display these characteristics in a manner that is relative to the interpretant to which they are displayed.

[73] Abraham J. Heschel, *Between God and Man,* ed. Fritz Rothschild (New York: Free Press, 1959), 61.

[74] "The Order of Nature" (1878), *CP* 6.417.

[75] "Pragmaticism: The Normative Sciences" (1903), *CP* 5.14-40, at 28.

[76] See *CP* 6.419 ("The Order of Nature" [1878]).

[77] His examination of reality with respect to these categories corresponded to Kant's verifying, through the deductions of the *Critique of Pure Reason,* the results of his Analytic.

[78] "Evolutionary Love" (1893), *CP* 6.302.

[79] "The Doctrine of Necessity Examined," *The Monist* 2 (1892), 321-37, repr. *CP* 6.59.

[80] John E. Smith, *Purpose and Thought,* 141.

[81] "The Reality of Thirdness" (1903), *CP* 5.93-119, at 119.

[82] *CP* 5.536 ("Consequences of Critical Common-Sensism" [1905]).

[83] *CP* 5.47 ("The Universal Categories" [1903]).

[84] As suggested by the Biblical appellation for God: *ani ehyeh asher ehyeh,* "I will be there as I will be there" (Ex. 3.14). Interpreting this translation, rather than "I am what I am," Martin Buber wrote:

> And the great narrator helps us to get out of our minds the meaning of "being" *(esse)* in the use of the word by repeating in accordance with Biblical style the word *ehyeh* in the sense of "being present" *(adesse):* he anticipates the "I will be" in question with the related "I will be with thee" (Ex. 3.12), and follows it with the related "I will be with thy mouth." Thus YHVH does not not say that He exists absolutely or eternally, but—without pledging himself to any particular way of revelation ("as I will be there"), by which He also makes it known that He cannot be bound by any conjuration—that He wants to remain with His people, to go with them, to lead them (Martin Buber, *The Prophetic Faith,* trans. C. Witton-Davies [New York: Harper & Row, 1960], 29).

[85] Michael Raposa, *Peirce's Philosophy of Religion,* 142-54.

[86] Technically, these symbols display what Peirce called the irremediable *vagueness* of reality, meaning that a real thing does not simply possess a determinate character, but displays its characters relative to the other real things with which it is in relationship at a given time.

[87] *CP* 5.317 ("Some Consequences of Four Incapacities" [1868]).

[88] *The Star of Redemption,* trans. from the German *(Der Stern der Erlösung)* by William Halo (New York: Holt, Rinehart and Winston, 1971).

[89] From chapter 3 of the unedited manuscript of Robert Gibbs' forthcoming book, *Correlations: Rosenzweig and Levinas.*

[90] Ibid., 26. Rosenzweig wrote, in *The Star of Redemption,* 180: "'I have sinned.' Thus speaks the soul and abolishes shame. By speaking thus, referring purely back into the past, it purifies the present from the weakness of the past. 'I have sinned' means I was a sinner. With this acknowledgement of having sinned, however, the soul clears the way for the acknowledgement 'I am a sinner.' And this second acknowledgement is already the full admission of love."

[91] "A Religion of Science," *The Open Court* 7 (1893), 3559-60, repr. *CP* 6.441.

[92] "Evolutionary Love," *CP* 6.294.

[93] Technically speaking, this hypothesis-making, or abduction, would correspond to a transcendental analysis of the conditions of community reformation.

[94] IV.A., Principle A1, above.

[95] Or, as suggested, Peirce may conflate the fourth and fifth steps.

[96] Even when informed by Peirce's principles of fallibilism and of pragmatic doubt, such a conception may prove to be a totalizing or dogmatic one, in that the "principle of community" operative here is an extension of one community's conception of its own principle of integration.

[97] Raposa, *Peirce's Philosophy of Religion,* 99.

[98] *CP* 6.443-48 ("A Religion of Science" [1893]). Is this language of war and of desire not the language of the "modernist who will belong again . . ." but has not yet located his reforming community?

Cheryl B. Torsney (essay date 1993)

SOURCE: "Henry James, Charles Sanders Peirce, and the Fat Capon: Homoerotic Desire in *The American,*" in *The Henry James Review,* Vol. 14, 1993, pp. 166-78.

[In the following excerpt, Torsney examines the writings of both Henry James and Peirce to further her assumption that the two men were sexually involved.]

I

Jonathan Dollimore opens *Sexual Dissidence,* his influential examination of politics, perversity, and homosexual aesthetics, with a short narrative, "Wilde and Gide in Algiers." Gide, Dollimore explains, spent considerable time in Wilde's company in Paris in late 1891, and Wilde encouraged Gide to liberate himself from the very core of the younger man's identity, which was "rooted . . . in a Protestant ethic and high bourgeois moral rigour and repression which generated a kind of conformity which Wilde scorned" (3). Gide reports: "Wilde, I think, did me nothing but harm. In his company I had lost the habit of thinking. I had more varied emotions, but had forgotten how to bring order into them" (4) The pages from his diary in which he detailed their time together have been ripped out. As Richard Ellman remarks, "The main document about the psychic possession of Gide by Wilde is an absent one—a truly symbolist piece of evidence" (Dollimore 3). When Gide and Wilde met again in Algiers a little over two years later, Wilde procured an Arab boy, who was the agent of Gide's sexual liberation.

Gide and Wilde were not the first intellectuals to have a significant encounter in the City of Light. I will argue that Paris had hosted a similarly homoerotic couple about fifteen years earlier in the persons of James and Charles Sanders Peirce and that the main document detailing their relationship is not a sequence of absent diary entries but rather chapter five of James's novel *The American.* Next, I will suggest that the case of unrequited love to be examined in the novel is *not* Newman's for Claire de Cintré but Babcock's for Newman (and perhaps Peirce's for James), that this is the love fetishized in the gift Newman gives to his comrade. Finally, I will propose that Dollimore's figuration of the Gide/Wilde relationship as the conflict between a transgressive ethic and transgressive aesthetic aptly describes the Newman/Babcock alliance, suggesting a related way to read the homoerotic subtext of *The American.*

II

The philosopher and semiotician, the scholar who coined the term "pragmatism," Charles Sanders Peirce first visited the writer Henry James on 17 November 1875 in Paris, after William James encouraged his friend Charles, who was then working for the United States Geographical Survey on a series of experiments involving pendulums, to stop to see his brother. According to Henry's letters, Peirce "took [James] up very vigorously" (*HJL* II, 7), but the feeling was undoubtedly mutual.[1] Several weeks later, on 3 December, Henry reports on Peirce in two letters that announce the friendship but protest, perhaps a bit too much, about the incomplete nature of their affinity. First, he tells his Aunt Catherine Walsh that they "have several times dined together and gone to the theatre" but that James does not find Peirce "of thrilling interest" (*HJL* II, 11). Then, in a letter to William, Henry details that he and Peirce "meet every two or three days to dine together; but tho' we get on very well, our sympathy is economical rather than intellectual" (*HJL* II, 13). James writes on 20 December to his father that Peirce "turns out quite a 'sweet' fellow" (*HJL* II, 16).

What William's biographer Ralph Barton Perry terms "echoes of this strange fellowship" came from Peirce's side as well in several letters to William (536). Of the person he calls "a fine fellow" (21 November 1875) and "a splendid fellow" (16 December 1875), Peirce writes: "I admire him greatly and have only discovered two faults in him. One is that his digestion isn't quite that of an ostrich and the other is that he isn't as fond of turning over questions as I am, but likes to settle them and have done with them. A manly trait too, but not a philosophic one" (537).

William offered his brother some revealing advice about dealing with the philosopher:

> I am amused that you should have fallen into the arms of C. S. Peirce, whom I imagine you find a rather uncomfortable bedfellow, thorny & spinous, but the way to treat him is after the fabled "nettle" receipt: grasp firmly, contradict, push hard, make fun of him, and he is as pleasant as anyone; but be overawed by his sententious manner and his paradoxical & obscure statements, wait upon them as it were, for light to dawn, and you will never get a feeling of ease with him any more than I did for years, until I changed my course & treated him more or less chaffingly. (Brent 103)

On 14 March 1876, Henry writes to William:

> *Apropos* of "intimacies," Charles Peirce departed a week since for Berlin—my intimacy with whom mother says "greatly amuses" you. It was no intimacy, for during the last two months of his stay I saw almost nothing of him. He is a very good fellow, and one must appreciate his mental ability; but he has too little social talent, too little art of making himself agreeable. He had however a very lonely and dreary winter here and I should think would detest Paris. I did what I could to give him society. (*HJL* II, 32)

The two intellectuals continued to see each other and to correspond, even after Peirce left Paris. They met again in July 1876, as detailed in Henry's letter to William: "[I] enjoyed . . . his profound first-class intellect reflected in his ardent eyes. It will amuse you to hear that he is an *extreme* admirer of *Roderick Hudson:* a conquest which flatters me" (Brent 103).[1] Nearly a year later, in a 1 May 1877 letter to William, Peirce notes that he, Charles, had recently received a letter from Henry. Why should the friendship not continue? As Leon Edel discreetly notes, James and Peirce "helped each other through certain hours of loneliness" that dark winter of 1875-76 (233).

During this European sojourn, Charles Sanders Peirce was still married to Harriet Melusina Fay Peirce, a talented writer and activist whom he had married in October, 1861. An advocate of cooperative housekeeping and political action to give women a public voice, Zina had investigated alternative housekeeping, particularly in Great Britain, where her 1868-69 articles on the topic for the *Atlantic Monthly* had been reprinted as a book in Edinburgh and London.[2] The couple had no children and suffered profound difficulties throughout the marriage. Their finances were always tenuous, Charles forgetting to leave addresses at which he could be paid, paying no mind to mounting debt. Throughout his life permanent academic posts eluded him because his reputation as difficult and explosive overrode his reputation for brilliance. Because Charles apparently drank and was physically abusive, Zina lived much of the winter of 1884-85 with her parents, after having charged Charles with adultery. Despite the troubled marriage, Zina nonetheless agreed to accompany her husband to Europe in 1875 so that he could investigate European gravimetrics. They landed in Liverpool in September, but by the end of the month, Zina had returned to Cambridge, citing both health and marital problems. Peirce returned to America in August 1876, and by 1 May 1877, he and Zina were separated.

On 3 March 1882, Peirce sued his wife for divorce on the grounds of desertion. The divorce was granted on 24 April 1883, and on 30 April, Peirce announced his marriage to Juliette Froissy Pourtalai although the ceremony had been performed two days before his divorce from Zina became final. Little is known about the second Mrs. Peirce, and her identity is considered "the chief single unsolved problem of the [Peirce] biography" (Ketner and Klosel 399). She was probably sixteen years old at the time of the marriage, twenty-seven years younger than her husband, whom she called "Papa." Early in the marriage she spoke no English though after learning the language, she studied acting. The few other details we do know suggest an eccentric, possibly delusional woman. As Joseph Brent's new biography of Peirce details, although Juliette claimed royal associations with the Hapsburgs, she went to a great deal of trouble to conceal her true identity, fabricating both her maiden name Froissy and the name of her putative first husband, Pourtalai. Rumor has it that she sold her jewels for subsistence since Peirce was unable to earn a living through permanent academic appointment.[3]

It is easy enough to infer an explanation for the Peirces' marital history. A paranoid personality with a self-destructive streak, threatened, on the one hand, by Henry James and the Parisian hedonism he represented, and on the other by Zina, an independent New Woman, Charles Sanders Peirce withdrew from society, living out his days in the Pennsylvania countryside with a child-like caretaker wife, with whom he had a *mariage blanc.* If

we probe more deeply, however, Peirce, and, as we will see, his fictionalized double, Benjamin Babcock, resemble the sort of homosexual Jamesian characters Kaja Silverman describes in *Male Subjectivity at the Margins.* Like Strether, Peirce (and Babcock) "is a man without (economic) means," who is financed by a woman (166).[4] Like John Marcher, Peirce (and Babcock) "is also a man without sexual means, foreclosed from start to finish from the scene of passion, *except through identification*" (171). Like Strether and Marcher, Peirce is a voyeur, whose occupation is watching pendulums swing. Babcock is a voyeur, come to Europe to view paintings, whose focus is narrowed to watching a capon hang.

III

During that brief period when Henry James and Charles Sanders Peirce were keeping company in the winter of 1875-76, the writer was completing *The American,* a novel about an American capitalist, Christopher Newman, whose attempts to marry a French woman are obstructed by her ultramontane family. In many ways a traditional romance verging on melodrama, the novel presents a single anomolous episode that fits definitions of neither genre. This strange interlude presents the narrative of Newman's relationship with Benjamin Babcock, the strait-laced, young Unitarian minister from Dorchester, Massachusetts, "with whom, for a time, [Newman] formed a sort of traveller's partnership" (*AM* 105). Their alliance evolves and dissolves within the short space of chapter five, and Babcock disappears from the action nearly as soon as he is introduced.

After William read the novel, he wrote to Henry about the novelist's creation of Babcock, whom he called "the morbid little clergyman": "I was not a little amused to find some of my own attributes in him—I think you found my 'moral reaction' excessive when I was abroad" (Perry 371). Clearly, William saw his own "moral reaction" replicated in Babcock's response to what he perceives as Newman's hedonism. Readers have taken William's judgment for granted, reading Henry's philosopher brother as the template for Babcock.[5]

While James's characterization of Babcock may owe something to the Cambridge pragmatists in general, the minister's earnest seriousness and the progress of his relationship with Newman seem to have distinctive resonances with James's own relationship with Charles Sanders Peirce. Babcock, we learn in the narrative of his relationship with Newman, is a Unitarian minister; Peirce was brought up as a Unitarian. Peirce complains in his letter to William of Henry's weak digestion, and in a comic turning of the tables, Henry has Newman complaining of Babcock's: the minister, we remember, survives on Graham bread and hominy, purchasing them during his Parisian sojourn at "an establishment which called itself an American Agency" (*AM* 105). Babcock, who "retire[s] to his room early in the evening for the express purpose of considering it [his relationship with Newman]," likes Newman but "the brevity of Newman's judgments very often shocked and discomposed him." As Babcock explains, "[Newman] had a way of damning people without farther appeal, or of pronouncing them capital company in the face of uncomfortable symptoms, which seemed unworthy of a man whose conscience had been properly cultivated" (*AM* 107-108). Peirce is "fond of turning over questions," while James "likes to settle them and have done with them" (Perry 537).

William James's biographer describes Peirce as "ill at ease, of uncertain temper . . . [a man who] found it increasingly difficult, as life went on, to associate with his fellow men" (Perry 538). Babcock is described as "gloomy and even a trifle irritable; he seemed moody, absent, preoccupied" (*AM* 108). He says of Newman's inability to understand his motives: "It's very distressing to me. It keeps me in a state of unrest. It irritates me; I can't settle anything . . . I am very uncomfortable" (*AM* 109). Babcock is, of course, the one who breaks off the partnership with Newman. The Unitarian minister, who is devoted to art, tries "to arrive at the truth about everything" (*AM* 109). Similarly, Peirce feels at home in the exact sciences "where a man might be sure of his ground, and where inaccuracy was the deadliest of sins" (Perry 538). Both James and Peirce and Newman and Babcock part, it first appears, because of irreconcilable philosophical differences. Babcock rejects what he reads as Newman's general conduct, returning to Milan to reconsider the paintings of Luini, over which the men had disagreed.[6] Similarly, a distinctly unhappy Peirce leaves James in early March 1876 to continue his pendulum research in Berlin. Later that year he has the first of the three mental breakdowns he experiences in three years.

Peirce attributed his poor mental health to a lack of "moral self-control" in his childhood. "He had as a result suffered long from lack of sovereignty over himself" (Holmes 113). In 1910, he stated that his own "failure in youth to regard good counsel about self-control led to [his] becoming a miserably unhappy man" (Holmes 114). The philosophic position of pragmatism was, he asserted, based on self-control, an experience "common to all grown men and women" (Holmes 115). Babcock's behavior can be limned by Peirce's explanation of the essential features of self-control, which encourages "critical comparison with previous decisions or with ideals, rehearsal in the imagination of future conduct on various possible occasions, and the formation or modification thereby of habits or dispositions of the occult something behind consciousness" (Holmes 117).[7] An unpublished manuscript in the Papers of Charles Sanders Peirce sums up the philosopher's obsession with self-control: "Reasoning properly means controlled thought, and the only possible control consists in critical review, or self-confession" (Holmes 117). Babcock leaves Newman because he fears a loss of self-control, which he confesses has already experienced. He has been seduced by Newman and his easy ways, which have led him, he confesses to an overestimation of Luini, whom Newman finds "enchanting." According the New-

man's evaluation, "There is something in [Luini's] genius that is like a beautiful woman" (*AM* 110).

How can we characterize this loss of self-control, this behavior that demands modification? Peirce's most recent biographer, Joseph Brent, implies that it is related to alcoholism, violence, and suicidal tendencies. He explains that "Peirce felt himself to be the victim of an overwhelming and uncontrollable passion. He found the same three traits in his formidable father that he found in himself: great mathematical ability, contentiousness bordering on the pathological, and exaggerated sensibility" (Brent 31). This exaggerated sensibility, along with a fear of strong new women and a dependence upon weak sisterly women, like Juliette Pourtalai, is a defining feature of the late nineteenth-century decadent male personality, which Elaine Showalter decodes as homosexual (Showalter 171). I would suggest, then, that the fear experienced by both Peirce and Babcock is a terror of the homoerotic, which may manifest itself as homosexual panic, defined by Eve Sedgwick as "the most private, psychologized form in which many twentieth-century western men experience their vulnerability to the social pressure of homophobic blackmail" (89).[8] This panic can be understood to have caused Peirce's 1876 nervous collapse, which Brent specifies as "conversion hysteria (also called dissociative reaction)," in which "the victim, unable to cope, retreats into complete physical impotence" (105). In 1880, Peirce voluntarily committed himself for possible insanity. Taken as a whole, this behavior would have been figured in the nineteenth century as the possible consequences of sexual inversion, with Peirce experiencing hysteria, a disease limited to women. Similarly, homosexual panic, I assert, precipitated Babcock's flight from his object of desire, Christopher Newman.

Whether we accept or reject the recent research grounding sexual preference in genetics, it is clear that the Peirce family was well acquainted with homosexuality. Brent comments that only one of the four Peirce sons experienced conventional marriage and employment and had children. Benjamin Mills Peirce, Brent explains, "lived a wild life far from his family and died young in circumstances and from causes hidden under . . . 'that queer blanket of obscurity' which the Peirces threw not only over the life of Charles, but over the lives of all three of their unusual sons" (78). James Mills Peirce, who became dean of the graduate school at Harvard, was a closeted homosexual whose letter defending gay love was excerpted in Havelock Ellis's *Sexual Inversion* (Brent 78). We can hear echoes of Charles's statements about the necessity of self-control in his brother's recommendations: "I have considered & enquired into this question for many years; and it has long been my settled conviction that no breach of morality is involved in homosexual love; that, like every other passion, it tends, when duly understood and *controlled by spiritual feeling* to the physical and moral health of the individual & the race" (Brent 78; my emphasis). That Peirce dressed the role of the dandy is not enough to signal irrevocably his sexual preference for men, nor is the fact that his heterosexual relationships were unhappy and unhealthy. We cannot know for certain whether Charles was, like his brother (or brothers), gay. What we can demonstrate, however, is that Peirce and Henry James floated together intimately on a sea of well-being, but that when their relationship went aground or drifted apart, Peirce's control wrecked.

What we can further suggest is that James's fictional portrayal of Peirce, Babcock, does not separate from Newman so much because of a distaste for his personal philosophy as because he suffers from a panic borne of his homoerotic attraction to Newman. After Babcock proposes that the Americans go their separate ways, the conventional language of a lovers' spat emerges, with the minister finally exasperated, complaining that Newman has not provided enough intellectual foreplay to satisfy his needs: "I try to arrive at the truth about everything. And then you go too fast. For me, you are too passionate, too extravagant" (*AM* 109). Following the dispute and Newman's promise to wait for Babcock anywhere, once he has received word that he is wanted, the two separate. Later, Newman receives a farewell note from Babcock, in which the minister confesses: "I know there is a great deal to be said for your way; I have felt its attraction, in your society, very strongly. But for this I should have left you long ago. But I was so perplexed. I hope I have not done wrong" (*AM* 111).[9] Dollimore describes one way homosocial desire functions in male bonding:

> the necessary identifications of male bonding—"I desire to be like you"—produce an intensity of admiration some of which just cannot help but transform into deviant desire for, rather than just honourable imitation of, "man's" most significant other (i.e. man). And it occurs so easily—almost passively—requiring little more than a relinquishing of the *effort* of emulation, the erasure of *"to be like"* and the surrender of what remains: *"I desire . . . you";* thus: "I desire (to be like) you" (305).

As Dollimore explains, this homosocial relationship is played out "within and against the very situations in which heterosexuality is most ardently pursued" (305), in this case, Newman's single-minded search for a wife. Babcock's departure is motivated by his own recognition that he has experienced that erasure of *'to be like'* and must leave because he now desires Newman.

IV

In response to Babcock's confession in his farewell note, which ends with the imperative, "only *do* remember that Life and Art *are* extremely serious" (*AM* 111), the American sends a gift:

> a grotesque little statuette in ivory, of the sixteenth century . . . [which] represented a gaunt, ascetic-looking monk, in a tattered gown and cowl, kneeling with clasped hands and pulling a portentiously

long face. It was a wonderfully delicate piece of carving and in a moment, through one of the rents of his gown, you espied a fat capon hung round the monk's waist. In Newman's intention what did the figure symbolise? Did it mean that he was going to try to be as "high-toned" as the monk looked at first, but that he feared he should succeed no better than the friar, on a closer inspection, proved to have done?" (*AM* 112)

Although these questions are left unanswered, Newman purchases the statuette as a narrative text in its own right and sends it to Babcock "without a commentary." But we get no indication that anyone is able to read the text, including the omniscient narrator, who can only comment in the negative: "It is *not* supposable that he intended a satire upon Babcock's own asceticism, for this would have been a truly cynical stroke" (*AM* 112; my emphasis). Rather than offering a simple satire of asceticism, the statue is a fetish that plays a key role in the sexual economy of the novel.

An artifact of anticlerical sentiment reminiscent of several of Chaucer's pilgrims or of the lascivious monks of gothic romance, the clergy and religious orders often took direct hits to their respectability, the charge being sexual indulgence. This ivory monk looks gaunt (spent in the medieval sense of the term?) and ascetic (repentant?) and represents an anomolously-gendered sexuality. He is dispossessed of any religious authority. Described as *delicate,* wearing a *gown,* its appearance pale, the monk may be seen as gendered female, previewing the fair-complected Claire, who is similarly described elsewhere in the novel as a statue. Is Newman, then, presenting his former companion with his, Newman's, image of Babcock as a woman? Or is this monk a figure who is wasted from lack of self-control?

The economy represented by the ivory monk is not simply sexual, however: it is specifically homoerotic. Just as the subtext interlineally presented in chapter five, a subtext represented by the ivory monk, subverts the marriage plot in *The American,* yet another body—the fat capon—defines this fetish.[10] According to Freud, we recall, the fetish is a supplementary phallus, which appears in the line of vision and onto which desire is displaced. Emily Apter explains further: "As the device that 'wards off' homosexuality, fetishism is also implicitly valorized by Freud as a kind of vaccination against a desire of man for man that he is incapable of recognizing in and for itself (that is, as anything other than a defense against the phantom of emasculation). Fetishism emerges then as homosexuality's repressive watchdog, an ensign of homophobia" (211). But, she adds, "it is not quite so simple": "Though Freud does indeed identify the fetish with the suppression of the visible cause of homosexuality, he also allows it to function as a visual incentive, a target for the gaze that loves to look (even as it looks away). It is thus becomes an ambivalent site on which the possibility of a homoerotic encounter is held out, *as well as* the mark of society's punishment for any *passage à l'acte*" (211). It could hardly be clearer that the "fat capon hung round the monk's waist" (*AM* 112) is the fetish's fetish.[11] Visible through the rent in the monk's gown, the capon answers "yes" to Roland Barthes's question "Is not the most erotic portion of a body *where the garment gapes?*" (9). The capon, rather than the monk's face, gives the statuette potential meaning.

What exactly is a capon, which a turn-of-the-century gastronomical history terms "the greatest favourite with the clergy" (Ellwanger 306)? According to Jessup Whitehead's *Hotel Meat Cooking:* "A capon is a young male chicken gelded, by making an opening in its side and then sewing it up again, in order to make it fatten" (345). As it matures, it becomes hen-like: "Its body becomes plump instead of angular, the quality of its flesh is much better than that of the cock" (Women's Institute Library of Cooking 12.4). Capons can be distinguished by the pale and shriveled appearance of the combs, the undeveloped condition of the spurs, and especially round, well-fleshed bodies" (Ward 102).[12] A capon is, in other words, a *Bad*cock.

The equation I am postulating is that castration=feminine=homosexual. There is no arguing that in the case of chickens, castration produces a feminized fowl. But because people are not poultry, we might want to shift the order of the terms in the equation. As Silverman outlines, various homosexual subcultures throughout history have used signifiers of femininity to define the gay male self. I would argue that castration, whose appearance can be fetishized, say, in the jock strap, and which effects the disappearance of the penis signals the feminine; and that since the feminine is figured both within and without any number of homosexual/social subcultures as homosexual, then castration, through the feminine, prefigures the homosexual.[13] As Leo Bersani explains in working with the middle term of my equation, "in occupying a female subject-position the gay man himself submits to a kind of castration" (Silverman 350).

The ivory monk Newman presents to Babcock, particularly with its eroticized capon hanging from its waist, embodies the castration anxiety inherent in the fetish, as defined by Freud.[14] It represents the loss of the sort of manhood and virility for which Newman stands, foreshadowing his own metaphoric castration by the Bellegardes, and also, potentially, with Babcock.[15] And while scholars generally agree that James's famous "obscure hurt" was little more than a bad back, the specter of James's own "castration" lurks.[16] The silent, delicately-carved ivory monk is itself a metonymic capon, an ironic figure of the unspeakable desires of the flesh that have been rendered sterile: it supplements desire only to replace it with a castrated chicken. The figure of the monk itself is, we recall, gaunt, yet the capon hanging so seductively from his waist is fat. Here is the displacement of desire onto the substitute phallus writ large.

In her discussion of the poetics of deviant detail and Gide's turn-of-the-century homotextual fetishism, Apter

explains how "the tropes of oscillation, uncertainty, displacement, and de-repressed negation that circle around a charged, eroticized object are decipherable as textual expressions of the epistemological affinities and tensions between homosexuality and fetishism" (212). Similarly, I have been arguing that Newman's gift of the ivory monk to Babcock precisely identifies the homosexual economy in which these two figures participate.

V

We do not know if James ever sent Peirce a gift after they parted ways. While we know that they, like Gide and Wilde, met again after their initial encounter, so far as we know, the Gide-Wilde analogy does not come full-circle with James (or his stand-in, Christopher Newman) procuring a young boy for Peirce (or his fictional double, Benjamin Babcock). We would not have expected that: Wilde's out-of-the-closet style did not at all appeal to James. But James and Peirce's adventures in Paris and their fictionalization in chapter five of *The American* suggest that rereading what Dollimore calls Gide's transgressive ethic and Wilde's transgressive aesthetic might prove valuable.

What separates the philosophy of the two intellects is their practice of transgression. According to Dollimore, "Wilde's experience of deviant desire . . . leads him not to escape the repressive ordering of society, but to a reinscription within it, and an inversion of the binaries upon which that ordering depends; desire, and the transgressive aesthetic which it fashions, reacts against, disrupts, and displaces from within" (14). Newman, accused by Babcock of being "immoral, a devotee of 'art for art'" (*AM* 116), is a harbinger of Wildean aesthetics, who inverts various binaries in order to reinscribe himself in French culture. As we learn early in the novel, he prefers artistic copies (and not very good ones) to originals. As an American, and a Californian at that, Newman is a product of colonial expansion who sets out to colonize the colonizer.

Gide, however, transgresses "in the name of a desire and identity rooted in the natural, the sincere, and the authentic" (Dollimore 14). Babcock deserts Newman, transgressing the laws of homosocial bonding, because, in effect, Newman displays what will come to be known as the Wildean sensibility. As Babcock explains in his farewell letter to Newman: "Art and life seem to me intensely serious things. . . . You seem to hold that if a thing amuses you for the moment, that is all you need ask for it; and your relish for mere amusement is also much higher than mine. You put, moreover, a kind of reckless confidence into your pleasure which at times, I confess, has seemed to me . . . almost cynical" (*AM* 111). Though seemingly opposed, both Wilde's and Gide's approaches to transgression are strategies designed to authenticate homosexual ways of being.

While similar transgressions exist both in the narratives of Newman and Babcock (and of James and Peirce), available meaning rests not in any clearly decipherable gay text but instead in that gap in the garment which is chapter five, an erotic interlude whose meaning is embodied in the figure of a castrated chicken. And if the disappearance of capons from our meat cases suggests anything, it may be that there are no more "bad cocks." I like to think that the transgressive efforts of writers and thinkers like James and Peirce and Wilde and Gide have liberated literature and philosophy for the twentieth century, giving voice to the homoerotic subtext and quieting the panic that surely must have been felt by all of those nineteenth-century "new men."

NOTES

[1] According to Perry, Peirce became a frequent visitor in the James home when the family moved to Cambridge in 1866; thus, he was undoubtedly acquainted with Henry before his Parisian sojourn (533).

[2] Interestingly, Alfred Habegger links Henry James, Sr.'s, use of the term "ardent" to his own homoerotic relationship with Ralph Waldo Emerson. It is good, too, to recall that *Roderick Hudson* features a thinly disguised homoerotic relationship between Hudson, the sculptor, and his older American mentor.

[3] In a letter to Henry James, Sr., dated 20 Dec. 1875, the Paris-based writer notes that his father has enclosed a letter from Mrs. Charles Peirce and then continues by saying that he "continue[s] to see C. Peirce himself" (*HJL* II, 16).

[4] For a short discussion of Zina's achievements, see Fisch (409). For what minimal information is available on Pourtalai, see both Ketner and Kloesel (311) and Lenzen (10, 11).

[5] As Brent notes, both Benjamin Peirce and his son "were very lonely men, dependent on women. In Peirce's case, this dependence may have been a direct result of his neuralgia, which made him a patient in search of the solace of a nurse, mother, lover, confidante, and scapegoat" (49).

[6] William Veeder makes a strong case for Henry's homosexual desire for his brother William, which would support my assertion of the erotic undercurrent of chapter five of *The American* (see especially pages 103-104). He, however, suggests that Babcock is nonetheless modeled on William, with Henry displacing his desire for his own brother onto his brother's friend, Charles Sanders Peirce.

[7] Babcock confesses, "I am afraid that I over-estimated [Luini]. I don't think that he is a painter of the first rank." Newman responds, "Why, he's enchanting—he's magnificent! There is something in his genius that is like a beautiful woman. It gives one the same feeling" (*AM* 110).

[8] One elaboration of the "occult something behind" consciousness is homosexual desire. See Silverman (esp. 174-81).

[9] Although I am dealing here with the last quarter of the nineteenth century, when conceptions of homophobia and homosexuality were rapidly changing (see Cohen), Sedgwick's definition nevertheless holds true.

[10] Carolyn Porter has made a case for a homoerotic relationship between Newman and Valentin de Bellegarde.

[11] For James's use of the marriage plot, see Joseph Boone.

[12] The capon is the perfect representation of, as Mulvey puts it, "the fact of fetishisation, concealing as it does, castration fear" (442).

[13] Brillat-Savarin, the celebrated gastronome, writes: "Three districts of ancient France rival for the honour of furnishing the finest poultry: Caux, le Mans, and la Bress. As to capons, there is always some doubt; the one a man has his fork in always appearing the best" (53).

[14] See Silverman, who cites Freud on the fetishization of the athletic support belt (46).

[15] For a fascinating reading of the body as embodiment, see Mark Seltzer's discussion of the chickens in Hawthorne's *The House of the Seven Gables:* "The chickens function as a 'symbol of the life of the old house,' 'embodying its interpretation' even as they 'embodied the traditionary peculiarities of their whole line of progenitors'" (142). James's fondness for Hawthorne goes without saying.

[16] It also suggests dishonesty and corruption, else why is the capon hanging *under* the gown? See the reference in Jaques's "Seven Ages of Man" speech in *As You Like It:* "And then the justice,/In fair round belly with good capon lined" (II.vii.52-53). For a reading of Newman's impotent masculinity, see Porter.

[17] For a complete discussion of various readings of the "obscure hurt," see Kirby.

KEY TO WORKS BY HENRY JAMES

AM—The American. Ed. William Spengemann. New York: Penguin, 1981.

HJL—Henry James Letters. Vol. 2, 1875-1883. Ed. Leon Edel. Cambridge: Harvard UP, 1975.

OTHER WORKS CITED

Apter, Emily. *Feminizing the Fetish: Psychoanalysis and Narrative Obsession in Turn-of-the-Century France.* Ithaca: Cornell U P, 1991.

Barthes, Roland. *The Pleasure of the Text.* Trans. Richard Miller. New York: Hill and Wang, 1975.

Boone, Joseph. "Modernist Manoeuvrings and the Marriage Plot: Breaking Ideologies of Gender and Genre in James's *The Golden Bowl.*" *PMLA* 101 (1986): 374-88.

Brent, Joseph. *Charles Sanders Peirce: A Life.* Bloomington: Indiana U P, 1993.

Brillat-Savarin, Jean Anthelme. *A Handbook of Gastronomy.* Boston: Houghton Mifflin, 1915.

Cohen, Ed. "Legislating the Norm: From Sodomy to Gross Indecency." *South Atlantic Quarterly* 88 (1989): 181-218.

Dollimore, Jonathan. *Sexual Dissidence: Augustine to Wilde, Freud to Foucault.* Oxford: Oxford U P, 1991.

Edel, Leon. *Henry James: The Conquest of London (1870-1881).* Philadelphia: Lippincott, 1962.

Ellwanger, George H. *The Pleasures of the Table: An Account of Gastronomy from Ancient Days to Present Times.* New York: Doubleday Page, 1902.

Fisch, Max H. *Peirce, Semeiotic, and Pragmatism: Essays by Max H. Fisch.* Ed. Kenneth Laine Ketner and Christian J. W. Kloesel. Bloomington: Indiana U P, 1986.

Habegger, Alfred. "The Sex of James's Parents." Rethinking Gender and Sexual Politics: Henry James in the New Century. New York City, 2 June 1993.

Holmes, Larry. "Peirce on Self-Control." *Transactions of the Charles Sanders Peirce Society* 2 (1966): 113-30.

Kirby, David. "The Sex Lives of the James Family." *Virginia Quarterly Review* 64 (1988): 56-73.

Lenzen, Victor F. "Reminiscences of a Mission to Milford, Pennsylvania." *Transactions of the Charles Sanders Peirce Society* 1 (1965): 3-11.

Mulvey, Laura. "Visual Pleasure and Narrative Cinema." *Feminisms: An Anthology of Literary Theory and Criticism.* Ed. Robin Warhol and Diane Price-Herndl. New Brunswick: Rutgers U P, 1991. 432-42.

Peirce, Charles Sanders. *Collected Papers: Elements of Logic.* Vol. 2. Ed. Charles Hartshorne and Paul Weiss. Cambridge: Harvard U P, 1932.

———. *Collected Papers: Reviews, Correspondence, Bibliography.* Vol. 8. Ed. Arthur W. Burks. Cambridge: Harvard U P, 1958.

Perry, Ralph Barton. *The Thought and Character of William James.* Vol. 1. London: Humphrey Milford, 1935.

Porter, Carolyn. "Gender and Value in *The American.*" *New Essays on* The American." Ed. Martha Banta. New York: Cambridge U P, 1987. 99-129.

Sedgwick, Eve Kosofsky. *Between Men: English Literature and Male Homosocial Desire.* New York: Columbia U P, 1985.

Seltzer, Mark. *Bodies and Machines.* New York: Routledge, 1992.

Showalter, Elaine. *Sexual Anarchy: Gender and Culture at the Fin De Siècle.* New York: Penguin, 1990.

Silverman, Kaja. *Male Subjectivity at the Margins.* New York and London: Routledge, 1992.

Veeder, William. "The Portrait of a Lack." *New Essays on* The Portrait of a Lady. Ed. Joel Porte. Cambridge: Cambridge U P, 1990. 95-122.

Ward, Artemas. *The Encyclopedia of Food.* 1882; New York: np, 1923.

Whitehead, Jessup. *Hotel Meat Cooking.* 1880; Chicago: Jessup Whitehead, 1893.

Woman's Institute Library of Cooking: Soup, Meat, Poultry and Game, Fish and Shellfish. Vol. 3.1918; Scranton, PA: Woman's Institute of Domestic Arts and Sciences, 1927.

Josiah Lee Auspitz (essay date 1994)

SOURCE: "The Wasp Leaves the Bottle: Charles Sanders Peirce," in *The American Scholar*, Vol. 63, Autumn, 1994, pp. 602-606, 608-610, 612-618.

[*In the following excerpt, Auspitz places Peirce among his list of the world's greatest philosophers, a distinction he credits to Peirce's consistent and rigorous thought.*]

In 1983, a review of the first two volumes of the new chronological edition of the Peirce papers noted that at Peirce's alma mater, Harvard, his name had appeared in the catalogue of philosophy courses only once in the previous five years, buried in fine print with the usual clutch of "American pragmatists." During the same period, two courses a year were usually devoted to the work of Wittgenstein, early and late.

In the intervening decade, the canon has changed little with respect to Wittgenstein, who in 1993 shared with Plato, Aristotle, Kant, and Hegel the distinction of being twice featured in the titles of Harvard philosophy courses. But Peirce is inching up. And when his name, too, at last breaks into the bold print of American university course catalogues, that outcome will owe much to the long-term institutional support evident in the volumes and series listed at the end of this essay.

Three of the books contain selections that introduce Peirce to serious students of philosophy (joining similar anthologies published in the past decade in German, Italian, Japanese, Portuguese, Romanian, and Spanish). Another three are scholarly editions of Peirce's writings, by theme and chronology. Five more collect by topic some of the three hundred essays from the 1989 Peirce Sesquicentennial Congress, at which world-renowned professors lent their luster to the devoted scholars who, working in unfashionable places, have been the mainstay of the Peirce revival. Finally, there are three secondary works of more general interest—the first full-length biography, a recent paperback edition of the best introductory survey, and a collection of historical essays setting Peirce in his nineteenth-century context—and a selection of six monographs from the more than forty book-length titles of the past seven years.

In all, the expanding bookshelf gives evidence that Peircean studies have completed an important decade in a growing movement of rediscovery. Taken together, the materials go far to establish Charles Sanders Peirce as the classic American philosopher—a difficult, ranging, and rigorous philosophical mind, as important as any that the English-speaking world has produced.

The point, moreover, at which Peirce diverges radically from the more celebrated Wittgenstein may now be working to Peirce's advantage. Wittgenstein posed the issue in the opening pages of his *Blue Book,* a collection of his lecture notes from the early 1930s. Here he departed from his usually restrained style to disparage the "craving for generality" that, as he saw it, had led philosophy astray. His disdain set a cleansing tone of scrupulous modesty in an age of ideological excess. It seemed to his followers to be vindicated in a new departure—the case method, focused not on metaphysical isms but on the minutious examination of both ordinary language and the "language games" that shape experience:

If we say thinking is essentially operating with signs, the first question you might ask is: "What are signs?"— Instead of giving any kind of *general* answer to this question, I shall propose to you to look closely at *particular cases* which we should call "operating with signs." (My italics)

Peirce, by contrast, tackled the question "What are signs?" head on, not because he was less fastidious than Wittgenstein in his craving for generality, but because his was a mind of greater speculative power. More rigorously trained than Wittgenstein as both mathematician and experimental scientist, and incomparably better read in the history of logic and philosophy, Peirce saw the case method as posing a problem for signs *in general.*

To recognize something as a case, an instance, always raised the question "a case of what?" As Peirce saw it, any sign can be viewed simultaneously in both general and particular aspects. His distinction between "token" and "type" went to the heart of the problem. (The young

Cambridge logician F. P. Ramsey had in fact commended it to Wittgenstein in a 1923 review of the *Tractatus*). A mark on a piece of paper may be viewed both as a physical inscription (and as such a particular instance or "token") and as a representation of more general attributes shared by any inscription of that "type." Further, the token-type distinction, now canonical among logicians, is but a partial rendering of one of many triadic divisions in a ramified theory of signs that Peirce developed from the mid-1860s until his death in 1914.

For Peirce actual signs are never univocal. It is in their general character that they may be construed variably and analyzed modally. Of Peirce's own divisions, icon-index-symbol is the most commonly used. Santayana took it up the moment he heard Peirce expound it, and the linguist Roman Jakobson, when he came upon it in late career, saw it as opening "new, urgent and far-reaching vistas to the science of language." In a computer age we are quick to see it as a modal classification with no pure referents in everyday experience.

Thus, as a portrait, Gainsborough's "Blue Boy" is an "icon," a self-sufficient sign that represents its object by resemblance. But we can also view it as an "index," pointing to something beyond itself that can be confirmed with collateral evidence, as when a physician sees in the pallor of Blue Boy's skin evidence that Gainsborough's model suffered from a nutritional deficiency. Or we might take it as a "symbol"—of youth, of British eighteenth-century portraiture, of the spirit of an age, or any other generality it may represent by convention or habit of association. And since the various modal classes need not exclude each other, a symbol may be further analyzed under the token-type distinction (a sign modality which is both symbol and token being in Peirce's lexicon a "replica").

Icon-index-symbol, tone-token-type, and the five dozen other Peircean classificatory terms are not grammatical or linguistic groupings but elements in a table of the modalities of signification. They are markers in a continuum of "semeiosis" (Peirce's punctilious transliteration of the Greek for what Wittgenstein called "operating with signs," or *Zeichenhandeln.*)

Peirce's categories proceed from a formal, three-way view of the semiotic relationship, in which a "sign" mediates between an "object" and an "interpretant," the interpreting effect that the sign produces upon, for example, a human mind. In exploring the myriad relations and gradations among these three correlates, Peirce's modalities make of every sign-event a moment pregnant with infinite possibility.

In so doing, they permit a more widely ranging phenomenology than that limited to the givens of actual experience. As constructs, they are judged not by the correspondence of each modality to some particular fact or utterance but by the explanatory power of the theory of signs as a whole. Like the elements of the periodic table,

Peirce's sign-modalities occur in experience mainly in combination. And, like the periodic table, they are meant to cover every possible compound. One of their advantages over natural language is that they can account for sciences of discovery. Because they are not limited to what exists, they are able, at least in principle, to accommodate whatever might be. And by including modal terms to explain, criticize, and justify the persistence of commonsense ideas, the Peircean system both encourages flexibility and guards against a merely frivolous deconstruction of experience.

Peirce, one of the founders of modern symbolic logic, thus introduces into the philosophy of language the premeditated artificiality that constitutes at once the power and limitation of modern science. Science leaps out of common sense into a rigorously defined language that it uses to model aspects of experience. Peirce pursues this habit to a philosophically conscious and self-critical level.

As Hegel, relatively early in the development of modern historiography, produced a philosophy that took wing from historical consciousness, Peirce, at the first stirrings of the American research university, became the philosopher par excellence to bring the reality posited by modern science to the point of reunion with experience as a whole.

Whether we wish, as protagonists, to give the fullest play to a scientific worldview or, as critical philosophers, to understand its conditionality, Peirce's work as a whole—independent of its still unexhausted technical achievements—is an indispensable port of call. And because he was profoundly learned in ancient and medieval logic, Peirce gives us a philosophy in the grand tradition, one that is genuinely post-rather than anti-Aristotelian.

Whence the headnote of Joseph Brent's pioneering biography, taken from one of Peirce's portentously self-referential manuscript pages:

> [I intend] to make a philosophy like that of Aristotle, that is to say, to outline a theory so comprehensive that, for a long time to come, the entire work of human reason, in philosophy of every school and kind, in mathematics, in psychology, in physical science, in history, in sociology, and in whatever other department there may be, shall appear as the filling up of its details.

Brent's narrative leans heavily on such direct quotations from unpublished manuscripts and epistolary material, so that one can appreciate that Brent's work was seriously retarded by the refusal of the Harvard Philosophy Department circa 1958 to grant him access to four boxes of Peirce family letters. When he gained knowledge of some of the contents from other archival sources—and quoted from them in a 1960 doctoral dissertation in history at UCLA—he incurred, as he reports it, the wrath of Harvard. He believes that this hostility more than any professional judgment on the quality of his work accounted for the failure of academic presses to publish his dissertation in the 1960s.

Happily, Brent's preface reports that in 1989 Indiana University Press paid him a small advance to bring up to date and reconsider the doctoral work of thirty years before. Without incident, Harvard gave permission to quote from its full collection, and the shroud of secrecy surrounding Peirce's personal life, maintained by surviving relatives as well as a decorous Harvard department, was officially broken.

The family archive does in fact contain dirt on Peirce, but the real scandal is more institutional than personal. It lies in the conduct of scientific rivals, who seized upon Peirce's weaknesses to deny him preferment, employment, and grants. Brent documents what others have also observed: that after the death of Peirce's main patron, his father Benjamin Peirce, Jr., a group closed in upon him; the movement was orchestrated at crucial junctures by Simon Newcomb, the noted astronomer who succeeded Peirce's father as the most influential American scientist of his generation. Such eminences as the university presidents Eliot of Harvard, Gilman of Johns Hopkins, and Butler of Columbia were among Charles Peirce's leading detractors. Though they sometimes claimed to be protecting innocent students from Peirce's allegedly baneful moral influence, they also took care to deny him opportunities for guest lectures and pure research that involved no student contact.

Peirce's family and publishing connections, his admitted brilliance, and his own and his wife's inherited income, until they lost it in the crash of 1893, were such that he could not be eliminated entirely from the intellectual scene. His supporters included William James, Josiah Royce, John Dewey, a few loyal students he had inspired in his four years at Johns Hopkins, some college classmates, and several important editors, officials, publishers, and men of means: Garrison of the *Nation,* Carus of the *Monist,* Cattell of *Popular Science Monthly,* Baldwin of the *Dictionary of Philosophy and Psychology,* Smith of the *Century Dictionary,* Langley of the Smithsonian, the publishers Putnam and Plimpton, the millionaires Pinchot and Morrison.

These admirers often came through in a pinch with a writing commission, a few lectures, a loan, or a direct subsidy. Charles's elder brother James Mills Peirce, a Harvard mathematics professor and dean of the graduate school, intervened to straighten out his financial affairs, and his younger brother Herbert, a career diplomat, used his Washington connections as well as those of Senator (and cousin) Henry Cabot Lodge on Charles's behalf.

But in the small university world of his day, Peirce's enemies controlled the heights. When Peirce was forty-five, Daniel C. Gilman abruptly dismissed him from Johns Hopkins upon receiving testimony that Peirce had lived with his second wife before the completion of the legal divorce from his first. After that Peirce was repeatedly blackballed from further university positions. When, in his mid-fifties, he began to reach, as philosophers often do, the full range of his powers, there was no institution to underwrite him, no body of students to take direct guidance from him.

Peirce's most enraging flaw was that he often seemed not to care. He was dedicated to making his mind a vessel through which reality might shine, and this gave him a childlike insouciance that was both a provocation and an easy target for academics bent on the more mundane aspects of their calling.

Charles had been raised in a hothouse environment in which intellectual excellence was prized above all else. His father, aunt, uncles, and family friends led lives largely devoted to science and mathematics. The elder Peirce was so completely concentrated upon intellectual achievement that, in the midst of the Civil War, he condoned slavery if used, as in ancient Greece, to free an elite for scientific inquiry. He began training his son early in mathematical games and in discrimination among the senses. When Charles was eleven he wrote **"A History of Chemistry."** At sixteen, father and son began regular readings in Kant's *Critique of Pure Reason;* at eighteen Charles worked with his father's sister on an English translation of the section on the Transcendental Analytic.

Both at Harvard and nationally, the Peirce circle was at the center of a movement dedicated to the proposition that intellectual excellence alone should determine appointments to scientific and scholarly positions. This meritocratic view, always of limited appeal, reflected a devotion to inquiry that became the guiding principle of Charles Peirce's life. It explains both the singleness of purpose and the resilience that enabled him to surmount many tribulations.

In charting Peirce's troubles, Brent does not flinch from the lugubrious or the sensational. He documents the facial neuralgia that caused Peirce excruciating physical pain for most of his life, the resulting addiction to narcotics, the violent outbursts, the periods of near madness, the (hetero-) sexual excesses, the financial crises, the petty mendacities and thefts. On slimmer evidence, Brent speculates on Peirce as a wife beater and on the earlier career of Peirce's second wife, Juliette, as a French courtesan. And, on Peirce's authority, he presents the philosopher's left-handedness as a disability comparable to neuralgia (Peirce attributed the incomprehensibility of his work to his "left-brained," diagrammatic way of thinking).

Brent is at his archival best, however, in tracing the bureaucratic proceedings that resulted in Peirce being severed from Johns Hopkins, ousted from the Coast and Geodetic Survey, and finally, denied an early Carnegie grant despite the support of the president of the United States, the secretary of war, a raft of the leading philosophers and editors, and Andrew Carnegie himself. At almost every turn Brent shows how Peirce's self-absorption and consequent obtuseness to his effect on others conspired to undercut his own cause.

As a consolation, Peirce, at age sixty-four, received the honor from the Harvard Corporation of allowing private funds raised by William James to be passed through it to pay him for a series of lectures—his one fleeting academic berth in all the years after the Johns Hopkins dismissal. The talks were given in Sever Hall, which stands on the site of the house where Peirce grew up (a bronze plaque noting this fact now graces the entry of the building).

Ever proving himself beholden to no one, Peirce opened the lectures with what must have appeared as chaffingly condescending remarks about the lively but mistaken pragmatism of William James, his most reliable friend and benefactor, who had generously credited Peirce with originating the philosophical doctrine. Peirce saw Jamesian pragmatism as exaggerating practicality into a metaphysical doctrine parading as an anti-metaphysics. (James, as Peirce saw it, took practical effect as a criterion of truth rather than as a razor for clarifying meaning, and Peirce would soon rename his own view "pragmaticism," the better to distinguish it from that of James.)

James reacted by firing off an uncharacteristically furious letter, not quoted by Brent, calling Peirce "a monster of desultory intellect . . . without even any intellectual residuum from his work that can be called a finished construction, only 'suggestions' and a begging old age." James subsequently discouraged publication of the Sever Hall lectures, but continued to stand by Peirce financially, raising a fund that assisted him in the mendicant, unusually productive final decade of his life.

In assessing Peirce as a philosopher, Brent has profited from the thirty years since his dissertation. Not only has the accumulating opinion on Peirce's philosophy helped to enrich the accepted view of it, but Brent modifies his earlier, callow thesis of a direct relation between Peirce's temperament and the allegedly failed architectonic of the Peircean system. Instead, he gives us, in his final chapter, a moving gloss on Peirce's own description of himself as a "wasp in a bottle," buzzing furiously in a glass cage formed by his own self-conception and the reaction of others to it.

Brent portrays Peirce as spurred by the ruins of his private life and scholarly career to a contrite, peculiarly scientific piety, in which the theoretical gift of hypothesis becomes man's best stab at entering into the mind of God. Brent argues also that the philosopher's belated attempt at a "moral reconstruction of pragmatism" should be read as a "direct result of Peirce's recognition of his own folly and the remorse consequent upon it."

A single-volume biography has understandable difficulty doing justice to Peirce's philosophical development. For this, one turns to the Peircean corpus itself and to the expanding literature of re-engagement with it. Notwithstanding Peirce's fame as a neglected genius, his work has always commanded the attention of serious thinkers. It can be argued that recognition of his importance has been retarded because major writers have been moved by his work to pursue, not a full and fair understanding of Peirce, but ambitious and sometimes original lines of their own.

Peirce's papers, certainly, have not wanted for distinguished editors. At his death in 1914, the manuscript materials not previously published were enough to fill seventy-five 500-page volumes of the sort now produced by Indiana University Press. Harvard paid his widow $250 for the lot. Josiah Royce took charge of the editing in the two years before his own death in 1916. In the early 1920s, the editorial task passed to Charles Irving Lewis, who had been brought to Harvard partly for this purpose after his *Survey of Symbolic Logic* (1918) proclaimed Peirce's contribution, on the basis of the published materials alone, to have been "the most considerable of any up to his time, with the doubtful exception of Boole."

Lewis spent two years immersed in the manuscripts and wrote an editorial plan before giving the project up to pursue his own work in modal logic. In the 1920s the fund-raising efforts of a student of James and Royce, Morris Raphael Cohen of the City College of New York, enabled Harvard to employ as editors two junior faculty members, Charles Hartshorne and Paul Weiss, who were themselves to become important professors of philosophy.

Their first volume, published in 1931, cast Peirce's work into a mold for philosophy propounded by Alfred North Whitehead in his Gifford Lectures of 1926-27 (published as *Process and Reality* in 1929), in which a philosophical system was seen as generated recursively by a few fundamental metaphysical categories. Peirce seemed to fit this model precisely. From his triadic divisions of signs to his metaphysical categories of Firstness, Secondness, and Thirdness, triadicity recurred throughout his writings. To lay bare the architectonic of his philosophy, the editors began their collection with a volume devoted to Peirce's writings on the categories, without regard to chronology, to suggest that all else was generated from them. By 1935 Harvard University Press had issued the first six volumes of an eventual eight-volume *Collected Papers,* organized thematically.

The Hartshorne-Weiss edition revolutionized the accepted view of Peirce. Previous to it even Peirce's staunchest admirers considered his work fragmentary and undeveloped. The "tragedy" of Peirce was thought to be that his erratic temperament and unfavorable circumstances had conspired to deprive the world of any connected piece of his reasoning. Even Cohen, who had compiled the first Peirce bibliography (1916) and had edited a well-selected anthology of a dozen of Peirce's published essays (1923), had placed him among the lonely pioneers of philosophy whose main influence was in the fruitful suggestions they gave to others.

The Harvard *Collected Papers,* by contrast, established Peirce as the author of a major philosophical system. But it also set him up for a fall. It seemed to have him claiming too much. A wave of contrarian scholarship arose showing the Peircean "system" to be quaint, or failed, or no single system at all but two incipient systems in conflict with each other, or a series of three or four of them each developing out of the collapse of the previous one. The author of the most thorough and influential of these critical works merely reflected academic common sense circa 1965 when he wrote, in the first issue of the quarterly *Transactions of the Charles S. Peirce Society,* that "so much of Peirce's writing is so bizarre that the reader clings for dear life to those few doctrines which, like pragmatism, have an aura of reasonableness about them."

It was not until 1958, with the publication of the seventh and eighth volumes of the *Collected Papers,* edited by Arthur W. Burks and underwritten by the Rockefeller Foundation, that the scholarly apparatus to the Harvard edition included a partial chronology enabling readers to date the various excerpts. And it was not until 1967 that Richard S. Robin's annotated catalogue of the Harvard manuscript materials was published. (The editorial introduction to the recent electronic edition of the *Collected Papers* recommends using its search features in conjunction with the Burks and Robin bibliographies to undo the "artificial dismemberment of the Peircean corpus" in the topical arrangement of the original editors.)

In 1973 increasing dissatisfaction with the captious cast of the secondary literature led a group of scholars from the Charles S. Peirce Society to call for a more comprehensive, critical edition of his work, chronologically arranged. Under Edward C. Moore, the founding director of the Peirce Edition Project, funds were raised from the National Science Foundation, the National Endowment for the Humanities, and (in a remarkable gesture for an out-of-state writer by a local elected body) the Indiana State Legislature. Work on the chronological edition began in 1975 on the Indianapolis campus of Indiana and Purdue universities. It took a team of scholars six years to decipher, date, collate, transcribe, select, verify, emend, and annotate manuscripts before the first critically edited volume was ready for press. After eighteen years, the fifth volume, just out, takes Peirce's writings only through the aftermath of the Johns Hopkins period.

To hasten the dissemination of the post-Hopkins materials—a *selection* of which is now projected at twenty-five further volumes—photocopies of the full collection of dated manuscripts were early made available in open file cabinets both at the Peirce Edition Project and at the Center for the Study of Pragmaticism at Texas Tech University in Lubbock. Both the Indiana and Texas centers have other research aids that attract international visitors. The directors of both have actively promoted a range of research and study materials (most recently, *The Essential Peirce,* two volumes edited for convenient classroom and scholarly use by the current and past directors of the Peirce Edition Project, Nathan Houser and Christian Kloesel). As a result, the chronological edition has already given rise to a new wave of scholarship on Peirce's development.

The doyen of this scholarly movement is Max H. Fisch, whose first contribution to the Peirce literature came in 1939. Named by the Harvard Philosophy Department in 1959 as the official biographer, Fisch set about methodically to collect all relevant archival materials. Beginning with Brent's contribution of his extensive dissertation notes, scholars added to the "Fisch Notes"—a twenty-thousand-card collation of Peirce materials from numerous family and governmental archives—which were made more widely available at the Indianapolis and Lubbock centers. In addition, Fisch assembled forty-nine file drawers of scholarly correspondence and offprints on Peirce and an extensive personal library, which now forms the basis of more than seven hundred linear feet of bookshelves lining the walls of the Peirce Edition Project. As Fisch proceeded, he issued strategically placed articles that illuminated aspects of Peirce's thought and milieu. His services to other scholars, however, impeded his own progress on a biography. A punctilious correspondent, he was also known (as this writer can testify) to open his office, his files, and his home for weeks at a time to visiting researchers.

When Fisch's advancing years (he is now ninety-four) put a biography beyond his grasp, the directors of the Indiana and Texas centers, Christian Kloesel and Kenneth Laine Ketner, performed the filial act of collecting most of his important writings on Peirce under the title *Peirce, Semeiotic and Pragmatism.*

A careful scholar, Fisch nevertheless had a bold thesis on the origins of Peirce's pragmatism. Though Peirce was almost wholly preoccupied with science and logic, Fisch early suggested that the origins and implications of Peirce's philosophy were social. In this he followed an insight from Vico, who in Fisch's translation of him presents even logical relations as reflections upon institutionally dominant habits of thought. In an essay not reprinted in the collection, Fisch sees philosophy itself as emerging from the "critique of institutions."

For Peirce's pragmatism the institutional and social origins are, Fisch argued, bound up with law. Peirce and James both traced the doctrine to the early 1870s in the meetings of the Cambridge Metaphysical Club. Of the six most active club members, three were lawyers. Whereas James credited Peirce with pragmatism, Peirce himself cited Nicholas St. John Green, among the founding group of professors of the Harvard Law School, as the "grandfather of pragmatism."

Oliver Wendell Holmes, Jr., in his time the leading American writer on jurisprudence, was another of the active lawyers in the Cambridge Metaphysical Club, and Fisch saw in Holmes's youthful "prediction theory of

law" the first application of pragmatism to the social sphere. Holmes's prediction theory defined law as what the legal system could be expected to enforce after whim and idiosyncrasy were winnowed out by successive review. This fit the pragmatic maxim as Peirce would later expound it, first in French and then in carefully convoluted English phrasing: "Consider what effects, which might conceivably have practical bearings, we conceive the object of our conception to have. Then, our conception of these effects is the whole of our conception of the object."

Notwithstanding Holmes's antipathy to Peirce's speculative tendencies, Fisch suggested in the 1942 article that opens his collected essays that a Peircean recasting of Holmes might supply a more systematic logical ground than Holmes himself could muster.

Fifty years later, in the midst of a self-described pragmatic movement in American law schools, few have taken up Fisch's suggestion. Among the lawyers, an attempt to fashion a Wittgensteinian pragmatism (for which Richard Rorty rather than Wittgenstein would appear to be the philosophical mentor) may have delayed a grasp of Peirce's thought. The adage attributed to Wittgenstein that "meaning is use" is often misread as a pithy substitute for Peirce's original pragmatic maxim.

The original of Wittgenstein's remark, however, is neither pithy nor pragmatic. The words "meaning . . . is . . . use" are extracted from a much longer sentence that Wittgenstein characteristically limits to "a *large* class of cases—though not for all—in which we use the word 'meaning.'" The abridgment encourages a merely empirical inquiry into the practices of identifiable communities of interpreters. Peirce's pragmatic maxim, by contrast, is cast in a bolder spirit. It identifies meaning with *conceivable* practical bearings, independent of actual usage. It thus extends the community of interpreters hypothetically and indefinitely into all conceivable futures.

Peirce's maxim is intended to make a place for the imaginative element in science—hypothesis, the hallmark of what he called the method of abduction. Transposed into legal thought it would emphasize the vision that distinguishes disciplined jurisprudential reasoning from that of the pedestrian practitioner.

On a factual standard of use, Holmes's prediction theory of law could be maintained without much discernment. It would merely assert—as in fact Holmes did assert—the doctrine that law is what those in authority can reasonably be expected to do when on good behavior. It would seek the ultimate locus of law in current professional canons, a quest with understandable appeal in the law schools. By contrast, if pragmatic meaning extends to conceivability, the circle of interpretation will be more open. A prediction theory of law must then take into account a range of conjectured futures, many of which may not accord with the profession's conventional norms. The theory might then lead—as Holmes was indeed led—to a supplementary doctrine of judicial restraint founded in the fallibility of the legal profession.

A Peircean pragmatism thus shifts emphasis from the actual to the potential; by adding a greater burden of foresight, it anticipates Holmes's more mature jurisprudence. Which is what Fisch meant to suggest: that a Peircean standpoint helps to make explicit the underlying coherence in Holmes's thought in a way that eluded Holmes himself and that provides a logical basis for a reconstructed legal pragmatism.

To repeat: Peirce's motive in providing explicitly for the free, forward play of mind was to give prominence to hypothesis in scientific discovery. Instead of stifling the bold, speculative leap, Peirce wished to find ways to encourage and discipline it. He did so out of a faith in the human capacity to guess correctly. As he saw it, the progress of science testified to a reality present in both the human mind and the order of the universe. Science did not proceed merely in small inductive increments but in imaginative theorizing in which our use of signs in their general aspects enabled us to participate in a natural order that was itself evolving toward greater generality.

If, then, as Fisch would have it, philosophy is rooted in the critique of institutions, the relevant institution for Peirce's philosophy as a whole is modern science. Indeed, Peirce may be profitably read in terms of a double burden he placed upon himself: creating a logic for science that would also embody, through philosophical critique, the self-restraint appropriate to the limits of science as an institution.

Recent thematic collections and secondary literature give prominence both to this dual theme and to Peirce's success in transcending it. There is, indeed, a growing scholarly consensus that Peirce advances the logic of scientific inquiry in the context of a broader philosophical criterion applicable elsewhere.

The extent of Peirce's immersion in the science of his day is evident in his reviews in the *Nation,* collected and indexed in four volumes by Kenneth Laine Ketner, and in his papers, grant applications, and publishers' prospectuses in the history and practice of science, collected by Carolyn Eisele, herself a pioneering scholar on Peirce's work in science and mathematics. Peirce often earned his daily bread with such writings, or at least tried to. They show him learned in the history of science, alert to new discoveries and trends, and remarkably prescient about fruitful lines of inquiry.

His more popular articles throw a few "sops to Cerberus," as he called the inevitable compromises in making theoretical issues accessible. Yet, since they were at times his only public medium, they often broach his most difficult ideas in deceptively fluent and abbreviated form. Viewed against the background of what Peirce was writing in his notebooks and suffering in his life, even a minor book notice may serve as a running

commentary on central issues that engaged him. Especially poignant is his preoccupation with the honors and material support conducive to the flowering of scientific genius.

The thematic collections have encouraged an increasingly respectful treatment of Peirce's main work in logical semiotic and philosophy. Instead of trying to trip him up in inconsistencies and reversals, scholars are now wont to fasten on a powerful core of interrelated conceptions that provide a standard for both assessing his development and explaining his uncanny relevance across a variety of philosophical schools and academic disciplines.

Whether one approaches Peirce through scientific method, the pragmatic maxim, the theory of signs, his view of continuity, his work on the categories, his concepts of evolution and chance, his notions of God and love, or his logic of relations, one soon finds that each topic involves the others in a complex of ideas that he integrated with increasing mastery as he grew older.

Several new guides to this development are now available, each with some distinctive emphasis. Christopher Hookway's *Peirce* (1985), recently reissued in paperback in the Arguments of the Philosophers series, has the advantage over most of the earlier surveys of following Peirce on his own terms. Though alive with interstitial criticism, it does not try to impose an overarching structure or thesis upon him. Its leitmotif is Peirce's attention to traditional philosophical questions and his determination to supersede Kant. C. F. Delaney's *Science, Knowledge, and Mind* addresses Peirce's philosophy of science, using Descartes as his foil and limiting the number of concepts treated in the interest of brevity and readability. Carl R. Hausman's *Charles S. Peirce's Evolutionary Philosophy* stresses the architectonic character of Peirce's thought. By informing a reading of the early writings with the later, more speculative work, it develops a coherent view of Peirce's project, which it compares favorably with the best current academic work.

There is also an expanding monographic literature that reconstructs aspects of Peirce for contemporary use. In this technical realm, the strongest claims for Peirce are often the most narrowly couched. A prime example is Robert W. Burch's *A Peircean Reduction Thesis: The Foundations of Topological Logic,* which attempts in ten chapters an algebraic reconstruction of Peirce's logic. Burch sets his terms to prove a thesis central to Peirce's thought: that all logical relations of more than three elements are reducible to triadic relations, but that triadic relations are not reducible to dyads and monads. As Peirce liked to point out, our everyday language, by distinguishing between direct and indirect objects, has a version of this logical insight built into its grammar. "John gives Mary a book" cannot be reduced to the three dyads John gives/Mary, John gives/book, and Mary/book, whereas the four elements in "John gives Mary a book and a candle" are reducible into two three-element sentences without loss of logical content.

In the course of his demonstration, Burch argues (chapter 7) that all dyadic and monadic relations are expressible in a triadically grounded form, and (chapter 8) that the entire body of quantificational logic, which rests on a dyadic notion of identity, can be translated into a neo-Peircean system. In other words, triadic logics are richer than dyadic ones (though precisely how much richer is by no means settled, and several papers in *Studies in the Logic of Charles Peirce* begin to address the technical issues).

In an eleventh, non-algebraic chapter, Burch presents some of the fruits of his construction in graphs. He takes his cue from Peirce's own graphical systems of notation, as explicated by Don D. Roberts, J. Jay Zeman, and others. He compares Peirce's achievement in combining topology and logic—in effect, freeing logic from an algebraic notation based on movable type—with Descartes's melding of algebra and geometry in the analytic geometry. Burch's reconstruction is so much more perspicuously expressed in a few diagrams as to persuade one that topology is indeed the natural medium for Peirce's logic of relations, and that the heuristic test will come not with further algebraic work but with computer-graphic and other imaging aids.

The implications of Burch's argument are far-reaching. Peirce's core example of a purely triadic relation comes from semiosis, which relates object, sign, and interpretant. Peirce's approach differs from that of Saussure, the other pioneer of modern semiotic, who proposed a two-pronged view connecting the signifier and the signified. Burch's argument could be extended to suggest that Peircean semiotic swallows up the rival school.

The same point prompts a reconsideration of work done in Peirce's own name. Many who accept Peirce's triadic view of the sign divide the analysis of it into three dyadically organized subfields: semantics (studying relations of sign and object), syntactics (studying relations of signs to each other), and pragmatics (studying relations of signs to their interpretants). Charles Morris, an American follower of Tarski and the Vienna Circle who established this terminology in the 1930s, traced his approach to Peirce's first (1867) paper on the topic. John Dewey and the political scientist Arthur Bentley objected vociferously that something essential in Peirce's project was lost in Morris's three-way partition. Burch's proof that a triad cannot be reduced to three dyads makes their criticism of Morris more exact. It suggests that Peirce should be viewed not merely as precursor and contributor to the mainstream of semiotics of the past half century, but also as having conceived a project of a more spacious kind.

Burch is more explicit in drawing this very conclusion for modern logic. Previous to his work, debate had centered on whether Peirce's reduction thesis might have exceptions. Quine and others influenced by Tarski directed attention to the purely algebraic issue of whether there might be tetrads that are irreducible to triads.

Burch concentrates instead on theses of more pointedly logical consequence: he argues that all relations of both more than and fewer than three elements may be rendered in triadic form without loss of *logical* content. He thus suggests that a three-way notion of identity ("teridentity") is what distinguishes logic from other branches of study expressible in mathematical form. If this is true, the achievements of twentieth-century logic, insofar as they are philosophically neutral, can be retained and superseded in a fully reconstructed Peircean scheme.

The issue is more than quantitative. The *tertium quid* that Peirce persistently provides for is the active role of interpreting mind. One may, as noted, use Peirce's semiotic to analyze signs without attending to their interpretants—as in a purely formal semantics treating the relations of signs to their objects. But we know in advance that, however compelling and precise such abstraction might seem, its clarity will be of an inferior grade. For, if meaning consists in conceivable practical bearings, an "uninterpreted" system is meaningless by definition, and a logic that prescinds the interpretant from its purview will be tempted to slip in hidden assumptions and covert interpretive judgments.

Among formal logicians (Peirce included), one accepted solution to this and other dilemmas is to stratify discourse, positing hierarchies of languages in which one interprets another. Peirce's elegant alternative is to provide for interpretation architectonically by casting logic as semiotic: He introduces interpretation from the bottom up, at the level of the sign-interpretant rather than only at the more inflated stratum of a metalanguage. Instead of pretending that formal logic and other branches of "pure" mathematics necessarily exclude interpretants, we are encouraged to analyze the modalities of interpretation peculiar to them. If the Peircean approach is accepted, a great deal of highly regarded twentieth-century work, including stock-in-trade notions that shape Burch's own presentation, would appear more narrowly applicable than previously thought.

A further technical topic with profound philosophical implications is to be found in Peirce's theory of the continuum. Peirce's father taught him the calculus as Leibniz had originally conceived it, as a continuum of infinitesimals. The Leibnizian view has been revived in late twentieth-century mathematics under the label "nonstandard." Nonstandard analysis, as well as his own work in modal logic and Cantor's work on orders of infinity, provides Hilary Putnam with a point of reference against which to reconstruct Peirce's view of continuity.

In the introduction to *Reasoning and the Logic of Things: The Cambridge Conferences Lectures of 1898* (jointly written with Kenneth Laine Ketner), Putnam shows that if we illustrate Peirce's continuum linearly, it can be grasped not simply as an uncountable infinity of points along a line, but as a potential explosion of infinitesimals at any point at which we may choose to cut the line. Or as Peirce puts it, a point "might burst into any discrete multitude of points whatever, and they would all have been one point before the explosion." As Putnam is acutely aware, this is not an isolated mathematical curiosity, but a technical way of presenting the metaphysical concept that led Peirce to call his later philosophy "synechism," the doctrine of continuity. Synechistic points are conceived *possibilia* of infinite (and infinitesimal) breadth and depth.

When we add to Putnam's analysis the reminder that semiosis provides Peirce with the prime case of continuity, the radical implications of his view are apparent. Peirce's sign relation, as we have seen, connects object, sign, and interpretant in an irreducible triad. But since every interpretant may also be viewed as a sign, to be registered upon the mind with its own interpretant, the continuity of signs will be unbroken. Moreover, since signs are open to modal analysis, not only does every sign-interpretant lead to others, but every sign is analyzable into a multitude of modalities.

Peirce's concept of continuity, in sum, when coupled with his view of semiosis, portrays the universe as both endlessly unfolding and susceptible to an inexhaustible plurality of representations, ready to "explode," as it were, at any point we care to examine. Within this picture, the organizing conceptions of much contemporary academic philosophy may be accommodated and delimited. For example, Peirce's microcosmic view of *possibilia* helps to situate larger talk about "possible worlds" in a context at once precise and metaphysical so that, as Putnam gently puts it, the possible-worlds theories of contemporary writers appear as a *facon de parler*.

A mind as powerfully kaleidoscopic as Peirce's is apt to neglect the contours of common experience. Peirce portrayed himself self-deprecatingly as physiologically prone to this failing. He at times attributed his genius for compact conceptions to his left-handedness, which disposed him to think diagrammatically, at times to the unusually small size of his brain, which limited the number of ideas he could entertain. Be that as it may, he was not bashful about suggesting how others might make up for his deficiencies within a structure that he set forth. In doing so, he sometimes slipped into what he called "triadomany," which is misconceived when it attempts to derive substantive classifications from three-way modal distinctions.

Peirce's program for inquiry as well as his underlying diagrammatic and triadic habits of thought are meticulously elucidated in Beverly Kent's *Charles S. Peirce: Logic and the Classification of the Sciences*. Treating what might be regarded as a dated, nineteenth-century curiosity—Peirce's neo-Comtean classifications of the sciences—Kent excavates a latticed structure reminiscent of Escher. (In a much sketchier appendix she also compares Peirce's iconic habits of thought to those of Einstein.) In her hands the fusty tables of the sciences are turned into the best exposition available of Peirce's

view of the place of logic in relation to mathematics, the positive sciences, and the several branches of philosophy. Kent traces the shifts in classification and terminology that reflect Peirce's approach to a fundamental dilemma: on the one hand, Peirce portrays *formal* logic as a branch of pure mathematics; on the other, he insists on the triadic and normative character of logical semiotic as against the diadic and non-normative character of mathematics. It follows that formal logic as a branch of mathematics will always fall short of representing the essential character of logic itself. This helps us to understand why for Peirce a logic of relations, even when expressed algebraically, must be classified as distinct from the algebra of relations. Far from being the passive follower of mathematical fashion, logic provides its own, inner dynamic for mathematical innovation. As Kent is aware, Peirce's deep admiration for Hegel's *Science of Logic*—remarkable in a pioneer of precise notation—follows from this underlying view of logic as always bursting the formal bounds in which it is cast.

Classification, moreover, raises questions central to Peirce's philosophy and, indeed, to any theoretical project that explains the world in terms of supersensible structures. Supposing Peirce's views of continuity and triadicity to hold, how would they affect the conduct of inquiry? Or, more broadly: Given a world of seamless continuity and unending possibility, how do we go about making the meaningful distinctions that are the stuff of science as it is practiced and of life as we live it?

Recent monographs attempt to show the way Peirce might address these questions on two crucial topics: inquiry and the self. In *Truth and the End of Inquiry*, C. J. Misak draws distinctions that sometimes elude latter-day pragmatists, as well as Peirce's analytic critics. To say, as Peirce does, that everything is relational need not mean that "all truth is relative" or merely situational. And to say that interpretation is integral to the sign relationship does not eliminate meaningful distinctions between knowledge and opinion.

Though Peirce's early pragmatic writings did not dwell upon what contemporary analytic philosophers call a theory of truth—he discussed most issues that concern them under the heading of "reality"—Misak performs an artful reconstruction to present the Peirce of the early, academic years as a figure who more than holds his own in contemporary debate.

Peirce, it should be said, had a way of putting the question that does not translate easily into current academic parlance. He saw "reality" as categorically distinct from "existence." (It is significant that in a famous essay he makes an argument for the reality, not the existence, of God.) What exists—brute materiality—forces itself upon us at the beginning of inquiry. Reality, on the other hand, is what we would believe at the completion of inquiry. (The notion of conceivability in the pragmatic maxim, we have seen, encourages us not only to consider what exists but also to form clear hypotheses about a reality that might be.) Adapting a notion from differential calculus, Peirce once called reality a "limit"—what would be believed by a community of inquirers after inquiry had run its course. By identifying truth with this hypothetical *consensus ad quem,* Misak constructs a "pragmatic theory of truth" that captures Peirce's streak of objectivity without sacrificing his vivid sense of the interpretative and communal element in science. Her account, which contains several important subtleties, errs, however, in speaking as if objectivity requires—and hence that a reconstruction of Peirce's system should somehow vindicate—a "bivalent" logic, in which propositions must be either true or false.

To the contrary, if we are to borrow terms about truth values from formal logic, Peirce's logic of inquiry would have as its mathematical complement a formal system of more than two values, in which, for example, a third value between true and false might accommodate the crucial no-man's-land of propositions that are unproven, unprovable, or open to reconsideration. (And it is no accident that Peirce developed the first matrix notation for many-valued logic in late, unpublished notebook entries, more than a decade before the logicians Lukasiewicz and Post independently published similar innovations.) As Peirce put it technically, in keeping with one aspect of his doctrine of continuity, a triadic logic has a third value to represent "the common limit of 'P' and 'not P.'"

Peirce's overall trademark, both technically and metaphysically, is to set his terms so that intellectual boundaries are open to continuing revision in the pursuit of an ever more general grasp of reality—where "reality" is both explicandum and criterion for the inquiring mind and, at the same time, a general condition in which mind participates.

This supple and initially difficult conception is illustrated at the level of the formation of personality in *Peirce's Approach to the Self,* a book of essays by Vincent Michael Colapietro. Peirce makes the topic of the self inescapable. By building the interpretant into the definition of a sign, he requires as a philosophical complement a highly developed account of self-consciousness, self-criticism, and self-control. How else are we to sift out what is merely idiosyncratic in interpretation?

As he grew older, Peirce incessantly invoked an ideal of "self-control." Yet since his scattered writings on the self are often inconsistent and overstated, his emphasis on self-control has been plausibly read as a cry of remorse at the ruins of his private life. His failings on the topic have seemed especially glaring when compared with the robust and seductive portrayal of the self that suffuses the work of William James.

Hence Colapietro's work fills a gap of more than archival interest. If it can be shown that Peirce had a theory of the self that explains how we retain a personal identity while entering into a general and publicly articulable order of nature and society—and further how we exercise some control over the world and ourselves through the use of signs—this would justify strong claims for his philosophy as a whole.

Colapietro takes Peirce a good distance toward such a theory. He understands Peirce's semiotic to address a central problem in the conception of human subjectivity: the opposition between an inner, private self and a communal self defined by its relations with others—a tension, as Colapietro puts it, between solitude and solidarity. If mind is defined as operating with signs, and if the meaning of a sign is to be found in its conceivable practical effects, it follows that a self can be meaningful to itself only to the extent that it thinks in terms of practices, which are, in turn, predicated upon relations with others.

Peirce does not deny that we have idiosyncratic feelings, thoughts, and actions; that they are entrenched in the habits that define our individuality; and that we must summon energy to redirect or correct them. But all such personal struggles with habit are part of a continuum of semiosis and, as such, of a web of sign relationships whose meaning resides in practical bearings that go beyond us. The stage on which human life is enacted—including the life of the hermit-philosopher—is indelibly public.

Thus, whereas James's *Principles of Psychology* asserted the completely personal character of consciousness, Peirce stressed its communicability. In an evocative portrayal of consciousness, James had written:

> The only states of consciousness that we naturally deal with are found in personal consciousness, minds, selves, concrete particular I's and you's. Each of these minds keeps its own thoughts to itself; there is no giving or bartering between them. . . . Absolute insulation, irreducible pluralism, is the law . . . every thought being owned. . . . The breaches among such thoughts are the most absolute breaches in nature.

To which Peirce responded: "Is not the direct contrary nearer the observed facts?" That is, is not consciousness better defined by what it shares than what it negates in its relation with others? Is not thought itself, even the most private, really a dialogue involving signs that have meaning only by virtue of their effects in a world of outward relations? And if this is so, is not our capacity to enter into more general relations through our use of signs the very definition of human personality? On Peirce's view, a being speaking a purely private language would have a self utterly devoid of humanity.

In his early writings, when he adopted somewhat polemical stances to make his philosophy accessible to a broader readership, Peirce was wont to cast his communal insights in opposition to the logical individualism underlying English nominalism; at later times he railed against the crass individualism of the Gilded Age. In such moods he sometimes denied the self altogether. Colapietro's service is to glean the best from Peirce's writings on the self, supplemented by his mature concepts of individuality, continuity, organism, substance, and mind, and to suggest that a fully elaborated Peircean account would subsume a doctrine of individual personality in a larger perspective. Colapietro also joins Peirce himself, Walker Percy, and others in believing that a philosophical psychology along Peircean lines would avoid confusions in psychology and brain science deriving from overly rigid subject-object and mind-body dichotomies.

Colapietro's reconstruction, however, stops short of the technical virtuosity that makes Peirce compelling in other fields. Colapietro is aware that Peirce's system provides the raw material for a still more precise treatment: The modalities of the interpretant include terms to describe the formation and reshaping of habits. Unfortunately, Peirce waited until too late in life to undertake the demanding task of refashioning his terms to account for "self-control" at the level of the sign-interpretant. To supply this gap would complete his project.

For it is integral to Peirce's view that the more general our grasp of reality becomes, the more precise and ramified will be our explanations. Far from submerging all distinctions in the Oneness of the All, his concept of continuity would have us proceed from a core of received, often fruitfully vague ideas to an ever more differentiated picture. Each new discovery leads to others. Each new concept is open to further elaboration. It is through the purposeful embrace of the public and communal character of semiosis that the self finds its ultimate meaning.

Does this vision, congenial to science, extend beyond the laboratory? Do the compact conceptions of Peirce's philosophy have the broader applicability he intended?

For the crucial core of Peirce's later philosophy—the theorizing that proceeds from the continuous sign relationship—the range of his relevance cannot be in doubt. Once we accept Wittgenstein's verdict that "all thinking is essentially operating with signs," it follows that theorizing about the power, presuppositions, and limits of semiosis has by definition a universal subject matter. It must apply to anything and everything that may occur to consciousness. Thus, had our discussion centered on the current scholarship that treats Peirce's significance for the arts, morals, religion, linguistics, anthropology, evolutionary biology, cognitive science, cinematography, information theory, or quantum physics, the same organizing concepts—semiosis, continuity, pragmatic meaning, modalities of signs, reality—would have come into play.

As a result, three tendencies in twentieth-century philosophy that have also claimed broad applicability require Peirce's perspective for their own completion. The linguistic turn that has dominated the English-speaking world is a subspecies of the semiotic approach that Peirce took. The phenomenological movement popular on the Continent is likewise insufficiently self-critical without a phenomenology of signs, the medium in which thought itself takes place (and Husserl's late metaphysical attempt in this direction in fact took a triadic, albeit ego-centered, form). The scientific trend in philosophy, insofar as it excludes the interpreting mind from its working definition of reality, is subsumed and reoriented in Peirce, who locates its abstractions in a more capacious yet no less exacting context. (Abner Shimony, the noted practitioner and philosopher of quantum physics, concludes the section on complex systems of his two-volume *Search for a Naturalistic Worldview* with this self-effacing credo: "It is honorable to be an epigone of Peirce.")

Admittedly, it seems extravagant to suggest that a blackballed, debt-ridden, small-brained, left-handed, pain-wracked, opium-eating, skirt-chasing, nineteenth-century recluse, by the simple device of including the sign-interpretant in the formal definition of the sign and by a life-long struggle to draw out the implications of this idea, may still have more to teach us than the contemporary discussions we have learned to regard as momentous.

But consider: From his first paper on the subject in 1867, Peirce returned repeatedly to the continuous sign relationship. For the last three decades of his life, Peirce worked in increasing isolation, writing prodigiously, publishing only a portion—buzzing furiously, as he put it, like a wasp in a bottle. His interests and his situation reinforced each other. He attended more and more to phenomena of common experience that could be examined without the benefit of colleagues or scientific instruments. Though the growth of the modern university has done great things for topics that can be cast into specialized departments, there is no reason to suppose that anyone in the past century would have duplicated, let alone superseded, Peirce's concentration on a few ineluctable and inter-related concepts. The only excuse for not taking him seriously is a skeptical dogmatism that would have us deny (on a priori grounds?) that some ideas may be more fundamental than others.

Peirce's chosen idioms were doubly demanding: on the one hand, metaphysics, in which contributions are judged against a tradition of 2,400 years; on the other, symbolic logic, then in its infancy, of which he was a pioneer in its algebraic, quantificational, and topological forms. He insisted that each must reflect the other. How many writers of the past century have had Peirce's aptitude for both prongs of this bilingual enterprise, or have matched his unrelenting fecundity in concurrent innovation in them into his seventies?

Now, eighty years after his death, Peirce has himself become a topic for specialized inquiry. New tools for scholarship and for pedagogy are giving him a delayed afterlife. The *consensus ad quem* is that we shall have to take him more fully into account. The wasp is out of the bottle. His sting remains to be felt.

BOOKS DISCUSSED IN THIS ESSAY

Writings of Charles S. Peirce: A Chronological Edition, Volume 5, *1884-1886.* Compiled by the Editors of the Peirce Edition Project. Indiana University Press, 1993.

Historical Perspectives on Peirce's Logic of Science: A History of Science. Edited by Carolyn Eisele. Mouton Publishers, 1985. 2 volumes,

Charles Sanders Peirce: Contributions to The Nation, *Part Four: Index.* Edited by Kenneth Laine Ketner. Texas Tech University Press, 1987.

The Essential Peirce: Selected Philosophical Writings, Volume 1, *1867-1893.* Edited by Nathan Houser and Christian J. W. Kloesel. Indiana University Press, 1992. Volume 2, forthcoming, 1995.

Reasoning and the Logic of Things: The Cambridge Conference Lectures of 1898 of Charles Sanders Peirce. Edited by Kenneth Laine Ketner, with an introduction by Kenneth Laine Ketner and Hilary Putnam. Harvard University Press, 1992.

Peirce on Signs: Writings on Semiotic. By Charles Sanders Peirce, edited by James Hoopes. University of North Carolina Press, 1991.

The Collected Papers of Charles Sanders Peirce. MS-DOS version, with an editorial introduction by John Deely. InteLex Corporation, 1994. 8 vols. on 7 MB.

Studies in the Logic of Charles Sanders Peirce. Edited by Nathan Houser, Don D. Roberts, and James Van Evra. Indiana University Press, forthcoming, 1995.

Peirce and Contemporary Thought: Philosophical Inquiries. Edited by Kenneth Laine Ketner. Fordham University Press, forthcoming, 1994.

Charles S. Peirce and the Philosophy of Science. Edited by Edward C. Moore. University of Alabama Press, 1993.

Peirce and Value Theory: On Peircean Ethics and Aesthetics. Edited by Herman Parret. Benjamins, North America, 1993.

Peirce and Law: Issues in Pragmatism, Legal Realism, and Semiotics. Edited by Roberta Kevelson. Peter Lang, 1991.

Charles Sanders Peirce: A Life. By Joseph Brent, with an introduction by Thomas Sebeok. Indiana University Press, 1993.

Peirce, Semeiotic and Pragmatism: Essays. By Max H. Fisch, edited by Kenneth Laine Ketner and Christian J. W. Kloesel. Indiana University Press, 1986.

Peirce. By Christopher Hookway. Routledge & Kegan Paul, 1985. Paper (1992),

A Peircean Reduction Thesis: The Foundations of Topological Logic. By Robert W. Burch. Texas Tech University Press, 1991.

Peirce's Approach to the Self: A Semiotic Perspective on Human Subjectivity. By Vincent M. Colapietro. State University of New York Press, 1989.

Science, Knowledge, and Mind: A Study in the Philosophy of C. S. Peirce. By C. F. Delaney. University of Notre Dame Press, 1993.

Charles S. Peirce's Evolutionary Philosophy. By Carl R. Hausman. Cambridge University Press, 1993.

Charles S. Peirce: Logic and the Classification of the Sciences. By Beverly Kent. McGill-Queen's University Press, 1987.

Truth and the End of Inquiry: A Peircean Account of Truth. By C. J. Misak. Oxford University Press, 1991.

G. B. Christensen (essay date 1994)

SOURCE: "Peirce's Transformation of Kant," in *The Review of Metaphysics,* Vol. XLVIII, No. 189, September, 1994, pp. 91-120.

[*In the following excerpt, Christensen discusses the critical relevancy of Peirce's philosophical contributions to pragmatism.*]

Although C. S. Peirce is generally regarded as the founder of American pragmatism, the fragmentary and incomplete character of many of his texts makes it hard to glimpse any systematic or coherent philosophy of pragmatism in them. One might respond to this state of affairs by interpreting Peirce in the light of the views of other pragmatists, in particular, of William James. While this interpretive strategy certainly gives one a handle on at least aspects of Peirce's philosophy, it has one decided disadvantage: it leads one to portray Peirce as simply the first in a line of thought which extends more or less continuously through James, Mead, and Dewey to Quine and even Richard Rorty. It is thus fated to obscure such discontinuities of philosophical intention and doctrine as might exist between Peirce and the later pragmatists. We have good reason to suspect the existence of such discontinuities. Late in his life Peirce himself felt that other writers who had begun calling themselves pragmatists had so misunderstood what he meant by the term that his own philosophy was in danger of being confused with theirs; in consequence, he renamed his doctrine "pragmaticism" in order to emphasize its difference from the doctrines of other so-called pragmatists.[1] This fact is a clear indication that we need another strategy of interpretation, one which will reveal a more systematic and coherent side to Peirce's philosophy, in the light of which the difference upon which Peirce himself insisted will become more clearly visible and intelligible.

In this paper, I seek to identify just such an alternative strategy and then to sketch with its help an alternative picture of Peirce. Specifically, I seek to show how one might interpret Peirce's philosophy as possessing a decidedly Kantian character or architectonic in virtue of which there must be a fundamental discontinuity between his thought and that of James and those later writers who see themselves as belonging to the one tradition of American pragmatism initiated by Peirce. I will do this by adopting and elaborating the interpretation of Peirce articulated by the contemporary German philosopher Karl-Otto Apel in his book, *Charles S. Peirce: From Pragmatism to Pragmaticism.*[2] My claim will not be that the Apel-inspired picture of Peirce which I wish to sketch here is the only possible one; the frequent difficulty and incompleteness of Peirce's texts presumably make it futile to hope for a single definitive interpretation of him. Nonetheless, I do believe, first, that such a view of Peirce finds support in at least some, if not all, of his texts; and second, that it portrays him as an interesting and original thinker who is attempting to overcome the traditional concept of theoretical knowledge as *epistēmē*[3] while not rejecting, as is currently fashionable, the very idea of theory as knowledge of how things really are. Much of what I say comes from Apel, and where that is the case, I have indicated it. At the same time, Apel's interpretation is itself rather scanty and even obscure; in order to overcome these difficulties, I have engaged in more than a little creative reconstruction of my own. In particular, the account I give in section III of what Peirce means by semiosis is not to be found in Apel, although many things he says suggest aspects of it. Nor does Apel ever explicitly describe Peirce's central problem in the way I do in section IV, namely, as the problem of showing how theoretical inquiry is possible once one has made that break with the traditional concept of theory as *epistēmē* which Apel calls Peirce's semiotic transformation of the theory of knowledge. The views expressed in sections VI and VII should not be attributed to Apel. This is particularly true of the claim I make in section VII, namely, that a consensus theory of truth, whether Peirce's or anyone else's, is best understood not as offering an *alternative* to the traditional correspondence theory, but rather as making this latter *criterially relevant.*

I

Why Apel is Interested in Peirce. In order to understand why Apel interprets Peirce in the particular way he does, one must understand why he concerns himself with Peirce at all. Two motives underlie Apel's interest in Peirce, a "scholarly" one and a deeper, more philosophical one.

On the surface, Apel is simply trying to correct conventional wisdom on Peirce and his philosophy. Conven-

tionally, Peirce is seen as an insightful philosopher but poor writer whose obscure doctrine of pragmatism had to be popularized by the literarily gifted, but philosophically shallow, William James. On this view, pragmatism is a doctrine which identifies meaning with operationalizability and truth with rational assertability in the here and now, or even with mere practical utility; it is radically empiricist, naturalistic, anti-Kantian, and ultimately antiintentional and behavioristic.[4] This is the pragmatism that ultimately leads to Richard Rorty.

Apel thinks that this is wrong. In particular, he believes that such popular pragmatism, whether it is that of James or not, is certainly not that of Peirce. He of course admits that aspects of Peirce's thought insinuate popular pragmatism. He also recognizes that these aspects explain why pragmatism could, in the hands first of James and Mead, and then of Dewey and Morris, become increasingly antiintentional, behavioristic, and ethically irrelevant. Apel, however, thinks that these aspects are just one side of Peirce's philosophy; they represent the Humean and positivist influence exerted on Peirce by people like Chauncey Wright, Nicholas Green, and through the latter, Alexander Bain. According to Apel, James and others exaggerated this side of Peirce at the expense of another, namely, that which derives from his early studies of Kant and Duns Scotus. Apel wants to correct this one-sided interpretation by showing that Peirce can be understood as giving a modernized version of Kant's Critical Philosophy and Transcendental Logic. Furthermore, he wants to show that and how the undoubted empiricist elements in Peirce's thought are but a part of his attempt to synthesize the fundamental motivations of Kant's philosophy with that orientation toward experimental method and empirical inquiry which constitutes the better side of empiricism.

Underlying this surface concern to correct the conventional view of Peirce there is a deeper objective. Apel believes that to understand Peirce properly is to see him as having anticipated and to some extent realized what Apel sees as the principal task for philosophy today: the task of a critical rehabilitation or, as Apel calls it, a *transformation* of Kant's transcendental philosophy. As Apel understands it, to transform Kant in this way is both to revive and revise him. In particular, it is to revive Kant's original idea that there are certain "transcendental" activities of the knowing subject which are not solely objects of study for either psychology, linguistics, sociology, or history, but rather for transcendental philosophy. At the same time, it is to revise this idea in two quite radical respects: first, these activities must be shown to be transcendental in the sense that they constitute not merely conditions of the possibility of objective knowledge but rather conditions of the possibility of all meaning and sense. Second, these activities must not be conceived in Kant's traditional way, namely, on the model of mental processes going on "in the head." In other words, Apel wants to overcome Kant's reliance on the traditional Cartesian model of consciousness, that is, his casting of transcendental philosophy in the shape of a rather bizarre transcendental psychology. In order thus to "de-psychologize" Kant, Apel wants to draw upon the linguistic turn taken by philosophy both on the continent and in Anglo-Saxon countries. The concepts forged and insights gained, for example, by analytic philosophy in its classic debates on the relation between logic and language, truth conditions, propositions and communication, language, rules, and forms of life are all to be used to relocate these transcendental activities, and with them, the subject of such activities, in concrete linguistic practices of interpretation, discussion, and debate. At the same time, he wants to draw upon the German tradition of philosophical hermeneutics in order to gain a richer understanding of the historical dimension and background of these practices than can be derived from the analytic tradition.

Why should one desire such a transformation of Kant in the first place? Because, says Apel, such a transformation offers an alternative both to traditional philosophical foundationalism and to philosophical minimalism in both its continental and analytic forms, namely, relativist hermeneuticism and the restriction of theoretical philosophy to discussing scientific method and conceptual questions thrown up by the latest scientific theories. Apel believes that the way out of this dilemma lies in a critical return to Kant. On the theoretical side, he sees such a return as offering the prospect of a mildly foundational epistemology which identifies and takes on board what is right about current antifoundational and detranscendentalizing critiques while avoiding their relativist and historicist consequences. On the practical side, he sees it as the point of departure for a rationally founded, deontological "ethics of discourse" which avoids the abstract and ultimately empty purism of Kant's ethics and at the same times leaves room for fundamentally subjective, individual conceptions of the good. Clearly, Apel is aiming high, perhaps too high. However this may be, the pursuit of these ambitious goals leads him to read Peirce in a way that is interesting in its own right. I turn now to elaborate and expand upon Apel's reading of Peirce as anticipating and partly realizing a transformation of Kant.

II

What Must be Shown. In order to substantiate the claim that Peirce's pragmatism and logic of inquiry is a critical revision of Kant's transcendental philosophy, one must identify within Peirce's works something at least akin to Kant's transcendental deduction of the objective validity of the categories.[5] It is this part of the *Critique of Pure Reason* that contains that uniquely kantian kind of argument which the analytic tradition has come to call "transcendental argument." Very roughly, such arguments argue for a certain epistemologically significant proposition by claiming that some undeniable fact, feature, or capacity would not be possible unless this proposition were true. In Kant's case, this undeniable feature is the ability to identify oneself as one and the same subject of diverse seeings, hearings, and other

experiencings extended in time and ordered in temporal relations of succession and simultaneity. Kant called this ability, or rather its *exercise,* "transcendental apperception";[6] he called its *product,* that is, a specific state of self-consciousness, the "synthetic unity of apperception" and went on to say that the ability to produce such synthetic unity is "that highest point to which one must ascribe all exercise of the understanding, indeed, of logic itself, hence of transcendental philosophy."[7] The proposition whose truth makes this ability, its exercise, and its product possible, and which thus forms the conclusion of Kant's transcendental argument, states that these diverse and temporally ordered experiencings have as their objects entities which have an intrinsic spatiotemporal substantiality and causality.

Kant proceeds to this conclusion by arguing for the following claims: First, transcendental apperception, that is, self-consciousness, is certainly possible for us. Second, transcendental apperception is only possible for a subject if it can determine the identity and temporal position of individual experiences within its "bundle of perceptions." Third, the subject can only determine this identity and position by identifying something as a distinct *object* of experience which, because it determines temporal relations of succession and simultaneity among the *objects* of diverse experiences, imposes such relations on the experiences themselves. Fourth, the object of experience can only determine such an objective temporal order if it is intrinsically subject to some kind of causal law which determines what must succeed or exist simultaneously with it. That is, it can only determine such an order if a genuinely causal substantiality and interconnection with other such objects is constitutive of its very identity. It now follows by *modus ponens* that the concepts of substance-and-accident, cause-and-effect, and the like cannot be just subjective principles for ordering one's experiences (*pace* Hume), but must also be objective features, that is, genuine ontological categories, of the *objects* of experience.[8] If Peirce is, as Apel maintains, engaging in some kind of reformed transcendental philosophy, it must be possible to identify within his work a structure of argumentation at least analogous to this. Such argumentation need not have precisely Kant's premise or conclusion, but it must have the overall structure and style of Kant's argument.

Clearly, the first thing one must identify in Peirce is something recognizably equivalent in function to Kant's starting point, namely, transcendental apperception and the synthetic unity of apperception. Then one must show how this Peircean equivalent leads in a recognizably "transcendental" way to some proposition of equal epistemological gravity and foundational significance to Kant's conclusion that the categories have real application to the objects of experience.

These requirements determine the course my paper takes from sections III to V: Apel maintains that one can see in Peirce's central concept of *semiosis*[9] a structural equivalent to Kant's transcendental apperception and synthetic unity of apperception. Thus, my first job must be to outline just what Peirce means by semiosis. This I do in the next section, section III. Then, in section IV, I give an account of what Apel calls Peirce's semiotic transformation of the theory of knowledge. In particular, I show how this transformation represents a break with the traditional conception of theory and consequently raises the rather Kantian question of how theoretical inquiry is possible once one has made this break. Then, in the first part of section V, I elaborate upon Apel's thesis that Peirce saw his famous pragmatic maxim as arising from this semiotic transformation as a method of revealing the true content of our ideas and concepts. It is upon this thesis that Apel rests his claim that Peirce's philosophy is critical in a Kantian sense. In the second part of this section I then flesh out Apel's conviction that Peirce proceeds from his pragmatic maxim via his well-known definitions of reality and truth to the conclusion that the forms of so-called synthetic inference, abduction and induction, are valid in the sense that their continual exercise in the course of empirical inquiry must bring us ever nearer to the truth.[10] Precisely this is Peirce's equivalent of Kant's "Transcendental Deduction," a transcendental argument which deduces the validity not of specific categories but of the procedures of inquiry taken at their most abstract.[11] If this constitutes a plausible reconstruction of Peirce, then Apel's general claim will have been shown to have its own plausibility.

III

Peirce's Concept of Semiosis. Peirce defines semiosis as the action or process of a sign;[12] it is a sign so to speak in movement, that is, caught in the process of behaving in a typically signlike way. The best example of semiosis is, at least as Apel reads Peirce,[13] the uttering of a sentence in some language, therein referring to some object, predicating some property of it, and perhaps asserting the proposition thereby expressed. According to Apel semiosis constitutes Peirce's equivalent to Kant's synthetic unity of apperception.[14] In order to understand how Apel can maintain this, we must understand the formal structure which Peirce attributes to semiosis: Peirce claims that "a sign has, as such, three references: first, it is a sign *to* some thought which interprets it; second, it is a sign *for* some object to which in that thought it is equivalent; third, it is a sign, *in* some respect or quality, which brings it into connection with its object."[15] Peirce here appears to be saying three things.

First, the process of sign use is one of interpretation; it involves recognizing or interpreting the *practical significance* of this particular sign's applying to this particular object. This practical significance consists in certain further meaningful signs which the subject of sign use could derive from the uttered sign on the basis of its semantic meaning. Peirce calls these further signs "logical interpretants" of the first sign. Crucially, such "logical interpretants" are, at least ultimately, counterfactual conditionals expressing what observable behavior the *object* of sign use would display were the *subject* of sign use to act upon this object in specific ways.

Second, the process of sign use involves reference to an object or objects, and such reference must, at least ultimately, be of the causal, nonconceptual, and ostensive kind which is realized in language by indexical expressions. No sign can refer simply in virtue of the general terms and bound variables, or even in virtue of the nondemonstrative singular referring terms, that it contains. Many signs do not contain indexicals; for example, the sentence "The King of France in 1789 was a good hunter but a poor ruler." Even so, such signs only refer to real objects in the world because they are embedded in a context of sign use which connects them up with indexical references to their referents. As Apel puts it, indexicals "allow us at all times to have real contact with the individual subjects of our sentences;"[16] without them language could not attach to the world.

Third, the process of sign use is in part iconical. The later Peirce quite often speaks of "certain qualities of feeling, such as the color of magenta, the odor of attar, the sound of a railway whistle, the taste of quinine, the quality of the emotion upon contemplating a fine mathematical demonstration, the quality of feeling love, etc."[17] He seems to associate the experiencing of immediate qualities such as these with the corresponding general terms.[18] Thus the general term "magenta" is somehow bound up with the sensuous experiencing of magenta, the general term "railway whistle" with the sensuous experiencing of a railway whistle, and the general term "love" with the experiencing of loving. What does Peirce mean by this? I suspect he is claiming two things: first, that mastery of any general term presupposes mastery of general terms of the concrete, sensuous kind just mentioned; and second, that one only has complete mastery of these latter terms if one knows what it is like to experience them in their application to objects.[19] Certainly Apel appears to interpret Peirce along these lines; he says, for example, that the iconic function of language has the task of connecting up the qualities of nature with the predicates of human perceptual judgment.[20] This is quite plausible, for it fits well with the first structural characteristic of semiosis, and in particular, with Peirce's notion of the "logical interpretant." The logical interpretant is a rule or, as Peirce calls it, a "habit" of behavior expressing what observable behavior the object would display in response to our interaction with it. When construed more subjectively, it is a practical rule or maxim for our interacting with the object in order to induce certain desired behavior in it.[21] Consequently, it presupposes that we have sensuous experience of the thing, for it is only through the way a thing shows itself qualitatively to us that we can recognize its behavior and on this basis rationally adjust our own behavior to it. It is only because we can *see how* the liquid in the test tube is turning green in the heat of the bunsen burner's flame that withdrawing it from the flame in response to this change becomes something we *correctly* or *rationally* do in the light of certain goals. This experiencing is an essential part of our behavior *qua* rationally assessable, self-guiding action in an experimental context.

In order to understand how Apel can see Peirce's concept of semiosis as playing the kind of role played by transcendental apperception and the synthetic unity of apperception in Kant's philosophy, we must appeal to a further aspect of Peircean doctrine: according to Peirce the process of semiosis is not restricted to strictly linguistic cases, that is, to utterings of signs in a language; it can also occur psychologically. In other words, certain psychological processes have the structure of semiosis. Throughout his whole life Peirce always maintained that thinking requires signs. Apel embraces this with enthusiasm, for he is resolutely opposed to the Cartesian picture of the subject as capable of cognition prior to all language and communication with other subjects. Unfortunately, Peirce gives no detailed account of the relation between thought and signs at all, nor does Apel ever indicate with any precision just what his own views are.[22] A little detective work is therefore necessary if we are to identify anything as what Apel might be claiming on behalf of Peirce.

In his essay "From Kant to Peirce" Apel makes a number of remarks on semiosis and cognition[22] which tacitly presuppose a certain critique of the traditional conception of perception which ultimately derives from, or is at least inspired by, Heidegger.[23] There is an alternative account of perception implicit in this critique, and by making this explicit one can perhaps identify what conception of thought and cognition as dependent upon language Apel both endorses himself and also attributes to Peirce.[24] The tradition characteristically saw the perception of objects as a two-place relation between a subject and object, according to such perfectly acceptable linguistic formulas as "*S* sees a tree," "I see a red plane surface," and so on. But this is not correct; these linguistic formulas obscure the true structure of perception, at least as it is had by the kind of self-conscious being which the tradition always had in mind. Such beings perceive objects *as* this or that, that is, *as* satisfying this or that concept or predicate. Note that the formula "*S* perceives *X* as a case of *F*" is not two-place, but three-place, and that it takes general terms in its third place. This suggests what Apel is getting at: self-conscious perceivers *know what it is that they perceive things to be;* one might say, perhaps rather incautiously, that their thought and perception allows quantification over concepts and, by extension, abstract entities generally, propositions in particular. Such beings can thus distinguish between their contents of thought and perception and what satisfies them or makes them true; relatedly, they have the "semantic" concepts of truth and falsity, the intentional concepts of getting things right and getting things wrong, and the ontological concepts of reality and unreality. Now the ability to grasp or to understand a concept or proposition *as such*—as opposed to just having it as the content of some psychological

state—is, I would argue,[25] only possible as a grasping or understanding of signs which express these concepts or propositions. If this is so, then at least self-conscious perception and cognition involves signs, or rather, knowledge and understanding of sings.

IV

The Semiotic Transformation. By extending the notion of semiosis to cognition generally, and to perception in particular, Peirce has wrought what Apel calls a semiotic transformation of the concept and theory of knowledge.[26] Apel gives this extension such a grandiloquent title because he believes that it represents a quite radical break with traditional epistemology. Unfortunately, Apel never makes quite clear just how or why it amounts to such a break with tradition. In this section, however, I will use Peirce's texts and a number of suggestive hints from Apel to show that it implicitly breaks with the whole idea of theory as *epistēmē*. In the section that follows I will sketch how it leads to an alternative conception of theory which contrasts markedly with that individualistic conception of ultimately Platonic and Cartesian origin which underlies most modern epistemology. Let us start with the more specific consequences of the view that cognition involves what Peirce himself calls "psychical semiosis."[27]

Clearly, if cognition and, in particular, perception are themselves cases of semiosis, then they must have the same triadic structure as the linguistic kind; they must contain or implicate the three aspects or components outlined above, namely, *interpretation* in terms of rules or habits of behavior; *indexical relation* to the world; and *iconic* or *phenomenal quality*. If this is so, then radical consequences follow for the concept of theoretical knowledge. In order to expose these, we need to understand Peirce's concept of iconic or phenomenal quality a little better. What phenomenal quality is can be illustrated as follows: imagine you are lying in bed at night in a strange house and that you suddenly hear what you would retrospectively describe as a pitter-patter. Perhaps a little reflection will make everything clear to you: you are hearing rain hitting the tin roof. But before you thus reflect, you are simply experiencing those phenomenal qualities which usually underlie your hearing rain hitting a tin roof and which together constitute the latter's phenomenal "feel" or "appearance." Visual examples are of course also possible. Here, the relevant qualities of feeling will be those structural and sensual properties which together constitute the immediate, perspectival "look" of the thing seen. Note that the immediate or perspectival look of a thing seen is a genuine, if relational, property of this object; it and the qualities that "compose" it are thus not sense data in the traditional sense.

Such qualities of feeling alone constitute what is actually given in the present moment of perceptual cognition. Yet clearly, because they themselves are nothing propositional in nature, they are not themselves perceptual cognition. Perceptual cognition requires something more, namely, that aspect of conceptual interpretation which consists in associating some rule or habit of behavior with the object referred to either in one's utterance or in one's cognition. In order to bring out these points, one can fairly resort to Wittgenstein's famous and presumably more familiar "duck/rabbit" drawing. Peirce, in fact, uses a very similar example in order to illustrate the interpretive character of perception.[28] In Wittgenstein's example what is strictly given is always the same shape and sensual appearance. Furthermore, this shape and appearance must first be interpreted before a sensing of it has that intentional character which makes it a genuine seeing *of* something—as is shown precisely by the fact that in this particular case the one shape and appearance can be seen in two different ways, either as a duck or as a rabbit. But if that element of conceptual interpretation which turns mere sensing of quality into propositionally determinate, hence cognitively relevant perception is not itself given in perception, where does it come from? What makes a perceiving out of a mere sensing of quality? Peirce suggests that it is the embeddedness of such sensing in a whole series of prior perceptions and interpretations.[29] Genuine perception therefore involves the bringing to bear of one's possibly quite distinctive cognitive history and background in the interpretation of present phenomenal quality. One might say that it is "interpretation-laden."[30]

If present perception is determined by past cognition, that is, if it is essentially "interpretation-laden," then it is essentially hypothetical. There can be no such thing as ultimate perceptual judgments in the sense envisaged by empiricism, namely, basic perceptual judgments of which all knowing subjects would be capable irrespective of their differing historical and cognitive backgrounds, and which could thus form the basis for certain theoretical knowledge of the world. Because the point here is pretty much one made much later by Wilfrid Sellars, we can say with Sellars that a propositionally structured perceptual given which impresses itself upon all minds irrespective of theoretical background, history, and tradition is a myth. And if the given is a myth, then so too is the old idea of scientific theory as *epistēmē*, at least in its empiricist or logically positivist forms. Relatedly, empirical cognition in general must be radically holistic and fallible; the whole idea of cognition's having an absolute and unconditional, categorical founding in perception no longer makes sense. This leads to a certain problem: if theory and theoretical knowledge are not *epistēmē*, at least in the empiricist sense, what are they? What can it now mean to speak of systematic theoretical inquiry in the traditional sense of an activity which enables us not merely to get around the world better, but also and primarily to know how things really are? This latter question is decidedly Kantian in spirit, for it asks in effect how science and theoretical inquiry generally are possible, given that what makes theory theory as opposed to "mere opinion" cannot be its resting on basic propositions to whose truth we have indubitable access. One can construe Apel

as claiming that Peirce's pragmatism and logic of inquiry is a Kant-inspired attempt to answer it.

V

Peirce's Transcendental Argument and Philosophy. If the semiotic transformation of the concept of knowledge creates the above mentioned problem for the traditional notion of theory, it is also what Peirce sees as the key to its solution. This transformation shows that nonlogical predicates and concepts have a depth-structure which points the way out of the difficulty. They do not merely have the intentional or semantic property of being true of this or that. They also have a practical meaning or significance which lies in their determining rules or, to use Peirce's word, "habits" as to how the objects in their extension would reveal themselves behaviorally to the subject who applies them should this subject interact with these objects in certain ways. Part of our concept of a diamond, for example, is the fact that a diamond is something we would observe to scratch glass were we to drag it across the surface of a piece of glass—and so on, apparently for indefinitely many further conditionals of this kind.[31] Such conditionals or "logical interpretants" define what it means *to us* for something to be in the extension of a given concept or predicate; as such, they are an essential aspect of our understanding of concepts and predicates. Thus, all concepts and predicates that we can in any way grasp must have this practical or pragmatic dimension.

Pragmatism as Critical Philosophy. If the conclusions just reached are right, then Peirce's famous pragmatic maxim appears in a new light. For these conclusions suggest that this maxim derives from, or is contained in, the concept of semiosis as a critical principle with which one can assess the true content and import of concepts. In its most well-known formulation, Peirce's maxim reads as follows:

> Consider what effect, that might conceivably have practical bearings, we conceive the object of our conception to have. Then, our conception of these effects is the whole of our conception of the object.[32]

This maxim has often been understood as some kind of reductive claim to the effect that the intentional properties of concepts and the semantic properties of linguistic predicates simply consist in sets of counterfactuals articulating the behavioral dispositions of that to which they apply. If Peirce is, however, engaging in a kind of Kant-inspired Critical Philosophy along the lines outlined, then one can see the pragmatic maxim both as arising integrally out of Peirce's whole philosophy and in quite another, quite nonreductive light. On this reading, the pragmatic maxim appears as a means, a criterion, for assessing and criticizing concepts:[33] it is, to use Peirce's own words, a way of making our ideas clear. It is not a suggestion as to how one might *analyze* the truth conditional or propositional character of concepts and predicates in terms of behavior, but rather a principle by means of which one might test one's concepts for whether their intrinsic claim to determining an extension is in fact genuine.[34] Thus understood, the pragmatic maxim has a decidedly critical character which makes it comparable to the critical maxim one could derive from Kant's claim that the categories of the understanding have no cognitive application beyond the bounds of possible experience. At the same time, it is more radical than any critical maxim one could extract from the *Critique of Pure Reason*. This latter is, strictly speaking, only a critique of certain kinds of truth-claim, those, namely, of metaphysics. But the pragmatic maxim enables a critique of concepts *qua* claimings to sense, and it was to such critical ends that Peirce formulated and wielded it.

Perhaps somewhat ironically, the concept against which Peirce deploys the pragmatic maxim is the quintessentially Kantian notion of the unknowable *Ding an sich*.[35] It seems that what motivates Peirce's desire to eliminate the unknowable thing-in-itself as a pseudoconcept is the desire to identify a conception of reality that allows one to specify in turn a conception of theoretical inquiry that, while avoiding the traditional notion of theory as *epistēmē*, nonetheless preserves the equally traditional notion of theory as the pursuit of truth; of knowledge of how things really are. Peirce's argument against the Kantian *Ding an sich* is simple: the pragmatic maxim implies that concepts and predicates only have genuine meaning, hence determine an extension at all, if members of this extension are capable of revealing themselves behaviorally in our experience.[36] Since an unknowable thing-in-itself is by definition something which cannot reveal itself in our experience, the concept itself is empty; it is a pseudoconcept which, although it seems to possess some content and hence seems to determine an extension, does not really do so.[37]

Peirce's "Transcendental Deduction." The strategic role of Peirce's argument against the thing-in-itself seems to be the following: Peirce thinks it eliminates as senseless any conception of the real as cognitively inaccessible to us. In particular, he thinks it shows that there is no other sense to the notion of reality than the one we acquire so to speak by negation when "we discovered that there was an unreal, an illusion; that is, when we first corrected ourselves."[38] Apparently, Peirce sees this experience of error as giving us a concept of the unreal or illusory as the truth conditions of a hypothesis which *must,* as things stand, eventually be disappointed in some experience. And this concept of the unreal must evidently determine a corresponding or correlative concept of the real, namely, as the truth conditions of a hypothesis which, as things stand, *cannot* be disappointed by any experience. What is important for Peirce about these concepts of the real and unreal is that both clearly contain a reference to the process of forming, and confirming or disconfirming, hypotheses about the real. When Peirce speaks of the experience of disappointment, he cannot mean just any old experience, for not all experiences could count as genuinely disconfirming a hy-

pothesis. No experience I might have while under the influence of drugs, for example, could genuinely disconfirm any hypothesis. By his talk of experiences which disappoint hypotheses Peirce must mean such as are had under ascertainably adequate conditions, that is to say, under conditions which make it reasonable to treat them as veridical. Thus, in these notions of the real and unreal there is, via their explicit reference to the experience of disappointment, an ineliminable implicit reference to systematic and methodologically controlled processes of ensuring and testing the reliability of experience. This implies in turn a reference to the overall process of forming hypotheses, deducing predictions from them, and testing these predictions against methodologically created and controlled experience.

According to Peirce the absurdity of Kant's unknowable thing-in-itself shows that we can have no other notion of the real and unreal than the two concepts just outlined.[39] The real *as such* must be defined with reference to the process of inquiring into and ascertaining it. Just this is what Peirce is saying when he says "there is no thing which is in-itself in the sense of not being relative to the mind, though things which are relative to the mind doubtless are, apart from that relation."[40] It is this conception of the real which Peirce sees as entitling the conclusion that in general the real is what corresponds to that opinion "which, sooner or later, information and reasoning would finally result in."[41] One may well ask whether this inference is valid. For our purposes, however, it is more interesting to ask just whose processes of information and reasoning Peirce has in mind here. His very next remark gives the answer: he says that our conception of reality "essentially involves the notion of a COMMUNITY, without definite limits, and capable of a definite increase of knowledge."[42] Peirce thus intends the processes of information and reasoning of a community, not of an individual. If he were asked to put his conception of the real in its fullest and most explicit form, he would say that the real is what corresponds to a hypothesis or opinion in which all possible subjects would eventually agree if they collectively investigated the claim long enough.[43] Such an opinion, one with respect to which there is such universal consensus, is what Peirce means by an ultimate opinion. But why does Peirce's conception of reality contain this reference to an indefinite community of investigators? Why are the processes of information and reasoning to which it implicitly refers essentially social? This is a direct consequence of Peirce's rejection of the given, and with it, of empiricist versions of theory as *epistēmē*. If there is no given, if perception is not unconditional and self-guaranteeing, but rather reflects the habits of perceptual interpretation which the perceiving subject has acquired in and through its cognitive life-history, then this subject needs some kind of methodological control or check upon its perceptual judgments. Such methodological controls are not themselves self-applying, however: their application itself requires perceptual judgment. Thus, while the subject can to some degree exercise critical control over its habits of perceptual judgment, in order to maximize its confidence in the veridicality of such judgments it must have these methodological controls applied by *other* subjects. Since theoretical inquiry into the world is in part a process of maximizing confidence in one's perceptual judgments, any subject engaged in theoretical inquiry must, therefore, ultimately seek the opinion of others similarly engaged. Only in this way can the suspicion of perceptual idiosyncrasy be tendentiously removed or confirmed—through either the agreement or disagreement of distinct perceptual judgments. Perceptions find their way to objectivity through discursive comparison with the perceptions of others. Note how this gives disagreement between perceptual judgments a fundamental role in the process of inquiry. Note, too, how essentially social and linguistic theoretical inquiry has become. We have here a model of cognition which breaks with the traditional model which derives from Plato via Descartes and is shared by practically every other philosopher except perhaps Hegel, Hamann, and Herder. On the traditional model, systematic empirical inquiry is seen as an activity which each individual subject could at least in principle, if not in fact, carry out on its own simply on the basis of its own perceptual experience.

We are now in a position to indicate a sense in which Peirce's whole argumentation can be regarded as a kind of transcendental deduction. Recall that Peirce started from the concept of semiosis. He then did two things. First, he extended the concept of semiosis to cognition and perception generally, thereby obtaining the result that the thought processes of a being capable of the "I think" display the structure of semiosis. Second, he claimed that from the concept of semiosis one could derive a principle of sense, namely, the pragmatic maxim, which eliminated Kant's unknowable thing-in-itself as senseless and showed that the real as such must be defined with reference to the process of inquiring into and ascertaining it. If the real as such must be defined with reference to the process of inquiry, namely, as that which corresponds to an opinion upon which practitioners in the process of inquiry would eventually converge, then this process must tend toward truth; it must tend toward the knowledge of how things really are. On this basis, then, an argument can be constructed which proceeds from the fact of semiosis of the psychological kind in particular to the conclusion that the process of inquiry tends to truth; hence to theoretical knowledge of the world. The general shape and premises of this argument are as follows:

1. Perceptual experience and thought have the structure of semiosis.

2. The structure of semiosis implies that principle of sense which Peirce calls the pragmatic maxim.

3. The pragmatic maxim shows the Kantian idea of an unknowable thing-in-itself to be empty; we thus have no other concept of reality than the one we acquire through the experience of error.

4. This concept of reality contains an implicit reference to the process of forming a hypothesis about the real, deducing predictions from it, and experiencing its disappointments or increasing confirmation.

5. The real is thus nothing more than what would correspond to that final or ultimate opinion in which all possible inquirers would in the long run come to agree; our only concept of reality is thus simply that asymptote which is implicit in the process of inquiry itself.

Therefore, the process of inquiry must tend asymptotically toward truth.

This is the general shape of a transcendental argument as defined above. It is a "transcendental deduction" of the validity not of specific categories, but of the three aspects of the process of inquiry, namely, the formation of hypotheses, the deduction of predictions from these hypotheses, and the test of these against experience. Because the process of inquiry possesses this validity irrespective of the fact that it lacks any absolute founding in some perceptual given, this argument also answers the quasi-Kantian question raised above, namely, how scientific inquiry can be theory while not relying on the traditional concept of theory as *epistēmē*. The argument shows that empirical inquiry can still legitimately aspire to theory in the sense of knowledge of how things really are. But it also shows that what makes inquiry theory is not any founding in certain basic propositions to whose truth we have indubitable access. Rather, what ensures the theoretical character of inquiry is its having resulted from institutionalized processes of conjecture, experimental elaboration, and provisional confirmation. Of course, this conception of theory must renounce the goal of absolute certainty; to this extent, theory is, as the sophist has always alleged, opinion. It is not, however, just *mere* opinion because in virtue of its conception of reality the process of inquiry has a tendency to truth built into it.

In the light of this reconstruction, Apel's general thesis that Peirce is engaging in a critical revision of Kant's transcendental philosophy certainly seems plausible. It makes Peirce's often fragmentary and confusing texts tell a coherent story; moreover, a story which is much more interesting than the conventional interpretation of Peirce. Whether it is correct, and whether Peirce's philosophy as thus interpreted is valid, are questions which I do not wish to raise *in toto* here. But there is one general objection which I would like to discuss, namely, the charge of verificationism.

VI

Peirce's Verificationism. Clearly, Peirce's concepts of reality and truth ultimately commit him to the view that whatever is true is so if and only if it is in some sense verifiable. As such and in this sense Peirce's understanding of reality and truth is verificationist.[44] The root of this verificationism of course lies in those original conceptions of the real and unreal which, according to Peirce, we acquire through the experience of error and which are the only ones we can have. These conceptions quite explicitly bind the real and unreal to hypotheses about the real; and hypotheses are by definition not just propositions, but rather testable truth-claimings. Furthermore, by binding the real to hypothesis and methods of ascertaining the real, one similarly binds the proposition, that which does or does not correspond to the real. However, given this bond, all propositions must be potential hypotheses, hence potentially testable and decidable with regard to truth-value. With this, we have reached a verificationism of some sort.

The question is, however, whether Peirce, in view of what he is trying to do, really needs to commit himself in this way. Apel never really considers this question, just as he never considers whether Peirce's remarks on meaning, reality, and truth—remarks which he by and large endorses—involve verificationism at all and, if so, whether this verificationism is acceptable or not. Thus, in even raising this question, I am moving well beyond the strict letter of Apel's interpretation of Peirce. I am, however, remaining well within its spirit, for it seems to me that by resolving this question one must confirm Apel's reading of Peirce as transforming Kant.

Now it seems to me that Peirce finds himself embroiled in verificationism because of an ambiguity in his notion of reality. It seems to me that Peirce does not distinguish carefully enough between "the real" in the sense of particular objects and states of affairs, and "the real" in the sense of those particular properties which are exemplified in, or which constitute, particular objects and states of affairs. Reality in this latter sense is what the Scholastics used to call the "whatness" or *realitas* of a thing, and Peirce was indeed immensely impressed by the Scholastics, in particular, by Duns Scotus. In fact, Peirce's pragmatic maxim itself reflects this latter, scholastic understanding of the notion. The point of this maxim is that any empirical "idea," that is, any empirical predicate or concept, articulates some real causal propensity of whatever it applies to—for which reason causal connections between things are, *pace* Hume, real. Moreover, this real causal propensity simply is that real property which, as Aristotle and Duns Scotus maintained, corresponds to the concept in the head or the predicate in the language. Evidently, the notion of reality operative in all these highly Peircean claims is that of the reality of universals, which was indeed a recurring *topos* in Peirce's work.

How does clearing up this ambiguity show that Peirce does not need to be verificationist? A close inspection of his argument against Kant's unknowable thing-in-itself reveals that it is in fact the latter sense of reality which is relevant: an unknowable thing-in-itself is absurd because it is absurd to conceive of something with properties which could never make a difference to the course of experience, which could never manifest themselves

and some instance of them in experience. Now *this* thesis certainly leaves room for objects and states of affairs which are incognizable, say, because the laws of the universe render it impossible for any kind of experimental method to get a grip on them. Certain events taking place in black holes, or at the subatomic level, might be examples. These kinds of things are not ruled out by this thesis. What this thesis rules out is the idea of properties which, because they do not connect up causally with the universe of experienceable, hence cognizable objects and states of affairs, are incognizable. Note that it is just such an incognizability of its properties that makes Kant's *Ding an sich* so problematic. A Kantian *Ding an sich* is only incognizable because of the kind of thing it is, and the kind of any thing is clearly a function of its properties.

Once one appreciates just what notion of reality is involved in Peirce's argument against the unknowable thing-in-itself, one can see his conception of the real, and thus his conception of truth, in a new light. Indeed, Peirce ought to have said that the real in the *first* sense is that whose reality in the *second* sense corresponds to that opinion upon which the process of inquiry would converge in the long run. That is, he ought to have said that the real in the sense of particular objects or states of affairs is that the nature or laws of which correspond to that general theory upon which the process of empirical inquiry will sooner or later converge. In short, what Peirce means by the real is the ultimate nature or lawfulness of things; it is this which implicitly refers to the process of inquiry through which it is uncovered. When one thinks about it, this is what Peirce must mean by reality, for the empirical process of inquiry he has in mind is not at all interested in the particular facts of the universe, but rather in its intrinsic laws. At any rate, these considerations should make clear that Peirce need not be committed to a proposition-by-proposition verificationism. He need not maintain that all propositions are potentially hypotheses in the sense of testable opinions, hence potentially verifiable. His true claim is that all concepts and predicates must ultimately determine general hypotheses through testing which their exemplification can be confirmed, and that otherwise they have no extension.

VII

Consensus as the Mark of Truth. In a certain sense it is only when one renounces the concept of theory as *epistēmē* (in its empiricist form) that truth becomes a problem at all. To throw out the idea of indubitable and self-warranting basic judgments of perception is to find oneself left with fallible criteria for assessing the veridicality of our perceptions and, as we have seen, these criteria must ultimately be wielded collectively. In saying this, however, we make a certain presupposition, namely, that the ability of one's perceptual judgments and judgments generally to find the agreement of other real subjects in finite situations is a fallible criterion or touchstone of their truth. If we did not presuppose this, we could hardly argue that the truth-seeker should seek confirmation of his or her perceptual judgments in the judgments of others. We would have no reason for maintaining that agreement in perceptual judgments is preferable to disagreement. In virtue of what, however, is this presupposition true?

At first, one might claim that its truth is ultimately just a consequence of the causal regularity of nature in its application to perceptual and cognitive mechanisms. That is, one might first want to say that this presupposition is true simply because all inquirers have basically similar perceptual mechanisms, which consequently have similar cognitive consequences under similar conditions. The argument would run as follows: Given the basic causal similarity of inquirers' perceptual and cognitive mechanisms, it follows that the more common or widespread a perceptual judgment is among diverse inquirers, the more likely it is in each individual case to be a "normal" perceptual judgment, that is, one had by a "normal" inquirer under "normal" conditions and circumstances. Furthermore a "normal" or "standard" perceptual judgment will more than likely be true or veridical, for no one could survive whose perceptual judgments were not standardly true or veridical. From these two premises we can now conclude that the more widespread a perceptual judgment is among diverse inquirers, the more likely it is in each individual case to be true or veridical. With this we have explained how finite intersubjective agreement can function as a criterion or yardstick for picking out or identifying those of one's perceptions and perceptual judgments which are veridical, or at least objective in the sense that they stand a good chance of presenting things as they really are. In short, it is the basic similarity of perceptual mechanisms (and of such background conditions as training, ability, and life-experience) which ensures that when, say, a doctor submits his or her interpretation of X-ray pictures to the critical assessment of colleagues, he or she will most likely be right if and only if his or her colleagues judge similarly. It is this similarity which ensures that the agreement of these colleagues constitutes a mark of truth for the doctor's perceptual judgment.

This argument is fallacious, however, just as the appeal to similarity of perceptual mechanisms upon which it rests is beside the point. It trades on an ambiguity in the notion of a "normal" or "standard" perceptual judgment, that is, on what it is to be a "normal" inquirer perceiving under "normal" circumstances. If the normality of perceptual judgment is tacitly *defined* in terms which involve any appeal to the truth or veridicality of such judgment, then clearly the argument just begs the question. If, however, it is not thus defined, then a perceptual judgment made under conditions and circumstances which induce perceptual error will be just as "normal," just as "standard," as any other; it will be just as much the product of perceptual and cognitive mechanisms functioning in their usual, causally regular way. It must thus be false to maintain, as does the second premise of the argument, that the "normality" of a given perceptual judgment in some way implies its truth or veridicality.

Moreover, by not interpreting the notion of "normality," of "standard" perceptual judgment, in terms which appeal to the concepts of truth or veridicality, one robs this notion of all relevant content. The first premise of the argument, to the extent that it retains any content at all, is reduced to the irrelevant claim that, given the basic causal similarity of inquirers' perceptual and cognitive mechanisms, the more widespread a perceptual judgment is among inquirers, the more likely it is to be one had by these inquirers under similar conditions and circumstances. Clearly, similarity of perceptual and cognitive mechanisms only guarantees that people judge alike, not that they judge correctly. It does guarantee that if I, for example, make a certain perceptual judgment which conflicts with the judgment made by the majority under the same or similar circumstances, then there is very likely some further idiosyncratic feature of my particular background conditions which causes me to make an idiosyncratic judgment. It does not, however, guarantee that this idiosyncratic feature is also a distorting one, that is, one which leads me not merely into perceptual idiosyncrasy, but also into perceptual error. Thus the appeal to similarity of perceptual and cognitive mechanisms does indeed miss the point; one does not explain why finite agreement in perceptual judgments is a mark of truth by pointing to a causally sufficient condition of such agreement.

It seems to me that when Peirce sets out to "define" reality, and thence truth, he does so on the following basis: having rejected the given and therewith the conception of theory as *epistēmē* in the empiricist sense, he has located the objectivity of perception in discursive procedures of comparing the diverse perceptual judgments of different inquirers with one another and adjusting them until they concur. But why should such discursive mediation enhance objectivity, that is, why should consensus constitute a criterion of truth? Whether Peirce appreciates the spuriousness of a causal answer to this question is hard to tell. Whatever the case may be, his actual answer to it is not causal or naturalistic at all. His reply to this question is in effect that the concept of reality, of that for the sake of knowing which one submits one's judgments to the test of possible consensus, itself contains a reference to the procedures and process of inquiry itself. Thus there is built into the process of inquiry itself "a general drift" toward "one general agreement, one catholic consent"—a drift which of course can and no doubt must be interrupted by new and productive disagreement.[45] In short, finite consensus is a mark of truth because reality is essentially that upon whose fundamental nature the process of inquiry tends to converge.

Although construing Peirce as concerned to show why finite consensus is a mark of truth is ultimately just another way of demonstrating his concern to solve the problems which ensue upon the renouncement of an absolute perceptual given, it does have the advantage of helping to make clear just what his interest in the concept of truth is. It shows that he is really not at all interested in defining or analysing truth in the sense of "giving the meaning" of the truth predicate. Thus, it shows the error of thinking that according to Peirce the predicate "is true" has the same meaning as the predicate "is an opinion upon which the process of inquiry would converge in the long run."

That Peirce is not in fact interested in "giving the meaning" of the truth predicate is also indicated by a striking feature of his conception of reality, namely, its implicit commitment to a correspondence definition of truth. Clearly, to speak of the real as what corresponds to a hypothesis or opinion which stands in the long run is simply to *presuppose* that the truth of hypotheses consists in correspondence to the real. Indeed, Peirce can derive the claim that a true hypothesis or opinion is one which stands in the long run only on the assumption that what is true is what corresponds to the real. Only on this assumption does this peculiarly Peircean claim follow from Peirce's conception of the real as what corresponds to a hypothesis or opinion which stands in the long run. Thus, if by a theory of truth one means something which "gives the meaning" of the truth predicate, then one must admit that Peirce's theory of truth is a standard correspondence one. True, Peirce renders correspondence a rather toothless notion because he embeds his correspondence theory of truth within a decidedly verificationist consensus theory of reality; it is this embedding which explains why he wrongly makes all propositions potential hypotheses capable of being tested.

What, then, is Peirce doing with the concept of truth? The answer is implicit in the following remark:

> That truth is the correspondence of a representation with its object is, as Kant says, merely the nominal definition of it. . . . But what does this correspondence . . . consist in?[46]

Here Peirce is apparently thinking of the following passage from *The Critique of Pure Reason:*

> The nominal definition of truth, namely, that it is the agreement of knowledge with its object, is granted and presupposed. One wants to know, however, what the universal and certain criterion of the truth of each and every cognition is.[47]

A nominal definition of truth is for both Kant and Peirce simply a theory of truth in the sense of a specification of the meaning of the truth predicate. Whereas Kant, at least in the *The Critique of Pure Reason,* did not think there could be any criterion of truth, and thus in the quoted passage was speaking only ironically of the desire for a "universal and certain criterion of the truth of each and every cognition," Peirce sees a real point to this desire. True, if one understands the concept of a criterion of truth as Kant seems to, namely, as some kind of decision-procedure which can be algorithmically applied to any proposition whatsoever, then one must agree with Kant that this desire is futile. One can, however, also see in Kant's merely ironically posed question

a quite legitimate protest against the inability of the correspondence theory to be anything more than a theory of truth in a purely definitional or nominal sense. That is, one can see in it a protest against the criterial irrelevance of the correspondence theory, that is, against its inability to determine some kind of criterion of truth which constitutes a genuinely usable and reliable, if not infallible, guide to truth.

Peirce's remark about truth thus suggests that we see him as attempting to answer this difficulty of the correspondence theory *qua* nominal definition. His answer is, as we have already seen, to forge a conceptual link between the objective *relatum* of the correspondence "relation" (that is, the real) and the process of cognizing this *relatum.*[48] As we have also seen, this answer must quite legitimately presuppose the nominal definition of truth as correspondence to the real. Of course, if Peirce is to be read in this way, then he can no more intend agreement in the long run as a definition or analysis of truth than he can intend the pragmatic maxim as a definition or analysis of the concept of meaning. On this reading, he seeks not a definition of truth, but rather *an explication of the standard definition itself.* He seeks to explicate the traditional conception of truth as correspondence to the real in such a way that it can be seen to connect up with some condition which, while preserving the transcendent character of truth which this traditional conception expresses so well, nonetheless explains how truth can be a goal for which we can sensibly strive. He perceives, rightly I think, that given the demise of theory as *epistēmē,* making this connection is the only way in which we can determine whether truth-seeking is a real possibility for us and whether those real human activities which we take to be processes of truth-seeking really are what we take them to be. The condition Peirce postulates is agreement in the long run. Such agreement is of course only a regulative ideal, for otherwise it would not preserve the transcendent character of truth. At the same time, however, it connects such transcendent truth with real processes of reaching finite and limited agreement, thereby explaining why ever widening and deepening finite agreement, which is something we can attain, is a mark of truth. In explaining this it shows that and how truth can be a possible goal for us: our actual processes of reasoning and reaching agreement tend toward truth, even though we can never be certain at any one time that we have reached the truth.

As has already been shown, Peirce ultimately entangles himself in some kind of verificationism, and this may be thought to endanger his whole approach to the philosophical problem of truth. In response to this I can only say that I think a solution to the problem of truth along the lines just outlined can avoid verificationism of a proposition by proposition kind. As we have seen, the sources of Peirce's verificationism lie in an ambiguity in his crucial notion of the real, and I suspect that by clearing this ambiguity up in the manner outlined one saves not only his conception of reality, but also his explication of truth, from the sin of verificationism.

But however this may be, at the very least, our remarks here show something that Apel is very much concerned to maintain, namely, that Peirce's conception of truth, hence of pragmatism, is different from the view popularly attributed to James. Let me end by stressing just how social theoretical cognition has become in Peirce's hands. While I can of course know certain things about the world without there being as a matter of fact any one else who knows them, the defeasible means or criterion by which I can check whether I am rationally entitled to regard myself as knowing these things, and thus as not in fact deluded, is ultimately whether what I believe would stand the test of rational examination by all others. Cognition is necessarily a social process of practitioners critically examining the truth-claims of other practitioners for whether they can agree with them. One can thus understand why Apel should regard Peirce as opening the way to a conception of the collective process of inquiry as a "transcendental" activity in which differing opinions are "synthesized" in agreement. Relatedly, one can understand why he regards the central position given by Peirce to the community of inquirers as the tacit rehabilitation of some kind of "transcendental subject."[49]

NOTES

[1] See *The Collected Papers of Charles S Peirce,* ed. Charles Hartshorne and Paul Weiss (Cambridge: Harvard University Press, 1931-58), vol. 5, par. 414; subsequently cited as ·*CP* followed by volume and paragraph numbers.

[2] Karl-Otto Apel, *Charles S. Peirce: From Pragmatism to Pragmaticism,* trans. John Michael Krois (Amherst: University of Massachusetts Press, 1981). The German original is Karl-Otto Apel, *Der Denkweg von Charles S. Peirce* (Frankfurt am Main: Suhrkamp Verlag, 1975).

[3] The classic statement of the conception of theoretical or scientific knowledge as *epistēmē* is to be found in Aristotle, for example, in *Posterior Analytics* 1.2.71b9-72b4. Truly scientific or theoretical knowledge consists in a system of general propositions resting upon certain ultimate premises which are in some way immediately and certainly known. The idea of immediately given, certain perceptual judgments, upon which general theoretical propositions are inductively founded, is the classical empiricist or logical positivist version of this conception.

[4] This kind of reading is particularly prevalent among the German authors with whom Apel is most familiar. See, for instance, Gadamer's comments on American Pragmatism in "Was ist Wahrheit," in Hans-Georg Gadamer, *Kleine Schriften,* (Tübingen: J. C. B. Mohr, 1967), 1:55.

[5] This shows why Apel's interpretation of Peirce as transforming Kant is not uncontroversial. While the influence of Kant on Peirce in his earlier days is undeniable, commentators such as Jürgen von Kempski re-gard Peirce as having deliberately rejected Kant's idea of a transcendental philosophy, and of a transcendental deduction in particular. See Jürgen von Kempski, *Ch. S. Peirce and der Pragmatismus* (Stuttgart: Kohlhammer, 1952), 55-60.

[6] See Kant, *Kritik der reinen Vernunft* (Frankfurt: Suhrkamp Verlag, 1976), A106-7.

[7] Kant, *Kritik der reinen Vernunft,* B134n—my (slightly free) translation.

[8] "Die Bedingungen der Möglichkeit der Erfahrung überhaupt sind zugleich Bedingungen der Möglichkeit der Gegenstände der Erfahrung." B197/A158; see also A111 for an almost identical formulation.

[9] See Karl-Otto Apel, "Von Kant zu Peirce," in *Transformationen der Philosophie,* (Frankfurt am Main: Suhrkamp Verlag, 1981), 2:170. There Apel describes the sign-relation, or semiosis, as Peirce's (provisional) equivalent to Kant's highest point; semiosis is only a *provisional* highest point because unlike Kant's transcendental ego the subject of semiosis turns out to be essentially related to other such subjects in a collective process of reaching agreement on empirical hypotheses. Thus, ultimately, it is the collective reaching of agreement on such hypotheses which turns out to be the ultimate "synthetic unity." See also p. 177, where Apel speaks of the semiotic transformation of knowledge as the highest point of transcendental logic.

[10] See *CP* 5.354.

[11] See Apel, "Von Kant zu Peirce," 174.

[12] See *CP* 5.473, 5.484.

[13] See Apel, *Charles S. Peirce,* 123.

[14] See Apel, "Von Kant zu Peirce," 170.

[15] *CP* 5.283. See also *CP* 2.228: "A sign, or representation, is something which stands to somebody for something in some respect or capacity."

[16] Apel, *Charles S. Peirce,* 99.

[17] *CP* 1.304. This is apparently an excerpt from the manuscript "Logic viewed as Semeiotics, Introduction Number 2, Phaneroscopy," written around 1904.

[18] In *CP* 5.119 he makes remarks that entail that the predicates of perceptual judgment immediately present, hence are associated with, such qualities of feeling.

[19] In *CP* 5.261 Peirce does indeed discount the semantic and hence cognitive significance of qualities of feeling. As Apel points out, however, these remarks occur in an essay written in 1868, at which time Peirce appears to have had a more rationalist view which either downplayed

or ignored the specific contribution of qualitative experience to cognition; see Apel, *Charles S. Peirce,* 122. On the more developed view considered here, qualities of feeling, while never themselves general or predicative in nature, and thus never themselves cognitions, nonetheless constitute the point of departure for that activity of interpretation which culminates in full-fledged perceptual cognition.

[20] See Apel, *Charles S. Peirce,* 104.

[21] See *CP* 5.135, 5.491; see also *CP* 5.18 for Peirce's claim that the logical interpretant is "a . . . practical maxim expressible as a conditional sentence having its apodosis in the imperative mood." At times Peirce speaks of the "logical interpretant" as a behavioral "habit" of the *object* to which the sign interpreted applies. At other times he speaks of it as a practical rule or maxim of behavior of the *subject* who uses the sign.

[22] It is very hard to extract any coherent account of the relation between thought and signs from Peirce's obscure comments and claims. Sometimes Peirce appears to be saying not just that a thinking being, at least insofar as it is capable of self-consciousness, must possess "words or other external symbols" (*CP* 7.587), but also that such a being's thoughts are *themselves* signs; see *CP* 5.253. Thought is thus in a quite literal sense "a silent speech of the soul with itself"; *Writings of Charles S. Peirce—A Chronological Edition,* ed. Max H. Fisch (Bloomington: Indiana University Press, 1982), 2:172. It is indeed a matter of manipulating "mental signs" (*CP* 5.476). In short, Peirce sometimes seems to advocate some kind of "language of thought."

[23] See, for instance, Martin Heidegger, *Sein und Zeit,* 15th ed. (Tübingen: Max Niemeyer Verlag, 1979), 32, p. 149.

[24] See Apel, "Von Kant zu Peirce," 170-2 in particular.

[25] I would argue for this claim by appeal to what is involved in knowing what must be the case for, say, a certain belief or assertion to be true. To know this is to know what the propositional content of the belief or assertion is. But propositions, like numbers, are "abstract objects"; thus, like numbers, which are only identifiable and distinguishable from one another via numerals, propositions are only identifiable and distinguishable from one another via the spatiotemporally locatable and distinguishable forms of their representation, that is, sentences. Consequently, to identify something *as* a propositional content, that is, *as* a proposition, is to identify something as *what is expressed by such and such a sentence.* If this is true, then, since the self-conscious ascription of a psychological state with a propositional content to oneself involves identifying the propositional content in question, such self-ascription and self-consciousness can be possible only for a being that disposes over the appropriate sentences.

[26] See Apel, *Charles S. Peirce,* 25, 105, and elsewhere.

[27] See *CP* 5.485.

[28] See *CP* 5.183 for other examples provided by Peirce himself, in particular, for an example similar to Wittgenstein's. See Ludwig Wittgenstein, *Philosophical Investigations,* trans. G. E. M. Anscombe (Oxford: Basil Blackwell, 1978), p. 194.

[29] See *CP* 5.183.

[30] Although Peirce, like many others, does not make this distinction, it seems to me that one should distinguish between the "interpretation-ladenness" uncovered here and so-called theory-ladenness. The interpretation involved here is a process of fitting present phenomenal quality into a coherent, narratively-structured life-experience; hence it presupposes not theories, but rather the story as thus far narrated itself.

[31] The inspiration for this example comes from Peirce himself; see *CP* 5.403. For Apel's critique of the specifics of Peirce's account here, see Apel, *Charles S. Peirce,* 77. See also *CP* 7.341, where Peirce says—improving on his remarks in *CP* 5.403—that the sentence "The inkstand upon the table is heavy" simply means "that if its support be removed it will fall to the ground. This may perhaps never happen to it at all—and yet we say that it is really heavy all the time."

[32] *CP* 5.402.

[33] See *CP* 5.196, where Peirce describes the pragmatic maxim as "a . . . maxim which, if sound must render needless any further rule as to the admissibility of hypotheses to rank as hypotheses." Significantly, in just this paragraph Peirce also says that providing such a criterion "is *all* that the maxim of pragmatism really pretends to do."

[34] See *CP* 5.391, where Peirce points out of Descartes that "the distinction between an idea *seeming* clear and really being so, never occurred to him." The pragmatic maxim gives one a way of making this distinction.

[35] See Apel, "Von Kant zu Peirce," 175 and n. 40.

[36] Note that this is not verificationist. This claim is perfectly compatible with there being entities which it is nomologically impossible for us to discover and investigate. The claim being made here actually concerns not the notion of truth, but the notions of meaning and understanding. What this claim rules out is that there could be a predicate or concept *F* such that we understand *F* and it is nomologically impossible for *any* instances of *F* to impinge upon us in lawlike ways through experience. If one wants a name for it, one might call this the exemplificationist theory of meaning, as opposed to any verificationist theory of meaning. Ultimately, the difference between this conception of meaning and the verificationist one is that the latter theory attempts to associate procedures of *verification* with

whole sentences (as their meaning), which means that it is true only if all propositions expressed by meaningful sentences are verifiable. But the theory here associates procedures or possibilities of *exemplification* with *predicates* and thus is not committed to the view that all sentences as such are verifiable, only that for all predicates *F* some sentences containing *F* are.

[37] See *CP* 5.525 for Peirce's actual argument.

[38] *CP* 5.311. See also Apel, "Von Kant zu Peirce," 173.

[39] See, for instance, *CP* 7.345.

[40] *CP* 5.311; see also *CP* 7.336.

[41] *CP* 5.311. See also *CP* 5.354, 2.654.

[42] *CP* 5.311. See also *CP* 2.654, 5.354.

[43] See *CP* 5.331, where Peirce implies that "reality consists in the agreement that the whole community would eventually come to."

[44] See *CP* 5.565 for an example of just how verificationist Peirce could be.

[45] *CP* 8.12.

[46] *CP* 5.553.

[47] Kant, *Kritik der reinen Vernunft*, A58/B82 (my translation).

[48] See *CP* 5.553.

[49] Thus Apel speaks of this community as a "quasi-transcendental subject"; see Apel, "Von Kant zu Peirce," 173.

Georg Behrens (essay date 1995)

SOURCE: "Peirce's 'Third Argument' for the Reality of God and Its Relation to Scientific Inquiry," in *The Journal of Religion*, Vol. 75, No. 2, April, 1995, pp. 200-218.

[In the following excerpt, Behrens evaluates the validity of Peirce's arguments for the existence of a supreme being.]

What I will call a "scientific argument" for the existence of God is an appeal to the logic and methodology of science in order to show that theism (the claim that there is a God) is epistemically warranted. Most commonly but not exclusively, such an argument may seek to establish theism by demonstrating its conformity to scientific standards for what constitutes a reliable or confidence-worthy hypothesis. Although scientific arguments for the existence of God are currently enjoying a renaissance in the philosophy of religion, it was not long ago that science and theism were more often than not regarded as being antagonistic, and philosophers sympathetic to religion were concerned most of all to stake out and preserve for it a domain in which the logic of science possessed no authority. As Murray G. Murphey has pointed out, Pragmatism arose in a period (the late 1860s and 1870s) when the relation between science and religion was regarded as being one of conflict. The rise of Darwinism together with its sundry philosophical and ideological offshoots represented the severest challenge yet faced by the theistic commitments of American philosophers. "The main thrust of the movement," Murphey writes regarding Pragmatism, "was the determination to construct an epistemology adequate for both science and religion."[1] Much of the time, the Pragmatists' concern was only to "make room for" religion within a worldview increasingly determined by science and its interpretations; to follow Kant in showing that science, properly understood, at least did not speak against religion, again properly understood. But on at least one occasion, Pragmatism anticipated the present vogue of scientific arguments for theism, with the humbler Kantian program giving way to the far more ambitious one of showing that when measured against norms and standards given in the logic of science, the theistic "hypothesis" turns out to be a scientifically justified hypothesis. This occasion was C. S. Peirce's 1908 publication in the *Hibbert Journal* of the essay **"A Neglected Argument for the Reality of God"** (hereafter abbreviated **"NARG"**).[2] Traditionally, Peirce scholarship has not paid much attention to the scientific theism of this article. Such interpreters of Peirce as Justus Buchler and Thomas Goudge have tended to downplay its significance, judging it a somewhat anomalous sideshow to Peirce's more important concern with the logic and methodology of science. Recently, however, the reception granted **"NARG"** has been more generous, and various attempts have surfaced to rehabilitate Peirce's theistic argument in the face of earlier critiques.[3] No doubt these attempts at rehabilitation have been buoyed in part by the general popularity which scientific arguments are now enjoying.

My purpose in this essay is to ground argumentatively the traditional suspicion that Peirce's scientific theism is a mixture of oil and water. I will claim that in **"NARG,"** Peirce selectively edits his own theory of science in order to develop the impression of a harmony between it and his theism. By calling attention to those aspects of Peirce's theory of science which he himself does not bring into immediate contact with the Neglected Argument, I will show that within the Peircean framework, a scientific argument is indeed anomalous. No rehabilitation of the kind envisaged by present-day friends of scientific theism is possible. In making this claim, I am *not* ruling out reinterpretations of Peirce's theism which downplay theoretical and emphasize practical, speculative, or fideistic themes. Certainly, there are enough indications that Peirce supported a strong separation between practical and theoretical concerns, and still further indications to allow the supposition that theism belongs wholly on the side of the practical.[4] I do not question the rationality of Peirce's theism, just the tenability of his *scientific* theism. Peirce sees himself as "an individual whose unbiased study of scientific logic has led him to conclusions not discordant with traditional dogmas" (6:446). I accept this claim but aim to show that Peirce's "unbiased study of scientific logic" does not provide support for theism either. Understood as a bona fide scientific argument, Peirce's defense of theism in **"NARG"** is invalid.

THE THREE ARGUMENTS FOR THE REALITY OF GOD

As Peirce himself points out, **"NARG"** actually contains a "nest" of three distinct arguments for the reality of God,[5] only one of which involves a direct appeal to the logic of science and presupposes a theory of the scientific method. However, this "scientific argument" is in face dependent in important ways on Peirce's other two nonscientific arguments, so that these, too, will have to be taken into consideration. Peirce occasionally uses the term "Neglected Argument" (N.A.) to refer to the "nest" of all three arguments but prefers to reserve it for the second alone (6:487). The first argument he calls the "Humble Argument" (H.A.), while the third does not seem to have been baptized at all. I will call it the "Third Argument" (Th.A.) for easy reference. Of the three, it alone is a "scientific argument."

The Humble Argument

The H.A. is no "argumentation" in the sense of a formal demonstration running from explicit premises to conclusion, but rather a description of a procedure for convincing oneself that God is real. As a mere description, it lacks proof value, but nonetheless (according to Peirce) is more effective than any formal argumentation in convincing people of God's reality (6:486).

The starting point is Pure Play, a "lively exercise" of one's mental faculties constrained by no rules. Left to itself, Pure Play eventually assumes the more specialized form of "Musement," which takes as its object "some wonder" in the world, "with Speculation concerning its cause" (6.458). This concern with causal explanation leads in turn to a discovery of the "Idea of God" as a means of accounting for the wonders found in the world. The muser may, Peirce suggests, begin by considering naturalistic explanations, but these always call for additional higher-order explanations. Only the Idea of God can provide full explanatory satisfaction; and as a result, "in the Pure Play of Musement the idea of God's Reality will be sure sooner or later to be found an attractive fancy" (6:465). Having thus discovered the Idea of God as a way of accounting for the world, the muser will begin to meditate earnestly on it, such meditation, according to Peirce, being the origin of "a truly religious Belief in His Reality and His nearness" (6:486).

The Neglected Argument

The N.A., so-called because it has been neglected by theologians (6:457), consists in "showing that the humble ar-

gument is the natural fruit of free meditation"; that, far from contrived, it results from "universal human nature"; and that "a latent tendency toward belief in God is a fundamental ingredient of the soul" (6:487). The N.A. presupposes, first, that certain kinds of human mental activity can be identified as "natural" (or "instinctive," as Peirce sometimes puts it); and second, that there is an epistemic presumption in favor of "natural" mental activity: that "natural" beliefs are especially plausible, that "natural" inferences are especially reliable, and so on. The N.A. amounts to the claim that there is an epistemic presumption in favor of theism, because musement on the three Universes leads naturally to the Idea of God, meditation on which in turn leads naturally to belief in God's Reality. Thus, the N.A. is a genuine "argumentation," an argument from explicit premises to the truth of theism. According to Peirce, however, it lacks the H.A.'s power to convince, "for it would only be an apology—a vindicating description—of the mental operations which the Humble Argument actually and actively lives out" (6:487).

The Third Argument

The Th.A. is analogous in some ways to the N.A. It, too, is an argumentation; and it, too, lacks the sheer power to convince possessed by the H.A. The assumption this time is that (not as in the N.A., instinctive beliefs and inferences, but) scientific conclusions and methods are especially reliable. The Th.A. appears in three variants. In the first, Peirce claims that the H.A. is like certain procedures necessary to any scientific inquiry; and hence, he thinks, there is a certain presumption in favor of its conclusions. In the second and third variants of the Th.A., Peirce shifts his attention from the H.A. to its upshot: the "hypothesis of God" (or "theistic hypothesis" as I will call it), claiming that it possesses certain traits which the logic of science recognizes as being indicators of probable truth. All three variants will be considered in greater detail below.

As is to be expected, Peirce begins his exposition of the Th.A. with a brief sketch of his thoughts on scientific inquiry (6:469 ff.), the suggestion being that this sketch will provide the reader with enough information to make plausible the contention that the H.A. is a characteristically scientific procedure. Inquiry, he holds, is always cycling through three stages. The first is concerned with the generation of hypotheses by reasoning from the given data. The proximate cause for inquiry is the noticing of some anomalous or unexpected phenomenon. What follows is a search for a hypothesis that is able to explain the noticed anomaly, so that if the hypothesis were true, the phenomenon in question would no longer be unexpected. Peirce claims that the same type of mental process is always involved whenever a hypothesis is generated to explain an anomaly, and that this process can be described as a specialized form of scientific reasoning—he calls it "retroduction." (Indeed, Peirce thinks that each of the three stages of scientific inquiry corresponds to a unique "formula of reasoning"

[6:469], used in that stage alone and formally distinguishable from other sorts of reasoning.) The second stage of inquiry is concerned with the derivation of observable consequences from the hypotheses generated in retroduction, with a view to testing them against experience; the form of reasoning characteristic of this stage is called "deduction." Finally, the third stage is concerned with the testing of hypotheses against experience, by comparing the observable consequences derived in the second stage with actual observations and by evaluating the hypotheses on the basis of such comparisons. The evaluation which occurs in the third stage leads to a hypothesis' being accepted as confirmed or rejected as disconfirmed; the form of reasoning employed in such evaluation Peirce calls "induction."

RETRODUCTION AND ABDUCTION

An interesting feature of Peirce's 1908 account of scientific inquiry is that the moment of "abduction," so critical in his earlier expositions of the subject, goes entirely unmentioned.[6] This puzzling feature of the account has perhaps not received the attention it should, because it is commonly assumed that Peirce uses the terms "retroduction" and "abduction" synonymously. The assumption is false. "Abduction" is the wider term, covering both the retroduction process of reasoning from the data to a hypothesis and the distinct process of reasoning involved in what some philosophers are now calling the comparative "prior assessment"[7] of hypotheses already generated, performed with a view to selecting some for further consideration. That Peirce in some discussions of abduction stresses only its former (retroductive) function is potentially misleading. For example, he writes in 1903, "Abduction must cover all the operations by which theories and conceptions are engendered" (5:590). And again in 1903, "Abduction is the process of forming explanatory hypotheses. It is the only logical operation which introduces any new idea" (5:172). At other points, however, he makes it clear that "abduction" includes also a second process of reasoning which must be distinguished carefully from that responsible for the generation of hypotheses. He writes in 1901: "The first starting of a hypothesis and the entertaining of it . . . is an inferential step which I propose to call *abduction.* This will include a preference for any one hypothesis over others which would equally explain the facts, so long as this preference is not based on any previous knowledge bearing upon the truth of the hypotheses, nor on any testing of any of the hypotheses, after having admitted them on probation. I call all such inference by the peculiar name, *abduction,* because its legitimacy depends upon altogether different principles from those of other kinds of inference" (6:525). The term "abduction" does double duty in Peirce's account of the scientific enterprise. It designates, on the one hand, the reasoning process operative in the generation of new hypotheses; and on the other, that operative in an initial or preliminary *comparative* evaluation of the hypotheses generated. But these are two distinct kinds of reasoning. Abductive evaluation determines the order in which the

researcher proposes to subject the hypotheses generated to the inductive testing procedures which are capable of determining their truth or falsehood. The ranking achieved is not arbitrary, but the result of a rational procedure, guided by rules and criteria. In this regard, abductive evaluation differs crucially from retroduction, which has no critical or comparative function, and is concerned strictly with the generation of explanatory hypotheses. Clearly, then, it would be in holding with Peirce's "ethics of terminology" (see 5:413) to restrict the use of "abduction" to the domain of prior assessment, while leaving hypothesis generation to be covered by the term "retroduction."[8] Accordingly, I will use the term "abduction" in the narrower sense from now on.

Peirce's 1908 account of scientific inquiry is incomplete, because it includes no mention at all of abduction in the narrow sense. I will argue that this omission is by no means insignificant, and that it is precisely the suppressed logic of abduction which must provide the key to our understanding and evaluation of the Th.A. as a piece of philosophical theism. I will begin by attempting to fill in some of the gaps in the 1908 account of scientific inquiry by drawing on materials found in Peirce's earlier reflections on abduction.

The reason abduction or prior assessment is a necessary part of scientific inquiry (and hence the reason a discussion of it cannot be omitted from a full account of scientific inquiry) is that the number of explanatory guesses which can be generated retroductively in response to any puzzle or anomaly is so high that not all of them can be subjected to serious scientific consideration. Peirce writes that "proposals for hypotheses inundate us in an overwhelming flood" (5:602), while the number which can actually be tested is quite low, due to constraints of time and the limited availability of resources. The function of abduction, then, is to pare down the number of hypotheses due for serious consideration, and it does so by evaluating explanatory proposals according to specifiable criteria (which constitute the subject matter for the logic of abduction). These criteria are of two sorts: first, there are identity criteria for hypotheses, criteria designed to select from among the explanatory guesses retroductively generated those which are to be accorded the status of genuine scientific hypotheses; and second, there are the criteria given in the Economy of Research, designed to select for testing those hypotheses whose contribution toward the attainment of scientific goals is highest per unit expenditure.

Peirce gives his primary account of the identity criteria for hypotheses in the Lowell Lectures of 1903. The first formal criterion which a retroductively generated guess must meet in order to count as a scientific hypothesis is that it must genuinely *explain* some surprising or puzzling phenomenon. "The hypothesis cannot be admitted, even as a hypothesis, unless it be supposed that it would account for the facts or some of them" (5:189). But this criterion is not yet stringent enough. Putative explanatory guesses can be produced which are nonetheless useless for scientific inquiry. The requirement that a hypothesis be explanatory must be supplemented by a "further rule as to the admissibility of hypotheses to rank as hypotheses" (5:196), a rule which Peirce identifies as the doctrine of Pragmatism. "Any hypothesis . . . may be admissible, in the absence of any special reasons to the contrary, provided it be capable of experimental verification, and only insofar as it is capable of such verification. This is approximately the doctrine of pragmatism" (5:197). In order for an explanatory guess to merit scientific attention, in order for it to be a candidate for testing, it must be the sort of proposition which *can* be tested (cf. 7:220). More precisely, it must be the sort of proposition which is amenable to the deductive derivation of observable consequences and the inductive evaluation which occupy the second and third stages of inquiry, respectively. It must have observable consequences which can be spelled out deductively; and those consequences must be of the sort which can be verified or falsified through testing. The scientist who considers seriously propositions which do not meet this requirement is wasting time. For truth, the aim of inquiry, is accessible only by means of an assiduous application of the scientific method.

The primary loci for Peirce's doctrine of economy are a paper from the 1870s entitled **"Note on the Theory of the Economy of Research"** (reprinted at 7:139 ff.) and a manuscript (ca. 1901) entitled **"On the Logic of Drawing History from Ancient Documents, Especially from Testimonies"** (reprinted at 7:164 ff., with the section on abduction beginning at 7:218). "The main problem," writes Peirce, "is, how, with a given expenditure of money, time, and energy, to obtain the most valuable addition to our knowledge" (7:140). Abduction or prior assessment is concerned with maximizing what I will call "expected scientific payoff," or ESP (Peirce himself uses such terms as "value" and "cognitive value"). At 7:220, he is concerned with listing some of the properties of genuine hypotheses which function as determinants of ESP. Significantly, the ESP of a hypothesis is determined in part by its assessed likelihood of being true; where the assessment of a hypothesis's likelihood depends on both "instinctive" and "reasoned" "marks of truth in the hypothesis." Salient among the former is the consideration that the human mind is naturally fitted to the truth and hence that we ought to prefer "hypotheses . . . as naturally recommend themselves to the mind" (7:220). Such hypotheses, when entertained, simply strike the researcher as being especially plausible; and Peirce suggests that the logic of abduction should honor such feelings. Reasoned considerations of a hypothesis's likelihood of being true include whether it is supported by the facts and whether it fits in with our preconceived ideas of what is the case. A hypothesis's ESP is determined also by systematic considerations, which do not themselves suggest that the hypothesis is likely to be true, but which suggest that the value of testing the hypothesis for the progress of science is very high. Such considerations concern "the relation of what is proposed to other projects"; and favorable traits to be maximized are "Caution, Breadth, and Incomplexity" (7:220), where "breadth" is to be understood roughly as what philosophers recently have been calling "explanatory power," and "incomplexity" as what has been called "simplicity" (not to be confused with what Peirce himself means by "simplicity").

THE THIRD ARGUMENT AND THE LOGIC OF SCIENCE

With this supplementary information concerning the logic of abduction in hand, we are ready to take a closer look at the workings of the Th.A. Ideally, what Peirce would like is to apply the scientific method in an investigation of the "hypothesis of God" and actually to confirm the hypothesis. But no such large-scale operation is on the agenda. Peirce admits that the H.A. is no "complete inquiry into the Reality of God," for such an inquiry must traverse all three stages: retroduction, deduction, and induction. The H.A. is an instance of only the first stage of inquiry (6:468). "The student . . . compares the process of thought of the Muser upon the Three Universes with certain parts of the work of scientific inquiry, and finds that the 'Humble Argument' is nothing but an instance of the first stage of all such work, the stage of observing the facts, or variously rearranging them, and of pondering them until, by their reactions with the results of previous scientific experience, there is 'evolved' . . . an explanatory hypothesis" (6:489). The point of the Th.A. (in its first variant) is to show that the theistic hypothesis is worthy of our confidence, because Musement, the process by which it is discovered, is an "instance" of retroduction. In the second and third variants of the argument, Peirce points to other properties of the theistic hypothesis which he thinks should, on scientific principles, recommend it to our confidence.

The Th.A. is crucially dependent on Peirce's theory of scientific inquiry. Only if this be true, at least in its relevant features, can that be regarded as valid. If the first variant, for example, is to have any chance of success, then at the very least Peirce's claims concerning retroduction must be true: it must indeed be the case that scientific inquiry begins with explanatory puzzles and that there is a special kind of reasoning which responds to such puzzles with explanatory guesses. Now it is beyond the scope of this article to attempt a critique of Peirce's theory of scientific inquiry or even of his theory of retroduction. I will ask instead: if the theory were true, would it lend the kind of support to the Th.A. which Peirce thinks it does? In order to answer this question, I will consider the particular way(s) in which Peirce thinks that the Th.A. is buttressed by his account of science. The overall aim, again, is to show that on Peirce's own understanding of the logic of science, the Th.A. is invalid. My argument to this effect will occupy the rest of this section (subsections 1-3). Each subsection will deal with one of the three variants for the Th.A.

Variant 1: The Appeal to Retroductive Origin

What warrant does the logic of science accord to a hypothesis in virtue of its having been generated retroductively?

Recall that hypotheses are evaluated at two junctures in scientific inquiry, in the abductive stage as well as the inductive stage. Thus, if the theistic hypothesis is to receive epistemic support in virtue of its retroductive origin, then either the logic of abduction or the logic of induction must recognize retroductive origin as a valid source of epistemic support for a hypothesis. To attempt a sketch here of Peirce's theory of induction would go beyond the scope of this article. Perhaps we can accept his word that the H.A. is not a full scientific inquiry and covers only the first stage of such an inquiry. Since induction is the type of reasoning typical of the third stage, we can be sure that Peirce did not think that an appeal to the logic of induction was essential to the Th.A.

Only the logic of abduction, and not the logic of induction, comes into question as a possible source of legitimation for the Th.A. But the suggested appeal to the logic of abduction runs immediately into the following difficulty: abductive support (the support given to a hypothesis in abductive evaluation) may not be the kind of support needed to establish an epistemic warrant for believing that a hypothesis is true. As we have seen, abductive evaluation is concerned with determining whether a guess is worthy of being treated as a hypothesis and whether we ought to accord it a certain priority for testing. It is not concerned at all with the confirmation of hypotheses. In fact, abduction provides no warrant for scientific acceptance of a hypothesis as true. It confers no probability whatsoever on its conclusion. According to Peirce, "Deduction proves that something *must* be; induction shows that something *actually is* operative; abduction merely suggests that something *might be*" (5:171). The difference here is not one of higher or lower probability, but of modality. Abduction establishes a mere possibility, from which no probability can be inferred. In abduction the "conclusion" is not considered to be so much as probable, but is only "entertained interrogatively" (6:524) as "a *may-be* (*may-be* and *may-be* not)" (8:238), since "probability proper [has] nothing to do with the validity of abduction" (2:102). In fact, it may not be proper to speak of "abductive inference" at all, since the term "inference" suggests the establishment of a conclusion. Accordingly, Peirce points out that even the expression "abductively inferred" is inappropriate and should be replaced by the expression "abductively suggested" (5:189). "For abduction commits us to nothing. It merely causes a hypothesis to be set down upon our docket of cases to be tried" (5:602).

Abduction, then, ratifies explanatory guesses as hypotheses and recommends hypotheses for further investigation, but it gives the scientist no license to accept hypotheses as true. Nevertheless, it might be thought, abduction grounds the evaluative preference of one hypothesis over another, and this is all the Th.A. requires: a suggestion that the logic of science itself underwrites some sort of preference for the theistic hypothesis. Now as we have seen, the logic of abduction consists of the doctrine of Pragmatism, which identifies the explana-

tory guesses worthy of being regarded as genuine hypothesis, and the Economy of Research, which ranks hypotheses according to their ESP. Among the criteria of abductive evaluation given in the Economy of Research, we can distinguish again between, on the one hand, criteria for selecting hypotheses which we *think* will be confirmed, and on the other hand, criteria for selecting hypotheses which we *hope* will be confirmed, because their confirmation would result in an especially high scientific payoff. For the purposes of the Th.A., it is clear that we must restrict our attention to the former set of criteria. If abduction tells us that a hypothesis is likely to be confirmed, because it exhibits characteristics typical of hypotheses which by and large tend to be confirmed, then perhaps we may adduce this fact to ground our contention that it is true; but if abductive preference for a hypothesis is grounded merely in hope, then no such maneuver is possible. The scientist is entitled to accord such a hypothesis a high ranking in the list of hypotheses to be tested, but she cannot cite its high abductive ranking as a reason for taking it to be true. For example, the logic of abduction tells us to prefer hypotheses which are explanatorily powerful (or "broad," to use Peirce's own term) over less powerful ones, because the scientific payoff of confirming a powerful hypothesis is higher than that of confirming a less powerful hypothesis. But the criterion of explanatory power, on which the theistic hypothesis fares rather well (for it explains the existence of the entire world), is irrelevant to the Th.A., because it is not an indicator of whether a hypothesis is likely to be confirmed, if tested. Of the criteria of abduction which Peirce cites, we are interested only in those which are determinants of expected cognitive payoff *because* they are determinants of expected confirmation.

Thus we are led to ask: does the doctrine of economy lead us to judge that the theistic hypothesis is likely to be confirmed, in virtue of its having been discovered by a process that is an instance of retroduction? The answer is that it does not, and Peirce never explicitly cites retroductive origin as a criterion of abductive evaluation. Nor does this represent an oversight on his part. Recall that abduction is a process of *comparative* evaluation. Abductive criteria must be such that it is possible for hypotheses not to meet them, else they would be useless for the purposes of comparison. According to Peirce, all scientific hypotheses are discovered retroductively. Retroductive origin establishes no more presumption in favor of the theistic hypothesis than in favor of its chief rivals, which might be called "atheistic hypotheses"; for both are the results of human guessing. What Peirce needs to show is that there is some relevant difference between the theistic and atheistic hypotheses, a difference which the logic of science can grasp in order to legitimate and to ground a definite preference for the theistic hypothesis.[9] In short: the logic of abduction cannot underwrite the variant of the Th.A. which relies on the claim that the H.A. is an instance of retroduction. But Peirce has two other variants of the Th.A. capable of avoiding just this difficulty.

Variant 2: The Appeal to Instinctiveness

The Th.A., it must be stressed, does not depend on the claim that musement is an instance of retroduction. In the second and third variants, Peirce gets the same mileage from the claim that there is instead some property of the theistic hypothesis (distinguishable from the property of having been produced through retroductive reasoning) which serves to recommend it in prior assessment. Two candidates suggest themselves in accordance with the economic criteria delineated above. The theistic hypothesis, Peirce tells us at various points, is especially trustworthy, first, because it is an "instinctive" hypothesis (and there is an abductive presumption in favor of instinctive hypotheses), and second, because when it is entertained, it strikes the muser as being especially "plausible" (there being an abductive presumption in favor of hypotheses the entertainment of which is accompanied by a feeling of plausibility). It will be observed that the first of these arguments is a close cousin to the N.A. The crucial difference is that the N.A. makes no direct appeal to the logic of science, while the Th.A. does. In the context of the Th.A., the claim that there is a presumption in favor of instinctive guesses is the claim that it is the logic of abduction which underwrites a presumption in favor of instinctive guesses. In the N.A. such an appeal is lacking.

As we have seen, the Economy of Research does instruct us to give special preference to guesses which are instinctive. The reason we should do so is established by well-known metascientific arguments, which we need not consider here in great depth.[10] Peirce discusses one such metascientific argument in "NARG" at 6:476-77, the gist of which is that astounding historical advances in human science and cognition are explicable only on the assumption that the human mind is specially adapted to know the ways of nature. But if the mind is so fitted, the story goes, then its guesses are trustworthy, and there is a slight presumption in favor of any particular guess generated by the human mind. Now what Peirce wants to say here is either that *all* human guesses are instinctive, and hence that there is a presumption in favor of *any* particular human guess; or that only some human guesses are instinctive, and that it is for these in particular that the metascientific arguments establish a presumption. On the first reading, instinctiveness, like retroductive origin, is of no help in the task of comparatively evaluating diverse hypotheses. Hence, it is only the second reading which can be adequate to Peirce's intention in "NARG." If instinctiveness is to be a useful criterion of abductive evaluation, then it must be possible to distinguish instinctively generated hypotheses from other sorts: a criterion which instructs us to trust all hypotheses is abductively useless.

Variant 3: The Appeal to Antecedent Plausibility

So how do we tell which of our guesses are instinctive? Peirce suggests that a reliable indicator of instinctiveness is to be found in antecedent plausibility: in the case of

a hypothesis, "the strength of the impulse [to believe that it is true] is a symptom of its being instinctive" (6:476). From here, it is only a short distance to the third variant of the Th.A., in which the acceptability of a hypothesis is grounded directly in its antecedent plausibility. The full story can be spelled out as follows: retroductive reasoning gives rise to an explanatory hypothesis held to be "plausible" in virtue of its explanatory properties. The hypothesis emerges into the mind of the researcher with a degree of acceptance or confidence that it is true. Some hypotheses arrive with a greater, some with a lesser, initial plausibility. The "hypothesis of God" always appears in the mind of the muser with an exceptionally high initial plausibility. "The Plausibility of the [theistic] hypothesis reaches an almost unparalleled height among deliberately formed hypotheses. . . . This very small Plausibility is undoubtedly an argument of no small weight in favor of the truth of the hypothesis" (6:488). The suggestion is that atheistic hypotheses do not arrive in the mind with the same degree of plausibility as the theistic hypothesis and that, therefore, the theistic hypothesis is to be preferred. And again, this preference is held to be underwritten by the logic of abduction.

The success of the Th.A. now seems to ride on whether antecedent plausibility (the level of confidence accompanying the initial entertainment of a hypothesis) is recognized by the logic of abduction as a legitimate criterion of prior assessment. Peirce takes this to be a matter of crucial importance. He addresses it at length in the Lowell Lectures of 1903. The point is to determine whether it is "good reasoning to say that a given hypothesis is good, as a hypothesis, because it is a natural one, or one readily embraced by the human mind. It must concern logic in the highest degree to ascertain precisely how far and under what limitations this maxim may be held. For of all beliefs, none is more natural than the belief that it is natural for man to err. The logician ought to find out what the relation is between these two tendencies" (5:592). The view which emerges from the lectures is that antecedent likelihood must be handled with great care. "It is a very grave mistake to attach much importance to the antecedent likelihood of hypotheses, except in extreme cases; because likelihoods are mostly merely subjective, and have so little real value, that considering the remarkable opportunities which they will cause us to miss, in the long run attention to them does not pay" (5:598). The likelihood with which a hypothesis strikes a researcher depends to such an extent not on the properties of the hypothesis, but on those of the researcher, that it is of limited value to inquiry.

Several years later, in his exposition of the Third Argument, Peirce suggests that there is a certain sense of confidence in a hypothesis which is genuinely reliable. "[A] certain altogether peculiar confidence in a hypothesis, not to be confused with rash cocksureness, has a very appreciable value as a sign of the truth of the hypothesis. . . . [The Humble Argument] excited this peculiar confidence in the very highest degree" (6:477).

But in the very same passage, he offers the following critical remarks: "Far from constituting, by itself, a logical justification such as it becomes a rational being to put forth, this pleading, that we *cannot help* yielding to the suggestion, amounts to nothing more than a confession of having failed to train ourselves to control our thoughts" (6:476). The very ambivalence expressed here can be traced through the rest of Peirce's writings on plausibility. Overall, however, the stronger theme is that of caution and reflective distance when dealing with such feelings, and Peirce issues many a warning against their potential deceptiveness, as here (ca. 1896): "For after all, what is a *likely* hypothesis? It is one which falls in with our preconceived ideas. But these may be wrong. Their errors are just what the scientific man is out gunning for most particularly" (1:120). Of course, Peirce's misgivings concerning our unreflective propensities toward certain hypotheses come most clearly to the forefront in his early essay **"The Fixation of Belief"** (1878; 5:358-87). There, we find him contrasting unfavorably the "a priori method" of fixing opinion with the genuinely inductive scientific method. The former is a method of arriving at belief by honoring one's "natural preferences," by believing what appears true to oneself, or "that which we find ourselves inclined to believe" (5:382). "The very essence of it is to think what one is inclined to think" (5:385). As such it is unreliable, Peirce claims, because our "natural preferences" are often more clearly indicative of psychosociological facts about ourselves than of the facts concerned by the hypotheses in question. A genuinely reliable method must show a greater willingness to be guided by the nature of the object itself, and a greater effort to gain reflective distance from subjective preferences and impressions.

The conclusion I would like to draw is that Peirce's theory of abductive evaluation does not recognize antecedent plausibility as a reliable source of recommendation for a hypothesis. My argumentative strategy in reaching this conclusion has been to interpret **"NARG"** by referring to other writings from various periods in Peirce's career. This strategy, unfortunately, appears to be open to the objection that Peirce's thought on antecedent likelihood and plausibility must be viewed developmentally and that doing so reveals a transition from the early Peirce's criticisms of the a priori method to a later espousal of "commonsensism" in the tradition of William Hamilton and Thomas Reid. "Commonsensism" is generally understood to be the view that there are basic beliefs, propositions which we cannot help but believe to be true.[11] The idea underlying such a developmental account would be that, for Peirce, our confidence in antecedently plausible hypotheses is only a weakened version of our being unable to doubt our basic beliefs and that, therefore, by making room for basic beliefs, Peirce was also expressing a newfound trust in feelings of antecedent plausibility. This idea is not without textual support. It is suggested, for example, at 6:480, where Peirce tells us in one breath that Pragmaticism "implies faith in common sense and instinct" and that the theistic hypothesis is "of the very highest Plausibil-

ity." But in fact it can be shown on Peirce's own terms that antecedent plausibility and indubitability are two rather different properties of propositions, to the extent that no proposition can be both antecedently plausible and indubitable. To say that there are basic beliefs is to say not that there are scientific hypotheses which we entertain with the greatest confidence, but to say that there are propositions which cannot become scientific hypotheses at all, because we inquire into the truth of a proposition only if we are at least capable of doubting its truth. A basic belief is not the sort of proposition which would emerge into the mind as an exceptionally plausible hypothesis; rather, it is the sort of proposition which would never achieve the status of a hypothesis at all.

Peirce drives home the point that indubitability and antecedent plausibility are two very different properties of propositions, by contending that the indubitability of basic beliefs depends on their characteristic "vagueness," a property which scientific hypotheses do not share. According to commonsensism, "all the veritably indubitable beliefs are *vague*" where "the *vague* might be defined as that to which the principle of contradiction does not apply" (5:505), by which Peirce means that it is unclear what should be thought to follow from a vague proposition, and likewise what should be thought to contradict it. An example of a basic belief is "our belief in the Order of Nature" (5:508). Taken in the vague sense, the proposition that there is an order of nature is indubitable; made suitably precise, it becomes contentious and eminently dubitable. Scientific hypotheses, of course, cannot be vague, for "it is a function of an explanatory hypothesis . . . to excite a clear image in the mind by means of which the clear consequences of ascertainable conditions may be predicted" (6:488). Since scientific hypotheses must be precise enough to have definite consequences testable against experience, they are by nature dubitable. What follows is that to be indubitable, a proposition must be vague, which precludes its being antecedently plausible; to be antecedently plausible, it must be precise, which precludes its being indubitable. Thus, Peirce's commonsensical plea in favor of basic beliefs gives him no reason to temper the critical attitude he takes toward antecedent plausibility.[12]

For Peirce, in sum, antecedent likelihood is nothing but an initial and highly subjective impression of the merits of a hypothesis, before the evidence for and against is properly scrutinized. Since it is so dependent on scientifically irrelevant subjective factors, its claim to legitimacy as a criterion of prior assessment is tenuous. Nevertheless, Peirce does think that plausibility has a role to play in the logic of abduction. The Economy of Research cannot ignore it completely. I submit it is the use to which Peirce himself puts the criterion of antecedent plausibility that is most telling here. In applying the criterion to specific examples (see esp. those at 2:662), his aim most often is not to recommend an especially plausible hypothesis for preferred treatment, but to dismiss an especially implausible one from consideration altogether. What the criterion tells us is that hypotheses which seem highly implausible or preposterous need not be considered in scientific inquiry. "For example, if a man came to me and pretended to be able to turn lead into gold, I should say to him, 'My dear sir, I haven't the time to make gold'" (5:600). The suggested hypothesis (that the man is able to turn lead into gold) is so implausible that Peirce feels entitled to reject it out of hand. If the example is representative, the abductive criterion of antecedent plausibility should properly be understood as a criterion of antecedent implausibility. Its role is negative: to eliminate wildly unpromising hypotheses from consideration, and it has no significant positive function of special recommendation.

We have explored three variants of the Th.A., assessing the adequacy of each in terms of the logic of abduction. First, we considered the claim that the theistic hypothesis should be trusted because it is of retroductive origin. We saw this suggestion shatter against Peirce's claim that all hypotheses are retroductive in origin. Second, we considered the claim that the theistic hypothesis is warranted because it is instinctive. We saw that this suggestion merely delays the problem, because we require a criterion of instinctiveness. Third and finally, we considered the claim that the theistic hypothesis is warranted in virtue of the high plausibility it attains in the mind of one who muses to it. We saw that this suggestion is problematic, because the logic of abduction does not univocally recognize plausibility as a decisive criterion of preference. Peirce's suggestion is that the Th.A. is an inference whose leading principle is drawn from the logic of science. We can reject this suggestion, for we have shown that the logic of science provides no such leading principle.

PRAGMATISM AND THE "HYPOTHESIS OF GOD"

There is one more account on which the Th.A. violates the logic of science. In **"NARG"** Peirce takes it for granted that the conclusion of the H.A., the reality of God, has the status of a scientific hypothesis. He calls it the "hypothesis of God," seemingly bypassing his own doctrine of Pragmatism and the formal criterion which it provides for determining what explanatory guesses are to be regarded as genuine hypotheses. Now as stated in the pragmatic maxim, a hypothesis must be verifiable. It must have observational consequences which can be spelled out deductively, tested against real observations and evaluated inductively. Peirce himself admits that the theistic hypothesis fails on this score, having few or no experiential consequences (6:489).[13] Strangely, however, he does not face the implications of this admission, claiming instead that the drawback of having no experiential consequences is somehow compensated for by the peculiar practical relevance of the theistic hypothesis: when believed to be true, it exerts a "commanding influence over the whole conduct of life of its believers" (6:490). "[The H.A.] is the First Stage of a scientific inquiry, resulting in a hypothesis of the very highest Plausibility, whose ultimate test must lie in its value in the self-controlled growth of man's conduct of

life" (6:480). That the "hypothesis of God" is immune from all empirical tests is of no consequence, Peirce suggests, because a different kind of test alone is appropriate to it.

Two important difficulties beset this special plea for the theistic hypothesis. The first is that it leads Peirce to contradict what he says elsewhere about the relation between conduct and the testability of beliefs. On the view advanced in the article **"What Pragmatism Is"** (1905; 5.411-37), it is impossible for a belief to be *both* action guiding *and* immune to any sort of empirical testing. "Whenever a man acts purposely, he acts under a belief in some strictly experimental phenomenon. Consequently, the sum of the experimental phenomena that a proposition implies makes up its entire bearing on human conduct" (5:427). Although the argument here is a non sequitur, the underlying gist is not hard to discern: a proposition which is not amenable at all to inductive verification can have no bearing on conduct. If the theistic hypothesis is a genuine hypothesis, then it falls under this general rule: lacking experimental consequences, it can have no bearing on conduct.

But granted even that Peirce may have had good reason to change his mind between 1905 and 1908 on the relation between action guidingness and verifiability, it remains the case that his special plea for the theistic hypothesis involves a concession that all but undermines the Th.A. By admitting that the test for the validity of the theistic hypothesis differs from the test applicable to more run-of-the-mill scientific hypotheses, Peirce in effect concedes that the theistic hypothesis is not a scientific hypothesis at all and abandons the project of securing the reality of God via what I have called a "scientific argument." Thus, it should come as no surprise that we find in **"NARG"** a competing tendency to describe theistic belief in terms appropriate to the description of basic belief: it is vague, irresistible, and so on. Such suggestions, like the one that theism can be vindicated on the basis of its "value in the self-controlled growth of man's conduct of life," having nothing to do with an analysis of and appeal to the logic and methodology of science. The Th.A. cannot build on them.

NOTES

[1] Murray G. Murphey, "Kant's Children: The Cambridge Platonists," *Transactions of the Charles S. Peirce Society* 4 (1968): 3-33. Further references to this journal will employ the standard abbreviation *TCPS*. The present reference is to p. 8.

[2] All references to Peirce's writings are from the *Collected Papers of Charles Sanders Peirce*, ed. C. Hartshorne, P. Weiss, and A. Burks (Cambridge, Mass: Harvard University Press, 1935; reprint, 1958). Citation is according to the following formula: volume number: page number. "NARG" is reprinted in the *Collected Papers* at 6:452-85. I will be referring also to Peirce's "Additaments" to the article, dated ca. 1910 and reprinted at 6:486-90.

[3] See, e.g., Bowman L. Clarke, "Peirce's Neglected Argument," *TCPS* 14 (1977): 277-87. See also chap. 5 of Michael L. Raposa, *Peirce's Philosophy of Religion* (Bloomington: Indiana University Press, 1989); John E. Smith, "The Tension between Direct Experience and Argument in Religion," *Religious Studies* 17 (1981): 487-97.

[4] But see Richard L. Trammell's critique of this view in his "Religion, Instinct and Reason in the Thought of Charles S. Peirce," *TCPS* 8 (1972): 3-25.

[5] Although Peirce treats all three terms of the expression "argument for the reality of God" (namely, "argument," "reality," and "God") as technical terms in need of definition, it is clear that his intent is *not* thereby to isolate himself from the long tradition leading from Aristotle to Swinburne concerned with proving the existence of God. Some scholars have even thought to discover traditional theistic arguments in "NARG." Smith ("The Tension between Direct Experience and Argument in Religion") thinks Peirce's line of reasoning analogous in certain respects to Anselm's ontological argument, while Clarke ("Peirce's Neglected Argument," p. 278) takes the Humble Argument to be an argument from design. My claim is weaker than that of either of these scholars: while maintaining that Peirce's overall project of argumentatively motivating belief in the reality of God is on the same footing with that of other prominent theistic philosophers, I am not concerned to investigate the precise logical parallels obtaining between Peirce's and more traditional arguments.

[6] Nor does he mention "abduction" in the "Additaments" of 1910. The editors' "Index of Subjects" is misleading in this regard. For the entry "Abduction," the index lists both 6:469-70 (from the 1908 article) and 6:488 (from the "Additaments"). In both places, however, Peirce uses only the term "retroduction." Nicholas Rescher, *Peirce's Philosophy of Science* (Notre Dame, Ind.: University of Notre Dame Press, 1978) recognizes a distinction between retroduction and abduction, but his account of the distinction differs from my own. See his pp. 41 ff.

[7] For an explication of the differences between "theory generation" (the concern of retroduction) and "prior assessment," see Martin Curd, "The Logic of Discovery: An Analysis of Three Approaches," in *Scientific Discovery, Logic, and Rationality,* ed. Thomas Nickles (Dordrecht: D. Reidel, 1980), pp. 210-19.

[8] Peirce has been criticized widely for failing to spell out this distinction. See, e.g., W. M. Brown, "The Economy of Peirce's Abduction," *TCPS* 19 (1983): 397-411; C. F. Delaney, "Peirce on 'Simplicity' and the Conditions of the Possibility of Science," in *History of Philosophy in the Making,* ed. Linus J. Thro (Washington, D.C.: University Press of America, 1982), pp. 177-94, esp. p. 178, and "Peirce on the Hypothesis of God," *TCPS* 28 (1992): 725-39; Thomas Kapitan, "In What Way Is Abductive

Inference Creative?" *TCPS* 26 (1990): 499-512; Larry Laudan, "Why Was the Logic of Discovery Abandoned?" in Nickles, ed., pp. 173-83. The ambiguity in Peirce's use of the term "abduction" is perhaps most clearly evident at 7:219-20.

[9] For a similar reason, retroductive origin cannot serve as a criterion of inductive assessment: induction is a critical process, concerned with accepting some hypotheses as confirmed, and rejecting others as disconfirmed. But all hypotheses inductively evaluated are retroductive in origin.

[10] See Timothy Shanahan, "The First Moment of Scientific Inquiry: C. S. Peirce on the Logic of Abduction," *TCPS* 12 (1986): 449-66. Shanahan distinguishes five different arguments advanced by Peirce to support his thesis that the human mind is somehow especially "attuned to the truth of things."

[11] In its explicit form, commonsensism is characteristic of Peirce's later writings, but a version of it can be made out in the criticism of Descartes in "The Fixation of Belief." An important later document is the manuscript entitled "The Basis of Pragmatism" dated ca. 1905 (5:497 ff.).

[12] For an alternative account of the relation in Peirce's thought between commonsense and the logic of science, see Christopher Hookway, *Peirce* (London: Routledge & Kegan Paul, 1985), pp. 229 ff. According to Hookway, Peirce thinks that "we have a stock of vague indubitable beliefs, and one function of science is to give them precise form. If a scientific theory is refuted, this does not refute common-sense certainties, but simply calls on us to give new precise formulations." So far, so good. If a vague belief is made precise, it can be treated as a scientific hypothesis, though, as we have seen, it thereby loses its indubitability. But Hookway goes on to write, "The intuitive commonsense embodied in our abductive sense, our sense of plausibility, recommends a vaguely formulated hypothesis" (p. 231). This cannot be right. To the extent that a hypothesis is vague, it does not have clear, testable consequences. As we have seen, the logic of abduction requires us to accept as hypotheses those propositions for which observable consequences can be spelled out. Were the logic of abduction to recommend vague hypotheses, therefore, it would contradict itself, instructing us at the same time to prefer vague hypotheses (because they inspire confidence) and precise hypotheses (because they are testable).

[13] At one point, Peirce seems to want to retract this claim. He writes, "The hypothesis of God's Reality is logically not so isolated a conclusion as it may seem. On the contrary, it is connected so with a theory of the nature of thinking that if this be proved so is that. Now there is no such difficulty in giving experiential consequences of this theory of thinking as there are in attempting directly to trace out other consequences of God's reality" (6:491). The idea here is that the theistic

hypothesis is entailed by some theory of thought, so that any observational evidence for this theory is at the same time evidence for the theistic hypothesis. Unfortunately, Peirce leaves this line of reasoning wholly undeveloped.

Terry Cochran (essay date 1995)

SOURCE: "History and the Collapse of Eternity," in *Boundary 2: An International Journal of Literature and Culture,* Vol. 22, No. 3, Fall, 1995, pp. 33-55.

[In the following excerpt, Cochran uses Peirce's essay "Evolutionary Love" to examine the latter's idealism and acknowledgement of historical materialism.]

1

Since the advent of the modern state, every cultural and political economy has required a coherent and compatible sense of the past, present, and future. This sometimes implicit historical understanding, with its attendant categories of knowledge and value, endows any present with stability by mediating between the need for continuity with the past and the inevitability of disruptive change. A quandary in historical understanding occurs when disruptive change outdistances the capacity to integrate it; at its most extreme, this quandary touches on the very concept of historical protagonist, a central element of all historical thought. In modernity, however, when a transcendent deity gradually ceased being viewed as the primary agent of human events, the notion of historical protagonist has achieved unparalleled prominence. As shorthand for a social and ideological process, "modernity" is synonymous with the search for a secular agent to propel the movement of history and with the secular epistemology that derives from it. Endowed with recognizable characteristics, the historical agency of modernity has most insistently been attributed to collectivities, whether they take the form of the state, the nation, the class, or the people, and to the knowing subject, whether considered as the monadic individual or the personified *Geist* of idealism. Instability in the modern economy of agency places into question not only the tenuous historical continuity it produces but also the multivalent organization of knowledge that ranges from empirical institutions, such as the university, to presuppositions about how an object of knowledge is constituted.

In this context, the unfathomable acceleration of contemporary historical change, which affects realms of existence, from the technological to the political, from the economic to the ecological, increasingly shows the impotence, if not the irrelevance, of traditional categories of knowledge. The incipient unraveling of traditional historical understanding can be readily pinpointed. In the words of a contemporary sociologist who has spent his entire professional career seeking to identify the shifting protagonists of history, "The Subject [in the sense of 'subjectivity'] is no longer the presence in

us of the universal, whether one calls it the laws of nature, the meaning of history, or divine creation."[1] This statement about our historical condition, so to speak, like so many others that express a similar view, can be interpreted in various ways. Most interpreters oscillate between condemnation of our inability to posit universals and see them embodied in single instances and celebration of the fact that today we live in a world of relative values. But the fundamental historical question is whether the currently misplaced universal results from a loss or from recognition that it existed only by virtue of massive social and political support.

While the perceived gravity and diffusion of the so-called historical problem is unprecedented, the issues involved in the collapse of otherworldly historical understanding have been openly debated since the emergence of industrialized states and the accompanying political economy. This has been particularly true in the United States, where its industrialization went hand in hand with its emergence as a global power. In fact, without the slightest hint of irony, one could affirm that the most coldly analytical response to today's historical disjuncture was written by the American philosopher Charles Sanders Peirce at the end of the nineteenth century. Peirce's aggressive essay on historical agency, published in 1893 under the title **"Evolutionary Love,"**[2] is the fifth and final installment of a series of essays in which he attempts to construct the backbone of his entire philosophy, including his theories of mind and habit, alongside his more widely known semiotic notions of firstness, secondness, and thirdness. Yet, the essay's greater significance lies in its thematic concern with history, especially historical understanding as it pertains to the nineteenth and, in the essay's own reference, to the latter part of the twentieth century.

As might be guessed from Peirce's extensive debt to the idealist tradition, his essay is a scarcely veiled polemic against materialist views of history. A critique of materialism is, of course, common among philosophers of history, who must make recourse to nebulous concepts, such as "peoples," "states," and "historical epochs," to narrate their histories of progress and decline. But the essay's uniqueness resides in its attention to the implications of opposing views of historical understanding. These implications have a striking relevance for historical understanding at the edge of the twenty-first century.

Peirce's analysis concedes, from the outset, that the form of historical understanding he endorses runs counter to the historical forces of his own time. To abstract his views from the historical present, therefore, Peirce describes the contemporary present through the eyes of future historians:

> The nineteenth century is now fast sinking into the grave, and we all begin to review its doings and to think what character it is destined to bear as compared with other centuries in the minds of future historians. It will be called, I guess, the Economical Century; for political economy has

more direct relations with all the branches of activity than has any other science. Well, political economy has its formula of redemption, too. It is this: Intelligence in the service of greed ensures the justest prices, the fairest contracts, the most enlightened conduct of all the dealings between men, and leads to the summum bonum, food in plenty and perfect comfort. Food for whom? Why, for the greedy master of intelligence. (192)

The polemical, even sarcastic tone of this passage is unmistakable, and what it calls here "political economy" bears the brunt of the critique. Yet, in characteristic fashion, Peirce's critique refrains from taking a narrowly construed political position. His attack on the centrality of political economy applies to capitalism no less than to Marxist critiques of it; although Peirce is far from a straightforward proponent of idealism, he shares with idealist philosophers a distaste for materialist views of history. In effect, this entire essay does not question the validity of political and economic conceptions in themselves but seeks to deny political economy as a basis for historical understanding. Peirce acknowledges that what he calls political economy, like universalizing theories of history, has a form of redemption. But that is precisely the problem: its redemptive moment does not transcend its own historical moment. It is, in fact, contrary to the logic of transcendence, because it has to do only with individual self-interest. Tying historical agency to individual action trivializes any attempt to explain historical change by referring to nonperishable, or eternal, truths and ideas.

This elevation of individual self-interest constitutes, for Peirce, the primary danger in giving precedence to political economy. Of course, what I am calling "self-interest" appears consistently in the essay as "greed," a term chosen for its obvious rhetorical power. But Peirce is clear about the repercussions of overemphasizing greed in explaining the individual's role in history. In addition to transforming values presumed to underlie Euro-American civilization, moving greed or self-interest into the foreground requires a shift in historical understanding. In his own words, it has resulted in "a philosophy which comes unwittingly to this, that greed is the great agent in the elevation of the human race and in the evolution of the universe" (193). Greed, in this instance, is the contrary of a universal concept that then becomes manifest in the individual. If this greed is a concept at all, it nonetheless has no otherworldly attributes. Greed as self-interest mediates between individuals and historical evolution. In this struggle that powers history, the more intelligent, aggressive, or perhaps simply the more fortunate wins. Fundamentally, this view of political economy embodies a theory of history based on perpetual conflict without the harmonizing force of universal ideals that transcend the individual.

Writing at the end of the nineteenth century, Peirce observed the contemporary effects of industrialized society to extrapolate the historical consequences of political economic thought. To flesh out other characteristics of this troubling conception of history, Peirce draws on Darwin's theory of evolution; as stated in the essay, Darwin's *Origin of Species* "merely extends politico-economical views of progress to the entire realm of animal and vegetable life" (196). Since an overarching idea does not guide history toward ever higher stages, the notion of progress is a qualified one at best.

This concern with progress, with the directionality of history, becomes the focus of the essay's comments on Darwin's work as exemplifying political economy. Peirce summarizes his critical judgment in one brief sentence: "Natural selection, as conceived by Darwin, is a mode of evolution in which the only positive agent of change in the whole passage from moner to man is fortuitous variation" (197). Darwin's notion of "fortuitous variation," change without causality and on the basis of no master plan, stands in opposition to Peirce's strong sense of developmental history, of history that proceeds from worse to better by means of a universal, non-historical idea. This apprehension about Darwin's theories was shared by many of Peirce's (and Darwin's) contemporaries, who were specifically perturbed by a historical conception that removed deities from intervention in evolutionary matters; others, some of whom Darwin mentioned in his reedition of *Origin of Species,* contained this implicit theory of history by integrating evolution into theological notions of historical change.

But Peirce's concern, which becomes even more apparent when he counterposes his own historical model, does not really have to do with Darwinian evolution but with a theory of history that unfolds oblivious to any logic of necessity. It posits historical change and powerfully explains the development from a mass of protoplasm to human beings. But it does not tie agency to any notion or individual action that is not subject to the historical process. Consequently, its interpretation of the historical passage from the past to the present is most troubling because the present human dominance, the end point of history, endows history with only a simulation of purposiveness. As a theory of history, however, it projects an endemically uncertain future; it is historical process without a center, an eternal point of reference. Unlike in theories of the unfolding of human consciousness, progress is far from absolute. From the perspective of human dominance, for example, evolution has made continuous progress, but it is doubtful that dinosaurs or other extinct species would agree. Even more to the point regarding Peirce's astute critique, contemporary zoobiologists—such as Claude Allègre—have begun to analyze the historical limit of human dominance, just as astrophysicists calculate the collapse of the solar system.[3] We are far removed from bickering about whether the heavens revolve around the earth or the sun.

Briefly, therefore, Peirce's formulation seeks to fill the conceptual gap left by political economy's refusal or inability to give agency an immutable face, to assign a purposiveness to historical change, and its assertion that individual self-interest is the motor of history. This portrait of political economy represents the framework of his historical questioning. In devising a coherent response, Peirce predictably draws on the Christian tradition and, in a gesture characteristic of modernity, the obscured precepts of Greek philosophy. As the essay opens, it immediately sets out the parameters of discussion, although their significance becomes manifest only later: "Philosophy," Peirce writes, "when just escaping from its golden pupa-skin, mythology, proclaimed the great evolutionary agency of the universe to be Love" (190). This early philosophical understanding of the domain of human consciousness runs through Christianity, as well. And although Peirce's argument would seem to have little in common with Christianity, he demonstrates its pertinence by interpreting the Gospel John's statement "God is love" as the "formula of an evolutionary philosophy" (192), which stands in opposition to the materialist view attributed to Darwin and political economy.

Nevertheless, even as he uses these modes of thought and belief, Peirce is no more interested in defending religious ideals than he is in debunking the Darwinian theory of evolution or challenging what he refers to as the "scientific character" of political economy. In the context of the essay's aims, it is thus not surprising that Lamarck's theory of evolution serves as the point of departure. It lends itself well to representing the historical agency of love because, unlike Darwinism, it is fundamentally an interpretive theory that closely resembles narrative history. When translated into the terms of historical and ideological development, Lamarck's theory of evolution works by taking "force," the movement toward change, and integrating it into already established history, even if this history refers to some generalized notion of biological heredity. Peirce uses several words to describe the workings of this "force," or agency:

> Habit is mere inertia, a resting on one's oars, not a propulsion. Now it is energetic projaculation . . . by which in the typical instances of Lamarckian evolution the new elements of form are first created. Habit, however, forces them to take practical shapes, compatible with the structures they affect, and, in the form of heredity and otherwise, gradually replaces the spontaneous energy that sustains them. (201)

The narrative sequentiality of this passage is readily evident. Habit, a concept that stands at the center of Peircean pragmatism, functions as a setting against which an event takes place. Yet, unlike many narratives, and contrary to the theory of history underlying Darwinian evolution, the events' outcome is unidirectional and irreversible, because it leads toward an always improving accommodation to the world. Although even the most cursory knowledge of today's biogenetics would place these premises into question, that is really irrelevant for the theory of history that Lamarckian evolution is asserted to exemplify. This essentially narrative structure of historical change, change that occurs as a result of individual agents challenging habit and hered-

ity only to have heredity incorporate the challenge, seems to mimic the model of tradition often associated with modernity.

Ultimately, however, Peirce's own conception of history differs from this both in its complexity and explanatory power. This difference becomes evident when the essay shifts to a more openly phenomenological description of the process: "Everybody knows that the long continuance of a routine of habit makes us lethargic, while a succession of surprises wonderfully brightens the ideas. Where there is motion, where history is a-making, there is the focus of mental activity" (202). Consonant with a view that seeks historical constants to drive historical change, history requires mental activity to happen or to be produced. The reference to mental activity, to mind, is significant not only because it abstracts historical agency from the muck of materialism. In fact, the essay goes on to affirm that "all matter is essentially mind" and that historical consciousness rests on "a continuity of mind" (201). The continuity of mind proves to be the key concept that posits transhistorical continuity while providing both the space and the meaning for individual action. This formulation unites the possibility for individual agency, which, in political economy, lacks historical purposiveness, and an inexorable grinding out of history that shares features of Hegel's philosophy of history, which Peirce finds, in his own words, "superb, almost sublime" but lacking "living freedom" (204).

The essay's countergospel of love, which stands over against the gospel of greed, concretely expresses this continuity of history and action. Peirce's well-known penchant for Greek-based neologisms refashions the theory in terms of *agape:* "The agapastic development of thought should, if it exists, be distinguished by its purposive character, this purpose being the development of an idea" (212). In a most general sense, this formulation exhibits a striking resemblance to Hegelian history, but the differences are more suggestive because they address the perceived deficiencies in Hegel's theory. While, here, history and thought unfold in accordance with the idea, it is not a nameless abstract idea but one Peirce designates as love. This so-called agapastic theory of history contains within it the relationship between self and other, but it has virtually nothing to do with the subject-object dialectic that underlies much of the politics of identity.

Just as in the assertion that love explains historical evolution more effectively than self-interest, historical agency is produced through harmony rather than conflict. Although this emphasis hints at the ideological basis of Peirce's analysis, it proves necessary for the historical conception he so rigorously describes. In the essay's own terms, the dynamics of this series of conceptual relationships can be stated succinctly: "The agapastic development of thought is the adoption of certain mental tendencies . . . by an immediate attraction for the idea itself, whose nature is divined before the mind possesses it, by the power of sympathy, that is, by virtue of the continuity of mind" (205). In typical

Peircean fashion, this view of history based on the idea (specifically, the idea of love because of love's conceptual characteristics) derives from Peirce's celebrated notion of thirdness. It offers a third way of historical understanding that incorporates purpose, absent from Darwin's theory of evolution, and the space of individual freedom, constricted in Hegelian idealism. Understood in this way, the idea of love, therefore, expresses the "continuity of mind" in time and in the individuals' bond to a community that transcends them, a bond here referred to as "sympathy." On this basis, the passage then proceeds to the idea's historical role, affecting the collective as a whole, or the "collective personality," the individual as a collective member, and the individual as individual.

Other of Peirce's essays treat in greater detail various of these issues, most notably the continuity of mind. But this essay essentially dissects the analytic of historical understanding that has characterized the modern era. Peirce lived in a century of mass movements that have been surpassed only by our own. His description of an ahistorical or transhistorical idea of love represents an attempt to explain individuals' belonging to mass groups, their like thinking, even when such thinking would seem beyond specific individuals (213). Ultimately, after this painstaking analysis, Peirce concludes with a test that, if realizable, would establish the historical truth he endorses: "If it could be shown directly that there is such an entity as the 'spirit of an age' or of a people, and that mere individual intelligence will not account for all the phenomena, this would be proof enough at once of agapasticism and of synechism [or the continuity of mind]. I must acknowledge that I am unable to produce a cogent demonstration of this" (212-13). The spirit of an age is significant not because it represents a collective dimension but because it assumes the role of historical agent. Interestingly, Peirce's linguistic knowledge and integrity prevent him from asserting outright the existence of historical spirits. Instead, the essay demonstrates how collectivities are constructed, filled with meaning, given a temporal existence, and assigned the power of historical protagonist.

In 1893, the **"Evolutionary Love"** essay was framed as a response to a conflictual, fragmented society. The dominance of political economy and what Peirce calls "Wall Street sharps" robbed history of its agency and its purpose. The essay indulges only once in historicizing, projecting toward a future where the conflict will be harmonized and agency restored to its rightful place. The future it refers to is our present: "The twentieth century, in its latter half, shall surely see the deluge-tempest burst upon the social order—to clear upon a world as deep in ruin as that greed-philosophy has long plunged it into guilt" (195). This apocalyptic vision appears quaint today; the world we live in has become Peirce's worst nightmare, where agency has become more dispersed than he could ever have imagined. In effect, contemporary understandings of agency are considerably more radical and have none of the utopian

hubris. For example, Pierre Lévy, a researcher on questions of technology and society, writes: "A disparate crowd of social agents explores new possibilities for their own benefit (and to the detriment of other agents) until a new situation is provisionally stabilized, with its local values, morals, and cultures."[4] The humanistic disciplines, with their attendant concern with values and culture, no longer provide the means for stability. Agency itself has been historicized, just as the sites of knowledge production and reproduction have been transformed, and agency's idealized guarantors, including the state and nationhood, are becoming less and less viable. In this context, nostalgic calls for a return to earlier concepts of social stability appear as ahistorical as the historical protagonists they seek to recuperate.

2

Even if Peirce's essay does not succeed in establishing the historical power of love, it unambiguously shows that the contemporary historical problem derives from an incommensurability between notions of agency and historical understanding. Although today the notion of agency is most often discussed as an attribute of subjectivity, it is closely linked to the much more widespread discussions about the disappearance of the universal, supposedly a condition of postmodernity. Postmodernity, perhaps best understood as a historical moment of profound instability, is further aggravated by the massive social and technological changes in the twentieth century. In the epoch of decolonization, which roughly corresponds to a recognition of the misplaced universal, histories have proliferated, most often striving to compensate for history's inability to grasp its own movement and drawing on ideas that are affirmed to reside outside of mundane time. These ideas have a broad range, including recourse to particularist ideas such as ethnicity and cultural identity, inevitably linked to affirmations of the present's historical continuity with the past and future. At the same time, however, a universalist concern with history still has its adherents, leading Alain Finkielkraut, for example, to resuscitate the notion of love in a historical formula not unlike that of Peirce.[5] In fact, this mechanism of historical understanding has defined the historical thought and practice of this century, from Peirce's drive to recenter historical agency down to the contemporary obsession with the historical agency of cultural difference. But these proliferating ideas, all of which contribute to, rather than resolve, the problem of fragmentation, do not attempt to account for the historical specificity of contemporary society but rather operate according to the logic of unity that has become historically impossible.

To state the issue bluntly, contemporary historical understanding faces an unavoidable disjuncture between the reigning historical conception in modernity and the explosion in materialist, secular knowledge. The concept of agency, of how to conceive a contemporary historical protagonist, is the pivotal question of that disjuncture. Viewed in this way, the question of agency casts a different light on the omnipresent historical concerns and debates of the twentieth century. In this conceptual landscape, Walter Benjamin's writings on history occupy a unique position for coming to terms with the conflicts and tensions in any theory of twentieth-century history. As has become increasingly recognized, Benjamin was, from the beginning, literally obsessed with the relationship between historical understanding and historical intervention, although it came to dominate other concerns only in his later writings. Interestingly, Benjamin's later work, much of it unpublished and in numerous versions, including important texts and notes that served as supporting material, has been problematic precisely because it does not seem to endorse any established theory of history. As a consequence, the multiple interests of his interpreters have determined the reception of his work. Benjamin's later theory of history is alternatively seen as a botched or successful attempt at either historical materialism or theological messianism, and sometimes as a productive or debilitating synthesis of the two.[6] This series of banal oppositions has, in fact, become the tradition of Benjaminian interpretation.[7]

Rather than determining Benjamin's filiation, the tradition that might have claims on him, it would seem more fruitful to understand the way in which Benjamin takes elements from mutually exclusive theories of history to advance a historical understanding he considers appropriate for the age of mechanical reproducibility. Anyone who reads Benjamin's theses "On the Concept of History" immediately identifies the conflicting historical views that Benjamin juxtaposes. In the context of a devastating critique of historicism, the theses describe a new theory of history that they designate as historical materialism, although its apparent messianic elements indicate that this materialist theory of history resists being reduced to the customary historical materialism of Marxism. With the availability of Benjamin's texts and notes for his massive project now known as the *Passagen-Werk,* the range of Benjamin's thinking about materialist history becomes more apparent, and the nature of its resistance, both to historical materialism and to its messianic counterimage, more precise.

As Peirce's analysis demonstrated, a theory of history always entails a theory of agency, a notion of the idealized protagonist or force that propels historical change. Benjamin's critique of historicism, which plots the concerns he will rearticulate in his view of history, focuses on the assumptions and concepts that generate historicist interpretations. First of all, "historicism posits an 'eternal' image (*Bild*) of the past."[8] The eternal, an immutable idea that resists the ravages of time, marks a theory of history that exempts the historian, the contemporary interpreter, from the historical interests of the present, past, or future. This idea, or image, of eternity—in the case of historicism, a secular eternity—serves to anchor the theory of objectivity that was so much a part of positivist history. But it has other consequences as well: "Historicism rightly culminates in

universal history, [which] has no theoretical apparatus. Its procedure is additive; it musters a mass of facts to fill homogeneous, empty time" (702; 262). From the universal perspective, all strife producing history disappears, including the relationship between the present and a past that coexists in the present, that exists only because it is not wholly past. Not only the historian but history itself is de-historicized: it becomes homogeneous and empty to enable the historicist interpreter to empty her mind and voyage into the idealized past. Theorizing universal history, which is the ultimate effect of Benjamin's analysis, means reintroducing the historical nature of all historical thinking and upsetting the chain of events that constitutes historicist accounts of history. Historicism's assumptions about historical continuity motivate its recourse to causality as a fundamental element of historical understanding: "Historicism contents itself with establishing a causal connection between various moments in history. But no fact that is a cause is for that very reason historical. It became historical posthumously, as it were, through events that may be separated from it by thousands of years" (704; 263). As part of its very conception, historicism must remain blind to the process of historical construction that underlies all history. Causality, and the historical narratives it structures, is no more historical than the homogeneous time that provides its context.

Homogeneous time, ready to be filled with a series of facts marshaled to express a causal development, is the companion to modernity's secular notion of historical agency. The idea of progress, of course, best summarizes modernity's mode of conceiving historical change, and both the *Passagen-Werk* and the theses **"On the Concept of History"** identify progress as the lowest common denominator in historicist thought: "The idea (*Vorstellung*) of the historical progress of humankind cannot be sundered from the idea of its progression through a homogeneous, empty time. A critique of the idea of such a progression must from the basis of any critique of the idea of progress itself" (701; 261). In the same passage, Benjamin lists the characteristics of historicist progress as manifest in social democratic theory. Progress implies: the progress of humankind itself; an open-ended temporality, corresponding to humankind's infinite perfectability; and a certain directionality. Progress anchors historical agency, the understanding of how historical change is propelled; not God but the very idea of human progress pushes along historical development. In somewhat tautological fashion—a consequence of all transcendental notions of agency—development is inevitable because that is the way that history plays itself out. And while today this may seem a naïve, even ahistorical notion of history, it offers a stable narrative structure for historical understanding: the present is firmly located between a past that has been superseded and a future that will supersede our present. In the context of this formulation, Peirce's critique of evolution stands in even sharper contrast: evolution has a theory of change, but not of the future and not of absolute progress. There are too many factors, including even the environment, moving at different rates but also shifting position with respect to one another, to predict, even hypothetically, a better future. This denial of absolute progress hints at the ultimate materialism (or, perhaps, anti-idealism) of the theory of evolution. For historicism, localizing the idea of agency in progress means assigning an idealized humankind the role of historical agent, for progress is always progress for humankind.

Benjamin's theory of history is articulated against this idea of historical progression and against the idealism that it implies. How is agency articulated in his materialist theory of history? In what might be called classical historical materialism, the proletariat embodied in the Communist party begins to exercise its collective will the moment it achieves self-consciousness as a historical protagonist.[9] But Benjamin explicitly rejects that historical conception. In an openly political reference, Benjamin remarks that the failure of the political opponents of fascism results from their misconstrued understanding of history: "This consideration proceeds from the insight that the politicians' stubborn faith in progress, their confidence in their 'mass basis,' and, finally, their servile integration in an uncontrollable apparatus have been three aspects of the same thing" (698; 258). Here, Benjamin's French version expresses more precisely the nature of the critique, which enumerates the leftists' "blind faith in progress, in the force, justice, and promptness of reactions formed within the masses, and in the party" (1263-64). The text calls for a break with this sort of historical thinking, which claims to draw its impetus from the ideal of progress, a collective identity, or a bureaucratic organization. Rather than breaking with the political realm, however, Benjamin proposes regrounding it with a different understanding of historical agency.

As is often the case with Benjamin's affirmations, his analysis of agency is at the same time subtle and uncompromising. The historical subject does not represent or embody agency; instead, it produces epistemological effects: "The subject of historical knowledge is the struggling, oppressed class itself" (700; 260). Benjamin's French version clarifies the nature of this subject by calling it "the artisan of historical knowledge" (1264). The link between historical action and historical knowledge is unmistakable, but the modalities of this relationship are not specified at this juncture. And once again, Benjamin seeks to demarcate his conception of history by referring to the historical theory elaborated by the social democrats. By adopting progress as the motor of historical change, the text notes, they misunderstand the forces of history and reverse even the temporality that they would adopt. From this perspective, today's oppressed class struggles in the name of a future that history relentlessly approaches. In this sense, the notion of progress domesticates a potentially quite different theory of history and of historical knowledge; action in the present is robbed of its own presumed agency because its meaning is perpetually postponed. An early draft of Benjamin's theses underscores the domesticat-

ing power of progress in conjunction with its ideal future: "The classless society is not the ultimate goal of historical progress but its so often failed, ultimately realized interruption" (1231). This displays only the faintest resemblance to historical materialism as it is generally understood.

In Benjamin's conception, conflict traverses history, just as the present wrests itself out of the past, the oppressed struggle against domination, and historical action disrupts the apparent historical continuity. Even historical consciousness itself is manifest only in the instant and cannot be sustained: "The awareness (*Bewusstsein*) of exploding the continuum of history is characteristic of the revolutionary classes at the instant of their action" (701; 261). Just as the oppressed class produces historical knowledge by virtue of its struggle, the revolutionary classes, multiples of the same historical conflict, become aware of the effects of their action as the action takes place. They are not, however, agents of historical change, nor are they protagonists in a historical idea that exceeds their own time. This irrepressible historical conflict inhabits both the material of history and its mode of transmission: "There is no document of culture that is not simultaneously a document of barbarism. And just as such a document is not free of barbarism, barbarism also taints the manner in which it was transmitted" (696; 256). In this instance, the conflict between culture and barbarism encompasses the two primary poles of European historical understanding. At the same time, however, the example indicates the spatial and temporal aspects of any notion of cultural tradition, never entirely separable from the historical theory that founds its interpretation. In a fragment from the *Passagen-Werk*, Benjamin affirms the conflictual nature of even the concepts of interpretation: "Barbarism is bound up with the very concept of culture, just as a treasure chest full of valuables is considered separate from the production process in which it endures, but not separate from the production process that created it."[10] This enigmatic attempt to juxtapose synchrony and diachrony, the treasure that both exists in the present and bears the marks of its conflictual production, serves as the dividing line between the historicist and the materialist. The "historical materialist" (696; 256) or the "materialist historian" (1262) refuses to be swayed by the lures of the treasure and does not lose sight of the conflict that inhabits it; the historicist, on the other hand, endorses the spoils of the historical victor. Yet, the materialist historian cannot escape the historical discontinuity and the knowledge it produces, just as all products of human history, from the immaterial concept to the material object, cannot be separated from the conflict that created and transmitted them.

In effect, the materialist historian, or the historical materialist, is a key element in Benjamin's theory of history. As if to underscore this link, recent interpretations of Benjamin's theory of history tend to include lengthy reflections on the role of the historian and interpreter. For example, Stéphane Mosès's *L'ange de l'histoire,* undoubtedly the most complete reading of this historical aspect of Benjamin's work, places the historian at the center of Benjamin's political theory of history.[11] In interpreting Benjamin's historical theory, Mosès draws extensively on the notion of "actualization," a process whereby the past and present collide in producing new constellations of meaning. For Mosès, the historian's "actualization" becomes the concept that unifies Benjamin's political materialism and the seemingly theological concepts of redemption (*Erlösung*), remembrance (*Eingedenken*), and the much discussed now-time (*Jetztzeit*). And Mosès's identification of actualization's importance cannot be overestimated. In the *Passagen-Werk* (in a passage that will be fundamental for Mosès's interpretation), Benjamin, in fact, counterposes the notion of actualization to that of historicism's progress. One of the *Passagen-Werk*'s aims, he remarks, was "to demonstrate a historical materialism that has annihilated in itself the idea of progress. Precisely in this respect historical materialism has cause to set itself off sharply from customary bourgeois thought. Its fundamental concept is not progress but actualization" (574). On its own terms, actualization is a problematic concept that seems to run counter to the affirmations of a materialist history that has dispensed with the eternal. Steeped in idealism, it tends to name the process by means of which something hidden becomes visible or, to render a temporal version, the process by means of which something past becomes present. And this nexus of synchrony and diachrony has a performative role in Benjamin's understanding of the workings of history. In the context of Benjamin's materialism, *actualization* refers to that instant when historical effects are produced, that moment when aspects of the past, which already belongs to the present, become contemporary. This instant has obvious epistemological implications, as indicated in **"On the Concept of History."**

Although the term *actualization* itself is rare in Benjamin's work, it describes the articulation of agency in his theory of history. As such, it expresses a moment of great instability in any historical conception based on the idea of continuity; theories of history, of course, emerged precisely in response to instabilities in order to explain them, render them understandable. Thus, historical theories tend to be totalizing, positing an origin, an ending, and a transcendental notion to power the course separating them.[12] It is difficult to appreciate the radical nature of Benjamin's historical theory, because language, and the concepts that organize thought, operates by assigning agency to linguistic constructions; in this sense, personification may be the single most important trope of modernity. But that is precisely the problem that Benjamin is grappling with in his theory of history and in the concept of actualization. Mosès, in fact, in what appears to be a startling departure from his own reading, ultimately advances a personified version of the materialist historian to whom he imputes historical choice, for all practical purposes making the historian the agent of actualization: "If this *actualization* of the past and future is necessarily political, it is because,

for Benjamin, it depends on a choice. The historian who saves this or that past moment from the conformism threatening to swallow it up, to endow it with a new meaning in light of his own present, acts because he feels *responsible* for the past."[13] In this view, the subjectivity of the historian, whose actions result from a personal decision with historical implications, stabilizes the historical discontinuities. It introduces predictability into the historical equation by making it a function of personal identity, with its attendant ethical and moral decisions.[14] Despite the inherent attraction of interpreting a form of engagement into Benjamin's theory of history, the magnetic pull toward personification in modernity keeps us from knowing if such an interpretation derives from the formulation of Benjamin's theory of history or simply from the interpreter's methodological and historical concerns.[15]

On the other hand, Benjamin's writings are filled with notes on the question of history, inevitably attempting to articulate his notions in contrast to other views of history, much in the vein of his discussion of historicism and certain understandings of historical materialism. One particularly significant note from the *Passagen-Werk,* in which Benjamin succinctly summarizes his theory of history and plots the differences between it and the then-prevailing notions of history, deserves citation in its entirety:

> What distinguishes figures (*Bilder*) from the "essences" (*"Wesenheiten"*) of phenomenology is their historical index. (Heidegger's abstract attempt to save history for phenomenology by means of "historicity" [*"Geschichtlichkeit"*] is in vain.) These figures are to be thoroughly distinguished from the "human sciences" categories, from so-called habitus, style, etc. The figures' historical index means not only that they belong to a specific time but above all that they become readable (*zur Lesbarkeit kommen*) only at a specific time. And in fact this "becoming readable" (*"zur Lesbarkeit" gelangen*) is a specific critical point of their inner movement. Each present is specified by the figures that are synchronic with it: Every Now is the Now of a specific knowability (*Erkennbarkeit*). In the Now, truth is loaded with time until it bursts. (This bursting is nothing more than the death of *intentio,* which also coincides with the birth of real historical time, the time of truth.) Thus it is not that the past sheds its light on the present or that the present sheds its light on the past, but rather in the figure what has been (*das Gewesene*) and the Now meet in a flash of lightning to make a configuration (*Konstellation*). In other words: the figure is the dialectic at a standstill. Thus while the present's relation to the past is purely temporal, the relation between what has been and the Now is dialectical: of a figural rather than temporal nature. Only dialectical figures are really historical, that is, not archaic figures. The read figure, the figure in the Now of knowability, bears to the highest degree the stamp of the critical, dangerous moment that forms the basis of all reading. (577-78)

This passage straightforwardly describes the disjuncture separating Benjamin's theory of history and the historical concepts at our disposal. Figurality describes the historical mode of his materialism. These figures are distinct from essences that exist outside of time, cannot be equated with Heidegger's historical events, resist reduction to human science (*geisteswissenschaftlichen*) categories, signal the death of intention, and cannot be expressed in a simple narrative that divides the past from the present. The characteristic of these figures is their readability, and reading itself serves as the epistemological model for the generation of historical time.[16] Reading describes an engagement with something that has material existence, to produce something that has a nonmaterial, though nonetheless historical, existence. This should not be mistaken for a hermeneutic moment, however: there is no community of interpretants, no unfolding of meaning in time, no sense of a temporal tradition. In sum, it indicates what seems to be an irresolvable contradiction: the absolute singularity of what can only be described as a historical action. In other words, readability is no less historical than the reading itself.

But how does one talk about agency in this context? The entire process that Benjamin describes, the actualization of historical time, does not lend itself to personification. A specific readability does correspond to a specific moment of the figures' "inner movement," but this movement merely opposes stasis—it is motion without direction or control. These figures, however, are distinguished by their "historical index" (*historischer Index*). The index, of course, has been a productive notion in theories of meaning, especially in modern semiotics. But at the outset, it was no more than a general rhetorical term; Quintilian, for example, sees the index as simply a variant of the sign: "The Latin equivalent of the Greek *semeion* is *signum,* a sign, though some have called it *indicium,* an indication, or *vestigium,* a trace. Such signs or indications enable us to infer that something else has happened; blood for instance may lead us to infer that a murder has taken place."[17] For Quintilian, the term belongs squarely in the juridical tradition that gave birth to rhetoric. In this context of speculation about a prior event, it merely offers an indication of what might have happened, as would any other sign. And although Quintilian's definition has no direct significance for Benjamin's use of the term, it serves as a backdrop for Peirce's theory of semiotics, which is built on a series of distinctions between the various categories of sign and signification. The index plays an important role in Peirce's semiotics by being a signifying function that produces actions without depending on "resemblance" or intellectual operations": "Anything which focuses the attention is an index. Anything which startles us is an index, in so far as it marks the junction between two portions of experience. Thus a tremendous thunderbolt indicates that *something* considerable happened, though we may not know precisely what the event was. But it may be expected to connect itself with some other experience."[18] The index ruptures continuity, breaks experience in two. And while it may point to an event, it does not specify what that event might have been and does not require interpretation, even if it poses

the problem that might give rise to one. The index, which operates, as Peirce says, "by blind compulsion," has epistemological impact without being grounded in the need for meaning. It occupies a peculiar status even in contemporary, formalized semiotics precisely because it exceeds the linguistic while remaining an essential element of linguistic understanding.[19] As is the case with epistemological operations that skirt the edge of conceptual categories, the index is most often personified to render it more stable. Thus, it is not surprising that Peirce inevitably personifies reactions to the index, although his descriptions of the index itself are more carefully nuanced. To cite one of his many examples, a "rap on the door" calls one to attention, but, according to his logic, the "rap" as index does not depend on assigning protagonists.

Moreover, Benjamin transposes the index into history. The index, as *historical* index, loses even its illusion of a controlling consciousness. In his theses "On the Concept of History," Benjamin articulates other aspects of the index:

> The past carries along a secret index (*heimlichen Index*) by which it is referred to redemption (*auf die Erlösung verwiesen wird*). For did not a breath of the air floating around us once surround those who preceded us? Are not our sounds, when we voice them, an echo of those long since silent? . . . If so, there is a secret rendezvous between past generations and ours. . . . Like every generation that came before us, we have been endowed with a *weak* messianic power, a power to which the past has a claim.[20] (693-94; 255)

Here, redemption is resolutely historical and firmly anchored in the indexical structure of history. This secret rendezvous or meeting between past and present takes place, as Benjamin never tires of repeating, in a figure that is historical but not temporal. It takes place in a configuration that stops time to become historical in Benjamin's sense. If we still breathe the same air, if we still hear the past in our utterances, then we have a historical relationship to that past. In other words, the past continues to be present, however diminished and fragmentary it might be. And redemption is simply the present's opportunity to "indicate" the past in a way that places a claim on the future. That is the weak messianic power of the present, always ensconced in the historical conflicts that not even a full-fledged Messiah can escape: "The Messiah comes not only as the redeemer; he comes as the subduer of the Antichrist" (695; 255). The Messiah, despite, or regardless of, the religious connotations, is a figure of the indexical structure of history.

For Benjamin, history is not an event, not a subject unfolding itself in time, and is not controlled or generated by agents, even omniscient ones. Rather, it is a process of figuration characterized by its historicity and readability. The figure's historical index depersonalizes historical agency while retaining the phenomenological moment; but this moment, this experience (*Erfahrung*) with a past, bears no relation to the eternal and to the temporal as produced in historical narratives (702; 262). As in Peirce's description of the index, this experience is produced with lightning quickness; it refers to "seizing hold of a memory (*Erinnerung*) as it flashes up at a moment of danger. For historical materialism the point is to grasp a figure (*Bild*) of the past whose appearance catches the historical subject unawares, at a moment of danger" (695; 255). The historical subject acts or, rather, reacts to an unpredictable relationship between the present and past. As noted in Benjamin's extensive quote on the process of figuration, that experience has to do with the historical process of reading the figure or producing it "in the Now of knowability." But, in the same passage, he also notes that one cannot separate the read figure from "the critical, dangerous moment that forms the basis of all reading." That danger is not personal, something that threatens the reader, even if such a threat is often enacted by the institutions charged with perpetuating social memory. For Benjamin, it is historical and has to do with the process of figuration itself.

As Benjamin stressed, the figure's primary distinction is its historical indexicality. Thus, depicting the nature of this danger requires a more precise understanding of the index's mode of signification. Peirce's theory of signs analytically describes the index's specific properties: "Such, for instance, is a piece of mould with a bullet-hole in it as sign of a shot; for without the shot there would have been no hole; but there is a hole there, whether anybody has the sense to attribute it to a shot or not" (170). The relationship of the index to its referent has no bearing on the existence of the index. In this characterization, a hole in the molding of a door frame exists as a mark, an index, by virtue of an event that is not so much lost as irrelevant, at least to the status of the index. When the house is remodeled or torn down, that index will exist as long as the wood it marks continues to exist, until the wood is consumed. Historicizing this indexical signaling gives an approximation of Benjamin's theory of history. But as a figure, the historical index does not escape the limitations posed by its readability. Figures have a specific historical existence: "they belong to a specific time" and they "become readable at a specific time." Furthermore, while the historical movement of this figuration operates independently, the historian has a role to play in it. In effect, Benjamin's frequent statement that the historian must bring the figures to a halt, reconstitute them into a new configuration, all of which is, of course, contingent on their historical readability, refers to one aspect of the historian's role. In other words, in reading that figure at the moment of its disruptive appearance, the historian constitutes a new figure. The danger resides precisely at that instant: the historian might fail to "save," to "indicate," to reconstitute and thereby relay the historical index. This danger, Benjamin remarks, "threatens the tradition's content as well as its receivers. The same threat hangs over both: that of becoming a tool of the ruling classes" (695; 255). Or, as Benjamin says it in his French version, it is "the danger of enlisting [tradition's content and receivers] in the service of oppression" (1262). This danger exceeds the concerns of representational history that seeks to offer counterhisto-ries to the dominant versions. Rather than interpreting indices, giving them a representation, the emphasis is on actualizing them, without ever knowing about the time of their (present or future) readability.

In Benjamin, the birth of historical time corresponds to the death of intention. Intention anchors the customary historical premise that agency, with its attendant willfulness, can be located in a subject, even if that subject is eternal rather than flesh and blood. This historical time distinguishes itself from the temporality of representational history because it is discontinuous, leads to no sure future, and cannot be grasped in a developmental narrative. Therefore, while Benjamin's concept of history advances a claim to truth, it is not the truth of epistemological verification. Benjamin's truth remains rigorously historical and is subject to the same process his concept of history attempts to render. Immediately following his elaboration of the figure's historical index, a *Passagen-Werk* entry remarks that "a decisive turn away from the concept of 'timeless truth' is called for. Nevertheless, truth is not only—as Marxism claims—a temporal function of knowing but is bound up with a time kernel that simultaneously inhabits the knower and the known. That is so true that the eternal is more ruffles on a dress than an idea" (578). Separating truth from the readability that actualizes history separates agency as well; that is why any theory of history is simultaneously a theory of knowing. And locating truth outside of history—a timeless truth—or asserting it to be a temporal manifestation of knowing—such as in Benjamin's reference to Marxism—has the same structure with regard to formulating historical agency. They each make history, or historical "truth," secondary to something that resides outside of it, a conceptual maneuver that allows the illusion that history can be grasped by personifying representations. The eternal is resolutely historical, attached to the cloth of history but not constitutive of it. The French version of the theses echoes this critique: "The immobile truth just waiting for whoever seeks it corresponds in no way to the concept of truth in the matter of history" (1261).

And the matter of history has to do with the specific relationship between the past and the present, itself the mechanism to produce a future that has no ideal existence: "The true figure of the past *flits* by. The past can be seized only as a figure that flashes up at the instant when it can be known (*im Augenblick seiner Erkennbarkeit*), never to be seen again" (695; 255). The historian, the materialist, or the historical subject, the names Benjamin gives to the indispensable reader in his conception of history, reads the figure, indicates the figure by reading it. This is all the future that Benjamin's historical understanding provides: rescuing by indicating what appears as a figural index. That is the context of Benjamin's angel, a powerful figure that has been subject to countless attempts at representation. It has its back to the future, the eternal's hiding place in any structure of temporality. Contrary to what appears to be a linear extension of events, of presents turning into pasts, the angel stares at historical time in its singularity. It reminds us not to confuse the temporal and the historical. The temporal lends itself to narrative, the historical only to figuration.

NOTES

[1] Alain Touraine, *Critique de la modernité* (Paris: Librairie Arthème Fayard, 1992), 244.

[2] In Charles S. Peirce, *Scientific Metaphysics,* vol. 6 of *Collected Papers* (Cambridge: Harvard University Press, 1935), 190-215. Subsequent page references to this essay refer to this edition. This essay also appears in the recent volume 1 of *The Essential Peirce: Selected Philosophical Writings,* ed. Nathan Houser and Christian Kloesel (Bloomington: Indiana University Press, 1992), 352-71.

[3] In Claude Allègre, *Introduction à une Histoire naturelle: Du big bang à la disparition de l'Homme* (Paris: Fayard, 1992).

[4] Pierre Lévy, *Les technologies de l'intelligence: L'avenir de la pensée à l'ère informatique* (Paris: Editions La Découverte, 1990), 17.

[5] Alain Finkielkraut, *La sagesse de l'amour* (Paris: Gallimard, 1984).

[6] Pierre Missac, in "Walter Benjamin: From Rupture to Shipwreck," in *On Walter Benjamin: Critical Essays and Recollections,* ed. Gary Smith (Cambridge: MIT Press, 1988), gives a brief overview of these divergent views of Benjamin's work on history. These differences in interpretation (and in the interpreters' agendas) are most visible with regard to efforts to understand the historical status of the "aura." In *Marxism and Form* (Princeton: Princeton University Press, 1971), for example, Fredric Jameson identifies the aura as a "Utopian component of Benjamin's thought" (77) to link it to Benjamin's presumed nostalgia. Gianni Vattimo's *La società transparente* (Milan: Garzanti Editore, 1989) interprets the aura as proof that the mass media have simply changed the way in which "art" reveals itself (64-65). In sum, the interpretation given to aura inevitably serves a theory of history; Jameson reads Benjamin through Lukács's notion of history, whereas Vattimo adopts the ontologizing history of Heidegger. Habermas, Scholem, Adorno, Wohlfarth, and others invest aura with differing meanings, but for each it is the historical question that proves troubling.

[7] These oppositions are so well ensconced that even the most unlikely critics adopt the terms of this opposition. Jacques Derrida, for example, in his reading of Benjamin's essay "Zur Kritik der Gewalt" [in his *Force de loi* (Paris: Galilée, 1994)], describes the essay as "révolutionnaire dans un style à la fois marxiste et messianique" (69); as characterized by "la greffe du langage de la révolution marxiste sur celui de la révolution messianique" (70); and as "une greffe de mystique néo-messianique juive sur un néo-marxisme post-sorelien (ou l'inverse)" (77).

[8] Walter Benjamin, "Über den Begriff der Geschichte," in vol. 1 of *Gesammelte Schriften* (Frankfurt am Main: Suhrkamp Verlag, 1974, 1980), 702; translated as "Theses on the Philosophy of History," in *Illuminations,* ed. Hannah Arendt, trans. Harry Zohn (New York: Schocken Books, 1969), 262. The textual questions about Benjamin's work are endless and frequently permit no definitive answer. In the case of "On the Concept of History," there is a final German text and an almost complete French version that Benjamin himself wrote. Both of these versions are published in volume 1 of Benjamin's *Gesammelte Schriften,* the German text on pages 691-704, and the French text, entitled "Sur le concept d'histoire," on pages 1260-66. In the discussion that follows, I will generally refer to the official English translation (of the German version), often modifying the translation; subsequent page references to this version, which indicate first the German original and then the English translation, will be included in the text. The occasional references to the French version, which offers some productive differences and clarifications of the German text that preceded it, also appear in the text; in these instances, the translations are mine.

[9] For a discussion of Gramsci's theory of historical agency, see my "Culture in Its Socio-historical Dimension," *boundary* 2 21, no. 2 (1994): 139-78.

[10] Walter Benjamin, *Das Passagen-Werk,* vol. 5 of *Gesammelte Schriften* (Frankfurt am Main: Suhrkamp, 1982), 584; my translation. Subsequent references to this work will appear in the text. Benjamin had long considered this conflictual notion of tradition and history; in his *Moskauer Tagebuch,* he wrote that "die Geschichte der «Gebildeten» müsse materialistisch als Funktion und im strengen Zusammenhange mit einer «Geschichte der Unbildung» dargestellt werden" (in vol. 6 of *Gesammelte Schriften* [Frankfurt am Main: Suhrkamp, 1986], 310 [see also the continuation on 311]). This particular set of concerns, with the "cultured" versus the "uncultured" layers of society, antedates Benjamin's attempts to dismember historical agency.

[11] Stéphane Mosès, *L'ange de l'histoire: Rosenzweig, Benjamin, Scholem* (Paris: le Seuil, 1992).

[12] Elsewhere in the *Passagen-Werk,* Benjamin will use this notion of totality to describe how the idea of progress extinguished the possibility of historical critique. See 598-99.

[13] Mosès, *L'ange de l'histoire,* 153; author's emphasis.

[14] Mosès, *L'ange de l'histoire,* 153-54.

[15] In fact, this assertion of the ethical permits Mosès to link Benjamin's theory of history to Jewish messianism (155-56) and thereby confirm Scholem's interpretation (180). The tradition of Benjaminian interpretation requires that one adopt a perspective with regard to his lines of intellectual heritage, often at the expense of Benjamin's inconclusive texts.

[16] *Bild,* which I render here with "figure," is most often translated as "image"; here, however, the emphasis on reading suggests that "figure" is more appropriate. Moreover, "image" bears a great deal of interpretive baggage that would make it an obstacle for understanding the specificity of Benjamin's theory of history.

[17] Quintilian, *Institutio Oratoria,* trans. H. E. Butler (Cambridge: Harvard University Press, 1921), V, ix, 9.

[18] In Charles S. Peirce, *Elements of Logic,* vol. 2 of *Collected Papers* (Cambridge: Harvard University Press, 1932), 161. Subsequent references to this work will be cited parenthetically in the text.

[19] See Umberto Eco, *A Theory of Semiotics* (Bloomington: Indiana University Press, 1976), 115-21.

[20] Much of this passage was omitted in the English translation.

Susan Haack (essay date 1997)

SOURCE: "'We Pragmatists . . .': Peirce and Roy in Conversation," in *Partisan Review,* Vol. 64, No. 1, Winter 1997, pp. 91-107.

[*In the following excerpt, Haack moderates a mock dialogue on the nature of knowledge and truth between philosophers Peirce and Richard Rorty, using original writings of the two men.*]

SUSAN HAACK: Let me begin by asking Professor Rorty to explain how he feels about philosophers like you, Mr. Peirce, who take themselves to be seeking the truth.

RICHARD RORTY: It is . . . more difficult than it used to be to locate a real live metaphysical prig. [But] you can still find [philosophers] who will solemnly tell you that they are seeking *the truth,* not just a story or a consensus but an honest-to-God, down-home, accurate representation of the way the world is . . . lovably old-fashioned prigs (EHO, p. 86).

SUSAN HAACK: Mr. Peirce?

CHARLES SANDERS PEIRCE: In order to reason well . . . , it is absolutely necessary to possess . . . such virtues as intellectual honesty and sincerity and a real love of truth (2.82). The cause [of the success of scientific inquirers] has been that the motive which has carried them to the laboratory and the field has been a craving to know how things really were . . . (1.34). [Genuine inquiry consists] in diligent inquiry into truth for truth's sake (1.44), . . . in actually drawing the bow upon truth with intentness in the eye, with energy in the arm (1.235).

[When] it is no longer the reasoning which determines what the conclusion shall be, but . . . the conclusion which determines what the reasoning shall be . . . this is sham reasoning. . . . The effect of this shamming is that men come to look upon reasoning as mainly decorative . . . The result of this state of things is, of course, a rapid deterioration of intellectual vigor . . . (1.57-8).

RR: "Justification" [is] a social phenomenon rather than a transaction between "the knowing subject" and "reality" (PMN, p.9), . . . not a matter of a . . . relation between ideas (or words) and objects, but of conversation, of social practice. . . . We understand knowledge when we understand the social justification of belief, and thus have no need to view it as accuracy of representation (p. 170).

CSP: The result [as I said] is, of course, a rapid deterioration of intellectual vigor. This is just what is taking place among us before our eyes. . . . Man loses his conceptions of truth and of reason (1.58, cont. and 1.59).

RR: I do not have much use for notions like . . . "objective truth" (TWO, p. 141). [The] pragmatist view [is] of rationality as civility, . . . [as] respect for the opinions of those around one, . . . of "true" as a word which applies to those beliefs upon which we are able to agree . . . (SS, pp. 44, 40, 45).

CSP: [As I was saying,] man loses his conceptions of truth and of reason. If he sees one man assert what another denies, he will, if he is concerned, choose his side and set to work by all means in his power to silence his adversaries. The truth for him is that for which he fights (1.59, cont.).

RR: Truth [is] entirely a matter of solidarity (ORT, p.32). There is nothing to be said about either truth or rationality apart from descriptions of the familiar procedures of justification which a given society—*ours*—uses . . . (SS, p.42).

CSP: You certainly opine that there is such a thing as Truth. Otherwise, reasoning and thought would be without a purpose. What do you mean by there being such a thing as Truth? You mean that something is SO . . . whether you, or I, or anybody thinks it is so or not. . . . The essence of the opinion is that there is *something* that is SO, no matter if there be an overwhelming vote against it (2.135). Every man is fully satisfied that there is such a thing as truth, or he would not ask any question. *That* truth consists in a conformity to something *independent of his thinking it to be so,* or of any man's opinion on that subject (5.211).

Truth [is] overwhelmingly forced upon the mind in experience as the effect of an independent reality (5.564). The essence of truth lies in its resistance to being ignored (2.139).

RR: Some philosophers . . . insist that natural science discovers truth rather than makes it. . . . Other philosophers [like myself] . . . have concluded that science is no more than the handmaiden of technology (CIS, pp.3-4).

CSP: There are certain mummified pedants who have never waked to the truth that the act of knowing a real object alters it. They are curious specimens of humanity, and . . . I am one of them . . . (5.555).

RR: My rejection of traditional notions of rationality can be summed up by saying that the only sense in which science is exemplary is that it is a model of human solidarity (SS, p.46).

CSP: Other methods of settling opinion have [certain advantages] over scientific investigation. A man should consider well of them; and then he should consider that, after all, he wishes his opinions to coincide with the fact . . . (5.387).

RR: . . . I think that the very idea of a "fact of the matter" is one we would be better off without (PDP, p.271).

CSP: . . . he should consider that, after all, he wishes his opinions to coincide with the fact, and . . . there is no reason why the results of those . . . [other] methods should do so (5.387, cont.).

RR: "True sentences work because they correspond to the way things are" . . . [is an] empty metaphysical compliment, . . . [a] rhetorical pat on the back. . . . [The pragmatist] drops the notion of truth as correspondence with reality altogether . . . (CP, p.xvii).

CSP: Truth is the conformity of a representamen to its object, *its* object, ITS object, mind you (5.554).

[However], that truth is the correspondence of a representation to its object is, as Kant says, merely the nominal definition of it. Truth belongs exclusively to propositions. A proposition has a subject (or set of subjects) and a predicate. The subject is a sign; the predicate is a sign; and the proposition is a sign that the predicate is a sign of that of which the subject is a sign. If it be so, it is true. But what does this correspondence . . . of the sign to its object consist in? The pragmaticist answers this question as follows. . . . If we can find out the right method of thinking and can follow it out . . . then truth can be nothing more nor less than the last result to which the following out of this method would ultimately carry us (5.553).

RR: There are . . . two senses apiece of 'true' and 'real' and 'correct representation of reality,' . . . the homely use of 'true' to mean roughly 'what you can defend against all comers,' . . . [the] homely and shopworn sense [and] the specifically 'philosophical' sense . . . which, like the Ideas of Pure Reason, [is] designed precisely to stand for the Unconditioned . . . (PMN, pp.308-9.)

CSP: That to which the representation should conform, is itself . . . utterly unlike a thing-in-itself (5.553).

RR: [A] pragmatist theory . . . says that Truth is not the sort of thing one should expect to have a philosophically interesting theory about . . . (CP, p.xiii), Pragmatists think that the history of attempts to . . . define the word "true" . . . supports their suspicion that there is no interesting work to be done in this area (p.xiv).

CSP: Truth is that concordance of an abstract statement with the ideal limit towards which endless investigation would tend to bring scientific belief. . . . The truth of the proposition that Caesar crossed the Rubicon consists in the fact that the further we push our archaeological and other studies, the more strongly will that conclusion force itself on our minds forever—or would do so, if study were to go on forever. . . . The same definitions equally hold in the normative sciences (5.565-6).

RR: I do not think . . . that [your account] is defensible . . . [It] uses a term—'ideal'—which is just as fishy as 'corresponds' (PDT, pp.337, 338).

CSP: [A] false proposition is a proposition of which some interpretant represents that, on an occasion which it indicates, a percept will have a certain character, while the immediate perceptual judgment on that occasion is that the percept has not that character. A true proposition is a proposition belief in which would never lead to such disappointment so long as the proposition is not understood otherwise than it was intended (5.569).

Prof. Royce [like you] seems to think that this doctrine is unsatisfactory because it talks about what would be. . . . It may be he is right in this criticism; yet to our apprehension this "would be" is readily resolved . . . (8.113). [The] most important reals have the mode of being of what the nominalist calls "mere" words, that is, general types and would-bes. [His] "mere" reveals a complete misunderstanding . . . (8.191). The *will be's,* the *actually is's,* and the *have beens* are not the sum of the reals. . . . There are besides *would be's* and *can be's* that are real (8.216).

SH: I suspect, Professor Rorty, that your sympathies lie with the nominalist . . .

RR: Nominalists like myself—those for whom language is a tool rather than a medium, and for whom a concept is just the regular use of a mark or noise— . . . see language as just human beings using marks and noises to get what they want. (EHO, pp. 126-7).

The right idea, according to us nominalists, is that "recognition of meaning" is simply ability to substitute sensible signs . . . for other signs, . . . and so on indefinitely. This . . . doctrine is found . . . in [your writings] . . . (TMoL, p.211).

CSP: The nominalistic *Weltanschauung* has become incorporated into what I will venture to call the very flesh and blood of the average modern mind. (5.61). Modern nominalists are mostly superficial men . . . (5.312).

[A] realist is simply one who knows no more recondite reality than that which is represented in a true representation (5.312, cont.). I am myself a scholastic realist of a somewhat extreme stripe (5.470). Nomenclature involves classification; and classification is true or false, and the generals to which it refers are either reals in the one case, or figments in the other (5.453).

Pragmaticism could hardly have entered a head that was not already convinced that there are real generals (5.503).

SH: I wonder how Professor Rorty feels about your references to "true representations" . . .

RR: Pragmatism [is] anti-representationalism (PPD, p. 1).

CSP: REPRESENT: to stand for, that is, to be in such a relation to another that for certain purposes it is treated by some mind as if it were that other. . . . When it is desired to distinguish between that which represents and the . . . relation of representing, the former may be termed the "representamen," the latter the "representation" (2.273).

A sign, or *representamen,* is something which stands to somebody for something in some respect or capacity. It . . . creates in the mind of that person an equivalent sign, or perhaps a more developed sign. That sign which it creates I call the *interpretant* of the first sign. The sign stands for something, its *object* . . . in reference to a sort of idea, which I have sometimes called the *ground* of the representamen (2.228).

RR: The notion of "accurate representation" is simply an . . . empty compliment which we pay to those beliefs which are successful in helping us do what we want to do (PMN, p.10).

CSP: It is as though a man should address a land surveyor as follows: "You do not make a true representation of the land; you only measure lengths from point to point . . . you have to do solely with lines. But the land is a surface . . . You, therefore, fail entirely to represent the land." The surveyor, I think, would reply, "Sir, you have proved that . . . my map *is not* the land. I never pretended that it was. But that does not prevent it from truly representing the land, as far as it goes" (5.329).

SH: I am beginning to think that you may disagree with each other not only about nominalism, but about the nature and status of metaphysics . . .

RR: The pragmatist . . . does not think of himself as *any* kind of a metaphysician . . . (CP, p.xxviii).

CSP: [The Pragmatic Maxim] will serve to show that almost every proposition of ontological metaphysics is either meaningless gibberish—one word being defined by other words, and they by still others, without any real conception ever being reached—or else is downright absurd; so that all such rubbish being swept away, what will remain of philosophy will be a series of problems capable of investigation by the observational methods of the true sciences. . . . So, instead of merely jeering at metaphysics . . . the pragmaticist extracts from it a precious essence . . . (5.423).

We should expect to find metaphysics . . . to be somewhat more difficult than logic, but still on the whole one of the simplest of sciences, as it is one whose main principles must be settled before very much progress can be gained either in psychics or in physics. Historically we are astonished to find that it has been a mere arena of ceaseless and trivial disputation. But we also find that it has been pursued in a spirit the very contrary of that of wishing to learn the truth, which is the most essential requirement. . . . *Metaphysics* is the proper designation for the third, and completing department of coenoscopy. . . . Its business is to study the most general features of reality and real objects. But in its present condition it is . . . a puny, rickety and scrofulous science. It is only too plain that those who pretend to cultivate it carry not the hearts of true men of science within their breast (6.4-6).

Here let us set down almost at random a small specimen of the questions of metaphysics which press . . . for industrious and solid investigation: Whether or no there be any real indefiniteness, or real possibility and impossibility? Whether there be any strictly individual existence? Whether there is any distinction . . . between fact and fancy? Or between the external and the internal worlds? What general . . . account can be given of the different qualities of feeling . . . ? Do all possible qualities of sensation . . . form one continuous system . . . ? . . . Is Time a real thing . . . ? How about Space . . . ? . . . Is hylozoism an opinion, actual or conceivable, rather than a senseless vocable . . . ? . . . What is consciousness or mind like . . . ? (6.6).

RR: Metaphysicians see [books] as divided according to disciplines, corresponding to different objects of knowledge. [We] ironists see them as divided according to traditions . . . (CIS, pp.75-6).

CSP: All science is either, A. Science of Discovery; B. Science of Review; or C. Practical Science. . . . Science of Discovery is either, I. Mathematics; II. Philosophy; or III. Idioscopy. . . . Philosophy is divided into *a.* Phenomenology; *b.* Normative Science; *c.* Metaphysics. . . . Phenomenology is . . . a single study. Normative Science has three widely separated divisions: i. Esthetics; ii. Ethics. iii. Logic. . . . Metaphysics may be divided into, i, General Metaphysics, or Ontology; ii, Psychical, or Religious, Metaphysics, concerned chiefly with the questions of 1, God, 2, Freedom, 3, Immortality; and iii, Physical Metaphysics, which discusses the real nature of time, space, laws of nature, matter, etc. (1.181-192).

SH: Could you please explain your reference to "ironists," Professor Rorty?

RR: [Ironists] take naturally to the line of thought developed in . . . [my] book. . . . The opposite of irony is common sense. (CIS, p.74).

CSP: Pragmaticism will be sure to carry critical common-sensism in its arms . . . (5.499).

RR: Sentences like . . . "Truth is independent of the human mind" are simply platitudes used to inculcate . . . the common sense of the West (CIS, p.76-7).

CSP: The Critical Common-sensist holds that all the veritably indubitable beliefs are *vague* . . . (5.505); [that they] refer to a somewhat primitive mode of life . . . (5.511); [he] has a high esteem for doubt (5.514); [he] criticizes the critical method (5.523).

RR: [We ironists emphasize] the spirit of playfulness . . . (CIS, p.39). [We are] never quite able to take [our]-selves seriously . . . (p.73).

CSP: [The Critical Common-sensist] is none of those overcultivated Oxford dons—I hope their day is over—whom any discovery that brought quietus to a vexed question would evidently vex because it would end the fun of arguing around it and about it and over it (5.520).

RR: . . . I have spent forty years looking for a coherent . . . way of formulating my worries about what, if anything, philosophy is good for (TWO, p.146).

CSP: It is true that philosophy is in a lamentably crude condition at present; . . . most philosophers set up a pretension of knowing all there is to know—a pretension calculated to disgust anybody who is at home in any real science. But all we have to do is to turn our backs upon all such truly vicious conduct, and we shall find ourselves enjoying the advantages of having an almost virgin soil to till, where a given amount of really scientific work will bring in an extraordinary harvest . . . of very fundamental truth of exceptional value from every point of view (1.128).

SH: How do you feel about Mr. Peirce's description of philosophy as "scientific work," Professor Rorty?

RR: [One] side of pragmatism has been scientific. . . . Let me call the claim that there is [a] "reliable [scientific] method" "scientism" . . . If one takes the core of pragmatism to be its attempt to replace the notion of true beliefs as representations . . . and instead to think of them as successful rules for action, then it becomes . . .

hard to isolate a "method" that will embody this attitude (PWM, pp.260-262).

CSP: It is far better to let philosophy follow perfectly untrammeled a scientific method. . . . If that course be honestly and scrupulously carried out, the results reached, even if they be not altogether true, even if they be grossly mistaken, can not but be highly serviceable for the ultimate discovery of truth (1.644). Rational methods of inquiry . . . will make that result as speedy as possible . . . (7.78).

The first problems to suggest themselves to the inquirer into nature are far too complex . . . for any early solution. . . . What ought to be done, therefore, . . . is at first to substitute for those problems others much . . . more abstract. . . . The reasonably certain solutions of these last problems will throw a light . . . upon more concrete problems. . . . This method of procedure is that Analytic Method to which modern physics owes all its triumphs. It has been applied with great success in psychical sciences also. . . . It is reprobated by the whole Hegelian army, who think it ought to be replaced by the "Historic Method," which studies complex problems in all their complexity, but which cannot boast any distinguished successes.

There are in science three fundamentally different kinds of reasoning, Deduction, . . . Induction, . . . and Retroduction . . . Analogy combines the characters of Induction and Retroduction (1.63-6).

SH: Do you share Mr. Peirce's high regard for logic, Professor Rorty?

RR: Rigorous argumentation . . . is no more *generally* desirable than blocking the road of inquiry is generally desirable (CP, p.xli).

CSP: There are two qualifications which every true man of science possesses. . . . First, the dominant passion of his whole soul must be to find out the truth in some department. . . . Secondly, he must have a natural gift for reasoning, for severely critical thought (7.605). Logic is the theory of *right* reasoning, of what reasoning ought to be . . . (2.7).

RR: We no longer think of ourselves as having reliable "sources" of knowledge called "reason" or "sensation" . . . (OE, p.531).

CSP: The data from which inference sets out and upon which all reasoning depends are the *perceptual facts,* which are the intellect's fallible record of the *percepts,* or "evidence of the senses" (2.143).

RR: Eventually I got over [my] worry about circular argumentation by deciding that the test of philosophical truth was overall coherence, rather than deducibility from unquestioned first principles. But this didn't help much (TWO, p.145).

Philosophy ought . . . to trust . . . to the multitude and variety of its arguments. . . . Its reasoning should not form a chain which is no stronger than the weakest link, but a cable whose fibers may be ever so slender, provided they are sufficiently numerous and intimately connected (5.265).

RR: But [as I said] this didn't help much. For coherence is a matter of avoiding contradictions, and St. Thomas' advice, "When you meet a contradiction, make a distinction," makes that pretty easy (TWO, p.145).

SH: How do you feel about Professor Rorty's observation that making distinctions is "pretty easy," Mr. Peirce?

CSP: . . . Kant's conception of the nature of necessary reasoning is clearly shown by the logic of relations to be utterly mistaken, and his distinction between analytic and synthetic judgments, . . . which is based on that conception, is so utterly confused that it is difficult or impossible to do anything with it (5.176).

SH: Perhaps, while we are on the subject of logic, you could explain your attitude to the principle of bivalence . . .

RR: The pragmatist . . . should not succumb to the temptation to . . . take sides on the issue of "bivalence" (CP, p.xxvi).

CSP: Triadic logic is universally true (**Logic Notebook** for 1909).

SH: Perhaps, Professor Rorty, it would be helpful if you would explain how you see the relation of philosophy to science . . .

RR: The pragmatist is betting that what succeeds the "scientific," positivist culture which the Enlightenment produced will be *better* (CP, p.xxxviii). Science as the source of "truth" . . . is one of the Cartesian notions which vanish when the ideal of "philosophy as strict science" vanishes (p.34). Pragmatism . . . views science as one genre of literature—or, put the other way around, literature and the arts as inquiries, on the same footing as scientific inquiries (p.xliii). Philosophy is best seen as a kind of writing. It is delimited, as is any literary genre, not by form or matter, but by tradition. . . . Philosophy as more than a kind of writing—is an illusion. . . . [One] tradition takes scientific truth as the center of philosophical concern (and scorns the notion of incommensurable scientific world-pictures). It asks how well other fields of inquiry conform to the model of science. The second [pragmatist] tradition takes science as one (not especially privileged nor interesting) sector of culture, a sector which . . . only makes sense when viewed historically (pp.92-3). Literature has now displaced religion, science, and philosophy as the presiding discipline of our culture . . . (p.155).

SH: Mr. Peirce?

CSP: [I] desire to rescue the good ship Philosophy for the service of Science from the hands of lawless rovers of the sea of literature . . . (5.449).

RR: A few [lovably old-fashioned prigs] will even claim to write in a clear, precise, transparent way, priding themselves on manly straightforwardness, on abjuring "literary" devices (EHO, p.86).

CSP: As for that phrase "studying in a literary spirit" it is impossible to express how nauseating it is to any scientific man . . . (1.33).

RR: As soon as a program to put philosophy on the secure path of science succeeds, it simply converts philosophy into a boring academic specialty (PMN, pp. 384-5).

CSP: In order to be deep it is requisite to be dull . . . The new pragmatists . . . are *lively* . . . (5.17). The apostle of Humanism [F. C. S. Schiller, like you] says that professional philosophists "have rendered philosophy like unto themselves, abstruse, arid, abstract, and abhorrent." But I conceive that some branches of science are not in a healthy state if they are *not* abstruse, arid, and abstract, in which case, . . . it will be as Shakespeare said . . .

> Not harsh and crabbèd, as dull fools suppose,
> But musical as is Apollo's lute . . .
>
> (5.537).

The reader may find the matter [of my **"Minute Logic"**] so dry, husky and innutritious to the spirit that he cannot imagine that there is any human good in it. . . . But the fault is his. It shall not be more tedious than the multiplication table, . . . and as the multiplication table is worth the pains of learning, . . . so shall this be . . . (2.15).

SH: Professor Rorty, your view of philosophy as a genre of literature puzzles me; surely pragmatism is a form of empiricism?

RR: Pragmatism has gradually broken the historical links that once connected it to empiricism . . . (PPD, p.4).

CSP: The kind of philosophy which interests me and must, I think, interest everybody is that philosophy, which uses the most rational methods it can devise, for finding out the little that can as yet be found out about the universe of mind and matter from those observations which every person can make in every hour of his waking life . . . laboratory-philosophy . . . (1.126, 129).

RR: From the radically anti-representationalist viewpoint I . . . commend . . . pragmatism can be seen as gradually . . . escaping from scientism (PPD, p.4).

CSP: [Philosophical theories] have the same sort of basis as scientific results have. That is to say, they rest on experience—on the total everyday experience of many generations. . . . Such experience is worthless for distinctively scientific purposes . . . although all science . .

CSP: [Philosophical theories] have the same sort of basis as scientific results have. That is to say, they rest on experience—on the total everyday experience of many generations. . . . Such experience is worthless for distinctively scientific purposes . . . although all science . . . would have to shut up shop if she should manage to escape accepting them. No "wisdom" could ever have discovered argon; yet within its proper sphere, . . . the instinctive result of human experience ought to have so vastly more weight than any scientific result, that to make laboratory experiments to ascertain, for example, whether there be any uniformity in nature or no, would vie with adding a teaspoonful of saccharine to the ocean in order to sweeten it (5.522).

RR: The basic motive of pragmatism was . . . a continuation of the Romantic reaction to the Enlightenment's sanctification of natural science (EHO, p.18).

CSP: [Science] embodies the epitome of man's intellectual development (7.49). Iconoclastic inventions are always cheap and often nasty (4.71).

SH: May we go back for a minute to Professor Rorty's reference to Romanticism?

RR: The Platonist and the positivist share a reductionist view of metaphor: They think metaphors are either paraphrasable or useless for the one serious purpose which language has, namely, representing reality. By contrast, the Romantic has an expansionist view . . . Romantics attribute metaphor to a mysterious faculty called the "imagination," a faculty they suppose to be at the very center of the self . . . (CIS, p.19).

CSP: When a man desires ardently to know the truth, his first effort will be to imagine what that truth can be . . . there is, after all, nothing but imagination that can every supply him an inkling of the truth. . . . For thousands of men a falling apple was nothing but a falling apple; and to compare it to the moon would by them be deemed "fanciful." It is not too much to say that next after the passion to learn there is no quality so indispensable to the successful prosecution of science as imagination. . . . There are, no doubt, kinds of imagination of no value in science, mere artistic imagination, mere dreaming of opportunities for gain. The scientific imagination dreams of explanation and laws (1.46-8).

Cuvier said that Metaphysics is nothing but Metaphor. . . . If metaphor be taken literally to mean an expression of a similitude when the sign of predication is employed instead of the sign of likeness—as when we say this man *is* a fox instead of this man is like a fox,—I deny entirely that metaphysicians are given to metaphor . . . but if Cuvier was only using a metaphor himself, and meant by metaphor broad comparison on the ground of characters of a formal and highly abstract kind,—then, indeed, metaphysics professes to be metaphor . . . (7.590).

RR: [A] philosopher . . . like myself . . . thinks of himself as auxiliary to the poet rather than to the physicist. . . . Interesting philosophy is . . . a contest between an entrenched vocabulary which has become a nuisance and a half-formed new vocabulary which vaguely promises great things. (CIS, pp.7-9).

SH: But I don't think Mr. Peirce would deny the importance of linguistic innovation . . .

CSP: Every symbol is a living thing, . . . its meaning inevitably grows, incorporates new elements and throws off old ones. . . . Science is continually gaining new conceptions; and every new *scientific* conception should receive a new word. . . . Different systems of expression are often of the greatest advantage (2.222).

RR: It is a feature of . . . science that the vocabulary in which problems are posed is accepted by all those who count as contributing to the subject. The vocabulary may be changed, but that is only because a new theory has been discovered. . . . The vocabulary in which the *explicanda* are described has to remain constant (CP, pp.141-2).

CSP: How much more the word *electricity* means now than it did in the days of Franklin; how much more the term planet means now than it did in the time of Hipparchus. These words have acquired information . . . (7.587).

Symbols grow. . . . In use and in experience, [the] meaning [of a symbol] grows. Such words as *force, law, wealth, marriage,* bear for us very different meanings from those they bore to our barbarous ancestors (2.302).

SH: I gather, Professor Rorty, from your references to "irony" and "playfulness," that you disapprove of too solemn an attitude to philosophy as a profession . . .

RR: I would welcome a culture dominated by "the Rich Aesthete, the Manager and the Therapist" so long as *everybody* who wants to gets to be an aesthete. . . . The ironic, playful intellectual is a desirable character-type. . . (FMR, pp.16, 15).

SH: Mr. Peirce?

CSP: We remark three classes of men. The first consists of those for whom the chief thing is the qualities of feelings. These men create art. The second consists of the practical men . . . The third class consists of men to whom nothing seems great but reason. . . . Those are the natural scientific men . . . (1.43).

It is infinitely better that men devoid of genuine scientific curiosity should not barricade the road of science with empty books and embarrassing assumptions . . . (1.645).

RR: Intellectual gifts—intelligence, judgment, curiosity, imagination, . . . kinks in the brain . . . provide these gifts . . . (CIS, pp.187-8).

CSP: There is a kink in my damned brain that prevents me from thinking as other people think . . .

RR: As we look about at the manly, aggressive and businesslike academics of our . . . time, . . . the well-funded professor[s], jetting home after a day spent advising men of power . . . [we see that the] American academic mind has long since discovered the joy of making its own special enterprise "greater and better organized and a mightier engine in the general life" (CP, p.61).

CSP: Wherever there is a large class of academic professors who are provided with good incomes and looked up to as gentlemen, scientific inquiry must languish. Wherever the bureaucrats are the more learned class, the case will be still worse (1.51).

SH: And how do you see the relation of philosophy to society?

RR: Pragmatism must be defined as the claim that the function of inquiry is, in Bacon's words, to "relieve and benefit the condition of man" . . . (EHO, p.27).

CSP: [A] modern reader who is not in awe of [Bacon's] grandiloquence is chiefly struck by the inadequacy of his view of scientific procedure. . . . "He wrote on science like a Lord Chancellor," indeed, as Harvey, a genuine man of science said (5.361).

RR: Philosophy [is] *in the service* of democratic politics . . . (CIS, p.196). We pragmatists commend our anti-essentialism and antilogocentrism on the ground of its harmony with the practices and aims of a democratic society . . . (EHO, p.135).

CSP: I must confess that I belong to that class of scallawags who purpose, with God's help, to look the truth in the face, whether doing so be conducive to the interests of society or not. Moreover, if I should ever attack that excessively difficult problem, 'What is for the true interest of society?' I should feel that I stood in need of a great deal of help from the science of legitimate inference . . . (8.143). Against the doctrine that social stability is the sole justification of scientific research . . . I have to object, first, that it is historically false . . . second, that it is bad ethics; and, third, that its propagation would retard the progress of science (8.135).

RR: [There have been in our century] three conceptions of the aim of philosophizing. They are the Husserlian (or 'scientistic') answer, the Heideggerian (or 'poetic') answer, and the pragmatist (or 'political') answer (EHO, p.9).

CSP: In my opinion, the present infantile condition of philosophy . . . is due to the fact that . . . it has chiefly been pursued by men who have not . . . been animated by the true scientific *Eros;* but who have . . . been inflamed with a desire to amend the lives of themselves and others . . . (1.620). The two masters, *theory* and *practice,* you cannot serve (1.642).

SH: It seems to me that the two of you have radically different conceptions of what pragmatism is . . .

RR: "Pragmatism" is a vague, ambiguous and overworked word (CP, p.160).

CSP: Many writers, . . . in spite of pragmatists' declarations, unanimous, reiterated, and most explicit, still remain unable to "catch on" to what we are driving at, and persist in twisting our purpose and purport all awry. . . . [Pragmatism] is merely a method of ascertaining the meanings of hard words and of abstract concepts (5.464).

RR: The pragmatist . . . must struggle with the positivist for the position of radical anti-Platonist. . . . At first glance he looks like just another variety of positivist. (CP, p.xvii).

CSP: Pragmaticism is a species of prope-positivism (5.423).

RR: My first characterization of pragmatism is that it is simply anti-essentialism applied to notions like "truth," "knowledge," "language," "morality," and similar objects of philosophical theorizing. . . . There is no wholesale, epistemological way to direct, or criticize, or underwrite, the course of inquiry (CP, p.162). [A] second characterization of pragmatism might go like this: there is no epistemological difference between truth about what ought to be and truth about what is, nor any metaphysical difference between facts and values, nor any methodological difference between morality and science (p.163). . . . The pragmatists tell us, it is the vocabulary of practice rather than of theory . . . in which one can say something useful about truth (p.162). [A] third . . . characterization of pragmatism [is]: it is the doctrine that there are no constraints on inquiry save conversational ones. . . . The only sense in which we are constrained to truth is that, as [you] suggested, we can make no sense of the notion that the view which can survive all objections might be false. But objections—conversational constraints—cannot be anticipated (p.165).

CSP: To satisfy our doubts, . . . it is necessary that a method should be found by which our beliefs may be determined by nothing human, but by some external permanency—by something upon which our thinking has no effect. . . . It must be something which affects, or might affect, every man. . . . The method must be such that the ultimate conclusion of every man shall be the same. Such is the method of science (5.384).

RR: Once human desires are admitted into the criterion of "truth," . . . we have become pragmatists. The pragmatist's claim is that to know your desires is to know the criterion of truth . . . (EHO, pp.30-31).

CSP: It is necessary to note what is essentially involved in the Will to Learn. . . . I can excuse a person who has lost a dear companion and whose reason is in danger of giving way under the grief, for trying, on that account, to believe in a future life. . . . [But] I myself would not adopt a hypothesis . . . simply because the idea was pleasing to me. . . . That would be a crime against the integrity of . . . reason . . . (5.583, 598).

RR: What I am calling "pragmatism" might also be called "left-wing Kuhnianism" (SS, p.41).

CSP: An opinion which has of late years attained some vogue among men of science, [is] that we cannot expect any physical hypothesis to maintain its ground indefinitely even with modifications, but must expect that from time to time there will be a complete cataclysm that shall utterly sweep away old theories and replace them by new ones. As far as I know, this notion has no other basis than the history of science. Considering how very, very little science we have attained, and how infantile the history of science still is, it amazes me that anybody should propose to base a theory of knowledge upon the history of science alone. An emmet is far more competent to discourse upon the figure of the earth than we are to say what future millennia and millionennia may have in store for physical theories . . . The only really scientific theory that can be called old is the Ptolemaic system; and that has only been improved in details, not revolutionized (2.150).

RR: [Your] contribution to pragmatism was merely to have given it a name . . . (CP, p.161).

CSP: It has probably never happened that any philosopher has attempted to give a general name to his own doctrine without that name's soon acquiring in common philosophical usage, a signification much broader than was originally intended. . . . [My] word "pragmatism" . . . begins to be met with occasionally in the literary journals, where it gets abused in the merciless way that words have to expect when they fall into literary clutches. . . . So, then, the writer, finding his bantling "pragmatism" so promoted, feels that it is time to kiss his child goodbye and relinquish it to its higher destiny; while to serve the precise purpose of expressing the original definition, he begs to announce the birth of the word "pragmaticism," which is ugly enough to be safe from kidnappers (5.143-4).

It is good economy for philosophy to provide itself with a vocabulary so outlandish that loose thinkers shall not be tempted to borrow its words. . . . Whoever deliberately uses a word . . . in any other sense than that which was conferred upon it by its sole rightful creator commits a shameful offense against the inventor of the symbol and against science, and it becomes the duty of the others to treat the act with contempt and indignation (2.223-4).

RR: Revolutionary movements within an intellectual discipline require a revisionist history of that discipline (CP, p.211).

CSP: It seems to me a pity [that the pragmatists of today] should allow a philosophy so instinct with life to become infected with seeds of death in such notions as that of . . . the mutability of truth . . . (6.485).

. . . . .

Except where otherwise indicated, Peirce's contributions are taken from:

Collected Papers, eds Hartshorne, C., Weiss, P. and Burks, A., Harvard University Press, Cambridge, MA, 1931-58; references by volume and paragraph number.

Peirce's comment about the kink in his brain is reported by E. T. Bell in *The Development of Mathematics,* McGraw-Hill, New York and London, 1949, p.519.

The quotation Peirce attributes to Shakespeare is actually from Milton's *Comus.*

. . . . .

Rorty's contributions to the conversation are taken from:

CIS: *Contingency, Irony and Solidarity,* Cambridge University Press, Cambridge, 1989.

CP: *Consequences of Pragmatism,* Harvester, Hassocks, Sussex, 1982.

EHO: *Essays on Heidegger and Others,* Cambridge University Press, Cambridge, 1991.

FMR: "Freud and Moral Reflection," in Smith, J.H. and Kerrigan, W., eds, *Pragmatism's Freud,* Johns Hopkins University Press, Baltimore and London, 1986, 1-27.

OE: "On Ethnocentrism: A Reply to Clifford Geertz," *Michigan Quarterly Review,* 25, 1986, 525-34.

ORT: *Objectivity, Relativism and Truth,* Cambridge University Press, Cambridge, 1991.

PDP: "The Priority of Democracy to Philosophy," in Peterson, Merrill D. and Vaughn, Robert C., eds, *The Virginia Statute for Religious Freedom,* Cambridge University Press, Cambridge, 1988, 257-82.

PDT: "Pragmatism, Davidson and Truth," in Lepore, E., ed., *Truth and Interpretation: Perspectives on the Philosophy of Donald Davidson,* Blackwell, Oxford, 1986, 333-54.

PPD: "Introduction" to Murphy, J.P., *Pragmatism from Peirce to Davidson,* Westview Press, Boulder, CO, 1990, 1-6,

PMN: *Philosophy and the Mirror of Nature,* Princeton University Press, Princeton, NJ, 1979.

PWM: "Pragmatism Without Method," in Kurtz, Paul, ed., *Sidney Hook: Philosopher of Democracy and Humanism,* Prometheus Books, Buffalo, NY, 1938, 259-74.

SS: "Science as Solidarity," in Nelson, John S., Megill, Allan, and McCloskey, Donald M., eds, *The Rhetoric of the Human Sciences,* University of Wisconsin Press, Madison, WI, 1987, 38-52.

TMoL: "Two Meanings of 'Logocentrism'," in Dasenbrock, Reed Way, ed., *Redrawing the Lines: Analytic Philosophy, Deconstruction, and Literary Theory,* Minnesota University Press, Minneapolis, MN, 1989, 204-16.

TWO: "Trotsky and the Wild Orchids," *Common Knowledge,* 1.3, 1992, 140-53.

FURTHER READING

Criticism

Alexander, Gary. "The Hypothesized God of C. S. Peirce and William James." *Journal of Religion* (July 1987): 304-21.
> Compares and contrasts Peirce's and James's definition of pragmatism in relation to their respective interpretations of God.

Anderson, Douglas R. *Creativity and the Philosophy of C. S. Peirce.* Dordrecht: Martinus Nijhoff, 1987, 177 p.
> Examines Peirce's writings on art and science to isolate the philosopher's view of creativity.

Anderson, Douglas R. *Strands of System: The Philosophy of Charles Peirce.* West Lafayette, Ind.: Purdue University Press, 1995, 204 p.
> Defends Peirce's reputation as a major philosopher, and presents the full text and exegesis of Peirce's "The Fixation of Belief" and "A Neglected Argument for the Reality of God."

Barnouw, Jeffrey. "'Aesthetic' for Schiller and Peirce: A Neglected Origin of Pragmatism." *Journal of the History of Ideas* (October-December 1988): 607-32.
> Defends Barnouw's assertion that Peirce's version of pragmatism has a direct antecedent in Friedrich Schiller's *Aesthetic Letters.*

Brunning, Jacqueline and Forster, Paul, eds. *The Rule of Reason: The Philosophy of Charles Sanders Peirce.* Toronto: University of Toronto Press, 1997, 316 p.
> Collects eight essays that pertain to Peirce and his relationship with pragmatism, logic, and semantics.

Corrington, Robert S. *An Introduction to C. S. Peirce.* Lanham, Md.: Rowman & Littlefield, 1993, 227 p.
> Pursues the various avenues of Peirce's philosophy in light of available biographical information.

Delaney, C. F.. *Science, Knowledge, and Mind: A Study in the Philosophy of C. S. Peirce.* Notre Dame, Ind.: Notre Dame Press, 1993, 183 p.
> Begins with the premise that Peirce is the single most important American philosopher due to his mastery of science and mathematics, as well as his visionary and creative writing.

Jacobson, Roman. "A Few Remarks on Peirce, Pathfinder in the Science of Language." *MLN* (December 1977): 1026-32.
> Discusses Peirce's contributions to semiotics.

Ketner, Kenneth Laine. "Peirce's 'Most Lucid and Interesting Paper:' An Introduction to Cenopythagoreanism." *International Philosophical Quarterly* (December 1986): 375-92.
> Examines Peirce's mathematical support for his philosophy of systems of realtions.

———, ed. *Peirce and Contemporary Thought: Philosophical Inquiries.* New York: Fordham University Press, 1995, 444 p.
> Features essays dedicated to four different topics— "Peirce and Logic," "Peirce and Science," "Peirce and Semeiosis," and "Peirce and Metaphysics."

Murphey, Murray G. *The Development of Peirce's Philosophy.* Cambridge, Mass.: Harvard University Press, 1961, 432 p.
> Attempts to place a Kantian archtectonic order to the collected philosophical writings of Peirce.

Orange, Donna. "Peirce's Falsifiable Theism." *American Journal of Semiotics* 2, Nos. 1-2 (1983): 121-27.
> Discusses Peirce's belief that God and the world are symbols that signify the existence of each other.

Rescher, Nicholas. *Essays in the History of Philosophy.* Brookfield, Vt.: Ashgate Publishing Co., 1995, 372 p.
> Discusses "Peirce on Abduction, Plausibility, and the Efficiency of Scientific Inquiry" in Chapter 18.

Russo, Elena. *Skeptical Selves: Empiricism and Modernity in the French Novel.* Stanford, Calif.: Stanford University Press, 1996, 225 p.
> Dedicates the fifth chapter of the study to "Peirce's Alternative to Linguistic Idealism."

White, Morton. *Science and Sentiment in America: Philosophical Thought from Jonathon Edwards to John Dewey.* New York: Oxford University Press, 1972, 358 p.
> Claims Peirce as the first contemporary philosopher, and offers a discussion of his views on logic, semiotics, and metaphysics.

Howard Pyle

1853-1911

Illustrator, teacher, designer, novelist, and author of children's books.

INTRODUCTION

Generally regarded as the founder of American illustration and the Brandywine School, much of Pyle's influence is felt through his famous students, most notably N. C. Wyeth and Maxfield Parrish. Pyle is best remembered for his retelling of the Robin Hood legends and for his innovations in total book design.

Biographical Information

Howard Pyle was born March 5, 1853, in the abolitionist Quaker community of Wilmington, Delaware, to William and Margaret Churchman Painter Pyle. His father was a small businessman and both parents had adopted a mixed Quaker-Swedenborgian faith. Pyle was educated at the local Friends' School and later at a private institution, Clark and Taylor's. The family lacked the means to send Howard to study in European museums and galleries, so he went instead to study with a Dutch émigré, F. A. Van der Weilen, in Philadelphia. Three years later, Pyle returned to his family and most likely would have followed his father into business; however, after a vacation visiting the Chincoteague Islands, off the coast of Virginia, Pyle was inspired to produce an illustrated write-up of the trip, which he submitted to *Scribner's Monthly* in 1876. Not only was the piece accepted, but one of the magazine's owners, Roswell Smith, wrote to Pyle personally, recommending that he come to New York to seek his fortune as a professional artist. Pyle relocated to New York in 1877, and began refining his technique at the Art Student's League. There he became acquainted with Edwin A. Abbey, Frederick S. Church, Arthur B. Frost, and Winslow Homer, among others. He made valuable connections, meeting Mary Mapes Dodge, editor of *St. Nicholas* magazine, who would go on to publish his work consistently; and Charles Parsons, art director for *Harper's Weekly*, who printed his first full page illustration in 1878, "A Wreck in the Offing." Pyle submitted the work expecting to receive, at best, fifteen dollars for it—Parsons paid him seventy-five. Having established himself as an illustrator, Pyle returned to Wilmington, and went on to marry a singer named Anne Poole on April 12, 1881, with whom he would have seven children: Sellers, Phoebe, Theodore, Howard, Eleanor, Godfrey, and Wilfrid. However, despite the increasing domesticity of his life, it wasn't until two years later that Pyle's career fully resolved: when he began writing and illustrating stories for children, to

appear primarily in *St. Nicholas* and *Harper's Young People*. It was in 1883, also, that Pyle published his most enduring and famous work, *The Merry Adventures of Robin Hood of Great Renown, in Nottinghamshire.* In 1889, the Pyles sailed for Jamaica, leaving their two children in the care of their grandmother. Sellers, the eldest, died suddenly during the trip, and was buried before his parents were able to return. In dealing with the death of his first son, Pyle would go on to write *The Garden Behind the Moon* (1895), an allegory of life and death for children. As a rule, Pyle's children's books were popular and successful. Based on these successes, Pyle began teaching a course in illustration, the first such course ever taught in the United States, at the Drexel Institute in Philadelphia, in 1894. This course, along with a summer course at Chadds Ford, he would teach for the rest of his life. In 1900, Pyle opened his own artists' studio, where he taught N. C. Wyeth, Frank Schoonover, Jessie Wilcox Smith, Maxfield Parrish, and other prominent "Brandywine School" artists. Much of Pyle's enduring fame is due to the great enthusiasm and love he evoked in his prominent students, who uniformly remembered him as an inspirational teacher and spiritual artist. All his life, Pyle placed solid emphasis on the development of an American Illustrational style, to bring American talent out from under the shadow of European art. He scrupulously avoided any exposure to "European influence" during the greater part of his career. However, he finally succumbed to the lure of Italy's art treasures late in 1910. While on his way to Florence, he suffered an attack of renal colic and died suddenly at the age of 58, on November 9, 1911. He was buried just outside the city.

Major Works

The most famous and well-received of Pyle's works was his first, *The Merry Adventures of Robin Hood of Great Renown, in Nottinghamshire* (1883). He based it on Joseph Ritson's collection of Robin Hood ballads, of 1795, but the overall presentation of the work was a complete innovation. Pyle not only wrote the text and drew the illustrations, he designed the entire book, with elaborate marginal detailing, calligraphic scrolls inserted into the illustrations, which were themselves adaptations of archaic woodcuts, just as the prose was an adaptation of archaic rhetoric. Pyle's historical research, his accuracy of detail, and his thorough familiarity with the legends, would become hallmarks of his artistic approach, but his total-design philosophy was most likely his most influential innovation. Pyle's Robin Hood stories are characterized by their human scope and moral flexibility, where Robin is selflessly heroic, the sheriff of Nottingham, a flawed, selfish person, rather than a one-dimensional villain. Pyle was in love with fairy tales, and was forever reworking old stories and composing new ones. He published several collections of these: *Pepper and Salt; or, Seasoning for Young Folk* (1885) and *The Wonder Clock; or, Four and Twenty Marvellous Tales, Being One for Each Hour of the Day* (1888) are the most well-known. Pyle's first proper novel, *Otto of the Silver Hand* (1888), had a darker flavor than the material that had come before, being a grim depiction of chivalry in medieval Germany: the boy hero, Otto, is caught in a familial power struggle and loses his hand through the treachery of his father. His world is torn between the brutal world of power-mongering barons and the serenity of the monastic life, toward which he finally turns. *Men of Iron* (1892) followed in a similar vein. A chivalric romance of Henry IV's era, its hero, Myles, is the scion of an unfairly disgraced family, trying to qualify for knighthood. *The Garden Behind the Moon: A Real Story of the Moon Angel* (1895) was Pyle's response to the death of his first son, Sellers. It is an allegorical tale of life and death, designed for children. Interestingly, it is perhaps the one occasion for Pyle to express his racial views—he consistently refused to use the term "negro," prevalent at the time, preferring the less pejorative "black"; and used the overview granted him from the perspective of the moon angel to look down upon the earth and see the gruesome injustices of racism, which were pointedly not perpetuated in the moon-realm of death: ". . . there is as much joy and gladness over one poor black woman

who enters into that place as there is over the whitest empress who ever walked the earth of Christendom." Pyle's final important project was a thorough retelling of Arthurian legend, published in four volumes: *The Story of King Arthur and His Knights* (1903), *The Story of the Champions of the Round Table* (1905), *The Story of Sir Launcelot and His Champions* (1907), and *The Story of the Grail and the Passing of Arthur* (1910). True to form, Pyle researched his subject extensively, drawing on Malory, the Mabinogion, Thomas Percy's *Reliques of Ancient English Poetry*, among other sources, to recreate both the historical era of Arthur and the appropriate prose and illustrative styles. The tone, with regard to chivalry, is the most affirmative of all treatments of this era in Pyle's works.

Critical Reception

Pyle's work was generally well-received during his lifetime, although most critics seemed to prefer his art and design to his prose. He was able to support himself through art and education and many of his works have remained consistently in print, especially *Robin Hood*, which was proclaimed a modern classic in its own time. Most of Pyle's ongoing reputation emanates from the fame of his students and their loyalty and glowing recollections of Pyle. As time passed, Pyle's historical position as the founder of a distinctly American school of illustration and art, as the innovator who introduced the total-design approach, and as the great reinventor of children's books, would outshine any single work he did, so that he is remembered less for any one project than for his overall stance. However, of his many works, *Robin Hood* has remained the most abidingly popular and highly-regarded, resorted to as Pyle's masterwork, and the best introduction to his distinct aesthetic.

PRINCIPAL WORKS

The Merry Adventures of Robin Hood of Great Renown, in Nottinghamshire (stories) 1883.
Within the Capes (stories) 1885.
Pepper and Salt; or, Seasoning for Young Folk (stories) 1885.
The Rose of Paradise (stories) 1888.
The Wonder Clock; or, Four and Twenty Marvellous Tales, Being One for Each Hour of the Day (stories) 1888.
Otto of the Silver Hand (novel) 1888.
Men of Iron (novel) 1892.
A Modern Aladdin; or, The Wonderful Adventures of Oliver Munier (stories) 1892.
Twilight Land (stories) 1895.
The Story of Jack Ballister's Fortunes (stories) 1895.
The Garden Behind the Moon: A Real Story of the Moon Angel (novel) 1895.
The Ghost of Captain Brand (stories) 1896.

A Catalogue of Drawings Illustrating the Life of Gen. Washington, and of Colonial Life (illustrations) 1897.

The Divinity of Labor. An Address Delivered at Commencement Exercises at Delaware College, June 16, 1897 (speech) 1898.

The Price of Blood: An Extravaganza of New York Life in 1807 (novel) 1899.

Rejected of Men: A Story of To-Day (novel) 1903.

The Story of King Arthur and His Knights (stories) 1903.

The Story of the Champions of the Round Table (stories) 1905.

Stolen Treasure (stories) 1907.

The Story of Sir Launcelot and His Champions (stories) 1907.

The Ruby of Kishmoor (novel) 1908.

The Story of the Grail and the Passing of Arthur (stories) 1910.

CRITICISM

Charles D. Abbott (essay date 1931)

SOURCE: "A Writing Illustrator," in *Careers in the Making: Modern Americans When They Were Young—and on Their Way,* edited by Iona M. R. Logie, MA., Harper & Brothers Publishers, 1931, pp. 83-99.

[*In the following essay, Abbott recounts Pyle's early career as a magazine illustrator.*]

Since Howard was . . . old enough [in 1861] to gain something by a little study, his parents sent him to school—first to the old Friends' School and then to Clark and Taylor's. Here, by his own confession, he was far more interested in drawing pictures on his slate or in the margins of his books, than he was in the intricacies of grammar or arithmetic. He continued to go for a number of years, but the training received at the hands of his mother during these same years was to prove far more valuable than that given by schools. One of the books to which his mother introduced him during this period was Percy's *Reliques of Ancient English Poetry,* which gave him a vigorous interest in Robin Hood, and which was soon followed by Ritson's charming old collection of popular ballads that centered around the life of England's outlaw hero. From these early introductions was to spring one of the best of children's books some twenty years later [*The Merry Adventures of Robin Hood*]. Other literature was occupying his attention—Malory's *Morte d'Arthur* and many collections of German folk and fairy tales—and through it all his pencil was seldom still. Rough, crude sketches surrounded the family on all sides.

He was not to any considerable extent a sociable boy. While he joined in the play of his school companions, and was popular in a way among them, he was easier when off by himself, sketching away with some romantic idea in his head, or when peacefully sitting at home, happily intent on some tale of the Middle Ages. These signs of a distinctive personality did not discourage or alarm his family, as they are so likely to do among more conventional people. His mother had visions of her son fulfilling the dreams she had had in her own childhood and youth, and was overjoyed that he was giving such manifestations of promise. He was allowed to sketch and to scribble away—for he wanted to write as well as to draw—as much as he pleased, and his mother was always ready to make suggestions and to criticize whatever he produced. Who would deny that such patience and such sympathy on the part of the mother had an incomparable effect on the development of the impulses already strong in the child? Of course, there were moments when more typically boyish ambitions stirred within him. There was a decided thrill in watching the locomotives come rushing through on the old Philadelphia, Wilmington, and Baltimore Railroad, and he dreamed of the glories of being a trained engineer. And those delightful years in the country had given a glamour to that sort of life, which made him occasionally look forward to being a farmer. This last may perhaps have been merely a result of family habit, for his ancestors had been for many generations farmers in the peaceful Pennsylvania and Delaware hills. Always, however, he came back to the continual sketching; there was scarcely ever a break of any considerable length of time.

Punch continued to be one of the principal reading supplies of the family. In his later letters, Howard speaks again and again of the pictures by Leech and Doyle and Tenniel, and the essays by Thackeray and Douglas Jerrold. These had an immeasurable influence on his work, especially that of his earliest period. It was at this time that he absorbed the spirit and purpose of those hearty Englishmen. And the illustrated books continued to delight him. *Barnaby Rudge, The Old Curiosity Shop,* and *The Newcomes,* read again and again, made a deep impression on his plastic mind and remained favorites during the rest of his life.

When Howard was about fifteen or sixteen years old, his parents decided that it would be best to send him to college. Then followed a weary time of preparation. Through many hours of Latin and algebra he was joyously uninterested. What did college mean to a youth who was more anxious to learn how to get a certain shady effect in the background of a pen-and-ink sketch, than he was in knowing what Cicero said in support of the Manilian Law? The parents struggled, and Howard remained unmoved and unconvinced. Mrs. Pyle felt that college would not harm his talent for drawing and that it might decidedly improve his literary instincts. But the struggle was in vain. She had to surrender at last, and Howard was permitted to go on with his drawing and scribbling—doing, perhaps, the very best thing for the strengthening of his imagination. Might not college have left an unfortunate and indelible sophistication on the mind that was to create the *Wonder Clock?*

Study with oneself, no matter how excellent it may be for a time, cannot go on forever without ending in a kind of futility. This was the opinion of the Pyle family when Howard had finally committed himself to a life of artistic endeavor. The pecuniary circumstances of the family were somewhat straitened at the time, and it was idle to dream of sending the boy off to Europe to study with Gérôme in Paris or Piloty in Munich. Besides, he had not been sufficiently trained in academic methods. Then, also, Americans were not so much in the habit of rushing off to Europe to find an art education as they are in these days. Still, it was obviously necessary for Howard to study somewhere, and Philadelphia seemed to present the greatest opportunities. There were two schools there where the young artist might conceivably do his work—the Academy of Fine Arts, where careful instruction could be obtained along general classical lines, and a little private school where a certain Mr. Van der Weilen conducted a small class. It was decided that Howard should go to the second of these. Had he gone to the Academy, he would unquestionably have met and been familiar with a young man, Edwin Austin Abbey, who was studying there at the time and who was later to be for a short period a companion and fellow-worker with him. The advantages of being in a small class, however, where each pupil would receive a great deal of attention from Mr. Van der Weilen himself, outweighed all other arguments, and Howard became a regular student, commuting back and forth from Wilmington to Philadelphia. This was a great and momentous step; it crystallized into more certain forms the ambitions which had been more or less inchoate before. He felt himself committed to a certain walk of life, and there is no question that he was satisfied with his choice.

Mr. Van der Weilen had graduated from the school at Antwerp with high honors, but in pursuing his studies too zealously had committed irreparable injury to his eyesight. He had been left in such a condition that it was impossible for him to think of doing any considerable amount of original work himself; yet he could see sufficiently well to be of inestimable service to those pupils who were placed with him. With all the advantages of a European training, with a full knowledge of accepted technique, he combined a real teaching skill, making every effort to cultivate and improve the imaginations of the young men in his class. But it was a stiff course of study that he prescribed; it was hard, almost never-ending work. There was slight opportunity for dreaming or building castles in the air. He was always there, always insisting vigorously upon a close attention to the matter in hand, and the consequence was that his pupils—at least one of them—thought at the time that such work was drudgery. The taskmaster, however, was too efficient to allow such feelings to interfere with the regular routine. He kept them busily at their sketching and painting, and succeeded magnificently in giving them a technique.

Howard continued his Philadelphia trips for three years, during which time he gathered a great deal of knowl-edge from the persistent teaching of Mr. Van der Weilen. This was the only systematic training that he ever had, for his later work at the Art Students' League was certainly too disconnected to be of the greatest value.

The Wilmington life went on. Sketching and scribbling could be done in the spare hours when there was nothing to do for Mr. Van der Weilen. And yet with it all Howard found time to help his father in the leather business, which was not prospering too well in those panic-ridden early 'seventies. Mrs. Pyle continued to encourage her son, giving him the whole sympathy and power of her ardent spirit, never for a moment losing sight of the ambition which she had for him. And there was no lack of good reading. Trollope had come into fashion, and had found loyal supporters among the members of the Pyle household. Carlyle was attempted, but thrown down with something of disgust in the gesture. William Dean Howells was beginning to appear above the horizon with *Their Wedding Journey* and *A Chance Acquaintance.* These Howard read with avidity; he took an unusual fancy to them, especially to the style in which they were written, and he conceived an intense admiration for Howells, which was later to ripen into a rich friendship. And there were discussions in the Pyle family, open-minded discussions in which such subjects as Darwinism were carefully weighed pro and con, while spiritualism and even metaphysics, not to mention Swedenborg, were topics of absorbing interest.

But after the "Van der Weilen course of sprouts," as Howard called his Philadelphia experiences, there began to be a waning in the young artist's dreams of a career. He was working almost steadily in the leather establishment, and was heavily occupied not only with business, but also with a variety of social activities. Wilmington was a gay little city and there were many affairs which attracted him. He began to look upon his earlier ambitions as things of the past; he was occupied more with things of the present. Yet the creative urge was strong within him, even if it did find its outlet in a desultory fashion. He spent numerous spare hours in composing rippling ballads, and in constructing short stories; he drew sketches to illustrate them, and then usually destroyed them, since they failed to measure up to his expectations. His artistic impulses were still strong, and growing stronger every day, but his ambition was almost dead. He needed a great awakening, and it came in the fall of 1876.

In the spring of that year he had gone on an expedition to a little island off the coast of Virginia known as Chincoteague, where there flourished a breed of wild ponies. He was there at the time when the owners penned and branded these horses, and was very greatly interested in the operation. He watched it all in detail—how the horses were caught, how the branding was accomplished—and he especially took notice of the people who did it. He grasped their personalities, learned all about them, caught the spirit of the local atmosphere. Then, when he returned to Wilmington, he wrote about it and made sketches to go with his essay. It was a good description. It showed a real knowledge of the island and a splendid grasp of the picturesque details. Mrs. Pyle immediately saw its value and advised him to send it off to *Scribner's Monthly,* which was in the habit of publishing such things. He had also written, not long before, a little poem entitled **"The Magic Pill."** It was a slight piece, rather after the manner of Oliver Wendell Holmes, but it was in creditable verse and was characterized by a somewhat novel idea. Moreover, the picture he had drawn for it was very good, and went with the verses most fittingly. Both these were sent off to *Scribner's* at once. And immediately the old ambitions began to burst forth anew and with added vigor.

It was not long before a pleasant little note came from *Scribner's Monthly* saying that both had been accepted— the poem for the Bric-à-brac section and the article for the body of the magazine. The editors were particularly pleased with the illustrations, although the ones for **"Chincoteague"** would have to be redrawn by their own staff of artists in order to be made suitable for purposes of reproduction. The Pyle family was delighted; everything began to look rosy for Howard. Then Mr. Roswell Smith, who was one of the owners of *Scribner's Monthly,* got into communication with Mr. Pyle and learned all the details about Howard. He advised that the young man come to New York, spend all his time in drawing and writing for the magazines, and develop his abilities until they should become of really great value. He implied that there would be no difficulty in getting plenty of work from *Scribner's,* and succeeded in persuading Mr. Pyle that nothing would be easier than for Howard to make a good living.

Of course, Howard himself, with his old fires rekindled by this sudden success, was not at all averse to plunging into the hurly-burly of New York. It was an opportunity not to be missed. Not only could he get a good start in the way of practical work for the periodicals, but he could also study again. There would be any number of good teachers there, and he could surely spare enough time from his work to be trained in the latest methods that had been brought over from Europe. Mrs. Pyle was a perfect mother in her devotion. She was deeply moved at the thought of her son's being alone in the great metropolis; she would have loved to have him always in Wilmington, but his career was uppermost in her mind. Nothing would matter so long as her son became an artist and thus fulfilled her own dreams. Mr. Pyle's circumstances, considerably reduced since the early days, could not permit of any great drain, but nevertheless it was decided that if Howard found it difficult to make his way at first, he should be supported from the family purse. Accordingly, then, about the middle of October 1876, he set out for New York, carrying with him the high hopes of his family and the glad confidence of young ambition.

. . . . .

The first thing to look for in New York was a place to board—not too expensive a place, for the income of a young artist could not easily be made to support one in luxurious surroundings. Howard knew very little of the city; he hadn't the remotest idea where the so-called art centers were. Had he known where other people who were following his profession lived, he would undoubtedly have sought a harbor somewhere in that vicinity. But it was all new and strange; he thought merely of finding a comfortable boarding-house, not too far from the offices of *Scribner's* and the other magazines, where he could work without interruption. But such a place was not easy to find. The nearer the prospective dwelling was to the offices, the higher price one had to pay for the privilege of living there. After considerable searching he finally found on Forty-eighth Street a vacant room in a boarding-house managed by two middle-aged ladies, the Misses Marshall. The odd thing about it was that these two women were former neighbors of his mother's. They immediately took a fancy to the young man and saw to it that he was well supplied with the usual appurtenances of a boarding-house. Even under such pleasant conditions, however, Forty-eighth Street was not exactly an ideal place for an artist to live in those days—too many hours had to be occupied with walking down to the much-frequented centers of the publishing business.

As soon as he was settled in his new quarters, he began to attend the theaters. Good plays had been something of a rarity in Wilmington, but in New York the drama was moving towards a new importance, and the playhouses were taking on the brilliance that characterizes them today. His letters home are full of allusions to the various productions which he saw—he evidently was greatly impressed with the possibilities of the stage.

He worked regularly either at short stories and fables or at the illustrations to go with them, and for a time he had little difficulty in getting them accepted. Mary Mapes Dodge, who was then the editor of *St. Nicholas,* saw a certain charm in the animal fables which he was continually pouring out, and published a number of them. In spite of the certainty, however, with which Mr. Smith had told Mr. Pyle that *Scribner's* would find plenty of work for Howard to do, it was not long before very little was forthcoming from that magazine. Still, this was no great matter to a young man of Howard's stamp—there were plenty of other periodicals. In fact, it was probably in the end a very lucky occurrence, for it threw him on his own initiative and made him fight his own battles. As he himself wrote many years later, "I took him [Mr. Smith] at his word and went there expecting to find employment with *Scribner's.* Fortunately for me, I found that I had to make my own way, and that it was not made for me by *Scribner's.*" But Mr. Smith himself was most kind and sympathetic. He did everything he could in a personal way—criticized manuscripts and gave extremely valuable advice. . . .

During the early part of his years in New York he (Howard) wrote diary-letters—many of them have been, unfortunately, lost—to his mother, which gave her full accounts of his activities every day. The letters draw such a vivid picture of these months that it seems best to quote from them those passages which describe his habits, his achievements, and his aspirations. . . .

NOVEMBER 17, 1876

I went down to *Scribner's* yesterday, to take my fables to Mrs. Dodge. There was, I believe, some little difficulty in regard to the blurring of the lines of my illustrations, since both the former and Mr. Drake, the Art Editor, suggested that I go down and see the Photo-engraving Company and obtain such suggestions as they might offer. I could not attend to it yesterday, but shall today.

I stopped in at Mr. Smith's to see if he could refer me to someone who would give me severe criticisms on my articles before I submitted them to the magazines; for I feel more and more acutely as time progresses and I begin to know enough to "know how little I know," the need of severe advice in chopping off excrescences. Mr. Smith was more than kind. He cordially invited me to come up to his house for dinner and read my MS. to him and Mrs. Smith afterward, and he said that even were his criticisms useless in a literary sense, they would at least be *frank*. . . .

NOVEMBER 24, 1876

. . . Says Mr. Drake, the art editor, "If you are going to try to make an artist sufficiently good to illustrate extensively for us, you'll have to give up society entirely for the present, and devote your whole attention to study." They desire young men on their force, and they have one now who is illustrating for them, having some designs in the holiday *St. Nicholas*, which will probably be in Wilmington on Monday. He has illustrated an article called "The Horse Hotel" in a way that has gained him much praise. He is an indefatigable worker and puts me to the blush whenever I hear of him. . . .

I have been thinking lately that stories from the life of Robin Hood might be an interesting thing for *St. Nicholas*. Children are very apt to know of Robin Hood without any very clear ideas upon his particular adventures. And then how gloriously they would illustrate. If thee would lend me thy volume of Percy and express it on to me, I would take great care of it and would make the attempt. I think if I am not mistaken, that his life is incomplete in that work; dost thee know any other one work wherein he appears in his early history and adventures?

I wonder how long it will be that I shall have to crawl in writing before I can begin to walk? At times I feel discouraged and then again the feeling rises strong within me that there *is* something in me that will produce, perhaps, worthy fruit in time. At present I am trammelled more than I can describe with stiffness in manner, crudeness in style, and self-consciousness (I do not know how else to describe it) in thought. The feet of my ideas seem clogged with the difficulties of expression; I can't open the flood-gates of my mind and pour out my thoughts onto the paper. The sentences will not "round up" so as to contain the shell of a few distinctly expressed words. I have to strike again and again with simile and hyperbole before I can crack that invisible, intangible wall that separates my internal thought from the perception of others. One reason I so enjoy and pleasure in my fables is that the thought finds, as it were, a more tangible form, rough though it be, and clad in the rude garb of brute life. But even in them, easy as that way is of exhibiting some of the innumerable variations of human nature, I find in reading them over that I have failed in laying my thought clear and undimmed by diffuseness of language. It is as though the particular thread in the woof of my thoughts broke in my fingers as I strive to draw it forth. . . .

NOVEMBER 25, 1876

I worked yesterday morning at correcting the fable illustrations for *St. Nicholas* and took them down town with me. . . . When I called on Mr. Drake, he said that Mr. Smith had been speaking about me, and urged me again to go down to Wills and take lessons under him. I did not, however, incline much to that plan.

Two of the illustrations of the fables I sent up to Mrs. Dodge, as she wished to see them before Mr. Drake put them in process.

I stopped in the editorial rooms of *Scribner's* to see an old Dutch painting that they have been having photographed. I did not see it, however, as Mr. Gilder had it home with him. Mr. Gilder had a long talk with me and *he* advised me to take a course of life study around at the Artists' League, giving me a letter of introduction to a young Mr. Church who has his studio on Thirteenth Street. He also advised me to join the League, as there is a sketch class there where each student poses in turn for the benefit of the others. Since two persons' advice is better than one, I shall most probably take advantage of Messrs. Gilder's and Church's, and join the League, albeit not an inexpensive operation.

I have been thinking lately of taking a studio down town if I could get one in conjunction with some other young artist, so lessening the expense. I have no opportunity at home for models, etc., comprising all those thousand little surroundings that go so far toward rendering work more easy and speedy. One cannot improve without study from models and nature, as all the good artists here do; and making pictures means making bread and butter to me for a while. . . .

NOVEMBER 28, 1876

I was at work today making some comic illustrations, as I want to make some money between now and Christmas. The first was called "Bliss"; it represents a diminutive gamin with his head buried under the sun-bonnet of as diminutive a little girl. The second was entitled "The Spirit Is Willing, but the Flesh Is Weak"—"Lemme carry your baggage, Mister," says a very small boy to a gentleman with a very large valise. I did not take them down to Mr. Drake, because it was raining and snowing, besides being rather late.

I paid a visit to the Art Students' League in the evening. Snowing as it was, there was quite a class assembled, sketching a temporary pose assumed by a young lady. This class is held every evening, and would be very useful indeed, I should think. One of the students poses every evening for half an hour. They wished me to begin with my studies last night; as I had nothing ready, however, I postponed joining until next Monday. It will cost me about fifteen dollars, I suspect. . . .

NOVEMBER 30, 1876

I finished writing the fable and story for Mrs. Dodge's two woodcuts and took them down this morning to the office. They paid me for my former two budgets of fables, comprising thirteen in all; for which they gave me *thirty dollars!*—a little less than two dollars and a half for each fable. I was far from satisfied at this, as thee may well imagine, but I had to swallow it as best I could and digest the hard case in my own inner consciousness. They rather have me. There is no other child's magazine of any worth in the country, and my writings are essentially for children. I try to make them as witty as I can, and at the same time indoctrinate a small lesson. I strive to hold the lesson in view and throw in the wit as an accessory. Perhaps if I do the best I can in this way, it may bear fruit at some time; but dear only knows! it does seem as though it would be slow work. We shall see what people say when my little writings make their appearance. . . .

Harper's did not accept the illustrations submitted to them, so that makes three I now have upon my hands.

DECEMBER 2, 1876

. . . I attended the life class last night and finished my pencil sketch from life. Mr. Wilmot said it was in some respects a very nicely conceived piece; the action was stiff and some parts were out of proportion, but the arms were very good. I myself, however, am not at all satisfied with it and hope to do better next time. It is pretty good pencil work for me, however, and I want to show it to Mr. Drake to see if it won't refute his opinion of the need of rudiments on my part.

DECEMBER 14, 1876

. . . I have met with constant disappointment this week, and am beginning to get scared with this way of going on. If it continues, I shall not be able to make expenses. I am meeting my first reverses now, and they taste very bitter. If I should fail now, wouldn't it be a humiliating come-down?

DECEMBER 15, 1876

Still more reverses, and worse than before! I went down to see Mrs. Dodge yesterday morning to find out whether she had accepted my fairy tale or not. Fortunately I did not receive an answer to *that* in this unlucky time. . . . But what worried me was the complaint made of my drawings for the fables; and they certainly did not look well in print. They seem coarse and cheap looking, more so than in the original drawings, for upon being reduced they blotted and came up black and heavy looking. . . .

This was my first rebuff. Next—*Harper's* declined my design for "Despair." It was very clever but they could not use it. Another small design that I had submitted at the same time was too "loud" for them, or in other words it was likely to be accused of coarseness. I then took them to Frank Leslie. The "loud" was not too loud for him and he took it.

This much for my diary this week. It is short and not over sweet. In fact it combines with its smallness all the bitterness of a quinine pill; and it may be beneficial in removing all unhealthy humours of conceit and self-satisfaction. Still, I do hope that affairs will look brighter by Christmas time, and that present reverses will prove only a salutary check on a course of life that was proving too prosperous. I can tell you, in the last two weeks my expenses have been less than heretofore; and after all, I have quite a sum laid by. One doesn't like to have a nasty little cankering trouble gnawing on one about Christmas time, so, as I say, I hope my luck will change.

I shall try some illustrations for St. Valentine's Day, next week. I have not any very clear ideas on the subject as yet, though I should like to make a silhouette for *St. Nicholas* and a pen-and-ink design for *Harper's*. I don't recollect anywhere that Shakespeare speaks of St. Valentine's Day except in *Hamlet* where Ophelia first goes crazy, and that is hardly admissible for illustration. . . .

To sum up: I am not yet bankrupt; I am improving in drawing; I yet have ideas and pen and ink; and having received a salutary check, let us hope that I may remove the taint of vulgarity that affects my work. . . .

The depression that marks the closing paragraphs of the diary-letters was not easily dispersed. The Christmas season came and went, and still it was difficult to get the magazines to accept anything. The truth of the matter was that *St. Nicholas* was overstocked; the editors had on hand enough of the fables to last them for many months, since it was not editorial policy to publish too many at once. Consequently there was nothing else for Howard to do but devote himself to some different line of work. This he did, and in doing so turned away from *Scribner's* and worked almost entirely for the Harper publications.

In the months that followed, the old mental struggle, which was so frequently mentioned in the diary-letters, went on—whether it was better to continue looking to literature as the goal of these apprentice years, or whether art was the more fitting choice. Both his father and mother—and his mother's advice always carried particular weight—approved of the artistic career. Church thought he had considerable talent, and even Mr. Drake admitted that his drawing was improving. Finally, but not without severe internal questionings and many delays, he decided that his abilities led him more naturally towards art. With this change in ambition it became necessary, of course, to have a studio where he could work from models, where he would not be impeded by the thousand little inconveniences of a boarding-house. Accordingly, in conjunction with two other young men, Durand and LeGendre, he rented a regular studio which was more conveniently located than the Forty-eighth Street room. Here he worked on picture after picture, gradually building up a method of attack which was entirely his own. His ideas were good and he had plenty of them.

Mr. Charles Parsons, the art editor for Harper & Brothers, had gathered around him and trained a most remarkable group of young illustrators, among whom were Abbey, Frost, and Reinhart, and with these young men he was building up the pictorial side of his magazines to a point which had never before been reached in this country. To him Howard would take his sketches, and since the ideas were very often good, Mr. Parsons would accept them; but since in his opinion the technical work did not come up to the standard, he would have one of his staff artists redraw the picture on wood. This was, of course, very humiliating to the young man whose fertile brain had devised the idea. His friend Church, the man who was later to do some of the charming pictures for Joel Chandler Harris's *Uncle Remus,* was continually saying that it was poor policy to drag other people's trains in the way in which young Pyle was doing. The matter rankled, and finally he aroused sufficient courage to ask Mr. Parsons for a chance to try his own hand at it. He tells the story himself:

> I took one day to *Harper's* an idea sketch which I had called "A Wreck in the Offing." It represented an alarm brought into the Life Saving Station, a man bursting open the door, with the cold and snow rushing in after him, and shouting and pointing out into the darkness, the others rising from the table where they were sitting at a game of cards.

> I begged Mr. Parsons to allow me to make the picture, instead of handing it over to Mr. Abbey or to Mr. Reinhart or Mr. Frost, or to some other of the young Olympians to elaborate into a real picture. With some hesitating reluctance he told me that I might try, and that in the event of my failure, *Harper's* would pay me ten dollars, I think it was, or fifteen—for the idea. I believe I worked upon it somewhat over six weeks, and I might indeed have been working upon it today (finding it impossible to satisfy myself with it) had I not,

what with the cost of my models and the expense of living in New York, reduced myself to my last five-cent piece in the world. Then it was that my fate or my poverty, or whatever you may choose to call it, forced me to take the drawing down to *Harper's,* instead of drawing it over as I should have liked to have done.

> I think it was not until I stood in the awful presence of the art editor himself that I realized how this might be the turning-point in my life— that I realized how great was to be the result of his decision on my future endeavor. I think I have never since passed such a moment of intense trepidation—a moment of such confused and terrible blending of hope and despair at the same time. I can recall just how the art editor looked at me over his spectacles, and to my perturbed mind it seemed that he was weighing in his mind (for he was a very tender man) how best he might break the news of my unsuccess. The rebound was almost too great when he told me that Mr. Harper had liked the drawing very much, and that they were going to use it in the *Weekly.* But when he said that they were not only going to use it, but were going to make of it a double-page cut, my exaltation was so great that it seemed to me I knew not where I was standing or what had happened to me. As I went away, I walked upon air—I seemed to float. I found a friend and took him to Delmonico's, and we had lunch of all the delicacies in season and out of season. . . .

This was late in 1877, and from that time everything moved more pleasantly. Harper & Brothers were well pleased with his work, he was associating with the people who most interested him, and he was slowly but none the less surely building up an excellent reputation.

Robert Vitz (essay date 1983)

SOURCE: "Howard Pyle's America," in *Children's Literature Association Quarterly,* Vol. 8, No. 2, Summer, 1983, pp. 15-16, 34.

[*In the following essay, Vitz discusses Pyle's meticulous depiction of American history in his work.*]

The mere mention of Howard Pyle arouses visions of Robin Hood and Little John, of King Arthur locked in mortal combat with the Sable Knight, of a host of splendid pirates and adventurers. But we must not allow these childhood memories to obscure the depictions of historical characters that made up almost a third of Pyle's total work. How much richer our sense of history is today because of Pyle's imaginative rendering of Bunker Hill, with the British regulars resolutely marching toward the American lines, or of Lexington Common on that fateful April morning in 1775. Whether or not this is the way it was, it is surely the way it should have been.

Nothing captures Pyle's interest more than the tension of physical action. His best subjects are caught in movement, muscles tensed, the ultimate outcome still in doubt. Pyle himself was a large man, and there is much of his own ruggedness in his characters, a ruggedness which he associated with the vitality of life. He looked for this vitality in his students also. Baseball and tennis, swimming parties, bicycle forays along dusty roads, and long rambles through the Brandywine countryside served to release the explosive energy of young muscles. There was more than mere Rooseveltian vigor in all this, however; Pyle wanted his students to experience aching muscles and straining limbs so that they could transfer these feelings onto canvas and paper. This concern for realism, coupled with a highly developed imagination, made Pyle the most important illustrator of his generation.

Born to Quaker parents in Wilmington, Delaware, Howard Pyle grew up amidst solid, middle-class respectability. Early exposure to the great outpouring of illustrated English books and periodicals provided a powerful visual stimulus for his imagination. Fireside reading included *Robinson Crusoe, Gulliver's Travels, The Arabian Nights,* and later, the *Illustrated London News* and *London Punch.* Supplementing this literary and artistic education were the absorbed sensations of "old" Wilmington. Cobblestone Streets, Delaware River wharves, Conestoga wagons and seventeenth century stone farmhouses, stories of Washington's army along the Brandywine, all extended a tangible link to the past. Since he was nurtured in Quaker abolitionism, the Civil War provided a dramatic excitement for the young Pyle, and he found the absorbing life around him far more stimulating than any formal schooling. Not surprisingly, poor grades in Latin and mathematics barred his path to college, and at the age of sixteen he headed for Philadelphia and a career in art.

Three years of the traditional emphasis on technique from the undistinguished Mr. Van der Weilen provided the necessary skill and discipline. Returning to Wilmington, Pyle worked at both writing and drawing, not yet certain how he would utilize his twin skills. Then, in 1876, his combined talents enticed three acceptance notices from the New York publishing world, one from *St. Nicholas* and two from *Scribner's Monthly.* With the encouragement of Roswell Smith, of *Scribner's,* an elated Pyle soon set off for New York City to become a writer and artist. Early disappointment in the hectic publishing center rapidly gave way to success. The distinguished house of Harper opened its doors to him, and he joined a stable of artists that already included Charles Stanley Reinhart, Edwin A. Abbey, Arthur B. Frost, and the "old man," Thomas Nast, all working under the editorial eye of Charles Parsons. Here, Pyle felt at one with the world of art. His keen mind absorbed the many lessons of illustration work, from the first sketch to the final printing. But whatever the attractions of New York for other artists, it was not the place to bring out Pyle's talents. The quieter, more familiar atmosphere of the Brandywine River Valley beckoned, and the now confident professional returned to Wilmington. Perhaps Pyle was never truly comfortable with

the emerging commercial world because his own work looked back to an earlier time. He found his America in the gentle Delaware countryside, a historic landscape that released the products of his imagination.

Howard Pyle found a reality in the past. His most familiar writing, the books about **Robin Hood** and **King Arthur,** dealt with quasi-historical figures, and even **Otto of the Silver Hand** is set against the backdrop of medieval Germany. He identified with historical subjects, both real and imagined, in an intensely personal way. "I have lived so long in the American past," he informed one interviewer, "that it is like a certain part of my life. My imagination dwells in it and at times . . . I forget the present and see the characters and things of those old days moving about me." Pyle's strength as an illustrator lay in his ability to feel the personality of his subject, much like an actor playing a role on stage. He once advised a student to "throw your heart into your picture and jump in after it." Pyle did just that.

Following the publication of **The Merry Adventures of Robin Hood** in 1883, Pyle turned more and more to the nation's past. The writings of George Bancroft and Francis Parkman stirred his historical sensibilities, and from his reading came the inspiration for pictures of colonial Quakers, Revolutionary soldiers, and ruthless pirates. Throughout the 1880s and 1890s, his historical images dominated the pages of the nation's family magazines. His eye for detail made his characters realistic, even to the buttons on their coats, and his battle scenes smelled of gunpowder. His concern for proper costumes was legendary. As early as 1878 he worried about the lack of "correct" costumes for his illustration of "Christmas in Old New York." Local costume shops could not satisfy his fastidious taste. "I know what is correct and I must have *that,*" he emphatically wrote his mother. Over the years Pyle accumulated a costume wardrobe that rivaled any stock theater company's, and that also served as an encouragement for the occasional student theatricals. This accuracy of detail, and Pyle's attention to time and place, gave an authenticity to his work rarely found in American illustration.

Pyle shared with many of his contemporaries an implicit confidence in the virtues of America, and he conveyed this faith to his audience. His history is romantic, traditional, and unabashedly patriotic. It is the spirit of 1776 and Jacksonian Democracy; it is the confidence of a man who had seen the country survive its greatest crisis. His illustrations made a perfect match with the outpouring of popular histories from the pens of Oliver Wendell Holmes, Charles Coffin, John Greenleaf Whittier, Woodrow Wilson, and others. To Pyle, history was the collective embodiment of a people's character, and he approached it uncritically. His death in 1911 spared him from the change in American historiography begun by Charles Beard in 1913.

Still, one must not depict Howard Pyle as a flag-waving, my-country-right-or-wrong American. One senses that he found his own age less than admirable; indeed, in his art he seldom depicted the nineteenth century, preferring to let the eighteenth century carry his message. His history was personal, not institutional. The individual did matter, and Pyle's America is most clearly seen in his sturdy yeoman. In the simple dignity of his characters the artist's love of country is revealed.

Howard Pyle emerged at a critical time in the development of American illustration. Rapid changes in the publishing industry during and following the Civil War had encouraged the new family-oriented magazines, including *Century Illustrated, Scribner's Magazine, Collier's Weekly, St. Nicholas,* and the several Harper's publications. The increased demand for illustration found a ready supplier in Pyle. By the eighteen-nineties, American illustrators not only rivaled their English counterparts; they also saw themselves as part of the vanguard of American art. Pyle took part in this burst of cultural nationalism. In his brief New York apprenticeship he had enjoyed the companionship of William Merritt Chase, Walter Shirlaw, J. Alden Weir, and other young artists who expressed a desire to found a native school of painting. Pyle's removal to Wilmington did not lessen his enthusiasm, and he continued to see in illustration an opportunity to force European recognition of the vitality of American art. Despite his obvious debt to European painting and drawing, particularly English and German illustration, it is significant that Pyle made no effort to visit Europe until 1910, when his doubts about his mural painting suggested a trip to Italy. This concern for distinct American art was not unique to Pyle. More than a half century before, the Hudson River painters had sought a uniquely American expression in their landscapes, and one is reminded of the poet William Cullen Bryant's admonition to Thomas Cole to "keep that earlier, wilder image bright," as the artist prepared to leave for Europe. And the so-called "Ash Can" painters, contemporaries of Pyle, professed their own stout Americanism.

Howard Pyle went a step further, however. In 1894, his desire to influence American art led him to Drexel Institute in Philadelphia, where he began his teaching career. Instantly popular, Pyle eventually found the classes too large, the students too raw. He wanted to concentrate his influence on a few talented individuals and not dilute his effectiveness through general teaching. The establishment of his own school in 1900 allowed Pyle to control the size and quality of his classes, and the Howard Pyle School of Art, at Wilmington and Chadds Ford, remains his most serious effort at shaping the development of American art. "For I believe that the painters of true American art are yet to be produced," he wrote his friend Edward Penfield. "Such men as Winslow Homer and [George] Fuller in figure painting, and a group of landscape painters headed by George Innes as yet are almost the only occupants of the field. To this end I regard magazine and book illustration as a ground from which to produce painters."

The success of the school during its half-dozen years of existence cannot be questioned. With almost no excep-

tion the Pyle students looked back upon those years with great fondness, as an experience of both artistic and personal significance. No tuition was charged, but all shared the basic expenses and contributed to the upkeep and management of the school, and this arrangement added to the camaraderie. Support from fellow students and the inspirational criticism of Howard Pyle compensated for the long hours at the easel, and the knowledge that more than a few of the students had already received commissions for illustration work provided further encouragement. Group activities and the familial atmosphere of the Pyle home diminished whatever homesickness existed. Pyle was at his best with this small, talented and congenial group of men and women. Not only did he succeed in training a generation of first-rate illustrators, but these early years of the twentieth century witnessed some of his own best work. In addition, the students soaked up the rich atmosphere of the region and learned to share the historical themes that fed Pyle's imagination. Pyle's own intimate knowledge of the American Revolution often served as a source for the students' work, and several of the most talented turned out promising historical works of their own during this time. Frank Schoonover's early works, Stanley Arthur's "General Harrison and Tecumseh at Vincennes," and the many historical themes captured by N. C. Wyeth's remarkable brush, reflect Pyle's influence. Some of the students emulated the master's style as well, although Pyle, aware of this tendency, always encouraged "individual vein and peculiarity."

Still, one detects a Howard Pyle mold. His reputation and forceful personality, the shared intensity of living and working at the school, and, above all, the conscious process of student selection all encouraged a similarity of viewpoint. The students shared a common faith in realism as the basis of art; they also agreed with Pyle's optimistic, uncritical acceptance of his country. They took America as it was and found the source of its greatness in its past. They viewed the world in simple terms. The simplicity and the faith they took from Pyle have remained the basis for the popularity of both Pyle and his students.

In one way, the Howard Pyle School of Art did not succeed. Whatever its influence on American illustration, it ultimately made but a faint impression on the mainstream of American art. American art changed rapidly after 1900. Impressionism had mounted only the first assault on the realist tradition which Pyle revered. New illustrators challenged Pyle's position, and even his own students began to compete with him. Public taste demanded new illustrative styles, and perhaps Pyle himself no longer found the necessary challenge in his work. Pyle undoubtedly sensed these changes, for in the last years of his life he attempted to reach out in new directions. His brief stint as art director for *McClure's Magazine,* weekly lectures at the Art Students League in New York, and his immersion in public murals, suggest a need to extend his influence in new ways. None succeeded. His five-month relationship with S. S. McClure failed disastrously, and it was his own dissatisfaction with his murals that led to his fatal trip to Italy.

To leave Howard Pyle on a note of despair, even of failure, is to do him a grave injustice. Twenty-five years of prominence as a writer and illustrator, several dozen successful students, and the enduring popularity of his work tell us something different. His illustrations spoke to the America of his day, and they still speak to us. The world Howard Pyle painted mirrored the secure middle class he came from. In his historical illustrations, which made up almost a third of his life's work, one finds a moral, stable world, based upon the goodness of man. Sober Quakers, rugged colonists, enduring patriots displayed a virility and self-reliance that reassured an age struggling with social turbulence. By focusing on the virtues of the past, Pyle asked his viewers not to lose faith in the future. The spirit of the nation, of the people would prevail. Howard Pyle exhibited a Rooseveltian enthusiasm about America, a sense of adventure, a confidence and pride that was deeply rooted in the nineteenth century. A generation that had harnessed the industrial revolution, and extended American influence across the Pacific sought a link between its heritage and its destiny. Howard Pyle did not disappoint it.

Malcolm Usrey (essay date 1983)

SOURCE: "A Milestone of Historical Fiction for Children: 'Otto of the Silver Hand'," in *Children's Literature Association Quarterly,* Vol. 8, No. 2, Summer, 1983, pp. 25-26, 34.

[*In the following essay, Usrey considers* Otto of the Silver Hand *a groundbreaking historical children's novel because of its development of believable characters and its historically accurate rendering of dialogue and setting.*]

Along with Mark Twain's *The Prince and the Pauper,* Howard Pyle's *Otto of the Silver Hand* is one of the first historical novels written for children by an American. It is also one of the most remarkable, and it set the standard for many novels written since. There are two kinds of historical novels: those using both actual and fictional historical events and people, and those that use a historical period with fictional people and events. With the exception of Rudolph I and King Ottocar of Bohemia, there are no actual historical people in *Otto of the Silver Hand;* but that *Otto* is more fiction than history does not lessen its significance. It has all the marks of a good historical novel: it has an exciting plot, with ample conflict and believable characters; it uses language and dialect appropriate to its setting and the characters; it has a significant, universal theme, and it presents the details of daily life in Germany of the thirteenth century accurately and unobtrusively, making the period real and alive.

The conflict between the feuding houses of Baron Conrad and Baron Henry, and the conflict between good and evil represented by the church and by the robber barons, generate the action and suspense of the novel. It focuses on the boy Otto, the innocent victim of the feud and the hope of a brighter, less cruel world, a hope nurtured by Otto's early years with the monks at St. Michaelsburg. Steeped in the plots of traditional folktales, Howard Pyle had learned well how to construct a story that would keep readers, young or old, swiftly turning pages "to see what happens next." Pyle is especially effective in creating suspense in the episodes in which Baron Henry burns Drachenhausen, in which One-eyed Hans rescues Otto from Trutz-drachen, and in which Baron Henry cuts off Otto's hand.

The characterization of *Otto* also seems to be modeled on traditional folktales. Nearly all the characters are all good or all bad; only Baron Conrad and One-eyed Hans have both good and bad traits. Pyle has portrayed the problem of good and evil on a symbolic canvas, flattening most of the characters and aligning them on the side of good or evil.

One of the problems all historical novelists have is to create a reasonable facsimile of the language suitable to the time of their settings that will still be comprehensible to their readers. A writer cannot recreate the language of a specific period, certainly not that of thirteenth century Germany; but if he wants to convey the mood and flavor of a particular historical period, he cannot use completely contemporary language. On the other hand, too many "quotha's," "beset's," and "eldritch's" will destroy a period mood and flavor. Pyle seems to have struck a happy mean in *Otto of the Silver Hand;* the language is neither too contemporaneous or too archaic. The speech of his characters is somewhat formal by our standards. As Baron Conrad bids his goodbye for the last time, he says, "My little child, try not to hate thy father when thou thinkest of him hereafter, even though he be hard and bloody as thou knowest." And a little earlier, he says to One-eyed Hans, "Then take thou this child, and with the others ride with all the speed that thou canst to St. Michaelsburg. Give the child into the charge of the Abbot Otto. Tell him how that I have sworn fealty to the Emperor, and what I have gained thereby—my castle burnt, my people slain, and this poor, simple child, my only son, mutilated by the enemy."

Ideally, themes of historical novels should reflect truths valid for both the time of the story and for the present time. The theme of *Otto of the Silver Hand* was as important to its time as it is for ours. When Drachenhausen is rebuilt, Otto places beneath the scutcheon over the great gate a new motto for the Vuelphs: "Better a hand of silver than a hand of iron." The novel deals majestically with the theme expressed in this last sentence. It might be reworded, "Better kindness than cruelty," though Pyle's version is more richly connotative and perhaps more reflective of the time and temper of the story. Throughout the story, Pyle has shown the results of both cruelty and kindness, particularly by the contrasts between the evil in the feud between Baron Conrad and Baron Henry and the goodness, kindness, and enlightenment of St. Michaelsburg. Most of all, the theme reflected in the character of Otto, whose right hand is literally and symbolically one of silver. Otto embodies the goodness and kindness he learns in his twelve years at the monastery, and he carries these virtues with him to the world of the robber barons and their feuds. With his silver hand, he brings peace and harmony to the world of the robber barons and finally unites the two feuding houses by marrying Pauline, the daughter of Baron Henry, who cut off his real hand and killed his father.

Among the primary requisites of historical fiction is that it make the period of the setting real and alive for readers. Readers should come away from a historical novel knowing how people dressed, what they ate, how they ate, slept, and worked—all the myriad details of daily living that make the past alive. But the historical data are secondary and must be worked naturally into the story, for the function "of a historical story is not to present the facts of history in readable form, but in going beyond historical data," to help us see and understand the past. In *Otto of the Silver Hand,* Howard Pyle fulfills this requirement of good historical fiction. "Through his reading and study he has absorbed medieval records and has made for himself a medieval world in his mind in which he is at home." Details from his great store of knowledge of the Middle Ages are so naturally a part of Otto that a reader is hardly aware of his or her absorption of them. When readers finish the novel they have seen and heard "in winter time the howling wolves cours[ing] their flying prey across the moonlit snow and under the net-work of black shadows from the naked boughs above." And they have witnessed the cruelty and savagery of medieval evil and the sweetness and light of medieval kindness and compassion. Pyle's intimate knowledge of the Middle Ages is broad enough to make Otto stand out as more than just a good historical novel.

The concrete realism of Pyle's depiction of medieval life is particularly impressive. Elizabeth Nesbitt says, "Pyle's scruples as to the susceptibilities of children did not prevent him from revealing some of the harshness of life in the Middle Ages, its ugliness as well as its beauty, and the result is a great book." Henry C. Pitz agrees:

> the book, published in 1888, was a clean break with the still prevailing reluctance of writers to deal with brutality and evil in books for children. It was Pyle's first contribution to historical fiction for children, and it was a bold one. It appeared at a time when, with only the fewest exceptions, children's authors timidly circled away from the bitterness of life or threw a veil over it.

Though somewhat mild in comparison with some parts of the novel, Pyle's description of breakfast in Castle Drachenhausen is hardly veiled:

> the long, heavy wooden table [was] loaded with coarse food—black bread, boiled cabbage, bacon, eggs, a great chine from a wild boar, sausages, . . . and flagons and jars of beer and wine. . . . Four or five slatternly women and girls served the others as they fed noisily at the table, moving here and there behind the men with wooden or pewter dishes of food. . . .

Pyle does not picture life in the castle as very easy, but life in the peasants' huts was even less pleasant and not at all picturesque:

> Fritz, the swineherd, sat eating his late supper of porridge out of a great, coarse, wooden bowl; wife Katherine sat at the other end of the table, and the half-naked little children played upon the earthen floor. A shaggy dog lay curled up in front of the fire, and a grunting pig scratched against a leg of the rude table. . . .

Nor does Pyle shun the horror of death by crossbow: "There was a sharp, jarring twang of the bow-string, the hiss of the flying bolt, and the dull thud as it struck its mark. The man gave a shrill, quavering cry, and went staggering back, and then fell all of a heap against the wall behind him."

Pyle's equally impressive descriptions of Castle Drachenhausen and of St. Michaelsburg reflect the most distinctive quality of the novel, the contrasts Pyle built it around. Pyle's language in describing the castle connotes darkness, hardness, massiveness, and coldness, and suggests a furtively evil isolation. His repetition of hard k's and g's reinforces his connotations:

> up from the gray rocks, rising sheer and bald and bare, stood the walls and towers of Castle Drachenhausen. A great gate-way, with a heavy iron-pointed portcullis hanging suspended in the dim arch above, yawned blackly upon the bascule or falling drawbridge that spanned a chasm between the blank stone walls and the roadway that ran winding down the steep rocky slope. . . . Within the massive stone walls through which the gaping gateway led, three great cheerless brick buildings, so forbidding that even the yellow sunlight could not light them into brightness, looked down, with row upon row of windows, upon three sides of the bleak, stone courtyard.

Pyle's picture of St. Michaelsburg connotes light, peace, harmony, and suggests a kind of sunny openness. Pyle's repetition of soft s's helps to create the mood of quiet peace the passage suggests:

> St. Michaelsburg, rising from the reedy banks of the stream [the Rhine River], sweeps up with a smooth swell until it cuts sharp and clear against the sky. Stubby vineyards covered its earthy breast, and field and garden and orchard crowned its brow, where lay the Monastery of St. Michaelsburg— *'The White Cross on the Hill.'* There within the white walls, where the warm yellow sunlight slept, all was peaceful quietness, broken only now and

then by the crowing of the cock or the clamorous cackle of a hen, the lowing of kine, or the bleating of goats, a solitary voice in prayer, the faint accord of distant singing, or the resonant toll of the monastery bell from the high-peaked belfry that overlooked the hill and the valley and the smooth, far-winding stream. No other sounds broke the stillness, for in this peaceful haven was never heard the clash of armor, the ring of iron-shod hoofs, or the hoarse call to arms.

In *From Primer to Pleasure in Reading*, Mary F. Thwaite suggests that Pyle "brought new renown to the craft of historical fiction for youth with . . . *Otto of the Silver Hand*." Pitz says that in this book, Pyle turns "his back upon the clichés and sweetly doctored prose of the great bulk of late Victorian children's literature. The book marked a turn of taste and conception." Historical fiction is certainly richer because Howard Pyle wrote *Otto of the Silver Hand*.

Alethea Helbig (essay date 1983)

SOURCE: "Winsome Period Pieces: The Poetry of Howard Pyle," in *Children's Literature Association Quarterly*, Vol. 8, No. 2, Summer, 1983, pp. 28-32.

[*In the following essay, Helbig examines Pyle's significant body of children's poetry.*]

Howard Pyle stands among the most influential illustrators in the history of literature for the young in America, and he is remembered also for his retellings from oral tradition, literary fairy tales, novels, and numerous essays. Few people recall, however, that Pyle also wrote poems intended for children. Yet he produced some four dozen poems for the young and it was through a poem for children that he first broke into print.

After Pyle's school years were over and he had entered the family leather business, he spent many happy hours writing and sketching for his own enjoyment. One of these products of his leisure time was a short, amusing, story poem called **"The Magic Pill,"** which his mother, an intelligent, well-read woman, thought had possibilities for publication. To the Pyles' delight, the poem was accepted, and in July of 1876, **"The Magic Pill"** appeared in the "Bric-à-Brac" section of *Scribner's Monthly*, together with the skillful sketches that Pyle had fashioned to go along with it. No literary giant nor even a gem, **"The Magic Pill"** is a momentarily intriguing story in verse, with a clever twist in plot and an underlying shot at human frailty. The poem tells how Parson Cook "in New England a long time ago" attends a dying, old woman, who is rumored to be a witch. She gives him a pill that will grant one wish. That night, while sitting by the fireside with his wife, the Parson reflects on the discomforts of growing old:

> He fingered the pill, and he sighed,
>   and said he,

> "There is something quite wrong
>   in our poor mortal life.
> If *I* had arranged it, it surely would be,
> That age should not have all the
>   bitterest strife.
> Ah me!" sighed the Parson; "I wish
>   I were young;"
> And the little round pill glided over
>   his tongue.

Since Parson Cook fails to indicate how young he chooses to become, he decreases steadily in age as the poem progresses, turning into a mischievous and disagreeable boy, and finally into an equally unlovable baby, who, mercifully for those with whom he lives, expires in a fit of colic.

In spite of technical faults like padded lines, unnecessary inversions, clichés, and too deliberate archaicisms, the poem proceeds with a buoyancy and an affection for subject, audience, and life that offset its awkwardness and its underlying didacticism. As a youth, Pyle had read, among others, the tales of the Brothers Grimm, the stories of King Arthur, Joseph Ritson's ballads, and Thomas Percy's *Reliques of Ancient English Poetry*. In **"The Magic Pill,"** he gives evidence of responding to the spirit of these old, orginally oral stories. In fact, **"The Magic Pill"** reveals qualities that are to appear over and over again in his subsequent poems: the reliance on old stories for ideas; the ability to tell a good story well and with clarity, the ability to paint pictures with words; careful attention to details; the use of the medieval and early American periods for settings; technical shortcomings that result in verse rather than true poetry; and the inability to resist taking advantage of the opportunity to moralize or at least give gentle advice. Already in **"The Magic Pill,"** Pyle shows the felicitous combination of romanticism and realism that his biographers, Abbott, Nesbitt, and Pitz, find so striking in his prose work. Pyle's ability to create that same happy combination in his poems gives the best of them great charm, and draws attention away from their technical limitations and lack of orginality.

Over the next few years, Pyle published several poems in *Harper's Weekly* and in *Harper's New Monthly*. These are mostly full-page, hand-lettered productions, upon which Pyle no doubt lavished many hours of painstaking effort. Four of them are set in the out-of-doors, drawing their inspiration from nature.

The musical, static **"The Sea-Gull's Song"** depends upon the accompanying illustration for much of its meaning and effect. A young woman sits alone by the seashore, pensively watching a sea gull soaring overhead, and wonders what message the gull may be bringing her:

> Does it speak of a lover that sails to me
> From over the misty, wonderful sea,
> With gold and silver, and silks that shine,
> To make me, perhaps, a lady fine?
> What does the sea gull say?

In the last stanza, she answers her own questions:

> A sailor lad is sailing so free,
> And the wealth he brings is his heart to me.
> This does the sea gull say.

This rather uninspired little poem does contain one fairly evocative image, that of the "restless, heaving sea."

"The Robin's Vesper" takes place at twilight, while frogs are piping and small birds seek rest. The robin voices his appreciation of the waning day, leading the speaker, according to the illustration a young woman, to proclaim,

> So I'd have my Soul to be.
> Singing clear
> Thro' the near
> Shadow of Eternity.

Just as romantic, just as commonplace, and even more sing-songy, is **"The Milkmaid's Song."** A milkmaid pauses by "the light of early day" to express her joy for the new day, concluding with a metaphorical observation:

> And so too life in its dawn of spring,
> Is rich with the promises it doth bring;
> What time Love comes like the sun of May,
> And brightens its dawn to a fuller day.

"The Song of the Whippoorwill" exudes an eerie and ominous tone, the only one of Pyle's poems that seems to envision the potential for evil in the world. To judge by the illustration, the speaker is one of two children who meet an old woman, called a witch in the poem, and poke fun at her.

> Then her eyes gleamed green and cold
> Like a serpent's in its wrath,
> While sang the Whip-poor-Will.
> "Whip-poor-will,
> Whip-poor-will."

Later the speaker reflects that the look of the witch made him "deathly chill," and "at dead of night I see her gloat/and hear that bird its lonely note," and is filled with dread. The twice-repeated description of the whippoorwill, creates a shivery, foreboding feeling that lingers in the mind:

> That witches' bird that silent flits,
> Thro' the dark, or crouching sits,
> And sings its song of omen ill,
> "Whip-poor-Will,
> Whip-poor-Will."

Two other early poems were the result of Pyle's deep and abiding interest in American history. **"Tilghman's Ride from Yorktown to Philadelphia,"** a long, stirring narrative poem in the vein of Longfellow's "Paul Revere's Ride," appeared in *Harper's New Monthly* in November of 1881, commemorating the victory over Cornwallis one hundred years earlier. In anapestic couplets, Tilghman gallops northward through an anxious countryside spreading the joyful news of the American victory in the war for independence:

> each muscle and vein
> Of his charger knots with the nervous strain
> As, with head stretched forward and streaming mane,
> It bends to the pace, its nostrils red,
> And flecks of foam on its breast and head,
> Galloping free, with the ringing sound
> Of iron hoofs on the solid ground.
> As they flash like a bolt past the eager crowd,
> The horseman rises and shouts aloud—
> While the Tories cower and slink away—
> "Cornwallis is taken at York today!"

The last line is a several-times-repeated refrain which adds to the unity and increases the patriotic air. Here, too, appears evidence of Pyle's fidelity to detail and his remarkable skill at capturing in words the pictures he saw in his head.

While **"Tilghman's Ride"** is a serious poem, **"Washington's Birth-Day,"** published in the first president's one hundred fiftieth year, lightheartedly records how our ancestors celebrated their repected leader's birthday. This long story-poem describes how young Jared Judd "in his Sunday best,/ With light blue coat and figured vest,/ And splatterdashers to the knee,"/ picks up his sweetheart, Patience, and carries her to town with him "pillion nigh" "on the dapple gray." The two pass butchers' stalls, thrill to the fifes and drums "playing loud," and observe

> the train-band stout
> All step about with measured tread,
> While Captain Green gives orders out,
> And marches boldly at their head.

Judge Dean "makes a speech" at the "ten-foot speeching-stand":

> Says he, "The train-band men will teach
> Our foes to shun our native land."

Then the cannon goes off, scaring Patience, who catches

> At Jared's arm and shook for fear;
> And so he took her by, and bought
> Her cooky-cakes and ginger-beer.

Holiday, and story, end on a romantic note, as

> He took her home, and said good-by,
> And kissed her near the garden gate.

Here are pleasing storytelling, a strong sense of scene, and gentle, good humor.

While these poems were coming out, Pyle was also working on a book he had long wanted to write, the product of his childhood reading in Percy and Ritson. *The Merry Adventures of Robin Hood* was published in 1883. Interspersed among the action-filled, good-humored exploits of the valiant fellowship of loyal bowmen are a dozen and a half poems, whose music and subject support most happily the stories' atmosphere of merriment and conviviality. These melodic, sometimes rousing verses are largely of Pyle's own invention, but a dip into Percy and Ritson quickly gives evidence that in them Pyle found source material not only for his retellings of the old stories but also for the poems that accompany and decorate them. Pyle himself acknowledges his debt in the preface to *Robin Hood*, where he says,

> There are a whole host of knights, priests, nobles, burghers, yeomen, pages, ladies, lasses, landlords, beggars, peddlers, and what not, all living the merriest of merry lives, and all bound by nothing but a few odd strands of certain old ballads (snipped and clipped and tied together again in a score of knots) which draw these jocund fellows here and there, singing as they go.

The very first poem, for example, the song of the tinker who has in mind to serve a warrant upon the elusive outlaw, is taken *verbatim* from Percy.

> In peascod time, when hound to horn
> Gives ear till buck be killed,
> And little lads with pipes of corn
> Sit keeping beasts afield.

In the long narrative, **"The Wooing of Sir Keith,"** Pyle stays very close to the ballad from the Arthur cycle about the loathly lady that, in Percy, stars Sir Gawain. In *Robin Hood*, the ballad is sung by Arthur the lanner and has a Sir Keith as the leading character:

> But suddenly a silence came
> About the Table Round,
> For up the hall there walked a dame
> Bent nigh unto the ground.
> Her nose was hooked, her eyes were
>   bleared,
> Her locks were lank and white;
> Upon her chin there grew a beard;
> She was a gruesome sight.

After King Arthur, Lancelot, Tristram, and others make excuses for not kissing the ugly creature as she requests, Sir Keith gallantly does so. He thus releases her from the spell into which she has been cast, and gains a beautiful bride with a large dower of land in the bargain.

Pyle relies upon Percy and Ritson for themes, characters, subjects, tone, and style, and sometimes even for lines. His poems tell of a deserted shepherdess, of a knight gone to war, of a maiden who weds a fairy prince, of pining lovers, warbling robins, and bubbling brooks. Some poems are pensive, some bantering, some mischievous, some robust, lusty, and loud. Some are long and detailed, others mere snatches of songs. One can hear the pastoralists from Percy in the conversation poem **"The Loving and the Scornful Maid"**

> HE
> "Ah, it's wilt thou come with me, my love?
> And it's wilt thou, love, be mine?
> For I will give unto thee, my love,
> Gay knots and ribbons so fine. . . ."
> SHE
> "Now get thee away, young man so fine;
> Now get thee away, I say. . . ."

"The Song of the Deserted Shepherdess," sung by the Sheriff of Nottingham's cook, reworks the popular old willow song, most familiar today from *Othello*:

> In Lenten time, when leaves wax green,
> And pretty birds begin to mate,
> When lark doth sing, and thrush, I ween,
> And stockdove cooeth soon and late,
> Fair Phillis sat beside a stone,
> And thus I heard her make her moan:
> 'O willow, willow, willow, willow . . .'.

The poem ends happily, however, when Pyle gives Phillis another lover, Corydon. The last poem in *Robin Hood* improvises melodically on the well-known ballad about Lord Randal:

> 'Oh where hast thou been, my
>   daughter?
> Oh where hast thou been this day,
> Daughter, my daughter?'
> 'Oh, I have been to the river's side,
> Where the waters lie all gray and wide. . . .'

Other verses are sprinkled plentifully with such phrases as "daisies pied," "prithee," and "cowslips fair," and refrains like "hey nonny nonny" and "sing hey my frisking Nan," which evoke the jolly, vigorous, outdoor life and spirit of freedom that characterize the retellings of the old tales.

The poems fit, they belong, and they convince, even though they are often weak in technique. Despite its frequent awkwardness, Allan a Dale's lyric for Queen Eleanor is precisely the right sort of tuneful and romantic song to fall from the famed minstrel's lips at that particular moment in the story:

> Gentle river, gentle river,
> Bright thy crystal waters flow,
> Sliding where the aspens shiver,
> Gliding where the lilies blow. . . .

With two short exceptions, these poems were omitted from the abbreviated version of Robin's exploits published later, *Some Merry Adventures of Robin Hood*. Those who know only this account of the roguish hero's exploits do not miss them, and they are not intrinsic to the enjoyment of the tales. But those of us who grew up loving the original version sense that much of the merriment, and in particular, the color and the texture, have been lost because the poems were left out.

In 1883, not long after **Robin Hood,** Pyle got the idea of composing little "fables" in verse to be decorated with pen and ink sketches. He hoped to complete about fifty of these as a small gift book for the young, perhaps to come out for Christmas the next year. Harper's liked his suggestion, and he set to work writing them. He found the form more difficult than he had expected and finished only about two dozen verses, which were printed in various issues of *Harper's Young People* and were followed by a series of amusing literary fairy tales that he also wrote. The verses are handlettered and inserted into nimble, full-page line drawings, which place the poems in the Middle Ages, and occasionally, in the seventeenth or eighteenth centuries. In 1885, these poems and eight of the fairy tales were published by Harper's in the collection titled **Pepper & Salt, or Seasoning for Young Folk.**

These poems are short narratives, economical of words, whose one or two characters are placed in situations of contrast that lead quickly to an obvious moral that is usually stated at the end. Although the verses make use of the structure and style of the traditional Aesopic fable, they also have affinities to the old folk tales, utilizing their magic, whimsey, and motifs; and they lack the sharp, biting tone of the Aesopic form. Pyle's "fables" in verse are gentle, happy, and filled with fun, and far more entertaining than the true fable.

The first poem, **"Two Opinions,"** which aptly introduces what follows, describes with a bouncing beat two scenes featuring a silly, unthinking magpie, who impulsively jumps to conclusions. Part one, "Ye first opinion," relates how the magpie encounters a signpost and tries to strike up a conversation with it:

> A noisy chattering Magpie once,
> A talking gabbling hairbrained dunce,
> Came by where a signpost stood,
> He nodded his head with a modish air,
> And said, "good-day," for he wasn't
>   aware,
> That the signpost pointing its finger there
> Was only a block of wood.

The magpie chatters on about inconsequential matters, and, taking the post's lack of response as agreement with his observations, concludes that the post is "an intelligent creature that." In the second half of the poem, the magpie comes along during a pouring rain and inquires of the signpost where he may find shelter. Receiving no answer, he observes grumpishly that the post is an utter dolt.

> And flirting his tail he walked away,
> "You'r [sic] a fool." (this under his
>   breath.) [sic]

A "L'Envoy" encapsulates the obvious moral in a tidy, lighthearted couplet:

> The moral that this story traces
> Is—Circumstances alter cases.

Now that he has set the pattern and tone, Pyle romps along with more of the same sort of thing. In **"Ye Song of Ye Foolish Old Woman,"** the speaker observes an aged crone giggling and chuckling with glee as she toils up a very steep hill bearing on her back "a load as heavy as sins in lent":

> "Oh! why do you chuckle, old woman;"
> says I, As you climb up the hill—side so
> steep and so high?"
> "Because, don't you see,
>
> I'll presently be,
> At the top of the hill. He! he!" says she.

The humor of irony continues when the speaker presently observes her descending the hill with groans and moans and inquires why:

> "High-ho! I am vexed,
> Because I expects,"
> Says she, "I shall ache in climbing the
>   next."

The moral appears on banners inserted in the accompanying illustration: "Hope in Adversity" and "Fear in Prosperity."

Another poem tells of three tradesmen, a shoemaker, a tailor, and a baker, who set out to seek their fortunes. The shoemaker soon meets and chooses to settle down with a pretty young lass, and the tailor weds a well-off widow, who keeps an inn. Meanwhile, the baker jogs on, endlessly seeking the fortune that never comes his way. Pyle moralizes good-humoredly in the final lines:

> It is better, on the whole,
> For an ordinary soul,
> (So I gather from this song I've tried
>   to sing,)
> For to take the luck that may
> Chance to fall within his way,
> Than to toil for an imaginary thing.
>   (**"Three Fortunes"**)

In other verses, a tailor, after slaying a mouse, challenges a knight who easily bests him, a dull-witted stork mistakenly delivers a baby prince to a cobbler's house, and a faggot maker, after being granted two wishes by an angel, promptly fritters them away. Pyle asserts in the moral:

> If we had had two wishes, granted by an
>   Angel thus,
> We would not throw away the good so
>   kindly given us.
> For first we'd ask for wisdom, which,
>   when we had in store,
> I'm very doubtful if we'd care to ask for
>   any more.
>   (**"Ye Two Wishes"**)

Another verse tells about a raja who is so intent on obliterating troublesome flies from his kingdom that he neglects his royal duties, loses his throne, and takes to begging to survive, while a particularly amusing one describes the ill-fated efforts of the old woman who unsuccessfully seeks to make a gentleman out of her "beautiful piggy," whose name was James. She fails, of course, "For, whatever his polish might be,/ Why, dear me!/ He was pig at the bottom, you see." Here are tiny stories in verse, lighthearted homilies that lead to quite obvious morals, stated gently at the end.

Two poems strongly recall themes from Aesop. **"Over-confidence"** describes what happens when a proud peacock, basking in the adulation of the townspeople who admire his beautiful plumage, decides to thrill them further with "a touch of my delicate voice." Upon hearing his "squalling,/ And catermawalling," the townspeople thrust "a fingertip into each ear" and beseech him to stop. The moral caps the merriment:

> You see ye poor dunce had attempted
>   to shine
> In a way that was out of his natural line.

Remaking the sour grapes theme is a conversation poem, **"A Disappointment,"** in which a young man is so struck by the beauty of the miller's daughter he has just met, that he promptly asks her to marry him. She thanks him kindly for the compliment, but declines his proposal and informs him that she is already married. Thereupon their conversation ceases, and Pyle describes the youth walking dejectedly away, compensating for his disappointment by listing to himself what he now perceives as gross imperfections in her appearance and behavior:

> "'Tis a bargain of which I am very
>   well rid;
> I am glad, on ye whole, I escaped as
>   I did."

Other poems are spoofs. **"A Victim to Science"** tells of "two wise physicians once, of glory and renown,/ Who went to take a little walk nigh famous Concord town." Along the way these learned gentlemen encounter a crow who is "a-setting on ye ground./ Ye Crow was very, very sick. . . ." The doctors discuss possible treatments, the one advocating pills, the other preferring tonic. While the two physicians argue "long and high, and on, and on, and on. . . . Ye Crow, not waiting for the end, incontently died." Pyle ends the story: "Ye Moral is apparent." In **"Fancy and Fact,"** he pokes gentle fun at the pastoralists (to whom, of course, he was much indebted for ideas and language) in telling the story of a shepherd and shepherdess who "dealt in Arcadee,/ And they were dressed in Watteau dress,/ Most charming for to see." The time of year is spring, and the shepherd catches lumbago and the shepherdess a cold from sitting on the damp ground. Pyle finishes the story, tongue-in-cheek, by drolly observing

> That the Poets often sing
> Of those joys which in the practice

Are another sort of thing.

"A Verse with a Moral But No Name" chides self-styled wise men:

> Down East there dwells a man, and he
> Is asking questions constantly,
> That none can answer, that I see;
> Yet he's a wise, wise man!

In the very last poem in the book, Pyle even spoofs himself. After describing how some wolves devour all but the tail of a tender little lamb in **"Ye Sad Story Concerning One Innocent Little Lamb and Four Wicked Wolves,"** Pyle remarks somewhat ruefully:

> So with me; when I am done,
> And the critics have begun,
> All they'll leave me of my fun
> 'Ll be the tale.

Upbeat in mood, the poems are intended to amuse, to add levity to an existence that even for children might otherwise become humdrum. In the preface to the book, Pyle likens himself to a court jester. For a brief moment, the jester lays aside the trappings of his trade and sits down to explain to his public what he is trying to do with his poems and stories:

> Yet listen! One must not look to have nothing but pepper and salt in this life of ours—no, indeed! At that rate we would be worse off than we are now. I only mean that it is a good and pleasant thing to have something to lend the more solid part a little savor now and then!

The gentle satire and the morals are part of the fun. If one learns a little about life from these story-poems, he seems to imply, well, that is all to the good, but he puts the morals so ingratiatingly and disarmingly that hardly anyone could feel preached at. He so obviously speaks with a twinkle in his eye. The humor of the stories is so uncruel, the language so whimsical, that surely no one could take offense at such mild-mannered didacticism.

Although the poems in *Pepper & Salt* show a polish the earlier poems lack, here, too, many lines are padded, and many words inverted to accommodate the meter or rhyme. Pyle lacked Lear's inventiveness and Carroll's skill with language. Most of the poems roll along on iambs or anapests with predictable rhyme. There is a steady mechanical beat that moves readers quickly through the story. Only occasionally does Pyle vary the rhythm for effect. When he describes how the geese are excited by the newspaper driven by the wind in **"A Newspaper Puff,"** we see their jerky, scared actions and hear their excited hissing and squawking in the short, choppy lines and the clusters of sibilants and dentals:

> Out of wits
> Nearly fell
> Into fits.
> Off they sped,

Helter-skelter,
'Till they'd fled
Under shelter.

But when Pyle is bad, he can be quite bad indeed. Consider the trite phrases and the ridiculous image conjured up in the first stanza of **"Play and Earnest,"** about a playful little breeze that grows into a destructive storm.

Over dewy hill and lea
Merrily
Rushed a mad-cap breeze at play;
And the daisies, like the bright
Stars at night,
Danced and twinkled in its way.

The personified breeze illogically becomes a full-blown tempest only because "it cared to play no longer." Later it flings leaves about and roars "as though with thunder." Logically the storm must either thunder or not thunder. Finally, the storm tears at a tree "Till, at last, it flung it down,/ Stripped, and bare, and torn asunder," and Pyle leaves us to struggle with the ambiguity of the "its."

Pyle was a minor poet; indeed, he was versifier rather than poet, a reworker of themes and forms rather than innovator. But while technically untrue, his verses resound with considerable truth in outlook, tone, atmosphere, and sheer storytelling and picture-making ability. There is about them an innocence and optimism, a zest for living, a faith in people, a good-natured humor, and a love and respect for children that in some measure compensate for their technical limitations, and give them a certain quaint, old-fashioned charm. They are winsome period pieces that cast additional light upon the contribution of one of the most versatile and prolific figures in the history of children's literature.

Jill P. May (essay date 1986)

SOURCE: "The Hero's Woods: Pyle's 'Robin Hood' and the Female Reader," in *Children's Literature Association Quarterly,* Vol. 2, No. 4, Winter, 1986-87, pp. 197-200.

[*In the following essay, May argues that Pyle's depiction of the mythical forest in* The Merry Adventures of Robin Hood *is inclusive of young female readers, unlike other books for children such as* Treasure Island *and* Peter Pan, *where girls are either explicitly left out or serve as young mother figures who perform household duties while the boys have real adventures.*]

Legend tells me that, when Robert Louis Stevenson wrote his *Treasure Island,* he honored his stepson's request that he leave out all women, in order to create a real pirate story. That does not set well with me: a woman, I was once a girl who, like Stevenson's stepson, also sought adventure is drama, in going to another place. But the children's literature of my youth showed me that the places girls usually get to go are not so very far from the stove or the nursery, while boys get to be

shipwrecked, to live as bandits in the forest, or to float down the river with a faithful friend.

I spent my childhood dreaming of forests. I was sure that the woods of my Wisconsin home were perfect for my dreams of Pocahontas; I pretended I was a swamp girl abandoned and left on my own initiative as I explored our swampy marshland. But what literature supported my dreams? Where were the classical girls' stories with heroines living alone in a pastoral world? I grew up before Scott O'Dell started writing, and Wendy of *Peter Pan* was no one I wanted to be. I soon found that females who moved into exciting pastoral places never appeared in my books, that I had to be satisfied with Jo in *Little Women* as my ideal of a spirited heroine leaving home.

Consequently, my adventurous blood and my appreciation for the glories of the forest drew me into Howard Pyle's kingdom of Robin Hood, a bandit of great renown who not only ruled his forest, but who made life as an outlaw seem real, who knew how to find his forest dwelling and who understood the pleasures of a pastoral landscape. The fact that Maid Marian was simply mentioned as Robin's favorite girl whom he dreamed about before becoming an outlaw did not bother me. As a young adventurer used to playing with boys, I could make Robin's world a part of mine, much as Howard Pyle had done.

As a youth Pyle had been introduced to the Robin Hood materials collected by Ritson. As a fledgling artist looking for material, he wrote his mother that he wanted to write stories of Robin Hood for *St. Nicholas Magazine,* because "Children are apt to know of Robin Hood without any clear ideas upon his particular adventures." Seven years later, his **The Merry Adventures of Robin Hood** was published in book form. Concerning Pyle's feat of pulling together his earlier Robin Hood drawings originally published with the serialized stories, Estelle Jussim comments, "Strictly speaking, since the illustrations for **Robin Hood** were designed for periodical publication first, can one say that Pyle was truly illustrating a *book?* Perhaps not in the modern sense, although . . . he did a magnificent job. . . ."

Indeed, it hardly seems possible that Pyle could have lost sight of his forest, of his "merry men," or of his overall mood when writing the various Robin Hood stories. The woods are too firmly established, the adventures too formulated to be mere accident. How did Pyle establish a woods, found only by Robin and his fellows, that lasted in the hearts of real boys and at least in one case, real girls, for years to come?

The reader must begin with Pyle's "Preface" in order to understand that this American author was both systematically developing a very real setting and conjuring a mystical woods. Pyle wrote:

Here you will find a hundred dull, sober, jogging

places, all tricked out with flowers and what not, till no one would know them in their fanciful dress . . . wherein no chill mists press upon our spirits, and no rain falls but what rolls off our backs . . . where flowers bloom forever and birds are always singing . . . and ale and beer and wine (such as muddle no wits) flow like water in a brook.

Already Pyle has told the reader what it is that makes his woods a ritualistic place which glorifies the pastoral life: Pyle's woods will be full of tricks performed by nature and by Robin's band, it will have perfect weather, and it will resound with feasting. By the end of the first half of *The Merry Adventures of Robin Hood,* Pyle has established his forest. It is this part of the book which Pyle used to set the mood and action. And it is this part which inspires boys to play at being Robin Hood.

Robin Hood is a strong male leader in this book. He is not bothered with women (though he promises not to harm them), and he is not subject to anyone else's dictates (though he claims loyalty to the king). Yet, his role as leader does not evolve from his ability to win fights. Prior to Robin's adventure out of the forest to visit London, he has been involved in four battle scenes with another man, and in each our hero loses. What makes Robin a leader is his "good sweet nature" and his ability to create a world so serene that neither the weather nor the men under his rule sour into rage or battle. All the fighting happens outside of Robin's realm.

Pyle describes Robin's fights as "merry" adventures or "lusty" encounters. He begins by describing the weather and the greenwood forest, the birds singing in the trees, the peacefulness of Robin and his men in their glen. He allows Robin to venture out on his own, always reminding the reader that Robin is carrying his trusty horn just in case he can't handle his problems by himself. Once Robin sees and talks to his opponent, he challenges him to hand-to-hand combat—a not very wise decision, since he has never won in the past—and a fight ensues. Pyle tells the reader each time that Robin fought well, and then he has Robin use his trusty horn to call reinforcements. Once Robin is saved, he commends his opponent, identifies himself, and asks his adversary to join his forces. Little John demands that Robin further prove himself in a shooting match before he joins forces, but all the others ask for instant acceptance into the clan. Once the offer to join is accepted, the merry men return to the glen and feast in celebration. These repeated actions create a routine for the band of robbers, one that is adventurous but predictable and one that is episodic.

Pyle used more than a pattern of episodes in his stories; he ritualistically employed words in the woodland scenes to establish the romantic setting as both real and symbolic. In the scenes depicting Robin's cudgel battles, for example, Pyle used the words "lusty," "tough," "stout" to describe all the opponents except Robin's cousin Will Scarlet. In the episodes of the first three defeats Pyle described Robin and his men as full of mirth and laughter. All the victorious fighters except Little John tell Robin that they have heard of his adventures. The Tinker joins Robin because he professes to love "a merry life," and he continues, "and I love thee, good master, though thou didst thwack my ribs and cheat me into the bargain." Young Will Scarlet says he has been seeking Robin Hood so that he might join his band, and adds, "I make my vow, had I known who thou wert, I would never have dared to lift hand against thee this day. I trust I did thee no harm." When Friar Tuck finds out that it is Robin Hood he has defeated, he apologizes, saying, "I ha' ft heard thy name both sung and spoken of, but I never thought to meet thee in battle. I crave thy forgiveness, and do wonder not that I found so stout a man against me." All, then, profess to be familiar with the early folk ballads which are the storehouse of Robin's activities.

On the practical side, Pyle has shown Robin's band as a united group of "lusty" fellows. In the case of the four battles, each of the victors is surrounded by Robin's men, so inevitably they *must* join the band if they hope to live. Probably the Tinker's comment that Robin is a "slyer man than I" is more honest. Yet it is a quick comment, never played upon in later encounters. The word "sly" is not one which Pyle uses when describing this band of robbers. Repeatedly he describes them as "merry," "sweet," "gay" and "stout" fellows, implying that they are fun-loving, fair playing, honest men. Even the robbing scenes are described as fair, with Robin playing host at "robbing feasts."

One such scene is described as so pleasant that the "guests" forgot their troubles and "laughed aloud again and again." Indeed, those who rob in Sherwood Forest do it in a ritualistic fashion. They only entertain those wealthy enough to have many riches to forfeit, and they always follow feasting with business matters. They never blindfold those they rob, yet their glen cannot be found by men of law. Only the truly baptized members of Robin's band can wander freely about the woods to return home at the end of their journey.

In fact, Pyle used language and scene to establish Robin Hood as the shepherd of his flock, the savior of the innocent who, once tested and found worthy, are feasted and welcomed into a life free of stress. He carefully created a pastoral scene which supports the antics of a male clan that closely resembles the best of comradeship, of the macho sense of fair play, trickery, and verbal and physical confrontation. Much like children of nature, Robin and his band live in harmony, forced only to while their idle hours away or to seek out adventure. If threatened, these men retreat into the forest. They are symbols of both pastoral freedom and fair play. J. W. Walker calls Robin Hood "the English ideal of the Middle Ages at its best and sweetest," and explains that Robin displayed the "simple and manly courtesy" typical of the English countryman who remains "sportsman to the backbone, gentle to all, servile to none."

Pyle's continual use of "merry" when describing the woods and the outlaws implies more than laughter. It implies a natural system kept in check by a code of honor and good weather. Furthermore, the scenes of Robin's adventures in the woods occur most often in May or early autumn; they never occur in winter. Robin's men are never seen as hungry, cold thieves. There is no real social bite to their thieving. These merry men are fun-loving boys who somehow keep the larder stocked. And, though Robin Hood talks of adventuring to "find sport," there are not many scenes of robbing feasts. But that does not mean that there is not a good deal of eating to be done. Like all growing boys who play hard, Robin loves to eat. Thus, while traveling on the outskirts of his forest, Robin says, "I would that I had somewhat to eat. Methinks a good loaf of white bread, with a piece of snow-white cheese, washed down with a draught of humming ale, were a feast for a king." This is a meal of peasant fare. The feasts in the glen sport much more hearty meals. Usually those outlaws not involved in Robin's venture have been hunting and have returned "with a brace of fat does" which are roasted over an open fire. Food and drink give the woods a congenial tone of partying and frolic. For dessert, Robin and his men turn to storytelling and ballad singing. Thus, when the bread, cheese and ale have been consumed Robin opens up the ritualistic entreaty for song, and is answered with a polite acceptance which contains its own entreaty for the merriment to continue. Pyle writes:

> "Now," quoth Robin, "I do feel myself another man, and would fain enjoy something pleasant before going farther upon our journey. I do bethink me, Will, that thou didst use to have a pretty voice, and one that tuned sweetly upon a song. Prythee, give us one ere we journey farther."
>
> "Truly, I do not mind turning a tune," answered Will Scarlet; "but I would not sing alone."
>
> "Nay others will follow. Strike up, lad," quoth Robin.
>
> "In that case, 't is well," said Will Scarlet.

When Robin is lazing about on a bright day with his followers in the glen under the greenwood tree, storytelling abounds, especially from Will Scathelock, who is "as full of tales and legends as an egg is of meat." The men are described as "being carried away by the tale of knightly daring and noble sacrifice." Fighting, singing and eating seem to be the major occupations of Robin and his men. The woods have weather that holds "the freshness of the dawn . . . and the song of the small birds," causing Robin to seek adventure. Almost all of his adventures bring new recruits who are able singers and heavy eaters.

When Robin first sees Friar Tuck seated "with his broad back against the rugged trunk of the willow tree . . . half hidden by the soft ferns around him" he is eating "a great pasty compounded of juicy meats of divers kinds made savory with tender young onions, both meat and onions being mingled with a good rich gravy," and he

is washing it down with "a great bottle of Malmsley." The good friar, once he has finished eating, talks himself into singing in the ritualistic manner so often used by Robin in earlier scenes. Watching the scene, Robin thinks that "this is the merriest feast, the merriest wight, the merriest place, and the merriest sight in all merry England." Pyle's repeated reference to scenes as "merry" creates an atmosphere of play which supports his romantic interpretation of Sherwood Forest.

Discussing the elements found in an all male romanticized scene of fair play and perpetual youth, Northrop Frye says:

> In literature this phase presents a pastoral and Arcadian world, generally a pleasant wooded landscape, full of glades, shaded valleys, murmuring brooks, the moon, and other images closely linked with the female or maternal aspect of sexual imagery . . . . It is often a world of magic or desirable law, and it tends to center on a youthful hero still overshadowed by parents, surrounded by youthful companions . . . . The archetype of erotic innocence is [displayed in] . . . the love of two boys for each other.

Robin's own followers constantly express love for him, and Robin in turn leads them into a fantasy world of youth and freedom where there are no adult concerns. Yet, they are overshadowed by knowing that they do not wish to offend their royal "father," the real ruler of those forests where they play.

This, then, could be *the forest* of my childhood dreams. It is a romantic place where nature is gentle and supportive. If the forest is symbolic of women, and of gentler sex, then the image Pyle provides of it is a positive one. Certainly Robin Hood could not have lived without his murmuring brooks, shaded glades, and moonlit parties.

But while it might be the forest, which makes the adventure possible, as a child I certainly did not wish to be identified with a forest. My nurturing strain was not so strong that I preferred to be Mother Earth. Rather, I wanted to wander with the band of young male rascals who were allowed to playfully hit each other, to climb trees and shoot at deer, to plan parties and to laze around in the shade singing songs and telling stories.

I do not contend that Pyle would have welcomed me into his forest. His sympathies, I am afraid, were closer to Frye's interpretation of the forest scene. His own lifestyle supported a growing macho clan, much like the one depicted in *The Merry Adventures of Robin Hood*. Pyle established an art school in Wilmington. The great master did not want monetary rewards for his teachings, but he did ask for spiritual support from his followers. Almost all of Pyle's art students were male, and almost all wrote glowing interpretations of the Wilmington experience. One student, John Vandercook, wrote:

> Many jolly evenings did we spend before his crackling log fires, eating nuts, telling stories or,

best of all listening to his reminiscences or stories.
. . . How can I tell in words the life of the thirty
or more who lived in these historic, picturesque,
rolling hills . . . . I loved it. And here the teacher
kept his class intact for five glorious summers.
Who of us does not count those as golden days?

Yet, I do not think that Pyle's world will invite boys
alone. I refuse to believe that all the real adventurers
into the Arcadian woods need be boys. Rather, my own
childhood experience tells me that one can see the adventurers as asexual, as those typical early adolescents
not yet interested in erotica.

What might I have seen about Pyle's woods as a child
that enthralled me enough to pique my return as an
adult? Why would Robin Hood appeal to me more than
the heroines found in J. M. Barrie's woods?

In Pyle there are no sex roles to suffer. Pyle's cook is
asked to join the band after he has proven himself in
battle with Little John. No real mention of his cooking
skills is made. Instead Little John proclaims, "thou art
the very best swordsman that ever mine eyes beheld. . . .
What sayst thou, jolly Cook, wilt thou go with me to
Sherwood Forest and join with Robin Hood's band?
Thou shalt live a merry life within the woodlands, and
seven score good companions shalt thou have, one of
whom is mine own self." The true balladeer is the only
person who enters Robin's glade without a fight. And he
is also the only one to marry. Yet, he is accepted into
the band. Robin says, "Truly I do feel my heart go out
toward thee with great love," and Allan a Dale answers
Robin's emotions with a kiss on the hand. Still, it would
never have occurred to me as a youth that this was a
display of erotic innocence. Youngsters of both sexes are
prone to throwing their arms about each other's shoulders and striding down the road as companions in adventure, and with no concern that they might be thought
of as anything other than friends and comrades.

Such a hero as Robin is much closer to my heart than
either of Barrie's two female heroines in *Peter Pan.* A
child dreaming romantically of Pocahontas and the un-
civilized U.S. eastern woods, I had no time for Barrie's
description of Tiger Lily as a "lovely creature" or his
use of broken English as an interpretation of "Indian
talk." A child who dreamed of high adventure in the
swamps, I could not respond to Wendy's games of playing mother at tea parties or her constant cooking, darn-
ing, cleaning, and harping. It was hard enough to take
Jo's constant self-effacing outbreaks in *Little Women,*
let alone remember that the farthest place she ever went
to was New York City, a place easily located on any
globe. Pyle's elusive romantic woods full of adventure
without fear of growing up and facing adult responsibility were much more appealing.

And so, though not a boy at all, I chose to travel into the
greenwood that Pyle established, to watch the birds sing,
see the people pass on their way to the market, watch
Robin's band save their leader in yet another fight, and

finally sit in the dark after a busy day in Sherwood
Forest, watching "crackling fires in the woodlands" with
everyone enjoying "a jolly feast in welcome to the new
members of the band," listening to "songs and jesting
and laughter that echoed through the deeper and more
silent nooks of the forest" until I was too tired from the
fresh air and adventure to stay awake one more moment.
Then, just like all the rest, I would seek my couch and
fall asleep. Is it any wonder that this hero's woods can
beckon a girl as easily as a boy?

Taimi M. Ranta (essay date 1987)

SOURCE: "Howard Pyle's 'The Merry Adventures of
Robin Hood': The Quintessential Children's Story," in
*Touchstones: Reflections on the Best in Children's Lit-
erature,* Volume Two: Fairy Tales, Fables, Myths, Legends, and Poetry, ChLA, 1987, pp. 213-20.

[*In the following essay, Ranta explains why* The Merry
Adventures of Robin Hood *is considered by many critics to
be one of the greatest children's books ever published.*]

If Bennett A. Brockman correctly defines children's literature as "imaginative literature marketed to children
and designed for their amusement as well as their edification," then *The Merry Adventures of Robin Hood*
stands at the apex of children's literature; indeed, the
author-illustrator Robert Lawson once called it "the
most perfect of children's books." It embodies all of the
significant ingredients of a successful story, regardless
of a reader's age. The language befitting the characters
of twelfth century England, the pastoral setting, and the
lyrical tone all elicit the involvement of a reader or
listener. The theme of good triumphing over evil helps
the story fuse into a memorable work of fiction. Moreover, Pyle's picturesque, detailed illustrations add special texture and fabric to the story; Selma Lane writes,
"There are lovers of fine books who feel Pyle's *Robin
Hood* represents the highwater mark of American book-
making."

The folk hero Robin Hood has been celebrated in popular tales and ballads as far back as the Middle Ages.
From this reservoir of unrelated, often conflicting ballads, Pyle, in his own words, "snipped, clipped and tied
together again in a score of knots" stories in a loose
episodic sequence which nevertheless forms an artistic
whole. The book has ten parts, each with two or three
chapters containing numerous single episodes of Robin
Hood's indefatigable courage, unmatched skill at archery, and daring deeds in his quest for justice for the
poor. They depict Robin Hood, the unifying element,
progressing merrily through life from the time he becomes an outlaw in the Prologue until his death in the
Epilogue. While the order of most of the episodes in the
cycle could be shifted without disturbing the sense of
wholeness, there is some progression because additional
characters are added as the story unfolds who then are
involved in later episodes. Also, some sense of chronol-

ogy is achieved by the succession of kings: Henry II, Richard I, and John. The underlying theme of the cycle is the glaring gap between legal and social justice which Robin Hood personally accepts as his life's challenge.

Born in 1853, Howard Pyle had his first success at the age of twenty-three, when *Scribner's Monthly* bought an illustrated story about the annual wild pony roundup on the island of Chincoteague. That same year, 1876, Pyle moved to New York City and took a job with *Harper's,* one of the great magazines of the day. He worked as their visual idea man, his rough sketches being developed by more experienced staff members. But Pyle was dissatisfied with this work, so he spent several weeks working on a melodramatic sketch, **"Wreck in the Offing,"** which publisher Henry Harper reproduced as a double page showpiece in the magazine. As a result, Pyle soon became the most popular and sought-after magazine illustrator in America.

Following this artistic and commercial success, Pyle left New York and returned to his home in Wilmington, Delaware, where he founded the Brandywine School of Illustrators. His school assisted the development of some of America's most renowned illustrators and painters, including N. C. Wyeth, Violet Oakley, Jessie Wilcox Smith, Maxfield Parrish, and Frank Schoonover. Pyle, meanwhile, devoted his free time to working on his epic masterpiece, the retelling and illustrating of *The Merry Adventures of Robin Hood.*

Although Pyle also completed the text and illustrations for such widely known books as *The Wonder Clock, The Story of King Arthur and His Knights,* and *Otto of the Silver Hand,* his work on *The Merry Adventures of Robin Hood* is his main gift to American Literature. Indeed, his Robin Hood is one of the all-time quixotic heroes, at once Sir Lancelot, Cyrano de Bergerac, Don Quixote, Huck Finn, Tom Sawyer—a Medieval English hero with surprising resemblances to the romantic outlaws of legendary America.

The opening sentences of the prologue to *The Merry Adventures of Robin Hood* lyrically sets the stage for this hero:

> In merry England in the times of old, when good King Henry the Second ruled the land, there lived within the green glades Sherwood Forest, near Nottingham Town, a famous outlaw whose name was Robin Hood. No archer ever lived that could speed a gray goose shaft with such skill and cunning as his nor were there ever such yeomen as the seven-score merry men that roamed with him through the greenwood shades. Right merrily they dwelt within the depths of Sherwood Forest, suffering neither care nor want.

It is Robin Hood's skill as an archer that first gets him into trouble with King Henry, and begins the action. At the age of eighteen, Robin unwittingly kills one of the King's deer, reason enough to cause him trouble. But when he kills one of the King's lackeys in the dispute that follows, not only does it make him an outlaw, it fills his heart with despair:

> Robin Hood ran through the greenwood. Gone was all the joy and brightness from everything, for his heart was sick within him, and it was borne in upon his soul that he had slain a man . . . (but) even in his trouble, he remembered the old saw that, "What is done is done; and the egg cracked cannot be cured."

The Sheriff of Nottingham pledges to bring Robin to justice for this dastardly deed done against the King and against the existing order of things—and also, against himself, for the man Robin slew was a relative of the Sheriff. Robin is mortified by his own deed.

> And so he came to dwell in the greenwood that was to be his home for many a year to come, never again to see the happy days with the lads and lasses of sweet Locksley Town; for he was outlawed, not only because he had killed a man, but also because he had poached upon the King's deer, and two hundred pounds were set upon his head, as a reward for whoever would bring him to the court of the King.

Many outcasts from the King's favor gather around Robin and choose him as their leader. They live by a code that deems they help poor people treated unjustly because of the exorbitant taxes, rents and fines levied by the King. In reprisal, Robin levies a toll upon any abbot, knight, or esquire who travels through Sherwood Forest.

In most children's books, there are one or two characters who stand out as memorable; in *The Merry Adventures of Robin Hood,* there are several imposing characters: " . . . Robin Hood lay hidden in Sherwood Forest for a year, and in that time there gathered around him many others like himself, cast out from other folk for this cause and for that . . . all, for one cause or another, had come to Sherwood to escape wrong and oppression." Among this "legion of damned" synonymous with Robin Hood in the annals of classic literature: Little John, Will Stutely, Will Scarlet, Arthur a Bland, Allan a Dale, and Friar Tuck. Each is distinctly drawn—what E. M. Forster called "round characters" as opposed to "flat characters." Their exploits make up the body of the story, in connecting episodes that tell of their merry outrages against the King, the Sheriff of Nottingham, and the existing social order.

Pyle's vigorous illustrations etch the main participants and events in the story into a reader's mind. These illustrations are detailed black and white pen and ink drawings, including many animated full-page plates with decorative borders that reflect Pyle's keen interest in nature, many delightful vignettes and head- and tail-pieces, and many illuminated initial letters. Each illustration enhances character and action, much like a word-picture. The ones of the merry Friar carrying Robin across the water on his back and of Robin on the log bridge looking down at the tall stranger struggling in the water up to his neck among the lily pads reflect the good humor that permeates the stories. Another illustration renders Robin as a Sir Lancelot-like warrior, standing next to a tree with his archery accoutrements strapped to his svelte body. It is a strong yet poetic figure, one which admirably expresses the romance of a warrior steadfast in his resolve to do battle against the forces of evil.

The language that makes up the story is in perfect harmony with the pictures, and often makes pictures itself:

> The day was bright and jocund, and the morning dew still lay upon the grass. Under the greenwood tree sat Robin Hood; on one side was Will Scarlet, lying at full length upon his back, gazing into the clear sky, with hands clasped behind his head; upon the other side sat Little John, fashioning a cudgel out of stout crab-tree limb.

This passage offers a vivid word-picture of this merry band of men relaxing in the idyllic setting of Sherwood Forest on a sultry day, a sort of "laid back" period of peace and restoration before striding forth once again to do battle against the foes who are opposed to better life for all of the people in the King's domain.

If imitation is the sincerest form of flattery, then parody may be the sincerest revelation of the importance of a work of fiction. Even before Pyle adapted them, stories of Robin Hood had been popular enough to parody. Mark Twain, for instance, showed how the fabled adventures of Robin Hood were grist for the individual drives of Tom Sawyer and Huck Finn against the constricture and hypocrisy of small town midwestern life. Although Tom and Huck are equipped with rapscallion qualities, they also manifest some of the positive values Robin Hood represents when they confront oppression. In Chapter Eight of *The Adventures of Tom Sawyer*, Mark Twain writes of Tom roaming through a glen and having illusions of Robin Hood, a scene of childhood fantasy that expresses the need of young people to escape from the literal world of adults:

> He (Tom) said cautiously—to an imaginary company: "Hold, my merry men! Keep hid till I blow."
>
> Now appeared Joe Harper, as airily clad and elaborately armed as Tom. Tom called: "Hold! Who comes here into Sherwood Forest without my pass?"
>
> "Guy of Guisborne wants no man's pass. Who art thou that—that—"
>
> "Dares to hold such language," said Tom, prompting—for they talked "by the book," from memory . . .

As Twain wrote, Tom and his merry band of young friends "would rather be outlaws a year in Sherwood Forest than the President of the United States forever."

High praise indeed by one of America's greatest writers for the ever-appealing Robin Hood material that Pyle would recreate a few years later.

If, as Tom Sawyer seems to do, one considers Robin Hood's exploits as a drive against social and political evil, then it is easy to see connections between the Robin Hood legend and the infamous outlaws who played an intricate part in the settling of the American West. Although most outlaws were involved in their lawless deeds for personal gain, there was a quixotic aura about the actions of some of these legendary personas. History and folklore tell us that some outlaws sensed a calling to aid people who were being coerced by powerful political elements. History tells us that Jesse James and "Billy the Kid" were in opposition to those who would pervert justice for their own personal gain, just as Robin Hood, in the twelfth century, was opposed to King Henry the Second and his repressive reign. In the case of Jesse James, and his brother Frank James, there is historical evidence that they returned to Missouri from the Civil War and discovered their home state overrun by predators of all sorts: carpetbaggers, greedy landowners, and Unionists. Much of this is conjecture, but it is worth considering when discussing the significance of the Robin Hood legend in the American consciousness—a significance implied in Twain's work and stated forcefully by Pyle.

Like all quixotic heroes in literature, Pyle's Robin Hood seems confronted by almost insurmountable forces in his drive for truth and justice. Although the King is the power behind those human forces, the personification of evil for Robin Hood is manifested in the person of Guy of Gisbourne. Robin had heard of Guy of Gisbourne and all his infamous deeds; when he actually meets him in Sherwood Forest, all of the tribulations that have beset Robin seem present in this man:

> . . . he pushed the cowl back from his head and showed a knit brow, a hooked nose, and a pair of fierce, restless, black eyes, which altogether made Robin think of a hawk as he looked on his face. But beside this there was something about the lines on the stranger's face, and his thin cruel mouth, and the hard glare of his eyes, that made one's flesh creep to look upon.

Following this stark characterization is a fight in which Robin Hood slays Guy of Gisbourne. Afterwards Robin becomes an [ally] to King Richard of the Lion's Heart. A favorite of the King, Robin Hood rises in rank to become chief of the yeomen, eventually regaining his rightful heritage as the Earl of Huntingdon. As in many movies and TV shows that express key elements of the American consciousness, one good man and his friends can eventually win out over corrupt, powerful forces.

The Merry Adventures of Robin Hood is still significant reading for children. The prose is such that it would interest even young readers who may not be accustomed to such a florid style; and the simplicity, gaiety, and morality of the story make this an incomparable book for teachers who wish to introduce their students to a classic milestone of children's literature. *The Merry Adventures of Robin Hood* is tasty enough to be palatable in and of itself but also complex enough to be a stepping-stone to many other great books in world literature.

Nevertheless, teachers may be bewildered by the number of collections of Robin Hood stories that are available, even editions of the Pyle version. A recent *Children's Catalog* (1981) lists both Pyle's *The Merry Adventures of Robin Hood of Great Renown in Nottinghamshire* and his *Some Merry Adventures of Robin Hood of Great Renown in Nottinghamshire,* which was adapted by Pyle himself from his longer work; it contains only twelve of the original twenty-two stories, and some of these Pyle shortened or condensed for easier reading, without losing the spirit of his masterpiece of epic re-telling. Nevertheless, the Dover edition of *The Merry Adventures of Robin Hood* is the best choice, for it is an unabridged and unaltered republication of the work originally published by Charles Scribner's in 1883. It includes Pyle's delightful borders for large full-page plates, his pleasing vignettes, and his decorative initial letters, all of which are such an integral part of the total illustration, and all of which were removed in the mutilated and still available 1946 edition. In the Brandywine Edition that Scribner's Sons issued in 1983 to celebrate the hundredth anniversary of the publication of *The Merry Adventures of Robin Hood,* Pyle's work is intruded upon by additional illustrations by former Pyle pupils. Many school versions are cheap substitutions that cheat the students out of a true experience of Pyle's work.

Children should become aware of the living, changing nature of language instead of thinking of it as a static entity; and teachers should use carefully selected pieces of choice literature to develop awareness of these changes. In my own teaching, Pyle's version of the Robin Hood stories has been a key example of such changes, specifically for the Middle English flavoring that Pyle sought to capture.

Yet students today are attuned to the greater dependence of our English upon word order for meaning than was the language of Robin Hood's day. So, Pyle's text may sound somewhat foreign to modern ears and be slower to read than recently published adventure fiction. But since the sometimes archaic language is part of the book's charm and authenticity, it lends itself to reading aloud, at least in part, by the teacher and by better readers in a fifth or sixth grade class. Many of the children will know Robin Hood as a hero, but usually only through screen renditions, lesser versions, or hearsay. Expressive oral reading will convey the spirit of the Pyle version and recreate some of the flavor of the original oral tradition from which the stories stem. I often follow my own presentation of Pyle's version to upper elementary or middle school children, and also to college students in children's literature classes, with a short pre-

sentation of ballads, first some that Pyle used as source material and then other folk and literary ballads, including some modern ones.

I often hear the lament, "Where have all our heroes gone?" Robin Hood is the very definition of the hero for children. He embodies the basic characteristics of the epic hero, those of courage, justice, and control. A book recommended for teaching should always say something important to students at that phase of their lives, and not be assigned merely to prepare them for some future goal in literary experience. Pyle's *The Merry Adventures of Robin Hood* does both. It involves the students in the exploits of an ageless hero of the people and leads them into the study of the ageless heroes like King Arthur, Beowolf, and Odysseus.

In summary, the study of *The Merry Adventures of Robin Hood* provides children with (1) the pleasure of reading a rollicking good adventure story, (2) an introduction to one of the great traditional folk cycles in English literature, (3) an opportunity to weigh values of courage, justice, honor, and loyalty without didactic overtones, (4) some awareness of how their mother tongue has evolved over the centuries, and (5) a natural steppingstone to other great literary experiences.

Writing some years ago in *A Critical History of Children's Literature,* Ruth Hill Viguers said, "Many fine books that deserve to be read generation after generation may be lost in the confusion of pendantry, technology, and good intentions that confounds the mid-century." They plague us even more in the late twentieth century. This must not happen to Pyle's Robin Hood. Children should be encouraged to follow the Piper when Pyle himself in his preface says, "And now I lift the curtain that hangs between here and No-man's-land. Will you come with me, sweet Reader? I thank you. Give me your hand."

In his introduction to the first edition of that same text on the history of children's literature, Henry Steele Commager quotes the great author-artist Howard Pyle himself: "My ambition in days gone by was to write a really notable adult book, but now I am glad that I have made literary friends of the children rather than the older folk. In one's mature years one forgets the books one reads but the stories of childhood leave an indelible impression, and their author always has a niche in the temple of memory from which the image is never cast out to be thrown into the rubbish-heap of things that are outgrown and outlived." *The Merry Adventures of Robin Hood* does leave an indelible impression, Mr. Pyle.

Jill P. May (essay date 1987)

SOURCE: "Howard Pyle's 'The Story of King Arthur and His Knights': A Backwards Look at Chivalry," in *Touchstones: Reflections on the Best in Children's Literature,* Volume Two: Fairy Tales, Fables, Myths, Legends, and Poetry, ChLA, 1987, pp. 221-227.

[In the following essay, May discusses Pyle's reinterpretation of the ancient legend of King Arthur, noting his adept updating and organizing of the tales for children.]

My fascination with Howard Pyle's version of the King Arthur legends began only after I had become an adult, so I cannot claim that I can remember their childhood appeal, and that I am now returning for a look in terms of my adult response. And since Lloyd Alexander once confessed to me that he had *never* read the versions by Pyle, I cannot even say that Pyle has been a direct influence on all later authors of fantasy. Yet I think that Pyle's King Arthur series indirectly established a tradition, for it was the first of many multiple-volumed sequential fantasy tales based upon new interpretations of Arthurian materials. And I believe that modern children's versions of these materials do contain adventures and characters similar to those found in Pyle's story. In fact, Pyle's historically significant role in the continual process of reinterpretation makes the first volume of his series on King Arthur (as well as the following ones) archetypal in children's literature.

Pyle took a backwards look at the old tales and created a new version for his modern audience. He sought to write a tale of Arthur which would be acceptable to his contemporaries. Today I look backwards at Pyle, knowing something about his sources, his plans, and his Arthur, and realize that I am looking at his work as an adult just as the adult Pyle looked at his own source materials when he determined to re-create Arthur for children. Like Pyle, I remember other versions of Arthur, only mine are both older and newer than his.

Northrop Frye once wrote, "We cannot in practice study a literary work without remembering that we have encountered many similar ones previously. Hence after following a narrative through to the end, our critical response includes the establishment of its categories, which are chiefly its conventions and its genre. In this way the particular story is seen as a *projection* of the theme, as one of the infinite number of ways of getting to the theme ("The Road of Excess"). Thinking about that comment I am struck by its similarity to Pyle's own belief in what he was doing with the King Arthur legends, and to his recognition that he was *reshaping* earlier mythic and historic legendary tales, transforming tales of chivalry not yet available to young readers of English either in North America or the British Isles into an American romance.

Pyle had already read much of what was available on Arthur in English; since he took German in grade school and since he owned some reference books in German, it is possible that he had read or heard other versions. Pyle wrote to Edith Dean Weir that there was much in the legends which disturbed him, much he planned to leave out, and went on to say that he hoped to develop a new version which would be enjoyed by his readers. He wrote: I must follow the thread of the better known legends, for it is not advisable for me to draw upon the less well-known narratives. So I try to represent those which are known in the best light.

Earlier, Pyle had woven the remnants of Robin Hood legend into a continual hero story. That book was extremely popular from the day of its release, for heroic legend was in vogue with American audiences. Pyle lived among fanatic readers of Sir Walter Scott; the Waverly novels were popular with the young boys of the Wilmington area. Pyle had probably read Scott's comment that the Arthurian tales were full of "dull repetition and uninteresting dialect" within a "confused story" as well as his judgement that, nevertheless, the stories contained "passages of interest" and "specimens of spirited and masculine writing" ("Essay on Romance"). Aware of Scott's popularity and encouraged by publishers, Pyle began to rewrite the loosely joined Arthurian legends into an easily followed chronological narrative. The episodes he chose are still those most often found in more recent children's versions of the Arthurian tales, and usually, the characters' personalities in these newer fantasies resemble the people in Pyle's version; for these reasons, the books must be considered archetypal in characterization.

The Story of King Arthur and His Knights was the first in a set of four books by Pyle about King Arthur's court and his knights. It sets up all of the patterns now familiar in questing hero stories. As such, it is the groundwork for establishing the courtly intrigue and the final collapse of Arthur's rule which are the subjects of the later books.

Each time Arthur or his knights go to battle during this first book, Pyle describes the countryside and the scene in detail. He sets most of the major battles between knights in glens within a woods, which the knights reach on horseback. The physical battles are not held inside the court; while help is sought from the court, the actual fighting occurs outside of the "civilization" of Arthur's rule. A knight on quest must leave Arthur's rule, travel into the unknown, seek adventure in the name of honor, and return home after an honorable fight. The highest battles are those which are fought to preserve the courtly system, save a damsel from disgrace, or revenge unknightly conduct. The low battles unworthy of glory are those involving power struggles between two knights. A knight will not fight a foe of lesser strength, and he cannot turn down a virtuous maiden's plea for help. In order to keep the peace established after a battle, Arthur takes the favorite son of his conquered enemy with him "to serve in court" (*or* to serve as ransom).

The covenant of the Round Table, Pyle writes, demands of the knights

> That they would be gentle unto the weak; that they would be courageous unto the strong; that they would do terrible unto the wicked and the evil-doer; that they would defend the helpless who should call upon them for aid; that all women should be held unto them sacred; that they would

stand unto the defense of one another whensoever such defense should be required; that they would be merciful unto all men; that they would be gentle of deed, true in friendship, and faithful in love.

Today's fantasy stories based on Arthurian traditions and written for children still contain questing male heroes who are gentle, faithful, true; Pyle did not say that a masculine hero needed to be intelligent, and no demands of intelligence are placed on later male heroes either. Taran, Lloyd Alexander's hero in the Prydain series, begins his quest with no knowledge concerning his adventure, gains friends he would defend at all costs, and in the end says, "I ask no reward . . . I want no friend to repay me for what I did willingly, out of friendship and my own honor." Alexander's hero fits into the code as easily as Pyle's heroes.

But knights are not all alike in Pyle's *The Story of King Arthur and His Knights*. Heroes are clearly differentiated from one another in the Pyle books. Many of these heroic personalities were already defined in the earlier versions, but Pyle reformed them to fit his needs. Within the first volume, for instance, Pyle establishes his character portrayals of Merlin, Sir Pellias, and Sir Gawaine. Each has a unique personality which is based in the earlier legends and is itself the basis for characters found in renditions created after Pyle's series.

Gawaine represents the earthy, hot headed young knight who is at times vain and brutal. The early French romances depicted Gawain as both knightly in battle skills and lascivious and cruel. Pyle realized that in his story of Gawaine, he must explain why so noble a hero would act in less than virtuous ways when dealing with others. He decided to "try to represent Gawaine as proud and passionate, quick to anger, but with a broad basis of generosity and nobility" and admitted that he would "modernize Sir Gawaine." Pyle lets his readers know that Gawaine is a proud young man full of high spirits by describing him as such, and by having the courtly action center on him during a balmy afternoon when he is the "most gayly clad" of the court and is busy entertaining the others with song. Suddenly the queen's favorite greyhound runs in, jumps up and soils Gawaine's clothes. Pyle writes: "At this Sir Gawaine was very wroth, wherefore he clinched his hand and smote the hound upon the head . . .". Thus, Gawaine's high spirits drive him away from the court when he displeases Guinevere. But even the queen does not break his will. Once Guinevere orders him away he complies, saying, "Nor will I return thitherward until thou art willing for to tell me that thou art sorry for the discourteous ways in which thou has entreated me now and other times before my peers." In the end it is a fay who tames Gawaine, with her devoted love. After Gawaine is wedded to duty, Pyle tells the reader, he is one of the most virtuous of knights. Nevertheless, the reader is likely to remember that Guinevere sent him away, and to hold some suspicions that the two are not true friends.

Sir Pellias, on the other hand, foreshadows two knights still to come: Launcelot and Galahad. Pyle calls Pellias "the gentle knight," and has him go questing for Queen Guinevere's sake. He is a noble young man who would hold that the queen's honor is sacred, yet, unlike Launcelot, he would not honor the queen above all womankind, and, unlike Galahad, he would not sacrifice his belief in the powers of the fay in honor of the Christian God. In Pellias, Pyle has established a prototype of the two noblest of knights, and he has given the reader a sense of what it means to be the greatest warrior of chivalry. In this first book, Pellias has fallen in love with a dishonorable maiden who has used magical powers to bewitch him; he is saved by a fay who gives him another magical element, the water of life. Once he receives it, Pellias declares, "Thou hast given life unto me again, now do I give that life unto thee forever." Sir Pellias travels with his companion to the land of Avalon, the self-same land where Arthur will go upon his death. Pellias is a representation of Pyle's own ambivalence concerning the Christian belief in eternity and the Celtic land of death—Avalon. Pyle's story continually brings the best of knights who express the old ideals of chivalry to Avalon. Pellias will be joined by Arthur; Gawaine is married to a fay who chooses to become human for his sake.

The other character who reflects Pyle's modern beliefs is Merlin. In Pyle's version, the magician decides to share his knowledge with Vivien, a decision which Pyle calls a misuse of his God-given powers (*The Story of King Arthur and His Knights*). Part of this may be Pyle's own philosophy; he had earlier expressed a disinterest in training women artists and sought to separate his creative world into two parts, one in which masculine peers worked side by side as artists, and the other the intellectual ambiance of the afternoon soirée attended by both sexes. Considering that, it is difficult when reading about Merlin's failing to decide whether Pyle objects to Merlin's sharing knowledge with Vivien because she is evil, or because she is female.

Pyle's attitude towards his heroines is always interesting; it is both a backwards look at earlier legends and a modernized Pyle interpretation of woman's role in society. His version of the quest valorizes the female as heroine at home or villain when traipsing about the countryside, the male as the quester in journey or the wise leader while at home, and magic as somehow amoral yet most appealing.

Pyle successfully weaves together the Celtic and the Christian tales, but he does it at the expense of his female characters. He chooses to ignore the fact that Arthur is the bastard younger brother of Morgana, and to separate the Lady of the Lake's powers from Morgana's by making the Lady and her fays' motives ambiguous, Morgana's evil. Yet, he has Morgana rule Avalon, and says, "This island of Avalon was a very strange, wonderful land, such as was not to be seen anywhere else in all the world. For it was like a Paradise for beauty. . . . Avalon would float from place to place according to the will of Queen Morgana le Fay, so that sometimes it would be here, and sometimes it would be there, as that royal lady willed it to be." In the end, he has Morgana return for Arthur upon his death and take him away with her to Avalon, implying some kind of sibling tie of loyalty or love. In this first book, however, Pyle calls Morgana cunning, and gives her no real motive for her outbursts of jealousy other than that she wishes to have power over Arthur's kingdom and respect from Arthur. Since the reader has no real knowledge of Morgana's claim to Arthur's throne, she seems petty and mean.

Pyle is not ignoring earlier legend in his retelling. Geoffrey of Monmouth in *Vita Merlin* had described Avalon as an "otherworld" and had named Morgan chief of the land, and Malory had laid most of the blame for the court's failure upon Guinevere, choosing to ignore the earlier legends that made Mordred Arthur's bastard son conceived with his half-sister. While Celtic legend had placed women enchantresses in esteemed positions, there is no evidence that Pyle had read these versions. What Pyle did was to represent "all that is noble and high and great" and omit "all that is cruel and mean and treacherous" in terms of male supremacy and the Christian masculine code of honor. And so, he depicted Morgana as the dark side of religious beliefs representing black magic, and placed the saving Christian graces in the male hero Galahad.

This interpretation is not new with Pyle, but it was solidified in children's literature by him. Pyle's tradition of a series which depicts an evil queen and a gentle but forceful male ruler is seen again in C. S. Lewis's Narnia series, and is also followed in Alexander's Prydain series. The pattern was not to be broken until women fantasy authors such as Cherry Wilder returned to the Celtic legends as source materials for their fantasy series.

Pyle's interpretations of women are never flattering. Even Guinevere is less than perfect. She knows that Arthur is more than a gardener's boy when he appears in her father's garden, and she purposely exposes him to her ladies in waiting. Pyle writes:

> And after that time, whenever the Lady Guinevere would come upon the gardener's lad in the garden, she would say unto her damsel in such a voice that he might hear her speech: "Lo! yonder is the gardener's lad who hath an ugly place upon his head so that he must always wear his cap for to hide it."

> Thus she spake openly, mocking at him; but privily she bade her damsels to say naught concerning these things . . .

Later, when she discovers that he is King Arthur and that she is to be wed to him, she says, "Lord, I am afeard of thy greatness." Pyle has Arthur play the per-

fect courtly gentleman when he replies, " . . . thy kind regard is dearer to me than anything else in the world, else had I not served for these twelve days as gardener's boy . . .".

The women, then, are more ornamental or meddlesome than they are comforting. The only noble spirits in this first volume are the fay, and they are aloof for the most part.

Pyle's Arthurian cycle is firmly established in the first book. He has created a court for his king, has established the women as troublemakers within the court, and has repeatedly shown the conduct of a worthy knight in battle. His choice of ignoring the Celtic and Welsh ideals of women as leaders and spiritual guides, and of showing Arthur as a hero "as pure as snow," probably stemmed from his background reading. He had read Malory and Scott; it is not certain that he read the *Mabinogian.* Even if he had, he knew that youngsters were reading Sir Walter Scott and his version of Robin Hood. His intended American audience, with its full blown optimism and its thirst for heroism, would have been more receptive to a manly version of the quest.

What Pyle established for future writers was a chronological adventure story which wove the various legends into a consistent story. Years later, English reading audiences would not only have newer versions in children's fantasy but also could see theatrical representations of the continuous story in *Camelot* and *Excalibur.* Pyle's books have inspired many young boys to play act knightly quests based, whether they knew it or not, upon his ritualistic pattern. Today's youth use these character types when they participate in Dungeons and Dragons.

Pyle's *The Story of King Arthur and His Knights* was greeted with high praise in his own time. It brought together old legends, and created a romantic adventure that captured the hearts of its readers. Full of jousts and courtly activity, it glorifies an aristocracy based on male honor and feminine beauty. Northrop Frye has called the medieval chivalric romance "a ritualized action expressing the ascendancy of a horse-riding aristocracy," one which "expresses that aristocracy's dreams of its own social function, and the idealized acts of protection and responsibility that it invokes to justify that function" (*The Secular Scripture*). Pyle's turn of the century volumes gave his youthful reading audience that tradition. The entire cycle was strongly conservative in its attitudes. It firmly supported the established code of ethics found within American society. Within his Arthurian cycle, Pyle was able to bring alive the old ideas of a code of honor, of the virtues in serving a worthy cause, and the glories of battle. He also sought to show male readers the pitfalls of putting trust in a woman's advice or becoming too infatuated with the woman you serve (unless she happens to be fay). And so, the questing hero was born in children's literature.

That hero is found several times on the ChLA list of Touchstones. Though he may look slightly different, he can be seen in Lloyd Alexander's books, in C. S. Lewis's Narnia series, and in T. H. White's *The Sword in the Stone.* As part of a literary tradition continuously being reinterpreted, Pyle's first children's version of Arthur is an essential beginning in our understanding of the Arthurian cycle and its significance in children's literature.

Susan F. Beegel (essay date 1993)

SOURCE: "Howard Pyle's Book of Pirates and Male Taciturnity in Hemingway's 'A Day's Wait'," in *Studies in Short Fiction,* Vol. 30, No. 4, Fall, 1993, pp. 535-41.

[*In the following essay, Beegel argues that the presence of Howard Pyle's Book of Pirates in Ernest Hemingway's short story "A Day's Wait" is significant because it serves as a subtext for what Beegel believes is really a story critical of male stoicism.*]

> Beyond the long arm of the Law,
> Close to a shipping road,
> Pirates in their island lairs
> Observe the pirate code.
> —W. H. Auden, "Islands"

The plot of "A Day's Wait" is deceptively simple. A young boy with influenza hears that his temperature is 102 degrees and mistakes the Fahrenheit reading for Centigrade, in which a temperature of 44 degrees is invariably fatal. The boy, called Schatz, spends a day bravely waiting to die before his father discovers and corrects his mistake. Many critics believe that this is all "A Day's Wait" is about, that the discovery of the boy's mistake is the climax of this story, an O. Henry-like "Wow!" at the end that resolves things rather too neatly. Other critics have read Schatz as a miniature code hero, a brave little man holding tight onto himself in the face of death, an innocent version of dissipated Harry in "The Snows of Kilimanjaro," staring at death at the foot of the bed. This is true as far as it goes, and gives real pathos to Schatz's stoic behavior, but it is also a rather unquestioning "boys' book" idea of courage and of this complex short story.

My purpose in this essay is to suggest that the revelation of the Fahrenheit/Centigrade mistake does not resolve the central misunderstanding in "A Day's Wait." Further, I believe that the story actually questions the very values of male stoicism and taciturnity that it seems to extol. *Howard Pyle's Book of Pirates,* the boy's book read by father to son in "A Day's Wait," provides a hitherto neglected allusive subtext that supports these observations, commenting ironically on the story's larger actions.

At the story's conclusion, the father/narrator reveals what he and we as readers have missed: his son has been in mortal terror from the earliest moments of "A Day's Wait." The superficial reason why—the Fahrenheit/Centigrade confusion—is inadequate to explain the story's central problem, Schatz's silent endurance, and the father's blindness to a child's fear.

Look at the multiple levels of misunderstanding inherent in just three lines of a dialogue initiated by Schatz with "You don't have to stay in here with me, Papa, if *it* bothers you" (my emphasis). This is male taciturnity, the code of remaining silent about deeply felt emotions, carried to extremes. Why? Because "it" is death. Simply translated, the boy is saying: "You don't have to stay in here with me, Papa, if *my dying* bothers you." When we remember that Schatz is addressing this sentence to a father who is calmly reading *Howard Pyle's Book of Pirates* and apparently waiting for him to die, this simple statement takes on disturbing dimensions. It becomes a question: "Does my dying bother you? Why don't you seem to be bothered? Don't you love me?" At the same time, Schatz offers to release his father from the necessity of being "bothered," from the extreme demands an emotional deathbed scene would doubtless make on their mutual stoicism.

The father, pleasurably occupied with the boy's book, gives this honest answer: "*It* doesn't bother me" (my emphasis). For the father, "it" means "staying with you." Simply translated: "Staying with you when you're sick doesn't bother me." That's a profession of loyalty and love, but Schatz, for whom "it" means death, hears his father say "*Your dying* doesn't bother me."

Too secure in his father's love to accept this "reading," Schatz assumes a misunderstanding and revises the tense of his speech to address not his present mild illness but his impending death: "No, I mean you don't have to stay in here if *it's going* to bother you" (my emphasis). Translation: "You don't have to stay in here when I *start to die* if *my dying* bothers you." Again, the boy seeks reassurance that his father *is* bothered by his death while offering to release him from that bother.

The obtuse father's response is potentially shattering. Believing that the boy is light-headed with fever, the father does not respond, but simply gives Schatz some pills and leaves on a hunting trip. For the child, his father's departure has only two possible interpretations, and neither is comforting. The exit either means "your dying *doesn't* bother me, so I'm going hunting" (corroborating the worst interpretation of the father's earlier remark), or it means "your dying *does* bother me, so I'm taking advantage of your offer and leaving" (corroborating Schatz's worst fear about his illness).

Hemingway, with his belief in the power of concrete language, knew well how to marry signifier and signified. "Bread is a fine word and still means bread," he would write in an early draft of *Death in the Afternoon,* "wheat means wheat, and cold means cold . . .". In "A Day's Wait," the misunderstanding between father and son results from a culpable failure to make meaning, a failure the more poignant as this confessional short story's father-narrator is presumably Nick Adams, a writer by profession. The road to *aporia* here is paved with indefinite pronoun reference—those shifty "its," signifying nothing, or anything.

The values of "code heroism," of stoic male behavior and taciturnity, are directly responsible for the linguistic and emotional isolation of father and son, for their apparent inability to pronounce words like "love" and "death." It is at this juncture that *Howard Pyle's Book of Pirates* comes into play as an important allusive subtext. The father's choice of the pirate book for distracting and entertaining his feverish child is painfully ironic. Chapter Three of that book, "With the Buccaneers," the story of a boy's first confrontation with death, has some interesting parallels with "A Day's Wait." To date, no critic has examined them.

A plantation owner's son, 16-year-old Harry Mostyn, runs away from home to seek adventure with pirate captain Henry Morgan. The boy accompanies Morgan and a handful of desperados on a cutting-out expedition. They seize a Spanish galleon and endeavor to sail the treasure-laden ship out of a heavily defended harbor. On the way, Morgan engages in desperate combat with a Spanish galley. The Spaniards concentrate all of their musket fire on the pirates' helmsman, and when the helmsman falls, fatally wounded, Morgan roars for someone to seize the wheel and keep the pirate ship from falling off the wind. Our boy-hero obliges:

> In the first moment of this effort [Harry] had reckoned of nothing but carrying out his captain's designs. He thought neither of cannon balls nor of bullets. But now . . . he came suddenly back to himself to find the galleries of the galley aflame with musket shots, and to become aware with the most horrible sinking of the spirits that all the shots therefrom were intended for him. *He cast his eyes about him in despair,* but *no one came to ease him of his task,* which, having undertaken, *he had too much spirit to resign from carrying through to the end,* though he was very well aware that the very next instant might mean his sudden and violent death. His ears hummed and rang, and *his brain swam light as a feather.* (my emphasis)

Thanks to Harry's courage, the pirate ship remains on course, ramming and sinking the enemy galley.

> And now . . . that all danger was past and gone, there were plenty to come running to help our hero at the wheel. As for Captain Morgan . . . he fetches the young helmsman a clap on the back. 'Well, Master Harry,' says he, 'and did I not tell you I would make a man of you?' Whereat our poor Harry fell a-laughing, but with a sad catch in his voice, for his hands trembled as with an ague, and were as cold as ice. As for his emotions, *God knows he was nearer crying than laughing, if Captain Morgan had but known it.* (my emphasis)

In this story Henry Morgan becomes a kind of savage surrogate father to young Harry Mostyn, introducing the boy to the world of piracy and to codes of behavior requiring a man to stand to the wheel in a hail of fire and shrug off his fear with no more comment than a forced laugh.

The father in "A Day's Wait" reads aloud to Schatz from *Howard Pyle's Book of Pirates* twice, both before and after the hunt. As Schatz struggles to confront death bravely, his father is, all unwittingly, catechizing him on courage, urging him to remain stoic and silent. Twice the father stops reading, thinking "I could see he was not following what I was reading . . . ," when in fact Schatz *is* following what his father is reading, following the pirate code of stoicism in the face of death as strictly as he can. We can sense Schatz's hurt when his father tells him to "Just take *it* easy" (my emphasis). The son believes his father is telling him to take *death* easy, which is exactly what he has been trying to do. From Schatz's point of view, his father obviously has not appreciated his courageous behavior.

There is additional irony in the father's sitting at the foot of the bed and reading to himself from *Howard Pyle's Book of Pirates* when he thinks he sees that Schatz is not following. The father becomes so engrossed in the boy's book account of young Harry's fictional courage that he overlooks the genuine courage of his own young son. Easily distracted by accounts of Spanish galleons and piratical doings, the "childish" father unintentionally exposes his own Schatz (Schatz is a German endearment meaning "my treasure") to an appearance of cruel paternal indifference.

At the end of "With the Buccaneers," Harry Mostyn's real father sends for him. A gentleman plantation owner, the real father is half "distracted" by his boy's part in the "terrible bloody and murthering business" of piracy. It is a children's book conclusion, in which young Harry, having undergone a frightening adventure and proved his courage and manliness, is returned safely to the fold of parental love and protection, rescued from the dark fatherhood of Captain Morgan.

"A Day's Wait" seems to have an equally comfortable conclusion. When the boy's confusion about temperature is at last revealed, the boy is restored to the familiar father who treasures and reassures him: "You poor Schatz . . . Poor old Schatz. It's like miles and kilometers. You aren't going to die." He is rescued, in effect, from the dark father who catechized him with pirate stories about being a man and taking death easy, who said things to a sick child that seemed to mean "Your dying doesn't bother me."

Yet despite relief and reconciliation, Schatz's "gaze at the foot of the bed relax[es] slowly." Staring fixedly at the foot of the bed, he is not only staring at the place where death lurked like the hallucinatory hyena that rests its head on the foot of Harry's cot in "The Snows of Kilimanjaro," but also at the place where his father sat reading *Howard Pyle's Book of Pirates,* and then at the emptiness left when his father abandoned him to go hunting, leaving the boy as alone in his wait for death as a pirate's victim marooned on a desert isle. None of these concepts—his own mortality, the piratical code of masculine behavior, his isolation from paternal consolation—is easy for "a very sick and miserable boy of nine years" to shake, and the extent of his trauma is made plain when, the next day, he cries "very easily at little things that were of no importance."

"The boys' books [have] a lot to answer for," asserts Jonathan Raban in *Hunting Mr. Heartbreak: A Discovery of America.* He goes on to deliver a powerful indictment of masculine ideals as espoused by American literature in general, and by Ernest Hemingway in particular:

> American men of my own and Red's generation had been raised on a kind of tribal literature that was a more suitable preparation for life as an Apache brave than it was for husband and fatherhood in the average American suburb. From the moment they could read, their teachers had fed them with Fenimore Cooper, Mark Twain, Hemingway. Out of school, they were suckled on the mythology of the western and the romance of the frontier. Their ideal of American masculinity was pitched somewhere between the characters of Buck Rogers, Harry Morgan, and Huckleberry Finn. Real life, according to these books and movies, always happened out of doors. It was essentially solitary. It was dangerous. It called for self-reliance above all other human qualities. Woodcraft and seamanship would stand you in far better stead than, say, the capacity to express affection. The books and movies heroized the rejection of the domestic life. . . .

Complaints like Raban's are made possible by critics who read "A Day's Wait" as though it were a child's pirate story, or who exclude "A Day's Wait" and other investigations of parenting from the Hemingway canon.

In truth, "A Day's Wait" indicts *Howard Pyle's Book of Pirates* and similar boys' books as poor models for American manhood, and questions the very ideals of masculinity Hemingway is most thought to valorize. Rejecting both Raban's "tribal literature" and its ethos of solitary self-reliance, "A Day's Wait" elects instead to heroize the domestic and explore the painful cost of failing to express affection.

FURTHER READING

Biography

Hawkes, Elizabeth H. "Drawn in Ink: Book Illustrations by Howard Pyle." *The American Illustrated Book in the Nineteenth Century*, edited by Gerald W. R. Ward, pp. 201-31. Wilmington, Del.: Henry Francis du Pont Winterthur Museum and Charlottesville: University Press of Virginia, 1987.
    Summarizes Pyle's life and career with special attention to his artistic techniques, influences, and use of symbolism.

Criticism

Agosta, Lucien. *Howard Pyle.* Boston: G. K. Hall, 1987, 162 p.
    Survey of Pyle's work as a fiction writer.

Nesbit, Elizabeth. *Howard Pyle.* London: Bodley Head, 1966, 72 p.
    Introductory overview of Pyle's work as a writer and illustrator.

Pitz, Henry C. *Howard Pyle: Writer, Illustrator, Founder of the Brandywine School.* New York: Clarkson N. Potter, 1975, 248 p.
    Comprehensive study of Pyle's development and achievements as a writer and artist.

The following sources published by Gale contain additional coverage of Pyle's life and career: *Children's Literature Review,* Vol. 22; *Contemporary Authors,* Vols. 109, 137; *Dictionary of Literary Biography,* Vols. 42, 188; *Dictionary of Literary Biography, Documentary Series,* Vol. 13; *Major Authors and Illustrators for Children and Young Adults*; *Something about the Author,* Vol. 16.

Ethelwyn Wetherald

1857-1940

(Full name Agnes Ethelwyn Wetherald; also wrote under the pseudonym Bel Thistlethwaite) Canadian poet, journalist, and novelist.

INTRODUCTION

Wetherald was a Canadian poet noted for her naturalistic imagery, which has earned her work comparisons with that of Emily Dickinson, and for the strong religious faith which permeates her verse. Likewise she is known for her good-humored optimism, and for her occasionally insightful treatment of erotic and romantic themes. By virtue of the era in which she wrote, as well as by her associations with such literary figures as Wilfred Campbell and Duncan Campbell Scott, Wetherald could be said to belong to the Confederation Group. The latter, a movement which helped to forge a national identity in literature for the newly formed Dominion of Canada, is also called the Group of '61 because several of its key figures—including Campbell, Scott, and Archibald Lampman, an admirer of Wetherald's work–were born in or around 1861. Wetherald's concerns, as displayed in poetic works such as *The House of the Trees and Other Poems* (1895), tended to be more personal; and as a woman writing in the late nineteenth and early twentieth centuries, much of her journalism was confined to magazines specifically for women. She nonetheless managed to develop a successful dual career as a poet and journalist, and earned the respect of numerous leading figures on both sides of the Canadian border.

Biographical Information

The sixth of eleven children, Wetherald was born in 1857 in Rockwood, Ontario, to Quaker parents. Her father founded and served as principal of Rockwood Academy, whose alumni included railway magnate James J. Hill and critic Archibald MacMurchy, who later included Wetherald in his *Handbook of Canadian Literature*. In 1864 her father resigned his post to become superintendent of Haverford College in Pennsylvania, where as Wetherald would later recall, she saw the passing of President Lincoln's funeral train. After a few years the family returned to Ontario, at which time her father became a Quaker minister, and the family settled on a farm near the town of Fenwick on the Niagara Peninsula. Despite a number of moves in her career as a journalist, Wetherald would return throughout her life to this place, site of "The House of the Trees" which she used as the title for her first book of poems. Wetherald had almost as much exposure to American life as to Canadian: she attended the Friends Boarding School in Union Springs, New York, for instance, and later spent a summer with relatives in Iowa. She also attended Pickering College in Ontario. In the 1880s, she began to work as a freelance journalist contributing in succession to *Rose-Belford's Canadian Monthly*, the Toronto *Globe* (often under the pseudonym Bel Thistlethwaite, her paternal grandmother's maiden name), and the *Week*. She had been publishing poetry, and getting paid for it, since the age of seventeen; and when she was twenty-nine, she brought out her only novel, *An Algonquin Maiden* (1886), cowritten with Graeme Mercer Adam. In 1889 John Cameron, Wetherald's editor at the *Globe*, founded a publication called *Wives and Daughters*, which advanced suffragist ideas and other feminist causes of the era. He invited Wetherald to move to London, Ontario, and write for the publication full-time, which she did until it ceased circulation in 1892. During this time she began to publish more poetry in both Canadian and American periodicals such as *Scribner's*, the Detroit *Free Press*, and the *Youth's Companion* of Boston. (The bulk of her poems in *The House of the Trees* first saw print in the latter publication.) In the mid-1890s, she worked in the United States as an editorial assistant, first at the *Ladies' Home Journal* in Philadelphia; and later with Charles Dudley Warner and Forrest Morgan on the final volumes of *A Library of the World's Best Literature*. Returning to Fenwick in the early years of the twentieth century, Wetherald published several books of verse and, though she never married, adopted a child, a daughter she named Dorothy. For Dorothy she wrote the children's verse contained in *Tree-Top Mornings* (1921), her last volume of new material. Said to be friendly and good-natured by a number of people who met her, Wetherald counted among her acquaintances a number of other Canadian writers, including the poets Helena Coleman and Marjorie Pickthall, and the journalist Laura Durand. Deaf in her latter years, she died in Fenwick in 1940, a few weeks short of her eighty-third birthday.

Major Works

Although she published numerous articles in periodicals of the day, including a series on Canadian female writers for the *Week* in the 1880s, Wetherald would perhaps have wanted to be remembered for her five volumes of verse. Certainly it appears that she did not wish to have her name associated with *An Algonquin Maiden*, a book many critics consider a stereotypical and sentimental portrait of an Indian girl; hence she asked John W. Garvin to leave out all mention of it in his editor's introduction to the collection *Lyrics and Sonnets* (1931). No doubt, then, she would have been both surprised and chagrined to discover that when the University Press of Toronto in 1973 republished one of her books, it was *Algonquin Maiden*. As for her books of poetry, they included *The House of the Trees, Tangled in Stars* (1902), *The Radiant Road* (1904), and *The Last Robin: Lyrics and Sonnets* (1907). The first of these earned the praise of Lampman, a leading figure in Canadian literature; and Governor General Earl Gray so admired *The Last Robin* that he wrote her an effusive letter, and purchased twenty-five copies of the book. Wetherald's themes can perhaps best be outlined by reference to the divisions Garvin accords them in *Lyrics and Sonnets*, starting with "Lyrics of the Seasons." A string of her titles reads like a calendar: "To February," "Leafless April," "A Summer Sleeping Room," "In August," and "October"; and many of her poems have clearly naturalistic themes such as "Among the Leaves," "The Fields of Dark," "The Fire-Weed," "A Rainy Morning," "The Screech Owl," and "The Woodside Way." In addition to "Lyrics of the Seasons," Garvin divides Wetherald's poems into "Bird Songs," "Love Songs," "Humorous Verse," "Lyrics of Life and Wisdom" (e.g., "The Failure," "Youth and Age"), "Sonnets," and "Rhymes for Children"—the latter drawn chiefly from *Tree-Top Mornings*.

PRINCIPAL WORKS

An Algonquin Maiden: A Romance of the Early Days of Upper Canada [with Graeme Mercer Adam] (novel) 1886
The House of the Trees and Other Poems (poetry) 1895
Tangled in Stars (poetry) 1902
The Radiant Road (poetry) 1904
The Last Robin: Lyrics and Sonnets (poetry) 1907
Tree-Top Mornings (children's poetry) 1921
Lyrics and Sonnets (poetry) 1931

CRITICISM

Archibald MacMurchy (essay date 1906)

SOURCE: *Handbook of Canadian Literature,* William Briggs, 1906, pp. 171-75.

[*In the following excerpt from a guide to notable Canadian writers of the day, MacMurchy provides a short overview of Wetherald's career up to the time of publication, and presents examples of her poetry.*]

Miss Ethelwyn Wetherald, journalist, poet, a native of the Province of Ontario, Canada, of English Quaker parentage, her father being the Rev. William Wetherald, who founded (about the middle of last century) the Rockwood Academy, where he had under his charge youths from many counties of Ontario. Educated at home, at a Friends' boarding school in New York State and at Pickering College, Ontario, Miss Wetherald has written for many of the best journals and magazines on this side of the Atlantic, and highly appreciative reviews of her poetic work have appeared in the best periodicals of Canada, the United States and England.

Author of *The House of the Trees, and Other Poems,* 1895; *Tangled in Stars, Poems,* 1902; *The Radiant Road,* 1904. In these volumes we have a delightful collection of sonnets, songs and verses, abounding in pure thoughts and bright picturesque descriptions expressed in truly poetic language. She stands in the foremost rank of our lyrists; as a sonnet writer she has few equals. Her best praise is her work.

The Woodside Way

"I wandered down the woodside way,
  Where branching doors ope with the breeze,
And saw a little child at play
  Among the strong and lovely trees;

The dead leaves rustled to her knees;
  Her hair and eyes were brown as they.
'Oh, little child,' I softly said,
  'You come a long, long way to me;
The trees that tower overhead
  Are here in sweet reality,
But you're the child I used to be,
  And all the leaves of May you tread.'"

At the Window

"How thick about the window of my life
  Buzz, insect-like, the tribe of petty frets;
Small cares, small thoughts, small trials and
    small strife,
  Small loves and hates, small hopes and small
    regrets.

"If 'mid this swarm of smallnesses remain
  A single undimmed spot, with wondering eye
I note before my freckled window-pane
  The outstretched splendor of the earth and sky."

These two poems are instances of the author's reminiscent and comforting moods.

Leafless April

"Leafless April chased by light,
  Chased by dark and full of laughter,
Stays a moment in her flight
  Where the warmest breezes waft her,
By the meadow brook to lean,
  Or where winter rye is growing,
Showing in a lovelier green
  Where her wayward steps are going.
"Blithesome April, brown and warm,
  Showing slimness through her tatters,
Chased by sun or chased by storm—
  Not a whit to her it matters.

Swiftly through the violet bed,
  Down to where the stream is flooding,
Light she flits—and round her head
  See the orchard branches budding!"

A Rainy Morning

"The low sky, and the warm, wet wind,
  And the tender light on the eyes;
A day like a soul that never sinned,
  New dropped from Paradise.

"And 'tis oh, for a long walk in the rain,
  By the side of the warm, wet breeze,
With the thoughts washed clean of dust and stain
  As the leaves on the shining trees."
—*The House of the Trees, and Other Poems.*

These stanzas express artistically her joy in out-door life.

Do we not all remember the joy of such an experience as we have so sweetly recalled by the lines following:

Among the Leaves

"The near sky, the under sky,
  The low sky that I love!
I lie where fallen leaves lie,
  With a leafy sky above,
And draw the colored leaves nigh,
And push the withered leaves by,
And feel the woodland heart upon me,
  Brooding like a dove.
"The bright sky, the moving sky,
  The sky that autumn weaves.
I see where scarlet leaves fly,
  The sky the wind bereaves.
I see the ling'ring leaves die,
I hear the dying leaves sigh,
And breathe the woodland breath made sweet
  Of all her scented leaves."

We quote a poem in which the gifted writer expresses her loving sympathies so gracefully, with respect to home:

Poverty's Lot

"Poverty bought our little lot,
  Flooded with daisy blooms;
Poverty built our little cot,
  And furnished all its rooms.

"Yet Peace leans over Labor's chair,
  Joys at the fireside throng,
While up and down on Poverty's stair
  Love sings the whole day long."

To the majority of readers the short poems will appeal most forcibly. They could more appropriately be called "thoughts," for each gives some truth in two or three verses. A striking instance is **"The Failure"**:

"A failure who had ne'er achieved
  Self-victory, at last lay dead.
'Poor failure!' thus his neighbors grieved.
  'Poor miserable wretch,' they said,

'His weakness was the worst of crimes—
  He failed at least a thousand times.'
"Meanwhile the failure gave to God
  His vain attempts. Remorsefully
And prostrate on the skyey sod,
  'I failed a thousand times,' said he.
'Welcome!' rang out the heavenly chimes,
'He strove—he strove a thousand times.'"
                                        —*The Radiant Road.*

Miss Wetherald has added a contribution of indisputable grace to the treasury of Canadian poetic literature. One great merit of her writing is that it is so decidedly, if spontaneously, Canadian in coloring and atmosphere.

John W. Garvin (essay date 1931)

SOURCE: "Ethelwyn Wetherald's Poetry, An Appreciation," in the *Canadian Bookman,* Vol. XIII, No. 10, October, 1931, pp. 199-201.

[*In the following essay, the editor of* Lyrics and Sonnets *presents an overview of the works contained in that volume.*]

It may be regarded as almost a truism that if a poet be placed in any environment, particularly of Nature, things of beauty will soon be observed and sung about. Most of her life Miss Wetherald has lived at what is now the old homestead in Pelham township, Niagara Peninsula, which is environed by every rural charm; and scarcely an object or phase of beauty thereabouts has escaped her observation and poetic expression. And human life as well, as she has seen it lived, or has read of it, or as her wisdom has interpreted it, has been given manifold utterance in rhythmical, musical poems. A complete edition of her lyrics and sonnets, three hundred and fifty in number, has just been issued by Nelson's —[*Lyrics and Sonnets.*]. Her 'Lyrics of the Seasons' are seventy-nine in number, and exquisite indeed are most of them. She was born in April; this may account in part for the warmth of feeling which inspired such lines as these:

When spring unbound comes o'er us like
  a flood,
  My spirit slips its bars
And thrills to see the trees break into bud
  As skies break into stars.

. . . . .

How shall we fasten the door of spring
  Wide, so wide that it cannot close?
  Though buds are filling and frogs
    are trilling
  And violets breaking and grass
    awaking,
  Yet doubtfully back and forth it blows
Till come the birds, and the woodlands
  ring
  With sharp beak stammer—

The sudden clamour
Of the woodpecker's hammer
At the door of spring.

. . . . .

A spirit through
My window came when earth was soft
    with dew,
Close at the tender edge of dawn, when
    all
The spring was new,

And bore me back
Along her rose-and-starry tinted track,
And showed me how the full-winged day
    emerged
From out the black.

Birds and their warblings have attracted poets the world over; and English poetry is rich in melodious lyrics, giving expression to their appeal. But no other Canadian poet has attained to the high level of excellence in songs about birds, reached by Miss Wetherald. **'The Indigo Bird'** will serve to illustrate:

When I see,
High on the tip-top of a tree,
Something blue by the breezes stirred,
But so far up that the blue is blurred,
So far up no green leaf flies
'Twixt its blue and the blue of the skies,
Then I know, ere a note be heard,
That is naught but the Indigo bird.

Blue on the branch and blue in the sky,
And naught between but the breezes high,
And naught so blue by the breezes stirred
As the deep, deep blue of the Indigo bird.

When I hear
A song like a bird laugh, blithe and clear,
As though of some airy jest he had heard
The last and the most delightful word:
A laugh as fresh in the August haze
As it was in the full-voiced April days;
Then I know that my heart is stirred
By the laugh-like song of the Indigo bird.

Joy on the branch and joy in the sky,
And naught between but the breezes high;
And naught so glad on the breezes heard
As the gay, gay note of the Indigo bird.

Miss Wetherald's love songs are replete with restrained passion, but as to their message a number are quite unusual in modern verse. They give emphasis to the danger of too close an intimacy:

Dearest, give your soul to me;
  Let it in your glances shine;
Let a path of ecstasy
  Stretch between your eyes and mine.
Should you press me to your heart,
    That enchanted,

That enchanted little pathway must
    depart.

. . . . .

If you love me, tell me so
  In your greeting, in your eyes,
In your footstep, swift or slow,
  In your tender-voiced replies.
    Love that stays in heart and blood
    Lives forever in the bud;
    Once in words 'tis past recall—
    Down the lovely petals fall.

The humorous poems for adults are fourteen in number. They are original and deliciously amusing. **'Self-Righteousness'** is a characteristic example:

Unto the diamond with a flaw
  The perfect pebble spake:
'Alas, poor sister, some great law
  Of heaven you did break,

Since Imperfection's curse I see
  Whene'er your form I view;
But cheer up! someday you may be
  A perfect pebble, too.

There is no other poet known to me whose heart is so charged with tender sympathy for all things that have life. There is no sentimentality or affectation in this. It is genuine affection. In Miss Wetherald's religion and philosophy, the kinship of all finite living things is unquestionable, for they are the creation of the One Loving All-Father.

The Screech Owl

Hearing the strange night-piercing sound
  Of woe that strove to sing,
I followed where it hid, and found
  A soft small-throated thing,
A feathered handful of gray grief,
Perched by the year's last leaf.

And heeding not that in the sky
  The lamps of peace were lit,
It sent abroad that sobbing cry,
  And sad hearts echoed it.
O hush, poor grief, so gray, so wild,
God still is with his child!

. . . . .

From **'The Song Sparrow's Nest'**:

Then in the summer night,
  When I awake with a start,
I think of the nest at the height—
  The leafy height of my heart;

I think of the mother love,
  Of the patient wings close furled,
Of the sky that broods above,
  Of the Love that broods on the world.

There are one hundred and twenty-two 'Lyrics of Life and Wisdom.' To be fully appreciated they must be read and re-read. The wisdom of an exalted personality, observing life with serenity but with keenness of vision, and with enduring faith in the supremacy of good over evil, is invariably expressed, and that with rare simplicity and beauty of art. Two short examples:

The Fire-Weed

Where forest fires have swept the land,
  The musing traveller sees
These little bright-faced flowers stand
  In crowded companies.

So in the heart that grief has charred
  New fairness decks the sod,
And every blackened life is starred
  With tender gifts from God.

Legacies

Unto my friends I give my thoughts,
  Unto my God my soul,
Unto my foe I leave my love—
  These are of life the whole.

Nay, there is something—a trifle—left;
  Who shall receive this dower?
See, Earth Mother, a handful of dust—
  Turn it into a flower.

Ethelwyn Wetherald is one of the best of Canada's sonnet writers. She has used the most difficult form of the Petrarchan or Italian School, yet the thoughts and lines flow with the same grace and freedom as in her lyrics. This is an unusual achievement. One example out of thirty-eight:

At Waking

When I shall go to sleep and wake again
  At dawning in another world than this,
  What will atone to me for all I miss?
The light melodious footsteps of the rain,
The press of leaves against my window-
    pane,
  The sunset wistfulness and morning
    bliss,
  The moon's enchantment, and the
    twilight kiss
Of winds that wander with me through the
    lane.

Will not my soul remember evermore
  The earthly winter's hunger for the
    spring,
    The wet sweet cheek of April, and
    the rush
Of roses through the summer's open door;
  The feelings that the scented woodlands
    bring
    At evening with the singing of the
    thrush?

In poems for children—sixty in number—this author also excels. Her happy rhythms and rhymes and the humour of which most of the verses are redolent, are a constant source of pleasure to young hearers and readers.

To illustrate:

The Baby Who Was Three-Fourths Good

'Now will you be good?' said little Bob
  Wood,
To his baby sister Sue,
As he lifted his hand with a look of
  command,
And the baby answered 'Goo.'

'You've sucked Noah's paint till he looks
  quite faint
And wrecked nearly all his crew.
Is that being good?' asked stern Bobby
  Wood,
And the baby gurgled out 'Goo!'

'You mean pretty well, so seldom you
  yell,
And you never were known to look blue;
But you're not always good—that's quite
  understood—
And the little one laughed and said 'Goo!'

'Goo is three-fourths of good,' said wise
  Bobby Wood,
'I suppose that's the best you can do;
But when you're as big as I am, you
  sprig,
You'll have to be good clear through.'

In conclusion let me say that I find no ground for adverse criticism. It is seldom one meets with such perfection in word, phrase and line. The thought is invariably original and the expression artistic and lucid. Indeed Ethelwyn Wetherald's poetry charms and delights all readers, from the University Professor down to the Kindergartner. And this, it seems to me, is the supreme test of genius.

John W. Garvin (essay date 1931)

SOURCE: An Introduction to *Lyrics and Sonnets,* by Ethelwyn Wetherald, Thomas Nelson & Sons, 1931, pp. v-xviii.

[*In the following excerpt from the introduction to* Lyrics and Sonnets, *Garvin surveys Wetherald's life and work.*]

Ethelwyn Wetherald is of English-Irish descent. Her paternal grandmother, née Isabel Thistlethwaite, died in Yorkshire, England, in 1826; and in 1834, grandfather Wetherald and several of his large family took ship for New York, on their way to Upper Canada. Such an ocean voyage in those days required nearly six weeks. The journey from New York, by way of Albany, Schenectady, Utica, Oswego, Kingston and Toronto, was also long and wearisome, but these travellers in a strange new land never lost their interest in sight-seeing.

John Wetherald bought a farm of one hundred acres in Puslinch township, near Guelph, the cost price of which was two hundred and fifty dollars for the settler's right and title, and in addition two hundred and seventy dollars to the Government agent in Toronto, payable in nine annual instalments. As one acre only was cleared, the family had to settle down to pioneering in earnest. The remaining children, with the exception of one daughter, Agnes, who had married in England, joined them the next year.

Miss Wetherald's maternal grandparents were natives of Ireland. Miss Sarah Harris was a refined and cultured governess in a wealthy family, in the north of Ireland when the attentions of a young and ardent wooer by the name of Balls, who was thirteen years her junior, so embarrassed and agitated her, that she sought escape by resigning and voyaging to Canada. The young man was not so easily shaken, however, for he promptly followed and succeeded shortly in making her a pioneer's wife. Later Mrs. Balls opened a backwoods school and received a grant from the Government. She was an excellent teacher and disciplinarian. . . . Her husband played the fiddle and was popular in his family and with the neighbours. He raised wheat, and about the year 1840 won a prize of nine dollars at the Guelph Fall Fair for the best bushel of that grain. Every kernel was handpicked by himself and his three children. Also he interested himself in raising chickens, making maple sugar, and in hunting and shooting wolves. . . . . Mrs. Balls was reticent and dignified. The old country custom of five o'clock tea was retained by her, and Miss Wetherald has still the teapot, 'cream ewer' and 'sugar shovel' that she used.

The maiden name of Miss Wetherald's mother was Jemima Harris Balls. She was born at Rockwood, a few miles from Guelph, and was married in her eighteenth year.

William Wetherald, the father of our poet, was the ninth of eleven children. He was born at Healaugh, Yorkshire, England, September 26, 1820. For four years before coming to Upper Canada, he attended Ackworth School, an institution of The Society of Friends. The discipline was severe and holidays were few, but notwithstanding, he left this school with a genuine love of knowledge and with his ambition aroused and quickened. As he was not strong physically it was his desire to become a teacher, and so he was detected sometimes in the fields working out mathematical problems while the team and plough were resting. For several years he taught a district school. After his marriage he opened a Boarding School at Rockwood. This was in 1851. (Four years later it became the Rockwood Academy with a large stone building,) In December, 1857, the Academy had fifty pupils enrolled, two or three assistant teachers, a capable housekeeper with several women helpers, and a

man to do the chores. It provided also an apartment for the Wetherald family and a beloved nurse.

A number of the students afterwards became distinguished men, among them the late James J. Hill, railway magnate; Hon. Arthur Sturgis Hardy, K.C., LL.D., Prime Minister of Ontario; and Archibald MacMurchy, M.A., LL.D., for many years principal of the Toronto Grammar School, later the Jarvis Street Collegiate Institute.

In September, 1864, Mr. Wetherald resigned his principalship to accept the position of superintendent of Haverford College, near Philadelphia. A few years later he returned to Ontario and bought a fruit and dairy farm, in Pelham township, near Fenwick, in the beautiful Niagara Peninsula.

In his later years, Mr. Wetherald became an ordained minister of The Society of Friends, and devoted himself almost exclusively to his religious duties. He travelled extensively and became widely known. By hard study and much reading of classical literature, this prominent educator and preacher gained a fine mastery of English, which he imparted to his children. His distinguished daughter acknowledges with loving gratitude her indebtedness to him.

Agnes Ethelwyn was born at Rockwood, April 26, 1857, the sixth of eleven children. Her early education was received at home. Later she attended The Friends Boarding School, at Union Springs, N.Y., and subsequently, Pickering College, Ontario.

As a writer, Miss Wetherald won her first prominence, in the years, 1887-'88-'89, when she contributed articles frequently to the Toronto *Globe.* Each article was about a column in length and was signed by the *nom de plume,* 'Bel Thistlethwaite,' a contraction of the maiden name of her paternal grandmother. . . . In June, 1889, when a member of the *Globe* staff, now a Canadian Senator, was about to take his holidays, Miss Wetherald was requested by the editor to come to the city to write 'Notes and Comments' and an occasional editorial. The editor was Mr. John Cameron.

The following year, Mr. Cameron resigned and returned to London, Ontario, as Managing Editor of the *Advertiser.* In September, 1890, he founded a small monthly magazine, entitled *Wives and Daughters,* with his wife as editor and Ethelwyn Wetherald as assistant. This little magazine continued publication for three years. Miss Wetherald wrote nearly all the editorials and they were creditable indeed. She wrote also most of the book reviews, in which she sought to make the reader acquainted with the particular characteristics, flavour and quality of each author and volume. She was responsible as well for the "Selected Poetry", "Children's Department", etc.

It was during those years in London, that Miss Wetherald began writing her exquisite lyrics and sonnets, which have since charmed so many readers. By 1895, she had enough for her first book, *The House of the Trees and Other Poems.* In 1902, appeared *Tangled In Stars;* and in 1904, *The Radiant Road.* In the autumn of 1907, a larger collection of her verse was published in Toronto, *The Last Robin; Lyrics and Sonnets.* It was this book, presented to him by Clara Kirchhoffer, wife of Senator Kirchhoffer, that attracted the attention of His Excellency, Earl Grey, at that time Governor-General of Canada. The poems appealed to him to such a degree that he wrote the author a lengthy, appreciative letter, and ordered twenty-five copies from the publishers to send as gifts to his friends.

It was Mrs. Kirchhoffer also who presented the copy to Sir Wilfred Laurier, from which he quoted in the House of Commons in 1911, while speaking in favour of unrestricted reciprocity with the United States, the lines:

> My orders are to fight
>   Then if I bleed, or fail,
> Or strongly win, what matters it?
>   God only doth prevail.
>
> The servant craveth naught
>   Except to serve with might.
> I was not told to win or lose,—
>   My orders are to fight.

This *Complete Edition* contains every poem that Miss Wetherald wishes preserved. There are three hundred and fifty in all, arranged in seven groups: 'Lyrics of the Seasons,' 'Bird Songs,' 'Love Songs,' 'Humorous Verse,' 'Lyrics of Life and Wisdom,' 'Sonnets' and 'Rhymes for Children'.

It would be difficult to criticize adversely any one of these charming lyrics and sonnets. In such fundamentals as clarity, melodious rhythm and rhyme, spontaneity and originality, they are uniformly excellent. Moreover, Miss Wetherald's poetry exemplifies to a marked degree "that artless simplicity which is very exquisite art".

Reminiscences of the Poet

[by Ethelwyn Wetherald]

As a child I was never robust enough to enjoy outdoor exercise, although I took pleasure in all-day excursions after wild raspberries among the hills of Rockwood, usually accompanied by several of our household. Large pails were brought back brimming with the perfumed fruit, which was 'put down pound for pound' (a pound of sugar to each pound of berries) to ensure freedom from mould. Long walks especially through the woods, which never had enough mosquitoes to frighten me away, were always a delight. . . . I am very fond of country life: less enthusiastic over farm activities. I was seven years old when we left Rockwood. Hills and rocks, woods and the smell of cedars, all come back in the name. (At the age of eight, accompanied by my sister and three brothers, I watched the slow-moving train

draped in black, passing by the railroad station near Haverford College bearing the dead body of President Lincoln. The aura of intense grief, nation-wide, and the sorrowful face of my father, made a deep impression.)

At school I had no love of mathematics and have always thought that for me to go beyond the multiplication table was a waste of time. . . . I have studied French and have taken private lessons from a native Frenchman, who shook his head over my hopelessly British accent. I attended Pickering College and shall never forget the endless patience of my favourite teacher, who would take me into her room in the evening and go over and over the mathematical puzzle that perplexed and baffled me, in a usually vain attempt to make it clear. Really in the realm of figures I am a hopeless moron. . . .

The very first cheque I received for verse was when I was seventeen and sent a string of stanzas to the *St. Nicholas* of New York, in which I described some of the antics of my two brothers, Lewis and Herbert, aged four and two respectively. I have forgotten the words. It was a mere rhyme, so I don't regret its oblivion; but I have some poems that I should have kept copies of. One was called **"The Fire Builders"**, which appeared in *Youth's Companion* in 1890—I think in July of that year. Another July contribution to *Youth's Companion*—I've forgotten the year,—dealt with the misunderstanding between two children, a Canadian and an American, one praising the 'glorious fourth' the other protesting it was the 'glorious first', and correcting each other very frequently. There was an editor's note at the end explaining that July 1st was Confederation Day in Canada. . . . Most of the poems in *The House of the Trees* appeared first in that periodical.

Just before moving to London, Ontario, in 1890, I sent **'The Wind of Death'** to the *Travellers Record* and when I showed the ten dollar cheque received for it to my fellow-boarders, they were openly astonished. To get real money for a string of verses seemed absurd. . . .

The impulse to write verse became irresistible between 1893, when I returned home, and 1896, when *The House of the Trees* appeared.

A humorous poem sent to *Munsey's Magazine* has been lost. The editor returned it with a note saying it was a dreadful mistake to make 'swan' rhyme with 'dawn', but if I would remove that defect he would gladly accept it.

Nearly all the verse I have had printed appeared between 1890 and 1900. . . . While I was in London, Ontario, I took lessons in horseback riding—the old fashioned side-saddle kind, and my friends and I often went for a twenty-mile ride in the moonlight. No mere motor-car could give such pleasure as that. . . . . Part of the summer of 1888 I spent with cousins on a large prairie farm in Iowa. There were two boys and three girls in the family, hospitable parents, numerous horses.

My favourite cousin, Clara, and I had many a horseback ride over the prairies. The farm and the congenial society of my relatives gave me a sense of peace and freedom.

Most of my journeys were in company with my brother Sam who was six years my senior. When he suffered from a nervous breakdown. I was his nurse, private secretary, companion and closest friend. When he recovered we went together to Florida, to Atlantic City, Philadelphia, Washington, on a 'pay trip' to Devil's Lake, while he was paymaster on the Great Northern, and to California.

Unless there is a direct inspiration I prefer discursive essay writing to writing stories. 'The Autocrat at the Breakfast Table' by Oliver Wendell Holmes, I have read again and again. Also his 'Professor and Poet' at the same unwearying table. . . . . I have had sketches accepted by the *Youth's Companion* and New York *Outlook* (formerly *Christian Union*). On appearance of the sketches one of the editors of the David Cook Company in Chicago wrote to me asking for stories for their Sunday School papers. I wrote a few for them, and several stories for young people in the Sunday Edition of a Philadelphia Daily. I also wrote a host of brief stories and articles for agricultural papers all of which brought modest sums. But I cared little for the work and much more enjoyed sending aphorisms and pointed paragraphs to the *Detroit Free Press,* to *Smart Set,* and to *Puck, Judge* and *Life* of New York. *The Star Weekly* of Toronto accepted a weekly column entitled *Reflections of an Old Maid.*

The house in the tree was built in March, 1910, and was blown down in a high gale in the fall of 1920. The old willow, being very much alive and steadily growing, seemed to work itself loose from the house fastened to its branches. The last nights I slept in it were memorable. Every joint and ligament shrieked and groaned in the wind; so finally when the dear thing was pulled away by the gale and fell to the ground, roof downward, I saw that *Finis* had been written. It was taken apart, but the old willow still survives. It is a lovely memory. Sam called it Camp Shelbi, a name made up of the first letters of the ten kinds of wood used: chestnut, ash, maple, pine, spruce, hemlock, elm, linden, birch, and ironwood. These and these only were the woods represented in my dear little tree house.

"The Tall Evergreens," the name of the Wetherald homestead came very naturally by its name. So many times friends of the family, coming for the first time to this neighbourhood and inquiring for us, would be told at the station (Fenwick), 'Take the next road south and go east a mile till you come to some tall evergreens: that's the place'. My father and Sam planted these spruces and pines in 1867.

I frequently met James J. Hill when I lived in St. Paul with my brothers, Sam and Charlie. They were employed in the Great Northern Railway office. Mrs. Hill's splendid team of blacks made a sensation in our quiet street on the occasions when she called on me. We spent pleasant evenings in their home. I recall the great gallery of famous paintings and the admonitory gesture with which Mrs. Hill checked her husband's rather too audible conversation while her three youngest children were saying their evening prayers at their mother's knee.

When I was nineteen I visited friends in New York who took me to their Unitarian Church to hear Dr. Bellows preach. I was less impressed by his discourse than by the fact that William Cullen Bryant was seated in the pew before me. I was thrilled by the thought that at my age he had written the wonderful poem, 'Thanatopsis'.

One of my classmates at Pickering College was the later internationally known Dr. Barker of Johns' Hopkins University in Baltimore. He was a small, slight, white-faced boy, known to all of us as Lewy Barker. He was easily first in everything, simply ate up knowledge, like a child at a candy box. His father, a Quaker, was superintendent at Pickering, and often preached in meeting.

Another noted man whom I knew was Lyman Abbott, successor to Beecher, who lectured in London in the fall of 1890, and was entertained by the Camerons when I was with them.

When Wilfred Campbell happened to be in London he called on me several times and read aloud to me from a sheaf of his poems. We had considerable argument, as I could not agree with his estimate of Lampman as a 'carver of cherry stones'.

I have always prized the friendship of Paul Peel. His was a very charming personality. I have his autograph on a picture he gave me.

I have been asked, frequently about my favourite books. In my teens I was fond of Emerson, Carlyle and Matthew Arnold, and can truthfully say that they have never wearied me. The New England poets and essayists, Holmes and Lowell, always delighted me. I had read all of Dickens before I was fifteen, and all of Shakespeare before I was twenty. I always enjoyed the prose of Swift and Addison, but disliked Dr. Johnson, because of his rough ways and the pleasure he evidently took in snubbing others. Cowper's gentle and sympathetic nature attracted me more than his poetry. Of course all the poets are dear to me, though of the Brownings I much prefer Elizabeth to Robert.

As for fiction I never cared for the realism of Zola; but there is a realism I greatly admire—that of Arnold Bennett, Jane Austen, W. D. Howells, Mary E. Wilkins, Booth Tarkington, George Eliot, and the class of novelists who tell what is going on in people's minds and show that character always compels destiny.

Most of the winter of '95-'96 I spent in Philadelphia as assistant to Francis Bellamy, the literary editor of the

Ladies' Home Journal. There I met Mr. Edward Bok, who always impressed me as a man just fresh from a bout with the punching bag and a cold shower. Also I met, and very much liked, Mrs. George T. Lanigan, managing editor, and widow of the famous author of 'The Ahkoond of Swat'. Mr. Lanigan, I fancy, did not shine as a money-maker, as she told me that, at the time of his death, she was left with five children and seven dollars. She was amazed to hear me say I would rather be the author of 'The Ahkoond of Swat' than of any other humorous poem in the English language, with the possible exception of Bret Harte's 'Heathen Chinee' and Oliver Wendell Holmes' 'One Hoss Shay' . . . My work was altogether critical—the reading of manuscripts which came in by the hundred every day, and writing out an estimate of worthwhile articles of their availability for the Journal. In some ways I enjoyed the experience, but it was a lasting dissatisfaction to feel, at the end of each day, that I was too tired to do any creative work of my own.

My chance to assist one of the editors of *The World's Best Literature* came about through correspondence. He had written in praise of my **'Wind of Death',** and we had corresponded for years before we met. If ever there was a human cyclopaedia it was Forrest Morgan. He did a tremendous amount of work on 'The World's Best'. When the mother of his assistant was so seriously ill that the girl had to give up her work and go home, Mr. Morgan wrote, urging me to take her place. I acted as his assistant for nearly a year, when the thirtieth and last volume of the series was published. This final volume consisted entirely of verse, and Charles Dudley Warner, editor-in-chief, included in it five or six little poems of my own. I was paid eighteen dollars a week. . . . When the work was finished Mr. Morgan offered me a position as first-class proofreader at a larger salary, but I longed for home. I was not homesick but there was an indefinable feeling that too much 'learned lumber in the head' must crush out whatever repressed spontaneous growth of my own was still surviving. Our correspondence ceased in 1923, just after his physician had told him he had only a few weeks to live. Certainly to know him was a liberal education.

Among the most memorable weeks of my life are two spent at Pinehurst, Helena Coleman's island home in the St. Lawrence, near Gananoque. It was an ideal spot for a vacation in that exceptionally hot July of 1911, as it consisted of a three-acre island, satisfyingly rough and rocky, with paths leading from the wide-verandaed residence to boat-house and bathing pool. We were a group of women and girls; Miss Coleman, her two nieces, a literary friend from Australia, Marjorie Pickthall and myself, not to mention the cook, who produced the outdoor meals we so much enjoyed. These were movable feasts, as, when the wind was fresh from the west, we moved to the east veranda, and when the sun was hot at the east the table was set at the other side. My sleeping-room was open on one side to the St. Lawrence, and when a great steamer moved past in the night, the impression was unforgettable. My choicest pleasure came in the morning, for, as the early light awakened Marjorie Pickthall in the room next to mine and Helena Coleman just across the hall, we fell into frequent talk and discussion before arising. How I wish I had taken notes of these impromptu exchanges of thought, fancy and opinion. I remember distinctly that Marjorie Pickthall did not argue. She questioned, mused awhile, differed gently, or expressed her differing attitude by a little laugh that was as charming as it was free from self-consciousness. She was a poet to the innermost fibre of her beautiful and totally unaffected nature. Her *Three Island Songs* I am confident were written at Pinehurst.

The amusements of these harmonious housemates were boating and bathing, rambles after wild berries, fishing, five-o'clock tea, discussion of just-read books and visiting of picturesque points of interest. I remember in particular the Sunday morning when the cook wished to go to church. Miss Coleman and I rowed her across to Gananoque and while she went to her place of worship, we waited outside in the boat and talked of churches and creeds, of Christianity and the meaning of existence, of things that remind us we are infinite. The best of herself is what Helena Coleman gives in her talk as in her written prose and poetry.

Clara Bernhardt (essay date 1940)

SOURCE: "Ethelwyn Wetherald," in *Saturday Night,* Vol. 55, No. 24, April 13, 1940, pp. 11.

[*In the following essay, Bernhardt offers an appreciation of Wetherald on the occasion of the author's death.*]

With the passing of Ethelwyn Wetherald, beloved Canadian poet, another of that shining company in Canadian literature, known as the Group of '61 (Carman, Lampman, Drummond, Pauline Johnson, and represented now only by Roberts) has crossed into the realm where beauty is eternal. To those who knew and loved her poetry, its singing heritage remains. And to those who knew and loved Ethelwyn Wetherald herself, there remains a vivid memory of a gallant soul and a sparkling personality.

Her intense zest for life is the thing about Miss Wetherald that will always stay with me. That and her scintillating wit and ready humor. Straight and slim as one of the tall evergreens marking the road to her home, Miss Wetherald's body, like her spirit, made little concession to advancing years. Deafness rather increased the solitude in which she lived at her country home near Fenwick, Ontario, but poetry lovers still found their way to her door. Only last summer she was garden party hostess to the Canadian Authors' Association in the quietude of "The Tall Evergreens"—an afternoon which will live long in the hearts of those privileged to attend

It was through requesting a hand-written copy of what is probably her most widely known and best loved poem, **"Legacies,"** that I first became acquainted with Miss Wetherald several years ago. In complying with characteristic graciousness, she remarked wistfully that she wished she too were young again, and at the beginning of a literary career. That this enthusiasm for life, which was amazing in one of her years, stayed with her to the very end, was evident in a letter written several weeks before her death.

"I am feeling divinely happy today, partly because light came early this morning, and will come earlier tomorrow. I am almost unnaturally well and feel correspondingly gay. I hope you too are going on your way rejoicing."

On her way rejoicing! What a rare and admirable attitude for a deaf, solitary old lady of eighty-three! People half her age might well envy this spirit. It was through keeping alive her interest in the changing work, and in the younger generation, that Miss Wetherald retained her youthful outlook and verve. She wanted to know what the younger Canadian writers were doing. For in the letter she wrote me just a week before her death, received with an autographed gift copy of the life of Homer Watson she wanted me to have, was this adjuration: "Tell me about the younger poets with whom you feel in closest affinity. I am always interested."

Then she spoke a few words of artistic perception, evoked by her reading of a review of my book of poems to which she had written the foreword last April: "After all, your own best critic is yourself. Your knowledge of your own aims, your own soul, your own invisible personality is greater than any attained by others." Words which any writer, surely, would do well to ponder.

And nowhere is Miss Wetherald's own "invisible personality" more evident than in the final lines from the personal poem with which she greeted her friends last Christmas:

> "Be thine the sense of wings, the
>   subtle call
> That comes from some bird-breasted
>   waterfall;
> The comradeship of trees, the hearts
>   of friends,
> And one Near Presence where the
>   footpath bends."

FURTHER READING

Criticism

Review of *Tree-Top Mornings*. *Canadian Bookman* IV, No. 4 (March 1922): 108.
    An approving review, which commends Wetherald's "playful-motherly attitude toward her readers."

"The Last Robin." *Canadian Magazine* 30, No. 3 (January 1908): 291.
    A favorable review of *The Last Robin*, in which the critic takes note of the book's "genial, optimistic tone."

"Recent Verse." *Nation* 87, No. 2,245 (9 July 1908): 34-35.
    A negative review of *The Last Robin* which in several places refers to the author as "Mr. Wetherald."

Payne, William Morton. "Recent Poetry." *Dial* XXXV, No. 418 (16 November 1903): 358.
    In a comparative review of recent works by female poets, Payne briefly assesses *Tangled in Stars*.

> The following source published by Gale contains additional coverage of Wetherald's life and career: *Dictionary of Literary Biography*, Vol. 99.

Hank Williams

1923-1953

(Full name Hiram Hank King Williams; also recorded under the pseudonym The Lonesome Drifter) American songwriter and singer.

INTRODUCTION

With Jimmy Rogers and Ernest Tubb, Williams is considered a seminal figure in the American Country and Western genre. Williams wrote and recorded songs that ensured him success in his lifetime, and eventually became musical standards for artists in every category of popular music. The result was the first Country and Western music to extend beyond regional success to national recognition due, in part, to such artists as Tony Bennett, Jo Stafford, and Frankie Lane recording his songs. Williams's recordings of his songs, as well as songs by obscure or unknown songwriters, also gained national prominence. Several of his songs are credited with inspiring such later musical styles as American Rockabilly and rock, as well as expanding the form and subject matter of Country and Western and folk music. Williams's songwriting displays his familiarity with such musical predecessors the Carter Family, Roy Acuff, and Ernest Tubb, as well as with African-American blues and gospel, American folk, and Tin-Pan Alley traditions. It is as a lyricist, however, that Williams is mostly admired. Unlike much Country and Western music that preceded it, Williams's employed music and melody as minimal devices in service of the songs's lyrics, which address topics of lost love, religious faith, and revelry. Williams's influence has been noted by critics in the music of such diverse artists as Buddy Holly, Bob Dylan, George Thorogood, and Tony Bennett; the latter who enjoyed his inaugural recording success with Williams's "Cold, Cold Heart."

Biographical Information

Williams was born in a log cabin in Mt. Olive, Alabama. His father was a veteran of World War I, who suffered from shell-shock. By the time Williams's was seven-years-old, his father had been admitted to a veteran's hospital and never returned to his family. The loss of Williams's father and the economic conditions of the Great Depression kept the Williams family living in near-poverty conditions. Williams's mother was an organist and singer in the Mt. Olive Baptist church choir, who also worked a variety of jobs to support the family. She exerted a strong musical influence on Williams throughout his life, beginning with his tenure in the church choir at the age of six, and buying him his first guitar in 1930. While still a child, Williams contributed to the family budget by shining shoes, and selling newspapers and peanuts. During this time, he accepted musical tutelage from Rufus Payne, an African-American street singer known as Tee-Tot who gave Williams singing and guitar lessons. When he was fourteen-years-old, Williams was writing songs, singing andplaying guitar for his own country band. In 1937, Williams won first-place in an amateur contest in Montgomery, Alabama, with a performance of a song he wrote: "W.P.A. Blues." In the next few years before World War II, Williams and his band The Drifting Cowboys performed in small clubs throughout the South with minimal success. Following the war, Williams and his first wife, Audrey, went to Nashville, Tennessee, to audition for music writer and publisher Fred Rose. Success was gradual; Williams performed regularly on the "Louisiana Hayride" radio program, and was eventually installed as a member of the Grand Ole Opry. Williams's success was mired, however, by his addiction to alcohol and painkillers, as well as his tempestuous relationship with Audrey. He suffered arrests, banishment from the Grand Ole Opry, and a divorce before his death at age twenty-nine in 1953, the result of heart complications from amphetamines, painkillers, and alcohol abuse.

Major Works

Williams's first gained major prominence in 1949 with "Lovesick Blues," a song written in the 1920s by Irving Mills and Cliff Friend. A performance of the song on the Grand Ole Opry led to his invitation to join the prestigious institution and the number-one selling Country and Western song of 1949. The popularity of "Lovesick Blues" spurred interest in several of Williams's previous compositions, including "Honky Tonkin'," "Move It on Over," "I Saw the Light," and "A Mansion on the Hill," which he co-wrote with Fred Rose. Because Williams could neither read nor write, some critics credit Rose with majority authorship of many songs. Other legends have Williams's buying songs and authorship rights from other songwriters for as little as five dollars apiece. Regardless, the collaboration between songwriter and performer Williams and producer and publisher Rose resulted in many subsequent Country and Western hit records, including "Long Gone Lonesome Blues," "I'm So Lonesome I Could Cry," "Cold, Cold Heart," "Hey, Good Lookin'," "Why Don't You Love Me," "Kaw-Liga," "Your Cheatin' Heart," "There's a Tear in My Beer," and "Jambalaya (On the Bayou)."

PRINCIPAL WORKS

Hank Williams's 40 Greatest Hits (songs) 1978
Hank Williams: The Original Singles Collection (songs) 1990
The Complete Hank Williams (songs) 1998

CRITICISM

Roger M. Williams (essay date 1975)

SOURCE: "Hank Williams," in *Stars of Country Music: Uncle Dave Mason to Johnny Rodriguez*, edited by Bill C. Malone and Judith McCulloh, University of Illinois Press, 1975, pp. 237-54.

[*The author of the Hank Williams's biography* Sing a Sad Song, *Williams examines in the following excerpt the influences of FredRose, Roy Acuff, Jimmie Rogers, and Ernest Tubb on Williams's music.*]

Although there is no means of objective measurement, Hank Williams has as strong a claim as anyone to the mythical title Greatest Figure in Country Music History. Certainly two related distinctions are his: Williams's music and popularity have outlived him in a manner unparalleled in country music and perhaps in all of American popular culture; his were the first songs firmly to bridge the gulf between country and pop music. Was Williams also country music's greatest songwriter? Almost certainly, yes. And when he was right (that is, half sober and in reasonably good health), he was one of its two or three best performers as well.

Yet these distinctions do not fully convey the impact and influence of Hank Williams. He was a legend in his time, and he has remained one ever since. Today, twenty-two years after his death, the legend can be measured in money (his royalties during this period exceed $5 million), in the international acceptance the best of his songs have won, and in the fact that the publishing and record companies that own the rights to his material have continued to bring out Williams products, new and old the new being songs fashioned from snippets of lyrics he left. Williams's impact on his fellow country music writers and performers is more difficult to measure. However, there is no doubt that he not only spawned a group of imitators including Ray Price and George Jones but also greatly furthered a simple, earthy style of songs and singing that has marked the best of country music ever since.

As much as with any other major figure in the field, Williams's music is linked with his life. His rural, broken-home upbringing and his tempestuous marriages were directly reflected in the songs he wrote. And his legend has been burnished by his swift rise and sudden, tragic fall, awash in liquor and drugs.

He was born Hiram Hank Williams on September 17, 1923, near the town of Georgiana, Alabama, some sixty miles south of Montgomery. All of his formative years were spent in that area. His father was a sometime lumber-train engineer, store owner, and berry grower who went into a Veterans Administration hospital and virtually out of Hank's life when the boy was seven. His mother, who raised him, was the dominant force in his life. Her name was Lilly, and she was large, mannish, and overbearing. As with so many country musicians' mothers, Lilly was a church organist, and the earliest stories of Hank Williams and music tell how he shared the bench with her while she pounded out the old four-square hymns.

Hank had guitars at an early age, and there are at least two men in Georgiana today who claim to have given him the first of them.He might never have escaped Georgiana, however, had he not encountered an elderly black street singer named Tee-Tot. It was Tee-Tot (Rufe Payne was his real name) who gave the initial shaping to what was to become the Hank Williams style. Tee-Tot's music was mostly blues, with a bit of jazz and pop thrown in. Hank did not learn fancy picking from him; he learned chords, chord progressions, bass runs, and the simple, uniform style of accompaniment that suited the songs he soon would be writing. Williams never took a music or guitar lesson from anyone else.

From Georgiana, Williams followed a fairly standard musical path. He played with various local bands in south Alabama and Montgomery. Rejected in his first try for the Grand Ole Opry, he wound up instead in the high minor leagues, the Louisiana Hayride. He might not even have reached the Hayride, let alone his subsequent stardom, without the help of Fred Rose and his son, Wesley.

The Roses, giants in the publishing part of the country music business, were the most important influences in Hank Williams's professional life. Fred Rose was a successful pop songwriter ("Red Hot Mama," "'Deed I Do") turned successful country music writer and publisher. In 1942, he teamed with Roy Acuff, already a star on the Opry, to form Nashville's first publishing firm. That was a bold challenge to an industry that traditionally had been controlled in the North, and it succeeded from the start. By the time Hank Williams joined Acuff-Rose, in 1946, the company had a stable of country writers that included Pee Wee King and Redd Stewart, Jenny Lou Carson, Paul Howard, Clyde Moody, and Mel Foree.

Williams had dabbled in songwriting almost from the day he first picked up a guitar. As a skinny teenager, he won fifteen dollars at a Montgomery amateur night by singing a ditty that included these lines:

> I got a home in Montgomery,
> A place I like to stay.
> But I have to work for the WPA,
> And I'm dissatisfied I'm dissatisfied.

That was the first performance-worthy song Williams wrote, and it was one of the few that bore a social message. Throughout his career, Hank Williams, along with almost every other country songwriter of his era, stuck with the standard categories: songs of unrequited love, funny songs, and country hymns. (A notable exception: his rambling, philosophical "Luke the Drifter" recitations.) In 1946, at the age of twenty-three, Williams figured he had assembled enough decent songs to get at least a few of them published. To him, there was only one place to go: Acuff-Rose. All the other publishers were up North, and he wasn't ready to cope with it or them.

As Wesley Rose remembers it, Hank and his first wife, Audrey, interrupted the Roses' lunchtime Ping-Pong game at Nashville's WSM radio studio. At a busier moment, the Roses might have turned the young country couple away. But they put down their paddles and listened to the lanky, sad-looking young man sing a half-dozen of his songs. Among them were **"When God Comes and Gathers His Jewels"** and **"Six More Miles to the Graveyard,"** both destined to become standards in the Williams songbook. A widely told story has it that Fred Rose, unsure of the stranger's real talent, sent him off by himself to compose a song and that Williams came back a short while later with the famous **"Mansion on the Hill."** The Roses needed no such test. They knew talent when they heard it, and they immediately signed Williams to a contract.

Fred Rose made critical contributions to Williams's songwriting career. Nashville people often talk about how Rose "polished" Williams's material, but his influence went far beyond polishing. Rose was a master craftsman, a veritable sculptor with the raw materials of music words and melodies. He could change an inflection here, a note there, a line of lyric somewhere else, and he could do it all so completely within the idiom of the original composer that no one would know the song had passed through another musical intelligence. The Rose contributions to Williams's material varied widely, because the material reached Rose in many different stages: as complete songs, as a couple of verses and a few lines of melody, as a chorus, or even less. In each case, Rose did whatever had to be done to make the song successful.

While Rose's most frequent contribution was smoothing out the lyrics of his semieducated protégé, he effected basic changes as well. For instance, he added the twist that made **"Kaw-Liga,"** one of Williams's novelty songs, a hit. The twist: substituting, within a theme of unrequited love, wooden Indians for the live Indians that Williams had used. The result was as catchy as it was humorous, and it raised an ordinary song to the rank of a lesser country classic. Rose's name appears as coauthor on **"Kaw-Liga"** and on five other songs commonly attributed to Williams alone including the celebrated **"I'll Never Get Out of This World Alive"** and **"Mansion on the Hill."** For the most part, however, he contented himself with the satisfactions, and the finan-

cial rewards, of a job well done. In all, the Williams-Rose collaboration was one of the most successful in American musical history. It was a perfect union: Williams's native genius, Rose's craftsmanship and sure sense of the market.

The Roses did a great deal more for Hank Williams than simply dress up his songs. They directed his entire career, from personal appearances to recordings. Fred Rose functioned as Williams's manager, and no country music star has ever had a more effective one. It was Rose who, buoyed by the sound of Williams's first recordings for little-known Sterling, secured for him a contract with a major label. The label was MGM, which until that time (the late 1940s) had had only one country artist, Bob Wills.

It was Rose, also, who supervised all of Williams's recording sessions getting the back-up musicians, selecting the songs, arranging the accompaniments. "No song was ever recorded by us without Mr. Rose's approval," said Frank Walker, president of MGM, some years ago. "Also, no record session was ever held without either Fred Rose or Wesley Rose being present. . . ." Williams's first MGM release, **"Move It On Over,"** sold several hundred thousand records (in those pre-LP days) and won for him the first of many places on the *Billboard* and *Cash Box* charts.

It was Rose, too, who, after the success of **"Move It On Over,"** decided to send Williams to the Louisiana Hayride. Making him a star as an in-person performer was essential if his songwriting and recording careers were to catch fire; in those days, perhaps more than now, country music fans demanded that their favorites be seen as well as heard. The Opry was, at that point, out of the question. Williams simply wasn't a big enough name. Of the other top radio shows of the day, Shreveport's Louisiana Hayride, Chicago's Barn Dance, and West Virginia's WWVA Jamboree, Rose preferred the Hayride. Says Wesley Rose: "My father knew he'd get a straight reaction to Hank in Shreveport. The people there are real country fans."

Finally, it was Rose who guided Williams's breakthrough into the prestigious and lucrative world of popular music. The breakthrough was made by Williams's songs, not by his performing talent. There was no chance of making ol' Hank, with his downhome speech and the warbling "tear" in his singing voice, palatable to the pop music followers of a quarter-century ago. The only possibility was to put Williams's songs into the throats of established pop singers. Today that is a simple matter, but it was a daring maneuver when the Roses executed it. To be sure, a number of country writers had breached the pop barrier with a tune or two: Jimmie Davis with "You Are My Sunshine"; Ernest Tubb with "Walking the Floor over You"; Stewart and King with "Tennessee Waltz," which Patti Page turned into a nearly-two-million seller. But no one broke the barrier over and again until Williams came along. He demolished it and, in the process, paved the way for the subtle, fruitful interchanges between pop and country that have become commonplace.

It was Wesley Rose who achieved the actual breakthrough. The Roses had been wrestling with the pop problem for some time, and when Williams wrote **"Cold, Cold Heart,"** they were convinced they had the means to solve it. **"Cold, Cold Heart"** had a universal theme with a twist a man trying to win over a sweetheart who still carries the torch for her last romance. More important, its lyrics were a good deal less countryfied than those of a typical Williams song. So Wesley Rose set off for the pop publishing houses of New York, with the sheet music to **"Cold, Cold Heart"** inhis briefcase. He met severe disappointment: "I beat on everybody's door, and I got the same answer everywhere: 'That's a hillbilly song.'" Finally Rose went to see Mitch Miller, the goateed arranger-conductor who was then in charge of pop music at Columbia Records. Miller bought the song and began shopping it around. Before long he placed it with an aspiring young pop singer named Tony Bennett. Bennett's 1951 recording of **"Cold, Cold Heart"** sold over a million copies and became number one on the pop charts, thereby launching his immensely successful career and dashing forever the artificial barriers between pop and country music.

Throughout the last several years of their respective lives (they died only a year apart), Hank Williams and Fred Rose maintained a relationship that not only covered all areas of Hank's career but often transcended it. Rose became a father figure for the young man who had sorely missed one. He loaned Williams money, helped manage his rapidly growing income, and made periodic efforts to help him rearrange what was fast becoming a chaotic and dangerous private life. In the last area, Rose's interventions were too few and too timid. Had he acted more resolutely, Rose might have forestalled the premature death of one of the authentic giants of American popular culture.

The odds are, however, that Rose could have done no such thing. Driven by loneliness, insecurity, and the burdens of a warped childhood, ravaged by a bitterly competitive marriage, addicted to alcohol and later to pills, Williams was bent on self-destruction. He began drinking before he was twelve, outside the dance halls of south Alabama mining camps. By the time he was twenty, he was virtually an alcoholic, and the remaining nine years of his life can be divided into periods when the boozing was under control and periods when it wasn't. Stories of Williams's drinking are legend in Nashville. They are not stories of great consumption, for the man had a low drunkenness threshold. Nor, with a few exceptions, are they funny stories, for he was not a particularly lovable drunk. Alcohol almost ruined Williams's career before it really took off in Montgomery, then again in Shreveport, where the Hayride found itself barely able to tolerate him.

Genius or not, the proper indeed, stuffy Grand Ole Opry of that day wanted no part of Hank Williams. It was not until he joined forces with a song called **"Lovesick Blues"** that the Opry decided it could no longer resist the Williams momentum. **"Lovesick Blues"** remains a curiosity because it was distinctly outside the country music pattern. Written about 1920 by a pop songwriter, Cliff Friend, **"Lovesick Blues"** was what Wesley Rose calls "a Broadway-type tune." It had a slick, show-business sound to it, along with chord progressions that must have dazzled the country strummer weaned on straight G-C-D with an occasional passing chord (in this instance, A) thrown in. In any event, when Williams began singing **"Lovesick Blues"** on the Louisiana Hayrideearly in 1949, it was an instant success. He cut a record of it, and when the record hit the charts, the Opry talent managers took a deep breath and invited him in for a guest shot. Williams's performance of June 11, 1949, still ranks as the most memorable debut in Opry history. A wildly cheering audience brought him back a half-dozen times to sing the closing line of **"Lovesick Blues":** "I'm lo-o-one-some, I got the lovesick blues." Master of ceremonies Red Foley had to plead with the crowd to cease howling for more and let the program proceed. Nothing could stop Hank Williams after that; nothing, that is, except himself. In the succeeding three years, he rose to and fell from the pinnacle of country music success. Six months later, he was dead.

To become an Opry star, Williams needed his own band. At the Hayride and even before that, he'd had one he called the Drifting Cowboys. Only one of the Cowboys came from Shreveport to Nashville with him, but he kept the band's name nonetheless. It was a smart move. The Drifting Cowboys became one of country music's most famous bands. Although always playing in their leader's shadow, they gained such a following that they were able, twenty years after his death, to resume their career under the same name. During the Williams glory years, the Drifting Cowboys consisted of Jerry Rivers, fiddle; Don Helms, steel guitar; Bob McNett and later Sammy Pruett, lead guitar; Hillous Butrum and later Cedric Rainwater, bass. At the time it was formed, this was hardly an all-star group. The members were young and little known. But they worked hard, blended well, and became a strong asset to Williams and his singing. Butrum, who has seen scores of bands come and go, says the Nashville version of the Drifting Cowboys was the equal of the best country ensembles of its day, which he lists as the Jimmy Dickens and Cowboy Copas bands, the Oklahoma Cowboys, and Ernest Tubb and his Texas Troubadours.

Although Rivers was a fine fiddler and Helms an outstanding steel man, the Drifting Cowboys' distinctiveness came from the head man himself. As soon as he stepped on stage, following a couple of introductory numbers, he was the unquestioned star of the show. The songs played were songs he selected and, four times out of five, songs he had written; he sang the only solos, with the group singing behind him in the old "boys-in-the-band" style. Except for the japes directed at the baggy-pants bass player, the repartee centered on Williams. He was not, however, particularly vain or selfish. He appreciated good instrumental work all the more so because he couldn't produce any himself and encouraged "the boys" to develop impressive instrumental "breaks," or solos. Further, Williams was receptive to innovation. There was usually an electric guitar in his recording sessions; there was sometimes a piano, played by Fred Rose, to add fullness and to smooth out the chunky sound of the string band. (Rose's piano work is audible on just one recording and only because Williams secretly arranged with the band to stop playing and singing a few notes from the end of the song. Rose, faithfully following thescore, played on alone. "I jest wanted to have you on records," Hank drawled.)

Williams's relationship with his Drifting Cowboys was a curious blend of intimacy and privacy. The barnstorming tour and one-night stand were then at their high point, and the Cowboys, like many another band, crisscrossed the country on bone-wearying auto trips to meet their "show date" obligations. By all accounts, the Cowboys were a highly congenial group. They genuinely liked Hank, and they made him the butt of many good-natured jokes. When essential, they acted resolutely to keep him off booze and to shape him up sufficiently to play a show. But none of them ever made a sustained effort to stop his headlong plunge toward self-destruction. In that time and place, such interference was considered an unwarranted invasion of The Leader's privacy. So the Cowboys literally fiddled while their world burned.

What of Hank Williams the entertainer? Even half-drunk, he was brilliant. (More than half, he was a disaster.) No single think about him was extraordinary, although his voice would be closest to it. His voice had no crooning qualities, highly prized by many of today's country artists, but it was strong and steady, and it had a cutting edge. Allan Rankin, who heard Williams sing around Montgomery, caught the essence of it when he wrote: "He had a voice that went through you like electricity, sent shivers up your spine, and made the hair rise on the back of your neck with the thrill. With a voice like that he could make you laugh or cry." Further, Williams had very good phrasing and timing. He could slide easily from note to note or one tempo to another, and he handled demanding songs like **"Lovesick Blues"** without difficulty.

In appearance, Williams was country handsome, with a bony, open face and a thoroughly disarming smile. Women found him extremely appealing, and not only for his looks: Williams pioneered the hunched-over, rocking, lightly gyrating posture that was to culminate, several years later, in Elvis Presley. "He had a real animal magnetism," says comedienne Minnie Pearl, who worked with Williams on many show dates. "He destroyed the women in the audience."

His on-stage style was about as natural as style can be. The jokes and banter were prearranged, but everything else was spontaneous, and Williams never played roles, never tried to create "moods" for particular songs, never pretended to be anything other than the country boy he was. He was outfitted by Nudie, the famous Hollywood country-and-western tailor, but his stage costumes were relatively conservative. And, heaven knows, he didn't dazzle anyone with his guitar playing. He was strictly a chord-and-rhythm man of the type that could easily have been eliminated. (In fact, Fred Rose suggested, at more than one recording session, that Williams leave the guitar work to theback-up men and concentrate on his singing. Hank's reply: "I paid good money for this old box, and I ain't gonna lay it down now.")

Above all, Williams had the infectious appeal common to all great performers. Minnie Pearl saw it often: "People used to tell me, 'We got boys who can sing three times as good as him.' Sure, but they'd never get that cataclysmic reaction from the audience that Hank got. Look at me. I'm not funny. But I've built up the fact that I love to perform, and the people know I love it. That sort of thing is contagious, and it's more valuable than being able to sing or being funny or anything else." Little Jimmy Dickens saw it too: "You could hear a pin drop when Hank was working. He just seemed to hypnotize those people. It was simplicity, I guess. He brought the people with him. He put himself on their level."

The Williams style was shaped in numberless honky-tonks of south Alabama. Williams learned early that the worst mistake a fellow could make in one of those places was to be uppity or to act like anything other than a good ol' boy. Sometimes even those precautions didn't help. Among the many stories of his days in the "blood buckets," as the musicians called the rougher honky-tonks, is one in which Williams got into a scuffle with a drunk who'd been baiting him all evening. The two of them tumbled onto the dance floor, Williams pounding his adversary with a steel fretting bar he'd grabbed from the band's steel guitar. The bar had served him well in the past, Hank later reminisced, "and he was about to go under. One more good blow woulda done it. But he reached out and bit a plug hair and all outta my eyebrow." Williams bore the scar from that fight for the rest of his life.

The young Williams listened to, and probably imitated, most of the great country singers, from Jimmie Rodgers on up. The only ones who seemed to have a lasting influence, however, were Roy Acuff and Ernest Tubb. Williams often said that his own style was a cross between theirs. He took, he said, a little from each: the wailing, stylized sound of Acuff and the phrasing of Tubb. "We were especially similar in presenting songs," Acuff says. "Each of us had a type of cry in our voice, and we sang with a lot of energy and feeling." Acuff adds, however, that the young singer he saw from time to time around Montgomery "didn't try to copy anybody much. He was developing a style of his own. He'd usually come by my dressing room, sit around, sing songs, and play the guitar. He was just a little fellow, and he just hunkered down in the corner, waiting for a chance to sing."

In all his travels, Williams went out of the United States only three times. Two of the times were to Canada, where he played before big, responsive crowds. The third time was a trip to Germany, in 1949, an Opry-sponsored tour of United States military bases. His most famous trip, and the one that demonstrates conclusively his broader-than-country appeal, was his 1951 American tour with the Hadacol Caravan. The caravan was the brainchild of super-salesman Dudley J. LeBlanc, the inventorof Hadacol, largest-selling patent medicine of all time. It brought together many of the brightest stars in American show business. The caravan played one-nighters across the Midwest and South, drawing standing-room-only crowds at every stop. Williams and his Drifting Cowboys, the only "country" act, were an immediate hit. Accordingly, the promoters moved them ever further down the program, toward the closing spots traditionally reserved for the stars. It was in the second-to-last spot on the show, in Louisville, that Williams upstaged none other than Bob Hope.

When Williams ended his set with **"Lovesick Blues,"** recalls Drifting Cowboy Jerry Rivers, "the packed stadium seemed to explode, the ovation was so great." When the master of ceremonies tried to introduce the last act, Hope, his words were lost in the cheers and shouts. Says Rivers: "They just brought him [Hope] on anyway and he stood there in front of the microphone for several minutes while the applauding gradually died down. When the roar was down to a point where his voice could be heard over the sound system, Bob pulled a big ragged cowboy hat down on his ears and said, 'Hello, folks, this is Hank Hope. . . . ' The roar went up again, and Bob Hope shared in some of Hank Williams' glory."

Performing brought out the best parts of Williams's personality his warmth and genuine I'm-just-folks modesty. Offstage, when he was not among close friends, he often became uncommunicative and moody. Discounting Fred Rose, who was practically a father to him, Williams had no close friends. The Drifting Cowboys, singer Ray Price (whose career Williams boosted), and a few country writers, like Vic McAlpin, were close to him in various ways, but none could ever engage him in serious discussions about himself or his problems. In a business whose practitioners talk a great deal about maintaining their privacy, Williams was one man who really did it. When a friend broached the subjects of alcohol or marital difficulties, Hank became so noncommittal or evasive that the conversation quickly faded.

Although Williams had as much formal education as many Nashville celebrities (he was a high-school drop-out), it had little effect on him. His grammar was bad, his syntax worse, and he slurred and misused words with blithe carelessness. Window was "winder," picture was "pitcher." When an interviewer once remarked on the prevalence of sad themes in his songs, he replied somberly, "Yes, I guess I always was a sadist." He doused everything with ketchup and avoided all but bland, familiar foods. He had little use for books or the world of ideas. His reading consisted almost entirely of comic books, newspaper sports pages, and an occasional cheap murder mystery.

While disinterested in formal religion perhaps a reaction to his fundamentalist upbringing he could on occasion become quite emotional about God and spiritual matters in general; certainly there is no lack of conviction in the numerous country hymns he wrote. Curiously, he had a strong antipathy to anyone's takingthe Lord's name in vain, although the general run of swearing was perfectly acceptable. He waged periodic campaigns against cursing among the Drifting Cowboys; before one road trip he cut a slit in the top of a cigar box and announced, "Anybody who uses the Lord's name in vain has gotta put a quarter in the box"; he himself wound up contributing $2.75.

As a performer, Hank Williams sang almost exclusively his own songs. That does not seem remarkable in the era of James Taylor, Kris Kristofferson, and Simon and Garfunkel, but in Williams's time it was unusual, for the simple reason that few singers had a sufficiently large supply of good and varied songs of their own. The fact that Williams had just such a supply is one mark of his songwriting greatness. A larger mark is the extraordinary number of truly memorable songs he turned out. Those songs transcend country music, or any category short of pop. They are part of America's musical heritage, and they elevate the man who wrote them to a very high rank among the nation's songwriters.

Mitch Miller calls Williams "an absolute original" and puts him in a class with Stephen Foster as an American songwriter. "He had a way of reaching your guts and your head at the same time," says Miller. "No matter who you were, a country person or a sophisticate, the language hit home. Nobody I know could use basic English so effectively. Every song socks you in the gut." That is a perceptive synthesis of Williams's songwriting genius. Williams's songs are a lesson in the use of simple language for profound emotional effect. His best work reaches the level of poetry folk poetry, to be sure, but it hardly needs the qualification. Take his most famous single verse, the opener to **"I'm So Lonesome I Could Cry"**:

> Did you ever see a robin weep
> When leaves began to die.
> That means he's lost the will to live,
> I'm so lonesome I could cry.

Those lines may have the Fred Rose touch, but knowing Williams through many others, almost as good, one concludes that it was a light touch at most. The sentiment is pure Williams, and it is distilled through the kind of everyday language he handled so ineptly in speech and so magnificently in song.

Without question, the keys to Williams's greatness as a writer were simplicity and sincerity. Everybody understands what a Hank Williams song means, and almost everyone senses the straightforward, bedrock emotion joy or anguish or both from which it springs. "Hank had the ability to write music that the average unmusical person could understand and yet was not trite," said Ken Nelson of Capitol Records several years ago. "His songs were accepted in the pop field because they were realistic, and they were melodically and lyrically understandable to everyone."

There is no point here in attempting a comprehensive listing of Williams's memorable songs. But one cannot write about the man without naming a few of the great ones: among the love ballads (in addition to **"I'm So Lonesome I Could Cry"**), **"Cold, Cold Heart," "I Can't Help It (If I'm Still in Love with You),"** and **"Your Cheatin' Heart"**; among the hymns, **"I Saw the Light"** and **"When God Comes and Gathers His Jewels"**; among the bouncy, good-natured songs, **"Hey, Good Lookin'," "Why Don't You Love Me (Like You Used to Do)?,"** and **"Move It On Over"**; and among the novelty songs, **"Jambalaya"** and **"Kaw-Liga."**

To Williams, as to many pop and country writers, songwriting was a catch-as-catch-can business. There were no office hours, no period when songs were "written"; instead, there were borrowed pencils, pieces of scrap paper, fragments of lyrics or melodies, sometimes only an idea that would later be coaxed into full flower as a song. Williams himself often said his songs "just come bustin' out." There was, of course, a lot more to it than that. An idea may bust out, but a lot of effort, and usually a lot of trial and error, are required to turn it into a song. In one of the few substantial quotations from him that has ever reached print, Williams elaborated on the inspiration, if not the process, that is involved. The secret, he said, is sincerity: "When a hillbilly sings a crazy song, he feels crazy. When he sings, **'I Laid My Mother Away,'** he sees her a-laying right there in the coffin. . . . What he is singing is the hopes and prayers and dreams of what some call the common people." In truth, the things Williams sang about concern uncommon people too. You don't have to be half-educated or work with your hands or eat at drive-ins to be touched by, and to love, a Hank Williams song. As Vic McAlpin says, "You've got a good song if the public, whether it's kids at Vanderbilt University or a farmer plowing a field in Murfreesboro, hear it three times and go around humming it."

McAlpin recalls how he and Williams used to "write" and swap songs while fishing near Nashville. "He didn't worry about melody. He knew that with ninety percent of all hits, country and pop too, the basic melody is familiar to the guy who hears it. Hell, if it wasn't familiar, nine out of ten people wouldn't buy it." McAlpin cites Jimmie Rodgers as evidence: "Every damn one of Rodgers' melodies is basically the same. All those 'Blue Yodels,' for instance. All they had was different words,

and they were the biggest sellers of their time." When Williams and McAlpin, on one of their fishing trips, concocted a promising song, Williams often bought it from his buddy outright; one song that was born in their boat is **"Long Gone Lonesome Blues,"** which became a Williams standard.

Much has been said, particularly in the years since Williams's death, about how his life and the problems that brought it to an end can be seen in his songs. Fights with his first wife, Audrey, for example, are supposed to have caused him to write this song or that. It is true that Williams, more than most country musicwriters, drew directly and incessantly on his own experiences and feelings. And there is little doubt that at least two of his songs, **"Mind Your Own Business"** and **"Be Careful of Stones That You Throw,"** were meant as pointed replies to gossips who spread the latest story about the drunken Hank or the unhappy Williams marriage. Williams knew intuitively that his problems and emotional responses were not his alone, but typified those faced by millions of other people, and that therefore they were good grist for his songwriting mill.

Unfortunately for Williams and for lovers of good songs, the mill became less and less able to handle the grist. By the fall of 1952, after a scant three years at the top of the country music business, Hank Williams was back in Shreveport. He had been fired from the Grand Ole Opry, and while his name was still magic to millions of fans, it was mud to dozens of promoters whose shows he had skipped or botched under the influence of alcohol. He had also been divorced by Audrey, who was shrewd enough to demand and receive half of all his future royalties. The last months of Williams's life abound in tragicomedy: his marriage to nineteen-year-old Billie Jean Jones Eshlimar, with two paid-admission wedding ceremonies at the New Orleans municipal auditorium; his attempts to kick the alcohol and pill habits and to convince the country music world that he could regain the heights; his pitiful "treatments" at the hands of a quack doctor named Toby Marshall.

The tragedy is heightened by the fact that he died at the very point when a comeback seemed possible. He and the Drifting Cowboys had been booked for a New Year's night show in Canton, Ohio. Williams hired a young man named Charles Carr to drive his Cadillac through a snowstorm from Montgomery to Canton. They never made it. Somewhere in Tennessee, without a sound, Williams died. He had been sleeping for a good deal of the trip, and Carr decided not to disturb him. But at Oak Hill, West Virginia, Carr tried to awaken his passenger and found him dead. The cause of death was, in modern medical parlance, alcoholic cardiomyopathy heart disease directly traceable to excessive drinking. The Canton show went on without Hank, but not without tears. The performers and members of the audience wept openly.

In addition to the many formal proclamations of grief, Williams in death received some strikingly individualistic tributes. MGM's Frank Walker wrote a highly sentimental "open letter" addressed to "Mr. Hank Williams, c/o Songwriter's Paradise"; the letter seemed so appropriate, and so suited to the promotion of record sales, that MGM ran it in full on the back of a Hank Williams memorial album issued soon after the singer's death. On January 2, the Montgomery *Advertiser* gave its entire front page to news of the event and reactions to it; ten days later, the *Advertiser* gave Williams another full page, most of it devoted to the reminiscences of south Alabamians who had or said they had known him.

There was a sudden boom in the sales of Williams's then-current recordings, which included, ironically, **"I'll Never Get Out of This World Alive."** There was also a rash of "tribute" records fifteen or so, almost certainly more than have been generated by the death of any other entertainer. Two were entitled The Death of Hank Williams (one of them sold well over 100,000 copies); among the others were "There's a New Star in Hillbilly Heaven" and "Hank Williams Meets Jimmie Rodgers."

Remarkable as they were, these tributes paled by comparison to the Williams funeral. Save only the awesome turnout for the martyred Dr. Martin Luther King, Jr., fifteen years later, it was the most spectacular funeral the South has ever seen. Twenty-five thousand people gathered in front of the Montgomery municipal auditorium. Several thousand of them managed to file by the casket, and some 2,750 of the privileged were given seats for the service. It was a country music spectacular. Ernest Tubb sang "Beyond the Sunset"; Roy Acuff, **"I Saw the Light"**; Red Foley, his voice breaking, "Peace in the Valley." Four women fainted; a fifth fell at the foot of the casket and was carried from the auditorium in hysterics. It is easy to be cynical about such goings-on. Without doubt there was phony emotion and a hefty portion of "the hype" the deliberate inflation of records and personalities in which Nashville excels. But the hype has not been invented that can get twenty-five thousand people to stand for hours on a cold winter day with nothing tangible to gain, not even a decent view of the proceedings.

There were numerous other events that were far more commercial clean-up than memorial tribute. Wives number one and two both hit the road to perform for audiences as "Mrs. Hank Williams." MGM brought out a movie version of Williams's life called *Your Cheatin' Heart.* It was frankly a cornball moneymaker, and although the singing (by Hank Williams, Jr.) was good, the story was a bowdlerized version of the man's life: no mention of drugs, nor of booze on the Canton trip; no mention of his divorce and subsequent remarriage. These shortcomings have not hindered the movie's commercial success. The most successful country music film ever made, it has earned ten times its original investment of $1.2 million.

Both MGM Records and Acuff-Rose have a strong continuing interest in Hank Williams. Acuff-Rose controls

all of Williams's songs, as well as those precious song snippets. Hank Williams, Jr., now a star in his own right, has turned a number of the snippets into full-dress songs and recorded them for MGM, of course under the title *Songs My Father Left Me.* Thirty LPs of Hank, Sr., are currently in print, and they continue to sell very well. The thirty include not only the inevitable "great hits" and "memorial" albums but more significantly albums that treat the "country" music with lush string arrangements. MGM has sold many millions of Hank Williams records (just how many it declines to say); other artists, from Ramsey Lewis to Ray Charles to Lawrence Welk, have together sold millions more of their renditions of his music. Purists may well deplore the commercialization of songs best sung by the man who created them, but there is no better proof of the songs' and the man's greatness. As the citation on Hank Williams's Country Music Hall of Fame plaque says: "The simple, beautiful melodies and straightforward, plaintive stories in his lyrics of life as he knew it will never die."

Kent Blaser (essay date 1985)

SOURCE: "'Pictures from Life's Other Side': Hank Williams, Country Music, and Popular Culture in America," in *South Atlantic Quarterly,* Vol. 84, Winter, 1985, pp. 12-26.

[In the following excerpt, Blaser examines Williams's life and work to gain insights into American popular culture.]

On 1 January 1953, Hank Williams, on an all night road trip to a New Years' Day performance at Canton, Ohio, died in the back seat of his limousine. He was 29 years old. The cause of death was cardiac arrest precipitated by a combination of drugs and alcohol. The week he died Williams had three songs on *Billboard*'s Top Ten Country Music chart. Twenty-five thousand people attended his funeral in Montgomery, Alabama. Montgomery and Nashville were focal points of a spasm of public mourning for an entertainer not seen again until the recent deaths of Elvis Presley and John Lennon. So ended the life of a man who would become one of the major legends of country music.

"Pictures From Life's Other Side" is one of William's songs. A sentimental, mawkish "talkie" about people defeated by life and "gone bad," it is not one of his better or more memorable efforts. In fact, the song was released under an alias, Luke the Drifter, a ploy Williams sometimes used for material that seemed in some way out of character or below his usual standards. But the importance of this particular title will become obvious as this study unfolds. It is my contention that Hank Williams's career and music offer some important insights into aspects of American society and popular culture that have been too much overlooked or ignored. A rather lengthy digression on American popular culture studies will help explain more precisely what I mean by that.

I

Something approaching a paradigm now shapes much of both the scholarly study and the public perception of American popular culture. From Hector St. Jean de Crevecoeur and Benjamin Franklin to Christopher Lasch and Tom Wolfe, there is and has been a broad consensus on the basic lineaments of the *mentalité* of the average American during most of American history.

A recent book, Conal Furay's *The Grass Roots Mind in America,* provides an exemplary illustration.[1] Furay's is a study of the American mind with the emphasis definitely on its popular components. Based on a wide variety of secondary sources, it is highly typical of current writing about American popular culture. Furay finds that the grass roots American mind tends to be antirational and responds more to common sense, "folkish" symbols, patterns, and associations than to articulated ideas, concepts, and philosophies; and that there is a permanence and stability to the basic *mentalité* that persists despite increasing but superficial change and innovation in American culture. The major bedrock qualities include: (1) a strong sense of individualism, (2) an adherence to traditional values sexual, social, moral, and otherwise, and (3) optimism, a specifically popular culture trait opposed to the fashionable pessimism of modern high culture, with examples such as the saccharine views of the *Reader's Digest* or the sugar-coated stories of Walt Disney suggested as typical evidence.[2]

The sources of this "paradigm" (proto-paradigm would perhaps be better) are not difficult to locate, and they are more than a little respectable. Alexis de Tocqueville is one of the patron saints of students of American culture. Much of *Democracy in America* now seems so familiar as to be commonsense knowledge. Tocqueville's Americans were overwhelmingly middle class bourgeois in the broadest sense "conscious that they are well off," and therefore confident, satisfied, and optimistic, sometimes to the point of smugness. His work also portrayed a people remarkably homogenous and homogenized. The American individual was paradoxically at the same time a conformist a sober, common-sense citizen with a devotion to order, the community, custom, tradition, propriety, and property. And finally, the American (male, at any rate) was a rather shallow, uncomplicated fellow unphilosophical, unconcerned with art or literature, at least of the high-brow variety, materialistic, practical, action-oriented, altogether not much given to brooding and pessimism about the darker side of life. Tocqueville marvelled that Americans had an unshakeable confidence in the "indefinite perfectability of man."[3]

Since Tocqueville, many others have added important features to the American portrait. A string of European visitors Harriet Martineau, Charles Dickens, Mrs. Trollope, Fanny Kemble, Lord Bryce concurred with the broad outlines sketched by Tocqueville, as did American sages like Whitman and Emerson.[4] Henry James made such themes central to some of the finest fiction in English literature (as had Cooper and Hawthorne earlier). And Frederick Jackson Turner developed a composite American that was as famous as Tocqueville's, and very similar. Turner's frontier-shaped American was, among other things, also middle-class, action-oriented, materialistic, practical, and civic-minded. And he was especially marked by a "bouyancy andexhuberence" about himself and his society.[5]

After World War II, exploring these "American character" themes became a major intellectual endeavor. Indeed, the postwar era occupies a special niche in two respects in the development of this intellectual tradition. These years were, first, a time when persistent, unique American traits seemed to stand out more dominantly than ever. This was the era of Willie Loman and the "man in the gray flannel suit," of William Whyte's "organization man" and Vance Packard's "status seekers," of Herbert Gans's "Levittowners," Betty Friedan's "feminine mystique" and Kenneth Keniston's "uncommitted" youth. It was also a time when the formulation of scholarly theories concerning American uniqueness was at a peak. They were at the heart of, but not restricted to, the new discipline of American Studies. David Riesman's *The Lonely Crowd,* R. W. B. Lewis's *The American Adam,* and Henry Steele Commager's *The American Mind* were just a few of the works suggesting the persistence of Tocqueville and Turner's themes of innocence and optimism, the triumph of the present and future over the past. Many other classic studies of American society and American culture were products of this era. One thinks quickly, as contributors, of Reinhold Niebuhr, Richard Hofstadter, C. Vann Woodward, Henry Nash Smith, David Potter, Louis Hartz, George Pierson, Seymour Martin Lipset, Daniel Boorstin, Daniel Bell, and a long list of others. Typical works included Bernard Rosenberg and David M. White's important anthology, *Mass Culture,* John Kenneth Galbraith's *Affluent Society,* Arthur Schlesinger, Jr.'s *Vital Center,* Denis Brogan's *American Character,* and two influential essays, John Higham's "The Cult of American Consensus" and Dwight Macdonald's "Mass Cult and Mid Cult." "Mass Culture," "affluence" and "consensus" were the key words for a decade that was being seen as more and more archetypally American.[6]

Almost willy-nilly certain elements of these works have played a critical role in shaping our understanding of American popular culture. Much of the national character debate, and indeed the entire American Studies endeavor, has recently become focused rather exclusively within the province of popular culture.[7] Recent studies, spanning several centuries of American society, have again and again been dominated by a few key words, concepts, and themes optimism, innocence, blandness, materialism, pragmatism (defined loosely as practicality), prosperity, and a uniquely American, nonideological blend of liberalism and conservatism.[8]

Specific studies of popular culture in the 1950s almost universally supported the broader synthesis, but a few examples will have to suffice. S. I. Hayakawa, in an important and influential article, "Popular Songs vs. the Facts of Life," characterized the decade's popular music as "sweetened, sentimentalized, and trivialized."[9] Herbert Goldberg, writing in the 1960s, agreed. Popular music in the 1950s was "stereotyped" and "infantile"; "conservative, non-controversial, and emotionally inauthentic"; dominated by "slick and smiling non-entities," "phony crooner types" with a "total conformity to blandness."[10] Another popular cultural specialist, Douglas T. Miller, found American popular culture in the 1950s "permeated by religiosity." But what Americans sought from their religion was a "sense of well-being." They did "not want religion to remind them of their frailties or to criticize the status quo." Popular religion of the Norman Vincent Peale-Billy Graham type was part of a broader "cult of reassurance." The American people would only "listen to someone who told them that everything would turn out all right." Like Hayakawa, Miller detected an "ostrich solution" for the real problems facing individuals and society.[11]

The above statements sometimes verge on caricature, but to a substantial degree they still represent our essential view of the 1950s. Slightly more moderate versions occur regularly in many history textbooks, along with scenes from a variety of Rock Hudson-Cary Grant-Doris Day movies, and comments on Eisenhower's golfing, Disneyland, Lawrence Welk, Norman Rockwell, and the Barbie doll phenomenon.[12] A recent wave of nostalgia for the 1950s, evident in the popularity of *Happy Days* and its many television spinoffs and movies like *Grease*, testifies to the breadth, if not the depth, of a popular stereotype of the postwar era.[13]

II

This essay proposes an alternative look at American society in the 1950s, using the career and popularity of Hank Williams as a vantage point from which to view the scene, and suggests that the postwar years are an apt focal point for reexamining the larger issue of American popular culture generally.

Williams's credentials as an important figure in American popular culture are perhaps familiar to some, but are worth reemphasizing.[14] He grew up in moderate poverty in his native, depression-ridden Alabama. After a stint as a struggling local musician in Montgomery, he went to Nashville shortly after World War II to sell some songs he had written, was sent by the Nashville moguls to perform for a popular radio program, the Louisiana Hayride out of Shreveport (the Hayride was a kind of minor league farm club for the Grand Old Opry; it was also the launching pad for Elvis Presley's career several years later) but was soon recalled to Nashville and stepped almost overnight into the national country-music spotlight in 1949, at age twenty-five, with a premiere appearance at the Opry that according to legend

and the memory of various eyewitnesses has never been equalled for its electricity and magnetism. His first big hit, **"Lovesick Blues,"** became the *Cashbox* country/western song of the year, and was followed by five other releases that made the charts that year. After that, in the words of one critic, "there was hardly a week when he didn't have a song in the top 10."[15] Often there were two or three. In the next four years Williams had seven number-one songs, including **"Cold, Cold Heart,"** still one of the longest running C&W singles on *Billboard*'s charts (at forty-six weeks), and a list of other classics including **"Jambalaya," "Hey, Good Lookin'," "Half as Much," "Kaw-Liga," "I'm So Lonesome I Could Cry,"** and **"Your Cheatin' Heart."**[16] Income from record sales and performances was enough to place Williams in the select "superstar" category of public idols who made several hundred thousand dollars a year.[17]

Chart comparisons, however, hardly tell the entire story. Hank Williams died after less than four years of national exposure and was incapacitated during part of those four years by a combination of alcoholism, pain killers, malnutrition, and poor health that left him dead at the age of twenty-nine. Recurring drinking sprees, bouts of depression connected especially with marital problems, and a general inability to handle wealth and fame were all chronic problems aggravated to a critical level by a bitter divorce and subsequent firing from the Opry. Yet millions of fans forgave broken engagements and occasional rude or incoherent appearances, because Williams's music said something important to them.

At the time of his death Hank Williams was already a legendary figure in some intangible sense beyond the level suggested by his record sales or place in the charts.[18] And the legend continued to grow. When the Country Music Hall of Fame opened in 1961, Williams was one of the first three people initiated. His name still dominates polls as the premiere country writer and singer of all time. Performers still make a living doing Hank Williams imitations. Perhaps most importantly, Williams is almost routinely invoked by professionals as the standard by which country writers and performers are measured.[19]

Another measure of Williams's influence lies in the recent popularity of "progressive" country music, which suggests many of the themes, values, and styles embodied by Williams. The current country-music boom, of course, is simply a small example of the obvious "westernizing" of main-stream American culture that has taken place in the last decade. From the popularity of country themes in night clubs and bars across the country (and a resulting spate of injuries inflicted by mechanical bulls) to the ubiquitousness of blue jeans and cowboy boots in pop fashion; from a wave of movies and television specials featuring country-music stars to the penultimate symbol of having arrived culturally, Willie Nelson's designer jeans "country" has become one of the current rages of American popular culture. Even academia has joined the bandwagon. Since 1970 both academic journals and nonacademic magazines catering to country tastes have proliferated, and scholarly journals from *Yale Review* to *Human Behavior* and nearly everywhere in between have had articles on the current country trend.[20]

Williams's reputation has been riding the crest of a much larger wave, then. But current influence and popularity are not the central issues here. Many historians have detected an important change in American popular culture in the 1960s and 1970s a breaking away from earlier traits occasioned by the Vietnam War, by racial turmoil, by Watergate, by the energy and economic crises of recent years that brought an end to the confidence and optimism and innocence that had been the hallmarks of American culture previously.[21] But my argument is that highly visible aspects of current American popular culture were also present, if largely unnoted by historians, to a substantial degree even in the 1950s. Williams, even then, was far more than a minor cult figure or a little known subculture hero. Establishing more firmly his place in American popular culture, however, will require some further background material on popular music, recording, and radio in the twentieth century.

III

The depression of the 1930s devastated the recording industry. There was a near 95 percent drop in record sales between 1927 and 1933. The smaller market that remained was decidedly older and more sophisticated than that of the 1920s; as a result popular music became more complex and refined. But after World War II, numerous forces contributed to a renewal of popular music and to the "plebianization" of popular music that had begun earlier in the twentieth century with ragtime and jazz. There was a marked shift from the dance-oriented big bands and instrumentalists of the 1930s towards a listener-oriented solo singer medium. Dinah Shore, Bing Crosby, Frank Sinatra, and Perry Como emerged from and eventually eclipsed the famous bands of the 1930s. A major reason for the change involved radio. Expanding rapidly after the war, but also facing critical competition in the form of television, radio moved dramatically in the late 1940s towards its typical current format. National network materials which had comprised up to 95 percent of prime time programming was phased out for an orientation and style that heavily emphasized local news and issues, popular music, and a disc jockey personality.[22]

Within this general setting, there was a nationwide boom in country music. Hillbilly songs, as they were mostly called, were the "current wonder of the music world," according to *Newsweek* in 1949.[23] Record sales had quintupled in the four years after the war. "Cool Water" and "Riders in the Sky" had been national best sellers for any kind of music. Million selling records were becoming more common. Two years later the staid *New York Times* reported a "revolution brewing in the

music business," and ran a feature article in their Sunday magazine on "Tin Pan Alley's Git-tar Blues," describing the frantic efforts on Tin Pan Alley to cash in on the Nashville phenomenon.[24] By then "Tennessee Waltz" by an unknown Oklahoman, Patti Page, had sold three million records in eight months and had pushed "White Christmas" off its perennial top seller pedestal.

Country music was truly "big business," as *Newsweek* noted in a second item on the theme.[25] Radio advertising revenues in the early 1950s over-shadowed those of television. Virtually every household in the country that had electricity had a radio (93 percent of all households), and the average listening time was more than five hours per day, per person.[26] Between 1945 and 1950 the number of AM radio stations more than doubled, to over 2,000. At least half of those stations had a country music orientation; 650 had featured live country music shows. A conference sponsored by WSM in Nashville drew 400 disc jockeys from around the nation, at their own expense, to learn more about country records and recording. WSM itself broadcast into 30 states, and its Grand Old Opry, still the longest running show on radio, had nearly 10 million regular listeners plus a consistently sold out live audience. In the late 1940s and early 1950s both the Opry and the Midwest Hayride from Cincinnati were on national television, and the Ozark Jubilee from Springfield, Missouri, garnered a 90-minute prime time slot on Saturday night from NBC.[27]

Top stars, including Williams, Red Foley, Eddy Arnold, and Roy Accuff, were making several hundred thousand dollars a year, a good figure for any entertainer or singer.[28] Some estimates put C&W record sales at rough parity with popular music, the two genres dividing the vast majority of the estimated total of almost 200 million records sold each year in the United States.[29] Again, however, record sales probably substantially understated the overall importance of country music as a popular culture medium. Most studies suggest that country music listeners were generally from lower income brackets, and quite likely purchased fewer records and did more radio listening than their counterparts in the popular music audience.[30]

Nor was the country audience as geographically constricted as is often assumed. When the Lovin' Spoonful lamented in their popular song from the 1960s, "Nashville Cats," the lack of interest in Nashville music north of the Mason-Dixon line, they may have been reflecting popular perceptions of the 1960s, but not the reality of the 1950s. Indeed, one of the most commented-upon features of the country music phenomenon after the war was its new, wider audience. *Newsweek* talked of its "nationwide sales field." *Good Housekeeping* noted that hillbilly music was leaving the hills for an urban audience. *Nations Business* ran an article titled "Country Music Goes to Town." Even the august Jacques Barzun felt compelled to comment on an emerging new cultural type, the "city-billy."[31] Opry road shows were a consistent success throughout the Midwest, West, and South, drawing live audiences of up to 50,000. Country-music radio stations, both local and regional, (50,000 watt), were distributed widely across the country, with the exception of the area east of the Hudson River. (The Opry itself moved to New York City for a summer experiment in 1952 without notable success, either critical or popular; New York was the last major market in the country to get a country music station.) The traditional association of country music with a strictly southern or Appalachian audience doesn't hold for the 1950s.[32]

So, Hank Williams was just the tip of the country music iceberg. He may have had fifteen or twenty million fans; he may have had many times that number of casual but frequent listeners; he may have been the undisputed "king of the hillbillies" (from a *Time* obituary article); but he was not an isolated or unique phenomenon. There is little excuse for the continued underestimation of country music as a major part of popular music and popular culture in the 1950s.[33]

IV

Accepting for the moment Williams's importance, trying to isolate the themes, ideas, and values that his music represented raises some further difficulties and questions. Generally it is true that content or "message" is only a small part of the total "package" that makes a particular song popular. Its impact depends on many factors other than lyrics, so one must be extremely circumspect in deriving broad statements on cultural values from the content of a selected group of popular songs.[34] Different songs, even by the same artist, may suggest different and even conflicting cultural values. Williams, for instance, wrote and sang hymns or "sacred music," and also songs with at least covert anti-religious implications.[35] In the end, given constraints of time and space, one can only argue, first, that Williams's music has enough coherence *in toto* so that certain fundamental themes, values, and beliefs may be derived from them; and secondly, that there is some acknowledged relationship, however tenuous and ill-defined, between a musician's popularity, the ideas or message of his music, and his listeners' values.[36]

In Williams's case, too, these problems are partly alleviated by several factors. First, lyrics play an especially important role in country music generally.[37] Secondly, Williams placed even more emphasis on lyrics than most country singers and writers. He was not an accomplished musician and was relatively unconcerned with the subtleties in melody and accompaniment. A book of advice to would-be country music writers and performers that he co-authored concentrated almost completely on lyric-writing, not on the music itself. He commented to a friend that "every damn one of [Jimmy] Rogers melodies is basically the same," and warned his back up band about "good guitar players who've educated themselves right out of a job." Most of all, however, Williams not only wrote his own music, he lived the kind of music he wrote. He himself argued that his success

could "be explained in just one word: 'sincerity.'" That word appears with uncanny frequency in other peoples' explanations of Williams's charisma and popular appeal as well. A friend noted his ability to "hypnotize" an audience by "putting himself on their level." After his European tour he attributed much of his success to his belief that he represented to both Europeans and American GI's "what everyday Americans are really like."[38] Whether that was true or not, there was nothing phony about the tragedy of his music his life was also tragic, and that was an essential part of his appeal.

Now, what about those themes?

The first impressions one is likely to receive from most of his music are sadness, lonesomeness, unhappiness, and a strong sense of fatalism. To make a difficult attempt at categorizing and quantifying intractible material, of fifty of Williams's most important songs, all but five deal with relationships between the sexes.[39] Of these forty-five, almost one third involve the protagonist being left by the woman with whom he is in love. Other major themes include marriages or relationships in which both members' love has grown cold (11 percent); failure to find love, or unrequited love (14 percent); and "evil woman" songs describing a kind of love-hate relationship with a woman who treats the singer badly (16 percent). There are a scattering of rambling or hobo songs, drinking songs, a prison song, hymns, and seven novelty or miscellaneous songs, of which four describe general martial or personal problems, like the broken romance between the two wooden Indians in **"Kaw-Liga."** Of the fifty total, eight are moderately cheerful, upbeat songs, but five of these are of the honky-tonk, let's-have-a-party-and-get-drunk genre. All in all, there are *three* songs that deal in a reasonably positive way with love and the prospects for future happiness.[40]

Williams's music, then, was hardly a paean to American optimism, innocence, and the good life. A pet phrase, which he used as a signature to close many of his concerts, was "don't worry about nothin', cause it ain't gonna be all right no how." Even his titles reveal deep roots in the blues, that southern black music that contradicts in almost every way the typical popular-culture image of the 1950s. His songs include **"Cold, Cold Heart," "The Blues Come Around," "Weary Blues From Waitin'," "Lovesick Blues," "Never Been So Lonesome," "Moanin' the Blues," "Long gone Lonesome Blues," "I Don't Care If Tomorrow Never Comes,"** and **"I'll Never Get Out of This World Alive."** The first known song he wrote was titled **"WPA Blues."**

Williams is especially associated with a kind of music called "honky-tonk," a blend of country and blues that emerged from the rural South in the 1920s and 1930s. The "honky-tonk hero" (to use a phrase from a recent hit) is one of the major figures in Williams's songs. And the values portrayed often suggest the kind of rebellion against bourgeois morality that supposedly became a part of popular music only with the emergence of folk music and the birth of rock and roll later in the 1950s and 1960s.[41] Casual romance, living from day to day, a rejection of traditional morality are all part of the honky-tonk life.

Indeed, in a variety of ways, Williams went out of his way to flaunt traditional ideas of "proper" behavior, marital bliss, and middle-class values generally. **"Mind Your Own Business"** relates the stormy relationship Williams had with his first wife and not too subtly chastizes people who pry into his private life. From the beginning authorities at the Opry worried that Williams's reputation would damage their clean-cut family image. Williams and the Opry maintained, at best, an uneasy relationship until he was finally fired for drunkenness and missed engagements.

Williams did, of course, partake of some of the traditional popular culture of the 1950s. He styled himself after that quintessential American symbol of individualism, innocence, and optimism the cowboy. He wore ostentatiously western clothes and called his band the Drifting Cowboys; he even ran away to join a rodeo as a teenager. All of this was perhaps sincere enough, but it was also almost entirely superficial. Williams sang almost no true western songs. Both his career and his music were a direct contradiction to the squeaky-clean cowboy image cultivated by the famous singing cowboys and western movie stars of the period Roy Rogers, Gene Autry, or William Boyd (Hopalong Cassidy). As mentioned earlier, Williams wrote religious music, but surprisingly for an era and audience usually viewed as extremely religious, Williams's sacred songs were not among his top sellers, even though some of them have later come to be recognized as classics of the genre. Most of Williams's listeners apparently preferred honky-tonking, drinking, and frustrated love as themes.

Of course, "somebody-done-somebody-wrong" songs and "look-how-rotten-things-are-let's-get-drunk" songs are standards of country music generally.[42] Williams was unique only in the intensity and talent with which he pursued the theme, and in his wide popularity. It hardly appears coincidental that blues, country music, and Hank Williams all originated in the rural South. This may support C. Vann Woodward's contention that the South was long atypical in having a sense of defeat, pessimism, and irony not present in most of American culture.[43] But the fact that Williams brought country blues to a receptive, national audience in the 1950s, an audience that cut through the sectional limitations of earlier traditional country music, suggests that more of the nation was ready to tune in to such emotions and ideas than has usually been recognized. If Williams had fifteen million devoted fans, it was because his music told them something many of them knew was true that life was not all easy and all right. Heartbreak and lonesomeness were part of it too, and people liked Williams for singing about it, and for living it.

V

So, where does all of this leave us in terms of popular culture in the 1950s? I certainly do not want to imply thatprevious perspectives on popular culture in the 1950s are wrong only that there are some important alternatives.

Significant insights might be gained here from other scholarly fields. Anthropologists, folklorists, and European social historians have found persistent conflicts between folk culture and the more official culture of the elites of society. Folk events, from premodern Europe through the nineteenth century, frequently provided an outlet for both suppressed sexuality and pent-up economic and social frustration. From the persistence of pagan beliefs and popular superstition at holidays like Mayday to the "world-turned-upside-down" motif and the Feast of Fools during Carnival, from bear-and-bull baiting and other popular "blood" sports to the sexuality of lower-class dance and song, heavy overtones of sex, violence, and class and generational tensions dominate much of Western folk and popular culture.[44] Much the same is almost certainly true of American folk culture in the eighteenth and nineteenth centuries.[45] We should not, of course, expect to see such themes displayed so obviously in twentieth-century America, when various subcultures *have* been much homogenized and bourgeois culture has become pervasive, through mass media, at all levels of society. But perhaps we have overemphasized such trends. Marshall McLuhan's persuasive characterization of mass culture and mass media as the "folk-lore of the common man" is in some ways seriously misleading. It has led to a major confusion of folk culture with mass media or popular culture. Post-World-War-II country music may not be genuine folk culture either though some scholars argue that it is but it is almost surely less distant, less manipulated and shaped by external forces and is closer to grass-roots feelings than most cultural media.[46]

Many fault lines cut, however obliquely, across the usual categories of American culture and society. There are distinctions between the "respectable" and "not-so-respectable" members of a community, between the church-goers and pool-hall frequenters of a small town, between the college-bound and noncollege-bound students of a high school. American popular culture studies are too often dominated by the former of these, whose values tend to monopolize official popular culture television, movies, mass media print that are the bread-and-butter sources of most popular culture studies.

Hank Williams's music gives us some "pictures from life's other side." His popularity suggests that sympathy with this "underground" aspect of popular culture was still significant in the 1950s, and more pervasive than is often realized. He had a wide appeal, and it was an appeal that penetrated to the supposed core of American culture small town, rural, middle class America. At the very least this should make us wary of stereotyping too glibly *the* popular mind or culture of American society. Some Americans in the 1950s may indeed have been listening to Lawrence Welk, Billy Graham, Norman Vincent Peale, or Walt Disney, and singing along to popular songs that urged them to "accentuate the positive." But many were also fans of Hank Williams getting drunk, grinding his hips and swooning on stage, exuding what one critic called "raw sexual primitivism,"[47] and singing songs like **"Mansion on the Hill"** and **"Wealth Won't Save Your Soul"** that had transparent class and social implications. Williams represents tensions, traditions, and currents of the 1950s that have been too much ignored. His songs at least remind us that there was indeed an "other side" to American society. The 1950s weren't "Happy Days" for everyone.

NOTES

[1] Conal Furay, *The Grass Roots Mind in America: The American Sense of Absolutes* (New Haven, Conn., 1977).

[2] Ibid., pp. 7-26, 32-58.

[3] Richard Heffiner, ed., *Democracy in America* (New York, 1956), pp. 5-38, 119-20, 156-57.

[4] See Edward Pessen, *Jacksonian America* (Homewood, Ill., 1969), pp. 5-38, and Seymour Martin Lipset's "Introduction" to Harriet Martineau's *Society in America* (New York, 1962).

[5] *The Significance of the Frontier in American History* (New York, 1963), p. 57.

[6] Political scientists, especially, armed with the new weapon of public opinion polls (and multinational ones at that) turned out work after work in the 1950s and early 1960s, corroborating the consensus view of the political culture of the average American citizen. Geoffrey Hodgson, *America in Our Time: From World War II to Nixon, What Happened and Why* (New York, 1976) contains a good summary, especially on pp. 67-69.

[7] See Robert Sklar, "The Problem of an American Studies 'Philosophy': A Bibliography of New Directions," *American Quarterly* (August 1975): 245-62; Karen Winkler, "For Scholars in American Studies, the Intellectual Landscape Is Changing," *Chronicle of Higher Education,* 10 March 1980.

[8] In addition to works already mentioned in the text, on American character see works by Ralph Gabriel, Michael Kammen, Irving Bartlett, and Paul Kurtz. For more specifically popular cultural interpretations, see John Kouwenhoven, Richard Schickel, William K. Schweinder, Alice Payne Hackett, Ruth M. Elson, William Brown, and Steven Piess. There have of course been exceptions to this view, but they represent a distinctly minority viewpoint. One of the more thorough recent revisionists is Lewis Saum, *The Popular Mind of Pre-Civil War America* (Westport, Conn., 1980).

[9] "Popular Songs vs. the Facts of Life," in *Mass Culture: The Popular Arts in America,* by Bernard Rosenberg and David M. White (Glencoe, Ill., 1957), pp. 393-402.

[10] "Contemporary Popular Music," *Journal of Popular Culture* (Winter 1971): 579-89.

[11] "Popular Religion of the 1950s: Norman Vincent Peale and Billy Graham," *Journal of Popular Culture* (Summer 1975): 66-67. For other similar interpretations, see Richard Hasbany, "Bromidic Parables: The American Musical Theatre During the Second World War," *Journal of Popular Culture* (Winter 1973): 642-65, and a contemporary study, Lee Coleman, 'What Is American? A Study of Alleged American Traits," *Social Forces* 19 (1941): 492-99.

[12] For examples, see William Leuchtenburg, *A Troubled Feast,* pp. 69-83 Conkin and Burner, *A History of Recent America,* pp. 620-29; Link and Catton, *American Epoch,* pp. 631-64.

[13] There was, of course, another darker side to the 1950s that was represented by Elvis and rock and roll, James Dean, the Beats, juvenile delinquency, and teenage gangs. But that is usually seen as a distinct undercurrent, a minority, youth-oriented subculture counterpoint to the main themes of the decade.

[14] The main source of biographical information for the following has been Roger M. Williams, *Sing a Sad Song: The Life of Hank Williams* (New York, 1970).

[15] Eli Waldron, "Country Music I: The Death of Hank Williams," *Reporter,* 19 May 1955, 37.

[16] Joel Whilburn, *Top Country and Western Records, 1949-71* (Menomonee Falls, Wis., 1972).

[17] Williams, *Sing a Sad Song,* pp. 220-54; "Country Music is Big Business," *Newsweek,* 11 August 1952, 82-85; "Hillbilly Heaven," *American Magazine,* March 1952, 121; Waldron, "Country Music I," 35-37.

[18] Williams was preeminently a live performer. His stage appeal was almost uncannily magnetic. He quickly became the favorite act on a military entertainment entourage to Europe in 1951. On a celebrity-studded touring show known as the Hadacol Caravan he upstaged such luminaries as Jack Benny, Milton Berle, and Bob Hope, and eventually took over the closing spot. Many of the people who listened to Hank Williams were not part of the affluent 1950s. They probably did not buy hi-fis or records with the same frequency as their wealthier neighbors with more sophisticated tastes in music. But they did have radios.

[19] Williams's influence has been pervasive in many areas ofpopular music. He was one of the first and most successful writers to span the gulf between country and "pop" music. His songs became popular hits for a vari-

ety of entertainers in the 1950s. Tributes to the influence of Hank Williams turn up in the songs and personal statements of artists in folk, blues, and rock and roll as well as country and western music. An informal impression finds Williams rivaled only by Elvis Presley and Woodie Guthrie. See *Sing a Sad Song,* pp. v-vii; Malone, *Country Music USA,* p. 232; and Dean and Nancy Tudor, *Grass Roots Music* (Littleton, Col., 1979), pp. 202-04.

[20] *The Journal of Country Music, Country Music, Country Music Review, Old Time Music, Mississippi Rag, Music City,* and *Country Music People,* all beginning publication between 1970 and 1975, are some examples.

[21] See, for examples, Robert Wiebe, *The Segmented Society* (New York, 1975); Frances Fitzgerald, *America Revised* (New York, 1979); C. Vann Woodward, *The Burden of Southern History* (Baton Rouge, 1970); and Sidney Nie et al., *The Changing American Voter* (Cambridge, Mass., 1976).

[22] H. F. Mooney, "Popular Music Since the 1920's: The Significance of Shifting Taste," *American Quarterly* (Spring 1968): 67; Martin W. Laforse and James A. Drake, *Popular Culture and American Life* (Chicago, 1981), pp. 7-64; Frederick Lewis Allen, *The Big Change* (New York, 1952), pp. 273-76; Kenneth Bartlett, "The Popularity of Pre-TV Radio," in *The History of Popular Culture Since 1815,* Norman F. Cantor and Michael S. Werthman, ed. (New York, 1968), pp. 193-95; Alan Havig, "Radio and American Life," *Reviews in American History* (September 1980): 403-07; and Eric Barnouw, *The Golden Web: A History of Broadcasting in the U.S.* (New York, 1968), Vol. 2.

[23] "Corn of Plenty," 13 June 1949, pp. 76-77. See also Malone, *Country Music USA,* p. 232.

[24] *New York Times Magazine,* 15 June 1951.

[25] "Country Music is Big Business," 11 August 1952.

[26] According to a survey by Paul Lazarsfeld and Harry Field, *The People Look at Radio* (Chapel Hill, N.C., 1946), p. 101.

[27] George O. Carney, "Country Music and the Radio: A Geographic Assessment," *Rocky Mountain Social Science Journal,* p. 21; Dean and Nancy Tudor, *Grass Roots Music,* pp. 202-04; Bartlett, "Pre-TV Radio," pp. 193-96; and "They Love Mountain Music," *Time,* 7 May 1956, 60.

[28] See *Newsweek,* 13 June 1949, 76-77; *Reporter,* 19 May 1955, 35-37; *American Magazine,* March 1952, 29-121.

[29] By contrast, in the mid-1960s the country music share of the total market had declined drastically, to as low as 10 percent; in the early 1970s it began climbing rapidly and is now back near parity with rock and roll. The number of country music radio stations was growing by about 20 percent per year in the late 1970s. L. M. Smith, "An Introduction to Bluegrass," and Ed Kahn, "Hillbilly Music; Source and Resource," both in *Journal of American Folklore,* (July-September 1965): 253, 264; "Who Listens to Country Music," *Human Behavior,* (November 1975): 63; *New York Times Magazine,* 15 July 1951, 36; *Newsweek,* 11 August 1952, 85; *American Magazine,* March 1952, 28.

[30] This is an important issue. Unfortunately, determining specifics for a radio audience is a very difficult problem and is generally beyond the scope of this study. Suggestive studies, however, include Charles F. Gritzner, "Country Music: A Reflection of Popular Culture" (Paper mailed to the author), "Who Listens to Country Music?," *Human Behavior;* Paul Dimaggie et al., "Country Music: Ballad of the Silent Majority," in R. S. Denisoff and R. A. Peterson *The Sounds of Social Change* (Chicago, 1972), and R. W. Hodge and D. J. Treman, "Class Identification in the U.S.," *American Journal of Sociology* (March 1968): 535-47.

[31] "Corn of Plenty" 13 June 1949, 76; "Hillbilly Music Leaves the Hills" June 1954, 18; February 1953, 41: 44-46; "A Kind Word for Pop, Bop, and Folk," *Reporter,* 17 May 1956, 36-39.

[32] Several reasons for the geographic dispersion of country music have been noted. The gigantic, so-called "X" stations operating from Mexican border areas (beginning with XER from Del Rio in 1930) broadcast to most of the U.S. and could sometimes be heard in Canada and Western Europe. Much of their programming included country music. The continuing migration of Southerners northward during and after the war probably also played a role. Country music was especially popular with men in the armed forces. Almost any area with a large concentration of service men, including Europe and Japan, was likely to be fertile ground for the spread of country music. See Carney, "Country Music and the Radio," pp. 20-22; Wilgus, "Hillbilly Music"; *Journal of American Folklore,* 1965; *Newsweek,* "Corn of Plenty: and "Country Music is Big Business"; "Country Music II," *Reporter;* John Greenway, "Country Western: The Music of America," *American West* (November 1968), 32-41.

[33] For specific examples, see Mooney, "Popular Music" and Hitchcock, *Music in the United States.* The quote is from *Time,* "King of the Hillbillies," 12 January 1953, p. 92. The estimated number of fans is from Williams, *Sad Song,* p. 244, and *Reporter,* "Country Music I," p. 12.

[34] An exemplary warning should be served by the popularity, at roughly the same time and with at least partly the same audience, of conservative/patriotic songs like Barry Sadler's "Ballad ofthe Green Beret" and Merle Haggard's "Fightin' Side of Me," and protest songs like Barry McGuire's "Eve of Destruction," Bob Dylan's "World War III Blues," and Crosby, Stills and Nash's "Chicago" and "Ohio." This problem is addressed in

R. Serge Denisoff and Mark H. Levine, "The One Dimensional Approach to Popular Music: A Research Note," *Journal of Popular Culture* (Spring 1971),: 911-19, and Mooney, "Popular Music," pp. 84-85.

[35] A particularly poignant anecdote: One of Williams's popular religious songs was "I Saw the Light." Near the end of his career, coming off the stage having just finished that song, Williams commented to a close friend, Minnie Pearl, that for him there wasn't any "light."

[36] For support for this side of the argument, see Alan Lomax, *Folk Song Style and Culture* (Washington, D.C., 1969), pp. 6-8; Clifford Geertz, "Art as a Cultural System," *MLN,* 1976, pp. 1473-99; Lawrence W. Levine, *Black Culture and Black Consciousness* (New York, 1977), pp. 270-97.

[37] See Tudor and Tudor, *Grass Roots Music,* p. 200; Ann Nietzke, "Doin' Somebody Wrong," *Human Behavior* (November 1975): 64-69; Gritzner, "Country Music."

[38] *Sad Song,* pp. 119, 115, 151, 162.

[39] The sources for the following are Melvin Shatack, ed., *The Songs of Hank Williams* (Nashville, n.d.); Whilburn, *Top Country and Western Records;* and the discography in Williams's *Sing a Sad Song.*

[40] This is almost identical to the findings of another study of the content of country songs generally. Dorothy A. Hortsman, *Sing Your Heart Out Country Boy* (New York, 1975).

[41] See Coldberg, "Contemporary Popular Music," and Miller and Novak, *The Fifties,* pp. 291-314.

[42] See Hortsman, "Sing Your Heart Out"; Tudor and Tudor, *Grass Roots Music;* Nietzke, "Doin' Somebody Wrong"; Waldron, "Country Music II"; and *Good Housekeeping,* "Hillbilly Music Leaves the Hills," for an interview with D. J. Nelson King.

[43] *Burden of Southern History,* p. 213-33.

[44] Good examples are works by Peter Burke, Robert W. Malcolmson, Leroy Emmanuel Ladurie, and Michel Foucault. Much of the very large volume of work focusing on modernization deals at least obliquely with this issue.

[45] Herbert S. Guttman, *Work, Culture and Society in Industrializing America, 1815-1919* (New York, 1977) is one of the best of many examples.

[46] See Gritzner, "Country Music," and Greenway, "Country Western," for the argument that country music is genuine folk art.

[47] Tudor and Tudor, *Grass Roots Music,* p. 215.

Richard Leppert and George Lipsitz (essay date 1990)

SOURCE: "'Everybody's Lonesome for Somebody': Age, the Body, and Experience in the Music of Hank Williams," in *Popular Music,* Vol. 9, No. 3, October, 1990, pp. 259-74.

[*In the following excerpt, Leppert and Lipsitz give credit to Williams's diverse musical background, which they assert increased the legitamacy of country music.*]

> 'He was so ordinary he merges with the crowd in my memory.' (Mrs Lilly McGill, teacher, Georgiana, Alabama, on her former pupil, Hank Williams.)

Houston Baker locates the blues at the crossroads of lack and desire, at the place where the hurts of history encounter determined resistance from people who know they are entitled to something better (Baker 1984, pp. 7, 150). Like the blues singers from whom he learned so much, Hank Williams (1923 to 1953) spent a lot of time at that particular intersection. There he met others whose own struggles informed and shaped his music. Williams's voice expressed the contradictions of his historical moment post Second World War America a time when diverse currents of resistance to class, race and gender oppressions flowed together to form a contradictory, but nonetheless real, unity of opposites. Standing at a crossroads in history, at a fundamental turning point for relationships between men and women, whites and blacks, capital and labour, Williams's songs about heartbreak and failed personal relations indentified the body and the psyche as crucial terrains of political struggle in the post-war era.

Hank Williams was an extraordinary artist, a songwriter with a gift for concise yet powerful expression, and a singer with exceptional phrasing and drama. Yet we miss the point if we view Williams solely as an individual genius who rose above the crowd; the real story of Hank Williams is how he remained part of the crowd by letting its diverse currents flow through him. His extraordinary popularity, his success at introducing country music to new audiences, and his influence on an astonishingly diverse range of popular musical artists and genres all stem from Williams's ability to understand and articulate the blasted hopes and repressed desires of his audience.

Above all, Hank Williams understood that the profound changes in American family life during the 1930s and 1940s had ushered in anew era, fundamentally altering old categories of age, gender and romance. His songs soared to popularity in the early 1950s, a time often hailed as the 'golden age' of the family (see May 1988; Mintz and Kellogg 1988). Yet Williams's narratives exuded a fatalism and despair about personal relationships. They resisted romantic optimism, and also avoided the kinds of closure and transcendence historically associated with male subjectivity. In this way, they expressed what Tania Modleski has described as a refusal to be oedipalised (Modleski 1982, p. 74), and what Fred Pfeil calls the 'deoedipalisation of American society' (Pfeil 1988, pp. 395-6).[1]

This is not to argue that Hank Williams found his way to an emancipatory political programme or even to a cultural vision completely free from dominant constructions of gender, sexuality and romance. Far from it. But it is to claim that Williams's music and lyrics represented a significant refusal to accept dominant cultural narratives, and that they gave voice to potentials for resistance that remain important to this day. People can be imprisoned by cultural stories as easily as by iron bars and stone walls. Indeed, the core insight of contemporary cultural studies has been the understanding that people are more frequently contained within cultural narratives than within jail cells. In this context, all refusals are important because they represent a challenge to the prisons of mind and spirit that repress emancipatory hopes. Our exploration of the music of Hank Williams focuses on the ways in which he gave an individual voice to collective fears and hopes about the body, romance, gender roles and the family. We wish to locate these issues variously, in the site/sight of his physical body, his voice, his lyrics and his music.

AGE AND HISTORICISATION OF THE BODY

Hank Williams began his career as a child prodigy and ended it as a still young man who appeared years older than his age. At thirteen, he won an 'amateur hour' contest in Montgomery, Alabama with a song protesting against the conditions facing labourers for the federal Works Progress Administration. Williams's singing and songwriting immediately earned him a spot as 'The Singing Kid' on a local radio show featuring 'Dad' Cryswell and his band (Caress 1979, p. 25). But his first recording session did not come until 11 December 1946 and he attained his first hit record in 1947 (Kingsbury and Axelrod 1988, p. 247). His last recording session occurred on 23 September 1952, slightly more than three months before his death in the early morning hours of 1 January 1953. Thus his career as a country singer spanned only six years, beginning when he was twenty-three and ending with his death at twenty-nine. Despite Williams's short life and the relative brevity of his career, among the more striking aspects of his work as a lyricist, composer and performer were the multiple and complex encodings of both age and experience as played out on the ground of the individual human body, both physically andpsychically. Significantly, he located his work within a context that invariably posited that body not in the transcendence of timeless/universal humanism, but in the history of rural southern poor and working class America in the mid-twentieth century.

The concept of youth is largely taken as a 'natural' and not constructed category in American middle-class culture today. But in the early post-war years (especially among the rural poor) the concept had little bearing on life as it was lived, as Williams's own typical experience as a child labourer illustrates. To be young was essentially to be an even less reliable wage slave than one's parents, in a setting when obtaining work at all ages was a necessity for survival. Hank Williams lived out his short life within this larger reality; he lived out his decade as an 'official' of-age adult under still more complex circumstances, during a decade of traumatic post-war change in America in general, and in the rural south in particular. In this respect, his experience paralleled that of a generation of young men and women who came of age during the war (where, in the field, a twenty-six-year-old might commonly be referred to as the Old Man) and who confronted the jolting realities of an atomic peace immediately re-defined in terms of Cold War and economic upheaval, massive migrations from the land to the emerging suburbs, and changing prescriptions for family life and for relations among races, classes and genders.

Hank Williams was heard as 'authentic' at a time when authenticity was a prime determinate in the success of in-person and radio performers. (Like other country singers of his time, Williams never pulled back from the live-performance circuit; audiences were built and maintained by visual contact and live radio, without which recording careers could not develop, and 'in his prime, Hank was doing two hundred one-nighters a year' (Koon 1983, p. 88; see also p. 93).) There are several interlocking reasons why this is so, among which the 'age' of the experiences his lyrics described and the 'age' of his voice were of special importance. At a more immediate and pre-musical level, his appearance played a part as well.

At twenty-three, as at twenty-nine, Williams was a chronologically young man long past youth indeed, a man who seemingly never experienced youth, as was borne out by his physical appearance. At six feet in height he was not especially tall, but his thin body (140 lbs), and the hats he perpetually wore (to cover his thinning hair about which he was sensitive [Williams 1981, p. 144), made him look taller: he stood out. Toward the end of his life he was haggard, gaunt, physically wrecked. He began drinking by the time he was eleven (*ibid.*, p. 15), a habit he continued with few interruptions for the rest of his life, compounded by drug use in his later years (amphetamines and Seconal, the sedative chloral hydrate, and morphine). He had a form of spina bifida which exacerbated his chronic back painand, near the end, hepatitis and a heart condition; and he suffered from malnutrition when drinking heavily he did not eat, sometimes for days on end (*ibid.*, pp. 175, 205, 207; Koon 1983, p. 50). His body could never properly fill out his expensive tailor-made suits (evident even in the posed publicity shots).

The appearance of Williams's body marked the urgency of age as a central category in his work, especially in a culture where increasingly prescriptive postwar expectations of bodily and behavioural propriety were being forged. It was well known that Hank Williams lived his life on the edge. His music masked none of it. His songs about failed love followed closely the dismal history of his marriages and his innumerable one-night stands just as his obsession with death and repentence (of which more follows) confirmed that he knew the price he was paying both in this life and, unless he was careful, likewise the next. Williams referred to himself as 'ole Hank' both on the air and in private.[2]

Audiences were by no means amused by or even tolerant of his most drunken performances, especially when he failed to remember lyrics (see Williams 1981, p. 180). His increasingly debilitating alcoholism culminated in his being thrown off the Grand Ole Opry in 1952 (*ibid.*, pp. 172-3, 191, 196-8); his trips to sanitariums for drying out 'became almost routine' (*ibid.*, p. 194). Nevertheless, audiences 'loved Hank partly *because* of his problems', according to Frank Page, associated with Shreveport's KWKH Louisiana Hayride (*ibid.*, p. 198).[3] For those who saw his live performances, drunk or sober, his physical vulnerability was both obvious and affecting. In body he confounded the model of the self-reliant, self-contained in-shape and battle-tested postwar male ('He'd come slopping and slouching out on stage, limp as a dishrag' [*ibid.*, p. 140, quoting *Montgomery Advertiser* columnist Allen Rankin]).

Hank Williams's lyrics and music, like his physical appearance, reflect age and the historicisation of the body in love songs and gospel numbers alike. In the first instance, his subjects invariably exude a spoken or unspoken history. His upbeat love songs (**"If You'll be a Baby (to Me)"**) characteristically refer to a rural timelessness, a pastoral imagery that pulls back from postwar futurism ('I can plow and milk the cow . . . [You] keep the homefires burnin'") but which, by recalling agrarian cyclical chronology, confront the sense of the real (not imagined) loss of that way of life.[4] To be sure, images of the man in the field and the woman in the kitchen correspond roughly to the Levittown ideal of suburban social organisation, but only to an urban/suburbanite. The rural reality encoded here is one of shared labours: the woman is not kept cosy by her man's work; she is a labourer as well. She heats her cookstove with wood and coal, and she does the wash with her bare knuckles. In this way Williams's lyrics, built on traditional domestic rural socialorganisation, incorporate simultaneously an ancient and recent past that his listeners clearly recognised, that most had lived or were still living, but which they also knew was ending in favour of a future that was profoundly uncertain. In this regard, Williams when he sang about love, voiced more than the desire for partnership: he voiced the pain of loss for a way of life that could already be described with the anxiety of ending.

As regards gospel, the fact that a young man in the 1940s might sing of Jesus (and in 20 per cent of his repertory [Koon 1983, p. 81]) is not in itself particularly surprising, at least in the rural south, though the num-bers of Williams's gospel tunes may be unusual (some were recorded under his own name, others under the pseudonym of his alter-ego Luke the Drifter). In many respects a tune like **"How Can You Refuse Him Now?"** is quite an ordinary, even conventional piece of white gospel. But in other ways, this song and others like it exceed conventions. Unlike contemporaneous southern black gospel, his tunes are seldom upbeat; neither musically nor lyrically do they convincingly encode happiness, let alone ecstasy. Instead, they fixate on death (as in **"We're Getting Closer to the Grave Each Day,"** recorded when he was twenty-six, and **"Mother is Gone"**) and on death rituals (**"The Funeral"**, in this instance that of a black child[5]). Williams's religious lyrics speak to life's suffering and failures, often without recourse to the promise of an afterlife. As such they tend to exceed and politically subvert the generic passivity encoded especially into much white gospel music. (The musical and performative vitality of black gospel, by contrast, acts to undercut the otherworldly fixation of the lyrics, re-establishing the physical present, as well as the spiritual future, in the lives of believers.) That is, once the hope of afterlife is pushed aside, the terrain that matters is located in the concrete personal and social body, not in the abstract soul. Thus even in **"I Saw the Light"**, perhaps his best known gospel song but certainly not his best the most Williams can offer for accepting Jesus fails to exceed this life, as it vaguely conjures up the rather tired imagery of smiling in the face of adversity (as the phrase now runs: 'Don't worry, be happy'). The text proffers consolation, and consolation is the only reward; the reserve with which Williams sings the words only confirms the limits of hope offered, all the more given his biological' youth from which conventional 'idealism' and future directedness are already stripped.

"Men with Broken Hearts", a Luke the Drifter (non-gospel) recitation (recorded 21 December 1950), locates the terrain of failure in particularly dismal (and unrelenting) fashion, calling forth rhetorically to God at the end, but without hope for redress. The text speaks of defeat in the metaphor of men's broken bodies stooped shoulders, heads 'bowed low', vacantly staring eyes walking allegories of what Williams calls 'living death', relief from which can only come via death itself.

At the level of an unconscious politics lies the gesture of recognition that to have failed in this life is to have failed: it carries its own punishment and there is nothing more beyond it, or at least nothing one can safely predict. In **"We're Getting Closer to the Grave Each Day"**, Williams reiterates the theology of Christ's redemptive death and, to be sure, he makes passing reference to the Judgement Day. But the image that incessantly repeats is that of the approach to the grave. In **"How Can You Refuse Him Now?"**, the image of Christ crucified is not that of the redeemer, but of a man suffering. It is His suffering that should trigger our response, not our own fear of death or a hope for afterlife. Christ, in essence, becomes one of us, a man in trouble.

Hank Williams's singing voice registers differently from his [FM!-] radio-perfect speaking voice. There is an aura of careworn exhaustion even in his quasi-upbeat tunes. Thus in the 56 second fragment **"If You'll Be a Baby (to Me)"**, a lyric essentially proposing marriage, Williams does not sound like a teenager in love, nor even a twenty-year-old. There is no sense of passionate sensuality in either the words or the voice. There is instead a textual promise of peace ('no quarrellin") and a vocal explicitly timbral expression of hope for refuge. That is, the putative subject of the tune has all the naivete of uncomplicated first-love-and-family aspirations ('I'll be your baby/ And I don't mean maybe'), but Williams's voice encodes something more complex. The delivery is subdued, the words slightly swallowed, the overall acoustical affect establishing associations less of first love than of trying-once-more. It is a voice of knowing, not anticipating, confined to a narrow range (a major sixth), middle register (the high note is A below middle C), and a middling dynamic. The enthusiasm presumed by the lyrics is undercut by the doubtfulness of the delivery.

In **"A House without Love is Not a Home"**, the narrative plays off a long-time relationship now failed, its imagery repeatedly referring to the passage of time and loss. The timbral difference from Williams's deep, resonant speaking voice is striking. The voice is thin and, characteristically, his pitch wavers on held notes, especially in the upper half of his narrow register. It is a voice lacking certainty but gaining thereby in credibility. The melodic structure produces a different affect from that of **"If You'll Be a Baby (to Me)"**. In the earlier tune, Williams's upper register is not called upon and most of the intervallic relationships are seconds, apart from the major/minor thirds and a single perfect fourth. In **"A House Without Love"** the range extends over a tenth (to E above middle C), and the tune is largely constructed around the interval of a fourth: that is, it is far more disjointed, providing the opportunity/ necessity for him to connect the two pitches of the interval with a slurred slide (in instances where the interval is falling, as the majority of them do). And though, to be sure, this is a musical gesture characteristic to much country music, it is a musicalpractice outside country music more commonly located in the singing of women than men. Combined with the other vocal features we have described, it registers uncertainty, vulnerability, and given the lyrics the sorts of failure that only age can produce.

Both tunes are in the key of C and neither uses any chromatic inflection: the melodies are musically straightforward, 'guileless'. Indeed, Williams characteristically keeps melodic, rhythmic and harmonic surprises to a minimum the arch-shape of his melodies is sufficiently predictable that committing the tunes to memory is easily accomplished on one or two hearings. All of this affects the reception of Williams's music. Taken together, the appeal is that of a boy-man; the musical vocabulary encodes a simplicity on the verge of the child-like; contrarily, the voice is marked by uncertain age. The contradiction results in the ambiguity and complexity of audience reactions, especially when combined with his physical performance image. He is to be mothered, but also to be erotically loved, and above all to be heard as one's own: a capsulised history of a self-consciously regionally-ghettoised people.

If we look at Williams's gospel tunes, the same features are found (**"We're Getting Closer to the Grave Each Day"**, **"How Can You Refuse Him Now?"**); indeed, the distinctions between these two primary genres of his work are few.[6] Notable among them are the frequent shift from the duple time characteristic of the secular tunes to a lilting 3/4 in gospel; in the religious tunes, he uses a more pronounced slur-slide on downward moving intervals; and here too the famous vocal 'tear' (as in both weeping and pulling apart) appears: the voice momentarily breaks, in a convention of pathos which Williams perfected (this device occurs repeatedly in **"We're Getting Closer to the Grave Each Day"**).

There was a considerable rift between Williams's deep, resonant speaking voice and the thinner, more nasal, crooning quality of his singing, a rift notably widened by the accompanying change in his physical appearance when, from standing before the microphone conversing, he shifted into song: 'It was like a charge of electricity had gone through him' (Allen Rankin, quoted in Williams 1981, p. 140). (Between songs Williams enjoyed folksy bantering with his audiences; indeed such contacts were conventional in gigs and radio shows alike. And many Luke the Drifter bits were essentially monologues with musical accompaniment.) Minnie Pearl was struck by his stage presence from the first time she encountered it: 'He had a real animal magnetism. He destroyed the women in the audience.' (*ibid.,* p. 144)[7] He knew how to use his body; hunching forward into the mike, 'He'd close his eyes and swing one of those big long legs, and the place would go wild' (*ibid.,* p. 145, quoting Don Helms).[8] He played on a sexuality that was exciting precisely because of the contradictions it contained. Minnie Pearl suggests that Williams appealed to women's maternal instincts. Others suggest afar more sensual dimension, though both reflected his true character a womaniser nevertheless dominated by his strong mother. This contradiction engenders an ambiguity of a simultaneously exciting but politically dangerous sort. It constitutes a partially masked refusal to adhere to standards of propriety established for a post-war culture of re-domestication, a culture built on self-contradictory and increasingly complex erotic economies of controlled role-playing. Williams like Elvis soon after him marked with his bodily gestures a language of difference and demand, just as one might expect (or hope for) in the young thereby accounting for the insistence then, as now, that youth be tightly controlled, especially physically. Yet his speaking and singing voices also referenced acoustics culturally characteristic of middle age and beyond, just as his love songs consistently dealt with the failures of middle age, and his gospel tunes with death. In sound and sight alike, he encompassed the experiences of life's full range of contradictions, hopes and failures for a society which unquestionably recognised in him both what they loved and hated of themselves.

GENDER DIFFERENCE AND SOCIAL CLASS: IDENTITY BY ALIENATION

> America as a social and political organization is committed to a cheerful view of life. (Film critic Robert Warshow)

> That's just it, Minnie, there ain't no light. (Hank Williams to Minnie Pearl)

Kent Blaser points out that forty-five of Williams's fifty most important songs deal with relationships between men and women, and that fifteen of these complain about being abandoned by one's partner (Blaser 1985, p. 23). From **"Lovesick Blues"** to **"Your Cheatin' Heart"**, his most popular songs articulate loneliness, frustration and despair as necessary parts of the search for love. This pessimism made a break with the traditional romantic optimism of popular music as crafted in Tin Pan Alley, but in the context of post-Second World War America it held special significance.

After the Second World War, Americans married earlier and in greater numbers and had more children than had been true in the past. This extraordinary increase in marriages and births brought with it an unprecedented focus on the family by both private capital and the state. The nuclear family emerged as the primary social unit, a unit whose true home was the suburban shopping mall (see Leo 1988, p. 31), and everything from the Cold War to the growth of suburbs to increases in private debt and consumer spending drew justification from uncritical celebrations of the nuclear family and heterosexual romance (see May 1989, p. 155). In that context, Hank Williams's fatalism and existential despair rebuked dominant social narratives and spoke directly to the internal psychic wounds generated by the gap between lived experience and an ideology that promised universal bliss through the emergence of romance and the family as unchallenged centres of personal life.

Hank Williams's own life experience allowed him precious few illusions about the nuclear family, and in that respect he exemplified a broader social and historical experience. The Great Depression of the 1930s had undermined both the theory and the practice of the nuclear family. Unemployed fathers deserted their families in large numbers; by 1940 1,500,000 married women lived apart from their husbands. Many families formed extended households by moving in with relatives, but in the mid-1930s an estimated 200,000 vagrant children roamed the country. Women and children once again entered the workforce in large numbers, and their earning power undercut the previously unchallenged authority of male breadwinners (Mintz and Kellogg 1988, pp. 137-8). Mobilisation for the Second World War accelerated these trends. During the war, six million women workers entered high-paying production jobs in industry. Sixteen million Americans left their homes to join the armed forces, and another fifteen million travelled to new jobs in war production centres. Under these conditions, old ties of family and community broke down, and Americans experimented with new gender and family roles (*ibid.*, p. 155).

Hank Williams's family life reflected these larger social trends. His father had suffered shell shock in combat during the First World War and, after a series of short-term jobs in the late 1920s, was committed in 1930 to the Veterans Administration Hospital in Biloxi, Mississippi where he stayed ten years. Thus for most of the time between his sixth and sixteenth birthday, Hank Williams was raised by his mother and his sister. His mother assumed an awesome presence in his life and career, supporting her children with her own labour during the hard years of the Great Depression, and managing her son's entry into show business. Like many working class children, he also spent considerable time with relatives outside his nuclear family, living for a year when he was six with his cousin J.C. in Monroe County, Alabama, so that J.C.'s sister could go to school in Georgiana by living with Hank's mother and sister (Caress 1979, p. 12). Lilly Williams moved her family to Montgomery in 1937 when Hank was fourteen, and she ran a boarding house there that exposed her son to yet another extended household.

There was little in Hank Williams's personal experience that conformed with the reigning cultural optimism about the nuclear family. He started dating Audrey Mae Sheppard, a married woman with a daughter at home and a husband overseas, in 1942. Sheppard's father threatened to kill Hank over the relationship, and when Hank first brought Audrey home to meet his mother, Lilly asked 'Where'd you get this whore?', a comment that provoked a fistfight between mother and son (*ibid.*, pp. 35-6. 38). In aculture that increasingly lauded motherhood in the abstract while imposing ever-greater burdens on it in practice, not every son could use the words Hank Williams employed to speak about his mother to Minnie Pearl, 'Minnie, there ain't nobody in the world I'd rather have alongside me in a fight than my mama with a broken beer bottle in her hand' (Pearl 1980, p. 213). Hank married Audrey in 1944 before a Justice of the Peace in a Texaco station in Andalusia, Alabama, but the marriage was illegal because it came too soon after Audrey's separation from her husband to satisfy the requirements of Alabama law (Koon 1983, p. 19). Hank and Audrey were divorced in 1948, but reconciled after the birth of their son Randall Hank (Hank Williams, Jr) in 1949 (*ibid.*, pp. 29-30). The tempestuous relationship led to another divorce, and his remarriage (in 1952) to Billie Jean Eshlimar (who had been abandoned by her first husband) led to constant bickering among Williams, his mother and both his wives (Caress 1979, p. 189).

Biographer Jay Caress locates the roots of Williams's personal problems in the singer's distance from the experience of a nuclear family, arguing that Williams 'never made the normal psychological transfer from what psychologists call dependent mother love to assertive, independent (father emulating) mother love' (*ibid.,* p. 12). Yet Hank Williams's experiences with strong-willed and competent women left him with a deep respect for women and a powerful desire for connection to them. His failure' to make the oedipal break led him to remain in dialogue with all of the significant women in his life, and led him away from the dominant 'heroic' image of masculinity.

In an age when cultural voices ranging from the masculinist rhetoric of Mickey Spillane novels and John Wayne films to the conformist and paternalistic pressures of outer-directed corporate culture to the hedonistic appeals of *Playboy* magazine all encouraged men to widen the distance between themselves and women, Williams presented a masculine voice that longed for reconnection with the feminine, that refused the oedipality of the dominant culture in favour of an almost pre-oedipal craving for intimacy, pleasure and reconnection with women (see Modleski 1982, pp. 72-9). Of course, even this refusal could be channelled into the kind of flight from the family and responsibility that Barbara Ehrenreich describes as an important factor in sexualising and engendering male consumer desire in the 1950s (Ehrenreich 1984). The pre-oedipal stage might be seen as the perfect model for the needy narcissism vital to consumer desire. As Fred Pfeil explains, 'the increasing number of de-Oedipalized middle-class male subjects, even ostensibly politically progressive ones, in no way guarantees any decrease in their fear of and hostility toward women' (Pfeil 1988, p. 396). But the rise of a de-oedipalised subjectivity does constitute the body and psyche as sites for political meaning, and it also evidences a kind of subjectivity that seeks connection rather than separation, that disconnects ego and identity from hatred of a(proximate) mother and identification with a (distant) father. Collective social problems can never be solved by purely individual responses, but individual predispositions can often disclose contradictions and interruptions in dominant ideology that prefigure the sites where resistance might emerge. In Hank Williams's case, resistance to the oedipal narrative reveals structural weaknesses within the idealised nuclear family and its promises of happiness, as well as the existence of a popular desire for something better.

Hank Williams not only refused a narrowly oedipal definition of masculinity, but in fact he spent most of his life as a fugitive from nearly any stable identity. As a child he attached himself to black street singers Rufus Payne (known as Tee Tot) and Connie McKee (known as Big Day) who became his first strong adult male role models. Before deciding on a life as a musician, he tried out for the rodeo, and while working as a shipfitter's helper in Mobile, Alabama took a secret trip to Portland, Oregon in 1944 to try his luck in the Kaiser ship-

yards in that city. Even after achieving stardom, he went to work under the pseudonym Herman P. Willis for Dallas nightclub owner (and later assassin of Lee Harvey Oswald) Jack Ruby (Koon 1983, p. 34). As a young musician, he formed a country and western band with 'Indian Joe' Hatcher on lead guitar and 'Mexican Charlie' Mayes on fiddle. He adopted the pseudonym 'Luke the Drifter' for a series of recitations, and repeated the 'drifting' theme by naming his band of Alabama-born musicians the 'Drifting Cowboys' (Caress 1979, pp. 20, 22, 26, 17; Koon 1983, p. 34). While on tour with his band, he loved to listen to baseball games on the car radio, but had no favourite team (Williams 1981, p. 135). He sang religious hymns to his audiences, but lived a decidedly non-religious life.[9] This refusal to accept any permanent identity also characterized Williams's view of class which he interpreted through the frame of gender. As Dorothy Horstman notes.

> The farmers and labourers who made up the original market for country music were for the most part dirt-poor, bypassed by the American dream and the means of achieving it. Burdened with poor land, a poor economy, and hostile natural forces beyond their control, many felt they were, indeed 'born to lose'. . . . . A tragic love affair, then, is the final insult and perhaps the focus for economic and social frustrations it would be unmanly to admit. (Horstman 1975, p. 140)

Country musicians in general, and Hank Williams in particular, locate the politics of gender on the terrain of social class difference, but less on the overt ground of society and its institutions than on the privatised body, particularly its psyche. In the process, Williams gives sight to the unseen, especially in love song laments about infidelity and failed relationships.

Marital cheating was a taboo subject in country music recordingsprior to the social upheavals of the 1940s, so that Hank Williams's **"Your Cheatin' Heart",** among the classics of the genre (recorded in his last session 23 September 1952 - together with another tune of the same sort, **"Take These Chains from My Heart",** and two others), was a type of song having a very short history. When Williams wrote these tunes, their subject rang true, not as repetitious or timeless commentaries, but as expressions of profound and shattering change. They caught on precisely because he was able to locate the societal in the most personal and private terrain of sexual love. It was not that infidelity never occurred in the rural south prior to Williams's generation; it was rather that infidelity was admitted for the first time among the expressible catalogue of failures. By inscribing the rising stakes of societal suffering in infidelity, by locating that suffering in the psyche, he undercut the final refuge for resistance. The soul of the privatised body could no longer be separated, refuge-like, from the larger social economy: cheating songs confirmed devolutionary change.[10]

Similarly, songs of unrequited love (**"I'm So Lonesome I Could Cry"**; **"Cold, Cold Heart"**), though excluding the sin of adultery, preserve the political essentials of songs about cheating, even if they accomplish their politics of emotion in a slightly different fashion. By emphasising a love that is never responded to, as opposed to a love that once was but is now lost, unrequited love songs fundamentally account for an equally defeating if not necessarily worse sort of failure: the inability to find love in the first place, to love but not be loved in return, to be rejected. It is in songs of unrequited love that the work of Hank Williams approaches black music most directly, and where it crosses gender lines into emotional ground more commonly occupied by women, and notably by women who are black (e.g. Billie Holiday, Nina Simone). As Billie Holiday, dying, gravel-voiced, movingly and pathetically sang in "Glad to Be Unhappy", one of her last recorded songs, when someone you adore fails to love you back, 'It's a pleasure to be sad'.

The emotional intensity that Billie Holiday accorded to this topic,[11] via her vocal/timbral inscription of failure (as well as by the words), bears a distinct similarity to that achieved by Hank Williams, though musically by quite different means. The difference can be stated quite simply: the musical and cultural traditions that would allow a black woman to produce this lament generally affect men in a quite dissimilar way. For a man to utter similar sentiments, in this society, reflects a more extreme degree of failure and frustration. The fact that Williams wrote and sang such tunes, in other words, produces affect by collapsing the distinction not only between genders, but between races as well (southern whites, after all, heard blues music). Not only with subject matter, but also with what might be termed the politics of timbre, an acoustic solidarity is implicitly forged: between genders, between the races, and among the poor. Black audiences recognised elements of their own culture inWilliams's music, and in large numbers attended the Louisiana Hayride when he was on the bill.[12] Blues singer B. B. King remembers paying special attention to the songs by Hank Williams that he heard on the radio while working on a Mississippi plantation because:

> Like Hank Williams, man, when he wrote **"Cold, Cold Heart"**, tunes like that, that carried me right back to my same old blues about 'don't answer the door' and all that kind of stuff. 'Cause this is a guy hurting. He's hurting from inside. And **"Your Cheating Heart"**, many things of this sort are just to me another form of blues sung by other people. (Redd 1974, p. 97)

The sound of a white man's voice singing about these subjects, hence crossing gender and racial boundaries, inscribes a socio-cultural disruption of the most encompassing finality, at precisely the instant that it offers the specifically *acoustic* opportunity to establish a relationship of resistance with another socially alienated group.

Finally, even in tunes of courtship or proposal, like **"If You'll Be a Baby (to Me)"**, conventional romantic love is not part of the equation;[13] instead there is an offer of a partnership for mutually-supporting labour, and the extent of the male singer's love is promised in terms of the work appropriate to her that he's willing to shoulder: if she cooks, he'll plow and *even* do the churning. He loves her and considers doing 'women's' work a gesture of his devotion.[14] This may not be in the de-politicised tradition of romantic love, but it *is* romantic love of the most meaningful and committed sort. It openly recognises the mutuality of marital labour and the urge to take on more than what society conventionally identifies as the man's share. (It is arguable that, under these conditions, what otherwise passes for romantic love might flourish past the stages of passion characterising young relationships.) Lyrics of this sort are all the more striking given the national phenomenon in the early post-war years of a return to 'traditional' pre-war gender divisions, articulated especially in the domestication of the suburb with its removal of women from the labour force, as well as in a broad range of popular cultural expressions built upon the assumption of innate antagonisms between men and women, ranging from commercial television programmes and film noir motion pictures to the lyrics of most popular songs.

Yet for all his shifting subjectivies, a remarkable consistency characterises Williams's voice, and that consistency is connected to his class and regional identity. There is no discernible difference between his earliest recordings and his last, and the same holds for his unsophisticated, elementary, essentially three-chord guitar strumming. The voice is common, untrained. The delivery is inevitably straightforward, without pretence, without acrobatics or tricks unless one counts the country-conventional vocal 'tear' mentioned earlier. The upper range, which Williamsuses to good effect in producing acoustic tension, is thin and often strained, the latter quality exacerbated by a notable and fast vibrato; the low and middle range is both rich and firm, like his speaking voice. Together these variant timbres produce a comfort in the latter, inevitably undercut by the vulnerability of that comfort in the former. Moreover, he typically gives accentual and dynamic emphasis to his high voice, that is, to that part of his range that semiotically undercuts the culturally coded paternal assuredness of the deeper male sounds.

Williams's slightly nasal twang is especially obvious in the higher register the locus of tension thus most evident in precisely the acoustic space that best identifies pain and its politics. The country twang, in other words, locates him as one of his listeners' own, a man who shares their experiences. Nasality in other circumstances provides the southern rural poor with subcultural/community identity, like any other accentual or dialectical effect. But in extra-regional popular culture (notably the movies, often in grotesquely exaggerated burlesques like *Ma and Pa Kettle,* and in later television shows like *Beverly Hillbillies*) that effect becomes a weapon for derision, a fact never lost on any poor person. Hank Williams exploited that sound in a timbral expression of class and regional solidarity, though to be sure he was not unique in this regard. To similar, if more obvious, purpose is his swallowing of word endings at phrase ends ('quarrellin'', 'churnin''), and regional pronounciations ('yer' for 'your' and so on). In his Luke the Drifter recitation **"Beyond the Sunset"** (recorded 10 January 1950), he tells of a man's vigilant loyalty to a woman preceding him in death; it is his memory of her that gives him the strength to go on. The recitation depends on an implicit understanding of the uses of memory as regards its connection to history, issues that go far beyond the narrower topic of this small piece. As **"Beyond the Sunset"** has it: 'Memory is a gift from God that death cannot destroy'. The politics embedded here grow from the fact that Williams recognised less that songs are social constructions and more that society itself is constructed by the songs we sing, the stories we tell, and the *sounds* we voice in the narration.

EVERYBODY'S LONESOME FOR SOMEBODY

> I'm so lonesome I could cry. (Hank Williams lyric)

> What prepares men [*sic*] for totalitarian domination in the non-totalitarian world is the fact that loneliness, once a borderline experience usually suffered in certain marginal social conditions like old age, has become an everyday experience of the ever-growing masses of our century. (Hannah Arendt in *The Origins of Totalitarianism*)

> Goodbye Hank Williams, my old friend, I didn't know you but I've been the places you've been. (Tim Hardin lyric)

> Hank Williams you wrote my life. (Moe Bandy lyric)

The extraordinary popularity of Hank Williams's songs in the late 1940s and early 1950s played a crucial role in transforming country music from a regional and class-bound genre to a staple of mass popular culture. Along with related developments in popular speech, dress and dance, the rise to national prominence of country music reflected the emergence of a prestige from below in which cultural hybrids emanating from intersections of race, class and gender articulated a new basis for American commercial culture.

Class, race and gender all contributed to the grounding of Williams's music in oppositional cultures and practices. His songs resonated with the materials memory forged in previous popular struggles against hierarchy and exploitation. But as a creation of a distinct historical moment, he added a new element to the historic struggle for the good life. In an age of renewed racism, he created a music that underscored the connections between whites and blacks. At a time of upward mobility and cultural assimilation for much of the working class, he affirmed his standpoint as a worker and an ordinary citizen. In an age of resurgent patriarchy, he lamented the schisms between men and women, resisted the dominant oedipal narrative, and sought closer connections to women. Finally, he foregrounded existential despair in an age of exuberant and uncritical 'progress', countering ubiquitous romantic invocations of the superiority of the nuclear family with honest words and deep emotions drawn from the hurts of history and the experiences of everyday life. As modern life became increasingly characterised by 'the policing of families' as part of capital's project to colonise the psyche and the body, Williams constituted his own voice and body as sites of resistance. Millions of fans could feel that he 'wrote their lives', because even when they did not know him, they could feel that he knew the places they had been.

NOTES

[1] We use psychoanalytic language here as a shorthand way of describing our culture's dominant narratives about the construction of subjectivity, not because we believe in any innate or transcendent human personality.

[2] See the examples quoted by Williams's second wife Billy Jean in Horstman 1975, p. 194.

[3] His chronic back problem, for example, was explained on a pre-recorded-for-broadcast apology that Williams produced from his hospital bed when he had to miss a December 1951 appearance in Baltimore. It is reproduced as the final cut on *Hank Williams: I Won't Be Home No More June 1952-September 1952,* Polydor ... volume 8, and the last, of Polydor's comprehensive, retrospective series of Williams's recordings.

[4] The loss of home through the upheavals of war and migration are a recurrent theme in Southern culture beginning with the Civil War, and become more intense after each of this century's two world wars. One price paid for migration was guilt for not remaining to 'share the common burden'. See Horstman 1975, pp. 3-5.

[5] See further Hume 1982, pp. 94-6, 'Dead Kids and Country Music'.

[6] The other genres being the Luke the Drifter accompanied monologues, and the occasional novelty songs like the slightly bizarre 'Indian' love song "Kaw Liga" or the famous "Jambalaya".

[7] On Williams's securing of women following show dates, see Ibid., p. 164. Nor was his stage presence effective only on women: 'He quickly became the favorite act on a military entertainment entourage to Europe in 1951. [Moreover, on a celebrity-studded touring show known as the Hadacol Caravan he upstaged such luminaries as Jack Benny, Milton Berle, and Bob Hope, and eventually took over the closing spot.' (Blaser 1985, p. 17, n. 18) For details of the Caravan tour, see Williams 1981, pp. 150-5; Koon 1983, pp. 36, 38.

[8] Cf. Frank Page: 'He was just electrifying on stage. . . . He had the people in the palm of his hands from the moment he walked out there'. (*ibid.*, p. 74) See also Koon 1983, p. 28.

[9] His contradictory relationship to religion is encapsulated in what is probably an apocryphal story about a young fan who admitted to not being a 'God-fearing boy', and found Hank piping up 'Don't let it trouble you none. I ain't afraid of God, either' (Caress 1979, pp. 81-2). Koon quotes the very authoritative Bob Pinson as saying that the Shestack interview, from which this story is taken, is 'all fiction; it never happened' (Koon 1983, p. 94). Yet the quotation seems to capture correctly something about Williams's view of religion. Roger M. Williams notes, 'Hank, after his childhood, never demonstrated an interest in organized religion. But he had flashes of intense personal feeling about spiritual matters, which led to some of the finest songs he ever wrote. Further, he knew that "sacred songs" always find a ready market in country music' (Williams 1981, p. 57).

[10] 'Inevitably, in the upheaval of a wartime society, with women working, husbands and wives separated, easy social and geographical mobility, and honky tonks no longer populated exclusively by women of easy virtue, country writers began to flirt with, then to address directly, the subject of cheating.' (Horstman 1975, p. 182; see also Hume 1982, pp. 84-5)

[11] See also the work of Nina Simone, ten years Hank Williams's junior, for example, on her live album, *Little Girl Blue,* especially "He Needs Me (He doesn't know it but he needs me)"

It is worth noting the correspondences and, especially, the differences between Hank Williams's songs of failed love and some of the early recordings of Patsy Cline (all songs written by others, whereas Williams mostly performed his own material). "If I Could Only Stay Asleep" moves slowly, underscoring the sense of loss inscribed by a vocal line repeatedly leaping to high notes only to slide back as if in defeat. "I'm Blue Again" registers the vocal 'tear' perfected by Williams to help mark a text entirely about loss, but this effect (and others) acts in contrast to the tempo, oddly upbeat, and to Cline's vocal delivery which breathes an air of confidence seriously undercutting the text's defeatism. Indeed, time and again in Cline's work, discrepancies occur between the putative subjects of the lyrics and her delivery of them. Among the reasons Patsy Cline is such an exciting singer is that, like Hank Williams, she pushed hard against the margins of musical conventions stretching semiotic possibilities, introducing contradictions and unexpected tensions, and, in particular, refusing to be bound by conventional expectations of vocal delivery located in gender distinction. Thus whereas Williams voices a feminine identity, mediating traditional masculine vocal qualities, Patsy Cline voices a masculine identity, notably by mediating the passivity that tunes of loss commonly inscribe lyrically and often musically. The loss of a man may be getting her down, so her words go, but she won't be down for long, so her voice encodes. She subscribes to the potential joys of men and women relating to each other but she refuses (not textually but vocally) to be overwhelmed by the absence or failure of the experience. It is very difficult to listen to "I've Loved and Lost Again" and really believe that the pain will be permanent. She will be up and dancing soon, playing a profoundly (vocally) liberated role: her vocal-gutteral growls on "Gotta Lot of Rhythm (In My Soul)", a thoroughly upbeat number, echo an effect heard commonly in early rock 'n' roll singers (both male and female).

[12] On these shows Williams typically included one or two Luke the Drifter recitations that specifically addressed black subjects, such as "The Funeral". This recitation, to the accompaniment of Hammond organ and steel guitar (recorded 10 January 1950), tells of the narrator, a white man, coming upon a humble country church and witnessing the funeral service for a black child. To be sure, Williams repeats racial stereotypes and dialogue embedded in southern racism (the child is described as having 'curly hair, protruding lips'; the black preacher's speech includes 'sho 'nough'); on the other hand, Williams in effect absents himself as narrator almost from the start, giving sole voice to the preacher whose sermon he repeats at length. That is, a white man takes a pew to witness a funeral and thereafter tells his story: he tells his (primarily white) audience that he has learned something from what he describes as the 'wisdom and ignorance of a crushed, undying race'. (See Williams 1981, pp. 74-5). Hank Williams's own funeral, held in Montgomery auditorium, included about two hundred blacks seated in the segregatedbalcony among the three thousand mourners who managed to squeeze inside; moreover, the music was provided in part by a black quartet, the Southwind Singers, in addition to various white country music luminaries (see Koon 1983, p. 54).

[13] Indeed, romantic love is generally in short supply in the country music of Williams's day, precisely because it could have had little ring of credibility in the circumstances of its hearers. See Horstman 1975, p. 119.

[14] Occasionally Williams confronted the politics of class more directly; perhaps the best example is "A Mansion on the Hill" recorded 7 November 1947). Audrey Williams has said that (Chicago, urban-bred) Fred Rose gave Hank the title and sent him off to see what he could do with it. The result was an explicit articulation of high-low class hierarchy invited by Rose's title the lyrics employ a binary opposition between the mansion on a hill and the narrator's cabin in a valley. See Horstman 1975, p. 165.)

REFERENCES

Baker, H. 1984. *Blues, Ideology, and Afro-American Literature: a Vernacular Theory* (Chicago)

Blaser, K. 1985. ' "Pictures from Life's Other Side": Hank Williams, country music, and popular culture in America', *The South Atlantic Quarterly,* 84 (1), pp. 12-26

Caress, J. 1979. *Hank Williams: Country Music's Tragic King* (New York)

Ehrenreich, B. 1984. *The Hearts of Men: American Dreams and the Flight from Commitment* (Garden City, NY)

Horstman, D. 1975. *Sing Your Heart Out, Country Boy* (New York)

Hume, M. 1982. *You're So Cold I'm Turnin' Blue: Martha Hume's Guide to the Greatest Country Music* (New York)

Kingsbury, P. and Axelrod, A., eds. 1988. *Country: The Music and the Musicians. Pickers, Slickers, Cheatin' Hearts & Superstars* (New York)

Koon, G. 1983. *Hank Williams: A Bio-Bibliography* (Westport, CT)

Leo, J. 1988. 'The familialism of man in American television melodrama', *The South Atlantic Quarterly,* 88 (1), pp. 31-51

May, E. T. 1988. *Homeward Bound* (New York)

May, E. T. 1989. 'Explosive issues: sex, women, and the bomb', in *Recasting America,* ed. L. May (Chicago), pp. 154-70

Mintz, S. and Kellogg, S. 1988. *Domestic Revolutions* (New York)

Modleski, T. 1982. 'Film theory's detour', *Screen,* 23 (5), pp. 72-9

Pearl, M., with Dew, J. 1980. *Minnie Pearl: An Autobiography* (New York)

Pfeil, F. 1988. 'Postmodernism as a "structure of feeling"', in *Marxism and the Interpretation of Culture,* ed. L. Grossberg and C. Nelson (Champaign), pp. 381-405

Redd, L. 1974. *Rock is Rhythm and Blues* (East Lansing)

Williams, R.M. 1981. *Sing a Sad Song: The Life of Hank Williams,* 2nd edn (Urbana)

Christopher Metress (essay date 1995)

SOURCE: "Sing Me a Song about Ramblin' Man: Visions and Revisions of Hank Williams in Country Music," in *South Atlantic Quarterly,* Vol. 94, No. 1, Winter, 1995, pp. 7-27.

[*In the following excerpt, Metress examines Williams's musical legacy as expressed in musical tributes since his death.*]

To get there you take I-65 straight south out of Nashville. The ride is good and gentle, and before you know it you're crossing the Tennessee River into the Heart of Dixie and you're starting to see more frequent signs for Birmingham, the only city that stands between you and Montgomery. After you pass through the Magic City, skirting it to the right, the land starts to flatten out as red iron mountains give way to rich black soil. In just over an hour, you will see Montgomery on the horizon. Stay on I-65 until you near the center of the city. You will exit here and work your way carefully through the streets, following the map on the passenger's seat beside you until you find the road with seven bridges.

Oakwood Cemetery Annex is tucked away in a modest section of the city, only a few blocks from the state capitol building. When you get there it's not hard to find his grave, for it's marked by an upright slab nearly twice the size of a man. Made of Vermont granite, it shines like marble in the afternoon sun. At the top of the slab you find the opening notes of **"I Saw the Light."** Below this and to the left, a bronze plaque shows him smiling and playing his guitar, and beside it, etched into the granite, sunshine pours through a thicket of layered clouds. A little further down, just above eye level, the name "Hank Williams" is cut deep and thick and clean into the memorial stone.[1]

Resting at the base of this slab is an exact replica of Hank's hat, surrounded by small granite squares where someone has chiseled the front-page sheet music to some of Hank's greatest songs. A few feet in front of all this lies a flat slab that marks the grave itself. The whole area is framed by a rectangular border of stone, and inside this frame stand two urns for decoration and two benches for rest. The grave is not busy at this time of day. A few wrappers and cigarette butts on the artificial turf around the plot let you know that others were here not long ago, but in the quiet of this particular afternoon you rest awhile on one of the benches and spend a few moments listening to the clouds move soundless as smoke overhead.

When it's time to go you might decide to walk out the way you came in. But you shouldn't. If you do, if you leave the grave the same way you approached it, you will miss something very important. So, instead of retracing your steps, you get off the bench and walk straight toward the upright slab. Take it in one last time the deep cut of his name, his sharp face molded in bronze, the clouds and sunshine etched into the granite like some fragile but palpable hope. Now move past the slab. Here, standing in the shadows at the back of the slender marker, you will find a poem entitled "Thank You, Darling." Unlike the lyrics and notes carved into the front of the stone, these words will be unfamiliar:

Thank you for all the love you gave me
There could be one no stronger
Thank you for the many beautiful songs
They will live long and longer

Thank you for being a wonderful father to
   Lycrecia
She loves you more than you knew
Thank you for our precious son
And thank God he looks so much like you

And now I can say:
There are no words in the dictionary
That can express my love for you
   Someday beyond the blue

The poem is signed "Audrey Williams."

At first, what is happening on the backside of Hank Williams's gravestone seems quite clear: Audrey Williams, the grieving widow, is paying her final tribute to her husband. But something makes you uncomfortable. Is it the disjunction between the simple lyrics chiseled on the front of the slab and the discordant poetry cut into its back? Perhaps, yet there is something so touching in what you've just read: the widow fighting through her pain to write a final song for her songwriting husband. Still, something bothers you. It's only after you've listened a little longer to the silence overhead that you remember Audrey Williams wasn't Hank's widow.

Now you begin to understand what's really happening here on the shadowy side of Hank's grave. Everything about the gravesite centers on Hank, or so it first appears. The marker has his name on it, those are his lyrics etched in stone, that's his image cast in bronze. They've let his name, his face, and his words speak for themselves. When you look behind the grave, however, you see that Hank hasn't had the final say. Hank's a legend, after all, and legends become legends because we don't let them have the last word. Rather, after they are gone we continue to speak for them, creating them, if not in our own image, then at least in an image that serves our own purposes. And that's what's happening here in Montgomery. Miz Audrey is staking her claim, making Hank Williams *her* Hank Williams because she knows that another Williams, Billie Jean, is out there trying to stake *her* own claim. When Miz Audrey writes, "Thank you for our precious son / And thank God he looks so much like you," you can almost hear the satisfaction, the legacy and the claims of inheritance that are asserted in those lines. The Hank Williams buried here isn't just any Hank Williams but *her* Hank Williams.

In 1975 Moe Bandy released a song by Paul Kraft entitled "Hank Williams You Wrote My Life." As true as these words are to many country music fans, they may blind us to another important fact: just as Hank Williams wrote our lives, we have written his. Audrey Williams's poem at the gravesite in Montgomery was not the first attempt to take hold of Hank's life and inscribe it in a certain way. And it definitely wasn't the

last. For instance, in 1953, the year Hank Williams died, every major recording studio in Nashville released a song about him, sixteen tributes in all.[2] The first to be released was Jack Cardwell's "Death of Hank Williams." A Montgomery disc jockey and singer for King Records, Cardwell knew Hank in his pre-*Opry* days. When he heard of Hank's death on New Year's Eve, he wrote a song about it that very night. A week later, on 8 January, King Records released "The Death of Hank Williams." It went as high as #2 on the charts, kept out of the top spot by one of Hank's own songs, **"Your Cheatin' Heart."** With more than 107,000 singles sold, "The Death of Hank Williams" may have been the most successful of all these tribute records, but it really wasn't that much different from the rest. Beginning with a peaceful image of Hank lying in the back of his car, "in a deep and dreamless sleep" from which he never awakens, Cardwell's song tries to reassure us that Hank Williams has "gone to a better land."

When listened to one after another, the sixteen tribute songs of 1953 construct a highly specific image of Hank Williams. A little more than a year before his death, remember, Hank had left Nashville in disgrace. In the tribute songs, however, there is little, if any, mention of the Hank Williams who got himself fired from the *Opry* for repeatedly embarrassing the Nashville establishment with his drunkenness and unreliability. Yes, Arthur Smith sings, in his "In Memory of Hank Williams," about how, "like all of us Hank had his faults," but those faults are notspecified in any of the tributes. What we get, rather, is a kind of hagiography, a portrait of Hank Williams as a country music saint who has gone peacefully to his just reward.[3] In "Hank Williams Meets Jimmie Rodgers," for instance, the Virginia Rounders sing of a "great meeting in Heaven" between the two kings of country music. In this song, Hank doesn't so much die as "answer his Maker's call" to perform with the angels. Jimmie Rodgers tells Hank that he and the angels needed some help in their "heavenly band," so they decided to call for the best singer on earth. In the end, we are assured that

    The voices of Rodgers and Williams,
    The greatest this world's ever known,
    Will blend up yonder forever
    Around that heavenly throne.

As if their point had not been made well enough in this song, the Virginia Rounders also released "There's a New Star in Hillbilly Heaven," in which they speculate that the angels called for Hank Williams because they needed "someone to write them new songs."

Jimmie Skinner's "Singing Teacher in Heaven" and Johnny Ryon's "That Heaven Bound Train" each maintains this comforting portrait of a singer called home to "his Maker." Skinner assures us that Hank has "traveled on to a house of gold" where "the saints of God abed." For Ryon, Hank "is riding to glory on that Heaven bound train," where he will find angels to sing "the many songs that [he] will bring." Moreover, both Skinner and Ryon imagine moments when they will join Hank in some unbroken circle in the sky. Ryon sings of how "someday we all will be with him again" when we are called upon to ride "that Heaven bound train," while Skinner prays for a reunion with Hank on the day when he himself must "join the heavenly choir."

In "Hank, It Will Never Be the Same Without You," Williams's good friend Ernest Tubb sings of how, from the start, Hank's life was full of "misery." But that misery doesn't matter now because, in his death, Hank has finally achieved that goal he struggled "so bravely for" in life: "eternal happiness." A similar sentiment is found in Jimmie Logsdon's "Hank Williams Sings the Blues No More," in which we are assured that Hank has now found "a new singing place / Where the sun shines on his face." In "The Last Letter," Jimmy Swan offers the most explicit assurance that the Ramblin' Man has indeed achieved eternal peace when he sings of how he dreamed one night of meeting Hank Williams in heaven. Swan's dream centers on an image of Hank holding tightly to a "little white Bible."

Many of these first tribute songs were written by artists who knew Hank well, so we certainly can't fault them for being sentimental portraits of a good friend. But as Hank Williams, Jr., said on one of his early albums: "In January of 1953, my father stopped being a man and became a legend."[4] These tribute songs initiated the construction of that legend. The man who died alone in the backseat of a car because his heart finally failed him after so many years of heavy drinking had now simply passed away in a "deep and dreamless sleep." This long night's sleep, more of a summons from heaven than an actual death, had finally allowed the Ramblin' Man to gain his rightful rest. Moreover, the man who had been fired from the *Opry* two years before no longer existed. Instead, Hank now sings forever with the angels in some kind of *Grand Ole Opry* in the sky, and we too will sing with him "someday beyond the blue." Hindsight has allowed Hank Jr. to understand exactly what was going on in 1953. In *Living Proof,* his 1979 autobiography, he wrote: "While [Daddy] was alive, he was despised and envied; after he died, he was some kind of saint. And that's exactly how Nashville decided to treat Daddy country music's first authentic saint."[5]

Nashville may have needed a saint, but Miz Audrey simply needed a husband. If the tribute songs served to smooth over the divorce between Hank and Nashville, Miz Audrey's songs served to smooth over her divorce from him. In a series of records released during the first two years after his death, Audrey Williams had her chance to write Hank's life the way she wanted it to be read. Fighting for custody of his memory as well as his estate, she was not only billing herself as "The One and Only Audrey (Mrs. Hank) Williams," she was singing about herself that way as well. On one of her early records, she tapped into the heaven imagery of the tribute songs, and just as the Nashville musicians imagined

a reunion with Hank in the great beyond, Miz Audrey imagined a heavenly reprise of her wedded bliss with Hank on earth. "Are you writing songs for me up in Heaven?" she asks Hank. "So when I meet you beyond the blue, / You'll say 'Come here and listen to me,' / Then I'll smile and listen just as we used to do." In another song, entitled "My Life with You," she sings of how she and Hank first met and of how, when they were later married, she wept with happiness. She notes, however, that their "happiness didn't last long" because people started "wagging their tongues," and in the next stanza, she describes their divorce in a way that, well, makes it seem like they never got divorced:

> Along about then, everything went wrong,
> Little did we know it wouldn't be long
> 'Til you'd be in Heaven no more to be blue,
> It's hard to go on without my life with you.

When she wasn't writing her own songs about Hank, Miz Audrey was recording songs that carefully wrote her back into Hank's life. In Lycrecia Williams's 1989 memoir, *Still in Love with You: The Story of Hank and Audrey Williams,* she recalled one of her mother's Decca recording sessions in August of 1953:

> Still backed by the Drifting Cowboys, but short one guitar player, [Mother] recorded three emotional numbers that day. First was a recitation of Daddy's **"To My Pal Bocephus,"** a poem filled with a father's hopes and concerns for his baby son. She read the words just as Daddy would have done, without changing the wording for the speaker as a "man" and a "father." Her second number, "I Forgot More Than You'll Ever Know About Him," a current hit . . . for the Davis Sisters, was so appropriate to her feelings about Billie Jean's claims to Daddy that it might have been written just for her. For the last song, Mother rewrote the lyrics to Daddy's **"Ramblin' Man"** to express some of her own thoughts:

> Some folks might say that I didn't care,
> But wherever you went I was always there.
> When I get lonely, at your grave I'll stand.
> So I'll be near my ramblin' man.
> I still love you honey and I can't understand
> I am a ramblin' gal that lost her ramblin' man.[6]

As Chet Flippo argued in *Your Cheatin' Heart: A Biography of Hank Williams,* those who knew Hank "revise[d] his history to sweeten their own."[7] And this, of course, was what Audrey Williams did when she decided to revise Hank's music in revising **"Ramblin' Man,"** she was revising *the* Ramblin' Man and sweetening her life with him. The two bitter divorces and the long separations never really happened because, in truth, wherever Hank Williams went, she was "always there."

As much as Miz Audrey was rewriting in song her husband's problematic past, she was also writing in life her son's promising future. Whereas other artists could only pen or perform tributes to Hank, Audrey Williams could turn her son into a living, singing tribute. And this she did. Although it was to a son named Randall Hank Williams that Audrey gave birth on 26 May 1949, she raised him as "Hank Williams, Jr." The boy's renaming was only the beginning. In his autobiography, Hank Jr. recalled those early years of careful refashioning: "Mother used to coach me in things Daddy said and then I'd go on stage and the audience would go crazy. They'd say I sounded just like ole Hank, and I guess I did."[8]

By age eleven, young Hank sounded enough like "ole Hank" to take the *Opry* stage and sing a few of his father's songs. Four years later, in 1964, he appeared on the *Ed Sullivan Show* and sang **"Long Gone Lonesome Blues,"** a cover of his father's #1 hit from 1950. Peaking at #5, the song gave fifteen-year-old Hank Jr. his first chart record. When he tried to follow up later in the year with two singles of his own songs, he reached no higher than #42 on the charts. To the young Hank Williams, the message couldn't have been clearer: "There'd be the people [at my concerts] who came looking for my daddy, who wanted to hear nothing but **'I'm So Lonesome I Could Cry'** and **'Jambalaya** and a crawfish pie-a and a me-o-my-o,' and would be bitterly disappointed when they found only me."[9]

Hank Jr. didn't break into the top ten with one of his own songs until "Standing in the Shadows" was released in 1966. While this wasn't a cover of one of his father's earlier hits, it was nevertheless a song about his father. In "Standing in the Shadows," Hank Jr. maintains that he's "just doin' the best [he] can," but that "it's hard" when you have to stand in the shadow "of a very great man." He recognizes the burden of his father's legacy, but he also makes it quite clear that he's happy to bear that burden because it allows his father's music to "live on and on and on." When he followed up "Standing in the Shadows" with "I Can't Take It No Longer" another one of his own songs Hank Jr. failed again to reach the top of the charts. His next single, "I'm in No Condition," peaked at #60 and was followed by "Nobody's Child," which managed to climb to #46. Hank's 1968 album, *My Songs,* produced only one chart single, "I Wouldn't Change a Thing About You (But Your Name)," which hit #31. The success of **"Long Gone Lonesome Blues"** and "Standing in the Shadows," coupled with the failure of every other song up to that point, made something else quite clear to Hank Jr.: if he sang his father's songs, or sang about how willing he was to carry on his father's legacy, he'd be accepted; if not, he'd flounder at the bottom of the charts. It's no wonder, then, that early in his career he released such albums as *Hank Williams, Jr. Sings the Songs of Hank Williams* and *Songs My Father Left Me: The Poems of Hank Williams Set to Music and Sung by Hank Williams, Jr.*

In the late 1960s and early 1970s, Hank Jr. the performer remained faithful to the country-music-saint image of his father created by the tribute records and by his mother. In recalling those years, however, Hank Jr.

admitted knowing that this image wouldn't last: "Essentially, what was happening [in the late 1960s] was that one myth of Hank Williams was getting ready to overtake the other. . . . While *Opry* folks were still praising Daddy's name . . . [a group of] young singers and songwriters had adopted a live fast, die young, and leave a beautiful corpse posture, and they talked about the way that Hank did it."[10] Unfortunately, what was happening in country music a shift from one Hank Williams myth to another, and from the sweet, respectable arrangements of the "Nashville Sound" to the hard-driving honky tonk tunes of the "Outlaw" movement was also being played out in Hank's personal life. In *Living Proof,* he wrote: "The years all run together '71, '72, '73, '74. An endless nightmare of bars and shows, of sick mornings and stoned nights and big chunks of time where there are no memories. Of Jim Beam and cheery, multicolored pills, and strange girls with vacant eyes." As a result, "people were starting to come to my shows to see if I would fall off stage. . . . For a measly five bucks you could step right up and see whether the son of the greatest country artist of all time could get through his set without dropping a guitar or forgetting the words to **'Cold, Cold Heart,'**"[11]

It was during these tough years that Hank Jr. began to questionin song the myth of Hank Williams. "Standing in the Shadows" pictures Hank Sr. as "a very great man," and that's all that is said; when Hank Jr. claims that "there'll never be another Hank Williams," we know he's thinking of the Hank Williams who's singing with Jimmie Rodgers in heaven. At one point in the song, Hank Jr. sings about how, when he is performing in concert, he will occasionally look up toward the ceiling to ask his father how he's doing, to receive, as it were, his father's heavenly blessing. But in "Hank," a 1973 release, Bocephus sings about a more complex Hank Williams: "They say Hank was a mighty heavy drinker, I don't know. / They say Hank was a mighty heavy thinker, I reckon that's so." The song continues in this vein, with Hank Jr. telling us first what "they say" and then whether he agrees or disagrees with that. For instance, when "they say" that whiskey wrecked his father's health, Hank disagrees, but when "they say" his father sang a "real good song," Hank agrees. If "Standing in the Shadows" expressed his certainty that there would "never be another Hank Williams," in "Hank" he's not certain how many Hank Williamses there were. What Hank Jr. is sure of, however, is that what "they say" must be confronted and, perhaps more importantly, contested.

Feeling trapped by the legacy of his father's music, Hank Jr. was saved by it, ironically enough. One afternoon in 1974, when Hank Jr. was racing his Ford truck along 1-65 at a hundred-plus miles per hour, he finally had to pull off the road for gas in Clarksville, Tennessee. The first pump he found was at a general store that doubled as a local bar. He went into the store, ordered a shot of Jim Beam, and headed for the jukebox. "I walked over to that jukebox like I owned the place,"

Hank Jr. remembered. "I dropped my quarter down the slot and started looking. What I found was my ghost, my inspiration, my daddy, this time in the form of Linda Ronstadt singing **'I Can't Help It If I'm Still In Love With You.'**" His own marriage having just recently collapsed, Hank Jr. broke into tears at the jukebox: "It was like Daddy reachin' out across the years, telling me he understood."[12]

Feeling "touched by some kind of C & W muse," Hank Jr. staggered back to his truck and in ten minutes wrote the lyrics to "Stoned at the Jukebox."[13] On one level, this song is about the breakup of his marriage. But on another level, it's about his coming to terms with his father's legacy. In "Stoned at the Jukebox," Hank Jr. not only recognizes his father's music for what it really is, "hurtin' music," but he also recognizes that, having been haunted by this hurtin' music all his life, he has begun to live it out. One myth of Hank Williams was indeed giving way to another Hank Jr. was becoming the Hank Williams that everyone talked about but no one dared to sing about.

After "Stoned at the Jukebox," he made a real effort to turn his life around, to get out from under the shadow of what "they" kept saying about his father. The first step was to get out of Nashville, which he did in 1974 when he moved to Cullman, Alabama. The second step was to put together a new album, which he also did, in 1975. *Hank Williams Junior and Friends* seemed to make good on his promise to himself to start over again, to make "*my* music, not Daddy's, not Mother's or anybody else's. . . . Music for 1974 instead of 1953."[14] Marking a new direction alright, this album included "Living Proof," a cut that Hank Jr. considered "the most important song I've ever written," a song that "was going to be the exclamation point at the end of the old Hank Williams Junior."[15] In "Living Proof," Hank Jr. laments having been "living for more than one man" all of his life and swears that he doesn't want to pay the price his father paid. Whereas in 1966 the Hank Jr. of "Standing in the Shadows" had been glad to bear the burden and keep his father's music living "on and on and on" for the old "fans and friends," by 1975 the Hank Jr. of "Living Proof" was vowing to "quit singing all them sad songs." When he asks at the end of the song why he has to be "the living proof" of his father's legend, we see that he's no longer willing to stand in that shadow. Moreover, as he sings elsewhere in the same song, he doesn't want to be a legend either he "just want[s] to be a man."

But as important as this song was, "Living Proof" did not really represent "the exclamation point" that Hank Jr. hoped it would be. Yes, he turned his life around in the mid-1970s, as he swore that he would not become the "Living Proof" of the "Williams Curse." But, contrary to his vow, Hank Jr. did not "quit singing all them sad songs." Nor did he stop singing about the Ramblin' Man who wrote those sad songs.[16] The change was not that Hank Jr. put his father behind him. Rather, what changed was Hank's attitude toward his father and the myths that "they," the Nashville establishment, had created about him.

Early in his career he knew that Nashville had made his father into "country music's first authentic saint." He knew as well that he himself was "the chosen one," designated to walk in the shadow of that saint.[17] In his teens and twenties, Hank Jr. played the role perfectly, practicing the patter and giving back to Nashville the ghost it wanted to see and hear. But when he started popping pills and drinking booze and running around all over town, Nashville turned on him, and it did so by using his father against him. Music City had Hank Jr. in a double bind: On the one hand, he was expected to be the model son of the "Singing Teacher in Heaven." Then, when he proved to be no son of a saint, Nashville sighed with resignation: What else could they expect from a (Hank) Williams? The first one had let them down, and the second one was sinking even lower. Whichever vision of Hank Sr. they held up before him country music saint or irredeemable sinner Hank Jr. couldn't win. He was shadowed by a myth that the *Opry,* not the Son of Ramblin' Man, controlled.

But by 1976 he had figured out a way to beat the myth. According to Hank Jr., after "Living Proof" was released, "ole Hank's reincarnation had finally hung up his guitar, and Hank Williams Junior had a story to tell."[18] But in the story Hank Jr. told about himself, his father was still a major character, if not the hero. Before 1975, Hank Jr. had let everyone else tell him who his father was and what his father's life meant. As long as he listened to others' stories, he was stuck with the role of either the son of a saint or the son of a cheatin', boozin', no-account failure. But after 1975, Hank Jr. hung up the two-hat legend of Hank Sr. that Nashville had fashioned and started writing his own version of his father's life. What he linked up with was a third myth of Hank Williams not the saint, not the sinful failure, but "the most wanted outlaw in the land."

In a steady series of revisionist songs, including "Feelin' Better," "Family Tradition," and "The Conversation," Hank Jr. took his lead from singer-songwriters like Kris Kristofferson and Waylon Jennings.[19] The Outlaw movement that began in the late 1960s and peaked in the mid-1970s had created an antiestablishment Hank Williams long before his son ever embraced that vision. While Hank Jr. was still trying to sort through all the things that "they" kept saying about his father, Kris Kristofferson began to tell Nashville that Hank Williams was an Outlaw, and, if "they" didn't like this image of Hank, well, "they" could kiss his ass. At the same time, Waylon Jennings was proudly proclaiming, "I'm A Ramblin' Man," thus offering himself up as the Second Coming of the original Outlaw. Moreover, Jennings had surveyed the Nashville music scene and wondered aloud, "Are You Sure Hank Done It This Way?" Seeing nothing in Nashville but "rhinestone suits and new shiny cars," Waylon concluded that country music needed to change. The change, of course, would come from the Outlaws themselves as the ones who were out there speeding their young lives away, they were the rightful heirs to the Hank Williams legacy. In the early 1970s, the Outlaws were trying to tell Nashville that it no longer understood what country music was all about, and the best way to accomplish this was to show Nashville that it had never really understood what Hank Williams was all about.

In "Feelin' Better," his 1977 follow-up to "Living Proof," Hank Jr. acknowledges his debt to the Outlaws, singing about how he had to get out of Nashville because the folks there "wouldn't let me sing nothing but them sad old songs." Thanks to "Waylon and Toy [Caldwell] and all the boys," however, he could sing his own stuff now, a kind of Southern country rock less suited to Nashville than to "Macon and Muscle Shoals." But in this new stage of his career, he was not just singing his own music; he was also writing his own version of his father's life. Nowhere was this done more forcefully, or more skillfully, than in two songs from 1979: the top-ten hit "Family Tradition" and the Waylon Jennings duet "The Conversation."

In "Family Tradition," Hank Jr. admits that he's changed direction in the last few years, and that in doing so he has broken with the Nashville tradition. But then he asks Nashville to think about his "unique position." If he drinks, smokes dope, lives a hard and tragic honky tonk life that runs counter to the Nashville tradition, well, that's just his "family tradition" after all. With this song, then, Hank Jr. was able to turn the tables on Nashville and the dictates of its tortuous logic: be like who we say your father was (the country music saint), but not too much like who we say your father also was (the irresponsible failure) or we'll run you out of town for not being the living proof of your father that we want, and need, you to be. In "Family Tradition," Hank Jr. created his own kind of tortuous logic and then turned it on Nashville: Yes, he admitted, there's a Nashville family tradition. Fine. But there's also a Williams family tradition. And his family tradition isn't like their family tradition, and he's the one named Williams here. So, if "you stop and think it over," the Nashville tradition and the Williams tradition are nothing alike. In 1952, Music City may have kicked Hank Williams out of the family, but, in 1979, his son was returning the boot.

In the opening stanza of "Family Tradition," Hank Jr. sings about how, lately, some of his Nashville "kinfolk have disowned a few others and me." Then, teaming up in "The Conversation" with one of those disowned others Waylon Jennings Hank Jr. took back the family inheritance. In fact, what Hank Jr. and Waylon did in this song was akin to what Audrey Williams had done in Oakwood Cemetery Annex back in the 1950s staking a claim to Hank Williams. First, these two disowned Outlaws set out to take control over what was said about Hank Williams. At the beginning of the song, they agree not to "talk about the habits / Just the music and the man." Next, having set the agenda, they set about exposing the hypocrisy of those who have staked false claims to Hank's memory. In their refrain, they both sing:

> Back then they called him crazy,
> Nowadays they call him a saint.
> Now the ones that called him crazy then
> Are still ridin' on his name.

The final revisionary step, of course, is to stake their own claim to Hank, to "write" and thus "ride" on his name. So when Waylon asks Hank Jr. whether his father would approve of the Outlaws if he were alive today, Hank assures Waylon that the original Ramblin' Man would be "right here by our side." The early tribute singers placed themselves beside Hank Williams in heaven; Miz Audrey claimed the same place with him "beyond the blue," where she would join Hank and he'd "say 'Come here and listen to me.'" Now, here were Hank Jr. and Outlaw Waylon claiming that the Ramblin' Man would "be the first one on [their] bus and ready to ride." "The Conversation," which begins with Waylon's invitation, "Hank, let's talk about your daddy," drives straight toward its calculated, revisionist conclusion, in which both voices are joined in proclaiming, "You know when we get right down to it, / He's still the most wanted outlaw in the land!"

Hank Jr., Waylon, and others continued to promote this outlaw image of Hank Williams well into the next decade, while some, like Charley Pride, in his 1980 release "I Got a Little Bit of Hank in Me," were reasserting the more sanitized, saintly vision of the Ramblin' Man.[20] In the 1980s and 1990s, however, yet another image of Hank Williams emerged, one that is best illustrated by two Top 10 songs: David Allan Coe's "The Ride" (1983) and Alan Jackson's "Midnight in Montgomery" (1992). In neither song is Hank portrayed as a saint or an outlaw, nor is he put on a heaven-bound train or the Outlaws' bus. Instead, the Ramblin' Man has become a weary ghost who cannot ride with either gang.[21]

"The Ride" (written by J. B. Detterline and Gary Gentry) sets out to revise every tribute song ever written about Hank by turning the "Singing Teacher in Heaven" into the tormented ghost of I-65. As Coe's recording of the song opens, he is making the same trek to Nashville that Hank made twenty years before. Thumbing his way north from Montgomery, he is offered a ride by a stranger in an "antique Cadillac." The Hank who had appeared to Jimmy Swan in a dream, holding a "little white Bible" in heaven, now appears as a "ghost white pale," "half drunk and hollow-eyed" stranger. No longer harmonizing with the angels in heaven, Hank is back on earth dispensing hard and bitter truths. In the song's haunting refrain, Hank warns the singer, "If you're big star bound, let me tell you it's a long hard ride." In the final stanza, Hank stops the car just south of Nashville and begins to cry: his passenger must get out here because Hank is going back to Alabama. We're not told why Hank Williams won't drive on into Music City. In an Outlaw song, he would probably be rejecting Nashville. Hank's tears in "The Ride," however, suggest not a defiance of Nashville, but a longing for home and, perhaps, acceptance. Envisioned in this song as a lonesome exile, Hank is doomed to ride the highway between Montgomery and Nashville, never finding rest, never gaining peace, never getting home. "The Ride" revises Hank Williams with its own hard and bitter truth: No matter how much we'd like to believe otherwise, Hank never got on Johnny Ryon's (or Cal Shrum's) "Heaven Bound Train," never found the "eternal happiness" that Ernest Tubb envisioned. Nor did he ever board the Outlaw's bus with Waylon and Hank Jr. The bitter truth? Hank Williams's life was a long hard ride, and so was his death.

At the beginning of "Midnight in Montgomery," Alan Jackson is headed in the opposite direction from Coe or so it first appears. Riding south on I-65, Jackson is not "big star bound," he's already a big star (witness the Silver Eagle). On his way from Nashville to Mobile for a "big New Year's Eve show," Jackson stops for just a moment in Montgomery to pay homage to Hank Williams. He is surprised when a "drunk man in a cowboy hat," with "haunted, haunted eyes," appears. This ghostly Hank haslittle to say to Jackson except to thank him for caring enough to visit. When Hank quickly disappears, Jackson wonders whether he was "ever really there." Still uncertain, Jackson reboards his bus, leaving Hank behind. If the implication of "The Ride" is that Hank must drive eternally up and down I-65, then Jackson's song implies that Hank can't ever get on I-65, or any other road, for that matter, neither heading for Provo on the Outlaws' bus nor bound for glory on a celestial train. Moreover, while the refrain of Jackson's song assures us that Hank will always be "singing there" in Montgomery, he won't be performing the way he did in the previous tribute songs. During the 1950s, Hank was said to be singing in the heavenly choir, while in the 1970s, he was still touring, in spirit at least, with the Outlaws. But Jackson's song leaves Hank to sing alone, at "midnight in Montgomery," with a "smell of whiskey in the air." Like Coe's "hollow-eyed" highwayman Jackson's "haunted"-eyed ghost stands side-by-side with no one, and no one stands side-by-side with him.

The developing visions of Hank Williams that I have mapped out here, from heavenly saint to defiant Outlaw to lonely ghost, should by no means suggest that every country artist has accepted this development, that Hank Williams's presence is now only that of a haunted, and haunting, apparition in country music. In "Me & Hank & Jumpin' Jack Flash," a song released in 1992, the same year as "Midnight in Montgomery," Marty Stuart dreams of a visit with Hank Williams in "hillbilly heaven." Stuart's Hank is still putting on concerts and giving his blessing to the truly authentic country singers (like Stuart himself). In fact, Stuart adds his own little twist to the narrative I've been tracing here when he implies that his entire album, *This One's*

Gonna Hurt You, is actually a revelation from Hank himself that Hank, not Marty, wrote all the songs.[22] Hank seems, to Marty Stuart at least, to still be the great "singing teacher in heaven."

In his biography of Hank Williams, however, Chet Flippo argues that this great singing teacher

> never really got it straight in his mind whether he was writing for Saturday night . . . or whether he was writing for Sunday morning. . . . He kept writing both kinds of songs and could never get it entirely straight in his own mind just where he belonged. He wanted to have Saturday night, drink it up and have a good time, but then he'd start to feel guilty and want to go back to Sunday morning and the sunlight and the white church and innocence.[23]

I think that much the same can be said for us. Just as Hank Williams struggled to figure out "where he belonged," we too have struggled to figure out what place he holds in country music. As soon as we have chiseled one version of Hank Williams's life we feel guilty, knowing that our song tells us more about ourselves than about the man. So we chisel another version. And thenanother. And yet another. Our own restlessness and uncertainty keep us on the road, on a constant journey between Nashville and Montgomery, between Music City and Hank's city, in search of an answer. But perhaps in the end there is no answer except this one: Hiram "Hank" Williams died on 1 January 1953, and, whether we want to admit it or not, we've all been writing on his back ever since.[24]

NOTES

[1] Those who have been to the grave in recent years will be aware of how, in the spirit of this essay, I have revised the scene (as indicated by my last photograph). My apologies to Miz Audrey.

[2] Here is a complete list of those 1953 songs (for recording information, see Selected Discography): "The Death of Hank Williams" (Jack Cardwell); "Hank, It Will Never Be the Same Without You" (Ernest Tubb); "Hank's Song" (Ferlin Husky); "Hank Williams Meets Jimmie Rodgers" (The Virginia Rounders); "Hank Williams Sings the Blues No More" (Jimmie Logsdon); "Hank Williams Will Live Forever" (Johnny and Jack); "(I Would Have Liked to Have Been) Hank's Little Flower Girl" (Little Barbara); "In Memory of Hank Williams" (Arthur Smith); "The Last Letter" (Jimmy Swan); "The Life of Hank Williams" (Hawkshaw Hawkins); "Singing Teacher in Heaven" (Jimmie Skinner); "That Heaven Bound Train" (Johnny Ryon; Cal Shrum); "There's a New Star in Hillbilly Heaven" (The Virginia Rounders); "Tribute to Hank Williams" (Joe Rumore); "A Tribute to Hank Williams, My Buddy" (Luke McDaniel).

[3] The one exception is Ferlin Husky's "Hank's Song."

4 See Hank Williams, Jr., *Insights Into Hank Williams* (MGM Records, 1974).

5 Hank Williams, Jr. (with Michael Bane), *Living Proof: An Autobiography* (New York, 1979), 64.

6 Lycrecia Williams, *Still in Love with You: The Story of Hank and Audrey Williams* (Nashville, 1989), 125.

7 Chet Flippo, *Your Cheatin' Heart: A Biography of Hank Williams* (New York, 1981), 240.

8 H. Williams, *Living Proof,* 37.

9 Ibid., 17.

10 Ibid., 129.

11 Ibid., 161, 163-64.

12 Ibid., 165.

13 Ibid., 166.

14 Ibid., 168.

15 Ibid., 181.

16 In 1979, for instance, Peter Guralnick wrote, "It is no accident . . . that [Hank Williams, Sr.] continues to be a dominant presence in [Hank Jr.'s] themes if not in his music or his writing, which is far more particular, or confessional anyway, than anything his father ever wrote. On *The New South* alone there are four songs that refer directly or indirectly to Hank Williams, and it seems an irony that Hank Junior will never escape, that the more he tries to pull away the more he will be reminded of his father's name." See his *Lost Highway: Journeys and Arrivals of American Musicians* (Boston, 1979), 230.

17 H. Williams, *Living Proof,* 24.

18 Ibid., 190.

19 These three songs, of course, do not represent a complete list of Hank Jr.'s revisionist songs, for example, "The Ballad of Hank Williams" or "A Whole Lotta Hank" (see Selected Discography). Note as well that Hank Sr. often appears in songs that are not devoted entirely to him. On *The New South,* for instance, several songs (e.g., "Montgomery in the Rain" and "The Blues Man") make reference to Hank Sr.

20 Hank Jr.'s 1983 release "A Whole Lotta Hank" seems to have been written in rebuttal to Pride's assertion that "I Got a Little Bit of Hank in Me." In "A Whole Lotta Hank," Hank Jr. is once again reclaiming his inheritance from those who would appropriate, and define, it for themselves.

21 For another song that manifests this third vision, see Robin and Linda Williams's "Rollin' and Ramblin' (The Death of Hank Williams)," on their 1988 album, *All Broken Hearts Are the Same* (see also Emmylou Harris's version of this song on her 1990 album, *Brand New Dance*).

22 The opening song on the album, "Me & Hank & Jumpin' Jack Flash," ends with the suggestion that the next song was sung by Hank Williams during Stuart's dream. The third cut no longer plays with this suggestion or so it appears. But the last song on side two is followed by fifteen seconds of silence, after which Stuart is heard to say, "And that's when I woke up," thus suggesting that the entire album was sung by Hank during Stuart's dream.

23 Flippo, *Your Cheatin' Heart,* 49.

24 Considerations of space and thesis have precluded discussionof every song ever written about Hank Williams. The following list, by no means definitive, covers songs not mentioned elsewhere in this essay and is intended to aid other scholars (for recording information, see Selected Discography): "The Car Hank Died In" (The Austin Lounge Lizards); "From Hank to Hendrix" (Neil Young); "The Ghost of Hank Williams" (The Kentucky Head Hunters); "Hank" (Jerry Bergonzi; Treat Her Right); "Hank Drank" (Bobby Lee Springfield); "Hank and George, Lefty and Me" (Tommy Cash); "Hank and Lefty Raised My Country Soul" (Stoney Edwards); "Hank, You Still Make Me Cry" (Boxcar Willie); "Hank Williams from His Grave" (Paleface); "Hank Williams Led a Happy Life" (The Geezinslaw Brothers); "Hank Williams's Guitar" (Freddy Hart); "Has Anybody Here Seen Hank?" (The Waterboys); "I Feel Like Hank Williams Tonight" (Jerry Jeff Walker); "I Remember Hank" (Lenny Breau); "I Think I Been Talkin' to Hank" (Mark Chestnutt); "The Night Hank Williams Came to Town" (Johnny Cash); "Wailin' with Hank" (Art Farmer Quintet); "When He Was Young, He Was Billed as the Next Hank Williams" (Jerry Farden).

FURTHER READING

Biography

Caress, Jay. *Hank Williams: Country Music's Tragic King.* New York: Stein and Day, 1979, 253 p.
Retells Williams's life, and presents a critical analysis of many of his songs.

Flippo, Chet. *Your Cheatin' Heart: A Biography of Hank Williams.* New York: Simon and Schuster, 1981, 251 p.

Employs elements of Gonzo Journalism to create a narrative retelling of Williams's life.

Williams, Hank Jr. with Bane, Michael. *Living Proof: An Autobiography*. New York: G.P. Putnam's Sons, 1979, 222 p.

Williams's son and a successful Country and Western performer in his own right, writes about his father's legacy and its sometimes negative effect on his own life and career.

Williams, Roger M. *Sing a Sad Song: The Life of Hank Williams*. New York: Doubleday & Co., 1970, 275 p.

Draws heavily on extensive interviews with Hank Williams's contemporaries and physicians specializing in alcoholism to re-create Williams's life and to support his thesis that Williams's talent was equal to his legend.

Criticism

Gleason, Ralph J. "Perspectives: Hank Williams, Roy Acuff and Then God!!" *Rolling Stone*, No. 36 (28 June 1969): 32.

Recalls meeting Williams and recounts his interview in which Williams divulges his musical influences and contemporaries he admires.

Moses, Mark. "Randy, Reba, and Hank." *The New Yorker* LXIV, No. 12 (9 May 1988): 110, 113-15.

Contrasting the body of work of Williams, Reba McIntyre, and Randy Travis, Moses asserts that Williams's songwriting and singing earned him his well-deserved status as a popular-music legend, and inspired a great deal of the popular music of different genres that was written and performed after his death.

Twentieth-Century
Literary Criticism

Cumulative Indexes
Volumes 1-81

How to Use This Index

The main references

Calvino, Italo
    1923–1985 .... CLC **5, 8, 11, 22, 33, 39,
                                73; SSC 3**

list all author entries in the following Gale Literary Criticism series:

BLC = *Black Literature Criticism*
CLC = *Contemporary Literary Criticism*
CLR = *Children's Literature Review*
CMLC = *Classical and Medieval Literature Criticism*
DA = *DISCovering Authors*
DAB = *DISCovering Authors: British*
DAC = *DISCovering Authors: Canadian*
DAM = *DISCovering Authors: Modules*
          DRAM: *Dramatists Module;* **MST**: *Most-Studied Authors Module;*
          MULT: *Multicultural Authors Module;* **NOV**: *Novelists Module;*
          POET: *Poets Module;* **POP**: *Popular Fiction and Genre Authors Module*
DC = *Drama Criticism*
HLC = *Hispanic Literature Criticism*
LC = *Literature Criticism from 1400 to 1800*
NCLC = *Nineteenth-Century Literature Criticism*
PC = *Poetry Criticism*
SSC = *Short Story Criticism*
TCLC = *Twentieth-Century Literary Criticism*
WLC = *World Literature Criticism, 1500 to the Present*

The cross-references

See also CANR 23; CA 85-88;
    obituary CA116

list all author entries in the following Gale biographical and literary sources:

AAYA = *Authors & Artists for Young Adults*
AITN = *Authors in the News*
BEST = *Bestsellers*
BW = *Black Writers*
CA = *Contemporary Authors*
CAAS = *Contemporary Authors Autobiography Series*
CABS = *Contemporary Authors Bibliographical Series*
CANR = *Contemporary Authors New Revision Series*
CAP = *Contemporary Authors Permanent Series*
CDALB = *Concise Dictionary of American Literary Biography*
CDBLB = *Concise Dictionary of British Literary Biography*
DLB = *Dictionary of Literary Biography*
DLBD = *Dictionary of Literary Biography Documentary Series*
DLBY = *Dictionary of Literary Biography Yearbook*
HW = *Hispanic Writers*
JRDA = *Junior DISCovering Authors*
MAICYA = *Major Authors and Illustrators for Children and Young Adults*
MTCW = *Major 20th-Century Writers*
NNAL = *Native North American Literature*
SAAS = *Something about the Author Autobiography Series*
SATA = *Something about the Author*
YABC = *Yesterday's Authors of Books for Children*

Literary Criticism Series
Cumulative Author Index

Aldanov, M. A.
 See Aldanov, Mark (Alexandrovich)
Aldanov, Mark (Alexandrovich) [1886(?)-1957]
  TCLC 23
 See also CA 118
Aldington, Richard [1892-1962] .... **CLC 49**
 See also CA 85-88; CANR 45; DLB 20, 36, 100,
  149
Aldiss, Brian W(ilson) [1925-]**CLC 5, 14, 40;**
  DAM NOV
 See also CA 5-8R; CAAS 2; CANR 5, 28, 64;
  DLB 14; MTCW; SATA 34
Alegria, Claribel [1924-] .... **CLC 75; DAM**
  MULT
 See also CA 131; CAAS 15; CANR 66; DLB
  145; HW
Alegria, Fernando [1918-] .... **CLC 57**
 See also CA 9-12R; CANR 5, 32; HW
Aleichem, Sholom .... **TCLC 1, 35**
 See also Rabinovitch, Sholem
Aleixandre, Vicente [1898-1984] **CLC 9, 36;**
  DAM POET; PC 15
 See also CA 85-88; 114; CANR 26; DLB 108;
  HW; MTCW
Alepoudelis, Odysseus
 See Elytis, Odysseus
Aleshkovsky, Joseph [1929-]
 See Aleshkovsky, Yuz
 See also CA 121; 128
Aleshkovsky, Yuz .... **CLC 44**
 See also Aleshkovsky, Joseph
Alexander, Lloyd (Chudley) [1924-] **CLC 35**
 See also AAYA 1; CA 1-4R; CANR 1, 24, 38,
  55; CLR 1, 5, 48; DLB 52; JRDA; MAICYA;
  MTCW; SAAS 19; SATA 3, 49, 81
Alexander, Samuel [1859-1938] ..... **TCLC 77**
Alexie, Sherman (Joseph, Jr.) [1966-]**CLC 96;**
  DAM MULT
 See also CA 138; CANR 65; DLB 175; NNAL
Alfau, Felipe [1902-] .... **CLC 66**
 See also CA 137
Alger, Horatio, Jr. [1832-1899] .... **NCLC 8**
 See also DLB 42; SATA 16
Algren, Nelson [1909-1981] .... **CLC 4, 10, 33**
 See also CA 13-16R; 103; CANR 20, 61;
  CDALB 1941-1968; DLB 9; DLBY 81, 82;
  MTCW
Ali, Ahmed [1910-] .... **CLC 69**
 See also CA 25-28R; CANR 15, 34
Alighieri, Dante
 See Dante
Allan, John B.
 See Westlake, Donald E(dwin)
Allan, Sidney
 See Hartmann, Sadakichi
Allan, Sydney
 See Hartmann, Sadakichi
Allen, Edward [1948-] .... **CLC 59**
Allen, Paula Gunn [1939-] ..... **CLC 84; DAM**
  MULT
 See also CA 112; 143; CANR 63; DLB 175;
  NNAL
Allen, Roland
 See Ayckbourn, Alan
Allen, Sarah A.
 See Hopkins, Pauline Elizabeth
Allen, Sidney H.
 See Hartmann, Sadakichi
Allen, Woody [1935-]**CLC 16, 52; DAM POP**
 See also AAYA 10; CA 33-36R; CANR 27, 38,
  63; DLB 44; MTCW
Allende, Isabel [1942-]**CLC 39, 57, 97; DAM**
  MULT, NOV; HLC; WLCS
 See also AAYA 18; CA 125; 130; CANR 51;
  DLB 145; HW; INT 130; MTCW
Alleyn, Ellen

 See Rossetti, Christina (Georgina)
Allingham, Margery (Louise) [1904-1966]
  CLC 19
 See also CA 5-8R; 25-28R; CANR 4, 58; DLB
  77; MTCW
Allingham, William [1824-1889] ... **NCLC 25**
 See also DLB 35
Allison, Dorothy E. [1949-] .... **CLC 78**
 See also CA 140; CANR 66
Allston, Washington [1779-1843] .... **NCLC 2**
 See also DLB 1
Almedingen, E. M. .... **CLC 12**
 See also Almedingen, Martha Edith von
 See also SATA 3
Almedingen, Martha Edith von [1898-1971]
 See Almedingen, E. M.
 See also CA 1-4R; CANR 1
Almqvist, Carl Jonas Love [1793-1866]**NCLC**
  42
Alonso, Damaso [1898-1990] .... **CLC 14**
 See also CA 110; 131; 130; DLB 108; HW
Alov
 See Gogol, Nikolai (Vasilyevich)
Alta [1942-] .... **CLC 19**
 See also CA 57-60
Alter, Robert B(ernard) [1935-] .... **CLC 34**
 See also CA 49-52; CANR 1, 47
Alther, Lisa [1944-] .... **CLC 7, 41**
 See also CA 65-68; CANR 12, 30, 51; MTCW
Althusser, L.
 See Althusser, Louis
Althusser, Louis [1918-1990] .... **CLC 106**
 See also CA 131; 132
Altman, Robert [1925-] .... **CLC 16**
 See also CA 73-76; CANR 43
Alvarez, A(lfred) [1929-] .... **CLC 5, 13**
 See also CA 1-4R; CANR 3, 33, 63; DLB 14,
  40
Alvarez, Alejandro Rodriguez [1903-1965]
 See Casona, Alejandro
 See also CA 131; 93-96; HW
Alvarez, Julia [1950-] .... **CLC 93**
 See also AAYA 25; CA 147; CANR 69
Alvaro, Corrado [1896-1956] .... **TCLC 60**
 See also CA 163
Amado, Jorge [1912-]**CLC 13, 40, 106; DAM**
  MULT, NOV; HLC
 See also CA 77-80; CANR 35; DLB 113;
  MTCW
Ambler, Eric [1909-] .... **CLC 4, 6, 9**
 See also CA 9-12R; CANR 7, 38; DLB 77;
  MTCW
Amichai, Yehuda [1924-] .... **CLC 9, 22, 57**
 See also CA 85-88; CANR 46, 60; MTCW
Amichai, Yehudah
 See Amichai, Yehuda
Amiel, Henri Frederic [1821-1881] . **NCLC 4**
Amis, Kingsley (William) [1922-1995]**CLC 1,**
  2, 3, 5, 8, 13, 40, 44; DA; DAB; DAC; DAM
  MST, NOV
 See also AITN 2; CA 9-12R; 150; CANR 8, 28,
  54; CDBLB 1945-1960; DLB 15, 27, 100,
  139; DLBY 96; INT CANR-8; MTCW
Amis, Martin (Louis) [1949-]**CLC 4, 9, 38, 62,**
  101
 See also BEST 90:3; CA 65-68; CANR 8, 27,
  54; DLB 14, 194; INT CANR-27
Ammons, A(rchie) R(andolph) [1926-]**CLC 2,**
  3, 5, 8, 9, 25, 57, 108; DAM POET; PC 16
 See also AITN 1; CA 9-12R; CANR 6, 36, 51;
  DLB 5, 165; MTCW
Amo, Tauraatua i
 See Adams, Henry (Brooks)
Anand, Mulk Raj [1905-] **CLC 23, 93; DAM**
  NOV
 See also CA 65-68; CANR 32, 64; MTCW
Anatol

 See Schnitzler, Arthur
Anaximander [c. 610B.C.-c. 546B.C.] **CMLC**
  22
Anaya, Rudolfo A(lfonso) [1937-] .. **CLC 23;**
  DAM MULT, NOV; HLC
 See also AAYA 20; CA 45-48; CAAS 4; CANR
  1, 32, 51; DLB 82; HW 1; MTCW
Andersen, Hans Christian [1805-1875]**NCLC**
  7; DA; DAB; DAC; DAM MST, POP; SSC
  6; WLC
 See also CLR 6; MAICYA; YABC 1
Anderson, C. Farley
 See Mencken, H(enry) L(ouis); Nathan, George
  Jean
Anderson, Jessica (Margaret) Queale [1916-]
  CLC 37
 See also CA 9-12R; CANR 4, 62
Anderson, Jon (Victor) [1940-]**CLC 9; DAM**
  POET
 See also CA 25-28R; CANR 20
Anderson, Lindsay (Gordon) [1923-1994]
  CLC 20
 See also CA 125; 128; 146
Anderson, Maxwell [1888-1959] ..... **TCLC 2;**
  DAM DRAM
 See also CA 105; 152; DLB 7
Anderson, Poul (William) [1926-] .... **CLC 15**
 See also AAYA 5; CA 1-4R; CAAS 2; CANR
  2, 15, 34, 64; DLB 8; INT CANR-15;
  MTCW; SATA 90; SATA-Brief 39
Anderson, Robert (Woodruff) [1917-] .. **C L C**
  23; DAM DRAM
 See also AITN 1; CA 21-24R; CANR 32; DLB
  7
Anderson, Sherwood [1876-1941]**TCLC 1, 10,**
  24; DA; DAB; DAC; DAM MST, NOV;
  SSC 1; WLC
 See also CA 104; 121; CANR 61; CDALB
  1917-1929; DLB 4, 9, 86; DLBD 1; MTCW
Andier, Pierre
 See Desnos, Robert
Andouard
 See Giraudoux, (Hippolyte) Jean
Andrade, Carlos Drummond de .... **CLC 18**
 See also Drummond de Andrade, Carlos
Andrade, Mario de [1893-1945] .... **TCLC 43**
Andreae, Johann V(alentin) [1586-1654] **L C**
  32
 See also DLB 164
Andreas-Salome, Lou [1861-1937] **TCLC 56**
 See also DLB 66
Andress, Lesley
 See Sanders, Lawrence
Andrewes, Lancelot [1555-1626] .... **LC 5**
 See also DLB 151, 172
Andrews, Cicily Fairfield
 See West, Rebecca
Andrews, Elton V.
 See Pohl, Frederik
Andreyev, Leonid (Nikolaevich) [1871-1919]
  TCLC 3
 See also CA 104
Andric, Ivo [1892-1975] .... **CLC 8**
 See also CA 81-84; 57-60; CANR 43, 60; DLB
  147; MTCW
Androvar
 See Prado (Calvo), Pedro
Angelique, Pierre
 See Bataille, Georges
Angell, Roger [1920-] .... **CLC 26**
 See also CA 57-60; CANR 13, 44; DLB 171,
  185
Angelou, Maya [1928-] . **CLC 12, 35, 64, 77;**
  BLC 1; DA; DAB; DAC; DAM MST,
  MULT, POET, POP; WLCS
 See also AAYA 7, 20; BW 2; CA 65-68; CANR
  19, 42, 65; DLB 38; MTCW; SATA 49

Baron, David
See Pinter, Harold
Baron Corvo
See Rolfe, Frederick (William Serafino Austin Lewis Mary)
Barondess, Sue K(aufman) [1926-1977]**CLC 8**
See also Kaufman, Sue
See also CA 1-4R; 69-72; CANR 1
Baron de Teive
See Pessoa, Fernando (Antonio Nogueira)
Barres, (Auguste-) Maurice [1862-1923]
TCLC 47
See also CA 164; DLB 123
Barreto, Afonso Henrique de Lima
See Lima Barreto, Afonso Henrique de
Barrett, (Roger) Syd [1946-] .... **CLC 35**
Barrett, William (Christopher) [1913-1992]
CLC 27
See also CA 13-16R; 139; CANR 11, 67; INT CANR-11
Barrie, J(ames) M(atthew) [1860-1937]**TCLC 2; DAB; DAM DRAM**
See also CA 104; 136; CDBLB 1890-1914; CLR 16; DLB 10, 141, 156; MAICYA; YABC 1
Barrington, Michael
See Moorcock, Michael (John)
Barrol, Grady
See Bograd, Larry
Barry, Mike
See Malzberg, Barry N(athaniel)
Barry, Philip [1896-1949] .... **TCLC 11**
See also CA 109; DLB 7
Bart, Andre Schwarz
See Schwarz-Bart, Andre
Barth, John (Simmons) [1930-]**CLC 1, 2, 3, 5, 7, 9, 10, 14, 27, 51, 89; DAM NOV; SSC 10**
See also AITN 1, 2; CA 1-4R; CABS 1; CANR 5, 23, 49, 64; DLB 2; MTCW
Barthelme, Donald [1931-1989]**CLC 1, 2, 3, 5, 6, 8, 13, 23, 46, 59; DAM NOV; SSC 2**
See also CA 21-24R; 129; CANR 20, 58; DLB 2; DLBY 80, 89; MTCW; SATA 7; SATA-Obit 62
Barthelme, Frederick [1943-] .... **CLC 36**
See also CA 114; 122; DLBY 85; INT 122
Barthes, Roland (Gerard) [1915-1980]. **C L C 24, 83**
See also CA 130; 97-100; CANR 66; MTCW
Barzun, Jacques (Martin) [1907-] .... **CLC 51**
See also CA 61-64; CANR 22
Bashevis, Isaac
See Singer, Isaac Bashevis
Bashkirtseff, Marie [1859-1884] .... **NCLC 27**
Basho
See Matsuo Basho
Bass, Kingsley B., Jr.
See Bullins, Ed
Bass, Rick [1958-] .... **CLC 79**
See also CA 126; CANR 53
Bassani, Giorgio [1916-] .... **CLC 9**
See also CA 65-68; CANR 33; DLB 128, 177; MTCW
Bastos, Augusto (Antonio) Roa
See Roa Bastos, Augusto (Antonio)
Bataille, Georges [1897-1962] .... **CLC 29**
See also CA 101; 89-92
Bates, H(erbert) E(rnest) [1905-1974] .. **C L C 46; DAB; DAM POP; SSC 10**
See also CA 93-96; 45-48; CANR 34; DLB 162, 191; MTCW
Bauchart
See Camus, Albert
Baudelaire, Charles [1821-1867]**NCLC 6, 29, 55; DA; DAB; DAC; DAM MST, POET; PC 1; SSC 18; WLC**
Baudrillard, Jean [1929-] .... **CLC 60**

Baum, L(yman) Frank [1856-1919] **TCLC 7**
See also CA 108; 133; CLR 15; DLB 22; JRDA; MAICYA; MTCW; SATA 18
Baum, Louis F.
See Baum, L(yman) Frank
Baumbach, Jonathan [1933-] .... **CLC 6, 23**
See also CA 13-16R; CAAS 5; CANR 12, 66; DLBY 80; INT CANR-12; MTCW
Bausch, Richard (Carl) [1945-] .... **CLC 51**
See also CA 101; CAAS 14; CANR 43, 61; DLB 130
Baxter, Charles (Morley) [1947-]**CLC 45, 78; DAM POP**
See also CA 57-60; CANR 40, 64; DLB 130
Baxter, George Owen
See Faust, Frederick (Schiller)
Baxter, James K(eir) [1926-1972] ..... **CLC 14**
See also CA 77-80
Baxter, John
See Hunt, E(verette) Howard, (Jr.)
Bayer, Sylvia
See Glassco, John
Baynton, Barbara [1857-1929] ...... **TCLC 57**
Beagle, Peter S(oyer) [1939-] ..... **CLC 7, 104**
See also CA 9-12R; CANR 4, 51; DLBY 80; INT CANR-4; SATA 60
Bean, Normal
See Burroughs, Edgar Rice
Beard, Charles A(ustin) [1874-1948]**TCLC 15**
See also CA 115; DLB 17; SATA 18
Beardsley, Aubrey [1872-1898] .... **NCLC 6**
Beattie, Ann [1947-] .. **CLC 8, 13, 18, 40, 63; DAM NOV, POP; SSC 11**
See also BEST 90:2; CA 81-84; CANR 53; DLBY 82; MTCW
Beattie, James [1735-1803] .... **NCLC 25**
See also DLB 109
Beauchamp, Kathleen Mansfield [1888-1923]
See Mansfield, Katherine
See also CA 104; 134; DA; DAC; DAM MST
Beaumarchais, Pierre-Augustin Caron de [1732-1799] .... **DC 4**
See also DAM DRAM
Beaumont, Francis [1584(?)-1616]**LC 33; DC 6**
See also CDBLB Before 1660; DLB 58, 121
Beauvoir, Simone (Lucie Ernestine Marie Bertrand) de [1908-1986]**CLC 1, 2, 4, 8, 14, 31, 44, 50, 71; DA; DAB; DAC; DAM MST, NOV; WLC**
See also CA 9-12R; 118; CANR 28, 61; DLB 72; DLBY 86; MTCW
Becker, Carl (Lotus) [1873-1945] .. **TCLC 63**
See also CA 157; DLB 17
Becker, Jurek [1937-1997] .... **CLC 7, 19**
See also CA 85-88; 157; CANR 60; DLB 75
Becker, Walter [1950-] .... **CLC 26**
Beckett, Samuel (Barclay) [1906-1989]**CLC 1, 2, 3, 4, 6, 9, 10, 11, 14, 18, 29, 57, 59, 83; DA; DAB; DAC; DAM DRAM, MST, NOV; SSC 16; WLC**
See also CA 5-8R; 130; CANR 33, 61; CDBLB 1945-1960; DLB 13, 15; DLBY 90; MTCW
Beckford, William [1760-1844] ...... **NCLC 16**
See also DLB 39
Beckman, Gunnel [1910-] .... **CLC 26**
See also CA 33-36R; CANR 15; CLR 25; MAICYA; SAAS 9; SATA 6
Becque, Henri [1837-1899] .... **NCLC 3**
See also DLB 192
Beddoes, Thomas Lovell [1803-1849]**NCLC 3**
See also DLB 96
Bede [c. 673-735] .... **CMLC 20**
See also DLB 146
Bedford, Donald F.
See Fearing, Kenneth (Flexner)
Beecher, Catharine Esther [1800-1878]**NCLC

30
See also DLB 1
Beecher, John [1904-1980] .... **CLC 6**
See also AITN 1; CA 5-8R; 105; CANR 8
Beer, Johann [1655-1700] .... **LC 5**
See also DLB 168
Beer, Patricia [1924-] .... **CLC 58**
See also CA 61-64; CANR 13, 46; DLB 40
Beerbohm, Max
See Beerbohm, (Henry) Max(imilian)
Beerbohm, (Henry) Max(imilian) [1872-1956]
TCLC 1, 24
See also CA 104; 154; DLB 34, 100
Beer-Hofmann, Richard [1866-1945] **T C L C 60**
See also CA 160; DLB 81
Begiebing, Robert J(ohn) [1946-] ..... **CLC 70**
See also CA 122; CANR 40
Behan, Brendan [1923-1964]**CLC 1, 8, 11, 15, 79; DAM DRAM**
See also CA 73-76; CANR 33; CDBLB 1945-1960; DLB 13; MTCW
Behn, Aphra [1640(?)-1689] ... **LC 1, 30; DA; DAB; DAC; DAM DRAM, MST, NOV, POET; DC 4; PC 13; WLC**
See also DLB 39, 80, 131
Behrman, S(amuel) N(athaniel) [1893-1973]
CLC 40
See also CA 13-16; 45-48; CAP 1; DLB 7, 44
Belasco, David [1853-1931] .... **TCLC 3**
See also CA 104; DLB 7
Belcheva, Elisaveta [1893-] .... **CLC 10**
See also Bagryana, Elisaveta
Beldone, Phil "Cheech"
See Ellison, Harlan (Jay)
Beleno
See Azuela, Mariano
Belinski, Vissarion Grigoryevich [1811-1848]
NCLC 5
See also DLB 198
Belitt, Ben [1911-] .... **CLC 22**
See also CA 13-16R; CAAS 4; CANR 7; DLB 5
Bell, Gertrude (Margaret Lowthian) [1868-1926] .... **TCLC 67**
See also DLB 174
Bell, James Madison [1826-1902] . **TCLC 43; BLC 1; DAM MULT**
See also BW 1; CA 122; 124; DLB 50
Bell, Madison Smartt [1957-] ... **CLC 41, 102**
See also CA 111; CANR 28, 54
Bell, Marvin (Hartley) [1937-] .... **CLC 8, 31; DAM POET**
See also CA 21-24R; CAAS 14; CANR 59; DLB 5; MTCW
Bell, W. L. D.
See Mencken, H(enry) L(ouis)
Bellamy, Atwood C.
See Mencken, H(enry) L(ouis)
Bellamy, Edward [1850-1898] .... **NCLC 4**
See also DLB 12
Bellin, Edward J.
See Kuttner, Henry
Belloc, (Joseph) Hilaire (Pierre Sebastien Rene Swanton) [1870-1953]**TCLC 7, 18; DAM POET**
See also CA 106; 152; DLB 19, 100, 141, 174; YABC 1
Belloc, Joseph Peter Rene Hilaire
See Belloc, (Joseph) Hilaire (Pierre Sebastien Rene Swanton)
Belloc, Joseph Pierre Hilaire
See Belloc, (Joseph) Hilaire (Pierre Sebastien Rene Swanton)
Belloc, M. A.
See Lowndes, Marie Adelaide (Belloc)
Bellow, Saul [1915-] **CLC 1, 2, 3, 6, 8, 10, 13,**

Bird, Cordwainer
See Ellison, Harlan (Jay)
Bird, Robert Montgomery [1806-1854]**NCLC 1**
Birney, (Alfred) Earle [1904-1995] **CLC 1, 4, 6, 11; DAC; DAM MST, POET**
See also CA 1-4R; CANR 5, 20; DLB 88; MTCW
Bishop, Elizabeth [1911-1979]**CLC 1, 4, 9, 13, 15, 32; DA; DAC; DAM MST, POET; PC 3**
See also CA 5-8R; 89-92; CABS 2; CANR 26, 61; CDALB 1968-1988; DLB 5, 169; MTCW; SATA-Obit 24
Bishop, John [1935-] .... **CLC 10**
See also CA 105
Bissett, Bill [1939-] .... **CLC 18; PC 14**
See also CA 69-72; CAAS 19; CANR 15; DLB 53; MTCW
Bitov, Andrei (Georgievich) [1937-] . **CLC 57**
See also CA 142
Biyidi, Alexandre [1932-]
See Beti, Mongo
See also BW 1; CA 114; 124; MTCW
Bjarme, Brynjolf
See Ibsen, Henrik (Johan)
Bjoernson, Bjoernstjerne (Martinius) [1832-1910] ....
TCLC 7, 37
See also CA 104
Black, Robert
See Holdstock, Robert P.
Blackburn, Paul [1926-1971] .... **CLC 9, 43**
See also CA 81-84; 33-36R; CANR 34; DLB 16; DLBY 81
Black Elk [1863-1950]**TCLC 33; DAM MULT**
See also CA 144; NNAL
Black Hobart
See Sanders, (James) Ed(ward)
Blacklin, Malcolm
See Chambers, Aidan
Blackmore, R(ichard) D(oddridge) [1825-1900]
TCLC 27
See also CA 120; DLB 18
Blackmur, R(ichard) P(almer) [1904-1965]
CLC 2, 24
See also CA 11-12; 25-28R; CAP 1; DLB 63
Black Tarantula
See Acker, Kathy
Blackwood, Algernon (Henry) [1869-1951]
TCLC 5
See also CA 105; 150; DLB 153, 156, 178
Blackwood, Caroline [1931-1996] . **CLC 6, 9, 100**
See also CA 85-88; 151; CANR 32, 61, 65; DLB 14; MTCW
Blade, Alexander
See Hamilton, Edmond; Silverberg, Robert
Blaga, Lucian [1895-1961] .... **CLC 75**
See also CA 157
Blair, Eric (Arthur) [1903-1950]
See Orwell, George
See also CA 104; 132; DA; DAB; DAC; DAM MST, NOV; MTCW; SATA 29
Blais, Marie-Claire [1939-]**CLC 2, 4, 6, 13, 22; DAC; DAM MST**
See also CA 21-24R; CAAS 4; CANR 38; DLB 53; MTCW
Blaise, Clark [1940-] .... **CLC 29**
See also AITN 2; CA 53-56; CAAS 3; CANR 5, 66; DLB 53
Blake, Fairley
See De Voto, Bernard (Augustine)
Blake, Nicholas
See Day Lewis, C(ecil)
See also DLB 77
Blake, William [1757-1827]**NCLC 13, 37, 57;**

DA; DAB; DAC; DAM MST, POET; PC 12; WLC
See also CDBLB 1789-1832; CLR 52; DLB 93, 163; MAICYA; SATA 30
Blasco Ibanez, Vicente [1867-1928]**TCLC 12; DAM NOV**
See also CA 110; 131; HW; MTCW
Blatty, William Peter [1928-] .. **CLC 2; DAM POP**
See also CA 5-8R; CANR 9
Bleeck, Oliver
See Thomas, Ross (Elmore)
Blessing, Lee [1949-] .... **CLC 54**
Blish, James (Benjamin) [1921-1975]**CLC 14**
See also CA 1-4R; 57-60; CANR 3; DLB 8; MTCW; SATA 66
Bliss, Reginald
See Wells, H(erbert) G(eorge)
Blixen, Karen (Christentze Dinesen) [1885-1962]
See Dinesen, Isak
See also CA 25-28; CANR 22, 50; CAP 2; MTCW; SATA 44
Bloch, Robert (Albert) [1917-1994] . **CLC 33**
See also CA 5-8R; 146; CAAS 20; CANR 5; DLB 44; INT CANR-5; SATA 12; SATA-Obit 82
Blok, Alexander (Alexandrovich) [1880-1921]
TCLC 5; PC 21
See also CA 104
Blom, Jan
See Breytenbach, Breyten
Bloom, Harold [1930-] .... **CLC 24, 103**
See also CA 13-16R; CANR 39; DLB 67
Bloomfield, Aurelius
See Bourne, Randolph S(illiman)
Blount, Roy (Alton), Jr. [1941-] .... **CLC 38**
See also CA 53-56; CANR 10, 28, 61; INT CANR-28; MTCW
Bloy, Leon [1846-1917] .... **TCLC 22**
See also CA 121; DLB 123
Blume, Judy (Sussman) [1938-] **CLC 12, 30; DAM NOV, POP**
See also AAYA 3; CA 29-32R; CANR 13, 37, 66; CLR 2, 15; DLB 52; JRDA; MAICYA; MTCW; SATA 2, 31, 79
Blunden, Edmund (Charles) [1896-1974]**CLC 2, 56**
See also CA 17-18; 45-48; CANR 54; CAP 2; DLB 20, 100, 155; MTCW
Bly, Robert (Elwood) [1926-]**CLC 1, 2, 5, 10, 15, 38; DAM POET**
See also CA 5-8R; CANR 41; DLB 5; MTCW
Boas, Franz [1858-1942] .... **TCLC 56**
See also CA 115
Bobette
See Simenon, Georges (Jacques Christian)
Boccaccio, Giovanni [1313-1375] **CMLC 13; SSC 10**
Bochco, Steven [1943-] .... **CLC 35**
See also AAYA 11; CA 124; 138
Bodel, Jean [1167(?)-1210] .... **CMLC 28**
Bodenheim, Maxwell [1892-1954] . **TCLC 44**
See also CA 110; DLB 9, 45
Bodker, Cecil [1927-] .... **CLC 21**
See also CA 73-76; CANR 13, 44; CLR 23; MAICYA; SATA 14
Boell, Heinrich (Theodor) [1917-1985]**CLC 2, 3, 6, 9, 11, 15, 27, 32, 72; DA; DAB; DAC; DAM MST, NOV; SSC 23; WLC**
See also CA 21-24R; 116; CANR 24; DLB 69; DLBY 85; MTCW
Boerne, Alfred
See Doeblin, Alfred
Boethius [480(?)-524(?)] .... **CMLC 15**
See also DLB 115
Bogan, Louise [1897-1970]**CLC 4, 39, 46, 93;**

DAM POET; PC 12
See also CA 73-76; 25-28R; CANR 33; DLB 45, 169; MTCW
Bogarde, Dirk .... **CLC 19**
See also Van Den Bogarde, Derek Jules Gaspard Ulric Niven
See also DLB 14
Bogosian, Eric [1953-] .... **CLC 45**
See also CA 138
Bograd, Larry [1953-]....................... **CLC 35**
See also CA 93-96; CANR 57; SAAS 21; SATA 33, 89
Boiardo, Matteo Maria [1441-1494] ..... **LC 6**
Boileau-Despreaux, Nicolas [1636-1711]**LC 3**
Bojer, Johan [1872-1959]................... **TCLC 64**
Boland, Eavan (Aisling) [1944-] **CLC 40, 67, 113; DAM POET**
See also CA 143; CANR 61; DLB 40
Boll, Heinrich
See Boell, Heinrich (Theodor)
Bolt, Lee
See Faust, Frederick (Schiller)
Bolt, Robert (Oxton) [1924-1995] .. **CLC 14; DAM DRAM**
See also CA 17-20R; 147; CANR 35, 67; DLB 13; MTCW
Bombet, Louis-Alexandre-Cesar
See Stendhal
Bomkauf
See Kaufman, Bob (Garnell)
Bonaventura .... **NCLC 35**
See also DLB 90
Bond, Edward [1934-]**CLC 4, 6, 13, 23; DAM DRAM**
See also CA 25-28R; CANR 38, 67; DLB 13; MTCW
Bonham, Frank [1914-1989] .... **CLC 12**
See also AAYA 1; CA 9-12R; CANR 4, 36; JRDA; MAICYA; SAAS 3; SATA 1, 49; SATA-Obit 62
Bonnefoy, Yves [1923-] **CLC 9, 15, 58; DAM MST, POET**
See also CA 85-88; CANR 33; MTCW
Bontemps, Arna(ud Wendell) [1902-1973]
CLC 1, 18; BLC 1; DAM MULT, NOV, POET
See also BW 1; CA 1-4R; 41-44R; CANR 4, 35; CLR 6; DLB 48, 51; JRDA; MAICYA; MTCW; SATA 2, 44; SATA-Obit 24
Booth, Martin [1944-] .... **CLC 13**
See also CA 93-96; CAAS 2
Booth, Philip [1925-] .... **CLC 23**
See also CA 5-8R; CANR 5; DLBY 82
Booth, Wayne C(layson) [1921-] .... **CLC 24**
See also CA 1-4R; CAAS 5; CANR 3, 43; DLB 67
Borchert, Wolfgang [1921-1947] ..... **TCLC 5**
See also CA 104; DLB 69, 124
Borel, Petrus [1809-1859] .... **NCLC 41**
Borges, Jorge Luis [1899-1986]**CLC 1, 2, 3, 4, 6, 8, 9, 10, 13, 19, 44, 48, 83; DA; DAB; DAC; DAM MST, MULT; HLC; PC 22; SSC 4; WLC**
See also AAYA 19; CA 21-24R; CANR 19, 33; DLB 113; DLBY 86; HW; MTCW
Borowski, Tadeusz [1922-1951] .... **TCLC 9**
See also CA 106; 154
Borrow, George (Henry) [1803-1881]**NCLC 9**
See also DLB 21, 55, 166
Bosman, Herman Charles [1905-1951]**TCLC 49**
See also Malan, Herman
See also CA 160
Bosschere, Jean de [1878(?)-1953] **TCLC 19**
See also CA 115
Boswell, James [1740-1795]**LC 4; DA; DAB; DAC; DAM MST; WLC**

Bronte, Charlotte [1816-1855]NCLC **3, 8, 33, 58; DA; DAB; DAC; DAM MST, NOV; WLC**
See also AAYA 17; CDBLB 1832-1890; DLB 21, 159, 199

Bronte, Emily (Jane) [1818-1848] NCLC **16, 35; DA; DAB; DAC; DAM MST, NOV, POET; PC 8; WLC**
See also AAYA 17; CDBLB 1832-1890; DLB 21, 32, 199

Brooke, Frances [1724-1789] .... **LC 6**
See also DLB 39, 99

Brooke, Henry [1703(?)-1783] .... **LC 1**
See also DLB 39

Brooke, Rupert (Chawner) [1887-1915] **TCLC 2, 7; DA; DAB; DAC; DAM MST, POET; WLC**
See also CA 104; 132; CANR 61; CDBLB 1914-1945; DLB 19; MTCW

Brooke-Haven, P.
See Wodehouse, P(elham) G(renville)

Brooke-Rose, Christine [1926(?)-] .... **CLC 40**
See also CA 13-16R; CANR 58; DLB 14

Brookner, Anita [1928-]CLC **32, 34, 51; DAB; DAM POP**
See also CA 114; 120; CANR 37, 56; DLB 194; DLBY 87; MTCW

Brooks, Cleanth [1906-1994]CLC **24, 86, 110**
See also CA 17-20R; 145; CANR 33, 35; DLB 63; DLBY 94; INT CANR-35; MTCW

Brooks, George
See Baum, L(yman) Frank

Brooks, Gwendolyn [1917-]CLC **1, 2, 4, 5, 15, 49; BLC 1; DA; DAC; DAM MST, MULT, POET; PC 7; WLC**
See also AAYA 20; AITN 1; BW 2; CA 1-4R; CANR 1, 27, 52; CDALB 1941-1968; CLR 27; DLB 5, 76, 165; MTCW; SATA 6

Brooks, Mel .... **CLC 12**
See also Kaminsky, Melvin
See also AAYA 13; DLB 26

Brooks, Peter [1938-] .... **CLC 34**
See also CA 45-48; CANR 1

Brooks, Van Wyck [1886-1963] .... **CLC 29**
See also CA 1-4R; CANR 6; DLB 45, 63, 103

Brophy, Brigid (Antonia) [1929-1995]CLC **6, 11, 29, 105**
See also CA 5-8R; 149; CAAS 4; CANR 25, 53; DLB 14; MTCW

Brosman, Catharine Savage [1934-] .. **CLC 9**
See also CA 61-64; CANR 21, 46

Brother Antoninus
See Everson, William (Oliver)

The Brothers Quay
See Quay, Stephen; Quay, Timothy

Broughton, T(homas) Alan [1936-] .. **CLC 19**
See also CA 45-48; CANR 2, 23, 48

Broumas, Olga [1949-] .... **CLC 10, 73**
See also CA 85-88; CANR 20, 69

Brown, Alan [1950-] .... **CLC 99**
See also CA 156

Brown, Charles Brockden [1771-1810]NCLC **22**
See also CDALB 1640-1865; DLB 37, 59, 73

Brown, Christy [1932-1981] .... **CLC 63**
See also CA 105; 104; DLB 14

Brown, Claude [1937-]CLC **30; BLC 1; DAM MULT**
See also AAYA 7; BW 1; CA 73-76

Brown, Dee (Alexander) [1908-] CLC **18, 47; DAM POP**
See also CA 13-16R; CAAS 6; CANR 11, 45, 60; DLBY 80; MTCW; SATA 5

Brown, George
See Wertmueller, Lina

Brown, George Douglas [1869-1902]TCLC **28**
See also CA 162

Brown, George Mackay [1921-1996] CLC **5, 48, 100**
See also CA 21-24R; 151; CAAS 6; CANR 12, 37, 67; DLB 14, 27, 139; MTCW; SATA 35

Brown, (William) Larry [1951-] .... **CLC 73**
See also CA 130; 134; INT 133

Brown, Moses
See Barrett, William (Christopher)

Brown, Rita Mae [1944-] ..... CLC **18, 43, 79; DAM NOV, POP**
See also CA 45-48; CANR 2, 11, 35, 62; INT CANR-11; MTCW

Brown, Roderick (Langmere) Haig-
See Haig-Brown, Roderick (Langmere)

Brown, Rosellen [1939-] .... **CLC 32**
See also CA 77-80; CAAS 10; CANR 14, 44

Brown, Sterling Allen [1901-1989]CLC **1, 23, 59; BLC 1; DAM MULT, POET**
See also BW 1; CA 85-88; 127; CANR 26; DLB 48, 51, 63; MTCW

Brown, Will
See Ainsworth, William Harrison

Brown, William Wells [1813-1884] NCLC **2; BLC 1; DAM MULT; DC 1**
See also DLB 3, 50

Browne, (Clyde) Jackson [1948(?)-] . **CLC 21**
See also CA 120

Browning, Elizabeth Barrett [1806-1861] **NCLC 1, 16, 61, 66; DA; DAB; DAC; DAM MST, POET; PC 6; WLC**
See also CDBLB 1832-1890; DLB 32, 199

Browning, Robert [1812-1889]NCLC **19; DA; DAB; DAC; DAM MST, POET; PC 2; WLCS**
See also CDBLB 1832-1890; DLB 32, 163; YABC 1

Browning, Tod [1882-1962] .... **CLC 16**
See also CA 141; 117

Brownson, Orestes (Augustus) [1803-1876] **NCLC 50**

Brownson, Orestes Augustus [1803-1876] **NCLC 50**
See also DLB 1, 59, 73

Bruccoli, Matthew J(oseph) [1931-] . **CLC 34**
See also CA 9-12R; CANR 7; DLB 103

Bruce, Lenny .... **CLC 21**
See also Schneider, Leonard Alfred

Bruin, John
See Brutus, Dennis

Brulard, Henri
See Stendhal

Brulls, Christian
See Simenon, Georges (Jacques Christian)

Brunner, John (Kilian Houston) [1934-1995] **CLC 8, 10; DAM POP**
See also CA 1-4R; 149; CAAS 8; CANR 2, 37; MTCW

Bruno, Giordano [1548-1600] .... **LC 27**

Brutus, Dennis [1924-]CLC **43; BLC 1; DAM MULT, POET**
See also BW 2; CA 49-52; CAAS 14; CANR 2, 27, 42; DLB 117

Bryan, C(ourtlandt) D(ixon) B(arnes) [1936-] **CLC 29**
See also CA 73-76; CANR 13, 68; DLB 185; INT CANR-13

Bryan, Michael
See Moore, Brian

Bryant, William Cullen [1794-1878]NCLC **6, 46; DA; DAB; DAC; DAM MST, POET; PC 20**
See also CDALB 1640-1865; DLB 3, 43, 59, 189

Bryusov, Valery Yakovlevich [1873-1924] **TCLC 10**
See also CA 107; 155

Buchan, John [1875-1940] .. TCLC **41; DAB;**

DAM POP
See also CA 108; 145; DLB 34, 70, 156; YABC 2

Buchanan, George [1506-1582] .... **LC 4**
See also DLB 152

Buchheim, Lothar-Guenther [1918-] . **CLC 6**
See also CA 85-88

Buchner, (Karl) Georg [1813-1837]NCLC **26**

Buchwald, Art(hur) [1925-] .... **CLC 33**
See also AITN 1; CA 5-8R; CANR 21, 67; MTCW; SATA 10

Buck, Pearl S(ydenstricker) [1892-1973]CLC **7, 11, 18; DA; DAB; DAC; DAM MST, NOV**
See also AITN 1; CA 1-4R; 41-44R; CANR 1, 34; DLB 9, 102; MTCW; SATA 1, 25

Buckler, Ernest [1908-1984] . CLC **13; DAC; DAM MST**
See also CA 11-12; 114; CAP 1; DLB 68; SATA 47

Buckley, Vincent (Thomas) [1925-1988] C L C **57**
See also CA 101

Buckley, William F(rank), Jr. [1925-]CLC **7, 18, 37; DAM POP**
See also AITN 1; CA 1-4R; CANR 1, 24, 53; DLB 137; DLBY 80; INT CANR-24; MTCW

Buechner, (Carl) Frederick [1926-]CLC **2, 4, 6, 9; DAM NOV**
See also CA 13-16R; CANR 11, 39, 64; DLBY 80; INT CANR-11; MTCW

Buell, John (Edward) [1927-] .... **CLC 10**
See also CA 1-4R; DLB 53

Buero Vallejo, Antonio [1916-] .. CLC **15, 46**
See also CA 106; CANR 24, 49; HW; MTCW

Bufalino, Gesualdo [1920(?)-] .... **CLC 74**
See also DLB 196

Bugayev, Boris Nikolayevich [1880-1934] **TCLC 7; PC 11**
See also Bely, Andrey
See also CA 104; 165

Bukowski, Charles [1920-1994] CLC **2, 5, 9, 41, 82, 108; DAM NOV, POET; PC 18**
See also CA 17-20R; 144; CANR 40, 62; DLB 5, 130, 169; MTCW

Bulgakov, Mikhail (Afanas'evich) [1891-1940] **TCLC 2, 16; DAM DRAM, NOV; SSC 18**
See also CA 105; 152

Bulgya, Alexander Alexandrovich [1901-1956] **TCLC 53**
See also Fadeyev, Alexander
See also CA 117

Bullins, Ed [1935-]CLC **1, 5, 7; BLC 1; DAM DRAM, MULT; DC 6**
See also BW 2; CA 49-52; CAAS 16; CANR 24, 46; DLB 7, 38; MTCW

Bulwer-Lytton, Edward (George Earle Lytton) [1803-1873] .... NCLC **1, 45**
See also DLB 21

Bunin, Ivan Alexeyevich [1870-1953]TCLC **6; SSC 5**
See also CA 104

Bunting, Basil [1900-1985] .. CLC **10, 39, 47; DAM POET**
See also CA 53-56; 115; CANR 7; DLB 20

Bunuel, Luis [1900-1983] CLC **16, 80; DAM MULT; HLC**
See also CA 101; 110; CANR 32; HW

Bunyan, John [1628-1688] LC **4; DA; DAB; DAC; DAM MST; WLC**
See also CDBLB 1660-1789; DLB 39

Burckhardt, Jacob (Christoph) [1818-1897] **NCLC 49**

Burford, Eleanor
See Hibbert, Eleanor Alice Burford

Burgess, AnthonyCLC **1, 2, 4, 5, 8, 10, 13, 15, 22, 40, 62, 81, 94; DAB**

Card, Orson Scott [1951-] ... **CLC 44, 47, 50; DAM POP**
See also AAYA 11; CA 102; CANR 27, 47; INT CANR-27; MTCW; SATA 83

Cardenal, Ernesto [1925-] .... **CLC 31; DAM MULT, POET; HLC; PC 22**
See also CA 49-52; CANR 2, 32, 66; HW; MTCW

Cardozo, Benjamin N(athan) [1870-1938] **TCLC 65**
See also CA 117; 164

Carducci, Giosue (Alessandro Giuseppe) [1835-1907] ....
TCLC 32
See also CA 163

Carew, Thomas [1595(?)-1640] .... **LC 13**
See also DLB 126

Carey, Ernestine Gilbreth [1908-] .... **CLC 17**
See also CA 5-8R; SATA 2

Carey, Peter [1943-] .... **CLC 40, 55, 96**
See also CA 123; 127; CANR 53; INT 127; MTCW; SATA 94

Carleton, William [1794-1869] .... **NCLC 3**
See also DLB 159

Carlisle, Henry (Coffin) [1926-] .... **CLC 33**
See also CA 13-16R; CANR 15

Carlsen, Chris
See Holdstock, Robert P.

Carlson, Ron(ald F.) [1947-] .... **CLC 54**
See also CA 105; CANR 27

Carlyle, Thomas [1795-1881] **NCLC 70; DA; DAB; DAC; DAM MST**
See also CDBLB 1789-1832; DLB 55; 144

Carman, (William) Bliss [1861-1929]**TCLC 7; DAC**
See also CA 104; 152; DLB 92

Carnegie, Dale [1888-1955] .... **TCLC 53**

Carossa, Hans [1878-1956] .... **TCLC 48**
See also DLB 66

Carpenter, Don(ald Richard) [1931-1995] **CLC 41**
See also CA 45-48; 149; CANR 1

Carpentier (y Valmont), Alejo [1904-1980] **CLC 8, 11, 38, 110; DAM MULT; HLC**
See also CA 65-68; 97-100; CANR 11; DLB 113; HW

Carr, Caleb [1955(?)-] .... **CLC 86**
See also CA 147

Carr, Emily [1871-1945] .... **TCLC 32**
See also CA 159; DLB 68

Carr, John Dickson [1906-1977] .... **CLC 3**
See also Fairbairn, Roger
See also CA 49-52; 69-72; CANR 3, 33, 60; MTCW

Carr, Philippa
See Hibbert, Eleanor Alice Burford

Carr, Virginia Spencer [1929-] .... **CLC 34**
See also CA 61-64; DLB 111

Carrere, Emmanuel [1957-] .... **CLC 89**

Carrier, Roch [1937-]**CLC 13, 78; DAC; DAM MST**
See also CA 130; CANR 61; DLB 53

Carroll, James P. [1943(?)-] .... **CLC 38**
See also CA 81-84

Carroll, Jim [1951-] .... **CLC 35**
See also AAYA 17; CA 45-48; CANR 42

Carroll, Lewis ..... **NCLC 2, 53; PC 18; WLC**
See also Dodgson, Charles Lutwidge
See also CDBLB 1832-1890; CLR 2, 18; DLB 18, 163, 178; JRDA

Carroll, Paul Vincent [1900-1968] ... **CLC 10**
See also CA 9-12R; 25-28R; DLB 10

Carruth, Hayden [1921-]**CLC 4, 7, 10, 18, 84; PC 10**
See also CA 9-12R; CANR 4, 38, 59; DLB 5, 165; INT CANR-4; MTCW; SATA 47

Carson, Rachel Louise [1907-1964] **CLC 71;**

DAM POP
See also CA 77-80; CANR 35; MTCW; SATA 23

Carter, Angela (Olive) [1940-1992]**CLC 5, 41, 76; SSC 13**
See also CA 53-56; 136; CANR 12, 36, 61; DLB 14; MTCW; SATA 66; SATA-Obit 70

Carter, Nick
See Smith, Martin Cruz

Carver, Raymond [1938-1988]**CLC 22, 36, 53, 55; DAM NOV; SSC 8**
See also CA 33-36R; 126; CANR 17, 34, 61; DLB 130; DLBY 84, 88; MTCW

Cary, Elizabeth, Lady Falkland [1585-1639] **LC 30**

Cary, (Arthur) Joyce (Lunel) [1888-1957] **TCLC 1, 29**
See also CA 104; 164; CDBLB 1914-1945; DLB 15, 100

Casanova de Seingalt, Giovanni Jacopo [1725-1798] ....**LC 13**

Casares, Adolfo Bioy
See Bioy Casares, Adolfo

Casely-Hayford, J(oseph) E(phraim) [1866-1930] ... **TCLC 24; BLC 1; DAM MULT**
See also BW 2; CA 123; 152

Casey, John (Dudley) [1939-] .... **CLC 59**
See also BEST 90:2; CA 69-72; CANR 23

Casey, Michael [1947-] .... **CLC 2**
See also CA 65-68; DLB 5

Casey, Patrick
See Thurman, Wallace (Henry)

Casey, Warren (Peter) [1935-1988] .. **CLC 12**
See also CA 101; 127; INT 101

Casona, Alejandro .... **CLC 49**
See also Alvarez, Alejandro Rodriguez

Cassavetes, John [1929-1989] .... **CLC 20**
See also CA 85-88; 127

Cassian, Nina [1924-] .... **PC 17**

Cassill, R(onald) V(erlin) [1919-] . **CLC 4, 23**
See also CA 9-12R; CAAS 1; CANR 7, 45; DLB 6

Cassirer, Ernst [1874-1945] .... **TCLC 61**
See also CA 157

Cassity, (Allen) Turner [1929-] ..... **CLC 6, 42**
See also CA 17-20R; CAAS 8; CANR 11; DLB 105

Castaneda, Carlos [1931(?)-] .... **CLC 12**
See also CA 25-28R; CANR 32, 66; HW; MTCW

Castedo, Elena [1937-] .... **CLC 65**
See also CA 132

Castedo-Ellerman, Elena
See Castedo, Elena

Castellanos, Rosario [1925-1974] ... **CLC 66; DAM MULT; HLC**
See also CA 131; 53-56; CANR 58; DLB 113; HW

Castelvetro, Lodovico [1505-1571] ..... **LC 12**

Castiglione, Baldassare [1478-1529] ...**LC 12**

Castle, Robert
See Hamilton, Edmond

Castro, Guillen de [1569-1631] ....**LC 19**

Castro, Rosalia de [1837-1885]**NCLC 3; DAM MULT**

Cather, Willa
See Cather, Willa Sibert

Cather, Willa Sibert [1873-1947]**TCLC 1, 11, 31; DA; DAB; DAC; DAM MST, NOV; SSC 2; WLC**
See also AAYA 24; CA 104; 128; CDALB 1865-1917; DLB 9, 54, 78; DLBD 1; MTCW; SATA 30

Catherine, Saint [1347-1380] .... **CMLC 27**

Cato, Marcus Porcius [234B.C.-149B.C.] **CMLC 21**

Catton, (Charles) Bruce [1899-1978]**CLC 35**

See also AITN 1; CA 5-8R; 81-84; CANR 7; DLB 17; SATA 2; SATA-Obit 24

Catullus [c. 84B.C.-c. 54B.C.] .... **CMLC 18**

Cauldwell, Frank
See King, Francis (Henry)

Caunitz, William J. [1933-1996] .... **CLC 34**
See also BEST 89:3; CA 125; 130; 152; INT 130

Causley, Charles (Stanley) [1917-] ..... **CLC 7**
See also CA 9-12R; CANR 5, 35; CLR 30; DLB 27; MTCW; SATA 3, 66

Caute, (John) David [1936-] ..**CLC 29; DAM NOV**
See also CA 1-4R; CAAS 4; CANR 1, 33, 64; DLB 14

Cavafy, C(onstantine) P(eter) [1863-1933] **TCLC 2, 7; DAM POET**
See also Kavafis, Konstantinos Petrou
See also CA 148

Cavallo, Evelyn
See Spark, Muriel (Sarah)

Cavanna, Betty .... **CLC 12**
See also Harrison, Elizabeth Cavanna
See also JRDA; MAICYA; SAAS 4; SATA 1, 30

Cavendish, Margaret Lucas [1623-1673] **L C 30**
See also DLB 131

Caxton, William [1421(?)-1491(?)] ...... **LC 17**
See also DLB 170

Cayer, D. M.
See Duffy, Maureen

Cayrol, Jean [1911-] .... **CLC 11**
See also CA 89-92; DLB 83

Cela, Camilo Jose [1916-]**CLC 4, 13, 59; DAM MULT; HLC**
See also BEST 90:2; CA 21-24R; CAAS 10; CANR 21, 32; DLBY 89; HW; MTCW

Celan, Paul .... **CLC 10, 19, 53, 82; PC 10**
See also Antschel, Paul
See also DLB 69

Celine, Louis-Ferdinand**CLC 1, 3, 4, 7, 9, 15, 47**
See also Destouches, Louis-Ferdinand
See also DLB 72

Cellini, Benvenuto [1500-1571] .... **LC 7**

Cendrars, Blaise [1887-1961] ... **CLC 18, 106**
See also Sauser-Hall, Frederic

Cernuda (y Bidon), Luis [1902-1963]**CLC 54; DAM POET**
See also CA 131; 89-92; DLB 134; HW

Cervantes (Saavedra), Miguel de [1547-1616] **LC 6, 23; DA; DAB; DAC; DAM MST, NOV; SSC 12; WLC**

Cesaire, Aime (Fernand) [1913-]**CLC 19, 32, 112; BLC 1; DAM MULT, POET**
See also BW 2; CA 65-68; CANR 24, 43; MTCW

Chabon, Michael [1963-] .... **CLC 55**
See also CA 139; CANR 57

Chabrol, Claude [1930-] .... **CLC 16**
See also CA 110

Challans, Mary [1905-1983]
See Renault, Mary
See also CA 81-84; 111; SATA 23; SATA-Obit 36

Challis, George
See Faust, Frederick (Schiller)

Chambers, Aidan [1934-] .... **CLC 35**
See also CA 25-28R; CANR 12, 31, 58; JRDA; MAICYA; SAAS 12; SATA 1, 69

Chambers, James [1948-]
See Cliff, Jimmy
See also CA 124

Chambers, Jessie
See Lawrence, D(avid) H(erbert Richards)

Chambers, Robert W(illiam) [1865-1933]

See Westlake, Donald E(dwin)

Clark, Eleanor [1913-1996] .... **CLC 5, 19**
See also CA 9-12R; 151; CANR 41; DLB 6

Clark, J. P.
See Clark, John Pepper
See also DLB 117

Clark, John Pepper [1935-] **CLC 38; BLC 1;**
DAM DRAM, MULT; DC 5
See also Clark, J. P.
See also BW 1; CA 65-68; CANR 16

Clark, M. R.
See Clark, Mavis Thorpe

Clark, Mavis Thorpe [1909-] .... **CLC 12**
See also CA 57-60; CANR 8, 37; CLR 30;
MAICYA; SAAS 5; SATA 8, 74

Clark, Walter Van Tilburg [1909-1971] **C L C**
28
See also CA 9-12R; 33-36R; CANR 63; DLB
9; SATA 8

Clarke, Arthur C(harles) [1917-]**CLC 1, 4, 13,**
18, 35; DAM POP; SSC 3
See also AAYA 4; CA 1-4R; CANR 2, 28, 55;
JRDA; MAICYA; MTCW; SATA 13, 70

Clarke, Austin [1896-1974] . **CLC 6, 9; DAM**
POET
See also CA 29-32; 49-52; CAP 2; DLB 10, 20

Clarke, Austin C(hesterfield) [1934-] **CLC 8,**
53; BLC 1; DAC; DAM MULT
See also BW 1; CA 25-28R; CAAS 16; CANR
14, 32, 68; DLB 53, 125

Clarke, Gillian [1937-] .... **CLC 61**
See also CA 106; DLB 40˙

Clarke, Marcus (Andrew Hislop) [1846-1881]
NCLC 19

Clarke, Shirley [1925-] .... **CLC 16**

Clash, The
See Headon, (Nicky) Topper; Jones, Mick;
Simonon, Paul; Strummer, Joe

Claudel, Paul (Louis Charles Marie) [1868-
1955] ....
TCLC 2, 10
See also CA 104; 165; DLB 192

Clavell, James (duMaresq) [1925-1994] **C L C**
6, 25, 87; DAM NOV, POP
See also CA 25-28R; 146; CANR 26, 48;
MTCW

Cleaver, (Leroy) Eldridge [1935-] .. **CLC 30;**
BLC 1; DAM MULT
See also BW 1; CA 21-24R; CANR 16

Cleese, John (Marwood) [1939-] ...... **CLC 21**
See also Monty Python
See also CA 112; 116; CANR 35; MTCW

Cleishbotham, Jebediah
See Scott, Walter

Cleland, John [1710-1789] .... **LC 2**
See also DLB 39

Clemens, Samuel Langhorne [1835-1910]
See Twain, Mark
See also CA 104; 135; CDALB 1865-1917; DA;
DAB; DAC; DAM MST, NOV; DLB 11, 12,
23, 64, 74, 186, 189; JRDA; MAICYA;
YABC 2

Cleophil
See Congreve, William

Clerihew, E.
See Bentley, E(dmund) C(lerihew)

Clerk, N. W.
See Lewis, C(live) S(taples)

Cliff, Jimmy .... **CLC 21**
See also Chambers, James

Clifton, (Thelma) Lucille [1936-]**CLC 19, 66;**
BLC 1; DAM MULT, POET; PC 17
See also BW 2; CA 49-52; CANR 2, 24, 42;
CLR 5; DLB 5, 41; MAICYA; MTCW; SATA
20, 69

Clinton, Dirk
See Silverberg, Robert

Clough, Arthur Hugh [1819-1861] **NCLC 27**
See also DLB 32

Clutha, Janet Paterson Frame [1924-]
See Frame, Janet
See also CA 1-4R; CANR 2, 36; MTCW

Clyne, Terence
See Blatty, William Peter

Cobalt, Martin
See Mayne, William (James Carter)

Cobb, Irvin S. [1876-1944] .... **TCLC 77**
See also DLB 11, 25, 86

Cobbett, William [1763-1835] .... **NCLC 49**
See also DLB 43, 107, 158

Coburn, D(onald) L(ee) [1938-] .... **CLC 10**
See also CA 89-92

Cocteau, Jean (Maurice Eugene Clement)
[1889-1963] ....
CLC 1, 8, 15, 16, 43; DA; DAB; DAC; DAM
DRAM, MST, NOV; WLC
See also CA 25-28; CANR 40; CAP 2; DLB
65; MTCW

Codrescu, Andrei [1946-] ...... **CLC 46; DAM**
POET
See also CA 33-36R; CAAS 19; CANR 13, 34,
53

Coe, Max
See Bourne, Randolph S(illiman)

Coe, Tucker
See Westlake, Donald E(dwin)

Coen, Ethan [1958-] .... **CLC 108**
See also CA 126

Coen, Joel [1955-] .... **CLC 108**
See also CA 126

The Coen Brothers
See Coen, Ethan; Coen, Joel

Coetzee, J(ohn) M(ichael) [1940-]**CLC 23, 33,**
66; DAM NOV
See also CA 77-80; CANR 41, 54; MTCW

Coffey, Brian
See Koontz, Dean R(ay)

Cohan, George M(ichael) [1878-1942]**T C L C**
60
See also CA 157

Cohen, Arthur A(llen) [1928-1986]**CLC 7, 31**
See also CA 1-4R; 120; CANR 1, 17, 42; DLB
28

Cohen, Leonard (Norman) [1934-]**CLC 3, 38;**
DAC; DAM MST
See also CA 21-24R; CANR 14, 69; DLB 53;
MTCW

Cohen, Matt [1942-] .... **CLC 19; DAC**
See also CA 61-64; CAAS 18; CANR 40; DLB
53

Cohen-Solal, Annie [19(?)-] .... **CLC 50**

Colegate, Isabel [1931-] .... **CLC 36**
See also CA 17-20R; CANR 8, 22; DLB 14;
INT CANR-22; MTCW

Coleman, Emmett
See Reed, Ishmael

Coleridge, M. E.
See Coleridge, Mary E(lizabeth)

Coleridge, Mary E(lizabeth) [1861-1907]
TCLC 73
See also CA 116; 166; DLB 19, 98

Coleridge, Samuel Taylor [1772-1834]**N C L C**
9, 54; DA; DAB; DAC; DAM MST, POET;
PC 11; WLC
See also CDBLB 1789-1832; DLB 93, 107

Coleridge, Sara [1802-1852] .... **NCLC 31**
See also DLB 199

Coles, Don [1928-] .... **CLC 46**
See also CA 115; CANR 38

Coles, Robert (Martin) [1929-] .... **CLC 108**
See also CA 45-48; CANR 3, 32, 66; INT
CANR-32; SATA 23

Colette, (Sidonie-Gabrielle) [1873-1954]
TCLC 1, 5, 16; DAM NOV; SSC 10

See also CA 104; 131; DLB 65; MTCW

Collett, (Jacobine) Camilla (Wergeland) [1813-
1895] ....
NCLC 22

Collier, Christopher [1930-] .... **CLC 30**
See also AAYA 13; CA 33-36R; CANR 13, 33;
JRDA; MAICYA; SATA 16, 70

Collier, James L(incoln) [1928-] ..... **CLC 30;**
DAM POP
See also AAYA 13; CA 9-12R; CANR 4, 33,
60; CLR 3; JRDA; MAICYA; SAAS 21;
SATA 8, 70

Collier, Jeremy [1650-1726] .... **LC 6**

Collier, John [1901-1980] .... **SSC 19**
See also CA 65-68; 97-100; CANR 10; DLB
77

Collingwood, R(obin) G(eorge) [1889(?)-1943]
TCLC 67
See also CA 117; 155

Collins, Hunt
See Hunter, Evan

Collins, Linda [1931-] .... **CLC 44**
See also CA 125

Collins, (William) Wilkie [1824-1889] **N C L C**
1, 18
See also CDBLB 1832-1890; DLB 18, 70, 159

Collins, William [1721-1759]**LC 4, 40; DAM**
POET
See also DLB 109

Collodi, Carlo [1826-1890] .... **NCLC 54**
See also Lorenzini, Carlo
See also CLR 5

Colman, George [1732-1794]
See Glassco, John

Colt, Winchester Remington
See Hubbard, L(afayette) Ron(ald)

Colter, Cyrus [1910-] .... **CLC 58**
See also BW 1; CA 65-68; CANR 10, 66; DLB
33

Colton, James
See Hansen, Joseph

Colum, Padraic [1881-1972] .... **CLC 28**
See also CA 73-76; 33-36R; CANR 35; CLR
36; MAICYA; MTCW; SATA 15

Colvin, James
See Moorcock, Michael (John)

Colwin, Laurie (E.) [1944-1992]**CLC 5, 13, 23,**
84
See also CA 89-92; 139; CANR 20, 46; DLBY
80; MTCW

Comfort, Alex(ander) [1920-] . **CLC 7; DAM**
POP
See also CA 1-4R; CANR 1, 45

Comfort, Montgomery
See Campbell, (John) Ramsey

Compton-Burnett, I(vy) [1884(?)-1969] **C L C**
1, 3, 10, 15, 34; DAM NOV
See also CA 1-4R; 25-28R; CANR 4; DLB 36;
MTCW

Comstock, Anthony [1844-1915] ... **TCLC 13**
See also CA 110

Comte, Auguste [1798-1857] .... **NCLC 54**

Conan Doyle, Arthur
See Doyle, Arthur Conan

Conde, Maryse [1937-] .. **CLC 52, 92; BLCS;**
DAM MULT
See also Boucolon, Maryse
See also BW 2

Condillac, Etienne Bonnot de [1714-1780]**L C**
26

Condon, Richard (Thomas) [1915-1996]**C L C**
4, 6, 8, 10, 45, 100; DAM NOV
See also BEST 90:3; CA 1-4R; 151; CAAS 1;
CANR 2, 23; INT CANR-23; MTCW

Confucius [551B.C.-479B.C.]**CMLC 19; DA;**
DAB; DAC; DAM MST; WLCS

Congreve, William [1670-1729]**LC 5, 21; DA;**

DAB; DAC; DAM DRAM, MST, POET; DC 2; WLC
See also CDBLB 1660-1789; DLB 39, 84

Connell, Evan S(helby), Jr. [1924-]**CLC 4, 6, 45; DAM NOV**
See also AAYA 7; CA 1-4R; CAAS 2; CANR 2, 39; DLB 2; DLBY 81; MTCW

Connelly, Marc(us Cook) [1890-1980]**CLC 7**
See also CA 85-88; 102; CANR 30; DLB 7; DLBY 80; SATA-Obit 25

Connor, Ralph .... **TCLC 31**
See also Gordon, Charles William
See also DLB 92

Conrad, Joseph [1857-1924]**TCLC 1, 6, 13, 25, 43, 57; DA; DAB; DAC; DAM MST, NOV; SSC 9; WLC**
See also CA 104; 131; CANR 60; CDBLB 1890-1914; DLB 10, 34, 98, 156; MTCW; SATA 27

Conrad, Robert Arnold
See Hart, Moss

Conroy, Donald Pat(rick) [1945-]**CLC 30, 74; DAM NOV, POP**
See also AAYA 8; AITN 1; CA 85-88; CANR 24, 53; DLB 6; MTCW

Conroy, Pat
See Conroy, Donald Pat(rick)

Constant (de Rebecque), (Henri) Benjamin [1767-1830] .... **NCLC 6**
See also DLB 119

Conybeare, Charles Augustus
See Eliot, T(homas) S(tearns)

Cook, Michael [1933-] .... **CLC 58**
See also CA 93-96; CANR 68; DLB 53

Cook, Robin [1940-] ..... **CLC 14; DAM POP**
See also BEST 90:2; CA 108; 111; CANR 41; INT 111

Cook, Roy
See Silverberg, Robert

Cooke, Elizabeth [1948-] .... **CLC 55**
See also CA 129

Cooke, John Esten [1830-1886] .... **NCLC 5**
See also DLB 3

Cooke, John Estes
See Baum, L(yman) Frank

Cooke, M. E.
See Creasey, John

Cooke, Margaret
See Creasey, John

Cook-Lynn, Elizabeth [1930-]**CLC 93; DAM MULT**
See also CA 133; DLB 175; NNAL

Cooney, Ray .... **CLC 62**

Cooper, Douglas [1960-] .... **CLC 86**

Cooper, Henry St. John
See Creasey, John

Cooper, J(oan) California .... **CLC 56; DAM MULT**
See also AAYA 12; BW 1; CA 125; CANR 55

Cooper, James Fenimore [1789-1851] **N C L C 1, 27, 54**
See also AAYA 22; CDALB 1640-1865; DLB 3; SATA 19

Coover, Robert (Lowell) [1932-]**CLC 3, 7, 15, 32, 46, 87; DAM NOV; SSC 15**
See also CA 45-48; CANR 3, 37, 58; DLB 2; DLBY 81; MTCW

Copeland, Stewart (Armstrong) [1952-]**C L C 26**

Copernicus, Nicolaus [1473-1543] .... **LC 45**

Coppard, A(lfred) E(dgar) [1878-1957]**TCLC 5; SSC 21**
See also CA 114; DLB 162; YABC 1

Coppee, Francois [1842-1908] .... **TCLC 25**

Coppola, Francis Ford [1939-] .... **CLC 16**
See also CA 77-80; CANR 40; DLB 44

Corbiere, Tristan [1845-1875] .... **NCLC 43**

Corcoran, Barbara [1911-] .... **CLC 17**
See also AAYA 14; CA 21-24R; CAAS 2; CANR 11, 28, 48; CLR 50; DLB 52; JRDA; SAAS 20; SATA 3, 77

Cordelier, Maurice
See Giraudoux, (Hippolyte) Jean

Corelli, Marie [1855-1924] .... **TCLC 51**
See also Mackay, Mary
See also DLB 34, 156

Corman, Cid [1924-] .... **CLC 9**
See also Corman, Sidney
See also CAAS 2; DLB 5, 193

Corman, Sidney [1924-]
See Corman, Cid
See also CA 85-88; CANR 44; DAM POET

Cormier, Robert (Edmund) [1925-] **CLC 12, 30; DA; DAB; DAC; DAM MST, NOV**
See also AAYA 3, 19; CA 1-4R; CANR 5, 23; CDALB 1968-1988; CLR 12; DLB 52; INT CANR-23; JRDA; MAICYA; MTCW; SATA 10, 45, 83

Corn, Alfred (DeWitt III) [1943-]..... **CLC 33**
See also CA 104; CAAS 25; CANR 44; DLB 120; DLBY 80

Corneille, Pierre [1606-1684] .. **LC 28; DAB; DAM MST**

Cornwell, David (John Moore) [1931-]**CLC 9, 15; DAM POP**
See also le Carre, John
See also CA 5-8R; CANR 13, 33, 59; MTCW

Corso, (Nunzio) Gregory [1930-] . **CLC 1, 11**
See also CA 5-8R; CANR 41; DLB 5, 16; MTCW

Cortazar, Julio [1914-1984]**CLC 2, 3, 5, 10, 13, 15, 33, 34, 92; DAM MULT, NOV; HLC; SSC 7**
See also CA 21-24R; CANR 12, 32; DLB 113; HW; MTCW

Cortes, Hernan [1484-1547] .... **LC 31**

Corwin, Cecil
See Kornbluth, C(yril) M.

Cosic, Dobrica [1921-] .... **CLC 14**
See also CA 122; 138; DLB 181

Costain, Thomas B(ertram) [1885-1965]**C L C 30**
See also CA 5-8R; 25-28R; DLB 9

Costantini, Humberto [1924(?)-1987]**CLC 49**
See also CA 131; 122; HW

Costello, Elvis [1955-] .... **CLC 21**

Cotes, Cecil V.
See Duncan, Sara Jeannette

Cotter, Joseph Seamon Sr. [1861-1949]**T C L C 28; BLC 1; DAM MULT**
See also BW 1; CA 124; DLB 50

Couch, Arthur Thomas Quiller
See Quiller-Couch, SirArthur (Thomas)

Coulton, James
See Hansen, Joseph

Couperus, Louis (Marie Anne) [1863-1923] **TCLC 15**
See also CA 115

Coupland, Douglas [1961-] ... **CLC 85; DAC; DAM POP**
See also CA 142; CANR 57

Court, Wesli
See Turco, Lewis (Putnam)

Courtenay, Bryce [1933-] .... **CLC 59**
See also CA 138

Courtney, Robert
See Ellison, Harlan (Jay)

Cousteau, Jacques-Yves [1910-1997] **CLC 30**
See also CA 65-68; 159; CANR 15, 67; MTCW; SATA 38, 98

Cowan, Peter (Walkinshaw) [1914-] . **SSC 28**
See also CA 21-24R; CANR 9, 25, 50

Coward, Noel (Peirce) [1899-1973]**CLC 1, 9, 29, 51; DAM DRAM**

See also AITN 1; CA 17-18; 41-44R; CANR 35; CAP 2; CDBLB 1914-1945; DLB 10; MTCW

Cowley, Abraham [1618-1667] .... **LC 43**
See also DLB 131, 151

Cowley, Malcolm [1898-1989] .... **CLC 39**
See also CA 5-8R; 128; CANR 3, 55; DLB 4, 48; DLBY 81, 89; MTCW

Cowper, William [1731-1800]**NCLC 8; DAM POET**
See also DLB 104, 109

Cox, William Trevor [1928-] . **CLC 9, 14, 71; DAM NOV**
See also Trevor, William
See also CA 9-12R; CANR 4, 37, 55; DLB 14; INT CANR-37; MTCW

Coyne, P. J.
See Masters, Hilary

Cozzens, James Gould [1903-1978]**CLC 1, 4, 11, 92**
See also CA 9-12R; 81-84; CANR 19; CDALB 1941-1968; DLB 9; DLBD 2; DLBY 84, 97; MTCW

Crabbe, George [1754-1832] .... **NCLC 26**
See also DLB 93

Craddock, Charles Egbert
See Murfree, Mary Noailles

Craig, A. A.
See Anderson, Poul (William)

Craik, Dinah Maria (Mulock) [1826-1887] **NCLC 38**
See also DLB 35, 163; MAICYA; SATA 34

Cram, Ralph Adams [1863-1942] .. **TCLC 45**
See also CA 160

Crane, (Harold) Hart [1899-1932]**TCLC 2, 5, 80; DA; DAB; DAC; DAM MST, POET; PC 3; WLC**
See also CA 104; 127; CDALB 1917-1929; DLB 4, 48; MTCW

Crane, R(onald) S(almon) [1886-1967] **C L C 27**
See also CA 85-88; DLB 63

Crane, Stephen (Townley) [1871-1900]**T C L C 11, 17, 32; DA; DAB; DAC; DAM MST, NOV, POET; SSC 7; WLC**
See also AAYA 21; CA 109; 140; CDALB 1865-1917; DLB 12, 54, 78; YABC 2

Crase, Douglas [1944-] .... **CLC 58**
See also CA 106

Crashaw, Richard [1612(?)-1649] .... **LC 24**
See also DLB 126

Craven, Margaret [1901-1980]**CLC 17; DAC**
See also CA 103

Crawford, F(rancis) Marion [1854-1909] **TCLC 10**
See also CA 107; DLB 71

Crawford, Isabella Valancy [1850-1887] **NCLC 12**
See also DLB 92

Crayon, Geoffrey
See Irving, Washington

Creasey, John [1908-1973] .... **CLC 11**
See also CA 5-8R; 41-44R; CANR 8, 59; DLB 77; MTCW

Crebillon, Claude Prosper Jolyot de (fils) [1707-1777] .... **LC 28**

Credo
See Creasey, John

Credo, Alvaro J. de
See Prado (Calvo), Pedro

Creeley, Robert (White) [1926-]**CLC 1, 2, 4, 8, 11, 15, 36, 78; DAM POET**
See also CA 1-4R; CAAS 10; CANR 23, 43; DLB 5, 16, 169; MTCW

Crews, Harry (Eugene) [1935-]**CLC 6, 23, 49**
See also AITN 1; CA 25-28R; CANR 20, 57; DLB 6, 143, 185; MTCW

Crichton, (John) Michael [1942-]CLC 2, 6, 54,
    90; DAM NOV, POP
    See also AAYA 10; AITN 2; CA 25-28R; CANR
    13, 40, 54; DLBY 81; INT CANR-13; JRDA;
    MTCW; SATA 9, 88
Crispin, Edmund .... CLC 22
    See also Montgomery, (Robert) Bruce
    See also DLB 87
Cristofer, Michael [1945(?)-] . CLC 28; DAM
    DRAM
    See also CA 110; 152; DLB 7
Croce, Benedetto [1866-1952] .... TCLC 37
    See also CA 120; 155
Crockett, David [1786-1836] .... NCLC 8
    See also DLB 3, 11
Crockett, Davy
    See Crockett, David
Crofts, Freeman Wills [1879-1957] TCLC 55
    See also CA 115; DLB 77
Croker, John Wilson [1780-1857] .. NCLC 10
    See also DLB 110
Crommelynck, Fernand [1885-1970] CLC 75
    See also CA 89-92
Cromwell, Oliver [1599-1658] .... LC 43
Cronin, A(rchibald) J(oseph) [1896-1981]
    CLC 32
    See also CA 1-4R; 102; CANR 5; DLB 191;
    SATA 47; SATA-Obit 25
Cross, Amanda
    See Heilbrun, Carolyn G(old)
Crothers, Rachel [1878(?)-1958] .... TCLC 19
    See also CA 113; DLB 7
Croves, Hal
    See Traven, B.
Crow Dog, Mary (Ellen) [(?)-] .... CLC 93
    See also Brave Bird, Mary
    See also CA 154
Crowfield, Christopher
    See Stowe, Harriet (Elizabeth) Beecher
Crowley, Aleister .... TCLC 7
    See also Crowley, Edward Alexander
Crowley, Edward Alexander [1875-1947]
    See Crowley, Aleister
    See also CA 104
Crowley, John [1942-] .... CLC 57
    See also CA 61-64; CANR 43; DLBY 82; SATA
    65
Crud
    See Crumb, R(obert)
Crumarums
    See Crumb, R(obert)
Crumb, R(obert) [1943-] .... CLC 17
    See also CA 106
Crumbum
    See Crumb, R(obert)
Crumski
    See Crumb, R(obert)
Crum the Bum
    See Crumb, R(obert)
Crunk
    See Crumb, R(obert)
Crustt
    See Crumb, R(obert)
Cryer, Gretchen (Kiger) [1935-] .... CLC 21
    See also CA 114; 123
Csath, Geza [1887-1919] .... TCLC 13
    See also CA 111
Cudlip, David [1933-] .... CLC 34
Cullen, Countee [1903-1946]TCLC 4, 37; BLC
    1; DA; DAC; DAM MST, MULT, POET;
    PC 20; WLCS
    See also BW 1; CA 108; 124; CDALB 1917-
    1929; DLB 4, 48, 51; MTCW; SATA 18
Cum, R.
    See Crumb, R(obert)
Cummings, Bruce F(rederick) [1889-1919]
    See Barbellion, W. N. P.

See also CA 123
Cummings, E(dward) E(stlin) [1894-1962]
    CLC 1, 3, 8, 12, 15, 68; DA; DAB; DAC;
    DAM MST, POET; PC 5; WLC 2
    See also CA 73-76; CANR 31; CDALB 1929-
    1941; DLB 4, 48; MTCW
Cunha, Euclides (Rodrigues Pimenta) da [1866-
    1909] ....
TCLC 24
    See also CA 123
Cunningham, E. V.
    See Fast, Howard (Melvin)
Cunningham, J(ames) V(incent) [1911-1985]
    CLC 3, 31
    See also CA 1-4R; 115; CANR 1; DLB 5
Cunningham, Julia (Woolfolk) [1916-] . C L C
    12
    See also CA 9-12R; CANR 4, 19, 36; JRDA;
    MAICYA; SAAS 2; SATA 1, 26
Cunningham, Michael [1952-] .... CLC 34
    See also CA 136
Cunninghame Graham, R(obert) B(ontine)
    [1852-1936] ....
TCLC 19
    See also Graham, R(obert) B(ontine)
        Cunninghame
    See also CA 119; DLB 98
Currie, Ellen [19(?)-] .... CLC 44
Curtin, Philip
    See Lowndes, Marie Adelaide (Belloc)
Curtis, Price
    See Ellison, Harlan (Jay)
Cutrate, Joe
    See Spiegelman, Art
Cynewulf [c. 770-c. 840] .... CMLC 23
Czaczkes, Shmuel Yosef
    See Agnon, S(hmuel) Y(osef Halevi)
Dabrowska, Maria (Szumska) [1889-1965]
    CLC 15
    See also CA 106
Dabydeen, David [1955-] .... CLC 34
    See also BW 1; CA 125; CANR 56
Dacey, Philip [1939-] .... CLC 51
    See also CA 37-40R; CAAS 17; CANR 14, 32,
    64; DLB 105
Dagerman, Stig (Halvard) [1923-1954]T C L C
    17
    See also CA 117; 155
Dahl, Roald [1916-1990] .... CLC 1, 6, 18, 79;
    DAB; DAC; DAM MST, NOV, POP
    See also AAYA 15; CA 1-4R; 133; CANR 6,
    32, 37, 62; CLR 1, 7, 41; DLB 139; JRDA;
    MAICYA; MTCW; SATA 1, 26, 73; SATA-
    Obit 65
Dahlberg, Edward [1900-1977] CLC 1, 7, 14
    See also CA 9-12R; 69-72; CANR 31, 62; DLB
    48; MTCW
Daitch, Susan [1954-] .... CLC 103
    See also CA 161
Dale, Colin .... TCLC 18
    See also Lawrence, T(homas) E(dward)
Dale, George E.
    See Asimov, Isaac
Daly, Elizabeth [1878-1967] .... CLC 52
    See also CA 23-24; 25-28R; CANR 60; CAP 2
Daly, Maureen [1921-] .... CLC 17
    See also AAYA 5; CANR 37; JRDA; MAICYA;
    SAAS 1; SATA 2
Damas, Leon-Gontran [1912-1978] .. CLC 84
    See also BW 1; CA 125; 73-76
Dana, Richard Henry Sr. [1787-1879] N C L C
    53
Daniel, Samuel [1562(?)-1619] .... LC 24
    See also DLB 62
Daniels, Brett
    See Adler, Renata
Dannay, Frederic [1905-1982]CLC 11; DAM

POP
    See also Queen, Ellery
    See also CA 1-4R; 107; CANR 1, 39; DLB 137;
    MTCW
D'Annunzio, Gabriele [1863-1938] TCLC 6,
    40
    See also CA 104; 155
Danois, N. le
    See Gourmont, Remy (-Marie-Charles) de
Dante [1265-1321] .. CMLC 3, 18; DA; DAB;
    DAC; DAM MST, POET; PC 21; WLCS
d'Antibes, Germain
    See Simenon, Georges (Jacques Christian)
Danticat, Edwidge [1969-] .... CLC 94
    See also CA 152
Danvers, Dennis [1947-] .... CLC 70
Danziger, Paula [1944-] .... CLC 21
    See also AAYA 4; CA 112; 115; CANR 37; CLR
    20; JRDA; MAICYA; SATA 36, 63; SATA-
    Brief 30
Dario, Ruben [1867-1916] .... TCLC 4; DAM
    MULT; HLC; PC 15
    See also CA 131; HW; MTCW
Darley, George [1795-1846] .... NCLC 2
    See also DLB 96
Darrow, Clarence (Seward) [1857-1938]
    TCLC 81
    See also CA 164
Darwin, Charles [1809-1882] .... NCLC 57
    See also DLB 57, 166
Daryush, Elizabeth [1887-1977] ...CLC 6, 19
    See also CA 49-52; CANR 3; DLB 20
Dasgupta, Surendranath [1887-1952] T C L C
    81
    See also CA 157
Dashwood, Edmee Elizabeth Monica de la Pas-
    ture [1890-1943]
    See Delafield, E. M.
    See also CA 119; 154
Daudet, (Louis Marie) Alphonse [1840-1897]
    NCLC 1
    See also DLB 123
Daumal, Rene [1908-1944] .... TCLC 14
    See also CA 114
Davenport, Guy (Mattison, Jr.) [1927-] C L C
    6, 14, 38; SSC 16
    See also CA 33-36R; CANR 23; DLB 130
Davidson, Avram [1923-]
    See Queen, Ellery
    See also CA 101; CANR 26; DLB 8
Davidson, Donald (Grady) [1893-1968] C L C
    2, 13, 19
    See also CA 5-8R; 25-28R; CANR 4; DLB 45
Davidson, Hugh
    See Hamilton, Edmond
Davidson, John [1857-1909] .... TCLC 24
    See also CA 118; DLB 19
Davidson, Sara [1943-] .... CLC 9
    See also CA 81-84; CANR 44, 68; DLB 185
Davie, Donald (Alfred) [1922-1995]CLC 5, 8,
    10, 31
    See also CA 1-4R; 149; CAAS 3; CANR 1, 44;
    DLB 27; MTCW
Davies, Ray(mond Douglas) [1944-] . CLC 21
    See also CA 116; 146
Davies, Rhys [1901-1978] .... CLC 23
    See also CA 9-12R; 81-84; CANR 4; DLB 139,
    191
Davies, (William) Robertson [1913-1995]CLC
    2, 7, 13, 25, 42, 75, 91; DA; DAB; DAC;
    DAM MST, NOV, POP; WLC
    See also BEST 89:2; CA 33-36R; 150; CANR
    17, 42; DLB 68; INT CANR-17; MTCW
Davies, W(illiam) H(enry) [1871-1940]T C L C
    5
    See also CA 104; DLB 19, 174
Davies, Walter C.

See Kornbluth, C(yril) M.

Davis, Angela (Yvonne) [1944-]**CLC 77; DAM MULT**
See also BW 2; CA 57-60; CANR 10

Davis, B. Lynch
See Bioy Casares, Adolfo; Borges, Jorge Luis

Davis, Harold Lenoir [1896-1960] ... **CLC 49**
See also CA 89-92; DLB 9

Davis, Rebecca (Blaine) Harding [1831-1910] **TCLC 6**
See also CA 104; DLB 74

Davis, Richard Harding [1864-1916]**TCLC 24**
See also CA 114; DLB 12, 23, 78, 79, 189; DLBD 13

Davison, Frank Dalby [1893-1970] .. **CLC 15**
See also CA 116

Davison, Lawrence H.
See Lawrence, D(avid) H(erbert Richards)

Davison, Peter (Hubert) [1928-] .... **CLC 28**
See also CA 9-12R; CAAS 4; CANR 3, 43; DLB 5

Davys, Mary [1674-1732] .... **LC 1**
See also DLB 39

Dawson, Fielding [1930-] .... **CLC 6**
See also CA 85-88; DLB 130

Dawson, Peter
See Faust, Frederick (Schiller)

Day, Clarence (Shepard, Jr.) [1874-1935] **TCLC 25**
See also CA 108; DLB 11

Day, Thomas [1748-1789] .... **LC 1**
See also DLB 39; YABC 1

Day Lewis, C(ecil) [1904-1972]**CLC 1, 6, 10; DAM POET; PC 11**
See also Blake, Nicholas
See also CA 13-16; 33-36R; CANR 34; CAP 1; DLB 15, 20; MTCW

Dazai Osamu [1909-1948] .... **TCLC 11**
See also Tsushima, Shuji
See also CA 164; DLB 182

de Andrade, Carlos Drummond
See Drummond de Andrade, Carlos

Deane, Norman
See Creasey, John

de Beauvoir, Simone (Lucie Ernestine Marie Bertrand)
See Beauvoir, Simone (Lucie Ernestine Marie Bertrand) de

de Beer, P.
See Bosman, Herman Charles

de Brissac, Malcolm
See Dickinson, Peter (Malcolm)

de Chardin, Pierre Teilhard
See Teilhard de Chardin, (Marie Joseph) Pierre

Dee, John [1527-1608] .... **LC 20**

Deer, Sandra [1940-] .... **CLC 45**

De Ferrari, Gabriella [1941-] .... **CLC 65**
See also CA 146

Defoe, Daniel [1660(?)-1731]**LC 1; DA; DAB; DAC; DAM MST, NOV; WLC**
See also CDBLB 1660-1789; DLB 39, 95, 101; JRDA; MAICYA; SATA 22

de Gourmont, Remy(-Marie-Charles)
See Gourmont, Remy (-Marie-Charles) de

de Hartog, Jan [1914-] .... **CLC 19**
See also CA 1-4R; CANR 1

de Hostos, E. M.
See Hostos (y Bonilla), Eugenio Maria de

de Hostos, Eugenio M.
See Hostos (y Bonilla), Eugenio Maria de

Deighton, Len .... **CLC 4, 7, 22, 46**
See also Deighton, Leonard Cyril
See also AAYA 6; BEST 89:2; CDBLB 1960 to Present; DLB 87

Deighton, Leonard Cyril [1929-]
See Deighton, Len
See also CA 9-12R; CANR 19, 33, 68; DAM

NOV, POP; MTCW

Dekker, Thomas [1572(?)-1632]**LC 22; DAM DRAM**
See also CDBLB Before 1660; DLB 62, 172

Delafield, E. M. [1890-1943] .... **TCLC 61**
See also Dashwood, Edmee Elizabeth Monica de la Pasture
See also DLB 34

de la Mare, Walter (John) [1873-1956]**TCLC 4, 53; DAB; DAC; DAM MST, POET; SSC 14; WLC**
See also CA 163; CDBLB 1914-1945; CLR 23; DLB 162; SATA 16

Delaney, Franey
See O'Hara, John (Henry)

Delaney, Shelagh [1939-] .... **CLC 29; DAM DRAM**
See also CA 17-20R; CANR 30, 67; CDBLB 1960 to Present; DLB 13; MTCW

Delany, Mary (Granville Pendarves) [1700-1788] .... **LC 12**

Delany, Samuel R(ay, Jr.) [1942-]**CLC 8, 14, 38; BLC 1; DAM MULT**
See also AAYA 24; BW 2; CA 81-84; CANR 27, 43; DLB 8, 33; MTCW

De La Ramee, (Marie) Louise [1839-1908]
See Ouida
See also SATA 20

de la Roche, Mazo [1879-1961] .... **CLC 14**
See also CA 85-88; CANR 30; DLB 68; SATA 64

De La Salle, Innocent
See Hartmann, Sadakichi

Delbanco, Nicholas (Franklin) [1942-]**CLC 6, 13**
See also CA 17-20R; CAAS 2; CANR 29, 55; DLB 6

del Castillo, Michel [1933-] .... **CLC 38**
See also CA 109

Deledda, Grazia (Cosima) [1875(?)-1936] **TCLC 23**
See also CA 123

Delibes, Miguel ....**CLC 8, 18**
See also Delibes Setien, Miguel

Delibes Setien, Miguel [1920-]
See Delibes, Miguel
See also CA 45-48; CANR 1, 32; HW; MTCW

DeLillo, Don [1936-]**CLC 8, 10, 13, 27, 39, 54, 76; DAM NOV, POP**
See also BEST 89:1; CA 81-84; CANR 21; DLB 6, 173; MTCW

de Lisser, H. G.
See De Lisser, H(erbert) G(eorge)
See also DLB 117

De Lisser, H(erbert) G(eorge) [1878-1944] **TCLC 12**
See also de Lisser, H. G.
See also BW 2; CA 109; 152

Deloney, Thomas [(?)-1600] .... **LC 41**
See also DLB 167

Deloria, Vine (Victor), Jr. [1933-] .. **CLC 21; DAM MULT**
See also CA 53-56; CANR 5, 20, 48; DLB 175; MTCW; NNAL; SATA 21

Del Vecchio, John M(ichael) [1947-] **CLC 29**
See also CA 110; DLBD 9

de Man, Paul (Adolph Michel) [1919-1983] **CLC 55**
See also CA 128; 111; CANR 61; DLB 67; MTCW

De Marinis, Rick [1934-] .... **CLC 54**
See also CA 57-60; CAAS 24; CANR 9, 25, 50

Dembry, R. Emmet
See Murfree, Mary Noailles

Demby, William [1922-]**CLC 53; BLC 1; DAM MULT**
See also BW 1; CA 81-84; DLB 33

de Menton, Francisco
See Chin, Frank (Chew, Jr.)

Demijohn, Thom
See Disch, Thomas M(ichael)

de Montherlant, Henry (Milon)
See Montherlant, Henry (Milon) de

Demosthenes [384B.C.-322B.C.] ... **CMLC 13**
See also DLB 176

de Natale, Francine
See Malzberg, Barry N(athaniel)

Denby, Edwin (Orr) [1903-1983] ...... **CLC 48**
See also CA 138; 110

Denis, Julio
See Cortazar, Julio

Denmark, Harrison
See Zelazny, Roger (Joseph)

Dennis, John [1658-1734] .... **LC 11**
See also DLB 101

Dennis, Nigel (Forbes) [1912-1989] .... **CLC 8**
See also CA 25-28R; 129; DLB 13, 15; MTCW

Dent, Lester [1904(?)-1959] .... **TCLC 72**
See also CA 112; 161

De Palma, Brian (Russell) [1940-] .... **CLC 20**
See also CA 109

De Quincey, Thomas [1785-1859] .... **NCLC 4**
See also CDBLB 1789-1832; DLB 110; 144

Deren, Eleanora [1908(?)-1961]
See Deren, Maya
See also CA 111

Deren, Maya [1917-1961] .... **CLC 16, 102**
See also Deren, Eleanora

Derleth, August (William) [1909-1971] **C L C 31**
See also CA 1-4R; 29-32R; CANR 4; DLB 9; SATA 5

Der Nister [1884-1950] .... **TCLC 56**

de Routisie, Albert
See Aragon, Louis

Derrida, Jacques [1930-] .... **CLC 24, 87**
See also CA 124; 127

Derry Down Derry
See Lear, Edward

Dersonnes, Jacques
See Simenon, Georges (Jacques Christian)

Desai, Anita [1937-] ... **CLC 19, 37, 97; DAB; DAM NOV**
See also CA 81-84; CANR 33, 53; MTCW; SATA 63

de Saint-Luc, Jean
See Glassco, John

de Saint Roman, Arnaud
See Aragon, Louis

Descartes, Rene [1596-1650] .... **LC 20, 35**

De Sica, Vittorio [1901(?)-1974] .... **CLC 20**
See also CA 117

Desnos, Robert [1900-1945] .... **TCLC 22**
See also CA 121; 151

Destouches, Louis-Ferdinand [1894-1961] **CLC 9, 15**
See also Celine, Louis-Ferdinand
See also CA 85-88; CANR 28; MTCW

de Tolignac, Gaston
See Griffith, D(avid Lewelyn) W(ark)

Deutsch, Babette [1895-1982] .... **CLC 18**
See also CA 1-4R; 108; CANR 4; DLB 45; SATA 1; SATA-Obit 33

Devenant, William [1606-1649] .... **LC 13**

Devkota, Laxmiprasad [1909-1959]**TCLC 23**
See also CA 123

De Voto, Bernard (Augustine) [1897-1955] **TCLC 29**
See also CA 113; 160; DLB 9

De Vries, Peter [1910-1993]**CLC 1, 2, 3, 7, 10, 28, 46; DAM NOV**
See also CA 17-20R; 142; CANR 41; DLB 6; DLBY 82; MTCW

Dexter, John

See Bradley, Marion Zimmer

Dexter, Martin
See Faust, Frederick (Schiller)

Dexter, Pete [1943-] **CLC 34, 55; DAM POP**
See also BEST 89:2; CA 127; 131; INT 131; MTCW

Diamano, Silmang
See Senghor, Leopold Sedar

Diamond, Neil [1941-] .... **CLC 30**
See also CA 108

Diaz del Castillo, Bernal [1496-1584] . **LC 31**

di Bassetto, Corno
See Shaw, George Bernard

Dick, Philip K(indred) [1928-1982] . **CLC 10, 30, 72; DAM NOV, POP**
See also AAYA 24; CA 49-52; 106; CANR 2, 16; DLB 8; MTCW

Dickens, Charles (John Huffam) [1812-1870]
NCLC 3, 8, 18, 26, 37, 50; DA; DAB; DAC; DAM MST, NOV; SSC 17; WLC
See also AAYA 23; CDBLB 1832-1890; DLB 21, 55, 70, 159, 166; JRDA; MAICYA; SATA 15

Dickey, James (Lafayette) [1923-1997]**CLC 1, 2, 4, 7, 10, 15, 47, 109; DAM NOV, POET, POP**
See also AITN 1, 2; CA 9-12R; 156; CABS 2; CANR 10, 48, 61; CDALB 1968-1988; DLB 5, 193; DLBD 7; DLBY 82, 93, 96, 97; INT CANR-10; MTCW

Dickey, William [1928-1994] .... **CLC 3, 28**
See also CA 9-12R; 145; CANR 24; DLB 5

Dickinson, Charles [1951-] .... **CLC 49**
See also CA 128

Dickinson, Emily (Elizabeth) [1830-1886]
NCLC 21; DA; DAB; DAC; DAM MST, POET; PC 1; WLC
See also AAYA 22; CDALB 1865-1917; DLB 1; SATA 29

Dickinson, Peter (Malcolm) [1927-] **CLC 12, 35**
See also AAYA 9; CA 41-44R; CANR 31, 58; CLR 29; DLB 87, 161; JRDA; MAICYA; SATA 5, 62, 95

Dickson, Carr
See Carr, John Dickson

Dickson, Carter
See Carr, John Dickson

Diderot, Denis [1713-1784] .... **LC 26**

Didion, Joan [1934-]**CLC 1, 3, 8, 14, 32; DAM NOV**
See also AITN 1; CA 5-8R; CANR 14, 52; CDALB 1968-1988; DLB 2, 173, 185; DLBY 81, 86; MTCW

Dietrich, Robert
See Hunt, E(verette) Howard, (Jr.)

Dillard, Annie [1945-]**CLC 9, 60; DAM NOV**
See also AAYA 6; CA 49-52; CANR 3, 43, 62; DLBY 80; MTCW; SATA 10

Dillard, R(ichard) H(enry) W(ilde) [1937-]
CLC 5
See also CA 21-24R; CAAS 7; CANR 10; DLB 5

Dillon, Eilis [1920-1994] .... **CLC 17**
See also CA 9-12R; 147; CAAS 3; CANR 4, 38; CLR 26; MAICYA; SATA 2, 74; SATA-Obit 83

Dimont, Penelope
See Mortimer, Penelope (Ruth)

Dinesen, Isak .... **CLC 10, 29, 95; SSC 7**
See also Blixen, Karen (Christentze Dinesen)

Ding Ling .... **CLC 68**
See also Chiang, Pin-chin

Disch, Thomas M(ichael) [1940-] . **CLC 7, 36**
See also AAYA 17; CA 21-24R; CAAS 4; CANR 17, 36, 54; CLR 18; DLB 8; MAICYA; MTCW; SAAS 15; SATA 92

Disch, Tom
See Disch, Thomas M(ichael)

d'Isly, Georges
See Simenon, Georges (Jacques Christian)

Disraeli, Benjamin [1804-1881] . **NCLC 2, 39**
See also DLB 21, 55

Ditcum, Steve
See Crumb, R(obert)

Dixon, Paige
See Corcoran, Barbara

Dixon, Stephen [1936-] .... **CLC 52; SSC 16**
See also CA 89-92; CANR 17, 40, 54; DLB 130

Doak, Annie
See Dillard, Annie

Dobell, Sydney Thompson [1824-1874]**NCLC 43**
See also DLB 32

Doblin, Alfred .... **TCLC 13**
See also Doeblin, Alfred

Dobrolyubov, Nikolai Alexandrovich [1836-1861] .... **NCLC 5**

Dobson, Austin [1840-1921] .... **TCLC 79**
See also DLB 35; 144

Dobyns, Stephen [1941-] .... **CLC 37**
See also CA 45-48; CANR 2, 18

Doctorow, E(dgar) L(aurence) [1931-]**CLC 6, 11, 15, 18, 37, 44, 65, 113; DAM NOV, POP**
See also AAYA 22; AITN 2; BEST 89:3; CA 45-48; CANR 2, 33, 51; CDALB 1968-1988; DLB 2, 28, 173; DLBY 80; MTCW

Dodgson, Charles Lutwidge [1832-1898]
See Carroll, Lewis
See also CLR 2; DA; DAB; DAC; DAM MST, NOV, POET; MAICYA; YABC 2

Dodson, Owen (Vincent) [1914-1983]**CLC 79; BLC 1; DAM MULT**
See also BW 1; CA 65-68; 110; CANR 24; DLB 76

Doeblin, Alfred [1878-1957] .... **TCLC 13**
See Doblin, Alfred
See also CA 110; 141; DLB 66

Doerr, Harriet [1910-] .... **CLC 34**
See also CA 117; 122; CANR 47; INT 122

Domecq, H(onorio) Bustos
See Bioy Casares, Adolfo; Borges, Jorge Luis

Domini, Rey
See Lorde, Audre (Geraldine)

Dominique
See Proust, (Valentin-Louis-George-Eugene-)Marcel

Don, A
See Stephen, SirLeslie

Donaldson, Stephen R. [1947-]**CLC 46; DAM POP**
See also CA 89-92; CANR 13, 55; INT CANR-13

Donleavy, J(ames) P(atrick) [1926-]**CLC 1, 4, 6, 10, 45**
See also AITN 2; CA 9-12R; CANR 24, 49, 62; DLB 6, 173; INT CANR-24; MTCW

Donne, John [1572-1631]**LC 10, 24; DA; DAB; DAC; DAM MST, POET; PC 1**
See also CDBLB Before 1660; DLB 121, 151

Donnell, David [1939(?)-] .... **CLC 34**

Donoghue, P. S.
See Hunt, E(verette) Howard, (Jr.)

Donoso (Yanez), Jose [1924-1996] . **CLC 4, 8, 11, 32, 99; DAM MULT; HLC**
See also CA 81-84; 155; CANR 32; DLB 113; HW; MTCW

Donovan, John [1928-1992] .... **CLC 35**
See also AAYA 20; CA 97-100; 137; CLR 3; MAICYA; SATA 72; SATA-Brief 29

Don Roberto
See Cunninghame Graham, R(obert) B(ontine)

Doolittle, Hilda [1886-1961]**CLC 3, 8, 14, 31, 34, 73; DA; DAC; DAM MST, POET; PC 5; WLC**
See also H. D.
See also CA 97-100; CANR 35; DLB 4, 45; MTCW

Dorfman, Ariel [1942-] ... **CLC 48, 77; DAM MULT; HLC**
See also CA 124; 130; CANR 67; HW; INT 130

Dorn, Edward (Merton) [1929-] **CLC 10, 18**
See also CA 93-96; CANR 42; DLB 5; INT 93-96

Dorris, Michael (Anthony) [1945-1997] **CLC 109; DAM MULT, NOV**
See also AAYA 20; BEST 90:1; CA 102; 157; CANR 19, 46; DLB 175; NNAL; SATA 75; SATA-Obit 94

Dorris, Michael A.
See Dorris, Michael (Anthony)

Dorsan, Luc
See Simenon, Georges (Jacques Christian)

Dorsange, Jean
See Simenon, Georges (Jacques Christian)

Dos Passos, John (Roderigo) [1896-1970]
CLC 1, 4, 8, 11, 15, 25, 34, 82; DA; DAB; DAC; DAM MST, NOV; WLC
See also CA 1-4R; 29-32R; CANR 3; CDALB 1929-1941; DLB 4, 9; DLBD 1, 15; DLBY 96; MTCW

Dossage, Jean
See Simenon, Georges (Jacques Christian)

Dostoevsky, Fedor Mikhailovich [1821-1881]
NCLC 2, 7, 21, 33, 43; DA; DAB; DAC; DAM MST, NOV; SSC 2; WLC

Doughty, Charles M(ontagu) [1843-1926]
TCLC 27
See also CA 115; DLB 19, 57, 174

Douglas, Ellen .... **CLC 73**
See also Haxton, Josephine Ayres; Williamson, Ellen Douglas

Douglas, Gavin [1475(?)-1522] .... **LC 20**
See also DLB 132

Douglas, George
See Brown, George Douglas

Douglas, Keith (Castellain) [1920-1944]
TCLC 40
See also CA 160; DLB 27

Douglas, Leonard
See Bradbury, Ray (Douglas)

Douglas, Michael
See Crichton, (John) Michael

Douglas, (George) Norman [1868-1952]
TCLC 68
See also CA 119; 157; DLB 34, 195

Douglas, William
See Brown, George Douglas

Douglass, Frederick [1817(?)-1895] **NCLC 7, 55; BLC 1; DA; DAC; DAM MST, MULT; WLC**
See also CDALB 1640-1865; DLB 1, 43, 50, 79; SATA 29

Dourado, (Waldomiro Freitas) Autran [1926-]
CLC 23, 60
See also CA 25-28R; CANR 34

Dourado, Waldomiro Autran
See Dourado, (Waldomiro Freitas) Autran

Dove, Rita (Frances) [1952-] ..... **CLC 50, 81; BLCS; DAM MULT, POET; PC 6**
See also BW 2; CA 109; CAAS 19; CANR 27, 42, 68; DLB 120

Doveglion
See Villa, Jose Garcia

Dowell, Coleman [1925-1985] .... **CLC 60**
See also CA 25-28R; 117; CANR 10; DLB 130

Dowson, Ernest (Christopher) [1867-1900]
TCLC 4
See also CA 105; 150; DLB 19, 135

Doyle, A. Conan
See Doyle, Arthur Conan

Echo
See Proust, (Valentin-Louis-George-Eugene-)
Marcel
Eckert, Allan W. [1931-] .... **CLC 17**
See also AAYA 18; CA 13-16R; CANR 14, 45;
INT CANR-14; SAAS 21; SATA 29, 91;
SATA-Brief 27
Eckhart, Meister [1260(?)-1328(?)] **CMLC 9**
See also DLB 115
Eckmar, F. R.
See de Hartog, Jan
Eco, Umberto [1932-]**CLC 28, 60; DAM NOV,
POP**
See also BEST 90:1; CA 77-80; CANR 12, 33,
55; DLB 196; MTCW
Eddison, E(ric) R(ucker) [1882-1945] **T C L C
15**
See also CA 109; 156
Eddy, Mary (Morse) Baker [1821-1910]
TCLC 71
See also CA 113
Edel, (Joseph) Leon [1907-1997] **CLC 29, 34**
See also CA 1-4R; 161; CANR 1, 22; DLB 103;
INT CANR-22
Eden, Emily [1797-1869] .... **NCLC 10**
Edgar, David [1948-] **CLC 42; DAM DRAM**
See also CA 57-60; CANR 12, 61; DLB 13;
MTCW
Edgerton, Clyde (Carlyle) [1944-] ... **CLC 39**
See also AAYA 17; CA 118; 134; CANR 64;
INT 134
Edgeworth, Maria [1768-1849] .**NCLC 1, 51**
See also DLB 116, 159, 163; SATA 21
Edmonds, Paul
See Kuttner, Henry
Edmonds, Walter D(umaux) [1903-] **CLC 35**
See also CA 5-8R; CANR 2; DLB 9; MAICYA;
SAAS 4; SATA 1, 27
Edmondson, Wallace
See Ellison, Harlan (Jay)
Edson, Russell .... **CLC 13**
See also CA 33-36R
Edwards, Bronwen Elizabeth
See Rose, Wendy
Edwards, G(erald) B(asil) [1899-1976] **C L C
25**
See also CA 110
Edwards, Gus [1939-] .... **CLC 43**
See also CA 108; INT 108
Edwards, Jonathan [1703-1758] .. **LC 7; DA;
DAC; DAM MST**
See also DLB 24
Efron, Marina Ivanovna Tsvetaeva
See Tsvetaeva (Efron), Marina (Ivanovna)
Ehle, John (Marsden, Jr.) [1925-] .... **CLC 27**
See also CA 9-12R
Ehrenbourg, Ilya (Grigoryevich)
See Ehrenburg, Ilya (Grigoryevich)
Ehrenburg, Ilya (Grigoryevich) [1891-1967]
CLC 18, 34, 62
See also CA 102; 25-28R
Ehrenburg, Ilyo (Grigoryevich)
See Ehrenburg, Ilya (Grigoryevich)
Ehrenreich, Barbara [1941-] .... **CLC 110**
See also BEST 90:4; CA 73-76; CANR 16, 37,
62; MTCW
Eich, Guenter [1907-1972] .... **CLC 15**
See also CA 111; 93-96; DLB 69, 124
Eichendorff, Joseph Freiherr von [1788-1857]
NCLC 8
See also DLB 90
Eigner, Larry .... **CLC 9**
See also Eigner, Laurence (Joel)
See also CAAS 23; DLB 5
Eigner, Laurence (Joel) [1927-1996]
See Eigner, Larry
See also CA 9-12R; 151; CANR 6; DLB 193

Einstein, Albert [1879-1955] .... **TCLC 65**
See also CA 121; 133; MTCW
Eiseley, Loren Corey [1907-1977] ...... **CLC 7**
See also AAYA 5; CA 1-4R; 73-76; CANR 6
Eisenstadt, Jill [1963-] .... **CLC 50**
See also CA 140
Eisenstein, Sergei (Mikhailovich) [1898-1948]
TCLC 57
See also CA 114; 149
Eisner, Simon
See Kornbluth, C(yril) M.
Ekeloef, (Bengt) Gunnar [1907-1968]**CLC 27;
DAM POET; PC 23**
See also CA 123; 25-28R
Ekelof, (Bengt) Gunnar
See Ekeloef, (Bengt) Gunnar
Ekelund, Vilhelm [1880-1949] .... **TCLC 75**
Ekwensi, C. O. D.
See Ekwensi, Cyprian (Odiatu Duaka)
Ekwensi, Cyprian (Odiatu Duaka) [1921-]
CLC 4; BLC 1; DAM MULT
See also BW 2; CA 29-32R; CANR 18, 42; DLB
117; MTCW; SATA 66
Elaine .... **TCLC 18**
See also Leverson, Ada
El Crummo
See Crumb, R(obert)
Elder, Lonne III [1931-1996] .... **DC 8**
See also BLC 1; BW 1; CA 81-84; 152; CANR
25; DAM MULT; DLB 7, 38, 44
Elia
See Lamb, Charles
Eliade, Mircea [1907-1986] .... **CLC 19**
See also CA 65-68; 119; CANR 30, 62; MTCW
Eliot, A. D.
See Jewett, (Theodora) Sarah Orne
Eliot, Alice
See Jewett, (Theodora) Sarah Orne
Eliot, Dan
See Silverberg, Robert
Eliot, George [1819-1880]**NCLC 4, 13, 23, 41,
49; DA; DAB; DAC; DAM MST, NOV; PC
20; WLC**
See also CDBLB 1832-1890; DLB 21, 35, 55
Eliot, John [1604-1690] .... **LC 5**
See also DLB 24
Eliot, T(homas) S(tearns) [1888-1965]**CLC 1,
2, 3, 6, 9, 10, 13, 15, 24, 34, 41, 55, 57, 113;
DA; DAB; DAC; DAM DRAM, MST,
POET; PC 5; WLC**
See also CA 5-8R; 25-28R; CANR 41; CDALB
1929-1941; DLB 7, 10, 45, 63; DLBY 88;
MTCW
Elizabeth [1866-1941] .... **TCLC 41**
Elkin, Stanley L(awrence) [1930-1995]**CLC 4,
6, 9, 14, 27, 51, 91; DAM NOV, POP; SSC
12**
See also CA 9-12R; 148; CANR 8, 46; DLB 2,
28; DLBY 80; INT CANR-8; MTCW
Elledge, Scott .... **CLC 34**
Elliot, Don
See Silverberg, Robert
Elliott, Don
See Silverberg, Robert
Elliott, George P(aul) [1918-1980] ..... **CLC 2**
See also CA 1-4R; 97-100; CANR 2
Elliott, Janice [1931-] .... **CLC 47**
See also CA 13-16R; CANR 8, 29; DLB 14
Elliott, Sumner Locke [1917-1991] .. **CLC 38**
See also CA 5-8R; 134; CANR 2, 21
Elliott, William
See Bradbury, Ray (Douglas)
Ellis, A. E. .... **CLC 7**
Ellis, Alice Thomas .... **CLC 40**
See also Haycraft, Anna
See also DLB 194
Ellis, Bret Easton [1964-] **CLC 39, 71; DAM
POP**
See also AAYA 2; CA 118; 123; CANR 51; INT
123
Ellis, (Henry) Havelock [1859-1939]**TCLC 14**
See also CA 109; DLB 190
Ellis, Landon
See Ellison, Harlan (Jay)
Ellis, Trey [1962-] .... **CLC 55**
See also CA 146
Ellison, Harlan (Jay) [1934-] **CLC 1, 13, 42;
DAM POP; SSC 14**
See also CA 5-8R; CANR 5, 46; DLB 8; INT
CANR-5; MTCW
Ellison, Ralph (Waldo) [1914-1994]**CLC 1, 3,
11, 54, 86; BLC 1; DA; DAB; DAC; DAM
MST, MULT, NOV; SSC 26; WLC**
See also AAYA 19; BW 1; CA 9-12R; 145;
CANR 24, 53; CDALB 1941-1968; DLB 2,
76; DLBY 94; MTCW
Ellmann, Lucy (Elizabeth) [1956-] ... **CLC 61**
See also CA 128
Ellmann, Richard (David) [1918-1987] **C L C
50**
See also BEST 89:2; CA 1-4R; 122; CANR 2,
28, 61; DLB 103; DLBY 87; MTCW
Elman, Richard (Martin) [1934-1997]**CLC 19**
See also CA 17-20R; 163; CAAS 3; CANR 47
Elron
See Hubbard, L(afayette) Ron(ald)
Eluard, Paul .... **TCLC 7, 41**
See also Grindel, Eugene
Elyot, Sir Thomas [1490(?)-1546] .... **LC 11**
Elytis, Odysseus [1911-1996]**CLC 15, 49, 100;
DAM POET; PC 21**
See also CA 102; 151; MTCW
Emecheta, (Florence Onye) Buchi [1944-]
CLC 14, 48; BLC 2; DAM MULT
See also BW 2; CA 81-84; CANR 27; DLB 117;
MTCW; SATA 66
Emerson, Mary Moody [1774-1863]**NCLC 66**
Emerson, Ralph Waldo [1803-1882]**NCLC 1,
38; DA; DAB; DAC; DAM MST, POET;
PC 18; WLC**
See also CDALB 1640-1865; DLB 1, 59, 73
Eminescu, Mihail [1850-1889] .... **NCLC 33**
Empson, William [1906-1984]**CLC 3, 8, 19, 33,
34**
See also CA 17-20R; 112; CANR 31, 61; DLB
20; MTCW
Enchi, Fumiko (Ueda) [1905-1986] .. **CLC 31**
See also CA 129; 121
Ende, Michael (Andreas Helmuth) [1929-1995]
CLC 31
See also CA 118; 124; 149; CANR 36; CLR
14; DLB 75; MAICYA; SATA 61; SATA-
Brief 42; SATA-Obit 86
Endo, Shusaku [1923-1996]**CLC 7, 14, 19, 54,
99; DAM NOV**
See also CA 29-32R; 153; CANR 21, 54; DLB
182; MTCW
Engel, Marian [1933-1985] .... **CLC 36**
See also CA 25-28R; CANR 12; DLB 53; INT
CANR-12
Engelhardt, Frederick
See Hubbard, L(afayette) Ron(ald)
Enright, D(ennis) J(oseph) [1920-] **CLC 4, 8,
31**
See also CA 1-4R; CANR 1, 42; DLB 27; SATA
25
Enzensberger, Hans Magnus [1929-] **CLC 43**
See also CA 116; 119
Ephron, Nora [1941-] .... **CLC 17, 31**
See also AITN 2; CA 65-68; CANR 12, 39
Epicurus [341B.C.-270B.C.] .... **CMLC 21**
See also DLB 176
Epsilon
See Betjeman, John

Ferguson, Samuel [1810-1886] ...... NCLC 33
See also DLB 32
Fergusson, Robert [1750-1774] .... LC 29
See also DLB 109
Ferling, Lawrence
See Ferlinghetti, Lawrence (Monsanto)
Ferlinghetti, Lawrence (Monsanto) [1919(?)-]
CLC 2, 6, 10, 27, 111; DAM POET; PC 1
See also CA 5-8R; CANR 3, 41; CDALB 1941-
1968; DLB 5, 16; MTCW
Fernandez, Vicente Garcia Huidobro
See Huidobro Fernandez, Vicente Garcia
Ferrer, Gabriel (Francisco Victor) Miro
See Miro (Ferrer), Gabriel (Francisco Victor)
Ferrier, Susan (Edmonstone) [1782-1854]
NCLC 8
See also DLB 116
Ferrigno, Robert [1948(?)-] .... CLC 65
See also CA 140
Ferron, Jacques [1921-1985] .. CLC 94; DAC
See also CA 117; 129; DLB 60
Feuchtwanger, Lion [1884-1958] ..... TCLC 3
See also CA 104; DLB 66
Feuillet, Octave [1821-1890] .... NCLC 45
See also DLB 192
Feydeau, Georges (Leon Jules Marie) [1862-
1921] ....
TCLC 22; DAM DRAM
See also CA 113; 152; DLB 192
Fichte, Johann Gottlieb [1762-1814]NCLC 62
See also DLB 90
Ficino, Marsilio [1433-1499] .... LC 12
Fiedeler, Hans
See Doeblin, Alfred
Fiedler, Leslie A(aron) [1917-]CLC 4, 13, 24
See also CA 9-12R; CANR 7, 63; DLB 28, 67;
MTCW
Field, Andrew [1938-] .... CLC 44
See also CA 97-100; CANR 25
Field, Eugene [1850-1895] .... NCLC 3
See also DLB 23, 42, 140; DLBD 13; MAICYA;
SATA 16
Field, Gans T.
See Wellman, Manly Wade
Field, Michael [1915-1971] .... TCLC 43
See also CA 29-32R
Field, Peter
See Hobson, Laura Z(ametkin)
Fielding, Henry [1707-1754]LC 1; DA; DAB;
DAC; DAM DRAM, MST; WLC
See also CDBLB 1660-1789; DLB 39, 84, 101
Fielding, Sarah [1710-1768] .... LC 1, 44
See also DLB 39
Fields, W. C. [1880-1946] .... TCLC 80
See also DLB 44
Fierstein, Harvey (Forbes) [1954-]. CLC 33;
DAM DRAM, POP
See also CA 123; 129
Figes, Eva [1932-] .... CLC 31
See also CA 53-56; CANR 4, 44; DLB 14
Finch, Anne [1661-1720] .... LC 3; PC 21
See also DLB 95
Finch, Robert (Duer Claydon) [1900-]CLC 18
See also CA 57-60; CANR 9, 24, 49; DLB 88
Findley, Timothy [1930-]CLC 27, 102; DAC;
DAM MST
See also CA 25-28R; CANR 12, 42, 69; DLB
53
Fink, William
See Mencken, H(enry) L(ouis)
Firbank, Louis [1942-]
See Reed, Lou
See also CA 117
Firbank, (Arthur Annesley) Ronald [1886-
1926] .... TCLC 1
See also CA 104; DLB 36
Fisher, M(ary) F(rances) K(ennedy) [1908-

1992] .... CLC 76, 87
See also CA 77-80; 138; CANR 44
Fisher, Roy [1930-] .... CLC 25
See also CA 81-84; CAAS 10; CANR 16; DLB
40
Fisher, Rudolph [1897-1934]TCLC 11; BLC 2;
DAM MULT; SSC 25
See also BW 1; CA 107; 124; DLB 51, 102
Fisher, Vardis (Alvero) [1895-1968] ... CLC 7
See also CA 5-8R; 25-28R; CANR 68; DLB 9
Fiske, Tarleton
See Bloch, Robert (Albert)
Fitch, Clarke
See Sinclair, Upton (Beall)
Fitch, John IV
See Cormier, Robert (Edmund)
Fitzgerald, Captain Hugh
See Baum, L(yman) Frank
FitzGerald, Edward [1809-1883] .... NCLC 9
See also DLB 32
Fitzgerald, F(rancis) Scott (Key) [1896-1940]
TCLC 1, 6, 14, 28, 55; DA; DAB; DAC;
DAM MST, NOV; SSC 6, 31; WLC
See also AAYA 24; AITN 1; CA 110; 123;
CDALB 1917-1929; DLB 4, 9, 86; DLBD 1,
15, 16; DLBY 81, 96; MTCW
Fitzgerald, Penelope [1916-] CLC 19, 51, 61
See also CA 85-88; CAAS 10; CANR 56; DLB
14, 194
Fitzgerald, Robert (Stuart) [1910-1985]C L C
39
See also CA 1-4R; 114; CANR 1; DLBY 80
FitzGerald, Robert D(avid) [1902-1987]C L C
19
See also CA 17-20R
Fitzgerald, Zelda (Sayre) [1900-1948] T C L C
52
See also CA 117; 126; DLBY 84
Flanagan, Thomas (James Bonner) [1923-]
CLC 25, 52
See also CA 108; CANR 55; DLBY 80; INT
108; MTCW
Flaubert, Gustave [1821-1880] .NCLC 2, 10,
19, 62, 66; DA; DAB; DAC; DAM MST,
NOV; SSC 11; WLC
See also DLB 119
Flecker, Herman Elroy
See Flecker, (Herman) James Elroy
Flecker, (Herman) James Elroy [1884-1915]
TCLC 43
See also CA 109; 150; DLB 10, 19
Fleming, Ian (Lancaster) [1908-1964]CLC 3,
30; DAM POP
See also CA 5-8R; CANR 59; CDBLB 1945-
1960; DLB 87; MTCW; SATA 9
Fleming, Thomas (James) [1927-] ...... CLC 37
See also CA 5-8R; CANR 10; INT CANR-10;
SATA 8
Fletcher, John [1579-1625] .... LC 33; DC 6
See also CDBLB Before 1660; DLB 58
Fletcher, John Gould [1886-1950] . TCLC 35
See also CA 107; DLB 4, 45
Fleur, Paul
See Pohl, Frederik
Flooglebuckle, Al
See Spiegelman, Art
Flying Officer X
See Bates, H(erbert) E(rnest)
Fo, Dario [1926-]CLC 32, 109; DAM DRAM
See also CA 116; 128; CANR 68; DLBY 97;
MTCW
Fogarty, Jonathan Titulescu Esq.
See Farrell, James T(homas)
Folke, Will
See Bloch, Robert (Albert)
Follett, Ken(neth Martin) [1949-] .. CLC 18;
DAM NOV, POP

See also AAYA 6; BEST 89:4; CA 81-84; CANR
13, 33, 54; DLB 87; DLBY 81; INT CANR-
33; MTCW
Fontane, Theodor [1819-1898] ...... NCLC 26
See also DLB 129
Foote, Horton [1916-]...... CLC 51, 91; DAM
DRAM
See also CA 73-76; CANR 34, 51; DLB 26; INT
CANR-34
Foote, Shelby [1916-] .. CLC 75; DAM NOV,
POP
See also CA 5-8R; CANR 3, 45; DLB 2, 17
Forbes, Esther [1891-1967] .... CLC 12
See also AAYA 17; CA 13-14; 25-28R; CAP 1;
CLR 27; DLB 22; JRDA; MAICYA; SATA 2
Forche, Carolyn (Louise) [1950-]CLC 25, 83,
86; DAM POET; PC 10
See also CA 109; 117; CANR 50; DLB 5, 193;
INT 117
Ford, Elbur
See Hibbert, Eleanor Alice Burford
Ford, Ford Madox [1873-1939] TCLC 1, 15,
39, 57; DAM NOV
See also CA 104; 132; CDBLB 1914-1945;
DLB 162; MTCW
Ford, Henry [1863-1947] .... TCLC 73
See also CA 115; 148
Ford, John [1586-(?)] ....DC 8
See also CDBLB Before 1660; DAM DRAM;
DLB 58
Ford, John [1895-1973] .... CLC 16
See also CA 45-48
Ford, Richard [1944-] .... CLC 46, 99
See also CA 69-72; CANR 11, 47
Ford, Webster
See Masters, Edgar Lee
Foreman, Richard [1937-] .... CLC 50
See also CA 65-68; CANR 32, 63
Forester, C(ecil) S(cott) [1899-1966] CLC 35
See also CA 73-76; 25-28R; DLB 191; SATA
13
Forez
See Mauriac, Francois (Charles)
Forman, James Douglas [1932-] .... CLC 21
See also AAYA 17; CA 9-12R; CANR 4, 19,
42; JRDA; MAICYA; SATA 8, 70
Fornes, Maria Irene [1930-] .... CLC 39, 61
See also CA 25-28R; CANR 28; DLB 7; HW;
INT CANR-28; MTCW
Forrest, Leon (Richard) [1937-1997] CLC 4;
BLCS
See also BW 2; CA 89-92; 162; CAAS 7; CANR
25, 52; DLB 33
Forster, E(dward) M(organ) [1879-1970]CLC
1, 2, 3, 4, 9, 10, 13, 15, 22, 45, 77; DA; DAB;
DAC; DAM MST, NOV; SSC 27; WLC
See also AAYA 2; CA 13-14; 25-28R; CANR
45; CAP 1; CDBLB 1914-1945; DLB 34, 98,
162, 178, 195; DLBD 10; MTCW; SATA 57
Forster, John [1812-1876] .... NCLC 11
See also DLB 144, 184
Forsyth, Frederick [1938-]CLC 2, 5, 36; DAM
NOV, POP
See also BEST 89:4; CA 85-88; CANR 38, 62;
DLB 87; MTCW
Forten, Charlotte L. .... TCLC 16; BLC 2
See also Grimke, Charlotte L(ottie) Forten
See also DLB 50
Foscolo, Ugo [1778-1827] .... NCLC 8
Fosse, Bob .... CLC 20
See also Fosse, Robert Louis
Fosse, Robert Louis [1927-1987]
See Fosse, Bob
See also CA 110; 123
Foster, Stephen Collins [1826-1864]NCLC 26
Foucault, Michel [1926-1984]CLC 31, 34, 69
See also CA 105; 113; CANR 34; MTCW

Gallico, Paul (William) [1897-1976] .. **CLC 2**
See also AITN 1; CA 5-8R; 69-72; CANR 23;
DLB 9, 171; MAICYA; SATA 13

Gallo, Max Louis [1932-] .... **CLC 95**
See also CA 85-88

Gallois, Lucien
See Desnos, Robert

Gallup, Ralph
See Whitemore, Hugh (John)

Galsworthy, John [1867-1933] . **TCLC 1, 45;
DA; DAB; DAC; DAM DRAM, MST,
NOV; SSC 22; WLC 2**
See also CA 104; 141; CDBLB 1890-1914;
DLB 10, 34, 98, 162; DLBD 16

Galt, John [1779-1839] .... **NCLC 1**
See also DLB 99, 116, 159

Galvin, James [1951-] .... **CLC 38**
See also CA 108; CANR 26

Gamboa, Federico [1864-1939] ..... **TCLC 36**

Gandhi, M. K.
See Gandhi, Mohandas Karamchand

Gandhi, Mahatma
See Gandhi, Mohandas Karamchand

Gandhi, Mohandas Karamchand [1869-1948]
TCLC 59; DAM MULT
See also CA 121; 132; MTCW

Gann, Ernest Kellogg [1910-1991] ... **CLC 23**
See also AITN 1; CA 1-4R; 136; CANR 1

Garcia, Cristina [1958-] .... **CLC 76**
See also CA 141

Garcia Lorca, Federico [1898-1936]**TCLC 1,
7, 49; DA; DAB; DAC; DAM DRAM,
MST, MULT, POET; DC 2; HLC; PC 3;
WLC**
See also CA 104; 131; DLB 108; HW; MTCW

Garcia Marquez, Gabriel (Jose) [1928-]**C L C
2, 3, 8, 10, 15, 27, 47, 55, 68; DA; DAB;
DAC; DAM MST, MULT, NOV, POP;
HLC; SSC 8; WLC**
See also AAYA 3; BEST 89:1, 90:4; CA 33-
36R; CANR 10, 28, 50; DLB 113; HW;
MTCW

Gard, Janice
See Latham, Jean Lee

Gard, Roger Martin du
See Martin du Gard, Roger

Gardam, Jane [1928-] .... **CLC 43**
See also CA 49-52; CANR 2, 18, 33, 54; CLR
12; DLB 14, 161; MAICYA; MTCW; SAAS
9; SATA 39, 76; SATA-Brief 28

Gardner, Herb(ert) [1934-] .... **CLC 44**
See also CA 149

Gardner, John (Champlin), Jr. [1933-1982]
**CLC 2, 3, 5, 7, 8, 10, 18, 28, 34; DAM NOV,
POP; SSC 7**
See also AITN 1; CA 65-68; 107; CANR 33;
DLB 2; DLBY 82; MTCW; SATA 40; SATA-
Obit 31

Gardner, John (Edmund) [1926-] ... **CLC 30;
DAM POP**
See also CA 103; CANR 15, 69; MTCW

Gardner, Miriam
See Bradley, Marion Zimmer

Gardner, Noel
See Kuttner, Henry

Gardons, S. S.
See Snodgrass, W(illiam) D(e Witt)

Garfield, Leon [1921-1996] .... **CLC 12**
See also AAYA 8; CA 17-20R; 152; CANR 38,
41; CLR 21; DLB 161; JRDA; MAICYA;
SATA 1, 32, 76; SATA-Obit 90

Garland, (Hannibal) Hamlin [1860-1940]
TCLC 3; SSC 18
See also CA 104; DLB 12, 71, 78, 186

Garneau, (Hector de) Saint-Denys [1912-1943]
TCLC 13
See also CA 111; DLB 88

Garner, Alan [1934-] ... **CLC 17; DAB; DAM
POP**
See also AAYA 18; CA 73-76; CANR 15, 64;
CLR 20; DLB 161; MAICYA; MTCW; SATA
18, 69

Garner, Hugh [1913-1979] .... **CLC 13**
See also CA 69-72; CANR 31; DLB 68

Garnett, David [1892-1981] .... **CLC 3**
See also CA 5-8R; 103; CANR 17; DLB 34

Garos, Stephanie
See Katz, Steve

Garrett, George (Palmer) [1929-] **CLC 3, 11,
51; SSC 30**
See also CA 1-4R; CAAS 5; CANR 1, 42, 67;
DLB 2, 5, 130, 152; DLBY 83

Garrick, David [1717-1779] ..... **LC 15; DAM
DRAM**
See also DLB 84

Garrigue, Jean [1914-1972] .... **CLC 2, 8**
See also CA 5-8R; 37-40R; CANR 20

Garrison, Frederick
See Sinclair, Upton (Beall)

Garth, Will
See Hamilton, Edmond; Kuttner, Henry

Garvey, Marcus (Moziah, Jr.) [1887-1940]
TCLC 41; BLC 2; DAM MULT
See also BW 1; CA 120; 124

Gary, Romain .... **CLC 25**
See also Kacew, Romain
See also DLB 83

Gascar, Pierre .... **CLC 11**
See also Fournier, Pierre

Gascoyne, David (Emery) [1916-] .... **CLC 45**
See also CA 65-68; CANR 10, 28, 54; DLB 20;
MTCW

Gaskell, Elizabeth Cleghorn [1810-1865]
NCLC 70; DAB; DAM MST; SSC 25
See also CDBLB 1832-1890; DLB 21, 144, 159

Gass, William H(oward) [1924-] **CLC 1, 2, 8,
11, 15, 39; SSC 12**
See also CA 17-20R; CANR 30; DLB 2; MTCW

Gasset, Jose Ortega y
See Ortega y Gasset, Jose

Gates, Henry Louis, Jr. [1950-] ...... **CLC 65;
BLCS; DAM MULT**
See also BW 2; CA 109; CANR 25, 53; DLB
67

Gautier, Theophile [1811-1872] **NCLC 1, 59;
DAM POET; PC 18; SSC 20**
See also DLB 119

Gawsworth, John
See Bates, H(erbert) E(rnest)

Gay, Oliver
See Gogarty, Oliver St. John

Gaye, Marvin (Penze) [1939-1984] .. **CLC 26**
See also CA 112

Gebler, Carlo (Ernest) [1954-] .... **CLC 39**
See also CA 119; 133

Gee, Maggie (Mary) [1948-] .... **CLC 57**
See also CA 130

Gee, Maurice (Gough) [1931-] .... **CLC 29**
See also CA 97-100; CANR 67; SATA 46

Gelbart, Larry (Simon) [1923-] . **CLC 21, 61**
See also CA 73-76; CANR 45

Gelber, Jack [1932-] .... **CLC 1, 6, 14, 79**
See also CA 1-4R; CANR 2; DLB 7

Gellhorn, Martha (Ellis) [1908-1998]**CLC 14,
60**
See also CA 77-80; 164; CANR 44; DLBY 82

Genet, Jean [1910-1986]**CLC 1, 2, 5, 10, 14, 44,
46; DAM DRAM**
See also CA 13-16R; CANR 18; DLB 72;
DLBY 86; MTCW

Gent, Peter [1942-] .... **CLC 29**
See also AITN 1; CA 89-92; DLBY 82

Gentlewoman in New England, A
See Bradstreet, Anne

Gentlewoman in Those Parts, A
See Bradstreet, Anne

George, Jean Craighead [1919-] ...... **CLC 35**
See also AAYA 8; CA 5-8R; CANR 25; CLR 1;
DLB 52; JRDA; MAICYA; SATA 2, 68

George, Stefan (Anton) [1868-1933]**TCLC 2,
14**
See also CA 104

Georges, Georges Martin
See Simenon, Georges (Jacques Christian)

Gerhardi, William Alexander
See Gerhardie, William Alexander

Gerhardie, William Alexander [1895-1977]
CLC 5
See also CA 25-28R; 73-76; CANR 18; DLB
36

Gerstler, Amy [1956-] .... **CLC 70**
See also CA 146

Gertler, T. .... **CLC 34**
See also CA 116; 121; INT 121

Ghalib .... **NCLC 39**
See also Ghalib, Hsadullah Khan

Ghalib, Hsadullah Khan [1797-1869]
See Ghalib
See also DAM POET

Ghelderode, Michel de [1898-1962]**CLC 6, 11;
DAM DRAM**
See also CA 85-88; CANR 40

Ghiselin, Brewster [1903-] .... **CLC 23**
See also CA 13-16R; CAAS 10; CANR 13

Ghose, Aurabinda [1872-1950] ...... **TCLC 63**
See also CA 163

Ghose, Zulfikar [1935-] .... **CLC 42**
See also CA 65-68; CANR 67

Ghosh, Amitav [1956-] .... **CLC 44**
See also CA 147

Giacosa, Giuseppe [1847-1906] .... **TCLC 7**
See also CA 104

Gibb, Lee
See Waterhouse, Keith (Spencer)

Gibbon, Lewis Grassic .... **TCLC 4**
See also Mitchell, James Leslie

Gibbons, Kaye [1960-]**CLC 50, 88; DAM POP**
See also CA 151

Gibran, Kahlil [1883-1931]**TCLC 1, 9; DAM
POET, POP; PC 9**
See also CA 104; 150

Gibran, Khalil
See Gibran, Kahlil

Gibson, William [1914-] **CLC 23; DA; DAB;
DAC; DAM DRAM, MST**
See also CA 9-12R; CANR 9, 42; DLB 7; SATA
66

Gibson, William (Ford) [1948-] **CLC 39, 63;
DAM POP**
See also AAYA 12; CA 126; 133; CANR 52

Gide, Andre (Paul Guillaume) [1869-1951]
**TCLC 5, 12, 36; DA; DAB; DAC; DAM
MST, NOV; SSC 13; WLC**
See also CA 104; 124; DLB 65; MTCW

Gifford, Barry (Colby) [1946-] .... **CLC 34**
See also CA 65-68; CANR 9, 30, 40

Gilbert, Frank
See De Voto, Bernard (Augustine)

Gilbert, W(illiam) S(chwenck) [1836-1911]
TCLC 3; DAM DRAM, POET
See also CA 104; SATA 36

Gilbreth, Frank B., Jr. [1911-] .... **CLC 17**
See also CA 9-12R; SATA 2

Gilchrist, Ellen [1935-] ... **CLC 34, 48; DAM
POP; SSC 14**
See also CA 113; 116; CANR 41, 61; DLB 130;
MTCW

Giles, Molly [1942-] .... **CLC 39**
See also CA 126

Gill, Patrick
See Creasey, John

See also Greve, Felix Paul (Berthold Friedrich)
See also DLB 92

Grubb
See Crumb, R(obert)

Grumbach, Doris (Isaac) [1918-]CLC **13, 22, 64**
See also CA 5-8R; CAAS 2; CANR 9, 42; INT CANR-9

Grundtvig, Nicolai Frederik Severin [1783-1872] ....
NCLC 1

Grunge
See Crumb, R(obert)

Grunwald, Lisa [1959-] .... CLC **44**
See also CA 120

Guare, John [1938-]CLC **8, 14, 29, 67; DAM DRAM**
See also CA 73-76; CANR 21, 69; DLB 7; MTCW

Gudjonsson, Halldor Kiljan [1902-1998]
See Laxness, Halldor
See also CA 103; 164

Guenter, Erich
See Eich, Guenter

Guest, Barbara [1920-] .... CLC **34**
See also CA 25-28R; CANR 11, 44; DLB 5, 193

Guest, Judith (Ann) [1936-]CLC **8, 30; DAM NOV, POP**
See also AAYA 7; CA 77-80; CANR 15; INT CANR-15; MTCW

Guevara, Che .... CLC **87; HLC**
See also Guevara (Serna), Ernesto

Guevara (Serna), Ernesto [1928-1967]
See Guevara, Che
See also CA 127; 111; CANR 56; DAM MULT; HW

Guild, Nicholas M. [1944-] .... CLC **33**
See also CA 93-96

Guillemin, Jacques
See Sartre, Jean-Paul

Guillen, Jorge [1893-1984] .... CLC **11; DAM MULT, POET**
See also CA 89-92; 112; DLB 108; HW

Guillen, Nicolas (Cristobal) [1902-1989]C L C **48, 79; BLC 2; DAM MST, MULT, POET; HLC; PC 23**
See also BW 2; CA 116; 125; 129; HW

Guillevic, (Eugene) [1907-] .... CLC **33**
See also CA 93-96

Guillois
See Desnos, Robert

Guillois, Valentin
See Desnos, Robert

Guiney, Louise Imogen [1861-1920]TCLC **41**
See also CA 160; DLB 54

Guiraldes, Ricardo (Guillermo) [1886-1927]
TCLC 39
See also CA 131; HW; MTCW

Gumilev, Nikolai (Stepanovich) [1886-1921]
TCLC 60
See also CA 165

Gunesekera, Romesh [1954-] .... CLC **91**
See also CA 159

Gunn, Bill .... CLC **5**
See also Gunn, William Harrison
See also DLB 38

Gunn, Thom(son William) [1929-] CLC **3, 6, 18, 32, 81; DAM POET**
See also CA 17-20R; CANR 9, 33; CDBLB 1960 to Present; DLB 27; INT CANR-33; MTCW

Gunn, William Harrison [1934(?)-1989]
See Gunn, Bill
See also AITN 1; BW 1; CA 13-16R; 128; CANR 12, 25

Gunnars, Kristjana [1948-] .... CLC **69**

See also CA 113; DLB 60

Gurdjieff, G(eorgei) I(vanovich) [1877(?)-1949]

TCLC 71
See also CA 157

Gurganus, Allan [1947-]CLC **70; DAM POP**
See also BEST 90:1; CA 135

Gurney, A(lbert) R(amsdell), Jr. [1930-]C L C **32, 50, 54; DAM DRAM**
See also CA 77-80; CANR 32, 64

Gurney, Ivor (Bertie) [1890-1937] TCLC **33**

Gurney, Peter
See Gurney, A(lbert) R(amsdell), Jr.

Guro, Elena [1877-1913] .... TCLC **56**

Gustafson, James M(oody) [1925-] CLC **100**
See also CA 25-28R; CANR 37

Gustafson, Ralph (Barker) [1909-] .. CLC **36**
See also CA 21-24R; CANR 8, 45; DLB 88

Gut, Gom
See Simenon, Georges (Jacques Christian)

Guterson, David [1956-] .... CLC **91**
See also CA 132

Guthrie, A(lfred) B(ertram), Jr. [1901-1991]
CLC 23
See also CA 57-60; 134; CANR 24; DLB 6; SATA 62; SATA-Obit 67

Guthrie, Isobel
See Grieve, C(hristopher) M(urray)

Guthrie, Woodrow Wilson [1912-1967]
See Guthrie, Woody
See also CA 113; 93-96

Guthrie, Woody .... CLC **35**
See also Guthrie, Woodrow Wilson

Guy, Rosa (Cuthbert) [1928-] .... CLC **26**
See also AAYA 4; BW 2; CA 17-20R; CANR 14, 34; CLR 13; DLB 33; JRDA; MAICYA; SATA 14, 62

Gwendolyn
See Bennett, (Enoch) Arnold

H. D. .... CLC **3, 8, 14, 31, 34, 73; PC 5**
See also Doolittle, Hilda

H. de V.
See Buchan, John

Haavikko, Paavo Juhani [1931-] CLC **18, 34**
See also CA 106

Habbema, Koos
See Heijermans, Herman

Habermas, Juergen [1929-] .... CLC **104**
See also CA 109

Habermas, Jurgen
See Habermas, Juergen

Hacker, Marilyn [1942-]CLC **5, 9, 23, 72, 91; DAM POET**
See also CA 77-80; CANR 68; DLB 120

Haeckel, Ernst Heinrich (Philipp August) [1834-1919] .... TCLC **83**
See also CA 157

Haggard, H(enry) Rider [1856-1925] T C L C **11**
See also CA 108; 148; DLB 70, 156, 174, 178; SATA 16

Hagiosy, L.
See Larbaud, Valery (Nicolas)

Hagiwara Sakutaro [1886-1942]TCLC **60; PC 18**

Haig, Fenil
See Ford, Ford Madox

Haig-Brown, Roderick (Langmere) [1908-1976]
CLC 21
See also CA 5-8R; 69-72; CANR 4, 38; CLR 31; DLB 88; MAICYA; SATA 12

Hailey, Arthur [1920-] .. CLC **5; DAM NOV, POP**
See also AITN 2; BEST 90:3; CA 1-4R; CANR 2, 36; DLB 88; DLBY 82; MTCW

Hailey, Elizabeth Forsythe [1938-] .. CLC **40**
See also CA 93-96; CAAS 1; CANR 15, 48;

INT CANR-15

Haines, John (Meade) [1924-] .... CLC **58**
See also CA 17-20R; CANR 13, 34; DLB 5

Hakluyt, Richard [1552-1616] .... LC **31**

Haldeman, Joe (William) [1943-] ..... CLC **61**
See also CA 53-56; CAAS 25; CANR 6; DLB 8; INT CANR-6

Haley, Alex(ander Murray Palmer) [1921-1992] CLC **8, 12, 76; BLC 2; DA; DAB; DAC; DAM MST, MULT, POP**
See also BW 2; CA 77-80; 136; CANR 61; DLB 38; MTCW

Haliburton, Thomas Chandler [1796-1865]
NCLC 15
See also DLB 11, 99

Hall, Donald (Andrew, Jr.) [1928-]CLC **1, 13, 37, 59; DAM POET**
See also CA 5-8R; CAAS 7; CANR 2, 44, 64; DLB 5; SATA 23, 97

Hall, Frederic Sauser
See Sauser-Hall, Frederic

Hall, James
See Kuttner, Henry

Hall, James Norman [1887-1951] .. TCLC **23**
See also CA 123; SATA 21

Hall, (Marguerite) Radclyffe [1886-1943]
TCLC 12
See also CA 110; 150

Hall, Rodney [1935-] .... CLC **51**
See also CA 109; CANR 69

Halleck, Fitz-Greene [1790-1867] . NCLC **47**
See also DLB 3

Halliday, Michael
See Creasey, John

Halpern, Daniel [1945-] .... CLC **14**
See also CA 33-36R

Hamburger, Michael (Peter Leopold) [1924-]
CLC 5, 14
See also CA 5-8R; CAAS 4; CANR 2, 47; DLB 27

Hamill, Pete [1935-] .... CLC **10**
See also CA 25-28R; CANR 18

Hamilton, Alexander [1755(?)-1804]NCLC **49**
See also DLB 37

Hamilton, Clive
See Lewis, C(live) S(taples)

Hamilton, Edmond [1904-1977] .... CLC **1**
See also CA 1-4R; CANR 3; DLB 8

Hamilton, Eugene (Jacob) Lee
See Lee-Hamilton, Eugene (Jacob)

Hamilton, Franklin
See Silverberg, Robert

Hamilton, Gail
See Corcoran, Barbara

Hamilton, Mollie
See Kaye, M(ary) M(argaret)

Hamilton, (Anthony Walter) Patrick [1904-1962] .... CLC **51**
See also CA 113; DLB 10

Hamilton, Virginia [1936-] .... CLC **26; DAM MULT**
See also AAYA 2, 21; BW 2; CA 25-28R; CANR 20, 37; CLR 1, 11, 40; DLB 33, 52; INT CANR-20; JRDA; MAICYA; MTCW; SATA 4, 56, 79

Hammett, (Samuel) Dashiell [1894-1961]CLC **3, 5, 10, 19, 47; SSC 17**
See also AITN 1; CA 81-84; CANR 42; CDALB 1929-1941; DLBD 6; DLBY 96; MTCW

Hammon, Jupiter [1711(?)-1800(?)]NCLC **5; BLC 2; DAM MULT, POET; PC 16**
See also DLB 31, 50

Hammond, Keith
See Kuttner, Henry

Hamner, Earl (Henry), Jr. [1923-] .... CLC **12**
See also AITN 2; CA 73-76; DLB 6

Hampton, Christopher (James) [1946-]CLC **4**

See also CA 25-28R; DLB 13; MTCW
Hamsun, Knut .... **TCLC 2, 14, 49**
See also Pedersen, Knut
Handke, Peter [1942-] . **CLC 5, 8, 10, 15, 38; DAM DRAM, NOV**
See also CA 77-80; CANR 33; DLB 85, 124; MTCW
Hanley, James [1901-1985] ... **CLC 3, 5, 8, 13**
See also CA 73-76; 117; CANR 36; DLB 191; MTCW
Hannah, Barry [1942-] .... **CLC 23, 38, 90**
See also CA 108; 110; CANR 43, 68; DLB 6; INT 110; MTCW
Hannon, Ezra
See Hunter, Evan
Hansberry, Lorraine (Vivian) [1930-1965]
CLC 17, 62; BLC 2; DA; DAB; DAC; DAM DRAM, MST, MULT; DC 2
See also AAYA 25; BW 1; CA 109; 25-28R; CABS 3; CANR 58; CDALB 1941-1968; DLB 7, 38; MTCW
Hansen, Joseph [1923-] .... **CLC 38**
See also CA 29-32R; CAAS 17; CANR 16, 44, 66; INT CANR-16
Hansen, Martin A. [1909-1955] ..... **TCLC 32**
Hanson, Kenneth O(stlin) [1922-] .... **CLC 13**
See also CA 53-56; CANR 7
Hardwick, Elizabeth [1916-] . **CLC 13; DAM NOV**
See also CA 5-8R; CANR 3, 32; DLB 6; MTCW
Hardy, Thomas [1840-1928] **TCLC 4, 10, 18, 32, 48, 53, 72; DA; DAB; DAC; DAM MST, NOV, POET; PC 8; SSC 2; WLC**
See also CA 104; 123; CDBLB 1890-1914; DLB 18, 19, 135; MTCW
Hare, David [1947-] .... **CLC 29, 58**
See also CA 97-100; CANR 39; DLB 13; MTCW
Harewood, John
See Van Druten, John (William)
Harford, Henry
See Hudson, W(illiam) H(enry)
Hargrave, Leonie
See Disch, Thomas M(ichael)
Harjo, Joy [1951-] ..... **CLC 83; DAM MULT**
See also CA 114; CANR 35, 67; DLB 120, 175; NNAL
Harlan, Louis R(udolph) [1922-] ...... **CLC 34**
See also CA 21-24R; CANR 25, 55
Harling, Robert [1951(?)-] .... **CLC 53**
See also CA 147
Harmon, William (Ruth) [1938-] ...... **CLC 38**
See also CA 33-36R; CANR 14, 32, 35; SATA 65
Harper, F. E. W.
See Harper, Frances Ellen Watkins
Harper, Frances E. W.
See Harper, Frances Ellen Watkins
Harper, Frances E. Watkins
See Harper, Frances Ellen Watkins
Harper, Frances Ellen
See Harper, Frances Ellen Watkins
Harper, Frances Ellen Watkins [1825-1911]
TCLC 14; BLC 2; DAM MULT, POET; PC 21
See also BW 1; CA 111; 125; DLB 50
Harper, Michael S(teven) [1938-] . **CLC 7, 22**
See also BW 1; CA 33-36R; CANR 24; DLB 41
Harper, Mrs. F. E. W.
See Harper, Frances Ellen Watkins
Harris, Christie (Lucy) Irwin [1907-]**CLC 12**
See also CA 5-8R; CANR 6; CLR 47; DLB 88; JRDA; MAICYA; SAAS 10; SATA 6, 74
Harris, Frank [1856-1931] .... **TCLC 24**
See also CA 109; 150; DLB 156, 197
Harris, George Washington [1814-1869]

NCLC 23
See also DLB 3, 11
Harris, Joel Chandler [1848-1908] **TCLC 2; SSC 19**
See also CA 104; 137; CLR 49; DLB 11, 23, 42, 78, 91; MAICYA; YABC 1
Harris, John (Wyndham Parkes Lucas) Beynon [1903-1969]
See Wyndham, John
See also CA 102; 89-92
Harris, MacDonald .... **CLC 9**
See also Heiney, Donald (William)
Harris, Mark [1922-] .... **CLC 19**
See also CA 5-8R; CAAS 3; CANR 2, 55; DLB 2; DLBY 80
Harris, (Theodore) Wilson [1921-] ... **CLC 25**
See also BW 2; CA 65-68; CAAS 16; CANR 11, 27, 69; DLB 117; MTCW
Harrison, Elizabeth Cavanna [1909-]
See Cavanna, Betty
See also CA 9-12R; CANR 6, 27
Harrison, Harry (Max) [1925-] .... **CLC 42**
See also CA 1-4R; CANR 5, 21; DLB 8; SATA 4
Harrison, James (Thomas) [1937-]**CLC 6, 14, 33, 66; SSC 19**
See also CA 13-16R; CANR 8, 51; DLBY 82; INT CANR-8
Harrison, Jim
See Harrison, James (Thomas)
Harrison, Kathryn [1961-] .... **CLC 70**
See also CA 144; CANR 68
Harrison, Tony [1937-] .... **CLC 43**
See also CA 65-68; CANR 44; DLB 40; MTCW
Harriss, Will(ard Irvin) [1922-] .... **CLC 34**
See also CA 111
Harson, Sley
See Ellison, Harlan (Jay)
Hart, Ellis
See Ellison, Harlan (Jay)
Hart, Josephine [1942(?)-]**CLC 70; DAM POP**
See also CA 138
Hart, Moss [1904-1961]**CLC 66; DAM DRAM**
See also CA 109; 89-92; DLB 7
Harte, (Francis) Bret(t) [1836(?)-1902]**TCLC 1, 25; DA; DAC; DAM MST; SSC 8; WLC**
See also CA 104; 140; CDALB 1865-1917; DLB 12, 64, 74, 79, 186; SATA 26
Hartley, L(eslie) P(oles) [1895-1972] **CLC 2, 22**
See also CA 45-48; 37-40R; CANR 33; DLB 15, 139; MTCW
Hartman, Geoffrey H. [1929-] .... **CLC 27**
See also CA 117; 125; DLB 67
Hartmann, Sadakichi [1867-1944] **TCLC 73**
See also CA 157; DLB 54
Hartmann von Aue [c. 1160-c. 1205] **CMLC 15**
See also DLB 138
Hartmann von Aue [1170-1210] ... **CMLC 15**
Haruf, Kent [1943-] .... **CLC 34**
See also CA 149
Harwood, Ronald [1934-] ...... **CLC 32; DAM DRAM, MST**
See also CA 1-4R; CANR 4, 55; DLB 13
Hasegawa Tatsunosuke
See Futabatei, Shimei
Hasek, Jaroslav (Matej Frantisek) [1883-1923]
TCLC 4
See also CA 104; 129; MTCW
Hass, Robert [1941-] **CLC 18, 39, 99; PC 16**
See also CA 111; CANR 30, 50; DLB 105; SATA 94
Hastings, Hudson
See Kuttner, Henry
Hastings, Selina .... **CLC 44**
Hathorne, John [1641-1717] .... **LC 38**

Hatteras, Amelia
See Mencken, H(enry) L(ouis)
Hatteras, Owen .... **TCLC 18**
See also Mencken, H(enry) L(ouis); Nathan, George Jean
Hauptmann, Gerhart (Johann Robert) [1862-1946] .... **TCLC 4; DAM DRAM**
See also CA 104; 153; DLB 66, 118
Havel, Vaclav [1936-] **CLC 25, 58, 65; DAM DRAM; DC 6**
See also CA 104; CANR 36, 63; MTCW
Haviaras, Stratis .... **CLC 33**
See also Chaviaras, Strates
Hawes, Stephen [1475(?)-1523(?)] .... **LC 17**
See also DLB 132
Hawkes, John (Clendennin Burne, Jr.) [1925-]
CLC 1, 2, 3, 4, 7, 9, 14, 15, 27, 49
See also CA 1-4R; CANR 2, 47, 64; DLB 2, 7; DLBY 80; MTCW
Hawking, S. W.
See Hawking, Stephen W(illiam)
Hawking, Stephen W(illiam) [1942-]**CLC 63, 105**
See also AAYA 13; BEST 89:1; CA 126; 129; CANR 48
Hawkins, Anthony Hope
See Hope, Anthony
Hawthorne, Julian [1846-1934] ..... **TCLC 25**
See also CA 165
Hawthorne, Nathaniel [1804-1864]**NCLC 39; DA; DAB; DAC; DAM MST, NOV; SSC 3, 29; WLC**
See also AAYA 18; CDALB 1640-1865; DLB 1, 74; YABC 2
Haxton, Josephine Ayres [1921-]
See Douglas, Ellen
See also CA 115; CANR 41
Hayaseca y Eizaguirre, Jorge
See Echegaray (y Eizaguirre), Jose (Maria Waldo)
Hayashi, Fumiko [1904-1951] .... **TCLC 27**
See also CA 161; DLB 180
Haycraft, Anna
See Ellis, Alice Thomas
See also CA 122
Hayden, Robert E(arl) [1913-1980]**CLC 5, 9, 14, 37; BLC 2; DA; DAC; DAM MST, MULT, POET; PC 6**
See also BW 1; CA 69-72; 97-100; CABS 2; CANR 24; CDALB 1941-1968; DLB 5, 76; MTCW; SATA 19; SATA-Obit 26
Hayford, J(oseph) E(phraim) Casely
See Casely-Hayford, J(oseph) E(phraim)
Hayman, Ronald [1932-] .... **CLC 44**
See also CA 25-28R; CANR 18, 50; DLB 155
Haywood, Eliza [1693(?)-1756] .... **LC 44**
See also DLB 39
Haywood, Eliza (Fowler) [1693(?)-1756]**LC 1, 44**
Hazlitt, William [1778-1830] .... **NCLC 29**
See also DLB 110, 158
Hazzard, Shirley [1931-] .... **CLC 18**
See also CA 9-12R; CANR 4; DLBY 82; MTCW
Head, Bessie [1937-1986]**CLC 25, 67; BLC 2; DAM MULT**
See also BW 2; CA 29-32R; 119; CANR 25; DLB 117; MTCW
Headon, (Nicky) Topper [1956(?)-] .. **CLC 30**
Heaney, Seamus (Justin) [1939-]**CLC 5, 7, 14, 25, 37, 74, 91; DAB; DAM POET; PC 18; WLCS**
See also CA 85-88; CANR 25, 48; CDBLB 1960 to Present; DLB 40; DLBY 95; MTCW
Hearn, (Patricio) Lafcadio (Tessima Carlos) [1850-1904] .... **TCLC 9**
See also CA 105; 166; DLB 12, 78

Hill, George Roy [1921-] .... CLC 26
See also CA 110; 122
Hill, John
See Koontz, Dean R(ay)
Hill, Susan (Elizabeth) [1942-] . CLC 4, 113;
DAB; DAM MST, NOV
See also CA 33-36R; CANR 29, 69; DLB 14,
139; MTCW
Hillerman, Tony [1925-] CLC 62; DAM POP
See also AAYA 6; BEST 89:1; CA 29-32R;
CANR 21, 42, 65; SATA 6
Hillesum, Etty [1914-1943] .... TCLC 49
See also CA 137
Hilliard, Noel (Harvey) [1929-] .... CLC 15
See also CA 9-12R; CANR 7, 69
Hillis, Rick [1956-] .... CLC 66
See also CA 134
Hilton, James [1900-1954] .... TCLC 21
See also CA 108; DLB 34, 77; SATA 34
Himes, Chester (Bomar) [1909-1984] CLC 2,
4, 7, 18, 58, 108; BLC 2; DAM MULT
See also BW 2; CA 25-28R; 114; CANR 22;
DLB 2, 76, 143; MTCW
Hinde, Thomas .... CLC 6, 11
See also Chitty, Thomas Willes
Hindin, Nathan
See Bloch, Robert (Albert)
Hine, (William) Daryl [1936-] .... CLC 15
See also CA 1-4R; CAAS 15; CANR 1, 20; DLB
60
Hinkson, Katharine Tynan
See Tynan, Katharine
Hinton, S(usan) E(loise) [1950-]CLC 30, 111;
DA; DAB; DAC; DAM MST, NOV
See also AAYA 2; CA 81-84; CANR 32, 62;
CLR 3, 23; JRDA; MAICYA; MTCW; SATA
19, 58
Hippius, Zinaida .... TCLC 9
See also Gippius, Zinaida (Nikolayevna)
Hiraoka, Kimitake [1925-1970]
See Mishima, Yukio
See also CA 97-100; 29-32R; DAM DRAM;
MTCW
Hirsch, E(ric) D(onald), Jr. [1928-] .. CLC 79
See also CA 25-28R; CANR 27, 51; DLB 67;
INT CANR-27; MTCW
Hirsch, Edward [1950-] .... CLC 31, 50
See also CA 104; CANR 20, 42; DLB 120
Hitchcock, Alfred (Joseph) [1899-1980] C L C
16
See also AAYA 22; CA 159; 97-100; SATA 27;
SATA-Obit 24
Hitler, Adolf [1889-1945] .... TCLC 53
See also CA 117; 147
Hoagland, Edward [1932-] .... CLC 28
See also CA 1-4R; CANR 2, 31, 57; DLB 6;
SATA 51
Hoban, Russell (Conwell) [1925-] CLC 7, 25;
DAM NOV
See also CA 5-8R; CANR 23, 37, 66; CLR 3;
DLB 52; MAICYA; MTCW; SATA 1, 40, 78
Hobbes, Thomas [1588-1679] .... LC 36
See also DLB 151
Hobbs, Perry
See Blackmur, R(ichard) P(almer)
Hobson, Laura Z(ametkin) [1900-1986] C L C
7, 25
See also CA 17-20R; 118; CANR 55; DLB 28;
SATA 52
Hochhuth, Rolf [1931-] CLC 4, 11, 18; DAM
DRAM
See also CA 5-8R; CANR 33; DLB 124; MTCW
Hochman, Sandra [1936-] .... CLC 3, 8
See also CA 5-8R; DLB 5
Hochwaelder, Fritz [1911-1986] ..... CLC 36;
DAM DRAM
See also CA 29-32R; 120; CANR 42; MTCW

Hochwaider, Fritz
See Hochwaelder, Fritz
Hocking, Mary (Eunice) [1921-] .... CLC 13
See also CA 101; CANR 18, 40
Hodgins, Jack [1938-] .... CLC 23
See also CA 93-96; DLB 60
Hodgson, William Hope [1877(?)-1918]TCLC
13
See also CA 111; 164; DLB 70, 153, 156, 178
Hoeg, Peter [1957-] .... CLC 95
See also CA 151
Hoffman, Alice [1952-] . CLC 51; DAM NOV
See also CA 77-80; CANR 34, 66; MTCW
Hoffman, Daniel (Gerard) [1923-]CLC 6, 13,
23
See also CA 1-4R; CANR 4; DLB 5
Hoffman, Stanley [1944-] .... CLC 5
See also CA 77-80
Hoffman, William M(oses) [1939-] ... CLC 40
See also CA 57-60; CANR 11
Hoffmann, E(rnst) T(heodor) A(madeus) [1776-
1822] ....
NCLC 2; SSC 13
See also DLB 90; SATA 27
Hofmann, Gert [1931-] .... CLC 54
See also CA 128
Hofmannsthal, Hugo von [1874-1929] T C L C
11; DAM DRAM; DC 4
See also CA 106; 153; DLB 81, 118
Hogan, Linda [1947-] CLC 73; DAM MULT
See also CA 120; CANR 45, 69; DLB 175;
NNAL
Hogarth, Charles
See Creasey, John
Hogarth, Emmett
See Polonsky, Abraham (Lincoln)
Hogg, James [1770-1835] .... NCLC 4
See also DLB 93, 116, 159
Holbach, Paul Henri Thiry Baron [1723-1789]
LC 14
Holberg, Ludvig [1684-1754] .... LC 6
Holden, Ursula [1921-] .... CLC 18
See also CA 101; CAAS 8; CANR 22
Holderlin, (Johann Christian) Friedrich [1770-
1843] ....
NCLC 16; PC 4
Holdstock, Robert
See Holdstock, Robert P.
Holdstock, Robert P. [1948-] .... CLC 39
See also CA 131
Holland, Isabelle [1920-] .... CLC 21
See also AAYA 11; CA 21-24R; CANR 10, 25,
47; JRDA; MAICYA; SATA 8, 70
Holland, Marcus
See Caldwell, (Janet Miriam) Taylor (Holland)
Hollander, John [1929-] .... CLC 2, 5, 8, 14
See also CA 1-4R; CANR 1, 52; DLB 5; SATA
13
Hollander, Paul
See Silverberg, Robert
Holleran, Andrew [1943(?)-] .... CLC 38
See also CA 144
Hollinghurst, Alan [1954-] .... CLC 55, 91
See also CA 114
Hollis, Jim
See Summers, Hollis (Spurgeon, Jr.)
Holly, Buddy [1936-1959] .... TCLC 65
Holmes, Gordon
See Shiel, M(atthew) P(hipps)
Holmes, John
See Souster, (Holmes) Raymond
Holmes, John Clellon [1926-1988] ... CLC 56
See also CA 9-12R; 125; CANR 4; DLB 16
Holmes, Oliver Wendell, Jr. [1841-1935]
TCLC 77
See also CA 114
Holmes, Oliver Wendell [1809-1894]NCLC 14

See also CDALB 1640-1865; DLB 1, 189;
SATA 34
Holmes, Raymond
See Souster, (Holmes) Raymond
Holt, Victoria
See Hibbert, Eleanor Alice Burford
Holub, Miroslav [1923-] .... CLC 4
See also CA 21-24R; CANR 10
Homer [c. 8th cent. B.C.-] CMLC 1, 16; DA;
DAB; DAC; DAM MST, POET; PC 23;
WLCS
See also DLB 176
Hongo, Garrett Kaoru [1951-] .... PC 23
See also CA 133; CAAS 22; DLB 120
Honig, Edwin [1919-] .... CLC 33
See also CA 5-8R; CAAS 8; CANR 4, 45; DLB
5
Hood, Hugh (John Blagdon) [1928-]CLC 15,
28
See also CA 49-52; CAAS 17; CANR 1, 33;
DLB 53
Hood, Thomas [1799-1845] .... NCLC 16
See also DLB 96
Hooker, (Peter) Jeremy [1941-] .... CLC 43
See also CA 77-80; CANR 22; DLB 40
hooks, bell .... CLC 94; BLCS
See also Watkins, Gloria
Hope, A(lec) D(erwent) [1907-] ..... CLC 3, 51
See also CA 21-24R; CANR 33; MTCW
Hope, Anthony [1863-1933] .... TCLC 83
See also CA 157; DLB 153, 156
Hope, Brian
See Creasey, John
Hope, Christopher (David Tully) [1944-]CLC
52
See also CA 106; CANR 47; SATA 62
Hopkins, Gerard Manley [1844-1889] N C L C
17; DA; DAB; DAC; DAM MST, POET;
PC 15; WLC
See also CDBLB 1890-1914; DLB 35, 57
Hopkins, John (Richard) [1931-] .... CLC 4
See also CA 85-88
Hopkins, Pauline Elizabeth [1859-1930]
TCLC 28; BLC 2; DAM MULT
See also BW 2; CA 141; DLB 50
Hopkinson, Francis [1737-1791] .... LC 25
See also DLB 31
Hopley-Woolrich, Cornell George [1903-1968]
See Woolrich, Cornell
See also CA 13-14; CANR 58; CAP 1
Horatio
See Proust, (Valentin-Louis-George-Eugene-)
Marcel
Horgan, Paul (George Vincent O'Shaughnessy)
[1903-1995] .... CLC 9, 53; DAM NOV
See also CA 13-16R; 147; CANR 9, 35; DLB
102; DLBY 85; INT CANR-9; MTCW;
SATA 13; SATA-Obit 84
Horn, Peter
See Kuttner, Henry
Hornem, Horace Esq.
See Byron, George Gordon (Noel)
Horney, Karen (Clementine Theodore
Danielsen) [1885-1952] .... TCLC 71
See also CA 114; 165
Hornung, E(rnest) W(illiam) [1866-1921]
TCLC 59
See also CA 108; 160; DLB 70
Horovitz, Israel (Arthur) [1939-] ... CLC 56;
DAM DRAM
See also CA 33-36R; CANR 46, 59; DLB 7
Horvath, Odon von
See Horvath, Oedoen von
See also DLB 85, 124
Horvath, Oedoen von [1901-1938] TCLC 45
See also Horvath, Odon von
See also CA 118

Horwitz, Julius [1920-1986] .... **CLC 14**
See also CA 9-12R; 119; CANR 12

Hospital, Janette Turner [1942-] ...... **CLC 42**
See also CA 108; CANR 48

Hostos, E. M. de
See Hostos (y Bonilla), Eugenio Maria de

Hostos, Eugenio M. de
See Hostos (y Bonilla), Eugenio Maria de

Hostos, Eugenio Maria
See Hostos (y Bonilla), Eugenio Maria de

Hostos (y Bonilla), Eugenio Maria de [1839-1903] ....
TCLC 24
See also CA 123; 131; HW

Houdini
See Lovecraft, H(oward) P(hillips)

Hougan, Carolyn [1943-] .... **CLC 34**
See also CA 139

Household, Geoffrey (Edward West) [1900-1988] .... **CLC 11**
See also CA 77-80; 126; CANR 58; DLB 87; SATA 14; SATA-Obit 59

Housman, A(lfred) E(dward) [1859-1936]
TCLC 1, 10; DA; DAB; DAC; DAM MST, POET; PC 2; WLCS
See also CA 104; 125; DLB 19; MTCW

Housman, Laurence [1865-1959] .... **TCLC 7**
See also CA 106; 155; DLB 10; SATA 25

Howard, Elizabeth Jane [1923-] ...**CLC 7, 29**
See also CA 5-8R; CANR 8, 62

Howard, Maureen [1930-] ...... **CLC 5, 14, 46**
See also CA 53-56; CANR 31; DLBY 83; INT CANR-31; MTCW

Howard, Richard [1929-] .... **CLC 7, 10, 47**
See also AITN 1; CA 85-88; CANR 25; DLB 5; INT CANR-25

Howard, Robert E(rvin) [1906-1936]**TCLC 8**
See also CA 105; 157

Howard, Warren F.
See Pohl, Frederik

Howe, Fanny [1940-] .... **CLC 47**
See also CA 117; CAAS 27; SATA-Brief 52

Howe, Irving [1920-1993] .... **CLC 85**
See also CA 9-12R; 141; CANR 21, 50; DLB 67; MTCW

Howe, Julia Ward [1819-1910] ...... **TCLC 21**
See also CA 117; DLB 1, 189

Howe, Susan [1937-] .... **CLC 72**
See also CA 160; DLB 120

Howe, Tina [1937-] .... **CLC 48**
See also CA 109

Howell, James [1594(?)-1666] .... **LC 13**
See also DLB 151

Howells, W. D.
See Howells, William Dean

Howells, William D.
See Howells, William Dean

Howells, William Dean [1837-1920]**TCLC 7, 17, 41**
See also CA 104; 134; CDALB 1865-1917; DLB 12, 64, 74, 79, 189

Howes, Barbara [1914-1996] .... **CLC 15**
See also CA 9-12R; 151; CAAS 3; CANR 53; SATA 5

Hrabal, Bohumil [1914-1997] .... **CLC 13, 67**
See also CA 106; 156; CAAS 12; CANR 57

Hroswitha of Gandersheim [c. 935-c. 1002]
CMLC 29
See also DLB 148

Hsun, Lu
See Lu Hsun

Hubbard, L(afayette) Ron(ald) [1911-1986]
CLC 43; DAM POP
See also CA 77-80; 118; CANR 52

Huch, Ricarda (Octavia) [1864-1947] **T C L C 13**
See also CA 111; DLB 66

Huddle, David [1942-] .... **CLC 49**
See also CA 57-60; CAAS 20; DLB 130

Hudson, Jeffrey
See Crichton, (John) Michael

Hudson, W(illiam) H(enry) [1841-1922]
TCLC 29
See also CA 115; DLB 98, 153, 174; SATA 35

Hueffer, Ford Madox
See Ford, Ford Madox

Hughart, Barry [1934-] .... **CLC 39**
See also CA 137

Hughes, Colin
See Creasey, John

Hughes, David (John) [1930-] .... **CLC 48**
See also CA 116; 129; DLB 14

Hughes, Edward James
See Hughes, Ted
See also DAM MST, POET

Hughes, (James) Langston [1902-1967] **C L C 1, 5, 10, 15, 35, 44, 108; BLC 2; DA; DAB; DAC; DAM DRAM, MST, MULT, POET; DC 3; PC 1; SSC 6; WLC**
See also AAYA 12; BW 1; CA 1-4R; 25-28R; CANR 1, 34; CDALB 1929-1941; CLR 17; DLB 4, 7, 48, 51, 86; JRDA; MAICYA; MTCW; SATA 4, 33

Hughes, Richard (Arthur Warren) [1900-1976]
CLC 1, 11; DAM NOV
See also CA 5-8R; 65-68; CANR 4; DLB 15, 161; MTCW; SATA 8; SATA-Obit 25

Hughes, Ted [1930-]**CLC 2, 4, 9, 14, 37; DAB; DAC; PC 7**
See also Hughes, Edward James
See also CA 1-4R; CANR 1, 33, 66; CLR 3; DLB 40, 161; MAICYA; MTCW; SATA 49; SATA-Brief 27

Hugo, Richard F(ranklin) [1923-1982]**CLC 6, 18, 32; DAM POET**
See also CA 49-52; 108; CANR 3; DLB 5

Hugo, Victor (Marie) [1802-1885]**NCLC 3, 10, 21; DA; DAB; DAC; DAM DRAM, MST, NOV, POET; PC 17; WLC**
See also DLB 119, 192; SATA 47

Huidobro, Vicente
See Huidobro Fernandez, Vicente Garcia

Huidobro Fernandez, Vicente Garcia [1893-1948] .... **TCLC 31**
See also CA 131; HW

Hulme, Keri [1947-] .... **CLC 39**
See also CA 125; CANR 69; INT 125

Hulme, T(homas) E(rnest) [1883-1917]**TCLC 21**
See also CA 117; DLB 19

Hume, David [1711-1776] .... **LC 7**
See also DLB 104

Humphrey, William [1924-1997] ...... **CLC 45**
See also CA 77-80; 160; CANR 68; DLB 6

Humphreys, Emyr Owen [1919-] ..... **CLC 47**
See also CA 5-8R; CANR 3, 24; DLB 15

Humphreys, Josephine [1945-] .. **CLC 34, 57**
See also CA 121; 127; INT 127

Huneker, James Gibbons [1857-1921] **T C L C 65**
See also DLB 71

Hungerford, Pixie
See Brinsmead, H(esba) F(ay)

Hunt, E(verette) Howard, (Jr.) [1918-]**CLC 3**
See also AITN 1; CA 45-48; CANR 2, 47

Hunt, Kyle
See Creasey, John

Hunt, (James Henry) Leigh [1784-1859]
NCLC 70; DAM POET
See also DLB 96, 110, 144

Hunt, (James Henry) Leigh [1784-1859]
NCLC 1; DAM POET

Hunt, Marsha [1946-] .... **CLC 70**
See also BW 2; CA 143

Hunt, Violet [1866(?)-1942] .... **TCLC 53**
See also DLB 162, 197

Hunter, E. Waldo
See Sturgeon, Theodore (Hamilton)

Hunter, Evan [1926-]**CLC 11, 31; DAM POP**
See also CA 5-8R; CANR 5, 38, 62; DLBY 82; INT CANR-5; MTCW; SATA 25

Hunter, Kristin (Eggleston) [1931-] . **CLC 35**
See also AITN 1; BW 1; CA 13-16R; CANR 13; CLR 3; DLB 33; INT CANR-13; MAICYA; SAAS 10; SATA 12

Hunter, Mollie [1922-] .... **CLC 21**
See also McIlwraith, Maureen Mollie Hunter
See also AAYA 13; CANR 37; CLR 25; DLB 161; JRDA; MAICYA; SAAS 7; SATA 54

Hunter, Robert [(?)-1734] .... **LC 7**

Hurston, Zora Neale [1903-1960] **CLC 7, 30, 61; BLC 2; DA; DAC; DAM MST, MULT, NOV; SSC 4; WLCS**
See also AAYA 15; BW 1; CA 85-88; CANR 61; DLB 51, 86; MTCW

Huston, John (Marcellus) [1906-1987]**CLC 20**
See also CA 73-76; 123; CANR 34; DLB 26

Hustvedt, Siri [1955-] .... **CLC 76**
See also CA 137

Hutten, Ulrich von [1488-1523] .... **LC 16**
See also DLB 179

Huxley, Aldous (Leonard) [1894-1963]**CLC 1, 3, 4, 5, 8, 11, 18, 35, 79; DA; DAB; DAC; DAM MST, NOV; WLC**
See also AAYA 11; CA 85-88; CANR 44; CDBLB 1914-1945; DLB 36, 100, 162, 195; MTCW; SATA 63

Huxley, T(homas) H(enry) [1825-1895]**NCLC 67**
See also DLB 57

Huysmans, Joris-Karl [1848-1907] **TCLC 7, 69**
See also CA 104; 165; DLB 123

Hwang, David Henry [1957-] **CLC 55; DAM DRAM; DC 4**
See also CA 127; 132; INT 132

Hyde, Anthony [1946-] .... **CLC 42**
See also CA 136

Hyde, Margaret O(ldroyd) [1917-] .. **CLC 21**
See also CA 1-4R; CANR 1, 36; CLR 23; JRDA; MAICYA; SAAS 8; SATA 1, 42, 76

Hynes, James [1956(?)-] .... **CLC 65**
See also CA 164

Ian, Janis [1951-] .... **CLC 21**
See also CA 105

Ibanez, Vicente Blasco
See Blasco Ibanez, Vicente

Ibarguengoitia, Jorge [1928-1983] ... **CLC 37**
See also CA 124; 113; HW

Ibsen, Henrik (Johan) [1828-1906]**TCLC 2, 8, 16, 37, 52; DA; DAB; DAC; DAM DRAM, MST; DC 2; WLC**
See also CA 104; 141

Ibuse, Masuji [1898-1993] .... **CLC 22**
See also CA 127; 141; DLB 180

Ichikawa, Kon [1915-] .... **CLC 20**
See also CA 121

Idle, Eric [1943-] .... **CLC 21**
See also Monty Python
See also CA 116; CANR 35

Ignatow, David [1914-1997] **CLC 4, 7, 14, 40**
See also CA 9-12R; 162; CAAS 3; CANR 31, 57; DLB 5

Ihimaera, Witi [1944-] .... **CLC 46**
See also CA 77-80

Ilf, Ilya .... **TCLC 21**
See also Fainzilberg, Ilya Arnoldovich

Illyes, Gyula [1902-1983] .... **PC 16**
See also CA 114; 109

Immermann, Karl (Lebrecht) [1796-1840]
NCLC 4, 49

King, Stephen (Edwin) [1947-]CLC 12, 26, 37, 61, 113; DAM NOV, POP; SSC 17
See also AAYA 1, 17; BEST 90:1; CA 61-64; CANR 1, 30, 52; DLB 143; DLBY 80; JRDA; MTCW; SATA 9, 55

King, Steve
See King, Stephen (Edwin)

King, Thomas [1943-] CLC 89; DAC; DAM MULT
See also CA 144; DLB 175; NNAL; SATA 96

Kingman, Lee .... CLC 17
See also Natti, (Mary) Lee
See also SAAS 3; SATA 1, 67

Kingsley, Charles [1819-1875] .... NCLC 35
See also DLB 21, 32, 163, 190; YABC 2

Kingsley, Sidney [1906-1995] .... CLC 44
See also CA 85-88; 147; DLB 7

Kingsolver, Barbara [1955-]CLC 55, 81; DAM POP
See also AAYA 15; CA 129; 134; CANR 60; INT 134

Kingston, Maxine (Ting Ting) Hong [1940-] CLC 12, 19, 58; DAM MULT, NOV; WLCS
See also AAYA 8; CA 69-72; CANR 13, 38; DLB 173; DLBY 80; INT CANR-13; MTCW; SATA 53

Kinnell, Galway [1927-]CLC 1, 2, 3, 5, 13, 29
See also CA 9-12R; CANR 10, 34, 66; DLB 5; DLBY 87; INT CANR-34; MTCW

Kinsella, Thomas [1928-] .... CLC 4, 19
See also CA 17-20R; CANR 15; DLB 27; MTCW

Kinsella, W(illiam) P(atrick) [1935-]CLC 27, 43; DAC; DAM NOV, POP
See also AAYA 7; CA 97-100; CAAS 7; CANR 21, 35, 66; INT CANR-21; MTCW

Kipling, (Joseph) Rudyard [1865-1936]TCLC 8, 17; DA; DAB; DAC; DAM MST, POET; PC 3; SSC 5; WLC
See also CA 105; 120; CANR 33; CDBLB 1890-1914; CLR 39; DLB 19, 34, 141, 156; MAICYA; MTCW; YABC 2

Kirkup, James [1918-] .... CLC 1
See also CA 1-4R; CAAS 4; CANR 2; DLB 27; SATA 12

Kirkwood, James [1930(?)-1989] .... CLC 9
See also AITN 2; CA 1-4R; 128; CANR 6, 40

Kirshner, Sidney
See Kingsley, Sidney

Kis, Danilo [1935-1989] .... CLC 57
See also CA 109; 118; 129; CANR 61; DLB 181; MTCW

Kivi, Aleksis [1834-1872] .... NCLC 30

Kizer, Carolyn (Ashley) [1925-] CLC 15, 39, 80; DAM POET
See also CA 65-68; CAAS 5; CANR 24; DLB 5, 169

Klabund [1890-1928]...................... TCLC 44
See also CA 162; DLB 66

Klappert, Peter [1942-] .... CLC 57
See also CA 33-36R; DLB 5

Klein, A(braham) M(oses) [1909-1972] C L C 19; DAB; DAC; DAM MST
See also CA 101; 37-40R; DLB 68

Klein, Norma [1938-1989] .... CLC 30
See also AAYA 2; CA 41-44R; 128; CANR 15, 37; CLR 2, 19; INT CANR-15; JRDA; MAICYA; SAAS 1; SATA 7, 57

Klein, T(heodore) E(ibon) D(onald) [1947-] CLC 34
See also CA 119; CANR 44

Kleist, Heinrich von [1777-1811]NCLC 2, 37; DAM DRAM; SSC 22
See also DLB 90

Klima, Ivan [1931-] CLC 56; DAM NOV
See also CA 25-28R; CANR 17, 50

Klimentov, Andrei Platonovich [1899-1951]
See Platonov, Andrei
See also CA 108

Klinger, Friedrich Maximilian von [1752-1831] NCLC 1
See also DLB 94

Klingsor the Magician
See Hartmann, Sadakichi

Klopstock, Friedrich Gottlieb [1724-1803] NCLC 11
See also DLB 97

Knapp, Caroline [1959-] .... CLC 99
See also CA 154

Knebel, Fletcher [1911-1993] .... CLC 14
See also AITN 1; CA 1-4R; 140; CAAS 3; CANR 1, 36; SATA 36; SATA-Obit 75

Knickerbocker, Diedrich
See Irving, Washington

Knight, Etheridge [1931-1991]CLC 40; BLC 2; DAM POET; PC 14
See also BW 1; CA 21-24R; 133; CANR 23; DLB 41

Knight, Sarah Kemble [1666-1727] ...... LC 7
See also DLB 24, 200

Knister, Raymond [1899-1932] ...... TCLC 56
See also DLB 68

Knowles, John [1926-]CLC 1, 4, 10, 26; DA; DAC; DAM MST, NOV
See also AAYA 10; CA 17-20R; CANR 40; CDALB 1968-1988; DLB 6; MTCW; SATA 8, 89

Knox, Calvin M.
See Silverberg, Robert

Knox, John [c. 1505-1572] .... LC 37
See also DLB 132

Knye, Cassandra
See Disch, Thomas M(ichael)

Koch, C(hristopher) J(ohn) [1932-] . CLC 42
See also CA 127

Koch, Christopher
See Koch, C(hristopher) J(ohn)

Koch, Kenneth [1925-] .. CLC 5, 8, 44; DAM POET
See also CA 1-4R; CANR 6, 36, 57; DLB 5; INT CANR-36; SATA 65

Kochanowski, Jan [1530-1584] .... LC 10

Kock, Charles Paul de [1794-1871]NCLC 16

Koda Shigeyuki [1867-1947]
See Rohan, Koda
See also CA 121

Koestler, Arthur [1905-1983] CLC 1, 3, 6, 8, 15, 33
See also CA 1-4R; 109; CANR 1, 33; CDBLB 1945-1960; DLBY 83; MTCW

Kogawa, Joy Nozomi [1935-]CLC 78; DAC; DAM MST, MULT
See also CA 101; CANR 19, 62

Kohout, Pavel [1928-] .... CLC 13
See also CA 45-48; CANR 3

Koizumi, Yakumo
See Hearn, (Patricio) Lafcadio (Tessima Carlos)

Kolmar, Gertrud [1894-1943] .... TCLC 40

Komunyakaa, Yusef [1947-] ...... CLC 86, 94; BLCS
See also CA 147; DLB 120

Konrad, George
See Konrad, Gyoergy

Konrad, Gyoergy [1933-] .... CLC 4, 10, 73
See also CA 85-88

Konwicki, Tadeusz [1926-] ..... CLC 8, 28, 54
See also CA 101; CAAS 9; CANR 39, 59; MTCW

Koontz, Dean R(ay) [1945-] ..CLC 78; DAM NOV, POP
See also AAYA 9; BEST 89:3, 90:2; CA 108; CANR 19, 36, 52; MTCW; SATA 92

Kopernik, Mikolaj

See Copernicus, Nicolaus

Kopit, Arthur (Lee) [1937-] .. CLC 1, 18, 33; DAM DRAM
See also AITN 1; CA 81-84; CABS 3; DLB 7; MTCW

Kops, Bernard [1926-] .... CLC 4
See also CA 5-8R; DLB 13

Kornbluth, C(yril) M. [1923-1958] . TCLC 8
See also CA 105; 160; DLB 8

Korolenko, V. G.
See Korolenko, Vladimir Galaktionovich

Korolenko, Vladimir
See Korolenko, Vladimir Galaktionovich

Korolenko, Vladimir G.
See Korolenko, Vladimir Galaktionovich

Korolenko, Vladimir Galaktionovich [1853-1921] .... TCLC 22
See also CA 121

Korzybski, Alfred (Habdank Skarbek) [1879-1950] .... TCLC 61
See also CA 123; 160

Kosinski, Jerzy (Nikodem) [1933-1991] C L C 1, 2, 3, 6, 10, 15, 53, 70; DAM NOV
See also CA 17-20R; 134; CANR 9, 46; DLB 2; DLBY 82; MTCW

Kostelanetz, Richard (Cory) [1940-] CLC 28
See also CA 13-16R; CAAS 8; CANR 38

Kostrowitzki, Wilhelm Apollinaris de [1880-1918]
See Apollinaire, Guillaume
See also CA 104

Kotlowitz, Robert [1924-] .... CLC 4
See also CA 33-36R; CANR 36

Kotzebue, August (Friedrich Ferdinand) von [1761-1819] .... NCLC 25
See also DLB 94

Kotzwinkle, William [1938-] .. CLC 5, 14, 35
See also CA 45-48; CANR 3, 44; CLR 6; DLB 173; MAICYA; SATA 24, 70

Kowna, Stancy
See Szymborska, Wislawa

Kozol, Jonathan [1936-] .... CLC 17
See also CA 61-64; CANR 16, 45

Kozoll, Michael [1940(?)-] .... CLC 35

Kramer, Kathryn [19(?)-] .... CLC 34

Kramer, Larry [1935-] CLC 42; DAM POP; DC 8
See also CA 124; 126; CANR 60

Krasicki, Ignacy [1735-1801] .... NCLC 8

Krasinski, Zygmunt [1812-1859] ..... NCLC 4

Kraus, Karl [1874-1936].................. TCLC 5
See also CA 104; DLB 118

Kreve (Mickevicius), Vincas [1882-1954] TCLC 27

Kristeva, Julia [1941-] .... CLC 77
See also CA 154

Kristofferson, Kris [1936-] .... CLC 26
See also CA 104

Krizanc, John [1956-] .... CLC 57

Krleza, Miroslav [1893-1981] .... CLC 8
See also CA 97-100; 105; CANR 50; DLB 147

Kroetsch, Robert [1927-]CLC 5, 23, 57; DAC; DAM POET
See also CA 17-20R; CANR 8, 38; DLB 53; MTCW

Kroetz, Franz
See Kroetz, Franz Xaver

Kroetz, Franz Xaver [1946-] .... CLC 41
See also CA 130

Kroker, Arthur (W.) [1945-] .... CLC 77
See also CA 161

Kropotkin, Peter (Alekseevich) [1842-1921] TCLC 36
See also CA 119

Krotkov, Yuri [1917-] .... CLC 19
See also CA 102

Krumb
See Crumb, R(obert)

Krumgold, Joseph (Quincy) [1908-1980]**CLC 12**
See also CA 9-12R; 101; CANR 7; MAICYA; SATA 1, 48; SATA-Obit 23

Krumwitz
See Crumb, R(obert)

Krutch, Joseph Wood [1893-1970] ... **CLC 24**
See also CA 1-4R; 25-28R; CANR 4; DLB 63

Krutzch, Gus
See Eliot, T(homas) S(tearns)

Krylov, Ivan Andreevich [1768(?)-1844] **NCLC 1**
See also DLB 150

Kubin, Alfred (Leopold Isidor) [1877-1959] **TCLC 23**
See also CA 112; 149; DLB 81

Kubrick, Stanley [1928-] .... **CLC 16**
See also CA 81-84; CANR 33; DLB 26

Kumin, Maxine (Winokur) [1925-]**CLC 5, 13, 28; DAM POET; PC 15**
See also AITN 2; CA 1-4R; CAAS 8; CANR 1, 21, 69; DLB 5; MTCW; SATA 12

Kundera, Milan [1929-]**CLC 4, 9, 19, 32, 68; DAM NOV; SSC 24**
See also AAYA 2; CA 85-88; CANR 19, 52; MTCW

Kunene, Mazisi (Raymond) [1930-] . **CLC 85**
See also BW 1; CA 125; DLB 117

Kunitz, Stanley (Jasspon) [1905-]**CLC 6, 11, 14; PC 19**
See also CA 41-44R; CANR 26, 57; DLB 48; INT CANR-26; MTCW

Kunze, Reiner [1933-] .... **CLC 10**
See also CA 93-96; DLB 75

Kuprin, Aleksandr Ivanovich [1870-1938] **TCLC 5**
See also CA 104

Kureishi, Hanif [1954(?)-] .... **CLC 64**
See also CA 139; DLB 194

Kurosawa, Akira [1910-] .... **CLC 16; DAM MULT**
See also AAYA 11; CA 101; CANR 46

Kushner, Tony [1957(?)-] .... **CLC 81; DAM DRAM**
See also CA 144

Kuttner, Henry [1915-1958] .... **TCLC 10**
See also Vance, Jack
See also CA 107; 157; DLB 8

Kuzma, Greg [1944-] .... **CLC 7**
See also CA 33-36R

Kuzmin, Mikhail [1872(?)-1936] ... **TCLC 40**

Kyd, Thomas [1558-1594] .... **LC 22; DAM DRAM; DC 3**
See also DLB 62

Kyprianos, Iossif
See Samarakis, Antonis

La Bruyere, Jean de [1645-1696] .... **LC 17**

Lacan, Jacques (Marie Emile) [1901-1981] **CLC 75**
See also CA 121; 104

Laclos, Pierre Ambroise Francois Choderlos de [1741-1803] .... **NCLC 4**

La Colere, Francois
See Aragon, Louis

Lacolere, Francois
See Aragon, Louis

La Deshabilleuse
See Simenon, Georges (Jacques Christian)

Lady Gregory
See Gregory, Isabella Augusta (Persse)

Lady of Quality, A
See Bagnold, Enid

La Fayette, Marie (Madelaine Pioche de la Vergne Comtes [1634-1693] .... **LC 2**

Lafayette, Rene

See Hubbard, L(afayette) Ron(ald)

Laforgue, Jules [1860-1887]**NCLC 5, 53; PC 14; SSC 20**

Lagerkvist, Paer (Fabian) [1891-1974]**CLC 7, 10, 13, 54; DAM DRAM, NOV**
See also Lagerkvist, Par
See also CA 85-88; 49-52; MTCW

Lagerkvist, Par .... **SSC 12**
See also Lagerkvist, Paer (Fabian)

Lagerloef, Selma (Ottiliana Lovisa) [1858-1940] ....
TCLC 4, 36
See also Lagerlof, Selma (Ottiliana Lovisa)
See also CA 108; SATA 15

Lagerlof, Selma (Ottiliana Lovisa)
See Lagerloef, Selma (Ottiliana Lovisa)
See also CLR 7; SATA 15

La Guma, (Justin) Alex(ander) [1925-1985] **CLC 19; BLCS; DAM NOV**
See also BW 1; CA 49-52; 118; CANR 25; DLB 117; MTCW

Laidlaw, A. K.
See Grieve, C(hristopher) M(urray)

Lainez, Manuel Mujica
See Mujica Lainez, Manuel
See also HW

Laing, R(onald) D(avid) [1927-1989]**CLC 95**
See also CA 107; 129; CANR 34; MTCW

Lamartine, Alphonse (Marie Louis Prat) de [1790-1869]**NCLC 11; DAM POET; PC 16**

Lamb, Charles [1775-1834] .. **NCLC 10; DA; DAB; DAC; DAM MST; WLC**
See also CDBLB 1789-1832; DLB 93, 107, 163; SATA 17

Lamb, Lady Caroline [1785-1828] **NCLC 38**
See also DLB 116

Lamming, George (William) [1927-]**CLC 2, 4, 66; BLC 2; DAM MULT**
See also BW 2; CA 85-88; CANR 26; DLB 125; MTCW

L'Amour, Louis (Dearborn) [1908-1988]**CLC 25, 55; DAM NOV, POP**
See also AAYA 16; AITN 2; BEST 89:2; CA 1-4R; 125; CANR 3, 25, 40; DLBY 80; MTCW

Lampedusa, Giuseppe (Tomasi) di [1896-1957] **TCLC 13**
See also Tomasi di Lampedusa, Giuseppe
See also CA 164; DLB 177

Lampman, Archibald [1861-1899] **NCLC 25**
See also DLB 92

Lancaster, Bruce [1896-1963] .... **CLC 36**
See also CA 9-10; CAP 1; SATA 9

Lanchester, John .... **CLC 99**

Landau, Mark Alexandrovich
See Aldanov, Mark (Alexandrovich)

Landau-Aldanov, Mark Alexandrovich
See Aldanov, Mark (Alexandrovich)

Landis, Jerry
See Simon, Paul (Frederick)

Landis, John [1950-] .... **CLC 26**
See also CA 112; 122

Landolfi, Tommaso [1908-1979] . **CLC 11, 49**
See also CA 127; 117; DLB 177

Landon, Letitia Elizabeth [1802-1838]**NCLC 15**
See also DLB 96

Landor, Walter Savage [1775-1864]**NCLC 14**
See also DLB 93, 107

Landwirth, Heinz [1927-]
See Lind, Jakov
See also CA 9-12R; CANR 7

Lane, Patrick [1939-] **CLC 25; DAM POET**
See also CA 97-100; CANR 54; DLB 53; INT 97-100

Lang, Andrew [1844-1912] .... **TCLC 16**
See also CA 114; 137; DLB 98, 141, 184; MAICYA; SATA 16

Lang, Fritz [1890-1976] .... **CLC 20, 103**
See also CA 77-80; 69-72; CANR 30

Lange, John
See Crichton, (John) Michael

Langer, Elinor [1939-] .... **CLC 34**
See also CA 121

Langland, William [1330(?)-1400(?)] **LC 19; DA; DAB; DAC; DAM MST, POET**
See also DLB 146

Langstaff, Launcelot
See Irving, Washington

Lanier, Sidney [1842-1881] .. **NCLC 6; DAM POET**
See also DLB 64; DLBD 13; MAICYA; SATA 18

Lanyer, Aemilia [1569-1645] .... **LC 10, 30**
See also DLB 121

Lao Tzu .... **CMLC 7**

Lapine, James (Elliot) [1949-] .... **CLC 39**
See also CA 123; 130; CANR 54; INT 130

Larbaud, Valery (Nicolas) [1881-1957]**TCLC 9**
See also CA 106; 152

Lardner, Ring
See Lardner, Ring(gold) W(ilmer)

Lardner, Ring W., Jr.
See Lardner, Ring(gold) W(ilmer)

Lardner, Ring(gold) W(ilmer) [1885-1933] **TCLC 2, 14**
See also CA 104; 131; CDALB 1917-1929; DLB 11, 25, 86; DLBD 16; MTCW

Laredo, Betty
See Codrescu, Andrei

Larkin, Maia
See Wojciechowska, Maia (Teresa)

Larkin, Philip (Arthur) [1922-1985]**CLC 3, 5, 8, 9, 13, 18, 33, 39, 64; DAB; DAM MST, POET; PC 21**
See also CA 5-8R; 117; CANR 24, 62; CDBLB 1960 to Present; DLB 27; MTCW

Larra (y Sanchez de Castro), Mariano Jose de [1809-1837] .... **NCLC 17**

Larsen, Eric [1941-] .... **CLC 55**
See also CA 132

Larsen, Nella [1891-1964] . **CLC 37; BLC 2; DAM MULT**
See also BW 1; CA 125; DLB 51

Larson, Charles R(aymond) [1938-] **CLC 31**
See also CA 53-56; CANR 4

Larson, Jonathan [1961-1996] .... **CLC 99**
See also CA 156

Las Casas, Bartolome de [1474-1566] **LC 31**

Lasch, Christopher [1932-1994] ..... **CLC 102**
See also CA 73-76; 144; CANR 25; MTCW

Lasker-Schueler, Else [1869-1945] **TCLC 57**
See also DLB 66, 124

Laski, Harold [1893-1950] .... **TCLC 79**

Latham, Jean Lee [1902-1995] .... **CLC 12**
See also AITN 1; CA 5-8R; CANR 7; CLR 50; MAICYA; SATA 2, 68

Latham, Mavis
See Clark, Mavis Thorpe

Lathen, Emma .... **CLC 2**
See also Hennissart, Martha; Latsis, Mary J(ane)

Lathrop, Francis
See Leiber, Fritz (Reuter, Jr.)

Latsis, Mary J(ane) [1927(?)-1997]
See Lathen, Emma
See also CA 85-88; 162

Lattimore, Richmond (Alexander) [1906-1984] **CLC 3**
See also CA 1-4R; 112; CANR 1

Laughlin, James [1914-1997] .... **CLC 49**
See also CA 21-24R; 162; CAAS 22; CANR 9, 47; DLB 48; DLBY 96, 97

Laurence, (Jean) Margaret (Wemyss) [1926-1987] **CLC 3, 6, 13, 50, 62; DAC; DAM**

Macdonald, Ross .... **CLC 1, 2, 3, 14, 34, 41**
See also Millar, Kenneth
See also DLBD 6
MacDougal, John
See Blish, James (Benjamin)
MacEwen, Gwendolyn (Margaret) [1941-1987]
CLC 13, 55
See also CA 9-12R; 124; CANR 7, 22; DLB
53; SATA 50; SATA-Obit 55
Macha, Karel Hynek [1810-1846] . **NCLC 46**
Machado (y Ruiz), Antonio [1875-1939]
TCLC 3
See also CA 104; DLB 108
Machado de Assis, Joaquim Maria [1839-1908]
TCLC 10; BLC 2; SSC 24
See also CA 107; 153
Machen, Arthur .... **TCLC 4; SSC 20**
See also Jones, Arthur Llewellyn
See also DLB 36, 156, 178
Machiavelli, Niccolo [1469-1527] .. **LC 8, 36;**
DA; DAB; DAC; DAM MST; WLCS
MacInnes, Colin [1914-1976] .... **CLC 4, 23**
See also CA 69-72; 65-68; CANR 21; DLB 14;
MTCW
MacInnes, Helen (Clark) [1907-1985] **CLC 27,**
39; DAM POP
See also CA 1-4R; 117; CANR 1, 28, 58; DLB
87; MTCW; SATA 22; SATA-Obit 44
Mackay, Mary [1855-1924]
See Corelli, Marie
See also CA 118
Mackenzie, Compton (Edward Montague)
[1883-1972] ....
CLC 18
See also CA 21-22; 37-40R; CAP 2; DLB 34,
100
Mackenzie, Henry [1745-1831] ...... **NCLC 41**
See also DLB 39
Mackintosh, Elizabeth [1896(?)-1952]
See Tey, Josephine
See also CA 110
MacLaren, James
See Grieve, C(hristopher) M(urray)
Mac Laverty, Bernard [1942-] .... **CLC 31**
See also CA 116; 118; CANR 43; INT 118
MacLean, Alistair (Stuart) [1922(?)-1987]
CLC 3, 13, 50, 63; DAM POP
See also CA 57-60; 121; CANR 28, 61; MTCW;
SATA 23; SATA-Obit 50
Maclean, Norman (Fitzroy) [1902-1990] **C L C**
78; DAM POP; SSC 13
See also CA 102; 132; CANR 49
MacLeish, Archibald [1892-1982] . **CLC 3, 8,**
14, 68; DAM POET
See also CA 9-12R; 106; CANR 33, 63; DLB
4, 7, 45; DLBY 82; MTCW
MacLennan, (John) Hugh [1907-1990] **CLC 2,**
14, 92; DAC; DAM MST
See also CA 5-8R; 142; CANR 33; DLB 68;
MTCW
MacLeod, Alistair [1936-] .... **CLC 56; DAC;**
DAM MST
See also CA 123; DLB 60
Macleod, Fiona
See Sharp, William
MacNeice, (Frederick) Louis [1907-1963]
CLC 1, 4, 10, 53; DAB; DAM POET
See also CA 85-88; CANR 61; DLB 10, 20;
MTCW
MacNeill, Dand
See Fraser, George MacDonald
Macpherson, James [1736-1796] .... **LC 29**
See also Ossian
See also DLB 109
Macpherson, (Jean) Jay [1931-] .... **CLC 14**
See also CA 5-8R; DLB 53
MacShane, Frank [1927-] .... **CLC 39**

See also CA 9-12R; CANR 3, 33; DLB 111
Macumber, Mari
See Sandoz, Mari(e Susette)
Madach, Imre [1823-1864] .... **NCLC 19**
Madden, (Jerry) David [1933-] ..... **CLC 5, 15**
See also CA 1-4R; CAAS 3; CANR 4, 45; DLB
6; MTCW
Maddern, Al(an)
See Ellison, Harlan (Jay)
Madhubuti, Haki R. [1942-] **CLC 6, 73; BLC**
2; DAM MULT, POET; PC 5
See also Lee, Don L.
See also BW 2; CA 73-76; CANR 24, 51; DLB
5, 41; DLBD 8
Maepenn, Hugh
See Kuttner, Henry
Maepenn, K. H.
See Kuttner, Henry
Maeterlinck, Maurice [1862-1949] . **TCLC 3;**
DAM DRAM
See also CA 104; 136; DLB 192; SATA 66
Maginn, William [1794-1842] .... **NCLC 8**
See also DLB 110, 159
Mahapatra, Jayanta [1928-] . **CLC 33; DAM**
MULT
See also CA 73-76; CAAS 9; CANR 15, 33, 66
Mahfouz, Naguib (Abdel Aziz Al-Sabilgi)
[1911(?)-]
See Mahfuz, Najib
See also BEST 89:2; CA 128; CANR 55; DAM
NOV; MTCW
Mahfuz, Najib .... **CLC 52, 55**
See also Mahfouz, Naguib (Abdel Aziz Al-
Sabilgi)
See also DLBY 88
Mahon, Derek [1941-] .... **CLC 27**
See also CA 113; 128; DLB 40
Mailer, Norman [1923-] **CLC 1, 2, 3, 4, 5, 8, 11,**
14, 28, 39, 74, 111; DA; DAB; DAC; DAM
MST, NOV, POP
See also AITN 2; CA 9-12R; CABS 1; CANR
28; CDALB 1968-1988; DLB 2, 16, 28, 185;
DLBD 3; DLBY 80, 83; MTCW
Maillet, Antonine [1929-] .... **CLC 54; DAC**
See also CA 115; 120; CANR 46; DLB 60; INT
120
Mais, Roger [1905-1955] .... **TCLC 8**
See also BW 1; CA 105; 124; DLB 125; MTCW
Maistre, Joseph de [1753-1821] ..... **NCLC 37**
Maitland, Frederic [1850-1906] ..... **TCLC 65**
Maitland, Sara (Louise) [1950-] .... **CLC 49**
See also CA 69-72; CANR 13, 59
Major, Clarence [1936-] **CLC 3, 19, 48; BLC 2;**
DAM MULT
See also BW 2; CA 21-24R; CAAS 6; CANR
13, 25, 53; DLB 33
Major, Kevin (Gerald) [1949-] **CLC 26; DAC**
See also AAYA 16; CA 97-100; CANR 21, 38;
CLR 11; DLB 60; INT CANR-21; JRDA;
MAICYA; SATA 32, 82
Maki, James
See Ozu, Yasujiro
Malabaila, Damiano
See Levi, Primo
Malamud, Bernard [1914-1986] **CLC 1, 2, 3, 5,**
8, 9, 11, 18, 27, 44, 78, 85; DA; DAB; DAC;
DAM MST, NOV, POP; SSC 15; WLC
See also AAYA 16; CA 5-8R; 118; CABS 1;
CANR 28, 62; CDALB 1941-1968; DLB 2,
28, 152; DLBY 80, 86; MTCW
Malan, Herman
See Bosman, Herman Charles; Bosman, Herman
Charles
Malaparte, Curzio [1898-1957] ..... **TCLC 52**
Malcolm, Dan
See Silverberg, Robert
Malcolm X .... **CLC 82; BLC 2; WLCS**

See also Little, Malcolm
Malherbe, Francois de [1555-1628] ...... **LC 5**
Mallarme, Stephane [1842-1898] **NCLC 4, 41;**
DAM POET; PC 4
Mallet-Joris, Francoise [1930-] .... **CLC 11**
See also CA 65-68; CANR 17; DLB 83
Malley, Ern
See McAuley, James Phillip
Mallowan, Agatha Christie
See Christie, Agatha (Mary Clarissa)
Maloff, Saul [1922-] .... **CLC 5**
See also CA 33-36R
Malone, Louis
See MacNeice, (Frederick) Louis
Malone, Michael (Christopher) [1942-] **C L C**
43
See also CA 77-80; CANR 14, 32, 57
Malory, (Sir) Thomas [1410(?)-1471(?)] .. **L C**
11; DA; DAB; DAC; DAM MST; WLCS
See also CDBLB Before 1660; DLB 146; SATA
59; SATA-Brief 33
Malouf, (George Joseph) David [1934-] **C L C**
28, 86
See also CA 124; CANR 50
Malraux, (Georges-)Andre [1901-1976] **C L C**
1, 4, 9, 13, 15, 57; DAM NOV
See also CA 21-22; 69-72; CANR 34, 58; CAP
2; DLB 72; MTCW
Malzberg, Barry N(athaniel) [1939-] . **CLC 7**
See also CA 61-64; CAAS 4; CANR 16; DLB
8
Mamet, David (Alan) [1947-] **CLC 9, 15, 34,**
46, 91; DAM DRAM; DC 4
See also AAYA 3; CA 81-84; CABS 3; CANR
15, 41, 67; DLB 7; MTCW
Mamoulian, Rouben (Zachary) [1897-1987]
CLC 16
See also CA 25-28R; 124
Mandelstam, Osip (Emilievich) [1891(?)-
1938(?)] ....
TCLC 2, 6; PC 14
See also CA 104; 150
Mander, (Mary) Jane [1877-1949] **TCLC 31**
See also CA 162
Mandeville, John [fl. 1350-] .... **CMLC 19**
See also DLB 146
Mandiargues, Andre Pieyre de .... **CLC 41**
See also Pieyre de Mandiargues, Andre
See also DLB 83
Mandrake, Ethel Belle
See Thurman, Wallace (Henry)
Mangan, James Clarence [1803-1849] **N C L C**
27
Maniere, J.-E.
See Giraudoux, (Hippolyte) Jean
Manley, (Mary) Delariviere [1672(?)-1724]
LC 1
See also DLB 39, 80
Mann, Abel
See Creasey, John
Mann, Emily [1952-] .... **DC 7**
See also CA 130; CANR 55
Mann, (Luiz) Heinrich [1871-1950] **TCLC 9**
See also CA 106; 164; DLB 66
Mann, (Paul) Thomas [1875-1955] **TCLC 2, 8,**
14, 21, 35, 44, 60; DA; DAB; DAC; DAM
MST, NOV; SSC 5; WLC
See also CA 104; 128; DLB 66; MTCW
Mannheim, Karl [1893-1947] .... **TCLC 65**
Manning, David
See Faust, Frederick (Schiller)
Manning, Frederic [1887(?)-1935] **TCLC 25**
See also CA 124
Manning, Olivia [1915-1980] .... **CLC 5, 19**
See also CA 5-8R; 101; CANR 29; MTCW
Mano, D. Keith [1942-] .... **CLC 2, 10**
See also CA 25-28R; CAAS 6; CANR 26, 57;

Maupassant, (Henri Rene Albert) Guy de [1850-1893] ....
NCLC 1, 42; DA; DAB; DAC; DAM MST; SSC 1; WLC
See also DLB 123

Maupin, Armistead [1944-] ... **CLC 95; DAM POP**
See also CA 125; 130; CANR 58; INT 130

Maurhut, Richard
See Traven, B.

Mauriac, Claude [1914-1996] .... **CLC 9**
See also CA 89-92; 152; DLB 83

Mauriac, Francois (Charles) [1885-1970] **CLC 4, 9, 56; SSC 24**
See also CA 25-28; CAP 2; DLB 65; MTCW

Mavor, Osborne Henry [1888-1951]
See Bridie, James
See also CA 104

Maxwell, William (Keepers, Jr.) [1908-]**C L C 19**
See also CA 93-96; CANR 54; DLBY 80; INT 93-96

May, Elaine [1932-] .... **CLC 16**
See also CA 124; 142; DLB 44

Mayakovski, Vladimir (Vladimirovich) [1893-1930] ....
TCLC 4, 18
See also CA 104; 158

Mayhew, Henry [1812-1887] .... **NCLC 31**
See also DLB 18, 55, 190

Mayle, Peter [1939(?)-] .... **CLC 89**
See also CA 139; CANR 64

Maynard, Joyce [1953-] .... **CLC 23**
See also CA 111; 129; CANR 64

Mayne, William (James Carter) [1928-]**C L C 12**
See also AAYA 20; CA 9-12R; CANR 37; CLR 25; JRDA; MAICYA; SAAS 11; SATA 6, 68

Mayo, Jim
See L'Amour, Louis (Dearborn)

Maysles, Albert [1926-] .... **CLC 16**
See also CA 29-32R

Maysles, David [1932-] .... **CLC 16**
See also CA 165

Mazer, Norma Fox [1931-] .... **CLC 26**
See also AAYA 5; CA 69-72; CANR 12, 32, 66; CLR 23; JRDA; MAICYA; SAAS 1; SATA 24, 67

Mazzini, Guiseppe [1805-1872] ..... **NCLC 34**

McAuley, James Phillip [1917-1976] **CLC 45**
See also CA 97-100

McBain, Ed
See Hunter, Evan

McBrien, William Augustine [1930-]**CLC 44**
See also CA 107

McCaffrey, Anne (Inez) [1926-]**CLC 17; DAM NOV, POP**
See also AAYA 6; AITN 2; BEST 89:2; CA 25-28R; CANR 15, 35, 55; CLR 49; DLB 8; JRDA; MAICYA; MTCW; SAAS 11; SATA 8, 70

McCall, Nathan [1955(?)-] .... **CLC 86**
See also CA 146

McCann, Arthur
See Campbell, John W(ood, Jr.)

McCann, Edson
See Pohl, Frederik

McCarthy, Charles, Jr. [1933-]
See McCarthy, Cormac
See also CANR 42, 69; DAM POP

McCarthy, Cormac [1933-]**CLC 4, 57, 59, 101**
See also McCarthy, Charles, Jr.
See also DLB 6, 143

McCarthy, Mary (Therese) [1912-1989]**C L C 1, 3, 5, 14, 24, 39, 59; SSC 24**
See also CA 5-8R; 129; CANR 16, 50, 64; DLB 2; DLBY 81; INT CANR-16; MTCW

McCartney, (James) Paul [1942-]**CLC 12, 35**

See also CA 146

McCauley, Stephen (D.) [1955-] .... **CLC 50**
See also CA 141

McClure, Michael (Thomas) [1932-] . **CLC 6, 10**
See also CA 21-24R; CANR 17, 46; DLB 16

McCorkle, Jill (Collins) [1958-] .... **CLC 51**
See also CA 121; DLBY 87

McCourt, Frank [1930-] .... **CLC 109**
See also CA 157

McCourt, James [1941-] .... **CLC 5**
See also CA 57-60

McCoy, Horace (Stanley) [1897-1955]**T C L C 28**
See also CA 108; 155; DLB 9

McCrae, John [1872-1918] .... **TCLC 12**
See also CA 109; DLB 92

McCreigh, James
See Pohl, Frederik

McCullers, (Lula) Carson (Smith) [1917-1967] **CLC 1, 4, 10, 12, 48, 100; DA; DAB; DAC; DAM MST, NOV; SSC 9, 24; WLC**
See also AAYA 21; CA 5-8R; 25-28R; CABS 1, 3; CANR 18; CDALB 1941-1968; DLB 2, 7, 173; MTCW; SATA 27

McCulloch, John Tyler
See Burroughs, Edgar Rice

McCullough, Colleen [1938(?)-]**CLC 27, 107; DAM NOV, POP**
See also CA 81-84; CANR 17, 46, 67; MTCW

McDermott, Alice [1953-] .... **CLC 90**
See also CA 109; CANR 40

McElroy, Joseph [1930-] .... **CLC 5, 47**
See also CA 17-20R

McEwan, Ian (Russell) [1948-] . **CLC 13, 66; DAM NOV**
See also BEST 90:4; CA 61-64; CANR 14, 41, 69; DLB 14, 194; MTCW

McFadden, David [1940-] .... **CLC 48**
See also CA 104; DLB 60; INT 104

McFarland, Dennis [1950-] .... **CLC 65**
See also CA 165

McGahern, John [1934-]**CLC 5, 9, 48; SSC 17**
See also CA 17-20R; CANR 29, 68; DLB 14; MTCW

McGinley, Patrick (Anthony) [1937-]**CLC 41**
See also CA 120; 127; CANR 56; INT 127

McGinley, Phyllis [1905-1978] .... **CLC 14**
See also CA 9-12R; 77-80; CANR 19; DLB 11, 48; SATA 2, 44; SATA-Obit 24

McGinniss, Joe [1942-] .... **CLC 32**
See also AITN 2; BEST 89:2; CA 25-28R; CANR 26; DLB 185; INT CANR-26

McGivern, Maureen Daly
See Daly, Maureen

McGrath, Patrick [1950-] .... **CLC 55**
See also CA 136; CANR 65

McGrath, Thomas (Matthew) [1916-1990] **CLC 28, 59; DAM POET**
See also CA 9-12R; 132; CANR 6, 33; MTCW; SATA 41; SATA-Obit 66

McGuane, Thomas (Francis III) [1939-]**C L C 3, 7, 18, 45**
See also AITN 2; CA 49-52; CANR 5, 24, 49; DLB 2; DLBY 80; INT CANR-24; MTCW

McGuckian, Medbh [1950-] .. **CLC 48; DAM POET**
See also CA 143; DLB 40

McHale, Tom [1942(?)-1982] .... **CLC 3, 5**
See also AITN 1; CA 77-80; 106

McIlvanney, William [1936-] .... **CLC 42**
See also CA 25-28R; CANR 61; DLB 14

McIlwraith, Maureen Mollie Hunter
See Hunter, Mollie
See also SATA 2

McInerney, Jay [1955-] . **CLC 34, 112; DAM POP**

See also AAYA 18; CA 116; 123; CANR 45, 68; INT 123

McIntyre, Vonda N(eel) [1948-] .... **CLC 18**
See also CA 81-84; CANR 17, 34, 69; MTCW

McKay, Claude**TCLC 7, 41; BLC 3; DAB; PC 2**
See also McKay, Festus Claudius
See also DLB 4, 45, 51, 117

McKay, Festus Claudius [1889-1948]
See McKay, Claude
See also BW 1; CA 104; 124; DA; DAC; DAM MST, MULT, NOV, POET; MTCW; WLC

McKuen, Rod [1933-] .... **CLC 1, 3**
See also AITN 1; CA 41-44R; CANR 40

McLoughlin, R. B.
See Mencken, H(enry) L(ouis)

McLuhan, (Herbert) Marshall [1911-1980] **CLC 37, 83**
See also CA 9-12R; 102; CANR 12, 34, 61; DLB 88; INT CANR-12; MTCW

McMillan, Terry (L.) [1951-]**CLC 50, 61, 112; BLCS; DAM MULT, NOV, POP**
See also AAYA 21; BW 2; CA 140; CANR 60

McMurtry, Larry (Jeff) [1936-] **CLC 2, 3, 7, 11, 27, 44; DAM NOV, POP**
See also AAYA 15; AITN 2; BEST 89:2; CA 5-8R; CANR 19, 43, 64; CDALB 1968-1988; DLB 2, 143; DLBY 80, 87; MTCW

McNally, T. M. [1961-] .... **CLC 82**

McNally, Terrence [1939-] . **CLC 4, 7, 41, 91; DAM DRAM**
See also CA 45-48; CANR 2, 56; DLB 7

McNamer, Deirdre [1950-] .... **CLC 70**

McNeile, Herman Cyril [1888-1937]
See Sapper
See also DLB 77

McNickle, (William) D'Arcy [1904-1977]**CLC 89; DAM MULT**
See also CA 9-12R; 85-88; CANR 5, 45; DLB 175; NNAL; SATA-Obit 22

McPhee, John (Angus) [1931-] .... **CLC 36**
See also BEST 90:1; CA 65-68; CANR 20, 46, 64, 69; DLB 185; MTCW

McPherson, James Alan [1943-]**CLC 19, 77; BLCS**
See also BW 1; CA 25-28R; CAAS 17; CANR 24; DLB 38; MTCW

McPherson, William (Alexander) [1933-]**CLC 34**
See also CA 69-72; CANR 28; INT CANR-28

Mead, Margaret [1901-1978] .... **CLC 37**
See also AITN 1; CA 1-4R; 81-84; CANR 4; MTCW; SATA-Obit 20

Meaker, Marijane (Agnes) [1927-]
See Kerr, M. E.
See also CA 107; CANR 37, 63; INT 107; JRDA; MAICYA; MTCW; SATA 20, 61

Medoff, Mark (Howard) [1940-] **CLC 6, 23; DAM DRAM**
See also AITN 1; CA 53-56; CANR 5; DLB 7; INT CANR-5

Medvedev, P. N.
See Bakhtin, Mikhail Mikhailovich

Meged, Aharon
See Megged, Aharon

Meged, Aron
See Megged, Aharon

Megged, Aharon [1920-] .... **CLC 9**
See also CA 49-52; CAAS 13; CANR 1

Mehta, Ved (Parkash) [1934-] .... **CLC 37**
See also CA 1-4R; CANR 2, 23, 69; MTCW

Melanter
See Blackmore, R(ichard) D(oddridge)

Melies, Georges [1861-1938] .... **TCLC 81**

Melikow, Loris
See Hofmannsthal, Hugo von

Melmoth, Sebastian

Miyamoto, Yuriko [1899-1951] ...... **TCLC 37**
See also DLB 180
Miyazawa, Kenji [1896-1933] .... **TCLC 76**
See also CA 157
Mizoguchi, Kenji [1898-1956] .... **TCLC 72**
See also CA 157
Mo, Timothy (Peter) [1950(?)-] .... **CLC 46**
See also CA 117; DLB 194; MTCW
Modarressi, Taghi (M.) [1931-] .... **CLC 44**
See also CA 121; 134; INT 134
Modiano, Patrick (Jean) [1945-] ...... **CLC 18**
See also CA 85-88; CANR 17, 40; DLB 83
Moerck, Paal
See Roelvaag, O(le) E(dvart)
Mofolo, Thomas (Mokopu) [1875(?)-1948]
TCLC 22; BLC 3; DAM MULT
See also CA 121; 153
Mohr, Nicholasa [1938-] .... **CLC 12; DAM
MULT; HLC**
See also AAYA 8; CA 49-52; CANR 1, 32, 64;
CLR 22; DLB 145; HW; JRDA; SAAS 8;
SATA 8, 97
Mojtabai, A(nn) G(race) [1938-]**CLC 5, 9, 15,
29**
See also CA 85-88
Moliere [1622-1673]**LC 28; DA; DAB; DAC;
DAM DRAM, MST; WLC**
Molin, Charles
See Mayne, William (James Carter)
Molnar, Ferenc [1878-1952]**TCLC 20; DAM
DRAM**
See also CA 109; 153
Momaday, N(avarre) Scott [1934-]**CLC 2, 19,
85, 95; DA; DAB; DAC; DAM MST,
MULT, NOV, POP; WLCS**
See also AAYA 11; CA 25-28R; CANR 14, 34,
68; DLB 143, 175; INT CANR-14; MTCW;
NNAL; SATA 48; SATA-Brief 30
Monette, Paul [1945-1995] .... **CLC 82**
See also CA 139; 147
Monroe, Harriet [1860-1936] .... **TCLC 12**
See also CA 109; DLB 54, 91
Monroe, Lyle
See Heinlein, Robert A(nson)
Montagu, Elizabeth [1917-] .... **NCLC 7**
See also CA 9-12R
Montagu, Mary (Pierrepont) Wortley [1689-
1762] .... **LC 9; PC 16**
See also DLB 95, 101
Montagu, W. H.
See Coleridge, Samuel Taylor
Montague, John (Patrick) [1929-]**CLC 13, 46**
See also CA 9-12R; CANR 9, 69; DLB 40;
MTCW
Montaigne, Michel (Eyquem) de [1533-1592]
LC 8; DA; DAB; DAC; DAM MST; WLC
Montale, Eugenio [1896-1981] **CLC 7, 9, 18;
PC 13**
See also CA 17-20R; 104; CANR 30; DLB 114;
MTCW
Montesquieu, Charles-Louis de Secondat
[1689-1755] .... **LC 7**
Montgomery, (Robert) Bruce [1921-1978]
See Crispin, Edmund
See also CA 104
Montgomery, L(ucy) M(aud) [1874-1942]
TCLC 51; DAC; DAM MST
See also AAYA 12; CA 108; 137; CLR 8; DLB
92; DLBD 14; JRDA; MAICYA; YABC 1
Montgomery, Marion H., Jr. [1925-] . **CLC 7**
See also AITN 1; CA 1-4R; CANR 3, 48; DLB
6
Montgomery, Max
See Davenport, Guy (Mattison, Jr.)
Montherlant, Henry (Milon) de [1896-1972]
CLC 8, 19; DAM DRAM
See also CA 85-88; 37-40R; DLB 72; MTCW
Monty Python

See Chapman, Graham; Cleese, John
(Marwood); Gilliam, Terry (Vance); Idle,
Eric; Jones, Terence Graham Parry; Palin,
Michael (Edward)
See also AAYA 7
Moodie, Susanna (Strickland) [1803-1885]
NCLC 14
See also DLB 99
Mooney, Edward [1951-]
See Mooney, Ted
See also CA 130
Mooney, Ted .... **CLC 25**
See also Mooney, Edward
Moorcock, Michael (John) [1939-]**CLC 5, 27,
58**
See also CA 45-48; CAAS 5; CANR 2, 17, 38,
64; DLB 14; MTCW; SATA 93
Moore, Brian [1921-]**CLC 1, 3, 5, 7, 8, 19, 32,
90; DAB; DAC; DAM MST**
See also CA 1-4R; CANR 1, 25, 42, 63; MTCW
Moore, Edward
See Muir, Edwin
Moore, George Augustus [1852-1933] **TCLC
7; SSC 19**
See also CA 104; DLB 10, 18, 57, 135
Moore, Lorrie .... **CLC 39, 45, 68**
See also Moore, Marie Lorena
Moore, Marianne (Craig) [1887-1972]**CLC 1,
2, 4, 8, 10, 13, 19, 47; DA; DAB; DAC;
DAM MST, POET; PC 4; WLCS**
See also CA 1-4R; 33-36R; CANR 3, 61;
CDALB 1929-1941; DLB 45; DLBD 7;
MTCW; SATA 20
Moore, Marie Lorena [1957-]
See Moore, Lorrie
See also CA 116; CANR 39
Moore, Thomas [1779-1852] .... **NCLC 6**
See also DLB 96, 144
Morand, Paul [1888-1976] . **CLC 41; SSC 22**
See also CA 69-72; DLB 65
Morante, Elsa [1918-1985] .... **CLC 8, 47**
See also CA 85-88; 117; CANR 35; DLB 177;
MTCW
Moravia, Alberto [1907-1990]**CLC 2, 7, 11, 27,
46; SSC 26**
See also Pincherle, Alberto
See also DLB 177
More, Hannah [1745-1833] .... **NCLC 27**
See also DLB 107, 109, 116, 158
More, Henry [1614-1687] .... **LC 9**
See also DLB 126
More, Sir Thomas [1478-1535] ..... **LC 10, 32**
Moreas, Jean .... **TCLC 18**
See also Papadiamantopoulos, Johannes
Morgan, Berry [1919-] .... **CLC 6**
See also CA 49-52; DLB 6
Morgan, Claire
See Highsmith, (Mary) Patricia
Morgan, Edwin (George) [1920-] ..... **CLC 31**
See also CA 5-8R; CANR 3, 43; DLB 27
Morgan, (George) Frederick [1922-] **CLC 23**
See also CA 17-20R; CANR 21
Morgan, Harriet
See Mencken, H(enry) L(ouis)
Morgan, Jane
See Cooper, James Fenimore
Morgan, Janet [1945-] .... **CLC 39**
See also CA 65-68
Morgan, Lady [1776(?)-1859] .... **NCLC 29**
See also DLB 116, 158
Morgan, Robin (Evonne) [1941-] .... **CLC 2**
See also CA 69-72; CANR 29, 68; MTCW;
SATA 80
Morgan, Scott
See Kuttner, Henry
Morgan, Seth [1949(?)-1990] .... **CLC 65**
See also CA 132

Morgenstern, Christian [1871-1914]**TCLC 8**
See also CA 105
Morgenstern, S.
See Goldman, William (W.)
Moricz, Zsigmond [1879-1942] ...... **TCLC 33**
See also CA 165
Morike, Eduard (Friedrich) [1804-1875]
NCLC 10
See also DLB 133
Moritz, Karl Philipp [1756-1793] .... **LC 2**
See also DLB 94
Morland, Peter Henry
See Faust, Frederick (Schiller)
Morren, Theophil
See Hofmannsthal, Hugo von
Morris, Bill [1952-] .... **CLC 76**
Morris, Julian
See West, Morris L(anglo)
Morris, Steveland Judkins [1950(?)-]
See Wonder, Stevie
See also CA 111
Morris, William [1834-1896] .... **NCLC 4**
See also CDBLB 1832-1890; DLB 18, 35, 57,
156, 178, 184
Morris, Wright [1910-] ... **CLC 1, 3, 7, 18, 37**
See also CA 9-12R; CANR 21; DLB 2; DLBY
81; MTCW
Morrison, Arthur [1863-1945] .... **TCLC 72**
See also CA 120; 157; DLB 70, 135, 197
Morrison, Chloe Anthony Wofford
See Morrison, Toni
Morrison, James Douglas [1943-1971]
See Morrison, Jim
See also CA 73-76; CANR 40
Morrison, Jim .... **CLC 17**
See also Morrison, James Douglas
Morrison, Toni [1931-]**CLC 4, 10, 22, 55, 81,
87; BLC 3; DA; DAB; DAC; DAM MST,
MULT, NOV, POP**
See also AAYA 1, 22; BW 2; CA 29-32R;
CANR 27, 42, 67; CDALB 1968-1988; DLB
6, 33, 143; DLBY 81; MTCW; SATA 57
Morrison, Van [1945-] .... **CLC 21**
See also CA 116
Morrissy, Mary [1958-] .... **CLC 99**
Mortimer, John (Clifford) [1923-]**CLC 28, 43;
DAM DRAM, POP**
See also CA 13-16R; CANR 21, 69; CDBLB
1960 to Present; DLB 13; INT CANR-21;
MTCW
Mortimer, Penelope (Ruth) [1918-] .... **CLC 5**
See also CA 57-60; CANR 45
Morton, Anthony
See Creasey, John
Mosca, Gaetano [1858-1941] .... **TCLC 75**
Mosher, Howard Frank [1943-] .... **CLC 62**
See also CA 139; CANR 65
Mosley, Nicholas [1923-] .... **CLC 43, 70**
See also CA 69-72; CANR 41, 60; DLB 14
Mosley, Walter [1952-]**CLC 97; BLCS; DAM
MULT, POP**
See also AAYA 17; BW 2; CA 142; CANR 57
Moss, Howard [1922-1987]**CLC 7, 14, 45, 50;
DAM POET**
See also CA 1-4R; 123; CANR 1, 44; DLB 5
Mossgiel, Rab
See Burns, Robert
Motion, Andrew (Peter) [1952-] .... **CLC 47**
See also CA 146; DLB 40
Motley, Willard (Francis) [1909-1965]**CLC 18**
See also BW 1; CA 117; 106; DLB 76, 143
Motoori, Norinaga [1730-1801] ..... **NCLC 45**
Mott, Michael (Charles Alston) [1930-] **C L C
15, 34**
See also CA 5-8R; CAAS 7; CANR 7, 29
Mountain Wolf Woman [1884-1960] **CLC 92**
See also CA 144; NNAL

See also CA 41-44R; CANR 14; JRDA; SATA 5, 77

Nexo, Martin Andersen [1869-1954]**TCLC 43**

Nezval, Vitezslav [1900-1958] .... **TCLC 44**
See also CA 123

Ng, Fae Myenne [1957(?)-] .... **CLC 81**
See also CA 146

Ngema, Mbongeni [1955-] .... **CLC 57**
See also BW 2; CA 143

Ngugi, James T(hiong'o) .... **CLC 3, 7, 13**
See also Ngugi wa Thiong'o

Ngugi wa Thiong'o [1938-] **CLC 36; BLC 3; DAM MULT, NOV**
See also Ngugi, James T(hiong'o)
See also BW 2; CA 81-84; CANR 27, 58; DLB 125; MTCW

Nichol, B(arrie) P(hillip) [1944-1988]**CLC 18**
See also CA 53-56; DLB 53; SATA 66

Nichols, John (Treadwell) [1940-] .... **CLC 38**
See also CA 9-12R; CAAS 2; CANR 6; DLBY 82

Nichols, Leigh
See Koontz, Dean R(ay)

Nichols, Peter (Richard) [1927-]**CLC 5, 36, 65**
See also CA 104; CANR 33; DLB 13; MTCW

Nicolas, F. R. E.
See Freeling, Nicolas

Niedecker, Lorine [1903-1970] .. **CLC 10, 42; DAM POET**
See also CA 25-28; CAP 2; DLB 48

Nietzsche, Friedrich (Wilhelm) [1844-1900] **TCLC 10, 18, 55**
See also CA 107; 121; DLB 129

Nievo, Ippolito [1831-1861] .... **NCLC 22**

Nightingale, Anne Redmon [1943-]
See Redmon, Anne
See also CA 103

Nik. T. O.
See Annensky, Innokenty (Fyodorovich)

Nin, Anais [1903-1977]**CLC 1, 4, 8, 11, 14, 60; DAM NOV, POP; SSC 10**
See also AITN 2; CA 13-16R; 69-72; CANR 22, 53; DLB 2, 4, 152; MTCW

Nishida, Kitaro [1870-1945] .... **TCLC 83**

Nishiwaki, Junzaburo [1894-1982] ..... **PC 15**
See also CA 107

Nissenson, Hugh [1933-] .... **CLC 4, 9**
See also CA 17-20R; CANR 27; DLB 28

Niven, Larry .... **CLC 8**
See also Niven, Laurence Van Cott
See also DLB 8

Niven, Laurence Van Cott [1938-]
See Niven, Larry
See also CA 21-24R; CAAS 12; CANR 14, 44, 66; DAM POP; MTCW; SATA 95

Nixon, Agnes Eckhardt [1927-] .... **CLC 21**
See also CA 110

Nizan, Paul [1905-1940]................. **TCLC 40**
See also CA 161; DLB 72

Nkosi, Lewis [1936-] . **CLC 45; BLC 3; DAM MULT**
See also BW 1; CA 65-68; CANR 27; DLB 157

Nodier, (Jean) Charles (Emmanuel) [1780-1844] .... **NCLC 19**
See also DLB 119

Noguchi, Yone [1875-1947] .... **TCLC 80**

Nolan, Christopher [1965-] .... **CLC 58**
See also CA 111

Noon, Jeff [1957-] .... **CLC 91**
See also CA 148

Norden, Charles
See Durrell, Lawrence (George)

Nordhoff, Charles (Bernard) [1887-1947] **TCLC 23**
See also CA 108; DLB 9; SATA 23

Norfolk, Lawrence [1963-] .... **CLC 76**
See also CA 144

Norman, Marsha [1947-] .... **CLC 28; DAM DRAM; DC 8**
See also CA 105; CABS 3; CANR 41; DLBY 84

Normyx
See Douglas, (George) Norman

Norris, Frank [1870-1902] .... **SSC 28**
See also Norris, (Benjamin) Frank(lin, Jr.)
See also CDALB 1865-1917; DLB 12, 71, 186

Norris, (Benjamin) Frank(lin, Jr.) [1870-1902] **TCLC 24**
See also Norris, Frank
See also CA 110; 160

Norris, Leslie [1921-] .... **CLC 14**
See also CA 11-12; CANR 14; CAP 1; DLB 27

North, Andrew
See Norton, Andre

North, Anthony
See Koontz, Dean R(ay)

North, Captain George
See Stevenson, Robert Louis (Balfour)

North, Milou
See Erdrich, Louise

Northrup, B. A.
See Hubbard, L(afayette) Ron(ald)

North Staffs
See Hulme, T(homas) E(rnest)

Norton, Alice Mary
See Norton, Andre
See also MAICYA; SATA 1, 43

Norton, Andre [1912-] .... **CLC 12**
See also Norton, Alice Mary
See also AAYA 14; CA 1-4R; CANR 68; CLR 50; DLB 8, 52; JRDA; MTCW; SATA 91

Norton, Caroline [1808-1877] .... **NCLC 47**
See also DLB 21, 159, 199

Norway, Nevil Shute [1899-1960]
See Shute, Nevil
See also CA 102; 93-96

Norwid, Cyprian Kamil [1821-1883]**NCLC 17**

Nosille, Nabrah
See Ellison, Harlan (Jay)

Nossack, Hans Erich [1901-1978] .... **CLC 6**
See also CA 93-96; 85-88; DLB 69

Nostradamus [1503-1566]..................... **LC 27**

Nosu, Chuji
See Ozu, Yasujiro

Notenburg, Eleanora (Genrikhovna) von
See Guro, Elena

Nova, Craig [1945-] .... **CLC 7, 31**
See also CA 45-48; CANR 2, 53

Novak, Joseph
See Kosinski, Jerzy (Nikodem)

Novalis [1772-1801] .... **NCLC 13**
See also DLB 90

Novis, Emile
See Weil, Simone (Adolphine)

Nowlan, Alden (Albert) [1933-1983]**CLC 15; DAC; DAM MST**
See also CA 9-12R; CANR 5; DLB 53

Noyes, Alfred [1880-1958] .... **TCLC 7**
See also CA 104; DLB 20

Nunn, Kem .... **CLC 34**
See also CA 159

Nye, Robert [1939-] **CLC 13, 42; DAM NOV**
See also CA 33-36R; CANR 29, 67; DLB 14; MTCW; SATA 6

Nyro, Laura [1947-] .... **CLC 17**

Oates, Joyce Carol [1938-]**CLC 1, 2, 3, 6, 9, 11, 15, 19, 33, 52, 108; DA; DAB; DAC; DAM MST, NOV, POP; SSC 6; WLC**
See also AAYA 15; AITN 1; BEST 89:2; CA 5-8R; CANR 25, 45; CDALB 1968-1988; DLB 2, 5, 130; DLBY 81; INT CANR-25; MTCW

O'Brien, Darcy [1939-] .... **CLC 11**
See also CA 21-24R; CANR 8, 59

O'Brien, E. G.

See Clarke, Arthur C(harles)

O'Brien, Edna [1936-]**CLC 3, 5, 8, 13, 36, 65; DAM NOV; SSC 10**
See also CA 1-4R; CANR 6, 41, 65; CDBLB 1960 to Present; DLB 14; MTCW

O'Brien, Fitz-James [1828-1862] .. **NCLC 21**
See also DLB 74

O'Brien, Flann .... **CLC 1, 4, 5, 7, 10, 47**
See also O Nuallain, Brian

O'Brien, Richard [1942-] .... **CLC 17**
See also CA 124

O'Brien, (William) Tim(othy) [1946-]**CLC 7, 19, 40, 103; DAM POP**
See also AAYA 16; CA 85-88; CANR 40, 58; DLB 152; DLBD 9; DLBY 80

Obstfelder, Sigbjoern [1866-1900] **TCLC 23**
See also CA 123

O'Casey, Sean [1880-1964]**CLC 1, 5, 9, 11, 15, 88; DAB; DAC; DAM DRAM, MST; WLCS**
See also CA 89-92; CANR 62; CDBLB 1914-1945; DLB 10; MTCW

O'Cathasaigh, Sean
See O'Casey, Sean

Ochs, Phil [1940-1976] .... **CLC 17**
See also CA 65-68

O'Connor, Edwin (Greene) [1918-1968]**C L C 14**
See also CA 93-96; 25-28R

O'Connor, (Mary) Flannery [1925-1964]**CLC 1, 2, 3, 6, 10, 13, 15, 21, 66, 104; DA; DAB; DAC; DAM MST, NOV; SSC 1, 23; WLC**
See also AAYA 7; CA 1-4R; CANR 3, 41; CDALB 1941-1968; DLB 2, 152; DLBD 12; DLBY 80; MTCW

O'Connor, Frank .... **CLC 23; SSC 5**
See also O'Donovan, Michael John
See also DLB 162

O'Dell, Scott [1898-1989] .... **CLC 30**
See also AAYA 3; CA 61-64; 129; CANR 12, 30; CLR 1, 16; DLB 52; JRDA; MAICYA; SATA 12, 60

Odets, Clifford [1906-1963] .. **CLC 2, 28, 98; DAM DRAM; DC 6**
See also CA 85-88; CANR 62; DLB 7, 26; MTCW

O'Doherty, Brian [1934-] .... **CLC 76**
See also CA 105

O'Donnell, K. M.
See Malzberg, Barry N(athaniel)

O'Donnell, Lawrence
See Kuttner, Henry

O'Donovan, Michael John [1903-1966] **C L C 14**
See also O'Connor, Frank
See also CA 93-96

Oe, Kenzaburo [1935-]**CLC 10, 36, 86; DAM NOV; SSC 20**
See also CA 97-100; CANR 36, 50; DLB 182; DLBY 94; MTCW

O'Faolain, Julia [1932-] . **CLC 6, 19, 47, 108**
See also CA 81-84; CAAS 2; CANR 12, 61; DLB 14; MTCW

O'Faolain, Sean [1900-1991]**CLC 1, 7, 14, 32, 70; SSC 13**
See also CA 61-64; 134; CANR 12, 66; DLB 15, 162; MTCW

O'Flaherty, Liam [1896-1984]**CLC 5, 34; SSC 6**
See also CA 101; 113; CANR 35; DLB 36, 162; DLBY 84; MTCW

Ogilvy, Gavin
See Barrie, J(ames) M(atthew)

O'Grady, Standish (James) [1846-1928] **TCLC 5**
See also CA 104; 157

O'Grady, Timothy [1951-] .... **CLC 59**

See also CA 138

O'Hara, Frank [1926-1966]CLC **2, 5, 13, 78; DAM POET**
See also CA 9-12R; 25-28R; CANR 33; DLB 5, 16, 193; MTCW

O'Hara, John (Henry) [1905-1970]CLC **1, 2, 3, 6, 11, 42; DAM NOV; SSC 15**
See also CA 5-8R; 25-28R; CANR 31, 60; CDALB 1929-1941; DLB 9, 86; DLBD 2; MTCW

O Hehir, Diana [1922-] .... CLC **41**
See also CA 93-96

Okigbo, Christopher (Ifenayichukwu) [1932-1967] ....
CLC **25, 84; BLC 3; DAM MULT, POET; PC 7**
See also BW 1; CA 77-80; DLB 125; MTCW

Okri, Ben [1959-] .... CLC **87**
See also BW 2; CA 130; 138; CANR 65; DLB 157; INT 138

Olds, Sharon [1942-] . CLC **32, 39, 85; DAM POET; PC 22**
See also CA 101; CANR 18, 41, 66; DLB 120

Oldstyle, Jonathan
See Irving, Washington

Olesha, Yuri (Karlovich) [1899-1960] CLC **8**
See also CA 85-88

Oliphant, Laurence [1829(?)-1888]NCLC **47**
See also DLB 18, 166

Oliphant, Margaret (Oliphant Wilson) [1828-1897] ....
NCLC **11, 61; SSC 25**
See also DLB 18, 159, 190

Oliver, Mary [1935-] .... CLC **19, 34, 98**
See also CA 21-24R; CANR 9, 43; DLB 5, 193

Olivier, Laurence (Kerr) [1907-1989]CLC **20**
See also CA 111; 150; 129

Olsen, Tillie [1913-] ... CLC **4, 13; DA; DAB; DAC; DAM MST; SSC 11**
See also CA 1-4R; CANR 1, 43; DLB 28; DLBY 80; MTCW

Olson, Charles (John) [1910-1970] CLC **1, 2, 5, 6, 9, 11, 29; DAM POET; PC 19**
See also CA 13-16; 25-28R; CABS 2; CANR 35, 61; CAP 1; DLB 5, 16, 193; MTCW

Olson, Toby [1937-] .... CLC **28**
See also CA 65-68; CANR 9, 31

Olyesha, Yuri
See Olesha, Yuri (Karlovich)

Ondaatje, (Philip) Michael [1943-] . CLC **14, 29, 51, 76; DAB; DAC; DAM MST**
See also CA 77-80; CANR 42; DLB 60

Oneal, Elizabeth [1934-]
See Oneal, Zibby
See also CA 106; CANR 28; MAICYA; SATA 30, 82

Oneal, Zibby .... CLC **30**
See also Oneal, Elizabeth
See also AAYA 5; CLR 13; JRDA

O'Neill, Eugene (Gladstone) [1888-1953]
TCLC **1, 6, 27, 49; DA; DAB; DAC; DAM DRAM, MST; WLC**
See also AITN 1; CA 110; 132; CDALB 1929-1941; DLB 7; MTCW

Onetti, Juan Carlos [1909-1994] CLC **7, 10; DAM MULT, NOV; SSC 23**
See also CA 85-88; 145; CANR 32, 63; DLB 113; HW; MTCW

O Nuallain, Brian [1911-1966]
See O'Brien, Flann
See also CA 21-22; 25-28R; CAP 2

Ophuls, Max [1902-1957] .... TCLC **79**
See also CA 113

Opie, Amelia [1769-1853] .... NCLC **65**
See also DLB 116, 159

Oppen, George [1908-1984] ... CLC **7, 13, 34**
See also CA 13-16R; 113; CANR 8; DLB 5, 165

Oppenheim, E(dward) Phillips [1866-1946]
TCLC **45**
See also CA 111; DLB 70

Opuls, Max
See Ophuls, Max

Origen [c. 185-c. 254] .... CMLC **19**

Orlovitz, Gil [1918-1973] .... CLC **22**
See also CA 77-80; 45-48; DLB 2, 5

Orris
See Ingelow, Jean

Ortega y Gasset, Jose [1883-1955] . TCLC **9; DAM MULT; HLC**
See also CA 106; 130; HW; MTCW

Ortese, Anna Maria [1914-] .... CLC **89**
See also DLB 177

Ortiz, Simon J(oseph) [1941-]CLC **45; DAM MULT, POET; PC 17**
See also CA 134; CANR 69; DLB 120, 175; NNAL

Orton, Joe .... CLC **4, 13, 43; DC 3**
See also Orton, John Kingsley
See also CDBLB 1960 to Present; DLB 13

Orton, John Kingsley [1933-1967]
See Orton, Joe
See also CA 85-88; CANR 35, 66; DAM DRAM; MTCW

Orwell, George . TCLC **2, 6, 15, 31, 51; DAB; WLC**
See also Blair, Eric (Arthur)
See also CDBLB 1945-1960; DLB 15, 98, 195

Osborne, David
See Silverberg, Robert

Osborne, George
See Silverberg, Robert

Osborne, John (James) [1929-1994]CLC **1, 2, 5, 11, 45; DA; DAB; DAC; DAM DRAM, MST; WLC**
See also CA 13-16R; 147; CANR 21, 56; CDBLB 1945-1960; DLB 13; MTCW

Osborne, Lawrence [1958-] .... CLC **50**

Oshima, Nagisa [1932-] .... CLC **20**
See also CA 116; 121

Oskison, John Milton [1874-1947]TCLC **35; DAM MULT**
See also CA 144; DLB 175; NNAL

Ossian [c. 3rd cent. -] .... CMLC **28**
See also Macpherson, James

Ossoli, Sarah Margaret (Fuller marchesa d') [1810-1850]
See Fuller, Margaret
See also SATA 25

Ostrovsky, Alexander [1823-1886] NCLC **30, 57**

Otero, Blas de [1916-1979] .... CLC **11**
See also CA 89-92; DLB 134

Otto, Whitney [1955-] .... CLC **70**
See also CA 140

Ouida .... TCLC **43**
See also De La Ramee, (Marie) Louise
See also DLB 18, 156

Ousmane, Sembene [1923-] . CLC **66; BLC 3**
See also BW 1; CA 117; 125; MTCW

Ovid [43B.C.-18(?)]CMLC **7; DAM POET; PC 2**

Owen, Hugh
See Faust, Frederick (Schiller)

Owen, Wilfred (Edward Salter) [1893-1918]
TCLC **5, 27; DA; DAB; DAC; DAM MST, POET; PC 19; WLC**
See also CA 104; 141; CDBLB 1914-1945; DLB 20

Owens, Rochelle [1936-] .... CLC **8**
See also CA 17-20R; CAAS 2; CANR 39

Oz, Amos [1939-]CLC **5, 8, 11, 27, 33, 54; DAM NOV**
See also CA 53-56; CANR 27, 47, 65; MTCW

Ozick, Cynthia [1928-]CLC **3, 7, 28, 62; DAM NOV, POP; SSC 15**
See also BEST 90:1; CA 17-20R; CANR 23, 58; DLB 28, 152; DLBY 82; INT CANR-23; MTCW

Ozu, Yasujiro [1903-1963] .... CLC **16**
See also CA 112

Pacheco, C.
See Pessoa, Fernando (Antonio Nogueira)

Pa Chin .... CLC **18**
See also Li Fei-kan

Pack, Robert [1929-] .... CLC **13**
See also CA 1-4R; CANR 3, 44; DLB 5

Padgett, Lewis
See Kuttner, Henry

Padilla (Lorenzo), Heberto [1932-] .. CLC **38**
See also AITN 1; CA 123; 131; HW

Page, Jimmy [1944-] .... CLC **12**

Page, Louise [1955-] .... CLC **40**
See also CA 140

Page, P(atricia) K(athleen) [1916-]CLC **7, 18; DAC; DAM MST; PC 12**
See also CA 53-56; CANR 4, 22, 65; DLB 68; MTCW

Page, Thomas Nelson [1853-1922] .... SSC **23**
See also CA 118; DLB 12, 78; DLBD 13

Pagels, Elaine Hiesey [1943-] .... CLC **104**
See also CA 45-48; CANR 2, 24, 51

Paget, Violet [1856-1935]
See Lee, Vernon
See also CA 104; 166

Paget-Lowe, Henry
See Lovecraft, H(oward) P(hillips)

Paglia, Camille (Anna) [1947-] .... CLC **68**
See also CA 140

Paige, Richard
See Koontz, Dean R(ay)

Paine, Thomas [1737-1809] .... NCLC **62**
See also CDALB 1640-1865; DLB 31, 43, 73, 158

Pakenham, Antonia
See Fraser, (Lady) Antonia (Pakenham)

Palamas, Kostes [1859-1943] .... TCLC **5**
See also CA 105

Palazzeschi, Aldo [1885-1974] .... CLC **11**
See also CA 89-92; 53-56; DLB 114

Paley, Grace [1922-]CLC **4, 6, 37; DAM POP; SSC 8**
See also CA 25-28R; CANR 13, 46; DLB 28; INT CANR-13; MTCW

Palin, Michael (Edward) [1943-] ...... CLC **21**
See also Monty Python
See also CA 107; CANR 35; SATA 67

Palliser, Charles [1947-] .... CLC **65**
See also CA 136

Palma, Ricardo [1833-1919] .... TCLC **29**

Pancake, Breece Dexter [1952-1979]
See Pancake, Breece D'J
See also CA 123; 109

Pancake, Breece D'J .... CLC **29**
See also Pancake, Breece Dexter
See also DLB 130

Panko, Rudy
See Gogol, Nikolai (Vasilyevich)

Papadiamantis, Alexandros [1851-1911]
TCLC **29**

Papadiamantopoulos, Johannes [1856-1910]
See Moreas, Jean
See also CA 117

Papini, Giovanni [1881-1956] .... TCLC **22**
See also CA 121

Paracelsus [1493-1541] ....LC **14**
See also DLB 179

Parasol, Peter
See Stevens, Wallace

Pardo Bazán, Emilia [1851-1921] ..... SSC **30**

Pareto, Vilfredo [1848-1923] .... TCLC **69**

Parfenie, Maria

See Codrescu, Andrei
Parini, Jay (Lee) [1948-] .... **CLC 54**
See also CA 97-100; CAAS 16; CANR 32
Park, Jordan
See Kornbluth, C(yril) M.; Pohl, Frederik
Park, Robert E(zra) [1864-1944] ... **TCLC 73**
See also CA 122; 165
Parker, Bert
See Ellison, Harlan (Jay)
Parker, Dorothy (Rothschild) [1893-1967]
CLC 15, 68; DAM POET; SSC 2
See also CA 19-20; 25-28R; CAP 2; DLB 11,
45, 86; MTCW
Parker, Robert B(rown) [1932-]**CLC 27; DAM
NOV, POP**
See also BEST 89:4; CA 49-52; CANR 1, 26,
52; INT CANR-26; MTCW
Parkin, Frank [1940-] .... **CLC 43**
See also CA 147
Parkman, Francis, Jr. [1823-1893] **NCLC 12**
See also DLB 1, 30, 186
Parks, Gordon (Alexander Buchanan) [1912-]
CLC 1, 16; BLC 3; DAM MULT
See also AITN 2; BW 2; CA 41-44R; CANR
26, 66; DLB 33; SATA 8
Parmenides [c. 515B.C.-c. 450B.C.]**CMLC 22**
See also DLB 176
Parnell, Thomas [1679-1718] .... **LC 3**
See also DLB 94
Parra, Nicanor [1914-] .... **CLC 2, 102; DAM
MULT; HLC**
See also CA 85-88; CANR 32; HW; MTCW
Parrish, Mary Frances
See Fisher, M(ary) F(rances) K(ennedy)
Parson
See Coleridge, Samuel Taylor
Parson Lot
See Kingsley, Charles
Partridge, Anthony
See Oppenheim, E(dward) Phillips
Pascal, Blaise [1623-1662] .... **LC 35**
Pascoli, Giovanni [1855-1912] .... **TCLC 45**
Pasolini, Pier Paolo [1922-1975] **CLC 20, 37,
106; PC 17**
See also CA 93-96; 61-64; CANR 63; DLB 128,
177; MTCW
Pasquini
See Silone, Ignazio
Pastan, Linda (Olenik) [1932-]**CLC 27; DAM
POET**
See also CA 61-64; CANR 18, 40, 61; DLB 5
Pasternak, Boris (Leonidovich) [1890-1960]
**CLC 7, 10, 18, 63; DA; DAB; DAC; DAM
MST, NOV, POET; PC 6; SSC 31; WLC**
See also CA 127; 116; MTCW
Patchen, Kenneth [1911-1972] **CLC 1, 2, 18;
DAM POET**
See also CA 1-4R; 33-36R; CANR 3, 35; DLB
16, 48; MTCW
Pater, Walter (Horatio) [1839-1894]**NCLC 7**
See also CDBLB 1832-1890; DLB 57, 156
Paterson, A(ndrew) B(arton) [1864-1941]
TCLC 32
See also CA 155; SATA 97
Paterson, Katherine (Womeldorf) [1932-]
CLC 12, 30
See also AAYA 1; CA 21-24R; CANR 28, 59;
CLR 7, 50; DLB 52; JRDA; MAICYA;
MTCW; SATA 13, 53, 92
Patmore, Coventry Kersey Dighton [1823-
1896] .... **NCLC 9**
See also DLB 35, 98
Paton, Alan (Stewart) [1903-1988]**CLC 4, 10,
25, 55, 106; DA; DAB; DAC; DAM MST,
NOV; WLC**
See also CA 13-16; 125; CANR 22; CAP 1;
MTCW; SATA 11; SATA-Obit 56

Paton Walsh, Gillian [1937-]
See Walsh, Jill Paton
See also CANR 38; JRDA; MAICYA; SAAS 3;
SATA 4, 72
Patton, George S. [1885-1945] .... **TCLC 79**
Paulding, James Kirke [1778-1860] **NCLC 2**
See also DLB 3, 59, 74
Paulin, Thomas Neilson [1949-]
See Paulin, Tom
See also CA 123; 128
Paulin, Tom .... **CLC 37**
See also Paulin, Thomas Neilson
See also DLB 40
Paustovsky, Konstantin (Georgievich) [1892-
1968] ....
CLC 40
See also CA 93-96; 25-28R
Pavese, Cesare [1908-1950] **TCLC 3; PC 13;
SSC 19**
See also CA 104; DLB 128, 177
Pavic, Milorad [1929-] .... **CLC 60**
See also CA 136; DLB 181
Payne, Alan
See Jakes, John (William)
Paz, Gil
See Lugones, Leopoldo
Paz, Octavio [1914-1998]**CLC 3, 4, 6, 10, 19,
51, 65; DA; DAB; DAC; DAM MST,
MULT, POET; HLC; PC 1; WLC**
See also CA 73-76; 165; CANR 32, 65; DLBY
90; HW; MTCW
p'Bitek, Okot [1931-1982] . **CLC 96; BLC 3;
DAM MULT**
See also BW 2; CA 124; 107; DLB 125; MTCW
Peacock, Molly [1947-] .... **CLC 60**
See also CA 103; CAAS 21; CANR 52; DLB
120
Peacock, Thomas Love [1785-1866]**NCLC 22**
See also DLB 96, 116
Peake, Mervyn [1911-1968] .... **CLC 7, 54**
See also CA 5-8R; 25-28R; CANR 3; DLB 15,
160; MTCW; SATA 23
Pearce, Philippa .... **CLC 21**
See also Christie, (Ann) Philippa
See also CLR 9; DLB 161; MAICYA; SATA 1,
67
Pearl, Eric
See Elman, Richard (Martin)
Pearson, T(homas) R(eid) [1956-] .... **CLC 39**
See also CA 120; 130; INT 130
Peck, Dale [1967-] .... **CLC 81**
See also CA 146
Peck, John [1941-] .... **CLC 3**
See also CA 49-52; CANR 3
Peck, Richard (Wayne) [1934-] .... **CLC 21**
See also AAYA 1, 24; CA 85-88; CANR 19,
38; CLR 15; INT CANR-19; JRDA;
MAICYA; SAAS 2; SATA 18, 55, 97
Peck, Robert Newton [1928-] .. **CLC 17; DA;
DAC; DAM MST**
See also AAYA 3; CA 81-84; CANR 31, 63;
CLR 45; JRDA; MAICYA; SAAS 1; SATA
21, 62
Peckinpah, (David) Sam(uel) [1925-1984]
CLC 20
See also CA 109; 114
Pedersen, Knut [1859-1952]
See Hamsun, Knut
See also CA 104; 119; CANR 63; MTCW
Peeslake, Gaffer
See Durrell, Lawrence (George)
Peguy, Charles Pierre [1873-1914] **TCLC 10**
See also CA 107
Peirce, Charles Sanders [1839-1914]**TCLC 81**
Pena, Ramon del Valle y
See Valle-Inclan, Ramon (Maria) del
Pendennis, Arthur Esquir

See Thackeray, William Makepeace
Penn, William [1644-1718] .... **LC 25**
See also DLB 24
PEPECE
See Prado (Calvo), Pedro
Pepys, Samuel [1633-1703]**LC 11; DA; DAB;
DAC; DAM MST; WLC**
See also CDBLB 1660-1789; DLB 101
Percy, Walker [1916-1990]**CLC 2, 3, 6, 8, 14,
18, 47, 65; DAM NOV, POP**
See also CA 1-4R; 131; CANR 1, 23, 64; DLB
2; DLBY 80, 90; MTCW
Perec, Georges [1936-1982] .... **CLC 56**
See also CA 141; DLB 83
Pereda (y Sanchez de Porrua), Jose Maria de
[1833-1906] .... **TCLC 16**
See also CA 117
Pereda y Porrua, Jose Maria de
See Pereda (y Sanchez de Porrua), Jose Maria
de
Peregoy, George Weems
See Mencken, H(enry) L(ouis)
Perelman, S(idney) J(oseph) [1904-1979]**CLC
3, 5, 9, 15, 23, 44, 49; DAM DRAM**
See also AITN 1, 2; CA 73-76; 89-92; CANR
18; DLB 11, 44; MTCW
Peret, Benjamin [1899-1959] .... **TCLC 20**
See also CA 117
Peretz, Isaac Loeb [1851(?)-1915] **TCLC 16;
SSC 26**
See also CA 109
Peretz, Yitzhok Leibush
See Peretz, Isaac Loeb
Perez Galdos, Benito [1843-1920] . **TCLC 27**
See also CA 125; 153; HW
Perrault, Charles [1628-1703] .... **LC 2**
See also MAICYA; SATA 25
Perry, Brighton
See Sherwood, Robert E(mmet)
Perse, St.-John
See Leger, (Marie-Rene Auguste) Alexis Saint-
Leger
Perutz, Leo [1882-1957] .... **TCLC 60**
See also DLB 81
Peseenz, Tulio F.
See Lopez y Fuentes, Gregorio
Pesetsky, Bette [1932-] .... **CLC 28**
See also CA 133; DLB 130
Peshkov, Alexei Maximovich [1868-1936]
See Gorky, Maxim
See also CA 105; 141; DA; DAC; DAM DRAM,
MST, NOV
Pessoa, Fernando (Antonio Nogueira) [1898-
1935] ....
TCLC 27; HLC; PC 20
See also CA 125
Peterkin, Julia Mood [1880-1961] .... **CLC 31**
See also CA 102; DLB 9
Peters, Joan K(aren) [1945-] .... **CLC 39**
See also CA 158
Peters, Robert L(ouis) [1924-] .... **CLC 7**
See also CA 13-16R; CAAS 8; DLB 105
Petofi, Sandor [1823-1849] .... **NCLC 21**
Petrakis, Harry Mark [1923-] .... **CLC 3**
See also CA 9-12R; CANR 4, 30
Petrarch [1304-1374]**CMLC 20; DAM POET;
PC 8**
Petrov, Evgeny .... **TCLC 21**
See also Kataev, Evgeny Petrovich
Petry, Ann (Lane) [1908-1997] **CLC 1, 7, 18**
See also BW 1; CA 5-8R; 157; CAAS 6; CANR
4, 46; CLR 12; DLB 76; JRDA; MAICYA;
MTCW; SATA 5; SATA-Obit 94
Petursson, Halligrimur [1614-1674] ..... **LC 8**
Phaedrus [18(?)B.C.-55(?)] .... **CMLC 25**
Philips, Katherine [1632-1664] .... **LC 30**
See also DLB 131

See also CA 107; 145; CANR 33, 61; MTCW
Pound, Ezra (Weston Loomis) [1885-1972]
**CLC 1, 2, 3, 4, 5, 7, 10, 13, 18, 34, 48, 50,
112; DA; DAB; DAC; DAM MST, POET;
PC 4; WLC**
See also CA 5-8R; 37-40R; CANR 40; CDALB
1917-1929; DLB 4, 45, 63; DLBD 15;
MTCW
Povod, Reinaldo [1959-1994] .... **CLC 44**
See also CA 136; 146
Powell, Adam Clayton, Jr. [1908-1972] **C L C
89; BLC 3; DAM MULT**
See also BW 1; CA 102; 33-36R
Powell, Anthony (Dymoke) [1905-]**CLC 1, 3,
7, 9, 10, 31**
See also CA 1-4R; CANR 1, 32, 62; CDBLB
1945-1960; DLB 15; MTCW
Powell, Dawn [1897-1965] .... **CLC 66**
See also CA 5-8R; DLBY 97
Powell, Padgett [1952-] .... **CLC 34**
See also CA 126; CANR 63
Power, Susan [1961-] .... **CLC 91**
Powers, J(ames) F(arl) [1917-]**CLC 1, 4, 8, 57;
SSC 4**
See also CA 1-4R; CANR 2, 61; DLB 130;
MTCW
Powers, John J(ames) [1945-]
See Powers, John R.
See also CA 69-72
Powers, John R. .... **CLC 66**
See also Powers, John J(ames)
Powers, Richard (S.) [1957-] .... **CLC 93**
See also CA 148
Pownall, David [1938-] .... **CLC 10**
See also CA 89-92; CAAS 18; CANR 49; DLB
14
Powys, John Cowper [1872-1963] . **CLC 7, 9,
15, 46**
See also CA 85-88; DLB 15; MTCW
Powys, T(heodore) F(rancis) [1875-1953]
TCLC 9
See also CA 106; DLB 36, 162
Prado (Calvo), Pedro [1886-1952] . **TCLC 75**
See also CA 131; HW
Prager, Emily [1952-] .... **CLC 56**
Pratt, E(dwin) J(ohn) [1883(?)-1964]**CLC 19;
DAC; DAM POET**
See also CA 141; 93-96; DLB 92
Premchand .... **TCLC 21**
See also Srivastava, Dhanpat Rai
Preussler, Otfried [1923-] .... **CLC 17**
See also CA 77-80; SATA 24
Prevert, Jacques (Henri Marie) [1900-1977]
CLC 15
See also CA 77-80; 69-72; CANR 29, 61;
MTCW; SATA-Obit 30
Prevost, Abbe (Antoine Francois) [1697-1763]
LC 1
Price, (Edward) Reynolds [1933-] . **CLC 3, 6,
13, 43, 50, 63; DAM NOV; SSC 22**
See also CA 1-4R; CANR 1, 37, 57; DLB 2;
INT CANR-37
Price, Richard [1949-] .... **CLC 6, 12**
See also CA 49-52; CANR 3; DLBY 81
Prichard, Katharine Susannah [1883-1969]
CLC 46
See also CA 11-12; CANR 33; CAP 1; MTCW;
SATA 66
Priestley, J(ohn) B(oynton) [1894-1984]**C L C
2, 5, 9, 34; DAM DRAM, NOV**
See also CA 9-12R; 113; CANR 33; CDBLB
1914-1945; DLB 10, 34, 77, 100, 139; DLBY
84; MTCW
Prince [1958(?)-] .... **CLC 35**
Prince, F(rank) T(empleton) [1912-] **CLC 22**
See also CA 101; CANR 43; DLB 20
Prince Kropotkin

See Kropotkin, Peter (Aleksieevich)
Prior, Matthew [1664-1721] .... **LC 4**
See also DLB 95
Prishvin, Mikhail [1873-1954] .... **TCLC 75**
Pritchard, William H(arrison) [1932-]**CLC 34**
See also CA 65-68; CANR 23; DLB 111
Pritchett, V(ictor) S(awdon) [1900-1997]**CLC
5, 13, 15, 41; DAM NOV; SSC 14**
See also CA 61-64; 157; CANR 31, 63; DLB
15, 139; MTCW
Private 19022
See Manning, Frederic
Probst, Mark [1925-] .... **CLC 59**
See also CA 130
Prokosch, Frederic [1908-1989] .... **CLC 4, 48**
See also CA 73-76; 128; DLB 48
Prophet, The
See Dreiser, Theodore (Herman Albert)
Prose, Francine [1947-] .... **CLC 45**
See also CA 109; 112; CANR 46
Proudhon
See Cunha, Euclides (Rodrigues Pimenta) da
Proulx, Annie
See Proulx, E(dna) Annie
Proulx, E(dna) Annie [1935-] **CLC 81; DAM
POP**
See also CA 145; CANR 65
**Proust, (Valentin-Louis-George-Eugene-)
Marcel** [1871-1922]**TCLC 7, 13, 33; DA;
DAB; DAC; DAM MST, NOV; WLC**
See also CA 104; 120; DLB 65; MTCW
Prowler, Harley
See Masters, Edgar Lee
Prus, Boleslaw [1845-1912] .... **TCLC 48**
Pryor, Richard (Franklin Lenox Thomas)
[1940-] .... **CLC 26**
See also CA 122
Przybyszewski, Stanislaw [1868-1927]**T C L C
36**
See also CA 160; DLB 66
Pteleon
See Grieve, C(hristopher) M(urray)
See also DAM POET
Puckett, Lute
See Masters, Edgar Lee
Puig, Manuel [1932-1990]**CLC 3, 5, 10, 28, 65;
DAM MULT; HLC**
See also CA 45-48; CANR 2, 32, 63; DLB 113;
HW; MTCW
Pulitzer, Joseph [1847-1911] .... **TCLC 76**
See also CA 114; DLB 23
Purdy, A(lfred) W(ellington) [1918-]**CLC 3, 6,
14, 50; DAC; DAM MST, POET**
See also CA 81-84; CAAS 17; CANR 42, 66;
DLB 88
Purdy, James (Amos) [1923-]**CLC 2, 4, 10, 28,
52**
See also CA 33-36R; CAAS 1; CANR 19, 51;
DLB 2; INT CANR-19; MTCW
Pure, Simon
See Swinnerton, Frank Arthur
Pushkin, Alexander (Sergeyevich) [1799-1837]
**NCLC 3, 27; DA; DAB; DAC; DAM
DRAM, MST, POET; PC 10; SSC 27;
WLC**
See also SATA 61
P'u Sung-ling [1640-1715] .... **LC 3; SSC 31**
Putnam, Arthur Lee
See Alger, Horatio, Jr.
Puzo, Mario [1920-]**CLC 1, 2, 6, 36, 107; DAM
NOV, POP**
See also CA 65-68; CANR 4, 42, 65; DLB 6;
MTCW
Pygge, Edward
See Barnes, Julian (Patrick)
Pyle, Ernest Taylor [1900-1945]
See Pyle, Ernie

See also CA 115; 160
Pyle, Ernie [1900-1945] .... **TCLC 75**
See also Pyle, Ernest Taylor
See also DLB 29
Pyle, Howard [1853-1911] .... **TCLC 81**
See also CA 109; 137; CLR 22; DLB 42, 188;
DLBD 13; MAICYA; SATA 16
Pym, Barbara (Mary Crampton) [1913-1980]
CLC 13, 19, 37, 111
See also CA 13-14; 97-100; CANR 13, 34; CAP
1; DLB 14; DLBY 87; MTCW
Pynchon, Thomas (Ruggles, Jr.) [1937-]**C L C
2, 3, 6, 9, 11, 18, 33, 62, 72; DA; DAB;
DAC; DAM MST, NOV, POP; SSC 14;
WLC**
See also BEST 90:2; CA 17-20R; CANR 22,
46; DLB 2, 173; MTCW
Pythagoras [c. 570B.C.-c. 500B.C.]**CMLC 22**
See also DLB 176
Q
See Quiller-Couch, SirArthur (Thomas)
Qian Zhongshu
See Ch'ien Chung-shu
Qroll
See Dagerman, Stig (Halvard)
Quarrington, Paul (Lewis) [1953-] ... **CLC 65**
See also CA 129; CANR 62
Quasimodo, Salvatore [1901-1968] .. **CLC 10**
See also CA 13-16; 25-28R; CAP 1; DLB 114;
MTCW
Quay, Stephen [1947-] .... **CLC 95**
Quay, Timothy [1947-] .... **CLC 95**
Queen, Ellery .... **CLC 3, 11**
See also Dannay, Frederic; Davidson, Avram;
Lee, Manfred B(ennington); Marlowe,
Stephen; Sturgeon, Theodore (Hamilton);
Vance, John Holbrook
Queen, Ellery, Jr.
See Dannay, Frederic; Lee, Manfred
B(ennington)
Queneau, Raymond [1903-1976]**CLC 2, 5, 10,
42**
See also CA 77-80; 69-72; CANR 32; DLB 72;
MTCW
Quevedo, Francisco de [1580-1645] .... **LC 23**
Quiller-Couch, SirArthur (Thomas) [1863-
1944] .... **TCLC 53**
See also CA 118; 166; DLB 135, 153, 190
Quin, Ann (Marie) [1936-1973] .... **CLC 6**
See also CA 9-12R; 45-48; DLB 14
Quinn, Martin
See Smith, Martin Cruz
Quinn, Peter [1947-] .... **CLC 91**
Quinn, Simon
See Smith, Martin Cruz
Quiroga, Horacio (Sylvestre) [1878-1937]
TCLC 20; DAM MULT; HLC
See also CA 117; 131; HW; MTCW
Quoirez, Francoise [1935-] .... **CLC 9**
See also Sagan, Francoise
See also CA 49-52; CANR 6, 39; MTCW
Raabe, Wilhelm [1831-1910] .... **TCLC 45**
See also DLB 129
Rabe, David (William) [1940-] **CLC 4, 8, 33;
DAM DRAM**
See also CA 85-88; CABS 3; CANR 59; DLB 7
Rabelais, Francois [1483-1553] ... **LC 5; DA;
DAB; DAC; DAM MST; WLC**
Rabinovitch, Sholem [1859-1916]
See Aleichem, Sholom
See also CA 104
Rachilde [1860-1953] .... **TCLC 67**
See also DLB 123, 192
Racine, Jean [1639-1699]**LC 28; DAB; DAM
MST**
Radcliffe, Ann (Ward) [1764-1823] **NCLC 6,
55**

See also CA 103; CANR 46

Rich, Adrienne (Cecile) [1929-] **CLC 3, 6, 7, 11, 18, 36, 73, 76; DAM POET; PC 5**
See also CA 9-12R; CANR 20, 53; DLB 5, 67; MTCW

Rich, Barbara
See Graves, Robert (von Ranke)

Rich, Robert
See Trumbo, Dalton

Richard, Keith .... **CLC 17**
See also Richards, Keith

Richards, David Adams [1950-]**CLC 59; DAC**
See also CA 93-96; CANR 60; DLB 53

Richards, I(vor) A(rmstrong) [1893-1979] **CLC 14, 24**
See also CA 41-44R; 89-92; CANR 34; DLB 27

Richards, Keith [1943-]
See Richard, Keith
See also CA 107

Richardson, Anne
See Roiphe, Anne (Richardson)

Richardson, Dorothy Miller [1873-1957] **TCLC 3**
See also CA 104; DLB 36

Richardson, Ethel Florence (Lindesay) [1870-1946]
See Richardson, Henry Handel
See also CA 105

Richardson, Henry Handel .... **TCLC 4**
See also Richardson, Ethel Florence (Lindesay)
See also DLB 197

Richardson, John [1796-1852]**NCLC 55; DAC**
See also DLB 99

Richardson, Samuel [1689-1761]... **LC 1, 44; DA; DAB; DAC; DAM MST, NOV; WLC**
See also CDBLB 1660-1789; DLB 39

Richler, Mordecai [1931-]**CLC 3, 5, 9, 13, 18, 46, 70; DAC; DAM MST, NOV**
See also AITN 1; CA 65-68; CANR 31, 62; CLR 17; DLB 53; MAICYA; MTCW; SATA 44, 98; SATA-Brief 27

Richter, Conrad (Michael) [1890-1968] **CLC 30**
See also AAYA 21; CA 5-8R; 25-28R; CANR 23; DLB 9; MTCW; SATA 3

Ricostranza, Tom
See Ellis, Trey

Riddell, Charlotte [1832-1906] ...... **TCLC 40**
See also CA 165; DLB 156

Riding, Laura .... **CLC 3, 7**
See also Jackson, Laura (Riding)

Riefenstahl, Berta Helene Amalia [1902-]
See Riefenstahl, Leni
See also CA 108

Riefenstahl, Leni .... **CLC 16**
See also Riefenstahl, Berta Helene Amalia

Riffe, Ernest
See Bergman, (Ernst) Ingmar

Riggs, (Rolla) Lynn [1899-1954] ... **TCLC 56; DAM MULT**
See also CA 144; DLB 175; NNAL

Riis, Jacob A(ugust) [1849-1914] .. **TCLC 80**
See also CA 113; DLB 23

Riley, James Whitcomb [1849-1916].. **TCLC 51; DAM POET**
See also CA 118; 137; MAICYA; SATA 17

Riley, Tex
See Creasey, John

Rilke, Rainer Maria [1875-1926] **TCLC 1, 6, 19; DAM POET; PC 2**
See also CA 104; 132; CANR 62; DLB 81; MTCW

Rimbaud, (Jean Nicolas) Arthur [1854-1891] **NCLC 4, 35; DA; DAB; DAC; DAM MST, POET; PC 3; WLC**

Rinehart, Mary Roberts [1876-1958] **T C L C 52**
See also CA 108; 166

Ringmaster, The
See Mencken, H(enry) L(ouis)

Ringwood, Gwen(dolyn Margaret) Pharis [1910-1984] .... **CLC 48**
See also CA 148; 112; DLB 88

Rio, Michel [19(?)-] .... **CLC 43**

Ritsos, Giannes
See Ritsos, Yannis

Ritsos, Yannis [1909-1990] ..... **CLC 6, 13, 31**
See also CA 77-80; 133; CANR 39, 61; MTCW

Ritter, Erika [1948(?)-] .... **CLC 52**

Rivera, Jose Eustasio [1889-1928] **TCLC 35**
See also CA 162; HW

Rivers, Conrad Kent [1933-1968] ...... **CLC 1**
See also BW 1; CA 85-88; DLB 41

Rivers, Elfrida
See Bradley, Marion Zimmer

Riverside, John
See Heinlein, Robert A(nson)

Rizal, Jose [1861-1896] .... **NCLC 27**

Roa Bastos, Augusto (Antonio) [1917-] **C L C 45; DAM MULT; HLC**
See also CA 131; DLB 113; HW

Robbe-Grillet, Alain [1922-]**CLC 1, 2, 4, 6, 8, 10, 14, 43**
See also CA 9-12R; CANR 33, 65; DLB 83; MTCW

Robbins, Harold [1916-1997] .. **CLC 5; DAM NOV**
See also CA 73-76; 162; CANR 26, 54; MTCW

Robbins, Thomas Eugene [1936-]
See Robbins, Tom
See also CA 81-84; CANR 29, 59; DAM NOV, POP; MTCW

Robbins, Tom .... **CLC 9, 32, 64**
See also Robbins, Thomas Eugene
See also BEST 90:3; DLBY 80

Robbins, Trina [1938-] .... **CLC 21**
See also CA 128

Roberts, Charles G(eorge) D(ouglas) [1860-1943] .... **TCLC 8**
See also CA 105; CLR 33; DLB 92; SATA 88; SATA-Brief 29

Roberts, Elizabeth Madox [1886-1941]**TCLC 68**
See also CA 111; 166; DLB 9, 54, 102; SATA 33; SATA-Brief 27

Roberts, Kate [1891-1985] .... **CLC 15**
See also CA 107; 116

Roberts, Keith (John Kingston) [1935-] **C L C 14**
See also CA 25-28R; CANR 46

Roberts, Kenneth (Lewis) [1885-1957]**T C L C 23**
See also CA 109; DLB 9

Roberts, Michele (B.) [1949-] .... **CLC 48**
See also CA 115; CANR 58

Robertson, Ellis
See Ellison, Harlan (Jay); Silverberg, Robert

Robertson, Thomas William [1829-1871] **NCLC 35; DAM DRAM**

Robeson, Kenneth
See Dent, Lester

Robinson, Edwin Arlington [1869-1935] **TCLC 5; DA; DAC; DAM MST, POET; PC 1**
See also CA 104; 133; CDALB 1865-1917; DLB 54; MTCW

Robinson, Henry Crabb [1775-1867]. **N C L C 15**
See also DLB 107

Robinson, Jill [1936-] .... **CLC 10**
See also CA 102; INT 102

Robinson, Kim Stanley [1952-] .... **CLC 34**
See also CA 126

Robinson, Lloyd
See Silverberg, Robert

Robinson, Marilynne [1944-] .... **CLC 25**
See also CA 116

Robinson, Smokey .... **CLC 21**
See also Robinson, William, Jr.

Robinson, William, Jr. [1940-]
See Robinson, Smokey
See also CA 116

Robison, Mary [1949-] .... **CLC 42, 98**
See also CA 113; 116; DLB 130; INT 116

Rod, Edouard [1857-1910] .... **TCLC 52**

Roddenberry, Eugene Wesley [1921-1991]
See Roddenberry, Gene
See also CA 110; 135; CANR 37; SATA 45; SATA-Obit 69

Roddenberry, Gene .... **CLC 17**
See also Roddenberry, Eugene Wesley
See also AAYA 5; SATA-Obit 69

Rodgers, Mary [1931-] .... **CLC 12**
See also CA 49-52; CANR 8, 55; CLR 20; INT CANR-8; JRDA; MAICYA; SATA 8

Rodgers, W(illiam) R(obert) [1909-1969]**CLC 7**
See also CA 85-88; DLB 20

Rodman, Eric
See Silverberg, Robert

Rodman, Howard [1920(?)-1985] ..... **CLC 65**
See also CA 118

Rodman, Maia
See Wojciechowska, Maia (Teresa)

Rodriguez, Claudio [1934-] .... **CLC 10**
See also DLB 134

Roelvaag, O(le) E(dvart) [1876-1931] **T C L C 17**
See also CA 117; DLB 9

Roethke, Theodore (Huebner) [1908-1963] **CLC 1, 3, 8, 11, 19, 46, 101; DAM POET; PC 15**
See also CA 81-84; CABS 2; CDALB 1941-1968; DLB 5; MTCW

Rogers, Samuel [1763-1855] .... **NCLC 69**
See also DLB 93

Rogers, Thomas Hunton [1927-] ...... **CLC 57**
See also CA 89-92; INT 89-92

Rogers, Will(iam Penn Adair) [1879-1935] **TCLC 8, 71; DAM MULT**
See also CA 105; 144; DLB 11; NNAL

Rogin, Gilbert [1929-] .... **CLC 18**
See also CA 65-68; CANR 15

Rohan, Koda .... **TCLC 22**
See also Koda Shigeyuki

Rohlfs, Anna Katharine Green
See Green, Anna Katharine

Rohmer, Eric .... **CLC 16**
See also Scherer, Jean-Marie Maurice

Rohmer, Sax .... **TCLC 28**
See also Ward, Arthur Henry Sarsfield
See also DLB 70

Roiphe, Anne (Richardson) [1935-]**CLC 3, 9**
See also CA 89-92; CANR 45; DLBY 80; INT 89-92

Rojas, Fernando de [1465-1541]..........**LC 23**

Rolfe, Frederick (William Serafino Austin Lewis Mary) [1860-1913] ...... **TCLC 12**
See also CA 107; DLB 34, 156

Rolland, Romain [1866-1944] .... **TCLC 23**
See also CA 118; DLB 65

Rolle, Richard [c. 1300-c. 1349] ... **CMLC 21**
See also DLB 146

Rolvaag, O(le) E(dvart)
See Roelvaag, O(le) E(dvart)

Romain Arnaud, Saint
See Aragon, Louis

Romains, Jules [1885-1972] .... **CLC 7**

See also CA 89-92

Schnitzler, Arthur [1862-1931]**TCLC 4; SSC
15**
See also CA 104; DLB 81, 118

Schoenberg, Arnold [1874-1951] ... **TCLC 75**
See also CA 109

Schonberg, Arnold
See Schoenberg, Arnold

Schopenhauer, Arthur [1788-1860]**NCLC 51**
See also DLB 90

Schor, Sandra (M.) [1932(?)-1990] ... **CLC 65**
See also CA 132

Schorer, Mark [1908-1977] .... **CLC 9**
See also CA 5-8R; 73-76; CANR 7; DLB 103

Schrader, Paul (Joseph) [1946-] .... **CLC 26**
See also CA 37-40R; CANR 41; DLB 44

Schreiner, Olive (Emilie Albertina) [1855-1920]

TCLC 9
See also CA 105; 154; DLB 18, 156, 190

Schulberg, Budd (Wilson) [1914-] **CLC 7, 48**
See also CA 25-28R; CANR 19; DLB 6, 26,
28; DLBY 81

Schulz, Bruno [1892-1942] **TCLC 5, 51; SSC
13**
See also CA 115; 123

Schulz, Charles M(onroe) [1922-] .... **CLC 12**
See also CA 9-12R; CANR 6; INT CANR-6;
SATA 10

Schumacher, E(rnst) F(riedrich) [1911-1977]
CLC 80
See also CA 81-84; 73-76; CANR 34

Schuyler, James Marcus [1923-1991] **CLC 5,
23; DAM POET**
See also CA 101; 134; DLB 5, 169; INT 101

Schwartz, Delmore (David) [1913-1966]**C L C
2, 4, 10, 45, 87; PC 8**
See also CA 17-18; 25-28R; CANR 35; CAP 2;
DLB 28, 48; MTCW

Schwartz, Ernst
See Ozu, Yasujiro

Schwartz, John Burnham [1965-] .... **CLC 59**
See also CA 132

Schwartz, Lynne Sharon [1939-] ...... **CLC 31**
See also CA 103; CANR 44

Schwartz, Muriel A.
See Eliot, T(homas) S(tearns)

Schwarz-Bart, Andre [1928-] .... **CLC 2, 4**
See also CA 89-92

Schwarz-Bart, Simone [1938-]**CLC 7; BLCS**
See also BW 2; CA 97-100

Schwob, (Mayer Andre) Marcel [1867-1905]
TCLC 20
See also CA 117; DLB 123

Sciascia, Leonardo [1921-1989] **CLC 8, 9, 41**
See also CA 85-88; 130; CANR 35; DLB 177;
MTCW

Scoppettone, Sandra [1936-] .... **CLC 26**
See also AAYA 11; CA 5-8R; CANR 41; SATA
9, 92

Scorsese, Martin [1942-] .... **CLC 20, 89**
See also CA 110; 114; CANR 46

Scotland, Jay
See Jakes, John (William)

Scott, Duncan Campbell [1862-1947]**TCLC 6;
DAC**
See also CA 104; 153; DLB 92

Scott, Evelyn [1893-1963] .... **CLC 43**
See also CA 104; 112; CANR 64; DLB 9, 48

Scott, F(rancis) R(eginald) [1899-1985] **C L C
22**
See also CA 101; 114; DLB 88; INT 101

Scott, Frank
See Scott, F(rancis) R(eginald)

Scott, Joanna [1960-] .... **CLC 50**
See also CA 126; CANR 53

Scott, Paul (Mark) [1920-1978] .... **CLC 9, 60**

See also CA 81-84; 77-80; CANR 33; DLB 14;
MTCW

Scott, Sarah [1723-1795] .... **LC 44**
See also DLB 39

Scott, Walter [1771-1832]**NCLC 15, 69; DA;
DAB; DAC; DAM MST, NOV, POET; PC
13; WLC**
See also AAYA 22; CDBLB 1789-1832; DLB
93, 107, 116, 144, 159; YABC 2

Scribe, (Augustin) Eugene [1791-1861]**NCLC
16; DAM DRAM; DC 5**
See also DLB 192

Scrum, R.
See Crumb, R(obert)

Scudery, Madeleine de [1607-1701] ...... **LC 2**

Scum
See Crumb, R(obert)

Scumbag, Little Bobby
See Crumb, R(obert)

Seabrook, John
See Hubbard, L(afayette) Ron(ald)

Sealy, I. Allan [1951-] .... **CLC 55**

Search, Alexander
See Pessoa, Fernando (Antonio Nogueira)

Sebastian, Lee
See Silverberg, Robert

Sebastian Owl
See Thompson, Hunter S(tockton)

Sebestyen, Ouida [1924-] .... **CLC 30**
See also AAYA 8; CA 107; CANR 40; CLR 17;
JRDA; MAICYA; SAAS 10; SATA 39

Secundus, H. Scriblerus
See Fielding, Henry

Sedges, John
See Buck, Pearl S(ydenstricker)

Sedgwick, Catharine Maria [1789-1867]
NCLC 19
See also DLB 1, 74

Seelye, John [1931-] .... **CLC 7**

Seferiades, Giorgos Stylianou [1900-1971]
See Seferis, George
See also CA 5-8R; 33-36R; CANR 5, 36;
MTCW

Seferis, George .... **CLC 5, 11**
See also Seferiades, Giorgos Stylianou

Segal, Erich (Wolf) [1937-] **CLC 3, 10; DAM
POP**
See also BEST 89:1; CA 25-28R; CANR 20,
36, 65; DLBY 86; INT CANR-20; MTCW

Seger, Bob [1945-] .... **CLC 35**

Seghers, Anna .... **CLC 7**
See also Radvanyi, Netty
See also DLB 69

Seidel, Frederick (Lewis) [1936-] ..... **CLC 18**
See also CA 13-16R; CANR 8; DLBY 84

Seifert, Jaroslav [1901-1986] **CLC 34, 44, 93**
See also CA 127; MTCW

Sei Shonagon [c. 966-1017(?)] .... **CMLC 6**

Selby, Hubert, Jr. [1928-]**CLC 1, 2, 4, 8; SSC
20**
See also CA 13-16R; CANR 33; DLB 2

Selzer, Richard [1928-] .... **CLC 74**
See also CA 65-68; CANR 14

Sembene, Ousmane
See Ousmane, Sembene

Senancour, Etienne Pivert de [1770-1846]
NCLC 16
See also DLB 119

Sender, Ramon (Jose) [1902-1982] ... **CLC 8;
DAM MULT; HLC**
See also CA 5-8R; 105; CANR 8; HW; MTCW

Seneca, Lucius Annaeus [4B.C.-65]**CMLC 6;
DAM DRAM; DC 5**

Senghor, Leopold Sedar [1906-]**CLC 54; BLC
3; DAM MULT, POET**
See also BW 2; CA 116; 125; CANR 47; MTCW

Serling, (Edward) Rod(man) [1924-1975]

CLC 30
See also AAYA 14; AITN 1; CA 162; 57-60;
DLB 26

Serna, Ramon Gomez de la
See Gomez de la Serna, Ramon

Serpieres
See Guillevic, (Eugene)

Service, Robert
See Service, Robert W(illiam)
See also DAB; DLB 92

Service, Robert W(illiam) [1874(?)-1958]
**TCLC 15; DA; DAC; DAM MST, POET;
WLC**
See also Service, Robert
See also CA 115; 140; SATA 20

Seth, Vikram [1952-]**CLC 43, 90; DAM MULT**
See also CA 121; 127; CANR 50; DLB 120;
INT 127

Seton, Cynthia Propper [1926-1982] **CLC 27**
See also CA 5-8R; 108; CANR 7

Seton, Ernest (Evan) Thompson [1860-1946]
TCLC 31
See also CA 109; DLB 92; DLBD 13; JRDA;
SATA 18

Seton-Thompson, Ernest
See Seton, Ernest (Evan) Thompson

Settle, Mary Lee [1918-] .... **CLC 19, 61**
See also CA 89-92; CAAS 1; CANR 44; DLB
6; INT 89-92

Seuphor, Michel
See Arp, Jean

**Sevigne, Marie (de Rabutin-Chantal) Marquise
de** [1626-1696] .... **LC 11**

Sewall, Samuel [1652-1730] .... **LC 38**
See also DLB 24

Sexton, Anne (Harvey) [1928-1974]**CLC 2, 4,
6, 8, 10, 15, 53; DA; DAB; DAC; DAM
MST, POET; PC 2; WLC**
See also CA 1-4R; 53-56; CABS 2; CANR 3,
36; CDALB 1941-1968; DLB 5, 169;
MTCW; SATA 10

Shaara, Michael (Joseph, Jr.) [1929-1988]
CLC 15; DAM POP
See also AITN 1; CA 102; 125; CANR 52;
DLBY 83

Shackleton, C. C.
See Aldiss, Brian W(ilson)

Shacochis, Bob .... **CLC 39**
See also Shacochis, Robert G.

Shacochis, Robert G. [1951-]
See Shacochis, Bob
See also CA 119; 124; INT 124

Shaffer, Anthony (Joshua) [1926-] . **CLC 19;
DAM DRAM**
See also CA 110; 116; DLB 13

Shaffer, Peter (Levin) [1926-] **CLC 5, 14, 18,
37, 60; DAB; DAM DRAM, MST; DC 7**
See also CA 25-28R; CANR 25, 47; CDBLB
1960 to Present; DLB 13; MTCW

Shakey, Bernard
See Young, Neil

Shalamov, Varlam (Tikhonovich) [1907(?)-
1982] .... **CLC 18**
See also CA 129; 105

Shamlu, Ahmad [1925-] .... **CLC 10**

Shammas, Anton [1951-] .... **CLC 55**

Shange, Ntozake [1948-] ..**CLC 8, 25, 38, 74;
BLC 3; DAM DRAM, MULT; DC 3**
See also AAYA 9; BW 2; CA 85-88; CABS 3;
CANR 27, 48; DLB 38; MTCW

Shanley, John Patrick [1950-] .... **CLC 75**
See also CA 128; 133

Shapcott, Thomas W(illiam) [1935-] **CLC 38**
See also CA 69-72; CANR 49

Shapiro, Jane .... **CLC 76**

Shapiro, Karl (Jay) [1913-] **CLC 4, 8, 15, 53**
See also CA 1-4R; CAAS 6; CANR 1, 36, 66;

DLB 48; MTCW

Sharp, William [1855-1905] .... **TCLC 39**
See also CA 160; DLB 156

Sharpe, Thomas Ridley [1928-]
See Sharpe, Tom
See also CA 114; 122; INT 122

Sharpe, Tom .... **CLC 36**
See also Sharpe, Thomas Ridley
See also DLB 14

Shaw, Bernard .... **TCLC 45**
See also Shaw, George Bernard
See also BW 1

Shaw, G. Bernard
See Shaw, George Bernard

Shaw, George Bernard [1856-1950] **TCLC 3, 9, 21; DA; DAB; DAC; DAM DRAM, MST; WLC**
See also Shaw, Bernard
See also CA 104; 128; CDBLB 1914-1945; DLB 10, 57, 190; MTCW

Shaw, Henry Wheeler [1818-1885] **NCLC 15**
See also DLB 11

Shaw, Irwin [1913-1984]**CLC 7, 23, 34; DAM DRAM, POP**
See also AITN 1; CA 13-16R; 112; CANR 21; CDALB 1941-1968; DLB 6, 102; DLBY 84; MTCW

Shaw, Robert [1927-1978] .... **CLC 5**
See also AITN 1; CA 1-4R; 81-84; CANR 4; DLB 13, 14

Shaw, T. E.
See Lawrence, T(homas) E(dward)

Shawn, Wallace [1943-] .... **CLC 41**
See also CA 112

Shea, Lisa [1953-] .... **CLC 86**
See also CA 147

Sheed, Wilfrid (John Joseph) [1930-]**CLC 2, 4, 10, 53**
See also CA 65-68; CANR 30, 66; DLB 6; MTCW

Sheldon, Alice Hastings Bradley [1915(?)-1987]
See Tiptree, James, Jr.
See also CA 108; 122; CANR 34; INT 108; MTCW

Sheldon, John
See Bloch, Robert (Albert)

Shelley, Mary Wollstonecraft (Godwin) [1797-1851] ....
NCLC 14, 59; DA; DAB; DAC; DAM MST, NOV; WLC
See also AAYA 20; CDBLB 1789-1832; DLB 110, 116, 159, 178; SATA 29

Shelley, Percy Bysshe [1792-1822]**NCLC 18; DA; DAB; DAC; DAM MST, POET; PC 14; WLC**
See also CDBLB 1789-1832; DLB 96, 110, 158

Shepard, Jim [1956-] .... **CLC 36**
See also CA 137; CANR 59; SATA 90

Shepard, Lucius [1947-] .... **CLC 34**
See also CA 128; 141

Shepard, Sam [1943-]**CLC 4, 6, 17, 34, 41, 44; DAM DRAM; DC 5**
See also AAYA 1; CA 69-72; CABS 3; CANR 22; DLB 7; MTCW

Shepherd, Michael
See Ludlum, Robert

Sherburne, Zoa (Morin) [1912-] .... **CLC 30**
See also AAYA 13; CA 1-4R; CANR 3, 37; MAICYA; SAAS 18; SATA 3

Sheridan, Frances [1724-1766] .... **LC 7**
See also DLB 39, 84

Sheridan, Richard Brinsley [1751-1816]
NCLC 5; DA; DAB; DAC; DAM DRAM, MST; DC 1; WLC
See also CDBLB 1660-1789; DLB 89

Sherman, Jonathan Marc .... **CLC 55**
Sherman, Martin [1941(?)-] .... **CLC 19**

See also CA 116; 123

Sherwin, Judith Johnson [1936-] .**CLC 7, 15**
See also CA 25-28R; CANR 34

Sherwood, Frances [1940-] .... **CLC 81**
See also CA 146

Sherwood, Robert E(mmet) [1896-1955]
TCLC 3; DAM DRAM
See also CA 104; 153; DLB 7, 26

Shestov, Lev [1866-1938] .... **TCLC 56**

Shevchenko, Taras [1814-1861] ..... **NCLC 54**

Shiel, M(atthew) P(hipps) [1865-1947]**TCLC 8**
See also Holmes, Gordon
See also CA 106; 160; DLB 153

Shields, Carol [1935-] ..... **CLC 91, 113; DAC**
See also CA 81-84; CANR 51

Shields, David [1956-] .... **CLC 97**
See also CA 124; CANR 48

Shiga, Naoya [1883-1971] ... **CLC 33; SSC 23**
See also CA 101; 33-36R; DLB 180

Shilts, Randy [1951-1994] .... **CLC 85**
See also AAYA 19; CA 115; 127; 144; CANR 45; INT 127

Shimazaki, Haruki [1872-1943]
See Shimazaki Toson
See also CA 105; 134

Shimazaki Toson [1872-1943] .... **TCLC 5**
See also Shimazaki, Haruki
See also DLB 180

Sholokhov, Mikhail (Aleksandrovich) [1905-1984] ....
CLC 7, 15
See also CA 101; 112; MTCW; SATA-Obit 36

Shone, Patric
See Hanley, James

Shreve, Susan Richards [1939-] .... **CLC 23**
See also CA 49-52; CAAS 5; CANR 5, 38, 69; MAICYA; SATA 46, 95; SATA-Brief 41

Shue, Larry [1946-1985] .... **CLC 52; DAM DRAM**
See also CA 145; 117

Shu-Jen, Chou [1881-1936]
See Lu Hsun
See also CA 104

Shulman, Alix Kates [1932-] .... **CLC 2, 10**
See also CA 29-32R; CANR 43; SATA 7

Shuster, Joe [1914-] .... **CLC 21**

Shute, Nevil .... **CLC 30**
See also Norway, Nevil Shute

Shuttle, Penelope (Diane) [1947-] .... **CLC 7**
See also CA 93-96; CANR 39; DLB 14, 40

Sidney, Mary [1561-1621] .... **LC 19, 39**

Sidney, Sir Philip [1554-1586]**LC 19, 39; DA; DAB; DAC; DAM MST, POET**
See also CDBLB Before 1660; DLB 167

Siegel, Jerome [1914-1996] .... **CLC 21**
See also CA 116; 151

Siegel, Jerry
See Siegel, Jerome

Sienkiewicz, Henryk (Adam Alexander Pius) [1846-1916] .... **TCLC 3**
See also CA 104; 134

Sierra, Gregorio Martinez
See Martinez Sierra, Gregorio

Sierra, Maria (de la O'LeJarraga) Martinez
See Martinez Sierra, Maria (de la O'LeJarraga)

Sigal, Clancy [1926-] .... **CLC 7**
See also CA 1-4R

Sigourney, Lydia Howard (Huntley) [1791-1865] .... **NCLC 21**
See also DLB 1, 42, 73

Siguenza y Gongora, Carlos de [1645-1700]
LC 8

Sigurjonsson, Johann [1880-1919] **TCLC 27**

Sikelianos, Angelos [1884-1951] .... **TCLC 39**

Silkin, Jon [1930-].................... **CLC 2, 6, 43**
See also CA 5-8R; CAAS 5; DLB 27

Silko, Leslie (Marmon) [1948-] . **CLC 23, 74; DA; DAC; DAM MST, MULT, POP; WLCS**
See also AAYA 14; CA 115; 122; CANR 45, 65; DLB 143, 175; NNAL

Sillanpaa, Frans Eemil [1888-1964] . **CLC 19**
See also CA 129; 93-96; MTCW

Sillitoe, Alan [1928-] **CLC 1, 3, 6, 10, 19, 57**
See also AITN 1; CA 9-12R; CAAS 2; CANR 8, 26, 55; CDBLB 1960 to Present; DLB 14, 139; MTCW; SATA 61

Silone, Ignazio [1900-1978] .... **CLC 4**
See also CA 25-28; 81-84; CANR 34; CAP 2; MTCW

Silver, Joan Micklin [1935-] .... **CLC 20**
See also CA 114; 121; INT 121

Silver, Nicholas
See Faust, Frederick (Schiller)

Silverberg, Robert [1935-]**CLC 7; DAM POP**
See also AAYA 24; CA 1-4R; CAAS 3; CANR 1, 20, 36; DLB 8; INT CANR-20; MAICYA; MTCW; SATA 13, 91

Silverstein, Alvin [1933-] .... **CLC 17**
See also CA 49-52; CANR 2; CLR 25; JRDA; MAICYA; SATA 8, 69

Silverstein, Virginia B(arbara Opshelor) [1937-
] ....
CLC 17
See also CA 49-52; CANR 2; CLR 25; JRDA; MAICYA; SATA 8, 69

Sim, Georges
See Simenon, Georges (Jacques Christian)

Simak, Clifford D(onald) [1904-1988]**CLC 1, 55**
See also CA 1-4R; 125; CANR 1, 35; DLB 8; MTCW; SATA-Obit 56

Simenon, Georges (Jacques Christian) [1903-1989] ....
CLC 1, 2, 3, 8, 18, 47; DAM POP
See also CA 85-88; 129; CANR 35; DLB 72; DLBY 89; MTCW

Simic, Charles [1938-] . **CLC 6, 9, 22, 49, 68; DAM POET**
See also CA 29-32R; CAAS 4; CANR 12, 33, 52, 61; DLB 105

Simmel, Georg [1858-1918] .... **TCLC 64**
See also CA 157

Simmons, Charles (Paul) [1924-] ...... **CLC 57**
See also CA 89-92; INT 89-92

Simmons, Dan [1948-] .. **CLC 44; DAM POP**
See also AAYA 16; CA 138; CANR 53

Simmons, James (Stewart Alexander) [1933-]
CLC 43
See also CA 105; CAAS 21; DLB 40

Simms, William Gilmore [1806-1870]**NCLC 3**
See also DLB 3, 30, 59, 73

Simon, Carly [1945-] .... **CLC 26**
See also CA 105

Simon, Claude [1913-1984] **CLC 4, 9, 15, 39; DAM NOV**
See also CA 89-92; CANR 33; DLB 83; MTCW

Simon, (Marvin) Neil [1927-] **CLC 6, 11, 31, 39, 70; DAM DRAM**
See also AITN 1; CA 21-24R; CANR 26, 54; DLB 7; MTCW

Simon, Paul (Frederick) [1941(?)-] ... **CLC 17**
See also CA 116; 153

Simonon, Paul [1956(?)-] .... **CLC 30**

Simpson, Harriette
See Arnow, Harriette (Louisa) Simpson

Simpson, Louis (Aston Marantz) [1923-]**CLC 4, 7, 9, 32; DAM POET**
See also CA 1-4R; CAAS 4; CANR 1, 61; DLB 5; MTCW

Simpson, Mona (Elizabeth) [1957-] . **CLC 44**
See also CA 122; 135; CANR 68

Simpson, N(orman) F(rederick) [1919-] **C L C**

29
See also CA 13-16R; DLB 13
Sinclair, Andrew (Annandale) [1935-]**CLC 2, 14**
See also CA 9-12R; CAAS 5; CANR 14, 38; DLB 14; MTCW
Sinclair, Emil
See Hesse, Hermann
Sinclair, Iain [1943-] .... **CLC 76**
See also CA 132
Sinclair, Iain MacGregor
See Sinclair, Iain
Sinclair, Irene
See Griffith, D(avid Lewelyn) W(ark)
Sinclair, Mary Amelia St. Clair [1865(?)-1946]
See Sinclair, May
See also CA 104
Sinclair, May [1863-1946] .... **TCLC 3, 11**
See also Sinclair, Mary Amelia St. Clair
See also CA 166; DLB 36, 135
Sinclair, Roy
See Griffith, D(avid Lewelyn) W(ark)
Sinclair, Upton (Beall) [1878-1968]**CLC 1, 11, 15, 63; DA; DAB; DAC; DAM MST, NOV; WLC**
See also CA 5-8R; 25-28R; CANR 7; CDALB 1929-1941; DLB 9; INT CANR-7; MTCW; SATA 9
Singer, Isaac
See Singer, Isaac Bashevis
Singer, Isaac Bashevis [1904-1991] **CLC 1, 3, 6, 9, 11, 15, 23, 38, 69, 111; DA; DAB; DAC; DAM MST, NOV; SSC 3; WLC**
See also AITN 1, 2; CA 1-4R; 134; CANR 1, 39; CDALB 1941-1968; CLR 1; DLB 6, 28, 52; DLBY 91; JRDA; MAICYA; MTCW; SATA 3, 27; SATA-Obit 68
Singer, Israel Joshua [1893-1944] . **TCLC 33**
Singh, Khushwant [1915-] .... **CLC 11**
See also CA 9-12R; CAAS 9; CANR 6
Singleton, Ann
See Benedict, Ruth (Fulton)
Sinjohn, John
See Galsworthy, John
Sinyavsky, Andrei (Donatevich) [1925-1997] **CLC 8**
See also CA 85-88; 159
Sirin, V.
See Nabokov, Vladimir (Vladimirovich)
Sissman, L(ouis) E(dward) [1928-1976] **C L C 9, 18**
See also CA 21-24R; 65-68; CANR 13; DLB 5
Sisson, C(harles) H(ubert) [1914-] ..... **CLC 8**
See also CA 1-4R; CAAS 3; CANR 3, 48; DLB 27
Sitwell, Dame Edith [1887-1964]**CLC 2, 9, 67; DAM POET; PC 3**
See also CA 9-12R; CANR 35; CDBLB 1945-1960; DLB 20; MTCW
Siwaarmill, H. P.
See Sharp, William
Sjoewall, Maj [1935-] .... **CLC 7**
See also CA 65-68
Sjowall, Maj
See Sjoewall, Maj
Skelton, Robin [1925-1997] .... **CLC 13**
See also AITN 2; CA 5-8R; 160; CAAS 5; CANR 28; DLB 27, 53
Skolimowski, Jerzy [1938-] .... **CLC 20**
See also CA 128
Skram, Amalie (Bertha) [1847-1905]**TCLC 25**
See also CA 165
Skvorecky, Josef (Vaclav) [1924-]**CLC 15, 39, 69; DAC; DAM NOV**
See also CA 61-64; CAAS 1; CANR 10, 34, 63; MTCW
Slade, Bernard .... **CLC 11, 46**

See also Newbound, Bernard Slade
See also CAAS 9; DLB 53
Slaughter, Carolyn [1946-] .... **CLC 56**
See also CA 85-88
Slaughter, Frank G(ill) [1908-] .... **CLC 29**
See also AITN 2; CA 5-8R; CANR 5; INT CANR-5
Slavitt, David R(ytman) [1935-] ...**CLC 5, 14**
See also CA 21-24R; CAAS 3; CANR 41; DLB 5, 6
Slesinger, Tess [1905-1945] .... **TCLC 10**
See also CA 107; DLB 102
Slessor, Kenneth [1901-1971] .... **CLC 14**
See also CA 102; 89-92
Slowacki, Juliusz [1809-1849] .... **NCLC 15**
Smart, Christopher [1722-1771] **LC 3; DAM POET; PC 13**
See also DLB 109
Smart, Elizabeth [1913-1986] .... **CLC 54**
See also CA 81-84; 118; DLB 88
Smiley, Jane (Graves) [1949-] ... **CLC 53, 76; DAM POP**
See also CA 104; CANR 30, 50; INT CANR-30
Smith, A(rthur) J(ames) M(arshall) [1902-1980] .... **CLC 15; DAC**
See also CA 1-4R; 102; CANR 4; DLB 88
Smith, Adam [1723-1790] .... **LC 36**
See also DLB 104
Smith, Alexander [1829-1867] .... **NCLC 59**
See also DLB 32, 55
Smith, Anna Deavere [1950-] .... **CLC 86**
See also CA 133
Smith, Betty (Wehner) [1896-1972] . **CLC 19**
See also CA 5-8R; 33-36R; DLBY 82; SATA 6
Smith, Charlotte (Turner) [1749-1806]**NCLC 23**
See also DLB 39, 109
Smith, Clark Ashton [1893-1961] ..... **CLC 43**
See also CA 143
Smith, Dave .... **CLC 22, 42**
See also Smith, David (Jeddie)
See also CAAS 7; DLB 5
Smith, David (Jeddie) [1942-]
See Smith, Dave
See also CA 49-52; CANR 1, 59; DAM POET
Smith, Florence Margaret [1902-1971]
See Smith, Stevie
See also CA 17-18; 29-32R; CANR 35; CAP 2; DAM POET; MTCW
Smith, Iain Crichton [1928-] .... **CLC 64**
See also CA 21-24R; DLB 40, 139
Smith, John [1580(?)-1631] .... **LC 9**
See also DLB 24, 30
Smith, Johnston
See Crane, Stephen (Townley)
Smith, Joseph, Jr. [1805-1844] .... **NCLC 53**
Smith, Lee [1944-] .... **CLC 25, 73**
See also CA 114; 119; CANR 46; DLB 143; DLBY 83; INT 119
Smith, Martin
See Smith, Martin Cruz
Smith, Martin Cruz [1942-] .. **CLC 25; DAM MULT, POP**
See also BEST 89:4; CA 85-88; CANR 6, 23, 43, 65; INT CANR-23; NNAL
Smith, Mary-Ann Tirone [1944-] ..... **CLC 39**
See also CA 118; 136
Smith, Patti [1946-] .... **CLC 12**
See also CA 93-96; CANR 63
Smith, Pauline (Urmson) [1882-1959] **T C L C 25**
Smith, Rosamond
See Oates, Joyce Carol
Smith, Sheila Kaye
See Kaye-Smith, Sheila
Smith, Stevie .... **CLC 3, 8, 25, 44; PC 12**

See also Smith, Florence Margaret
See also DLB 20
Smith, Wilbur (Addison) [1933-] ...... **CLC 33**
See also CA 13-16R; CANR 7, 46, 66; MTCW
Smith, William Jay [1918-] .... **CLC 6**
See also CA 5-8R; CANR 44; DLB 5; MAICYA; SAAS 22; SATA 2, 68
Smith, Woodrow Wilson
See Kuttner, Henry
Smolenskin, Peretz [1842-1885] ..... **NCLC 30**
Smollett, Tobias (George) [1721-1771] . **LC 2**
See also CDBLB 1660-1789; DLB 39, 104
Snodgrass, W(illiam) D(e Witt) [1926-]**CLC 2, 6, 10, 18, 68; DAM POET**
See also CA 1-4R; CANR 6, 36, 65; DLB 5; MTCW
Snow, C(harles) P(ercy) [1905-1980]**CLC 1, 4, 6, 9, 13, 19; DAM NOV**
See also CA 5-8R; 101; CANR 28; CDBLB 1945-1960; DLB 15, 77; MTCW
Snow, Frances Compton
See Adams, Henry (Brooks)
Snyder, Gary (Sherman) [1930-]**CLC 1, 2, 5, 9, 32; DAM POET; PC 21**
See also CA 17-20R; CANR 30, 60; DLB 5, 16, 165
Snyder, Zilpha Keatley [1927-] .... **CLC 17**
See also AAYA 15; CA 9-12R; CANR 38; CLR 31; JRDA; MAICYA; SAAS 2; SATA 1, 28, 75
Soares, Bernardo
See Pessoa, Fernando (Antonio Nogueira)
Sobh, A.
See Shamlu, Ahmad
Sobol, Joshua .... **CLC 60**
Socrates [469B.C.-399B.C.] .... **CMLC 27**
Soderberg, Hjalmar [1869-1941] ... **TCLC 39**
Sodergran, Edith (Irene)
See Soedergran, Edith (Irene)
Soedergran, Edith (Irene) [1892-1923]**TCLC 31**
Softly, Edgar
See Lovecraft, H(oward) P(hillips)
Softly, Edward
See Lovecraft, H(oward) P(hillips)
Sokolov, Raymond [1941-] .... **CLC 7**
See also CA 85-88
Solo, Jay
See Ellison, Harlan (Jay)
Sologub, Fyodor .... **TCLC 9**
See also Teternikov, Fyodor Kuzmich
Solomons, Ikey Esquir
See Thackeray, William Makepeace
Solomos, Dionysios [1798-1857] .... **NCLC 15**
Solwoska, Mara
See French, Marilyn
Solzhenitsyn, Aleksandr I(sayevich) [1918-] **CLC 1, 2, 4, 7, 9, 10, 18, 26, 34, 78; DA; DAB; DAC; DAM MST, NOV; WLC**
See also AITN 1; CA 69-72; CANR 40, 65; MTCW
Somers, Jane
See Lessing, Doris (May)
Somerville, Edith [1858-1949] .... **TCLC 51**
See also DLB 135
Somerville & Ross
See Martin, Violet Florence; Somerville, Edith
Sommer, Scott [1951-] .... **CLC 25**
See also CA 106
Sondheim, Stephen (Joshua) [1930-]**CLC 30, 39; DAM DRAM**
See also AAYA 11; CA 103; CANR 47, 68
Song, Cathy [1955-] .... **PC 21**
See also CA 154; DLB 169
Sontag, Susan [1933-]**CLC 1, 2, 10, 13, 31, 105; DAM POP**
See also CA 17-20R; CANR 25, 51; DLB 2,

Stevens, Wallace [1879-1955]TCLC 3, 12, 45;
DA; DAB; DAC; DAM MST, POET; PC
6; WLC
See also CA 104; 124; CDALB 1929-1941;
DLB 54; MTCW

Stevenson, Anne (Katharine) [1933-] CLC 7,
33
See also CA 17-20R; CAAS 9; CANR 9, 33;
DLB 40; MTCW

Stevenson, Robert Louis (Balfour) [1850-1894]
NCLC 5, 14, 63; DA; DAB; DAC; DAM
MST, NOV; SSC 11; WLC
See also AAYA 24; CDBLB 1890-1914; CLR
10, 11; DLB 18, 57, 141, 156, 174; DLBD
13; JRDA; MAICYA; YABC 2

Stewart, J(ohn) I(nnes) M(ackintosh) [1906-
1994] ....
CLC 7, 14, 32
See also CA 85-88; 147; CAAS 3; CANR 47;
MTCW

Stewart, Mary (Florence Elinor) [1916-]C L C
7, 35; DAB
See also CA 1-4R; CANR 1, 59; SATA 12

Stewart, Mary Rainbow
See Stewart, Mary (Florence Elinor)

Stifle, June
See Campbell, Maria

Stifter, Adalbert [1805-1868] NCLC 41; SSC
28
See also DLB 133

Still, James [1906-] .... CLC 49
See also CA 65-68; CAAS 17; CANR 10, 26;
DLB 9; SATA 29

Sting
See Sumner, Gordon Matthew

Stirling, Arthur
See Sinclair, Upton (Beall)

Stitt, Milan [1941-] .... CLC 29
See also CA 69-72

Stockton, Francis Richard [1834-1902]
See Stockton, Frank R.
See also CA 108; 137; MAICYA; SATA 44

Stockton, Frank R. .... TCLC 47
See also Stockton, Francis Richard
See also DLB 42, 74; DLBD 13; SATA-Brief
32

Stoddard, Charles
See Kuttner, Henry

Stoker, Abraham [1847-1912]
See Stoker, Bram
See also CA 105; 150; DA; DAC; DAM MST,
NOV; SATA 29

Stoker, Bram [1847-1912] ..... TCLC 8; DAB;
WLC
See also Stoker, Abraham
See also AAYA 23; CDBLB 1890-1914; DLB
36, 70, 178

Stolz, Mary (Slattery) [1920-] .... CLC 12
See also AAYA 8; AITN 1; CA 5-8R; CANR
13, 41; JRDA; MAICYA; SAAS 3; SATA 10,
71

Stone, Irving [1903-1989]CLC 7; DAM POP
See also AITN 1; CA 1-4R; 129; CAAS 3;
CANR 1, 23; INT CANR-23; MTCW; SATA
3; SATA-Obit 64

Stone, Oliver (William) [1946-] .... CLC 73
See also AAYA 15; CA 110; CANR 55

Stone, Robert (Anthony) [1937-]CLC 5, 23, 42
See also CA 85-88; CANR 23, 66; DLB 152;
INT CANR-23; MTCW

Stone, Zachary
See Follett, Ken(neth Martin)

Stoppard, Tom [1937-]CLC 1, 3, 4, 5, 8, 15, 29,
34, 63, 91; DA; DAB; DAC; DAM DRAM,
MST; DC 6; WLC
See also CA 81-84; CANR 39, 67; CDBLB
1960 to Present; DLB 13; DLBY 85; MTCW

Storey, David (Malcolm) [1933-] CLC 2, 4, 5,
8; DAM DRAM
See also CA 81-84; CANR 36; DLB 13, 14;
MTCW

Storm, Hyemeyohsts [1935-] ... CLC 3; DAM
MULT
See also CA 81-84; CANR 45; NNAL

Storm, (Hans) Theodor (Woldsen) [1817-1888]
NCLC 1; SSC 27
See also DLB 129

Storni, Alfonsina [1892-1938]TCLC 5; DAM
MULT; HLC
See also CA 104; 131; HW

Stoughton, William [1631-1701] .... LC 38
See also DLB 24

Stout, Rex (Todhunter) [1886-1975] .. CLC 3
See also AITN 2; CA 61-64

Stow, (Julian) Randolph [1935-] CLC 23, 48
See also CA 13-16R; CANR 33; MTCW

Stowe, Harriet (Elizabeth) Beecher [1811-1896]
NCLC 3, 50; DA; DAB; DAC; DAM MST,
NOV; WLC
See also CDALB 1865-1917; DLB 1, 12, 42,
74, 189; JRDA; MAICYA; YABC 1

Strachey, (Giles) Lytton [1880-1932]TCLC 12
See also CA 110; DLB 149; DLBD 10

Strand, Mark [1934-]CLC 6, 18, 41, 71; DAM
POET
See also CA 21-24R; CANR 40, 65; DLB 5;
SATA 41

Straub, Peter (Francis) [1943-]CLC 28, 107;
DAM POP
See also BEST 89:1; CA 85-88; CANR 28, 65;
DLBY 84; MTCW

Strauss, Botho [1944-] .... CLC 22
See also CA 157; DLB 124

Streatfeild, (Mary) Noel [1895(?)-1986] C L C
21
See also CA 81-84; 120; CANR 31; CLR 17;
DLB 160; MAICYA; SATA 20; SATA-Obit
48

Stribling, T(homas) S(igismund) [1881-1965]
CLC 23
See also CA 107; DLB 9

Strindberg, (Johan) August [1849-1912]
TCLC 1, 8, 21, 47; DA; DAB; DAC; DAM
DRAM, MST; WLC
See also CA 104; 135

Stringer, Arthur [1874-1950] .... TCLC 37
See also CA 161; DLB 92

Stringer, David
See Roberts, Keith (John Kingston)

Stroheim, Erich von [1885-1957]... TCLC 71

Strugatskii, Arkadii (Natanovich) [1925-1991]
CLC 27
See also CA 106; 135

Strugatskii, Boris (Natanovich) [1933-] C L C
27
See also CA 106

Strummer, Joe [1953(?)-] .... CLC 30

Stuart, Don A.
See Campbell, John W(ood, Jr.)

Stuart, Ian
See MacLean, Alistair (Stuart)

Stuart, Jesse (Hilton) [1906-1984] . CLC 1, 8,
11, 14, 34; SSC 31
See also CA 5-8R; 112; CANR 31; DLB 9, 48,
102; DLBY 84; SATA 2; SATA-Obit 36

Sturgeon, Theodore (Hamilton) [1918-1985]
CLC 22, 39
See also Queen, Ellery
See also CA 81-84; 116; CANR 32; DLB 8;
DLBY 85; MTCW

Sturges, Preston [1898-1959] .... TCLC 48
See also CA 114; 149; DLB 26

Styron, William [1925-]CLC 1, 3, 5, 11, 15, 60;
DAM NOV, POP; SSC 25

See also BEST 90:4; CA 5-8R; CANR 6, 33;
CDALB 1968-1988; DLB 2, 143; DLBY 80;
INT CANR-6; MTCW

Su, Chien [1884-1918]
See Su Man-shu
See also CA 123

Suarez Lynch, B.
See Bioy Casares, Adolfo; Borges, Jorge Luis

Suckow, Ruth [1892-1960] .... SSC 18
See also CA 113; DLB 9, 102

Sudermann, Hermann [1857-1928] TCLC 15
See also CA 107; DLB 118

Sue, Eugene [1804-1857] .... NCLC 1
See also DLB 119

Sueskind, Patrick [1949-] .... CLC 44
See also Suskind, Patrick

Sukenick, Ronald [1932-] ..... CLC 3, 4, 6, 48
See also CA 25-28R; CAAS 8; CANR 32; DLB
173; DLBY 81

Suknaski, Andrew [1942-] .... CLC 19
See also CA 101; DLB 53

Sullivan, Vernon
See Vian, Boris

Sully Prudhomme [1839-1907] ...... TCLC 31

Su Man-shu .... TCLC 24
See also Su, Chien

Summerforest, Ivy B.
See Kirkup, James

Summers, Andrew James [1942-] ..... CLC 26

Summers, Andy
See Summers, Andrew James

Summers, Hollis (Spurgeon, Jr.) [1916-]C L C
10
See also CA 5-8R; CANR 3; DLB 6

Summers, (Alphonsus Joseph-Mary Augustus)
Montague [1880-1948] .... TCLC 16
See also CA 118; 163

Sumner, Gordon Matthew [1951-] ... CLC 26

Surtees, Robert Smith [1803-1864]NCLC 14
See also DLB 21

Susann, Jacqueline [1921-1974] .... CLC 3
See also AITN 1; CA 65-68; 53-56; MTCW

Su Shih [1036-1101] .... CMLC 15

Suskind, Patrick
See Sueskind, Patrick
See also CA 145

Sutcliff, Rosemary [1920-1992]CLC 26; DAB;
DAC; DAM MST, POP
See also AAYA 10; CA 5-8R; 139; CANR 37;
CLR 1, 37; JRDA; MAICYA; SATA 6, 44,
78; SATA-Obit 73

Sutro, Alfred [1863-1933] .... TCLC 6
See also CA 105; DLB 10

Sutton, Henry
See Slavitt, David R(ytman)

Svevo, Italo [1861-1928]TCLC 2, 35; SSC 25
See also Schmitz, Aron Hector

Swados, Elizabeth (A.) [1951-] .... CLC 12
See also CA 97-100; CANR 49; INT 97-100

Swados, Harvey [1920-1972] .... CLC 5
See also CA 5-8R; 37-40R; CANR 6; DLB 2

Swan, Gladys [1934-] .... CLC 69
See also CA 101; CANR 17, 39

Swarthout, Glendon (Fred) [1918-1992]C L C
35
See also CA 1-4R; 139; CANR 1, 47; SATA 26

Sweet, Sarah C.
See Jewett, (Theodora) Sarah Orne

Swenson, May [1919-1989]CLC 4, 14, 61, 106;
DA; DAB; DAC; DAM MST, POET; PC
14
See also CA 5-8R; 130; CANR 36, 61; DLB 5;
MTCW; SATA 15

Swift, Augustus
See Lovecraft, H(oward) P(hillips)

Swift, Graham (Colin) [1949-] ... CLC 41, 88
See also CA 117; 122; CANR 46; DLB 194

Swift, Jonathan [1667-1745]LC 1; DA; DAB; DAC; DAM MST, NOV, POET; PC 9; WLC
See also CDBLB 1660-1789; DLB 39, 95, 101; SATA 19
Swinburne, Algernon Charles [1837-1909] TCLC 8, 36; DA; DAB; DAC; DAM MST, POET; WLC
See also CA 105; 140; CDBLB 1832-1890; DLB 35, 57
Swinfen, Ann .... CLC 34
Swinnerton, Frank Arthur [1884-1982] C L C 31
See also CA 108; DLB 34
Swithen, John
See King, Stephen (Edwin)
Sylvia
See Ashton-Warner, Sylvia (Constance)
Symmes, Robert Edward
See Duncan, Robert (Edward)
Symonds, John Addington [1840-1893]NCLC 34
See also DLB 57, 144
Symons, Arthur [1865-1945] .... TCLC 11
See also CA 107; DLB 19, 57, 149
Symons, Julian (Gustave) [1912-1994]CLC 2, 14, 32
See also CA 49-52; 147; CAAS 3; CANR 3, 33, 59; DLB 87, 155; DLBY 92; MTCW
Synge, (Edmund) J(ohn) M(illington) [1871-1909] ....
TCLC 6, 37; DAM DRAM; DC 2
See also CA 104; 141; CDBLB 1890-1914; DLB 10, 19
Syruc, J.
See Milosz, Czeslaw
Szirtes, George [1948-] .... CLC 46
See also CA 109; CANR 27, 61
Szymborska, Wislawa [1923-] .... CLC 99
See also CA 154; DLBY 96
T. O., Nik
See Annensky, Innokenty (Fyodorovich)
Tabori, George [1914-] .... CLC 19
See also CA 49-52; CANR 4, 69
Tagore, Rabindranath [1861-1941] TCLC 3, 53; DAM DRAM, POET; PC 8
See also CA 104; 120; MTCW
Taine, Hippolyte Adolphe [1828-1893]N C L C 15
Talese, Gay [1932-] .... CLC 37
See also AITN 1; CA 1-4R; CANR 9, 58; DLB 185; INT CANR-9; MTCW
Tallent, Elizabeth (Ann) [1954-] .... CLC 45
See also CA 117; DLB 130
Tally, Ted [1952-] .... CLC 42
See also CA 120; 124; INT 124
Tamayo y Baus, Manuel [1829-1898]NCLC 1
Tammsaare, A(nton) H(ansen) [1878-1940] TCLC 27
See also CA 164
Tam'si, Tchicaya U
See Tchicaya, Gerald Felix
Tan, Amy (Ruth) [1952-]........ CLC 59; DAM MULT, NOV, POP
See also AAYA 9; BEST 89:3; CA 136; CANR 54; DLB 173; SATA 75
Tandem, Felix
See Spitteler, Carl (Friedrich Georg)
Tanizaki, Jun'ichiro [1886-1965] CLC 8, 14, 28; SSC 21
See also CA 93-96; 25-28R; DLB 180
Tanner, William
See Amis, Kingsley (William)
Tao Lao
See Storni, Alfonsina
Tarassoff, Lev
See Troyat, Henri

Tarbell, Ida M(inerva) [1857-1944]TCLC 40
See also CA 122; DLB 47
Tarkington, (Newton) Booth [1869-1946] TCLC 9
See also CA 110; 143; DLB 9, 102; SATA 17
Tarkovsky, Andrei (Arsenyevich) [1932-1986] CLC 75
See also CA 127
Tartt, Donna [1964(?)-] .... CLC 76
See also CA 142
Tasso, Torquato [1544-1595] .... LC 5
Tate, (John Orley) Allen [1899-1979]CLC 2, 4, 6, 9, 11, 14, 24
See also CA 5-8R; 85-88; CANR 32; DLB 4, 45, 63; MTCW
Tate, Ellalice
See Hibbert, Eleanor Alice Burford
Tate, James (Vincent) [1943-] .. CLC 2, 6, 25
See also CA 21-24R; CANR 29, 57; DLB 5, 169
Tavel, Ronald [1940-] .... CLC 6
See also CA 21-24R; CANR 33
Taylor, C(ecil) P(hilip) [1929-1981].. CLC 27
See also CA 25-28R; 105; CANR 47
Taylor, Edward [1642(?)-1729] .. LC 11; DA; DAB; DAC; DAM MST, POET
See also DLB 24
Taylor, Eleanor Ross [1920-] .... CLC 5
See also CA 81-84
Taylor, Elizabeth [1912-1975] .. CLC 2, 4, 29
See also CA 13-16R; CANR 9; DLB 139; MTCW; SATA 13
Taylor, Frederick Winslow [1856-1915]TCLC 76
Taylor, Henry (Splawn) [1942-] .... CLC 44
See also CA 33-36R; CAAS 7; CANR 31; DLB 5
Taylor, Kamala (Purnaiya) [1924-]
See Markandaya, Kamala
See also CA 77-80
Taylor, Mildred D. .... CLC 21
See also AAYA 10; BW 1; CA 85-88; CANR 25; CLR 9; DLB 52; JRDA; MAICYA; SAAS 5; SATA 15, 70
Taylor, Peter (Hillsman) [1917-1994] CLC 1, 4, 18, 37, 44, 50, 71; SSC 10
See also CA 13-16R; 147; CANR 9, 50; DLBY 81, 94; INT CANR-9; MTCW
Taylor, Robert Lewis [1912-] .... CLC 14
See also CA 1-4R; CANR 3, 64; SATA 10
Tchekhov, Anton
See Chekhov, Anton (Pavlovich)
Tchicaya, Gerald Felix [1931-1988]CLC 101
See also CA 129; 125
Tchicaya U Tam'si
See Tchicaya, Gerald Felix
Teasdale, Sara [1884-1933] .... TCLC 4
See also CA 104; 163; DLB 45; SATA 32
Tegner, Esaias [1782-1846] .... NCLC 2
Teilhard de Chardin, (Marie Joseph) Pierre [1881-1955] .... TCLC 9
See also CA 105
Temple, Ann
See Mortimer, Penelope (Ruth)
Tennant, Emma (Christina) [1937-] CLC 13, 52
See also CA 65-68; CAAS 9; CANR 10, 38, 59; DLB 14
Tenneshaw, S. M.
See Silverberg, Robert
Tennyson, Alfred [1809-1892] NCLC 30, 65; DA; DAB; DAC; DAM MST, POET; PC 6; WLC
See also CDBLB 1832-1890; DLB 32
Teran, Lisa St. Aubin de .... CLC 36
See also St. Aubin de Teran, Lisa
Terence [195(?)B.C.-159B.C.]CMLC 14; DC 7

Teresa de Jesus, St. [1515-1582] .... LC 18
Terkel, Louis [1912-]
See Terkel, Studs
See also CA 57-60; CANR 18, 45, 67; MTCW
Terkel, Studs .... CLC 38
See also Terkel, Louis
See also AITN 1
Terry, C. V.
See Slaughter, Frank G(ill)
Terry, Megan [1932-] .... CLC 19
See also CA 77-80; CABS 3; CANR 43; DLB 7
Tertullian [c. 155-c. 245] .... CMLC 29
Tertz, Abram
See Sinyavsky, Andrei (Donatevich)
Tesich, Steve [1943(?)-1996] .... CLC 40, 69
See also CA 105; 152; DLBY 83
Teternikov, Fyodor Kuzmich [1863-1927]
See Sologub, Fyodor
See also CA 104
Tevis, Walter [1928-1984] .... CLC 42
See also CA 113
Tey, Josephine .... TCLC 14
See also Mackintosh, Elizabeth
See also DLB 77
Thackeray, William Makepeace [1811-1863] NCLC 5, 14, 22, 43; DA; DAB; DAC; DAM MST, NOV; WLC
See also CDBLB 1832-1890; DLB 21, 55, 159, 163; SATA 23
Thakura, Ravindranatha
See Tagore, Rabindranath
Tharoor, Shashi [1956-] .... CLC 70
See also CA 141
Thelwell, Michael Miles [1939-] .... CLC 22
See also BW 2; CA 101
Theobald, Lewis, Jr.
See Lovecraft, H(oward) P(hillips)
Theodorescu, Ion N. [1880-1967]
See Arghezi, Tudor
See also CA 116
Theriault, Yves [1915-1983] . CLC 79; DAC; DAM MST
See also CA 102; DLB 88
Theroux, Alexander (Louis) [1939-]CLC 2, 25
See also CA 85-88; CANR 20, 63
Theroux, Paul (Edward) [1941-]CLC 5, 8, 11, 15, 28, 46; DAM POP
See also BEST 89:4; CA 33-36R; CANR 20, 45; DLB 2; MTCW; SATA 44
Thesen, Sharon [1946-] .... CLC 56
See also CA 163
Thevenin, Denis
See Duhamel, Georges
Thibault, Jacques Anatole Francois [1844-1924]
See France, Anatole
See also CA 106; 127; DAM NOV; MTCW
Thiele, Colin (Milton) [1920-] .... CLC 17
See also CA 29-32R; CANR 12, 28, 53; CLR 27; MAICYA; SAAS 2; SATA 14, 72
Thomas, Audrey (Callahan) [1935-] . CLC 7, 13, 37, 107; SSC 20
See also AITN 2; CA 21-24R; CAAS 19; CANR 36, 58; DLB 60; MTCW
Thomas, D(onald) M(ichael) [1935-]CLC 13, 22, 31
See also CA 61-64; CAAS 11; CANR 17, 45; CDBLB 1960 to Present; DLB 40; INT CANR-17; MTCW
Thomas, Dylan (Marlais) [1914-1953] T C L C 1, 8, 45; DA; DAB; DAC; DAM DRAM, MST, POET; PC 2; SSC 3; WLC
See also CA 104; 120; CANR 65; CDBLB 1945-1960; DLB 13, 20, 139; MTCW; SATA 60
Thomas, (Philip) Edward [1878-1917]T C L C 10; DAM POET

See also CA 106; 153; DLB 19

Thomas, Joyce Carol [1938-] .... **CLC 35**
See also AAYA 12; BW 2; CA 113; 116; CANR 48; CLR 19; DLB 33; INT 116; JRDA; MAICYA; MTCW; SAAS 7; SATA 40, 78

Thomas, Lewis [1913-1993] .... **CLC 35**
See also CA 85-88; 143; CANR 38, 60; MTCW

Thomas, Paul
See Mann, (Paul) Thomas

Thomas, Piri [1928-] .... **CLC 17**
See also CA 73-76; HW

Thomas, R(onald) S(tuart) [1913-]**CLC 6, 13, 48; DAB; DAM POET**
See also CA 89-92; CAAS 4; CANR 30; CDBLB 1960 to Present; DLB 27; MTCW

Thomas, Ross (Elmore) [1926-1995] **CLC 39**
See also CA 33-36R; 150; CANR 22, 63

Thompson, Francis Clegg
See Mencken, H(enry) L(ouis)

Thompson, Francis Joseph [1859-1907] **TCLC 4**
See also CA 104; CDBLB 1890-1914; DLB 19

Thompson, Hunter S(tockton) [1939-]**CLC 9, 17, 40, 104; DAM POP**
See also BEST 89:1; CA 17-20R; CANR 23, 46; DLB 185; MTCW

Thompson, James Myers
See Thompson, Jim (Myers)

Thompson, Jim (Myers) [1906-1977(?)] **C L C 69**
See also CA 140

Thompson, Judith .... **CLC 39**

Thomson, James [1700-1748] . **LC 16, 29, 40; DAM POET**
See also DLB 95

Thomson, James [1834-1882]**NCLC 18; DAM POET**
See also DLB 35

Thoreau, Henry David [1817-1862] **NCLC 7, 21, 61; DA; DAB; DAC; DAM MST; WLC**
See also CDALB 1640-1865; DLB 1

Thornton, Hall
See Silverberg, Robert

Thucydides [c. 455B.C.-399B.C.] .. **CMLC 17**
See also DLB 176

Thurber, James (Grover) [1894-1961]**CLC 5, 11, 25; DA; DAB; DAC; DAM DRAM, MST, NOV; SSC 1**
See also CA 73-76; CANR 17, 39; CDALB 1929-1941; DLB 4, 11, 22, 102; MAICYA; MTCW; SATA 13

Thurman, Wallace (Henry) [1902-1934] **TCLC 6; BLC 3; DAM MULT**
See also BW 1; CA 104; 124; DLB 51

Ticheburn, Cheviot
See Ainsworth, William Harrison

Tieck, (Johann) Ludwig [1773-1853]**NCLC 5, 46; SSC 31**
See also DLB 90

Tiger, Derry
See Ellison, Harlan (Jay)

Tilghman, Christopher [1948(?)-] .... **CLC 65**
See also CA 159

Tillinghast, Richard (Williford) [1940-]**C L C 29**
See also CA 29-32R; CAAS 23; CANR 26, 51

Timrod, Henry [1828-1867] .... **NCLC 25**
See also DLB 3

Tindall, Gillian (Elizabeth) [1938-].... **CLC 7**
See also CA 21-24R; CANR 11, 65

Tiptree, James, Jr. .... **CLC 48, 50**
See Sheldon, Alice Hastings Bradley
See also DLB 8

Titmarsh, Michael Angelo
See Thackeray, William Makepeace

Tocqueville, Alexis (Charles Henri Maurice Clerel Comte) [1805-1859] **NCLC 7, 63**

Tolkien, J(ohn) R(onald) R(euel) [1892-1973] **CLC 1, 2, 3, 8, 12, 38; DA; DAB; DAC; DAM MST, NOV, POP; WLC**
See also AAYA 10; AITN 1; CA 17-18; 45-48; CANR 36; CAP 2; CDBLB 1914-1945; DLB 15, 160; JRDA; MAICYA; MTCW; SATA 2, 32; SATA-Obit 24

Toller, Ernst [1893-1939] .... **TCLC 10**
See also CA 107; DLB 124

Tolson, M. B.
See Tolson, Melvin B(eaunorus)

Tolson, Melvin B(eaunorus) [1898(?)-1966] **CLC 36, 105; BLC 3; DAM MULT, POET**
See also BW 1; CA 124; 89-92; DLB 48, 76

Tolstoi, Aleksei Nikolaevich
See Tolstoy, Alexey Nikolaevich

Tolstoy, Alexey Nikolaevich [1882-1945] **TCLC 18**
See also CA 107; 158

Tolstoy, Count Leo
See Tolstoy, Leo (Nikolaevich)

Tolstoy, Leo (Nikolaevich) [1828-1910]**T C L C 4, 11, 17, 28, 44, 79; DA; DAB; DAC; DAM MST, NOV; SSC 9, 30; WLC**
See also CA 104; 123; SATA 26

Tomasi di Lampedusa, Giuseppe [1896-1957]
See Lampedusa, Giuseppe (Tomasi) di
See also CA 111

Tomlin, Lily .... **CLC 17**
See also Tomlin, Mary Jean

Tomlin, Mary Jean [1939(?)-]
See Tomlin, Lily
See also CA 117

Tomlinson, (Alfred) Charles [1927-]**CLC 2, 4, 6, 13, 45; DAM POET; PC 17**
See also CA 5-8R; CANR 33; DLB 40

Tomlinson, H(enry) M(ajor) [1873-1958] **TCLC 71**
See also CA 118; 161; DLB 36, 100, 195

Tonson, Jacob
See Bennett, (Enoch) Arnold

Toole, John Kennedy [1937-1969]**CLC 19, 64**
See also CA 104; DLBY 81

Toomer, Jean [1894-1967] . **CLC 1, 4, 13, 22; BLC 3; DAM MULT; PC 7; SSC 1; WLCS**
See also BW 1; CA 85-88; CDALB 1917-1929; DLB 45, 51; MTCW

Torley, Luke
See Blish, James (Benjamin)

Tornimparte, Alessandra
See Ginzburg, Natalia

Torre, Raoul della
See Mencken, H(enry) L(ouis)

Torrey, E(dwin) Fuller [1937-] .... **CLC 34**
See also CA 119

Torsvan, Ben Traven
See Traven, B.

Torsvan, Benno Traven
See Traven, B.

Torsvan, Berick Traven
See Traven, B.

Torsvan, Berwick Traven
See Traven, B.

Torsvan, Bruno Traven
See Traven, B.

Torsvan, Traven
See Traven, B.

Tournier, Michel (Edouard) [1924-] . **CLC 6, 23, 36, 95**
See also CA 49-52; CANR 3, 36; DLB 83; MTCW; SATA 23

Tournimparte, Alessandra
See Ginzburg, Natalia

Towers, Ivar
See Kornbluth, C(yril) M.

Towne, Robert (Burton) [1936(?)-] .. **CLC 87**
See also CA 108; DLB 44

Townsend, Sue .... **CLC 61**
See also Townsend, Susan Elaine
See also SATA 55, 93; SATA-Brief 48

Townsend, Susan Elaine [1946-]
See Townsend, Sue
See also CA 119; 127; CANR 65; DAB; DAC; DAM MST

Townshend, Peter (Dennis Blandford) [1945-] **CLC 17, 42**
See also CA 107

Tozzi, Federigo [1883-1920] .... **TCLC 31**
See also CA 160

Traill, Catharine Parr [1802-1899]**NCLC 31**
See also DLB 99

Trakl, Georg [1887-1914] .... **TCLC 5; PC 20**
See also CA 104; 165

Transtroemer, Tomas (Goesta) [1931-] . **C L C 52, 65; DAM POET**
See also CA 117; 129; CAAS 17

Transtromer, Tomas Gosta
See Transtroemer, Tomas (Goesta)

Traven, B. [(?)-1969] .... **CLC 8, 11**
See also CA 19-20; 25-28R; CAP 2; DLB 9, 56; MTCW

Treitel, Jonathan [1959-] .... **CLC 70**

Tremain, Rose [1943-] .... **CLC 42**
See also CA 97-100; CANR 44; DLB 14

Tremblay, Michel [1942-]**CLC 29, 102; DAC; DAM MST**
See also CA 116; 128; DLB 60; MTCW

Trevanian .... **CLC 29**
See also Whitaker, Rod(ney)

Trevor, Glen
See Hilton, James

Trevor, William [1928-] **CLC 7, 9, 14, 25, 71; SSC 21**
See also Cox, William Trevor
See also DLB 14, 139

Trifonov, Yuri (Valentinovich) [1925-1981] **CLC 45**
See also CA 126; 103; MTCW

Trilling, Lionel [1905-1975] ... **CLC 9, 11, 24**
See also CA 9-12R; 61-64; CANR 10; DLB 28, 63; INT CANR-10; MTCW

Trimball, W. H.
See Mencken, H(enry) L(ouis)

Tristan
See Gomez de la Serna, Ramon

Tristram
See Housman, A(lfred) E(dward)

Trogdon, William (Lewis) [1939-]
See Heat-Moon, William Least
See also CA 115; 119; CANR 47; INT 119

Trollope, Anthony [1815-1882] **NCLC 6, 33; DA; DAB; DAC; DAM MST, NOV; SSC 28; WLC**
See also CDBLB 1832-1890; DLB 21, 57, 159; SATA 22

Trollope, Frances [1779-1863] .... **NCLC 30**
See also DLB 21, 166

Trotsky, Leon [1879-1940] .... **TCLC 22**
See also CA 118

Trotter (Cockburn), Catharine [1679-1749] **LC 8**
See also DLB 84

Trout, Kilgore
See Farmer, Philip Jose

Trow, George W. S. [1943-] .... **CLC 52**
See also CA 126

Troyat, Henri [1911-] .... **CLC 23**
See also CA 45-48; CANR 2, 33, 67; MTCW

Trudeau, G(arretson) B(eekman) [1948-]
See Trudeau, Garry B.
See also CA 81-84; CANR 31; SATA 35

Trudeau, Garry B. .... **CLC 12**
See also Trudeau, G(arretson) B(eekman)
See also AAYA 10; AITN 2

Truffaut, Francois [1932-1984] **CLC 20, 101**
See also CA 81-84; 113; CANR 34

Trumbo, Dalton [1905-1976] .... **CLC 19**
See also CA 21-24R; 69-72; CANR 10; DLB 26

Trumbull, John [1750-1831] .... **NCLC 30**
See also DLB 31

Trundlett, Helen B.
See Eliot, T(homas) S(tearns)

Tryon, Thomas [1926-1991]**CLC 3, 11; DAM POP**
See also AITN 1; CA 29-32R; 135; CANR 32; MTCW

Tryon, Tom
See Tryon, Thomas

Ts'ao Hsueh-ch'in [1715(?)-1763].......... **LC 1**

Tsushima, Shuji [1909-1948]
See Dazai Osamu
See also CA 107

Tsvetaeva (Efron), Marina (Ivanovna) [1892-1941] ....
TCLC 7, 35; PC 14
See also CA 104; 128; MTCW

Tuck, Lily [1938-] .... **CLC 70**
See also CA 139

Tu Fu [712-770] .... **PC 9**
See also DAM MULT

Tunis, John R(oberts) [1889-1975] ... **CLC 12**
See also CA 61-64; CANR 62; DLB 22, 171; JRDA; MAICYA; SATA 37; SATA-Brief 30

Tuohy, Frank .... **CLC 37**
See also Tuohy, John Francis
See also DLB 14, 139

Tuohy, John Francis [1925-]
See Tuohy, Frank
See also CA 5-8R; CANR 3, 47

Turco, Lewis (Putnam) [1934-] ... **CLC 11, 63**
See also CA 13-16R; CAAS 22; CANR 24, 51; DLBY 84

Turgenev, Ivan [1818-1883] .. **NCLC 21; DA; DAB; DAC; DAM MST, NOV; DC 7; SSC 7; WLC**

Turgot, Anne-Robert-Jacques [1727-1781]**LC 26**

Turner, Frederick [1943-] .... **CLC 48**
See also CA 73-76; CAAS 10; CANR 12, 30, 56; DLB 40

Tutu, Desmond M(pilo) [1931-]**CLC 80; BLC 3; DAM MULT**
See also BW 1; CA 125; CANR 67

Tutuola, Amos [1920-1997] ... **CLC 5, 14, 29; BLC 3; DAM MULT**
See also BW 2; CA 9-12R; 159; CANR 27, 66; DLB 125; MTCW

Twain, MarkTCLC **6, 12, 19, 36, 48, 59; SSC 6, 26; WLC**
See also Clemens, Samuel Langhorne
See also AAYA 20; DLB 11, 12, 23, 64, 74

Tyler, Anne [1941-]**CLC 7, 11, 18, 28, 44, 59, 103; DAM NOV, POP**
See also AAYA 18; BEST 89:1; CA 9-12R; CANR 11, 33, 53; DLB 6, 143; DLBY 82; MTCW; SATA 7, 90

Tyler, Royall [1757-1826] .... **NCLC 3**
See also DLB 37

Tynan, Katharine [1861-1931]......... **TCLC 3**
See also CA 104; DLB 153

Tyutchev, Fyodor [1803-1873] .... **NCLC 34**

Tzara, Tristan [1896-1963] .... **CLC 47; DAM POET**
See also CA 153; 89-92

Uhry, Alfred [1936-] **CLC 55; DAM DRAM, POP**
See also CA 127; 133; INT 133

Ulf, Haerved
See Strindberg, (Johan) August

Ulf, Harved

See Strindberg, (Johan) August

Ulibarri, Sabine R(eyes) [1919-] ..... **CLC 83; DAM MULT**
See also CA 131; DLB 82; HW

Unamuno (y Jugo), Miguel de [1864-1936]
TCLC 2, 9; DAM MULT, NOV; HLC; SSC 11
See also CA 104; 131; DLB 108; HW; MTCW

Undercliffe, Errol
See Campbell, (John) Ramsey

Underwood, Miles
See Glassco, John

Undset, Sigrid [1882-1949] ..... **TCLC 3; DA; DAB; DAC; DAM MST, NOV; WLC**
See also CA 104; 129; MTCW

Ungaretti, Giuseppe [1888-1970]**CLC 7, 11, 15**
See also CA 19-20; 25-28R; CAP 2; DLB 114

Unger, Douglas [1952-] .... **CLC 34**
See also CA 130

Unsworth, Barry (Forster) [1930-] .. **CLC 76**
See also CA 25-28R; CANR 30, 54; DLB 194

Updike, John (Hoyer) [1932-]**CLC 1, 2, 3, 5, 7, 9, 13, 15, 23, 34, 43, 70; DA; DAB; DAC; DAM MST, NOV, POET, POP; SSC 13, 27; WLC**
See also CA 1-4R; CABS 1; CANR 4, 33, 51; CDALB 1968-1988; DLB 2, 5, 143; DLBD 3; DLBY 80, 82, 97; MTCW

Upshaw, Margaret Mitchell
See Mitchell, Margaret (Munnerlyn)

Upton, Mark
See Sanders, Lawrence

Urdang, Constance (Henriette) [1922-] **C L C 47**
See also CA 21-24R; CANR 9, 24

Uriel, Henry
See Faust, Frederick (Schiller)

Uris, Leon (Marcus) [1924-]**CLC 7, 32; DAM NOV, POP**
See also AITN 1, 2; BEST 89:2; CA 1-4R; CANR 1, 40, 65; MTCW; SATA 49

Urmuz
See Codrescu, Andrei

Urquhart, Jane [1949-] .... **CLC 90; DAC**
See also CA 113; CANR 32, 68

Ustinov, Peter (Alexander) [1921-]..... **CLC 1**
See also AITN 1; CA 13-16R; CANR 25, 51; DLB 13

U Tam'si, Gerald Felix Tchicaya
See Tchicaya, Gerald Felix

U Tam'si, Tchicaya
See Tchicaya, Gerald Felix

Vachss, Andrew (Henry) [1942-] .... **CLC 106**
See also CA 118; CANR 44

Vachss, Andrew H.
See Vachss, Andrew (Henry)

Vaculik, Ludvik [1926-] .... **CLC 7**
See also CA 53-56

Vaihinger, Hans [1852-1933] .... **TCLC 71**
See also CA 116; 166

Valdez, Luis (Miguel) [1940-] **CLC 84; DAM MULT; HLC**
See also CA 101; CANR 32; DLB 122; HW

Valenzuela, Luisa [1938-]**CLC 31, 104; DAM MULT; SSC 14**
See also CA 101; CANR 32, 65; DLB 113; HW

Valera y Alcala-Galiano, Juan [1824-1905]
TCLC 10
See also CA 106

Valery, (Ambroise) Paul (Toussaint Jules) [1871-1945]**TCLC 4, 15; DAM POET; PC 9**
See also CA 104; 122; MTCW

Valle-Inclan, Ramon (Maria) del [1866-1936]
TCLC 5; DAM MULT; HLC
See also CA 106; 153; DLB 134

Vallejo, Antonio Buero

See Buero Vallejo, Antonio

Vallejo, Cesar (Abraham) [1892-1938]**TCLC 3, 56; DAM MULT; HLC**
See also CA 105; 153; HW

Vallette, Marguerite Eymery
See Rachilde

Valle Y Pena, Ramon del
See Valle-Inclan, Ramon (Maria) del

Van Ash, Cay [1918-] .... **CLC 34**

Vanbrugh, Sir John [1664-1726]**LC 21; DAM DRAM**
See also DLB 80

Van Campen, Karl
See Campbell, John W(ood, Jr.)

Vance, Gerald
See Silverberg, Robert

Vance, Jack .... **CLC 35**
See also Kuttner, Henry; Vance, John Holbrook
See also DLB 8

Vance, John Holbrook [1916-]
See Queen, Ellery; Vance, Jack
See also CA 29-32R; CANR 17, 65; MTCW

Van Den Bogarde, Derek Jules Gaspard Ulric Niven [1921-]
See Bogarde, Dirk
See also CA 77-80

Vandenburgh, Jane .... **CLC 59**

Vanderhaeghe, Guy [1951-] .... **CLC 41**
See also CA 113

van der Post, Laurens (Jan) [1906-1996]**CLC 5**
See also CA 5-8R; 155; CANR 35

van de Wetering, Janwillem [1931-] **CLC 47**
See also CA 49-52; CANR 4, 62

Van Dine, S. S. .... **TCLC 23**
See also Wright, Willard Huntington

Van Doren, Carl (Clinton) [1885-1950]**TCLC 18**
See also CA 111

Van Doren, Mark [1894-1972] ...... **CLC 6, 10**
See also CA 1-4R; 37-40R; CANR 3; DLB 45; MTCW

Van Druten, John (William) [1901-1957]
TCLC 2
See also CA 104; 161; DLB 10

Van Duyn, Mona (Jane) [1921-]**CLC 3, 7, 63; DAM POET**
See also CA 9-12R; CANR 7, 38, 60; DLB 5

Van Dyne, Edith
See Baum, L(yman) Frank

van Itallie, Jean-Claude [1936-] .... **CLC 3**
See also CA 45-48; CAAS 2; CANR 1, 48; DLB 7

van Ostaijen, Paul [1896-1928] ...... **TCLC 33**
See also CA 163

Van Peebles, Melvin [1932-]**CLC 2, 20; DAM MULT**
See also BW 2; CA 85-88; CANR 27, 67

Vansittart, Peter [1920-] .... **CLC 42**
See also CA 1-4R; CANR 3, 49

Van Vechten, Carl [1880-1964] .... **CLC 33**
See also CA 89-92; DLB 4, 9, 51

Van Vogt, A(lfred) E(lton) [1912-] ...... **CLC 1**
See also CA 21-24R; CANR 28; DLB 8; SATA 14

Varda, Agnes [1928-] .... **CLC 16**
See also CA 116; 122

Vargas Llosa, (Jorge) Mario (Pedro) [1936-]
CLC 3, 6, 9, 10, 15, 31, 42, 85; DA; DAB; DAC; DAM MST, MULT, NOV; HLC
See also CA 73-76; CANR 18, 32, 42, 67; DLB 145; HW; MTCW

Vasiliu, Gheorghe [1881-1957]
See Bacovia, George
See also CA 123

Vassa, Gustavus
See Equiano, Olaudah

Vassilikos, Vassilis [1933-] .... **CLC 4, 8**
  See also CA 81-84
Vaughan, Henry [1621-1695] .... **LC 27**
  See also DLB 131
Vaughn, Stephanie .... **CLC 62**
Vazov, Ivan (Minchov) [1850-1921]**TCLC 25**
  See also CA 121; DLB 147
Veblen, Thorstein B(unde) [1857-1929]**TCLC 31**
  See also CA 115; 165
Vega, Lope de [1562-1635] .... **LC 23**
Venison, Alfred
  See Pound, Ezra (Weston Loomis)
Verdi, Marie de
  See Mencken, H(enry) L(ouis)
Verdu, Matilde
  See Cela, Camilo Jose
Verga, Giovanni (Carmelo) [1840-1922]
  TCLC 3; SSC 21
  See also CA 104; 123
Vergil [70B.C.-19B.C.] **CMLC 9; DA; DAB; DAC; DAM MST, POET; PC 12; WLCS**
Verhaeren, Emile (Adolphe Gustave) [1855-1916] .... **TCLC 12**
  See also CA 109
Verlaine, Paul (Marie) [1844-1896] **NCLC 2, 51; DAM POET; PC 2**
Verne, Jules (Gabriel) [1828-1905] **TCLC 6, 52**
  See also AAYA 16; CA 110; 131; DLB 123; JRDA; MAICYA; SATA 21
Very, Jones [1813-1880] .... **NCLC 9**
  See also DLB 1
Vesaas, Tarjei [1897-1970] .... **CLC 48**
  See also CA 29-32R
Vialis, Gaston
  See Simenon, Georges (Jacques Christian)
Vian, Boris [1920-1959] .... **TCLC 9**
  See also CA 106; 164; DLB 72
Viaud, (Louis Marie) Julien [1850-1923]
  See Loti, Pierre
  See also CA 107
Vicar, Henry
  See Felsen, Henry Gregor
Vicker, Angus
  See Felsen, Henry Gregor
Vidal, Gore [1925-]**CLC 2, 4, 6, 8, 10, 22, 33, 72; DAM NOV, POP**
  See also AITN 1; BEST 90:2; CA 5-8R; CANR 13, 45, 65; DLB 6, 152; INT CANR-13; MTCW
Viereck, Peter (Robert Edwin) [1916-]**CLC 4**
  See also CA 1-4R; CANR 1, 47; DLB 5
Vigny, Alfred (Victor) de [1797-1863] **NCLC 7; DAM POET**
  See also DLB 119, 192
Vilakazi, Benedict Wallet [1906-1947]**TCLC 37**
Villa, Jose Garcia [1904-1997] .... **PC 22**
  See also CA 25-28R; CANR 12
Villaurrutia, Xavier [1903-1950] ... **TCLC 80**
  See also HW
Villiers de l'Isle Adam, Jean Marie Mathias Philippe Auguste, Comte de [1838-1889]
  NCLC 3; SSC 14
  See also DLB 123
Villon, Francois [1431-1463(?)] .... **PC 13**
Vinci, Leonardo da [1452-1519] .... **LC 12**
Vine, Barbara .... **CLC 50**
  See also Rendell, Ruth (Barbara)
  See also BEST 90:4
Vinge, Joan D(ennison) [1948-]**CLC 30; SSC 24**
  See also CA 93-96; SATA 36
Violis, G.
  See Simenon, Georges (Jacques Christian)
Virgil

See Vergil
Visconti, Luchino [1906-1976] .... **CLC 16**
  See also CA 81-84; 65-68; CANR 39
Vittorini, Elio [1908-1966] .... **CLC 6, 9, 14**
  See also CA 133; 25-28R
Vizenor, Gerald Robert [1934-] .... **CLC 103; DAM MULT**
  See also CA 13-16R; CAAS 22; CANR 5, 21, 44, 67; DLB 175; NNAL
Vizinczey, Stephen [1933-] .... **CLC 40**
  See also CA 128; INT 128
Vliet, R(ussell) G(ordon) [1929-1984]**CLC 22**
  See also CA 37-40R; 112; CANR 18
Vogau, Boris Andreyevich [1894-1937(?)]
  See Pilnyak, Boris
  See also CA 123
Vogel, Paula A(nne) [1951-] .... **CLC 76**
  See also CA 108
Voigt, Cynthia [1942-] .... **CLC 30**
  See also AAYA 3; CA 106; CANR 18, 37, 40; CLR 13,48; INT CANR-18; JRDA; MAICYA; SATA 48, 79; SATA-Brief 33
Voigt, Ellen Bryant [1943-] .... **CLC 54**
  See also CA 69-72; CANR 11, 29, 55; DLB 120
Voinovich, Vladimir (Nikolaevich) [1932-]
  CLC 10, 49
  See also CA 81-84; CAAS 12; CANR 33, 67; MTCW
Vollmann, William T. [1959-] **CLC 89; DAM NOV, POP**
  See also CA 134; CANR 67
Voloshinov, V. N.
  See Bakhtin, Mikhail Mikhailovich
Voltaire [1694-1778]**LC 14; DA; DAB; DAC; DAM DRAM, MST; SSC 12; WLC**
von Daeniken, Erich [1935-] .... **CLC 30**
  See also AITN 1; CA 37-40R; CANR 17, 44
von Daniken, Erich
  See von Daeniken, Erich
von Heidenstam, (Carl Gustaf) Verner
  See Heidenstam, (Carl Gustaf) Verner von
von Heyse, Paul (Johann Ludwig)
  See Heyse, Paul (Johann Ludwig von)
von Hofmannsthal, Hugo
  See Hofmannsthal, Hugo von
von Horvath, Odon
  See Horvath, Oedoen von
von Horvath, Oedoen
  See Horvath, Oedoen von
von Liliencron, (Friedrich Adolf Axel) Detlev
  See Liliencron, (Friedrich Adolf Axel) Detlev von
Vonnegut, Kurt, Jr. [1922-]**CLC 1, 2, 3, 4, 5, 8, 12, 22, 40, 60, 111; DA; DAB; DAC; DAM MST, NOV, POP; SSC 8; WLC**
  See also AAYA 6; AITN 1; BEST 90:4; CA 1-4R; CANR 1, 25, 49; CDALB 1968-1988; DLB 2, 8, 152; DLBD 3; DLBY 80; MTCW
Von Rachen, Kurt
  See Hubbard, L(afayette) Ron(ald)
von Rezzori (d'Arezzo), Gregor
  See Rezzori (d'Arezzo), Gregor von
von Sternberg, Josef
  See Sternberg, Josef von
Vorster, Gordon [1924-] .... **CLC 34**
  See also CA 133
Vosce, Trudie
  See Ozick, Cynthia
Voznesensky, Andrei (Andreievich) [1933-]
  CLC 1, 15, 57; DAM POET
  See also CA 89-92; CANR 37; MTCW
Waddington, Miriam [1917-] .... **CLC 28**
  See also CA 21-24R; CANR 12, 30; DLB 68
Wagman, Fredrica [1937-] .... **CLC 7**
  See also CA 97-100; INT 97-100
Wagner, Linda W.
  See Wagner-Martin, Linda (C.)

Wagner, Linda Welshimer
  See Wagner-Martin, Linda (C.)
Wagner, Richard [1813-1883] .... **NCLC 9**
  See also DLB 129
Wagner-Martin, Linda (C.) [1936-] . **CLC 50**
  See also CA 159
Wagoner, David (Russell) [1926-]**CLC 3, 5, 15**
  See also CA 1-4R; CAAS 3; CANR 2; DLB 5; SATA 14
Wah, Fred(erick James) [1939-] .... **CLC 44**
  See also CA 107; 141; DLB 60
Wahloo, Per [1926-1975] .... **CLC 7**
  See also CA 61-64
Wahloo, Peter
  See Wahloo, Per
Wain, John (Barrington) [1925-1994]**CLC 2, 11, 15, 46**
  See also CA 5-8R; 145; CAAS 4; CANR 23, 54; CDBLB 1960 to Present; DLB 15, 27, 139, 155; MTCW
Wajda, Andrzej [1926-] .... **CLC 16**
  See also CA 102
Wakefield, Dan [1932-] .... **CLC 7**
  See also CA 21-24R; CAAS 7
Wakoski, Diane [1937-]**CLC 2, 4, 7, 9, 11, 40; DAM POET; PC 15**
  See also CA 13-16R; CAAS 1; CANR 9, 60; DLB 5; INT CANR-9
Wakoski-Sherbell, Diane
  See Wakoski, Diane
Walcott, Derek (Alton) [1930-]**CLC 2, 4, 9, 14, 25, 42, 67, 76; BLC 3; DAB; DAC; DAM MST, MULT, POET; DC 7**
  See also BW 2; CA 89-92; CANR 26, 47; DLB 117; DLBY 81; MTCW
Waldman, Anne (Lesley) [1945-] .... **CLC 7**
  See also CA 37-40R; CAAS 17; CANR 34, 69; DLB 16
Waldo, E. Hunter
  See Sturgeon, Theodore (Hamilton)
Waldo, Edward Hamilton
  See Sturgeon, Theodore (Hamilton)
Walker, Alice (Malsenior) [1944-]**CLC 5, 6, 9, 19, 27, 46, 58, 103; BLC 3; DA; DAB; DAC; DAM MST, MULT, NOV, POET, POP; SSC 5; WLCS**
  See also AAYA 3; BEST 89:4; BW 2; CA 37-40R; CANR 9, 27, 49, 66; CDALB 1968-1988; DLB 6, 33, 143; INT CANR-27; MTCW; SATA 31
Walker, David Harry [1911-1992] .... **CLC 14**
  See also CA 1-4R; 137; CANR 1; SATA 8; SATA-Obit 71
Walker, Edward Joseph [1934-]
  See Walker, Ted
  See also CA 21-24R; CANR 12, 28, 53
Walker, George F. [1947-] **CLC 44, 61; DAB; DAC; DAM MST**
  See also CA 103; CANR 21, 43, 59; DLB 60
Walker, Joseph A. [1935-] ...... **CLC 19; DAM DRAM, MST**
  See also BW 1; CA 89-92; CANR 26; DLB 38
Walker, Margaret (Abigail) [1915-]**CLC 1, 6; BLC; DAM MULT; PC 20**
  See also BW 2; CA 73-76; CANR 26, 54; DLB 76, 152; MTCW
Walker, Ted .... **CLC 13**
  See also Walker, Edward Joseph
  See also DLB 40
Wallace, David Foster [1962-] .... **CLC 50**
  See also CA 132; CANR 59
Wallace, Dexter
  See Masters, Edgar Lee
Wallace, (Richard Horatio) Edgar [1875-1932]
  TCLC 57
  See also CA 115; DLB 70
Wallace, Irving [1916-1990]**CLC 7, 13; DAM**

NOV, POP
See also AITN 1; CA 1-4R; 132; CAAS 1; CANR 1, 27; INT CANR-27; MTCW

Wallant, Edward Lewis [1926-1962] **CLC 5, 10**
See also CA 1-4R; CANR 22; DLB 2, 28, 143; MTCW

Walley, Byron
See Card, Orson Scott

Walpole, Horace [1717-1797] .... **LC 2**
See also DLB 39, 104

Walpole, Hugh (Seymour) [1884-1941]**T C L C 5**
See also CA 104; 165; DLB 34

Walser, Martin [1927-] .... **CLC 27**
See also CA 57-60; CANR 8, 46; DLB 75, 124

Walser, Robert [1878-1956]**TCLC 18; SSC 20**
See also CA 118; 165; DLB 66

Walsh, Jill Paton .... **CLC 35**
See also Paton Walsh, Gillian
See also AAYA 11; CLR 2; DLB 161; SAAS 3

Walter, Villiam Christian
See Andersen, Hans Christian

Wambaugh, Joseph (Aloysius, Jr.) [1937-]
CLC 3, 18; DAM NOV, POP
See also AITN 1; BEST 89:3; CA 33-36R; CANR 42, 65; DLB 6; DLBY 83; MTCW

Wang Wei [699(?)-761(?)] .... **PC 18**

Ward, Arthur Henry Sarsfield [1883-1959]
See Rohmer, Sax
See also CA 108

Ward, Douglas Turner [1930-] .... **CLC 19**
See also BW 1; CA 81-84; CANR 27; DLB 7, 38

Ward, Mary Augusta
See Ward, Mrs. Humphry

Ward, Mrs. Humphry [1851-1920] **TCLC 55**
See also DLB 18

Ward, Peter
See Faust, Frederick (Schiller)

Warhol, Andy [1928(?)-1987] .... **CLC 20**
See also AAYA 12; BEST 89:4; CA 89-92; 121; CANR 34

Warner, Francis (Robert le Plastrier) [1937-]
CLC 14
See also CA 53-56; CANR 11

Warner, Marina [1946-] .... **CLC 59**
See also CA 65-68; CANR 21, 55; DLB 194

Warner, Rex (Ernest) [1905-1986] ... **CLC 45**
See also CA 89-92; 119; DLB 15

Warner, Susan (Bogert) [1819-1885]**NCLC 31**
See also DLB 3, 42

Warner, Sylvia (Constance) Ashton
See Ashton-Warner, Sylvia (Constance)

Warner, Sylvia Townsend [1893-1978]**CLC 7, 19; SSC 23**
See also CA 61-64; 77-80; CANR 16, 60; DLB 34, 139; MTCW

Warren, Mercy Otis [1728-1814] ... **NCLC 13**
See also DLB 31, 200

Warren, Robert Penn [1905-1989]**CLC 1, 4, 6, 8, 10, 13, 18, 39, 53, 59; DA; DAB; DAC; DAM MST, NOV, POET; SSC 4; WLC**
See also AITN 1; CA 13-16R; 129; CANR 10, 47; CDALB 1968-1988; DLB 2, 48, 152; DLBY 80, 89; INT CANR-10; MTCW; SATA 46; SATA-Obit 63

Warshofsky, Isaac
See Singer, Isaac Bashevis

Warton, Thomas [1728-1790] ..**LC 15; DAM POET**
See also DLB 104, 109

Waruk, Kona
See Harris, (Theodore) Wilson

Warung, Price [1855-1911] .... **TCLC 45**

Warwick, Jarvis
See Garner, Hugh

Washington, Alex
See Harris, Mark

Washington, Booker T(aliaferro) [1856-1915]
TCLC 10; BLC 3; DAM MULT
See also BW 1; CA 114; 125; SATA 28

Washington, George [1732-1799] .... **LC 25**
See also DLB 31

Wassermann, (Karl) Jakob [1873-1934]
TCLC 6
See also CA 104; DLB 66

Wasserstein, Wendy [1950-] **CLC 32, 59, 90; DAM DRAM; DC 4**
See also CA 121; 129; CABS 3; CANR 53; INT 129; SATA 94

Waterhouse, Keith (Spencer) [1929-]**CLC 47**
See also CA 5-8R; CANR 38, 67; DLB 13, 15; MTCW

Waters, Frank (Joseph) [1902-1995] **CLC 88**
See also CA 5-8R; 149; CAAS 13; CANR 3, 18, 63; DLBY 86

Waters, Roger [1944-] .... **CLC 35**

Watkins, Frances Ellen
See Harper, Frances Ellen Watkins

Watkins, Gerrold
See Malzberg, Barry N(athaniel)

Watkins, Gloria [1955(?)-]
See hooks, bell
See also BW 2; CA 143

Watkins, Paul [1964-] .... **CLC 55**
See also CA 132; CANR 62

Watkins, Vernon Phillips [1906-1967]**CLC 43**
See also CA 9-10; 25-28R; CAP 1; DLB 20

Watson, Irving S.
See Mencken, H(enry) L(ouis)

Watson, John H.
See Farmer, Philip Jose

Watson, Richard F.
See Silverberg, Robert

Waugh, Auberon (Alexander) [1939-] **CLC 7**
See also CA 45-48; CANR 6, 22; DLB 14, 194

Waugh, Evelyn (Arthur St. John) [1903-1966]
CLC 1, 3, 8, 13, 19, 27, 44, 107; DA; DAB; DAC; DAM MST, NOV, POP; WLC
See also CA 85-88; 25-28R; CANR 22; CDBLB 1914-1945; DLB 15, 162, 195; MTCW

Waugh, Harriet [1944-] .... **CLC 6**
See also CA 85-88; CANR 22

Ways, C. R.
See Blount, Roy (Alton), Jr.

Waystaff, Simon
See Swift, Jonathan

Webb, (Martha) Beatrice (Potter) [1858-1943]
TCLC 22
See also Potter, (Helen) Beatrix
See also CA 117

Webb, Charles (Richard) [1939-] .... **CLC 7**
See also CA 25-28R

Webb, James H(enry), Jr. [1946-] .... **CLC 22**
See also CA 81-84

Webb, Mary (Gladys Meredith) [1881-1927]
TCLC 24
See also CA 123; DLB 34

Webb, Mrs. Sidney
See Webb, (Martha) Beatrice (Potter)

Webb, Phyllis [1927-] .... **CLC 18**
See also CA 104; CANR 23; DLB 53

Webb, Sidney (James) [1859-1947] **TCLC 22**
See also CA 117; 163; DLB 190

Webber, Andrew Lloyd .... **CLC 21**
See also Lloyd Webber, Andrew

Weber, Lenora Mattingly [1895-1971]**CLC 12**
See also CA 19-20; 29-32R; CAP 1; SATA 2; SATA-Obit 26

Weber, Max [1864-1920] .... **TCLC 69**
See also CA 109

Webster, John [1579(?)-1634(?)] **LC 33; DA; DAB; DAC; DAM DRAM, MST; DC 2;**

WLC
See also CDBLB Before 1660; DLB 58

Webster, Noah [1758-1843] .... **NCLC 30**

Wedekind, (Benjamin) Frank(lin) [1864-1918]
TCLC 7; DAM DRAM
See also CA 104; 153; DLB 118

Weidman, Jerome [1913-] .... **CLC 7**
See also AITN 2; CA 1-4R; CANR 1; DLB 28

Weil, Simone (Adolphine) [1909-1943]**T C L C 23**
See also CA 117; 159

Weinstein, Nathan
See West, Nathanael

Weinstein, Nathan von Wallenstein
See West, Nathanael

Weir, Peter (Lindsay) [1944-] .... **CLC 20**
See also CA 113; 123

Weiss, Peter (Ulrich) [1916-1982] **CLC 3, 15, 51; DAM DRAM**
See also CA 45-48; 106; CANR 3; DLB 69, 124

Weiss, Theodore (Russell) [1916-]**CLC 3, 8, 14**
See also CA 9-12R; CAAS 2; CANR 46; DLB 5

Welch, (Maurice) Denton [1915-1948]**T C L C 22**
See also CA 121; 148

Welch, James [1940-] .. **CLC 6, 14, 52; DAM MULT, POP**
See also CA 85-88; CANR 42, 66; DLB 175; NNAL

Weldon, Fay [1931-]**CLC 6, 9, 11, 19, 36, 59; DAM POP**
See also CA 21-24R; CANR 16, 46, 63; CDBLB 1960 to Present; DLB 14, 194; INT CANR-16; MTCW

Wellek, Rene [1903-1995] .... **CLC 28**
See also CA 5-8R; 150; CAAS 7; CANR 8; DLB 63; INT CANR-8

Weller, Michael [1942-] .... **CLC 10, 53**
See also CA 85-88

Weller, Paul [1958-] .... **CLC 26**

Wellershoff, Dieter [1925-] .... **CLC 46**
See also CA 89-92; CANR 16, 37

Welles, (George) Orson [1915-1985]**CLC 20, 80**
See also CA 93-96; 117

Wellman, John McDowell [1945-]
See Wellman, Mac
See also CA 166

Wellman, Mac [1945-] ......:................ **CLC 65**
See also Wellman, John McDowell; Wellman, John McDowell

Wellman, Manly Wade [1903-1986] . **CLC 49**
See also CA 1-4R; 118; CANR 6, 16, 44; SATA 6; SATA-Obit 47

Wells, Carolyn [1869(?)-1942] .... **TCLC 35**
See also CA 113; DLB 11

Wells, H(erbert) G(eorge) [1866-1946]**T C L C 6, 12, 19; DA; DAB; DAC; DAM MST, NOV; SSC 6; WLC**
See also AAYA 18; CA 110; 121; CDBLB 1914-1945; DLB 34, 70, 156, 178; MTCW; SATA 20

Wells, Rosemary [1943-] .... **CLC 12**
See also AAYA 13; CA 85-88; CANR 48; CLR 16; MAICYA; SAAS 1; SATA 18, 69

Welty, Eudora [1909-]**CLC 1, 2, 5, 14, 22, 33, 105; DA; DAB; DAC; DAM MST, NOV; SSC 1, 27; WLC**
See also CA 9-12R; CABS 1; CANR 32, 65; CDALB 1941-1968; DLB 2, 102, 143; DLBD 12; DLBY 87; MTCW

Wen I-to [1899-1946] .... **TCLC 28**

Wentworth, Robert
See Hamilton, Edmond

Werfel, Franz (Viktor) [1890-1945] **TCLC 8**
See also CA 104; 161; DLB 81, 124

Wergeland, Henrik Arnold [1808-1845]
NCLC 5

Wersba, Barbara [1932-] .... **CLC 30**
See also AAYA 2; CA 29-32R; CANR 16, 38;
CLR 3; DLB 52; JRDA; MAICYA; SAAS 2;
SATA 1, 58

Wertmueller, Lina [1928-] .... **CLC 16**
See also CA 97-100; CANR 39

Wescott, Glenway [1901-1987] .... **CLC 13**
See also CA 13-16R; 121; CANR 23; DLB 4,
9, 102

Wesker, Arnold [1932-] . **CLC 3, 5, 42; DAB;**
DAM DRAM
See also CA 1-4R; CAAS 7; CANR 1, 33;
CDBLB 1960 to Present; DLB 13; MTCW

Wesley, Richard (Errol) [1945-] .... **CLC 7**
See also BW 1; CA 57-60; CANR 27; DLB 38

Wessel, Johan Herman [1742-1785] ...... **LC 7**

West, Anthony (Panther) [1914-1987] **CLC 50**
See also CA 45-48; 124; CANR 3, 19; DLB 15

West, C. P.
See Wodehouse, P(elham) G(renville)

West, (Mary) Jessamyn [1902-1984] **CLC 7, 17**
See also CA 9-12R; 112; CANR 27; DLB 6;
DLBY 84; MTCW; SATA-Obit 37

West, Morris L(anglo) [1916-] ...... **CLC 6, 33**
See also CA 5-8R; CANR 24, 49, 64; MTCW

West, Nathanael [1903-1940] **TCLC 1, 14, 44;**
SSC 16
See also CA 104; 125; CDALB 1929-1941;
DLB 4, 9, 28; MTCW

West, Owen
See Koontz, Dean R(ay)

West, Paul [1930-] .... **CLC 7, 14, 96**
See also CA 13-16R; CAAS 7; CANR 22, 53;
DLB 14; INT CANR-22

West, Rebecca [1892-1983] . **CLC 7, 9, 31, 50**
See also CA 5-8R; 109; CANR 19; DLB 36;
DLBY 83; MTCW

Westall, Robert (Atkinson) [1929-1993] **CLC 17**
See also AAYA 12; CA 69-72; 141; CANR 18,
68; CLR 13; JRDA; MAICYA; SAAS 2;
SATA 23, 69; SATA-Obit 75

Westlake, Donald E(dwin) [1933-] **CLC 7, 33;**
DAM POP
See also CA 17-20R; CAAS 13; CANR 16, 44,
65; INT CANR-16

Westmacott, Mary
See Christie, Agatha (Mary Clarissa)

Weston, Allen
See Norton, Andre

Wetcheek, J. L.
See Feuchtwanger, Lion

Wetering, Janwillem van de
See van de Wetering, Janwillem

Wetherald, Agnes Ethelwyn [1857-1940]
TCLC 81
See also DLB 99

Wetherell, Elizabeth
See Warner, Susan (Bogert)

Whale, James [1889-1957] .... **TCLC 63**

Whalen, Philip [1923-] .... **CLC 6, 29**
See also CA 9-12R; CANR 5, 39; DLB 16

Wharton, Edith (Newbold Jones) [1862-1937]
TCLC 3, 9, 27, 53; DA; DAB; DAC; DAM
MST, NOV; SSC 6; WLC
See also AAYA 25; CA 104; 132; CDALB 1865-
1917; DLB 4, 9, 12, 78, 189; DLBD 13;
MTCW

Wharton, James
See Mencken, H(enry) L(ouis)

Wharton, William (a pseudonym) **CLC 18, 37**
See also CA 93-96; DLBY 80; INT 93-96

Wheatley (Peters), Phillis [1754(?)-1784] **LC 3; BLC 3; DA; DAC; DAM MST, MULT, POET; PC 3; WLC**

See also CDALB 1640-1865; DLB 31, 50

Wheelock, John Hall [1886-1978] .... **CLC 14**
See also CA 13-16R; 77-80; CANR 14; DLB 45

White, E(lwyn) B(rooks) [1899-1985] **CLC 10, 34, 39; DAM POP**
See also AITN 2; CA 13-16R; 116; CANR 16,
37; CLR 1, 21; DLB 11, 22; MAICYA;
MTCW; SATA 2, 29; SATA-Obit 44

White, Edmund (Valentine III) [1940-] **CLC 27, 110; DAM POP**
See also AAYA 7; CA 45-48; CANR 3, 19, 36,
62; MTCW

White, Patrick (Victor Martindale) [1912-1990]
CLC 3, 4, 5, 7, 9, 18, 65, 69
See also CA 81-84; 132; CANR 43; MTCW

White, Phyllis Dorothy James [1920-]
See James, P. D.
See also CA 21-24R; CANR 17, 43, 65; DAM
POP; MTCW

White, T(erence) H(anbury) [1906-1964] **CLC 30**
See also AAYA 22; CA 73-76; CANR 37; DLB
160; JRDA; MAICYA; SATA 12

White, Terence de Vere [1912-1994] **CLC 49**
See also CA 49-52; 145; CANR 3

White, Walter F(rancis) [1893-1955] **TCLC 15**
See also White, Walter
See also BW 1; CA 115; 124; DLB 51

White, William Hale [1831-1913]
See Rutherford, Mark
See also CA 121

Whitehead, E(dward) A(nthony) [1933-] **CLC 5**
See also CA 65-68; CANR 58

Whitemore, Hugh (John) [1936-] ..... **CLC 37**
See also CA 132; INT 132

Whitman, Sarah Helen (Power) [1803-1878]
NCLC 19
See also DLB 1

Whitman, Walt(er) [1819-1892] **NCLC 4, 31;**
DA; DAB; DAC; DAM MST, POET; PC 3; WLC
See also CDALB 1640-1865; DLB 3, 64; SATA
20

Whitney, Phyllis A(yame) [1903-] .. **CLC 42; DAM POP**
See also AITN 2; BEST 90:3; CA 1-4R; CANR
3, 25, 38, 60; JRDA; MAICYA; SATA 1, 30

Whittemore, (Edward) Reed (Jr.) [1919-] **CLC 4**
See also CA 9-12R; CAAS 8; CANR 4; DLB 5

Whittier, John Greenleaf [1807-1892] **NCLC 8, 59**
See also DLB 1

Whittlebot, Hernia
See Coward, Noel (Peirce)

Wicker, Thomas Grey [1926-]
See Wicker, Tom
See also CA 65-68; CANR 21, 46

Wicker, Tom .... **CLC 7**
See also Wicker, Thomas Grey

Wideman, John Edgar [1941-] **CLC 5, 34, 36, 67; BLC 3; DAM MULT**
See also BW 2; CA 85-88; CANR 14, 42, 67;
DLB 33, 143

Wiebe, Rudy (Henry) [1934-] **CLC 6, 11, 14; DAC; DAM MST**
See also CA 37-40R; CANR 42, 67; DLB 60

Wieland, Christoph Martin [1733-1813]
NCLC 17
See also DLB 97

Wiene, Robert [1881-1938] .... **TCLC 56**

Wieners, John [1934-] .... **CLC 7**
See also CA 13-16R; DLB 16

Wiesel, Elie(zer) [1928-] **CLC 3, 5, 11, 37; DA; DAB; DAC; DAM MST, NOV; WLCS 2**

See also AAYA 7; AITN 1; CA 5-8R; CAAS 4;
CANR 8, 40, 65; DLB 83; DLBY 87; INT
CANR-8; MTCW; SATA 56

Wiggins, Marianne [1947-] .... **CLC 57**
See also BEST 89:3; CA 130; CANR 60

Wight, James Alfred [1916-1995]
See Herriot, James
See also CA 77-80; SATA 55; SATA-Brief 44

Wilbur, Richard (Purdy) [1921-] **CLC 3, 6, 9, 14, 53, 110; DA; DAB; DAC; DAM MST, POET**
See also CA 1-4R; CABS 2; CANR 2, 29; DLB
5, 169; INT CANR-29; MTCW; SATA 9

Wild, Peter [1940-] .... **CLC 14**
See also CA 37-40R; DLB 5

Wilde, Oscar (Fingal O'Flahertie Wills) [1854(?)-1900] ... **TCLC 1, 8, 23, 41; DA; DAB; DAC; DAM DRAM, MST, NOV; SSC 11; WLC**
See also CA 104; 119; CDBLB 1890-1914;
DLB 10, 19, 34, 57, 141, 156, 190; SATA 24

Wilder, Billy .... **CLC 20**
See also Wilder, Samuel
See also DLB 26

Wilder, Samuel [1906-]
See Wilder, Billy
See also CA 89-92

Wilder, Thornton (Niven) [1897-1975] **CLC 1, 5, 6, 10, 15, 35, 82; DA; DAB; DAC; DAM DRAM, MST, NOV; DC 1; WLC**
See also AITN 2; CA 13-16R; 61-64; CANR
40; DLB 4, 7, 9; DLBY 97; MTCW

Wilding, Michael [1942-] .... **CLC 73**
See also CA 104; CANR 24, 49

Wiley, Richard [1944-] .... **CLC 44**
See also CA 121; 129

Wilhelm, Kate .... **CLC 7**
See also Wilhelm, Katie Gertrude
See also AAYA 20; CAAS 5; DLB 8; INT
CANR-17

Wilhelm, Katie Gertrude [1928-]
See Wilhelm, Kate
See also CA 37-40R; CANR 17, 36, 60; MTCW

Wilkins, Mary
See Freeman, Mary Eleanor Wilkins

Willard, Nancy [1936-] .... **CLC 7, 37**
See also CA 89-92; CANR 10, 39, 68; CLR 5;
DLB 5, 52; MAICYA; MTCW; SATA 37, 71;
SATA-Brief 30

Williams, C(harles) K(enneth) [1936-] . **CLC 33, 56; DAM POET**
See also CA 37-40R; CAAS 26; CANR 57; DLB
5

Williams, Charles
See Collier, James L(incoln)

Williams, Charles (Walter Stansby) [1886-
1945] .... **TCLC 1, 11**
See also CA 104; 163; DLB 100, 153

Williams, (George) Emlyn [1905-1987] **CLC 15; DAM DRAM**
See also CA 104; 123; CANR 36; DLB 10, 77;
MTCW

Williams, Hank [1923-1953] .... **TCLC 81**

Williams, Hugo [1942-] .... **CLC 42**
See also CA 17-20R; CANR 45; DLB 40

Williams, J. Walker
See Wodehouse, P(elham) G(renville)

Williams, John A(lfred) [1925-] .. **CLC 5, 13; BLC 3; DAM MULT**
See also BW 2; CA 53-56; CAAS 3; CANR 6,
26, 51; DLB 2, 33; INT CANR-6

Williams, Jonathan (Chamberlain) [1929-]
CLC 13
See also CA 9-12R; CAAS 12; CANR 8; DLB
5

Williams, Joy [1944-] .... **CLC 31**
See also CA 41-44R; CANR 22, 48

Literary Criticism Series
Cumulative Topic Index

This index lists all topic entries in Gale's *Classical and Medieval Literature Criticism, Contemporary Literary Criticism, Literature Criticism from 1400 to 1800, Nineteenth-Century Literature Criticism,* and *Twentieth-Century Literary Criticism.*

Topic Index

Topic Index

Topic Index

Twentieth-Century Literary Criticism
Cumulative Nationality Index

Herzl, Theodor **36**
Horvath, Oedoen von **45**
Jozsef, Attila **22**
Karinthy, Frigyes **47**
Mikszath, Kalman **31**
Molnar, Ferenc **20**
Moricz, Zsigmond **33**
Radnoti, Miklos **16**

ICELANDIC
Sigurjonsson, Johann **27**

INDIAN
Chatterji, Saratchandra **13**
Dasgupta, Surendranath **81**
Gandhi, Mohandas Karamchand **59**
Ghose, Aurabinda **63**
Iqbal, Muhammad **28**
Naidu, Sarojini **80**
Premchand **21**
Tagore, Rabindranath **3, 53**

INDONESIAN
Anwar, Chairil **22**

IRANIAN
Hedayat, Sadeq **21**

IRISH
A.E. **3, 10**
Baker, Jean H. **3, 10**
Cary, (Arthur) Joyce (Lunel) **1, 29**
Dunsany, Lord **2, 59**
Gogarty, Oliver St. John **15**
Gregory, Isabella Augusta (Persse) **1**
Harris, Frank **24**
Joyce, James (Augustine Aloysius) **3, 8, 16,
   35, 52**
Ledwidge, Francis **23**
Martin, Violet Florence **51**
Moore, George Augustus **7**
O'Grady, Standish (James) **5**
Shaw, Bernard **45**
Shaw, George Bernard **3, 9, 21**
Somerville, Edith **51**
Stephens, James **4**
Stoker, Bram **8**
Synge, (Edmund) J(ohn) M(illington) **6, 37**
Tynan, Katharine **3**
Wilde, Oscar (Fingal O'Flahertie Wills) **1, 8,
   23, 41**
Yeats, William Butler **1, 11, 18, 31**

ITALIAN
Alvaro, Corrado **60**
Betti, Ugo **5**
Brancati, Vitaliano **12**
Campana, Dino **20**
Carducci, Giosue (Alessandro Giuseppe) **32**
Croce, Benedetto **37**
D'Annunzio, Gabriele **6, 40**
Deledda, Grazia (Cosima) **23**
Giacosa, Giuseppe **7**
Jovine, Francesco **79**
Lampedusa, Giuseppe (Tomasi) di **13**
Malaparte, Curzio **52**
Marinetti, Filippo Tommaso **10**
Mosca, Gaetano **75**
Papini, Giovanni **22**
Pareto, Vilfredo **69**
Pascoli, Giovanni **45**
Pavese, Cesare **3**
Pirandello, Luigi **4, 29**

Saba, Umberto **33**
Svevo, Italo **2, 35**
Tozzi, Federigo **31**
Verga, Giovanni (Carmelo) **3**

JAMAICAN
De Lisser, H(erbert) G(eorge) **12**
Garvey, Marcus (Moziah Jr.) **41**
Mais, Roger **8**
McKay, Claude **7, 41**
Redcam, Tom **25**

JAPANESE
Akutagawa, Ryunosuke **16**
Dazai Osamu **11**
Futabatei, Shimei **44**
Hagiwara Sakutaro **60**
Hayashi, Fumiko **27**
Ishikawa, Takuboku **15**
Masaoka Shiki **18**
Miyamoto, Yuriko **37**
Miyazawa, Kenji **76**
Mizoguchi, Kenji **72**
Nagai Kafu **51**
Natsume, Soseki **2, 10**
Nishida, Kitaro **83**
Noguchi, Yone **80**
Rohan, Koda **22**
Santoka, Taneda **72**
Shimazaki Toson **5**
Yokomitsu Riichi **47**
Yosano Akiko **59**

LATVIAN
Rainis, Janis **29**

LEBANESE
Gibran, Kahlil **1, 9**

LESOTHAN
Mofolo, Thomas (Mokopu) **22**

LITHUANIAN
Kreve (Mickevicius), Vincas **27**

MEXICAN
Azuela, Mariano **3**
Gamboa, Federico **36**
Gonzalez Martinez, Enrique **72**
Nervo, (Jose) Amado (Ruiz de) **11**
Reyes, Alfonso **33**
Romero, Jose Ruben **14**
Villaurrutia, Xavier **80**

NEPALI
Devkota, Laxmiprasad **23**

NEW ZEALANDER
Mander, (Mary) Jane **31**
Mansfield, Katherine **2, 8, 39**

NICARAGUAN
Dario, Ruben **4**

NORWEGIAN
Bjoernson, Bjoernstjerne (Martinius) **7, 37**
Bojer, Johan **64**
Grieg, (Johan) Nordahl (Brun) **10**
Hamsun, Knut **2, 14, 49**
Ibsen, Henrik (Johan) **2, 8, 16, 37, 52**
Kielland, Alexander Lange **5**
Lie, Jonas (Lauritz Idemil) **5**
Obstfelder, Sigbjoern **23**

Skram, Amalie (Bertha) **25**
Undset, Sigrid **3**

PAKISTANI
Iqbal, Muhammad **28**

PERUVIAN
Palma, Ricardo **29**
Vallejo, Cesar (Abraham) **3, 56**

POLISH
Asch, Sholem **3**
Borowski, Tadeusz **9**
Conrad, Joseph **1, 6, 13, 25, 43, 57**
Peretz, Isaac Loeb **16**
Prus, Boleslaw **48**
Przybyszewski, Stanislaw **36**
Reymont, Wladyslaw (Stanislaw) **5**
Schulz, Bruno **5, 51**
Sienkiewicz, Henryk (Adam Alexander Pius) **3**
Singer, Israel Joshua **33**
Witkiewicz, Stanislaw Ignacy **8**

PORTUGUESE
Pessoa, Fernando (Antonio Nogueira) **27**
Sa-Carniero, Mario de **83**

PUERTO RICAN
Hostos (y Bonilla), Eugenio Maria de **24**

ROMANIAN
Bacovia, George **24**
Caragiale, Ion Luca **76**
Rebreanu, Liviu **28**

RUSSIAN
Aldanov, Mark (Alexandrovich) **23**
Andreyev, Leonid (Nikolaevich) **3**
Annensky, Innokenty (Fyodorovich) **14**
Artsybashev, Mikhail (Petrovich) **31**
Babel, Isaak (Emmanuilovich) **2, 13**
Bagritsky, Eduard **60**
Balmont, Konstantin (Dmitriyevich) **11**
Bely, Andrey **7**
Berdyaev, Nikolai (Aleksandrovich) **67**
Bergelson, David **81**
Blok, Alexander (Alexandrovich) **5**
Bryusov, Valery Yakovlevich **10**
Bulgakov, Mikhail (Afanas'evich) **2, 16**
Bulgya, Alexander Alexandrovich **53**
Bunin, Ivan Alexeyevich **6**
Chekhov, Anton (Pavlovich) **3, 10, 31, 55**
Der Nister **56**
Eisenstein, Sergei (Mikhailovich) **57**
Esenin, Sergei (Alexandrovich) **4**
Fadeyev, Alexander **53**
Gladkov, Fyodor (Vasilyevich) **27**
Gorky, Maxim **8**
Gumilev, Nikolai (Stepanovich) **60**
Gurdjieff, G(eorgei) I(vanovich) **71**
Guro, Elena **56**
Hippius, Zinaida **9**
Ilf, Ilya **21**
Ivanov, Vyacheslav Ivanovich **33**
Khlebnikov, Velimir **20**
Khodasevich, Vladislav (Felitsianovich) **15**
Korolenko, Vladimir Galaktionovich **22**
Kropotkin, Peter (Aleksieevich) **36**
Kuprin, Aleksandr Ivanovich **5**
Kuzmin, Mikhail **40**
Lenin, V. I. **67**
Mandelstam, Osip (Emilievich) **2, 6**
Mayakovski, Vladimir (Vladimirovich) **4, 18**

TCLC-81 Title Index

ISBN 0-7876-2741-0

90000

9 780787 627416